Travel Discount Coupon

This coupon entitles you to special discounts when you book your trip through the

GLOBAL TRAVEL NETWORK®
RESERVATION SERVICE

Hotels ♦ Airlines ♦ Car Rentals ♦ Cruises
All Your Travel Needs

Here's what you get: *

♦ A discount of $50 USD on a booking of $1,000** or more for two or more people!

♦ A discount of $25 USD on a booking of $500** or more for one person!

♦ Free membership for three years, and 1,000 free miles on enrollment in the unique Miles-to-Go™ frequent-traveler program. Earn one mile for every dollar spent through the program. Earn free hotel stays starting at 5,000 miles. Earn free roundtrip airline tickets starting at 25,000 miles.

♦ Personal help in planning your own, customized trip.

♦ Fast, confirmed reservations at any property recommended in this guide, subject to availability.***

♦ Special discounts on bookings in the U.S. and around the world.

♦ Low-cost visa and passport service.

♦ Reduced-rate cruise packages.

Visit our website at http://www.travnet.com/Frommer or call us globally at 201-567-8500, ext. 55. In the U.S., call toll-free at 1-888-940-5000, or fax 201-567-1838. In Canada, call toll-free at 1-800-883-9959, or fax 416-922-6053. In Asia, call 60-3-7191044, or fax 60-3-7185415.

* To qualify for these travel discounts, at least a portion of your trip must include destinations covered in this guide. No more than one coupon discount may be used in any 12-month period, for destinations covered in this guide. Cannot be combined with any other discount or program.

**These are U.S. dollars spent on commissionable bookings.

***A $10 USD fee, plus fax and/or phone charges, will be added to the cost of bookings at each hotel not linked to the reservation service. Customers must approve these fees in advance.

Valid until December 31, 1998. Terms and conditions of the Miles-to-Go™ program are available on request by calling 201-567-8500, ext 55.

NEN123

Frommer's®

Spain

Including Majorca, Minorca & Ibiza

by Darwin Porter & Danforth Prince

Macmillan • USA

About the Authors

North Carolina-born **Darwin Porter** and **Danforth Prince,** a native of Ohio, are the coauthors of several bestselling Frommer guides—notably to the Caribbean, England, France, Italy, and Germany. Porter, who worked in television advertising and was a former bureau chief for *The Miami Herald,* wrote the first-ever Frommer's guide to Spain while still a student. Prince, who began his association with Porter in 1982, worked for the Paris bureau of *The New York Times.* Both of these writers know their destination well, and have made countless annual trips through the cities and countryside of Spain to share their discoveries with you.

MACMILLAN TRAVEL

A Simon & Schuster Macmillan Company
1633 Broadway
New York, NY 10019

Find us online at **http://www.mgr.com/travel** or
on America Online at Keyword: **Frommer's.**

ISBN 0-02-861202-7
ISSN 1091-2827

Editor: Kelly Regan
Production Editor: Carol Sheehan
Design by Michele Laseau
Map Editor: Doug Stallings
Digital Cartography by Ortelius Design and Roberta Stockwell

Manufactured in the United States of America

Contents

6 Excursions from Madrid 178

7 Old Castile & León 212

8 Extremadura 235

List of Maps

An Invitation to the Reader

In researching this book, we discovered many wonderful places—hotels, inns, restaurants, shops, and more. We're sure you'll find others. Please tell us about them, so we can share the information with your fellow travelers in upcoming editions. If you were disappointed with a recommendation, we'd love to know that, too. Please write to:

Darwin Porter & Danforth Prince
Frommer's Spain, 17th Edition
Macmillan Travel
1633 Broadway
New York, NY 10019

An Additional Note

Please be advised that travel information is subject to change at any time—and this is especially true of prices. We therefore suggest that you write or call ahead for confirmation when making your travel plans. The authors, editors, and publisher cannot be held responsible for the experiences of readers while traveling. Your safety is important to us, however, so we encourage you to stay alert and be aware of your surroundings. Keep a close eye on cameras, purses, and wallets, all favorite targets of thieves and pickpockets.

What the Symbols Mean

✪ Frommer's Favorites

Hotels, restaurants, attractions, and entertainment you should not miss.

$ Super-Special Values

Hotels and restaurants that offer great value for your money.

The following abbreviations are used for credit cards:

AE	American Express	EU	Eurocard
CB	Carte Blanche	JCB	Japan Credit Bank
DC	Diners Club	MC	MasterCard
DISC	Discover	V	Visa
ER	enRoute		

The Best of Spain

1

Spain presents visitors with an embarrassment of riches; you may find yourself bewildered with all the choices you'll have to make when planning a trip. We've scoured the country in search of the best places and experiences, and in this chapter we'll share some of our very personal and opinionated choices. Seek out a Picasso masterwork. Ogle the "hanging houses" in clifftop Cuenca. Chase a bull down the cobblestone streets of Pamplona. From cave dwelling to tapas tasting, we hope these picks will give you some ideas to get you started.

1 The Best Travel Experiences

- **An Afternoon at the Bullfights:** Based on origins as old as pagan Spain, the art of bullfighting is more closely associated with the Iberian temperament and passions than any other pastime. Detractors cite the sport as cruel, bloody, violent, hot, and savage. Aficionados view bullfighting as a microcosm of death, catharsis, and rebirth, and defend it as one of the most evocative and memorable events in Spain. Head for the *plaza de toros* (bullring) in any major city—notably Madrid, Seville, or Granada. Amid feverish crowds, observe the ballet of the *banderilleros,* the thundering fury of the bull, the arrogance of the matador—all leading to "death in the afternoon."
- **Listening to the Sound of Flamenco:** It's best heard in some old tavern, in a ghetto like the Barrio de Triana in Seville. But from the lowliest *taberna* to the poshest nightclub, you can hear the heel clicking, foot stamping, castanet rattling, hand clapping, and sultry guitar and tambourine sound—this is flamenco. Some say its origins lie deep in Asia, but the Spanish gypsy has given it an original and unique style, a dance to dramatize inner conflict and pain. Performed by a great artist, flamenco can tear your heart out with its soulful and throaty singing.
- **Feasting on Tapas in the Tascas:** It's reason enough to go to Spain! Spanish tapas are so good their once-secret recipes have been broadcast around the world, but they always taste better on home turf. The *tapeo* is the equivalent of the pub crawl in London—that is, going from one tapas bar to another. Each has a different specialty. Tapas bars—called *tascas* —are the quintessential Spanish experience, be it in Galicia, Andalusia, Catalonia,

or Castile. Originally tapas were cured ham or *chorizo* (spicy sausage). Today they are likely to include everything— *gambas* (deep-fried shrimp), anchovies marinated in vinegar, stuffed peppers, a cooling gazpacho, or hake salad. To go really native, try lamb's sweetbreads or bull's testicles. These dazzling spreads will fortify you until the fashionable 10pm dining hour.

- **Visiting the Prado:** It's one of the world's supreme art museums, ranking up there with the Louvre. The Prado is home to some 4,000 masterpieces, many of them acquired by Spanish kings. The wealth of Spanish art is staggering—everything from Goya's *Naked Maja* to the celebrated *Las Meninas* (*The Maids of Honor*) by Velázquez (our favorite). Masterpiece after masterpiece unfolds before your eyes: You can wander in Hieronymus Bosch's *Garden of Earthly Delights* or thrill to the horror of Goya's *Disasters of War* etchings. When the Spanish artistic soul gets too dark, escape to the Italian salons and view canvases by "the divine" Caravaggio, Fra Angelico, and Botticelli. It would take a lifetime to savor the Prado's wonders. See Chapter 5.
- **Wine Tasting at Jerez de la Frontera:** In Spain, sherry is *Jerez,* a major industry and an entire subculture in its own right. Hispanophiles compare its flavors to the finest wines produced in France and make pilgrimages to the bodegas in Andalusia that ferment this amber-colored liquid that's been called the potent lifeblood of Spain. More than a hundred bodegas are available for visits, tours, and tastings, and most open their gates to oenophiles interested in a process that's as old as the country's Roman occupation of long ago. See Chapter 9.
- **Wandering Through Barcelona's Barri Gòtic:** Long before Madrid was even founded, the kingdom of Catalonia was a bastion of art and architecture. Whether the Gothic Quarter is truly Gothic is the subject of endless debate, but the Ciutat Vella, or old city, of Barcelona is one of the most evocative sites in Spain. Its richly textured streets, with their gurgling fountains, vintage stores, and ancient fortifications inspired such artists as Pablo Picasso and Joan Miró (who was born in this *barrio*). See Chapter 13.
- **Going Gaga over Gaudí:** No architect in Europe was as fantastical as Antoni Gaudí y Cornet. The city of Barcelona is studded with the architectural works of this extraordinary artist—in fact, UNESCO now lists all his creations among the World Trust Properties. No two buildings of this eccentric genius are alike—he conceived buildings as "visions." A recluse and a celibate bachelor, he lived out his own fantasy. Nothing is more stunning than his Sagrada Familia, Barcelona's best-known landmark, a cathedral on which Gaudí labored for the last 43 years of his life before he was run over by a tram in 1926. It was never completed. In Barcelona, the question is not "to be or not to be" but "to finish or not to finish." If it's ever finished, "The Sacred Family" will be Europe's largest cathedral. See Chapter 13.
- **Running with the Bulls in Pamplona:** The Fiesta de San Fermín in July is the most dangerous ritual in Spain, made even worse by the large amounts of wine consumed by its many participants and observers. Broadcast live on TV throughout Spain and the rest of Europe, and originally exposed to North American audiences by Ernest Hemingway, the festival features herds of furious bulls that charge down medieval streets, sometimes trampling and goring some of the hundreds of youths who opt to run beside them. Few other rituals in Spain are as breathtaking and foolhardy. Few others are as memorable. See Chapter 17.
- **Following the Pilgrim Route to Santiago:** Tourism as we know it began during the Middle Ages as thousands of European pilgrims journeyed to the shrine

of Santiago (Saint James) in Galicia in northwestern Spain. Even if you're not motivated by faith to visit, you should come to see some of the most dramatic landscapes and the grandest scenery in Spain, by crossing the northern tier of the country—all the way from the Pyrenees to Santiago de Compostela. Some of the country's most stunning architecture can be viewed along the way, including gems in Roncevalles, Burgos, and León. The deluxe Hostal de Los Reyes Católicos in Santiago awaits the weary pilgrim at the end of the journey. See Chapter 20.

2 The Most Romantic Getaways

- **Arcos de la Frontera:** Fleeing overcrowded and overrun Andalusia, you arrive at this old Arab town—now a historical monument—20 miles (32km) east of Jerez de la Frontera, the town that sherry put on the map. Lodged comfortably in the Parador Casa del Corregidor (an old vicar's home), you can set out to explore this lofty place, hemmed in on three sides by the Guadalete River. The parador is perched along the edge of a cliff, and you can take many walks in several directions, viewing this *pueblo blanco* (white village) of whitewashed Andalusian houses. Spectacular vistas open in all directions, and in this retreat you can absorb the unique feeling of Andalusia without having to face the urban stresses of Seville. See Chapter 9.
- **Nerja:** On the Costa del Sol at the Balcón de Europa (Balcony of Europe), this is one of the gems of the Mediterranean coastline, with a palm-shaded promenade that juts out into the sea. Lined with antique iron lampposts, the village overlooks a pretty beach and the fishing fleet. The resort town lies on a sloping site at the foot of a wall of jagged coastal mountains. You can snuggle up here in the parador or in one of the little inns on the narrow streets. See Chapter 10.
- **Sitges:** South of Barcelona is Spain's most romantic Mediterranean resort, with a 1½-mile-long sandy beach (La Ribera) and a promenade studded with flowers and palm trees. Such famous artists as Picasso have lived here. Wander its little lanes and inspect the old villas of its Casco Antiguo, the old quarter. When not at the beach, you can view three good art museums, including one in the former studio of artist Santiago Rusiñol (1861–1931). Nowadays, thousands of gay men and women flock to Sitges, but there's a wide spectrum of visitors of all persuasions. See Chapter 14.
- **Santillana del Mar:** Jean-Paul Sartre called it "the prettiest village in Spain." Only six blocks long and just three miles (5km) from the sea, Santillana del Mar perfectly encapsulates the spirit of Cantabria. It's also near the Cuevas de Altamira, often called "the Sistine Chapel of prehistoric art." Romanesque houses and mansions line the ironstone streets. People still sell fresh milk from their stable doors, as if the Middle Ages had never ended. But you can live in comfort at one of Spain's grandest paradors, Parador de Santillana del Mar, a converted 17th-century mansion. See Chapter 19.
- **Deià:** On the island of Majorca—one of Spain's Balearic Islands—you'll find this lovely old village (also spelled Deyá), where the poet Robert Graves lived until his death, in 1985. Following in his footsteps, artists and writers flock to this haven of natural beauty, 17 miles (27km) northwest of Palma. The views here are panoramic, both of sea and mountains. Gnarled and ancient olive trees dot the landscape. You can book into cozy nests of luxury like La Residencia or Es Molí. See Chapter 21.

3 The Best Offbeat Experiences

- **Living in a Monastery:** Many monasteries in Spain have been turned into deluxe paradors. But if you want a taste of the true monastic life, you can experience that too. Most monasteries allow men only, but some accept women as well. You don't need to be Catholic, but you must respect the tranquil monastic atmosphere and follow a few simple rules. Among the most evocative monasteries are the following: **Nuestra Señora de los Angeles** (Asturias; ☎ **98/526-49-95**), a spartan hill convent in undulating countryside that accepts women and an occasional man. More opulent is **Monasterio de Santo Domingo de Silos** (Burgos; ☎ **947/38-07-68**), which is fabulously rich and famous for its school of Gregorian chant. Men only are accepted here. **Monasterio de Leyre** (Leyre; ☎ **948/88-41-37**), is a Cistercian monastery with a history dating to the 18th century. Its Romanesque church and crypt are among the oldest in Spain. This comfortable guest house serves hearty Navarrese cooking and accepts both men and women. **Monasterio de San Pedro de Cardena** (Burgos; ☎ **947/29-00-33**), another Cistercian monastery, claims to be the resting place of El Cid. Only men are accepted, and they must be silent at mealtime. **Real Monasterio de Guadalupe** (Cáceres; ☎ **927/36-70-00**), is Franciscan. Even royalty has stayed here—notably Ferdinand and Isabella, who ordered the construction of Hostal Real, with its Zurbarán paintings and stunning Gothic facade. Men and women are accepted.
- **Ballooning in Spain:** Hot-air balloon rides are now possible in the most scenic regions of Spain—from flights over Catalonia to flights over some of Spain's great historic cities of the heartland, as well as flights over Andalusia. More and more adventurers are finding it the ideal way to see medieval villages, scenic valleys, and mountain ranges. You can even view Segovia's famous castle while ballooning over the mountains. Champagne breakfasts usually follow the landing. It's most definitely an endeavor for early risers, as the best time for ballooning is just after dawn when the air is calm and cool—though there are night flights over Marbella on the Costa del Sol. For a list of hot-air ballooning outfitters, refer to "The Active Vacation Planner" in Chapter 3.
- **Exploring the High Pyrenees:** Spain is great walking country, and the Pyrenees in northern Spain are among the most desirable places for a hiking adventure, equaled only by the Picos de Europa. Hiking tours provide sensational scenery and memorable experiences: roam through forgotten villages, taste great country food, take part in local fiestas, and see rare birds and other animals. Most tours take in the High Pyrenees, the western valleys, and the eastern Pyrenean foothills. One company offers a trio of different tours, lasting from 9 to 15 days, but participants can also choose to join a tour only for a week. Lodgings are found in country homes and remote hotels with scenic settings. These tours are scheduled throughout the year except in winter, when inclement weather makes hiking impossible. Contact Alto Aragón at 2 Linstead Way, Southfields, London SW18 5QA in England (☎ **0181/788-5417**). In Spain call **974/37-50-36** for more information.
- **Living in a Cave:** Fourteen caves are now available for rent in the mountain village of Galera, Granada. The caves are available on a daily or weekly basis, with prices ranging from approximately 3,750 pesetas ($30) per day or 21,250 pesetas ($170) per week for a one-bedroom cave for two guests, to approximately 8,750 pesetas ($70) per day or 51,000 pesetas ($408) per week for a five-bedroom underground apartment that can accommodate seven people with two doubles and three singles. The caves come fully equipped with running water,

electricity, and plumbing. The indoor temperature hovers around 68° F year-round, so no air-conditioning is required. Life underground is nothing new in the clay hillsides of the Andalusian provinces of Jaén and Granada. Here several communities of cave dwellers still enjoy all the comforts of modern life, with the added advantage of being able to expand the size of their homes with just a hammer and a chisel. For further information contact Turismo Rural Casas Cuevas, Promociones Turísticas de Galera (Granada), Avenida Nicasio Tomás 12, 18440 Granada (☎ or fax **958/73-90-68**).

- **Experiencing the Peasant Life:** If you grew up in a city and didn't learn all those skills like milking cows and herding goats, you now have your chance. At an Andalusian farm in the Valle de Abdelajis, north of Málaga, you can till the fields (following a mule-drawn plow, naturally) or try your hand at milking a goat. It's not all work; you're allowed to hike through the countryside and enjoy the good country cooking at lunch—all for 3,500 pesetas ($28). Should you wish to spend the night on the farm, the cost goes up to 5,500 pesetas ($44). For more information, contact Colin Dean, Peasant Adventure, Plaza del Sol 4, 29240 Valle de Abdelajis (Málaga; ☎ **95/248-55-81**).
- **Cruising the Ebro in a Houseboat:** A unique adventure in Catalonia is to rent a houseboat and cruise the waters of the province's Ebro River. The smallest boat in the fleet accommodates four adults and two children. The biggest can shelter up to eight adults and a child in a trio of spacious cabins. The bases of the houseboat fleet are at Riba-roya d'Erbe, close to Tarragona's frontier with Aragón, and at Amposta, on the Ebro delta. The company will plot a choice of itineraries for you, and you don't need previous navigation experience. Some of the most beautiful and least discovered scenery in Spain is along these river routes. Fishers will delight in learning that some of the largest catfish in Europe live in the Ebro. Contact Badia Tucana at Ctra. De Faió, 43790 Ribaroja d'Ebra (Tarragona; ☎ **977/41-65-49**) for more information.

4 The Best Castles & Palaces

- **Palacio Real, Madrid:** No longer occupied by royalty, but used for state occasions, the Palacio Real (Royal Palace) stands in the heart of Madrid on the bank of the Manzanares River. It was built in the mid-18th century over the site of a former palace. It's not Versailles, but mighty impressive, with 2,000 some rooms, many of them palatial. No one has lived here since the king fled in 1931, but the chandeliers, marble columns, and ornate, gilded borders, paintings, and objets d'art, including Flemish tapestries and Tiepolo ceiling frescoes, are still well preserved. The empty thrones of King Juan Carlos and Queen Sofia are among the highlights of the tour. They live in Zarzuela Palace, on the outskirts of Madrid. See Chapter 5.
- **El Alcázar, Segovia:** Once the most impregnable castle in Spain, it rises dramatically from a rock spur near the ancient heart of town. Isabella married Ferdinand within this foreboding site, surrendering rights that eventually led to the unification of Spain. Today, it's the single most photographed, evocative, and dramatic castle in Iberia. See Chapter 6.
- **Palacio Real, Aranjuez:** Built at enormous expense by the Bourbon cousins of the rulers of France, it was designed to emulate the glories of Versailles. Today, only a handful of other royal buildings in Spain so effectively replicate the 18th-century neoclassicism then prevalent in Europe. The gardens are more fascinating than the palace. The gem of the complex is the Casita del Labrador, an annex as

unbelievably rich and ornate as its model—Marie Antoinette's Petit Trianon at Versailles. See Chapter 6.

- **Alhambra, Granada:** Originally conceived by the Muslims as a fortified pleasure pavilion, its allure was instantly recognized by Catholic monarchs after the Reconquest. Despite the presence in its center of a decidedly European palace, begun in 1526, the setting remains one of the most exotic (and Moorish) in all of Europe. Ironically, the European palace that rises from the center of the complex was paid for with a tax imposed upon the city's Moorish population after their defeat. See Chapter 9.
- **Alcázar, Seville:** The oldest royal residence in Europe still in use was built by Peter the Cruel (1350–69) in 1364—78 years after the Moors left Seville. One of the purest examples of the Mudéjar, or Moorish, style, its decoration is based on that of the Alhambra in Granada. Ferdinand and Isabella once lived here. A multitude of Christian and Islamic motifs are combined architecturally in this labyrinth of gardens, halls, and courts, none more notable than the Patio de las Doncellas (Court of the Maidens). Although he doesn't live in the Royal Palace in Seville, King Carlos stays here when he visits Seville. See Chapter 9.

5 The Best Museums

The Prado in Madrid is no mere museum, but a travel experience. It's worth a journey to Spain just to visit it (see above).

- **Museo Lázaro Galdiano, Madrid:** This rare collection demonstrates the evolution of enamel and ivory crafts from the Byzantine era to 19th-century Limoges. Of almost equal importance are the displays of superb medieval gold and silver work along with the Italian Renaissance jewelry. The museum also contains galleries with rare paintings, everything from Flemish primitives to works by Spanish masters of the golden age, including El Greco, Murillo, and Zurbarán. There are also paintings from Goya's "Black Period" and from such English and Italian masters as Constable and Tiepolo. See Chapter 5.
- **Thyssen-Bornemisza Museum, Madrid:** Madrid's acquisition of this treasure trove of art in the 1980s was one of the greatest art coups in European history. Amassed by a Central European connoisseur beginning around 1920, and formerly displayed in Lugano, Switzerland, its 700 canvasses are arranged in chronological order in a way that rivals the legendary holdings of the Queen of England herself. Works by artists ranging from El Greco to Picasso decorate the walls. See Chapter 5.
- **Museo de Arte Abstracto Español, Cuenca:** The angular medieval architecture of the town that contains it is an appropriate foil for a startling collection of modern masters. A group of some of Europe's most celebrated artists settled in Cuenca in the 1950s and 1960s. They included Fernando Zobel, Antoni Tàpies, Eduardo Chillida, Luis Feito, and Antonio Saura. Their works are on display here. See Chapter 6.
- **Museo de Santa Cruz, Toledo:** This is the most important museum in New Castile. Built as a hospital for the poor and orphaned by the archbishop of Toledo, this museum is known for its plateresque architecture, notably for its intricate facade, and for the wealth of art inside. Among its noteworthy collection of 16th- and 17th-century paintings are 18 works by El Greco. Don't miss his *Altarpiece of the Assumption,* completed in 1613 during his final period. His figures are elongated as never before. The gallery is also known for its collection of primitive paintings. See Chapter 6.

- **Museo Nacional de Escultura, Valladolid:** The greatest collection of gilded polychrome sculpture—an art form that reached its pinnacle in Valladolid—is on display here in the 15th-century San Gregorio College, the city's greatest Isabelline monument. Figures are first carved in wood, then painted with great artistry to achieve a lifelike appearance. The most remarkable exhibit is an altarpiece designed by Alonso Berruguete for the Church of San Benito. Also seek out his *Martyrdom of St. Sebastian.* See Chapter 7.
- **Museo Nacional de Arte Romano, Mérida:** A museum that makes most archaeologists salivate, this modern building contains hundreds of pieces of ancient Roman sculpture discovered in and around this dried-out, sun-baked Extremaduran town. The treasures built here by the Romans include theaters, amphitheaters, racecourses, and hundreds of tombs full of art objects, many of which are on display here. See Chapter 8.
- **Museo Provincial de Bellas Artes de Sevilla, Seville:** The Prado doesn't own all the great Spanish art in the country. Located in the early 17th-century convent of La Merced, this Andalusian museum is famous for its works by such Spanish masters as Valdés Leal, Zurbarán, and Murillo. Spain's golden age is best exemplified by Murillo's monumental *Immaculate Conception* and Zurbarán's *Apotheosis of St. Thomas Aquinas,* which is stunning in its play of light and shade. See Chapter 9.
- **Museu Picasso, Barcelona:** Picasso, who spent much of his formative years as an artist in Barcelona, in 1970 donated some 2,500 of his paintings, drawings, and engravings to launch this museum. Seek out his notebooks, which contain many sketches of Barcelona scenes. Here is a rare chance to see Picasso's genius developing in his early works; numerous portraits of his family, as well as examples from both his Blue Period and Rose Period are on display. His *Las Meninas* series—painted in 1959—offers exaggerated variations of the theme of the famous picture by Velázquez hanging in Madrid's Prado Museum. See Chapter 13.
- **Teatre Museu Dalí, Figueres:** The "divine" Salvador Dalí is showcased here as nowhere else. The crazed surrealist artist—known for everything from lobster telephones to *Rotting Mannequin in a Taxicab*—is presented here as theater. Dalí's mustache-antennae, dandyism, and often brilliant clowning live on here in his art. But, be warned: As Dalí's final joke, he wanted the museum to spew forth "false information." See Chapter 15.

6 The Best Cathedrals

- **Cabildo Catedral de Segovia, Segovia:** Even though Renaissance architecture was in full flower when this cathedral was built between 1515 and 1558, the builders clung to the time-favored Gothic style. Thus, the edifice became the last Gothic cathedral built in Spain. Standing on the historic plaza where Isabella I was proclaimed Queen of Castile, it is affectionately called *la dama de las catedrales.* A massive pile, it nevertheless has many architectural grace notes, including golden stones, stepped pinnacles, a tall tower, and delicate balustrades. See Chapter 6.
- **Catedral de Ávila, Ávila:** One of the earliest Gothic cathedrals in Castile, this rugged and plain edifice was called "a soldier's church." A brooding, granite monolith, which in some ways resembles a fortress, it is the centerpiece of a city that produced St. Teresa, the most famous mystic of the Middle Ages. In contrast with the foreboding exterior, the interior of the cathedral, with its High Gothic nave, is filled with notable works of art, including many plateresque statues. Its sandstone patches of red and yellow are startling. See Chapter 6.

- **Catedral de Toledo, Toledo:** Ranked among the greatest of all Gothic structures, this cathedral was built on the site of an old Arab mosque. A vast pile from the 13th through the 15th centuries, it has an interior filled with masterpieces—notably an immense polychrome retable carved in the flamboyant style and magnificent 15th- and 16th-century choir stalls. In the treasury is a splendid 16th-century silver and gilt monstrance, weighing about 500 pounds. See Chapter 6.
- **Real Monasterio de San Lorenzo de El Escorial, San Lorenzo de El Escorial:** It was commissioned in the 1530s by one of the most powerful monarchs in history, Philip II, who envisioned it as a monastic fortress against the distractions of the secular world. Frightening in its severe dignity, and more awesome than beautiful, it's the world's best example of the semifanatical religious devotion of Renaissance Spain. This huge granite fortress, the burial place for Spanish kings, houses a wealth of paintings and tapestries—works by everyone from Titian to Velázquez. See Chapter 6.
- **Catedral de León, León:** Filled with more sunlight than any other cathedral in Spain, this edifice was begun in 1250 with a design pierced with 125 stained-glass windows and 57 oculi, the oldest of which date from the 13th century. This architectural achievement, unique in Spain, is stunning but also dangerous. The sheer mass endangers the resistance of the walls. Architects fear that an urgent restoration is needed to strengthen the walls to prevent collapse. Even without the stained glass, the cathedral is filled with such treasures as well-preserved cloisters. See Chapter 7.
- **Catedral de Santa María, Burgos:** After its cornerstone was laid in 1221, it became the beneficiary of creative talent imported from England, Germany, and France. It is the third-largest cathedral in Spain, after Seville and Toledo. Art historians view it as the medieval religious building with the most diverse spectrum of sculpture in Gothic Spain—so diverse that a special name has been conjured up to describe it: the School of Burgos. El Cid is buried here. See Chapter 7.
- **Catedral Vieja & Catedral Nueva, Salamanca:** Set side by side near the banks of the Tormes River, these sibling churches date from the 1100s and the 1500s, respectively. The older and smaller Romanesque building is partially concealed by the more ostentatious bulk of the newer one. Fortunately, the later building respected the integrity of the older structure's design and merely concealed, rather than destroyed, it. The combination of the two buildings offers a rare opportunity to admire the progression of Spanish building designs within their historic settings. See Chapter 7.
- **Real Monasterio de Santa María de Guadalupe, Guadalupe:** Established by Alfonso XI in 1340, and dedicated to the "Dark Virgin" he prayed to before winning a decisive battle against the Moors, this complex of buildings grew during the 14th and early 15th centuries into one of the richest monasteries in Spain. Part of its charm derives from the needs of the builders to cram as much as possible into the cramped perimeter of fortifications built to fend off the Moors. Abandoned in 1835, then restored beginning in 1908 by the Franciscans, it's loaded with art treasures worthy of most major museums. See Chapter 8.
- **Catedral de Sevilla, Seville:** The Christians are not the only occupants of Seville who considered this site holy; an enormous mosque stood here before the *Réconquista.* To quote the Christians who built it, they planned a cathedral "so immense that everyone, on beholding it, will take us for madmen." They succeeded without a glitch: After St. Peter's in Rome and St. Paul's in London, the cathedral of this Andalusian capital is the largest in Europe. Among its most important features are the tomb of Columbus, the Patio de los Naranjos (Courtyard of the

Orange Trees), the Giralda Tower, and the Capilla Real (Royal Chapel). In the almost unbelievably rich chancel is an immense Flemish altarpiece of delicate carving, an ecclesiastical treasure. See Chapter 9.

- **Mezquita-Catedral de Córdoba, Córdoba:** In the 1500s, the Christian rulers of Spain tried to gracefully convert one of the largest and most elaborate mosques in the Muslim world, the Mezquita, into a Catholic cathedral. The result, a bizarre amalgam of Gothic and Muslim architecture, is an awesomely proportioned cultural compromise that defies categorization. In its 8th-century heyday, the Mezquita was the crowning Muslim architectural achievement in the West, rivaled only by the Mosque at Mecca. See Chapter 9.
- **Catedral de Barcelona, Barcelona:** One of the most impressive of Spain's cathedrals, this church was completed in 1450 and grew to represent the spiritual power of the Catalán empire. With its 270-foot facade and flying buttresses and gargoyles, it is the Gothic Quarter's most stunning monument. The interior is in the Catalán Gothic style with slender pillars. See Chapter 13.
- **Monestir de Poblet, near Tarragona:** It was founded by the patriarch of Catholic Catalonia (Ramón Berenguer IV) in thanks for delivering the region from the Moors. Entrusted to the Cistercians, who were known for their successful draining of marshes and development of farmland throughout neighboring France, it is today the largest Cistercian monastery in the world, and the pantheon (burial place) of several royal families. In 1835, as revolution swept through Spain, the building's artworks were sold and the monks ousted. The community of Cistercian monks who now inhabit the medieval premises has been there only since 1940. See Chapter 14.
- **Montserrat, near Barcelona:** Since its inauguration in the 9th century by Benedictine monks, it's been the preeminent religious shrine of Catalonia and the site of the legendary statue of La Moreneta (The Black Madonna). Its inhabitants have included musicians, poets, and a savvy abbot who was eventually elected as Pope Julius II, patron of the Renaissance in Italy. Its glory years ended abruptly in 1812, when it was sacked by the armies of Napoleon. Today, sitting atop a 4,000-foot mountain 7 miles long and 3$^1/_2$ miles wide, it is one of the three most important pilgrimage sites in Spain and the most popular day excursion from Barcelona. See Chapter 14.
- **Catedral de Santiago de Compostela, Santiago de Compostela:** During the Middle Ages, this verdant city on the northwestern tip of Iberia attracted thousands of religious pilgrims, who walked hundreds of miles through hostile terrain seeking salvation at the tomb of St. James. The cathedral itself shows the architectural influences of nearly 800 years of religious conviction, much of it financed by donations from exhausted pilgrims. A harmonious hybrid of styles, the cathedral is a virtual textbook in the history of Western art and architecture. Its two most stunning features are its Obradoiro facade, a baroque masterpiece, and its carved Doorway of Glory behind the facade. The immense Romanesque cathedral in which pilgrims crowded in the Middle Ages has remained more or less intact. See Chapter 20.

7 The Best Vineyards & Wineries

Here's a list of visitable bodegas in regions that include some old favorites as well as some bright newcomers that are quickly gaining international recognition. For more information about the 10 regions—and the 39 officially recognized wine-producing *Denominatións de Origen* scattered across those regions—contact **Wines from Spain,** c/o the Commercial Office of Spain, 405 Lexington Avenue, 44th Floor, New York, NY 10174-0331 (☎ **212/661-4818**).

RIBERA DEL DUERO

Set halfway between Madrid and Santander, this region near Burgos is the fastest-developing wine district in the country and the beneficiary of massive investments in the last few years. Cold nights, sunny days, the highest altitudes of any wine-producing region in Spain, and a fertile alkaline soil produce an award-winning wine with unusual flavors. Among the noteworthy individual vineyards is:

- **Bodegas Señorio de Nava, Nava de Roa** (☎ **947/55-00-03**): This is one of the region's best examples of a once-sleepy, now-booming vintner whose growth has exploded since an influx of investment. Merlot and Cabernet Sauvignon grapes are cultivated, as well as such more obscure local varieties as *Tinta del País* (also known as the *Tempranillo*) and *Garnacha* (or *grenache,* as it's called across the border in France). Some of the wines bottled here are distributed under the brand name Vega Cubillas.

JEREZ DE LA FRONTERA

This town of 200,000 inhabitants (most of whom work in the wine trade) is surrounded by a sea of vineyards, which thrive in the hot, chalky soil. Ninety-five percent of the region is planted with the hardy and flavorful *Palomino fino* to produce sherry, a wine fortified by high-alcohol additives and long one of the most beloved products of Spain. Few other regions contain so many bodegas, any of which can be visited as part of active public relations programs that are the most accommodating in Spain. Some of the outstanding choices (see also Chapter 9) include:

- **Agustín Blazquez, Jerez de la Frontera** (☎ **956/34-82-50**): Established in 1795, its products have been judged among the finest in the region since the 1980s. Connoisseurs consider this sherry a perfect accompaniment for tapas, for which the town of Jerez is well known.
- **Emilio Lustau, Jerez de la Frontera** (☎ **956/34-37-84**): This bodega was established in 1896 as a hobby of a local lawyer, and ever since has invested time and money in exotic forms of sherry snapped up as collectors' items by aficionados everywhere. In 1990 it acquired additional vineyards.
- **Antonio Barbadillo, Sanlúcar de Barrameda** (☎ **956/36-12-42**): This firm controls 70% of the sherry produced in the region around Sanlúcar, a town just 15 miles (25km) north of Jerez. Venerable and respected, it boasts one of the most impressive headquarters of any distillery in the south—a palace originally conceived as a residence for a local bishop. Although established in 1821, it remained a sleepy, small-time player until the 1960s, when production and quality zoomed upward. Some of its wine is distributed in Britain as Harvey's of Bristol.
- **González Byass, Jerez de la Frontera** (☎ **956/34-00-00**): Flourishing since 1835, this bodega has gained enormous recognition from one of the most famous brand names in the world, Tío Pepe, today the world's best-selling sherry. It isn't as picturesque as you might have hoped, since modernization has added some rather bulky concrete buildings to its historic core, but it's nonetheless one of the most visible names in the industry.
- **Pedro Domecq, Jerez de la Frontera** (☎ **956/15-15-00**): This, the oldest of all the large sherry houses, was established by an Irishman, Patrick Murphy, in 1730. Its bodega contains casks whose contents were once destined for such sherry lovers as William Pitt, Lord Nelson, and the Duke of Wellington. If you visit this

sprawling compound, look for *La Mezquita* bodega, whose many-columned interior somewhat resembles the famous mosque in Córdoba.

PENEDÉS

In ancient times, thousands of amphorae of wine were shipped from this region, near the French border, to fuel the orgies of the Roman Empire. Much of the inspiration for the present industry was developed in the 19th century by French vintners, who found the climate and soil similar to those of Bordeaux. The region produces still wines, as well as 98% of Spain's sparkling wine (*cava*), which stands an excellence chance of supplanting French champagne in the minds of celebrants throughout the world. Some of the largest producers of these regions are also the most hospitable.

- **Cordoníu, Sant Sadurní d'Anoia (☎ 93/818-32-32)**: With a history going back to the mid-1500s, this vineyard became famous after its owner, Josep Raventós, produced Spain's first version of sparkling wine. During the harvest, more than 2.2 million pounds of grapes, collected from about 1,000 growers, are pressed daily. The company's headquarters, designed around the turn of the century by Puig i Cadafalch, a student of Gaudí, sit above the 19 miles of underground tunnels where the product is aged.
- **Freixenet, Sant Sadurní d'Anoia (☎ 93/818-32-00)**: Cordoníu's largest and most innovative competitor began in 1889 as a family-run wine business, which quickly changed its production process to incorporate the radical developments in sparkling *cava*. Today, although still family-owned, it's an awesomely efficient factory pressing vast numbers of grapes, with at least a million cases sold to the United States every year. Award-winning brand names include Cordon Negro Brut and Carta Nevada Brut.
- **Miguel Torres, Vilafranca del Penedés (☎ 93/890-01-00)**: This winery was established in 1870 by a local son (Jaime Torres), who returned to his native town after making a fortune trading petroleum and oil in Cuba. On the premises today, you can see what was once the world's largest wine vat (132,000 gallons); its interior was used as the site of a banquet for 50 held in honor of the Spanish king. Today, thanks to generations of management by French-trained specialists, it's one of the most sophisticated and advanced vineyards in the region. It's also close enough to Barcelona, the beach resort of Sitges, and the ancient monastery of Montserrat to permit a side trip.

LA RIOJA

Set in the foothills of the Pyrenees, close to the French border, La Rioja turns out wines that compete with the best in the world. The region produced millions of gallons during the regime of the ancient Romans, and it boasts quality-control laws that were promulgated by a local bishop in the 9th century. Here are some of the most visitable vineyards:

- **Hérederos de Marqués de Riscal, Elciego (☎ 941/10-60-00)**: This vineyard was founded around 1850 by a local entrepreneur who learned much of his winegrowing techniques after a prolonged exile in France. Ironically, the modern-day enterprise still bases most of its income on the 492 acres acquired by the organization's founding father. Despite several disappointing years between 1975 and 1985, the site is one of the most respected in the region.
- **Bodegas Riojanas, Cenicero (☎ 941/570-66-04)**: Set on the main street of the wine-growing hamlet of Cenicero, this century-old bodega expanded massively in the 1980s, and upgraded its visitor information program. You'll be received in a

mock-feudal tower complete with crenellations, where you can grasp the nuances of the wine industry.

- **Bodegas Muga, Haro (☎ 941/31-04-98)**: This bodega adheres more to the 19th-century Old World craftsmanship than any of its competitors. The winery contains an assortment of old-fashioned casks made from American or French oak. Production is small, eclectic, and choice.
- **La Rioja Alta, Haro (☎ 941/31-03-46)**: Another bodega in the wine-growing community of Haro, this one is set near the railway station. Founded in 1890, it has all the dank and atmospheric cellars you'd expect, and was graced in 1984 by a visit from Spain's royal family. About 85% of the production at this small but quality outfit is bottled as *reservas* (aged at least three years) and *gran reservas (aged at least five years).*

GALICIA

This Celtic outpost, set in the northwestern corner of Spain, produces white wines that connoisseurs praise as almost flawless accompaniments to the seafood hauled from local estuaries. (The marketing name for the product, appropriately, is "El Vino del Mar," whereas the *Denominación de Origen* includes the appellations "Rias Baixas" and "Ribeiro.") Since wine consumption in Galicia, per capita, is significantly higher than anywhere in Spain, much of what was produced in the past was consumed locally. Massive investments during the 1980s changed all that, as you'll note after visits to the region's most viable wineries, such as:

- **Bodega Morgadio, Albeos-Crecente (☎ 986/66-61-50)**: This vineyard, near Pontevedra, launched the D.O. "Rias Baixas" in 1984. Then, four friends whom locals referred to as "madmen" bought 70 acres of land that, with the Albariño grape, they transformed into one of the most respected and award-winning vineyards in the district. Fertilizers for each year's crop comes from the bodega's own flock of sheep. The success of old-fashioned farming methods coupled with state-of-the-art fermentation tanks is a model of entrepreneurial courage in an otherwise economically depressed outpost of Spain.

8 The Best Luxury Hotels

- **Villa Magna, Madrid (☎ 91/587-12-34)**: Although it looks like a House of Parliament, it is a pocket of posh in the Spanish capital—regal, sedate, and with the aura of a country estate. Fine furnishings, beautiful linen, and such designer toiletries as fragrant Maja soaps are part of the exquisite guest rooms. Surrounded by beautiful gardens, the hotel dates only from the 1970s but looks older because of its traditional architecture. Guests are coddled. See Chapter 4.
- **Hotel Ritz, Madrid (☎ 91/521-28-57)**: Discretion and professional service unequaled in Madrid are the hallmarks of this, the capital's most distinguished hostelry. Antiques, gracious marble baths, and elegant detailing characterize the bedrooms. This Edwardian grand hotel is mellower than ever before, the old haughtiness of former managements gone with the wind—it long ago rescinded its policy of not allowing movie stars as guests. See Chapter 4.
- **Hotel Alfonso XIII, Seville (☎ 95/422-28-50)**: Built to house visitors for the Iberoamerican Exposition of 1929, this grand hotel features Moorish-style rooms, with doors opening onto little balconies overlooking a Spanish courtyard with a bubbling fountain and potted palms. Set in front of the city's fabled Alcázar, the Alfonso XIII is one of the most legendary hotels of Spain. Hand-painted tiles,

marble, and mahogany can overwhelm, but a welcoming bowl of oranges adds a human touch. See Chapter 9.

- **La Bobadilla, Loja (☎ 958/32-18-61)**: The most luxurious retreat in the south of Spain, this secluded oasis lies in the foothills of the Sierra Nevada, an hour's drive northeast of Málaga. Whitewashed *casas* cluster around a tower and a church. Each individually designed *casa* is complete with a roof terrace and balcony overlooking olive groves. Guests live in luxury within the private compound of 1,750 acres. See Chapter 10.
- **Marbella Club, Marbella (☎ 95/282-22-13)**: Built during the "golden age" of the Costa del Sol (the 1950s), this bastion of chic is composed of ecologically conscious clusters of garden pavilions, bungalows, and small-scale annexes. Luxurious rooms are taken from the pages of a European design magazine. It has many competitors, but remains an elite retreat. See Chapter 10.
- **Puente Romano, Marbella (☎ 95/282-09-00)**: On manicured and landscaped grounds facing the beach, Puente Romano evokes a highly stylized Andalusian village. Exotic bird life flutters its way through the lush gardens, planted with banana trees and other vegetation. Villas are spacious and beautifully furnished, with marble floors and baths, big mirrors, and tasteful wood furnishings. The pampered life holds forth here; in summer the flamenco dancers come in to entertain. See Chapter 10.
- **Hotel Ritz, Barcelona (☎ 93/318-52-00)**: A 1919 *grand luxe* hotel, this is one of the finest in Spain, if not all of Europe. Guests are wrapped in dazzling elegance, with all the gilt, marble, and fresh flowers they would ever want. Classic Belle Epoque detailing extends to the plush guest quarters, many of which have high, ornate ceilings and gold bathroom fixtures. See Chapter 12.
- **Hotel María Cristina, San Sebastián (☎ 943/42-49-00)**: One of the country's great Belle Epoque treasures, this quintessential Old World seafront hotel has sheltered discriminating guests since 1912. Oriental rugs, antiques, potted palms, high ceilings, formal lounges, marble pillars, and marble floors show off a turn-of-the-century glamour. The bedrooms, naturally, are traditional with wood furnishings and tasteful pastel fabrics. There's nothing in the Basque country that measures up to this old charmer. See Chapter 18.
- **La Residencia, Deià, Majorca (☎ 971/63-90-11)**: Set amid 30 acres of citrus and olive groves, this tranquil hotel was converted from two Renaissance-era manor houses. Jasmine-scented terraces open onto stunning views of the surrounding villages and mountains. Pampered guests are served a creative cuisine that features local produce. Leisure facilities include a swimming pool fed by mountain spring water. Many of the bedrooms have regal four-poster beds. It's a haven from the rest of the overcrowded Majorca. See Chapter 21.

9 The Best Affordable Hotels

- **Hostal del Cardenal, Toledo (☎ 925/22-49-00)**: The summer residence of Toledo's 18th-century Cardinal Lorenzano, built into the walls of the old city next to the Bisagra Gate, just happens to be Toledo's best restaurant. But the setting—rose gardens, cascading vines, and Moorish fountains—makes it an ideal place to stay as well. Spanish furniture and a scattering of antiques recapture the aura of Castile. See Chapter 6.
- **Posada de San José, Cuenca (☎ 969/21-13-00)**: This hotel, located in the oldest part of medieval Cuenca, is a remarkable bargain. In the 17th century, it sheltered sisters of a convent; the rooms, now decorated in *rústica* style, have been converted

to receive guests. Views are superb; the *posada* sits atop a cliff, overlooking the forbidding depths of a gorge and the river below. See Chapter 6.

- **Hostería Real de Zamora, Zamora (☎ 980/53-45-45)**: It was once the dreaded headquarters of the local Spanish Inquisition; today the welcome is far friendlier. Hotel guests enjoy coffee on the patio and the pleasure of a garden planted along the city's medieval fortifications. If these 15th-century walls could talk . . . See Chapter 7.
- **Hotel Doña María, Seville (☎ 95/422-49-90)**: Near the fabled cathedral, this hotel boasts a rooftop terrace with unmatched views of the Andalusian capital. A private villa that dates from the 1840s, the Doña María has a swimming pool ringed with garden-style lattices and antique wrought-iron railings. Bedrooms are uniquely designed with tasteful Iberian antiques. See Chapter 9.
- **Hotel Reina Victoria, Ronda (☎ 95/287-12-40)**: This country-style hotel is best known as the place where the German poet Rainer Maria Rilke wrote *The Spanish Trilogy.* Its terrace, perched on a dramatic precipice, offers commanding views of the countryside. An Englishman built this Victorian charmer in 1906 to honor his recently deceased monarch, Queen Victoria. Ernest Hemingway, a frequent visitor, suggested the setting was ideal for a honeymoon. See Chapter 9.
- **Hotel América, Granada (☎ 958/22-74-71)**: This onetime private villa, located within the walls of the Alhambra, is one of the most popular small hotels in Granada. Its homey bedrooms are filled with reproductions of Andalusian antiques. Plants cascade down the white plaster walls and entwine with ornate grillwork on the shady patio. Good-tasting, inexpensive meals are served in the hotel restaurant. See Chapter 9.
- **Hotel Mijas, Mijas (☎ 95/248-58-00)**: The most charming of the "affordable" hotels along the Costa del Sol. It's designed in the typical Andalusian style with flowering terraces, wrought-iron accents, and sun-flooded bedrooms. Though built in the 1970s, it blends in perfectly with the region's gleaming white buildings. See Chapter 10.
- **Huerto del Cura, Elche (☎ 96/545-80-40)**: From your bedroom you'll have a panoramic view of Priest's Grove, a formidable, and quite famous, date-palm forest. Between Alicante and Murcia, this is one of the choice addresses in the south of Spain. Bedrooms are handsomely maintained and beautifully furnished, and a swimming pool separates the palm grove from the rooms. The regional cuisine in the hotel's restaurant is excellent. See Chapter 11.
- **Mesón Castilla, Barcelona (☎ 93/318-21-82)**: This two-star charmer with an art nouveau facade lies right in the heart of Barcelona. It is a well-maintained and well-managed hotel with prices that are blessedly easy on the wallet. Comfortable rooms often come with large terraces. Only breakfast is served, but there are many nearby taverns with excellent food. See Chapter 12.
- **Hotel Pampinot, Fuenterrabía (☎ 943/64-06-00)**: The Infanta María Teresa stayed at this 16th-century aristocratic mansion on a journey to France for her eventual marriage to the Sun King, Louis XIV. Now a stately hotel, it's on a quiet side street in this Basque seaside resort, near the French border. Behind a richly textured stone facade and Renaissance detailing are bedrooms furnished with both antiques and reproductions. See Chapter 18.

10 The Best Paradors

Funded and maintained by the government, Spain's paradors (*paradores* in Spanish) showcase a building or setting of important cultural and historic interest. Some are, admittedly, much older, grander, and more interesting than others. Here are the country's most interesting and unusual.

- **Parador de Ávila, Ávila (☎ 920/21-13-40)**: Built as an enlargement of a 15th-century palace (Palacio de Piedras Albas, also known as the Palacio de Benavides), it features gardens that flank the northern fortifications of this well-preserved, 11th-century walled city. Only some of the comfortable, airy bedrooms lie within the original palace—but it's still the region's most intriguing hotel. In the parador restaurant, try the roast suckling pig, a specialty of the region. See Chapter 6.
- **Parador de Turismo de Cuenca, Cuenca (☎ 969/23-23-20)**: This 16th-century building, once a Dominican convent, is one of the most recently inaugurated paradors in Spain. Like the medieval houses for which Cuenca is famous, the balconies of this parador jut out over rocky cliffs, overlooking swift-moving rivers below. The sight of the *casas colgadas,* or "suspended houses," is simply unforgettable. An adjoining restaurant specializes in seasonal wild game. See Chapter 6.
- **Parador Nacional de Conde Orgaz, Toledo (☎ 925/22-18-50)**: This is a relatively modern building, though the architecture subtly evokes much older models. Views from the windows, boasting a faraway glimpse of the city's historic core, evoke the scenes El Greco painted in his *View of Toledo.* A swimming pool comes as a welcome relief in sultry Toledo. Such regional dishes as stewed partridge are featured in the hotel restaurant. See Chapter 6.
- **Parador Nacional Enrique II, Ciudad Rodrigo (☎ 923/46-01-50)**: Few lodgings in Europe evoke such a vivid sense of the feudal ages. This 12th-century castle is a sprawling mass of battlements, turrets, and impossibly thick masonry, all restored by the Spanish government. The bedrooms are severe and dignified, and the views over the undulating fields are soothing. The stone-arched dining room serves excellent roasts, Iberian sausages, and hams—all specialties of the region. See Chapter 7.
- **Parador San Marcos, León (☎ 987/23-73-00)**: Originally home to the Order of Santiago, a group of knights charged with protecting pilgrims who journeyed across northern Spain in the 12th century, the building was expanded and embellished into a monastery some 400 years later. These days, it's one of Spain's most deluxe paradors—set beside the Bernesga River and including a lavishly decorated church on the grounds. With a dramatic lobby, grand entranceway, huge cast-iron chandelier, and stone staircases, the public areas are a model of medieval grandeur. See Chapter 7.
- **Parador Turistico de Zamora, Zamora (☎ 980/51-44-97)**: Among the most beautiful and richly decorated paradors in Spain is this onetime Moorish fortress, turned Renaissance palace. A medieval aura is reflected in the details: armor, coats-of-arms, tapestries, and attractive four-poster beds. A swimming pool enhances the tranquil rear garden. Such Castilian cookery as stuffed roast veal typifies the restaurant's offerings. See Chapter 7.
- **Parador de Cáceres, Cáceres (☎ 927/21-17-59)**: Live like royalty at this palace, built in the 1400s on the site of Arab fortifications. The parador lies in the city's old quarter, recently declared a World Heritage Site. The spacious public areas are decorated with soft cream shades and rough-hewn ceiling beams. Venison with Casar cheese and roast kid with rosemary are typical of the varied Extremaduran cuisine served in the parador restaurant. See Chapter 8.
- **Parador Nacional de Trujillo, Trujillo (☎ 927/32-13-50)**: A parador set in the inviting 16th-century convent of Santa Clara. Originally built in a combination of medieval and Renaissance styles, the building was transformed into a hotel in

1984. The bedrooms are considerably more lavish than they were during their stint as nun's cells. The cuisine is the best in town. See Chapter 8.

- **Parador Vía de la Plata, Mérida (☎ 924/31-38-00)**: A 16th-century building that was, at various times, a convent and a prison, this parador once hosted a meeting between the much-hated dictators of Spain (Franco) and Portugal (Salazar) in the 1960s. Mudéjar, Roman, and Visigothic elements adorn the interior in unusual but stunning juxtaposition. The inner courtyard and Mozarabic gardens add a grace note. The kitchen serves the best of the area, including gazpacho, *calderetas extremeñas* (stews), and the famous Almoharin figs. See Chapter 8.
- **Parador Castillo de Santa Catalina, Jaén (☎ 953/23-00-00)**: In the 10th century, Muslims built this foreboding fortress on a cliff high above town. After the *Réconquista,* the Christians added Gothic vaulting and touches of luxury, which remain in place thanks to a renovation by the government. Bedrooms provide sweeping views over Andalusia. A swimming pool is a welcome retreat from the burning sun. Sample such dishes as cold garlic soup and partridge salad in the panoramic restaurant. See Chapter 9.
- **Parador de Santillana del Mar, Santillana del Mar (☎ 942/81-80-00)**: This bucolic parador recalls the manor houses that dotted northern Spain's verdant hillsides more than 400 years ago. Composed of thick stone walls and heavy timbers, it's pleasantly isolated and elegantly countrified. An added bonus: its proximity to what has been called "the Sistine Chapel of prehistoric art"—the Caves of Altamira. See Chapter 19.
- **Parador El Molino Viejo, Gijón (☎ 98/537-05-11)**: As the name implies, this hotel grew up around the decrepit remains of a cider mill (and the antique presses are still on hand). Close to San Lorenzo Beach, it's the only parador in the northern province of Asturias. The dining room serves up typical Asturian cuisine, including the famous *fabada,* a rich white bean and pork stew. See Chapter 19.
- **Parador Nacional Casa del Barón, Pontevedra (☎ 986/85-58-00)**: The building is a 16th-century Renaissance palace built on foundations that are at least 200 years older than that. It's most famous, however, for being one of Spain's first paradors. Inaugurated in 1955, its success led to the amplification of the parador program. The parador is still alluring today, with its delightful terrace garden and stately dining room, which serves the fresh fish and seafood for which Galicia is known. See Chapter 20.
- **Hostal de Los Reyes Católicos, Santiago de Compostela (☎ 981/58-22-00)**: The best for last—this is one of the most spectacular hotels in Europe. Originally a hospice for wayfaring pilgrims, it boasts a lavish 16th-century facade, four open-air courtyards, and a bedchamber once occupied by Franco. Today the hotel is a virtual museum, with Gothic, Renaissance, and baroque architectural elements. There are four cloisters of immense beauty, elegant public areas, and spectacular bedrooms. See Chapter 20.

11 The Best Luxury Restaurants

- **El Amparo, Madrid (☎ 91/431-64-56):** In the old days of Franco, gastronomes flocked to Jockey or Horcher. Today their savvy sons and daughters head to El Amparo, the trendiest of Madrid's gourmet restaurants. It serves mainly haute Basque cuisine, and it does so against a backdrop of cosmopolitan glamor. Patrons sample everything from cold marinated salmon with a tomato sorbet to ravioli stuffed with seafood. See Chapter 4.

- **Chez Victor, Salamanca (☎ 923/21-31-23)**: In the historic center of this university town, this is the most glamorous and continental restaurant around. Chef Victoriano Salvador gives customers terrific value for their pesetas with his imaginative, oft-renewed menus. The freshly prepared fish and his traditional version of roast lamb are especially tempting. Regionally rooted but modern in outlook, Salvador has a finely honed technique and isn't afraid to be inventive on occasion. See Chapter 7.
- **Jaume de Provenca, Barcelona (☎ 93/430-00-29)**: The Catalán capital has more starred restaurants than even Madrid. At the western end of the Eixample district, this Catalán/French restaurant is the domain of one of the city's most talented chefs, Jaume Bargués. He serves modern interpretations of traditional Catalán and southern French cuisine—such dishes as pig's trotters with plums and truffles or crabmeat lasagne. The cooking from his personal repertoire is distinctive, and occasionally new taste sensations are created when he's feeling experimental. See Chapter 12.
- **Botafumiero, Barcelona (☎ 93/218-42-30)**: The city's best seafood is prepared here, in a glistening, modern kitchen visible from the dining room. The King of Spain is a frequent patron, enjoying paellas, *zarzuelas,* or any of the hundred or so ultrafresh seafood dishes. The chef's treatment of the fish is the most intelligent and subtle in town—but don't expect cheap prices. See Chapter 12.
- **Ampurdán, Figueres (☎ 972/50-05-62)**: Although ordinary on the outside, this hotel restaurant is one of the finest on the Costa Brava. It was a favorite of Salvador Dalí, who once wrote his own cookbook. Haute Catalán cuisine is the specialty—everything from duck foie gras with Armagnac to suprême of sea bass with flan. The flavors are refined yet definite, and the food here warms our hearts. See Chapter 15.
- **Akelare, San Sebastián (☎ 943/21-20-52)**: San Sebastián owner/chef Pedro Sabijana pioneered the school of *nueva cocina vasco* (modern Basque cuisine). His restaurant has attracted gourmets from around Europe. Sabijana transforms such seemingly simple dishes as fish cooked on a griddle with garlic and parsley into something magical. No other eatery in northern Spain comes close to equaling the superb viands dispensed here. There are those—and we are among them—who consider Subijana the best chef in Spain. See Chapter 18.

12 The Best Affordable Restaurants

- **Sobrino de Botín, Madrid (☎ 91/366-42-17)**: Since 1725, this restaurant—so beloved by Hemingway, who mentioned it in *The Sun Also Rises* —has been celebrated for its roast suckling pig, prepared in a tile oven that dates back two centuries. The roast Segovian lamb is equally delectable. There is little subtlety of flavor here—only food prepared by time-tested recipes that have appealed to kings as well as Castilian peasants. And the aromas waft clear across Madrid's old town. See Chapter 4.
- **Mesón de Candido, Segovia (☎ 921/42-59-11)**: Gastronomes from around the country flock to this 19th-century Spanish inn, "The House of Candido," for one dish: roast suckling pig, acclaimed the best in Spain (even by Hemingway, who might otherwise be seen at Botín in Madrid). In Spanish it's called *cochinillo asado,* and it's delectable—prepared according to a century-old recipe. Here's our secret: the *cordero asado,* or roast baby lamb, is equally flavorful. See Chapter 6.
- **Mesón Casa Colgadas, Cuenca (☎ 969/22-35-09)**: Without a doubt the most spectacularly sited restaurant in Spain—a "hanging house" suspended over a

precarious precipice. The cookery is Spanish and international, with an emphasis on regional ingredients. The dishes can be ingenious, but the culinary repertoire usually reflects time-tested classics that might have pleased your grandparents. See Chapter 6.

- **El Caballo Rojo, Córdoba (☎ 957/47-53-75)**: Begin your evening with a sherry in the popular bar, followed by a visit to the traditional dining room. Not only Andalusian dishes are served here; some classics are based on ancient Sephardic and Mozarabic specialties. Most guests begin with a soothing gazpacho and wash everything down with locally produced sangría. Finish off the meal with one of the homemade ice creams, especially pistachio. See Chapter 9.
- **Galbis, Valencia (☎ 96/380-94-73)**: Crowds come for the good Valenciano cuisine, the filling portions, and the reasonable prices. The cuisine is traditional and unassuming but excellent in texture and flavor. Try the salad of roasted peppers with duck or the roast lamb flavored with Mediterranean herbs. Of course, since Valencia is the home of paella, you might want to try that dish on its home turf. See Chapter 11.
- **Los Caracoles, Barcelona (☎ 93/302-31-85)**: Legend has it that this restaurant is so old it was around to welcome the Roman armies. Actually it's been feeding hungry locals only since 1835. But any restaurant that has thrived that long must be doing something right. These days, a young, sophisticated crowd of food lovers has discovered the full array of hearty Catalán and Spanish dishes served here. The namesake snails are always worth a try. See Chapter 12.

13 The Best Festivals

- **The Autumn Festival, Madrid:** Held in October and November, it's the best music festival in Spain, with a line-up that attracts the cream of the European and South American musical communities. The usual roster of chamber music, symphonic pieces, and orchestral works is supplemented by a program of *zarzuela* (musical comedy), as well as Arabic and Sephardic pieces that were composed during the Middle Ages. For information and tickets, call **91/580-25-75.**
- **Feria del Caballo (Horse Fair), Jerez de la Frontera:** Few events show off Spain's equestrian traditions in such a flattering light. Costumes are appropriately ornate; riders demonstrate the stern, carefully controlled movements developed during countless medieval battles; and the entire city of Jerez (otherwise famous for its sherry) becomes one enormous riding ring for the presentation of dressage and jumping events. Horse buying and trading is commonplace at this May event; especially coveted is a graceful type of white horse (*Cartujanos*) first bred by the Moors. For information, contact the Office of Tourism in Jerez de la Frontera (**☎ 956/33-11-50**).
- **Los Hogueres de Sant Joan (St. John's Bonfires), Alicante:** Bonfires blaze through the night on June 20 as a celebration of a festival revered by the Celtic pagans and Romans alike—the summer solstice. Stacks of flammable objects, including discarded finery and cardboard replicas of sinners and witches, are set ablaze in a ceremony that reminds some observers of the auto-da-fés during the Inquisition. The bonfire signals the beginning of five days of nightly fireworks and daily parades during which normal business comes virtually to a standstill. For information, contact the Office of Tourism in Alicante (**☎ 96/520-00-00**).
- **Misteri d'Elx (The Mystery of Elche), Elche:** Based on the reputed mystical powers of an ancient, black-faced statue of the Virgin, the citizens of Elche have staged a mystery play in the local church every year for more than six centuries. The

chanting and songs that accompany the plot line are in an archaic dialect that even the Castilians can barely understand. Competition is fierce for seats during the August event, and celebrations precede and follow the play. For information, contact the Tourist Office in Elche (☎ **96/545-27-47**).

- **Moros y Cristianos (Moors and Christians), Alcoy, near Alicante:** The agonizing, century-long process of evicting the Moors from Iberia is re-created during two days of simulated, vaudeville-style fighting between "Moors" and "Christians" every April (dates vary). Circus-style costumes worn by the Moors are as absurdly anachronistic as possible. When the Christians win, a statue of the Virgin is carried proudly through the city as proof of Alcoy's staunchly passionate defense of its role as a bastion of Christianity. For information, contact the Tourist Office in Alicante (☎ **96-520-00-00**).
- **A Rapa das Bestas (The Capture of the Beasts), San Lorenzo de Sabuceno, Galicia:** In the verdant hills of northwestern Spain, horses graze at will, oblivious to boundary markers and borders. On the first weekend of July, they are rounded up and herded into a corral, in a ritual that evokes the Wild West. There, each is branded, then released back into the wild after a few days of medical observation. For information, contact the Office of Tourism in Pontevedra (☎ **986/85-08-14**).

14 The Best Beach Coasts

Though it is flanked to the east by France and the Pyrenees and to the west by Portugal, most of Spain is completely ringed with rock, sand, and seawater. That, coupled with almost endless sunshine, has attracted million of beachgoers. Here are the best bets.

- **Costa de la Luz:** Ths stretch of coastline in southwestern Andalusia boasts long stretches of sand deposited by four important rivers, and the almost constant sunlight for which the coast is named. The blue, though sometimes rough, Atlantic waters are enticement enough, as is the region's proximity to several historic cities. Foremost of the coastal cities is Cádiz, and Seville is just a short drive inland. Despite the region's allure, it's less developed than equivalent beaches along the more popular, and more frenetic, Costa del Sol. See Chapter 9.
- **Costa del Sol:** Stretching east from Gibraltar along the southernmost coast of Spain, the Costa del Sol is the most famous, most risqué, and most overdeveloped string of beaches in Iberia. The beaches are superbly sandy, and the Mediterranean waters are calm and warm throughout most of the year. But these charms have brought throngs of upscale emigrants (many of whom are European retirees) and beachgoers, who make this the most congested group of coastal resorts in Europe. The most important resorts are Marbella, Torremolinos, Málaga, and Nerja. Look for soaring, ugly skyscrapers; bikinis and monokinis that stretch the limits of decency; a sophisticated internationalism, one of the most pronounced in Spain; lots of sunlight; and interminable traffic jams. See Chapter 10.
- **Costa Blanca:** This southeastern coast embraces the industrial city of Valencia, but its best-known resorts are Benidorm and Alicante, both of which are packed with northern European sun-seekers every year. The surrounding scenery isn't particularly dramatic—flat, sunbaked terrain bathed in a stark white light. But the water is turquoise, the sand is white, and a low annual rainfall virtually guarantees a sunny holiday. See Chapter 11.
- **Costa Brava:** Rockier, more serpentine, and without the long stretches of sand that mark the Costa Blanca, the cliff-edged Costa Brava stretches from Barcelona to the French border. Charming, sandy-bottomed coves proliferate. Although there are

fewer "undiscovered" beaches here than along Spain's Atlantic coast, the Costa Brava still retains a sense of the rocky wilderness that inspired its name, which translates as the "Wild Coast." One of the more eccentric-looking villas along this coast belonged to the late Salvador Dalí, the region's most famous modern son. See Chapter 15.

- **Costa Verde:** Radically different from the sunbaked and desiccated coastline of Andalusia, the rocky Costa Verde (Green Coast) resembles a sunnier version of Ireland's western shore. It's temperate in summer, when the rest of Spain can be unbearably hot. Much of the coast is contained within the ancient province of Asturias, a region rife with Romanesque architecture and medieval pilgrimage sites— and one that has not yet been overwhelmed with tourism. Premier resorts include some districts of Santander, Gijón, and—a short distance inland—Oviedo. See Chapter 19.
- **Balearic Islands:** Just off the coast of Catalonia, this rocky, sand-fringed archipelago has attracted English poets, urban refugees seeking ultraviolet rays, jet-set glitterati, and Eurotrashy exhibitionists in scanty beachwear. The Mediterranean climate is warmer here than on the mainland. Although worthy beaches stretch for miles around all the islands, Palma de Majorca has the greatest number of high-rises and the most crowded shorelines. Sleepy Menorca and the southern coast of Ibiza offer more isolation. See Chapter 21.

15 The Best Small Villages

- **Cuenca:** Set amid a landscape of rugged limestone outcroppings at the junction of two rivers, Cuenca is a fascinating combination of medieval masonry and cantilevered balconies that seem to float above the vertiginous gorges far below. The architecture's angularity is said to have inspired early versions of cubism, a fact commemorated in a village museum, the Museo de Arte Abstracto Español,which is often called one of the finest modern art museums in Spain. See Chapter 6.
- **Zafra:** The cubists are said to have been inspired by the angular, stark white architecture of Zafra, whose cattle graze in sunbaked fields in ways that evoke similar scenes many hundreds of years ago. Although sleepier today than during its years of glory, its 15th-century castle is the largest and best preserved in the region, set within an architectural pearl. See Chapter 8.
- **Baeza:** After it was wrenched away from the Moors in 1227, it became a frontier town between the Christian and Moorish worlds, a diehard symbol of the Catholic ambition to occupy all of Iberia. Today, despite the town's general sleepiness, a wealth of architecture survives as evidence of the acquisitive passions that once fueled Iberian dynasties. See Chapter 9.
- **Carmona:** Pint-sized, sleepy Carmona—usually visited from Seville—packs a historical wallop and lots of references to the Roman occupation of Iberia. The town claims an architectural legacy from every occupying force dating back to 206 B.C., when a Roman general demolished the resident Carthaginian army. Fortunately, an economic slump in the early part of this century prevented "modernization" from destroying the town's Andalusian authenticity. See Chapter 9.
- **Ronda:** The site appears inhospitable—a gorge slices through the town center, its twin halves (the newer of which dates from around 1500) interconnected with bridges that are antiques in their own right. But the winding streets of this old Moorish town are perfect for wandering (and getting lost), and with Ronda's unusual vantage point, the views of the surrounding Andalusian countryside are

stupendous. Ronda is also revered by bullfighting aficionados, both because of its bullring (the oldest and most beautiful in Spain) and the region's skill in breeding what are considered the fiercest bulls in the country. See Chapter 9.

- **Mijas:** The town itself, rather than any particular monument within it, is the attraction here. The allure involves wandering through streets and alleyways known in ages past to the Phoenicians, the Celts, and the Moors. Today, it offers a welcome dose of medieval flair to a Costa del Sol otherwise filled with mostly modern and often ugly resort hotels. See Chapter 10.
- **Elche:** These days, in this place favored by every major wave of society since the Celts, you can see date palms said to have been planted originally by the Phoenicians and a mystery play celebrating the Assumption of the Virgin, which has been performed in the village church every year since the 1300s. Although famed as a charming medieval village, Elche is best known as the excavation site of one of the premier sculptures of the Roman Empire in Iberia, *La Dama de Elche,* now exhibited in Madrid's archaeological museum. See Chapter 11.
- **Cadaqués:** The 16th-century church that dominates this town from a nearby hilltop isn't particularly noteworthy. But Cadaqués—on the Costa Brava near the French border—still charms, with a combination of Catalán nostalgia and whitewashed, fishing-village simplicity. The azure waters of the Mediterranean appealed to surrealist master Salvador Dalí, who built a suitably bizarre villa in the adjoining hamlet of Lligat. See Chapter 15.

16 The Best of Roman Spain

- **Segovia:** The Roman aqueduct here is one of the finest left in the world. Amazingly, this elegant structure—constructed during the reign of Trajan in the 1st century A.D.—is still operating. The 2,388-foot-long aqueduct carries water from the Río Acebeda in the Sierra de Fuenfria to the upper part of Segovia. Constructed of mortarless granite, it has 118 arches. In one two-tiered section, it rises to its highest point of 95 feet. Castilians proudly call it *El Puente* ("The Bridge"). See Chapter 6.
- **Mérida:** Studded with ancient monuments, Mérida was founded in 25 B.C.; the Romans named it Augusta Emerita. It lay at the crossroads linking Salamanca and Seville and Toledo and Lisbon. A splendid city in its Roman heyday, Mérida was in fact called a "miniature Rome." Evidence of those glory days remain: its Roman bridge, stretching for half a mile with 64 arches, is the longest in Spain. The Anfiteatro Romano, from the 1st century B.C., could hold 15,000 spectators, who came to watch the chariot races. Gladiator combats and mock sea battles were also held here. A third major attraction is the Museo Nacional de Arte Romano, containing more than 30,000 artifacts from the ancient capital Augusta Emerita. See Chapter 8.
- **Tarragona:** This ancient port city, south of Barcelona, stands on a rocky bluff above the Mediterranean. Often called the "second city" of Catalonia, it was captured by the Romans as early as 218 B.C. At its peak, Tarragona had a population of some one million living behind its 40-mile-long city walls. Today, among the city's best preserved monuments is the Amfiteatre Romà, carved out of a cliff rising from the beach. In the 2nd century A.D., thousands were entertained here. The Museu Nacional Arqueològic contains the best collection of Roman relics, notably a mesmerizing *Head of Medusa,* much reproduced in art books. Finally, visit the Necròpolis, one of the most important burial grounds in Spain, used by Christians from the 3rd through the 5th centuries. See Chapter 14.

2 Getting to Know Spain

The once-accepted adage that "Europe ends at the Pyrenees" is no longer true. Today, the two countries forming the Iberian Peninsula at the southwestern end of the continent—Spain and Portugal—are totally integrated in Europe as members of the European Union, with democratic governments and vibrant economies of their own. In fact, Spain has the fastest-growing economy in the EU; new industries and an expanding infrastructure continue to alter its ancient landscape.

The political changes adopted after the death of Gen. Francisco Franco—Europe's last prewar dictator—in 1975 contributed to a remarkable cultural renaissance, known as *la movida.* This rebirth has transformed Spain's two largest cities—Madrid, the capital, and Barcelona—into major European centers of artistic and intellectual activity. Here, amid some of the world's most innovative architecture, contemporary movements in art, literature, the cinema, and fashion are constantly finding new and original expression; and at night the cafés and bars hum with animated discussions on politics, the economy, society. In every aspect of urban life, a visitor can feel the Spanish people's reawakened self-confidence and pride in their newfound prosperity.

The vitality and excitement of today's Spain have made it a popular place to visit. Indeed, this land of jeweled Moorish palaces, sun-drenched beaches, terraced vineyards, sleepy fishing villages, primeval *corridas* (bullfights) and sensuous flamenco has become the sophisticated "playground of Europe."

These developments contrast with Spain's unhappy experiences at other periods in this century, particularly during the devastating Civil War of 1936–39 and Franco's subsequent long rule. During the Franco years, political and intellectual freedom was limited, and Spain was snubbed by most of Europe.

Earlier in its history, Spain had played a major role in the Mediterranean world. In the 16th century it was the seat of a great empire; the Spanish monarchy dispatched fleets that conquered the New World, returning with its riches. Columbus sailed to America and Balboa to the Pacific Ocean; Cortés conquered Mexico for glory; and Pizarro brought Peru into the Spanish fold.

The conquistadors too often revealed the negative side of the Spanish character, including an adoption of brutality in the name of honor and glory. These adventurers, however, also embodied the positive side, the belief that the "impossible dream" was possible. No character in Spain's literary history has better embodied this idealism than Don Quixote, whose tilting at windmills on the plains of La Mancha has served for centuries as a parable of the Spanish soul.

It's difficult to visit this country without recalling its golden past: those famous "castles in Spain" really do exist. Yet to many, Spain isn't a single country but a series of nations, united the way Yugoslavia used to be. Many groups, especially the Basques, the Cataláns, and the Gallegos in the northeast, are asserting their individuality in everything from culture to language. Despite these independence movements, Castile and Andalusia, in the south, remain quintessentially Spanish, at least to the foreign visitor.

As the inheritors of a great and ancient civilization dating from before the Roman Empire, Spaniards live in a land as culturally rich as it is geographically varied, with wooded sierras, arid plateaus, and sandy beaches. It is this exciting variety in landscape, as well as in art, architecture, music, and cuisine, that makes Spain one of the top countries in the world to visit. In the number of foreign tourists who make a cultural pilgrimage to its soil, Spain ranks alongside France, Italy, and England.

1 Regions in Brief

Three times the size of Illinois, with a population of nearly 40 million, Spain faces the Atlantic Ocean and the Bay of Biscay to the north and the Mediterranean Sea to the south and east. Portugal borders on the west, whereas the high Pyrenees separate Spain from France and the rest of Europe. The southern coastline is only a few sea miles from the north coast of Africa. One finds it almost impossible to generalize about Spain because it is composed of so many regions—50 provinces in all—each with its own physical makeup, history, and culture. The country's topography divides it into many regions: The Cantabrian Mountains in the north, those of Cuenca in the east, and the Sierra Morena in the south mark off a high central tableland that itself is cut across by other hills.

Madrid & Environs Set on a high and arid plateau near the geographic center of Iberia, Madrid was created by royal decree in the 1600s, long after the much older kingdoms of León, Navarre, Aragón, and Catalonia, and long after the final Moor was ousted by Catholic armies. Since its debut, all roads within Spain have radiated outward from its precincts, and as the country's most important airline and railway hub, it's likely to be your point of arrival.

Despite the city's increasingly unpleasant urban sprawl, its paralyzing traffic jams, and prices that, in the 1990s, roared upward to compete with those of London and Paris, Madrid packs a lot of bang for your tourist peseta. Take in the Prado, the Thyssen-Bornemisza Museum, and perhaps the Royal Palace. Walk through historic neighborhoods around the Plaza Mayor (though beware of muggers). Devote time to one of the city's greatest pastimes, a round of tapas tasting.

Plan on at least two days to explore the city and another three for trips to the attractions beyond the capital. Almost more important than Madrid is a day trip to the imperial city of Toledo—brimming with monuments and paintings by El Greco and home to one of Spain's greatest cathedrals. Other worthy excursions include a view of the Roman aqueduct at Segovia, tours through such monuments to religious and political megalomania as El Escorial, and a visit to the "hanging village" of Cuenca, site of a world-class museum of modern art.

Spain

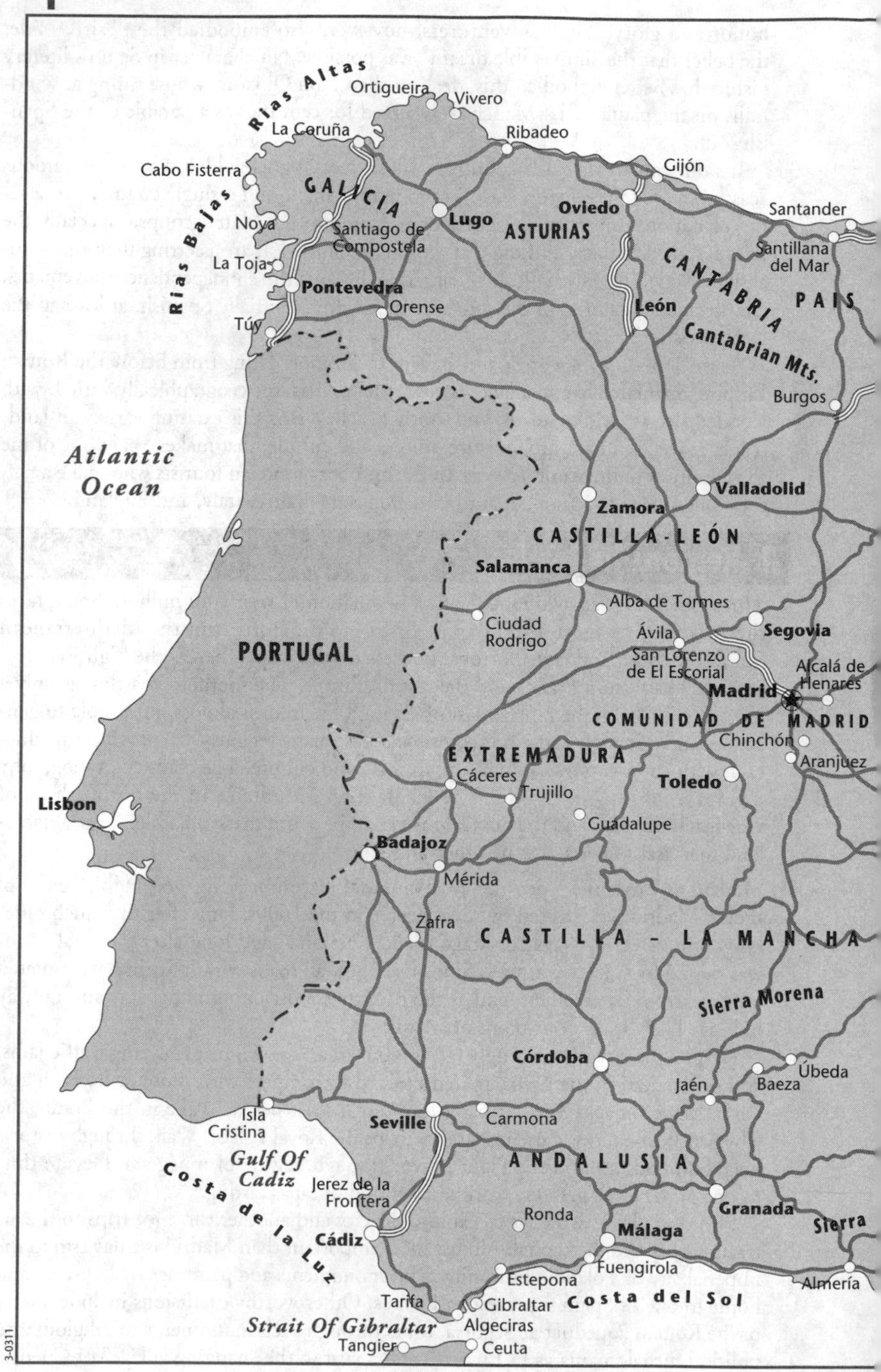

Rias Altas
Ortigueira
Vivero
La Coruña
Ribadeo
Cabo Fisterra
Gijón
GALICIA
Oviedo
Santander
Rias Bajas
Noya
Lugo
ASTURIAS
Santiago de Compostela
Santillana del Mar
La Toja
CANTABRIA
Pontevedra
PAIS
Orense
León
Túy
Cantabrian Mts.
Burgos
Atlantic Ocean
Valladolid
Zamora
CASTILLA-LEÓN
Salamanca
Alba de Tormes
Ciudad Rodrigo
Segovia
Ávila
PORTUGAL
San Lorenzo de El Escorial
Alcalá de Henares
Madrid
COMUNIDAD DE MADRID
Chinchón
EXTREMADURA
Aranjuez
Cáceres
Toledo
Trujillo
Lisbon
Guadalupe
Badajoz
Mérida
Zafra
CASTILLA - LA MANCHA
Sierra Morena
Córdoba
Úbeda
Baeza
Jaén
Isla Cristina
Seville
Carmona
Gulf Of Cadiz
ANDALUSIA
Costa de la Luz
Jerez de la Frontera
Granada
Ronda
Sierra
Cádiz
Málaga
Fuengirola
Estepona
Almería
Tarifa
Gibraltar
Costa del Sol
Strait Of Gibraltar
Algeciras
Tangier
Ceuta
3-0311

0
100 mi
160 km
N
Bay
Of
Biscay
FRANCE
Laredo
Ondárroa
San
Sebastián
Bilbao
VASCO
NAVARRA
Vitoria-
Gasteiz
Pamplona
Logroño
Pyrenees
LA
RIOJA
Sos del Rey
Católico
Ribera
de Cardós
Andorra
GULF
OF
LIONS
Tudela
Tarazona
Figueres
Cadaqués
ARAGÓN
Zaragoza
CATALUNYA
Girona
Lérida
Calatayud
Tossa de Mar
Montserrat
Lloret de Mar
Tarragona
Barcelona
Costa Brava
Guadalajara
Sitges
Costa Dorada
COMUNIDAD
VALENCIANA
Teruel
Cuenca
Costa del Azahar
Minorca
Balearic Islands
Majorca
Palma
Valencia
Ibiza
Benidorm
MURCIA
Elche
Alicante
Murcia
Costa Blanca
Lorca
Nevada
Cartagena
Mediterranean Sea
Costa Calida

Did You Know?

- Spanish artist Pablo Picasso was the world's most prolific painter: 13,500 paintings or sketches, 34,000 illustrations, and 100,000 etchings.
- A Spaniard, Josep Grugués, cooked the world's largest sausage, measuring 3 miles (5km) long.
- A recent survey revealed that 60% of the Spanish people have no interest in bullfighting.
- The palm was introduced into Europe by Muslim monarch Abd-al-Rahman I, who planted seedlings on the palace grounds at Córdoba.
- In 1762 Charles III ordered that all nudes in the royal collection be burned. Court painter Anton Raphael Mengs didn't obey, thereby rescuing many masterpieces for posterity.
- Ernest Hemingway himself never ran in the *encierro* (running of the bulls) held during the festival in Pamplona.

Old Castile & León The proud kingdoms of Castile and León in north-central Iberia are part of the core from which modern Spain developed. Some of their greatest cathedrals and monuments were erected during a time when each was staunchly independent. But León's annexation by Queen Isabella of Castile in 1474 (five years after her politically advantageous but unhappy marriage to Ferdinand of Aragón) irrevocably linked the two regions.

Be alert to the confusion that reigns even within Spain regarding the appellations of Old Castile (as it's presented within Chapter 7) and New Castile, which is a modern linguistic and governmental concept that includes a territory much larger than the medieval entity known by Isabella and her subjects. Despite the presence of direct rail lines to and from Madrid, we don't recommend any of the regions' highlights as day trips from Madrid, but rather as overnight destinations in their own right.

Architectural and cultural highlights include Burgos (the ancient "cradle" of Castile), Salamanca (a medieval Castilian university town), and León, glittering capital of the district bearing its name and site of one of the most unusual cathedrals in Iberia. If time remains, consider an overnight at the extraordinary parador in Ciudad Rodrigo, as well as trips to Zamora, known for its stunning Romanesque churches, and Valladolid, whose monuments suffered severe damage after its heyday under Isabella and Ferdinand.

Extremadura Far from the mainstream of urbanized Spain, Extremadura lives within a time warp where references to the Middle Ages and ancient Rome crop up unexpectedly beside sun-baked highways and the roar of diesel trucks. Many conquistadores who pillaged the Indian civilizations of the New World came from this hard, granitic land.

Be prepared for hot, arid landscapes and smoking trucks carrying heavy loads across this once-turbulent corridor between Madrid and Lisbon. Devote two days to the region, stopping off at such sites as Guadalupe, whose Mudéjar monastery revolves around the medieval cult of the Dark (or Black) Virgin, and Trujillo, where many of the monuments were built with gold sent home by native sons like Pizarro, Peru's conqueror. Also worthwhile is Cáceres, a fortified city with one foot planted firmly in the Middle Ages, and Zafra, where evidence of the Moorish occupation is stronger than anywhere in Spain outside of Andalusia.

Andalusia In A.D. 711 Muslim armies swept into Iberia from strongholds in what is now Morocco. Since then, Spain's southernmost district has been enmeshed in the mores, art, and architecture of the Muslim world. During the 900s, Andalusia blossomed into a sophisticated society—advanced in philosophy, mathematics, and trading—that far surpassed a feudal Europe still trapped in the Dark Ages. Moorish domination ended completely in 1492, when Granada was captured by the armies of Isabella and Ferdinand. Today, the region offers more insight into the Muslim occupation of Iberia than any other area of Spain. Andalusia is an arid district that, despite such economically rejuvenating events as Seville's Expo, isn't highly prosperous.

The major cities of Andalusia deserve at least a week, with overnights in Seville (hometown of Carmen, Don Giovanni, and the famous opera about a barber); Córdoba, site of the Mezquita, one of history's most versatile religious edifices; and Cádiz, a venerable seaport where thousands of ships embarked on their colonization of the New World. Perhaps greatest of all is Granada, a town of such impressive artistry that it inspired many of the works by the 20th-century romantic poet Federico García Lorca.

The Costa del Sol The Costa del Sol sprawls across the southernmost edge of Spain between Algeciras to the west—a few miles from the rocky heights of British-controlled Gibraltar—and Almería to the east. En route, it encompasses more traffic jams, suntan oil, sun-bleached high-rises, and almost-naked flesh than any piece of terrain in Iberia. The beaches here are some of the best in Europe. But be warned: Your greatest inconveniences will be human congestion and crime, which is regrettably on the rise.

Unless you travel by car or rail from Madrid, chances are that you'll arrive by plane via Málaga, the district's most historic city. The coast's largest resort town is distinctive, Renaissance-era Marbella, the centerpiece of 17 miles of beaches. Nerja is just one of the booming resorts that has kept an out-of-the-way, fishing-village feel. The most overcrowded and activity-packed resort is Torremolinos. One modern development that has managed to remain distinctive is Puerto Banús, a neo-Moorish village that curves around a sheltered marina, where the wintering wealthy dock their yachts.

Valencia & the Costa Blanca Valencia, the third-largest city in Spain, is rarely visited by foreign tourists because of the heavy industry that surrounds its inner core. More alluring are such resorts as Alicante and Benidorm or the medieval hamlet of Elche (where some of the world's most famous ancient Roman statues were discovered).

Unless you opt to skip Valencia completely (and many travelers do), plan to see the city's cathedral, the exterior of its Palacio de la Generalidad, and as many of its three important museums as you can fit into a one-day trip. To visit the Costa Blanca, allow as much or as little time as your budget and your interest in the beach permit.

Barcelona & Catalonia Its history is older than that of its rival, Madrid, its streets filled with the gothic and medieval buildings that Spain's relatively newer capital lacks. During the 1200s, Barcelona rivaled the trading prowess of such cities as Genoa and Pisa, and it became the Spanish city that most resembled other great cities of Europe.

Allow yourself at least three days to explore the city, with stops at the Picasso Museum, the Joan Miró foundation, the Catalonian Museum, the Gothic quarter, and a crowning triumph of early modernist architecture, the Eixample District. Make time for a stroll—during daylight hours only, as nighttime explorations tend to be unsafe—along Les Rambles, one of the most delightful outdoor promenades in Spain.

Don't overlook the allure of Catalonia's hinterlands. A short drive to the south is Sitges, a stylish beach resort that caters to a diverse clientele ranging from freewheeling nudists to fun-seeking families. Other worthy destinations are Tarragona, one of ancient Rome's district capitals, and Montserrat, site of one of Europe's best-preserved medieval monasteries.

The Costa Brava It's Spain's "other" Riviera, a region with a deep sense of medieval history and a topography that's rockier and more interesting than that of the Costa del Sol. The "Wild Coast" stretches from the resort of Blanes, just north of Barcelona, along 95 miles (153km) of dangerously winding clifftop roads that bypass peninsulas and sheltered coves on their way to the French border. Despite hordes of midsummer visitors, the Costa Brava resorts still manage to feel less congested and less spoiled than equivalent ones along the Costa del Sol.

Sun-worshipers usually head for the twin beachfront resorts of Lloret de Mar and Tossa de Mar. Persons interested in the history of 20th-century painting head for Figueres; Salvador Dalí was born here, in 1904, and a controversial and bizarre museum is devoted exclusively to his surrealist works.

Aragón Except for Aragón's association with Ferdinand, the unsavory, often unethical husband of Queen Isabella, few foreign visitors ever thought much about this northeastern quadrant of Iberia. A land of ancient references, noteworthy Mudéjar architecture, and high altitudes that guarantee cool midsummer temperatures, it's also one of the foremost bull-breeding regions of Spain.

Aragón is best visited as a stopover on the heavily traveled highways between Barcelona and Madrid. Stay overnight in Zaragoza, the district capital, and take a series of day trips to Tarazona ("The Toledo of Aragón"), Calatayud, and Daroca, all important Moorish and Roman military outposts; and Nuévalos/Piedra, the site of an extraordinary riverside hotel built in 1194 as a Cistercian monastery. Also worth a trip is Sos del Rey Católico, the rocky, relatively unspoiled village where Ferdinand was born.

Navarre & La Rioja This strategic province, one of the four original Christian kingdoms in Iberia, shares a border—and numerous historical references—with France. One of France's Renaissance kings, Henri IV "de Navarre," was linked to the province's royal family. Many Navarre customs, and some of its local dialect, reflect the influence of its passionately politicized neighbors, the Basques. Celtic pagans, Romans, Christians, and Arabs have all left architectural reminders of their presence.

The province contains nine points where traffic is funneled into and out of Spain, so if you're driving or riding the train, say, from Paris to Madrid, chances are you'll get a fast overview of Navarre. The province's best-known site is Pamplona, the district capital and annual host for the bull-running Fiesta de San Fermín.

One small corner of Navarre is comprised of La Rioja, the smallest *autonomía* (semi-autonomous province) of Spain. Irrigated by the Ebro River, it produces some of the country's finest wines. If wine tasting appeals to you, head for the town of Haro, and drop in on several bodegas to sample local vintages.

The Basque Country This is the native land Europe's oldest traceable ethnic group. The Basque people have been more heavily persecuted than any other within Spain, by Madrid regimes determined to shoehorn their unusual language and culture into that of mainstream Spain. The region of rolling peaks and fertile, sunny valleys hugs the Atlantic coast adjacent to the French border. It also boasts the best regional cuisine in Spain.

Unless you're devoted to beachgoing, allow three leisurely days for this unusual district. Visit San Sebastián (Donostia) for its international glamour, Fuenterrabía (Hondarribía) for its medieval history, Guernica for a sobering reminder of past atrocity, and Lekeitio for its simple fishing-village charm.

Cantabria & Asturias Positioned on Iberia's north-central coastline, these are the most verdant regions of Spain. In the Middle Ages pilgrims passed through here on their way to Santiago de Compostela—a legacy evident from the wealth of Romanesque churches and abbeys in the vicinity. Come for beaches that are rainier, but much less crowded, than those along Spain's southern coasts.

Enjoy such beach resorts as El Sardinero and Laredo, as well as the rugged beauty of Los Picos de Europa, a dramatic mountain range that is home to rich colonies of wildlife. Sites of interest include the Caves of Altamira (called "the Sistine Chapel of prehistoric art," though admission is strictly regulated), the pre-Romanesque town of Oviedo (Uviéu), and the architecturally important old quarter of Gijón (Xixón). The region's largest city, Santander, lies amid a maze of peninsulas and estuaries favored by boaters. In summer it becomes a major beach resort, although San Sebastián is more fashionable.

Galicia A true Celtic outpost in northwestern Iberia, Galicia's landscape is often compared to rainy, windswept Ireland. Known for a coastline that's indented with granite-edged estuaries akin to Norway's fjords, the region is wild and relatively underpopulated.

Spend at least two days here, enjoying some of the most scenic drives in Iberia. Stop at such historic and religious sites as Santiago de Compostela; Lugo, an ancient Roman outpost, also merits a visit. The region's greatest city is La Coruña, the point of embarkation for Spain's tragic Armada, sunk by the English army on its way to invade Britain in the late 16th century.

The Balearic Islands Part of their appeal derives from their isolated position off the Costa Blanca and Costa Brava. "Discovered" by English Romantics in the early 19th century, and long known as a strategic naval outpost in the western Mediterranean, they're sunny, subtropical, mountainous, and more verdant than the Costa del Sol. They have their pockets of style and posh, although Majorca and Ibiza are overrun in summer. Minorca is more fashionable. But know before you go: Getting here is part of the inconvenience—and part of the fun.

2 Spain Today

Tourism continues to dominate the Spanish economy as never before. In 1995 a record 63.5 million visitors were reported, a 3% increase over the previous year. No longer interested in the "lager lout" image its coastal resorts such as Benidorm earned in the 1970s and 1980s, Spain has reached out to a more upmarket visitor. Bargain Spain on $5 a day is now a distant memory, as prices have skyrocketed. The government is trying to lure visitors away from the overcrowded coasts (especially Majorca, the Costa del Sol, and the Costa Brava) and steer them to the country's less-traveled, but more historic, destinations. Government paradors and other improved tourist facilities, better restaurants, and spruced-up attractions, have sent out the message.

Dateline

- **11th** c. B.C. Phoenicians settle Spain's coasts.
- **650** B.C. Greeks colonize the east.
- **600** B.C. Celts cross the Pyrenees and settle in Spain.
- **6th–3rd** c. B.C. Carthaginians make Cartagena their colonial capital, driving out the Greeks.
- **2nd** c. B.C.–A.D. **2nd** c. Rome controls most of Iberia. Christianity spreads.
- **218–201** B.C. Second Punic War: Rome defeats Carthage.

continues

- **5th c.** Vandals, then Visigoths, invade Spain.
- **8th c.** Moors conquer most of Spain.
- **1214** More than half of Iberia is regained by Catholics.
- **1469** Ferdinand of Aragón marries Isabella of Castile.
- **1492** Catholic monarchs seize Granada, the last Moorish stronghold. Columbus lands in the New World.
- **1519** Cortés conquers Mexico. Charles I is crowned Holy Roman Emperor, as Charles V.
- **1556** Philip II inherits throne and launches the Counter-Reformation.
- **1588** England defeats Spanish Armada.
- **1700** Philip V becomes king. War of Spanish Succession follows.
- **1713** Treaty of Utrecht ends war. Spain's colonies reduced.
- **1759** Charles III ascends throne.
- **1808** Napoleon places brother Joseph on the Spanish throne.
- **1813** Wellington drives French out of Spain; the monarchy is restored.
- **1876** Spain becomes a constitutional monarchy.
- **1898** Spanish-American War leads to Spain's loss of Puerto Rico, Cuba, and the Philippines.
- **1923** Primo de Rivera forms military directorate.
- **1930** Right-wing dictatorship ends; Primo de Rivera exiled.
- **1931** King Alfonso XIII abdicates; Second Republic is born.
- **1933–35** Falange party formed.
- **1936–39** Civil War between the governing Popular Front and the Nationalists led by Franco.

continues

Still, Spain faces many economic woes, including a slow recovery from a deep recession. In the 1980s Spain spent recklessly, living far beyond its means. Now the government is trying to maintain growth—but at a more sustainable rate. The most critical issue remains the staggering 24.2% unemployment rate. Spain's civil service is incredibly bloated, and one in four salaried employees works for the state in one form or another. Many a Spaniard—too many in fact—dreams of a safe, cushy government job with a pension to follow.

The birth rate—surprisingly in a Catholic country—remains low, and the population is aging. More and more Spaniards are going to be entitled to pensions, and there will be less younger people working to support them. The average Spaniard lives to the age of 77—a year longer than the average American.

Between 1995 and 1999 Spain is set to receive some $23 billion from the European Union. Most of this money is slated for infrastructure investment such as road building. Although many politicians have rejoiced at the largesse, other savvy economists have warned that these funds will one day have to be paid back, at great cost to Spain.

In March of 1996, the conservative party, which has roots in the Franco dictatorship, won Spain's general elections. This ended the 13-year rule of the scandal-plagued Socialist party under Prime Minister Felipe González. His government, however, was credited with ushering Spain into the modern age following the dim years of the Franco dictatorship. José Maria Aznar, leader of the victorious Popular party, took over as Spain's prime minister. He claimed his party would be one "of the center."

Spain today continues to attract world attention, especially in 1992, which was called "the jamboree year." Barcelona hosted the Olympics, Seville had its Expo, and Madrid was named the European Community's "Capital of Culture." At the same time, the whole country celebrated the Columbus quincentennial.

Spain continues to change as it moves toward the millennium. A drug culture and escalating crime—something virtually unheard of in Franco's day—are an unfortunate sign of Spain's entry into the modern world. The most remarkable advance has been in the legal status of women, who now have access to contraception, abortion, and divorce. Sights once thought "unimaginable" are now taking place: an annual lesbian "kiss-in" at Madrid's Puerto del Sol and women officiating as governors of men's prisons.

At least for the moment, Spain's monarchy seems to be working. England's House of Windsor might well use the Court of Borbón—presided over by King Juan Carlos and Queen Sofia—as role models. In 1975, when the king assumed the throne after the death of Franco, he was called "Juan Carlos the Brief," implying that his reign would be short. But almost overnight he distanced himself from Franco's dark legacy and became a hardworking and serious sovereign. He staved off a coup attempt in 1981, and he and the other Spanish royals remain popular. Juan Carlos even makes do on a meager $7 million salary—less than one-tenth of what England's Queen Elizabeth is reputed to earn in a year.

Author John Hooper, in an updated version of his 1986 bestseller, *The New Spaniards,* remains optimistic about the future of Spain, in spite of its problems. He suggests Spaniards not forget that "to be true to themselves they may need to be different from others." Hooper believes that the new Spain will have arrived at adulthood "not on the day it ceases to be different from the rest of Europe, but on the day that it acknowledges that it is."

- **1939** Franco establishes dictatorship, which will last 36 years.
- **1941** Spain technically stays neutral in World War II, but Franco favors Germany.
- **1955** Spain joins the United Nations.
- **1969** Franco names Juan Carlos as his successor.
- **1975** Juan Carlos becomes king.
- **1978** New, democratic constitution initiates reforms.
- **1981** Coup attempt by right-wing officers fails.
- **1982** Socialists gain power after 43 years of right-wing rule.
- **1986** Spain joins the European Community (now the European Union).
- **1992** Barcelona hosts the Summer Olympics; Seville hosts Expo '92.
- **1996** A conservative party defeats Socialist party, ending 13-year rule. José Maria Aznar chosen prime minister.

3 A Look at the Past

ANCIENT TIMES Ancestors of the Basques may have been the first settlers in Spain 10,000 to 30,000 years ago, followed, it is believed, by Iberians from North Africa. They, in turn, were followed by Celts, who crossed the Pyrenees around 600 B.C. These groups melded into a Celtic-Iberian people who inhabited central Spain.

Others coming to the Iberian Peninsula in ancient times were the Phoenicians, who took over coastal areas on the Atlantic beginning in the 11th century B.C. Cádiz, originally the Phoenician settlement of Gades, is perhaps the oldest town in Spain. The Greeks came roughly 500 years after the Phoenicians, lured by the peninsula's wealth of gold and silver. The Greeks established colonies before they were conquered by Carthaginians from North Africa.

Around 200 B.C. the Romans vanquished the Carthaginians and laid the foundations of the present Latin culture. Traces of Roman civilization can still be seen today. By the time of Julius Caesar, Spain (Hispania) was under Roman law and began a long period of peace and prosperity.

BARBARIAN INVASIONS, THE MOORISH KINGDOM & THE RECONQUEST When Rome fell in the 5th century, Spain was overrun, first by the Vandals and then by the Visigoths from eastern Europe. The chaotic rule of the Visigothic kings lasted about 300 years, but the barbarian invaders did adopt the language of their new country and tolerated Christianity as well.

In A.D. 711 Moorish warriors led by Tarik crossed over into Spain and conquered the disunited country. By 714 they controlled most of it, except for a few mountain regions around Asturias. For eight centuries the Moors occupied their new land, which they called *al-Andalus,* or Andalusia, with Córdoba as the capital. A great intellectual center, Córdoba became the scientific capital of Europe; notable advances were made in agriculture, industry, literature, philosophy, and medicine. The Jews were welcomed by the Moors, often serving as administrators, ambassadors, and financial officers. But the Moors quarreled with one another, and soon the few Christian strongholds in the north began to advance south.

The Reconquest, the name given to the Christian efforts to rid the peninsula of the Moors, slowly reduced the size of the Muslim holdings, with Catholic monarchies forming in northern areas. The three powerful kingdoms of Aragón, Castile, and León were joined in 1469, when Ferdinand of Aragón married Isabella of Castile. Catholic kings, as they were called, launched the final attack on the Moors and completed the Reconquest in 1492 by capturing Granada.

That same year Columbus, the Genoese sailor, landed on the West Indies, laying the foundations for a far-flung empire that brought wealth and power to Spain during the 16th and 17th centuries.

The Spanish Inquisition, begun under Ferdinand and Isabella, sought to eradicate all heresy and secure the primacy of Catholicism. Non-Catholics, Jews, and Moors were mercilessly persecuted, and many were driven out of the country.

THE GOLDEN AGE & LATER DECLINE Columbus's voyage to America and the conquistadors' subsequent exploration of that land ushered Spain into its golden age.

In the first half of the 16th century, Balboa discovered the Pacific Ocean, Cortés seized Mexico for Spain, Pizarro took Peru, and a Spanish ship (initially commanded by the Portuguese Magellan, who was killed during the voyage) circumnavigated the globe. The conquistadors took Catholicism to the New World and shipped cargoes of gold back to Spain. The Spanish Empire extended all the way to the Philippines. Charles V, grandson of Ferdinand and Isabella, was the most powerful prince in Europe—King of Spain and Naples, Holy Roman Emperor and lord of Germany, Duke of Burgundy and the Netherlands, and ruler of the New World territories.

But much of Spain's wealth and human resources was wasted in religious and secular conflicts. First Jews, then Muslims, and finally Moriscos (Catholicized Moors) were driven out—and with them much of the country's prosperity. When Philip II ascended the throne in 1556, Spain could indeed boast vast possessions: the New World colonies; Naples, Milan, Genoa, Sicily, and other portions of Italy; the Spanish Netherlands (modern Belgium and the Netherlands); and portions of Austria and Germany. But the seeds of decline had already been planted.

Philip, a fanatic Catholic, devoted his energies to subduing the Protestant revolt in the Netherlands and to becoming the standard bearer for the Counter-Reformation. He tried to return England to Catholicism, first by marrying Mary I ("Bloody Mary") and later by wooing her half sister, Elizabeth I, who rebuffed him. When, in 1588, he resorted to sending the Armada, it was ignominiously defeated; and that defeat symbolized the decline of Spanish power.

In 1700 a Bourbon prince, Philip V, became king, and the country fell under the influence of France. Philip V's right to the throne was challenged by a Hapsburg archduke of Austria, thus giving rise to the War of the Spanish Succession. When it ended, Spain had lost Flanders, its Italian possessions, and Gibraltar (still held by the British today).

During the 18th century, Spain's direction changed with each sovereign. Charles III (1759–88) developed the country economically and culturally. Charles IV became embroiled in wars with France, and the weakness of the Spanish monarchy allowed Napoleon to place his brother Joseph Bonaparte on the throne in 1808.

THE 19TH & 20TH CENTURIES Although Britain and France had joined forces to restore the Spanish monarchy, the European conflicts encouraged Spanish colonists to rebel. Ultimately, this led the United States to free the Philippines, Puerto Rico, and Cuba from Spain in 1898.

In 1876 Spain became a constitutional monarchy. But labor unrest, disputes with the Catholic Church, and war in Morocco combined to create political chaos. Conditions eventually became so bad that the Cortés, or parliament, was dissolved in 1923, and Gen. Miguel Primo de Rivera formed a military directorate. Early in 1930 Primo de Rivera resigned, but unrest continued.

On April 14, 1931, a revolution occurred, a republic was proclaimed, and King Alfonso XIII and his family were forced to flee. Initially the liberal constitutionalists ruled, but soon they were pushed aside by the socialists and anarchists, who adopted a constitution separating church and state, secularizing education, and containing several other radical provisions (for example, agrarian reform and the expulsion of the Jesuits).

The extreme nature of these reforms fostered the growth of the conservative Falange party (*Falange española,* Spanish Phalanx), modeled after Italy's and Germany's fascist parties. By the 1936 elections, the country was divided equally between left and right, and political violence was common. On July 18, 1936, the army, supported by Mussolini and Hitler, tried to seize power, igniting the Spanish Civil War. Gen. Francisco Franco, coming from Morocco to Spain, led the Nationalist (rightist) forces in the two years of fighting that ravaged the country. Towns were bombed and many atrocities were committed. Early in 1939, Franco entered Barcelona and went on to Madrid; thousands of republicans were executed. Franco became chief of state, remaining so until his death in 1975.

Although Franco adopted a neutral position during World War II, his sympathies obviously lay with Germany and Italy, and Spain gave aid to the Axis powers as a nonbelligerent. This action intensified the diplomatic isolation into which the country was forced after the war's end—in fact, it was excluded from the United Nations until 1955.

Before his death, General Franco selected as his successor Juan Carlos de Borbón y Borbón, son of the pretender to the Spanish throne. After the 1977 elections, a new constitution was approved by the electorate and the king; it guaranteed human and civil rights, as well as free enterprise, and canceled the status of the Roman Catholic Church as the church of Spain. It also granted limited autonomy to several regions, including Catalonia and the Basque provinces, both of which, however, are still clamoring for complete autonomy.

In 1981 a group of right-wing military officers seized the Cortés and called upon Juan Carlos to establish a Francoist state. The king, however, refused, and the

Impressions

I thought that I should never return to the country I love more than any other, except for my own.

—Ernest Hemingway

Three Spaniards, four opinions.

—Old Spanish Proverb

The Spectacle of Death

Many consider bullfighting cruel and shocking. But as Ernest Hemingway pointed out in Death in the Afternoon: "The bullfight is not a sport in the Anglo-Saxon sense of the word, that is, it is not an equal contest or an attempt at an equal contest between a bull and a man. Rather it is a tragedy: the death of the bull, which is played, more or less well, by the bull and the man involved and in which there is danger for the man but certain death for the bull." Hemingway, of course, was an aficionado.

When the symbolic drama of the bullfight is acted out, some think it reaches a higher plane. Some people argue that it is not a public exhibition of cruelty at all, but rather a highly skilled art requiring great qualities of survival, courage, showmanship, and gallantry.

Regardless of how you view it, this spectacle is an authentically Spanish experience and, as such, has much to reveal about the character of the land and its people. The season of the *corridas* (bullfights) lasts from early spring until around mid-October. Fights are held in a *plaza de toros* (bullring), ranging in location from the oldest ring in remote Ronda to the big-time Plaza de Toros in Madrid. Sunday is corrida day in most major Spanish cities, although Madrid and Barcelona may also have fights on Thursday.

Tickets fall into three classifications: *sol* (sun), the cheapest; *sombra* (shade), the most expensive; and *sol y sombra* (a mixture of sun and shade), the medium-price range.

The corrida begins with a parade. For many viewers, this may be the high point of the afternoon's festivities, as all the bullfighters are clad in their *trajes de luce,* or "suits of light."

Bullfights are divided into *tercios* (thirds). The first is the tercio de *capa* (cape), during which the matador tests the bull with various passes and gets acquainted with him. The second portion, the tercio de *varas* (sticks), begins with the lance-carrying picadores on horseback, who weaken, or "punish," the bull by jabbing him in the shoulder area. The horses are sometimes gored, even though they wear protective padding, or the horse and rider may be tossed into the air by the now-infuriated bull. The picadores are followed by the banderilleros, whose job it is to puncture the bull with pairs of boldly colored darts.

In the final tercio de muleta the action narrows down to the lone fighter and the bull. Gone are the fancy capes. Instead, the matador uses a small red cloth known as a *muleta,* which, to be effective, requires a bull with lowered head. (The picadores and banderilleros have worked to achieve this.) Using the muleta as a lure, the matador wraps the bull around himself in various passes, the most dangerous of which is the natural; here, the matador holds the muleta in his left hand, the sword in his right. Right-hand passes pose less of a threat, since the sword can be used to spread out the muleta, making a larger target for the bull. After a number of passes, the time comes for the kill, the "moment of truth." A truly skilled fighter may dispatch the bull in one thrust.

After the bull dies, the highest official at the ring may award the matador an ear from the dead bull, or perhaps both ears, or ears and tail. For a truly extraordinary performance, the hoof is sometimes added. The bullfighter may be carried away as a hero, or if he has displeased the crowd, he may be chased out of the ring by an angry mob. At a major fight, usually six bulls are killed by three matadors in one afternoon.

conspirators were arrested. The fledgling democracy overcame its first test. Its second major accomplishment—under the Socialist administration of Prime Minister Felipe González, the country's first leftist government since 1939—was to gain Spain's entry into the European Community (now Union) in 1986.

Further proof that the new Spain was now fully accepted by the international community came in 1992. In that *annus mirabilis,* as many Spaniards regarded it, Spain was designated by the EU as the Cultural Capital of Europe for the year; but more significant, the Summer Olympics were held successfully in Barcelona and a world's fair, Expo '92, was mounted in Seville, in Andalusia.

In March of 1996, more than 78% of Spain's 32 million registered voters cast ballots, ending the 13-year rule of the scandal-plagued Socialist party of Prime Minister Felipe González, even though he is credited with ushering Spain into the modern world. A conservative party with roots in the Franco dictatorship was swept into power, lead by José Maria Aznar, leader of the Popular party, who pledged to represent "all Spain." González, although congratulating the Popular party, took the defeat bitterly, alleging that the vote "was a step back to the fascist dictatorship of Franco."

4 Architecture 101

FROM THE ROMANS TO THE MOORISH INVASION The roots of architecture in Spain began with the Romans, who built aqueducts and more than 12,000 miles of roads and bridges as a means of linking their assorted Iberian holdings. The greatest of these, the Via Augusta, followed the Costa Brava, Costa Blanca, and Costa del Sol to carry armies and supplies between Cádiz and the Pyrenees.

This Hispano-Roman style involves prolific use of the vault and the arch—obvious in such marvels as the aqueduct at Segovia, the triumphal arch at Tarragona, and the rectilinear, carefully planned community at Mérida (whose Roman monuments are among the best preserved in Europe).

Historians mark A.D. 409 as the end of the Roman age in Iberia, the beginning of political anarchy, and the migration into Spain of thousands of immigrants (Vandals, Alans, Suevians, and Visigothic tribespeople) from central Europe. The newcomers, recent converts to some kind of Christianity, built crude chapels and fortresses based on a mishmash of aesthetic ideals from northern Europe and Byzantium, using engineering principles copied from the ancient Romans.

Spain's Romanesque style began to develop around A.D. 800 from the legacy of these crude Visigothic buildings (see below). Meanwhile, a major new aesthetic was forcibly imposed upon Spain from the south.

HISPANO-MOORISH ARCHITECTURE (711–1492) The Moors gained control of the Iberian Peninsula in the 8th century, and their 600-year rule left an architectural legacy that is among the most exotic and colorful in Europe. Regrettably, only a handful of *alcazars* (palaces), *alcazabas* (fortresses), and converted mosques remain intact today. Moorish buildings tended to be relatively flimsy and heavily accented with decorations. Many have collapsed (or were deliberately destroyed) in the Catholic zeal to "re-Christianize" Iberia.

The most visible traits of the Saracenic style included the use of forests of (sometimes mismatched) columns within mosques, each of which was used to support a network of horseshoe-shaped arches. These interconnected to support low, flat roofs. Some arches were scalloped, then decorated with geometric designs or calligraphic inscriptions from the Koran.

MOZARABIC ARCHITECTURE Mozárabes were Christian Spaniards who retained their religion under the Muslim rule. They successfully blended Gothic and Moorish styles in their art and architecture. The few structures that remain intact from this period can be found in Toledo and include the Monastery of El Cristo de la Luz, originally built in the 900s as a mosque; a 12th-century synagogue, now the church of Santa María de la Blanca; and the churches of Santiago del Arrabal and San Román. A secular example of the style in Toledo is the Puerto del Sol, an ornate gate built into the walls that surround the old city. Constructed around 1200, about 150 years after Toledo's reconquest by Christian forces, it combines the distinctive Moorish horseshoe arch with feudal battlements and Christian iconography.

MUDÉJAR ARCHITECTURE Equivalent in some ways to the above-mentioned Mozárabe style (with which it is frequently confused), Mudéjar refers to the architectural and decorative style developed by Spanish Muslims living in Christian territories after the Réconquista. A mix of Gothic and Moorish influences, it reached its peak between 1275 and 1350, made frequent use of brick instead of stone, and specialized in elaborate woodcarvings that merged the Moorish emphasis on geometrics and symmetry with Christian themes. Regrettably, after the final Moorish stronghold fell to the Christians in 1492, Spanish monarchs did everything they could to purge any artistic legacy left by the Moors. Mudéjar influences, however, still cropped up in rural pockets of Spain until the middle of the 18th century, and, in some cases, even merged subtly with ornate features of the baroque.

PRE-ROMANESQUE & ROMANESQUE ARCHITECTURE (700–1290) Ensconced in Asturias, feudal rulers of the Christian Visigothic tribes refined their architectural tastes. Stonework became better crafted than the crude models of the previous two centuries, and arches became more graceful. Under the rule of Alfonso the Chaste (791–842), dozens of pre-Romanesque churches were built in Oviedo, and a body believed to be that of Saint James was "discovered" in a field in Galicia. Thus was born Santiago de Compostela ("St. James of the Field"), the eventual site of a great cathedral and one of the most famous pilgrimage sites in the Christian world.

From these beginnings, and based on money and cultural influences from the floods of pilgrims pouring in from Italy, France, and other parts of Europe, a trail of Romanesque churches, shelters, monasteries, and convents sprang up across northern Spain, especially in Catalonia, Aragón, and northern Castile. The style is known for semicircular arches, small windows, crude but evocative carvings, and thick walls. It is best represented in the church of San Gil in Zaragoza and the cloisters of San Pedro, near Pamplona in the town of Estella.

SPANISH GOTHIC This style surged across provinces adjacent to the French border (Catalonia and Navarre) beginning around 1250. By the late 1200s, churches that had been initiated in the Romanesque style (such as the cathedral at Burgos) were completed as sometimes flamboyant Gothic monuments. During the 1300s and 1400s, bishops in León, Toledo, and Burgos even imported architects and masons from Gothic strongholds in other parts of Europe to design their cathedrals. In Spain, the Gothic style included widespread use of the *ogive* (high-pointed) arches and vaults, clustered pilasters, an opening up of walls to incorporate large, usually stained-glass, windows.

THE RENAISSANCE After the expulsion of the Moors from Iberia, and Columbus's first landings in the New World in 1492, Spain found itself caught up in a vivid, emphatic sense of its own manifest destiny. Searching for a national style of architecture, the Spanish monarchs adapted the aesthetic trends of Renaissance Italy into a "Hispanicized" style. Foremost among these was the 16th-century

Impressions

Now you have two homes.

—Traditional Spanish Farewell

Idiocy proliferates in Spain, from politics to culture.

—Nobel Prize winner Camilo José Cela

plateresque, which emulated in stone the finely worked forms that a silversmith might have hammered into silver plate. The style is best viewed in the exterior of the University of Salamanca and the Chapel of the New Kings inside the cathedral at Toledo.

CLASSICAL SPANISH ARCHITECTURE The austere regime of Philip II welcomed (and demanded) a less ornate national style from the country's architects. Fervently religious and obsessively ambitious for the advancement of Spanish interests, he embraced the austere ancient Roman forms that had been revived during Italy's late Renaissance. The style's most megalomaniacal manifestation within Spain came with Juan de Herrera's gargantuan, brooding, and military-looking monastery and palace at El Escorial (1563–84) on an isolated and windswept plateau outside Madrid. Philip II considered the style an appropriate manifestation of the stern principles of the Counter-Reformation and the new Inquisition that followed.

Later during the Renaissance, Herrera's rectilinear gridirons were replaced with the curved lines of the baroque. This style was avidly embraced by the Jesuits, one of the most powerful religious orders in Spain at the time, whose austere religious bent stood in marked contrast to their flamboyant architectural tastes. The baroque style appears at its most ornate in Andalusia, a region enjoying a building boom at the time thanks to the wealth that poured into its ports from the gold mines of Mexico and Peru.

Ironically, baroque was the style most enthusiastically embraced by the Spanish colonies in South America. Spain's interpretation of Italian baroque architecture is sometimes referred to as Churrigueresque, after José Churriguera (1665–1725), designer to the kings of Spain and architect of Salamanca's New Cathedral. The style is characterized by its dense concentrations of busy ornamentation that often completely disguised the basic form of the building itself. An example of baroque style in Spain is the wedding-cake facade of the cathedral at Murcia.

FROM BAROQUE TOWARD MODERN Under the Spanish Bourbon rulers of the 18th century, the favored style embraced the baroque and neoclassical influences of aristocratic France. El Pardo, Riofrio, and Aranjuez were all built as Europeanized hideaways. Even the design of the Royal Palace in Madrid was modeled after Versailles.

In the 19th century the Romantic age encouraged a revolt against the ideals of balance and reason that had defined upscale European architecture during the late 1700s. Spanish architecture throughout the 19th century was torn between the value of the individual architect's eclectic, personalized, and sometimes flamboyant vision, and the inevitable reactions that swung the pendulums of public taste back toward greater restraint and symmetry. There developed a new respect for the Gothic, as many 500-year-old Gothic cathedrals were adapted or altered with neo-Gothic alterations that modern art historians sometimes view with horror.

Out of this tension emerged one of Spain's most widely recognized architectural giants, Antonio Gaudí (1852–1926). His idiosyncratic, organic style coincided neatly with the most intense building boom ever experienced within his hometown of Barcelona. His curiously curved and sinuous buildings are genius-quality precursors of 20th-century modernism. One of the best examples of his ideas can be seen in Barcelona's Casa Milá.

ARCHITECTURE TODAY Other than occasional models of genuine inspiration, such as the whimsical and surrealist buildings devised by Salvador Dalí, much of modern Spain's architecture is derived from the older, tried-and-true sources that span the country's distinguished range of architectural traditions. When it comes to recycling the feudal or Renaissance monuments of yesteryear, Spain has no equal, as evidenced by the country's network of historic paradors. Regrettably, some areas of modern Spain, including many neighborhoods of Madrid and long stretches of the Costa del Sol, have bristled with high-rise, concrete-and-glass apartment houses. Few boast any distinguishing features, provoking laments from traditionalists.

5 Art 101

EARLY ROOTS Spain's art has always been characterized by a curious mixture of passion and austerity that makes it one of the most unusual and riveting contributions from Europe.

Some of the best examples of prehistoric art were discovered in Spanish caves, including the hunting scenes within the caves of Altamira and Puente Viesgo, and the mysterious dolmens that stand like Celtic sentinels at Antequera, near Málaga. Equivalent dolmens (known locally as *talayots* and *navetas*) were erected on the Balearics between around 2500 and 1000 B.C.

By 1000 B.C. Spain became a crossroads of civilizations, a role it would play for the next 3,000 years. Many of the most prized artifacts in Spanish museums date from this era; the statue *The Lady of Elche,* the lions of Córdoba, and the bulls (*toros*) of Guisando all reflect the influence of ancient Greeks and Phoenicians, who used Spain's coast as a port of call on their trade routes. In such port cities as Cádiz, for example, rows of Phoenician sarcophagi have been unearthed.

ANCIENT & EARLY MEDIEVAL SPAIN The Romans, who took an uncharacteristically long 200 years to subdue the natives of Iberia, were noted more for their architectural legacy (see "Architecture 101," above) than for their paintings and sculpture. Their buildings incorporated elaborate mosaics that depicted heroic or mythic themes, often entwined with leaves, flowers, vines, and symbols of the natural world, which later Visigothic and Romanesque artists adapted for their own use.

HISPANO-MOORISH ART Beginning in A.D. 711, when the first Moorish armies poured into Andalusia, the preconceptions of Spanish art changed forever. Forbidden by religious law to portray human or animal forms, Muslim artists restricted themselves to geometric patterns, ornate depictions of plant life, and calligraphic renderings of verses from the Koran. Their works influenced the Mozárabes, who brought these themes within a Christian context. The Moors also excelled at landscape architecture—the symmetrical placement of fountains, plants, and statues in some of the greatest gardens and pleasure pavilions ever built (see "Architecture 101," above).

ROMANESQUE ART Other than its architecture, the greatest artistic legacy of the Romanesque age, which began around A.D. 1000, was its sculpture. A vast number of churches and abbeys sprang up along the medieval world's most famous pilgrimage route (St. James's way across Asturias and Galicia), and each house of worship required sculpture to adorn the columns and altars. San Juan de la Peña was a master of the carved form, and his students branched out across the pilgrimage route, carving crude but symbolic references to apocryphal tales.

In Catalonia, aggressive merchants appropriated aesthetic ideals from Italy and France and had paintings executed on fresh plaster. Several of the most memorable of these Romanesque frescoes that remain today are credited to a mysterious painter, the Master of Tahull, who may have trained as far away as Byzantium. By 1300, Catalonia had been home to more than 1,000 artists, many of whom were inspired by this mysterious master.

GOTHIC ART Beginning around 1250, as the Gothic aesthetic trickled from France into Spain, the production of painting and sculpture accelerated. Works followed religious themes, often rendered in the form of polychrome triptychs and altarpieces that stretched toward the soaring heights of a cathedral's ceiling. Many painters took their inspiration from such contemporary pre-Renaissance Italians as Giotto; others looked to France and Flanders, and the attention their painters paid to naturalistic, and sometimes stylized, detail. Eventually, the slumbering figures atop funerary sarcophagi came to resemble, in sometimes ghoulish detail, the living body of the person buried within, and decorative adornments became almost obsessive.

RENAISSANCE, BAROQUE & BEYOND The defeat of the Muslims in 1492, and the colonialization the same year of the New World, marked the debut of the Renaissance in Spain. Choir stalls, altarpieces, funerary sarcophagi, and historical statues became commonplace throughout the newly united Spain. The popularity of gilding was a direct result of the precious metals flooding into the country from the mines of the New World. The cathedrals of Burgos and Barcelona and some of the chapels within the cathedral at Granada are fine examples of the heights to which Renaissance sculpture rose. A new technique, *estofado,* was introduced, whereby multiple colors were applied over a base of gold leaf, then rubbed or scratched to expose subtly gilded highlights in a way that prefigured the eventual rise of the baroque.

The greatest Spanish painter of the Renaissance was El Greco (Domenico Theotocopoulos, born in Crete in 1541), whose interpretation of Iberian mysticism reached deeper into the Spanish soul than any painter before or since. He was well versed in classical references and trained in all the methods popular in both Italy (especially Venice) and Byzantium. His was an intensely personal vision—amplified emotion, elongated limbs, and characters that were lifted bodily, and ecstatically, toward heaven. His style, known today as mannerism, met with violent criticism and lawsuits from disgruntled patrons.

After El Greco, the leading Spanish painter was Diego de Silva y Velázquez (1599–1660). Appointed court painter to the vain and self-indulgent monarch Philip IV, he painted 40 portraits of Philip, and dozens of other members of the royal family. Influenced by Rubens, who urged him to travel to Italy, his craftsmanship improved to the point where he has been hailed as the single greatest painter in the lexicon of Spanish art. Other important painters of this baroque period included José Ribera (1591–1652) and Francisco de Zurbarán (1598–1664). Bartolomé Murillo (1617–82) produced religious paintings that appealed, 200 years after his death, to the sentimentalism of the English Victorians.

The mantle of greatness was next passed to Francisco de Goya y Lucientes (1746–1828), an artist whose skill as a draftsman produced everything from tapestries to portraits of noble ladies. Rendered deaf in 1792 after a serious illness, Goya adopted a style of dark and brooding realism that many critics view as at least a century ahead of his contemporaries. In his work are vivid precursors of such future trends as romanticism and the psychological intricacies of expressionism. Victim of the political incompetencies of the Spanish regime, he was forced to flee in 1824 to Bordeaux, where he died, dejected, embittered, and broken.

MODERNISM & SURREALISM Around the turn of the 20th century, artists of note were so frustrated by the official repression of the Spanish establishment, that they emigrated, almost en masse to Paris. Such outstanding innovators as Joan Miró, Salvador Dalí, and Juan Gris were among this group, whose names later became as closely associated with France as with Spain.

The most influential of these expatriates was Pablo Picasso, born in Málaga in 1881. Before the end of his extraordinary career, he would become the most famous artist of the 20th century, mastering a variety of styles and in defining such major schools of art as cubism.

A divergent school, surrealism, was developed by Catalonia-born Dalí. His sometimes authentic, sometimes fraudulent commercial endeavors explored the subconscious levels of the human mind, using dream sequences whose content might have appealed to Jung and Freud.

Among the important Spanish abstract painters are Antoni Tàpies, a pioneer in the use of texture and geometric placement of shapes and forms, and Juan José Tharrats. Major sculptors include Jorge Otieza, Eduardo Chillida (whose abstract works bear almost no resemblance to the human form), and Andréu Alfaro, whose works hang in influential galleries in such cities as Barcelona and Madrid.

6 The Cuisine: Tapas to Paella & Sangría

The food in Spain is varied; the portions are immense, but the prices, by North American standards, are high. Whenever possible, try the regional specialties, particularly when you visit the Basque country or Galicia. Many of these regional dishes, including Andalusian gazpacho and Valencian paella, have become great dishes of the world.

MEALS

Breakfast In Spain the day starts with a continental breakfast of coffee, hot chocolate, or tea, with assorted rolls, butter, and jam. A typical Spanish breakfast consists of *churros* (fried fingerlike doughnuts) and a hot chocolate that is very sweet and thick. The coffee is usually strong and black, served with hot milk. Some Americans consider it too strong and bitter for their taste and therefore ask for instant coffee.

Lunch An important meal in Spain, lunch is comparable to the farm-style noonday "dinner" in America. It usually includes three or four courses, beginning with a choice of soup or several dishes of hors d'oeuvres called *entremeses.* Often a fish or an egg dish is served after this, then a meat course with vegetables. Wine is always on the table. Dessert is usually pastry, custard, or assorted fruit—followed by coffee. Lunch is served from 1 to 3:30pm, with "rush hour" at 2pm.

Tapas After the early-evening promenade, many Spaniards head for their favorite *tascas,* or bars, where they drink wine and sample assorted *tapas,* or snacks, such as bits of fish, eggs in mayonnaise, or olives.

Dinner Another extravaganza. A typical meal starts with a bowl of soup, followed by a second course, often a fish dish, and by another main course, usually veal, beef, or pork, accompanied by vegetables. Again, desserts tend to be fruit, custard, or pastries.

Wine is always available. Afterward, you might have a demitasse and a fragrant Spanish brandy. The chic dining hour, even in one-donkey towns, is 10 or 10:30pm. (In well-touristed regions and hardworking Catalonia, you can usually dine by 8pm.) In most middle-class establishments, people dine no later than 9:30pm. The choice is up to you.

Dining Customs Most restaurants in Spain close on Sunday, so be sure to check ahead. Hotel dining rooms are generally open seven days, and there's always a food dispenser open in such big cities as Madrid and Barcelona or such well-touristed areas as the Costa del Sol.

Generally, reservations are not necessary, except at popular, top-notch restaurants.

Some Health/Diet Tips North Americans who plunge wholeheartedly into the Spanish routine may experience digestive trouble, particularly if they also drink more wine than usual. By the third day they will invariably be in the grip of "Toledo trot." To stop this malady, purchase Tanagel, sold in all pharmacies.

Two heavy Spanish meals a day are definitely not recommended. For lighter fare, patronize the cafeterias that are not self-service.

As a final caution, if you do eat a large lunch, don't rush out into the noonday sun for a round of sightseeing. Do as the Spaniard does: Take a siesta. Or you can take your large meal at lunch and have a light snack at a tapas bar in the evening.

THE CUISINE

Soups & Appetizers Soups are usually served in big bowls. Cream soups, such as asparagus and potato, can be fine; sadly, however, they are too often made from powdered envelope soups such as Knorr and Liebig. Served year-round, chilled gazpacho, on the other hand, is tasty and particularly refreshing during the hot months. The combination is pleasant: olive oil, garlic, ground cucumbers, and raw tomatoes with a sprinkling of croûtons. Spain also offers several varieties of fish soup—*sopa de pescado*—in all its provinces, and many of these are superb.

In the paradors (government-run hostelries) and top restaurants, as many as 15 tempting hors d'oeuvres are served. In lesser-known places, avoid these *entremeses,* which often consist of last year's sardines and shards of sausage left over from the Moorish conquest.

Eggs These are served in countless ways. A Spanish omelet, a *tortilla española,* is made with potatoes. A simple omelet is called a *tortilla francesa.* A *tortilla portuguésa* is similar to the American Spanish omelet.

Fish Spain's fish dishes tend to be outstanding and vary from province to province. One of the most common varieties is sweet white hake (*merluza*). *Langosta,* a variety of lobster, is seen everywhere—it's a treat but terribly expensive. The Portuguese in particular, but some Spaniards, too, go into raptures at the mention of barnacles. Gourmets relish their seawater taste; others find them tasteless. *Rape* is the Spanish name for monkfish, a sweet, wide-boned ocean fish with a scalloplike texture. Also try a few dozen half-inch baby eels. They rely heavily on olive oil and garlic for their flavor, but they taste great. Squid cooked in its own ink is suggested only to those who want to go native. Charcoal-broiled sardines, however, are a culinary delight—a particular treat in the Basque provinces. Trout Navarre is one of the most popular fish dishes, usually stuffed with bacon or ham.

Paella You can't go to Spain without trying its celebrated paella. Flavored with saffron, paella is an aromatic rice dish usually topped with shellfish, chicken, sausage, peppers, and local spices. Served authentically, it comes steaming hot from the kitchen in a metal pan called a *paellera.* (Incidentally, what is known in America as Spanish rice isn't Spanish at all. If you ask an English-speaking waiter for Spanish rice, you'll be served paella.)

Meats Don't expect Kansas City steak, but do try the spit-roasted suckling pig, so sweet and tender it can often be cut with a fork. The veal is also good, and the Spanish *lomo de cerdo,* loin of pork, is unmatched anywhere. As for chicken, it will

From Vineyards to the Bodegas

Wines were first cultivated in Spain more than 2,000 years ago by ancient Greeks and Romans. Great emphasis came to be placed on the export of wines for both the orgies of the late Roman Empire and the celebration of communion during the early years of the Christian church.

Some of the country's vintages have been acknowledged as superb since the turn of the century, when vintners from Bordeaux, fleeing the phylloxera epidemic that had devastated many of the vineyards of France, carried their expertise to such regions as La Rioja, Navarre, and Catalonia. Beginning about a century earlier, others, most notably the vintners of such Andalusian regions as Jerez, grew rich on exporting sherries to the dinner tables of faraway Britain.

Today, Spain devotes more acreage to the cultivation of vineyards than any other nation in the world. For many years, however, because of trade restrictions and economic stagnation during the Franco regime, the output from many of these acres was not considered the equivalent of top wines from such competing regions as France, Italy, Chile, and California. Connoisseurs, when faced with a Spanish wine list, tended to focus rather narrowly on the wines of Jerez, La Rioja, and the Penedés region of Catalonia.

Thanks to some of the most aggressive and enlightened marketing in Europe, however, all of that is changing. Beginning in the 1990s, based partly on subsidies and incentives from the European Union, Spanish vintners have scrapped most of the country's obsolete wine-making equipment, hired new talent, and poured time and money into the improvement and promotion of wines from even high-altitude or arid regions not previously suitable for the drink's production. Thanks to irrigation, improved grape varieties, technological developments, and the expenditure of billions of pesetas, bodegas and vineyards are sprouting up throughout the country, opening their doors to visitors interested in how the stuff is grown, fermented, and bottled. These wines are now earning awards at wine competitions around the world for their quality and bouquet.

Interested in impressing a newfound Spanish friend over a wine list? Consider bypassing the usual array of Riojas, sherries, and sparkling Catalonian cavas in favor of, say, a Galician white from Rias Baixas, which some connoisseurs consider the perfect accompaniment for seafood. Among reds, make a beeline for vintages from the fastest-developing wine region of Europe, the arid, high-altitude district of Ribera del Duero, near Burgos, whose alkaline soil, cold nights, and sunny days have earned unexpected praise from wine makers (and encouraged massive investments) in the past five years.

For more information about these and others of the 10 wine-producing regions of Spain (and the 39 officially recognized wine-producing *Denominatións de Origen* scattered across those regions), contact **Wines from Spain,** c/o the Commercial Office of Spain, 405 Lexington Avenue, 44th Floor, New York, NY 10174-0331 (**☎ 212/661-4818**).

sometimes qualify for the Olympics because it is stringy and muscular. Spit-roasted chicken, however, often can be flavorful.

Vegetables & Salads Through more sophisticated agricultural methods, Spain now grows more of its own vegetables, which are available year-round, unlike days of yore, when canned vegetables were used all too frequently. Both potatoes and rice are a staple of the Spanish diet, the latter a prime ingredient, of course, in the famous paella originating in Valencia. Salads don't usually get the attention they do in California, and are often made simply with just lettuce and tomatoes.

Desserts The Spanish do not emphasize dessert. Flan, a home-cooked egg custard, appears on all menus—sometimes with a burnt-caramel sauce. Ice cream appears on nearly all menus as well. But the best bet is to ask for a basket of fresh fruit, which you can wash at your table. Homemade pastries are usually moist and not too sweet. As a dining oddity, many restaurants serve fresh orange juice for dessert. Madrileños love it!

Olive Oil & Garlic Olive oil is used lavishly in Spain. You may not want it in all dishes. If, for example, you prefer your fish grilled in butter, the word is *mantequilla.* In some instances, you'll be charged extra for the butter. Garlic is also an integral part of the Spanish diet, and even if you love it, you may find the Spaniard loves it more than you do and uses it in the oddest dishes.

. . . AND WHAT TO DRINK

Water It is generally safe to drink water in all major cities and tourist resorts in Spain. If you're traveling in remote areas, play it safe and drink bottled water. One of the most popular noncarbonated bottled drinks in Spain is Solares. Nearly all restaurants and hotels have it. If you'd like your water with a little kick, then ask for *agua mineral con gas.* Note that bottled water often costs more than the regional wine.

Soft Drinks In general, avoid the carbonated citrus drinks on sale everywhere. Most of them never saw an orange, much less a lemon. If you want a citrus drink, order old, reliable Schweppes. An excellent noncarbonated drink for the summer is called Tri-Naranjus, which comes in lemon and orange flavors. Your cheapest bet is a liter bottle of gaseosa, which comes in various flavors. In summer you should also try a drink that we've never had outside Spain, *horchara*—a nutty, sweet milklike beverage made of tubers called *chufas.*

Coffee Even if you are a dedicated coffee drinker, you may find the *café con leche* (coffee with milk) a little too strong. We suggest *leche manchada,* a little bit of strong, freshly brewed coffee in a glass that's filled with lots of frothy hot milk.

Milk In the largest cities you get bottled milk, but it loses a great deal of its flavor in the process of pasteurization. In all cases, avoid untreated milk and milk products. About the best brand of fresh milk is Lauki.

Beer Although not native to Spain, beer (*cerveza*) is now drunk everywhere. Domestic brands include San Miguel, Mahou, Aguila, and Cruz Blanka.

Wine Sherry (*vino de Jerez*) has been called "the wine with a hundred souls." Drink it before dinner (try the topaz-colored *finos,* a very pale sherry) or whenever you drop in to some old inn or bodega for refreshment; many of them have rows of kegs with spigots. Manzanilla, a golden-colored medium-dry sherry, is extremely popular. The sweet cream sherries (Harvey's Bristol Cream, for example) are favorite after-dinner wines (called *olorosos*). While the French may be disdainful of Spanish table wines, they can be truly noble, especially two leading varieties, Valdepeñas and Rioja, both from Castile. If you're fairly adventurous and not too demanding in your tastes, you can always ask for the *vino de la casa* (wine of the house) wherever you dine. The Ampurdan of Catalonia is heavy. From Andalusia comes the fruity Montilla. There are also some good local champagnes (*cavas*) in Spain, such as Freixenet. One brand, Benjamin, also comes in individual-sized bottles.

Sangría The all-time favorite refreshing drink in Spain, sangría is a red-wine punch that combines wine with oranges, lemons, seltzer, and sugar.

Whiskey & Brandy Imported whiskeys are available at most Spanish bars but at a high price. If you're a drinker, switch to brandies and cognacs, where the Spanish reign supreme. Try Fundador, made by the Pedro Domecq family in Jerez de la Frontera. If you're seeking a smooth cognac, ask for the "103" white label.

Planning a Trip to Spain

3

This chapter is devoted to the where, when, and how of your trip—the advance planning required to get it together and take it on the road.

After they've decided where to go, most people have two fundamental questions: What will it cost, and how do I get there? This chapter addresses these concerns and such other important issues as when to go, what entry requirements there are, what alternative travel vacations to consider, what pretrip preparations are needed, where to obtain more information about Spain, and much more.

1 Information & Required Documents

SOURCES OF VISITOR INFORMATION

In the United States For information before you go, contact the Tourist Office of Spain, 666 Fifth Ave., 5th Floor, New York, NY 10103 (☎ 212/265-8822), which can provide sightseeing information, calendars of events, train and ferry schedules, maps, and much, much more. Elsewhere in the United States, branches of the Tourist Office of Spain are located at: 8383 Wilshire Blvd., Suite 960, Beverly Hills, CA 90211 (☎ 213/658-7188); 845 N. Michigan Ave., Suite 915 E., Chicago, IL 60611 (☎ 312/642-1992); and 1221 Brickell Ave., Miami, FL 33131 (☎ 305/358-1992).

In Canada Write to the Tourist Office of Spain, 102 Bloor St. W., 14th Floor, Toronto, ON M5S 1M9 (☎ 416/961-3131).

In Australia Write to Spanish Tourist Information, 203 Castlereagh St., Suite 21A, P.O. Box 675, Sydney, NSW 2000 (☎ 612/264-7966).

In Great Britain Contact the Spanish National Tourist Office, 57 St. James's St., London SW1 (☎ 0171/499-0901).

REQUIRED DOCUMENTS

PASSPORTS A valid passport is all that an American, British, Canadian, or New Zealand citizen needs to enter Spain, and one can be secured as follows. (Australians need a visa—see below.)

In the United States You can apply for passports in person at one of 13 regional offices or by mail. To apply, you'll need a passport application form, available at U.S. post offices and federal court offices, and proof of citizenship, such as a birth certificate or naturalization papers; an expired passport is also accepted. First-time applicants for passports pay $65 ($40 if under 18 years of age) Persons 18 or older who have an expired passport that's not more than 12 years old can reapply by mail. The old passport must be submitted along with new photographs and a pink renewal form (DSP-82)

If your expired passport is more than 12 years old, or if it was granted to you before your 16th birthday, you must apply in person. The fee is $55. Call **202/647-0518** at any time for information. You can also write to Passport Service, Office of Correspondence, Department of State, 1111 19th St., NW, Suite 510, Washington, DC 20522-1075.

You'll wait the longest to receive your passport between mid-March and mid-September; in winter it usually takes about two weeks by mail. Passports can sometimes be issued quickly in an emergency, provided you present a plane ticket with a confirmed seat—but keep in mind it's more expensive.

In Canada Citizens may go to one of 28 regional offices located in major cities. Alternatively, you can mail your application to the Passport Office, External Affairs and International Trade Canada, Ottawa, ON K1A 0G3. Post offices have application forms. Passports cost CAN$60, and proof of Canadian citizenship is required, along with two signed identical passport-size photographs. Passports are valid for five years. For more information, call **800/567-6868.**

In Great Britain British subjects may apply to one of the regional offices in Liverpool, Newport, Glasgow, Peterborough, Belfast, or London. You can also apply in person at a main post office. The fee is £18, and the passport is good for 10 years. Two photos must accompany the application.

In Australia Citizens may apply at the nearest post office. Provincial capitals and other major cities have passport offices. Application fees are subject to review every three months. Telephone **02/13-12-32** for the latest information. Australians must pay for a departure tax stamp costing AUS$20 at a post office or airport; children 11 and under are exempt.

In New Zealand Citizens may go to their nearest consulate or passport office to obtain an application, which may be filed in person or by mail. To obtain a 10-year passport, proof of citizenship is required, plus a fee of NZ$80. Passports are processed at the New Zealand Passport Office, Documents of National Identity Division, Department of Internal Affairs, P.O. Box 10-526, Wellington (☎ **04/474-81-00**).

In Ireland Contact the passport office at Setna Centre, Molesworth St., Dublin 2 (☎ **01/671-16-33**). The charge is IR£45. Applications are sent by mail. Irish citizens living in North America can contact the Irish Embassy, 2234 Massachusetts Ave., NW, Washington, DC 20008 (☎ **202/462-3939**). The embassy can issue a new passport or direct you to one of three North American consulates that have jurisdiction over a particular region; the charge is US$80. If you apply in person, you'll get a $5 discount.

VISAS Visas are not needed by U.S., Canadian, Irish, or British citizens for visits of less than three months. Citizens of Australia and South Africa do need to obtain a visa and should apply in advance at the Spanish Consulate in their home country.

CUSTOMS You can take into Spain most personal effects and the following items duty free: two still cameras and 10 rolls of film per camera, tobacco for personal use, one liter each of liquor and wine, a portable radio, a tape recorder, a typewriter, a bicycle, sports equipment, fishing gear, and two hunting weapons with 100 cartridges each.

In the United States Returning to the United States from Spain, American citizens may bring in U.S.$400 worth of merchandise duty free, provided that they have not made a similar claim within the past 30 days. Remember to keep your receipts for purchases made in Spain. For more specific guidance, write to the U.S. Customs Service, P.O. Box 7407, Washington, DC 20044, and request the free pamphlet "Know Before You Go."

In Canada For total clarification Canadians can write for the booklet "I Declare," issued by Revenue Canada, Communications Branch, 875 Heron Rd., Ottawa, ON K1A 0L8. Canada allows its citizens a CAN$500 exemption after an absence of seven days or more. They can bring back, duty free, 200 cigarettes, 400 grams of manufactured tobacco, 50 cigars or cigarillos, and 30 ounces of liquor. In addition, they're allowed to mail unsolicited gifts (except alcohol or tobacco) to Canada from abroad at the rate of CAN$60 or less. On the package, mark "Unsolicited Gift, Under $60 Value." All valuables you own and take with you should be declared before you depart from Canada on the Y-38 form, including serial numbers.

In Great Britain Members of European Union (formerly Community) countries do not necessarily have to go through Customs when returning home, provided that their travel was exclusively within the EU. Of course, Customs officers reserve the right to search a traveler if they're suspicious. However, there are certain EU guidelines for returning passengers who can bring in 400 cigarillos, 200 cigars, 800 cigarettes, and 1 kilogram of smoking tobacco.

They can also bring in 10 liters of spirits, 20 liters of fortified wine, 90 liters of wine, and 110 liters of beer. Persons exceeding these limits may be asked to prove that excess is either for one's personal use or gifts for friends. For further details on United Kingdom Customs, contact: HM Customs and Excise, Advice Centre, Dorset House, Stamford St., London SE1 9NG (☎ **0171/202-4227**).

In Australia The duty-free allowance in Australia is AUS$400 or, for those under 18, AUS$200. Personal property mailed back from Spain should be marked "Australian goods returned," to avoid payment of duty. Upon returning to Australia, citizens can bring in 200 cigarettes or 250 grams of loose tobacco and a liter of alcohol. If you're returning with valuable goods you already own, such as foreign-made cameras, you should file Form B263. A helpful brochure, available from Australian consulates or Customs offices, is "Customs Information for All Travelers." For more information, contact the Australian Customs Service, 5 Constitution Ave., Canberra, ACT 2601 (☎ **6/275-62-55**).

In New Zealand The duty-free allowance is NZ$700. Citizens over 16 years of age can bring in 200 cigarettes (or 250 grams of loose tobacco) or 50 cigars, 4.5 liters of wine or beer, or 1.125 liters of liquor. New Zealand currency does not carry restrictions regarding import or export. A Certificate of Export, listing valuables taken out of the country, allows you to bring them back without paying duty. Most questions are answered in a free pamphlet, "New Zealand Customs Guide for Travellers," available at New Zealand consulates and Customs offices. For more information, contact New Zealand Customs, 50 Anzac Ave., P.O. Box 29, Auckland (☎ **9/377-35-20**).

2 Money

CASH/CURRENCY The basic unit of Spanish currency is the **peseta** (abbreviated pta.), currently worth about 8/10 of a cent in U.S. currency. One dollar is worth about 125 pesetas. Coins come in 1, 5, 25, 50, 100, 200, and 500 pesetas. Notes are issued in 500; 1,000; 5,000; and 10,000 pesetas.

The Spanish Peseta

For American Readers At this writing, $1 = approximately 125 ptas. (or 1 pta. = 8/10 of 1 U.S. cent). This was the rate of exchange used to calculate the dollar equivalents given throughout this edition.

For British Readers At this writing, £1 = approximately 188 ptas. (or l pta. = half a pence). This was the rate of exchange used to calculate the pound values in the table below.

peseta	US$	UK£	peseta	US$	UK£
50	0.40	0.27	20,000	160.00	106.00
100	0.80	0.53	25,000	200.00	132.50
300	2.40	1.59	30,000	240.00	159.00
500	4.00	2.65	35,000	280.00	185.50
700	5.60	3.71	40,000	320.00	212.00
1,000	8.00	5.30	45,000	360.00	238.50
1,500	12.00	7.95	50,000	400.00	265.00
2,000	16.00	10.60	100,000	800.00	530.00
3,000	24.00	15.90	125,000	1,000.00	662.50
4,000	32.00	21.20	150,000	1,200.00	795.00
5,000	40.00	26.50	200,000	1,600.00	1,060.00
7,500	60.00	39.75	250,000	2,000.00	1,325.00
10,000	80.00	53.00	500,000	4,000.00	2,650.00
15,000	120.00	79.50	1,000,000	8,000.00	5,300.00

All world currencies fluctuate, so you should be aware that the amounts appearing in this book are not exact. Currency conversions are presented only to give you a rough idea of the price you'll pay in U.S. dollars. There is no way to predict exactly what the rate of exchange will be when you visit Spain. Check the newspaper or ask at your bank for last-minute quotations.

Be advised that rates of exchange vary, depending on where you convert your money. In general, you'll get the best exchange rate by using your credit card or withdrawing cash from an ATM machine. Banks also offer competitive rates, but keep in mind they charge a commission for cashing traveler's checks. You'll get the worst rates of exchange at your hotel, as well as at point-of-entry sites like an airport or train station.

ATM NETWORKS PLUS, Cirrus, and other networks connecting automated-teller machines operate in Spain. If your bank card has been programmed with a PIN (Personal Identification Number), it is likely that you can use your card at ATMs abroad to withdraw money directly from your home bank account. Check with your bank to see if your PIN code must be reprogrammed for usage in Spain. Before leaving, always determine the frequency limits for withdrawals, and what fees—if any—your bank will assess. For Cirrus locations abroad, call **800/424-7787;** also, Cirrus ATM locations in selected cities are available on MasterCard's Internet site (www.mastercard.com). For PLUS usage abroad, contact your local bank or check Visa's page on the World Wide Web (www.visa.com).

TRAVELER'S CHECKS Though ATM usage is becoming increasingly commonplace, many people prefer the security of traveler's checks. Purchase them before leaving home and arrange to carry some ready cash (usually about $250, depending on your needs). In the event of theft, if the checks are properly documented, the value of your checks will be refunded. Most large banks sell traveler's checks, charging fees that average between 1% and 2% of the value of the checks you buy, although some out-of-the-way banks, in rare instances, have charged as much as 7%. If your bank wants more than a 2% commission, call the traveler's check issuers directly for the address of outlets where this commission will cost less.

American Express (☎ **800/221-7282** in the U.S. and Canada) is one of the largest and most immediately recognized issuers of traveler's checks. No commission is charged to members of the AAA and to holders of certain types of American Express credit cards. The company issues checks denominated in U.S. dollars, Canadian dollars, and British pounds, among other currencies. The vast majority of checks sold in North America are denominated in U.S. dollars. For questions or problems that arise outside the U.S. or Canada, contact any of the company's many regional representatives.

Citicorp (☎ **800/645-6556** in the U.S. and Canada, or 813/623-1709, collect, from anywhere else in the world) issues checks in U.S. dollars as well as British pounds.

Thomas Cook (☎ **800/223-7373** in the U.S., or 609/987-7300, collect, from other parts of the world) issues MasterCard traveler's checks denominated in U.S. dollars, British pounds, Spanish pesetas, and Australian dollars. Depending

What Things Cost in Madrid	U.S. $
Taxi from airport to Puerta del Sol	20.00
Public transportation within the city	1.05
Local telephone call	.20
Double room at the Palace (very expensive)	320.00
Double room at Aristos (moderate)	128.00
Double room at Hostal Principado (inexpensive)	46.40
Lunch for one, without wine, at Alkalde (expensive)	27.20
Lunch for one, without wine, at Foster's Hollywood (inexpensive)	14.00
Dinner for one, without wine, at El Cabo Mayor (expensive)	32.00
Dinner for one, without wine, at Sobrino de Botín (moderate)	19.90
Dinner for one, without wine, at Taberna Carmencita (inexpensive)	9.90
Coca-Cola in a restaurant	1.60
Cup of coffee	2.00
Glass of wine or beer	2.40
Admission to the Prado	3.20
Roll of ASA 100 color film, 36 exposures	8.00
Movie ticket	6.40
Theater ticket	11.20

on individual banking laws in each of the various states, some of the above-mentioned currencies may not be available in every outlet.

Interpayment Services (☎ **800/221-2426** in the U.S. or Canada, or 212/858-8500 from most other parts of the world) sells Visa checks sponsored by a consortium of member banks and the Thomas Cook organization. Traveler's checks can be denominated in U.S. or Canadian dollars or British pounds.

MoneyGram If you find yourself out of money, a new wire service provided by American Express can help you tap willing friends and family for emergency funds. Through MoneyGram, 6200 S. Quebec St., P.O. Box 5118, Englewood, CO 80155 (☎ **800/926-9400**), money can be sent around the world in less than 10 minutes. Senders should call AmEx to learn the address of the closest outlet that handles MoneyGrams. Cash, credit card, and the occasional personal check (with ID) are acceptable forms of payment. AmEx's fee for the service is $10 for the first $300 with a sliding scale for larger sums. The service includes a short telex message and a three-minute phone call from sender to recipient. The beneficiary must present a photo ID at the outlet where money is received.

CREDIT CARDS **American Express, Visa,** and **Diners Club** are widely recognized in Spain. If you see the **Eurocard** or **Access** sign on an establishment, it means that it accepts **MasterCard. Discover** cards are accepted only in the U.S.

CURRENCY EXCHANGE Many hotels in Spain do not accept dollar- or pound-denominated checks; those that do will almost certainly charge for the conversion. In some cases, they'll accept countersigned traveler's checks or a credit card, but if you're prepaying a deposit on hotel reservations, it's cheaper and easier to pay with a check drawn on a Spanish bank.

If you need a check payable in pesetas, call Ruesch's toll-free number, describe what you need, and note the transaction number given to you. Mail your dollar-denominated personal check (payable to Ruesch International) to their office in Washington, D.C. Upon receiving this, the company will mail a check denominated in pesetas for the financial equivalent, minus the $2 charge. The company can also help you with many different kinds of wire transfers and conversions of VAT (Value-Added Tax, known as IVA in Spain), refund checks, and also will mail brochures and information packets on request. Britishers can go to Ruesch International Ltd., 18 Savile Row, London W1X 2AD (☎ **0171/734-2300**).

3 When to Go: Climate, Holidays & Events

CLIMATE

May and October are the best months, weatherwise and crowdwise. In fact, spring and fall are ideal times to visit nearly all of Spain, with the possible exception of the Atlantic coast, which experiences heavy rains in October and November.

In summer it's hot, hot, and hot again, with the cities in Castile (Madrid) and Andalusia (Seville and Córdoba) stewing up the most scalding brew. Madrid has dry heat; the temperature can hover around 84°F in July, 75° in September. Seville has the dubious reputation of being about the hottest part of Spain in July and August, often baking under temperatures that average around 93°.

Barcelona is humid. Midsummer temperatures in Majorca often reach 91°. The overcrowded Costa Brava has temperatures around 81° in July and August. The Costa del Sol has an average of 77° in summer. The coolest spot in Spain is the Atlantic coast from San Sebastián to La Coruña, with temperatures in the 70s in July and August.

August remains the major vacation month in Europe. The traffic from France to Spain becomes a veritable migration, and low-cost hotels along the coastal areas are virtually impossible to find. To compound the problem, many restaurants and shops also decide that it's time for a vacation, thereby limiting the visitor's selections for both dining and shopping.

In winter, the coast from Algeciras to Málaga is the most popular, with temperatures reaching a warm 60° to 63°. Madrid gets cold, as low as 34°. Majorca is warmer, usually in the 50s, but it often dips into the 40s. Some mountain resorts can experience extreme cold.

HOLIDAYS

Holidays include January 1 (New Year's Day), January 6 (Feast of the Epiphany), March 19 (Feast of St. Joseph), Good Friday, Easter Monday, May 1 (May Day), June 10 (Corpus Christi), June 29 (Feast of St. Peter and St. Paul), July 25 (Feast of St. James), August 15 (Feast of the Assumption), October 12 (Spain's National Day), November 1 (All Saints' Day), December 8 (Immaculate Conception), and December 25 (Christmas).

No matter how large or small, every city or town in Spain also celebrates its local saint's day. In Madrid it's May 15 (St. Isidro). You'll rarely know what the local holidays are in your next destination in Spain. Try to keep money on hand, because you may arrive in town only to find banks and stores closed. In some cases, intercity bus services are suspended on holidays.

SPAIN CALENDAR OF EVENTS

The dates given below may not be precise. Sometimes the exact days are not announced until six weeks before the actual festival. Check with the National Tourist Office of Spain (see "Information & Required Documents" at the beginning of this chapter) if you're planning to attend a specific event.

January

- **Granada Reconquest Festival,** Granada. The whole of Granada celebrates the Christians' victory over the Moors in 1492. The highest tower at the Alhambra is open to the public on January 2. For information, contact the Tourist Office of Granada (☎ **958/22-66-88**). January 1–2.
- **Día de los Reyes (Three Kings Day),** throughout Spain. Parades are held around the country on the eve of the Festival of thc Epiphany. Various "kings" dispense candies to children. January 6.
- **St. Anthony's Day (La Puebla),** Majorca. Bonfires, dancing, revelers dressed as devils, and other riotous events honor St. Anthony on the eve of his day. January 17.

February

- **ARCO** (Madrid's International Contemporary Art Fair), Madrid. One of the biggest draws in Spain's cultural calendar, this exhibit showcases the best in contemporary art from Europe and America. At the Crystal Pavilion of the Casa de Campo, the exhibition presents both regional and internationally known artists. Dates vary.
- **Bocairente Festival of Christians and Moors,** Bocairentc (Valencia). Fireworks, colorful costumes, parades, and a reenactment of the struggle between Christians and Moors mark this exuberant festival. A stuffed effigy of Mohammed is blown to bits. February 1–15.

- **Carnivales de Cádiz,** Cádiz. The oldest and best-attended carnival in Spain has been called "rampant madness." Costumes, parades, strolling troubadours, and drum beating—it's all fun and games. February 22–March 4.
- **Madrid Carnival,** Madrid. The carnival kicks off with a big parade along the Paseo de la Castellana, culminating in a masked ball at the Círculo de Bellas Artes on the following night. Fancy-dress competitions last until February 28, when the festivities end with a tear-jerking "burial of a sardine" at the Fuente de los Pajaritos in the Casa de Campo. This is followed that evening by a concert in the Plaza Mayor. Dates vary.

March

- **Fallas de Valencia,** Valencia. Going back to the 1400s, this fiesta centers around the burning of papier-mâché effigies of winter demons. Burnings are preceded by bullfights, fireworks, and parades. March 19.

April

✪ **Feria de Sevilla (Seville Fair).** This is the most celebrated week of revelry in all of Spain, with all-night flamenco dancing, merrymaking in *casetas* (entertainment booths), bullfights, horseback riding, flower-decked coaches, and dancing in the streets. You'll need to reserve a hotel early for this one. For general information and exact festival dates, contact the Office of Tourism in Seville (☎ **95/422-14-04**). Mid-April.

✪ **Semana Santa (Holy Week),** Seville. Though many of the country's smaller towns stage similar celebrations, the festivities in Seville are by far the most elaborate. From Palm Sunday until Easter Sunday, a series of processions with hooded penitents moves to the piercing wail of the *saeta,* a love song to the Virgin or Christ. *Pasos* (heavy floats) bear images of the Virgin or Christ. Again, make hotel reservations way in advance. Call the Seville Office of Tourism for details (☎ **95/422-14-04**). Mid-April.

May

- **Festival de los Patios,** Córdoba. At this famous fair residents flamboyantly decorate their patios with cascades of flowers. Visitors wander from patio to patio. First two weeks in May.
- **Romería del Rocio (Pilgrimage of the Virgin of the Dew),** El Rocio (Huelva). The most famous pilgrimage in Andalusia attracts a million people. Fifty men carry the statue of the Virgin nine miles to Almonte for consecration. May 11–14.

✪ **Fiesta de San Isidro,** Madrid. Madrileños run wild with a 10-day celebration honoring their city's patron saint. Food fairs, Castilian folkloric events, street parades, parties, music, dances, bullfights, and other festivities mark the occasion. Make hotel reservations early. Expect crowds and traffic (and beware of pickpockets). For information, write to Oficina Municipal de Información y Turismo, Plaza Mayor, 3, 28014 Madrid. May 12–21.

- **Jerez Horse Fair,** Jerez de la Frontera. "Horses, wine, women, and song," according to the old Andalusian ditty, make this a stellar event at which some of the greatest horses in the world go on parade. May 13–20.

June

- **Veranos de la Villa,** Madrid. Called "the summer binge" of Madrid, this program presents folkloric dancing, pop music, classical music, zarzuelas, and flamenco at various venues throughout the city. Open-air cinema is a feature in the Parque del Retiro. Ask at the various tourist offices for complete details (the program changes every summer). Sometimes admission is charged, but often these events are free. All summer long.

- **Corpus Christi,** all over Spain. A major holiday on the Spanish calendar, this event is marked by big processions, especially in such cathedral cities as Toledo, Málaga, Seville, and Granada. June 14.
- ✪ **International Music and Dance Festival,** Granada. In its 47th year (1997), Granada's prestigious program of dance and music attracts international artists who perform at the Alhambra and other venues. It's a major event on the cultural calendar of Europe. Reserve well in advance. For a complete listing and to reserve tickets, contact El Festival Internacional de Música y Danza de Granada (☎ **958/22-00-22**). June 21–July 7.
- **Verbena de Sant Joan,** Barcelona. This traditional festival occupies all Cataláns. Barcelona literally "lights up"—with fireworks, bonfires, and dances until dawn. The highlight of the festival is the fireworks show at Montjuïc. June 24.

July

- **Festival of St. James,** Santiago de Compostela. Pomp and ceremony mark this annual pilgrimage to the tomb of St. James the Apostle in Galicia. Galician folklore shows, concerts, parades, and the swinging of the *botafumeiro* (a mammoth incense burner) mark the event. Mid- to late July.
- **San Sebastián Jazz Festival,** San Sebastián. Celebrating its 32nd year (1997), this festival brings together the jazz greats of the world at the pavilion of the Anoeta Sport Complex. Other programs take place al fresco at the Plaza de Trinidad in the old quarter. Last two weeks in July.
- ✪ **Fiesta de San Fermín,** Pamplona. Vividly described in Ernest Hemingway's novel *The Sun Also Rises,* the "running of the bulls" through the streets of Pamplona is the most popular celebration in Spain. The celebration also includes wine tasting, fireworks, and, of course, bullfights. Reserve months in advance. ("Papa" Hemingway paid a man a yearly stipend to secure the best tickets and hotel rooms.) For more information, such as a list of accommodations, contact the Office of Tourism, Duque de Ahumada, 3, 31002 Pamplona (☎ **948/22-07-41**). July 6–14.

August

- **Santander International Festival of Music and Dance,** Santander. The repertoire includes classical music, ballet, contemporary dance, chamber music, and recitals. Most performances are staged at the Plaza de la Porticada. For further information, contact Festival Internacional de Santander (☎ **942/210-345**). Throughout August.
- **Fiestas of Lavapiés and La Paloma,** Madrid. These two fiestas begin with the Lavapiés on August 1 and continue through the hectic La Paloma celebration on August 15, the day of the Virgen de la Paloma. Thousands of people race through the narrow streets. Apartment dwellers hurl buckets of cold water onto the crowds below to cool them off. There are children's games, floats, music, flamenco, and zarzuelas, along with street fairs. August 1–15.
- **The Mystery Play of Elche,** Elche. This sacred drama is reenacted in the 17th-century Basilica of Santa María in Elche (near Alicante). It represents the Assumption and the Crowning of the Virgin. Tickets may be obtained from the Office of Tourism in Elche (☎ **96/545-27-47**). August 11–15.
- **Feria de Málaga** (Málaga Fair). One of the longest summer fairs in southern Europe (generally lasting for 10 days), this celebration kicks off with fireworks displays and is highlighted by a parade of Arab horses pulling brightly decorated carriages. Participants are dressed in colorful Andalusian garb. Plazas rattle with castanets, and wine is dispensed by the gallon. Usually begins around mid-August.

September

- **Diada,** Barcelona. This is the most significant festival in Catalonia. It celebrates the region's autonomy from the rest of Spain, following years of repression under the dictator Franco. Demonstrations and other "flag-waving" events take place. The *senyera,* the flag of Catalonia, is much in evidence. Not your typical tourist fare, but interesting nevertheless. September 11.
- ✪ **Autumn Festival,** Madrid. Both Spanish and international artists participate in this cultural program, with a series of operatic, ballet, dance, music, and theatrical performances. From Strasbourg to Tokyo, this event is a premier attraction, yet tickets are reasonable. Make hotel reservations early, and write for tickets to Festival de Otoño, Plaza de España, 8, 28008 Madrid (☎ **91/580-25-75**). Mid-September to mid-November.
- **Cádiz Grape Harvest Festival,** Jerez de la Frontera. The major wine festival in Andalusia (which means Spain as well) honors the famous sherry of Jerez, with five days of processions, flamenco dancing, bullfights, livestock on parade, and, of course, sherry drinking. Mid-September (dates vary).
- **International Film Festival San Sebastián.** The premier film festival of Spain takes place in the Basque capital, often at the Victoria Eugenia Theater, a belle epoque masterpiece. Retrospectives are often featured, and week-long screenings are shown. Second half of September (dates vary).
- **Setmana Cran,** Barcelona. As the summer draws to an end, Barcelona stages week-long *verbenas* (carnivals) and *sardana* dances to honor its patron saint, the Virgin of Merced. Parades, concerts, various theatrical and musical events, and even sports competitions mark this event. Bullfights are also part of the festival. Look for the "parade of giants" through the streets, culminating at Plaça de Sant Jaume in front of the city hall. Dates vary.

October

- **St. Teresa Week,** Ávila. *Verbenas* (carnivals), parades, singing, and dancing honor the patron saint of this walled city. Dates vary.

November

- **All Saints' Day,** all over Spain. This public holiday is reverently celebrated, as relatives and friends lay flowers on the graves of the dead. November 1.

December

- **Día de los Santos Inocentes,** all over Spain. This equivalent of April Fools' Day is an excuse for people to do "loco" things. December 28.

4 The Active Vacation Planner

BIKING No one would ever recommend pedaling down the overcrowded highways of the Costa del Sol. But the tawny-colored landscape of Andalusia is perfect mountain-biking country. One of the best outfitters is **Mountain Bike Aventura,** Pueblo Platero, 8, Bloque 1, Elviria-Las Chapas, 29600 Marbella (Málaga) (☎ **95/283-12-04**). The leading U.S.-based competitor is **Easy Rider Tours,** P.O. Box 228, Newburyport, MA 01950 (☎ **508/463-6955**). Their tours average between 30 and 50 miles a day; the most appealing follows the route trod by medieval pilgrims on their way to Santiago. The bike tours offered by **Backroads,** 1516 5th St., Berkeley, CA 94710 (☎ **800/GO-ACTIVE**) carry participants through Spain's most verdant and Celtic province, Galicia, into its northern Portuguese counterpart, the Minho region.

In England, the **Cyclists' Touring Club,** 60 Meadrow, Godalming, Surrey GU7 3HS (☎ **01483/417-217**), charges £25 a year for membership; part of the fee provides for information and suggested cycling routes through Spain and dozens of other countries.

CROSS-COUNTRY SKIING A few companies organize cross-country ski expeditions. **Crestas y Llanos,** Edificio España, Gran Vía, 86, 28013 Madrid (☎ **91/548-04-75**) focuses on tours to northern Spain's dramatic Picos de Europa region. A specialist in ski tours on the south-facing slopes of Andalusia is **Nevadensis,** Calle Verónica, s/n, 18411 Pampaneira, Granada (☎ **958/76-31-27**). Finally, a company well versed in cross-country skiing in the foothills of Catalonia's Pyrenees is **Viajes Geosud,** Calle Modesto Lafuente, 18, bajo B, 28003 Madrid (☎ **091/593-28-50**). All these companies offer advice and tour packages.

GOLF Spain's emergence as a second home for thousands of British retirees has encouraged the introduction of dozens of new golf courses. Although the Costa Blanca has become an increasingly popular venue, more than a third of the country's approximately 160 courses lie within its southern tier, within a short drive of the Costa del Sol. Guaranteed playing time on some of the country's finest courses, as well as the requisite airfares and hotel accommodations, can be arranged through such firms as: **Golf International** (☎ **800/833-1389** in the U.S.), **Spanish Golf Adventures** (☎ **800/772-6465** in the U.S. and Canada), **Marsans International** (☎ **800/777-9110** in the U.S.), **Central Holidays** (☎ **800/935-5000** in the U.S. and Canada), **PGA Travel** (☎ **404/455-8019**), and **Comtours** (☎ **800/248-1331** in the U.S.).

What are the two most-talked-about golf sites in Spain? The well-established Valderrama on the Costa del Sol, a Robert Trent Jones–designed course carved out of an oak plantation in the 1980s, and Hyatt's new La Manga Club on the Costa Blanca near Murcia. It's the site of three golf courses, one of which was recently remodeled by Arnold Palmer.

HIKING & HILL CLIMBING If you're drawn to the idea of combining hiking with stopovers at inns whose kitchens and bars are well stocked in locally produced wines, contact **Winetrails,** Greenways, Vann Lake, Ockley, Dorking EH5 5NT, UK (☎ **01306/712-111**). This U.K.-based company conducts 10-day treks through northern Spain's wine districts. To venture into the more rugged countrysides of Catalonia, Andalusia's valley of the Guadalquivir, or the arid, beautiful Extremaduran plains, contact **Ramblers Holidays,** P.O. Box 43, Welwyn Garden AL8 6PQ, UK (☎ **01707/331-133**). Walking tours through the Pyrenees, the region around Alicante, and across the eerie volcanic expanses of the Canary Islands are conducted by **Waymark Holidays,** 44 Windsor Rd., Slough SL1 2EJ, UK (☎ **01753/516-477**).

An outfit known for its carriage-trade tours through esoteric territories is Chicago-based **Abercrombie & Kent International,** 1520 Kensington Rd., Oak Brook, IL 60521 (☎ **800/323-7308**). They conduct a nine-day "Walking the Pyrenees" tour on the Spanish side of the mountainous border with France. Special emphasis is placed on the medieval churches that provided rest and hope to 10th-century pilgrims on their way to Santiago.

HORSEBACK RIDING If you want to tour the arid countryside like caballeros of old, consider signing up for a tour that combines bird-watching with horseback riding. **Gourmet Birds,** Windrush, Coles Lane, Brasted, Westerham, Kent TN16 1NN, UK (☎ **01959/562-906**), offers tours every May that begin in Gibraltar, travel across Andalusia, and focus on birdlife near the once Moorish citadel of Ronda.

Other tours travel across Asturia and Galicia on their way to the medieval religious shrine at Santiago de Compostela. Lodging, the use of a horse, and all necessary equipment are included in the price. For information and reservations, contact the **Centro Hipico "O Castelo,"** Calle Urzáiz, 91, #5-A Vigo, Spain (☎ **986/42-59-37**).

A well-known equestrian center that conducts tours of the arid Alpujarras highlands is **Cabalgar,** Rutas Alternativas, Bubión, Granada (☎ **958/76-31-35**). The farm is best known for its weekend treks through the scrub-covered hills of southern and central Spain, though longer tours are also available.

HOT-AIR BALLOONING If you want to soar silently over the windmills of Don Quixote, a growing number of Spanish entrepreneurs can help arrange it. Laws of physics require that flights occur in the cool of either the morning or evening. Most rides last about an hour and, in some cases, include a picnic (usually breakfast) after landing. Here's a list of companies that can carry you sky-high:

In Catalonia, contact **Ultra Magic,** Aerodrom Igualada-Odena, Apartado 171, 08700 Igualada (Barcelona; ☎ **93/804-22-02**). Such royal sites as Aranjuez and Segovia can be viewed from balloons maintained by **Flying Circus,** Calle Peñalara, 11, 28002 Madrid (☎ **91/416-58-37**). In Andalusia, arrange rides through **Aviación del Sol,** Apartado 344, 29400 Ronda (Málaga; ☎ **95/287-72-49**). One local Balearic outfitter is **Mallorca Balloons,** Calle Caín Melis, 22, 07590 Cala Rejada, Majorca (☎ **971/81-81-82**).

SAILING An agency based in Seville offers weeklong cruises along the coast of Andalusia and the Algarve. Their three-masted, 42-foot sailing yacht departs from the Andalusian port of Huelva. For reservations and information, contact **Alventus,** Calle Imagen, 6, 41003 Sevilla (☎ **95/421-00-62**).

In northern Spain, consider a waterborne sojourn arranged by **Voyages Jules Verne,** 21 Dorset Sq., London NW1 6QG, UK (☎ **0171/616-1000**). Their guided holidays take in Galicia, its Portuguese neighbors, Trás-os-Montes and the Minho district, and Porto, the second-largest city in Portugal. The trips end with a boat ride up the Douro River back into Spain.

SKIING Few would associate the blazing heat of Spain with anything that approaches worthwhile skiing. But Iberia's mountain ranges provide some surprising opportunities for schussing downhill. And because skiers in Spain tend to keep the same late hours as their Madrileño siblings, slopes are noticeably less crowded between 9am and 11am, and between 1pm and 3pm—presumably the time when holidaymaking skiers are sleeping off a night of clubbing or enjoying a late lunch.

Besides the usually crowded facilities in Andorra, Spain's most successful and best-equipped resorts include Sierra Nevada, an Andalusian ski resort that was formally launched in the 1960s; Baqueira-Beret, in the Pyrenees, a favorite of Spain's royal family; and Alto Campo, in Cantabria.

For information about how and where to ski, call the **Ski Resort's Association of Spain** (ATUDEM) in Madrid at **91/350-20-20.** For information from Spain's oldest ski club, contact the **Sierra Nevada Club,** Edificio Cetursa, Plaza de Andalucia, 18196 Sierra Nevada (Granada; ☎ **958/24-91-11**). For information on the slopes in Andorra, contact **Andorra's Oficina de Turismo,** Calle Maria Cubi, 159, 08021 Barcelona (☎ **93/200-06-55**).

TENNIS A consortium of Spanish and English tennis enthusiasts organizes tennis holidays at a well-accessorized, relatively new resort, La Manga, in Murcia, on the Costa Blanca. Tennis packages include at least three hours of professional instruction per day; golf, horseback riding, and swimming facilities are also available. For more information on tennis holidays in Spain, contact **La Manga Connexions,** Atlas Partnership, Ltd., Clock House, High Street, Cuckfield, West Sussex RH17 5LB, UK (☎ **01444/417-299**).

5 Special Interest & Educational Travel

Offbeat, alternative modes of travel often cost less and can be an enriching way to travel. *Note:* The inclusion of an oganization in this section is in no way to be interpreted as a guarantee. Information about the organization is presented only as a preview, to be followed by your own investigation.

LEARNING VACATIONS An international series of programs for persons over 50 who are interested in combining travel and learning is offered by **Interhostel,** developed by the University of New Hampshire. Each program lasts two weeks, is led by a university faculty or staff member, and is arranged in conjunction with a host college, university, or cultural institution. Participants may stay longer if they wish. Interhostel offers programs in Spain that consist of cultural and intellectual activities, with field trips to museums and other centers of interest. For information, contact the University of New Hampshire, Division of Continuing Education, 6 Garrison Ave., Durham, NH 03824 (☎ **800/733-9753** or 603/862-1147).

STUDYING SPANISH IN SPAIN Your trip to Spain will be enriched and made easier by a basic understanding of the language.

Salminter, Calle Toro, 34–36, 37002 Salamanca (☎ **923/21-18-08;** fax 923/26-02-63), conducts courses in conversational Spanish, with optional courses in business Spanish, translation techniques, and Spanish culture. Classes contain no more than 10 persons. There are courses of two weeks, one month, and three months at seven progressive levels. The school can arrange housing with Spanish families or in furnished apartments shared with other students. For reservations and information, write or fax school officials at the address or number above.

Another good source of information about courses in Spain is the **American Institute for Foreign Study (AIFS),** 102 Greenwich Ave., Greenwich, CT 06830 (☎ **800/727-2437** or 203/869-9090). This organization can set up transportation and arrange for summer courses, with bed and board included. It can help you arrange study programs at either the University of Salamanca, one of Europe's oldest academic centers, or the University of Granada.

The biggest organization dealing with higher education in Europe is the **Institute of International Education (IIE),** 809 United Nations Plaza, New York, NY 10017 (☎ **212/883-8200**). A few of its booklets are free; but for $36.95, plus $4 for postage, you can purchase the more definitive *Vacation Study Abroad.* Visitors to New York may use the resources of its Information Center, which is open to the public Tuesday through Thursday from 11am to 4pm. The institute is closed on major holidays.

One well-recommended clearinghouse for academic programs throughout the world is the **National Registration Center for Study Abroad (NRCSA),** 823 N. 2nd St., P.O. Box 1393, Milwaukee, WI 53201 (☎ **414/278-0631**). The organization maintains language-study programs throughout Europe, including those within about 10 cities throughout Spain. Most popular are the organization's programs in Seville, Salamanca, and Málaga, where language courses last between four and six hours a day. With lodgings within private homes included as part of the price and part of the experience, tuition begins at around $800 for an intensive two-week language course. Courses of six weeks, eight weeks, a semester, and a full academic year are also available. NRCSA warns that the diplomas awarded by these Spanish schools are not always applicable toward an undergraduate degree at every North American university. (Some colleges will, however, accept successful completion of the curricula as independent studies.) Courses accept participants aged 17 to 80.

A clearinghouse for information on at least nine different Spain-based language schools is **Lingua Service Worldwide,** 216 E. 45th St., 17th Floor, New York, NY 10017 (☎ **800/394-LEARN** or 212/867-1225). Maintaining information about learning programs in 10 languages in 17 countries outside the United States, it represents organizations devoted to the teaching of Spanish and culture in 11 cities of Spain, including one in the Canary Islands.

The **Education Office of Spain,** 150 Fifth Ave., Suite 918, New York, NY 10011 (☎ **212/741-5144**), whose funding comes from the Spanish Ministry of Education, offers information on Spanish-language schools within the universities and privately funded schools of Spain. Information is provided free.

One well-recommended Spain-based language school that manages to combine a resort setting with intensive linguistic immersion is the **Escuela de Idiomas Nerja,** Calle Almirante Ferrándiz, 73, 29780 Nerja, Málaga (☎ **952/52-16-87**). Offering sessions of between 2 and 20 weeks, it charges a basic tuition of 43,000 pesetas ($344) for 2 weeks and 62,000 pesetas ($496) for 4 weeks. Also offered are one-on-one courses, refresher courses for teachers, and Spanish for business. Classes are limited to a maximum of 10 students each.

For more information about study abroad, contact the **Council on International Educational Exchange (CIEE),** 205 E. 42nd St., New York, NY 10017 (☎ **212/661-1450**).

HOMESTAYS **Friendship Force,** 57 Forsyth St. NW, Suite 900, Atlanta, GA 30303 (☎ **404/522-9490**), is a nonprofit organization that fosters and encourages friendship among people worldwide. Dozens of branch offices throughout North America arrange en masse visits, usually once a year. Because of group bookings, the airfare to the host country is usually less than the cost of individual APEX tickets. Each participant spends two weeks in the host country, one as a guest in the home of a family and the second traveling in the host country.

Servas, 11 John St., New York, NY 10038 (☎ **212/267-0252**), is an international nonprofit, nongovernmental, interfaith network of travelers and hosts whose goal is to help promote world peace, goodwill, and understanding. (Its name means "to serve" in Esperanto.) Servas hosts offer travelers hospitality for two days. Travelers pay a $55 annual fee and a $25 list deposit after filling out on application and being approved by an interviewer (interviewers are located across the United States). They then receive Servas directories listing the names and addresses of Servas hosts.

HOME EXCHANGES One of the most exciting breakthroughs in modern tourism is the home exchange, whereby the Diego family of Ávila can exchange their home with the Brier family's in North Carolina. Sometimes the family automobile is included. Of course, you must be comfortable with the idea of having relative strangers in your home, and you must be content to spend your vacation in one place.

Home exchanges cut costs. You don't pay hotel bills, and you can also save money by shopping in markets and eating in. One potential problem, though, is that you may not get a home in the area you request.

Intervac, U.S., P.O. Box 590504, San Francisco, CA 94159 (☎ **800/756-HOME** or 415/435-3497), is part of the largest worldwide exchange network. It publishes four catalogs a year, containing more than 10,000 homes in more than 36 countries. Members contact each other directly. The cost is $65 plus postage, which includes the purchase of three of the company's catalogs (which will be mailed to you), plus the inclusion of your own listing in whichever one of the three catalogs you select. A fourth catalog costs an extra $21. If you want to publish a photograph of your home, there is an additional charge of $11.

The Invented City, 41 Sutter St., Suite 1090, San Francisco, CA 94104 (☎ **800/788-CITY** or 415/252-1141), is another international home-exchange agency. Home-exchange listings are published three times a year—in February, May, and November. The $75 membership fee allows you to list your home, with your own description; you can also give your preferred time to travel, your occupation, and your hobbies.

Vacation Exchange Club, P.O. Box 650, Key West, FL 33041 (☎ **800/638-3841** or 305/294-1448), will send you five directories a year for $78. You'll be listed in one of the directories.

EARTHWATCHING IN SPAIN Many travelers appreciate the ability to merge a firsthand exposure to the cultures of Spain with a positive contribution to the ecology and cultural preservation of Europe. Founded in 1971, **Earthwatch,** 680 Mount Auburn St., P.O. Box 403, Watertown, MA 02272-9924 (☎ **617/926-8200**), is a nonprofit organization that recruits ordinary people to work as paying volunteers for university professors on field expeditions throughout the world. On two- to three-week programs, team members may learn to excavate, map, photograph, observe animal behavior, gather data, conduct oral-history interviews, assist diving operations, lend mechanical expertise, and share all other field chores associated with professional expedition research. Volunteers are almost never specialists in any particular field but interested "intergenerational" participants. Note that only 10% of volunteers are students; many are senior citizens. Ongoing Spain-centered projects include participation in monitoring the S'Albufera wetlands on the island of Majorca, excavating on Majorca a cluster of Bronze Age villages believed to have been occupied for a longer consecutive period than any other prehistoric site in western Europe, and researching the remains of another Bronze Age Iberian village near Borja in Aragón.

Participation in Earthwatch's two- or three-week Spanish projects involves a tax-deductible contribution of between $1,600 and $2,000, depending on the project, plus airfare to Spain. Living arrangements, as well as all meals and drinks at the organization's Saturday-night beer parties, are provided.

Earthwatch Europe, 57 Woodstock Rd., Delsyre Court, Oxford OX2 6HU, UK (☎ **01865/311-600**), is another highly respected organization, whose more than 150 programs are designed and supervised by well-qualified academic and ecological authorities. At any time, at least 50 of these programs welcome lay participants for hands-on experience in preserving or documenting historical, archaeological, or ecological phenomena of interest.

BIRD-WATCHING Ornithologists know that the Iberian Peninsula lies directly across migration routes or species that travel with the seasons between Africa and Europe. Some of the most comprehensive studies on these migratory patterns are conducted by Spain's **Centro de Migración de Aves,** SEO/BirdLife, Carretera de Humera 63-1, 28224 Pozuelo (Madrid; ☎ **91/351-10-45**). Based at a rustic outpost near Gibraltar, their summer work camps and field projects appeal to participants who want to identify, catalog, and "ring" (mark with an identifying leg band) some of the millions of birds that nest on Spanish soil every year. Participants are expected to pay for their "tuition," room, and board, but can often use the experience toward university credits, especially in such fields as zoology and ecology.

PLANT-WATCHING & BOTANIC TOURS Why not add a primer of lessons about Spanish botany to your roster of terms about Spanish art and architecture?

Travel specialist **Cox & Kings,** St. James Court, 45 Buckingham Gate, London SW1E SF, UK (☎ **0171/834-7422**) leads two-week treks in search of wild orchids, unusual ferns, and samples of the varied flora that grow in the damp but sunny foothills of the Pyrenees in the ancient province of Aragón. The firm also conducts other organized tours through Spain.

COOKING SCHOOLS One organization devoted to training Hispanophiles in the fine art of the nation's cuisine is the **Escuela de Cocina Juan Altimiras,** Calle de la Incarnación, 2, Madrid (☎ **91/547-88-27**). Established by Clara María González de Amezúa in 1973, it offers a series of lectures and demonstrations that benefit even professional chefs.

If your field of interest is not covered by any of the tours above, contact the London headquarters of the **International Association of Travel Agencies (IATA),** 133A St. Margaret's Road, Twickenham, Middlesex TW1 1RG, UK (☎ **0181/744-9280**). It may be able to provide you with the names of tour operators that specialize in travel relating to your particular interest.

6 Health & Insurance

HEALTH Spain should not pose any major health hazards. The overly rich cuisine—garlic, olive oil, and wine—may give some travelers mild diarrhea, so take along some antidiarrhea medicine, moderate your eating habits, and even though the water is generally considered safe, drink mineral water only. Fish and shellfish from the horrendously polluted Mediterranean should only be eaten cooked.

If you need a doctor, ask your hotel to locate one for you. You can also obtain a list of English-speaking doctors in Spain from the **International Association for Medical Assistance to Travelers (IAMAT),** in the United States at 417 Center St., Lewiston, NY 14092 (☎ **716/754-4883**); in Canada, at 40 Regal Rd., Guelph, ON N1K 1B5 (☎ **519/836-0102**).

If you have a chronic medical condition, talk to your doctor before taking the trip. For conditions such as epilepsy, heart condition, and diabetes, wear a Medic Alert Identification Tag, which will immediately alert any doctor to your condition and provide a 24-hour hotline phone number, so that a foreign doctor can obtain medical records for you. The initial membership costs $35. There is a $15 yearly fee. Contact the **Medic Alert Foundation,** P.O. Box 1009, Turlock, CA 95381-1009 (☎ **800/432-5378**).

Take all vital medicines with you in your carry-on luggage, and bring enough to last you during your stay. Also bring copies of each prescription written with the generic name—not the brand name—of the drug you're taking. It's a good idea to bring a sunscreen with a high SPF, since the sun can be intense in southern Spain.

INSURANCE Before purchasing any additional insurance, check your homeowner's, automobile, and medical insurance policies, as well as the insurance provided by your credit card companies and auto and travel clubs. You may have adequate off-premises theft coverage.

Remember: Medicare only covers U.S. citizens traveling in Mexico and Canada.

Also note that to submit any claim you must always have thorough documentation, including all receipts, police reports, medical records, and such.

If you are prepaying for your vacation or are taking a charter or any other flight that has cancellation penalties, look into cancellation insurance. Most companies listed below offer insurance packages that include provisions for lost luggage, medical coverage, emergency evacuation, accidental death, and trip cancellation. Call for policy specifics. (Also, check if your credit card company provides cancellation coverage if the ticket is paid for with a credit card.)

Among the firms to try: **Travel Guard International,** 1145 Clark St., Stevens Point, WI 54481 (☎ **800/826-1300**); **Mutual of Omaha** (Tele-Trip), Mutual of Omaha Plaza, Omaha, NE 68175 (☎ **800/228-9792**); **Healthcare Abroad (MEDEX)**, c/o Wallach & Co., 107 W. Federal St. (P.O. Box 480), Middleburg, VA 22117-0480 (☎ **800/237-6615** or **540/687-3166**); **Access America,** 6600 W. Broad St., Richmond, VA 23230 (☎ **800/284-8300**); **Travel Assistance International** by Worldwide Assistance Services, Inc., 1133 15th St., NW, Suite 400, Washington, DC 20005 (☎ **800/821-2828** or **202/331-1596**); and **Travel Insured International, Inc.,** P.O. Box 280568, East Hartford, CT 06128-0568 (☎ **800/243-3174** in the U.S., or **860/528-7663**).

7 Tips for Travelers with Special Needs

FOR PEOPLE WITH DISABILITIES Because of Spain's many hills and endless flights of stairs, disabled visitors may have difficulty getting around the country. But conditions are slowly improving. Newer hotels are more sensitive to the needs of the disabled; and the more expensive restaurants, in general, are wheelchair-accessible. (In Madrid, the capital, there is even a museum designed for the blind and sight impaired—see the section "More Attractions" in Chapter 5, "Madrid Attractions.") However, since most places have limited, if any, facilities for people with disabilities, consider taking an organized tour specifically designed to accommodate travelers with disabilities.

For the names and addresses of tour operators as well as other related information, write to the **Society for the Advancement of Travel for the Handicapped,** 347 Fifth Ave., New York, NY 10016 (☎ **212/447-7248**). Annual membership dues are $45, or $25 for senior citizens and students.

FEDCAP Rehabilitation Services (formerly Federation of the Handicapped), 154 W. 14th St., New York, NY 10011 (☎ **212/727-4200**), operates summer tours to Europe and elsewhere for its members. Membership costs $4 yearly.

You can also obtain, free, a copy of "Air Transportation of Handicapped Persons," published by the U.S. Department of Transportation, by writing: Free Advisory Circular No. AC12032, Distribution Unit, U.S. Department of Transportation, Publications Division, M-4332, Washington, DC 20590.

For the blind or visually impaired, the best source is the **American Foundation for the Blind,** 15 W. 16th St., New York, NY 10011 (☎ **800/232-5463** for ordering of information kits and supplies, or **212/502-7600**). It offers information on travel and various requirements for the transport and border formalities for seeing-eye dogs. It also issues identification cards to those who are legally blind.

The **Information Center for Individuals with Disabilities,** Fort Point Place, 27–43 Wormwood St., Boston, MA 02210 (☎ **800/462-5015** or 617/727-5540), is another good source. It has lists of travel agents who specialize in tours for persons with disabilities.

One of the best organizations serving the needs of persons with disabilities (wheelchairs and walkers) is **Flying Wheels Travel,** 143 West Bridge, P.O. Box 382, Owatonna, MN 55060 (☎ **800/535 6790** or 507/451-5005), offering various escorted tours and cruises internationally.

For a $25 annual fee, consider joining **Mobility International USA,** P.O. Box 10767, Eugene, OR 97440 (☎ **541/343-1284** voice & TDD). It answers questions on various destinations and also offers discounts on videos, publications, and programs it sponsors.

The **Airport Transport Users Council,** 5/F Kingsway House, 103 Kingsway, London WC2B 6QX (☎ **0171/242-3882**), publishes a free pamphlet, "Flight Plan—A Passenger's Guide to Planning and Using Air Travel," which is packed with information for all travelers.

FOR GAYS & LESBIANS In 1978 Spain legalized homosexuality among consenting adults. In April 1995 the parliament of Spain banned discrimination based on sexual orientation. Madrid and Barcelona are the major gay centers of the country. The leading gay resort is Sitges, south of Barcelona. There's also a large gay colony that frequents Torremolinos. Ibiza is the leading gay-oriented island in the Balearics.

To learn about gay and lesbian travel in Spain, you can secure publications or join data-dispensing organizations before you go. Men can order *Spartacus,* the international gay guide ($32.95), or *Odysseus 1997, The International Gay Travel Planner,* a guide to international gay accommodations ($25). Both lesbians and gay men may want to pick up a copy of *Gay Travel A to Z* ($16), which specializes in general information, as well as listing bars, hotels, restaurants, and places of interest for gay travelers throughout the world. These books and others are available from **Giovanni's Room,** 1145 Pine St., Philadelphia, PA 19107 (☎ **215/923-2960**).

Our World, 1104 N. Nova Rd., Suite 251, Daytona Beach, FL 32117 (☎ **904/441-5367**), is a magazine devoted to options and bargains for gay and lesbian travel worldwide. It costs $35 for 10 issues. ***Out and About,*** 8 W. 19th St., Suite 401, New York, NY 10011 (☎ **800/929-2268**), has been hailed for its "straight" reporting about gay travel. It profiles the best gay or gay-friendly hotels, gyms, clubs, and other places, with coverage of destinations throughout the world. Cost is $49 a year for 10 information-packed issues. Praised everywhere from *Travel & Leisure* to the *New York Times,* it aims for the more upscale gay male traveler.

The **International Gay Travel Association (IGTA),** P.O. Box 4974, Key West, FL 33041 (☎ **800/448-8550** voice mailbox, or 305/292-0217), encourages gay and lesbian travel worldwide. With around 1,200 member agencies, it specializes in networking travelers with the appropriate gay-friendly service organization or tour specialist. It offers a quarterly newsletter, marketing mailings, and a membership directory that is updated four times a year. Travel agents who are IGTA members are tied into this organization's vast information resources.

FOR SENIORS Many discounts are available for seniors, but often you need to be a member of an association to obtain them.

For information before you go, write for a free booklet, "101 Tips for the Mature Traveler," available from **Grand Circle Travel,** 347 Congress St., Suite 3A, Boston, MA 02210 (☎ **800/221-2610** or 617/350-7500).

One of the most dynamic travel organizations for seniors is **Elderhostel,** 75 Federal St., Boston, MA (☎ **617/426-7788**), established in 1975, which operates an array of programs throughout Europe, including Spain. Most courses last around three weeks and represent good value, since they include airfare, accommodations in student dormitories or modest inns, all meals, and tuition. Courses involve no homework, are ungraded, and are often liberal arts–oriented. These aren't luxury vacations, but they're fun and fulfilling. Participants must be at least 55 years old. A companion must be at least 50 years old; spouses may participate regardless of age.

SAGA International Holidays, 222 Berkeley St., Boston, MA 02116 (☎ **800/343-0273**), runs tours for seniors, 50 and older. Many tours are all-inclusive, covering air transfers and accommodations. Insurance, both baggage and medical, is also included in the net price of the tour.

In the United States, the best organization to belong to is the **AARP (American Association of Retired Persons),** 601 E St. NW, Washington, DC 20049 (☎ **202/434-AARP**). Members are offered discounts on car rentals, hotels, and airfares. The association's group travel is provided by the AARP Travel Experience from American Express. Tours may be purchased through any American Express office or travel agent, or by calling **800/927-0111.** Flights to the various destinations are handled by the toll-free number as part of land arrangements.

Information is also available from the **National Council of Senior Citizens,** 1331 F St. NW, Washington, DC 20005-1171 (☎ **202/347-8800**), which charges $12 per person or couple, for which you receive a monthly newsletter, part of which is devoted to travel tips. Reduced discounts on hotel and auto rentals are available.

If you're 45 or older and need a companion to share your travel and leisure with, **Golden Companions,** P.O. Box 5249, Reno, NV 89513 (☎ **702/324-2227**), may provide the answer. Founded in 1987, this helpful service has found companions for hundreds of mature travelers from all over the U.S. and Canada. Members meet through a confidential mail network and once they have connected make their own travel plans. Benefits include bimonthly membership updates as well as a newsletter, "The Golden Gateways." Membership for a full year is $94. A free brochure is available and sample newsletters are $2.

Uniworld, 16000 Ventura Blvd., Encino, CA 91436 (☎ **800/733-7820** or 818/382-7820), specializes in single tours for the mature person. It arranges for you to share an accommodation with another single person or gets you a low-priced single supplement. Uniworld specializes in travel to certain districts of England, France, Spain, Italy, and Scandinavia.

Mature Outlook, P.O. Box 10448, Des Moines, IA 50306 (☎ **800/336-6330**), is a membership program for people over 50. Members are offered discounts at ITC-member hotels and will receive a bimonthly magazine. The annual membership fee of $14.95 entitles its members to free coupons for discounts at Sears & Roebuck Co. Savings are also offered on selected auto rentals and restaurants.

FOR SINGLES It's no secret that the travel industry caters to people who are not traveling alone. Double rooms, for example, are usually much more reasonably priced than singles. One company, **Travel Companion,** has had great success in matching single travelers with like-minded companions. Its founder, Jens Jurgen, charges $99 for a six-month listing. New applicants desiring a travel companion fill out a form stating their preferences and needs. They then receive a list of people who might be suitable. Companions of the same age or opposite sex can be requested. A bimonthly newsletter averaging 46 large pages also gives numerous money-saving travel tips of special interest to solo travelers. A sample copy is available for $5. For an application and more information, write to Jens Jurgen, Travel Companion, P.O. Box P-833, Amityville, NY 11701 (☎ **516/454-0880**).

Another agency to check is **Grand Circle Travel,** 347 Congress St., Boston, MA 02110 (☎ **800/221-2610** or 617/350-7500), which offers escorted tours and cruises for retired people, including singles.

Since single-supplements on tours usually carry a hefty price tag, a way to get around paying the supplement is to find a tour company that allows you to share a room with a hitherto unknown fellow traveler. One company offering a "guaranteed-share plan" for its tours within Spain is **Cosmos** (an affiliate of Globus Tours). Upon your arrival in Spain, a suitable roommate will be assigned to you from among the tour's other participants. Double occupancy rates are guaranteed; if a roommate is unavailable, you do not pay the single-occupancy supplement. The company has offices at 5301 S. Federal Circle, Littleton, CO 80123 (☎ **800/221-0090**). You can obtain information about its tours through any travel agency.

Dedicated independent travelers may want to check out **The Globetrotters Club,** BCM/Roving, London WCIN 3XX, which enables members to exchange information and generally assist each other in traveling as cheaply as possible. Persons in the United States, and elsewhere outside the United Kingdom and Europe, pay $23 for the first year and an $18 annual renewal fee. Residents of the United Kingdom or citizens of Europe pay £12 for the first year and £9 for each year's renewal.

FOR FAMILIES "Family Travel Times" is a newsletter about traveling with children. The cost is $40 for four issues. Subscribers can also call in with travel questions, but only on Wednesday from 10am to 1pm Eastern Standard Time. Contact **TWYCH** (which stands for "Travel with Your Children"), 40 Fifth Ave., New York, NY 10011 (☎ **212/447-5524**).

FOR STUDENTS **Council Travel** is America's largest student, youth, and budget travel group, with more than 60 offices worldwide. It also sells publications for young people considering traveling abroad. For a copy of *Student Travels* magazine—which provides information on all of Council Travel's services as well as on programs and publications of the Council on International Educational Exchange—send $1 in postage.

Council Travel has offices throughout the United States, including the main office at 205 E. 42nd St., New York, NY 10017-5706 (☎ **888/COUNCIL**). Call that number to find the location nearest you.

The most commonly accepted form of identification is also an "open sesame" to bargains. An **International Student Identity Card (ISIC)** gets you such benefits as special student airfares to Europe, medical insurance, and many special discounts. In Spain the card secures you free entrance into state museums, monuments, and archaeological sights. Domestic train fares in Spain are also reduced for students. The card, which costs $18, is available at Council Travel offices nationwide, as well as on hundreds of college and university campuses across the country. Proof of student status and a passport-size photograph (2 in. by 2 in.) are necessary. For the ISIC-issuing office nearest you, contact the Council on International Educational Exchange, 205 E. 42nd St., New York, NY 10017 (☎ **800/GET AN ID**).

The **IYHF** (International Youth Hostel Federation) was designed to provide bare-bones overnight accommodations for budget-conscious travelers. For information, contact HI-AYH (Hostelling International/American Youth Hostels), 733 15th St. NW, No. 840, Washington, DC 20005 (☎ **800/444-6111** or 202/783-6161). Membership costs $25 annually, except for those under 18, who pay $10, and those 54 or more, who pay $15.

8 Getting There

BY PLANE FROM NORTH AMERICA

Flights from the U.S. East Coast to Spain take six to seven hours, depending on the season and the prevailing winds.

THE MAJOR AIRLINES

The airline industry has recently undergone upheavals. For last-minute conditions, including a rundown on carriers flying into Spain, check with your travel agent or the individual airlines. Here is the current status on flights from North America:

The national carrier of Spain, **Iberia Airlines** (☎ **800/772-4642**), has more routes into and within Spain than any other airline. It offers daily nonstop service to Madrid from both New York and Miami. Iberia also flies daily to Madrid from Los Angeles, with a brief stop in Miami. In addition, Iberia has service to Madrid from Toronto (through Montreal), which is provided between two and three times a week, depending on the season. Also available are attractive rates on fly-drive programs within Iberia and Europe; these can substantially reduce the cost of both the air ticket and the car rental.

A noteworthy cost-cutting option is Iberia's EuroPass. Available only to passengers who simultaneously arrange for transatlantic passage on Iberia and a minimum of two additional flights, it allows passage on any flight within Iberia's European or Mediterranean dominion for $250 for the first two flights and $125 for each additional flight (prices are subject to change). This is especially attractive for passengers wishing to combine trips to Spain with, for example, visits to such far-flung destinations as Cairo, Tel Aviv, Istanbul, Moscow, and Munich. For details, ask Iberia's phone representative.

Iberia's main Spain-based competitor is **Air Europa (☎ 888/238-7672)**, which offers nonstop service from New York's JFK Airport to Madrid, with continuing service to major cities within Spain. Fares are competitive.

Employee-owned **Trans World Airlines (☎ 800/221-2000)** operates separate daily nonstop flights to both Barcelona and Madrid from JFK. Like its competitors, TWA offers access to its trip-planning service (in this case, the Getaway Vacation desk) and can arrange fly-drive holidays, land packages at Spanish hotels, and escorted motorcoach tours.

American Airlines (☎ 800/433-7300) offers daily nonstop service to Madrid from its massive hub in Miami, with excellent connections from there to the rest of the airline's impressive North and South American network.

Delta (☎ 800/241-4141) maintains daily nonstop service from Atlanta (centerpiece of its worldwide network) to Madrid, with continuing service (and no change of equipment) to Barcelona. Delta's Dream Vacation department maintains access to fly-drive programs, land packages, and escorted bus tours through the Iberian Peninsula.

Since 1991, **United Airlines (☎ 800/538-2929)** has flown passengers nonstop to Madrid every day from Washington, D.C.'s Dulles Airport, with connecting flights to the West Coast. United also offers fly-drive programs and escorted motorcoach tours.

Continental Airlines (☎ 800/231-0856) offers between six and seven nonstop flights per week, depending on the season, to Madrid from Newark, New Jersey, an airport many New York residents prefer.

USAir (☎ 800/428-4322) offers daily nonstop service between Philadelphia and Madrid. USAir also has connecting flights to Philadelphia from more than 50 cities throughout the U.S., Canada, and the Bahamas.

GOOD-VALUE CHOICES

Most airlines divide their year roughly into seasonal slots, with the least expensive fares between November 1 and March 14, excluding holidays. The shoulder season (spring and early fall) is only slightly more expensive and includes October, which many veteran tourists consider the ideal time to visit Spain. Summer, of course, is the most expensive time.

Special Promotional Fares Many airlines occasionally offer promotional fares to Europe. To take advantage of this, you need to have a good travel agent or to do a lot of shopping or calling around yourself to learn what's available at the time of your intended trip.

Charter Flights A charter flight is one reserved months in advance for a one-time-only transit to a predetermined destination. For reasons of economy, some travelers choose this option.

Before paying for a charter, check the restrictions on your ticket or contract. You may be asked to purchase a tour package and pay far in advance. You'll pay a stiff penalty (or forfeit the ticket entirely) if you cancel. Charters are sometimes canceled if the tickets don't sell out. In some cases the charter-ticket seller will offer you an insurance policy for your own legitimate cancellation (proving illness with a hospital certificate, or having a death in the family, for example).

There is no way to predict whether a charter or a bucket-shop flight will be cheaper. You'll have to investigate this at the time of your trip.

Among charter-flight operators is **Council Charter,** a subsidiary of the Council on International Educational Exchange (CIEE), 205 E. 42nd St., New York, NY 10017 (☎ **212/822-2700**). This outfit can arrange charter seats to most major European cities, including Madrid, on regularly scheduled aircrafts.

One of the biggest New York charter operators is **Travac,** 989 Sixth Ave., 16th floor, New York, NY 10018 (☎ **800/TRAV-800** or 212/563-3303).

Be warned: Some charter companies have proved unreliable in the past.

Bucket Shops Bucket shops—or consolidators, as they are also called—exist in many shapes and forms. In their purest sense, they act as a clearinghouse for blocks of tickets that airlines discount and consign during normally slow periods of air travel. Charter operators and bucket shops used to perform separate functions, but today many perform both functions.

Ticket prices vary, sometimes going for as much as 35% off full fare. Terms of payment can be anywhere from 45 days before departure to the last minute.

Bucket shops abound from coast to coast, but just to get you started, here are some recommendations. (Look also for ads in your local newspaper's travel section.)

One of the biggest U.S. consolidators is **Travac,** 989 Sixth Ave., New York, NY 10018 (☎ **800/TRAV-80** or 212/563-3303). It offers discounted seats from points throughout the United States to most cities in Europe, including Madrid, on TWA, United, Delta, and other major airlines.

Also in New York, try **TFI Tours International,** 34 W. 32nd St., 12th Floor, New York, NY 10001 (☎ **212/736-1140** in New York State, or **800/745-8000** elsewhere in the U.S.). This tour company offers service to 177 cities worldwide, including Madrid and Barcelona.

UniTravel, 1177 N. Warson Rd., St. Louis, MO 63132 (☎ **800/325-2222**), offers tickets to Madrid and elsewhere in Europe at prices that may be lower than what airlines charge if you order tickets directly from them. UniTravel is best suited to providing discounts for passengers who want (or need) to get to Europe on short notice.

Headquartered in the Midwest is **Travel Avenue,** 10 S. Riverside Plaza, Suite 1404, Chicago, IL 60606 (☎ **800/333-3335**), a national agency. Its tickets are often cheaper than those sold by most shops.

Another possibility is **TMI** (Travel Management International), 3617 Dupont Ave. S., Minneapolis, MN 55409 (☎ **800/245-3672**). It offers a variety of discounts, including youth fares and student fares, as well as access to other kinds of air-related discounts. Madrid is one of its destinations.

You can also try **800-FLY-4-LESS,** RFA Building, 5440 Morehouse Dr., San Diego, CA 92121. Travelers unable to buy their tickets three weeks in advance can utilize this service to obtain low discounted fares with no advance purchase requirements. 800-FLY-4-LESS is a nationwide airline reservation and ticketing service that specializes in finding only the lowest fares.

A final option, suitable for clients with flexible travel plans, is available through **Airhitch,** 2472 Broadway, Suite 20, New York, NY 10025 (☎ **212/864-2000**). You let Airhitch know which five consecutive days you're available to fly to Europe, and Airhitch agrees to fly you there within those five days. It arranges for departures from the East or West Coast, the Midwest, and the Southeast and tries, but cannot guarantee, to fly you from and to the cities of your choice.

Rebators Another competitor in the low-cost airfare market, rebators pass along to the passenger part of their commission, although many assess a fee for their services. Most rebators offer discounts that range from 10% to 25%, plus a $25 handling charge. Although not the same as travel agents, they sometimes offer similar services, including discounted land arrangements and car rentals.

Two rebators are **Travel Avenue,** 10 S. Riverside Plaza, Suite 1404, Chicago, IL 60606 (☎ **800/333-3335** or 312/876-1116), and **The Smart Traveller,** 3111 SW 27th Ave. (P.O. Box 330010), Miami, FL 33133 (☎ **800/448-3338** or 305/448-3338). The Smart Traveller also offers discount tours, hotel packages, and fly-drive packages.

Travel Clubs Yet another possibility for low-cost air travel is the travel club, which supplies an unsold inventory of tickets offering discounts of 20% to 60%.

After you pay an annual fee, you're given a "hotline" number to call in order to find out what discounts are available. Many discounts become available several days, or sometimes as much as a month, before departure. So you have to be fairly flexible.

Moment's Notice, 7301 New Utrecht Ave., Brooklyn, NY 11228 (☎ **212/486-0500**), has a 24-hour hotline and charges a $25 yearly fee.

Sears Discount Travel Club, 3033 S. Parker Rd., Suite 900, Aurora, CO 80014 (☎ **800/433-9383**), offers members, for $50, a catalog (issued quarterly), maps, discounts at select hotels, and a 5% cash bonus on purchases.

Encore Travel Club, 4501 Forbes Blvd., Lanham, MD 20706 (☎ **800/638-8976**), charges $49.95 a year for membership and offers up to a 50% discount at more than 4,000 hotels, sometimes during off-peak periods; it also offers substantial discounts on airfare, cruises, and car rentals through its volume-purchase plans. Membership includes a travel package outlining the company's many services and use of a toll-free telephone number for advice and information.

REGULAR FARES

If your schedule does not permit you one of the options discussed above, you can opt for a regular fare. Economy class is the cheapest regular fare, followed by business class, and then by first class, obviously the most expensive ticket. All three of these fares have one thing in common: You can book them at the last minute and can depart and return when you wish. Of course, you'll pay more for the lack of restrictions.

Most airlines offer a consistently popular APEX (Advance Purchase Excursion) fare that often requires a 14-day advance payment and an obligatory stay of between 7 and 90 days, depending on the carrier. In most cases, this ticket is not completely refundable if you change flight dates or destination, so it pays to ask lots of questions before you book.

BY TRAIN

If you're already in Europe, you may want to go to Spain by train, especially if you have a Eurailpass. Even without a pass, you'll find that the cost of a train ticket is relatively moderate. Rail passengers who visit from Britain or France should make couchette and sleeper reservations as far in advance as possible, especially during the peak summer season.

Since Spain's rail tracks are of a wider gauge than those used for French trains (except for the TALGO and Trans-Europe-Express trains), you'll probably have to change trains at the border unless you're on an express train (see below). For long journeys on Spanish rails, seat and sleeper reservations are mandatory.

The most comfortable and the fastest trains in Spain are the TER, TALGO, and Electrotren. However, you pay a supplement to ride on these fast trains. Both first- and second-class fares are sold on Spanish trains. Tickets can be purchased in either the United States or Canada at the nearest office of Rail Europe, Inc. or from any reputable travel agent. Confirmation of your reservation will take about a week.

If you want your car carried, you must travel Auto-Expreso in Spain. This type of auto transport can be booked only through travel agents or rail offices once you arrive in Europe.

BY BUS

Bus travel to Spain is possible but not popular—it's quite slow. But coach services do operate regularly from major capitals of western Europe, and once in Spain, usually head for Madrid or Barcelona.

BY CAR

If you're touring the rest of Europe in a rented car, you might, for an added cost, be allowed to drop off your vehicle in a major city such as Madrid or Barcelona.

Motor approaches to Spain are across France on expressways. The most popular border crossing is near Biarritz, but there are 17 other border stations between Spain and France. If you're planning to visit the north or west of Spain (Galicia), the Hendaye-Irún border is the most convenient frontier crossing. If you're going to Barcelona or Catalonia and along the Levante coast (Valencia), take the expressway in France to Toulouse, then the A-61 to Narbonne, and then the A-9 toward the border crossing at La Junquera. You can also take the RN-20, with a border station at Puigcerda.

BY ORGANIZED TOUR

Some people prefer that a tour operator make all of their travel arrangements. There are many such companies, each offering transportation to and within Spain, prearranged hotel space, and such extras as bilingual tour guides and lectures. Many of these tours to Spain include excursions to Morocco or Portugal.

Some of the most unusual tours are run by **Abercrombie & Kent International, Inc.,** 1520 Kensington Rd., Oak Brook, IL 60521 (☎ **800/323-7308** or 708/954-2944), a Chicago-based company that specializes in glamorous tours around the world. It offers deluxe 7-, 12-, and 18-day tours of the Iberian Peninsula by train. Despite all the extras that are included, the tours cost less than any personally arranged tours with equivalent facilities and services.

On Abercrombie & Kent's "Great Spain & Portugal Express" tour by train, participants spend their nights in some of the most elegant paradors of Spain. (Run by the government and chosen for their historic and/or cultural interest, these hostelries include some of the most famous castles and medieval monasteries.) Tours depart in May and October; the cost is from $2,750 per person, double occupancy, with single supplements from $420 per person.

American Express Vacations, P.O. Box 1525, Fort Lauderdale, FL 33302 (☎ **800/446-6234** in the U.S. and Canada), offers some of the most comprehensive programs available to Spain, including Madrid as the major stopover.

Sun Holidays, 7280 W. Palmetto Park Rd., Suite 301, Boca Raton, FL, 33433 (☎ **800/422-8000** or 407/367-0105), has been specializing in extended vacations for senior citizens since 1980. The company features excursions to the Costa del Sol in Spain and the Algarve and Cascais/Lisbon areas of Portugal. The company also sponsors fully escorted motorcoach tours of Spain and Portugal.

Trafalgar Tours, 11 E. 26th St., Suite 1300, New York, NY 10010 (☎ **212/689-8977**) offers two 10-day tours of southern Spain. The itineraries are identical, but the prices differ according to season. Tours include visits to Granada, Seville, Córdoba, as well as free time on the Costa del Sol. "The Real Spain," departs on Fridays, from January 6 to March 24. Prices range from $550 for land only, to $950, including airfare. "Spanish Discovery" departs on Fridays from April 7 to December 8. Land-only packages cost from $799; land plus airfare costs from $1,425 to $1,598.

Insight International's "Highlights of Spain" is a 10-day tour that begins in Barcelona, sweeps along the southern and eastern coasts, and concludes in Madrid. Sights of interest include Seville, the peaks of the Sierra Nevada, and Cervantes's famed plains of La Mancha. The company offers the tour for $1,655 including airfare, accommodations, and some meals. Tours run weekly, April 7 through November 26. For information, contact your travel agent or Insight International (☎ **800/582-8380**).

Alternative Travel Group Ltd., 69–71 Banbury Rd., Oxford OX2 6PE, UK (☎ **01865/310-399**), organizes walking and cycling holidays, plus wine tours in Spain, Italy, and France. Tours explore the scenic countryside and medieval towns of each country.

9 Getting Around

BY PLANE

Three fiscally interconnected airlines operate within Spain: the well-recommended **Iberia** and its smaller cousins, **Aviaco** and **Binter Air.** (For reservations on any of these, call **800/772-4642** in the U.S.) By European standards, domestic flights within Spain are relatively inexpensive, and considering the vast distances within the country, flying between distant points sometimes makes sense.

If you plan to travel to a number of cities and regions, Iberia's **"Visit Spain"** ticket, priced between $279 and $349, depending on the season, makes flying even more economical. Sold only in conjunction with a transatlantic ticket and valid for any airport within Spain and the Balearic Islands, it requires that passengers identify in advance up to four different cities that they want to visit and the order of these stops. Restrictions forbid flying immediately back to the city of departure, instead encouraging far-flung visits to widely scattered regions of the peninsula. Only one change within the preset itinerary is permitted once the ticket is issued. The dates and departure times of the actual flights, however, can be determined or changed without penalty once you arrive in Spain. Also, passengers who want to exceed the predesignated number of stops (four) included within the basic ticket can add additional cities to their itineraries for $50 each. Children under 2 travel for 10% of the adult fare, and children 2 to 11 travel for 50% of the adult fare. The ticket is valid for up to 60 days after your initial transatlantic arrival in Spain.

BY TRAIN

If you plan to travel a great deal on the European railroads, it's worth securing a copy of the *Thomas Cook European Timetable of European Passenger Railroads.* It's available exclusively in North America from **Forsyth Travel Library,** P.O. Box 2975, Shawnee Mission, KS 66201 (☎ **800/FORSYTH**), at a cost of $27.95, plus $4.50 postage priority airmail in the United States or plus $2 (U.S.) for shipments to Canada.

The most economical way to travel in Spain is on the **Spanish State Railways (RENFE).** Most main long-distance connections are served with night express trains having first- and second-class seats as well as beds and bunks. There are also comfortable high-speed daytime trains of the TALGO, TER, and Electrotren types. There is a general fare for these trains; bunks, beds, and certain superior-quality trains cost extra. Nevertheless, the Spanish railway is one of the most economical in Europe; in most cases, this is the best way to go.

Direct trains connect Madrid with Paris and Lisbon, and Barcelona with Paris and Geneva; and international connections are easily made on the frontiers, at Valencia de Alcantara-Marvâo (Portugal), Irún-Hendaye, and Port Bou-Cerbère (France). There is also a direct express from Algeciras to Hendaye.

RAIL PASSES RENFE, the national railway of Spain, offers the **Spain Flexipass,** a discounted rail pass. Spain is crisscrossed with a detailed network of rail lines, connecting most of its large- and medium-sized cities into a coherent whole. Hundreds of trains depart every day for points around the country, including the fast TALGO and the more recent AVE trains, which reduce rail time between Madrid and Seville to only 2½ hours.

Flexipasses are usually chosen by passengers who prefer to stop and savor the cultural riches of Spain's cities for several days between train rides. Flexipasses permit a predesignated number of travel days within a predetermined time block—for example, 3 or 5 days in a predesignated block of one month or 10 days in two months.

You must buy these passes in the United States prior to your departure. For more information, consult a travel agent or **Rail Europe, Inc.** (☎ **800/4-EURAIL**).

VE Tours offers a computerized link to RENFE with its "instant purchase ticketing." By calling **800/222-8383,** travelers can reserve seats for travel between various cities within Spain and on journeys on RENFE to neighboring countries. The network includes access to the Intercity, Estrella, and Tren Hotel lines, as well as access to the AVE, Spain's high-speed network.

Eurailpass Many in-the-know travelers take advantage of the great travel bargain known as the Eurailpass, which permits unlimited first-class travel in any country in western Europe, except the British Isles (good in Ireland). The Eurailpass also entitles you to discounts on some bus and steamship lines. Passes are available for 15 days or as long as three months and are strictly nontransferable.

Children under 4 travel free, provided they don't occupy a seat of their own (otherwise, they're charged half fare); children 4 to 12 pay half fare. If you're under 26, you can purchase a **Eurail Youthpass,** which entitles you to unlimited second-class travel, for either 15 days, one month, or two months.

The **Eurail Saverpass** provides discounted 15-day travel for groups of three people traveling continuously together between April and September or two people between October and March. The price of a Saverpass, valid all over Europe is good for first class only.

The **Eurail Flexipass** allows passengers to visit Europe with more flexibility. It's valid in first class and offers the same privileges as the Eurailpass. However, it provides a number of individual travel days that can be used over a much longer period of consecutive days. That makes it possible to stay in one city and yet not lose a single day of travel. The pass entitles you, within a two-month period, to 10 or 15 days of travel.

With similar qualifications and restrictions, travelers under 26 can purchase a **Eurail Youth Flexipass.** It also allows, within a two-month period, for 10 or 15 days of travel.

Europass In the mid-1990s, yet another option was added to the several deals available from Rail Europe. Like its more comprehensive cousin, Eurailpass, the Europass offers the most favorable rates only to buyers who purchase it outside of Europe.

Depending on the fee, Europass allows unlimited rail travel within and between three and five European countries with shared (contiguous) borders, arranged into several different price tiers. The countries participating in the Europass plan include Italy, France, Germany, Switzerland, and Spain. The terrain covered by the Europass plan is deliberately less broad-based than that honored by the 17 countries within the Eurail network.

If you opt for five to seven days of first-class train travel in three of the above-mentioned countries (Italy plus two contiguous countries on the list), you'll have up to two months to complete your travel.

If you opt for 8 to 10 days of travel within any two-month period, you'll be able to add a fourth country from the above-cited list, and if you opt for 11 to 15 days of travel within any two-month period, you can travel through all five of the above-mentioned countries while using the pass.

You can reduce costs with this means of transport by sharing your trip with another adult, who will receive a 50% discount on each of the above-mentioned fares.

Note: You can add what Europass refers to as an "associate country" (Austria, Benelux, Greece, or Portugal) to the reach of your Europass by paying a surcharge.

If you're under 26 at the time you plan to use the pass, you're eligible for a **Europass Youth,** which is less expensive than the adult Europass, but limits you to the second-class compartment of every train. Most of the same stipulations and benefits apply, but at a discount of about 35% off the above-mentioned fares, so it's a worthwhile investment. Unlike the adult Europass, however, there is no discount for your companion if you opt to travel as a pair.

Europasses can be purchased from any travel agent, or arranged over the phone by dialing **800/4-EURAIL.**

VINTAGE TRAIN TRAVEL **Al Andalus Expreso** (or simply Al Andalus) is a restored vintage train that travels through some of the most historic destinations in Andalusia.

The train retains an atmosphere and level of service that recall the first three decades of this century. The passenger and dining cars boast panels of inlaid marquetry, hardwoods, brass fittings, and etched glass that could well be found in the Edwardian parlor of a private mansion; beneath the antique veneers, state-of-the-art engineering maintains comfortably high speeds. The train offers fine dining and such amenities as individual showers on wheels.

The Al Andalus consists of 13 carriages manufactured in Britain, Spain, or France between 1929 and 1930, which were collected and restored by railway historians at RENFE. Included are two restaurant cars, a games and lounge car, a bar car where live piano music and evening flamenco dances are presented, five sleeping carriages, and two shower cars. All carriages (except the shower cars) are air-conditioned and heated.

For reservations, contact your travel agent. For additional brochures and information, contact **Marketing Ahead,** 433 Fifth Ave., New York, NY 10016 (☎ **800/223-1356** or 212/686-9213).

BY BUS

Bus service in Spain is extensive, low-priced, and comfortable enough for short distances. You'll rarely encounter a bus terminal in Spain. The "station" might be a café, a bar, the street in front of a hotel, or simply a spot at an intersection.

A bus may be the cheapest mode of transportation, but it's not really feasible for distances of more than 100 miles. On long hauls, buses are slow and often uncomfortable. Another major drawback might be a lack of toilet facilities, though rest stops are frequent. It's best for one-day excursions outside of a major tourist center such as Madrid. In the rural areas of the country, bus networks are more extensive than the railway system; they go virtually everywhere, connecting every village. In general, a bus ride between two major cities in Spain, such as from Córdoba to Seville, is about two-thirds the price of a train ride.

BY CAR

A car offers the greatest flexibility while you're touring, even if you limit your explorations to the environs of Madrid. Don't, however, plan to drive in Madrid—it's too congested. Theoretically, rush hour is Monday to Saturday from 8 to 10am, 1 to 2pm, and 4 to 6pm. In reality, it's always busy.

CAR RENTALS Many of North America's biggest car-rental companies, including Avis, Budget, and Hertz, maintain offices throughout Spain. Although several Spain-based car-rental companies will try to entice you to their facilities, letters from readers of previous editions have shown that the resolution of billing irregularities and insurance claims tends to be less complicated with the U.S.-based rental firms.

Avis (☎ **800/331-2112**) maintains about a hundred branches throughout Spain, including about a dozen in Madrid, eight in Barcelona, a half-dozen in Seville, and four in the provincial city of Murcia. If you reserve and pay your rental by telephone at least two weeks prior to your departure from North America, you'll qualify for the company's best rate, with unlimited kilometers included, plus 15% tax, for the company's smallest and least-accessorized car, a Ford Fiesta or Renault 5. At Avis, as at its major competitors, prepaid rates do not include the taxes, which are settled in separate transactions once you reach the rental kiosk.

For its smallest car (a Ford Fiesta or Peugeot 106), **Hertz** (☎ **800/654-3001**) also requires prepayment; if a renter has access to a fax machine for the receipt of vouchers, only 24 hours advance notification is necessary. Hertz charges a value-added tax of 15% and an $8 airport surcharge, both of which are paid separately on Spanish soil.

Also attractive is **Budget Rent-a-Car** (☎ **800/527-0700**), whose least expensive car sometimes costs a bit more than those of its competitors (plus 15% VAT and, if applicable, the airport surcharge), but whose mid-priced cars are often less expensive than those of Avis or Hertz. Budget does not charge a supplement if you drop off its car in another Spanish city. But although you may drive a Budget car to another country in Europe, you have to return it to one of the company's drop-off points in Spain.

All three companies require that drivers be at least 21 years of age and, in some cases, not older than 72. To be able to rent a car, you must have a passport and a valid driver's license; you must also have a valid credit card or a prepaid voucher (if neither, you'll be asked to make a substantial cash deposit). An international driver's license is not essential, but you might want to present it if you have one; it's available from any North American office of the American Automobile Association (AAA).

Insurance options at each of the companies are complicated, but it's well worth the trouble to ask questions and understand your options before you depart from home. Some companies will include, for a higher net rate, insurance (both liability and collision damage) and taxes into a car's weekly rental fee. A collision-damage waiver costs $14 to $21 extra per day for most small- and medium-sized cars. Unless you're covered through independent insurance (such as that provided free by some credit card companies when their cards are used to pay for a rental), it's usually an excellent idea to accept the extra insurance. In some cases, you might also be offered theft insurance to protect the contents of your rented car. Know in advance that filing a claim for stolen goods requires lots of paperwork and, in many cases, a police report. Buy this insurance if it's available and if you think it's necessary, but remember that the best way to protect against theft is by emptying your car of all luggage when you're not traveling, or at least locking objects in the car's trunk, away from public view.

GASOLINE Gasoline, or petrol, is easily obtainable—but expensive—throughout Spain, with regular fuel normally being used in rented cars. The average Spanish vehicle gets close to 45 miles per gallon. Arrange an itinerary and set up hotels along the way so that you won't have to empty the tank while looking for a room. Try to leave early in the day to avoid the endless traffic lines that form on major arteries of Spanish cities during rush hours.

DRIVING RULES Spaniards drive on the right side of the road. Drivers should pass on the left; local drivers sound their horns when passing another car. Autos coming from the right have the right-of-way.

Spain's express highways are known as *autopistas,* which charge a toll, and *autovías,* which don't. To exit in Spain, follow the *salida* sign, except in Catalonia, where the word is *sortida.* On most express highways, the speed limit is 75 mph (120kmph). On other roads speed limits range from 56 mph (90kmph) to 62 mph (100kmph).

Most accidents in Spain are recorded along the notorious Costa del Sol highway, the Carretera de Cádiz.

If you must drive through a Spanish city, try to do so between 3 and 5pm, when many motorists are having a siesta. Never park your car facing oncoming traffic, as that is against the law. If you are fined by the highway patrol (Guardia Civil de Tráfico), you must pay on the spot. Penalties for drinking and driving are very stiff.

MAPS For one of the best overviews of the Iberian Peninsula (Spain and Portugal), obtain a copy of Michelin map number 990 (for a folding version) or number 460 for the same map in a spiral-bound version. For more detailed looks at Spain, Michelin has a series of six maps (nos. 441–446), showing specific regions, complete with many minor roads.

For extensive touring, purchase *Mapas de Carreteras–España y Portugal,* published by Almax Editores and available at most leading bookstores in Spain. This cartographic compendium of Spain provides an overview of the country and includes road and street maps of some of its major cities as well.

The American Automobile Association (☎ **800/222-4357**) publishes a regional map of Spain that's available free to members at most AAA offices in the United States. Also available free to members is a guide of approximately 60 pages, *Motoring in Europe,* that gives helpful information about road signs and speed limits, as well as insurance regulations and other relevant matters. Incidentally, the AAA is associated with the **Real Automóvil Club de España,** José Abascal, 10, Madrid 28003 (☎ **91/447-32-00**). This organization will provide helpful information about road conditions in Spain, including tourist and travel data. It will also provide limited road service, in an emergency, if your car breaks down.

BREAKDOWNS These can be a serious problem. If you're driving a Spanish-made vehicle, you'll probably be able to find spare parts, if needed. But if you have a foreign-made vehicle, you may be stranded. Have the car checked out before setting out on a long trek through Spain. On a major motorway you'll find strategically placed emergency phone boxes. On secondary roads, call for help by asking the operator to locate the nearest Guardia Civil, which will put you in touch with a garage that can tow you to a repair shop.

BY FERRY

Travel by ferry is not normally associated with Spain; however, this method of transportation might be convenient at times. For example, the least expensive way to travel from Spain to Morocco is by ferry connections from the Spanish port of Algeciras. Several other boat links also exist between Spain and Tangier and between mainland Spain and the Spanish enclave in Morocco, Ceuta.

Many boat and ferry links connect mainland Spain and the Balearics (Majorca, Minorca, and Ibiza).

SUGGESTED ITINERARIES

The number of places and sights to see in Spain is staggering. It takes at least two months to see all the major cities, and even that calls for some fast moving. Most of us don't have that much time, however, and will need to get the most out of Spain in a shorter time.

The following cities are particularly worth visiting: Barcelona, Córdoba, Granada, Madrid, Salamanca, Santiago de Compostela, Segovia, Seville, and Toledo.

If You Have One Week

Days 1–2 Spend your first two days in Madrid (one to recover from the flight or drive there, another to see the sights, including the Prado).

Day 3 Leave Madrid and drive south to Aranjuez to see its Palacio Real (Royal Palace), then move on to Toledo for the night.

Day 4 Spend a full day and night in Toledo, seeing its cathedral, El Greco paintings, and Alcázar.

Day 5 Leave Toledo and drive north toward Madrid, taking the bypass west to reach El Escorial, Philip II's giant palace. Spend the night there.

Day 6 Proceed west from El Escorial to the walled city of Ávila for an overnight stay.

Day 7 Leave Ávila and drive northeast toward Segovia to visit its Alcázar and Roman aqueduct. Spend the night there before returning to Madrid. (If time remains the next morning, see the Bourbon summer palace at La Granja before returning to Madrid.)

If You Have Two Weeks

Days 1–2 Spend these days as outlined above.

Day 3 While still in Madrid, take a trip to Toledo, with a possible morning stopover at Aranjuez.

Day 4 Make a morning visit to El Escorial and spend the afternoon at Segovia.

Day 5 Drive south to Córdoba, arriving in time to view its world-famous mosque.
Day 6 Leave Córdoba and drive west to Seville, the capital of Andalusia, for an overnight stay.
Day 7 Go south to the sherry town of Jerez, perhaps pressing on to the Atlantic seaport of Cádiz for the night.
Day 8 Drive on to Algeciras, east of Cádiz, with an afternoon visit to Gibraltar.
Day 9 From either port, you could spend a day in Tangier.
Days 10–11 Bask in the sun at one of the resorts, such as Marbella, along the Costa del Sol.
Days 12–13 Drive inland north to see Granada and its Alhambra.
Day 14 Return to Madrid, or travel to Málaga and catch a flight there.

A Themed Itinerary: St. James's Way

Six centuries ago pilgrims used to make the 500-mile trek from the Pyrenees to the shrine of St. James in Santiago de Compostela. The original route, suggested in the 1130 guidebook *Liber Sancti Jacobi,* can't be followed anymore, so here is a modern-day itinerary from the Basque country to Santiago de Compostela.

Day 1 Cross from the Basque country of France and drive into Spain. Before Irún, cut south on C-133 to Pamplona, the capital of the old kingdom of Navarre and the setting of the famous "running of the bulls" (see "Spain Calendar of Events" earlier in this chapter).
Day 2 After an overnight stay in Pamplona, drive northwest to San Sebastián, a Belle Epoque resort just 12 miles (19km) from the French border.
Day 3 After swimming at the Playa de la Concha continue west to Ondárroa, the most attractive fishing village in Spain, for lunch. In the afternoon continue west to Guernica, setting of Picasso's famous painting. Guernica lies 52 miles (83km) from San Sebastián. After a visit there, drive to Bilbao for the night.
Days 4–5 After a morning tour of Bilbao, drive west to Santander and relax in the afternoon at El Sardinero beach, 1 1/2 miles (2 1/2km) from the capital. Santander is a resort city of summer festivals. The next day, while still based at Santander, drive 18 miles (29km) southwest to visit Santillana del Mar, a medieval village near the site of the prehistoric cave paintings of Altamira. Return to Santander.
Day 6 Drive west from Santander to Oviedo, capital of the province of Asturias. Stay overnight there.
Day 7 Drive all the way from Oviedo to Santiago de Compostela, revered as the burial site of St. James, patron saint of Spain. Spend as much time as you have. There are daily flights to Madrid, plus train and bus service; otherwise, it's a 390-mile (625km) drive.

10 For British Travelers

GETTING THERE

BY PLANE

A regular fare from the United Kingdom to Spain is extremely high, so savvy Britons usually call a travel agent for a "deal"—either a charter flight or some special air-travel promotion. Such a deal is always available, because of great interest in Spain as a tourist destination. If one is not possible for you, then you may find that an APEX (Advance Payment Excursion) ticket is the best way to keep costs trimmed. Although an APEX ticket must be reserved in advance, it offers a discount without the strict booking restrictions experienced with a charter airline. You might also ask the airlines about a Eurobudget ticket, which carries such restrictions as length-of-stay requirements.

British Airways (☎ **0171/897-4000** in London) and **Iberia** (☎ **0171/437-5622** in London) are the two major carriers flying between England and Spain. More than a dozen daily flights, either on BA or Iberia, depart from London's Heathrow and Gatwick airports. The Midlands is served by flights from Manchester and Birmingham, two major airports that can also be used by Scottish travelers flying to Spain. There are about seven flights a day from London to Madrid and back and at least six to Barcelona (trip time: 2–2½ hours). From either the Madrid airport or the Barcelona airport, you can tap into Iberia's domestic network—flying, for example, to Seville or the Costa del Sol (centered at the Málaga airport). The best air deals on scheduled flights from England are those requiring a Saturday night stopover.

Most vacationing Britons, however, go charter, at least those looking for air flight bargains. Delays are frequent (some may last two whole days and nights), and departures are often at inconvenient hours. Booking conditions can also be severe; you should therefore read the fine print carefully and deal only with a reputable travel agent. Stays rarely last a month, and booking must sometimes be made at least a month in advance, although a two-week period is sometimes possible.

British newspapers are always full of classified advertisements touting "slashed" fares to Spain. A good source is *Time Out,* a magazine published in London. London's *Evening Standard* has a daily travel section, and the Sunday editions of most papers are full of charter deals. A travel agent can always advise what the best values are at the time of your intended departure.

Charter flights leave from most British regional airports with a destination in mind (for example, Málaga), bypassing the congestion at the Barcelona and Madrid airports. Figure on saving approximately 10% to 15% on regularly scheduled flight tickets. But check carefully. Recommended companies include **Trailfinders** (☎ **0171/937-5400** in London) and **Avro Tours** (☎ **0181/543-0000** in London), which operate charters.

In London, there are many bucket shops, around Victoria Station and Earls Court, that offer cheap fares. Make sure that the company you deal with is a member of the IATA, ABTA, or ATOL. These umbrella organizations will help you out if anything goes wrong.

CEEFAX, a British television information service, runs details of package holidays and flights to Europe and beyond. Just switch to your CEEFAX channel and you'll find travel information.

Make sure you understand the bottom line on any special deal you purchase. Ask whether all surcharges, including airport taxes and other hidden costs, are cited before committing yourself to purchase. Upon investigation, you may find that some of these "deals" are not as attractive as advertised. Also, make sure you understand what the penalties are if you're forced to cancel at the last minute.

By Train

To go from London to Spain by rail, you'll need to change not only the train but also the rail terminus in Paris. In Paris it's worth the extra bucks to purchase a TALGO express or a "Puerta del Sol" express—that way, you can avoid having to change trains once again at the Spanish border. Trip time from London to Paris is about 6 hours; from Paris to Madrid, about 15 hours or so, which includes two hours spent in Paris just changing trains and stations. Many different rail passes are available in the United Kingdom for travel in Europe. Stop in at **Wasteels,** at Victoria Station, opposite platform 2, London, SW1V 1JZ (☎ **0171/834-6744**). They can help you find the best option for the trip you're planning.

BY BUS

The busiest routes are from London and are run by **Eurolines Limited,** 23 Crawley Rd., Luton LU1 1HX, Bedfordshire (☎ **01582/404-511** or 0171/730-8235). The journey from London's Victoria Station to Madrid is provided by two services: Service 180 departs from London daily at 9pm and arrives in Madrid the following day at 9:30pm; Service 181 leaves London at 9pm on Day 1 and arrives in Madrid at 12:30am on Day 3.

Other bus trips can be arranged from London to Barcelona, Alicante, Benidorm, and Marbella.

Julia Tours of Barcelona (☎ **93/490-40-00** in Barcelona) operates a coach that departs from London's Victoria Station on Monday, Wednesday, and Saturday. It leaves London at 11am and gets into Barcelona the following morning at 10:45. An English-speaking staff in Barcelona can make reservations for you and supply more details.

BY CAR

If you're driving from Britain, make sure you have a cross-Channel reservation, as traffic tends to be very heavy, especially in summer. The major ferry crossings connect Dover and Folkestone with Dunkirk. Newhaven is connected with Dieppe, and the British city of Portsmouth with Roscoff. One of the fastest crossings is by Hovercraft from Dover to Boulogne or Calais. It costs more than the ferry, but it takes only about half an hour.

As of 1994, however, you can take the "Chunnel," the underwater Channel Tunnel linking Britain (Folkestone) and France (Calais) by road and rail—a great engineering feat that was first envisioned by Napoleon way back in 1802. Travel time between the English and French highway systems is about one hour.

TIPS FOR TRAVELERS WITH SPECIAL NEEDS

FOR TRAVELERS WITH DISABILITIES

RADAR (the Royal Association for Disability and Rehabilitation), Unit 12, City Forum, 250 City Rd., London EC1V 8AF (☎ **0171/250-3222**), publishes two annual holiday guides for travelers with disabilities. "Holidays and Travel Abroad," costs £5, whereas "Holidays in the British Isles" goes for £7. RADAR (whose patroness is Elizabeth, the Queen Mother), also provides a number of holiday information packets on such subjects as sports and outdoor holidays, insurance, financial arrangements for persons with disabilities, and accommodations within nursing care units for groups or for the elderly. Each of these fact sheets is available for £2. Fact sheets or the above-mentioned holiday guides can be mailed outside the U.K. for a nominal mailing fee.

Another good resource is the **Holiday Care Service,** Imperial Buildings, 2nd Floor, Victoria Rd., Horley, Surrey RH6 7PZ (☎ **01293/774-535**; fax 01293/784-647), a national charity that advises on accessible accommodations for elderly people or those with disabilities. Annual membership costs £10 (U.K. residents) and £25 (abroad). Members receive a newsletter and have access to a free reservations network for hotels throughout Britain and, to a lesser degree, Europe and the rest of the world.

For Singles

Single people feel comfortable traveling with other singles. A tour operator whose groups are usually composed at least 50% of unattached persons is **Explore Worldwide, Ltd.,** 1 Frederick St., Aldershot, Hampshire GU11 1LQ (☎ **01252/344-161**), with a well-justified reputation for assembling offbeat tours. Groups rarely include more than 20 participants, and children under 14 are not allowed.

For Seniors

Wasteels, Victoria Station, opposite platform 2, London SW1V 1JY (☎ **0171/834-7066**), currently provides an over-60s Rail Europe Senior Card. Its price is £5 to any British person with government-issued proof of his or her age, and £19 to anyone with a certificate of age not issued by the British government. With this card, discounts are sometimes available on certain trains within Britain and the rest of Europe.

For Families

The best deals for British families are often package tours put together by some of the giants of the British travel industry. Foremost among these is **Thomsons Tour Operators.** Through its subsidiary, **Skytours** (☎ **0171/387-9321**), it offers dozens of air/land packages to Spain that have a predesignated number of airline seats reserved for free use by children under 18 who accompany their parents. To qualify, parents must book airfare and hotel accommodations lasting two weeks or more, and book as far in advance as possible. Savings for families with children can be substantial.

For Students

Campus Travel, 52 Grosvenor Gardens, London SW1W 0AG (☎ **0171/730-3402**), provides a wealth of information for the student traveler, ranging from route planning to flight insurance, including rail cards.

The International Student Identity Card (ISIC) is an internationally recognized proof of student status that will entitle you to savings on flights, sightseeing, food, and accommodation. It costs only £5 and is well worth the cost. Always show your ISIC when booking a trip—you may not get a discount without it.

Youth hostels are the place to stay if you're a student or, in some cases, if you're traveling on an ultra-tight budget. You'll need an International Youth Hostels Association card, which you can purchase from either of London's youth hostel retail outlets. Housed near Covent Garden at 14 Southampton St., London WC23 7HY (☎ **0171/836-1036**), or within the same building as the previously recommended Campus Travel, 52 Grosvenor Gardens, London SW1W OAG (☎ **0171/823-4739**), they sell rucksacks, hiking boots, maps, and all the paraphernalia a camper, hiker, or shoestring traveler might need. To apply for a membership card, take both your passport and some passport-sized photos of yourself, plus a membership fee of £9. For membership by mail from outside of London, call the IYHA membership offices at 0171/730-5769.

The Youth Hostel Association puts together a *YHA Budget Accommodations Guide* (Volumes 1 and 2), which lists the address, phone number, and admissions policy for every youth hostel in the world. (Volume 1 covers Europe and the Mediterranean; volume 2 covers the rest of the globe.) The cost is £6.99 per volume, and either can be purchased at the retail outlets listed above. If ordering by mail, add 61p for postage within the U.K.

In summer, many youth hostels are full, so book ahead. In London, you can make advance reservations at the membership department at 14 Southampton St. (see above).

TRAVEL INSURANCE

Most big travel agents offer their own insurance, and will probably try to sell you their package when you book a holiday. Think before you sign. Britain's Consumers' Association recommends that you insist on seeing the policy and reading the fine print before buying travel insurance.

You should also shop around for better deals. You might call **Columbus Travel Insurance Ltd.** (☎ **0171/375-0011** in London) or, for students, **Campus Travel** (☎ **0171/730-3402** in London).

11 Tips on Accommodations

TYPES OF ACCOMMODATIONS From castles converted into hotels to modern high-rise resorts overlooking the Mediterranean, Spain has some of the most varied hotel accommodations in the world—with equally varied price ranges. Accommodations are broadly classified as follows:

One- to Five-Star Hotels The Spanish government rates hotels by stars. A five-star hotel is truly deluxe with deluxe prices; a one-star hotel is the most modest accommodation officially recognized as a hotel by the government. A four-star hotel offers first-class accommodations; a three-star hotel is moderately priced; and a one- or two-star hotel is inexpensively priced. The government grants stars based on such amenities as elevators, private bathrooms, and air-conditioning. If a hotel is classified as a *residencia,* it means that it serves breakfast (usually) but no other meals.

Hostals Not to be confused with a hostel for students, a *hostal* is a modest hotel without services, where you can save money by carrying your own bags and the like. You'll know it's a hostal if a small *s* follows the capital letter *H* on the blue plaque by the door. A hostal with three stars is about the equivalent of a hotel with two stars.

Pensions These boarding houses are among the least expensive accommodations, but you're required to take either full board (three meals) or demipension, which is breakfast plus lunch or dinner. The latter is the best option.

Casas Huespedes & Fondas These are the cheapest places in Spain and can be recognized by the light-blue plaques at the door displaying *CH* and *F,* respectively. These are invariably basic but respectable establishments.

Youth Hostels Spain has about 140 hostels (*albergues de juventud*). In theory, those 25 or under have the first chance at securing a bed for the night, but these places are certainly not limited to young people. Some of them are equipped for persons with disabilities. Most hostels impose an 11pm curfew. For information, write **Red Española de Alberques Juveniles,** Calle José Ortega y Gasset, 71, 28006 Madrid (☎ **91/344-77-78**).

Paradors The Spanish government in 1926 launched a series of unique state-owned inns called paradors (*paradores* in Spanish), which now blanket the country. Deserted castles, monasteries, palaces, and other buildings have been taken over and converted into hotels. Today there are 86 paradors in all, and they're documented in a booklet called "Visiting the Paradores," available at Spanish Tourist offices (see "Information & Required Documents" at the beginning of this chapter).

At great expense, modern baths, steam heat, and the like have been added to these buildings, yet classic Spanish architecture, where it existed, has been retained. Establishments are often furnished with antiques or at least good reproductions and decorative objects typical of the country.

Meals are also served in these government-owned inns. Usually, typical dishes of the region are featured. Paradors are likely to be overcrowded in the summer months, so advance reservations, arranged through any travel agent, are wise.

The government also operates a type of accommodation known as *albergues:* these are comparable to motels, standing along the roadside and usually built in hotel-scarce sections for the convenience of passing motorists. A client is not allowed to stay in an albergue for more than 48 hours, and the management doesn't accept reservations.

In addition, the government runs *refugios,* mostly in remote areas, attracting hunters, fishers, and mountain climbers. A final state-sponsored establishment is the *hostería,* or specialty restaurant, such as the one at Alcalá de Henares, near Madrid. Hosterías don't offer rooms; decorated in the style of a particular province, they serve regional dishes at reasonable prices.

The central office of paradors is **Paradores de España,** Requena, 3, 28013 Madrid (☎ **91/516-66-66**). The U.S. representative for the Paradores of Spain is **Marketing Ahead,** 433 5th Ave., New York, NY 10016 (☎ **800/223-1356**). Travel agents in the United States, Canada, and Britain can also arrange reservations.

SEASONAL & OTHER DISCOUNTS In theory, the maximum rate established by a hotel for its rooms is charged for its better rooms during peak season, but in fact the maximum rate is often in effect all year. At some resorts in the slow season, rates may be lowered by the management to attract business. Always ask for a discount if you sense that business is slow.

If there are three or more in your party, ask for an additional bed in your room. In a double an extra bed usually costs 35% or less than the maximum price for the room.

If you're traveling on a budget, don't expect to roll into a city after dark and secure the bargains—they will already have been grabbed by the early birds.

CENTRHOTEL operates a network of independent budget hotels, located throughout 11 Spanish cities. Ideal for families, business travelers, or any other budget-conscious traveler, the accommodations are two- to three-star hotels located in the heart of such cities as Seville, Barcelona, and Segovia. For information, contact CENTRHOTEL in Barcelona (☎ **93/451-44-56**).

HOUSES & APARTMENTS If you rent a home or an apartment, you can save money on accommodations and dining and still take daily trips to see the surrounding area.

Apartments in Spain generally fall into two different categories: hotel *apartamientos* and *residencia apartamientos.* The hotel apartments have full facilities, with chamber service, equipped kitchenettes, and often restaurants and bars. The residencia apartments, also called *apartamientos turisticos,* are fully furnished with kitchenettes but lack the facilities of the hotel complexes. They are cheaper, however.

Companies in the United States arranging such rentals include **At Home Abroad,** 405 E. 56th St., Suite 6H, New York, NY 10022 (☎ **212/421-9165**). It offers deluxe two- to four-bedroom apartments, packaged with a self-drive car, on the Costa del Sol. The estates on which the apartments are located have swimming pools for the residents, and the beach is at the end of the gardens.

A company that has proved helpful to those seeking to rent houses, condominiums, and private apartments in Spain is **Hometours International, Inc.,** P.O. Box

11503, Knoxville, TN 37939 (☎ **800/367-4668** or 423/588-8722). Most of the agency's Spanish inventory lies in Andalusia, which attracts more European sunseekers than any other region of Spain. To obtain their 260-page color catalog with descriptions and pictures, send $8 for postage and handling, $4 for their bed-and-breakfast catalog of small family-run hotels, or $3 for descriptive literature about any other location. Units are rented for a minimum of seven days; and for the most part, they lie in white-walled villages in such places as the Ronda Sierras of Andalusia, near the cultural and tourist attractions of Málaga, Gibraltar, and Marbella. Hometours also has a variety of offerings in neighboring Portugal and in Britain, France, Italy, and elsewhere in Europe, as well as in Israel.

Another agency willing to match prospective renters with empty real estate in Spain is **ILC (International Lodging Corp.),** 300 First Ave., Suite 7C, New York, NY 10009 (☎ **800/SPAIN-44** or 212/228-5900). The company specializes in rentals of privately owned apartments, houses, and villas, for a period of a week or more. It also offers access to suites in well-known hotels for stays of a week or longer, sometimes at rates lower than those that a traveler may have been given when contacting the hotel directly. (This service especially appeals to families with children and to business travelers intending to stay a month or more.) Rental units, regardless of their size, usually contain a kitchen. The company's listings cover accommodations in Madrid, Barcelona, Seville, and Granada, as well as on the Balearic island of Majorca.

FAST FACTS: Spain

Business Hours Banks are open Monday to Friday from 9:30am to 2pm and Saturday from 9:30am to 1pm. Most offices are open Monday to Friday from 9am to 5 or 5:30pm; the longtime practice of early closings in summer seems to be dying out. In restaurants, lunch is usually 1 to 4pm and dinner 9 to 11:30pm or midnight. There are no set rules for the opening of bars and taverns, many opening at 8am, others at noon; most stay open until 1:30am or later. Major stores are open Monday to Saturday from 9:30am to 8pm; smaller establishments, however, often take a siesta, doing business from 9:30am to 1:30pm and 4:30 to 8pm. Hours can vary from store to store.

Climate See "When to Go" earlier in this chapter.

Currency See "Money" earlier in this chapter.

Customs See "Information & Required Documents" earlier in this chapter.

Driving Rules See "Getting Around" earlier in this chapter.

Drugstores To find an open pharmacy outside of normal business hours, check the list of stores posted on the door of any drugstore. The law requires drugstores to operate on a rotating system of hours so that there's always a drugstore open somewhere, even Sunday at midnight.

Electricity Most establishments have 220 volts AC. Some older places have 110 or 125 volts. Carry your adapter with you, and always check at your hotel desk before plugging in any electrical appliance. It's best to travel with battery-operated equipment.

Embassies/Consulates If you lose your passport, fall seriously ill, get into legal trouble, or have some other serious problem, your embassy or consulate will probably have the means to provide assistance. These are the Madrid addresses and hours: The United States Embassy, Calle Serrano, 75 (☎ **91/577-40-00,** metro: Núñez de Balboa), is open Monday to Friday from 9:30am to 1pm and 2:30 to 5pm. In addition, there's a consular agency, which can provide limited services, in Fuengirola, near Málaga on the Costa del Sol: U.S. Consular Agency, Centrol Comerical Las Rampas, Fase II, 1, locales 12G7/12G8 Fuengirola, Málaga (☎ **952/47-48-91**). Office hours are 10am to 1pm Monday through Friday. The Canadian Embassy, Núñez de Balboa, 35 (☎ **91/431-43-00,** metro: Velázquez), is open Monday to Friday from 8:30am to 5pm. The United Kingdom Embassy, Fernando el Santo, 16 (☎ **91/319-02-00,** metro: Colón), is open Monday to Friday from 9am to 2pm and 3:30 to 6pm. The Republic of Ireland has an embassy at Claudio Coello, 73 (☎ **91/576-35-00,** metro: Serrano); it's open Monday to Friday from 10am to 2pm. The Australian Embassy, Paseo de la Castellana, 143 (☎ **91/579-04-28,** metro: Cuzco), is open Monday through Thursday 8:30am to 1:30pm and 2:30 to 5pm, Friday 8:30am to 2pm. Citizens of New Zealand have an embassy at Plaza de la Lealtad, 2 (☎ **91/523-02-26,** metro: Banco de España); it's open Monday through Friday 9am to 1:30pm and 2:30 to 5:30pm.

Emergencies The national emergency number for Spain (except the Basque country) is **006;** in the Basque country it is **088.**

Film Negra makes both black-and-white and color film. Valca is another popular brand.

Holidays See "When to Go" earlier in this chapter.

Information See "Information & Required Documents" earlier in this chapter, as well as individual city chapters for local information offices.

Language The official language in Spain is Spanish (Castilian, actually), the third most widely spoken language in the world after Chinese and English. Although Spanish is spoken in every province of Spain, local tongues reasserted themselves with the restoration of democracy in 1975. After years of being outlawed during the Franco dictatorship, Catalán has returned to Barcelona and Catalonia, even appearing on street signs; this language and its derivatives are also spoken in the Valencia area and in the Balearic Islands, including Majorca. The Basque language is widely spoken in the Basque region (the northeast, near France), which is seeking independence from Spain. Likewise, the Gallego language has enjoyed a renaissance in Galicia (the northwest). Of course, English is spoken in most hotels, restaurants, and shops. The best phrase book is *Spanish for Travellers* by Berlitz; it has a menu supplement and a 12,500-word glossary of both English and Spanish. Another way of communicating, if you don't speak Spanish, is through a visual translator called Kwikpoint, which allows you to communicate by pointing at various pictures. This four-panel brochure contains some 500 color illustrations of such everyday items as a pay phone and gasoline. It costs $6; you can order it by calling **703/548-8794** in the United States or by writing to Gaia Communications Inc., Dept. 102, P.O. Box 238, Alexandria, VA 22313-0238.

Laundry In most top hotels, fill out your laundry and dry-cleaning list and present it to your maid or valet. Same-day service usually costs from 25% to 50% more. To save money, go to a Laundromat; your hotel reception desk can advise you of the nearest one. Sometimes these establishments are self-service; others request that you drop off your laundry and pick it up later. See major cities for listings of Laundromats.

Liquor Laws The legal drinking age is 18. Bars, taverns, and cafeterias usually open at 8am, and many serve alcohol until around 1:30am or later. Generally, you can purchase alcoholic beverages in almost any market.

Mail Airmail letters to the United States and Canada cost 87 pesetas (70¢) up to 15 grams, and letters to Britain or other EU countries cost 60 pesetas (50¢) up to 20 grams; letters within Spain cost 30 pesetas (25¢). Postcards have the same rates as letters. Allow about eight days for delivery to North America, generally less to the United Kingdom; in some cases, letters take two weeks to reach North America. Rates change frequently, so check at your hotel before mailing anything. As for surface mail to North America, forget it. Chances are that you'll be home before your letter arrives.

Maps See "By Car" under Section 9, "Getting Around," earlier in this chapter.

Passports See "Information & Required Documents" earlier in this chapter.

Pets It's best to leave them at home. If you don't, you must bring any licenses and proof of vaccinations to your nearest Spanish consulate before you leave. Normally, pets aren't welcome in public places; certain hotels will accept them, however. But these arrangements should be made in advance. Don't forget to check vaccine regulations affecting your animal upon your return. Guide dogs, however, are always excluded from such rigid rules. For the pamphlet "Pets and Wildlife," write the U.S. Customs Service, P.O. Box 7407, Washington, DC 20044, or call **202/927-5580.**

Police The national emergency number is **006** throughout Spain, except in the Basque country, where it is **088.**

Radio/TV Every television network broadcasts in Spanish, but on radio you can listen to the voice of the American Armed Forces—news, music, sports, and local weather.

Restrooms In Spain they're called *aseos* and *servicios* and labeled *caballeros* for men and *damas* or *señoras* for women. If you can't find any, go into a bar, but you should order something.

Safety Pickpockets and purse snatchers flourish throughout Spain. They're particularly active in the large cities, such as Madrid and Barcelona, but also in smaller tourist attractions, such as Seville (actually throughout Andalusia, which takes in the Costa del Sol). In the wake of so many robberies, visitors have taken to leaving their passports at the hotel. But here's a catch-22 situation: Identification checks are common by Spanish police, who are actually cracking down on illegal immigrants. Police officers or plainclothes agents can stop you at any time of the day or night and demand to see your passport. You can be arrested, as many visitors are, if you can't produce yours. Carry your passport with you but carefully conceal it on your body, perhaps in a safety belt.

Taxes The internal sales tax (known in Spain as IVA) ranges between 7% and 33%, depending on the commodity being sold. Food, wine, and basic necessities are taxed at 7%; most goods and services (including car rentals) at 13%; luxury items (jewelry, all tobacco, imported liquors) at 33%; and hotels at 7%.

Telephones If you don't speak Spanish, you'll find it easier to telephone from your hotel, but remember that this is often very expensive because hotels impose a surcharge on every operator-assisted call. In some cases this can be as high as 40% or more. On the street, phone booths (known as *cabinas*), have dialing instructions in English; you can make locals calls by inserting a 25-peseta coin (20¢) for three minutes. In Spain many smaller establishments, especially bars, discos, and a few low-cost restaurants, don't have phones. Further, many summer-only bars and discos secure a phone for the season only, then get a new number the next season.

Many sightseeing attractions, such as small churches or even minor museums, have no staff to receive inquiries from the public.

Time Spain is six hours ahead of Eastern Standard Time in the United States. Daylight Saving Time is in effect from the last Sunday in March to the last Sunday in September.

Tipping Don't overtip. The government requires restaurants and hotels to include their service charges—usually 15% of the bill. However, that doesn't mean you should skip out of a place without dispensing some extra pesetas. The following are some guidelines:

Your hotel porter should get 50 pesetas (40¢) per bag and never less than 100 pesetas (80¢), even if you have only one suitcase. Maids should be given 100 pesetas (80¢) per day, more if you're generous. Tip doormen 100 pesetas (80¢) for assisting with baggage and 40 pesetas (30¢) for calling a cab. In top-ranking hotels the concierge will often submit a separate bill, showing charges for newspapers and other services; if he or she has been particularly helpful, tip extra. For cab drivers, add about 10% to 15% to the fare as shown on the meter. At airports, such as Barajas in Madrid and major terminals, the porter who handles your luggage will present you with a fixed-charge bill.

In both restaurants and nightclubs, a 15% service charge is added to the bill. To that, add another 3% to 5% tip, depending on the quality of the service. Waiters in deluxe restaurants and nightclubs are accustomed to the extra 5%, which means you'll end up tipping 20%. If that seems excessive, you must remember that the initial service charge reflected in the fixed price is distributed among all the help.

Barbers and hairdressers expect a 10% to 15% tip. Tour guides expect 200 pesetas ($1.60), although a tip is not mandatory. Theater and bullfight ushers get from 50 pesetas (40¢).

Tourist Offices See "Information & Required Documents" earlier in this chapter. See also specific city entries.

Visas See "Information & Required Documents" earlier in this chapter.

Settling into Madrid

4

Madrid was conceived, planned, and built when Spain was at the peak of its confidence and power, the solid and severely dignified seat of a great empire that stretched around the world. It's a monumental city that glitters almost as much as Paris, Rome, or London. Although the city lacks the spectacular Romanesque or Gothic monuments that pepper the landscape of older Spanish cities, it never fails to convey a sense of raw and rarely subtle power.

Madrid has the highest altitude of any European capital, with a climate that's blisteringly hot in summer but often quite cold in winter. Traffic roars down wide, exhaust-polluted boulevards that stretch for miles—from the narrow streets of the city's historic 17th-century core to the ugly concrete suburbs that have mushroomed in recent years.

Don't expect a city that looks classically Iberian. True, many of the older buildings of the historic core look as severely dignified and "Spanish" as those you might have encountered in rural towns across the plains of La Mancha. However, a great number of the monuments and palaces mirror the architecture of France—an oddity that reflects the genetic link between the royal families of Spain and the Bourbons and Bonapartes of France.

Most striking is how the city has blossomed since Franco's demise. Madrid was at the forefront of *la movida* (the movement), Spain's drive to resuscitate its artistic tradition after years of creative repression. Today, despite stiff competition from such smaller cities as Seville and Barcelona, Madrid reigns as the country's artistic and creative centerpiece.

More world-class art is concentrated in the neighborhood around the stellar Prado than within virtually any equivalent area in the world: the Caravaggios and Rembrandts at the Thyssen-Bornemisza; the El Grecos and Velázquezes at the Prado itself; and the Dalís and Mirós—not to mention Picasso's wrenching *Guernica*—at the Reina Sofia. Ironically, much of the city's art was collected by 18th-century Spanish monarchs whose artistic sense was frequently more astute than their political savvy.

Regrettably, within the city limits you'll also find sprawling expanses of concrete towers, sometimes paralyzing traffic, a growing incidence of street crime, and entire districts that, as in every other metropolis, bear virtually no historic or cultural interest for a temporary visitor. So, seek out the city's gems: the opulent grandeur of the Palacio Real, the uncontained bustle of El Rastro's flea market, the sultry fever of late-night flamenco. And when urban bustle starts to overwhelm, seek respite in the Parque del Retiro, a vast, verdant oasis in the heart of the city.

If your time within Spain is limited, a stopover in Madrid—coupled with day trips to its environs—can provide a primer in virtually every major period and school of Spanish art and architecture dating back to the Roman occupation. At least nine world-class destinations are less than 100 miles away, including Toledo, one of the most successful blends of medieval Arab, Jewish, and Christian cultures in the world; and Segovia, site of a well-preserved ancient Roman aqueduct and monuments commemorating Queen Isabella's coronation in 1474. Ávila is perhaps the most perfectly preserved medieval fortified city in Iberia, with its 11th-century battlements and endless references to Catholicism's most down-to-earth mystic, St. Theresa. The palace and monuments at Aranjuez, San Lorenzo de El Escorial, and El Pardo (Franco's favorite hangout) provide insight into the tastes and manias that inspired rulers of Spain throughout history. The neofascist monument at El Valle de los Caídos is a powerful testament to those who died in the Spanish Civil War. To see rural Iberia at its most charming, head for Chinchón or, better yet, the clifftop village of Cuenca, where a lavish homage to modern art and music has recently been installed. For more information on these day trips, see Chapter 6, "Excursions from Madrid."

1 Orientation

ARRIVING

BY PLANE Barajas, Madrid's international airport, lying nine miles east of the center, has two terminals—one international, the other domestic. A conveyor belt connects the two. For Barajas Airport information, call **91/305-83-43.**

Air-conditioned yellow airport buses take you from the arrival terminal to the bus depot under the Plaza de Colón. You can also get off at stops along the way, provided that your baggage isn't stored in the hold. The fare is 325 pesetas ($2.60), and the buses leave every 15 minutes, either to or from the airport.

If you go into town by taxi, expect to pay 2,500 pesetas ($20) and up, plus surcharges (in either direction), for the trip to the airport and for baggage handling. If you take an unmetered limousine, negotiate the price in advance.

BY TRAIN Madrid has three major railway stations: **Atocha** (Avenida Ciudad de Barcelona; metro: Atocha RENFE), for trains to Lisbon, Toledo, Andalusia, and Extremadura; **Chamartín** (in the northern suburbs at Augustín de Foxá, metro: Chamartín), for trains to and from Barcelona, Asturias, Cantabria, Castille-León, the Basque country, Aragón, Catalonia, Levante (Valencia), Murcia, and the French frontier; and **Estación Príncipe Pío** or Norte (Paseo del Rey 30; metro: Norte), for trains to and from northwest Spain (Salamanca and Galicia). For information about connections from any of these stations, call RENFE (Spanish Railways) at **91/328-90-20** daily from 7am to 11pm.

For tickets, go to the principal office of **RENFE,** Alcalá, 44 (☎ **91/328-90-20;** metro: Banco de España). The office is open Monday to Friday from 9am to 8pm.

BY BUS Madrid has at least eight major bus terminals, including the large **Estacíon Sur de Autobuses,** Calle Canarias, 17 (☎ **91/468-45-11;** metro: Palos de la Frontera). Most buses pass through this station.

BY CAR All highways within Spain radiate outward from Madrid. The following are the major highways into Madrid, with information on driving distances to the city:

Highways to Madrid

Route	From	Distance to Madrid
N-I	Irún	315 miles (505km)
N-II	Barcelona	389 miles (622km)
N-III	Valencia	217 miles (347km)
N-IV	Cádiz	388 miles (625km)
N-V	Badajoz	254 miles (409km)
N-VI	Galicia	374 miles (598km)

VISITOR INFORMATION

The most convenient tourist office is on the ground floor of the 40-story **Torre de Madrid,** Plaza de España (☎ **91/541-23-25;** metro: Plaza de España); it's open Monday to Friday from 9am to 7pm and Saturday from 9:30am to 1:30pm. Ask for a street map of the next town on your itinerary, especially if you're driving. The staff here can give you a list of hotels and hostals but cannot recommend any particular establishment.

CITY LAYOUT

In modern Spain all roads, rails, and telephone lines lead to Madrid. The capital has outgrown all previous boundaries and is branching out in all directions.

MAIN ARTERIES & SQUARES Every new arrival must find the **Gran Vía,** which cuts a winding pathway across the city beginning at **Plaza de España,** where you'll find one of Europe's tallest skyscrapers, the Edificio España. On this principal avenue is the largest concentration of shops, hotels, restaurants, and movie houses in the city. **Calle de Serrano** is a runner-up.

South of the avenue lies **Puerta del Sol.** All road distances within Spain are measured from this square. However, its significance has declined, and today it is a prime hunting ground for pickpockets and purse snatchers. Here **Calle de Alcalá** begins and runs for 2½ miles.

Plaza Mayor is the heart of Old Madrid, an attraction in itself with its mix of French and Georgian architecture. (Again, be wary, especially late at night.) Pedestrians pass under the arches of the huge square onto the narrow streets of the old town, where you can find some of the capital's most intriguing restaurants and *tascas,* serving tasty tapas with drinks. On the colonnaded ground level of the plaza are shops, many selling souvenir hats of turn-of-the-century Spanish sailors or army officers.

The area south of Plaza Mayor—known as *barrios bajos*—merits exploration. The narrow cobblestone streets are lined with 16th- and 17th-century architecture. Directly south of the plaza is the **Arco de Cuchilleros,** a street packed with markets, restaurants, flamenco clubs, and taverns.

The Gran Vía ends at Calle de Alcalá, and at this juncture lies **Plaza de la Cibeles,** with its fountain to Cybele, "the mother of the gods," and what has become known as "the cathedral of post offices." From Cibeles, the wide **Paseo de Recoletos** begins a short run to **Plaza de Colón.** From this latter square rolls the serpentine **Paseo de la Castellana,** flanked by expensive shops, apartment buildings, luxury hotels, and foreign embassies.

Back at Cibeles again: Heading south is **Paseo del Prado,** where you'll find Spain's major attraction, the Museo del Prado, as well as the Jardín Botánica (Botanical Garden). The *paseo* also leads to the Atocha Railway Station. To the west of the garden lies **Parque del Retiro,** once reserved for royalty, with restaurants, nightclubs, a rose garden, and two lakes.

FINDING AN ADDRESS Madrid is a city of grand boulevards that extend for long distances and cramped meandering streets that seem to follow no plan. Finding an address can sometimes be a problem, primarily because of the way buildings are numbered.

On most streets, the numbering begins on one side and runs consecutively until the end, then it resumes on the other side, going in the opposite direction, rather as a farmer plows a field—up one side, down the other. Thus, number 50 could be opposite number 250. But there are many exceptions to this system of numbering. That's why it's important that you know the cross street as well as the number of the address you're looking for. To complicate matters, some addresses don't have a number at all. What they have instead is the designation *s/n,* meaning *sin númerô* (without number). For example, the address of the Panteón de Goya (Goya's Tomb) is Glorieta de San Antonio de la Florida, s/n (see Chapter 5, "Madrid Attractions"). Note also that in Spain, as in many other European countries, the building number comes after the street name.

NEIGHBORHOODS IN BRIEF Madrid can be divided into three principal districts—Old Madrid, which holds the most tourist interest; Ensanche, the new district, often with the best shops and hotels; and the periphery, which is of little interest to visitors.

Plaza Mayor/Puerta del Sol This is the heart of Old Madrid, often called "the tourist zone." Filled with taverns and bars, it is bounded by Carrera de San Jerónimo, Calle Mayor, Cava de San Miguel, Cava Baja, and Calle de la Cruz. From Plaza Mayor, the Arco de Cuchilleros is filled with Castilian restaurants and taverns; more *cuevas* lie along the Cava de San Miguel, Cava Alta, and Cava Baja. To the west of this old district is the Manzanares River. Muslim Madrid centers on the present-day Palacio de Oriente and Las Vistillas. What is now Plaza de la Paja was the heart of the city and its main marketplace during the medieval and Christian period. In 1617 Plaza Mayor became the hub of Madrid, and it remains the nighttime center of tourist activity, more so than the Puerta del Sol.

The Salamanca Quarter Ever since Madrid's city walls came tumbling down in the 1860s, the district of Salamanca to the north has been a fashionable address. Cutting through it is Calle de Serrano, a street lined with stores and boutiques. The U.S. Embassy is also here.

Gran Vía/Plaza de España Gran Vía is the city's main street, lined with cinemas, department stores, and the headquarters of banks and corporations. It begins at the Plaza de España, with its bronze figures of Don Quixote and his faithful squire, Sancho Panza.

Argüelles/Moncloa The university area is bounded by Pintor Rosales, Cea Bermúdez, Bravo Murillo, San Bernardo, and Conde Duque. Students haunt its famous ale houses.

Chueca This is an old and decaying area north of the Gran Vía. Its main streets are Hortaleza, Infantas, Barquillo, and San Lucas. It is the center of gay nightlife, with many clubs and cheap restaurants. It can be dangerous at night, although police presence has increased.

Castellana/Recoletos/Paseo del Prado Not a real city district, this is Madrid's north-south axis, its name changing along the way. The Museo del Prado and some of the city's more expensive hotels are found here. Many restaurants and other hotels are located along its side streets. In summer the several open-air terraces are filled with animated crowds. The most famous café is the Gran Café Gijón (see "Dining" later in this chapter).

STREET MAPS Arm yourself with a good map before setting out. The best is published by **Falk,** and it's available at most newsstands and kiosks in Madrid. Those given away free by tourist offices and hotels aren't adequate, as they don't list the maze of little streets.

2 Getting Around

Getting around Madrid is not easy, because everything is spread out. Even many Madrileño taxi drivers, often new arrivals from a foreign country, are unfamiliar with their own city once they're off the main boulevards.

BY SUBWAY The metro system is easy to learn. The central converging point is the Puerta del Sol. The fare is 130 pesetas ($1.05) for a one-way trip. The metro operates from 6am to 1:30am. Avoid rush hours. For information, call **91/552-49-00.** You can save money on public transportation by purchasing a 10-trip ticket known as a *bonos*—for the metro it costs 645 pesetas ($5.15).

BY BUS A bus network also services the city and suburbs, with routes clearly shown at each stop on a schematic diagram. Buses are fast and efficient because they travel along special lanes. Both red and yellow buses charge 130 pesetas ($1.05) per ride.

For 645 pesetas ($5.15) you can also purchase a 10-trip ticket (but without transfers) for Madrid's bus system. It's sold at **Empresa Municipal de Transportes,** Plaza de la Cibeles (☎ **91/401-99-00**), where you can also purchase a guide to the bus routes. The office is open daily from 8am to 8:30pm.

BY TAXI Even though cab fares have risen recently, they're still reasonable. When you flag down a taxi, the meter should register 170 pesetas ($1.35); for every kilometer thereafter, the fare increases by 50 to 75 pesetas (40¢–60¢). A supplement is charged for trips to the railway station or the bullring, as well as on Sundays and holidays. The ride to Barajas Airport carries a 325-peseta ($2.60) surcharge and a 160-peseta ($1.30) supplement from railway stations. In addition, there is a 150-peseta ($1.20) supplement on Sundays and holidays, plus a 150-peseta ($1.10) supplement at night. It's customary to tip at least 10% of the fare.

Warning: Make sure that the meter is turned on when you get into a taxi. Otherwise, some drivers will "assess" the cost of the ride, and their assessment, you can be sure, will involve higher mathematics.

Also, there are unmetered taxis that hire out for the day or the afternoon. These are legitimate, but some drivers will operate as gypsy cabs. Since they're unmetered, they can charge high rates. They are easy to avoid, though—take either a black taxi with horizontal red bands or a white one with diagonal red bands instead.

If you take a taxi outside the city limits, the driver is entitled to charge you twice the rate shown on the meter.

To call a taxi, dial **91/445-90-08** or **91/447-51-80.**

BY CAR Driving is a nightmare and potentially dangerous in congested Madrid. It always feels like rush hour in Madrid (theoretically, rush hours are 8 to 10am, 1 to 2pm, and 4 to 6pm Monday to Saturday). Parking is next to impossible, except in expensive garages. About the only time you can drive around Madrid with a minimum of hassle is in hot August, when thousands of Madrileños have taken their automobiles and headed for Spain's vacation oases. Save your car rentals (see "Fast Facts: Madrid," below) for one-day excursions from the capital. If you drive into Madrid from another city, ask at your hotel for the nearest garage or parking possibility and leave your vehicle there until you're ready to leave.

BY BICYCLE Ever wonder why you see so few people riding bicycles in Madrid? Those who tried were overcome by the traffic pollution. It's better to walk.

ON FOOT This is the perfect way to see Madrid, especially the ancient narrow streets of the old town. If you're going to another district—and chances are that your hotel will be outside the old town—you can take the bus or metro. For such a large city, Madrid can be covered amazingly well on foot, because so much of what will interest a visitor lies in various clusters.

FAST FACTS: Madrid

American Express For your mail or banking needs, you can go to the American Express office at the corner of Marqués de Cubas and Plaza de las Cortés, 2, across the street from the Palace Hotel (☎ **91/322-55-00;** metro: Gran Vía). Open Monday to Friday from 9am to 5:30pm and Saturday from 9am to noon.

Area Code For phone calls within Spain, Madrid's area code is **91.** If you're calling from the United States, dial **011,** the country code (**34**), Madrid's city code (**1**), and then the local number.

Babysitters Most major hotels can arrange for babysitters, called *canguros* in Spanish. Usually the concierge keeps a list of reliable nursemaids and will contact them for you, provided that you give adequate notice. Rates vary considerably but are fairly reasonable. Although many babysitters in Madrid speak English, don't count on it. You may also want to contact La Casa de la Abuela (☎ **91/574-30-94**). Located in the prestigious Barrio Salamanca, "grandmother's house," basically a children's hotel, offers childcare combined with creative exercises and workshops in a child-friendly environment. It is open year-round; prices vary.

Bookstores Turner's, Genova, 3 & 5 (☎ **91/319-28-67;** metro: Alonso Martínez), has one of the largest collections of English-language books in the city, as well as a good selection of Spanish CDs. Open Monday through Friday from 10am to 8pm and Saturday from 10am to 2pm.

Car Rentals For more information on renting a car before you leave home, see "Getting Around" in Chapter 3. Should you want to rent one while in Madrid, you'll have several choices. In addition to its office at Barajas Airport (☎ **91/305-42-73**), Avis has a main office downtown at Gran Vía, 60 (☎ **91/348-03-48**). Hertz, too, has an office at Barajas Airport (☎ **91/305-84-52**) and another in the heart of Madrid in the Edificio España, Gran Vía, 88 (☎ **91/542-58-05**). Budget Rent-a-Car maintains its headquarters at Gran Vía, 49 (☎ **91/401-12-54**).

Climate See "When to Go" in Chapter 3.

Crime See "Safety," below.

Currency Exchange The currency exchange at Chamartín railway station (metro: Chamartín) is open 24 hours and gives the best rates in the capital. If you exchange money at a bank, ask about the minimum commission charged.

Madrid Metro

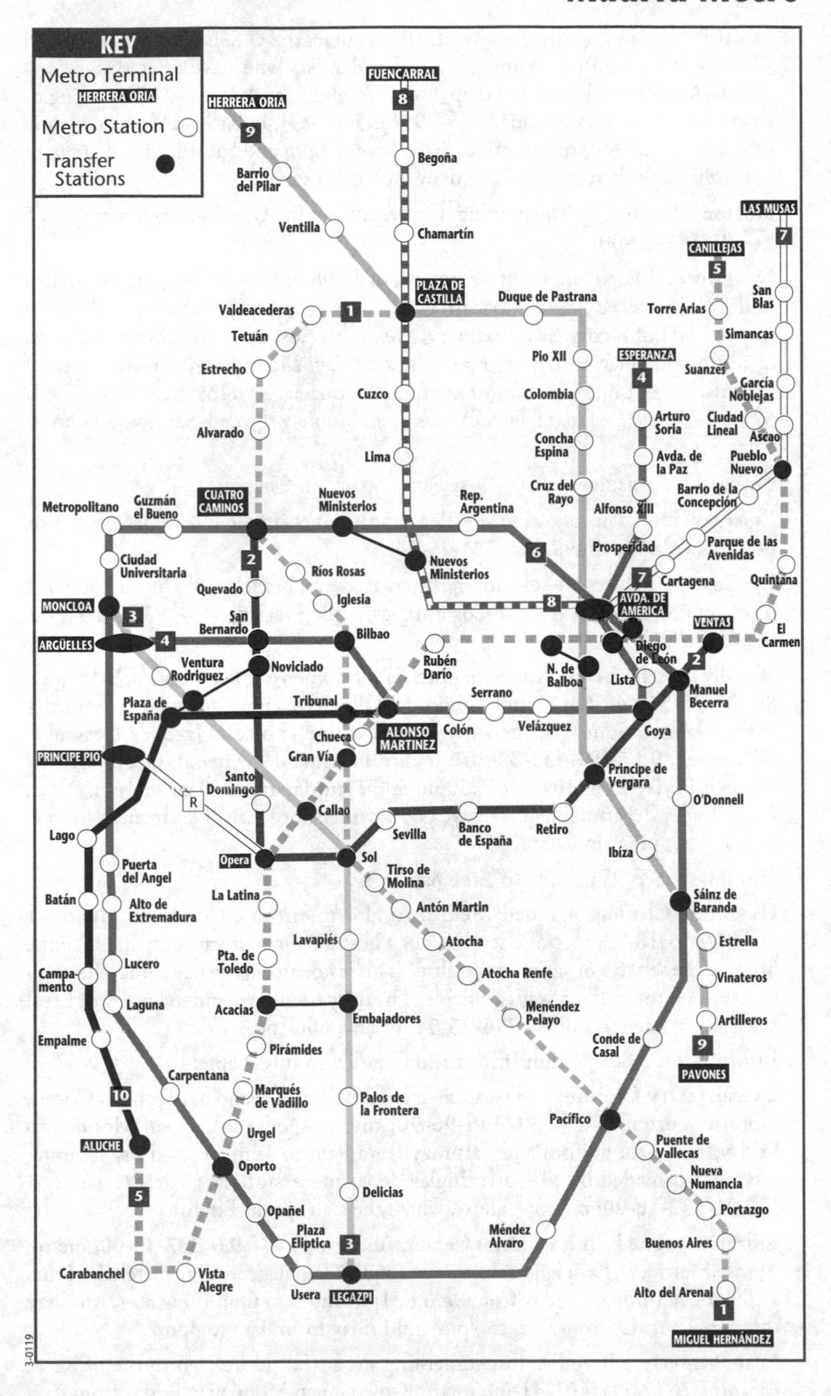

Dentist For an English-speaking dentist, contact the U.S. Embassy, Serrano, 75 (☎ **91/587-22-00**); it maintains a list of dentists who have offered their services to Americans abroad. For dental services, also consult Unidad Médica Anglo-Americana, Conde de Arandá, 1 (☎ **91/435-18-23**), in back of Plaza de Colón. Office hours are Monday to Friday from 9am to 8pm and Saturday from 10am to 1pm, although there is a 24-hour daily answering service.

Doctor For an English-speaking doctor, contact the U.S. Embassy, Serrano, 75 (☎ **91/587-22-00**).

Drugstores For a late-night pharmacy, dial **098** or look in the daily newspaper under *Farmacias de Guardia* to learn what drugstores are open after 8pm. Another way to find out is go to any pharmacy, even if it's closed—it will always post a list of nearby pharmacies that are open late that day. Madrid contains hundreds of pharmacies, but one of the most central is Farmacia Gayoso, Arenal, 2 (☎ **91/521-28-60;** metro: Puerta del Sol). It is open Monday through Saturday, 24 hours a day.

Embassies/Consulates See "Fast Facts: Spain" in Chapter 3.

Emergencies The following are telephone numbers to call in an emergency: fire, **080;** police, **091;** ambulance, **734-25-54.**

Eyeglasses Glasses are sold and repaired at several branches of Optica 2000, the most central of which is at El Corte Inglés, Calle Preciados (☎ **91/532-18-00;** metro: Callao).

Hairdressers/Barbers A good hairdresser for women or men is Galico, Velázquez, 89 (☎ **91/563-47-63;** metro: Núñez de Balboa); it's open Monday to Saturday from 10am to 6pm. For men or women, a fine choice is Jacques Dessange, O'Donnell, 9 (☎ **91/435-32-20**); metro: Príncipe de Vergara). Open Monday through Friday from 10am to 6:30pm and Saturday from 10am to 1pm. All El Corte Inglés department stores have good barbershops (see "Department Stores" under "Shopping" in Chapter 5).

Holidays See "When to Go" in Chapter 3.

Hospitals/Clinics Unidad Médica Anglo-Americana, Conde de Arandá, 1 (☎ **91/435-18-23;** metro: Usera), is not a hospital but a private outpatient clinic, offering the services of various specialists. This is not an emergency clinic, although someone on the staff is always available. The daily hours are 9am to 8pm. For a real medical emergency, call **91/734-25-54** for an ambulance.

Information See "Visitor Information" earlier in this chapter.

Laundry/Dry Cleaning Try a self-service facility, Lavandería Donoso Cortés, Donoso Cortés, 17 (☎ **91/446-96-90;** metro: Quevedo). Open Monday to Friday from 9am to 7pm and Saturday from 9am to 1pm. A good dry-cleaning service is provided by El Corte Inglés department store at Calle Preciados, 3 (☎ **91/532-18-00;** metro: Callos), where the staff speaks English.

Libraries The British Cultural Center, Almagro, 5 (☎ **91/ 337-35-00;** metro: Alonso Martínez), has a large selection of English-language reading material. Hours are Monday through Friday from 9am to 1pm and 3 to 6pm (in winter, Monday through Thursday from 9am to 7pm and Friday from 9am to 3pm).

Lost Property If you've lost something on a Madrid bus, go to the office at Alcántra, 26 (☎ **91/401-31-00;** metro: Goya), open Monday to Friday from 8am to 2pm. If you've lost something on the metro, go at any time to the Cuatro Caminos station (☎ **91/ 552-49-00**). For objects lost in a taxi, go to Plaza de Chamberí (☎ **91/448-79-26;** metro: Chamberí), open Monday to Friday from 9am to 2pm and Saturday 9am to 1pm. For objects lost anywhere else, go to the Palacio de Comunicaciones at the Plaza de la Cibeles (☎ **91/532-93-52;** metro: Banco de España), open Monday to Friday from 9am to 2pm and Saturday from 9am to 1pm. Don't call—show up in person.

Luggage Storage/Lockers These can be found at both the Atocha and Chamartín railway terminals, as well as the major bus station at the Estación Sur de Autobuses, Calle Canarías, 17 (☎ **91/468-45-11;** metro: Palos de la Frontera). Storage is also provided at the air terminal underneath the Plaza de Colón.

Newspapers/Magazines The Paris-based *International Herald Tribune* is sold at most major newsstands in the tourist districts, as is *USA Today,* plus the European editions of *Time* and *Newsweek. Guía del Ocio,* a small magazine sold in newsstands, contains entertainment listings and addresses, but in Spanish only.

Photographic Needs Kodak and other popular brands of film are sold in Madrid, but they're much more expensive than in the United States. For a Spanish film, try Valca (black and white) or Negra (black and white or color). Ask before photographing in churches or museums because photography is often not permitted. Your photographic needs can be serviced by El Corte Inglés department store at Calle Preciados, 3 (☎ **91/532-18-00;** metro: Callao).

Police Dial 091.

Post Office If you don't want to receive your mail at your hotel or the American Express office, direct it to *Lista de Correos* at the central post office in Madrid. To pick up mail, go to the window marked *Lista,* where you'll be asked to show your passport. Madrid's central office is in "the cathedral of the post offices" at Plaza de la Cibeles (☎ **91/536-01-11**).

Radio/TV During the day on shortwave radio you can hear the Voice of America and the BBC. An English-language radio program in Madrid called "Buenos Días" (Good Morning) airs many useful hints for visitors; it's broadcast on Monday through Friday from 6 to 8am on 657 megahertz. Radio 80 broadcasts news in English on Monday to Saturday from 7 to 8am on 89 FM. Some TV programs are broadcast in English in the summer months. Many hotels—but regrettably not most of our budget ones—also bring in satellite TV programs in English.

Restrooms Some public restrooms are available, including those in the Parque del Retiro and on Plaza de Oriente across from the Palacio Real. Otherwise, you can always go into a bar or *tasca,* but you should order something. The major department stores, such as Galerías Preciados and El Corte Inglés, have good, clean restrooms.

Safety Because of an increasing crime rate in Madrid, the U.S. Embassy has warned visitors to leave valuables in a hotel safe or another secure place when going out. Your passport may be needed, however, as the police often stop foreigners for identification checks. See "Safety" under "Fast Facts: Spain" in Chapter 3 for more details about this requirement. The embassy advises against carrying purses and suggests that you keep valuables in front pockets and carry only enough cash for the day's needs. Be aware of those around you and keep a separate record of your passport number, traveler's check numbers, and credit card numbers.

Purse snatching is common, and the criminals often work in pairs, grabbing purses from pedestrians, cyclists, and even from cars. A popular scam involves one miscreant's smearing the back of the victim's clothing, perhaps with mustard, ice cream, or something worse. An accomplice pretends to help clean up the mess, while picking all the victim's pockets.

Every car can be a target, parked or just stopped at a light, so don't leave anything in sight in your car. If a vehicle is standing still, a thief may open the door or break a window in order to snatch a purse or package, even from under the seat. Place valuables in the trunk when you park and always assume that someone is watching you to see whether you're putting something away for safekeeping. Keep the car locked while you're driving.

Shoe Repairs In an emergency, go to one of the "Mister Minit" shoe-repair centers at any El Corte Inglés department store. The flagship store of this chain is on the Calle Preciados, 3 (☎ **91/532-18-00;** metro: Callao), near the Puerta del Sol.

Taxes There are no special city taxes for tourists, except for the VAT (central government tax; known as IVA in Spain) levied nationwide on all goods and services, ranging from 7% to 33%. In Madrid the only city taxes are for home and car owners, which need not concern the visitor.

Taxis See "Getting Around" earlier in this chapter.

Telegrams/Telex/Fax Cables may be sent at the central post office building in Madrid at Plaza de la Cibeles (☎ **91/536-01-11**). To send a telegram by phone, dial **91/522-20-00.** In Spain it's cheaper to telephone within the country than to send a telegram. You can send telex and fax messages from the same central post office and from all major hotels.

Telephone To make calls in Madrid, follow the instructions in "Fast Facts: Spain" in Chapter 3. However, for long-distance calls, especially transatlantic ones, it may be best to go to the main telephone exchange, Locutorio Gran Vía, Gran Vía, 30; or Locutorio Recoletos, Paseo de Recoletos, 37–41. You may not be lucky enough to find an English-speaking operator, but you can fill out a simple form that will facilitate the placement of a call.

Transit Information For metro information, call **91/552-49-00.**

3 Accommodations

Madrid's hotels, though expensive, are among the finest in the world. The city's much-maligned reputation, earned in the days of Franco, is but a distant, unpleasant memory: No more rooms last renovated in 1870 or food that tastes of acidic olive oil left over from the Spanish-American War.

More than 50,000 hotel rooms blanket the city—from *grand luxe* bedchambers fit for a prince to bunker-style beds in the hundreds of neighborhood *hostales* and *pensiones* (low-cost boarding houses). Three-quarters of our recommendations are modern, yet many guests prefer the landmarks of yesteryear, including those grand old establishments, the Ritz and the Palace (ca. 1910–12). *But beware:* Many older hostelries in Madrid haven't kept abreast of the times; a handful haven't added improvements or overhauled bedrooms substantially since the 1960s.

Traditionally, hotels are clustered around the Atocha Railway Station and the Gran Vía. In our search for the most outstanding hotels, we've almost ignored these two popular, but noisy, districts. The newer hotels have been built away from the center, especially on residential streets jutting off from Paseo de la Castellana. Bargain seekers, however, will still find great pickings along the Gran Vía and in the Atocha district.

RESERVATIONS Most hotels require at least a day's deposit before they will reserve a room for you. Preferably, this can be accomplished with an international money order or, if agreed to in advance, with a personal check or credit card number. You can usually cancel a room reservation one week ahead of time and get a full refund. A few hotelkeepers will return your money three days before the reservation date, but some will take your deposit and never return it, even if you cancel far in advance. Many budget hotel owners operate on such a narrow margin of profit that they find just buying stamps for airmail replies too expensive by their standards. Therefore, it's most important that you enclose a prepaid International Reply Coupon with your payment, especially if you're writing to a budget hotel. Better yet, call and speak to the hotel of your choice or send a fax.

If you're booking into a chain hotel, such as a Hyatt or a Forte, you can call toll free in North America and easily make reservations over the phone. Whenever such a service is available, toll-free numbers are indicated in the individual hotel descriptions.

If you arrive without a reservation, begin your search for a room as early in the day as possible. If you arrive late at night, you have to take what you can get, often for a much higher price than you'd like to pay.

A Note on Making Hotel Reservations The telephone area code for Madrid is **91** if you're calling from within Spain. If you're calling from the United States, dial **011,** the country code (**34**), Madrid's city code (**1**), and then the local number.

PRICE CLASSIFICATIONS The following prices are for double rooms with private baths. Hotels rated "very expensive" charge from 30,000 pesetas ($240) for a double, although some establishments in this bracket, including the Villa Magna, the Santo Mauro, and the Ritz, can ask twice that price. Hotels judged "expensive" ask from 17,000 to 30,000 pesetas ($136–$240) for a double, and "moderate" hotels—at least moderate in the sense of Madrid's hotel price scale—charge from a low of 10,000 pesetas ($80) to a high of 17,300 pesetas ($138.40) for a double. Hotels considered "inexpensive"—again, by Madrid's pricing standards—ask 10,000 pesetas ($80) and under for a double.

Note: All hotels in the "very expensive" and "expensive" categories include private baths with their guest rooms unless otherwise specified. Hotels in the other categories may or may not include baths, and that information is supplied for each entry. Also, breakfast is not included in the quoted rates unless otherwise specified. A 7% government room tax is added to all rates.

RATINGS Spain officially rates its hotels by star designation, from one to five stars. Five stars is the highest rating in Spain, signaling a deluxe establishment complete with all the amenities and the high tariffs associated with such accommodations.

Most of the establishments recommended in this guide are three- and four-star hotels falling into that vague "middle-bracket" category. Hotels granted one and two stars, as well as pensions (guest houses), are far less comfortable, with limited plumbing and other physical facilities, although they may be perfectly clean and decent places. The latter category is strictly for dedicated budgeters.

PARKING As mentioned, this is a serious problem, as so few hotels have garages; many buildings turned into hotels were constructed before the invention of the automobile. Street parking is rarely available, and even if it is, you run the risk of having your car broken into. If you're driving into Madrid, most hotels (or most police) will allow you to park in front of the hotel long enough to unload your luggage. Someone on the staff will pinpoint the location of the nearest garage in the

Accommodations in Central Madrid

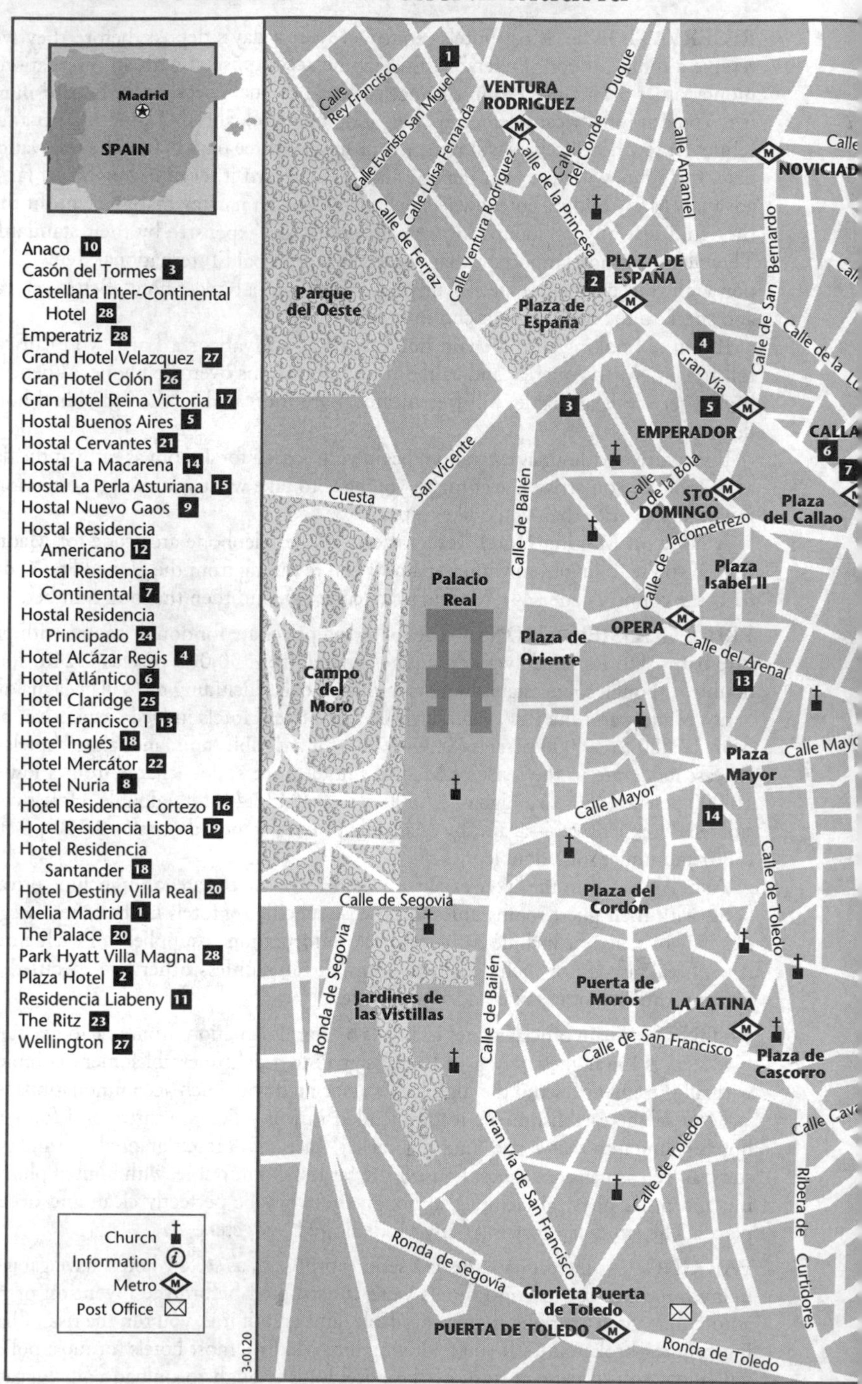

Madrid
SPAIN
Anaco 10
Casón del Tormes 3
Castellana Inter-Continental Hotel 28
Emperatriz 28
Grand Hotel Velazquez 27
Gran Hotel Colón 26
Gran Hotel Reina Victoria 17
Hostal Buenos Aires 5
Hostal Cervantes 21
Hostal La Macarena 14
Hostal La Perla Asturiana 15
Hostal Nuevo Gaos 9
Hostal Residencia Americano 12
Hostal Residencia Continental 7
Hostal Residencia Principado 24
Hotel Alcázar Regis 4
Hotel Atlántico 6
Hotel Claridge 25
Hotel Francisco I 13
Hotel Inglés 18
Hotel Mercátor 22
Hotel Nuria 8
Hotel Residencia Cortezo 16
Hotel Residencia Lisboa 19
Hotel Residencia Santander 18
Hotel Destiny Villa Real 20
Melia Madrid 1
The Palace 20
Park Hyatt Villa Magna 28
Plaza Hotel 2
Residencia Liabeny 11
The Ritz 23
Wellington 27
Church
Information
Metro
Post Office
3-0120
Calle Rey Francisco
Calle Evaristo San Miguel
Calle Luisa Fernanda
VENTURA RODRIGUEZ
Duque
Calle del Conde
Calle de la Princesa
Calle Ventura Rodríguez
Calle de Ferraz
Calle Amaniel
NOVICIAD
Calle de San Bernardo
PLAZA DE ESPAÑA
Plaza de España
Parque del Oeste
Gran Vía
Calle de la Lu
EMPERADOR
CALLA
San Vicente
Cuesta
Calle de la Bola
STO. DOMINGO
Plaza del Callao
Calle de Jacometrezo
Calle de Bailén
Palacio Real
Plaza Isabel II
OPERA
Calle del Arenal
Plaza de Oriente
Campo del Moro
Plaza Mayor
Calle Mayor
Calle de Segovia
Plaza del Cordón
Calle de Toledo
Ronda de Segovia
Jardines de las Vistillas
Puerta de Moros
LA LATINA
Calle de San Francisco
Plaza de Cascorro
Gran Vía de San Francisco
Calle de Toledo
Calle Cava
Ribera de Curtidores
Ronda de Segovia
Glorieta Puerta de Toledo
PUERTA DE TOLEDO
Ronda de Toledo

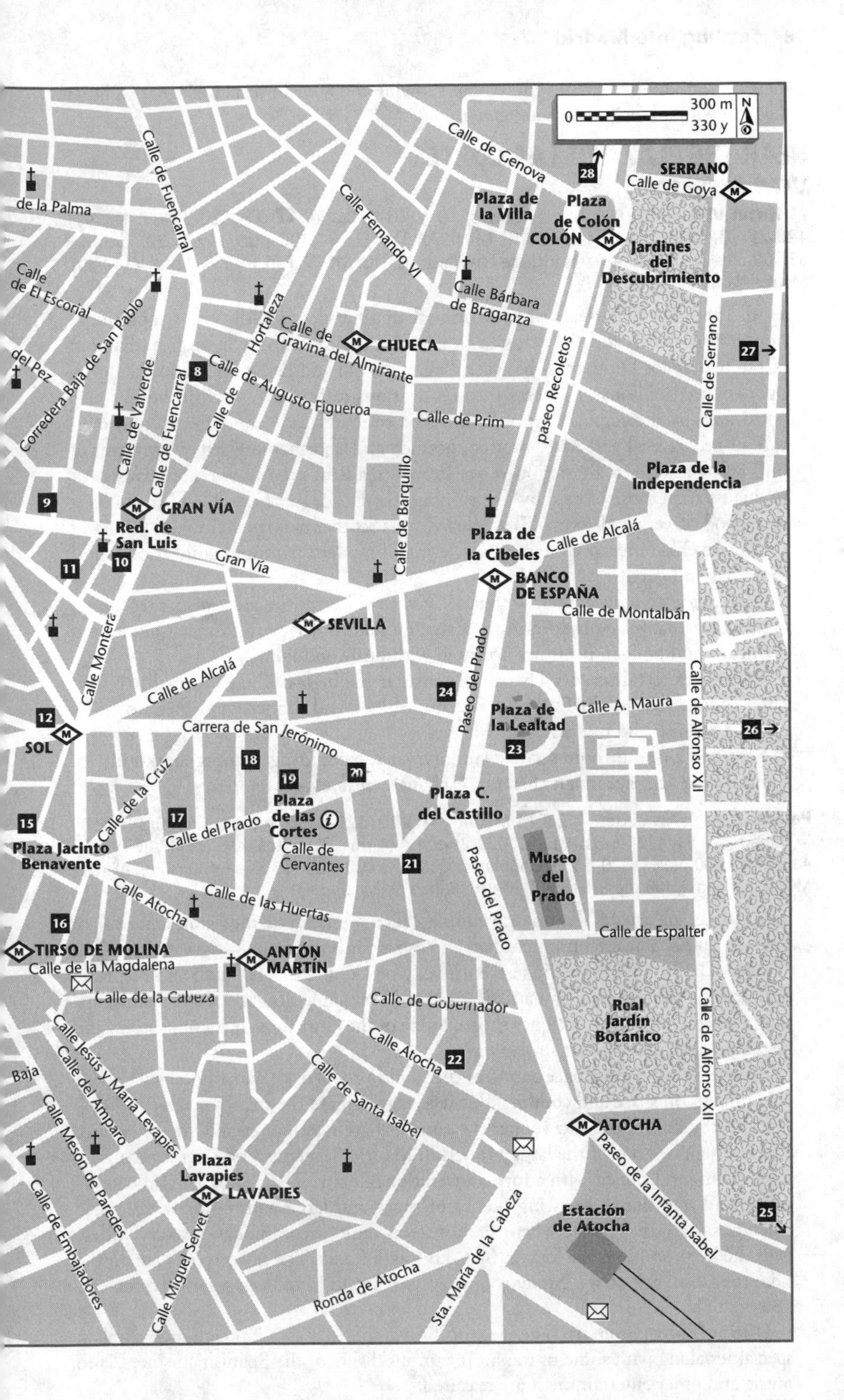
300 m
330 y
N
Calle de Genova
SERRANO
Calle de Goya
Plaza de la Villa
Plaza de Colón
COLÓN
Jardines del Descubrimiento
Calle Fernando VI
Calle de Fuencarral
de la Palma
Calle de El Escorial
Corredera Baja de San Pablo
del Pez
Calle Bárbara de Braganza
Calle de Hortaleza
Calle de Gravina del Almirante
CHUECA
Calle de Augusto Figueroa
Calle de Valverde
Calle de Fuencarral
Calle de Prim
paseo Recoletos
Calle de Serrano
Calle de Barquillo
Plaza de la Independencia
GRAN VÍA
Red. de San Luis
Gran Vía
Plaza de la Cibeles
Calle de Alcalá
BANCO DE ESPAÑA
Calle de Montalbán
SEVILLA
Calle Montera
Calle de Alcalá
Paseo del Prado
Plaza de la Lealtad
Calle A. Maura
Calle de Alfonso XII
SOL
Carrera de San Jerónimo
Calle de la Cruz
Plaza de las Cortes
Plaza C. del Castillo
Calle del Prado
Plaza Jacinto Benavente
Calle de Cervantes
Museo del Prado
Calle Atocha
Calle de las Huertas
Paseo del Prado
Calle de Espalter
TIRSO DE MOLINA
ANTÓN MARTÍN
Calle de la Magdalena
Calle de la Cabeza
Calle de Gobernador
Real Jardín Botánico
Calle Atocha
Calle de Alfonso XII
Calle Jesús y María Levapiés
Calle del Amparo
Baja
Calle de Santa Isabel
Calle Mesón de Paredes
ATOCHA
Paseo de la Infanta Isabel
Plaza Lavapies
LAVAPIES
Calle de Embajadores
Estación de Atocha
Calle Miguel Servet
Sta. María de la Cabeza
Ronda de Atocha

neighborhood, often giving you a map showing the way. In instances where a hotel has its own parking, charges are given.

NEAR THE PLAZA DE LAS CORTÉS

VERY EXPENSIVE

✪ **Hotel Villa Real.** Plaza de las Cortés, 10, 28014 Madrid. ☎ **91/420-37-67.** Fax 91/420-25-47. 115 rms, 19 suites. A/C MINIBAR TV TEL. 34,400 ptas. ($275.20) double; 65,000 ptas. ($520) suite. Rates include breakfast. AE, DC, MC, V. Parking 1,600 ptas. ($12.80). Metro: Plaza de la Cibeles.

Until 1989, the Villa Real was little more than a run-down 19th-century apartment house auspiciously located across a three-sided park from the Spanish parliament (Congreso de los Diputados) between Puerta del Sol and Paseo del Prado. Its developers poured billions of pesetas into renovations to produce a stylish hotel today patronized by the cognoscenti of Spain. The eclectic facade combines an odd mixture of neoclassical and Aztec motifs; footmen and doormen dressed in uniforms of buff and forest green are stationed out front. Villa Real's rooms are more consistent in quality than those offered by its neighbor, the Palace (see below), which can have very good or very bad rooms. But Villa Real lacks the mellow charm and patina of the Palace. The interior contains a scattering of modern paintings amid neoclassical moldings and details.

Each of the accommodations offers a TV with video movies and satellite reception, a safe for valuables, soundproofing, a sunken salon filled with leather-upholstered furniture, and built-in furniture accented with burlwood inlays.

Dining/Entertainment: The social center is the high-ceilinged formal bar. The hotel's formal restaurant Europa serves both lunch and dinner, with meals consisting of a Spanish and international cuisine.

Services: 24-hour room service, laundry/valet, babysitting, express checkout.

Facilities: Sauna, foreign currency exchange, business center.

Palace. Plaza de las Cortés, 7, 28014 Madrid. ☎ **800/325-3535** in the U.S., 800/325-3589 in Canada, or 91/429-75-51. Fax 91/429-86-55. 424 rms, 31 suites. A/C MINIBAR TV TEL. 40,000–46,000 ptas. ($320–$368) double; 75,000–175,000 ptas. ($600–$1,400) suite. AE, DC, MC, V. Parking 2,300 ptas. ($18.40). Metro: Banco de España.

The Palace, an ornate Victorian wedding cake, is known as the "grand *dueña*" of Spanish hotels. The establishment had an auspicious beginning, inaugurated by King Alfonso XIII in 1912. Covering an entire city block, it faces the Prado and Neptune Fountain, in the historical and artistic area, within walking distance of the main shopping center and the best antiques shops. Some of the city's most intriguing *tascas* and restaurants are only a short stroll away.

Architecturally, the Palace captures the grand pre–World War I hotel style, with an emphasis on space and comfort. But it doesn't achieve the snobby appeal and chic of its nearby sibling, the Ritz (under the same management), or even of the Villa Real. Even though it is one of the largest hotels in Madrid, it retains first-class service. The hotel is air-conditioned with a formal, traditional lobby. The rooms are also conservative and traditional, boasting plenty of space and large bathrooms with lots of amenities. As was the style when the hotel was built, accommodations vary widely with the best rooms on the fourth, fifth, and sixth floors. The noisy rooms are on the side; they also lack views. Many rooms appear not to have been renovated for two decades or so.

Dining/Entertainment: The elegant dining choice is La Cupola, serving Italian specialties along with some of the more famous dishes of the Spanish cuisine. Piano music and other entertainment are featured.

Services: 24-hour room service, laundry/valet, babysitting, express checkout. **Facilities:** Foreign currency exchange, business center.

Inexpensive

$ **Hostal Cervantes.** Cervantes, 34, 28014 Madrid. ☎ **91/429-27-45.** 12 rms. 6,000 ptas. ($48) double. No credit cards. Metro: Banco de España.

One of Madrid's most pleasant family-run hotels, the Cervantes has been widely appreciated by our readers for years. You'll take a tiny birdcage-style elevator to the immaculately maintained second floor of this stone-and-brick building. Each accommodation contains a bed and spartan furniture. No breakfast is served, but the owners, the Alfonsos, will direct you to a nearby café. The establishment is convenient to the Prado, Retiro Park, and the older sections of Madrid.

NEAR THE PLAZA ESPAÑA

Expensive

Plaza Hotel. Plaza de España, 8, 28013 Madrid. ☎ **91/547-12-00.** Fax 91/548-23-89. 231 rms, 75 suites. A/C MINIBAR TV TEL. 21,200 ptas. ($169.60) double; from 25,600 ptas. ($204.80) suite. AE, DC, MC, V. Parking 2,500 ptas. ($20). Metro: Plaza de España.

Atop a city garage, the Plaza Hotel, built in 1953, could be called the Waldorf-Astoria of Spain. A massive rose-and-white structure, it soars upward to a central tower that's 26 stories high. It is a landmark visible for miles around and one of the tallest skyscrapers in Europe. Once one of the best hotels in Spain, the Plaza has declined in recent years in spite of a 1992 renovation. It's aging and a bit dreary, and not at all in the same class as the hotels previously recommended. The hotel's accommodations include conventional doubles as well as luxurious suites, each of which contains a sitting room and abundant amenities. Each accommodation, regardless of its size, has a marble bathroom. Furniture is usually of a standardized modern style, in harmonized colors. The quieter rooms are on the upper floors.

Dining/Entertainment: The Azalea Restaurant offers either buffet or à la carte dining, and the Express Bar provides a complete buffet breakfast—even a "diet corner." There's also a piano bar.

Service: Room service, laundry, money exchange, medical service, hairdresser. **Facilities:** Shopping arcade.

Moderate

$ **Casón del Tormes.** Calle del Río, 7, 28013 Madrid. ☎ **91/541-97-46.** Fax 91/541-18-52. 63 rms. A/C TV TEL. 12,000 ptas. ($96) double; 15,300 ptas. ($122.40) triple. MC, V. Parking 1,200 ptas. ($9.60). Metro: Plaza de España.

The attractive three-star Casón del Tormes is around the corner from the Royal Palace and Plaza de España. Set behind a four-story red-brick facade with stone-trimmed windows, it overlooks a quiet one-way street. The long, narrow lobby contains vertical wooden paneling, a marble floor, and a bar opening into a separate room. The bedrooms are not spectacular, but generally roomy and comfortable. Motorists appreciate the public parking lot near the hotel. Laundry service is provided.

ON OR NEAR THE GRAN VÍA

Moderate

Hotel Atlántico. Gran Vía, 38, 28013 Madrid. ☎ **800/528-1234** in the U.S. and Canada, or 91/522-64-80. Fax 91/531-02-10. 80 rms. A/C MINIBAR TV TEL. 13,305 ptas. ($106.45) double. Rates include breakfast. AE, DC, MC, V. Metro: Gran Vía.

Refurbished in stages between the late 1980s and 1994, this hotel occupies five floors of a grand turn-of-the-century building on one of Madrid's most impressive avenues.

Established in 1989 as a Best Western affiliate, it offers security boxes in relatively unadorned but well-maintained bedrooms, which have been insulated against noise. Accommodations are rather small. The hotel contains an English-inspired bar serving drinks and snacks that's open 24 hours a day. Don't judge the hotel by its rather bleak check-in area or the rather shabby third-floor lounge.

Residencia Liabeny. Salud, 3, 28013 Madrid. ☎ **91/531-90-00.** Fax 91/532-74-21. 224 rms. A/C MINIBAR TV TEL. 9,600–14,000 ptas. ($76.80–$112) double; 16,000–21,000 ptas. ($128–$168) triple. AE, MC, V. Parking 1,400 ptas. ($11.20). Metro: Puerta del Sol, Callao, or Gran Vía.

This hotel, behind a stone-sheathed, austere rectangular facade, is in a prime location midway between the tourist highlights of the Gran Vía and Puerta del Sol. Named after the original owner of the hotel, it contains seven floors of comfortable, contemporary bedrooms, which even though newly redecorated are a bit too pristine for our taste. The cocktail bar is more warming, although in a rather macho style, and the dining room is strictly for convenience. A coffee shop is also on the premises, and good laundry service and rather personalized attention from the staff add to the allure of the place.

INEXPENSIVE

Anaco. Tres Cruces, 3, 28013 Madrid. ☎ **91/522-46-04.** Fax 91/531-64-84. 39 rms. A/C TV TEL. 9,000–9,500 ptas. ($72–$76) double; 10,500–12,000 ptas. ($84–$96) triple. AE, DC, MC, V. Metro: Gran Vía, Callao, or Puerta del Sol.

A modest yet modern hotel, the Anaco is just off the main shopping thoroughfare, the Gran Vía. Opening onto a tree-shaded plaza, it attracts those seeking a clean resting place. The bedrooms are compact and contemporary, with built-in headboards, reading lamps, and lounge chairs. *A useful tip:* Ask for one of the five terraced rooms on the top floor, which rent at no extra charge. The hotel has a bar/cafeteria/restaurant open daily. English is spoken here. Nearby is a municipally operated garage.

Hostal Buenos Aires. Gran Vía, 61, 28013 Madrid. ☎ **91/542-01-02.** Fax 91/542-28-69. 25 rms. A/C TV TEL. 7,000 ptas. ($56) double. AE, DC, MC, V. Metro: Plaza de España. Bus: 1, 2, or 44.

To reach this place, you pass through a marble-covered street-floor lobby within a 1955 building, then take the elevator to the second floor. The hostal occupies two floors. One of its best features is a wood-sheathed café/bar that's open 24 hours a day. Bedrooms are comfortable, modern, and clean, although a bit small, with safety deposit boxes, balconies, and hair dryers.

Hostal Nuevo Gaos. Calle Mesonero Romanos, 14, 28013 Madrid. ☎ **91/532-71-07.** Fax 91/522-70-98. 23 rms. A/C MINIBAR TV TEL. 6,200–7,500 ptas. ($49.60–$60) double. AE, DC, MC, V. Metro: Callao. Bus: 1, 2, or 44.

On the second, third, and fourth floors of a 1930s building just off the Gran Vía, this residencia offers guests the chance to enjoy a comfortable standard of living at moderate rates. The place lies directly north of Puerta del Sol, across the street from the popular flamenco club Torre Bermejas. Breakfast can be taken at a nearby café.

$ **Hostal-Residencia Continental.** Gran Vía, 44, 28013 Madrid. ☎ **91/521-46-40.** Fax 91/521-46-49. 29 rms. TV TEL. 5,000 ptas. ($40) double. AE, DC, MC, V. Metro: Callao. Bus: 1, 2, 36, or 46.

Sprawling over the third and fourth floors of Gran Vía, 44, this hostal is a bit more expensive than the other accommodations in the building, but the rooms are comfortable, tidy, and renovated. The desk clerk speaks English. The Continental is in a virtual "casa of budget hotels," a 19th-century building filled exclusively with small hotels and pensions. If no room is available at the Continental, you can ring the doorbells of the other establishments because this "house of hotels" is a good bet for the budget tourist. No breakfast is served.

Hotel Alcázar Regis. Gran Vía, 61, 28013 Madrid. ☎ **91/547-93-17.** 25 rms (none with bath). 5,500 ptas. ($44) double; 7,000 ptas. ($56) triple. AE. Metro: Plaza de España or Santo Domingo.

Conveniently located in the midst of Madrid's best shops is this post–World War II building, complete with a circular Greek-style temple as its crown. On the building's fifth floor, you'll find long and pleasant public rooms, wood paneling, leaded-glass windows, parquet floors, crystal chandeliers, and high-ceilinged guest rooms, each with hot and cold running water.

Hotel Nuria. Fuencarral, 52, 28004 Madrid. ☎ **91/531-92-08.** Fax 91/532-90-05. 80 rms. TV TEL. 6,200–6,350 ptas. ($49.60–$50.80) double. Rates include breakfast. AE, DC, MC, V. Metro: Gran Vía or Tribunal. Bus: 3, 7, or 40.

Hotel Nuria, just three blocks from the Gran Vía, has some bedrooms with especially interesting views of the capital. Furnishings are simple and functional. A bar, restaurant, and TV lounge are available to guests. The hotel was last renovated in 1986.

NEAR THE PUERTA DEL SOL

EXPENSIVE

Gran Hotel Reina Victoria. Plaza Santa Ana, 14, 28012 Madrid. ☎ **91/531-45-00.** Fax 91/522-03-7. 197 rms, 4 suites. A/C MINIBAR TV TEL. From 21,900 ptas. ($175.20) double; from 55,100 ptas. ($440.80) suite. (Breakfast included). AE, DC, MC, V. Parking 1,700 ptas. ($13.60). Metro: Tirso de Molina or Puerta del Sol.

This establishment is about as important to the legends of Madrid as the famous bullfighter Manolete himself. He used to stay here, giving lavish parties in one of the reception rooms and attracting mobs in the square below when he went out on his balcony for morning coffee. Since the recent renovation and upgrading of this property by Spain's Tryp Hotel Group, it's less staid and more impressive than ever.

Originally built in 1923 and named after the grandmother of the present King of Spain, Juan Carlos, the hotel sits behind an ornate and eclectic stone facade, which the Spanish government protects as a historic monument. Although it's located in a congested and noisy neighborhood in the center of town, the Reina Victoria opens onto its own sloping plaza, once a meeting place for 17th-century intellectuals. Today the area is usually filled with flower vendors, older people reclining in the midafternoon sun, and young persons resting between bouts at the dozens of neighborhood tapas bars.

Each of the hotel's bedrooms contains sound-resistant insulation, a safe for valuables, and a private bathroom with many amenities.

Dining/Entertainment: Guests enjoy the hotel's stylish and popular lobby bar, the Manuel Gonzalez Manolete; the lavishly displayed bullfighting memorabilia and potent drinks add another attraction to an already memorable hotel. The in-house restaurant is El Ruedo.

Services: 24-hour room service, concierge, babysitting.

Facilities: Because of the hotel's position in one of Madrid's most interesting neighborhoods, almost anything is available within a few minutes' walk.

INEXPENSIVE

$ Hostal la Macarena. Cava de San Miguel, 8, 28005 Madrid. ☎ **91/365-92-21.** Fax 91/364-27-57. 18 rms. TEL. 6,000 ptas. ($48) double; 7,500 ptas. ($60) triple; 8,000 ptas. ($64) quad. MC, V. Metro: Puerta del Sol, Opera, or La Latina.

Known for its reasonable prices and praised by readers for the warmth of its reception, this unpretentious, clean hostal is run by the Ricardo González family. Its 19th-century facade, accented with Belle Epoque patterns, stands in ornate contrast to the chiseled simplicity of the ancient buildings facing it. The location is one of the hostal's assets: It's on a street (an admittedly noisy one) immediately behind Plaza Mayor, near one of the best clusters of *tascas* in Madrid. Windows facing the street have double panes.

Hostal la Perla Asturiana. Plaza de Santa Cruz, 3, 28012 Madrid. ☎ **91/366-46-00.** Fax 91/366-46-08. 33 rms. TV TEL. 4,900 ptas. ($39.20) double; 7,000 ptas. ($56) triple. AE, DC, MC, V. Metro: Puerta del Sol.

Ideal for those who want to stay in the heart of old Madrid (one block off Plaza Mayor and two blocks from Puerta del Sol), this small family-run establishment has a courteous staff member at the desk 24 hours a day for security and convenience. You can socialize in the small, comfortable lobby that's adjacent to the reception desk. The bedrooms are clean and simple, but often cramped, with fresh towels supplied daily. Many inexpensive restaurants and tapas bars are nearby. No breakfast is served.

Hostal Residencia Americano. Puerta del Sol, 11, 28013 Madrid. ☎ **91/522-28-22.** 43 rms. TV TEL. 4,700 ptas. ($37.60) double; 7,000 ptas. ($56) triple; 8,000 ptas. ($64) quad. No credit cards. Metro: Puerta del Sol.

Hostal Residencia Americano, on the third floor of a five-floor building, is suitable for those who want to be in Puerta del Sol. Owner/manager A. V. Franceschi has refurbished all the guest rooms, most of them outside chambers with balconies facing the street. Mr. Franceschi promises hot and cold running water 24 hours a day. No breakfast is served.

$ Hostal-Residencia Principado. Zorrilla, 7, 28014 Madrid. ☎ **91/429-81-87.** 15 rms. TV. 5,800 ptas. ($46.40) double. AE, MC, V. Metro: Sevilla or Banco de España. Bus: 5, 9, or 53.

The two-star Hostal-Residencia Principado is a real find. Located in a well-kept town house, it is run by a gracious owner, who keeps everything clean and inviting. New tiles, attractive bedspreads, and curtains give the guest rooms a fresh look. Safety boxes are provided. For breakfast, you can go to a nearby café. English is spoken.

Hotel Francisco I. Arenal, 15, 28013 Madrid. ☎ **91/548-43-14.** Fax 91/542-28-99. 58 rms. TV TEL. 9,700 ptas. ($77.60) double. Rates include breakfast. MC, V. Metro: Puerta del Sol or Ópera.

Here you can rent modern, clean rooms. There's a pleasant lounge and a bar, and on the sixth floor you'll find a comfortable, rustically decorated restaurant. The hotel was considerably modernized in 1993, with the addition of new bathrooms as well as air-conditioning in most of the bedrooms. The hotel provides 24-hour room service and laundry and valet service.

$ Hotel Inglés. Calle Echegaray, 8, 28014 Madrid. ☎ **91/429-65-51.** Fax 91/420-24-23. 50 rms, 8 suites. TV TEL. 10,000 ptas. ($80) double; 13,600 ptas. ($108.80) suite. AE, DC, MC, V. Parking 1,200 ptas. ($9.60). Metro: Puerta del Sol or Sevilla.

You'll find the Hotel Inglés on a central street lined with *tascas,* although the hotel operates its own 24-hour cafeteria. It's more modern and impersonal than it was when Virginia Woolf made it her address in Madrid. Behind its red-brick facade you'll find unpretentious and contemporary bedrooms, all well maintained. The comfortable armchairs in the TV lounge are likely to be filled with avid soccer fans. The lobby is air-conditioned, although the guest rooms are not. Guests who open their windows at night are likely to hear noise from the enclosed courtyard, so light sleepers beware.

Hotel Residencia Lisboa. Ventura de la Vega, 17, 28014 Madrid. ☎ **91/429-98-94.** Fax 91/369-41-96. 27 rms. 6,000 ptas. ($48) double. AE, DC, MC, V. Metro: Puerta del Sol.

The Lisboa, on Madrid's most famous restaurant street, can be a bit noisy, but that's our only complaint. The hotel is a neat, modernized town house with compact rooms and central heating in the cooler months. The staff members speak five languages. The Lisboa does not serve breakfast, but it is surrounded by budget dining rooms, cafés, and *tascas.*

Hotel Residencia Santander. Calle Echegaray, 1, 28014 Madrid. ☎ **91/429-95-51.** 38 rms. TEL. 7,000 ptas. ($56) double. MC, V. Metro: Puerta del Sol.

A snug little hotel just off Puerta del Sol, the Santander is a refurbished 1930 house with adequate rooms, some of which contain TVs. Although it's on a teeming street, you might appreciate the nonstop local atmosphere. Restaurants and bars in the area are active day and night. No breakfast is served.

NEAR ATOCHA STATION

MODERATE

Hotel Mercátor. Calle Atocha, 123, 28012 Madrid. ☎ **91/429-05-00.** Fax 91/369-12-52. 89 rms, 3 suites. MINIBAR TV TEL. 11,350 ptas. ($90.80) double; 12,750 ptas. ($102) suite. AE, DC, MC, V. Parking 1,320 ptas. ($10.55). Metro: Atocha or Antón Martín.

Only a three-minute walk from the Prado, Centro de Arte Reina Sofía, and the Thyssen-Bornemisza Museum, the Mercátor draws a clientele seeking a good hotel—orderly, well run, and clean, with enough comforts and conveniences to please the weary traveler. The public rooms are simple, outfitted in a vaguely modern type of minimalism. Some of the guest rooms are more inviting than others, especially those with desks and armchairs. Twenty-one units are air-conditioned. The Mercátor is a residencia—that is, it offers breakfast only and does not have a formal restaurant for lunch and dinner; however, it has a bar and cafeteria serving light meals, such as *platos combinados* (combination plates). The hotel has a garage and is within walking distance of American Express. Laundry service is provided, plus room service from 7am to 10pm.

INEXPENSIVE

Hotel Residencia Cortezo. Doctor Cortezo, 3, 28012 Madrid. ☎ **91/369-01-01.** Fax 91/369-37-74. 86 rms, 4 suites. A/C MINIBAR TV TEL. 10,000 ptas. ($80) double; 14,750 ptas. ($118) suite. AE, MC, V. Parking 1,000 ptas. ($8). Metro: Tirso de Molina.

Just off Calle de Atocha, which leads to the railroad station of the same name, the Cortezo is a short walk from Plaza Mayor and Puerta del Sol. The accommodations are comfortable but very simply furnished, with contemporary baths. The beds are springy, the colors are well chosen, and the furniture is pleasantly modern; often there is a sitting area with a desk and armchair. The public rooms match the guest rooms in freshness. The hotel was built in 1959 and last renovated in 1989.

NEAR RETIRO/SALAMANCA

VERY EXPENSIVE

✪ **Park Hyatt Villa Magna.** Paseo de la Castellana, 22, 28046 Madrid. ☎ **800/223-1234** in North America, or 91/587-12-34. Fax 91/431-22-86. 164 rms, 18 suites. A/C MINIBAR

TV TEL. 42,000 ptas. ($336) double; from 78,000 ptas. ($624) suite. Weekend packages: 2 nights in a double room for 40,000 ptas. ($320). AE, DC, MC, V. Parking 2,000 ptas. ($16). Metro: Rubén Darío.

One of the finest hotels in Europe, the nine-story Park Hyatt is faced with slabs of rose-colored granite and set behind a bank of pines and laurels on the city's most fashionable boulevard. It was already a supremely comfortable and elegant modern hotel when Hyatt International took over its management in 1990. Today it is an even finer choice than the Palace or Villa Real and is matched in luxury, ambience, and tranquillity only by the Ritz, which has a greater patina since it's much older.

It was originally conceived when a handful of Spain's elite teamed up to create a setting in which their special friends, along with an array of discriminating international visitors, would be pleased to live and dine. They hired an architect, imported a French decorator (whose style is a contemporary version of neoclassicism), planted gardens, and put the staff through an intensive training program.

Separated from the busy boulevard by a parklike garden, its facade has contemporary lines. In contrast, its interior recaptures the style of Carlos IV, with paneled walls, marble floors, and bouquets of fresh flowers. Through the lobby and drawing rooms passes almost every film star shooting on location in Spain.

This luxury palace has plush but dignified bedrooms decorated in Louis XVI, English Regency, or Italian provincial style. Each comes with fresh flowers and a TV with video movies and satellite reception (including news broadcasts beamed in from the United States).

Dining/Entertainment: A pianist provides entertainment in the lobby-level champagne bar. The in-house restaurant, the Berceo, serves international food in a glamorous setting. The hotel is known for its summer terraces, Calalú and Berceo, set in gardens. One of them, Calalú, is the only terrace in Madrid where you can enjoy live jazz performed from Tuesday through Saturday.

Services: 24-hour room service, concierge, same-day laundry and dry cleaning, limousine service, babysitting.

Facilities: Business center, car rentals, barber and beauty shop, the boutique "Villa Magna," availability of both tennis and golf (15 and 25 minutes from the hotel, respectively).

✪ **Ritz.** Plaza de la Lealtad, 5, 28014 Madrid. ☎ **800/225-5843** in the U.S. and Canada, or 91/521-28-57. Fax 91/532-87-76. 154 rms, 29 suites. A/C MINIBAR TV TEL. 52,000–63,500 ptas. ($416–$508) double; 92,500–185,000 ptas. ($740–$1,480) suite. AE, DC, MC, V. Parking 2,000 ptas. ($16). Metro: Banco de España.

An international rendezvous point of legendary renown, the Ritz is the most famous hotel in Spain and the most prestigious address in Madrid. Its name has appeared countless times in the Spanish-language tabloids that document the comings and goings of its glamorous guests. Encased in a turn-of-the-century shell of soaring ceilings and graceful columns, it contains all the luxuries and special attentions that world travelers have come to expect of a grand hotel. Billions of pesetas have been spent on renovations since its acquisition in the 1980s by the British-based Forte chain. The result is a bastion of glamour where, despite modernization, great effort was expended to retain the hotel's Belle Epoque character and architectural details.

No other Madrid hotel, except for the Palace, has a more varied history. One of *Les Grand/Hôtels Européens,* the Ritz was built at the command of King Alfonso XIII, with the aid of César Ritz, in 1908. It looks out onto the circular Plaza de la Lealtad in the center of town, near 300-acre Retiro Park, facing the Prado, the adjacent Palacio de Villahermosa, and the Stock Exchange. The Ritz was constructed when costs were relatively low and when spaciousness, luxury, and comfort were the standard. Its facade has been designated a historic monument.

Family-Friendly Hotels

Meliá Castilla *(see p. 110)* Children can spend hours and all that extra energy in the hotel's swimming pool and gymnasium. On the grounds is a showroom exhibiting the latest European automobiles. Hotel services include babysitting, providing fun for kids and parents too.

Novotel Madrid *(see p. 106)* Children under 16 stay free in their parents' room, where the sofa converts into a comfortable bed. Kids delight in the open-air swimming pool and the offerings of the bountiful breakfast buffet.

Tirol *(see p. 111)* This centrally located three-star hotel is a favorite of families seeking good comfort at moderate price. It also has a cafeteria.

Bedrooms contain fresh flowers, well-accessorized marble bathrooms, and TVs with video movies and satellite reception.

Dining/Entertainment: The hotel maintains a formal dining room decorated in shades of cream, blue, and gold, which is lined with mirrors and 16th-century Flemish tapestries. Chefs present an international menu featuring a paella that is the most elaborate in Madrid. In time-honored Spanish tradition, guests tend to dress up here, sometimes even for breakfast. (Management stresses that this is not a resort hotel.) Guests looking for a more casual eatery usually head for the Jardín Ritz.

Services: 24-hour room service with everything from good nutty Jabugo ham to fresh hake, laundry/valet, express checkout.

Facilities: Fitness center, car-rental kiosk, business center, foreign currency exchange.

Wellington. Velázquez, 8, 28001 Madrid. ☎ **91/575-44-00.** Fax 91/576-4164. 280 rms, 10 suites. A/C MINIBAR TV TEL. 33,250 ptas. ($266) double; from 48,500 ptas. ($388) suite. AE, DC, MC, V. Parking 2,200 ptas. ($17.60). Metro: Retiro or Velázquez.

The Wellington, with its somber antique-tapestried entrance, is one of Madrid's more sedate deluxe hotels, built in the mid-1950s but substantially remodeled since, although the atmosphere remains heavy. Set within the Salamanca residential area near Retiro Park, the Wellington offers redecorated but rather staid guest rooms, each with cable TV and movie channels, music, two phones (one in the bathroom), and a guest-operated combination safe. Units are furnished in English-inspired mahogany reproductions, and the bathrooms (one per accommodation) are modern and immaculate, with marble sheathing and fixtures. Doubles with private terraces (at no extra charge) are the most sought-after accommodations. This is the major bullfighter hotel of Madrid. On bullfight days camp followers show up.

Dining/Entertainment: An added bonus here is the El Fogón grill room, styled like a 19th-century tavern, where many of the provisions for the typically Spanish dishes are shipped in from the hotel's own ranch. The pub-style Bar Inglés is a hospitable rendezvous. Lighter meals are served in the Las Llaves de Oro (Golden Keys) cafeteria.

Services: 24-hour room service, same-day dry cleaning and laundry.

Facilities: Outdoor swimming pool in summer, garage, beauty parlor.

EXPENSIVE

Emperatriz. López de Hoyos, 4, 28006 Madrid. ☎ **91/563-80-88.** Fax 91/563-98-04. 153 rms, 5 suites. A/C MINIBAR TV TEL. 24,000 ptas. ($192) double; 60,000 ptas. ($480) suite. AE, DC, MC, V. Parking 1,500 ptas. ($12) nearby. Metro: Rubén Darío.

This hotel lies just off the wide Paseo de Castellana, only a short walk from some of Madrid's most deluxe hotels, but it charges relatively reasonable rates. Built in the 1970s, it was last renovated in 1995, although the bedrooms remain much finer than the rather dowdy public rooms. Rooms are comfortable and classically styled, with TVs that receive many different European channels. If one is available, ask for a room on the seventh floor, where you'll get a private terrace at no extra charge. On the premises are a beauty salon, a barbershop, and well-upholstered lounges, where you're likely to meet fellow globe-trotting Americans. Laundry and valet service are provided.

Grand Hotel Velázquez. Calle de Velázquez, 62, 28001 Madrid. ☎ **91/575-28-00.** Fax 91/575-28-09. 71 rms, 75 suites. A/C MINIBAR TV TEL. 21,970 ptas. ($175.75) double; from 29,160 ptas. ($233.30) suite. AE, DC, MC, V. Parking 1,700 ptas. ($13.60). Metro: Retiro.

Opened in 1947 on an affluent residential street near the center of town, this hotel has a 1930s style art deco facade and a 1940s interior filled with well-upholstered furniture and richly grained paneling. Several public rooms lead off a central oval area; one of them includes a bar. As in many hotels of its era, the bedrooms vary, with some large enough for entertaining, with a small but separate sitting area for reading or watching TV. All contain piped-in music. This is one of the most attractive medium-size hotels in Madrid, with plenty of comfort and convenience. The in-house restaurant, Las Lanzas, features both international and Spanish cuisine. Parking is available on the premises.

Novotel Madrid. Calle Albacete, 1 (at the corner of Avenida Badajos), 28027 Madrid. ☎ **800/221-4542** in North America, or 91/405-46-00. Fax 91/404-11-05. 236 rms. A/C MINIBAR TV TEL. 17,500 ptas. ($140) double. Children under 16 free in parents' room. Weekend rate: 13,800 ptas. ($110.40) double. AE, DC, MC, V. Free parking. Metro: Concepción. Exit from the M-30 at Barrio de la Concepción/Parque de las Avenidas, just before reaching the city limits of central Madrid, then look for the chain's trademark electric-blue signs.

Novotel was originally intended to serve the hotel needs of a cluster of multinational corporations with headquarters 1½ miles east of the center of Madrid, but its guest rooms are so comfortable and its prices so reasonable that tourists have begun using it as well. Opened in 1986, it is located on the highway, away from the maze of sometimes confusing inner-city streets, which makes it attractive to motorists.

Bedrooms are laid out in a standardized format whose popularity in Europe has made it one of the hotel industry's most notable success stories. Each contains a well-designed bathroom, in-house movies, a radio, a TV, and soundproofing. The sofas, once their bolster pillows are removed, can be transformed into comfortable beds where children can sleep. The English-speaking staff is well versed in both sightseeing attractions and solutions to most business-related problems.

MODERATE

Gran Hotel Colón. Pez Volador, 11, 28007 Madrid. ☎ **91/573-59-00.** Fax 91/573-08-09. 380 rms. A/C MINIBAR TV TEL. 17,600 ptas. ($140.80) double. AE, DC, MC, V. Parking 1,500 ptas. ($12). Metro: Sainz de Baranda.

East of Retiro Park, the Gran Hotel Colón is a few minutes from the city center by subway. Built in 1966, it offers comfortable yet moderately priced accommodations in one of Madrid's modern hotel structures. More than half of the accommodations have private balconies, and all contain comfortably traditional furniture, much of it built-in.

Other assets include two dining rooms, a covered garage, and bingo games. One of the Colón's founders was an accomplished interior designer, which accounts for the unusual stained-glass windows and murals in the public rooms and the paintings by Spanish artists in the lounge.

Hotel Claridge. Plaza Conde de Casal, 6, 28007 Madrid. ☎ **91/551-94-00.** Fax 91/501-03-85. 148 rms, 2 suites. A/C TV TEL. 14,950 ptas. ($119.60) double; 19,000 ptas. ($152) suite. AE, MC, V. Free parking. Metro: Conde Casal.

This contemporary building, last renovated in 1994, is beyond Retiro Park, about five minutes from the Prado by taxi or subway. The bedrooms are well organized and pleasantly styled: small and compact, with coordinated furnishings and colors. You can take your meals in the hotel's cafeteria and also relax in the modern lounge.

CHAMBERÍ

VERY EXPENSIVE

Castellana Inter-Continental Hotel. Paseo de la Castellana, 49, 28046 Madrid. ☎ **800/327-0200** in the U.S., or 91/310-02-00. Fax 91/319-58-53. 270 rms, 35 suites. A/C MINIBAR TV TEL. 41,000–47,000 ptas. ($328–$376) double; from 76,500 ptas. ($612) suite. AE, DC, MC, V. Parking 2,100 ptas. ($16.80). Metro: Rubén Darío.

Solid, spacious, and conservatively modern, this is one of Madrid's more reliable hotels. Originally built in 1963 as the then-most-prestigious hotel on this famous boulevard, the Castellana Inter-Continental lies behind a barrier of trees within a neighborhood of apartment houses and luxury hotels. Its high-ceilinged public rooms provide a welcome refuge from the Madrileño heat. They're a tribute to the art of Spanish masonry, with terrazzo floors and a large-scale collection of angular abstract murals pieced together from multicolored stones and tiles. Most of the accommodations have private balconies and traditional furniture, each with a color TV with in-house videos and many channels beamed in from across Europe. Some rooms are in need of rejuvenation.

Dining/Entertainment: The La Ronda Bar offers drinks near the elegant Los Continentes Restaurant, serving both a creative and Mediterranean cuisine. In addition, El Jardín is a retreat in summer, with candlelit dinners and live soft background music. Good cookery and thrifty prices are found at El Sarracín, yet another restaurant.

Services: There's a helpful concierge and a travel agent who will book theater tickets, rental cars, and airline connections; there's also 24-hour room service, laundry, and babysitting.

Facilities: Kiosks and boutiques, hairdresser/barbershop, business center, top floor gym with sauna and outdoor solarium.

Miguel Angel. Miguel Angel, 29–31, 28010 Madrid. ☎ **91/442-81-99.** Fax 91/442-53-20. 278 rms, 26 suites. A/C MINIBAR TV TEL. 35,700–42,500 ptas. ($285.60–$340) double; 42,400–105,000 ptas. ($339.20–$840) suite. AE, DC, MC, V. Parking 1,800 ptas. ($14.40). Metro: Rubén Darío.

Just off Paseo de la Castellana, Miguel Angel, sleekly modern, opened its doors in 1975 and has been renovated and kept up to date periodically ever since. It has much going for it—ideal location, contemporary styling, good furnishings and art objects, an efficient staff, and plenty of comfort. Behind its facade is an expansive sun terrace on several levels, with clusters of garden furniture surrounded by paintings of semitropical scenes.

The soundproof bedrooms contain radios, TVs, color-coordinated fabrics and carpets, and in many cases reproductions of classic Iberian furniture.

Dining/Entertainment: The Farnesio bar is decorated in a Spanish Victorian style, and piano music is played beginning at 8pm. A well-managed restaurant on the premises is the Florencia. Dinner is also served until around 3am in the Zacarias boîte restaurant, where you can dine while watching an occasional cabaret or musical performance.

Services: 24-hour room service, same-day laundry/valet.

Facilities: Indoor heated swimming pool, saunas, hairdressers, and a drugstore. Art exhibitions are sponsored in the arcade of boutiques.

✪ **Santo Mauro Hotel.** Calle Zurbano, 36, 28010 Madrid. ☎ **91/319-6900.** Fax 91/308-5417. 31 rms, 6 suites. A/C MINIBAR TV TEL. 44,000 ptas. ($352) double; from 49,000 ptas. ($392) suite. AE, DC, MC, V. Parking 1,950 ptas. ($15.60). Metro: Rubén Darío or Alonso Martínez.

This hotel opened in 1991 within the once-decrepit neoclassical walls of a villa that was originally built in 1894 for the Duke of Santo Mauro. Set within a garden and reminiscent of the kind of architecture you'd expect to find in France, it contains a mixture of rich fabrics and art deco art and furnishings. Staff members outnumber rooms by two to one. Each of the bedrooms contains an audio system with a wide choice of tapes and CDs as well as many coordinated decor notes, which may include curtains of raw silk, Persian carpets, and jewel-toned colors.

Dining/Entertainment: The Belagua Restaurant is reviewed separately later in this chapter. An elegant bar is located off the main lobby, and tables are set up beneath the garden's large trees for drinks and snacks.

Services: 24-hour room service, laundry/valet, reception staff trained in the procurement of practically anything.

Facilities: Indoor swimming pool, health club with sauna and massage.

MODERATE

Conde Duque. Plaza Conde Valle de Súchil, 5, 28015 Madrid. ☎ **91/447-70-00.** Fax 91/448-35-69. 136 rms, 7 suites. A/C MINIBAR TV TEL. 18,200–22,850 ptas. ($145.60–$182.80) double; from 30,600 ptas. ($244.80) suite. Rates include breakfast. AE, DC, MC, V. Metro: San Bernardo.

The modern three-star Conde Duque, near a branch of the Galerías Preciados department store, opens onto a tree-filled plaza in a residential neighborhood that's near the Glorieta Quevado. The hotel is 12 blocks north of the Plaza de España, off Calle de San Bernardo, which starts at the Gran Vía. The walk to the plaza is too long, but a subway stop is nearby. Guest-room furnishings include built-in modern headboards and reproductions of 19th-century English pieces, plus bedside lights and telephones. Room service is provided 24 hours.

Hotel Escultor. Miguel Angel, 3, 28010 Madrid. ☎ **91/310-42-03.** Fax 91/319-25-84. 17 rms, 38 suites. A/C MINIBAR TV TEL. From 12,000 ptas. ($96) double; from 21,000 ptas. ($168) suite. AE, DC, MC, V. Parking 2,300 ptas. ($18.40) nearby. Metro: Rubén Darío.

Originally built in 1975, this comfortably furnished hotel provides fewer services and offers fewer facilities than others within its category, but it compensates with larger accommodations. Each guest unit has its own charm and contemporary styling—with video films; a private bathroom; and an efficient, logical layout. The hotel is fully air-conditioned, and the staff provides information about facilities in the neighborhood.

Dining/Entertainment: The hotel has a small but comfortable bar that's open nightly, and a traditional restaurant, the Señorio de Erazu, which closes on Saturday at lunchtime and all day on Sunday.

Services: Room service is offered at breakfast only, from 7 to 11am.

Residencia Bréton. Bréton de los Herreros, 29, 28003 Madrid. ☎ **91/442-83-00.** Fax 91/441-38-16. 55 rms, 2 suites. A/C MINIBAR TV TEL. 13,000 ptas. ($104) double; 20,000 ptas. ($160) suite. AE, DC, MC, V. Parking 1,500 ptas. ($12) nearby. Metro: Ríos Rosas.

You'll find this modern hotel, well furnished with reproductions of Iberian pieces, on a side street several blocks from Paseo de la Castellana. As a residencia, it doesn't offer a major dining room, but it does have a little bar and breakfast room adjoining the reception lounge. All the guest rooms have wood-frame beds, wrought-iron electrical fixtures, wall-to-wall curtains, comfortable chairs, and ornate tilework in the bathrooms.

INEXPENSIVE

Hostal Residencia Don Diego. Calle de Velázquez, 45, 28001 Madrid. ☎ **91/435-07-60.** Fax 91/431-42-63. 58 rms. A/C TV TEL. 8,500 ptas. ($68) double; 11,475 ptas. ($91.80) triple. MC, V. Metro: Velázquez.

On the fifth floor of a building with an elevator, Don Diego is in a combination residential/commercial neighborhood that's relatively convenient to many of the city monuments. The vestibule contains an elegant winding staircase accented with iron griffin heads supporting its balustrade. The hotel is warm and inviting, filled with leather couches and comfortable, no-nonsense angular but attractive furniture. A bar stands at the far end of the main sitting room. The hotel's cafeteria serves breakfast from 7:45 to 11am. From 7 to 11pm daily, you can also order drinks and snacks, especially sandwiches and omelets. Laundry service is provided, and room service is available daily from 8am to midnight.

CHAMARTÍN

EXPENSIVE

Cuzco. Paseo de la Castellana, 133, 28046 Madrid. ☎ **91/556-06-00.** Fax 91/556-03-72. 320 rms, 8 suites. A/C MINIBAR TV TEL. 21,600 ptas. ($172.80) double; from 28,000 ptas. ($224) suite. AE, DC, MC, V. Parking 1,800 ptas. ($14.40). Metro: Cuzco.

Popular with businesspeople and tour groups, Cuzco lies in a commercial neighborhood of big buildings, government ministries, spacious avenues, and the main Congress Hall. The Chamartín railway station is a 10-minute walk north, so it's a popular and convenient address.

This 15-floor structure, set back from Madrid's longest boulevard, has been redecorated and modernized many times since it was completed in 1967. The architect of the Cuzco allowed for spacious bedrooms, each with a separate sitting area, video movies, and a private bathroom. The decorator provided modern furnishings and patterned rugs.

There is a bilevel snack bar and cafeteria. The lounge is a forest of marble pillars and leather armchairs, its ambience enhanced by contemporary oil paintings and tapestries. Facilities include free parking, a beauty parlor, a sauna, massage, a gymnasium, and a cocktail bar.

Eurobuilding. Calle Padre Damián, 23, 28036 Madrid. ☎ **91/345-45-00.** Fax 91/345-45-76. 420 rms, 100 suites. A/C MINIBAR TV TEL. 29,500 ptas. ($236) double; from 34,700 ptas. ($277.60) suite. AE, DC, MC, V. Parking 2,500 ptas. ($20). Metro: Cuzco.

Even while the Eurobuilding was on the drawing boards, the rumor was that this five-star sensation of white marble would provide, in the architect's words, "a new concept in deluxe hotels." It is actually two hotels linked by a courtyard, away from the city center but right in the midst of apartment houses, boutiques, nightclubs, first-class restaurants, tree-shaded squares, and the modern Madrid business world.

The more glamorous of the twin buildings is the main one, named Las Estancias de Eurobuilding; it contains only suites, all of which were recently renovated in luxurious pastel shades. Here, drinks await you in your refrigerator. Ornately carved gold-and-white beds, background music, roomwide terraces for breakfast and cocktail entertaining—all are tastefully coordinated. Across the courtyard, the neighbor Eurobuilding contains less impressive, but still very comfortable, double rooms, many with views from private balconies of the formal garden and swimming pool below. All the accommodations have TVs with video movies and satellite reception, security doors, and individual safes.

Dining/Entertainment: Le Relais Coffee Shop is suitable for a quick bite, and Le Relais Restaurant offers buffets at both breakfast and lunch. For more formal dining, La Taberna at both lunch and dinner features a selection of Spanish and international cuisine, specializing in seafood and various paella dishes.

Services: Laundry/valet, concierge, 24-hour room service, babysitting.

Facilities: Health club with sauna, outdoor swimming pool.

Meliá Castilla. Calle Capitán, Haya, 43, 28020 Madrid. ☎ **800/336-3542** in the U.S., or 91/567-50-00. Fax 91/571-2210. 896 rms, 14 suites. A/C MINIBAR TV TEL. 29,900 ptas. ($239.20) double; from 55,000 ptas. ($440) suite. AE, DC, MC, V. Parking 6,240 ptas. ($49.90). Metro: Cuzco.

This mammoth hotel qualifies, along with the above-recommended Palace, as one of the largest in Europe. Loaded with facilities and built primarily to accommodate huge conventions, the Meliá Castilla also caters to the needs of the individual traveler. Everything is larger than life here: You need a floor plan to direct yourself around its precincts. The lounges and pristine marble corridors are vast—there is even a landscaped garden as well as a showroom full of the latest-model cars.

Each twin-bedded room comes with a private bath, a radio, a color TV, and modern furniture. Some lower rooms are quite noisy. The Meliá Castilla is in the north of Madrid, about a block west of Paseo de la Castellana, a short drive from the Chamartín railway station.

Dining/Entertainment: The hotel has a coffee shop, a seafood restaurant, a restaurant specializing in paella and other rice dishes, cocktail lounges, and the Trinidad nightclub. In addition, there's the restaurant/show Scala Meliá Castilla.

Services: 24-hour room service, hairdresser/barbershop, concierge, babysitting, laundry/valet.

Facilities: Swimming pool, shopping arcade with souvenir shops and bookstore, saunas, gymnasium, parking garage.

MODERATE

Aristos. Avenida Pío XII, 34, 28016 Madrid. ☎ **91/345-04-50.** Fax 91/345-10-23. 24 rms. A/C TV TEL. 18,000–20,500 ptas. ($144–$164) double. AE, DC, MC, V. Parking 1,500 ptas. ($12). Metro: Pío XII.

This three-star hotel is in an up-and-coming residential area of Madrid, not far from the Eurobuilding (see above). Its main advantage is a front garden where you can lounge, have a drink or order a complete meal. The hotel's restaurant, El Chaflán, is popular with neighborhood residents. Each of the bedrooms has a small terrace and an uncomplicated collection of modern furniture.

Hotel Chamartín. Estacíon de Chamartín, 28036 Madrid. ☎ **91/323-30-87.** Fax 91/733-02-14. 378 rms, 18 suites. A/C MINIBAR TV TEL. 13,800 ptas. ($110.40) double; from 25,000 ptas. ($200) suite. AE, DC, MC, V. Parking 2,000 ptas. ($16) in nearby garage. Metro: Chamartín. Bus: 5.

This brick-sided hotel soars nine stories above the northern periphery of Madrid. It's part of the massive modern shopping complex attached to the Chamartín railway station, although once you're inside your soundproofed room, the noise of the railway station will seem far away. The owner of the building is RENFE, Spain's government railway system, but the nationwide chain that administers it is HUSA Hotels. The hotel lies 15 minutes by taxi from both the airport and the historic core of Madrid and is conveniently close to one of the capital's busiest metro stops. Especially oriented to the business traveler, the Chamartín offers a currency exchange kiosk, a travel agency, a car-rental office, and a lobby video screen that posts the arrival and departure of all of Chamartín's trains.

A coffee bar serves breakfast daily, and room service is available from 7am to midnight. The hotel restaurant, Cota 13, serves an international cuisine. A short walk from the hotel lobby, within the railway-station complex, are a handful of shops and movie theaters, a roller-skating rink, a disco, and ample parking.

ARGÜELLES/MONCLOA

VERY EXPENSIVE

Husa Princesa. Serrano Jover, 3, 28015 Madrid. ☎ **91/542-35-00.** Fax. 91/559-4665. 275 rms, 12 suites. A/C TV TEL. 31,200 ptas. ($249.60) double; from 61,500 ptas. ($492) suite. AE, DC, MC, V. Parking 3,000 ptas. ($24). Metro: Argüelles.

Originally built during the mid-1970s and radically renovated after its takeover in 1991 by the nationwide chain Husa, the Princesa is a sprawling hotel designed with a series of massive rectangular sections clustered into an angular whole. The concrete-and-glass facade overlooks busy boulevards in the center of Madrid.

The hotel is patronized by both businesspersons and groups of visiting tourists; each of the bedrooms contains comfortable, contemporary furniture and a modernized bathroom.

Dining/Entertainment: The hotel's restaurant is called Ricón de Argüelles. There is also a bar, the Bar Royal.

Services: 24-hour room service, concierge, babysitting.

Facilities: The interior contains a large assortment of conference rooms, an underground garage, and a hairdressing salon.

EXPENSIVE

Meliá Madrid. Princesa, 17, 28008 Madrid. ☎ **800/336-3542** in the U.S., or 91/541-82-00. Fax 91/541-19-05. 260 rms, 5 suites. A/C MINIBAR TV TEL. 29,800 ptas. ($238.40) double; from 58,000 ptas. ($464) suite. AE, DC, MC, V. Parking 1,600 ptas. ($12.80). Metro: Rodríguez.

Here you'll find one of the most modern yet uniquely Spanish hotels in the country. Its 23 floors of wide picture windows have taken a permanent position in the capital's skyline. Each of the bedrooms is comfortable, spacious, and filled with contemporary furnishings plus a TV with video movies and many channels from across Europe. Most offer views over the skyline of Madrid. The chalk-white walls dramatize the flamboyant use of color accents; the bathrooms are sheathed in marble.

Dining/Entertainment: Restaurante Princesa is elegant and restful; equally popular is Don Pepe Grill. The cuisine in both restaurants is international and includes an array of Japanese and Indian dishes. There are also three bars and a coffee shop.

Services: 24-hour room service, concierge, babysitting, hairdresser/barber, laundry.

Facilities: A gallery that includes souvenir shops and bookstores, health club with sauna and massage.

MODERATE

Tirol. Marqués de Urquijo, 4, 28008 Madrid. ☎ **91/548-19-00.** Fax 91/541-39-58. 97 rms, 4 suites. A/C TEL. 10,850 ptas. ($86.80) double; 14,750 ptas. ($118) suite. MC, V. Parking 1,975 ptas. ($15.80). Metro: Argüelles. Bus: 2 or 21.

A short walk from Plaza de España and the swank Meliá Madrid hotel (see above), the Tirol is a good choice for clean, unpretentious comfort. Furnishings in this three-star hotel are simple and functional. Eight of the guest rooms have private terraces. A cafeteria and a parking garage are within the hotel.

4 Dining

After you've settled in, begin the search for a restaurant. Even more than Barcelona, Madrid boasts the most varied cuisine and the widest choice of dining opportunities in Spain. A post-1992 recession forced many neighborhood restaurants to lower their prices, meaning more bang for your dining buck. At the fancy tourist restaurants, however, prices are still comparable to those in New York, London, or Paris.

It's the custom in Madrid to consume the big meal of the day from 2 to 4pm. After a recuperative siesta, Madrileños then enjoy tapas—and indeed, no culinary experience would be complete without a tour of the city's many tapas bars (see "An Early Evening Tapeo," below, and "Best of the Tascas," at the end of this chapter).

All this nibbling is followed by dinner—more likely a light supper—in a restaurant, usually from 9:30pm to as late as midnight. Many restaurants, however, start serving dinner at 8pm to accommodate visitors from other countries who don't like to dine late.

Many of Spain's greatest chefs have opened restaurants in Madrid, energizing the city's culinary scene. Gone are the days when mainly Madrileño food was featured, which meant Castilian specialties such as *cocido* (a chickpea-and-sausage stew) or roasts of suckling pig or lamb. Now, you can take a culinary tour of the country while remaining in Madrid—from Andalusia with its gazpacho and braised bull's tails to Asturias with its *fabada* (a rich pork stew) and *sidra* (cider) to the Basque country, which has the most sophisticated cuisine in Spain. There are also a host of Galician and Mediterranean restaurants in Madrid. Amazingly, though Madrid is a landlocked city surrounded by a vast arid plain, you can order some of the freshest seafood in the country here.

Prices in Madrid's first-class and deluxe restaurants shock first-time visitors—at least those who don't live in such expensive cities as Tokyo, Oslo, London, and Paris.

Meals include service and tax (ranging from 7% to 12%, depending on the restaurant) but not drinks, which add to the tab considerably. The restaurants listed below that are categorized as "very expensive" charge from 6,000 pesetas ($48) per person for a meal. The restaurants that are rated "expensive" ask from 4,000 to 6,000 pesetas ($32–$48) per person for a meal; "moderate," from 2,000 to 4,000 pesetas ($16–$32); and "inexpensive," less than 2,000 pesetas ($16) per person.

If you can't afford the prices charged by most first-class restaurants in Madrid, there are numerous budget dining options to keep your bill down.

Don't overtip; follow the local custom. Theoretically, service is included in the price of the meal, but it's customary to leave an additional 10%.

For more details on dining (such as when and what to eat), see "The Cuisine" in Chapter 2.

Menú del Día and Cubierto Order the *menú del día* (menu of the day) or *cubierto* —both fixed-price menus based on what is fresh at the market that day. They are the dining bargains in Madrid, although often lacking the quality of more expensive à la carte dining. Usually each will include a first course, such as fish soup or hors d'oeuvres, followed by a main dish, plus bread, dessert, and the wine of the house. You won't have a large choice. The *menú turístico* is a similar fixed-price menu, but for many it's too large, especially at lunch. Only those with large appetites will find it the best bargain.

An Early Evening Tapeo

What's more fun than a pub crawl in London or Dublin? In Madrid, it's a *tapeo,* and you can drink just as much or more than in those far northern climes. A tapeo —one of the pleasures of a visit to Madrid—is strolling from one tapas bar to another, the way to keep yourself amused and fed before the fashionable Madrileño dining hour of 10pm.

Most of the world knows that tapas are Spain's delectable appetizer foods, and hundreds of restaurants in England and the United States now serve them. In Madrid they're served in tabernas, tascas, bars, and cafés.

Although Madrid took to tapas with a passion, they may have originated in Andalusia, especially around Jerez de la Frontera, where they were traditionally served to accompany the sherry produced there. The first tapa (which means a cover or lid) was probably *chorizo* (a spicy sausage) or a slice of cured ham perched over the mouth of a glass to keep the flies out. Later, the government mandated bars to serve a "little something" in the way of food with each drink to dissipate the effects of the alcohol. This was important when drinking a fortified wine like sherry, as its alcohol content is more than 15% higher than that of normal table wines. A selection of tapas will help preserve sobriety.

Tapas can be relatively simple: toasted almonds; slices of ham, cheese, or sausage; potato omelets; or the inevitable olives. But they can also be more elaborate: a succulent veal roll; herb-flavored snails; *gambas* (fried shrimp); a saucer of peppery *pulpo* (octopus); stuffed peppers; delicious *anguila* (eel); *cangrejo* (crabmeat salad); hake salad flavored with sweet red peppers, garlic, and cumin—and even bull testicles.

Each bar in Madrid gains a reputation for its rendition of certain favorite foods. One bar, for example, specializes in very garlicky grilled mushrooms, usually washed down with pitchers of sangría. Another will specialize in gambas. Most chefs are men in Madrid, but at tapas bars or *tascas,* the cooks are most often women—perhaps the mother or sister of the owner, but usually the wife.

Louis Armstrong, Manolete, Ava Gardner, or even Orson Welles may no longer be around Madrid to accompany you on a tapeo, but the tradition lives on. For a selection of our favorite bars, see "Best of the Tascas" later in this chapter. There are literally hundreds of others, many of which you'll discover on your own during your strolls around Madrid.

Cafeterias These are not self-service establishments but restaurants serving light, often American, cuisine. Go for breakfast instead of dining at your hotel, unless it's included in the room price. Some cafeterias offer no hot meals, but many feature combined plates of fried eggs, french fries, veal, and lettuce-and-tomato salad, which make adequate fare, or snacks like hot dogs and hamburgers.

NEAR THE PLAZA DE LAS CORTÉS

EXPENSIVE

El Espejo. Paseo de Recoletos, 31. ☎ **91/308-23-47.** Reservations required. *Menú del día* 2,750 ptas. ($22). AE, DC, MC, V. Sun–Fri 1–4pm, daily 9pm–1am. Metro: Colón. Bus: 27. INTERNATIONAL.

Here you'll find good-tasting food and one of the most perfectly crafted art nouveau decors in Madrid. If the weather is good, you can choose one of the outdoor tables,

Dining in Central Madrid

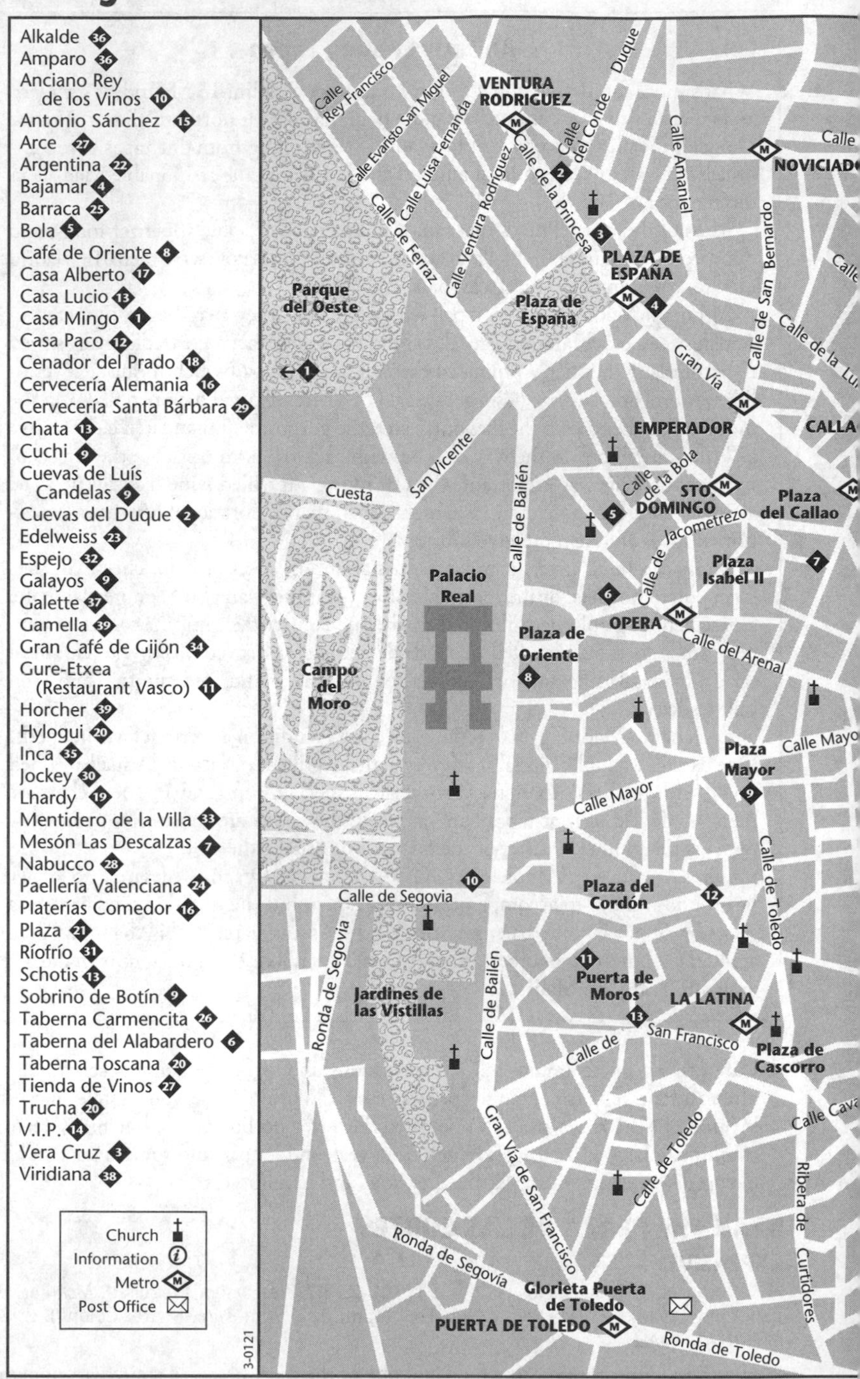
Alkalde 36
Amparo 36
Anciano Rey de los Vinos 10
Antonio Sánchez 15
Arce 27
Argentina 22
Bajamar 4
Barraca 25
Bola 5
Café de Oriente 8
Casa Alberto 17
Casa Lucio 13
Casa Mingo 1
Casa Paco 12
Cenador del Prado 18
Cervecería Alemania 16
Cervecería Santa Bárbara 29
Chata 13
Cuchi 9
Cuevas de Luís Candelas 9
Cuevas del Duque 2
Edelweiss 23
Espejo 32
Galayos 9
Galette 37
Gamella 39
Gran Café de Gijón 34
Gure-Etxea (Restaurant Vasco) 11
Horcher 39
Hylogui 20
Inca 35
Jockey 30
Lhardy 19
Mentidero de la Villa 33
Mesón Las Descalzas 7
Nabucco 28
Paellería Valenciana 24
Platerías Comedor 16
Plaza 21
Ríofrío 31
Schotis 13
Sobrino de Botín 9
Taberna Carmencita 26
Taberna del Alabardero 6
Taberna Toscana 20
Tienda de Vinos 27
Trucha 20
V.I.P. 14
Vera Cruz 3
Viridiana 38
Church
Information
Metro
Post Office
3-0121
VENTURA RODRIGUEZ
NOVICIADO
PLAZA DE ESPAÑA
Plaza de España
Parque del Oeste
EMPERADOR
CALLAO
STO. DOMINGO
Plaza del Callao
Plaza Isabel II
OPERA
Palacio Real
Plaza de Oriente
Campo del Moro
Plaza Mayor
Plaza del Cordón
Puerta de Moros
LA LATINA
Plaza de Cascorro
Jardines de las Vistillas
Glorieta Puerta de Toledo
PUERTA DE TOLEDO
Calle Rey Francisco
Calle Evaristo San Miguel
Calle Luisa Fernanda
Calle Ventura Rodriguez
Calle de Ferraz
Calle de la Princesa
Calle del Conde Duque
Calle Amaniel
Calle de San Bernardo
Calle de la Luna
Gran Vía
Cuesta San Vicente
Calle de Bailén
Calle de la Bola
Calle de Jacometrezo
Calle del Arenal
Calle Mayor
Calle de Segovia
Calle de Toledo
Ronda de Segovia
Calle de San Francisco
Gran Vía de San Francisco
Calle Cava
Ribera de Curtidores
Ronda de Toledo

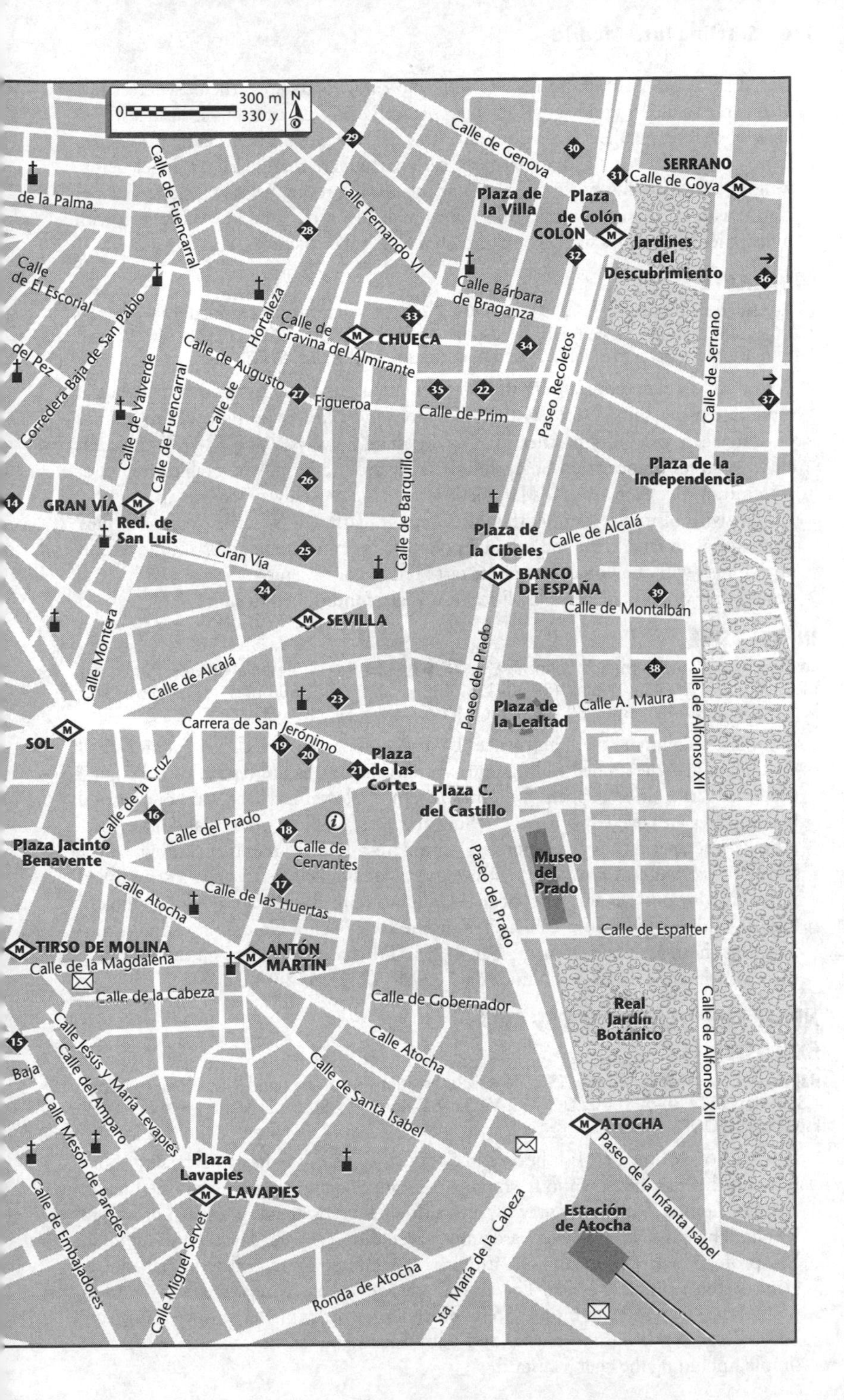
0
300 m
330 y
N
Calle de Fuencarral
de la Palma
Calle de El Escorial
Corredera Baja de San Pablo
del Pez
Calle de Valverde
Calle de Fuencarral
Calle de Hortaleza
Calle de Augusto
Figueroa
Calle de Gravina del Almirante
CHUECA
Calle Fernando VI
Calle de Genova
Plaza de la Villa
Plaza de Colón
COLÓN
SERRANO
Calle de Goya
Jardines del Descubrimiento
Calle Bárbara de Braganza
Paseo Recoletos
Calle de Prim
Calle de Barquillo
Calle de Serrano
Plaza de la Independencia
GRAN VÍA
Red. de San Luis
Gran Vía
Plaza de la Cibeles
Calle de Alcalá
BANCO DE ESPAÑA
Calle de Montalbán
SEVILLA
Calle Montera
Calle de Alcalá
Paseo del Prado
Plaza de la Lealtad
Calle A. Maura
Calle de Alfonso XII
SOL
Carrera de San Jerónimo
Plaza de las Cortes
Plaza C. del Castillo
Calle de la Cruz
Calle del Prado
Calle de Cervantes
Plaza Jacinto Benavente
Museo del Prado
Calle Atocha
Calle de las Huertas
Paseo del Prado
Calle de Espalter
TIRSO DE MOLINA
Calle de la Magdalena
ANTÓN MARTÍN
Calle de la Cabeza
Calle de Gobernador
Real Jardín Botánico
Calle Atocha
Calle de Alfonso XII
Baja
Calle Jesús y María Levapiés
Calle del Amparo
Calle de Santa Isabel
ATOCHA
Calle Mesón de Paredes
Plaza Lavapies
LAVAPIES
Paseo de la Infanta Isabel
Calle de Embajadores
Calle Miguel Servet
Ronda de Atocha
Sta. María de la Cabeza
Estación de Atocha
14
15
16
17
18
19
20
21
22
23
24
25
26
27
28
29
30
31
32
33
34
35
36
37
38
39

served by a battery of uniformed waiters who carry food across the busy street to a green area flanked with trees and strolling pedestrians. We prefer a table inside, within view of the tile maidens with vines and flowers entwined in their hair. After entering, you'll find yourself in a charming café/bar, where many visitors linger before walking down a hallway toward the spacious dining room. Dishes include grouper ragoût with clams, steak tartare, guinea fowl with Armagnac, and lean duck meat with pineapple. Profiteroles with cream and chocolate sauce make a delectable dessert.

Moderate

Edelweiss. Jovelianos, T. ☎ **91/521-03-26.** Reservations recommended. Main courses 1,200–2,600 ptas. ($9.60–$20.80); fixed-price menu 1,900 ptas. ($15.20). AE, MC, V. Daily 1–4pm, Mon–Sat 8pm–midnight. Closed Aug. Metro: Sevilla. Bus: 5. GERMAN.

Edelweiss is a German standby that has provided good-quality food and service at moderate prices since World War II. You are served hearty portions of food, mugs of draft beer, and fluffy pastries; that's why there's always a wait. *Tip:* To beat the crowds, go for dinner at un-Spanish hours, say around 9pm, when tables are not at a premium. But even when it's jammed, service is almost always courteous.

Start with Bismarck herring, then dive into goulash with spaetzle or *Eisbein* (pigs' knuckles) with sauerkraut and mashed potatoes, the most popular dish at the restaurant. Finish with the homemade apple tart. The decor is vaguely German, with travel posters and wood-paneled walls. Edelweiss is air-conditioned in summer.

Inexpensive

La Trucha. Manuel Fernandez Gonzalez, 3. ☎ **91/429-58-33.** Reservations recommended. Main courses 1,200–3,200 ptas. ($9.60–$25.60); *menú del día* 2,800 ptas. ($22.40). AE, MC, V. Mon–Sat 2:30–4pm and 7:30–midnight. Metro: Sevilla. SPANISH/SEAFOOD.

With its Andalusian tavern ambience, La Trucha boasts a street-level bar and small dining room—the arched ceiling and whitewashed walls are festive with hanging braids of garlic, dried peppers, and onions. On the lower level the walls of a second bustling area are covered with eye-catching antiques, bullfight notices, and other bric-a-brac. The specialty is fish; there's a complete à la carte menu including *trucha* (trout), *verbenas de abumados* (a "street party" of smoked delicacies), a stew called *fabada* ("glorious"; made with beans, Galician ham, black sausage, and smoked bacon), and a *comida casera rabo de toro* (home-style oxtail). No one should miss nibbling on the *tapas variadas* in the bar. If this Trucha turns out to be too crowded, there's another La Trucha at Núñez de Arce, 6 (☎ **91/532-08-82**).

NEAR THE PLAZA DE ESPAÑA

Expensive

Bajamar. Gran Vía, 78. ☎ **91/559-59-03.** Reservations recommended. Main courses 1,850–4,500 ptas. ($14.80–$36). AE, DC, MC, V. Daily 1–4pm and 8pm–midnight. Metro: Plaza de España. SEAFOOD.

Bajamar, one of the best fish houses in Spain, is right in the heart of the city. Both fish and shellfish are flown in fresh daily, the prices depending on what the market charges. Lobster, king crab, prawns, and soft-shell crabs are all priced according to weight. There is a large array of reasonably priced dishes as well. The service is smooth and professional. The menu is in English. For an appetizer, order the half-dozen giant oysters or rover crayfish. The special seafood soup is a most satisfying meal in itself. Try also the lobster bisque. Some of the noteworthy main courses include turbot Gallego style, seafood paella, and baby squid cooked in its ink. Desserts are simple, including the chef's custard.

Moderate

Las Cuevas del Duque. Princesa, 16. ☎ **91/559-50-37.** Reservations required. Main courses 1,875–3,000 ptas. ($15–$24). AE, DC, MC, V. Mon–Fri 1–4pm, daily 8pm–midnight. Metro: Ventura Rodríguez. Bus: 1, 2, or 42. SPANISH.

In front of the Duke of Alba's palace, a short walk from Plaza de España, is Las Cuevas del Duque, with an underground bar and a small, 20-table mesón that serves such simple Spanish fare as roast suckling pig, sirloin, tiny grilled lamb cutlets, and a few seafood dishes, including hake in garlic sauce and sole cooked in cider. In fair weather a few tables are set outside, beside a tiny triangular garden. Other tables line the Calle de la Princesa side and make an enjoyable roost for an afternoon drink.

Inexpensive

$ **Vera Cruz.** San Leonardo, 5. ☎ **91/547-11-50.** Main courses 400–950 ptas. ($3.20–$7.65); fixed-price menu 950 ptas. ($7.65). No credit cards. Daily 1–5pm and 8pm–midnight. Metro: Plaza de España. SPANISH.

Behind the landmark Edificio España, you'll find this old standby for hungry budget-minded visitors. It's a simple *económico,* but the food is acceptable and the service polite. The *menú del día* usually includes soup or appetizer, followed by a meat or fish dish, then cheese or fruit, plus bread and wine. The Vera Cruz also has daily specials like paella and *cocido,* a typical Madrid dish made of chickpeas, sausage, cabbage, and potatoes.

ON OR NEAR THE GRAN VÍA

Moderate

Arce. Augusto Figueroa, 32. ☎ **91/522-59-13.** Reservations recommended. Main courses 2,500–3,500 ptas. ($20–$28). AE, DC, MC, V. Mon–Fri 1:30–4pm, Mon–Sat 9pm–midnight. Closed week before Easter and Aug 15–31. Metro: Colón. BASQUE.

Arce has brought some of the best modern interpretations of Basque cuisine to the palates of Madrid, thanks to the enthusiasm of owner/chef Iñaki Camba and his wife, Theresa. Within a comfortably decorated dining room, you can enjoy simple dishes made of the finest ingredients; natural flavors are designed to dominate your taste buds. Examples include a salad of fresh scallops and an oven-baked casserole of fresh boletus mushrooms, seasoned lightly so the woodsy vegetable taste shines through. Look for unusual preparations of hake and seasonal variations of such game dishes as pheasant and woodcock.

La Barraca. Reina, 29–31. ☎ **91/532-71-54.** Reservations recommended. Main courses 1,800–3,000 ptas. ($14.40–$24); fixed-price menu 3,500 ptas. ($28). AE, DC, MC, V. Daily 1–4pm and 8:30pm–midnight. Metro: Gran Vía or Sevilla. Bus: 1, 2, or 74. VALENCIAN.

La Barraca is like a country inn right off the Gran Vía, and it's been a longtime local favorite. The food, frankly, used to be better, but perhaps our tastes have changed since our student days. This Valencian-style restaurant is a well-managed establishment recommendable for its tasty Levante cooking. There are four different dining rooms, three of which lie one flight above street level; they're colorfully cluttered with ceramics, paintings, photographs, Spanish lanterns, flowers, and local artifacts. The house specialty, paella à la Barraca, is made with pork and chicken. House specialties in the appetizer category include *desgarrat* (a salad made with codfish and red peppers), mussels in a white-wine sauce, and shrimp sautéed with garlic. In addition to the recommended paella, you can select at least 16 rice dishes, including black rice and queen paella. Main-dish specialties include brochette of angler fish and prawns and rabbit with fines herbes. Lemon-and-vodka sorbet brings the meal to a fitting finish.

El Mentidero de la Villa. Santo Tomé, 6. ☎ **91/308-12-85.** Reservations required. Main courses 1,950–2,400 ptas. ($15.60–$19.20). AE, DC, MC, V. Mon–Fri 1:30–4pm, Mon–Sat 9pm–midnight. Closed last 2 weeks of Aug. Metro: Alonso Martínez, Colón, or Gran Vía. Bus: 37. SPANISH/FRENCH.

This "Gossip Shop" (its name in English) is certainly a multicultural experience. The owner describes the cuisine as "modern Spanish with Japanese influence and a French cooking technique." That may sound confusing, but the end result is an achievement; each ingredient in every dish manages to retain its distinct flavor. The kitchen plays with such adventuresome combinations as veal liver in sage sauce, a type of spring roll filled with fresh shrimp and leeks, noisettes of veal with tarragon, filet steak with a sauce of mustard and brown sugar, and medaillons of venison with purées of chestnut and celery. Sherry trifle is but one of the notable desserts. The postmodern decor includes softly trimmed trompe l'oeil ceilings, exposed wine racks, ornate columns with unusual lighting, and a handful of antique carved horses from long-defunct merry-go-rounds.

INEXPENSIVE

Paellería Valenciana. Caballero de Gracia, 12. ☎ **91/531-17-85.** Reservations recommended. Main courses 1,250–2,500 ptas.($10–$20); fixed-price menus 1,250–1,600 ptas. ($10–$12.80). AE, MC, V. Mon–Sat 1:30–4:30pm. Metro: Gran Vía. SPANISH.

This lunch-only restaurant ranks as one of the best values in the city. The specialty is paella, which you must order by phone in advance. Once you arrive, you might begin with a homemade soup or the house salad, then follow with the paella, served in an iron skillet. At least two must order this rib-sticking fare. Among the desserts, the chef's special pride is razor-thin orange slices flavored with rum, coconut, sugar, honey, and raspberry sauce. A carafe of house wine comes with the set menu, and after lunch the owner comes around dispensing free cognac.

V.I.P. Gran Vía, 43. ☎ **91/559-64-57.** Main courses 750–1,400 ptas. ($6–$11.20). AE, DC, MC, V. Daily 9am–3am. Metro: Callao. FAST FOOD.

This place looks like a bookstore emporium from the outside, but in back it is a cafeteria serving fast food. You might begin with a cup of soothing gazpacho. There are more than a dozen V.I.P.s scattered throughout Madrid, but this is the most central one. Hamburgers are the rage here. Service leaves a lot to be desired.

NEAR THE PUERTA DEL SOL

EXPENSIVE

Lhardy. Carrera de San Jéronimo, 8. ☎ **91/521-33-85.** Reservations recommended in the upstairs dining room. Main dishes 1,900–5,000 ptas. ($15.20–$40). AE, DC, MC, V. Mon–Sat 1–3:30pm and 9–11:30pm. Closed Aug. Metro: Puerta del Sol. SPANISH/INTERNATIONAL.

Lhardy has been a Madrileño legend since it opened in 1839 as a gathering place for the city's literati and political leaders. In 1846 it entertained Dumas. On street level is what might be the most elegant snack bar in Spain. Within a dignified and antique setting of marble and varnished hardwoods, cups of steaming consommé are dispensed from silver samovars into delicate porcelain cups, and rows of croquettes, tapas, and sandwiches are served to stand-up clients who pay for their food at a cashier's kiosk near the entrance. Virtually anything you select (tapas, sandwiches, pastries, whatever) will cost around 90 pesetas (70¢). The ground-floor deli and takeaway service is open daily from 9am to 3pm and 5pm to 9:30pm.

The real culinary skill of the place, however, is found on Lhardy's second floor, where you'll find a formal restaurant decorated in the ornate Belle Epoque style of Isabel Segunda. Specialties of the house include fish, pork and veal, tripe in a

Family-Friendly Restaurants

Children visiting Spain will delight in patronizing any of the restaurants at the Parque de Atracciones in the **Casa de Campo** (see "Especially for Kids" in Chapter 5). Another good idea is to go on a picnic (see "Picnic Fare & Where to Eat It" later in this chapter).

For a taste of home, there are always the fast-food chains: McDonald's, Burger King, and Kentucky Fried Chicken. Remember, however, that the burgers and chicken will have a slightly different taste from those served back home.

Try taking the family to a local *tasca,* where children are bound to find something they like from the wide selection of tapas.

Foster's Hollywood *(see p. 125)* This restaurant has juicy hamburgers, plus lots of fare familiar to American kids.

V.I.P. *(see p. 118)* This chain spread across Madrid serves fast food, hamburgers, and other foodstuffs that kids go for in a big way, especially the ice cream concoctions.

garlicky tomato and onion wine sauce, and *cocido,* the celebrated chickpea stew of Madrid. *Soufflé sorpresa* (baked Alaska) is the dessert specialty.

Platerías Comedor. Plaza de Santa Ana, 11. ☎ **91/429-70-48.** Reservations recommended. Main courses 1,000–5,000 ptas. ($8–$40). AE, DC, MC, V. Mon–Fri 2:30–4pm, Mon–Sat 9pm–midnight. Metro: Puerta del Sol. SPANISH.

One of the most charming dining rooms in Madrid, Platerías Comedor has richly brocaded walls evocative of 19th-century Spain. Busy socializing may take place on the plaza outside, but this serene oasis makes few concessions to the new generation in its food, decor, or formally attired waiters. Specialties include beans with clams, stuffed partridge with cabbage and sausage, duck liver with white grapes, tripe à la Madrid, veal stew with snails and mushrooms, and guinea hen with figs and plums. Follow up any of these with the passionfruit sorbet. Many restaurants have sprouted up in recent years that serve better food, but Platerías Comedor continues to thrive as a culinary tradition; its old-fashioned atmosphere is hard to come by.

MODERATE

Café de Oriente. Plaza de Oriente, 2. ☎ **91/541-39-74.** Reservations recommended (in restaurant only). Café: tapas 850 ptas. ($6.80), coffee 650 ptas. ($5.20). Restaurant: main courses 1,700–3,950 ptas. ($13.60–$31.60). AE, DC, MC, V. Daily 1–4pm and 9pm–1:30am. Metro: Ópera. FRENCH/SPANISH.

The Oriente is a café-and-restaurant complex, the former being one of the most popular in Madrid. From the café tables on its terrace, there's a spectacular view of the Palacio Real (Royal Palace) and the Teatro Real. The dining rooms—Castilian upstairs, French Basque downstairs—are frequented by royalty and diplomats. Typical of the refined cuisine are vichyssoise, fresh vegetable flan, and many savory meat and fresh-fish offerings; service is excellent. Most visitors, however, patronize the café, trying if possible to get an outdoor table. The café is decorated in turn-of-the-century style, with banquettes and regal paneling, as befits its location. Pizza, tapas, and drinks (including Irish, Viennese, Russian, and Jamaican coffees) are served.

Casa Paco. Plaza Puerta Cerrada, 11. ☎ **91/366-31-66.** Reservations required. Main courses 1,100–3,800 ptas. ($8.80–$30.40); fixed-price menu 3,300 ptas. ($26.40). DC. Mon–Sat

1:30–4pm and 8:30pm–midnight. Closed Aug. Metro: Puerta del Sol, Ópera, or La Latina. Bus: 3, 21, or 65. STEAK.

Madrileños defiantly name Casa Paco, just beside the Plaza Mayor, when someone has the "nerve" to denigrate Spanish steaks. They know that here you can get the thickest, juiciest, tastiest steaks in Spain, which are priced according to weight. Señor Paco was the first in Madrid to sear steaks in boiling oil before serving them on plates so hot that the almost-raw meat continues to cook, preserving the natural juices. Located in the Old Town, this two-story restaurant has three dining rooms—but reservations are imperative. If you face a long wait, while away the time sampling the tapas at the *tasca* in front. Around the walls are autographed photographs of such notables as Frank Sinatra.

Casa Paco isn't just a steakhouse. You can start with a fish soup and proceed to grilled sole, baby lamb, or *Casa Paco cocido,* Madrid's famous chickpea and pork soup. You might top it off with one of the luscious desserts, but know that Paco no longer serves coffee. It made customers linger, keeping tables occupied while potential patrons had to be turned away.

✪ **El Cenador del Prado.** Prado, 4. ☎ **91/429-15-61.** Reservations recommended. Main courses 850–1,950 ptas. (46.80–$15.60); fixed-price menu 3,200 ptas. ($25.60). AE, DC, MC, V. Mon–Fri 1:45–4pm, Mon–Sat 9pm–midnight. Closed Aug 12–19. Metro: Puerta del Sol. INTERNATIONAL.

This restaurant is deceptively elegant. In the simple anteroom, an attendant will check you coat and packages in an elaborately carved armoire and the maître d' will usher you into one of a trio of rooms. Two of the rooms, done in tones of peach and sepia, have cove moldings and English furniture, as well as floor-to-ceiling gilded mirrors. A third room, the most popular, is ringed with lattices and flooded with sun from a skylight.

The food reflects a basically French influence, with the occasional Asian flourish. Many of the Spanish dishes are innovative. You can enjoy such well-flavored specialties as crêpes with salmon and Iranian caviar, a salad of crimson peppers and salted anchovies, a casserole of snails and oysters with mushrooms, a ceviche of salmon and shellfish, potato-leek soup studded with tidbits of hake and clams, sea bass with candied lemons, veal scaloppine stuffed with asparagus and garlic sprouts, and medaillons of venison served with pepper-and-fig chutney. Jackets and ties are recommended for men.

Inexpensive

Casa Alberto. Huertas, 18. ☎ **91/429-93-56.** Reservations recommended. Main courses 650–2,250 ptas. ($5.20–$18). AE, V. Tues–Sun 1–4pm, Tues–Sat 8:30–midnight. Metro: Antón Martín. CASTILIAN.

One of the oldest *tascas* in the neighborhood, Casa Alberto was originally established in 1827, and has thrived ever since. It lies on the street level of the house where Miguel de Cervantes lived briefly in 1614, and contains an appealing mixture of bullfighting memorabilia, engravings, and reproductions of Old Master paintings. Many visitors opt only for the tapas, which are continually replenished from platters on the bartop, but there's also a sit-down dining area for more substantial meals. Specialties include fried squid, shellfish in vinaigrette sauce, *chorizo* (sausage) in cider sauce, and several versions of baked or roasted lamb.

Hylogui. Ventura de la Vega, 3. ☎ **91/429-73-57.** Reservations recommended. Main courses 1,000–2,200 ptas. ($8–$17.60); fixed-price menus 1,400–1,700 ptas ($11.20–$13.60). AE, MC, V. Daily 1–4:30pm, Mon–Sat 9pm–midnight. Metro: Sevilla. SPANISH.

Hylogui, a local legend, is one of the largest dining rooms along Ventura de la Vega, but there are many arches and nooks for privacy. One globe-trotting American wrote enthusiastically that he took all his Madrid meals here, finding the soup pleasant and rich, the flan soothing, and the regional wine dry. The food is old-fashioned Spanish home-style cooking.

Mesón las Descalzas. Postigo San Martín, 3. ☎ **91/522-72-17.** Reservations recommended. Main courses 1,600–1,800 ptas. ($12.80–$14.40); fixed-price menu 1,200 ptas. ($9.60). AE, DC, MC, V. Daily noon–4pm and 8pm–midnight. Metro: Callao. SPANISH.

Las Descalzas, a recommended tavern-style restaurant, has a massive tapas bar that's often crowded at night. Behind a glass-and-wood screen is the restaurant section, its specialties including kidneys with sherry, *sopa castellana,* seafood soup, Basque-style hake, crayfish, shrimp, oysters, clams, and paella with shellfish—in other words, all that good food beloved during the Franco era. For entertainment, there is folk music.

✪ **La Plaza.** La Galería del Prado, Plaza de las Cortés, 7. ☎ **91/429-65-37.** Buffet 1,200–1,500 ptas. ($9.60–$12). Metro: Sevilla. SPANISH.

This restaurant serves as the underground centerpiece of one of Madrid's shopping complexes, La Galería del Prado. Surrounded by thick marble-sheathed walls, its bunker-style position eliminates the possibility of natural sunlight streaming through windows. Still, it's an attractive option for light, refreshing buffet meals within the expensive neighborhood near the Prado. Some of the tables overflow into the rotunda of the shopping mall, but most diners sit within a glossy series of lattices that form a garden-inspired enclave near a well-stocked salad bar (visits here are priced according to the portions you take). You might begin with Serrano ham or a mountain-fermented goat cheese, perhaps a homemade pâté. Daily specials include such dishes as ragoût of veal. Platters of pasta are another zesty way to fill up.

Taberna del Alabardero. Felipe V, 6. ☎ **91/547-25-77.** Reservations required for restaurant only. Bar: tapas 450–1,200 ptas. ($3.60–$9.60); glass of house wine 200 ptas. ($1.60). Restaurant: main courses 800–2,900 ptas. ($6.40–$23.20). AE, DC, V. Daily 1–4pm and 9–midnight. Metro: Ópera. BASQUE/SPANISH.

Because of its proximity to the Royal Palace, most patrons visit this little Spanish classic for its selection of tasty tapas, ranging from squid cooked in wine to fried potatoes dipped in hot sauce. Photographs of former patrons, including Nelson Rockefeller and the race-car driver Jackie Stewart, line the walls. The restaurant in the rear is said to be one of the city's best-kept secrets. Decorated in typical tavern style, it serves a savory Spanish and Basque cuisine with market-fresh ingredients.

RETIRO/SALAMANCA

VERY EXPENSIVE

✪ **La Gamella.** Alfonso XII, 4. ☎ **91/532-45-09.** Reservations required. Main courses 2,300–4,200 ptas. ($18.40–$33.60). AE, DC, MC, V. Mon–Fri 1:30–4pm, Mon–Sat 9pm–midnight. Closed 2 weeks around Easter and 2 weeks in Aug. Metro: Retiro. Bus: 19. CALIFORNIAN/CASTILIAN.

La Gamella established its gastronomic reputation shortly after it opened, several years ago, in less imposing quarters in another part of town. In 1988 its Illinois-born owner, former choreographer Dick Stephens, moved his restaurant into the 19th-century building where the Spanish philosopher Ortega y Gasset was born. The prestigious Horcher, one of the capital's legendary restaurants (see below), is just across the street—but the food at La Gamella is better. The russet-colored, high-ceilinged design invites customers to relax. Mr. Stephens has prepared his delicate and light-textured specialties for the King and Queen of Spain, as well as for Madrid's most talked-about artists and merchants, many of whom he knows and greets personally between sessions in his kitchen.

Typical menu items include a ceviche of Mediterranean fish, sliced duck liver in truffle sauce, a dollop of goat cheese served over caramelized endives, duck breast with peppers, and an array of well-prepared desserts, among which is an all-American cheesecake. Traditional Spanish dishes such as chicken with garlic have been added to the menu, plus what has been called "the only edible hamburger in Madrid." Because of the intimacy and the small dimensions of the restaurant, reservations are important.

Horcher. Alfonso XII, 6. ☎ **91/532-35-96.** Reservations required. Jackets and ties for men. Main courses 3,400–8,000 ptas. ($27.20–$64). AE, DC, MC, V. Mon–Fri 1:30–4pm, Mon–Sat 8:30pm–midnight. Metro: Retiro. GERMAN/INTERNATIONAL.

Horcher originated in Berlin in 1904. In 1943, prompted by a tip from a high-ranking German officer that Germany was losing the war, Herr Horcher moved his restaurant to Madrid. For years, it was known as the best dining room in the city, until culinary competition overtook that stellar position. Nevertheless, the restaurant has continued its grand European traditions, including excellent service.

Where to start? You might try the skate or shrimp tartare or the distinctive warm hake salad. Both the venison stew with green pepper and orange peel and the crayfish with parsley and cucumber are typical of the elegant fare served with impeccable style. Spanish artistocrats often come here in autumn to sample game dishes, including venison, wild boar, or roast wild duck. Other main courses include veal scaloppine in tarragon and sea bass with saffron. For dessert, the house specialty is crêpes Sir Holden, prepared at your table, with fresh raspberries, cream, and nuts.

EXPENSIVE

Alkalde. Jorge Juan, 10. ☎ **91/576-33-59.** Reservations required. Main courses 1,550–5,600 ptas. ($12.40–$44.80); fixed-price menu from 4,750 ptas. ($38). AE, DC, MC, V. Daily 1–4:30pm and 8:30pm–midnight. Closed Sat and Sun in July–Aug. Metro: Retiro or Serrano. Bus: 8, 20, 21, or 53. BASQUE/INTERNATIONAL.

For decades, Alkalde has been known for serving top-quality Spanish food in an old tavern setting. Decorated like a Basque inn, it has beamed ceilings and hams hanging from the rafters. Upstairs is a large *típico* tavern; downstairs is a maze of stone-sided cellars that are pleasantly cool in summer (though the whole place is air-conditioned).

Basque cookery is the best in Spain, and Alkalde honors that noble tradition. Begin with the cream of crabmeat soup, followed by *gambas a la plancha* (grilled shrimp) or *cigalas* (crayfish). Other well-recommended dishes include *mero salsa verde* (brill in a green sauce), trout Alkalde, stuffed peppers, and chicken steak. The dessert specialty is *copa Cardinal* (ice cream topped with fruit).

✪ **El Amparo.** Callejón de Puígcerdá, 8 (at corner of Jorge Juan). ☎ **91/431-64-56.** Reservations required. Main courses 3,000–4,000 ptas. ($24–$32); fixed-price menu 9,500 ptas. ($76). AE, MC, V. Mon–Fri 1:30–3:30pm, Mon–Sat 9:30–11:30pm. Closed week before Easter and in Aug. Metro: Goya. Bus: 21 or 53. BASQUE.

Behind the cascading vines on El Amparo's facade is one of Madrid's most elegant gastronomic enclaves. Inside, three tiers of roughly hewn wooden beams surround tables set with pink napery and glistening silver for a touch of cosmopolitan glamour. A sloping skylight floods the interior with sun by day; at night, pinpoints of light from the high-tech hanging lanterns create intimate shadows. Polite, uniformed waiters serve well-prepared nouvelle cuisine versions of cold marinated salmon with a tomato sorbet, cold cream of vegetable and shrimp soup, bisque of shellfish with Armagnac, ravioli stuffed with seafood, roast lamb chops with garlic purée, breast of duck, ragoût of sole, a platter of steamed fish of the day, roulades of lobster with soy sauce, and steamed hake with pepper sauce.

El Pescador. Calle José Ortega y Gasset, 75. ☎ **91/402-12-90.** Reservations required. Main courses 5,000–15,000 ptas. ($40–$120); fixed-price menu 6,250 ptas. ($50). MC, V. Mon–Sat 1:30–4pm and 8:30pm–midnight. Closed Aug. Metro: Lista. SEAFOOD.

El Pescador is a well-patronized fish restaurant that has become a favorite of Madrileños who appreciate the more than 30 kinds of fish prominently displayed in a glass case. Many of these are unknown in North America, and some originate off the coast of Galicia. The management air-freights them in and prefers to serve them grilled (*a la plancha*).

You might precede your main course with a spicy fish soup and accompany it with one of the many good wines from northeastern Spain. If you're not sure what to order (even the English translations might sound unfamiliar), try one of the many varieties and sizes of shrimp. These go under the names *langostinos, cigalas, santiaguinos,* and *carabineros.* Many of them are expensive and priced by the gram, so be careful when you order.

✪ **Viridiana.** Juan de Mena 14. ☎ **91/523-44-78.** Reservations recommended. Main courses 3,000–4,000 ptas. ($24–$32). AE, MC, V. Mon–Sat 1:30pm–4pm and 9pm–midnight. Closed 1 week at Easter and in Aug. Metro: Banco. INTERNATIONAL.

Viridiana is praised as one of the up-and-coming restaurants of Madrid, known for the creative imagination of its chef and part-owner, Abraham García. Menu specialties are usually contemporary adaptations of traditional recipes, and they change frequently according to the availability of the ingredients. Examples include a salad of exotic lettuces served with smoked salmon, guinea fowl stuffed with herbs and wild mushrooms, baby squid with curry served on a bed of lentils, roasted lamb served in puff pastry with fresh basil, and carpaccio of beef with a mousseline of white truffles.

INEXPENSIVE

Gran Café de Gijón. Paseo de Recoletos, 21. ☎ **521-54-25.** Reservations needed for restaurant. Main courses 3,000–5,000 ptas. ($24–$40); fixed-price menu 1,500 ptas. ($12). MC, V. Mon–Fri and Sun 9am–1:30am, Sat 9am–2am. Metro: Banco de España, Colón, or Recoletos. SPANISH.

Each of the old European capitals has a coffeehouse that traditionally attracts the literati—in Madrid it's the Gijón, which opened in 1888 in the heyday of the city's Belle Epoque. Artists and writers still patronize this venerated old café, many of them spending hours over one cup of coffee. Ernest Hemingway made the place famous for Americans, and such notables as Ava Gardner and Truman Capote followed in his footsteps in the 1950s. Open windows look out onto the wide paseo; the large terrace is perfect for sun worshippers and bird-watchers. Along one side of the café is a stand-up bar, and on the lower level is a restaurant. Food is prepared the "way it used to be" in Madrid. Patrons liked it then, and they come back for the same dishes enjoyed in their youth. In summer you can sit in the garden to enjoy a *blanco y negro* (black coffee with ice cream) or a mixed drink.

CHAMBERÍ

VERY EXPENSIVE

✪ **Las Cuatro Estaciones.** General Ibémñez Ibero, 5. ☎ **91/553-63-05.** Reservations required. Main courses 1,500–5,000 ptas. ($12–$40); fixed-price dinner 4,500 ptas. ($36). AE, DC,

MC, V. Mon–Fri 1:30–4pm and 9pm–midnight, Sat 9–11:30pm. Closed Aug. Metro: Guzmán el Bueno. MEDITERRANEAN.

Las Cuatro Estaciones is placed by gastronomes and horticulturists alike among their favorite Madrid dining spots, and it's become a neck-and-neck rival with the prestigious Jockey. In addition to superb food, the establishment prides itself on the masses of flowers that change with the season. Depending on the time of year, the mirrors surrounding the multilevel bar near the entrance reflect thousands of hydrangeas, chrysanthemums, or poinsettias. Even the napery matches whichever colors the resident botanist has chosen as the seasonal motif. Each person involved in food preparation spends a prolonged apprenticeship at restaurants in France before returning home to try their talents on the tastebuds of aristocratic Madrid.

Representative specialties include crab bisque, a petite marmite of fish and shellfish, a salad of eels, fresh asparagus and mushrooms in puff pastry with parsley-butter sauce, and a nouvelle cuisine version of blanquette of monkfish so tender that it melts in your mouth. The "festival of desserts" includes the specials the chef has concocted that day, a selection of which is brought temptingly to your table.

✪ **Jockey.** Amador de los Ríos, 6. ☎ **91/319-24-35.** Reservations required. Main courses 2,000–5,000 ptas. ($16–$40). AE, DC, MC, V. Mon–Sat 1–4pm and 9–11:30pm. Closed Aug. Metro: Colón. INTERNATIONAL.

For decades this was the premier restaurant of Spain, though that title is hotly contested today. The favorite of international celebrities, diplomats, and heads of state, it was once known as the "Jockey Club," although "Club" was eventually dropped because it suggested exclusivity. The restaurant, with tables on two levels, isn't large. Wood-paneled walls and colored linen provide warmth. Against the paneling are a dozen prints of jockeys mounted on horses—hence the name of the place.

Since Jockey's establishment shortly after World War II, the chef has prided himself on coming up with new and creative dishes. Sheiks can still order Beluga caviar from Iran, but others might settle happily for the goose-liver terrine or slices of Jabugo ham. Cold melon soup with shrimp is soothing on a hot day, especially when followed by grill-roasted young pigeon from Talavera or sole filets with figs in Chardonnay. Stuffed small chicken Jockey style is a specialty, as is *tripe Madrileña,* a local dish. Desserts are sumptuous.

✪ **Restaurante Belagua.** In the Hotel Palacio Santo Mauro, Calle Zurbano, 36. ☎ **91/319-69-00.** Reservations recommended. Main courses 2,300–3,900 ptas. ($18.40–$31.20). AE, DC, MC, V. Mon–Sat 1–4pm and 8:30–11:30pm. Closed national holidays. Metro: Rubén Darío or Alonso Martínez. BASQUE.

This glamorous restaurant was originally built in 1894 as a small palace in the French neoclassical style. In 1991 Catalán designer Josep Joanpere helped transform the building into a carefully detailed hotel (the Santo Mauro), which we've recommended separately (see above). On the hotel premises is this highly appealing postmodern restaurant, today one of the capital's finest.

Assisted by the well-mannered staff, you'll select from a menu whose inspiration and ingredients change with the seasons. Examples include watermelon-and-prawn salad, light cream of cold ginger soup, haddock baked in a crust of potatoes tinted with squid ink, filet of monkfish with prawn-and-zucchini sauce, and duck with honey and black cherries. Depending on the efforts of the chef, dessert might include miniature portions of flan with strawberry sauce plus an array of the day's pastries. The restaurant's name, incidentally, derives from a village in Navarre known for its natural beauty.

Inexpensive

La Bola. Calle de la Bola, 5. ☎ **91/547-69-30.** Reservations required. Main courses 1,400–2,200 ptas. ($11.20–$17.60); fixed-price menu 2,125 ptas. ($17). No credit cards. Mon–Sat 1–4pm and 9pm–midnight. Metro: Plaza de España or Ópera. Bus: 1 or 2. MADRILEÑA.

This is just the taberna in which to savor the 19th century. Just north of the Teatro Real, it's one of the few restaurants (if not the only one) left in Madrid with a blood-red facade; at one time, nearly all fashionable restaurants were so coated. La Bola hangs on to tradition like a tenacious bull. Time has passed, but not inside this restaurant: The soft, traditional atmosphere; the gentle and polite waiters; the Venetian crystal; the Carmen-red draperies; and the aging velvet preserve the 1870 ambience. Ava Gardner, with her entourage of bullfighters, used to patronize this establishment, but that was long before La Bola became so well known to tourists. Grilled sole, filet of veal, and roast veal are regularly featured. Basque-style hake and grilled salmon also are well recommended. A host of refreshing dishes to begin your meal include grilled shrimp, red-pepper salad, and lobster cocktail.

Foster's Hollywood. Magallanes, 1. ☎ **91/448-91-65.** Main courses 600–1,000 ptas. ($4.80–$8). AE, DC, MC, V. Sun–Thurs 1pm–midnight, Fri–Sat 1pm–2am. Metro: Quevedo. AMERICAN.

When Foster's opened its doors in 1971, it was not only the first American restaurant in Spain, it was one of the first in Europe. Since those early days it has grown to 15 restaurants in Madrid, and has even opened restaurants in Florida. A popular hangout for both locals and visiting Yanks, it offers a choice of dining venues, ranging from "classical club American" to studios, the latter evoking a working movie studio with props. Its varied menu includes Tex-Mex selections, ribs, steaks, sandwiches, freshly made salads, and, as its signature product, hamburgers grilled over natural charcoal in many variations. The *New York Times* once claimed that it had "probably the best onion rings in the world."

Locations where you can have a direct hook-up to the U.S.A. in Madrid are: Paseo de la Castellana, 116–118 (☎ **91/564-63-08**); Padre Damián, 38 (☎ **91/457-36-42**) next to the Eurobuilding hotel; Apolonio Morales, 3 (☎ **91/345-10-36**), in the Castellana area; Avenida de Brasil, 14 (☎ **91/597-16-74**), near the Meliá Castilla hotel; Princesa, 13(☎ **91/559-19-14**), near Plaza de España; Velázquez, 80 (☎ **91/435-61-28**), in the Serrano shopping area; Tamayo y Baus, 1 (☎ **91/531-51-15**), close to Plaza de la Cibeles and the Prado; Plaza Sagrado Corazón de Jesús, 2 (☎ **91/564-66-50**), next to the National Music Auditorium; Centro Comercial Arturo Soria (☎ **91/759-73-42**); and Centro Comercial La Vaguada (☎ **91/738-12-67**).

Ríofrío. Centro Colón; Plaza de Colán, 1. ☎ **91/319-29-77.** Main courses 700–3,200 ptas. ($5.60–$25.60); fixed-price menu 2,500 ptas. ($20); sandwiches 525–900 ptas. ($4.20–$7.20). AE, DC, MC, V. Daily 7:30am–2am. Metro: Colón. Bus: 5, 14, 21, 27, or 45. INTERNATIONAL.

Overlooking Madrid's version of New York's Columbus Circle, this is a sort of all-purpose place for drinking, eating, dining, or nightclubbing. The least-expensive way to eat here is to patronize one of two self-service cafeterias, where average meals run from 1,000 to 1,500 pesetas ($8–$12). There's also a large restaurant with an international cuisine, serving meals averaging 3,500 pesetas ($28), plus yet another dining room for informal lunches, dinners, snacks, or aperitifs. The spacious glassed-in terrace, open year-round, is known for serving some of the best paella in Madrid. Finally, there's even a nightclub, El Descubrimiento, should you desire to make an evening of it. The club serves dinner costing from 4,500 pesetas ($36), which includes not only the meal but a show to follow. Sandwiches are also available throughout the day if you'd like just a light bite in the hot Madrid sun.

CHAMARTÍN

VERY EXPENSIVE

✪ **Zalacaín.** Alvarez de Baena, 4. ☎ **91/561-48-40.** Reservations required. Main courses 3,500–5,000 ptas. ($28–$40). AE, DC, MC, V. Mon–Fri 1:30–3:30pm, Mon–Sat 9–11:30pm. Closed week before Easter and in Aug. Metro: Rubén Darío. INTERNATIONAL.

Outstanding in both food and decor, Zalacaín opened in 1973 and introduced nouvelle cuisine to Spain. It is reached by an illuminated walk from Paseo de la Castellana and housed at the garden end of a modern apartment complex. In fact, it's within an easy walk of such deluxe hotels as the Castellana and the Miguel Angel. The name of the restaurant comes from the intrepid hero of Basque author Pío Baroja's 1909 novel, *Zalacaín El Aventurero.* Zalacaín is small, exclusive, and expensive. It has the atmosphere of an elegant old mansion: The walls are covered with textiles, and some are decorated with Audubon-type paintings. Men should wear jackets and ties.

The menu features many Basque and French specialties, often with nouvelle cuisine touches. It might offer a superb sole in a green sauce, but it also knows the glory of grilled pig's feet. Among the most recommendable main dishes are a stew of scampi in cider sauce; crêpes stuffed with smoked fish; ravioli stuffed with mushrooms, foie gras, and truffles; Spanish bouillabaisse; and veal escalopes in orange sauce. For dessert, we'd suggest baked apples stuffed with cinnamon-flavored custard.

EXPENSIVE

Asador Errota-Zar. Corazón de Maria, 32. ☎ **91/413-52-24.** Reservations required. Main courses 1,500–3,000 ptas. ($12–$24). AE, DC, MC, V. Mon–Sat 1–4pm and 9pm–midnight. Closed Aug; Dec 24, 25, 31; Jan 1; and Easter. Metro: Alfonso XIII or Cartagena. Bus: 43. BASQUE.

An *asador* is a kind of Spanish restaurant that typically roasts meat on racks or spits over an open fire, and the Errota-Zar is one of Madrid's best. (The technique is said to have been brought to the Basque country by repatriated emigrés who learned it in Argentina and Uruguay a century ago. Since then, the Basques have claimed it as their own and presumably do it better than anyone else.) Asador Errota-Zar, contained behind the stucco-and-stone walls of an antique mill, is managed by Basque-born Segundo Olano and his wife, Eugenia.

You might begin your meal with slices of pork loin, grilled spicy sausage, scrambled eggs with boletus mushrooms, a savory soup made from Basque kidney beans, or red peppers stuffed with codfish. The real specialties of the house are the succulent cuts of beef, fish, or pork—first gently warmed, then seared, then cooked by the expert hand of Sr. Olano himself. The restaurant is at its most interesting when groups of friends arrive, sharing portions of several different appetizers among themselves before concentrating on a main course. The offerings of meat tend to be very fresh but rather limited. The culinary variety here lies in the appetizers.

El Bodegón. Pinar, 15. ☎ **91/562-31-37.** Reservations required. Main courses 3,400–4,000 ptas. ($27.20–$32); fixed-price dinner 4,900 ptas. ($39.20). AE, DC, MC, V. Mon–Fri 1:30–4pm, Mon–Sat 9pm–midnight. Closed holidays and Aug. Metro: Rubén Darío. INTERNATIONAL/BASQUE/SPANISH.

El Bodegón is imbued with the atmosphere of a gentleman's club for hunting enthusiasts. International globe-trotters are attracted here, especially in the evening, as the restaurant is near such deluxe hotels as the Castellana and the Miguel Angel. King Juan Carlos and Queen Sofía have dined here.

Waiters in black and white, with gold braid and buttons, bring dignity to the food service. Even bottled water is served champagne style, chilled in a silver floor stand. There are two main dining rooms—both conservative and oak-beamed in the country-inn style.

We recommend cream of crayfish bisque or velvety vichyssoise to launch your meal. Main-course selections include grilled filet mignon with classic béarnaise sauce and venison bourguignonne. Other main-course selections include shellfish au gratin Escoffier, quails Fernand Point, tartare of raw fish marinated in parsley-enriched vinaigrette, and smoked salmon.

✪ **El Cabo Mayor.** Juan Ramón Jiménez, 37. ☎ **91/350-87-76.** Reservations recommended. Main courses 2,000–3,400 ptas. ($16–$27.20). AE, DC, MC, V. Mon–Fri 1:30–5pm and 9pm–1:30am, Sat 9pm–1:30am. Closed 1 week at Easter and in Aug. Metro: Cuzco. SEAFOOD.

In the prosperous northern edges of Madrid, El Cabo Mayor is not far from the city-within-a-city of Chamartín Station. This is one of the best, most popular, and most stylish restaurants in Madrid, attracting on occasion the King and Queen of Spain. The open-air staircase leading to the entranceway descends from a manicured garden on a quiet side street. A battalion of uniformed doormen stand ready to greet arriving taxis. The restaurant's decor is a nautically inspired mass of hardwood panels, brass trim, old-fashioned pulleys and ropes, a tile floor custom-painted with sea-green and blue replicas of waves, and hand-carved models of fishing boats. In brass replicas of portholes, some dozen bronze statues honoring fishers and their craft are displayed in illuminated positions of honor.

Menu choices include paprika-laden peppers stuffed with fish, a salad composed of Jabugo ham and foie gras of duckling, fish soup from Cantabria, stewed sea bream with thyme, asparagus mousse, salmon in sherry sauce, and loin of veal in cassis sauce. Desserts include such selections as a mousse of rice with pine-nut sauce.

✪ **El Olivo Restaurant.** General Gallegos, 1. ☎ **91/359-15-35.** Reservations recommended. Main courses 2,950–3,500 ptas. ($23.60–$28); fixed-price meals 3,850–5,600 ptas. ($30.80–$44.80). AE, DC, MC, V. Tues–Sat 1–4pm and 9pm–midnight. Closed Aug 15–31 and 4 days around Easter. Metro: Plaza de Castilla. MEDITERRANEAN.

Locals praise the success of a non-Spaniard (in this case, French-born Jean Pierre Vandelle) in recognizing the international appeal of two of Spain's most valuable culinary resources, olive oil and sherry. His likable restaurant, located in northern Madrid, pays homage to the glories of the Spanish olive. Designed in tones of green and amber, it is the only restaurant in Spain that wheels a trolley stocked with 40 regional olive oils from table to table. From the trolley, diners select a variety to soak up with chunks of rough-textured bread that is, according to your taste, seasoned with a dash of salt.

Menu specialties include grilled filet of monkfish marinated in herbs and olive oil, then served with black-olive sauce over a compote of fresh tomatoes, and four preparations of codfish arranged on a single platter and served with a *pil-pil* sauce. (Named after the sizzling noise it makes as it bubbles on a stove, *pil-pil* sauce is composed of codfish gelatin and herbs that are whipped into a mayonnaise-like consistency with olive oil.) Desserts might be one of several different chocolate pastries. A wide array of reasonably priced Bordeaux and Spanish wines can accompany your meal.

A final note: Many clients deliberately arrive early as an excuse to linger within El Olivo's one-of-a-kind sherry bar. Although other drinks are offered, the bar features more than a hundred brands of *vino de Jerez,* more than practically any other establishment in Madrid. Priced at 300 to 800 pesetas ($2.40–$6.40) per glass, they make the perfect aperitif.

MODERATE

O'Pazo. Calle Reina Mercedes, 20. ☎ **91/553-23-33.** Reservations required. Main courses 2,000–3,000 ptas. ($16–$24). MC, V. Mon–Sat 1–4pm and 8:30pm–midnight. Closed Aug. Metro: Nuevos Ministerios or Alvarado. Bus: 3 or 5. GALICIAN/SEAFOOD.

O'Pazo is a deluxe Galician restaurant, viewed by local cognoscenti as one of the top seafood places in the country. The fish is flown in daily from Galicia and much of it is priced by weight, depending on market rates. In front is a cocktail lounge and bar, all in polished brass, with low sofas and paintings. Carpeted floors, cushioned Castilian furniture, soft lighting, and colored-glass windows complete the picture. O'Pazo lies north of the center of Madrid, near the Chamartín Station.

The fish and shellfish soup is delectable, although others gravitate to the seaman's broth as a beginning course. Natural clams are succulent, as are *cigalas* (a kind of crayfish), spider crabs, and Jabugo ham. Main dishes range from baby eels to sea snails, from scallops Galician style to *zarzuela* (a seafood and casserole).

INEXPENSIVE

Alfredo's Barbacoa. Juan Hurtado de Mendoza, 11. ☎ **91/345-16-39.** Reservations recommended. Main courses 700–2,000 ptas. ($5.60–$16). AE, DC, MC, V. Mon–Sat 1–5pm and 8:30pm–midnight. Metro: Cuzco. AMERICAN.

Alfredo's is a popular rendezvous for Americans longing for home-style food. Al arrives at his bar/restaurant wearing boots, blue jeans, and a 10-gallon hat; his friendly welcome has made the place a center for both his friends and newcomers to Madrid. You *can* have hamburgers here, but they are of the barbecued variety, and you might prefer the barbecued spareribs or chicken. The salad bar is an attraction. And it's a rare treat to be able to have corn on the cob in Spain.

The original Alfredo's Barbacoa, Lagasca, 5 (☎ **91/576-62-71**), is still in business, and also under Al's auspices. Metro: Retiro.

CHUECA

INEXPENSIVE

$ La Argentina. Gravina, 19. ☎ **91/531-91-17.** Main courses 800–1,250 ptas. ($6.40–$10); fixed-price menu 1,200 ptas. ($9.60). No credit cards. Tues–Sun noon–4pm, Tues–Sat 9pm–midnight. Closed July 25–Aug 31. Metro: Chueca. INTERNATIONAL.

La Argentina is run under the watchful eye of the owner, Andres Rodríguez. The restaurant has only 16 tables, but the food is well prepared, sort of Spanish family-style. The best bets are cannelloni Rossini, noodle soup, creamed spinach, and meat dishes, including entrecôte and roast veal. All dishes are served with mashed or french-fried potatoes. For dessert, have a baked apple or rice pudding. The decor is simple and clean, and you're usually served by one of the two waitresses who have been here for years.

$ El Inca. Gravina, 23. ☎ **91/532-77-45.** Reservations required on weekends. Main courses 1,800–3,500 ptas. ($14.40–$28); fixed-price menu 1,800 ptas. ($14.40) available at lunch. AE, DC, V. Tues–Sat 1:30–5pm and 9pm–1am, Sun 1:30-5pm. Closed Aug. Metro: Chueca. PERUVIAN.

For a taste of South America, try El Inca, decorated with Incan motifs and artifacts. Since it opened in the early 1970s, it has hosted its share of diplomats and celebrities, although you're more likely to see families and local office workers. The house cocktail is a deceptively potent *pisco* sour—the recipe comes straight from the Andes. Many of the dishes contain potatoes, the national staple of Peru. The salad of potatoes and black olives is given unusual zest with a white-cheese sauce. Other specialties are the *ceviche de merluza* (raw hake marinated with onions) and *aji de gallina* (a chicken-and-rice dish made with peanut sauce), a Peruvian favorite.

Nabucco. Calle Hortaleza, 108. ☎ **91/310-06-11.** Reservations recommended. Pizza 595–825 ptas. ($4.75–$6.60); main courses 720–1,380 ptas. ($5.75–$11.05). AE, DC, MC, V. Mon–Sat 1:30–4pm, Mon–Thurs 8:45pm–midnight, Fri–Sat9pm–1am. Metro: Alonso Martínez. Bus: 7 or 36. ITALIAN.

In a neighborhood of Spanish restaurants, the Italian format here comes as a welcome change. The decor resembles a postmodern update of an Italian ruin, complete with trompe l'oeil walls painted like marble. Roman portrait busts and a prominent bar lend a dignified air. Menu choices include cannelloni, a good selection of veal dishes, and such main courses as osso buco. You might begin your meal with a selection of antipasti.

Taberna Carmencita. Libertad, 16. ☎ **91/531-66-12.** Reservations recommended. Main courses 900–2,500 ptas. ($7.20–$20); fixed-price menu 1,200 ptas. ($9.60) available only at lunch. AE, DC, MC, V. Mon–Fri 1–4pm, Mon–Sat 9pm–midnight. Metro: Chueca. SPANISH/ BASQUE.

Carmencita, founded in 1840 and exquisitely restored, is a street-corner enclave of old Spanish charm, filled with 19th-century detailing and tilework. It was a favorite hangout for the poet Federico García Lorca, as well as a meeting place for intelligentsia in the pre–Civil War days. Meals might include entrecôte with green pepper sauce, escalope of veal, braised mollusks with port, filet of pork, codfish with garlic, and Bilbao-style hake. Every Thursday the special dish is a complicated version of Madrid's famous cocido. Patrons wax lyrical over this regional stew; at least the chefs have had decades to get it right.

Tienda de Vinos. Augusto Figueroa, 35. ☎ **91/521-70-12.** Main courses 600–2,000 ptas. ($4.80–$16); fixed-price menu 1,100 ptas. ($8.80). No credit cards. Mon–Sat 9am–4:30pm and 8:30pm–midnight. Metro: Chueca. SPANISH.

Officially this restaurant is known as the "Wine Store," but ever since the 1930s Madrileños have called it "El Comunista." Its now-deceased owner was a fervent Communist, and many locals who shared his political beliefs patronized the establishment. This rickety old wine shop with a few tables in the back is quite fashionable with actors and journalists looking for Spanish fare without frills. There is a menu, but no one ever looks at it—just ask what's available. Nor do you get a bill; you're just told how much to pay. You sit at simple wooden tables with wooden chairs and benches; walls are decorated with old posters, calendars, pennants, and clocks. Start with garlic or vegetable soup or lentils, followed by lamb chops, tripe in a spicy sauce, or meatballs and soft-set eggs with asparagus.

OFF THE PLAZA MAYOR

Expensive

Casa Lucio. Cava Baja 35. ☎ **91/365-32-52.** Reservations recommended. Main courses 2,000–3,500 ptas. ($16–$28). AE, DC, MC, V. Sun–Fri 1–4pm, daily 9pm–midnight. Closed Aug. Metro: La Latina. CASTILIAN.

Set on a historic street whose edges once marked the perimeter of Old Madrid, this is a venerable tasca with all the requisite antique accessories. Dozens of cured hams hang from hand-hewn beams above the well-oiled bar. Among the clientele is a stable of sometimes surprisingly well-placed public figures—even perhaps, the King of Spain. The two dining rooms, each on a different floor, have whitewashed walls, tile floors, and exposed brick. A well-trained staff offers classic Castilian food, which might include Jabugo ham with broad beans, shrimp in garlic sauce, hake with green sauce, several types of roasted lamb, and a thick steak served sizzling hot on a heated platter, *churrasco de la casa*.

Las Cuevas de Luís Candelas. Calle de Cuchilleros, 1. ☎ **91/366-54-28.** Reservations required. Main courses 1,400–3,400 ptas. ($11.20–$27.20). DC, MC, V. Daily 1–4pm and 8pm–midnight. Metro: Puerta del Sol. SPANISH/INTERNATIONAL.

Right down the steps from the popular but very touristy Mesón del Corregidor, a competitor restaurant, is the even-better-known Las Cuevas de Luís Candelas, housed in a building dating from 1616. The restaurant opened its doors at the turn of the century. Enter through a doorway under an arcade, on steps leading to the Calle de Cuchilleros—the nightlife center of Madrid that teems with restaurants, flamenco clubs, and rustic taverns. The restaurant is named after Luís Candelas, an 18th-century bandit who's sometimes known as the "Spanish Robin Hood." He is said to have hidden out in this maze of *cuevas* (dens). Although the menu is in English, the cuisine is authentically Spanish. Specialties include the chef's own style of hake. To begin your meal, you might try another house dish, *sopa de ajo Candelas* (garlic soup). Roast suckling pig and roast lamb, as in the other restaurants on the Plaza Mayor, are featured, but we prefer these two dishes at Botín (see below).

El Schotis. Cava Baja, 11. ☎ **91/365-32-30.** Reservations recommended. Main courses 1,000–2,550 ptas. ($8–$20.40); fixed-price menu 3,150 ptas. ($25.20). AE, DC, MC, V. Tues–Sun 1–4pm, Tues–Sat 9pm–midnight. Closed 2 weeks in Aug. Metro: Puerta del Sol or La Latina. SPANISH.

El Schotis was established in 1962 within a solid stone building on one of Madrid's oldest and most historic streets. A series of large and pleasingly old-fashioned dining rooms is the setting for an animated crowd of Madrileños and foreign visitors, who receive ample portions of conservative, well-prepared vegetables, salads, soups, fish, and above all, meat. Specialties of the house include roasted baby lamb, grilled steaks and veal chops, shrimp with garlic, fried hake in green sauce, and traditional desserts. Although one reader found everything but the gazpacho "ho-hum," this local favorite pleases thousands of diners annually. There's a bar near the entrance for tapas and before- or after-dinner drinks.

Moderate

Los Galayos. Calle Botoneras, 5. ☎ **91/366-30-28.** Reservations recommended. Main courses 1,160–3,875 ptas. ($9.30–$31). AE, MC, V. Daily 12:30pm–12:45am. Metro: Puerta del Sol. SPANISH.

Its location is among the most desirable in the city, on a narrow side street about three steps from the arcades of Plaza Mayor. Set within two separate houses, the restaurant has flourished on this site since 1894. In summer, cascades of vines accent a series of tables and chairs on the cobblestones outside, perfect for tapas sampling and people watching. Some visitors consider an evening here among the highlights of their trip to Spain.

The ambience inside evokes Old Castile; the several dining rooms sport vaulted or beamed ceilings. The Grande family, your multilingual hosts, prepare traditional versions of fish, shellfish, pork, veal, and beef in time-tested ways. Suckling pig, baby goat, and roasted lamb are almost always featured.

Gure-Etxea (Restaurante Vasco). Plaza de la Paja, 12. ☎ **91/365-61-49.** Reservations recommended. Main courses 1,425–3,000 ptas. ($11.40–$24); fixed-price menu 3,500 ptas. ($28). AE, DC, MC, V. Tues–Sat 1:30–4pm, Mon–Sat 9pm–midnight. Closed Aug. Metro: La Latina. BASQUE.

This restaurant is housed in a stone-walled building that was the convent for the nearby Church of San Andres before the Renaissance. Today, amid a decor enhanced by Romanesque arches, vaulted tunnels, and dark-grained paneling, you can enjoy selections from a small but choice menu. Specialties include *lomo de merluza* (hake), *calamares en su tinta* (squid in its own ink), Gure-Etxea's special filet of sole, and *bacalau al pil-pil* (codfish in a fiery sauce).

✪ **Sobrino de Botín.** Calle de Cuchilleros, 17. ☎ **91/366-42-17.** Reservations required. Main courses 800–3,000 ptas. ($6.40–$24); fixed-price menu 3,700 ptas. ($29.60). AE, DC, MC, V. Daily 1–4pm and 8pm–midnight. Metro: La Latina or Ópera. SPANISH.

Ernest Hemingway made this restaurant famous. In the final two pages of his novel *The Sun Also Rises,* Jake invites Brett to Botín for the Segovian specialty of roast suckling pig, washed down with Rioja Alta.

By merely entering its portals, you step back to 1725, the year the restaurant was founded. You'll see an open kitchen, with a charcoal hearth, hanging copper pots, an 18th-century tile oven for roasting the suckling pig, and a big pot of regional soup whose aroma wafts across the tables. Your host, Don Antonio, never loses his cool—even when he has 18 guests standing in line waiting for tables.

The two house specialties are roast suckling pig and roast Segovian lamb. From the à la carte menu, you might try the fish-based "quarter-of-an-hour" soup. Good main dishes include baked Cantabrian hake and filet mignon with potatoes. The dessert list features strawberries (in season) with whipped cream. You can wash down your meal with Valdepeñas or Aragón wine, although most guests order sangría.

INEXPENSIVE

La Chata. Cava Baja, 24. ☎ **91/366-14-58.** Reservations recommended. Main dishes 1,500–2,300 ptas. ($12–$18.40). AE, MC, V. Daily 12:30–5pm; Mon–Sat 7pm–midnight or 2am, Sun 7pm–midnight. Metro: La Latina. SPANISH.

The cuisine here is Castilian, Galician, and northern Spanish. Set behind a heavily ornamented tile facade, the place has a stand-up tapas bar at the entrance and a formal restaurant in a side room. Many locals linger at the darkly paneled bar, which is framed by hanging Serrano hams, cloves of garlic, and photographs of bullfighters. Full meals might include such dishes as roast suckling pig, roast lamb, *calamares en su tinta* (squid in its own ink), grilled filet of steak with peppercorns, and omelets flavored with strips of eel.

El Cuchi. Calle de Cuchilleros, 3. ☎ **91/366-44-24.** Reservations required. Main courses 1,500–3,000 ptas. ($12–$24). AE, DC, MC, V. Tues–Sun 1–4pm, daily 8pm–midnight. Metro: Puerta del Sol. MEXICAN/SPANISH.

A few doors down from Botín (see above), El Cuchi defiantly claims that "Hemingway never ate here." However, just about everybody else has, attracted by both its low prices and its labyrinth of dining rooms. A European link in Mexico's famous Carlos 'n Charlie's chain, the Madrid restaurant stands off a corner of Plaza Mayor. Ceiling beams and artifacts suggest rusticity. Menu specialties include black bean soup, ceviche, guacamole, stuffed trout, and roast suckling pig (much cheaper than that served at Botín).

NEAR PLAZA DE CUZCO

Chez Lou Crêperie. Pedro Munguruza, 6. ☎ **91/350-34-16.** Reservations required on weekends. Crêpes 800–1,800 ptas. ($6.40–$14.40). No credit cards. Mon–Fri 1:30–4pm and 8pm–midnight. Metro: Plaza de Castilla. Bus: 27 or 147. FRENCH.

Near the Eurobuilding in the northern sector of Madrid, Chez Lou stands near the huge mural by Joan Miró, which would be worth the trek up here alone. Come here if you're seeking a light supper when it's too hot for one of those table-groaning Spanish meals. In this intimate setting, you get well-prepared and reasonably priced French food. The restaurant serves pâté as an appetizer, then a large range of crêpes with many different fillings. Folded envelope style, the crêpes are not tearoom size, and they're perfectly adequate as a main course. We've sampled several variations, finding the ingredients nicely blended yet distinct enough to retain their identity. A favorite is the large crêpe stuffed with minced onions, cream, and smoked salmon. The ham-and-cheese crêpe is also tasty.

NEAR RECOLETOS

La Galette. Conde de Aranda, 11. ☎ **91/576-06-41.** Reservations recommended. Main courses 1,100–1,700 ptas. ($8.80–$13.60); fixed-price menu 2,500 ptas. ($20). AE, DC, MC, V. Mon–Sat 2–4pm and 9pm–midnight. Metro: Retiro. VEGETARIAN/INTERNATIONAL.

La Galette was one of Madrid's first vegetarian restaurants, and it remains one of the best. Small and charming, it lies in a residential and shopping area in the exclusive Salamanca district, near Plaza de la Independencia and the northern edge of Retiro Park. There is a limited selection of meat dishes, but the true allure lies in this establishment's imaginative preparation of vegetables. Examples include baked stuffed peppers, omelets, eggplant croquettes, and even vegetarian "hamburgers." Some of the dishes are macrobiotic. The place is also noted for its mouth-watering pastries. The same owners also operate La Galette II, in the same complex.

BEST OF THE TASCAS

Don't starve waiting around for Madrid's fashionable 9:30 or 10pm dinner hour. Throughout the city you'll find *tascas,* bars that serve wine and platters of tempting hot and cold hors d'oeuvres known as tapas: mushrooms, salads, baby eels, shrimp, lobster, mussels, sausage, ham—and, in one establishment at least, bull testicles. Below we've listed our favorite tapas bars. Keep in mind that you can often save pesetas by ordering at the bar rather than occupying a table.

Antonio Sánchez. Mesón de Parades, 13. ☎ **91/539-78-26.** Tapas (in the bar) 200–600 ptas. ($1.60–$4.80); main courses 1,200–2,500 ptas. ($9.60-$20); fixed-price menu 1,200 ptas. ($9.60) available at lunch Mon–Fri. MC, V. Daily noon–4pm, Mon–Sat 8pm–midnight. Metro: Tirso de Molina. SPANISH.

Named in 1850 after the founder's son, who was killed in the bullring, Antonio Sánchez is full of bullfighting memorabilia, including the stuffed head of the animal that gored young Sánchez. Also featured on the dark paneled walls are three works by the Spanish artist Zuloaga, who had his last public exhibition in this restaurant near Plaza Tirso de Molina. A limited array of tapas, including garlic soup, are served with Valdepeñas wine drawn from a barrel—though many guests ignore the edibles in favor of smoking cigarettes and arguing the merits of this or that bullfighter. A restaurant in the back serves Spanish food with a vaguely French influence.

$ **Casa Mingo.** Paseo de la Florida, 2. ☎ **91/547-79-18.** Main courses 550–1,200 ptas. ($4.40–$9.60). No credit cards. Daily 11am–midnight. Metro: Norte, then 15-minute walk. SPANISH.

Picnic Fare & Where to Eat It

On a hot day, do as the Madrileños do: Secure the makings of a picnic lunch and head for Casa de Campo (metro: El Batán), those once-royal hunting grounds in the west of Madrid across the Manzanares River. Children delight in this adventure, as they can also visit a boating lake, the Parque de Atracciones, and the Madrid zoo.

Your best choice for picnic fare is **Mallorca,** Velázquez, 59 (☎ **91/431-99-00;** metro: Velázquez). This place has all the makings for a deluxe picnic. It's open daily from 9am to 9pm.

Another good bet is **Rodilla,** Preciados, 25 (☎ **91/522-57-01;** metro: Callao), where you can find sandwiches, pastries, and takeaway tapas. Sandwiches, including vegetarian, meat, and fish, begin at 80 pesetas (65¢). It's open daily from 8:30am to 10:30pm.

Casa Mingo has been known for decades for its Asturian cider, both still and bubbly. The perfect accompanying tidbit is a piece of the local Asturian *cabrales* (goat cheese), but the roast chicken is the specialty of the house, with an unbelievable number of helpings served daily. There's no formality here, since customers share big tables under the vaulted ceiling in the dining room. In summer the staff sets up tables and wooden chairs out on the sidewalk. This is not so much a restaurant but a bodega/taverna that serves food.

Cervecería Alemania. Plaza de Santa Ana, 6. ☎ **91/429-70-33.** Beer 100–200 ptas. (80¢–$1.60); tapas 200–1,800 ptas. ($1.60–$14.40). No credit cards. Wed–Thurs and Sun–Mon 10am–12:30am, Fri Sat 10am–2am. Metro: Alonso Martín or Sevilla. TAPAS.

Hemingway used to frequent this casual spot with the celebrated bullfighter Luís Miguel Dominguín—ask the waiter to point out "Hemingway's table." However, it earned its name because of its long-ago German clients. Opening directly onto one of the liveliest little plazas in Madrid, it clings to its turn-of-the-century traditions. Young Madrileños are fond of stopping in for a mug of draft beer. You can sit at one of the tables, leisurely sipping beer or wine, since the waiters make no attempt to hurry you along. To accompany your beverage, try the fried sardines or a Spanish omelet.

Cervecería Santa Bárbara. Plaza de Santa Bárbara, 8. ☎ **91/319-04-049.** Beer 150–290 ptas. ($1.20–$2.30); tapas 1,000–3,750 ptas. ($8–$30). No credit cards. Daily 11am–11:30pm. Metro: Alonzo or Martínez. Bus: 3, 7, or 21. TAPAS.

Unique in Madrid, Cervecería Santa Bárbara is an outlet for a beer factory, and the management has spent a lot to make it modern and inviting. Hanging globe lights and spinning ceiling fans create an attractive ambience, as does the black-and-white checkerboard marble floor. You go here for beer, of course: *cerveza negra* (black beer) or *cerveza dorada* (golden beer). The local brew is best accompanied by homemade potato chips or by fresh shrimp, lobster, crabmeat, or barnacles. You can either stand at the counter or go directly to one of the wooden tables for waiter service.

Taberna Toscana. Ventura de la Vega, 22. ☎ **91/429-60-31.** Beer 120 ptas. (95¢), glass of wine 90 ptas. (70¢); tapas 200–4,000 ptas. ($1.60–$32). V. Tues–Sat noon–4pm, Mon and Wed–Sat 8pm–midnight. Closed Aug. Metro: Puerta del Sol or Sevilla. TAPAS.

Many Madrileños begin their nightly *tasca* crawl here. The aura is that of a village inn that's far removed from 20th-century Madrid. You sit on crude country stools, under sausages, pimientos, and sheaves of golden wheat that hang from the age-darkened beams. The long, tiled *tasca* bar is loaded with tasty tidbits, including the house specialties: *lacón y cecina* (boiled ham), *habas* (broad beans) with Spanish ham, and *chorizo* (a sausage of red peppers and pork)—all are almost meals in themselves. Especially delectable are the kidneys in sherry sauce and the snails in hot sauce.

5 Madrid Attractions

Madrid has changed drastically in recent years. No longer is it fair to say that it has only the Prado and after you see that you should head for Toledo or El Escorial. As you will discover, Madrid has something to amuse and delight everyone.

SUGGESTED ITINERARIES

If You Have One Day

If you have just arrived in Spain after a long flight, don't tackle too much on your first day. Spend the morning at the Prado, one of the world's great art museums, arriving when it opens at 9am (remember, it's closed on Mondays). Have lunch and then visit the Palacio Real (Royal Palace). Have an early dinner near the Plaza Mayor.

If You Have Two Days

Spend Day 1 as described above. On Day 2 take a trip to Toledo, where you can visit El Greco's House and Museum, the Santa Cruz Museum, the Church of Santo Tomé, and the Alcázar. Return to Madrid in the evening.

If You Have Three Days

Follow the suggestions for Days 1 and 2. On Day 3 take a one-hour train ride to the Monastery of San Lorenzo del Escorial, in the foothills of the Sierra de Guadarrama. Return to Madrid in the evening.

If You Have Five Days

Follow the suggestions for Days 1 to 3. Day 4 would be a very busy day indeed if you visited the Thyssen-Bornemisza Museum in the morning (it opens at 10am), took a walking tour of Medieval Madrid (see below), and toured the Museo Nacional Centro de Arte Reina Sofía in the late afternoon or early evening (it closes at 9pm on most nights). Here you can see Picasso's *Guernica,* as well as other great 20th-century art. Have dinner once again at one of the many restaurants off the Plaza Mayor. On Day 5 take a trip to Segovia, in Old Castile. Its Alcázar, Roman aqueduct, and cathedral are the major attractions. Sample regional specialties at lunch and return to Madrid for dinner in the old town.

1 The Top Attractions

MAJOR MUSEUMS

✪ **Museo del Prado.** Paseo del Prado. ☎ **91/420-28-36.** Admission 450 ptas. ($3.60). Tues–Sat 9am–7pm, Sun and holidays 9am–2pm. Closed Jan 1, Good Friday, May 1, and Dec 25. Metro: Banco de España or Atocha. Bus: 10, 14, 27, 34, 37, or 45.

With more than 7,000 paintings, the Prado is one of the most important repositories of art in the world. It began as a royal collection and was enhanced by the Hapsburgs, especially Charles V, and later the Bourbons. In paintings of the Spanish school the Prado has no equal; on your first visit, concentrate on the Spanish masters (Velázquez, Goya, El Greco, and Murillo).

Most major works are exhibited on the first floor. You'll see art by Italian masters—Raphael, Botticelli, Mantegna, Andrea del Sarto, Fra Angelico, and Correggio. The most celebrated Italian painting here is Titian's voluptuous Venus being watched by a musician who can't keep his eyes on his work.

The Prado is a trove of the work of El Greco (c. 1541 –1614), the Crete-born artist who lived much of his life in Toledo. You can see a parade of "The Greek's" saints, Madonnas, and Holy Families—even a ghostly *John the Baptist.*

You'll find a splendid array of works by the incomparable Diego Velázquez (1599–1660). The museum's most famous painting, in fact, is his *Las Meninas,* a triumph in the use of light effects. The faces of the queen and king are reflected in the mirror in the painting itself. The artist in the foreground is Velázquez, of course.

The Flemish painter Peter Paul Rubens (1577–1640), who met Velázquez while in Spain, is represented by the peacock-blue *Garden of Love* and by the *Three Graces.* Also worthy is the work of José Ribera (1591–1652), a Valencia-born artist and contemporary of Velázquez whose best painting is the *Martyrdom of St. Philip.* The Seville-born Bartolomé Murillo (1617–82)—often referred to as the "painter of Madonnas"—has three *Immaculate Conceptions* on display.

The Prado has an outstanding collection of the work of Hieronymus Bosch (1450?–1516), the Flemish genius. *The Garden of Earthly Delights,* the best-known work of "El Bosco," is here. You'll also see his *Seven Deadly Sins* and his triptych *The Hay Wagon. The Triumph of Death* is by another Flemish painter, Pieter Breughel the Elder (1525?–69), who carried on Bosch's ghoulish vision.

Francisco de Goya (1746–1828) ranks along with Velázquez and El Greco in the trio of great Spanish artists. Hanging here are his unflattering portraits of his patron, Charles IV, and his family, as well as the *Clothed Maja* and the *Naked Maja.* You can also see the much-reproduced *Third of May* (1808), plus a series of Goya sketches (some of which, depicting the decay of 18th-century Spain, brought the Inquisition down on the artist) and his expressionistic "black paintings."

✪ **Thyssen-Bornemisza Museum.** Palacio de Villahermosa, Paseo del Prado, 8. ☎ **91/369-01-51.** Admission 650 ptas. ($5.20). Tues–Sun 10am–7pm. Metro: Banco de España. Bus: 1, 2, 5, 9, 10, 14, 15, 20, 27, 34, 45, 51, 52, 53, 74, 146, or 150.

Until around 1985, the contents of this museum virtually overflowed the premises of a legendary villa near Lugano, Switzerland. One of the most frequently visited sites of Switzerland, the collection had been laboriously amassed over a period of about 60 years by the Thyssen-Bornemisza family, scions of a shipping, banking, mining, and chemical fortune whose roots began around 1905 in Holland, Germany, and Hungary. Experts had proclaimed it as one of the world's most extensive and valuable privately owned collections of paintings, rivaled only by the legendary holdings of Queen Elizabeth II.

For tax and insurance reasons, and because the collection had outgrown the boundaries of the lakeside villa that contained it, the collection was discreetly marketed in the early 1980s to the world's major museums. Amid endless intrigue, a litany of glamorous supplicants from eight different nations came calling. Among them were Margaret Thatcher and Prince Charles; trustees of the Getty Museum in Malibu, California; the president of West Germany; the Duke of Badajoz, brother-in-law of King Carlos II; even emissaries from Walt Disney World in Orlando, Florida, all hoping to acquire the collection for their respective countries or entities.

Eventually, thanks partly to the lobbying by Baron Hans Heinrich Thyssen-Borne-misza's fifth wife, a Spanish-born beauty (and former Miss Spain) named Tita, the collection was awarded to Spain for $350 million. Controversies over the public cost of the acquisition raged for months. Despite the brouhaha, various estimates have placed the value of this collection at anywhere between one and three billion dollars.

To house the collection, an 18th-century building adjacent to the Prado, the Villahermosa Palace, was retrofitted with the appropriate lighting and security devices, and renovated at a cost of $45 million. Rooms are arranged numerically so that by following the order of the various rooms (numbers 1 through 48, spread out over three floors), a logical sequence of European painting can be traced from the 13th through the 20th centuries. The nucleus of the collection consists of 700 world-class paintings. They include works by, among others, El Greco, Velázquez, Dürer, Rembrandt, Watteau, Canaletto, Caravaggio, Hals, Memling, and Goya.

Unusual among the world's great art collections because of its eclecticism, the Thyssen group also contains goodly numbers of 19th- and 20th-century paintings by many of the notable French impressionists, as well as works by Picasso, Sargent, Kirchner, Nolde, and Kandinsky—artists whose previous absence within Spanish museums had become increasingly obvious. This museum has attracted many millions of visitors since its long-awaited opening; be prepared for magnificent art but long lines.

✪ **Museo Nacional Centro de Arte Reina Sofía.** Santa Isabel, 52. ☎ **91/467-50-62.** Admission 450 ptas. ($3.60). Mon and Wed–Sat 10am–9pm, Sun 10am–2:30pm. Metro: Atocha. Bus: 6, 14, 26, 27, 32, 45, 57, or C.

Filling for the world of modern art the role that the Prado has filled for traditional art, the "MOMA" of Madrid (its nickname) is the greatest repository of 20th-century art in Spain. Set within the echoing, futuristically renovated walls of the former General Hospital, originally built between 1776 and 1781, the museum is a sprawling, high-ceilinged showplace named after the Greek-born wife of Spain's present king. Once designated as "the ugliest building in Spain" by Catalán architect Oriol Bohigas, the Reina Sofía has a design that hangs in limbo somewhere between the 18th and the 21st centuries. It incorporates a 50,000-volume art library and database, a café, a theater, a bookstore, Plexiglas-sided elevators, and systems that calibrate security, temperature, humidity, and the quality of light surrounding the exhibits.

Special emphasis is paid to the great artists of 20th-century Spain: Juan Gris, Salvador Dalí, Joan Miró, and Pablo Picasso (the museum has been able to acquire a handful of his works). What many critics claim as Picasso's masterpiece, *Guernica,* now rests at this museum after a long and troubling history of traveling. Banned in Spain during Franco's era (Picasso refused to have it displayed here anyway), it hung until 1980 at New York's Museum of Modern Art. The fiercely antiwar painting immortalizes the town's shameful blanket bombing by the German Luftwaffe, who were fighting for Franco during the Spanish Civil War. Guernica was the cradle of the Basque nation, and Picasso's canvas made it a household name around the world.

Madrid Attractions

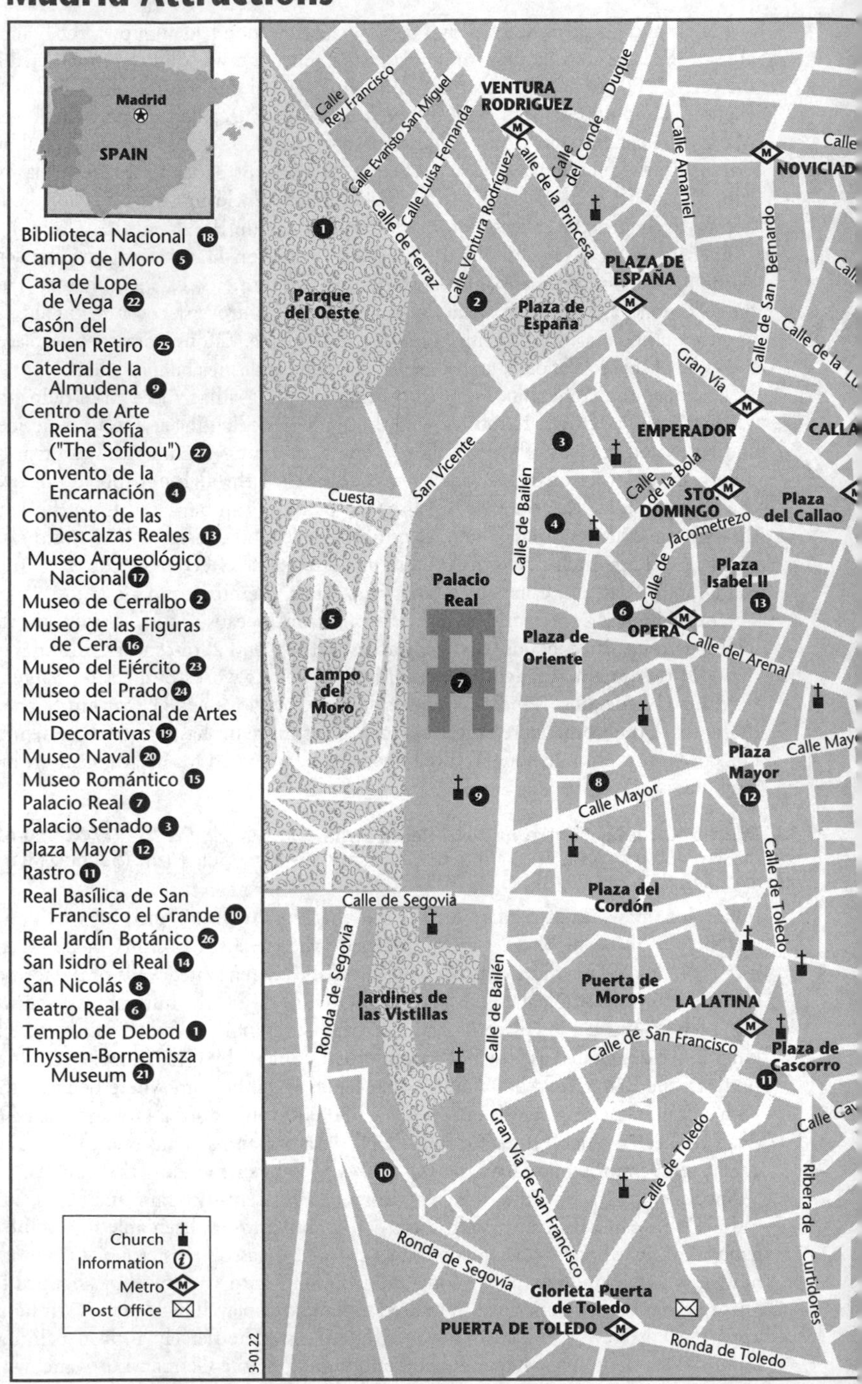

0
300 m
330 y
N
Calle de Genova
Calle de Fuencarral
de la Palma
Calle Fernando VI
Plaza de la Villa
Plaza de Colón
COLÓN
SERRANO
Calle de Goya
Jardines del Descubrimiento
Calle de El Escorial
Calle Baja de San Pablo
Calle de Hortaleza
Calle Bárbara de Braganza
Calle de Gravina del Almirante
CHUECA
Calle de Augusto Figueroa
del Pez
Corredera Baja de San Pablo
Calle de Valverde
Calle de Fuencarral
Calle de Prim
Paseo Recoletos
Calle de Serrano
Calle de Barquillo
Plaza de la Independencia
GRAN VÍA
Red. de San Luis
Gran Vía
Plaza de la Cibeles
Calle de Alcalá
BANCO DE ESPAÑA
SEVILLA
Calle de Montalbán
Calle Montera
Calle de Alcalá
Paseo del Prado
Plaza de la Lealtad
Calle A. Maura
SOL
Carrera de San Jerónimo
Calle de Alfonso XII
Calle de la Cruz
Plaza de las Cortes
Plaza C. del Castillo
Calle del Prado
Plaza Jacinto Benavente
Calle de Cervantes
Parque del Retiro
Paseo del Prado
Calle Atocha
Calle de las Huertas
Museo del Prado
Calle de Espalter
TIRSO DE MOLINA
ANTÓN MARTÍN
Calle de la Magdalena
Calle de la Cabeza
Calle de Gobernador
Real Jardín Botánico
Calle Jesús y María Levapiés
Calle del Amparo
Calle Atocha
Baja
Calle de Santa Isabel
Calle Mesón de Paredes
Calle de Alfonso XII
ATOCHA
Plaza Lavapies
LAVAPIES
Paseo de la Infanta Isabel
Calle de Embajadores
Calle Miguel Servet
Ronda de Atocha
Sta. María de la Cabeza
Estación de Atocha
14
15
16
17
18
19
20
21
22
23
24
25
26
27

Museo de la Real Academia de Bellas Artes de San Fernando (Fine Arts Museum). Alcalá, 13. ☎ **91/522-1491.** Tues–Fri admission 200 ptas. ($1.60) adults, free for children and adults over 60; free on Sat–Sun. Tues–Fri 9am–7pm, Sat–Mon 9am–2:30pm. Metro: Puerta del Sol or Sevilla. Bus: 15, 20, 51, 52, 53, or 150.

An easy stroll from Puerta del Sol, the Fine Arts Museum is located in the restored and remodeled 17th-century baroque palace of Juan de Goyeneche. The collection—more than 1,500 paintings and 570 sculptures, ranging from the 16th century to the present—was started in 1752 during the reign of Fernando VI (1746–59). It emphasizes works by Spanish, Flemish, and Italian artists. You can see masterpieces by El Greco, Rubens, Velázquez, Zurbarán, Ribera, Cano, Coello, Murillo, Goya, and Sorolla.

Museo Taurino (Bullfighting Museum). Plaza de Toros de las Ventas, Alcalá, 237. ☎ **91/725-18-57.** Free admission. Mar–Oct, Tues–Fri and Sun 9:30am–2:30pm; Nov–Feb, Mon–Fri 9:30am–2:30pm. Bus: 12, 21, 38, 53, 146, M1, or M8.

This museum might serve as a good introduction to bullfighting for those who want to see the real event. Here you'll see the death costume of Manolete, the *traje de luces* (suit of lights) that he wore when he was gored to death at age 30 in Linares's bullring.

Other memorabilia evoke the heyday of Juan Belmonte, the Andalusian who revolutionized bullfighting in 1914 by performing close to the horns. Other exhibits include a Goya painting of a matador, as well as photographs and relics that trace the history of bullfighting in Spain from its ancient origins to the present day.

✪ **Museo Lázaro Galdiano.** Serrano, 122. ☎ **91/561-60-84.** Admission 300 ptas. ($2.40). Tues–Sun 10am–2pm. Closed holidays and Aug. Metro: Avenida de América. Bus: 9, 16, 19, 51, or 89.

Imagine 37 rooms in a well-preserved 19th-century mansion bulging with artworks—including many by the most famous old masters of Europe. Most visitors take the elevator to the top floor and work down, lingering over such artifacts as 15th-century handwoven vestments, swords and daggers, royal seals, 16th-century crystal from Limoges, Byzantine jewelry, Italian bronzes from ancient times to the Renaissance, and medieval armor.

One painting by Bosch evokes his own peculiar brand of horror, his canvases peopled with creepy fiends devouring human flesh. The Spanish masters are the best represented—El Greco, Velázquez, Zurbarán, Ribera, Murillo, and Valdés-Leal.

One section is devoted to works by the English portrait and landscape artists Reynolds, Gainsborough, and Constable. Italian artists exhibited include Tiepolo and Guardi. Salon 30—for many, the most interesting—is devoted to Goya and includes paintings from his "black period."

NOTABLE BUILDINGS

✪ **Palacio Real (Royal Palace).** Plaza de Oriente, Calle de Bailén, 2. ☎ **91/542-00-59.** Admission 900 ptas. ($7.20); Museo de las Carruajes (Carriage Museum) 200 ptas. ($1.60). Mon–Sat 9am–6pm, Sun 9am–3pm. Metro: Ópera or Plaza de España.

This huge palace was begun in 1738 on the site of the Madrid Alcázar, which burned to the ground in 1734. Some of its 2,000 rooms—which that "enlightened despot" Charles III called home—are open to the public; others are still used for state business. The palace was last used as a royal residence in 1931, before King Alfonzo XIII and his wife, Victoria Eugénie, fled Spain.

You'll be taken on a guided tour that includes the Reception Room, the State Apartments, the Armory, and the Royal Pharmacy. To get an English-speaking guide, say "*Inglés*" to the person who takes your ticket.

Did You Know?

- Sobrino de Botín, a Hemingway favorite founded in 1725, claims to be the world's oldest restaurant.
- The only public statue anywhere dedicated to the Devil stands in Madrid's Retiro Park.
- A Mexican composer wrote the unofficial anthem "Madrid, Madrid, Madrid"—and he had never been to Madrid.

The Reception Room and State Apartments should get priority here if you're rushed. They embrace a rococo room with a diamond clock; a porcelain salon; the Royal Chapel; the Banquet Room, where receptions for heads of state are still held; and the Throne Room.

The rooms are literally stuffed with art treasures and antiques—salon after salon of monumental grandeur, with no apologies for the damask, mosaics, stucco, Tiepolo ceilings, gilt and bronze, chandeliers, and paintings.

If your visit falls on the first Wednesday of the month, look for the changing of the guard ceremony, which occurs at noon and is free to the public.

In the Armory, you'll see the finest collection of weaponry in Spain. Many of the items—powder flasks, shields, lances, helmets, and saddles—are from the collection of Charles V (Charles of Spain). From here, the comprehensive tour takes you into the Pharmacy.

You may want to visit the **Museo de las Carruajes (Carriage Museum),** also at the Royal Palace, to see some of the grand old relics used by Spanish aristocrats. Afterward, stroll through the Campo del Moro, the gardens of the palace.

Panteón de Goya (Goya's Tomb). Glorieta de San Antonio de la Florida. ☎ **91/542-07-22.** Admission 300 ptas. ($2.40). Tues–Fri 10am–2pm and 4–8pm, Sat–Sun 10am–2pm. Metro: Norte. Bus: 41, 46, 75, or C.

In a remote part of town beyond the North Station lies Goya's tomb, containing one of his masterpieces—an elaborately beautiful fresco depicting the miracles of St. Anthony on the dome and cupola of the little hermitage of San Antonio de la Florida. This has been called Goya's Sistine Chapel. Already deaf when he began the painting, Goya labored dawn to dusk for 16 weeks, painting with sponges rather than brushes. By depicting common street life—stone masons, prostitutes, and beggars—Goya raised the ire of the nobility who held judgment until the patron, Carlos IV, viewed it. When the monarch approved, the formerly "outrageous" painting was deemed acceptable.

The tomb and fresco are in one of the twin chapels (visit the one on the right) that were built in the latter part of the 18th century. Discreetly placed mirrors will help you see the ceiling better.

✪ **Monasterio de las Descalzas Reales.** Plaza de las Descalzas Reales, s/n. ☎ **91/542-00-59.** Admission 650 ptas. ($5.20) adults, 350 ptas. ($2.80) children. Sat and Tues–Thurs 10:30am–12:30pm and 4–5:30pm, Fri 10:30am–12:30pm, Sun 11am–1:30pm. Bus: 1, 2, 5, 20, 46, 52, 53, 74, M1, M2, M3, or M5. From Plaza del Callao, off Gran Vía, walk down Postigo de San Martín to Plaza de las Descalzas Reales; the convent is on the left.

In the mid-16th century, aristocratic women—either disappointed in love or "wanting to be the bride of Christ"—stole away to this convent to take the veil. Each brought a dowry, making this one of the richest convents in the land. By the mid-20th century the convent sheltered mostly poor women. True, it still contained a priceless collection of art treasures, but the sisters were forbidden to auction anything; in fact, they were literally starving. The state intervened, and the pope granted special dispensation to open the convent as a museum. Today the public can look behind the walls of what was once a mysterious edifice on one of the most beautiful squares in Old Madrid.

An English-speaking guide will show you through. In the Reliquary are the noblewomen's dowries, one of which is said to contain bits of wood from Christ's Cross; another, some of the bones of St. Sebastian. The most valuable painting is Titian's *Caesar's Money.* The Flemish Hall shelters other fine works, including paintings by Hans de Beken and Breughel the Elder. All of the tapestries were based on Rubens's cartoons, displaying his chubby matrons.

Real Fábrica de Tapices (Royal Tapestry Factory). Fuenterrabía, 2. ☎ **91/551-34-00.** Admission 250 ptas. ($2). Mon–Fri 9am–12:30pm. Closed Aug and holidays. Metro: Menéndez Pelayo. Bus: 10, 14, 26, 32, 37, C, or M9.

At this factory, the age-old process of making exquisite (and very expensive) tapestries is still carried on with consummate skill. Nearly every tapestry is based on a cartoon of Goya, who was the factory's most famous employee. Many of these patterns—such as *The Pottery Salesman* —are still in production today. (Goya's original cartoons are in the Prado.) Many of the other designs are based on cartoons by Francisco Bayeu, Goya's brother-in-law.

2 More Attractions

MAINLY MUSEUMS

Museo Arqueológico Nacional. Serrano, 13. ☎ **91/577-79-12.** Admission 400 ptas. ($3.20), free for children and adults over 60; free on Sat 2:30–8:30pm and Sun. Tues–Sat 9:30am–8:30pm, Sun 9:30am–2:30pm. Metro: Serrano or Retiro. Bus: 1, 9, 19, 51, 74, or M2.

This stately mansion is a storehouse of artifacts from the prehistoric to the baroque. One of the prime exhibits here is the Iberian statue *The Lady of Elche,* a piece of primitive carving (from the 4th century B.C.), discovered on the southeastern coast of Spain. Finds from Ibiza, Paestum, and Rome are on display, including statues of Tiberius and his mother, Livia. The Islamic collection from Spain is outstanding. There are also collections of Spanish Renaissance lusterware, Talavera pottery, Retiro porcelain, and some rare 16th- and 17th-century Andalusian glassware.

Many of the exhibits are treasures that were removed from churches and monasteries. A much-photographed choir stall from the palace of Palencia dates from the 14th century. Also worth a look are the reproductions of the Altamira cave paintings (chiefly of bison, horses, and boars), discovered near Santander in northern Spain in 1868.

Museo de América (Museum of the Americas). Avenida de los Reyes Catolicos, 6. ☎ **91/549-2641.** Admission 400 ptas. ($3.20) adults, 200 ptas. ($1.60) children. Tues–Sat 10am–3pm, Sat–Sun 10am–2:30pm. Metro: Moncloa.

This museum, situated near the university campus, houses an outstanding collection of pre-Columbian, Spanish-American, and Native American art and artifacts. Various exhibits chronicle the progress of the inhabitants of the New World, from the Paleolithic period to the present day. One exhibit, "Groups, Tribes, Chiefdoms, and States," focuses on the social structure of the various peoples of the Americas. Another display outlines the various religions and deities associated with them. Also included in the museum is an entire exhibit dedicated to communication, highlighting written as well as nonverbal expressions of art.

Frommer's Favorite Madrid Experiences

Tasca Hopping. The quintessential Madrid experience and the fastest way for a visitor to tap into the local scene. *Tascas* are Spanish pubs serving tapas, those tantalizing appetizers. You can go from one to the other, sampling each tavern's special dishes and wines.

Eating "Around Spain." The variety of gastronomic experiences is staggering: You can literally restaurant-hop from province to province without ever leaving Madrid.

Viewing the Works of Your Favorite Artist. Spend an afternoon at the Prado, savoring the works of your favorite Spanish artist, devoting all your attention to his work.

Bargain Hunting at El Rastro. Madrid has one of the greatest flea markets in Europe, if not the world. Wander through its many offerings to discover that hidden treasure you've been searching for.

A Night of Flamenco. Flamenco folk songs (*cante*) and dances (*baile*) are an integral part of the Spanish experience. Spend at least one night in a flamenco tavern, listening to the heart-rending laments of gypsy sorrows, tribulations, hopes, and dreams.

Outdoor-Café Sitting. This is a famous experience for the summertime, when Madrileños come alive again on their terrazas. The drinking and good times can go on until dawn. From glamorous hangouts to lowly street corners, the café scene takes place mainly along the axis formed by the Paseo de la Castellana, Paseo del Prado, and Paseo de Recoletos (all of which make up one contiguous street).

Museo del Ejército (Army Museum). Méndez Núñez, 1. ☎ **91/522-89 77.** Admission 100 ptas. (80¢) adults, free for children under 18 and adults over 65. Tues–Sun 10am–2pm. Metro: Banco de España.

This museum, in the Buen Retiro Palace, houses outstanding exhibits from military history, including El Cid's original sword. In addition, you can see the tent used by Charles V in Tunisia, relics of Pizarro and Cortés, and an exceptional collection of armor. Look for the piece of the cross that Columbus carried when he landed in the New World. The museum had a notorious founder: Manuel Godoy, who rose from relative poverty to become the lover of Maria Luisa of Parma, wife of Carlos IV.

Museo Municipal. Fuencarral, 78. ☎ **91/588-86-72.** Admission 300 ptas. ($2.40). Tues–Fri 9:30am–8pm, Sat–Sun 10am–2pm. Metro: Bilbao or Tribunal. Bus: 3, 7, 40, 147, or 149.

After years of restoration, the Museo Municipal displays collections on local history, archaeology, and art, with an emphasis on the Bourbon Madrid of the 18th century. Paseos with strolling couples are shown on huge tapestry cartoons. Paintings from the royal collections are here, plus period models of the best-known city squares and a Goya that was painted for the Town Hall.

Museo Nacional de Artes Decorativas. Calle de Montalbán, 12. ☎ **91/532-64-99.** Admission 400 ptas. ($3.20). Tues–Fri 9:30am–3pm, Sat–Sun 10am–2pm. Metro: Banco de España. Bus: 14, 27, 34, 37, 45, or M6.

In 62 rooms spread over several floors, this museum, near the Plaza de la Cibeles, displays a rich collection of furniture, ceramics, and decorative pieces. Emphasizing the 16th and 17th centuries, the eclectic collection includes Gothic carvings, alabaster figurines, festival crosses, elaborate dollhouses, elegant baroque four-poster beds, a chapel covered with leather tapestries, and even kitchens from the 18th century. Two new floors focusing on the 18th and 19th centuries have recently been added to the museum.

Museo Naval. Paseo del Prado. 5. ☎ **91/379-52-99.** Free admission. Tues–Sun 10:30am–1:30pm. Closed Aug. Metro: Banco de España. Bus: 10, 14, 27, 34, 37, 45, or M6.

The history of nautical science and the Spanish navy, from the time of Isabella and Ferdinand until today, comes alive at the Museo Naval. The most fascinating exhibit is the map made by the *Santa María's* first mate to show the Spanish monarchs the new discoveries. There are also souvenirs of the Battle of Trafalgar.

Museo Romántico. San Mateo, 13. ☎ **91/448-10-71.** Admission 400 ptas. ($3.20) adults, 200 ptas. ($1.60) children. Tues–Sat 9am–3pm, Sun 10am–2pm. Closed Aug. Metro: Alonso Martínez.

Geared toward those seeking the romanticism of the 19th century, the museum is housed in a mansion decorated with numerous period pieces—crystal chandeliers, faded portraits, oils from Goya to Sorolla, opulent furnishings, and porcelain. Many exhibits date from the days of Isabella II, the high-living, fun-loving queen who was forced into exile and eventual abdication.

Museo Sorolla. General Martínez Campos, 37. ☎ **91/310-15-84.** Admission 400 ptas. ($3.20). Tues–Sat 10am–3pm, Sun 10am–2pm. Metro: Iglesia or Rubén Darío. Bus: 5, 16, 61, 40, or M3.

From 1912, painter Joaquín Sorolla and his family occupied this elegant Madrileño town house off Paseo de la Castellana. His widow turned it over to the government, and it is now maintained as a memorial. Much of the house remains as Sorolla left it, right down to his stained paintbrushes and pipes. In the museum wing a representative collection of his works is displayed.

Although Sorolla painted portraits of Spanish aristocrats, he was essentially interested in the common people, often depicting them in their native dress. On view are the artist's self-portrait and the paintings of his wife and their son. Sorolla was especially fond of painting beach scenes of the Costa Blanca.

Museo Tiflológico. La Coruña, 18. ☎ **91/571-12-36.** Free admission. Tues–Fri 11am–2pm and 5–8pm, Sat 11am–2pm. Metro: Estrecho. Bus: 3, 42, 43, 64, or 124.

This museum is designed for sightless and sight-impaired visitors. Maintained by Spain's National Organization for the Blind, it's one of the few museums in the world that emphasizes tactile appeal. All the exhibits are meant to be touched and felt; to that end, the museum provides audiotapes, in English and Spanish, to guide visitors as they move their hands over the object on display. It also offers pamphlets in large type and Braille.

One section of the museum features small-scale replicas of such architectural wonders as the Mayan and Aztec pyramids of Central America, the Eiffel Tower, and the Statue of Liberty. Another section contains paintings and sculptures created by blind artists, such as Miguel Detrel and José António Braña. A third section outlines the status of blind people throughout history, with a focus on the sociology and technology that led to the development of Braille during the 19th century.

Real Basilica de San Francisco el Grande. Plaza de San Francisco el Grande, San Buenaventura, 1. ☎ **91/365-38-00.** Admission 50 ptas. (40¢). Tues–Sat 10am–1pm and 4–6pm. Metro: La Latina or Puerta del Toledo. Bus: 3, 60, C, or M4.

Ironically, Madrid, the capital of cathedral-rich Spain, does not itself possess a famous cathedral—but it does have an important church, with a dome larger than that of

St. Paul's in London. This 18th-century church is filled with a number of ecclesiastical works, notably a Goya painting of St. Bernardinus of Siena. A guide will show you through.

Templo de Debod. Paseo de Rosales. No phone. Admission 300 ptas. ($2.40) adults, 150 ptas. ($1.20) children under 16; free on Wed and Sun. Tues–Fri 10am–1pm and 4–7pm, Sat–Sun 10am–1pm. Metro: Plaza de España or Ventura Rodríguez. Bus: 25, 33, 39, 46, or 74.

This Egyptian temple near Plaza de España once stood in the Valley of the Nile, 19 miles from Aswan. When the new dam threatened the temple, the Egyptian government dismantled and presented it to Spain. Taken down stone by stone in 1969 and 1970, it was shipped to Valencia and taken by rail to Madrid, where it was reconstructed and opened to the public in 1971. Photos upstairs depict the temple's long history.

PARKS & GARDENS

For a touch of green in Madrid's sprawling gray urban expanse, visit one of the following:

Casa de Campo (metro: Lago or Batán) is the former royal hunting grounds—miles of parkland lying south of the Royal Palace across the Manzanares River. You can see the gate through which the kings rode out of the palace grounds, either on horseback or in carriages, on their way to the tree-lined park. A lake contained within Casa de Campo is usually filled with rowers. You can have drinks and light refreshments around the water or go swimming in a municipally operated pool. Children will love both the zoo and the Parque de Atracciones (see "Especially for Kids," below). The Casa de Campo can be visited daily from 8am to 9pm.

Parque de Retiro (metro: Retiro), originally a royal playground for the Spanish monarchs and their guests, extends over 350 acres. The huge palaces that once stood here were destroyed in the early 19th century; only the former dance hall, the Cáson del Buen Retiro (housing the modern works of the Prado) and the building containing the Army Museum remain. The park boasts numerous fountains and statues, plus a large lake. There are also two exposition centers, the Velásquez and Crystal palaces (built to honor the Phillipines in 1887), and a lakeside monument, erected in 1922 in honor of King Alfonso XII. In summer, the rose gardens are worth a visit, and you'll find several places for inexpensive snacks and drinks. The park is open daily 24 hours, but it is safest from 7am to 8:30pm.

Across Calle de Alfonso XII, at the southwest corner of Parque de Retiro, is the **Real Jardin Botánico (Botanical Garden)** (metro: Atocha. Bus: 10, 14, 19, 32, or 45). Founded in the 18th century, the garden contains more than 104 species of trees and 3,000 types of plants. Also on the premises are an exhibition hall and a library specializing in botany. The park is open daily from 10am to 8pm; admission is 200 pesetas ($1.60).

3 Especially for Kids

Aquápolis. Villanueva de la Canada, Carretera de El Escorial. ☎ **91/815-69-11.** Admission 3,500 ptas. ($28) adults, 1,500 ptas. ($12) children. Daily 10am–8pm. Closed Oct–Apr. Free bus at 10am, 11am, and noon, leaving Madrid from Calle de los Reyes, next to Coliseum Cinema, on eastern edge of Plaza de España.

Sixteen miles northwest of Madrid lies a watery attraction where the kids can cool off. Scattered amid shops, a picnic area, and a barbecue restaurant are water slides, wave-making machines, and tall slides that spiral children into a swimming pool below.

Museo de Cera de Madrid (Wax Museum). Paseo de Recoletas, 41. ☎ **91/319-26-49.** Admission 900 ptas. ($7.20) adults, 600 ptas. ($4.80) children. Daily 10:30am–1:30pm and 4–8pm. Metro: Colón. Bus: 27, 45, or 53.

The kids will enjoy seeing a lifelike wax Columbus calling on Ferdinand and Isabella, as well as Jackie Onassis having champagne at a supper club. The 450 wax figures also include heroes and villains of World War II. Two galleries display Romans and Arabs from the ancient days of the Iberian Peninsula; a show in multivision gives a 30-minute recap of Spanish history from the Phoenicians to the present.

Parque de Atracciones. Casa de Campo. ☎ **91/463-29-00.** Admission 450 ptas. ($3.60) adults; an all-inclusive ticket—good for all rides—is 9,000 ptas. ($72). Apr–June, Tues–Fri noon–9pm, Sat–Sun noon–1am; July–Aug, Tues–Fri 6pm–1am, Sat 6pm–2am, Sun noon–1am; Sept, Tues–Sun (variable hours—call to check before going there); Oct–Mar, Sat noon–8pm (sometimes 9pm), Sun 11am–8pm (sometimes 9pm). Take Teleférico cable car (see below); at end of this ride, "microbuses" take you the rest of the way. Alternatively, take suburban train from Plaza de España and stop near entrance to park (Entrada de Batán).

The park was created in 1969 to amuse the young at heart with an array of rides and concessions. The former include a toboggan slide, a carousel, pony rides, an adventure into "outer space," a walk through a transparent maze, a visit to "jungleland," a motor-propelled series of cars disguised as a tail-wagging dachshund puppy, and a gyrating whirligig clutched in the tentacles of an octopus named El Pulpo. The most popular rides are a pair of roller coasters named "7 Picos" and "Jet Star."

The park also has many diversions for adults. See "Madrid After Dark" later in this chapter for details.

Planetarium. Parque Tierno Galván, Méndez Alvaro. ☎ **91/467-34-61.** Admission 450 ptas. ($3.60) adults, 250 ptas. ($2) children under 14. Tues–Sun shows at 11:30am and 12:45, 5:30, 6:45, and 8pm. Closed 2 weeks in Jan. Metro: Méndez Alvaro. Bus: 148.

This planetarium has a projection room with optical and electronic equipment—including a multivision system—designed to reproduce outer space.

Teleférico. Paseo del Pintor Rosales, s/n. ☎ **91/541-74-40.** Fare 354 ptas. ($2.85) one way, 500 ptas. ($4) round-trip. Mar–Oct, daily noon–9pm; Nov–Feb, Sat–Sun noon–9pm. Metro: Plaza de España or Argüelles. Bus: 74.

Strung high above several of Madrid's verdant parks, this cable car was originally built in 1969 as part of a public fairgrounds (Parque de Atracciones) modeled vaguely along the lines of Disneyland. Today, even for visitors not interested in visiting the park, the *teleférico* retains an allure of its own as a high-altitude method of admiring the cityscape of Madrid. The cable car departs from Paseo Pintor Rosales at the eastern edge of Parque del Oeste (at the corner of Calle Marqués de Urquijo) and carries you high above two parks, railway tracks, and over the Manzanares River to a spot near a picnic ground and restaurant in Casa de Campo. Weather permitting, there are good views of the Royal Palace along the way. The ride takes 11 minutes.

Zoo Aquarium de la Casa de Campo. Casa de Campo. ☎ **91/711-99-50.** Admission 1,500 ptas. ($12) adults, 1,210 ptas. ($9.70) children 3–8, free for children 2 and under. Daily 10am–sunset. Metro: Batán. Bus: 33.

This modern, well-organized facility allows you to see wildlife from five continents, with about 3,000 animals on display. Most are in simulated natural habitats, with moats separating them from the public. There's a petting zoo for the kids and a show presented by the Chu-Lin band. The zoo/aquarium complex includes a 520,000-gallon tropical marine aquarium, a dolphinarium, and a parrot club.

FRANÇAISE
REPUBLIQUE
5 CENTS
CANADA 1978
PESOS
LIBERTY
VINGT FRANCS
FB 747022 T
LIRE

AMERICAN EXPRESS
Express Cash

And just in case.

We're here with American Express® Travelers Cheques and Cheques *for Two*.® They're the safest way to carry money on your vacation and the surest way to get a refund, practically anywhere, anytime.

Another way we help you...

do more

Travelers Cheques

4 Special-Interest Sightseeing

FOR THE LITERARY ENTHUSIAST

Casa de Lope de Vega. Cervantes, 11. ☎ **91/429-92-16.** Admission 200 ptas. ($1.60). Tues–Thurs 9:30am–2pm, Sat 10am–1:30pm. Closed Aug. Metro: Anton Martín.

Felix Lope de Vega, a prolific Madrid-born author, dramatized Hapsburg Spain as no one had before, earning a lasting position in Spanish letters. A reconstruction of his medieval house stands on a narrow street—ironically named for Cervantes, his competitor for the title of the greatest writer of the golden age of Spain. The dank, dark house is furnished with relics of the period, although one can't be sure that any of the furnishings or possessions actually belonged to this 16th-century genius.

HEMINGWAY HAUNTS

Chicote. Gran Vía, 12. ☎ **91/532-67-37.** Beer 550 ptas. ($4.40), whiskey and soda 1,000 ptas. ($8). Mon–Sat 5pm–2am. Metro: Gran Vía.

Ernest Hemingway used Chicote as a setting for his only play, *The Fifth Column.* He would sit here night after night, gazing at the *putas* (it was a famed hooker bar back then) as he entertained friends with such remarks as "Spain is a country for living and not for dying." The bar still draws a lively crowd.

Museo del Prado. Paseo del Prado. ☎ **91/420-28-36.**

Of the Prado, A. E. Hotchner wrote in his *Papa Hemingway:* "Ernest loved the Prado. He entered it as he entered cathedrals." More than any other, one picture held him transfixed, Andrea del Sarto's *Portrait of a Woman.* (For further details about the Prado, see "The Top Attractions" earlier in this chapter.)

Sobrino de Botín. Cuchilleros, 17. ☎ **91/366-42-17.**

In the final two pages of Hemingway's novel *The Sun Also Rises,* Jake invites Brett here for roast suckling pig and red wine. In another book, *Death in the Afternoon,* Hemingway told his mythical "Old Lady": "I would rather dine on suckling pig at Botín's than sit and think of casualties my friends have suffered." Since that time, thousands upon thousands of Americans have eaten at Botín (see Chapter 4 for details), a perennial favorite of all visiting Yankees.

FOR THE ARCHITECTURE ENTHUSIAST

✪ **Plaza Mayor.** Metro: Puerta del Sol.

In the heart of Madrid, this famous square was known as the Plaza de Arrabal in medieval times, when it stood outside the city wall.

The original architect of Plaza Mayor itself was Juan Gómez de Mora, who worked during the reign of Philip III. Under the Hapsburgs, the square rose in importance as the site of public spectacles, including the abominable autos-da-fé, in which "heretics" were burned. Bullfights, knightly tournaments, and festivals were also staged here.

Three times the buildings on the square burned—in 1631, 1672, and 1790—but each time the plaza bounced back. After the last big fire, it was completely redesigned by Juan de Villanueva.

Nowadays a Christmas fair is held around the equestrian statue of Philip III (dating from 1616) in the center of the square. On summer nights the Plaza Mayor becomes the virtual living room of Madrid, as tourists sip sangría at the numerous cafés and listen to the music performances, many of which are spontaneous.

Puerta de Toledo. Metro: Puerta de Toledo.

Puerta de Toledo is one of the two surviving town gates (the other is Puerta de Alcalá). Constructed during the brief and unpopular rule of Joseph I Bonaparte, this one marks the spot where citizens used to set out for the former imperial capital of Toledo. On an irregularly shaped square, it stands at the intersection of the Ronda de Toledo and Calle de Toledo. Its original purpose was a triumphal arch to honor Napoleon Bonaparte. In 1813 it became a symbol of Madrid's fierce independence and the loyalty of its citizens to their Bourbon rulers, who had been restored to the throne in the wake of the Napoleonic invasion.

WALKING TOUR 1
The Prado in Two Hours

Start: Velázquez door (western entrance).
Finish: Room 57A.
Time: 2 hours.
Best Times: At 9am opening.
Worst Times: From 12:30 to 3pm (too crowded); Monday, when it's closed.

The greatest cultural institution in all of Spain and the root of a deep-seated pride in the country's artistic heritage, the Prado places Madrid firmly on the artistic map of Europe. It is also one of the capital's most consistently reliable tourist attractions, as witnessed by the more than two million visitors who shuffle through its corridors every year.

But because of the Prado's *embarras de richesses* (only a third of the collection can be displayed at any given time), you may need some guidance to see at least some of the world-acclaimed masterpieces. You could devote weeks to the Prado, but regrettably many visitors have only two hours. Here's how to make the most of that limited time.

Because the lines there tend to be shorter, we usually prefer to enter via the:

1. **Velázquez door,** the Prado's western (central) entrance, near the larger-than-life bronze statue of the seated artist, one of Spain's most famous painters. Ignoring (for the time being) the riches of the museum's street level, climb to the upper floor, using the building's central (western) staircase, which lies a short distance to the right of the entrance turnstile. At the top of the stairs, walk down the short hall that will deposit you in the museum's famous:
2. **Long Gallery.** Although referred to as a gallery, it is more technically the interconnected series of rooms 24 through 32. Echoing, marble-sheathed, and often very crowded, these rooms are the main traffic artery of the Prado's second showcase floor. Walk south through rooms 28 and 29, admiring the large-scale works by mainly Italian Renaissance painters as you go. Specific artworks will include representations by Raphael, Titian, Tintoretto, and Fra Angelico. The gallery will eventually funnel into an octagonal room (no. 32), which contains:
3. **Oil paintings by Goya,** including his most famous portraits: the cruel depictions of the family of King Carlos IV. You are standing amid the museum's densest concentration of oils by Goya. The best of these lie a few steps to the east. With your back to the previously mentioned Long Gallery, turn left into the long and narrow room 31. At the end of room 31, turn left into room 22. This and four of its neighbors (specifically, rooms 19 to 23, which lie in a straight, uninterrupted line) contain many of the cartoons (sketches for tapestries) Goya designed for eventual execution by teams of weavers. Walk southward into room 18 to see:

Walking Tour: The Prado in Two Hours

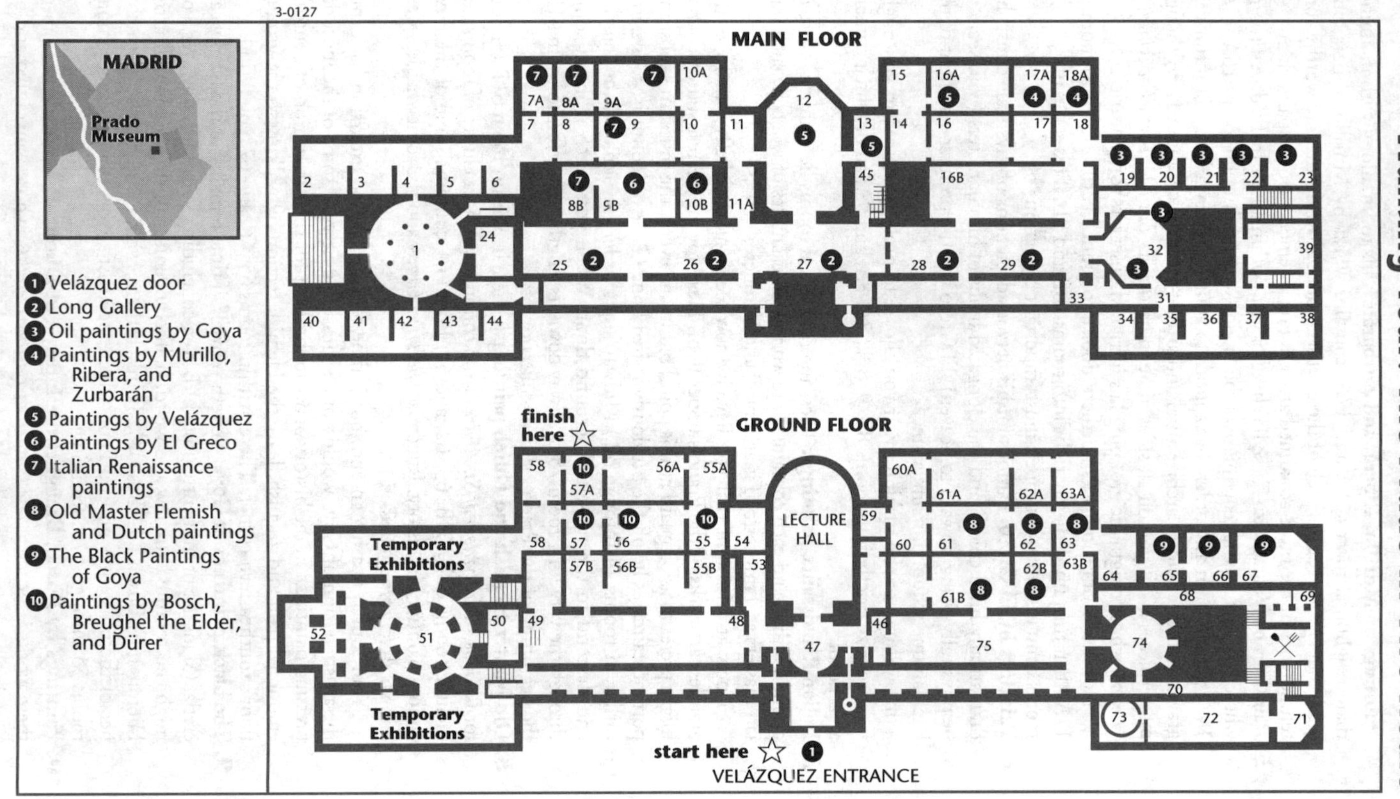

3-0127
MADRID
Prado Museum
1 Velázquez door
2 Long Gallery
3 Oil paintings by Goya
4 Paintings by Murillo, Ribera, and Zurbarán
5 Paintings by Velázquez
6 Paintings by El Greco
7 Italian Renaissance paintings
8 Old Master Flemish and Dutch paintings
9 The Black Paintings of Goya
10 Paintings by Bosch, Breughel the Elder, and Dürer
MAIN FLOOR
GROUND FLOOR
LECTURE HALL
Temporary Exhibitions
Temporary Exhibitions
finish here
start here
VELÁZQUEZ ENTRANCE

4. **Paintings by Murillo, Ribera, and Zurbarán.** This room, along with its immediate neighbors, rooms 18A and 17A, contains works by Murillo, Ribera, and Zurbarán (1598–1664). Each of these artists produced works that are worthy contemporaries of the most-acclaimed artwork ever to emerge from Spain, the:
5. **Paintings by Velázquez.** These lie ahead of you, within about half a dozen rooms whose contents are the centerpiece of the Prado. Wander through rooms 16A, 15A, 14, 16, and 13, in any order that appeals to your roving eye. You will intuitively gravitate to the Prado's architectural and artistic centerpiece, room 12. Although masterpieces await you on all sides, note in particular *Las Meninas* (*The Maids of Honor*), whose enigmatic grouping has intrigued observers for centuries.

   Now exit from room 12's northern door into room 11, turn left into room 11A, then turn immediately right into rooms 10B and 9B. This series of rooms contains one of Europe's most important collections of:
6. **Paintings by El Greco.** Famous for his nervous depictions of mystical ecstasy, his dramatically lurid colors, and the elongated limbs of his characters (who seem to be physically rising upward to heaven), El Greco was the premier exponent of the late baroque school of mannerism.

   Time will by now be rushing by. If you choose to prolong your visit, you might want to gaze briefly into rooms 8B, 9, 8, 7, 7A, 8A, and 9A, all of which contain an array of:
7. **Italian Renaissance paintings.** These interconnected rooms lie within a few steps of one another, and each contains more world-class examples of works by such Italian masters as Tintoretto, Titian, and Paolo Veronese.

   Know at this point that you have by now seen—albeit briefly—many of the grandest artworks of the Prado's upper floor. Head for the nearest staircase. (You might prefer to ask a guard at this point, but in any event, the museum's most important staircases lie off the previously visited Long Gallery—comprised, as stated earlier, of rooms 24 through 32.) Midway along its length, look for the staircase and descend to the museum's ground floor. When you reach it, head south through the very long room 75. Midway down its length, turn left into room 61B, the beginning of the Prado's superb collection of:
8. **Old Master Flemish and Dutch paintings.** These lie within room 61B (famous for Rubens's *Martyrdom of St. Andrew*) and continue within a cluster of rooms that include rooms 62B, 63B, 63, 62, and 61. Room 61 contains some of the most famous paintings in history: Rubens's *The Three Graces* and the somewhat less well-known *Judgment of Paris.*

   Your tour is nearing an end, but if time remains, a final excursion back into the artistic vision of Goya would not be amiss. For views of some of the most depressing paintings in the history of Spain, brilliant for their evocation of neurotic emotional pain and anguish, leave the Flemish section by walking to the ground floor's southeastern corner. There, within rooms 65, 66, and 67, you'll find:
9. **The black paintings of Goya.** Refresh yourself, if time remains, at the nearby cafeteria. (Signs are prominently posted.) Before concluding your tour, however, you might be tempted to view the weird, hallucinogenic paintings of Dutch artist Hieronymus Bosch ("El Bosco,"). To reach them, walk to the northeastern corner of the museum's ground floor, where the artist's works lie scattered among rooms 55 through 57A, featuring:
10. **Paintings by Bosch, Breughel the Elder, and Dürer.** The most important of these works is Bosch's *The Garden of Earthly Delights,* whose convoluted and bizarre images have provided fodder for the nightmares of generations of children. Also nearby are works by Flemish painter Rogier van der Weyden.

WALKING TOUR 2
Hapsburg Madrid

Start: Southeastern corner of the Palacio Real.
Finish: Calle del Arenal.
Time: 3 hours.
Best Times: Saturday or Sunday, when you can also visit the flea market of El Rastro.
Worst Times: Monday through Saturday 7:30 to 9:30am and 5 to 7:30pm—because of heavy traffic.

This tour encompasses 16th- and 17th-century Madrid, including the grand plazas and traffic arteries that the Hapsburg families built to transform a quiet town into a world-class capital.

The tour begins at the:

1. **Palacio Real (Royal Palace),** at the corner of Calle de Bailén and Calle Mayor. The latter was built by Philip II in the 1560s to provide easy access from the palace to his preferred church, San Jerónimo el Real.

    Walk east on:

2. **Calle Mayor,** on the south side of the street. Within a block, you'll reach a black bronze statue of a kneeling angel, erected in 1906 to commemorate the aborted assassination of King Alfonso XIII (grandfather of the present king, Juan Carlos).

    Across the street from the kneeling angel is the:

3. **Palacio de Abrantes,** Calle Mayor, 86, today occupied by the Italian Institute of Culture.

    On the same side of the street as the kneeling angel, to the statue's left, is the:

4. **Palacio de Uceda,** Calle Mayor, 79, today the headquarters of the Spanish military (their version of the U.S. Pentagon). Both of these palaces are among the best examples of 17th-century civil architecture in Madrid.

    Walk half a block east, crossing to the north side of Calle Mayor and detouring about 20 yards to the left, down narrow Calle de San Nicolás. You'll come to the somber facade of the oldest church in Madrid, the 12th-century:

5. **Church of San Nicolás,** Plaza de San Nicolás. Only a brick tower remains from the original building, one of the few examples of the Mudéjar style in the capital. The reredos at the high altar is the work of Juan de Herrera, also the architect of El Escorial.

    Retrace your steps to Calle Mayor. Turn left and continue to walk east. You'll pass Plaza de la Villa on your right, and, one block later:

6. **Plaza de San Miguel,** an iron-canopied meat-and-vegetable market. Here, you might stock up on ingredients for a picnic. (The market is open Monday to Friday from 9am to 2pm and 5 to 8pm, Saturday from 9am to 2pm.)

    Leave Plaza de San Miguel by Ciudad Rodrigo (there might not be a sign), which leads under a soaring granite archway and up a sloping street to the northwestern corner of:

7. **Plaza Mayor,** the landmark square that is at the heart of Old Madrid.

TAKE A BREAK **Café Bar Los Galayos,** Plaza Mayor, 1 (☎ 91/366-30-28), has long been one of the best places for tapas along this square. If you're taking the walking tour during the day, you may want to return to this café/bar at night, when it is most lively. In summer you can select one of the outdoor tables for your drinks and tapas. The café is open daily from noon to 1am.

Walking Tour: Hapsburg Madrid

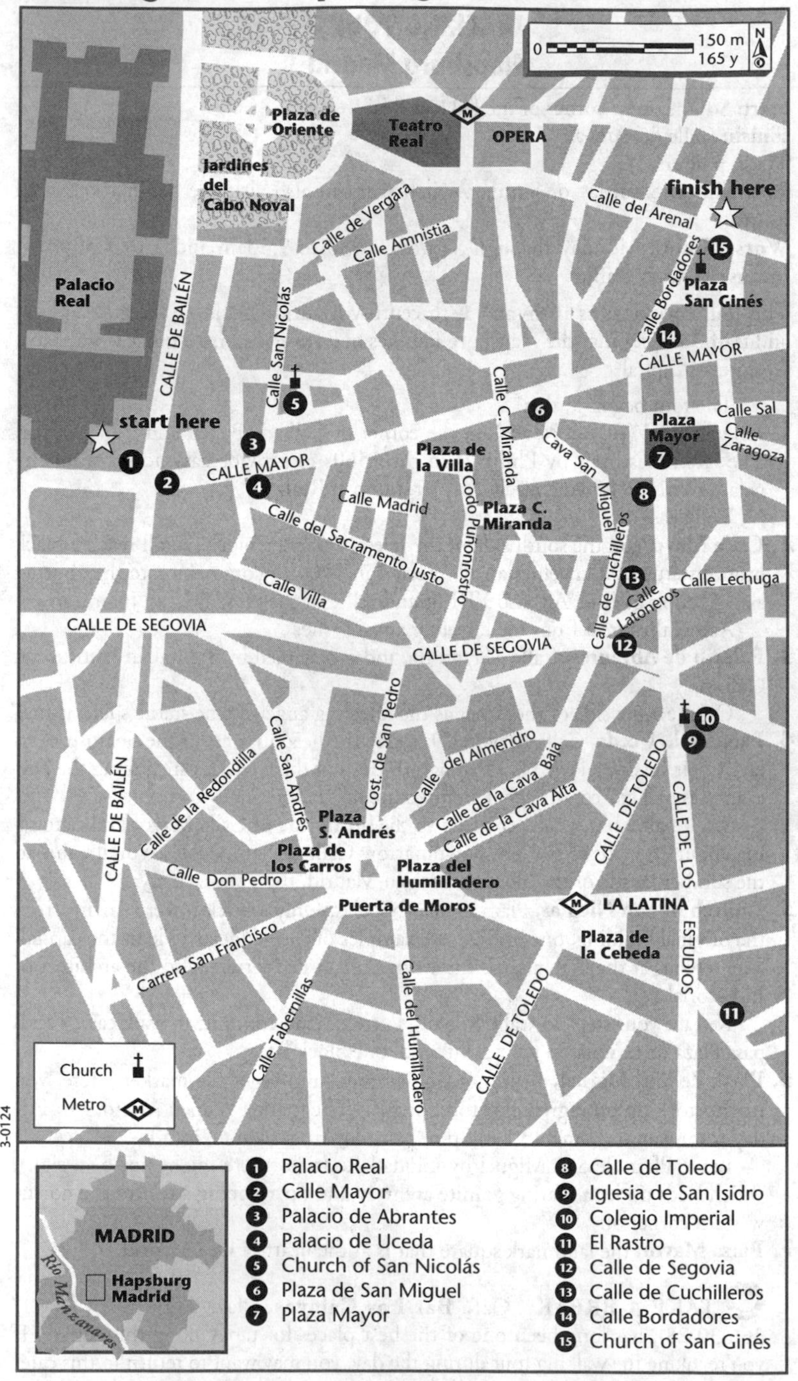

Stroll through Plaza Mayor, crossing it diagonally and exiting at the closer of its two southern exits. A dingy steep flight of stone stairs leads down to the beginning of the:

8. **Calle de Toledo.** Note in the distance the twin domes of the yellow stucco-and-granite:
9. **Iglesia de San Isidro,** legendary burial place of Madrid's patron saint and his wife, Santa Maria de la Cadeza. The church lost its status as a cathedral in 1992, when the honor went to the larger Church of La Almudena.

   Adjacent to San Isidro is the baroque facade of the:
10. **Colegio Imperial,** which was also run by the Jesuits. Lope de Vega, Calderón, and many other famous men studied at this institute.

    If your tour takes place on a Saturday or Sunday before 3pm, visit:
11. **El Rastro,** Madrid's world-famous flea market. Continue along Calle de Toledo, then fork left onto Calle Estudios and proceed to Plaza de Cascorro, named after a hero of the Cuban wars. El Rastro begins here. If your tour takes place Monday to Friday, skip the Rastro neighborhood. Instead, turn right onto:
12. **Calle de Segovia,** which intersects Calle de Toledo just before it passes in front of the Iglesia de San Isidro. Walk one block and turn right onto the first street:
13. **Calle de Cuchilleros.** Follow it north past 16th- and 17th-century stone-fronted houses. Within a block, a flight of granite steps forks to the right. Climb the steps (a sign identifies the new street as Calle Arco de Cuchilleros) and you'll pass one of the most famous *mesones* (typical Castilian restaurants) of Madrid, the Cueva de Luís Candelas.

    Once again you will have entered Plaza Mayor, this time on the southwestern corner. Walk beneath the southernmost arcade and promenade counterclockwise beneath the arcades, walking north underneath the square's eastern arcade. Then walk west beneath its northern arcade. At the northwest corner, exit through the archway onto Calle 7 de Julio. Fifty feet later, cross Calle Mayor and take the right-hand narrow street before you. This is:
14. **Calle Bordadores,** which during the 17th century housed Madrid's embroidery workshops, staffed exclusively by men.

    As you proceed, notice the 17th-century brick walls and towers of the:
15. **Church of San Ginés,** Arenal, 15. The church of one of Madrid's oldest parishes owes its present look to the architects who reconstructed it after a devastating fire in 1872.

    At the end of this tour, you'll find yourself on traffic-congested Calle del Arenal, at the doorstep of many interesting old streets.

WALKING TOUR 3
Bourbon Madrid

Start: Puerta de Alcalá.
Finish: Plaza de Oriente.
Time: 3 hours.
Best Times: Early morning or late afternoon in summer (or any sunny day in winter).
Worst Times: Monday through Saturday 7:30 to 9:30am and 5 to 7:30pm—because of heavy traffic.

By the time the Bourbons came to power in Spain, Madrid was firmly ensconced as a political and cultural center, proud of its role as head of a centralized government. This tour shows off the broad boulevards, spectacular fountains, and interconnected plazas that put Madrid on a par architecturally with other European capitals. Much of this tour goes through neighborhoods planned by Carlos III in the 18th century.

Begin at:

1. **Puerta de Alcalá (Alcalá Gate),** Plaza de la Independencia. One of the grand landmarks of Madrid, the Alcalá Gate was designed by Francesco Sabatini and built from 1769 to 1778. In the neoclassical style, it replaced a baroque arch that used to mark the entry into the city; with its five arched passages, it soon became a symbol of the new Bourbon "enlightenment" that swept over Madrid. Today it guards the approach to the major artery leading to northwestern Spain and on to France.

   Walk west, slightly downhill, along Calle de Alcalá to:

2. **Plaza de la Cibeles,** the most beautiful square in Madrid. In the center of the square is the Fuente de Cibeles, showing the Roman goddess Cybele driving an elaborate chariot pulled by two docile lions, which symbolize elegance and harmony. José Hermosilla and Ventura Rodríguez, architects of Paseo del Prado (see below), designed the fountain. To your left, on the corner of Calle de Alcalá and Plaza de la Cibeles, is the most magnificent post office in Europe, the Palacio de Comunicaciones. Its lavish embellishments give it the air of an ecclesiastical palace. It dates from 1904.

   From Plaza de la Cibeles you'll see two monuments—the pink-sided Palacio de Buenavista, the army headquarters of Spain, on the right side of the square; and immediately opposite you on the far side of the square, the Banco de España. You are now at the beginning of the most monumental part of Bourbon Madrid. Stroll beneath the leafy canopy of the:

3. **Paseo del Prado,** which incorporates two busy one-way streets separated by a wide pedestrian's promenade. Walk south down the world-famed promenade, passing shrubbery, trees, and benches. Paseo del Prado links Plaza de la Cibeles with Plaza del Emperador Carlos V, site of Atocha Train Station, the paseo's southern terminus. It is part of the busy north-south axis of the city. This whole section, called the Salón del Prado, incorporates more world-class art masterpieces than any other area of similar size in the world—not simply at the Prado but also at the Thyssen-Bornemisza Museum at Paseo del Prado, 8.

   On your left, as you head south toward Plaza de la Lealtad, you'll pass the:

4. **Museo Naval,** Paseo del Prado, 5. Adjacent to it, behind a gracefully angled row of neoclassical columns, stands the Madrid stock exchange (La Bolsa), dating from the 19th century.

   Continue down Paseo del Prado to the:

5. **Monument to the Heroes of the Second of May.** This 19th-century obelisk, on your left behind a barrier of trees, honors the "unknown soldiers" who fell in the Napoleonic wars of independence.

   To your right, a few paces later, is the:

6. **Palacio de Villahermosa,** Paseo del Prado, 8. This neoclassical palace holds one of the world's greatest artistic bequests, the Thyssen-Bornemisza Museum. In the center of Plaza Canovas del Castillo (also called Plaza de Neptuno) is a fountain dedicated to the Roman god Neptune.

   Continue walking south to reach the:

7. **Museo del Prado,** Paseo del Prado, one of the world's great art museums. The original core of paintings, which came from royal palaces throughout Spain, were substantially supplemented in the 19th century by private bequests. In the late 1700s, Carlos III commissioned the construction of a neoclassical brick-and-stone palace to house a Natural History Museum, named El Prado de San Jerónimo

Walking Tour: Bourbon Madrid

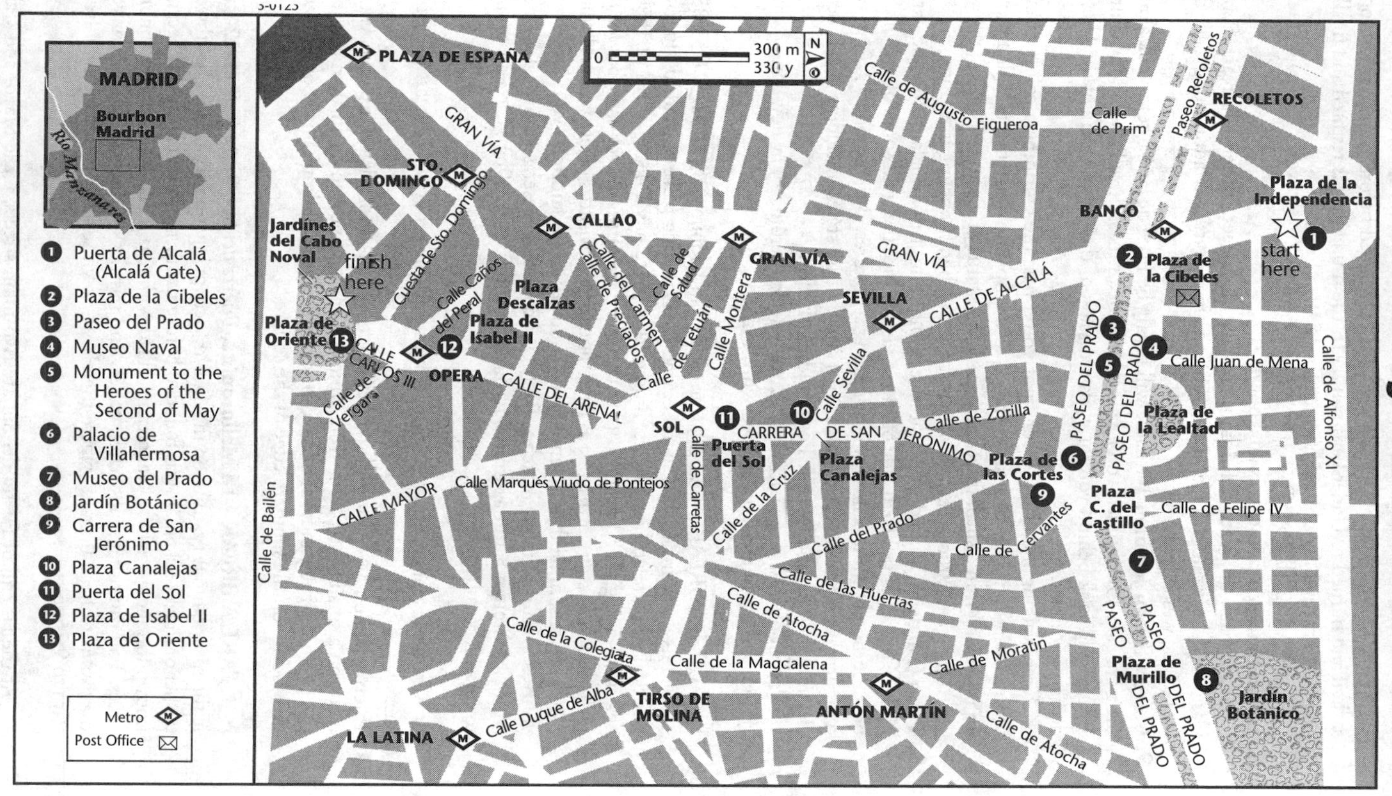

(St. Jerome's Meadow). It had barely been completed before Napoleon's troops sacked and burned it. Under Ferdinand VII, the museum was restored and finally opened to the public as an art musuem in 1819.

Continue south along Paseo del Prado to the:

8. Jardín Botánico, a fine oasis on a hot day.

Head back up Paseo del Prado, crossing the street. When you reach Plaza Cánovas del Castillo, turn left toward the ancient heart of Madrid along Calle de las Cortes, which leads into:

9. Carrera de San Jerónimo (its name will briefly be Plaza de las Cortés). Walk along the right side. On your left you'll pass the facade of the deluxe Palace Hotel. Turn around and look behind you for a distant view of the Gothic spire of the Iglesia de San Jerónimo.

Keep walking uphill. On your right you'll pass the Corinthian columns and bronze twin lions, flanking the entrance to the Spanish parliament, built around 1850. Facing it in a small three-sided park is a statue of Cervantes.

At this point, the street will narrow considerably, funneling itself into:

10. Plaza Canalejas, around which sit several buildings from the late 19th and early 20th centuries. On the left side of the square, notice the twin spires of one of the neighborhood's most whimsically appealing structures. Built around 1920, it was designed as an eclectic combination of 17th-century styles, including shells, neoclassical obelisks, and heraldic lions holding shields.

Pass along this square back onto Carrera de San Jerónimo, by now a busy, congested, and commercial street lined with stores.

TAKE A BREAK **Lhardy,** Carrera de San Jerónimo, 8 (☎ **91/521-33-85**), opened its doors in 1839. It soon became the gathering place of Madrid's literati, political leaders, and executives. Today this place has a decor called "Isabella Segundo" and gives off an aura of another era. Upstairs is a restaurant, but for refueling you can stop downstairs, as have thousands of visitors before you, and enjoy a cup of consommé from a large silver samovar; or, in summer, you can refresh yourself with soothing gazpacho. Each cup costs 200 pesetas ($1.60). It's open Monday through Saturday from 1 to 3:30pm and 9 to 11:30pm. Closed late July to early September.

Continue along Carrera de San Jerónimo to the geographical heart of Spain, the:

11. Puerta del Sol. Two-thirds of the way along its half-moon-shaped expanse, you'll come on a small brass plaque from which all the distances in Spain are measured, placed immediately in front of a red-brick municipal building called Comunidade de Madrid, on the southern edge of the square.

TAKE A BREAK **La Mallorquina,** Puerta del Sol, 8 (☎ **91/521-12-01**), is the most famous pastry shop in Madrid, occupying a position at the southwest corner of Puerta del Sol. It was founded before the turn of the century and became known for one specialty, a Napoletana, filled with cream and studded with almond slices. You can order sandwiches, coffee, and pastries on the ground floor, or you may want to head upstairs, where there's sit-down service. It is open daily from 9am to 9:15pm.

At the far end of Puerta del Sol are two main streets, Calle Mayor and Calle del Arenal, forking off to the right. Take Arenal, passing the red-brick neoclassical facade of the Iglesia de San Ginés on your left.

Within a short distance, you'll come on:

12. Plaza de Isabel II, graced with a bronze statue of the 19th-century music-loving queen, whose efforts helped construct an opera house for Madrid, the Teatro Real.

Follow the Calle del Arenal, now called Calle Carlos III, around the southern edge of the opera house to:

13. Plaza de Oriente, with its view of the Palacio Real (Royal Palace).

5 Organized Tours

A large number of agencies in Madrid book organized tours and excursions to sights and attractions both within and outside the city limits. Although your mobility and freedom might be somewhat hampered, some visitors appreciate the ease, convenience, and efficiency of being able to visit so many sights in a single efficiently organized day.

Many of the city's hotel concierges, and all of the city's travel agents, will book anyone who asks for a guided tour of Madrid or its environs with one of Spain's largest tour operators, Pullmantours, Plaza de Oriente, 8 (☎ **91/541-18-07**). Regardless of their destination and duration, virtually every tour departs from the Pullmantour terminal, at that address. Half-day tours of Madrid include an artistic tour priced at 4,950 pesetas ($39.60) per person, which includes entrance to a selection of the city's museums, and a panoramic half-day tour for 2,750 pesetas ($22).

Southward treks to Toledo are the most popular full-day excursions outside the city limits. They cost 7,650 pesetas ($61.20). These tours (including lunch) depart daily at 8:30am from the above-mentioned departure point, last all day, and include ample opportunities for wandering at will through the city's narrow streets. You can, if you wish, take an abbreviated morning tour of Toledo, without stopping for lunch, for 5,000 pesetas ($40).

Another popular tour stops briefly in Toledo and continues on to visit both the monastery at El Escorial and the Valley of the Fallen (Valle de los Caídos) before returning the same day to Madrid. With lunch included, this all-day excursion costs 10,700 pesetas ($85.60).

Other worthwhile full-day tours include visits to Segovia and the Bourbon dynasty's 18th-century palace of La Granja costing 6,200 pesetas ($49.60) without lunch and 9,400 pesetas ($75.20) with lunch. A half-day tour of Aranjuez and Chinchón, without lunch, costs 5,900 pesetas ($47.20).

The hop-off, hop-on **Madrid Vision Bus** lets you set your own pace and itinerary. A scheduled panoramic tour lasts a half hour, providing you don't get off the bus. Otherwise, you can opt for an unlimited number of stops, exploring at your leisure. The Madrid Vision makes four complete tours daily, two in the morning and two in the afternoon; on Sunday and Monday buses depart only in the morning. Check with Trapsa Tours (☎ **91/542-66-66**) for times of your departure, which are variable. The panoramic tour (without your getting off the bus) costs 600 pesetas ($4.80); the full-day tour with unlimited stops, 1,200 pesetas ($9.60). You can board the bus at the Madrid tourist office.

6 Outdoor Activities

SPECTATOR SPORTS

THE BULLFIGHT Madrid draws the finest matadors in Spain. If a matador hasn't proved his worth in the **Plaza Monumental de Toros de las Ventas,** Alcalá,

237 (☎ **91/356-22-00;** metro: Ventas), he just hasn't been recognized as a top-flight artist. The major season begins during the Fiestas de San Isidro, patron saint of Madrid, on May 15. This is the occasion for a series of fights, during which talent scouts are in the audience. Matadors who distinguish themselves in the ring are signed up for Majorca, Málaga, and other places.

For tickets to this biggest bullfight stadium in Madrid, go to its box office (open Fri–Sun 10am–2pm and 5–8pm). Admission usually ranges between 400 and 15,000 pesetas ($3.20–$120). Many hotels also have good seats that you can buy. Front-row seats are known as *barreras. Delanteras*—third-row seats—are available in both the *alta* (high) and the *baja* (low) sections. The cheapest seats sold, *filas,* afford the worst view and are in the sun (*sol*) during the entire performance. The best seats are in the shade (*sombra*). Bullfights are held on Sunday and holidays throughout most of the year, and every day during certain festivals, which tend to last around three weeks, usually in the late spring. Starting times are adjusted according to the anticipated hour of sundown on the day of a performance, usually 7pm from March through October, and at 5pm during late autumn and early spring. Late-night fights by neophyte matadors are sometimes staged under spotlights on Saturday around 11pm.

HORSE RACING There are two seasons—spring (February through June) and fall (mid-September to early December). Races, often six or seven, are generally held on Sunday and holidays (11am), with a series of night races (11pm) held on weekends in July and August. A restaurant and bar are at the **Hipódromo de la Zarzuela,** Carretera de la Coruña, Kilometer 7.8 (☎ **91/207-01-40**). The hippodrome is 11 miles (18km) from the center of Madrid (N-VI); take the free bus that leaves from Moncloa, across from the Air Ministry. Admission is 500 pesetas ($4).

SOCCER *Futbol* is played with a passion all year in Madrid. League matches, on Saturday or Sunday, run from September through May, culminating in the annual summer tournaments. Madrid has two teams in the top division.

The team Real Madrid plays home games at the Estadio Santiago Bernabéu, Concha Espina, 1 (☎ **91/344-00-52;** metro: Lima). Tickets, which run from 1,500 to 15,000 pesetas ($12–$120), can be obtained at the stadium. The Club Atlético de Madrid plays at the Estadio Vicente Calderón, Paseo de la Virgen del Puerto, 67 (☎ **91/366-47-07;** metro: Pirámides). Tickets are sold at the stadium, costing from 1,500 to 15,000 pesetas ($12–$120). Both box offices are open daily from noon to 1:30pm and 5 to 7pm.

RECREATION

FITNESS CENTERS Although Madrid has scores of gyms, bodybuilding studios, and aerobic-exercise centers, many of them are private. For one open to the public, try Atenas, Victor de la Serna, 37 (☎ **91/345-16-75;** metro: Colombia). This facility for men and women has an indoor swimming pool, workout equipment, a sauna, and such personal services as massage. It's open Monday through Friday from 7:30am to 10pm and Saturday from 9am to 2pm.

JOGGING Both the Parque del Retiro and Casa de Campo have jogging tracks. For details on how to get there, see below and also refer to "Parks & Gardens" in "More Attractions" earlier in this chapter.

SWIMMING & TENNIS The best swimming and tennis facilities are found at the Casa de Campo, Avenida del Angel (☎ **91/463-00-50;** metro: Lago or Batán), a 4,300-acre former royal hunting preserve that lies on the right bank of the Manzanares River. Today it is a public park, serving as a playground for Madrileños.

7 Shopping

Seventeenth-century playwright Tirso de Molina called Madrid "a shop stocked with every kind of merchandise," and it's true—an estimated 50,000 stores sell everything from high-fashion clothing to flamenco guitars to art and ceramics.

If your time is limited, go to one of the big department stores (see below). They all carry a "bit of everything."

THE SHOPPING SCENE

SHOPPING AREAS **The Center** The sheer diversity of shops in Madrid's center is staggering. Their densest concentration lies immediately north of Puerta del Sol, radiating out from Calle del Carmen, Calle Montera, and Calle Preciados.

Calle Mayor & Calle del Arenal Unlike their more stylish neighbors to the north of Puerta del Sol, shops in this district to the west tend toward the small, slightly dusty enclaves of coin and stamp dealers, family-owned souvenir shops, clockmakers, sellers of military paraphernalia, and an abundance of stores selling musical scores.

Gran Vía Conceived, designed, and built in the 1910s and 1920s as a showcase for the city's best shops, hotels, and restaurants, the Gran Vía has since been eclipsed by other shopping districts. Its art nouveau/art deco glamour still survives in the hearts of most Madrileños, however. The bookshops here are among the best in the city, as are outlets for fashion, shoes, jewelry, furs, and handcrafted accessories from all regions of Spain.

El Rastro It's the biggest flea market in Spain, drawing collectors, dealers, buyers, and hopefuls from throughout Madrid and its suburbs. The makeshift stalls are at their most frenetic on Sunday morning. For more information, refer to the "Flea Markets" section, below.

Plaza Mayor Under the arcades of the square itself are exhibitions of lithographs and oil paintings, and every weekend there's a loosely organized market for stamp and coin collectors. Within three or four blocks in every direction you'll find more than the average number of souvenir shops.

On Calle Marqués Viudo de Pontejos, which runs east from Plaza Mayor, is one of the city's headquarters for the sale of cloth, thread, and buttons. Also running east, on Calle de Zaragoza, are silversmiths and jewelers. On Calle Postas you'll find housewares, underwear, soap powders, and other household items.

Near the Carrera de San Jerónimo Several blocks east of Puerta del Sol is Madrid's densest concentration of gift shops, crafts shops, and antiques dealers—a decorator's delight. Its most interesting streets include Calle del Prado, Calle de las Huertas, and Plaza de las Cortés. The neighborhood is pricey—so don't expect bargains here.

Northwest Madrid A few blocks east of Parque del Oeste is an upscale neighborhood that's well stocked with luxury goods and household staples. Calle de la Princesa, its main thoroughfare, has shops selling shoes, handbags, fashion, gifts, and children's clothing. Thanks to the presence of the university nearby, there's also a dense concentration of bookstores, especially on Calle Isaac Peral and Calle Fernando el Católico, several blocks north and northwest, respectively, from the subway stop of Argüelles.

Salamanca District It's known throughout Spain as the quintessential upper-bourgeois neighborhood, uniformly prosperous, and its shops are correspondingly exclusive. They include outlets run by interior decorators, furniture shops, fur and jewelry shops, several department stores, and design headquarters whose output ranges from the solidly conservative to the high-tech. The main streets of this district are Calle de Serrano and Calle de Velázquez. The district lies northeast of the center of Madrid, a few blocks north of Retiro Park. Its most central metro stops are Serrano and Velázquez.

HOURS & SHIPPING Major stores are open (in most cases) Monday to Saturday from 9:30am to 8pm. Many small stores take a siesta between 1:30 and 4:30pm. Of course, there is never any set formula, and hours can vary greatly from store to store, depending on the idiosyncracies and schedules of the owner.

Many art and antiques dealers will crate and ship bulky objects for an additional fee. Any especially large or heavy item, such as a piece of furniture, should be sent by ship. Every antiques dealer in Spain maintains lists of reputable maritime shippers. One reliable option is **Emery Ocean Freight,** which maintains branch offices in Barcelona, Alicante, Madrid, Málaga, Bilboa, and Valencia. To contact their main office in Madrid, call **91/747-5533.** For more information, either before your departure or when checking the whereabouts of your shipment in transit from Spain, call Emery in the U.S. at ☎ **800/488-9451.**

For most small- and medium-sized shipments, air freight isn't much more expensive than shipping. **Iberia's Air Cargo Division** (☎ **800/221-6002** in the U.S.) offers air-freight service from Spain to either New York, Miami, or Los Angeles. For a shipment under 300 pounds from either Barcelona or Madrid to New York, the cost is 333 pesetas ($2.65) per pound. The per pound price goes down as the weight increases, reaching 269 pesetas ($2.15) per pound for shipments more than 1,000 pounds. Regardless of what you ship, there's a minimum charge of 8,500 pesetas ($68).

For an additional fee, Iberia or one of its representatives will pick up your package. For a truly precious cargo, ask the seller to build a crate for it. For information within Spain about air-cargo shipments, call Iberia's cargo division at Madrid's Barajas Airport (☎ **91/587-3307**) or at Barcelona's airport (☎ **93/401-3426**).

Remember that your air-cargo shipment will need to clear Customs after it's brought into the United States. This involves some additional paperwork, costly delays, and in some cases a trip to the airport where the shipment first entered the U.S. It's usually easier (and in some cases, much easier) to hire a commercial customs broker to do the work for you. Emery Worldwide, a division of CF Freightways, can clear your goods for around $125 for most shipments, which you'll pay in addition to any applicable duty you owe your home government. For information, you can call **800/323-4685** within the United States.

TAX & HOW TO RECOVER IT If you are not a European Union resident and make purchases in Spain worth more than 86,520 pesetas ($692.15), you can get a tax refund. (The internal tax, known as VAT in most of Europe, is called IVA in Spain.) Depending on the goods, the rate usually ranges from 7% to 12% of the total worth of your merchandise. Luxury items are taxed at 33%.

To get this refund, you must complete three copies of a form that the store will give you, detailing the nature of your purchase and its value. Citizens of non-EU countries show the purchase and the form to the Spanish Customs Office. The shop is supposed to refund the amount due you. Inquire at the time of purchase how they will do so and discuss in what currency your refund will arrive.

TRADITIONAL SALES The best sales are usually in summer. Called *rebajas,* they start in July and go through August. As a general rule, merchandise is marked down even more in August to make way for the new fall wares in most stores.

DUTY-FREE—WORTH IT OR NOT? Before you leave home, check the regular retail price of items that you're most likely to buy. Duty-free prices vary from one country to another and from item to item. Sometimes you're better off purchasing an item in a discount store at home. If you don't remember prices back home, you can't tell when you're getting a good deal.

BARGAINING The days of bargaining are, for the most part, long gone. Most stores have what is called *precio de venta al público* (PVP), a firm retail price not subject to negotiation. With street vendors and flea markets, it's a different story because haggling *a la española* is expected. However, you'll have to be very skilled to get the price reduced a lot, as most of these street-smart vendors know exactly what their merchandise is worth and are old hands at getting that price.

SHOPPING A TO Z

Spain has always been known for its craftspeople, many of whom still work in the time-honored and labor-intensive traditions of their grandparents. It's hard to go wrong if you stick to the beautiful handcrafted Spanish objects—hand-painted tiles, ceramics, and porcelain; handwoven rugs; handmade sweaters; and intricate embroideries. And, of course, Spain produces some of the world's finest leather. Jewelry, especially gold set with Majorca pearls, represents good value and unquestioned luxury.

Some of Madrid's art galleries are known throughout Europe for discovering and encouraging new talent. Antiques are sold in highly sophisticated retail outlets. Better suited to the budgets of many travelers are the weekly flea markets.

Spain continues to make inroads into the fashion world. Its young designers are regularly featured in the fashion magazines of Europe. Excellent shoes are available, some highly fashionable. But be advised that prices for shoes and quality clothing are generally higher in Madrid than in the United States.

ANTIQUES

In addition to the shops listed below, these are sold at the flea market (see El Rastro, below).

Centro de Anticuarios Lagasca. Lagasca, 36. No phone. Metro: Serrano or Velázquez.

You'll find about a dozen antiques shops here, clustered into one covered arcade. They operate as individual businesses, although by browsing through each you'll find an impressive assemblage of antique furniture, porcelain, and whatnots. Open Monday to Saturday from 10am to 1:30pm and 5 to 8pm.

Centro de Arte y Antigüedades. Serrano, 5. ☎ **91/576-96-82.** Metro: Retiro. Bus: 9 or 15.

Housed in a mid-19th-century building are several unusual antiques dealers (and a large carpet emporium as well). Each establishment maintains its own schedule, although the center itself has overall hours. Open Monday through Saturday from 11am to 2pm and 5 to 8:30pm.

ART GALLERIES

Galería Kreisler. Hermosilla, 6. ☎ **91/431-42-64.** Metro: Serrano. Bus: 27, 45, or 150.

One successful entrepreneur on Madrid's art scene is Ohio-born Edward Kreisler, whose gallery, now run by his son Juan, specializes in figurative and contemporary paintings, sculptures, and graphics. The gallery prides itself on occasionally displaying and selling the works of artists who are critically acclaimed and displayed in museums in Spain. Open Monday through Saturday from 10:30am to 2pm and 5 to 9pm. Closed Saturday afternoon July 15 to September 15 and August.

Capes

Capas Seseña. Cruz, 23. ☎ **91/531-68-40.** Metro: Sevilla or Puerta del Sol. Bus: 5, 51, or 52.

Founded shortly after the turn of the century, this shop manufactures and sells wool capes for both women and men. The wool comes from the mountain town of Béjar, near Salamanca. Celebrities who have been spotted donning Seseña capes include Picasso, Hemingway, Miró, and recently, First Lady Hillary Clinton and daughter Chelsea. Open Monday through Friday from 10am to 1:30pm and 5 to 8pm, Saturday from 10am to 1:30pm.

Carpets

Ispahan. Serrano, 5. ☎ **91/575-20-12.** Metro: Retiro. Bus: 1, 2, 9, and 15.

In this 19th-century building, behind bronze handmade doors, are three floors devoted to carpets from around the world, notably Afghanistan, India, Nepal, Iran, Turkey, and the Caucasus. One section features silk carpets. In addition, the Art Gallery of the Louvre, Ispahan II, displays both old masters and contemporary art. Open Monday through Saturday from 10am to 2pm and 4:30 to 8:30pm.

Ceramics

Antigua Casa Talavera. Isabel la Católica, 2. ☎ **91/547-34-17.** Metro: Santo Domingo. Bus: 1, 2, 46, 70, 75, or 148.

"The first house of Spanish ceramics" has wares that include a sampling of regional styles from every major area of Spain, including Talavera, Toledo, Manises, Valencia, Puente del Arzobispa, Alcora, Granada, and Seville. Sangría pitchers, dinnerware, tea sets, plates, and vases are all handmade. Inside one of the showrooms is an interesting selection of tiles, painted with reproductions of scenes from bullfights, dances, and folklore. There's also a series of tiles depicting famous paintings in the Prado. At its present location since 1904, the shop is only a short walk from Plaza de Santo Domingo. Open Monday through Friday from 10am to 1:30pm and 5 to 8pm, Saturday from 10am to 1:30pm.

Crafts

El Arco de los Cuchilleros Artesania de Hoy. Plaza Mayor, 9 (basement level). ☎ **91/365-26-80.** Metro: Puerta del Sol.

Set within one of the 17th-century vaulted cellars of Plaza Mayor, this shop is entirely devoted to unusual craft items derived from throughout Spain. The merchandise is unusual, one of a kind, and in most cases contemporary; it includes a changing array of pottery, leather, textiles, wood carvings, glassware, wickerwork, papier mâché, and silver jewelry. The hardworking owners deal directly with the artisans who produce each item, ensuring a wide inventory of handcrafts. The staff is familiar with the rituals of applying for tax-free status of purchases here, and speak several different languages. It's open January through September, Monday through Saturday from 11am to 8pm; October through December, Monday through Saturday from 11am to 9pm.

Department Stores

El Corte Inglés. Preciados, 3. ☎ **91/532-18-00.** Metro: Puerta del Sol.

This flagship of the largest department-store chain in Madrid sells hundreds of souvenirs and Spanish handcrafts—damascene steelwork from Toledo, flamenco dolls, and embroidered shawls. Some astute buyers report that it also sells glamorous fashion articles, such as Pierre Balmain designs, for about a third less than equivalent items in most European capitals. Services include interpreters, currency-exchange windows, and parcel delivery either to a local hotel or overseas. Open Monday through Saturday from 10am to 9pm.

EMBROIDERIES

Casa Bonet. Núñez de Balboa, 76. ☎ **91/575-09-12.** Metro: Núñez de Balboa.

The intricately detailed embroideries produced in Spain's Balearic Islands (especially Majorca) are avidly sought for bridal chests and elegant dinner settings. A few examples of the store's extensive inventory are displayed on the walls. Open Monday through Friday from 9:45am to 2pm and 5 to 8pm, Saturday from 10:15am to 2pm.

ESPADRILLES

Casa Hernanz. Toledo, 18. ☎ **91/366-54-50.** Metro: Puerta del Sol, Ópera, or La Latina.

A brisk walk south of Plaza Mayor delivers you to this store, in business since the 1840s. In addition to espadrilles, they sell shoes in other styles, as well as hats. Open Monday through Friday 9am to 1:30pm and 4:30 to 8pm, Saturday from 10am to 2pm.

FANS & UMBRELLAS

Casa de Diego. Puerta del Sol, 12. ☎ **91/522-66-43.** Metro: Puerta del Sol.

Here you'll find a wide inventory of fans, ranging from plain to fancy, from plastic to exotic hardwood, from cost-conscious to lavish. Some fans tend to be a bit overpriced; shopping around may increase your chances of finding a real bargain. In summer Casa de Diego is open Monday through Saturday from 9:30am to 8pm; in winter, Monday through Saturday from 9:30am to 1:30pm and 5 to 8pm.

FASHIONS FOR MEN

For the man on a budget who wants to dress reasonably well, the best outlet for off-the-rack men's clothing is one of the branches of the Corte Inglés department-store chain (see above). Most men's boutiques in Madrid are very expensive and may not be worth the investment.

FASHIONS FOR WOMEN

Don Carlos. Serrano, 92. ☎ **91/575-75-07.** Metro: Núñez de Balboa.

This boutique has a limited but tasteful array of clothing for women (and a somewhat smaller selection for men). Open Monday through Saturday from 10am to 2pm and 5 to 8:30pm.

Herrero. Preciados, 7. ☎ **91/521-29-90.** Metro: Puerta del Sol or Callao.

The sheer size and buying power of this popular retail outlet for women's clothing make it a reasonably priced emporium for all kinds of feminine garb as well as various articles for gentlemen. It is open Monday through Saturday from 10:30am to 8pm; some Sundays from noon to 8pm. Additional outlets lie on the same street at no. 16 and at Calle de Carrestas, 10. Both stores are open Monday through Saturday from 10:30am to 2pm and 4:30 to 8pm.

Modas Gonzalo. Gran Vía, 43. ☎ **91/547-12-39.** Metro: Callao or Puerta del Sol.

This boutique's baroque, gilded atmosphere evokes the 1940s, but its fashions are strictly up to date, well made, and intended for stylish adult women. No children's garments are sold. Open Monday through Saturday from 10am to 1:30pm and 4:30 to 8pm.

Flea Markets

El Rastro. Plaza Cascorro and Ribera de Curtidores. Metro: La Latina. Bus: 3 or 17.

Foremost among markets is El Rastro (translated as either flea market or thieves' market), occupying a roughly triangular district of streets and plazas a few minutes' walk south of Plaza Mayor. Its center is Plaza Cascorro and Ribera de Curtidores. This market will delight anyone attracted to a mishmash of fascinating junk interspersed with bric-a-brac and paintings. *Note:* Thieves are rampant here (hustling more than just antiques), so secure your wallet carefully, be alert, and proceed with caution. Open Tuesday through Sunday from 9:30am to 1:30pm and 5 to 8pm.

Food & Wine

Majorca. Velázquez, 59. ☎ **91/431-99-09.** Metro: Velásquez.

Madrid's best-established gourmet shop opened in 1931 as an outlet selling a pastry called *ensaimada,* and this is still one of the store's most famous products. Tempting arrays of cheeses, canapés, roasted and marinated meats, sausages, and about a dozen kinds of pâté—these accompany a spread of tiny pastries, tarts, and chocolates. Don't overlook the displays of Spanish wines and brandies. A stand-up tapas bar is always clogged with clients three deep, sampling the wares before they buy larger portions to take home. Tapas cost from 250 to 300 pesetas ($2–$2.40) per *ración* (portion). Open daily from 9am to 9pm.

Hats & Headgear

Casa Yustas. Plaza Mayor, 30. ☎ **91/366-50-84.** Metro: Puerta del Sol.

Founded in 1894, this extraordinary hat emporium is very popular. Want to see yourself as a Congo explorer, a Spanish sailor, an officer in the kaiser's army, or even Napoleon? Open Monday through Friday from 9:45am to 1:30pm and 4:30 to 8pm, Saturday from 9:45am to 1:30pm.

Leather

Loewe. Gran Vía, 8. ☎ **91/522-68-15.** Metro: Banco de España.

Since 1846 this has been the most elegant leather store in Spain. Its gold-medal-winning designers have always kept abreast of changing tastes and styles, but the inventory still retains a timeless chic. The store sells luggage, handbags, and jackets for men and women (in leather or suede). Open Monday through Saturday from 9:30am to 8pm.

Musical Instruments

Real Musical. Carlos III, no. 1. ☎ **91/541-30-07.** Metro: Ópera.

You'll find the best selection here—everything from a Spanish guitar to a piano, along with string and wind instruments. The place also has excellent Spanish records and sheet music. Open Monday through Friday from 9:30am to 2pm and 5 to 8pm, Saturday from 10am to 2pm.

Perfumes

Perfumería Padilla. Preciados, 17. ☎ **91/522-66-83.** Metro: Puerta del Sol.

This store sells a large and competitively priced assortment of Spanish and international scents for women. They also maintain a branch at Calle del Carmen, 78 (same phone). Both branches are open Monday through Saturday from 10am to 8:30pm.

Urguiola. Mayor, 1. ☎ **91/521-59-05.** Metro: Puerta del Sol.

Located at the western edge of the Puerta del Sol, this time-tested shop carries one of the most complete stocks of perfume in Madrid—both national and international brands. It also sells gifts, souvenirs, and costume jewelry. Open Monday through Saturday from 10am to 8pm.

PORCELAIN

Lasarte. Gran Vía, 44. ☎ **91/521-49-22.** Metro: Callao.

This store is an imposing outlet for Lladró porcelain, devoted almost exclusively to its distribution. The staff can usually tell you about new designs and releases the Lladró company is planning for the near future. Open Monday through Friday from 9:30 to 8pm, Saturday from 10am to 8pm.

SHOPPING MALLS

Galería del Prado. Plaza de las Cortes, 7. Metro: Banco de España or Atocha.

Spain's top designers are represented in this marble-sheathed concourse below the Palace Hotel. It opened in 1989 with 47 different shops, many featuring *moda joven* (fashions for the young). Merchandise changes with the season, but you will always find a good assortment of fashions, Spanish leather goods, cosmetics, perfumes, and jewelry. You can also eat and drink in the complex. The entrance to the gallery is in front of the hotel, facing the broad tree-lined Paseo del Prado across from the Prado itself. Open Monday through Saturday from 10am to 9pm.

8 Madrid After Dark

Madrid abounds with dance halls, *tascas,* cafés, theaters, movie houses, music halls, and nightclubs. You'll have to proceed carefully through this maze, as many of these offerings are strictly for the residents or for Spanish-speakers.

Because dinner is served late in Spain, nightlife doesn't really get under way until after 11pm, and it generally lasts until around 3am—Madrileños are so fond of prowling around at night that they are known around Spain as *gatos* (cats). If you arrive at 9:30pm at a club, you'll have the place all to yourself.

In most clubs a one-drink minimum is the rule: Feel free to nurse one drink through the entire evening's entertainment.

In summer Madrid becomes a virtual free festival because the city sponsors a series of plays, concerts, and films. Pick up a copy of the *Guía del Ocio* (available at most newsstands) for listings of these events. This guide also provides information about occasional discounts for commercial events, such as the concerts that are given in Madrid's parks. Also check the program of *Fundación Juan March,* Calle Castello, 77 (☎ **91/435-42-40;** metro: Núñez de Balboa), which frequently stages free concerts.

Flamenco in Madrid is geared mainly to tourists with fat wallets, and nightclubs are expensive. But since Madrid is preeminently a city of song and dance, you can often be entertained at very little cost—in fact, for the price of a glass of wine or beer, if you sit at a bar with live entertainment.

Like flamenco clubs, discos tend to be expensive, but they often open for what is erroneously called "afternoon" sessions (from 7 to 10pm). Although discos charge entry fees, at an "afternoon" session the cost might be as low as 300 pesetas ($2.40), rising to 2,000 pesetas ($16) and beyond for a "night" session—that is, beginning at 11:30pm and lasting until the early morning hours. Therefore, go

The Sultry Sound of Flamenco

The lights dim and the flamenco stars clatter rhythmically across the dance floor. Their lean bodies and hips shake and sway to the music. The word *flamenco* has various translations, meaning everything from "gypsified Andalusian" to "knife," from "blowhard" to "tough guy."

Accompanied by stylized guitar music, castanets, and the fervent clapping of the crowd, dancers are filled with tension and emotion. Flamenco dancing, with its flash, color, and ritual, is evocative of Spanish culture.

Its origins remain mysterious, however. Experts disagree as to where it came from, but most seem to claim Andalusia as its seat of origin. Although its influences were both Jewish and Islamic, it was the gypsy artist who perfected both the song and the dance. Gypsies took to flamenco like "rice to paella," in the word of the historian, Fernando Quiñones.

The deep song of flamenco represents a fatalistic attitude to life. Marxists used to say it was a deeply felt protest of the lower classes against their oppressors, but this seems unfounded. Protest or not, rich patrons—often young, brash young men—over the centuries liked the sound of flamenco and booked artists to stage *juergas* or fiestas. Dancer-prostitutes became the "erotic extras." The style had reached its present format by the early 17th century. Flamenco was linked with pimping, prostitution, and lots and lots of drinking, both from the audience and the artists.

By the mid-19th century flamenco had gone legitimate and was heard in theaters and *café cantantes.* By the 1920s even the pre-Franco Spanish dictator, Primo de Rivera, was singing the flamenco tunes of his native Cádiz. The poet Federico García Lorca and the composer Manuel de Falla prefered a purer form, attacking what they viewed as the degenerate and "ridiculous" burlesque of *flamenquismo,* the jazzed-up, audience-pleasing form of flamenco. The two artists launched a Flamenco Festival in Grenada in 1922. Of course, in the decades since, their voices have been drowned out, and flamenco is more *flamenquismo* than ever.

In his 1995 book *Flamenco Deep Song,* Thomas Mitchell draws a parallel to flamenco's "lowlife roots" and the "orgiastic origins" of jazz. He notes that early jazz, like flamenco, was "associated with despised ethnic groups, gangsters, brothels, free-spending bluebloods, and whoopee hedonism." By disguising their origins, Mitchell notes, both jazz and flamenco have entered the musical mainstream.

early, dance until 10pm, then proceed to dinner (you'll be eating at the fashionable hour).

Nightlife is so plentiful in Madrid that the city can be roughly divided into the following "night zones."

Plaza Mayor/Puerta del Sol The most popular areas from the standpoint of both tradition and tourist interest, they can also be dangerous, so explore them with caution, especially late at night. They are filled with tapas bars and *cuevas* (drinking "caves"). Here it is customary to begin a *tasca* crawl, going to tavern after tavern, sampling the wine in each, along with a selection of tapas. The major streets for such a crawl are Cava de San Miguel, Cava Alta, and Cava Baja. You can order *pinchos y raciones* (tasty snacks and tidbits).

Gran Vía This area contains mainly cinemas and theaters. Most of the after-dark action takes place on little streets branching off the Gran Vía.

Plaza de Isabel II/Plaza de Oriente This is another area much frequented by tourists. Many restaurants and cafés flourish here, including the famous Café de Oriente.

Chueca Embracing such streets as Hortaleza, Infantas, Barquillo, and San Lucas, this is the gay nightlife district, with many clubs. Cheap restaurants, along with a few female striptease joints, are also found here. This area can also be dangerous at night, so watch for pickpockets and muggers. As of late, there has been greater police presence at night.

Argüelles/Moncloa For university students, this part of town sees most of the action. Many dance clubs are found here, along with ale houses and fast-food joints. The area is bounded by Pintor Rosales, Cea Bermúdez, Bravo Murillo, San Bernardo, and Conde Duque.

THE PERFORMING ARTS

There are within Madrid a number of theaters, opera companies, and dance companies. To discover where and when specific cultural events are being performed, pick up a copy of *Guía del Ocio* at any city newsstand. The sheer volume of cultural offerings might stagger you; for concise summary of the highlights, see below.

Tickets to dramatic and musical events usually range in price from 700 to 3,000 pesetas ($5.60–$24), with discounts of up to 50% granted on certain days of the week (usually Wednesday and early performances on Sunday).

The concierges at most major hotels can usually get you tickets to specific concerts, if you are clear about your wishes and needs. They, of course, charge a considerable markup, part of which is passed along to whichever agency originally booked the tickets. You'll save money if you go directly to the box office to buy tickets. In the event your choice is sold out, you may be able to get tickets (with a considerable markup) at **Localidades Galicia** at Plaza del Carmen (**☎ 91/531-27-32;** metro: Puerta del Sol). This agency also markets tickets to bullfights and sports events. It is open Tuesday through Saturday from 9:30am to 1:30pm and 4:30 to 7:30pm; Sunday from 9:30am to 1:30pm.

Here follows a grab bag of nighttime diversions that might amuse and entertain you. First, the cultural offerings:

MAJOR PERFORMING ARTS COMPANIES

For those who speak Spanish, the **Compañía Nacional de Nuevas Tendencias Escénicas** is an avant-garde troupe that performs new (often controversial) works by undiscovered writers. On the other hand, the **Compañía Nacional de Teatro Clásico,** as its name suggests, is devoted to the Spanish classics, including works by the ever-popular Lope de Vega or Tirso de Molina.

Among dance companies, the national ballet of Spain—devoted exclusively to Spanish dance—is the **Ballet Nacional de España.** Their performances are always well attended. The national lyrical ballet company of the country is the **Ballet Lírico Nacional.**

World-renowned flamenco sensation Antonio Canales and his troup, **Ballet Flamenco Antonio Canales,** offer high-energy, spirited performances. Productions are centered around Canales's impassioned *Torero,* his interpretation of a bullfighter and the physical and emotional struggles within the man. For tickets and information, call **91/401-28-25.**

Madrid's opera company is the **Teatro de la Opera,** and its symphony orchestra is the outstanding **Orquesta Sinfónica de Madrid.** The national orchestra of Spain—widely acclaimed on the continent—is the **Orquesta Nacional de España,** which pays particular homage to Spanish composers.

Classical Music

Auditorio Nacional de Música. Príncipe de Vergara, 146. ☎ **91/337-01-00.** Tickets 1,000–6,000 ptas. ($8–$48). Metro: Cruz del Rayo.

Sheathed in slabs of Spanish granite, marble, and limestone and capped with Iberian tiles, this hall is the ultramodern home of both the National Orchestra of Spain and the National Chorus of Spain. Standing just north of Madrid's Salamanca district, it ranks as a major addition to the competitive circles of classical music in Europe. Inaugurated in 1988, it is devoted exclusively to the performances of symphonic, choral, and chamber music. In addition to the Auditorio Principal (Hall A), whose capacity is almost 2,300, there's a hall for chamber music (Hall B), as well as a small auditorium (seating 250) for intimate concerts.

Auditorio del Parque de Atracciones. Casa de Campo. Metro: Lago or Batán.

The schedule of this 3,500-seat facility might include everything from punk-rock musical groups to the more high-brow warm-weather performances of visiting symphony orchestras. Check with Localidades Galicia to see what's on at the time of your visit (see "The Performing Arts" above).

Auditorio del Real Conservatorio de Música. Plaza Isabel II. ☎ **91/337-01-00.** Tickets 1,500–7,500 ptas. ($12–$60). Metro: Ópera.

This is one of the home bases of the Spanish Philharmonic Orchestra, which presents its concerts between September and May. When it's not performing, the space is sometimes lent to relatively unknown musical newcomers, who perform at admission-free concerts. The auditorium also presents concerts by chamber music ensembles visiting from abroad. Containing only about 400 seats, the hall is sometimes sold out long in advance, especially for such famous names as Plácido Domingo.

Fundación Juan March. Castelló, 77. ☎ **91/435-42-40.** Metro: Núñez de Balboa.

This foundation sometimes holds free concerts at lunchtime. The advance schedule is difficult to predict, so call for information.

Ballet

Centro Cultural de la Villa. Plaza de Colón. ☎ **91/575-60-80.** Tickets, depending on event, 1,200–4,000 ptas. ($9.60–$32). Metro: Serrano or Colón.

Spanish-style ballet is presented at this cultural center. Tickets go on sale five days before the event of your choice, and performances are usually presented at two evening shows (8 and 10:30pm).

Flamenco

Café de Chinitas. Torija, 7. ☎ **91/559-51-35.** Dinner and show 8,500 ptas. ($68); cover charge for show without dinner (but with one drink included) 3,900 ptas. ($31.20). Metro: Santo Domingo. Bus: 1 or 2.

One of the best flamenco clubs in town, the Café de Chinitas is set one floor above street level in a 19th-century building midway between the Ópera and the Gran Vía.

It features an array of (usually) gypsy-born flamenco artists from Madrid, Barcelona, and Andalusia, with acts and performers changing about once a month.

You can arrange for dinner before the show, although many Madrileños opt for dinner somewhere else and then arrive just for drinks and the flamenco. Open Monday through Saturday, with dinner served from 9 to 11pm and the show lasting from 10:30pm to 2am. Reservations are recommended.

Casa Patas. Calle Cañizares 10. ☎ **91/369-04-96.** Admission 1,500–2,000 ptas. ($12–$16). Metro: Tirso de Molina.

This club is now one of the best places to see "true" flamenco as opposed to the more tourist-oriented version presented at Corral de la Moreria (see below). It is also a bar and restaurant, with space reserved in the rear for flamenco. Shows are presented midnight on Thursday, Friday, and Saturday and during Madrid's major fiesta month of May. The best flamenco in Madrid (on occasions) is presented here. Proof of the pudding is that flamenco singers and dancers often hang out here after hours. Tapas—rather pricey—are available at the bar. The club is open daily from 9pm to 5am.

Corral de la Morería. Morería, 17. ☎ **91/365-84-46.** Cover one-drink minimum 4,000 ptas. ($32); 9,500 ptas. ($76) with dinner. Metro: La Latina or Puerta del Sol.

In the old town, the Morería—meaning "where the Moors reside"—sizzles with flamenco. Strolling performers, colorfully costumed, warm up the audience around 11pm; a flamenco show follows, with at least 10 dancers. It's much cheaper to eat somewhere else first, paying only the one-drink minimum. Open daily from 9pm to 3am.

THEATER

Madrid offers many different theater performances, useful to you only if your Spanish is very fluent. If it isn't, check the *Guía del Ocia* for performances by English-speaking companies on tour from Britain or select a concert or subtitled movie instead.

In addition to the major ones listed below, there are at least 30 other theaters, including one devoted almost entirely to children's plays, the **Sala la Bicicleta,** in the Ciudad de los Niños at Casa de Campo. Dozens of other plays are staged by nonprofessional groups in such places as churches.

Teatro Calderón. Atocha, 18. ☎ **91/369-14-34.** Tickets 2,000–3,500 ptas. ($16–$28). Metro: Tirso de Molina.

This is the largest theater in Madrid, with a seating capacity of 1,700. It's known for its popular revues, performances of popular Spanish plays, and flamenco.

Teatro de la Comedia. Príncipe, 14. ☎ **91/521-49-31.** Tickets 1,500–2,600 ptas. ($12–$20.80); 50% discount on Thurs. Metro: Sevilla. Bus: 15, 20, or 150.

This is the home of the Compañía Nacional de Teatro Clásico. Here, more than anywhere else in Madrid, you're likely to see performances from the classic repertoire of great Spanish drama. Closed on Thursday and in July and August. The box office is open daily from 11:30am to 1:30pm and 5 to 6pm.

Teatro Español. Príncipe, 25. ☎ **91/429-62-97.** Tickets 200–2,000 ptas. ($1.60–$16); 50% discount on Wed. Metro: Sevilla.

The company is funded by Madrid's municipal government, its repertoire a time-tested assortment of great and/or favorite Spanish plays. The box office is open daily from 11:30am to 1:30pm and 5 to 6pm.

Teatro María Guerrero. Tamayo y Baus, 4. ☎ **91/319-47-69.** Tickets 1,600–2,600 ptas. ($12.80–$20.80); 50% discount on Wed. Metro: Banco de España or Colón.

Also funded by the government, it works in cooperation with the Teatro Español (see above) for performances of works by such classic Spanish playwrights as Lope de Vega and García Lorca. The theater was named after a much-loved Spanish actress. The box office is open daily from 11:30am to 1:30pm and 5 to 6pm.

Teatro Lírico Nacional de la Zarzuela. Jovellanos, 4. ☎ **91/524-54-00.** Tickets 1,800–13,200 ptas. ($14.40–$105.60). Metro: Sevilla.

Near Plaza de la Cibeles, this theater of potent nostalgia produces ballet and an occasional opera in addition to zarzuela. Show times vary. The box office is open daily from noon to 5pm.

Teatro Nuevo Apolo. Plaza de Tirso de Molina, 1. ☎ **91/369-14-67.** Cover usually 2,800 ptas. ($22.40). Metro: Tirso de Molina.

The Nuevo Apolo is the permanent home of the renowned Antología de la Zarzuela company. It is on the restored site of the old Teatro Apolo, where these musical variety shows have been performed since the 1930s. Prices and times depend on the show. The box office is open daily from 11:30am to 1:30pm and 5 to 6pm; show times vary.

THE CLUB & MUSIC SCENE

CABARET

Madrid's nightlife is no longer steeped in prudishness, as it was (at least officially) during the Franco era. You can now see glossy cabarets and shows with lots of nudity.

Café del Foro. Calle San Andres, 38. ☎ **91/445-37-52.** No cover (but may be imposed for a specially booked act). Metro: Bilboa. Bus: 40, 147, 149, or N19.

This oldtime favorite in the Malasaña district has suddenly in the mid-1990s become one of the most fashionable places in Madrid to hang out after dark. Patronizing the club are members of the literati along with a large student clientele. You never know exactly what the venue for the evening will be, although live music of some sort generally starts at 11:30pm. Cabaret is often featured, along with live merengue and salsa. There's a faux starry sky above the stage arena. Open daily from 7pm to 2am.

China Club. Calle Amor de Dios, 13. ☎ **91/429-74-24.** Admission 1,000 ptas. ($8), including first drink. Metro: Antón Martín.

The most outrageous cabaret acts in Madrid are performed here, with the performers often in drag. These acts don't start until 12:30am, however. Follow the dark passage into a spacious main arena. Tubes and pipes form part of the modernist architecture. In the words of the club manager, this place attracts "all kinds—everybody is welcome." Those "all kinds" get up to dance to a wide variety of sounds after the show is over. The club is open daily from 10:30pm to 3am.

Las Noches de Cuple. La Palma, 51. ☎ **91/533-71-15.** Cover 3,000 ptas. ($24), including first drink. Metro: Noviciado.

If you don't mind going to bed at sunrise, you might enjoy this updated version of a once-celebrated Madrileño cabaret. Its entrance is on a narrow, crowded street. Inside, in a long room with a vaulted ceiling and a tiny stage, Señora Olga Ramos conducts an evening of Iberian song. The charm of her all-Spanish act is increased by the discreet humor of an octogenarian accompanist with an ostrich-feather tiara and a fuchsia-colored boa. Open Monday through Saturday from 9:30pm to 2am; shows at midnight. Drinks begin at 1,100 pesetas ($8.80); dinner from 7,500 pesetas ($60).

Scala Melía Castilla. Calle Capitán Haya, 43 (entrance at Rosario Pino, 7). ☎ **91/571-44-11.** Cover 5,100 ptas. ($40.80), including first drink. Metro: Cuzco.

Madrid's most famous dinner show is a major Las Vegas–style spectacle, with music, water, light, and color. The program is varied—you might see international or Spanish ballet, magic acts, ice skaters, whatever. Most definitely you'll be entertained by a live orchestra. It is open Monday through Saturday from 8:30pm to 3am. Dinner is served beginning at 9pm; the show is presented at 10:30pm. The show with dinner costs 9,550 pesetas ($76.40), and if you partake you don't have to pay the cover charge above, as it's included in the show/dinner price. Reservations are needed.

JAZZ

Café Central. Plaza del Angel, 10. ☎ **91/369-41-43.** Cover charge Tues–Sun 1,000 ptas. ($8), Mon 800 ptas. ($6.40)—but prices vary depending on show. Metro: Antón Martín.

Off the Plaza de Santa Ana, beside the famed Gran Hotel Victoria, the Café Central has a vaguely art deco interior, with an unusual series of stained-glass windows. Many of the customers read newspapers and talk at the marble-top tables during the day, but the ambience is far more animated during the nightly jazz sessions. Open Sunday through Thursday from 1:30pm to 2:30am, Friday and Saturday from 1:30pm to 3:30am; live jazz is offered daily from 10pm to midnight. Drinks begin at 400 pesetas ($3.20).

Café Populart. Calle Huertas, 22. ☎ **91/429-84-07.** Metro: Antón Martín or Sevilla. Bus: 6 or 60.

This club is known for its exciting jazz groups, who encourage the audience to dance. It specializes in Brazilian, Afro-bass, reggae, and "new African wave" music. When the music starts, the prices of drinks are nearly doubled. Open daily from 6pm to 2 or 3am. Beer is 250 pesetas ($2) when live music isn't playing, 600 pesetas ($4.80) when a band is playing.

Clamores. Albuquerque, 14. ☎ **91/445-79-38.** Cover Tues–Sat usually 500–800 ptas. ($4–$6.40), but varies with act; no cover Sun–Mon. Metro: Bilbao.

With dozens of small tables and a huge bar in its dark and smoky interior, Clamores is the largest and one of the most popular jazz clubs in Madrid. Established in the early 1980s, it has thrived because of the diverse roster of American and Spanish jazz bands who have appeared here. The place is open daily from 6pm to around 3am, but jazz is presented only Tuesday through Saturday. Tuesday through Thursday, performances are at 11pm and again at 1am; Saturday, performances begin at 11:30pm, with an additional show at 1:30am. There are no live performances on Sunday or Monday nights, when the format is recorded disco music. Regardless of the night of the week you consume them, drinks begin at around 700 pesetas ($5.60) each.

DANCE CLUBS

The Spanish dance club takes its inspiration from those of other Western capitals. In Madrid most clubs are open from around 6pm to 9pm, reopening around 11pm. They generally start rocking at midnight or thereabouts.

Aqualung. Paseo de la Ermita del Santo. ☎ **91/526-5904.** Admission 1,200 ptas. ($9.60), including first drink. Metro: Puerto de Toledo.

This is one of the new, relatively ephemeral clubs of the sort that tend to open, thrive briefly, then disappear into the mists of forgotten Madrileño nightclubs. The entrance is behind a tawdry pizza and hamburger complex, all part of an indoor waterpark and leisure center. Able to hold 2,000 patrons, it is the hottest spot in town for live music. If the scene heats up too much, you can always jump into the pool. Currently, the venue is youthful, high energy, and late night in this concert hall cum disco. Clients have a good time enjoying the funky music, acid rock, and cool jazz. Open Monday through Thursday from 11pm to 3am and Friday through Sunday from 11:30pm to 5:30am.

Archy. Calle Marqués de Riscal. ☎ **91/308-31-62.** No cover. Metro: Colón.

In the cellar of an old apartment building, this art deco–style dance club manages to remain fashionable despite several years within that difficult role. Many of the women might remind you of Cher in her more youthful days, and virtually everyone seems to make some effort to dress the part of the young, the beautiful, and the restless. Hours are from 10pm to 5am Thursday to Sunday. Drinks begin at around 850 pesetas ($6.80) each.

Joy Eslava. Arenal, 1. ☎ **91/366-37-33.** Admission 1,500 ptas. ($12), including first drink. Metro: Puerta del Sol.

Set near the Puerto del Sol, this place has survived the passing fashions of Madrileño nightlife with more style than many of its (now-defunct) competitors. Virtually everyone in Madrid is likely to show up here, ranging from traveling sales reps in town from Düsseldorf to the youthful members of the Madrileño *movida.* Open nightly from 11:30pm to dawn. Drinks are 1,200 pesetas ($9.60) each.

Kapital. Atocha, 125. ☎ **91/420-29-06**. Admission 1,000–1,500 ptas. ($8–$12), including first drink. Metro: Antón Martín.

This is the most sprawling, labyrinthine, and multicultural disco in Madrid at the moment. Set within what was originally conceived as a theater, it contains seven different levels, each of which sports at least one bar and an ambience that's often radically different from the one you just left on a previous floor. Voyeurs of any age, take heart—there's a lot to see at the Kapital, with a mixed crowd that pursues whatever form of sexuality seems appropriate at the moment. Open Thursday through Sunday 11:30pm to 5:30am. Second drinks from 1,000 pesetas ($8) each.

Ku Madrid. Princesa, 1 (Plaza de España). No phone. Admission 1,400 ptas. ($11.20). Metro: Argüelles.

The decor is showplace modern, obviously the result of a cadre of decorators hired to make an important decorative statement. Its reputation is as a hip but potentially fleeting late-night venues for young and not-so-young night owls who enjoy a permissive and sophisticated ambience. Open Tuesday through Sunday from midnight to 5am. Drinks cost from 850 pesetas ($6.80) each.

Long Play. Plaza Vasquez de Mella, 2. ☎ **91/531-01-11.** Admission 1,000 ptas. ($8), including first drink. Metro: Gran Vía.

Catering to crowds of all ages, it manages to combine disco music with long stretches of bars, comfortable tables and chairs, and a crowd with seemingly nothing to do but dance, dance, dance. Recorded music sometimes intersperses itself with live bands. Open Tuesday through Sunday from 7pm to 3am.

Pachá. Calle Barcelo, 11. ☎ **91/446-01-37.** Admission 1,200 ptas. ($9.60), including first drink. Metro: Tribunal.

The carefully contrived setting is pseudo-opulent, and the drinks sometimes hard to get because of the milling crowds. Despite that, the place thrives as one of the late-night staples in Madrid for the mid-20s to late-40s clientele (a crowd that often segregates themselves by age into distinctly different areas of the place). More than other nightclubs in Madrid, this has been the subject of complaints from neighbors about late-night noise. It's open Tuesday through Sunday 11pm to 5am.

THE BAR SCENE

PUBS & BARS

Balmoral. Hermosilia, 10. ☎ **91/431-41-33.** Metro: Serrano.

Its exposed wood and comfortable chairs evoke a London club. The clientele tends toward journalists, politicians, army brass, owners of large estates, bankers, diplomats, and the occasional literary star. *Newsweek* magazine once dubbed it one of the "best bars in the world." No food other than tapas is served. Open Monday through Saturday from noon to midnight or 1am. Beer is 500 pesetas ($4); drinks are from 900 pesetas ($7.20).

Balneario. Juan Ramón Jiménez, 37. ☎ **91/350-87-76.** Metro: Cuzco.

Clients enjoy potent drinks in a setting with fresh flowers, white marble, and a stone bathtub that might have been used by Josephine Bonaparte. Near Chamartín Station on the northern edge of Madrid, Balneario is one of the most stylish and upscale bars in the city. It is adjacent to and managed by one of Madrid's most elegant and prestigious restaurants, El Cabo Mayor, and often attracts that dining room's clients for aperitifs or after-dinner drinks. Tapas include endive with smoked salmon, asparagus mousse, and anchovies with avocado. Open Monday through Saturday from noon to 2:30am. Drinks are 650 to 1,500 pesetas ($5.20–$12); tapas cost 550 to 1,750 pesetas ($4.40–$14).

Bar Cock. De la Reina, 16. ☎ **91/532-28-26.** Metro: Gran Vía.

This bar attracts some of the most visible artists, actors, models, and filmmakers in Madrid. The name comes from the word *cocktail,* or so they say. The decoration is elaborately unique, in contrast to the hip clientele. Open daily from 7pm to 3am; closed December 24 to 31. Drinks are 700 pesetas ($5.60).

Chicote. Gran Vía, 12. ☎ **91/532-67-37.** Metro: Gran Vía.

Beloved by Hemingway, who had quite a few drinks here, this is Madrid's most famous cocktail bar. It's a classic, with the same 1930s interior design it had when the foreign press came to sit out the Civil War, although the sound of artillery shells along the Gran Vía could be heard at the time. Even the seats are the same ones that held such luminaries as Don Ernesto, Grace Kelly, and Ava Gardner. Long a favorite of artists and writers, the bar became a haven for prostitutes in the late Franco era. No more. It's back in the limelight again, a sophisticated and much-frequented rendezvous. Open 11am to 3am daily. Drinks cost from 1,000 pesetas ($8), but the waiters serve them with such grace you don't mind.

Los Gabrieles. Echegaray, 17. ☎ **91/429-62-61.** Metro: Tirso de Molina.

Located in the heart of one of Madrid's most visible warrens of narrow streets, in a district that pulsates with after-dark nightlife options, this historic bar served throughout most of the 19th century as the sales outlet for a Spanish wine merchant. In the 1980s its two rooms were transformed into a bar and café, where you can admire lavishly tiled walls with detailed scenes of courtiers, dancers, and Andalusian maidens peering from behind mantillas and fans. Open Monday through Friday from noon to 2am; Saturday and Sunday from noon to 3am. Beer costs 200 to 400 pesetas ($1.60–$3.20).

Hanoi. Hortaleza, 81. ☎ **91/319-66-72.** Cover 1,200 ptas. ($9.60), including first drink. Metro: Alonso Martinez.

Its setting is stylish and minimalist—stainless steel, curving lines, and sharp angles—and its clients are youthful, attractive, and warmly sentimental about the memories that remain from the heady, early days of Madrid's *movida.* They include a bevy of male and female models who seem as mobile and changeable as the *movida* itself. The atmosphere is comfortable for attendees of any conceivable form of sexuality. At least a half-dozen video screens show films from long-defunct TV series, and the music reflects what's happening in London, Los Angeles, and New York. It's open Wednesday to Saturday from 9pm to 4am. Beer costs around 600 pesetas ($4.80).

Hispano Bar/Buffet. Paseo de la Castellana, 78. ☎ **91/411-48-76.** Metro: Nuevos Ministerios.

This establishment does a respectable lunch trade every day for members of the local business community, who crowd in to enjoy the amply portioned *platos del día.* These might include a platter of roast duck with figs or orange sauce, or a suprême of hake. After around 5pm, however, the ambience becomes that of a busy after-office bar, patronized by stylishly dressed women and many local entrepreneurs. The hubbub continues on into the night. Open daily from 1:30pm to 1:30am. Full meals at lunchtime cost from around 4,000 pesetas ($32), while beer, depending on the time of day you order it, ranges from 300 pesetas ($2.40) to 350 pesetas ($2.80).

Mr. Pickwick's. Marqués de Urquijo, 44 (at corner of Paseo del Pintor Rosales). ☎ **91/559-51-85.** Metro: Argüelles.

For homesick English expatriates, no other establishment in Madrid better captures the pub atmosphere than Mr. Pickwick's, a 10-minute walk from the Plaza de España. Although only a few of the staff speak fluent English, the decor includes everything you would expect in London: framed prints of Dickens's characters, brass hunting horns, and pewter and ceramic beer mugs. Loners can drink at the bar, or you can sit at one of the small tables, sinking into the soft sofas and armchairs. Open daily from 6pm to 1am. Beer begins at 360 pesetas ($2.90), whiskey at 750 pesetas ($6).

Oliver Piano Bar. Almirante, 12. ☎ **91/521-73-79.** Metro: Chueca. Bus: 70.

Oliver Piano Bar, off the Paseo de la Castellana, is a pub-style hangout for show-biz people, with a good sprinkling of foreign personalities. The bar feels like a drawing room or library, and there are two club rooms, each with its own personality. The first floor has sofas and comfortable armchairs arranged for conversational gatherings. Reached by a curving stairway, the downstairs room is more secluded. On either side of the fireplace are shelves with an eclectic collection of records (you can pick the ones you want played) and books on theater, movies, and painting. Open Monday through Friday from 4pm to 3:30am; Saturday from 6pm to 3:30am. Beer is 400 pesetas ($3.20).

Palacio Gaviria. Calle del Arenal, 9. ☎ **91/526-6069.** Cover 1,500 ptas. ($12), including first drink. Metro: Puerta del Sol or Ópera.

Its construction in 1847 was heralded as the architectural triumph of one of the era's most flamboyant aristocrats, the Marqués de Gaviria. Famous as one of the paramours of Queen Isabella II, he outfitted his palace with the ornate jumble of neoclassical and baroque styles that later became known as *Isabelino.* In 1993, after extensive renovations, the building was opened to the public as a concert hall for the occasional presentation of classical music and as a late-night cocktail bar. Ten high-ceilinged rooms now function as richly decorated, multipurpose areas for guests to wander in, drinks in hand, reacting to whatever, or whomever, happens to be there at the time. (One room is discreetly referred to as the bedroom-away-from-home of the queen herself.) No food is served, but the libations include a stylish list of cocktails and wines. The often-dull music doesn't match the elegance of the decor. Thursday through Saturday are usually dance nights, everything from the tango to the waltz. Cabaret is usually featured on most other nights. Open Monday through Friday from 10:30pm to 3am; Saturday and Sunday from 10:30pm to 5am. Second drinks start at 1,200 pesetas ($9.60).

Viva Madrid. Manuel Fernández y González, 7. ☎ **91/410-55-35.** Metro: Antón Martín.

A congenial and sudsy mix of students, artists, foreign tourists, and visiting Yanks cram into its turn-of-the-century interior, where antique tile murals and blatant Belle Epoque nostalgia contribute to an undeniable charm. Crowded and noisy, it's a place where lots of beer is swilled and spilled. It's set within a neighborhood of antique houses and narrow streets near the Plaza de Santa Ana. Open Friday from noon to 1am, Saturday from noon to 2am. Beer costs 500 pesetas ($4); whiskey begins at 875 pesetas ($7).

Gay & Lesbian Bars

Alves. Calle Veneras 2. ☎ **91/548-20-22.** Admission 1,200–1,500 ptas. ($9.60–$12), including one drink. Metro: Santo Domingo.

No longer Madrid's leading gay disco, Alves still attracts a widely diversified crowd of various sexual persuasions. Dance arenas are spread across three floors, and there's also a dark room for more amorous diversions. The bars offer surprisingly good food. Upstairs you can dance the *sevillana,* or dance to "rave" music on the lower levels. On Sundays there is sometimes a cabaret. Open midnight to 6am daily, but at its hottest from 3am to 5am.

Black and White. Gravina (at corner of Libertad). ☎ **91/531-11-41.** Metro: Chueca.

This is the major gay bar of Madrid, located in the center of the Chueca district. A guard will open the door to a large room—painted, as you might expect, black and white. There's a disco in the basement, but the street-level bar is the premier gathering spot, featuring drag shows Thursday through Sunday, male striptease, and videos. Old movies are shown against one wall. Open Monday through Friday from 8pm to 4am; Saturday and Sunday from 8pm to 5am. Beer is 500 pesetas ($4); whiskey costs 850 pesetas ($6.80).

Café Figueroa. Augusto Figueroa, 17 (at corner of Hortaleza). ☎ **91/521-16-73.** Metro: Chueca.

This turn-of-the-century café attracts a diverse clientele, including a large number of gay men and lesbians. It's one of the city's most popular gathering spots for drinks and conversations. Open Monday through Friday from 3pm to 1am; Saturday and Sunday from 3pm to 2:30am. Drinks are 650 pesetas ($5.20); beer from 275 pesetas ($2.20).

Cruising. Perez Galdos, 5. ☎ **91/521-51-43.** Metro: Chueca.

One of the predominant gay bars of Madrid, a center for gay consciousness-raising and gay cruising (as its name suggests), this place has probably been visited at least once by virtually every gay male in Castile. It doesn't get crowded or lively until late at night. Open Monday through Friday from 8pm to 3am; Saturday and Sunday from 8pm to 4:30am. Beer costs from 250 pesetas ($2).

Refugio. Calle Doctor Cortezo, 1. ☎ **91/308-14-62.** Cover 1,200–1,500 ptas. ($9.60–$12). Metro: Tirso de Molina.

This is one of the hottest venues for gays meeting gays in Madrid. It's eqivalent would be Soho in London or Sound Factory in New York. Spacious and lively, it's often a venue for theme parties during the week. Open midnight to 5am daily.

Summer Terrazas

At the first of the spring weather, Madrileños rush outdoors to drink, talk, and sit at a string of open-air cafés throughout the city. The best ones—and also the most expensive—are along Paseo de la Castellana between Plaza de la Cibeles and Plaza Emilio Castelar, but there are dozens more throughout the city.

You can wander up and down the boulevard, selecting one that appeals to you; if you get bored, you can go on later to another one. Sometimes these terrazas are called *chirinquitos.* You'll also find them along other paseos, the Recoletos and the Prado, both fashionable areas, although not as hip as the Castellana. For old, traditional atmosphere, the terrazas at Plaza Mayor win out. The terrazas of Plaza Santa Ana also have several atmospheric choices within the old city. Friday and Saturday are the most popular nights for drinking; many locals sit here all night.

Cave Crawling

To capture a peculiar Madrid joie de vivre of the 18th century, visit some mesones and cuevas, many found in the barrios bajos. From Plaza Mayor, walk down the Arco de Cuchilleros until you find a gypsylike cave that fits your fancy. Young people love to meet in the taverns and caves of Old Madrid for communal drinking and songfests. The sangría flows freely, the atmosphere is charged, and the room usually is packed; the sounds of guitars waft into the night air. Sometimes you'll see a strolling band of singing students (*tuna*) going from bar to bar, colorfully attired, with ribbons fluttering from their outfits.

Mesón del Champiñón. Cava de San Miguel, 17. No phone. Metro: Puerta del Sol or Ópera.

The bartenders keep a brimming bucket of sangría behind the long stand-up bar as a thirst quencher for the crowd. The name of the establishment in English is Mushroom, and that is exactly what you'll see depicted in various sizes along sections of the vaulted ceilings. A more appetizing way to experience a *champiñón* is to order a *ración* of grilled, stuffed, and salted mushrooms, served with toothpicks, for 575 pesetas ($4.60). Two tiny, slightly dark rooms in the back are where Spanish families go to hear organ music performed. Unless you want to be exiled to the very back, don't expect to get a seat. Practically everybody prefers to stand. Open daily from 6pm to 2am. Sangría is 1,400 pesetas ($11.20); tapas begin at 600 pesetas ($4.80).

Mesón de la Guitarra. Cava de San Miguel, 13. ☎ **91/559-95-31.** Metro: Puerta del Sol or Ópera.

Our favorite cueva in the area, Mesón de la Guitarra is loud and exciting on any night of the week, and it's as warmly earthy as anything you'll find in Madrid. The decor combines terra-cotta floors, antique brick walls, hundreds of sangría pitchers clustered above the bar, murals of gluttons, old rifles, and faded bullfighting posters. Like most things in Madrid, the place doesn't get rolling until around 10:30pm, although you can stop in for a drink and tapas earlier. Don't be afraid to start singing an American song if it has a fast rhythm—60 people will join in, even if they don't know the words. Open daily from 7pm to 1:30am. Beer is 200 to 250 pesetas ($1.60–$2); wine is from 150 pesetas ($1.20); tapas are 700 to 900 pesetas ($5.60–$7.20).

Sesamo. Príncipe, 7. ☎ **91/429-65-24.** Metro: Sevilla or Puerta del Sol.

In a class by itself, this cueva, dating from the early 1950s, draws a clientele of young painters and writers with its bohemian ambience. Hemingway was one of those early visitors (a plaque commemorates him). At first you'll think you're walking into a tiny snack bar—and you are. But proceed down the flight of steps to the cellar. Here, the walls are covered with contemporary paintings and quotations. At squatty stools and tables, an international assortment of young people listens to piano music and sometimes folk singing or guitar playing. Open daily from 6:30pm to 2am. A pitcher of sangría (for four) is 1,100 pesetas ($8.80); beer costs 300 pesetas ($2.40).

MORE ENTERTAINMENT

MOVIES Cinematic releases from Paris, New York, Rome, and Hollywood come quickly to Madrid, where an avid audience often waits in long lines for tickets. Most foreign films are dubbed into Spanish, unless they're indicated as VO (original version).

Madrid boasts at least 90 legitimate movie houses (many of which have several theaters under one roof) and many others with adult entertainment only. The premier theaters of the city are the enormous, slightly faded movie palaces of the Gran Vía, whose huge movie marquees announce in lurid colors whichever romantic or adventure *espectáculo* happens to be playing at the moment. For listings, consult *Guía de Ocio* or *Guía de Diario 16* (both available at newsstands), or a newspaper.

If you want to see a film while in Madrid, one of the best places is the quadruplex **Alphaville,** Martín de los Heros, 14 (☎ **91/559-38-36;** metro: Plaza de España). It shows English-language films with Spanish subtitles as well as other foreign language films such as French and German. If the film is not too long, there are four daily showings at 4:30pm, 6:30pm, 8:30pm, and 10:30pm. On Saturday and Sunday, there's a midnight show at 12:30am. Admission is 700 pesetas ($5.60). The complex also includes a bookstore and a café decorated in art deco style.

For classic revivals and foreign films, check the listings at Filmoteca in the *Cine Doré,* Santa Isabel, 3 (☎ **91/369-11-25;** metro: Antón Martín). Movies here tend to be shown in their original language. Tickets cost 225 pesetas ($1.80). There is a bar and a simple restaurant.

A CASINO The **Casino Gran Madrid** is at km 28,300, Apartado 62, of the Carretera Nacional VI-Madrid-La Coruña, (☎ **91/856-11-00**). Even nongamblers sometimes make the trek here from the capital; the casino's many entertainment facilities are considered by some to be the most exciting thing around. Its scattered attractions include two restaurants, four bars, and a nightclub. The casino is open daily from 4pm to 5am. For an entrance fee of 500 pesetas ($4), you can sample the action in the gaming rooms, including French and American roulette, blackjack, punto y banco, baccarat, and chemin de fer.

An à la carte restaurant in the French Gaming Room offers international cuisine, with dinners costing from 7,000 pesetas ($56). A buffet in the American Gaming Room will cost around 3,000 pesetas ($24). The restaurants are open from 9:15pm to 2am. The casino is about 18 miles (29km) northwest of Madrid, along the Madrid–La Coruña N-VI highway. If you don't feel like driving, the casino has buses that depart from Plaza de España, 6, every afternoon and evening at 4:30, 6, 7:30, and 9pm. Note that between October and June, men must wear jackets and ties; T-shirts and tennis shoes are forbidden in any season. To enter, European visitors must present an identity card and non-European visitors must present a passport.

6 Excursions from Madrid

Madrid makes an ideal base for excursions because it's surrounded by some of Spain's major attractions. The day trips listed below to both New Castile and Old Castile range from 9 miles to 100 miles (14–161km) outside Madrid, allowing you to leave in the morning and be back by nightfall. In case you choose to stay overnight, however, we've included a selection of hotels in each town.

The satellite cities and towns around Madrid include Toledo, with its El Greco masterpieces; the wondrous El Escorial monastery; Segovia's castles that "float" in the clouds; and the Bourbon palaces at La Granja. Cuenca, which is actually in La Mancha, is the longest excursion; so unless you want to spend a good part of the day getting there and back, you should consider it an overnight trip. For a selection of other cities in Old Castile—each of which is better visited on an overnight stopover rather than a day trip from Madrid—refer to Chapter 7.

EXPLORING THE REGION BY CAR

The speed of the itinerary below can be achieved only by car. Using public transportation would take twice as long. Therefore, if you have only a week and don't have a car, travel by train or bus from Madrid, taking in only the most important attractions: Toledo, El Escorial, Segovia, and Ávila, in that order.

Day 1 Leave Madrid and drive south to Aranjuez, visiting the Bourbon palace and gardens and continuing southwest to Toledo for the night.

Day 2 Spend the day and night in Toledo, which is hardly enough to get acquainted with the city, but it may be all the time you have. You'll at least have enough time to visit the Alcázar, the cathedral at Toledo, and El Greco's house and museum.

Day 3 In the morning head northwest for Ávila, exploring its attractions in the afternoon. These include Ávila Cathedral, Basilica de San Vicente, Monasterio de Santo Tomas, and Convento de Santa Teresa. Stay overnight.

Day 4 Drive northeast to Segovia. A wealth of architectural treasures await here, along with the specialty of the region: roast suckling pig so beloved by Hemingway. In one day you can cover such attractions as the Alcázar, the Roman aqueduct, the Cabildo Cathedral de Segovia, and the Iglesia de la Vera Cruz. Stay overnight.

Day 5 Still in Segovia, spend the day at La Granja, then drive through the snowcapped Guadarrama Mountains.
Day 6 Head southeast toward Madrid. Spend the day exploring the monastery of San Lorenzo de El Escorial, with a side trip to the Valley of the Fallen. Stay overnight in El Escorial (limited accommodations) or return to Madrid.

1 Toledo

42 miles (68km) SW of Madrid, 85 miles (137km) SE of Ávila

If you have only one day for an excursion outside Madrid, go to Toledo—a place made special by its Arab, Jewish, Christian, and even Roman and Visigothic elements. Declared a national landmark, the city that so inspired El Greco in the 16th century has remained relatively unchanged. You can still stroll through streets barely wide enough for a man and his donkey—much less for an automobile.

Surrounded on three sides by a bend in the Tagus River, Toledo stands atop a hill overlooking the arid plains of New Castile—a natural fortress in the center of the Iberian Peninsula. It was a logical choice for the capital of Spain, though it lost its political status to Madrid in the 1500s. Toledo remained the country's religious center, as the seat of the Primate of Spain.

If you're driving, the much-painted skyline of Toledo will come into view about 3½ miles (6km) from the city. But when you cross the Tagus River on the 14th-century Puente San Martín, the scene is reminiscent of El Greco's moody, storm-threatened *View of Toledo,* which hangs in New York's Metropolitan Museum of Art. The artist reputedly painted that view from a hillside that is now the site of Parador Nacional de Conde Orgaz. If you arrive at the right time, you can enjoy an aperitif on the parador's terrace and watch one of the famous "violet sunsets" of Toledo (see "Where to Stay," below).

Another Toledan highlight is the **Carretera de Circunvalación,** the route that threads through the city and runs along the Tagus. Clinging to the hillsides are rustic dwellings, the *cigarrales* of the Imperial City, immortalized by 17th-century dramatist Tirso de Molina, who named his trilogy *Los Cigarrales de Toledo.*

GETTING THERE **By Train** RENFE trains run here frequently every day. Those departing Madrid's Atocha Railway Station for Toledo run daily from 7am to 8:25pm; those leaving Toledo for Madrid run daily from 7am to 9pm. Traveling time is approximately two hours. For train information in Madrid call **91/468-45-11;** in Toledo call **925/22-30-99.**

By Bus Bus transit between Madrid and Toledo is faster and more convenient than travel by train. Buses are maintained by several companies, the largest of which include Continental or Galiano. They depart from Madrid's Estación Sur de Autobuses (South Bus Station), Canarias 17 (☎ **91/527-29-61** for information), every day between 6:30am and 10pm at 30-minute intervals. The fastest leave Monday through Friday on the hour. Those that depart weekdays on the half hour, and those that run on weekends, take a bit longer. Travel time, depending on whether the bus stops at villages en route, is between 1 hour and 1 hour 20 minutes. One-way transit costs 580 pesetas ($4.65).

Once you reach Toledo, you'll be deposited at the Estacíon de Autobuses, which lies beside the river, about ¾ of a mile from the historic center. Although many visitors opt to walk, be advised that the ascent is steep. Bus numbers 5 and 6 run from the station uphill to the center, charging 110 pesetas (90¢) for the brief ride. Pay the driver directly.

By Car Exit Madrid via Cibeles (Paseo del Prado) and take the N-401 south.

VISITOR INFORMATION The tourist information office is at Puerta de Bisagra (☎ **925/22-08-43**). It's open Monday through Friday from 9am to 2pm and 4 to 6pm, Saturday from 9am to 3pm and 4 to 7pm, and Sunday from 9am to 3pm.

WHAT TO SEE & DO

✪ **Cathedral.** Arcos de Palacio. ☎ **925/22-22-41.** Free admission to cathedral; Treasure Room, 500 ptas. ($4). Daily 10:30am–1pm and 3:30–6pm (until 7pm in summer). Bus: 5 or 6.

Ranked among the greatest of Gothic structures, the cathedral actually reflects several styles, since more than two and a half centuries elapsed during its construction (1226–1493). Many historic events transpired here, including the proclamation of Joanna the Mad and her husband, Philip the Handsome, as heirs to the throne of Spain.

Among its art treasures, the *transparente* stands out—a wall of marble and florid baroque alabaster sculpture overlooked for years because the cathedral was too poorly lit. Sculptor Narcisco Tomé cut a hole in the ceiling, much to the consternation of Toledans, and now light touches the high-rising angels, a *Last Supper* in alabaster, and a Virgin in ascension.

The 16th-century Capilla Mozárabe, containing works by Juan de Borgona, is another curiosity of the cathedral. Mass is still held here using Mozarabic liturgy.

The Treasure Room has a 500-pound 15th-century gilded monstrance—allegedly made with gold brought back from the New World by Columbus—that is still carried through the streets of Toledo during the feast of Corpus Christi.

Other highlights of the cathedral include El Greco's *Twelve Apostles* and *Spoliation of Christ* and Goya's *Arrest of Christ on the Mount of Olives.*

Alcázar. Calle General Moscardó, 4, near the Plaza de Zocodover. ☎ **925/22-30-38.** Admission 125 ptas. ($1) adults, free for children under 10. Tues–Sun 10am–1:30pm and 4–5:30pm (6:30pm July–Sept). Bus: 5 or 6.

The Alcázar, located at the eastern edge of the old city, dominates the Toledo skyline. It became world famous at the beginning of the Spanish Civil War, when it underwent a 70-day siege that almost destroyed it (see "The Siege of the Alcázar," below). Today it has been rebuilt and turned into an army museum, housing such exhibits as a plastic model of what the fortress looked like after the Civil War, electronic equipment used during the siege, and photographs taken during the height of the battle. A walking tour gives a realistic simulation of the siege. Allow an hour for a visit.

✪ **Museo de Santa Cruz.** Miguel de Cervantes, 3. ☎ **925/22-10-36.** Admission 200 ptas. ($1.60) adults, free for children. Tues–Sat 10am–6:30pm, Sun 10am–2pm, Mon 10am–2pm and 4–6:30pm. Bus: 5 or 6. Pass beneath the granite archway on the eastern edge of the Plaza de Zocodover and walk about one block.

Today a museum of art and sculpture, this was originally a 16th-century Spanish Renaissance hospice, founded by Cardinal Mendoza—"the third King of Spain"—who helped Ferdinand and Isabella gain the throne. The facade is almost more spectacular than any of the exhibits inside. It's a stunning architectural achievement in the classical plateresque style. The major artistic treasure inside is El Greco's *The Assumption of the Virgin,* his last known work. Paintings by Goya and Ribera are also on display along with gold items, opulent antique furnishings, Flemish tapestries, and even Visigothic artifacts. In the patio of the museum you'll stumble across various fragments of carved stone and sarcophagi lids. One of the major exhibits is of a large

Environs of Madrid

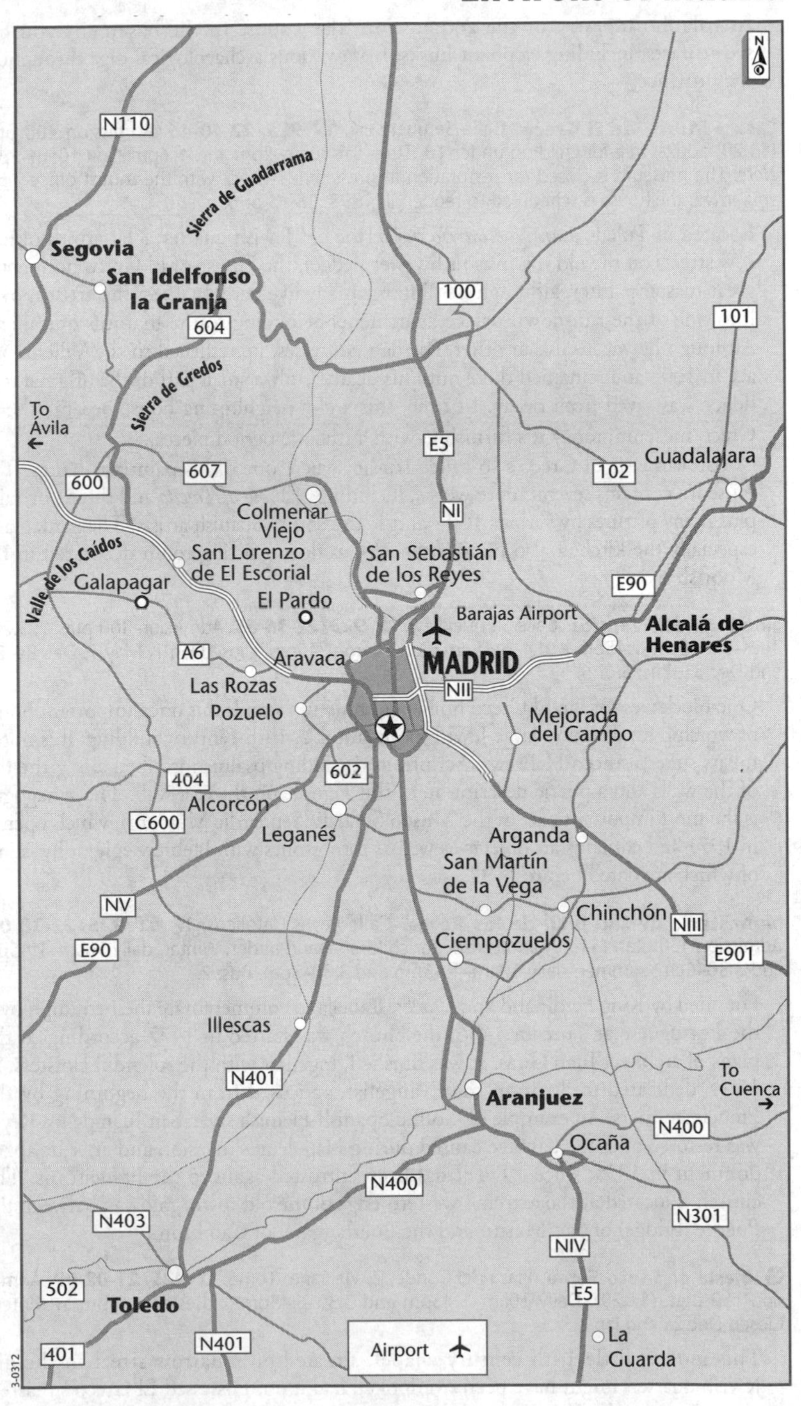

N110
Sierra de Guadarrama
Segovia
San Idelfonso la Granja
604
100
101
Sierra de Gredos
To Ávila
E5
Guadalajara
600
607
102
Colmenar Viejo
NI
Valle de los Caídos
San Lorenzo de El Escorial
San Sebastián de los Reyes
Galapagar
E90
El Pardo
Barajas Airport
Alcalá de Henares
A6
Aravaca
MADRID
Las Rozas
NII
Pozuelo
Mejorada del Campo
602
404
Alcorcón
C600
Leganés
Arganda
San Martín de la Vega
NV
Chinchón
NIII
E90
Ciempozuelos
E901
Illescas
N401
Aranjuez
To Cuenca
N400
Ocaña
N400
N403
N301
NIV
502
E5
Toledo
La Guarda
401
N401
Airport
3-0312

Astrolablio tapestry of the zodiac from the 1400s. In the basement you can see artifacts, including elephant husks, from various archaeological digs throughout the province.

Casa y Museo de El Greco. Calle Samuel Leví. ☎ **925/22-40-46.** Admission 400 ptas. ($3.20) adults, free for children under 10. Tues–Sat 10am–2pm and 4–6pm, Sun 10am–2pm. *Note:* The museum is closed for restoration at press time—check with the tourist office when you arrive; the house is scheduled to reopen in 1998. Bus: 5 or 6.

Located in Toledo's *antiguo barrio judio* (the old Jewish quarter, a labyrinth of narrow streets on the old town's southwestern edge), the House of El Greco honors the great master painter, although he didn't actually live here. In 1585 the artist moved into one of the run-down palace apartments belonging to the marquís of Villena. Although he was to live at other Toledan addresses, he returned to the Villena palace in 1604 and remained there until his death. Only a small part of the original residence was saved from decay. In time, this and a neighboring house became the El Greco museum; today it's furnished with authentic period pieces.

You can visit El Greco's so-called studio, where one of his paintings hangs. The museum contains several more works, including *A View of Toledo* and three portraits, plus many pictures by various 16th- and 17th-century Spanish artists. The garden and especially the kitchen also merit attention, as does a sitting room decorated in the Moorish style.

Sínagoga del Tránsito. Calle Samuel Leví. ☎ **925/22-36-65.** Admission 400 ptas. ($3.20). Tues–Sat 10am–1:45pm and 4–5:45pm, Sun 10am–1:45pm. Closed Jan 1, May 1, Dec 24–25, and Dec 31. Bus: 5 or 6.

One block west of the El Greco home and museum stands this once-important house of worship for Toledo's large Jewish population. A 14th-century building, it is noted for its superb stucco Hebrew inscriptions, including psalms inscribed along the top of the walls and a poetic description of the Temple on the east wall. The synagogue is the most important part of the **Museo Sefardí** (Sephardic Museum), which opened in 1971 and contains art objects as well as tombstones with Hebrew epigraphy, some of which are dated before 1492.

Monasterio de San Juan de los Reyes. Calle Reyes Católicos, 17. ☎ **925/22-38-02.** Admission 150 ptas. ($1.20) adults, free for children 8 and under. Winter, daily 10am–1:45pm and 3:30–6pm; summer, daily 10am–1:45pm and 3:30–7pm. Bus: 2.

Founded by King Ferdinand and Queen Isabella to commemorate their triumph over the Portuguese at Toro in 1476, the church was started in 1477 according to the plans of architect Juan Guas. It was finished, together with the splendid cloisters, in 1504, dedicated to St. John the Evangelist, and used from the beginning by the Franciscan friars. An example of Gothic-Spanish-Flemish style, San Juan de los Reyes was restored after the damage caused during Napoleon's invasion and after its abandonment in 1835; since 1954 it has been entrusted again to the Franciscans. The church is located at the extreme western edge of the old town, midway between the Puente (bridge) of San Martín and the Puerta (gate) of Cambron.

✪ **Iglesia de Santo Tomé.** Plaza del Conde, 2, Vía Santo Tomé. ☎ **925/21-02-09.** Admission 150 ptas. ($1.20). Daily 10am–1:45pm and 3:30–6:45pm (closes at 5:45pm in winter). Closed Dec 25 and Jan 1.

This modest little 14th-century chapel, situated on a narrow street in the old Jewish quarter, might have been overlooked had it not possessed El Greco's masterpiece *The Burial of the Count of Orgaz,* created in 1586.

The Siege of the Alcázar

Although the Alcázar of Toledo has suffered many a siege, one particularly dramatic encounter, in 1936, made world headlines. The Republicans were fighting to gain control of conservative, staunchly Catholic Toledo. Franco's rebel troops were commanded by one tough officer, Colonel José Moscardó. Not only were his troops inside the Alcázar, but women and children were holed up here as well. The Alcázar, although under heavy attack, withstood 70 days of bombardment.

On July 23, a Republican officer reached Moscardó by telephone within the Alcázar. The colonel was informed that Republican forces had kidnapped Luis, his 16-year-old son. Moscardó was told that unless he immediately surrendered the fortress, Luis would be executed.

To show that they did indeed have the child, they put Luis on the phone to his father. "Papa!" he shouted, "They say they are going to shoot me if you don't surrender."

Without hesitation, Moscardó told his son: "Then commend your soul to God, shout '*Viva España!*' and die like a hero."

The Republicans were good to their word. Luis was shot in the head. The fortress was surrendered in September of that year. In the Alcázar today hangs the wall phone on which the colonel spoke to his son for the last time.

Sínagoga de Santa María La Blanca. Calle Reyes Católicos, 2. ☎ **925/22-72-57.** Admission 150 ptas. ($1.20). Apr–Sept, daily 10am–2pm and 3:30–7pm; Oct–Mar, daily 10am–2pm and 3:30–6pm. Bus: 2.

In the late 12th century, the Jews of Toledo erected an important synagogue in the *almohade* style, which employs graceful horseshoe arches and ornamental horizontal moldings. Although by the early 15th century it had been converted into a Christian church, much of the original remains, including the five naves and elaborate Mudéjar decorations, mosquelike in their effect. The synagogue lies on the western edge of the city, midway between the El Greco museum and San Juan de los Reyes.

Hospital de Tavera. Hospital de Tavera, 2. ☎ **925/22-04-51.** Admission 500 ptas. ($4). Daily 10:30am–1:30pm and 3:30–6pm.

This 16th-century Greco-Roman palace north of the medieval ramparts of Toledo was originally built by Cardinal Tavera; it now houses a private art collection. Titian's portrait of Charles V hangs in the banqueting hall. The museum owns five paintings by El Greco: *The Holy Family, The Baptism of Christ,* and portraits of St. Francis, St. Peter, and Cardinal Tavera. Ribera's *The Bearded Woman* also attracts many viewers. The collection of books in the library is priceless. In the nearby church is the mausoleum of Cardinal Tavera, designed by Alonso Berruguete.

ENJOYING THE OUTDOORS

FISHING

Fishers wanting to try their luck in the Tagus River often head for Toledo, since the river forms a natural moat around the city. The Spanish government has introduced black bass at Finisterre Dam, which lies some 28 miles (45km) southeast of the city. In various reservoirs, large pike and carp can be caught. To fish these waters, you must obtain a permit in Madrid at either ICONA, Gran Vía de San Francisco, 4 (☎ **91/347-6000**), or from the Federación Española de Pesca, Navas de Tolosa 3 (☎ **91/532-83-53**).

SWIMMING

The best place for swimming is the Parador Nacional de Conde Orgaz (see below), but its pool is available only to house guests. The best outdoor pool—and a welcome relief in Toledo in July and August—is at the Camping Circo Romano, Calle Circo Romano, 21 (☎ **925/22-04-42**), a campground just north of the old city walls.

TENNIS

This sport in summer is best practiced either before noon or after 4pm. Club de Tenis de Toledo, Calle Navalpino, km 49 (☎ **925/22-42-78**), is private but will accept guests who call to make arrangements in advance.

SHOPPING

In swashbuckling days, the swordsmiths of Toldeo were renowned. They're still around and still turning out swords, although Errol Flynn in green tights is long gone. Toledo is equally renowned for its *damasquinado,* or damascene work, the Moorish art of inlaying gold, even copper or silver threads, against a matte black steel backdrop. Today Toledo is filled with souvenir shops hawking damascene. The price depends on whether the item is handcrafted or machine made. Sometimes machine-made damascene is passed off as the more expensive handcrafted item, so you have to shop carefully. Bargaining is perfectly acceptable in Toledo, but once and if you get the price down, you can't pay with a credit card—only cash.

Marzipan (called *mazapán* locally) is often prepared by nuns and is a local specialty. Many shops in town specialize in this treat made of sweet almond paste.

The province of Toledo is also renowned for its pottery, which is sold in so many shops at competitive prices that it's almost unnecessary to recommend specific branches hawking these wares. However, over the years we've found that the prices at the large roadside emporiums on the outskirts of town on the main road to Madrid often have better bargains than the shops within the city walls, where rents are higher.

Better yet, for the best deals, and if you're interested in buying a number of items, consider a trip to Talavera la Reina, 47 miles (76km) west of Toledo, where most of the pottery is made. Since Talavera is the largest city in the province, it is hardly a picture-postcard little potter's village. Most of the shops lie along the main street of town, where you'll find store after store selling this distinctive pottery in mutilcolored designs.

Pottery hunters also flock to Puente del Arzobispo, another ceramic center, known for its green-hued pottery. From Talavera drive west on the N-V to Oropesa, then south for 9 miles (14km) to a fortified bridge across the Tagus. In general, ceramics here are cheaper than those sold in Toledo.

Just past Oropesa at the turnoff to Lagartera is a village where the highly renowned and sought after embroidery of La Mancha originates. Virtually every cottage displays samples of this free-form floral stitching, shaped into everything from skirts to tablecloths. Of course, shops in Toledo are filled with samples of this unique embroidery.

Casa Bermejo. Calle Airosas, 5. ☎ **925/22-03-46.**

Established in 1910, this factory and store employs almost 50 artisans, whom you can observe at work as part of the drama of a visit to its premises. The outlet carries a wide array of damascene objects fashioned into Toledo's traditional Mudéjar designs. These include swords, platters, pitchers, and other gift items. Don't think, however, that everything this place manufactures follows the inspiration of the medieval Arabs. The outfit engraves many of the ornamental swords that are awarded to graduates of West Point in the United States, as well as the decorative, full-dress military accessories used by the armies of various countries of Europe, including France. Open Monday through Friday from 8am to noon and 4 to 8pm.

Casa Telesforo. Plaza de Zocodover, 17. ☎ **925/22-33-79.**

Many long-time residents of Toledo remember this place as the outfit that supplied the marzipan consumed at their childhood birthday parties and celebrations. A specialist in the almond-and-sugar confection whose origins go back hundreds of years, it sells the best marzipan in town, cunningly configured into such whimsical shapes as hearts, diamonds, flowers, and fish. It's open daily from l0am to 2pm and 4 to 9pm.

Felipe Suarez. Paseo de los Canónigos, 19. ☎ **925/22-56-15.**

Established in the 1920s, this outfit has manufactured damascene work in various forms ranging from unpretentious souvenir items to art objects of rare museum-quality beauty that sell for as much as 2,000,000 pesetas ($16,000). You'll find swords, straight-edged razors, pendants, fans, and an array of pearls. The shop maintains extended hours throughout the year, daily from 9:30am to 7pm.

Santiago Sanchez Martin. Calle Rio Llano, 15. ☎ **925/22-77-57.**

This is one of the most painstaking and prestigious manufacturers of damascene work in Toledo. It specializes in the elaborately detailed arabesques whose techniques are as old as the Arab conquest of Iberia. Look for everything from decorative tableware (platters, pitchers, etc.) to mirror frames, jewelry, letter openers, and ornamental swords. It's open Monday through Friday from 8am to noon and 4 to 8pm.

WHERE TO STAY

EXPENSIVE

✪ **Parador Nacional de Conde Orgaz.** Cerro del Emperador, 45002 Toledo. ☎ **925/22-18-50.** Fax 925/22-51-66. 76 rms, 2 suites. MINIBAR TV TEL. 19,500 ptas. ($156) double; 24,000 ptas. ($192) suite. AE, DC, MC, V. Free parking. Drive across Puente San Martín and head south for 2½ miles (4km).

You'll have to make reservations well in advance to stay at this parador, which is built on the ridge of a rugged hill where El Greco is said to have painted his *View of Toledo.* That view is still there, and it is without a doubt one of the grandest in the world. The main living room/lounge has fine furniture—old chests, brown leather chairs, and heavy tables—and leads to a sunny terrace overlooking the city. On chilly nights you can sit by the public fireplace. The guest rooms are the most luxurious in all of Toledo, far superior to those at Maria Cristina. Spacious and beautifully furnished, they contain private baths and reproductions of regional antique pieces.

Dining/Entertainment: See the restaurant recommendation in "Where to Dine," below.

Services: Room service, laundry/valet.

Facilities: Outdoor swimming pool.

MODERATE

✪ **Hostal del Cardenal.** Paseo de Recaredo, 24, 45003 Toledo. ☎ **925/22-49-00.** Fax 925/22-29-91. 27 rms, 2 suites. A/C TV TEL. 10,800 ptas. ($86.40) double; 15,000 ptas. ($120) suite. AE, DC, MC, V. Bus: 2 from rail station.

Although long acclaimed as the best restaurant in Toledo (see below), the fact that this establishment has rooms available is still a well-kept secret. They're not as grand as those at the parador, but they are choice nevertheless, sought by those wanting to capture an old Toledan atmosphere. The entrance to this unusual hotel is set into the stone fortifications of the ancient city walls, a few steps from the Bisagra Gate. To enter the hotel, you must climb a series of terraces to the top of the crenellated walls of the ancient fortress. There, grandly symmetrical and very imposing, is the hostal, the former residence of the 18th-century cardinal of Toledo, Señor Lorenzana. Just beyond the entrance, still atop the city wall, you'll find flagstone walkways, Moorish fountains, rose gardens, and cascading vines. The establishment has tiled walls; long, narrow salons; dignified Spanish furniture; and a smattering of antiques. Each room has a private bath.

Hotel Carlos V. Calle Trastamara, 1, 45001 Toledo. ☎ **925/22-21-00.** Fax 925/22-21-05. 69 rms. A/C TEL. 11,555–12,000 ptas. ($92.45–$96) double. AE, DC, MC, V. Bus: 5 or 6.

In Franco's day, this was *the* place to stay in Toledo. But increasing competition from such newer hotels such as Maria Cristina and Alfonso VI has relegated it to second-tier status. It's still going strong and filling up many a night, even though some readers have complained of the "unhelpful staff." The parador (see above) is outside of town, requiring frequent taxi rides, but Carlos V is right in the center of the action, between the cathedral and the Alcázar. Inside a masculine aura prevails, with brown leather chairs in the lounges. Rooms are also decorated in a rather severe masculine style. An outdoor bar is a summer feature. Standard Castilian meals are served in the dining room, which has a Mudéjar decorative motif.

Hotel Maria Cristina. Marqués de Mendigorría, 1, 45003 Toledo. ☎ **925/21-32-02.** Fax 925/21-26-50. 60 rms, 3 suites. A/C TV TEL. 10,800 ptas. ($86.40) double; 16,500 ptas. ($132) suite. AE, DC, MC, V. Parking 650 ptas. ($5.20).

Adjacent to thc historic Hospital de Tavera and near the northern perimeter of the old town, this stone-sided, awning-fronted hotel resembles a palatial country home. If you're willing to forgo the view from the parador and the charm of Hostal del Cardenal, this hotel is generally cited as *numero segundo* in Toledo. Originally built as a convent and later used as a hospital, it was transformed into this comfortable hostelry in the early 1980s. Sprawling, historic, and generously proportioned, it contains clean, amply sized, attractively furnished bedrooms, each with a private bath.

Dining/Entertainment: On site is the very large and well-recommended restaurant, El Abside, where fixed-price lunches and dinners are served. There's also a bar. The food is much better, however, at Hostal del Cardenal.

Services: 24-hour room service, laundry, concierge, babysitting.

Facilities: Tennis courts.

$ **Hotel Pintor El Greco.** Alamillos del Tránsito, 13, 45002 Toledo. ☎ **925/21-42-50.** Fax 925/21-58-19. 33 rms. A/C TV TEL. 12,000 ptas. ($96) double. AE, DC, MC, V.

In the old Jewish quarter, one of the most tradition-laden and historic districts of Toledo, this hotel was converted from a typical *casa Toledana,* which had once been used as a bakery. With careful restoration, especially of its ancient facade, it was transformed into one of Toledo's best and most atmospheric small hotels—the only one to match the antique charm of Hostal del Cardenal, although it seems relatively unknown. Decoration in both the public rooms and bedrooms is in a traditional Castilian style. Automatic phones, piped-in music, air-conditioning, satellite TV, and individual security boxes have been added to the immaculately kept bedrooms. At the doorstep of the hotel are such landmarks as the Monasterio de San Juan de los Reyes, Sínagoga de Santa María la Blanca, Sínagoga del Tránsito, Casa y Museo de El Greco, and Iglesia de Santo Tomé.

Hotel Residencia Alfonso VI. Calle General Moscardó, 2, 45001 Toledo. ☎ **925/22-26-00.** Fax 925/21-44-58. 85 rms, 3 suites. A/C TV TEL. 11,990–13,000 ptas. ($95.90–$104) double; 19,185–19,500 ptas. ($153.50–$156) suite. AE, DC, MC, V. Bus: 5 or 6.

Although built in the early 1970s, this hotel has been kept up to date. Run by the same management as Carlos V, it is a superior hotel with better appointments and comfort, though a few of the public rooms appear so faux Castilian they look like movie sets. It sits near a great concentration of souvenir shops in the center of the old city, at the southern perimeter of the Alcázar. Inside you'll discover a high-ceilinged, marble-trimmed decor with a scattering of Iberian artifacts, copies of Spanish provincial furniture, and dozens of leather armchairs. There's also a stone-floored dining room, where fixed-price meals are served.

Inexpensive

Hotel Residencia Imperio. Calle de las Cadenas, 5, 45001 Toledo. ☎ **925/22-76-50.** Fax 925/25-31-83. 21 rms. A/C TV TEL. 6,000 ptas. ($48) double. MC, V.

Just off Calle de la Plata, one block west of Plaza de Zocodover, the Imperio is the best bet for those on a tight budget. The rooms are clean and comfortable but small and lackluster, showing the wear of their years. Most overlook a little church with a wall overgrown with wisteria.

Hotel Maravilla. Plaza de Barrio Rey, 7, 45001 Toledo. ☎ **925/22-33-00.** Fax 925/25-05-58. 18 rms. A/C TV TEL. 6,600 ptas. ($52.80) double. AE, MC, V. Bus: 5 or 6.

If you enjoy hotels with lots of local color, then this little place might please you. It's only one block south of Plaza de Zocodover and opens directly onto its own cobblestone plaza. Semi-modernized in 1995, the building has many bay windows; the bedrooms are modest but adequate, the furnishings so-so. You can hang your laundry on the roof and use an iron in the downstairs laundry room.

NEARBY PLACES TO STAY

La Almazara. Carretera Toledo-Argés-Cuerva, km 3400, 45080 Toledo. ☎ **925/22-38-66.** 21 rms. TEL. 5,900 ptas. ($47.20) double. AE, MC, V. Closed Dec 10–Mar 10. Free parking. Follow the road to the parador of Ciudad Real, then take the C-781 to Cuerva.

For readers who have a car or who don't mind one or two taxi rides a day, there are some excellent lodgings across the Tagus. Taking its name from an olive-oil mill that used to stand here, La Almazara offers some of the most offbeat accommodations around. Hidden away in the hills, this old-fashioned country villa, with its own courtyards and vineyards, exudes the atmosphere of old Spain, far removed from city life. It has an exceptional view of Toledo. Request one of the spacious chambers in the main house rather than a room in the less comfortable annex.

Hotel los Cigarrales. Carretera Circunvalacíon, 32, 45004 Toledo. ☎ **925/22-00-53.** Fax 925/21-55-46. 36 rms. A/C TEL. 5,980 ptas. ($47.85) double. MC, V. Free parking. Bus: Chamartín from rail station.

About a mile south of the city center, this hotel is for those seeking quiet seclusion. Built in the 1960s in traditional red brick, it looks like a private villa with a garden; the friendliness of the family of owners adds to this feeling. Most of the interior is covered with blue and green tiles. The guest rooms are clean, sunny, and decorated with heavy Spanish furniture, a bit sterile but comfortable. Some of the rooms have balconies with panoramic views. From the flower-filled terrace of the cozy bar, you can see the towers of medieval Toledo.

WHERE TO DINE

Moderate

Asador Adolfo. La Granada, 6. ☎ **925/22-73-21.** Reservations recommended. Main courses 1,850–2,500 ptas. ($14.80–$20); fixed-price menu 3,400 ptas. ($27.20). AE, DC, MC, V. Daily 1–4pm, Mon–Sat 8pm–midnight. Bus: 5 or 6. SPANISH.

Located less than a minute's walk north of the cathedral, at the corner of Calle Hombre de Palo behind an understated sign, Asador Adolfo is considered by many locals to be the finest restaurant in town. We, however, rate it under the Hostal del Cardenal. Sections of the building were first constructed during the 1400s, although the thoroughly modern kitchen has recently been renovated. The dining room ceilings are supported by massive beams, and here and there the rooms contain faded frescoes dating from the original building.

Game dishes are a house specialty; such dishes as partridge with white beans and venison consistently rate among the best anywhere. Nongame offerings include hake flavored with local saffron as well as a wide array of beef, veal, or lamb dishes. To start, try the *pimientos rellenos* (red peppers stuffed with pulverized shellfish). The house dessert is marzipan, prepared in a wood-fired oven and noted for its lightness.

Casa Aurelio. Calle Sínagoga, 6. ☎ **925/22-20-97.** Reservations recommended. Main courses 2,500–4,000 ptas. ($20–$32); fixed-price menu 3,250 ptas. ($26). AE, DC, MC, V. Daily 1–4pm and 8–11:30pm. Bus: 5 or 6. CASTILIAN.

Established in the late 1940s, Casa Aurelio occupies two separate but neighboring dining rooms, with two separate entrances, near the northern edge of the cathedral. It's one of the restaurant staples of Toledo, with its generous portions, Castilian ambience, and efficient service. Traditional versions of *sopa castellana*, grilled hake, *lubina à la sal* (whitefish cooked in salt), fresh salmon, and roast lamb are on the menu. Note that the main outlet of this restaurant (Calle Sínagoga, 6) is usually closed every Wednesday, although the smaller of the restaurant's two dining rooms (Calle Snagoga, 1) remains open.

✪ **Hostal del Cardenal.** Paseo de Recaredo, 24. ☎ **925/22-08-62.** Reservations required. Main courses 800–2,600 ptas. ($6.40–$20.80); fixed-price menu 2,550 ptas. ($20.40). AE, DC, MC, V. Daily 1–4pm and 8:30–11:30pm. Bus: 2 from rail station. SPANISH.

Treat yourself to Toledo's best-known restaurant, owned by the same people who run Madrid's Sobrino de Botín, so beloved by Hemingway (see Chapter 4). The chef prepares regional dishes with flair and originality. Choosing from a menu very similar to that of the fabled Madrid eatery, begin with "quarter of an hour" (fish) soup or white asparagus, then move on to curried prawns, baked hake, filet mignon, or smoked salmon. Roast suckling pig is a specialty, as is partridge in casserole. Arrive early to enjoy a sherry in the bar or in the courtyard.

Parador Nacional de Conde Orgaz. Cerro del Emperador. ☎ **925/22-18-50.** Reservations not accepted. Main courses 1,000–2,500 ptas. ($8–$20); fixed-price menu 3,500 ptas. ($28). AE, DC, MC, V. Daily 1–4pm and 8:30–11pm. Drive across Puente San Martín and head south for 2½ miles (4km). CASTILIAN.

Sturdy Castilian cuisine is enhanced by one of the most panoramic views from any restaurant in Europe. Located in a fine parador (recommended above), this restaurant is on the crest of a hill—said to be the spot that El Greco chose for his *View of Toledo.* The place is somewhat tourist trodden, and the food doesn't quite match the view, but it's a worthy choice, nonetheless. The fixed-price meal might include tasty Spanish tapas, hake, then perhaps either veal or beef grilled on an open fire, and dessert. If you're dining lightly, try a local specialty, *tortilla española con magra* (potato omelet with ham or bacon). There is a bar on the upper level.

Venta de Aires. Circo Romano, 35. ☎ **925/22-05-45.** Reservations recommended. Main courses 1,500–2,500 ptas. ($12–$20); fixed-price menu 2,500 ($20). AE, DC, MC, V. Daily 1–4pm, Mon–Sat 8–11pm. SPANISH.

Just outside the city gates, southwest of the Circo Romano (Roman Circus), Venta de Aires has served Toledo's pièce de résistance—*perdiz* (partridge)—since 1891, when the place was just a tiny roadside inn. This dish is best eaten with the red wine of Méntrida. For dessert, try the marzipan, an institution in Toledo. On your way out, take note of former President Richard Nixon's entry in the guest book (he dined here in 1963)—believe or not, they're still talking about the visit.

INEXPENSIVE

El Emperador. Carretera del Valle, 1. ☎ **925/22-46-91.** Reservations recommended. Main courses 1,200–1,800 ptas. ($9.60–$14.40); fixed-price menu 1,400 ptas. ($11.20). V. Tues–Sun 2–4:30pm and 8–11pm. Bus: Carretera Valle. SPANISH.

A modern restaurant on the outskirts of Toledo, southwest of the historic core of the town, near the parador, El Emperador is reached via an arched bridge. Its terraces overlook the river and the towers of Toledo; the tavern-style interior has leather-and-wood chairs, heavy beams, and wrought-iron chandeliers. Service at this family-owned establishment is attentive. The fixed-price menu might include a choice of soup (beef, vegetable, or noodle), followed by a small steak with french fries, then fresh fruit, plus wine. Although the dishes are decently prepared from fresh ingredients, it is the economical prices that make this such an appealing choice.

La Parilla. Horno de los Bizcochos, 8. ☎ **925/21-22-45.** Main courses 1,100–1,775 ptas. ($8.80–$14.20); fixed-price menu 1,400 ptas. ($11.20). AE, DC, MC, V. Daily 1–4pm and 8–11pm. Bus: 5 or 6. SPANISH.

Go here for some real Franco-era dishes. This classic Spanish restaurant, lying within a thick-walled medieval building, stands on a cobbled street near the Hotel Alfonso VI, just east of the cathedral. The menu offers no surprises, but it's reliable. Likely inclusions on the bill of fare are roast suckling pig, spider crabs, Castilian baked trout, stewed quail, baked kidneys, and La Mancha rabbit. This is the type of heavy fare so beloved by Castilians, who still frequent the place in great numbers.

Maravilla. Plaza de Barrio Rey, 7. ☎ **925/22-33-00.** Reservations not accepted. Main courses 1,200–1,600 ptas. ($9.60–$12.80); fixed-price menus 1,075–1,800 ptas. ($8.60–$14.40). AE, MC, V. Tues–Sun 1–4pm and 8–11pm. Bus: 5 or 6. SPANISH.

Maravilla is in the Barrio Rey, a small square off the historic Plaza de Zocodover filled with budget restaurants and cafés that change their names so often it's virtually impossible to keep track. Here, you'll get the best all-around dining bargain. Its kitchen serves a typically Castilian menu, specializing in the area's famous *perdiz* (partridge) but also preparing *cordero asado* (roast lamb).

A TAPAS BAR

Bar Ludeña. Plaza de la Horn Madelena, 13, Corral de Don Diego, 10. ☎ **925/22-33-84.** Reservations not accepted. Tapas 250–800 ptas. ($2–$6.40). No credit cards. Thurs–Tues 10am–midnight. TAPAS.

A loyal clientele comes for the delectable tapas served here. Glasses of wine are sometimes passed through a small window to clients who are standing outside enjoying the view of the square. The bar is little more than a narrow corridor, serving *raciónes* of tapas that are so generous they make little meals, especially when served with bread. The roasted red peppers in olive oil are quite tasty, along with the stuffed crabs and *calamares* (squid). Huge dishes of pickled cucumbers, onions, and olives are available. A tiny dining room behind a curtain at the end of the bar serves inexpensive fare.

2 Aranjuez

29 miles (47km) S of Madrid, 30 miles (48km) NE of Toledo

This Castilian town, at a confluence of the Tagus and Jarama Rivers, was once home to Bourbon kings in the spring and fall. With the manicured shrubbery, stately elms, fountains, and statues of the Palacio Real and surrounding compounds, Aranjuez remains a regal garden oasis in what is otherwise an unimpressive agricultural flatland known primarily for its strawberries and asparagus.

GETTING THERE **By Train** Trains depart about every 20 minutes from Madrid's Atocha Railway Station to make the 50-minute trip to Aranjuez. Trains run less often along the east-west route to and from Toledo (a 40-minute ride). The Aranjuez station lies about a mile outside town. You can walk it in about 15 minutes, but taxis and buses line up on Calle Stuart (two blocks from the city tourist office). The bus that makes the run from the center of Aranjuez to the railway station is marked "N–Z."

By Bus Buses for Aranjuez depart every 30 minutes from 7:30am to 10pm from Madrid's Estación Sur de Autobuses, Canarias, 17. In Madrid, call **91/468-45-11** for information. Buses arrive in Aranjuez at the City Bus Terminal, Calle Infantas, 8 (☎ **91/891-01-83**).

By Car Driving is easy and takes about 30 minutes once you reach the southern city limits of Madrid. To reach Aranjuez, follow the signs to Aranjuez and Granada, taking highway N-IV.

VISITOR INFORMATION The tourist information office is at Plaza de San Antonio, 9 (☎ **91/891-04-27**). Open Monday through Friday from 10am to 2pm and 3 to 5pm and on Saturday from 10am to 2pm.

WHAT TO SEE & DO

Palacio Real. Plaza Palacio. ☎ **91/891-07-40.** Admission 500 ptas. ($4) adults, 250 ptas. ($2) students and children. Apr–Sept, Tues–Sun 10am–6:30pm; Oct–Mar, Tues–Sun 10am–5:30pm. Bus: Routes from the rail station converge at the square and gardens at the westernmost edge of the palace.

As you enter the cobblestoned courtyard, you can tell just by the size of the palace that it's going to be spectacular. Ferdinand and Isabella, Philip II, Philip V, and Charles III all made their way through here. The structure you see today dates from 1778 (the previous buildings were destroyed by fire). Its salons show the opulence of a bygone era, with room after room of royal extravaganza. Many styles are blended: Spanish, Italian, Moorish, and French. And, of course, no royal palace would be complete without a room reflecting the rage for chinoiserie that once swept over Europe. The Porcelain Salon is also of special interest. A guide conducts you through the huge complex (a tip is expected).

Jardín de la Isla. Directly northwest of the Palacio Real. No phone. Free admission. Apr–Sept, daily 8am–8:30pm; Oct–Mar, daily 8am–6:30pm.

After the tour of the Royal Palace, wander through the Garden of the Island. Spanish impressionist Santiago Rusiñol captured its evasive quality on canvas, and one Spanish writer said that you walk here "as if softly lulled by a sweet 18th-century sonata." A number of fountains are remarkable: the "Ne Plus Ultra" fountain, the black-jasper fountain of Bacchus, the fountain of Apollo, and the ones honoring Neptune (god of the sea) and Cybele (goddess of agriculture).

You may also stroll through the Jardín del Parterre, located in front of the palace. It's much better kept than the Garden of the Island but not as romantic.

Casita del Labrador. Calle Reina, Jardín del Príncipe. ☎ **91/891-13-44.** Admission 425 ptas. ($3.40). Apr–Sept, Tues–Sun 10am–6:30pm; Oct–Mar, Tues–Sun 10am–5:30pm.

"The Little House of the Worker," modeled after the Petit Trianon at Versailles, was built in 1803 by Charles IV, who later abdicated in Aranjuez. The queen came here with her youthful lover, Godoy (whom she had elevated to the position of prime minister), and the feeble-minded Charles didn't seem to mind a bit. Surrounded by beautiful gardens, the "bedless" palace is lavishly furnished in the grand style of the 18th and 19th centuries. The marble floors represent some of the finest workmanship of that day; the brocaded walls emphasize the luxurious lifestyle; and the royal toilet is a sight to behold (in those days, royalty preferred an audience). The clock here is one of the treasures of the house. The *casita* lies half a mile east of the Royal Palace; those with a car can drive directly to it through the tranquil Jardin del Príncipe.

WHERE TO STAY

Hostal Castilla. Carretera Andalucia, 98, 28300 Aranjuez. ☎ **91/891-26-27.** 17 rms. MINIBAR TV TEL. 5,600 ptas. ($44.80) double. AE, DC, MC, V.

On one of the town's main streets north of the Royal Palace and gardens, the Castilla consists of the ground floor and part of the first floor of a well-preserved early-18th-century house. Most of the accommodations overlook a courtyard with a fountain and flowers. Owner Joaquin Suarez, who speaks English fluently, suggests that reservations be made at least a month in advance. There are excellent restaurants nearby, and the hostal has an arrangement with a neighboring bar to provide guests with an inexpensive lunch. This is a good location from which to explore either Madrid or Toledo on a day trip.

WHERE TO DINE

Casa Pablo. Almibar, 42. ☎ **91/891-14-51.** Reservations recommended. Main courses 1,900–2,500 ptas. ($15.20–$20); four-course fixed-price menu 3,000 ptas. ($24). AE, MC, V. Daily 1–4:30pm and 8pm–midnight. Closed Aug. SPANISH.

An unpretentious and well-managed restaurant near the bus station in the town center, Casa Pablo was established in 1941. At tables set outside under a canopy, you can dine while enjoying red and pink geraniums along the tree-lined street; in cooler weather you eat either upstairs or in the cozy and clean rear dining room. The fixed-price menu includes four courses, a carafe of wine, bread, and gratuity. If it's hot and you don't want a heavy dinner, try a shrimp omelet or half a roast chicken; once we ordered just a plate of asparagus in season, accompanied by white wine. If you want a superb dish, try a fish called *mero* (Mediterranean pollack of delicate flavor), grilled over an open fire.

La Rana Verde. Reina, 1. ☎ **91/891-32-38.** Reservations recommended. Main courses 900–2,200 ptas. ($7.20–$17.60); fixed-price menu 2,200 ptas. ($17.60). MC, V. Daily 6–11pm. SPANISH.

"The Green Frog," just east of the Royal Palace and next to a small bridge spanning the Tagus, is still the traditional choice for many. Opened in 1905 by Tomas Diaz Heredero, it is still owned and run by a third-generation member of the family, who has decorated it in 1920s style. The restaurant looks like a summerhouse, with its high-beamed ceiling and soft ferns drooping from hanging baskets. The preferred tables are in the nooks overlooking the river. As in all the restaurants of Aranjuez, asparagus is a special feature. Game, particularly partridge, quail, and pigeon, can be recommended in season; fish, too, including fried hake and fried sole, makes a good choice. Strawberries are served with sugar, orange juice, or ice cream.

3 San Lorenzo de El Escorial

30 miles (48km) W of Madrid, 32 miles (52km) SE of Segovia

Aside from Toledo, the most important excursion from Madrid is to the austere royal monastery of San Lorenzo de El Escorial. Philip II ordered the construction of this granite-and-slate behemoth in 1563, two years after he moved his capital to Madrid. Once the haunt of aristocratic Spaniards, El Escorial is now a resort where hotels and restaurants flourish in summer, as hundreds come to escape the heat of the capital. Aside from the appeal of its climate, the town of San Lorenzo itself is not very noteworthy. But because of the monastery's size, you might decide to spend a night or two at San Lorenzo—or more if you have the time.

San Lorenzo makes a good base for visiting nearby Segovia and Ávila, the royal palace at La Granja, the Valley of the Fallen—and even the more distant university city of Salamanca.

GETTING THERE **By Train** More than two dozen trains depart daily from Madrid's Atocha, Nuevos Ministerios, and Chamartín train stations. During the summer extra coaches are added.

The railway station for San Lorenzo de El Escorial is located about a mile outside of town. The Herranz bus company meets all arriving trains with a shuttle bus that ferries arriving passengers to and from the Plaza Virgen de Gracia, about a block east of the entrance to the monastery.

By Bus The Office of Empresa Herranz, Calle Reina Victoria, 3, in El Escorial (☎ **91/890-41-22** or **91/890-41-25**) runs some 40 buses per day back and forth between Madrid and El Escorial. On Sunday service is curtailed to 10 buses. Trip time is an hour, and a round-trip fare costs 720 pesetas ($5.75). The same company also runs three buses a day to El Valle de los Caídos. They leave El Escorial at 11:15am, 1:15pm, and 3:15pm with returns at 2:15pm, 4:15pm, and 6:15pm. The ride takes only 15 minutes, and a round-trip fare is 830 pesetas ($6.65).

By Car Follow the N-VI highway (marked on some maps as A-6) from the northwest perimeter of Madrid toward Lugo, La Coruña, and San Lorenzo de El Escorial. After about a half hour, fork left onto the C-505 toward San Lorenzo de El Escorial. Driving time from Madrid is about an hour.

VISITOR INFORMATION The tourist information office is at Floridablanca, 10 (☎ **91/890-15-54**). It is open Monday through Friday from 10am to 2pm and 3 to 5pm, Saturday from 10am to 2pm.

WHAT TO SEE & DO

✪ **Real Monasterio de San Lorenzo de El Escorial.** Calle San Lorenzo de El Escorial, 1. ☎ **91/890-59-02.** Comprehensive ticket 850 ptas. ($6.80) adults, 350 ptas. ($2.80) children. Apr–Sept, Tues–Sun 10am–6pm; Oct–Mar, Tues–Sun 10am–5pm.

This huge granite fortress houses a wealth of paintings and tapestries and also serves as a burial place for Spanish kings. Foreboding both inside and out because of its sheer size and institutional look, El Escorial took 21 years to complete, a remarkably short time considering the bulk of the building and the primitive construction methods of the day. After his death, Juan Bautista de Toledo, the original architect, was replaced by Juan de Herrera, the greatest architect of Renaissance Spain, who completed the structure.

Philip II, who collected many of the paintings exhibited here in the New Museums, did not appreciate El Greco and favored Titian instead. But you'll still find El Greco's *The Martyrdom of St. Maurice,* rescued from storage, and his *St. Peter.* Other superb works include Titian's *Last Supper* and Velázquez's *The Tunic of Joseph.*

The Royal Library houses a priceless collection of 60,000 volumes—one of the most significant in the world. The displays range from the handwriting of St. Teresa to medieval instructions on playing chess. See, in particular, the Muslim codices and a Gothic *Cantigas* from the 13th-century reign of Alfonso X ("The Wise").

You can also visit the Philip II Apartments; these are strictly monastic, and Philip called them the "cell for my humble self" in this "palace for God." Philip became a religious fanatic and requested that his bedroom be erected overlooking the altar of the 300-foot-high basilica, which has four organs and whose dome is based on Michelangelo's drawings for St. Peter's. The choir contains a crucifix by Cellini. By comparison, the Throne Room is simple. On the walls are many ancient maps.

The Apartments of the Bourbon Kings are lavishly decorated, in contrast to Philip's preference for the ascetic. They are closed at present for restoration; check to see when they will reopen.

Under the altar of the church you'll find one of the most regal mausoleums in the world, the Royal Pantheon, where most of Spain's monarchs—from Charles I to Alfonso XII, including Philip II—are buried. In 1993 Don Juan de Borbón, the count of Barcelona and the father of King Juan Carlos (Franco "passed over" the count and never allowed him to ascend to the throne) was interred nearby. On a lower floor is the "Wedding Cake" tomb for children.

Allow at least three hours for a visit.

Casa de Príncipe (Prince's Cottage). Calle Reina, s/n. ☎ **91/891-03-05.** Admission included in comprehensive ticket to El Escorial, see above. Apr–July and Sept, Sat–Sun and holidays 10am–5:45pm; Aug, Tues–Sun 10am–5:45pm; Oct–Mar, Sat–Sun and holidays 10am–6:45pm.

This small but elaborately decorated 18th-century palace near the railway station was originally a hunting lodge built for Charles III by Juan de Villanueva. Most visitors stay in El Escorial for lunch, visiting the cottage in the afternoon.

El Valle de los Caídos (Valley of the Fallen). ☎ **91/890-56-11.** Admission 650 ptas. ($5.20). Apr–Sept, Tues–Sun 9:30am–7pm; Oct–Mar, Tues–Sun 10am–6pm. Bus: Tour buses from Madrid usually include an excursion to the Valley of the Fallen on their one-day trips to El Escorial (see "By Bus," above).

By Car Drive to the valley entrance, about 5 miles (8km) north of El Escorial in the heart of the Guadarrama Mountains. Once there, drive 3½ miles (6km) west along a wooded road to the underground basilica.

This is Franco's El Escorial, an architectural marvel that took two decades to complete, dedicated to those who died in the Spanish Civil War. Its detractors say that it represents the worst of neofascist design; its admirers say they have found renewed inspiration by coming here.

A gargantuan cross nearly 500 feet high dominates the Rock of Nava, a peak of the Guadarrama Mountains. Directly under the cross is a basilica with a vault in mosaic, completed in 1959. Here José Antonio Primo de Rivera, the founder of the Falange party, is buried. When this Nationalist hero was buried at El Escorial, many, especially influential monarchists, protested that he was not a royal. Infuriated, Franco decided to erect another monument. Originally it was slated to honor the dead on the Nationalist side only, but the intervention of several parties led to a decision to include all the *caídos* (fallen). In time the mausoleum claimed Franco as well; his body was interred behind the high altar.

A funicular extends from near the entrance to the basilica to the base of the gigantic cross erected on the mountaintop above (where there's a superb view). The fare is 300 pesetas ($2.40), and the funicular runs daily from 10:30am to 1:15pm and 4 to 6pm.

On the other side of the mountain is a Benedictine monastery that has sometimes been dubbed "the Hilton of monasteries" because of its seeming luxury.

WHERE TO STAY

MODERATE

Hotel Victoria Palace. Calle Juan de Toledo, 4, 28200 San Lorenzo de El Escorial. ☎ **91/890-15-11.** Fax 91/890-12-48. 90 rms. TV TEL. 13,500–15,800 ptas. ($108 –$126.40) double. AE, DC, MC, V. Free parking.

The Victoria Palace, with its view of El Escorial, is the finest hotel in town, a traditional establishment that has been modernized without losing its special aura of style and comfort. It is surrounded by beautiful gardens and has an outdoor swimming pool. The rooms (some with private terraces) are well furnished and maintained. The rates are reasonable enough, and a bargain for a four-star hotel. The dining room serves some of the best food in town.

INEXPENSIVE

$ **Hostal Cristina.** Juan de Toledo, 6, 28200 San Lorenzo de El Escorial. ☎ **91/890-19-61.** 16 rms. 6,000 ptas. ($48) double. MC, V.

An excellent budget choice, this hotel is run by the Delgado family, who opened it in the mid-1980s. It doesn't pretend to compete with comfort and amenities of the Victoria Palace or even the Miranda & Suizo (see below), but it has its devotees nonetheless. About 50 yards from the monastery, it stands in the center of town, offering clean and comfortable but simply furnished rooms. The helpful staff will direct you to the small garden. Since the food served in the restaurant is both good and plentiful, many Spanish visitors prefer to book here for a summer holiday.

Miranda & Suizo. Calle Floridablanca, 20, 28200 San Lorenzo de El Escorial. ☎ **91/890-47-11.** Fax 91/890-43-58. 50 rms, 2 suites. TV. 9,000 ptas. ($72) double; 12,000 ptas. ($96) suite. AE, DC, MC, V.

On a tree-lined street in the heart of town, within easy walking distance of the monastery, this excellent middle-bracket establishment ranks as a leading two-star hotel. It is the "second choice" in town, with rooms not quite as comfortable as those at the Victoria Palace. The Victorian-style building, nevertheless, has good guest rooms, some with terraces; 10 contain TVs. The furnishings are comfortable, the beds often made of brass; sometimes you'll find fresh flowers on the tables. In summer, there is outside dining.

WHERE TO DINE

MODERATE

Charolés. Calle Floridablanca, 24. ☎ **91/890-59-75.** Reservations required. Main courses 2,650–3,650 ptas. ($21.20–$28.50). AE, DC, MC, V. Daily 1–4pm and 9pm–midnight. SPANISH/INTERNATIONAL.

The thick and solid walls of this establishment date, according to its managers, "from the monastic age"—and probably predate the town's larger and better-known monastery of El Escorial. The restaurant contained within was established around 1980, and has been known ever since as the best dining room in town. It has a flower-ringed outdoor terrace for use during clement weather. The cuisine doesn't quite rate a star, but chances are you'll be satisfied. The wide choice of menu items based entirely on fresh fish and meats includes such dishes as grilled hake with green or hollandaise sauce, shellfish soup, pepper steak, a *pastel* (pie) of fresh vegetables with crayfish, and herb-flavored baby lamb chops. Strawberry or kiwi tart is a good dessert choice.

INEXPENSIVE

Mesón la Cueva. San Antón, 4. ☎ **91/890-15-16.** Reservations recommended. Main courses 850–2,500 ptas. ($6.80–$20); *menú del día* 1,800 ptas. ($14.40). No credit cards. Tues–Sun 1–4pm and 8:30–11:30pm. CASTILIAN.

Founded in 1768, this restaurant captures the world of Old Castile, and it lies only a short walk from the monastery. A *mesón típico* built around an enclosed courtyard, "the Cave" boasts such nostalgic accents as stained-glass windows, antique chests, a 19th-century bullfighting collage, faded engravings, paneled doors, and iron balconies. The cooking is on target, and the portions are generous. Regional specialties include Valencian paella and *fabada asturiana* (pork sausage and beans), but fresh trout broiled in butter is the best of all. The menu's most expensive items are Segovian roast suckling pig and roast lamb (tender inside, crisp outside). Off the courtyard through a separate doorway is La Cueva's *tasca,* filled with Castilians quaffing their favorite before-dinner drinks.

NEAR THE VALLEY OF THE FALLEN

Hostelerie Valle de los Caídos. Valle de los Cádos. ☎ **91/890-55-11.** Reservations not accepted. Main courses 600–1,300 ptas. ($4.80–$10.40); fixed-price menu 1,250 ptas. ($10). No credit cards. Daily 9–10am, 2–3:30pm, and 9–10pm. Closed Dec 15–Jan 15. SPANISH.

This restaurant is the most likely bet for those heading up into the Valley of the Fallen. Set amid an arid but dramatic landscape halfway along the inclined access road leading to Franco's monuments, and reachable only by car or bus, it's a mammoth modern structure with wide terraces, floor-to-ceiling windows, and a well-established pattern of feeding busloads of foreign tourists, mainly from tour groups. The *menú del día* usually includes such dishes as cannelloni Rossini, pork chops with potatoes, a dessert choice of flan or fruit, and wine. The typical fare of roast chicken, roast lamb, shellfish, and paella is somewhat cafeteria style in nature. View it mainly as a "feeding station" for the hundreds flocking to this attraction.

4 Segovia

54 miles (91km) NW of Madrid, 42 miles (68km) NE of Ávila

Less commercial than Toledo, Segovia, more than anywhere else, typifies the glory of Old Castile. Wherever you look, you'll see reminders of a golden era—whether it's the most spectacular Alcázar on the Iberian Peninsula or the well-preserved, still-functioning Roman aqueduct.

Segovia lies on the slope of the Guadarrama Mountains, where the Eresma and Clamores Rivers converge. This ancient city stands in the center of the most castle-rich part of Castile. Isabella was proclaimed Queen of Castile here in 1474.

The narrow, winding streets of this hill city must be covered on foot to fully view the Romanesque churches and 15th-century palaces along the way.

GETTING THERE **By Train** Nine trains leave Madrid's Chamartín Railway Station every day and arrive two hours later in Segovia, where you can board bus number 3, which departs every quarter hour for the Plaza Mayor. The station lies on the Paseo Obispo Quesada, s/n (☎ **921/42-07-74**), a 20-minute walk southeast of the town center.

By Bus Buses arrive and depart from the Estacionamiento Municipal de Autobuses, Paseo de Ezequile González, 10 (☎ **921/43-30-10**), near the corner of the Avenida Fernández Ladreda and the steeply sloping Paseo Conde de Sepúlveda. There are 10 to 15 buses a day to and from Madrid (which depart from Paseo de la Florida, 11; metro: Norte), and about four a day traveling between Ávila, Segovia, and Valladolid. One-way tickets from Madrid cost around 765 pesetas ($6.10).

By Car Take the N-VI (on some maps it's known as the A-6) or the Autopista del Nordeste northwest from Madrid, toward León and Lugo. At the junction with Route 110 (signposted Segovia), turn northeast.

VISITOR INFORMATION The tourist information office is at Plaza Mayor, 10 (☎ **921/46-03-34**). It is open daily from 10am to 2pm and 5 to 8pm.

WHAT TO SEE & DO

✪ **El Alcázar.** Plaza de La Reina Victoria Eugenia. ☎ **921/43-01-76.** Admission 375 ptas. ($3) adults, 175 ptas. ($1.40) children 8–14, free for children 7 and under. Apr–Sept, daily 10am–7pm; Oct–Mar, daily 10am–6pm. Bus: 3. Take either Calle Vallejo, Calle de Velarde, Calle de Daoiz, or Paseo de Ronda.

View the Alcázar first from below, at the junction of the Clamores and Eresma Rivers. It is on the west side of Segovia, and you may not spot it when you first enter the city. But that's part of the surprise.

The castle dates back to the 12th century, but a large segment—which contained its Moorish ceilings—was destroyed by fire in 1862. Restoration has continued over the years.

Royal romance is associated with the Alcázar. Isabella first met Ferdinand here, and today you can see a facsimile of her dank bedroom. Once married, she wasn't foolish enough to surrender her rights, as replicas of the thrones attest—both are equally proportioned. Philip II married his fourth wife, Anne of Austria, here as well.

Walk the battlements of this once-impregnable castle, from which its occupants hurled boiling oil onto the enemy below. Ascend the hazardous stairs of the tower, originally built by Isabella's father as a prison, for a panoramic view of Segovia.

✪ **Roman Aqueduct.** Plaza del Azoguejo.

This architectural marvel, built by the Romans nearly 2,000 years ago, is still used to carry water. Constructed of mortarless granite, it consists of 118 arches, and in one two-tiered section it soars 95 feet to its highest point. The Spanish call it El Puente. It spans the Plaza del Azoguejo, the old market square, stretching nearly 800 yards. When the Moors took Segovia in 1072, they destroyed 36 arches, which were later rebuilt under Ferdinand and Isabella in 1484.

✪ **Cabildo Catedral de Segovia.** Plaza Catedral, Marqués del Arco. ☎ **921/43-53-25.** Free admission to cathedral; cloisters, museum, and chapel room 250 ptas. ($2) adults, 50 ptas. ($0.40) children. Spring and summer, daily 9am–7pm; off-season, daily 9:30am–1pm and 3–6pm.

Constructed between 1515 and 1558, this is the last Gothic cathedral built in Spain. Fronting the historic Plaza Mayor, it stands on the spot where Isabella I was proclaimed Queen of Castile. Affectionately called *la dama de las catedrales,* it contains numerous treasures, such as the Blessed Sacrament Chapel (created by the flamboyant Churriguera), stained-glass windows, elaborately carved choir stalls, and 16th- and 17th-century paintings, including a reredos portraying the deposition of Christ from the cross by Juan de Juni. The cloisters are older than the cathedral, dating from an earlier church that was destroyed in the so-called War of the Communeros. Inside the cathedral museum you'll find jewelry, paintings, and a collection of rare antique manuscripts.

Iglesia de la Vera Cruz. Carretera de Zamarramala. ☎ **921/43-14-75.** Admission 175 ptas. ($1.40). Apr–Sept, Tues–Sun 10:30am–1:30pm and 3:30–7pm; Oct–Mar, Tues–Sun 10:30am–1:30pm and 3:30–6pm.

Built in either the 11th or the 12th century by the Knights Templar, this is the most fascinating Romanesque church in Segovia. It stands in isolation outside the walls of the old town, overlooking the Alcázar. Its unusual 12-sided design is believed to have been copied from the Church of the Holy Sepulchre in Jerusalem. Inside you'll find an inner temple, rising two floors, where the knights conducted nightlong vigils as part of their initiation rites.

Monasterio del Parral. Calle del Marqués de Villena (across the Eresma River). ☎ **921/43-23-98.** Free admission. Daily 10am–2pm and 4–6:30pm. Take Ronda de Sant Lucía, cross the Eresma River, and head down Calle del Marqués de Villena.

The restored "Monastery of the Grape" was established for the Hieronymites by Henry IV, a Castilian king (1425–74) known as "The Impotent." The monastery lies across the Eresma River about a half mile north of the city. The church is a medley of styles and decoration—mainly Gothic, Renaissance, and plateresque. The facade was never completed, and the monastery itself was abandoned when religious orders were suppressed in 1835. Today it's been restored and is once again the domain of the *jerónimos,* Hieronymus priests and brothers. Inside, a robed monk will show you the various treasures of the order, including a polychrome altarpiece and the alabaster tombs of the Marquis of Villena and his wife—all the work of Juan Rodríguez.

WHERE TO STAY

MODERATE

Los Arcos. Paseo de Ezequiel González, 26, 40002 Segovia. ☎ **800/528-1234** in the U.S., or 921/43-74-62. Fax 921/42-81-61. 59 rms. A/C MINIBAR TV TEL. 12,350 ptas. ($98.80) double. AE, DC, MC, V. Parking 900 ptas. ($7.20).

This concrete-and-glass five-story structure opened in 1987 and is generally cited as the best in town, although you may prefer Los Linajes instead (see below). Well run and modern, it attracts the business traveler, although tourists frequent the place in droves as well. Rooms are generally spacious but furnished in a standard international bland way, except for the beautiful rug-dotted parquet floors. Built-in furnishings and tiny combination baths are part of the offering, along with private safes. Rooms are well-kept, although some furnishings look worn.

Even if you don't stay here, consider dining at the hotel's La Cocina de Segovia, which is the only hotel dining room that competes successfully with Mesón de Cándido (see below). As at the nearby competitors, roast suckling pig and roast Segovia lamb—perfectly cooked in specially made ovens—are the specialties. There's also a tavernlike café and a bar. In all, it's a smart, efficiently run, and pleasant choice, if not a terribly exciting one.

Hotel Los Linajes. Dr. Velasco, 9, 40003 Segovia. ☎ **921/46-04-75.** Fax 921/46-04-79. 55 rms, 10 suites. TV TEL. 10,500 ptas. ($84) double; from 13,200 ptas. ($105.60) suite. AE, DC, MC, V. Parking 800 ptas. ($6.40). Bus: 1.

In the historical district of St. Stephen at the northern edge of the old town stands this hotel, the former home of a Segovian noble family. While the facade dates from the 11th century, the interior is modern, except for some Castilian decorations. Following a 1996 renovation, the hotel looks a bit brighter and fresher than Los Arcos. One of the best hotels in town, Los Linajes offers gardens and patios where guests can enjoy a panoramic view over the city. The hotel also has a bar/lounge, coffee shop, disco, and garage.

✪ **Parador de Segovia.** Carretera Valladolid, s/n (N-601), 40003 Segovia. ☎ **921/44-37-37.** Fax 921/43-73-62. 113 rms, 7 suites. A/C MINIBAR TV TEL. 16,500 ptas. ($132) double; from 25,000 ptas. ($200) suite. AE, DC, MC, V. Parking 900 ptas. ($7.20).

This 20th-century tile-roofed parador sits on a hill two miles (3km) northeast of Segovia (take the N-601). It stands on an estate called El Terminillo, which used to be famous for its vines and almond trees, a few of which still survive. If you have a car and can get a reservation, book in here; the comfort level dwarfs that found at either Los Arcos or Los Linajes. The guest rooms are deluxe, containing such extras as private safes and tiled combination baths. Furnishings are tasteful (often in "blond" pieces), and large windows open onto panoramic views of the countryside. Some of the older rooms here are a bit dated, however, with a lackluster decor. The vast lawns and gardens contain two lakelike swimming pools, and there is also an indoor pool. Other facilities include saunas and tennis courts.

INEXPENSIVE

Gran Hotel las Sirenas. Juan Bravo, 30, 40001 Segovia. ☎ **921/43-40-11.** Fax 921/43-06-33. 39 rms. A/C TV TEL. 8,000 ptas. ($64) double. AE, DC, MC, V.

Standing on the most charming old plaza in Segovia, opposite the Church of St. Martín, this hotel was built around 1950, and has been renovated several times. However, it has long since lost its Franco-era supremacy to Los Arcos (see above). It's modest and clean, and decorated in a conservative style. Each bedroom is well maintained and filled with functional, simple furniture. Breakfast is the only meal served, but the staff at the reception desk can direct clients to cafés and *tascas* nearby.

WHERE TO DINE

INEXPENSIVE

$ **El Bernardino.** Cervantes, 2. ☎ **921/43-32-25.** Reservations recommended. Main courses 1,300–2,350 ptas. ($10.40–$18.80); fixed-price menu 2,750 ptas. ($22). AE, DC, MC, V. Daily 1–4pm and 7:30–11:30pm. CASTILIAN.

El Bernardino, a three-minute walk west of the Roman aqueduct, is built like an old tavern. Lanterns hang from beamed ceilings, and the view over the red-tile rooftops of the city is delightful. The *menú del día* might include a huge paella, roast veal with potatoes, flan or ice cream, plus bread and wine. You might begin your meal with *sopa castellana* (made with ham, sausage, bread, egg, and garlic). The roast dishes are exceptional here, including roast suckling pig, from a special oven, and roast baby lamb. You can also order grilled rib steak or stewed partridge.

Casa Duque. Calle Cervantes, 12. ☎ **921/43-05-37.** Reservations recommended. Main courses 600–2,500 ptas. ($4.80–$20); fixed-price menu 1,875 ptas. ($15). AE, DC, MC, V. Daily 12:30–5pm and 8–11:30pm. CASTILIAN.

Duque—the *maestro asador,* as he calls himself—supervises the roasting of the pig, the house specialty, in this *mesón típico* founded in 1895. Waitresses wearing the traditional garb of the mayoress of Zamarramala will serve you other Segovian gastronomic specialties, such as *sopa castellana* or a cake known as *ponche alcázar.* There is a tavern below so that you may enjoy a predinner drink.

José María. Cronista Lecea, 11. ☎ **921/46-11-11.** Reservations recommended. Main courses 1,200–2,800 ptas. ($9.60–$22.40); fixed-price menu 3,800 ptas. ($30.40). AE, DC, MC, V. Daily 1–4pm and 8–11:30pm. SEGOVIAN.

This centrally located bar and restaurant, one block east of the Plaza Mayor, serves quality regional cuisine in a rustic stucco-and-brick dining room. Before dinner, locals crowd in for tapas at the bar, then move into the dining room for such Castilian specialties as roast suckling pig, rural-style conger eel, and freshly caught sea bream. Try the cream of crabmeat soup, roasted peppers, salmon with scrambled eggs, house-style hake, or grilled veal steak. For dessert, a specialty is ice cream tart with a whiskey sauce.

✪ **Mesón de Candido.** Plaza del Azoguejo, 5. ☎ **921/42-59-11.** Reservations recommended. Main courses 1,300–2,500 ptas. ($10.40–$20); fixed-price menu 2,500 ptas. ($20). AE, DC, MC, V. Daily 12:30–4:30pm and 8–11:30pm or midnight. CASTILIAN.

For years this beautiful old Spanish inn, standing on the eastern edge of the old town, has maintained a monopoly on the tourist trade. Apart from the hotels—specifically La Cocina de Segovia at the Los Arcos—it is the town's finest dining choice. The Candido family took it over in 1905, and fourth- and fifth-generation family members still run the place, having fed, over the years, everybody from Hemingway to Nixon. The oldest part of the restaurant dates from 1822, and the restaurant has gradually been enlarged since then. The proprietor of the House of Candido is known as *mesonero mayor de Castilla* (the major innkeeper of Castile). He's been decorated with more medals and honors than paella has grains of rice. The restaurant's popularity can be judged by the crowds of hungry diners who fill every seat in the six dining rooms. The à la carte menu includes those two regional staples: *cordero asado* (roast baby lamb) and *cochinillo asado* (roast suckling pig).

Mesón el Cordero. Calle de Carmen, 4. ☎ **921/43-51-96.** Reservations recommended. Main courses 1,000–1,800 ptas. ($8–$14.40); fixed-price menus 2,200–3,500 ptas. ($17.60–$28). AE, DC, MC, V. Daily 12:30–4:30pm and 8–11:30pm. CASTILIAN/IBERIAN.

Originally constructed in the 1800s as a Carmelite convent, near the base of the town's aqueduct, Mesón el Cordero was substantially enlarged in the 1970s by two hardworking partners who added dozens of rustic artifacts to create the charming eatery you see today. This restaurant is known for its flavorful roasted meats. One noteworthy specialty, *cordero lechal* (roasted suckling lamb), is served on the bone and seasoned with fresh herbs, including ample amounts of rosemary and thyme. The wine list includes an array of suitably robust reds from Rioja, Rivera, and southern France.

La Oficina. Calle Cronista Lecea, 10. ☎ **921/46-02-83.** Reservations not required. Main courses 600–1,700 ptas. ($4.80–$13.60); fixed-price menu 1,200 ptas. ($9.60). AE, DC, MC, V. Wed–Mon 1–4:30pm and 7–11:30pm. Closed 3 weeks in Nov. CASTILIAN.

Established in 1893, La Oficina has been maintained by three subsequent generations of the original owner's family. As such, it has virtually welcomed every resident of Segovia into the thick brick and stone walls that give it its distinctive Castilian flavor. Few changes, other than repairs, seem to have been made to the decor since its founding, a fact that contributes significantly to its charm. Set adjacent to Plaza Mayor, a short walk east of the cathedral, it offers a stand-up bar accessible through a separate entrance, where locals usually meet for an aperitif before beginning their meal. The owners have won awards for their roast suckling pig, which is prepared and served with suitable pomp and ceremony by the well-trained staff.

AN EASY EXCURSION TO LA GRANJA

To reach La Granja, seven miles (11km) southeast of Segovia, you can take a 20-minute bus ride from the center of the city. About 12 buses a day leave from Paseo Conde de Sepulveda at Avenida Fernández Ladreda.

✪ **Palacio Real de La Granja.** Plaza de España, 17, San Ildefonso (Segovia). ☎ **921/47-00-19.** Admission 650 ptas. ($5.20) adults, 250 ptas. ($2) children 5–14, free for children 4 and under. Apr–May, Mon–Fri 10am–1:30pm and 3–5pm, Sat–Sun 10am–6pm; June–Sept, daily 10am–6pm; Oct–Mar, Mon–Sat 10am–1:30pm and 3–5pm, Sun 10am–2pm.

San Ildefonso de la Granja was the summer palace of the Bourbon kings of Spain, who replicated the grandeur of Versailles in the province of Segovia. Set against the snowcapped Sierra de Guadarrama, the slate-roofed palace dominates the village that grew up around it (which, these days, is a summer resort).

The founder of La Granja was Philip V, grandson of Louis XIV and the first Bourbon King of Spain (his body, along with that of his second queen, Isabel de Fernesio, is interred in a mauseoleum in the Collegiate Church). Philip V was born at Versailles on December 19, 1683, which may explain why he wanted to re-create that atmosphere at Segovia.

At one time a farm stood on the grounds of what is now the palace—hence its totally incongruous name *la granja,* meaning "the farm" in Spanish.

The palace was built in the first part of the 18th century. Inside you'll find valuable antiques (many in the Empire style), paintings, and a remarkable collection of Flemish tapestries, as well as those based on Goya cartoons from the Royal Factory in Madrid.

Most visitors, however, seem to find a stroll through the gardens more pleasing, so allow adequate time for that. The fountain statuary is a riot of cavorting gods and nymphs, hiding indiscretions behind jets of water. The gardens are studded with chestnuts and elms. A spectacular display takes place when the water jets are turned on.

5 Alcalá de Henares

18 miles (29km) E of Madrid

History has been unfair to this ancient town, which once flourished with colleges, monasteries, and palaces. When a university was founded here in the 15th century, Alcalá became a cultural and intellectual center. Europe's first polyglot Bible (supposedly with footnotes in the original Greek and Hebrew) was published here in 1517. But the town declined during the 1800s when the university moved to Madrid. Today Alcalá is one of the main centers of North American academics in Spain, cooperating with the Fullbright Commission, Michigan State University, and Madrid's Washington Irving Center. Overall, the city has taken on new life. Commuters have turned it into a virtual suburb, dubbing it "the bedroom of Madrid."

GETTING THERE **By Train** Trains travel between Madrid's Atocha or Chamartín station and Alcalá de Henares every day and evening. Service is every 15 minutes (trip time: half an hour), and a round-trip fare from Madrid costs 580 pesetas ($4.65). The train station (☎ **91/888-01-96**) in Alcalá is at Paseo Estación.

By Bus Buses from Madrid depart from Avenida América, 18 (Metro: América), every 15 minutes. A one-way fare is 240 pesetas ($1.90). Bus service is provided by Continental-Auto, and the Alcalá bus station is on Avenida Guadalajara, 36 (☎ **91/888-16-22**), two blocks past Calle Libreros.

By Car Alcalá lies adjacent to the main national highway (N-11), connecting Madrid with eastern Spain. As you leave central Madrid, follow signs for Barajas Airport and Barcelona.

VISITOR INFORMATION The tourist information office is at Callejón de Santa María, 1 (☎ **91/899-26-94**). It will provide a map locating all the local attractions. Open daily 10am to 2pm and 4 to 6:30pm.

WHAT TO SEE & DO

Museo Casa Natal de Cervantes. Calle Mayor, 48. ☎ **91/889-96-54.** Free admission. Tues–Fri 10am–1:30pm and 4–6:30pm, Sat–Sun 10am–1:30pm.

Visitors come to see the birthplace of Spain's literary giant Miguel de Cervantes, the creator of *Don Quixote,* who may have been born here in 1547. This 16th-century Castilian house was reconstructed in 1956 around a beautiful little courtyard, which has a wooden gallery supported by pillars with Renaissance-style capitals, plus an old well. The house contains many Cervantes manuscripts and, of course, copies of *Don Quixote,* one of the world's most widely published books (in all languages).

Colegio Mayor de San Ildefonso. Plaza San Diego. ☎ **91/885-40-00.** Admission 250 ptas. ($2). Tues–Sat, tours (mandatory) at 11am, 11:45am, 12:30pm, 1:15pm, 4pm, 4:45pm, 5:30pm, and 6:15pm.

Adjacent to the main square, the Plaza de Cervantes, is the Colegio Mayor de San Ildefonso, where Lope de Vega and other famous Spaniards studied. You can see some of their names engraved on plaques in the examination room. The old university's plateresque facade dates from 1543. From here you can walk across the Patio of Saint Thomas (from 1662) and the Patio of the Philosophers to reach the Patio of the Three Languages (from 1557), where Greek, Latin, and Hebrew were once taught. Here is the *Paraninfo* (great hall or old examination room), which is now used for special events. The hall has a Mudéjar carved-panel ceiling. The Paraninfo is entered through a restaurant, Hostería del Estudiante (see "Where to Dine," below).

Capilla de San Ildefonso. Pedro Gumíelz. ☎ **91/885-40-00.** Admission included in tour of Colegio (see above). Hours same as Colegio (see above).

Next door to the Colegio is the Capilla de San Ildefonso, the 15th-century chapel of the old university. It also houses the Italian marble tomb of Cardinal Cisneros, the founder of the original university. This chapel also has an *artesonado* ceiling and intricately stuccoed walls.

WHERE TO DINE

Hostería del Estudiante. Calle Colegios, 3. ☎ **91/888-03-30.** Reservations recommended. Main courses 1,800–2,900 ptas. ($14.40–$23.20); fixed-price menus 2,500–3,500 ptas. ($20–$28). AE, DC, MC, V. Daily 1–4pm and 9–11:30pm. Closed for dinner in July–Aug. CASTILIAN.

Located within the university complex, this remarkable example of a 1510 building is an attraction in its own right. It opened as a restaurant in 1929, and its typically Castilian recipes haven't been altered since. In the cooler months, if you arrive early you can lounge in front of a 15-foot open fireplace. Oil lamps hang from the ceiling: pigskins are filled with locally made wine; and rope-covered chairs and high-backed carved settees capture the spirit of the past. Run by the Spanish parador system, the restaurant offers a tasty (and huge) three-course set-price lunch or dinner featuring such regional specialties as *cocido madrileño* (the hearty stew of Madrid), roast baby lamb, and trout Navarre style. For dessert, try the cheese of La Mancha.

6 El Pardo

8 miles (13 km) N of Madrid

After visiting Alcalá de Henares, spend an afternoon in El Pardo, the place Franco called home. During the Civil War many Spaniards died here, and much of the town was destroyed during the famous advance toward University City. But there's no trace of destruction today, and the countryside, irrigated by the Manzanares River, is lush and peaceful. If possible, go to the top of the hill and take in the view.

GETTING THERE **By Bus** Local city buses depart every 15 minutes from Madrid's Paseo de Moret (metro: Moncloa).

By Car Driving can be confusing on the minor roads. Head north from the city limits, following signs to La Coruña, then branch off to the west in the direction of "El Monte de El Pardo."

VISITOR INFORMATION Spring and fall can be chilly, so dress accordingly. The Manzanares River flows nearby, but there are no convenient rail lines.

WHAT TO SEE & DO

Palacio de El Pardo. Avenida de La Guardia. ☎ **91/376-15-00.** Admission (including palace, Casita del Príncipe, and Palacio de la Quinta) 650 ptas. ($5.20) adults, 250 ptas. ($2) children. Daily 10:30am–5pm.

A royal residence since medieval times, this was Franco's home until his death, when his body lay in state in front of the palace. When the palace was opened to the public in 1976, it quickly became one of the most popular sights around Madrid. The interior is lavishly furnished with Empire pieces, and Franco's ornate gilt throne reveals his royal pretensions. Many family mementos are displayed, including an extensive wardrobe; be sure to see the 10 wax dummies modeling Franco's important state uniforms.

Highlights of the 45-minute tour include the Tapestry Room, many of its 18th-century pieces based on cartoons by Goya, Bayeu, Aguirre, and González Ruiz; and the Salon de Consejos, with its 19th-century coved ceiling and Franco's most prized possession—a 15th-century sideboard that once belonged to Queen Isabella.

Behind the palace stands the 18th-century **Casita del Príncipe (Prince's Cottage),** a small hunting lodge built during the reign of Charles III. It was actually commissioned either by his son, the prince, or by his wife, who often needed trysting places. It was designed by López Corona. The Casita del Príncipe is presently closed for restoration.

At the **Palacio de la Quinta,** taken over by the Crown in 1745 from the Duke of Arcos, you can view the palace's gardens and fountains, but its elegant interior is also closed for restoration.

WHERE TO DINE

La Marquesita. Avenida de la Guardia, 4. ☎ **91/376-1915.** Reservations recommended. Main courses 1,200–2,600 ptas. ($9.60–$20.80); fixed-price menu 1,700 ptas. ($13.60). AE, DC, MC, V. Daily 12:30pm–1am. CASTILIAN.

Established in 1926, and still run by the same family, within a building erected in the 1840s, this restaurant has successfully weathered the passage of several of Spain's most tenacious political regimes. Set on the city's main boulevard, across from the palace gardens of El Pardo, it offers alfresco dining in summer and cozy meals in front of a fireplace in winter. The front room functions as a *tasca,* where diners traditionally order a Tío Pepe sherry before beginning their meal. The decor is that of a typical rustic Castilian tavern, with rows of Serrano hams hanging from a beamed ceiling. The house specialties, prepared over glowing coals and flavored with oils and herbs, usually involve grilled meat or fish—roast suckling pig, baby lamb, entrecôte of beef, filets of monkfish or salmon, wild rabbit, or braised venison, in season, with red wine sauce.

7 Chinchón

32 miles (52km) SE of Madrid, 16 miles (26km) NE of Aranjuez

The main attraction of Chinchón is the ***cuevas*** **(caves),** where Anis de Chinchón, an aniseed liqueur, is manufactured. You can buy bottles of the liqueur in Plaza Mayor, at the center of town.

Wander along the town's steep and narrow streets, past the houses with large bays and spacious carriageways. Although closed to the public, the 15th-century **Chinchón Castle,** seat of the Condes of Chinchón, can be viewed from outside. The most interesting church, **Nuestra Señora de la Asunción,** dating from the 16th and 17th centuries, contains a painting by Goya.

GETTING THERE **By Bus** From Madrid's Place del Condé de Casal, buses run hourly to and from Chinchón, where the terminal is about 300 yards from the center of town. The bus trip takes about an hour each way.

By Car Drive from Alcalá to Toledo, bypassing Madrid by taking the C-300 in a southwesterly arc around the capital. About halfway there, follow signs to "Cuevas de Chinchón." Another option is to take the E-901 southeast of Madrid toward Valencia, turning southwest at the turnoff for Chinchón.

WHERE TO STAY

Parador de Chinchón. Avenida Generalísimo, 1, Chinchón 28370 Madrid. ☎ **91/894-08-36.** Fax 91/894-09-08. 36 rms, 2 suites. A/C MINIBAR TV TEL. 16,000 ptas. ($128) double; 20,000 ptas. ($160) suite. AE, DC, MC, V.

Set near the town center, this hotel lies within the carefully restored 17th-century walls of what was originally an Augustinian convent. After a stint as both a civic jail and a courthouse, it was transformed in 1972 into a government-run parador and is the only really acceptable place to stay in town. A team of architects and designers converted it handsomely, with glass-walled hallways opening onto a stone-sided courtyard. The hotel contains two bars and two dining halls. Bedrooms, which are clean, simple, and severely dignified, still manage to convey their ecclesiastical origins. Facilities include an outdoor swimming pool, open in summertime only.

WHERE TO DINE

MODERATE

Mesón Cuevas del Vino. Benito Horteliano, 13. ☎ **91/894-02-06.** Reservations recommended on holidays. Main courses 1,800–3,600 ptas. ($14.40–$28.80); fixed-price menu 3,200 ptas. ($25.60). No credit cards. Wed–Mon 1:30–4pm and 8–11:30pm. Closed Aug 1–20. SPANISH.

This establishment is famous for its wine cellars, and you can sample the stock at lunch or dinner. Hams, hanging from the rafters, have been cured by the owners, and the flavorful spiced sausages are homemade. Chunks of the ham and sausage cooked in oil, plus olives and crunchy bread, are served. The *morteruelo* (warm pâté) is a good beginning, and a popular dessert is *hojuelas* (soft pastry with honey). Specialties include lamb and suckling pig roasted in a wood oven. The wines, or the dry or sweet anisette that is the main export of Chinchón, help make the meal more enjoyable.

Venta Reyes. Ronda de Mediodía, 18. ☎ **91/894-09-40.** Reservations required on holidays. Main courses 1,800–3,500 ptas. ($14.40–$28). No credit cards. Wed–Mon 1:30–4pm and 8pm–midnight. CASTILIAN/ANDALUSIAN.

With a decor of hanging lamps, tiles, and wicker furniture, this is clearly the most elegant dining choice in the area. In a garden setting, with swans gliding across the pool, Venta Reyes offers romance Sevillian style. In fair weather, you can dine in the garden. Many recipes are based on ancient dishes that have virtually faded from the Spanish culinary repertoire. Game fowl, grown on the premises, is a specialty—for example, partridge prepared Toledan style. Begin with Andalusian gazpacho or fish and shellfish soup, then follow with hen cooked with almonds, garlic, parsley, and saffron. Baked salmon and veal cooked in its own juice are other popular dishes. The savory cuisine is enhanced by more than 100 varieties of wine from all the regions of Spain.

8 Ávila

68 miles (110km) NW of Madrid, 41½ miles (67km) SW of Segovia

The ancient city of Ávila is completely encircled by well-preserved 11th-century walls, which are among the most important medieval relics in Europe. The city has been declared a national landmark, and there is little wonder why. The walls aren't the only attraction, however. Ávila has several Romanesque churches, Gothic palaces, and a fortified cathedral. It is among some 80 cities or so designated by UNESCO as World Heritage Sites. (Six of these cities are in Spain; the other five are Santiago de Compostela, Segovia, Toledo, Cáceres, and Salamanca.)

Ávila's spirit and legend are most linked to St. Teresa, who was born here in 1515. This Carmelite nun, who helped defeat the Reformation and founded a number of convents, experienced visions of the devil and angels piercing her heart with burning hot lances. She was eventually imprisoned in Toledo. Many legends sprang up after her death, including the belief that a hand severed from her body could perform miracles. Finally, in 1622 she was declared a saint (see "A Saint and Her City," below).

GETTING THERE **By Train** There are more than two dozen trains leaving daily from Madrid for Ávila, about a 1½- to 2-hour trip each way. Depending on their schedule, trains depart from Chamartín, Atocha, and Príncipe (Norte) railway stations. The 8am train from Atocha, arriving in Ávila at 9:26am, is a good choice, considering all that there is to see. Tickets cost from 850 to 1,400 pesetas ($6.80–$11.20). The Ávila station lies at Avenida Portugal, 17 (☎ **920/25-02-02**), about a mile east of the Old City.

By Bus Buses leave Madrid daily from Paseo Florida, 11 (metro: Norte), in front of Norte Railway Station. In Ávila the bus terminal (☎ **920/22-01-54**) is at the corner of Avenida Madrid and Avenida Portugal, northeast of the center of town. A round-trip ticket from Madrid costs 1,290 pesetas ($10.30).

By Car Exit Madrid from its northwest perimeter, and head northwest on highway N-VI (A-6), toward La Coruña, eventually forking southwest to Ávila. Driving time is around 1½ hours.

Taxis You can find taxis lined up in front of Ávila's railway station and at the more central Plaza Santa Teresa. For information, call **920/21-19-59** or 920/22-01-49.

VISITOR INFORMATION The tourist information office is at Plaza Catedral, 4 (☎ **920/21-13-87**). It is open daily from 10am to 2pm and 4 to 8pm. *Note:* Bring warm clothes if you're visiting in the early spring.

A Saint & Her City

The walled city of Ávila is forever linked with the legend of St. Teresa, one of the most famous of all Catholic saints. She is most often cited as a mystic but was an adventurer, pioneer, poet, and reformer. She was born in 1515 into a large Jewish family and christened Teresa de Cepeda y Ahumada. Her birth was 12 years before the reign of Philip II, who ruled from 1527 to 1598, presiding over Spain's "Golden Century."

Taking the Carmelite veil at 18, she is reported to have had her first vision at the age of 40. She toured Castile, seeking reforms and hoping to return the Carmelite order to its original vows of poverty and piety. For example, she advocated that the nuns discard shoes and wear sandals, which led to the misnomer "the Barefoot Carmelites." She founded her first Carmelite convent in 1562 and, in time, opened 16 other convents. It is said that her unfailing sense of humor and her abundant gift for friendship saved her from the dreaded Inquisition, which imprisoned her friend, mentor, and fellow Ávilan, St. John of the Cross. Many of her reforms were abandoned upon her death in 1582. She was canonized by the church, although she remained a controversial figure, and many church leaders opposed making her a saint.

Ávila abounds with Teresian memorabilia. She was fond of playing drums and bells and was always proclaiming, "God deliver me from sullen saints." If you'd like to pay homage to St. Teresa, you can order her favorite dish, partridge. It's a local specialty served in many of Ávila's restaurants. A servant was once perplexed at her obvious enjoyment of a large helping of partridge. He felt she was demonstrating too much pleasure in eating it. "My child," she said to him, "there is a time for penitence, but there is also a time for partridge."

But we doubt if the saint herself could have tolerated one highly touted local specialty: a sticky-sweet candy called *yemas de Santa Teresa.* We recommend that you avoid this glob as surely St. Teresa herself would have. She'd probably push it away from the table and order more partridge.

WHAT TO SEE & DO

Begun on orders of Alfonso VI as part of the general reconquest of Spain from the Moors, the 11th-century ✪ **Walls of Ávila,** built over Roman fortifications, took nine years to complete. They average 33 feet in height, have 88 semicircular towers, and more than 2,300 battlements. Of the nine gateways, the two most famous are the St. Vincent and the Alcázar, both on the eastern side. In many respects the walls are best viewed from the west. Whatever your preferred point of view, you can drive along their entire length: 1½ miles (2km).

Convento de Santa Teresa. Plaza de la Santa. ☎ **920/21-10-30.** Free admission. Daily 8:30am–1:30pm and 3:30–9pm. Bus: 1, 3, or 4.

This 17th-century convent and baroque church, two blocks southwest of the Plaza de la Victoria, is at the site of St. Teresa's birth. It contains a number of relics, including a finger from her right hand. Look also for the fine sculpture by Gregorio Hernández.

Catedral de Ávila. Plaza Catedral. ☎ **920/21-16-41.** Admission 300 ptas. ($2.40) adults, free for children under 8. May–Sept, daily 10am–1pm and 4:30–7pm; Oct–Apr, daily 10am–1pm and 3:30–5pm.

Built into the old ramparts of Ávila, this cold, austere cathedral and fortress (begun in 1099) bridges the gap between the Romanesque and the Gothic, and, as such, enjoys a certain distinction in Spanish architecture. One local writer compared it to a granite mountain. The interior is unusual, built with a mottled red-and-white stone.

Like most European cathedrals, Ávila lost its purity of design through the years as new chapels and wings—one completely in the Renaissance mode—were added. A Dutch artist, Cornelius, designed the seats of the choir stalls, also in Renaissance style, and the principal chapel holds a reredos showing the life of Christ by Pedro Berruguete, Juan de Borgoña, and Santa Cruz. Behind the chapel the tomb of Bishop Alonso de Madrigal—nicknamed "El Tostado" ("The Parched One") because of its brownish color—is Vasco de Zarza's masterpiece. The Cathedral Museum contains a laminated gold ceiling, a 15th-century triptych, a copy of an El Greco painting, as well as vestments and 15th-century songbooks.

Basilica de San Vicente. Plaza de San Vicente. ☎ **920/25-52-30.** Admission 50 ptas. (40¢). Daily 10am–2pm and 4–8pm.

Outside the city walls, at the northeast corner of the medieval ramparts, this Romanesque-Gothic church in faded sandstone encompasses styles from the 12th to the 14th century. It consists of a huge nave and a trio of apses. The eternal struggle between good and evil is depicted on a cornice on the southern portal. The western portal, dating from the 13th century, contains Romanesque carvings. Inside is the tomb of St. Vincent, martyred on this site in the 4th century. The tomb's medieval carvings, which depict his torture and subsequent martyrdom, are fascinating.

Monasterio de Santo Tomas. Plaza Granada. ☎ **920/22-04-00.** Admission to museum, 100 ptas. (80¢); cloisters, 50 ptas. (40¢). Museum, Mon–Sat 10am–1pm and 4–7pm, Sun 4–7pm; cloisters, Mon–Sat 10am–1pm and 4–8pm, Sun 4–8pm. Bus: 1, 2, or 3.

This 15th-century Gothic monastery was once the headquarters of the Inquisition in Ávila. For three centuries it housed the tomb of Torquemada, the first General Inquisitor, whose zeal in organizing the Inquisition made him a notorious figure in Spanish history. Legend has it that after the friars were expelled from the monastery in 1836, a mob of Torquemada-haters ransacked the tomb and burned the remains somewhere outside the city walls. His final burial site is unknown.

Prince John, the only son of Ferdinand and Isabella, was also buried here, in a sumptuous sepulchre in the church transept. The tomb was desecrated during a French invasion; now, only an empty crypt remains.

Visit the Royal Cloisters, in some respects the most interesting architectural feature of the place. In the upper part of the third cloister, you'll find the Museum of Far Eastern Art, which exhibits Vietnamese, Chinese, and Japanese art and handcrafts.

Carmelitas Descalzas de San José. Las Madres, 4 ☎ **920/22-21-27.** Admission to museum, 50 ptas. (40¢). Tues–Sun 10am–1pm and 4–7pm. From Plaza de Santa Teresa and its nearby Church of San Pedro, follow Calle del Duque de Alba for about two blocks.

Also known as the Convento de las Madres (Convent of the Mothers), this is the first convent founded by St. Teresa, who started the Reform of Carmel in 1562. Two churches are here—the primitive one, where the first Carmelite nuns took the habit; and one built by Francisco de Mora, architect of Philip III, after the saint's death. The museum displays many relics, including, of all things, St. Teresa's left clavicle.

WHERE TO STAY

Ávila is a summer resort—a refuge from Castilian heat—but the hotels are few in number, and the Spanish book nearly all the hotel space in July and August. Make sure to have a reservation in advance. Mesón El Sol y Residencia Santa Teresa (see "Where to Dine," below) also rents rooms.

EXPENSIVE

✪ **Gran Hotel Palacio de Valderrábanos.** Plaza Catedral, 9, 05001 Ávila. ☎ **800/528-1234** in the U.S. and Canada, or 920/21-10-23. Fax 920/25-16-91. 70 rms, 3 suites. A/C MINIBAR TV TEL. 14,000 ptas. ($112) double; 25,000 ptas. ($200) suite. AE, DC, MC, V. Free parking. Bus: 1, 2, or 3.

Set immediately adjacent to the front entrance of the cathedral, behind an entryway that is a marvel of medieval stonework, this is one of the most elegant and historic hotels of Castile. Originally built in the 1300s as a private home by an early bishop of Ávila (and a member of the Valderrábanos family), it contains a once-fortified lookout tower (whose circumference encloses one of the suites), high-beamed ceilings, intricately chiseled stonework, and a vivid sense of long-ago Spain. The public rooms have a somber elegance, with baronial furniture whose tassels and slightly faded upholstery add to the old-fashioned feeling. If at all possible, ask for a bedroom overlooking the cathedral.

Dining/Entertainment: The restaurant El Fogón de Santa Teresa is a high-ceilinged bastion of formality serving traditional Castilian meals.

Services: Concierge, laundry/valet, babysitting.

Meliá Palacio de Los Velada. Plaza de la Catedral, 10, 05001 Ávila. ☎ **800/336-3542** in the U.S. and Canada, or 920/25-51-00. Fax 920/25-49-00. 84 rms. A/C MINIBAR TV TEL. 16,000 ptas. ($128) double. AE, DC, MC, V. Parking 900 ptas. ($7.20).

When the Spanish chain Meliá opened this splendid gem to guests in 1995, it overnight became the most sought-after accommodation in the province, surpassing the government-run paradors. Four centuries ago, this palace sheltered the likes of Charles V and Philip II. Arrayed around a central courtyard, today's hotel offers a luxury that was unimaginable when those kings spent the night.

The styling in the public rooms and the luxuriously furnished bedrooms make even the paradors look like they need a face-lift. Enjoying the best location in town—right in the center near the cathedral—the hotel receives guests in the setting of a medieval palace, with massive stones and antiques throughout. All the modern conveniences, including freshly painted closets and wide, comfortable beds, have been installed along with state-of-the-art plumbing. The bright, helpful staff eases your adjustment into Ávila, and the elegant dining room serves some of the town's finest meals, including game (on occasion), succulent lamb, and excellent steaks. Service in the dining room is supremely efficient as well as courtly.

Parador de Ávila. Marqués de Canales de Chozas, 2, 05001 Ávila. ☎ **920/21-13-40.** Fax 920/22-61-66. 62 rms, 1 suite. MINIBAR TV TEL. 14,000 ptas. ($112) double; 20,000 ptas. ($160) suite. AE, DC, MC, V. Parking 1,000 ptas. ($7.10).

Lying two blocks northwest of Plaza de la Victoria, this two- and three-story parador stands on a ridge overlooking the banks of the Adaja River. Once it was known as the Palace of Benavides, with a history going back to the 15th century. Its facade forms part of the square. The palace has a dignified entranceway, and most of its public lounges open onto a central courtyard with an inner gallery of columns. The recently refurbished rooms contain tasteful furnishings: a tall stone fireplace, highly polished tile floors, old chests, leather armchairs, paintings, and sculptures. The dining room, with its leaded-glass windows opening onto a terraced garden, serves passable Castilian dishes.

MODERATE

$ Hosteria de Bracamonte. Bracamonte 6, 05001 Ávila. ☎ **920/25-12-80.** 17 rms. TV TEL. 10,000 ptas. ($80) double. MC, V.

The most tranquil spot in town is this little gem decorated in a classic Castilian style. It lies one block north of Plaza de Victoria, the main square within the city walls. A restful and quiet oasis, it has a number of charming features, including a lovely patio. A dark-wood Castilian motif is used throughout. Converted to a small inn in 1989, the *hosteria* retains some of its aristocratic origins as the town house of Governor Don Juan Teherán y Monjaraz. Rooms often contain whitewashed walls, and some have fireplaces and four-poster beds.

INEXPENSIVE

El Rastro. Plaza del Rastro, 1, 05001 Ávila. ☎ **920/21-12-18.** Fax 920/25-00-00. 10 rms. 5,000 ptas. ($40) double. AE, DC, MC, V.

Situated near the junction of Calle Caballeros and Calle Cepadas is the best choice for the bargain hunter. Few tourists know that they can spend the night at this old Castilian inn built into the city walls. The guest rooms are basic and clean. El Rastro is one of our dining recommendations too (see "Where to Dine," below).

WHERE TO DINE

$ Mesón El Sol y Residencia Santa Teresa. Avenida 18 de Julio, 25, 05003 Ávila. ☎ **920/22-02-11.** Fax 920/22-41-13. Reservations recommended. Main courses 950–2,300 ptas. ($7.60–$18.40); fixed-price menu 1,700 ptas. ($13.60). No credit cards. Daily 1–4pm and 8:30–11:30pm. Bus: 12. CASTILIAN.

You may be distracted by the aromas emanating from the kitchen of the lowest-priced inn in Ávila—a place known for its good food, moderate prices, and efficient service. Full meals may include seafood soup, fried hake, veal with garlic, and house-style flan. The inn also rents 15 simply furnished bedrooms, a double going for 7,500 pesetas ($60).

$ El Rastro. Plaza del Rastro, 1. ☎ **920/21-12-19.** Reservations required on weekends only. Main courses 1,800 ptas. ($14.40); fixed-price menu 1,400 ptas. ($11.20). AE, DC, MC, V. Daily 1–4pm and 9–11pm. CASTILIAN.

An old inn built into the 11th-century town walls, El Rastro serves typical Castilian dishes, with more attention given to freshness and preparation than to culinary flamboyance. Roast baby lamb and tender white veal are house specialties. Dessert recipes have been passed down from Ávila's nuns. Try, if you dare, the highly touted *yemas de Santa Teresa* (St. Teresa's candied egg yolk), although when we once dined here with travel expert Arthur Frommer he found this a particularly horrible dessert—and we concur. Yet, Ávila residents keep praising it as a specialty. To our taste, there are far better selections on the menu.

9 Cuenca

100 miles (161km) E of Madrid, 202 miles (325km) SW of Zaragoza

This medieval town, once dominated by the Arabs, is a spectacular sight with its *casas colgadas,* the cliff-hanging houses set on multiple terraces that climb up the impossibly steep sides of a ravine. The Júcar and Huécar Rivers meet at the bottom.

GETTING THERE **By Train** Trains leave Madrid's Atocha Railway Station about eight times throughout the day. Trains arrive in Cuenca at Paseo del Ferrocarril in the new city (☎ **969/22-07-20**), after a journey lasting anywhere from 2½ to 3 hours. A one-way ticket from Madrid costs 1,215 pesetas ($9.70).

By Bus There are about eight buses from Madrid every day. Buses arrive at Calle Fermín Caballero, s/n (☎ **969/22-70-87** for information and schedules). A one-way fare costs 1,260 pesetas ($10.10).

By Car Cuenca is the junction for several highways and about a dozen lesser roads that connect it to towns within its region. From Madrid, take the N-III to Tarancon, then the N-400, which leads directly into Cuenca.

VISITOR INFORMATION The tourist information office is at San Pedro, 6 (☎ **969/23-21-19**). Open Monday through Friday from 9am to 2pm and 4 to 7pm, Saturday and Sunday from 9am to 2pm and 4 to 8pm.

WHAT TO SEE & DO

The chief sight of Cuenca is the town itself. Isolated from the rest of Spain, it requires a northern detour from the heavily traveled Valencia-Madrid road. Deep gorges give it an unreal quality, and eight old bridges spanning two rivers connect the ancient parts of town with the growing new sections. One of the bridges is suspended over a 200-foot drop.

Cuenca's streets are narrow and steep, often cobbled, and even the most athletic tire quickly. But you shouldn't miss it, even if you have to stop and rest periodically. At night you're in for a special treat when the *casas colgadas* are illuminated. Also, try to drive almost to the top of the castle-dominated hill. The road gets rough as you approach the end, but the view makes the effort worthwhile.

Cathedral de Cuenca Plaza. Pío XII. Free admission. Daily 8:45am–2pm and 4–7pm (closes at 6pm in winter). Bus: 1 or 2.

Begun in the 12th century, the Gothic cathedral was influenced by England's Norman style, becoming the only Anglo-Norman cathedral in Spain. Part of it collapsed in this century, but it has been restored. A national monument filled with religious art treasures, the cathedral is a 10-minute walk from the Plaza Mayor, up Calle Palafox. The cathedral's *museo diocesano* exhibits two canvases by El Greco, a collection of Flemish tapestries (some beautifully designed), and a statue of the Virgin del Sagrario from the 1100s.

✪ **Museo de Arte Abstracto Español.** Calle los Canónigos, s/n. ☎ **969/21-29-83.** Admission 300 ptas. ($2.40). Tues–Fri 11am–2pm and 4–8pm, Sat 11am–2pm and 4–8pm, Sun 11am–2:30pm. Bus: 1 or 2.

North of Plaza Mayor, housed in a cliff-hanging dwelling, this ranks as one of the finest museums of its kind in Spain. It was conceived by painter Fernando Zóbel, who donated it in 1980 to the Juan March Foundation. The most outstanding abstract Spanish painters are represented, including Rafael Canogar (especially his *Toledo*), Luís Feito, Zóbel himself, Tápies, Eduardo Chillida, Gustavo Torner, Gerardo Rueda, Millares, Sempere, Cuixart, and Antonio Saura (see his grotesque Geraldine Chaplin and his study of Brigitte Bardot, a vision of horror, making the French actress look like an escapee from Picasso's *Guernica*).

WHERE TO STAY

$ **Hotel Avenida.** Carretería, 39, 16004 Cuenca. ☎ **969/21-43-43.** Fax 969/21-23-35. 49 rms. TEL. 4,500 ptas. ($36) double. Parking 900 ptas. ($7.20). MC, V.

A good value for the money, this hotel lies in Cuenca's modern commercial center, about a block southwest of Parque de San Julian. Built in 1971 and renovated in 1991, it offers tidy rooms with simple amenities and access to a helpful staff. Only a handful of rooms have air-conditioning; the rest are on the shaded side of the building and—at least according to management—don't seem to get very hot. No meals are served other than breakfast, but the staff can direct its clients to the nearby Calle Colón, where many different restaurants in various price ranges are ready, willing, and able to feed foreign visitors. Parking, incidentally, is within a nearby parking lot maintained by Cuenca's municipal government.

Hotel Figón de Pedro. Calle Cervantes, 15, 16004 Cuenca. ☎ **969/22-45-11.** Fax 969/23-11-92. 28 rms. TEL. 6,000 ptas. ($48) double. AE, DC, MC, V.

Figón de Pedro lies south of the old city, a short walk north of the bus and rail stations. The hotel (with elevator) is immaculate but not stuffy, since the staff keeps the atmosphere pleasantly informal. On the second floor you'll find a lounge with TV, and the hotel boasts a country-style dining room, with a *tasca* in front. Wood beams, fresh linen on the tables, and personal service all make this an inviting place for meals.

✪ **Parador de Turismo de Cuenca.** Convento de San Pablo, Paseo de la Hoz del Huécar, 16001 Cuenca. ☎ **969/23-23-20.** Fax 969/23-25-84. 62 rms, 1 suite. A/C MINIBAR TV TEL. 16,500 ptas. ($132) double; 26,000 ptas. ($208) suite. AE, DC, MC, V. Parking 805 ptas. ($6.45).

This government-sponsored hotel occupies the dignified premises of what was originally built, in 1523, as a Dominican monastery. A noteworthy example of late Gothic architecture, it lies on a hillside above Cuenca, about a half-mile northwest of the town's historic center. It is clearly the town's prestige address. Opened for business after extensive renovations in 1992, its three stories contain masses of intricately chiseled 16th-century stonework (some enhanced with glass panels overlooking the river), a church, a severely beautiful cloister, a sense of timeless solidity, and a swimming pool. There's a bar, a high-ceilinged restaurant, and two floors of bedrooms which, despite comfortably traditional furniture and modern bathrooms, richly convey their ecclesiastical origins.

$ **Posada de San José.** Julián Romero, 4, 16001 Cuenca. ☎ **969/21-13-00.** Fax 969/23-03-65. 30 rms (16 with bath). 3,800–4,600 ptas. ($30.40–$36.80) double without bath; 6,600–8,900 ptas. ($52.80–$71.20) double with bath. AE, DC, MC, V. Bus: 1 or 2.

Posada de San José stands in the oldest part of Cuenca, a short walk north of the cathedral. The 17th-century cells that used to shelter the sisters of this former convent now house overnight guests who consider its views of the old city the best in town. It sits atop a cliff, overlooking the forbidding depths of a gorge. Owners Antonio and Jennifer Cortinas renovated this place into one of the most alluring hotels of the region, with the bar perhaps the most charming of its well-decorated public rooms.

WHERE TO DINE

Mesón Casa Colgadas. Canónigos, 3. ☎ **969/22-35-09.** Reservations recommended. Main courses 1,750–2,800 ptas. ($14–$22.40); fixed-price menus 3,300–3,800 ptas. ($26.40–$30.40). AE, DC, MC, V. Daily 1:30–4pm, Wed–Mon 9–11pm. SPANISH/INTERNATIONAL.

One of the most spectacular dining rooms in Spain stands on one of the most precarious precipices in Cuenca. Established in the late 1960s, it occupies a 19th-century house, five stories high, with sturdy supporting walls and beams. Pine balconies and windows overlook the ravine below and the hills beyond. In fact, it's the most photographed "suspended house" in town, and dinner here is worth every céntimo. The menu includes regional dishes and a wide variety of well-prepared international cuisine. Drinks are served in the tavern room on the street level, so even if you're not dining here, you may want to drop in for a drink and the view. You'll find the Mesón Casa Colgadas just south of the cathedral and near the Museum of Spanish Abstract Art.

Togar. Avenida República Argentina, 3. ☎ **969/22-01-62.** Reservations required. Main courses 900–1,950 ptas. ($7.20–$15.60); fixed-price menu 1,500 ptas. ($12). AE, MC, V. Daily 1–4pm, Mon–Sat 8–11pm. Closed 1 week in July (dates vary). Bus: 1 or 6. SPANISH.

Rich with local flavor and aggressively cost-conscious, this is a simple but likable *tasca* on the southwestern periphery of town. Established in 1955, and set within an angular building erected the same year, it offers homemade cookery whose inspiration derives from the various regions of Spain. One of the specialties is *revuelto Togar,* an egg, ham, and shrimp dish served with herbs and crusty bread. Also available are well-peppered versions of pork, several kinds of rich soups, and various beef and fish dishes.

AN EASY EXCURSION TO CIUDAD ENCANTADA

If you're staying over in Cuenca, or otherwise have the time, you can easily visit what its citizens call their ✪ **Ciudad Encantada (Enchanted City),** Carretera de la Sierra, about 25 miles (40km) to the northeast. Storms and underground waters have created a city here out of large rocks and boulders, shaping them into bizarre designs: a seal, an elephant, a Roman bridge. Take CU-912, turning northeast onto CU-913. Ciudad Encantada is signposted.

7 Old Castile & León

Spain owes much to Castile, Aragón, and León, since these three kingdoms helped forge the various regions of the country into a unified whole. Modern Spain was conceived when Isabella of Castile married Ferdinand of Aragón on October 19, 1469. Five years later she was proclaimed Queen of Castile and of León. The Moors were eventually driven out of Granada, the rest of Spain was conquered, and Columbus sailed to America—all during the reign of these two Catholic monarchs.

This proud but controversial queen and her unscrupulous husband fashioned an empire whose influence extended throughout Spain, Europe, and the New World. The power once held by Old Castile shifted long ago to Madrid, but today there are many reminders of its storied past.

The ancient kingdom of León, which was eventually annexed to Castile, embraced three cities: Salamanca, Zamora, and the provincial capital of León. Today the district is known for its many castles.

In Old Castile, we'll cover the inland provincial capital of Valladolid, where Isabella married Ferdinand and where a brokenhearted Columbus died on May 19, 1506. From there we'll move on to Burgos, once the capital of Old Castile. Vivar, a small town near here, produced El Cid, Spain's greatest national hero, who conquered the Moorish kingdom of Valencia. For other destinations in the region, refer to Chapter 6, "Excursions from Madrid."

EXPLORING THE REGION BY CAR

Day 1 Those wishing to see the major capitals of the old provinces should head west from Madrid to Salamanca for two nights. You'll need a good part of the first day just to get there. On your first night in Salamanca, head for the Plaza Mayor, the heartbeat square of the city and one of the most beautiful public plazas in Spain. During La Alberca celebrations (August 15–16), crowds in folkloric dress converge on the plaza.

Day 2 While still based in Salamanca, see as much of the city's architectural treasures as you have time for, including both its old and new cathedrals, the Universidad de Salamanca, and the Convento de San Esteban, plus a selection of museums, including the Museo de Salamanca. Also make time for the Casa de las

Old Castile & León

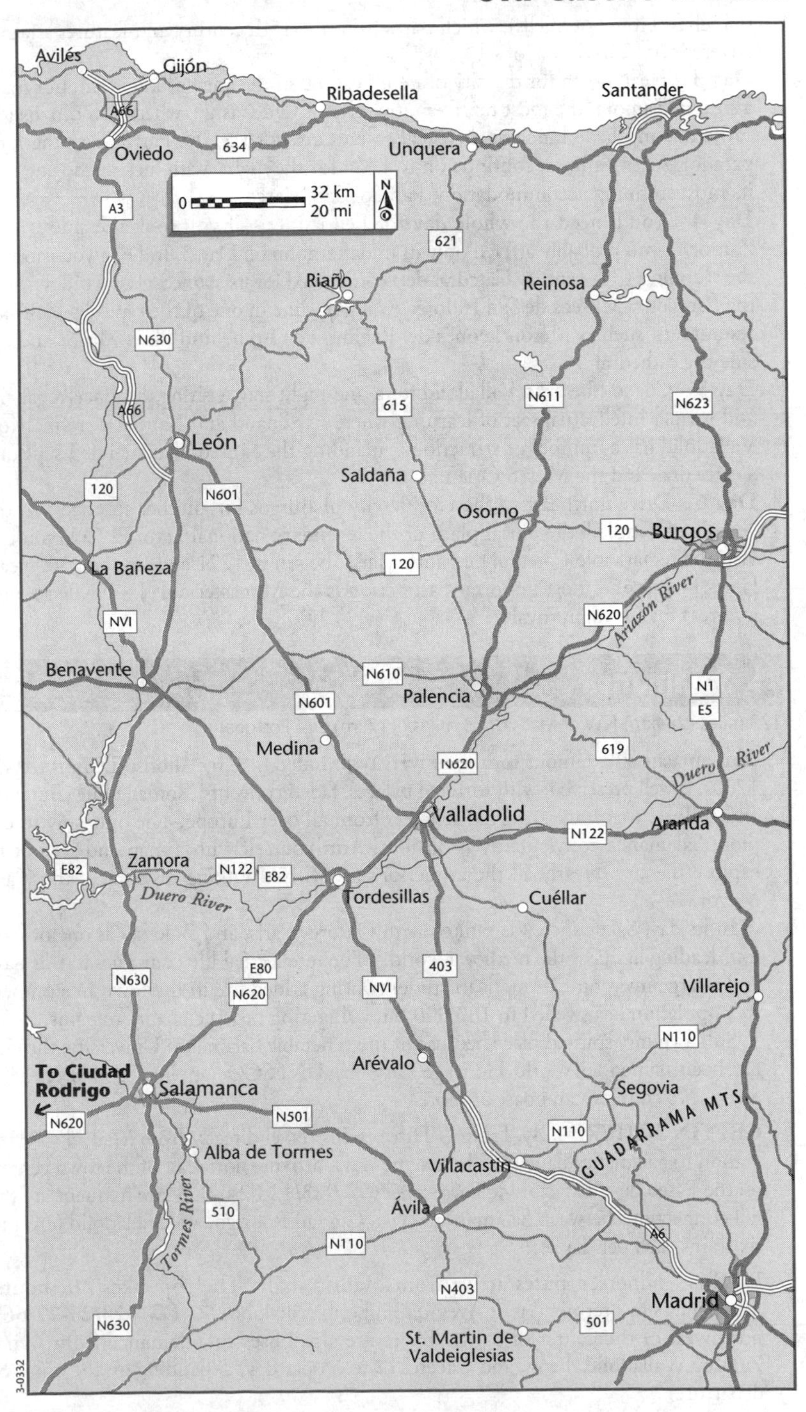

Conchas (House of Shells), which dates from the 15th century and features a facade covered with carved scallops.

Day 3 Head north for the city of León, capital of the ancient kingdom, but make a stop in Zamora, the most representative city of Old Castile, where you can visit its cathedral and have lunch at a typical restaurant, such as the París, or at the local parador. After Zamora, continue on to León for the night, with luck anchoring into its most stunning accommodation, Parador San Marcos.

Day 4 You'll need the whole day for León since—if you took the side trip to Zamora—you probably arrived only in midafternoon on Day 3. In León you can visit the stunning 13th-century Catedral de León, fabled for its stained-glass windows, and the Pantéon y Museos de San Isidoro. At night, dine in one of the typically Castilian restaurants, such as Mesón Leonés del Racimo de Oro behind Plaza Mayor and beside the cathedral.

Day 5 Cut southeast to Valladolid for a one-night stay, visiting this once-royal city and former intellectual seat of learning where Ferdinand and Isabella were married. Valladolid has a number of attractions, including the Museo Nacional de Escultura, a cathedral, and the Museo Oriental.

Day 6 Drive northeast to the Gothic city of Burgos for another stopover. In the "cradle of Castile," the burial place of the legendary national hero, El Cid, you can visit the remarkable Catedral de Santa Maria, begun in 1221 and finished 300 years later. The second most important attraction is the Monasterio de las Huelgas, once a retreat for Castilian royalty.

1 Salamanca

127 miles (204km) NW of Madrid, 73 miles (117km) E of Portugal

This ancient city, famous for the university founded here by Alfonso IX in the early 1200s, is well preserved, with turreted palaces, faded convents, Romanesque churches, and colleges that once attracted scholars from all over Europe. The only way to explore Salamanca conveniently is on foot. Arm yourself with a map and set out to explore the city. Nearly all the attractions are within walking distance of the Plaza Mayor.

In its day, Salamanca was ranked with Oxford, Paris, and Bologna as one of "the four leading lights of the medieval world." The intellectual life continues to this day, and a large invasion of American students bring added life to the town in summer. Its population has swelled to 180,000 but a lingering provincial aura remains.

Still a young, spirited place because of the venerable Salamanca University, the city has been named a "World Heritage City" by UNESCO, one of six such cities in Spain. No country can boast of more.

GETTING THERE **By Train** Three trains travel directly from Madrid's North Station to Salamanca daily (3½ hours one way), arriving northeast of the town center, on the Paseo de la Estación de Ferrocarril (☎ 923/12-02-02). More frequent are the rail connections between Salamanca, Ávila, Ciudad Rodrigo, and Valladolid (around six trains each per day).

By Bus Nineteen buses arrive from Madrid daily. The trip takes 2½ hours. Salamanca's bus terminal is at Avenida Filiberto Villalobos, 71 (☎ **923/23-22-66**), northwest of the center of town. There are also buses to Salamanca from Ávila, Zamora, Valladolid, León, and Caceres (2 to 13 per day, depending on the point of departure).

By Car Salamanca is not located on a national highway, but there is a good network of roads that converge on Salamanca from such nearby cities as Ávila, Valladolid, and Ciudad Rodrigo. One of the most heavily trafficked highways is the N-620, leading into Salamanca from both Barcelona and Portugal. From Madrid, take the N-VI northwest, forking off to Salamanca on the N-501.

VISITOR INFORMATION The tourist information office is at Gran Vía, 41 (☎ **923/26-85-71**). Open daily from 10am to 2pm and 5 to 8pm.

SEEING THE SIGHTS

To start, spend as much time as you can at the ✪ **Plaza Mayor,** an 18th-century baroque square acclaimed as the most beautiful public plaza in Spain. No trip to the university city is complete unless you walk through the arcaded shops and feast your eyes on the honey-colored buildings. After this you'll understand why the *plaza mayor,* a town's main square, is an integral part of Spanish life. If it's a hot day and you want what everybody else in the Plaza Mayor is drinking, stop in a café and order *leche helado,* an icy vanilla and almond milkshake that's very refreshing and not too filling.

Even before reaching Plaza Mayor, you may want to stop and admire the facade of the landmark **Casa de las Conchas,** or House of Shells, which appears as you walk north from the Patio de las Escuelas (site of the Universidad de Salamanca, see below) on Calles de Libreros and San Isidro. This much-photographed building is at the corner of Rua Mayor and Calle de la Compañía. The restored 1483 house is noted for its facade of 400 simulated scallop shells. A professor of medicine at the university and a doctor at the court of Isabella created the house as a monument to Santiago de Compostela, the renowned pilgrimage site. The shell is the symbol of the Order of Santiago.

Casa Museo Unamuno. Calle de Libreros, 25. ☎ **923/29-44-00.** Free admission. Daily 9am–2pm. Closed Aug. Bus: 1.

The poet and philosopher Miguel de Unamuno—and one of the world's most renowned scholars—lived from 1900 to 1914 in this 18th-century home beside the university. Here he wrote many of the works that made him famous. You can see some of his notebooks and his library, along with many personal mementos.

Catedral Nueva (New Cathedral). Plaza Juan XXII. ☎ **923/21-74-76.** Free admission. Daily 10am–1:30pm and 4–7:30pm. Bus: 1.

The origins of the "new" cathedral date from 1513. It took more than 200 years to complete it, so the edifice represents many styles: It's classified as late Gothic, but you'll see baroque and plateresque features as well. José Churriguera contributed some rococo elements, too. The building has a grand gold-on-beige sandstone facade, elegant chapels, the best-decorated dome in Spain, and bas-relief columns that look like a palm-tree cluster. Unfortunately, its stained glass is severely damaged. The cathedral lies in the southern section of the old town, about five blocks south of Plaza Mayor at the edge of Plaza de Anaya.

Catedral Vieja (Old Cathedral). Plaza Juan XXII. ☎ **923/21-74-76.** Admission 300 ptas. ($2.40). Daily 10am–1:30pm and 4–7:30pm. Bus: 1.

Adjoining the New Cathedral is this older Spanish Romanesque version, begun in 1140. Its simplicity provides a dramatic contrast to the ornamentation of its younger but bigger counterpart. After viewing the interior, stroll through the enclosed cloisters with their Gothic tombs of long-forgotten bishops. The chapels are of special architectural interest. In the Capilla de San Martín, the frescoes date from 1242, and in the Capilla de Santa Bárbara, final exams for Salamanca University students were given. The Capilla de Santa Catalina is noted for its gargoyles.

Museo Art Nouveau–Art Deco. Calle Gilbraltar, 14. ☎ **923/12-14-25.** Admission 300 ptas. ($2.40). Tues–Sun 11am–2pm and 5–9pm.

The Art Nouveau–Art Deco Museum contains more than 1,500 pieces, all part of the collection of the Manuel Ramos Andrade Foundation. Spanning the late 19th century to the 1930s, the collection includes both bronze and marble figurines, jewelry, furniture, paintings, and a collection of some 300 porcelain dolls. Numerous works by Emile Gallé and René Lalique are on display.

Museo de Salamanca (Casa de los Doctores de la Reina). Patio de las Escuelas, 2. ☎ **923/21-22-35.** Admission 200 ptas. ($1.60). Mon–Sat 10am–2pm and 4:30–7:30pm, Sun 10am–2pm. Bus: 1.

Built in the late 15th century by Queen Isabella's physician, this structure, located near the university, is a fine example of the Spanish plateresque style. The Fine Arts Museum is housed here, boasting a collection of paintings and sculptures dating from the 15th to the 20th century.

Convento de las Dueñas. Plaza del Concillo de Trento. ☎ **923/21-54-42.** Admission 100 ptas. (80¢). June–Sept, daily 10am–1pm and 4–7pm; Oct–May, daily 10:30am–1pm and 4–5:30pm.

Across Calle Buenaventura from San Esteban is one of the most popular sights of Salamanca, a former Mudéjar palace of a court official. The cloisters date from the 16th century, and are, in the opinion of some of Spain's architectural critics, the most beautiful in Salamanca. Climb to the upper gallery for a close inspection of the carved capitals, which are covered with demons and dragons, saints and sinners, and animals of every description—some from the pages of *The Divine Comedy.* There is also a portrait of Dante.

Convento de San Esteban. Plaza del Concilio de Trento. ☎ **923/21-50-00.** Admission 200 ptas. ($1.60). Daily 9am–1pm and 4–8pm.

Of all the old religious sites of Salamanca, St. Stephen's Convent is one of the most dramatic. The golden-brown plateresque facade of this late Gothic church competes with the cathedral in magnificence. Inside, José Churriguera in 1693 created a high altar that is one of Salamanca's greatest art treasures. The Claustro de los Reyes (Cloisters of the King) is both plateresque and Gothic in style. The convent lies two blocks east of the New Cathedral on the opposite side of busy Calle San Pablo at the southern terminus of Calle de España (Gran Vía).

Universidad de Salamanca. Patio de las Escuelas, 1. ☎ **923/29-44-00.** Admission 350 ptas. ($2.80). Mon–Fri 9:30am–1pm and 4–7pm, Sat 4–6pm, Sun 9:30am–1pm. Enter from Patio de las Escuelas, a widening of Calle de Libreros.

The oldest university in Spain was once the greatest in Europe. In front of the plateresque facade of the building, a statue honors Hebrew scholar Fray Luís de León. Arrested for heresy, Fray Luís was detained for five years before being cleared. When he returned, he began his first lecture: "As I was saying yesterday . . ." Fray Luís's remains are kept in the chapel, which is worth a look. You can also visit a dim 16th-century classroom, cluttered with crude wooden benches, but the library upstairs is closed to the public. The university lies two blocks from the cathedral in the southern section of the old town.

Impressions

Now the traveller has re-entered the bald regions of Old Castile, and the best thing is to get out of them again as quickly as possible.

—Richard Ford, *A Handbook for Travellers in Spain* (1855)

WHERE TO STAY

EXPENSIVE

Gran Hotel. Plaza Poeta Iglesias, 5, 37001 Salamanca. ☎ **923/21-35-00.** Fax 923/21-35-00. 107 rms, 6 suites. A/C MINIBAR TV TEL. 14,000–18,500 ptas. ($112–$148) double; 31,800 ptas. ($254.40) suite. AE, DC, MC, V. Parking 1,200 ptas. ($9.60).

Because of both its location and the legends that surround it, this hotel has been a favorite since its original construction in 1930. Set on the southeast corner of the Plaza Mayor, it became the traditional favorite of bull breeders and matadors, as well as of the literati of this ancient university town. Because its owners have kept it up to date, the hotel is still going strong, although accommodations at the parador (see below) are better appointed. In 1994 the hotel was completely renovated, with modern plumbing and accessories added, but with much of the old-fashioned charm left intact. Each bedroom is well maintained and clean. Castilian-style meals are served à la carte in the hotel's Restaurante Feudal. Service in both the hotel and the restaurant could stand some improvement.

✪ **Hotel Rector.** Rector Esperabé, 10, 37008 Salamanca. ☎ **923/21-84-82.** Fax 923/21-40-08. 14 rms. A/C TV TEL. 16,000 ptas. ($128) double. AE, DC, MC, V. Parking 1,200 ptas. ($9.60).

Far better than either the parador or the Gran Hotel, this small little inn has become the prestige address in Salamanca, where nothing matches it either in atmosphere or tranquillity. Located just beyond the Roman bridge, it was a private mansion until the owners, who live on the upper floors, converted it into a hotel in 1990. The rooms are not really hotel quarters, but resemble the elegantly furnished and spacious bedrooms you'd find in the home of a grand Spanish don. Because of the circumstances, don't expect all the amenities found in a full-service hotel, although the staff here is extremely professional and polite. Breakfast is the only meal served. Since this place is such a gem and eagerly sought out, reservations are important.

Parador Nacional de Salamanca. Teso de la Feria, 2, 37008 Salamanca. ☎ **923/26-87-00.** Fax 923/21-54-38. 104 rms, 4 suites. A/C MINIBAR TV TEL. 15,000 ptas. ($120) double; 24,000 ptas. ($192) suite. AE, DC, MC, V. Free parking.

Situated just across the Tormes River, this multilevel parador with a modern facade opened in the early 1980s, at a point less than a mile south of the historic center of town. Today it provides the most luxurious accommodations in town, although the public areas are looking a bit worn. Each of the well-furnished and comfortable bedrooms has two or three framed lithographs, as well as a mirador-style balcony and a private bath. On the premises are a garden, a parking garage, and an outdoor swimming pool.

MODERATE

Hotel Monterray. Azafrand, 2, 37001 Salamanca. ☎ **923/21-44-01.** Fax 923/21-44-00. 141 rms, 3 suites. TV TEL. 10,000–17,500 ptas. ($80–$140) double; 25,000 ptas. ($200) suite. AE, DC, MC, V. Parking 1,200 ptas. ($9.60).

A companion to the Gran (see above), this hotel is an acceptable alternative, although its sibling is better. It comes as a bit of a letdown after the Rector as well, but the location not far from the Plaza Mayor is ideal and its wood and velvet lobby is inviting. The conservatively and simply furnished guest rooms, although not as well appointed as those of the Gran, are still quite comfortable. The price, especially of the cheaper rooms, is a good value for Salamanca. Many Castilian specialties are served in the fine restaurant, El Fogón; there's also an inviting café.

Hotel las Torres. Plaza Mayor, 26 (at the intersection of Calle Concejo), 37002 Salamanca. ☎ **923/21-21-00.** Fax 923/21-21-01. 42 rms, 2 suites. A/C MINIBAR TV TEL. 9,100–11,000 ptas. ($72.80–$88) double; 12,500–14,500 ptas. ($100-$116) suite. AE, DC, MC, V. Parking 1,250 ptas. ($10).

Well-maintained, dignified, and respectable, this fading hotel occupies an enviable position near the northwestern corner of Plaza Mayor. A recent restoration of a historic monument, the hotel has a narrow reception area sheathed with polished marble and a congenial staff. The modern, if somewhat depressing, bedrooms are not overly large but are comfortably upholstered. Each contains a well-designed bathroom accented with marble and tile, a safe, and, in many cases, views over the plaza. There's an unpretentious restaurant on the premises. Additional seating spills over beneath the arcades of the plaza, allowing indoor-outdoor dining and lots of opportunities for people-watching. In spite of its drawbacks, including a seedy appearance, this place has its diehard fans.

INEXPENSIVE

$ **Hostal Laguna.** Consuelo, 19, 37001 Salamanca. ☎ **923/21-87-06.** 13 rms (6 with bath). 3,000 ptas. ($24) double without bath; 4,280 ptas. ($34.25) double with bath. MC, V.

This unpretentious hotel lies in the center of the historic core of Salamanca, close to both cathedrals and next to the Torre del Clavero. It is also near Plaza Mayor and the university. Its facade is traditional, with distinctive balustrades. The interior has been recently renovated, making for spartan but large, comfortable, and clean doubles.

Hostal Mindanao. Paseo de San Vicente; 2, 37007 Salamanca. ☎ **923/26-30-80.** 30 rms. 3,600 ptas. ($28.80) double. No credit cards.

Set within an angular and somewhat nondescript modern building that dates from the early 1980s, this unpretentious hostal is especially popular with students and, from time to time, their visiting parents. Bedrooms have private baths or showers, but absolutely no frills. No meals are served, but numerous cafés are nearby, making a trek out for morning coffee relatively painless. The hotel lies along the southwestern edge of the busy traffic peripheral ringing the town center, within a 12-minute walk of Plaza Mayor.

WHERE TO DINE

El Botín Charro. Calle Hovohambre, 6–8. ☎ **923/21-64-62.** Main courses 975–2,500 ptas. ($7.80–$20); fixed-price menu 2,500 ptas. ($20). AE, DC, MC, V. Daily 1:30–4pm, Mon–Sat 8:30–midnight. CASTILIAN/INTERNATIONAL.

A well-managed restaurant with some of the best food in town, this establishment has thrived in Salamanca since it was established in 1975. The building in which it is housed dates from the 1790s. Originally a private house, it lies on a narrow street off Plaza del Mercado, and contains a sampling of artifacts and antiques from the era of its construction. A polite staff prepares several types of grilled meats with well-rehearsed ceremony in the Castilian style. The chef works hard at diversifying into modern and creative interpretations of Spanish cuisine as well. Menu choices change with the seasons, but make ample use of autumn and winter game dishes, fresh and exotic mushrooms and asparagus, freshly culled herbs, and fresh seafood.

✪ **Chez Victor.** Espoz y Mina, 26. ☎ **923/21-31-23.** Reservations required. Main courses 2,000–3,200 ptas. ($16–$25.60). AE, DC, MC, V. Tues–Sun 2–3:30pm, Tues–Sat 9:30–11:30pm. Closed Aug. CONTINENTAL.

Set within the historic center of town, this is the most glamorous and Europeanized restaurant around. Its food is far superior to that of any other establishment in town, as the owner/chef Victoriano Salvador spent some 15 years in France learning and perfecting his innovative cuisine. He returned home to open this restaurant, which won the only star Michelin has ever granted to a Salamanca restaurant. Amid a monochromatic and deliberately understated modern decor, you'll enjoy dishes prepared with market-fresh ingredients.

Specialties include freshly prepared fish—perhaps sea wolf in black squid sauce, broiled turbot in a hot vinaigrette sauce, or, even better, tuna blue steak in sesame seeds. Try the chef's calf's medallions in lemon sauce and, if it's offered, ribs of pork stuffed with prunes and served with a honey-mustard sauce. Despite the modernity of the cuisine, the portions are ample and well suited to Spanish tastes.

Río de la Plata. Plaza del Poso, 1. ☎ **923/21-90-05.** Reservations recommended. Main courses 1,000–3,000 ptas. ($8–$24); *menú del día* 2,000 ptas. ($16). MC, V. Tues–Sun 1:30–4:30pm and 9pm–midnight. Closed July. CASTILIAN.

This tiny basement restaurant, two blocks south of Plaza Mayor on a small side square formed by the junction of Plaza Poeta Iglesia and Calle San Justo, has thrived since 1958. The kitchen uses fresh ingredients, preparing a traditional but simple *cocida castellana* (Castilian stew), house-style sole, roast baby goat, many varieties of fish, and pungently flavored sausages. Although a modest place, good-quality ingredients go into the dishes served. The linen is crisply ironed, the service usually impeccable. On a wintery night in Salamanca, this is one of the most inviting places in the city, with its cozy dark wood and fireplace. Locals fill up the place every night, which is endorsement enough.

AN EASY SIDE TRIP TO ALBA DE TORMES

Admirers of St. Teresa may want to make the 11-mile (18km) pilgrimage southeast of Salamanca to visit the medieval village of Alba de Tormes. Follow highway C-510. Cross a bridge with 22 arches spanning the Tormes River. Head between the Iglesia de San Pedro and the Basilica de Santa Teresa to Plaza de Santa Teresa, where you will come upon the **Convento de las Carmelitas** (☎ **923/30-00-43**) and the **Iglesia de Santa Teresa,** Plaza de Santa Teresa, 4. The church is a medley of Gothic, Renaissance, and baroque styles. The marble vault over the altar contains the ashes of Spain's most beloved saint, St. Teresa of Ávila, who died here in 1582. One of the two reliquaries flanking the altar is said to contain her arm; the other is said to hold the remains of her heart. Opposite the entrance door in the rear of the church is a grating through which you can look at the cell in which she died. Pope John Paul II visited Alba de Tormes in 1982 on the occasion of the 400th anniversary of St. Teresa's death. Admission is free. The church is open daily from 9am to 2pm and 4 to 8pm.

2 Ciudad Rodrigo

54 miles (87km) SW of Salamanca, 177 miles (285km) W of Madrid

A walled town dating from Roman days, Ciudad Rodrigo is known for its 16th- and 17th-century town houses, built by followers of the conquistadors. It was founded in the 12th century by Count Rodriguez González and today has been designated a national monument. Located near the Portuguese frontier, it stands high on a hilltop and is known for the familiar silhouette of the square tower of its Alcázar.

The ramparts were built in the 12th century along Roman foundations. Several stairways lead up to a mile-long sentry path. You can wander these ramparts at leisure and then walk through the streets with their many churches and mansions. It is not one chief monument that is the allure, but rather the city as a whole.

The town's major attraction is its cathedral, **Casco Viejo,** built between 1170 and 1230. It can be reached going east of Plaza Mayor through Plaza de San Salvador. Subsequent centuries saw more additions. The Renaissance altar on the north aisle is an acclaimed work of ecclesiastical art; look also for the Virgin Portal, at the west door, which dates from the 1200s. For 200 pesetas ($1.60), you'll be admitted to the cloisters, which have a medley of architectural styles, including a plateresque door. Hours are daily from 9am to 1pm and 4 to 6pm.

The **Plaza Mayor** is a showpiece of 17th-century architecture, with two Renaissance palaces. This is the main square of the city.

Your transportation in Ciudad Rodrigo will be your trusty feet, as walking is the only way to explore the city. Pick up a map at the tourist office (see below).

GETTING THERE **By Bus** Because train service is infrequent from Salamanca and the train station is a long way from the walls of the old city, the bus is preferred. The bus station is at Calle Campo de Toledo (☎ **923/46-10-09**). Monday through Friday eight buses arrive from Salamanca; on Saturday, five buses; and on Sunday, three. The trip takes an hour and costs 690 pesetas ($5.50) one way.

By Car The N-620 is the town's main link to both Salamanca and Portugal. Driving time from Salamanca is about 1 1/4 hours.

VISITOR INFORMATION The tourist information office is at Arco de Amayuelas, 5 (☎ **923/46-05-61**). Open Monday through Friday from 9:30am to 2pm and 5 to 8pm; Saturday and Sunday, from 10am to 2pm and 4 to 7pm.

SPECIAL EVENTS Carnival festivities in February in Ciudad Rodrigo feature a running of the bulls, traditional dances, and costumes.

WHERE TO STAY

Conde Rodrigo I. Plaza de San Salvador, 9, 37500 Ciudad Rodrigo. ☎ **923/46-14-04.** Fax 923/46-14-08. 35 rms. A/C TV. 6,200 ptas. ($49.60) double. AE, DC, MC, V.

Its central location next to the cathedral is one of this two-star hotel's advantages. Although much less desirable than the parador (see below), it was renovated a year ago. The location on the town's cathedral square is unbeatable. Try for a bedroom opening onto the square. The rooms are comfortable, but totally devoid of style. The building itself has some of the flavor of the medieval era, with its thick walls of chiseled stone. The hotel restaurant is a good buy, offering well-prepared Castilian food, such as roast meats, spicy sausages, and fresh fish.

✪ **Parador Nacional Enrique II.** Plaza del Castillo, 1, 37500 Ciudad Rodrigo. ☎ **923/46-01-50.** Fax 923/46-04-04. 27 rms, 1 suite. A/C MINIBAR TV TEL. 13,500 ptas. ($108) double; 16,500 ptas. ($132) suite. AE, DC, MC, V.

This completely restored building was an embattled castle in the 12th century, constructed by Enrique II of Trastamara on a hill overlooking Río Agueda. The Torre del Homenaje (keep) defines the profile of Ciudad Rodrigo, and once it was the seat of the feudal court. The parador has several gates and what the Spanish call *miradores*—platforms offering panoramic views. Sunset watching is a popular pastime.

The Gothic entrance bears the royal coat-of-arms and a plaque in Gothic letters. The tastefully furnished rooms offer more style and comfort than any other hotel in town, including the Conde Rodrigo. There is an underfloor heating system in all the bathrooms. Try for a bedroom overlooking the garden that runs down to the Agueda River. The food in the restaurant is well prepared, and the service polite.

WHERE TO DINE

Estoril. Traversia Talavera, 1. ☎ **923/46-05-50.** Reservations recommended. Main courses 1,200–1,800 ptas. ($9.60–$14.40); *menú del día* 1,400 ptas. ($11.20). AE, DC, MC, V. Daily 1–4pm and 8:30pm–midnight. CASTILIAN/BASQUE.

Lying only a short walk from Plaza Mayor, this popular restaurant was established in 1967, within a building constructed that year. The air-conditioned interior is decorated in a typical regional style, with bullfight photographs. Specialties of the house include roasted meats, such as roast suckling pig, with a special emphasis on roasted goat. Seafood, such as sole and hake, is presented in the Basque style. The seafood soup is particularly good. Everything is washed down with a variety of regional wines, including Cosechero Rioja.

Mayton. La Colada, 9. ☎ **923/46-07-20.** Reservations recommended. Main courses 800–2,250 ptas. ($6.40–$18); fixed-price menu 1,400–2,250 ptas. ($11.20–$18). AE, DC, MC, V. Daily noon–3:30pm and 8–11:30pm. CASTILIAN.

Adjacent to Plaza Mayor, within a 17th century building, Mayton is the best restaurant in the city. The walls of the antique and well-preserved bodega in which it stands reverberate with atmosphere and legend. The menu specializes in fresh fish and shellfish, and does so exceedingly well. Try the *sopa castellana* (Castilian soup) for an appetizer, followed by *merluza* (hake) in green sauce. You can also order veal, as tender as that of Ávila. The place is air-conditioned.

3 Zamora

40 miles (64km) N of Salamanca, 148 miles (238km) NW of Madrid

Little-known to North American visitors, Zamora (pronounced "Tha-*mor*-a") is the most representative city of Old Castile, blending ancient and modern, but noted mainly for its Romanesque architecture. In fact, Zamora is often called a "Romanesque museum." A medieval frontier city, it rises up starkly from the Castile flatlands, a reminder of an era of conquering monarchs and forgotten kingdoms.

You can explore Zamora's highlights in about four hours. Stroll along the main square, dusty Plaza Canovas; cross the arched Romanesque bridge from the 1300s; and take in at least some of the Romanesque churches for which the town is known. Many of them date from the 12th century. The cathedral is the best example, but others include **Iglesia de la Magdelena,** Rua de los Francos, and **Iglesia de San Ildefonso,** Calle Ramos Carrión. You might also want to look at **Iglesia de Santa María la Nueva,** Plaza de Santa María, and **Iglesia de Santiago el Burgo,** Calle Santa Clara.

The crowning achievement, however, at the far west end of Zamora, is the **cathedral,** Plaza Castillo o Pio XII, open daily from 11am to 1pm. It is topped by a gold-and-white Eastern-looking dome. Inside, you'll find rich hangings, interesting chapels, two 15th-century Mudéjar pulpits, and intricately carved choir stalls. Later architectural styles, including Gothic, have been added to the original Romanesque features, but this indiscriminate mixing of periods is typical of Spanish cathedrals. Inside the cloister, the Museo de la Catedral possesses ecclesiastical art, historical documents, church documents, and an unusual collection of "Black Tapestries" dating from the 1400s. The cathedral is free but admission to the museum costs 200 pesetas ($1.60) for adults, 100 pesetas (80¢) for children. The cathedral can generally be visited throughout the day. The museum is open June through September, Monday through Friday from 11am to 2pm and 5 to 8pm, Sunday from 11am to 2pm; October through May, Monday through Saturday from 11am to 2pm and 4 to 6pm, Sunday from 11am to 2pm.

GETTING THERE **By Train** There are four trains to and from Madrid every day and two to and from La Coruña (the trips take three and six hours, respectively). The railway station is at Calle Alfonso Peña, 3 (☎ **980/52-19-56**), about a 15-minute walk from the edge of the old town. Follow Avenida de las Tres Cruces northeast of the center of town.

By Bus More than 12 connections a day from Salamanca make this the easiest way to get in and out of town. Travel time between the cities is an hour. There are about six to seven buses a day from Madrid; the trip takes 3½ hours and costs 1,980 pesetas ($15.85) one way. The town's bus station lies a few paces from the railway station, at Calle Alfonso Peña, 3 (☎ **980/52-12-81**).

By Car Zamora is at the junction of eight different roads and highways. Most of the traffic from northern Portugal into Spain comes through Zamora. Highways headed north to León, south to Salamanca, and east to Valladolid are especially convenient. From Madrid, take the A-6 superhighway northwest toward Valladolid, cutting west on the N-VI and west again at the turnoff onto 122.

VISITOR INFORMATION The tourist information office is at Santa Clara, 20 (☎ **980/53-18-45**). Open Monday through Friday from 10am to 2pm and 5 to 8pm, Saturday from 9am to 2:30pm, and Sunday from 10am to 2pm.

SPECIAL EVENTS Holy Week, the week before Easter, in Zamora is a celebration known throughout the country. Street processions, called *pasos,* are among the most spectacular in Spain. If you plan to visit at this time, secure hotel reservations well in advance.

WHERE TO STAY

$ **Hostal Chiqui.** Benavente, 2, 49002 Zamora. ☎ **980/53-14-80.** 14 rms. 4,200 ptas. ($33.60) double. No credit cards.

If you're looking for a bargain and don't mind a few minor inconveniences, try this simple second-floor pension. The guest rooms are spartan but clean, with almost no accessories. No breakfast is served, but cafés are within walking distance. Chiqui lies behind the post office in the northwest section of the old town, near a corner of busy Calle Santa Clara.

✪ **Hostería Real de Zamora.** Cuesta de Pizarro, 7, 49027 Zamora. ☎ or fax **980/53-45-45.** 17 rms, 1 suite. MINIBAR TV TEL. 8,976 ptas. ($71.80) double; 9,976 ptas. ($79.80) suite. Rates include breakfast. AE, DC, MC, V. Parking 750 ptas. ($6).

The most charming small hotel in town, sporting walls that date from the 1400s, this establishment occupies the long-ago headquarters of Zamora's dreaded Inquisition. (Prior to that, ironically, the site housed a Jewish-owned building reputed to have been the home of the explorer Pizarro.) Today, the outstanding historical features of the building include a medieval reservoir, a patio perfect for enjoying a cup of tea or coffee, and a verdant garden that lies along the city's medieval fortifications. An excellent example of a tastefully modernized aristocratic villa, it stands a few steps to the west of the northern embankment of the city's most photographed bridge, the

Stone Bridge. Bedrooms contain simple but solid furnishings and offer safety-deposit boxes.

Dining/Entertainment: The restaurant Pizarro, with the air of a baronial private dining room, offers three-course fixed-price meals. Adjacent to it is the Restaurante Hostería Real, offering basically the same menu and a bar.

Services: 24-hour room service, laundry, babysitting.

✪ **Parador Turistico de Zamora.** Plaza de Viriato, 5, 49001 Zamora. ☎ **980/51-44-97.** Fax 980/53-00-63. 25 rms, 2 suites. MINIBAR TV TEL. 15,000 ptas. ($120) double; 17,000 ptas. ($136) suite. AE, DC, MC, V. Parking 800 ptas. ($6.40).

The site of this parador has always fulfilled a legendary role within Zamora. Originally fortified as an *Alcazaba* by the Moors during their occupation of Zamora, it was later expanded into a palace during the late Middle Ages. Most of that original monument was demolished and rebuilt upon its ancient foundations in 1459 by the Count of Alva y Aliste, and today the structure retains the severe, high-ceilinged dignity of its 15th-century Gothic form. Renovated by the Spanish government in the late 1960s, it is today one of the most beautiful and desirable paradors in Spain, and obviously the best and most tranquil place to stay in town.

Set two blocks south of Plaza Mayor, near the junction of Plaza de Viriato and Calle Ramos Carrión, the parador is richly decorated with medieval armor, antique furniture, tapestries, and potted plants. In winter, glass partitions close off a large inner patio centered around an antique well; baronial fireplaces provide much-appreciated warmth. Bedrooms are white walled, clean, and tastefully decorated with conservative furniture.

Dining/Entertainment: The sumptuous but rustic dining room has a view of the swimming pool and surrounding countryside. There's also a cozy bar.

Services: Room service, laundry/valet, babysitting.

Facilities: Swimming pool.

WHERE TO DINE

París. Avenida de Portugal, 14. ☎ **980/51-43-25.** Reservations recommended. Main dishes 1,600–2,600 ptas. ($12.80–$20.80); fixed-price menu 1,900 ptas. ($15.20). AE, DC, MC, V. Daily 1:30–4pm and 8:45pm–midnight. SPANISH/INTERNATIONAL.

This elegantly decorated, air-conditioned restaurant is known for its fish, often made with a regionally inspired twist. Well-prepared specialties include vegetable flan, braised oxtail, Zamora-style clams, and a delectable hake. Dishes, of course, change with the seasons. Most critics rate this restaurant number one in town. It is on the main traffic artery (Avenida de Portugal) that funnels traffic south to Salamanca.

Serafín. Plaza Maestro Haedo, 10. ☎ **980/53-14-22.** Main courses 900–2,800 ptas. ($7.20–$22.40); fixed price menus 1,800–2,500 ptas. ($14.40–$20). AE, DC, MC, V. Daily 1–5pm and 8:30pm–midnight. SPANISH.

At the northeast edge of the old town, about a block south of the busy traffic hub of Plaza Alemania and Avenida de Alfonso IX, this air-conditioned haven with an attractive bar makes a relaxing retreat from the sun. The specialties change with the season but might include seafood soup Serafín, paella, fried hake, Iberian ham, and a savory *cocido* (stew).

ZAMORA AFTER DARK

Calle Los Herreros, or Calle de Vinos, contains more bars per square foot than any street in Zamora—about 16 of them in all. Each is willing to accommodate a stranger with a leisurely glass of wine or beer and a selection of tapas. Calle Los Herreros is a narrow street at the southern end of the old town, about two blocks north of the Duero River, within the shadow of the Ayuntamiento Viejo (Old Town Hall), one block south of Plaza Mayor.

4 León

203 miles (327km) NW of Madrid, 122 miles (196km) N of Salamanca

Once the leading city of Christian Spain, this old cathedral town was the capital of a centuries-old empire that declined after uniting with Castile. León today is the gateway from Old Castile to the northwestern routes of Galicia. It is a sprawling city, but nearly everything of interest to visitors—monuments, restaurants, and hotels—can be covered on foot, once you arm yourself with a good map.

Today, León, once the heartbeat of a great kingdom, is a sleepy provincial city off the beaten track. But its wealth of old monuments, its top-notch accommodations, and a certain regal quality in the air still make the town feel like a capital.

The outlying mountain villages offer their own architectural gems, fine ski runs, and tasty concoctions of local trout and meat. Also, the region is particularly renowned for its soft-spoken and pristine Castilian accent. In sum, León is an excellent place to experience the tranquillity of the Spanish heartland, as well as an obligatory stop for students of medieval architecture.

GETTING THERE **By Train** León has good rail connections to the rest of Spain—five trains daily arrive from Madrid. The station, Estación del Norte, Avenida de Astorga, 2 (☎ **987/27-02-02**), lies on the western bank of the Bernesga River. Cross the bridge near Plaza de Guzmán el Bueno. The *rápido* train from Madrid takes five hours, the *TALGO* only four. A one-way ticket from Madrid ranges from 3,125 to 3,300 pesetas ($25–$26.40).

By Bus Most of León's buses arrive and depart from the Estación de Autobuses, Paseo Ingeniero Saenz de Miera (☎ **987/21-10-00**). Three to five buses per day link León with Zamora and Salamanca, and there are 10 per day from Madrid (trip time: 4½ hours). A one-way ticket on a regular bus from Madrid is 2,600 pesetas ($20.80), rising to 4,000 pesetas ($32) on a direct bus.

By Car León lies at the junction of five major highways coming from five different regions of Spain. From Madrid's periphery, head northwest on the N-VI superhighway toward La Coruña. At Benavente, bear right onto the N-630.

VISITOR INFORMATION The tourist information office is at Plaza de Regla, 4 (☎ **987/23-70-82**). Open Monday through Friday from 10am to 2pm and 5 to 7:30pm, Saturday and Sunday from 10am to 2pm.

EXPLORING THE TOWN

✪ **Catedral de León (Santa Maria de Regla).** Plaza de Regla. ☎ **987/23-00-60.** Admission to cathedral, free; cloisters and museum, 300 ptas. ($2.40). Cathedral, daily 8:30am–1:30pm and 4–7pm; cloisters and museum, Mon–Sat 9:30am–12:45pm and 4–6:30pm. Bus: 4 or 9.

The usual cathedral elements are virtually eclipsed here by the awesome stained-glass windows—some 125 in all (plus 57 oculi), the oldest dating from the 13th century. They are so heavy they have strained the walls of the cathedral. Look for a 15th-century altarpiece depicting the Entombment in the Capilla Mayor, as well as a Renaissance *trascoro* by Juan de Badajoz. The nave dates from the 13th and 14th centuries; the Renaissance vaulting is much later. Almost as interesting as the stained-glass windows are the cloisters, dating in part from the 13th and 14th

Luminous in León

In the church-building sweepstakes of the Middle Ages, every Gothic cathedral vied to distinguish itself with some superlative trait. Milan Cathedral was the biggest, Chartres had the most inspiring stained-glass windows, Palma de Majorca had the largest rose window, and so on.

Structurally speaking, the boldest cathedral was at León. This edifice set the record for the highest proportion of window space, with stained-glass windows soaring 110 feet to the vaulted ceiling, framed by the slenderest of columns, occupying 18,000 square feet, or almost all the space where you'd expect the walls to be.

The roof is held up not by walls but by flying buttresses on the exterior. Inside, even medievalists are astonished by the profusion of light and the illusion of weightlessness. The architects Juan Pérez and Maestro Enrique, who designed the cathedral in the 13th century, were, in effect, a premonition of Mies van der Rohe, seven centuries before the age of steel girders draped with plate-glass curtain walls.

centuries and containing faded frescoes and Romanesque and Gothic tombs; some capitals are carved with starkly lifelike scenes. Visitors can also see a museum containing valuable art and artifacts, including a Bible from the 10th century, notable sculptures, and a collection of romantic images of the Virgin Mary. The cathedral is on the edge of the old city, seven blocks east of the town's most central square, Plaza de Santo Domingo.

Panteón y Museos de San Isidoro. Plaza San Isidoro, 4. ☎ **987/22-96-08.** Admission 350 ptas. ($2.80). Tues–Sat 10am–1:30pm and 4–6:30pm, Sun 10am–1:30pm. Bus: 4 or 9.

This church, just a short walk northwest of the cathedral, was dedicated to San Isidoro de Sevilla in 1063 and contains 23 tombs of Leonese kings. One of the first Romanesque buildings in León and Castile, it was embellished by Ferdinand I's artists. The columns are magnificent, the capitals splendidly decorated; covering the vaults are murals from the 12th century. Unique in Spain, the Treasury holds rare finds—a 10th-century Scandinavian ivory, an 11th-century chalice, and an important collection of 10th- to 12th-century cloths from Asia. The library contains many ancient manuscripts and rare books, including a Book of Job from 951, a Visigothic Bible, and an 1162 Bible, plus dozens of miniatures.

WHERE TO STAY

$ Guzmán El Bueno. López Castrillón, 6, 24003 León. ☎ **987/23-64-12.** 29 rms (20 with bath). 3,000 ptas. ($24) double without bath, 4,800 ptas. ($38.40) double with bath. No credit cards. Walk up Calle Generalísimo from Plaza de Santo Domingo, turn left onto Calle de Cid; López Castrillón is a pedestrian-only street, branching off to the right.

The most inexpensive, comfortable accommodation in León is the no-frills Guzmán El Bueno, on the second floor of a centrally located boardinghouse. In all, it's a safe destination, widely known among international student travelers, who are drawn to its low prices. Some rooms have phones; all are clean. Be warned in advance that the staff speaks only Spanish.

Hotel Quindós. Avenida José Antonio, 24, 24002 León. ☎ **987/23-62-00.** Fax 987/24-22-01. 96 rms. TV TEL. 9,625 ptas. ($77) double. AE, DC, MC, V. Bus: 4 or 9.

This rather functional hotel has been tastefully decorated with modern paintings, which enhance the establishment considerably. The snug, comfortable, and well-maintained rooms are a good value. The hotel offers two restaurants, one with menus typical of Old Castile, another more elegant dining room serving an international cuisine. You can, for example, enjoy fish of the day baked in an oven, sirloin with onion jelly, and marinated pigeon. The Quindós lies three blocks south of Plaza de San Marcos, in the central commercial district in the northwest quadrant of the old town.

✪ **Parador San Marcos.** Plaza de San Marcos, 7, 24001 León. ☎ **987/23-73-00.** Fax 987/23-34-58. 251 rms, 2 suites. A/C TV TEL. 16,500–19,500 ptas. ($132–$156) double; 44,500 ptas. ($356) suite. AE, DC, MC, V. Free parking.

A top tourist attraction, this 16th-century former monastery with its celebrated plateresque facade is one of the most spectacular hotels in Spain. The government has remodeled it at great expense, installing extravagant authentic antiques and quality reproductions as well as improving the facade. Before its monastery days, the old "hostal" used to put up pilgrims bound for Santiago de Compostela in the 12th century. The parador also contains a church with a scallop-shell facade and an archaeological museum. The guest rooms are sumptuous, each with private bath. The parador is located northwest of the cathedral on the outskirts of the old town, on the east bank of the Bernesga River.

WHERE TO DINE

Albina. Condesa de Sagasta, 24. ☎ **987/22-19-12.** Reservations recommended. Main courses 1,300–2,000 ptas. ($10.40–$16); *menú del día* 1,500 ptas. ($12). AE, MC, V. Tues–Sun 1–4pm and 8:30pm–midnight. Bus: 4 or 9. FRENCH/SPANISH.

Outside the city center, a 15-minute walk northwest of the cathedral, adjacent to the Parador San Marcos, is this contemporary restaurant much favored by local residents. Within a modern and monochromatic interior, the owner supervises the preparation of fresh fish and meat dishes that are loosely based on French and Spanish models. Signature dishes include *lubina a la sal* (whitefish cooked in a salt crust), filet steak with pepper, carefully seasoned filets of pork, and roast duck in orange sauce. A long wine list is available, and the room is air-conditioned.

Casa Pozo. Plaza San Marcelo, 15. ☎ **987/22-30-39.** Reservations recommended. Main courses 1,200–2,300 ptas. ($9.60–$18.40); fixed price menus 1,900–2,575 ptas. ($15.20–$20.60). AE, DC, MC, V. Mon–Sat 12:30–4pm and 8–11:45pm. Closed Christmas. Bus: 4 or 9. SPANISH.

Located two blocks south of the busy traffic hub of Plaza Santo Domingo and across from city hall, this unpretentious restaurant is a long-enduring favorite with locals who appreciate its unassuming style and flavorful cuisine. Habitués call owner Gabriel del Pozo Alvarez "Pin," and he's the reason behind the success of the place. Specialties, all made from fresh ingredients, include peas with salty ham, shrimp with asparagus, roast pork or lamb laden with herbs and spices, and a delicate smothered sole known as *estofado*. Twelve varieties of fresh fish are available. The restaurant offers an excellent selection of Rioja wines.

Mesón Leonés del Racimo de Oro. Caño Badillo, 2. ☎ **987/25-75-75.** Reservations required. Main courses 1,000–1,600 ptas. ($8–$12.80); fixed-price menu 1,400 ptas. ($11.20). AE, MC, V. Wed–Sat 1:45–4pm and 9pm–midnight, Sun 1:45–4pm. CASTILIAN.

Behind Plaza Mayor and beside the cathedral, this bodega is housed in a structure from the early 1700s, and even it was built on older foundations. As such, it is one of the two or three oldest inns in León, and a lot of food and wine have been consumed on this site over the centuries. The building is what the Spanish call a *mesón típico* (house built in the regional style), and its tables overlook a patio.

The food is consistently good, with the owner specializing in a regional cuisine—*mollejas con rabo de toro* (oxtail), for example, or *merluza* (hake) house style. You might begin with an appetizer of Serrano ham or clams, then follow with one of the roast meats, such as roast suckling lamb cooked in a wood-fired clay oven. The service is attentive.

5 Valladolid

125 miles (201km) NW of Madrid, 83 miles (133km) SE of León

From the 13th century until its eventual decay in the early 17th century, Valladolid was a royal city and an intellectual center that attracted saints and philosophers. Isabella and Ferdinand were married here; Philip II was born here; and Columbus died here on May 19, 1506, broken in spirit and body after Isabella had died and Ferdinand refused to reinstate him as a governor of the Indies.

Valladolid is bitterly cold in winter, sweltering in summer. Today, after years of decline, the city is reviving economically and producing, among other things, flour, ironware, and cars. Consequently, it's polluted and noisy, and many of the old buildings have been replaced by utilitarian ones, although there are many attractions remaining.

From the tourist office (see below), you can pick up a map—*plano de la ciudad*—that marks all the major monuments of Valladolid. These attractions can be covered on foot, although you may want to take a taxi to the two most distant points recommended—the Museo Nacional de Escultura and the Museo Oriental.

GETTING THERE **By Plane** Flights to Valladolid land at Vallanubla Airport, Highway N-601 (☎ **983/41-54-00**), a 15-minute taxi ride from the center of town. Aviaco routes daily flights to and from Barcelona and Madrid. The local Aviaco/Iberia office is located at Gamazo, 17 (☎ **983/56-01-62**).

By Train Valladolid is well serviced by some two dozen daily trains to and from Madrid (trip time: 4 hours). A one-way fare costs 3,000 pesetas ($24). Other cities with train links to Valladolid include Salamanca (8 trains per day) and Burgos (11 trains per day). The train station (Estación del Norte), Calle Recondo, s/n (☎ **983/20-02-02**), is about one mile south of the historic center of town, one block southwest of Campo Grande park. There's a RENFE office selling tickets at Divina Pastora, 6 (☎ **983/21-09-28**). Phone reservations can be made daily from 9:30am to 1:30pm and 4:30 to 7:30pm.

By Bus The bus station lies within an eight-minute walk of the railway station, at Puente Colgante, 2 (☎ **983/23-63-08**), at the southern edge of town. There are more than a dozen buses every day to and from Madrid, 2½ hours away. Two buses per day arrive from Zamora (trip time: 40 minutes), and 11 buses per day from Burgos (2 hours).

By Car Valladolid lies at the center of the rectangle created by Burgos, León, Segovia, and Salamanca and is connected to each with good highways. From Madrid, driving time is about 2¼ hours. Take superhighway A-6 northwest from Madrid, turning north on 403.

VISITOR INFORMATION The tourist information office is at Plaza de Zorilla, 3 (☎ **983/35-18-01**). Open daily 10am to 2pm and 5 to 8pm.

SEEING THE SIGHTS

✪ **Museo Nacional de Escultura (National Museum of Sculpture).** Colegio de San Gregorio, Calle Cadeñas de San Gregorio, I. ☎ **983/25-03-75.** Admission 400 ptas. ($3.20), free for children under 18 and adults over 65. Tues–Sat 10am–2pm and 4–6pm, Sun 10am–2pm.

Located near Plaza de San Pablo, the museum displays a magnificent collection of gilded polychrome sculpture, an art form that reached its pinnacle in Valladolid. The figures were first carved from wood, then painted with consummate skill and grace to assume lifelike dimensions. See, especially, the works by Alonso Berruguete (1480–1561), son of Pedro, one of Spain's great painters. From 1527 to 1532 the younger Berruguete labored over the altar of the Convent of San Benito—a masterpiece now housed here. In particular, see his *Crucifix with the Virgin and St. John* in Room II and his *St. Sebastian and the Sacrifice of Isaac* in Room III. Works by Juan de Juni and Gregorio Fernández are also displayed.

After visiting the galleries, explore the two-story cloisters. The upper level is florid, with jutting gargoyles and fleurs-de-lis. See the chapel where the confessor to Isabella I (Fray Alonso de Burgos) was buried—and be horrified by the gruesome sculpture *Death*.

Cathedral. Calle Arrive, 1. ☎ **983/30-43-62.** Admission to cathedral, free; museum, 250 ptas. ($2). Cathedral and museum, Tues–Fri 10am–1:30pm and 4:30–7pm, Sat–Sun 10am–2pm.

In 1580 Philip II commissioned Juan de Herrera, architect of El Escorial, to construct this monument in the city where he was born. When Philip died in 1598, work came to a stop for 18 years. Alberto Churriguera resumed construction, drawing up more flamboyant plans, especially for the exterior, in an unharmonious contrast to the severe lines of his predecessor. The classical, even sober, interior conforms more with Herrera's designs. A highlight is the 1551 altarpiece in the main apsidal chapel, the work of Juan de Juni. Art critics have commented that his polychrome figures are "truly alive." The cathedral is in the heart of the city, east of Plaza Mayor and north of Plaza de Santa Cruz.

Iglesia de San Pablo. Plaza San Pablo, 4. ☎ **983/35-17-48.** Free admission. Daily 7am–2pm and 6–9pm.

Once a 17th-century Dominican monastery, San Pablo, with its Isabelline-Gothic facade, is very impressive. Flanked by two towers, the main entrance supports levels of lacy stone sculpture. The church lies six blocks north of the cathedral, one block south of busy Avenida Santa Teresa. Daily masses are held, with eight masses on Sunday.

Museo Oriental. Paseo de Filipinos, 7. ☎ **983/30-68-00.** Admission 350 ptas. ($2.80), free for children 9 and under. Mon–Sat 4–7pm, Sun 10am–2pm.

Located in the Royal College of the Augustinian Fathers, near Campo Grande park, the museum has 14 rooms: 10 Chinese and 4 Filipino. It has the best collection of Asian art in Spain, with bronzes from the 7th century B.C. to the 18th century A.D., wooden carvings, 100 fine porcelain pieces, paintings on paper and silk from the 12th century to the 19th, and ancient Chinese coins, furniture, jade, and ivory. In the Filipino section, ethnological and primitive art is represented by shields and arms. Eighteenth-century religious art can be admired in extraordinary ivories, embroideries, paintings, and silversmiths' work. Popular art of the 19th century includes bronzes, musical instruments, and statuary.

Casa de Cervantes. Calle del Rastro, s/n. ☎ **983/30-88-10.** Admission 400 ptas. ($3.20), free on Sun. Tues–Sun 9:30am–3:30pm.

Now a museum, this house was once occupied by Miguel de Cervantes, author of *Don Quixote,* who did much of his writing in Valladolid. Here the author remained for the last years of his life. Behind its white walls, the house is simply furnished, as it was in his day. It lies half a block south of the cathedral, two blocks north of the city park, Campo Grande.

WHERE TO STAY

Ⓢ Enara. Plaza de España, 5, 47001 Valladolid. ☎ **983/30-03-11.** Fax 983/30-03-11. 25 rms. TV TEL. 5,936 ptas. ($47.50) double. AE, MC, V. Closed Dec 24–25. Parking 1,000 ptas. ($8).

Located about a quarter mile south of the cathedral, near the junction of Avenida 2 de Mayo and Paseo Miguel Iscar, Enara is arguably the best inexpensive accommodation in Valladolid. Its central location is backed up by contemporary, pleasantly furnished guest rooms. The decoration is in the typical Castilian style with some antiques. There is no restaurant, but a continental breakfast is offered, and you'll be near many low-cost dining rooms and cafés. Originally built in the 19th century as a private house, it was converted into a hotel in the mid-1970s. Two of its three stories are devoted to simple but well-maintained bedrooms, and the ground floor contains the breakfast area.

Felipe IV. Calle de Gamazo, 16, 47004 Valladolid. ☎ **983/30-70-00.** Fax 983/30-86-87. 129 rms, 3 suites. A/C TV TEL. 13,550 ptas. ($108.40) double; 26,000 ptas. ($208) suite. AE, DC, MC, V. Parking 1,300 ptas. ($10.40).

When it was built, the Felipe IV was one of the grandest hotels in the city, although that position has now been usurped by the Meliá chain (see below). Each of its bedrooms is modernized, guaranteeing its ranking as one of Valladolid's solidly acceptable establishments. A garage provides parking for motorists. The hotel is south of the busy traffic hub of Plaza de Madrid, a few blocks north of the rail station, near the eastern edge of the city park, Campo Grande. It attracts many business travelers, as a visit to the hotel dining room at night will reveal. A standard Spanish cuisine—nothing special—is served.

Hotel Meliá Parque. Joaquin Garcia Morato, 17, 47007 Valladolid. ☎ **800/336-3542** in the U.S., or 983/22-00-00. Fax 983/47-50-29. 291 rms, 9 suites. A/C TV TEL. 10,379 ptas. ($83.05) double; 21,347 ptas. ($170.80) suite. AE, DC, MC, V. Parking 1,400 ptas. ($11.20).

Completed in 1982, this modern chain hotel lies two blocks west of the rail station on the city outskirts. It's popular with business travelers unwilling to negotiate the labyrinth of Valladolid's central streets. Although an acceptable choice in every way, it is not as luxuriously appointed or as comfortable as the Old Meliá (see below). The guest rooms are comfortable and functionally furnished—with no surprises and few disappointments. It also provides special rooms and facilities for people with disabilities. The hotel has a restaurant featuring average Castilian meals.

Hotel Old Meliá. Plaza San Miguel, 10, 47003 Valladolid. ☎ **800/336-3542** in the U.S., or 983/35-72-00. Fax 983/33-68-28. 204 rms, 7 suites. A/C MINIBAR TV TEL. 14,595 ptas. ($116.75) double; 24,500–36,000 ptas. ($196–$288) suite. AE, DC, MC, V. Parking 1,875 ptas. ($15).

Set in the heart of the historic zone, about five blocks northwest of the cathedral, this is a modern hotel whose original construction in the early 1970s has been upgraded throughout the public rooms with a postmodern gloss. The bedrooms are the most comfortable in town, filled with heavy Iberian furniture that seems to suit the hotel's neighborhood.

Dining/Entertainment: There's an in-house restaurant floored with cool slabs of polished stone, as well as a bar.

Services: Room service (available from 7am to 11pm), laundry, babysitting.

Facilities: Hairdresser/barber.

WHERE TO DINE

✪ **La Fragua.** Paseo de Zorilla, 10. ☎ **983/33-87-85.** Reservations recommended. Main courses 1,400–3,500 ptas. ($11.20–$28). AE, DC, MC, V. Tues–Sun 1:30–3:45pm, Tues–Sat 9–11:45pm. Closed Aug. CASTILIAN.

Amid rustic decor you'll enjoy beautifully prepared Castilian dishes, the best in town, at this restaurant just north of the rail station across busy Paseo de Zorilla. You might begin with spicy sausage, followed by beef, chicken, or lamb, each carefully seasoned and served in a generous portion. A wide variety of fish is imported daily. The huge wine list offers many regional vintages, one of which the steward will choose for you if you request it. Dessert could include a cheese tart or a melt-in-your-mouth chocolate truffle. Owner Antonio Garrote proudly displays his culinary diplomas.

Mesón Cervantes. Rastro, 6. ☎ **983/30-61-38.** Reservations recommended. Main courses 1,325–2,900 ptas. ($10.60–$23.20). AE, DC, MC, V. Mon–Sat 1–4pm and 9pm–midnight. Closed Aug. SPANISH/INTERNATIONAL.

Opened in 1973, this restaurant is regarded by some fans as the finest in the city. The owner, Alejandro, works the dining room and is capably complemented in the kitchen by his wife, Julia. Neighborhood residents favor this place for its lack of pretension and its delectable cuisine. Two particular favorites are sole with pine nuts and seasonal river crabs. Many other fish dishes, including hake and monkfish, are available. Roast suckling pig and roast lamb are also popular. Other specialties include peppers stuffed with crabmeat; tender veal scaloppini "Don Quixote," served with a piquant sauce; and *arroz con liebre* (herb-laden rice studded with chunks of roasted wild rabbit, in season). The restaurant stands beside the Casa de Cervantes, half a mile south of the cathedral.

Mesón Panero. Marina Escobar, 1. ☎ **983/30-70-19.** Reservations required. Main courses 1,900–2,500 ptas. ($15.20–$20); fixed-price menu 3,500 ptas. ($28). AE, DC, MC, V. Daily 1–4pm and 9pm–midnight; July–Aug, closed Sun. CASTILIAN/INTERNATIONAL.

The chef of this imaginative restaurant, Angel Cuadrado, can turn even the most austere traditional Castilian recipes into sensual experiences. Set near the water, this 1960s establishment lures diners with fresh fish, including a succulent brochette of sole and hake with fresh asparagus. Every week brings a featured favorite: *cocida castellana,* the famous regional stew. Roast lamb and suckling pig are also available, plus a selection of well-chosen wines. The Mesón Panero is near the Casa de Cervantes, just a short walk from the tourist office.

6 Burgos

150 miles (242km) N of Madrid, 75 miles (121km) NE of Valladolid

Founded in the 9th century, this Gothic city in the Arlanzón River valley lives up to its reputation as the "cradle of Castile." Just as the Tuscans are credited with speaking the most perfect Italian, so the citizens of Burgos, with their distinctive lisp ("El Theed "for "El Cid"), supposedly speak the most eloquent Castilian.

El Cid Campeador, Spain's greatest national hero immortalized in the epic *El Cantar de Mío Cid,* is forever linked to Burgos. He was born near here, and his remains lie in the city's grand cathedral.

Like all the great cities of Old Castile, Burgos declined seriously in the 16th century, only to be revived later. In 1936, during the Civil War, the right-wing city was Franco's Nationalist army headquarters.

Today, Burgos no longer enjoys its historical glory, but is a provincial city along the *meseta,* or plateau, of Spain. Dry as a desert in summer and burning hot during the day, it comes alive at night and is filled with smoky cafés and dance clubs. Most of the bars, frequented by students, are in the area around the cathedral. Many of them don't start to party seriously until after 10pm, so it's a late-night town.

GETTING THERE **By Train** Burgos is well connected to Madrid (8 trains daily make the 3- to 5-hour trip), Barcelona (4 trains daily, 8- to 9-hour trip), the French border (9 daily), and Valladolid (12 to 15 daily). Depending on the train, one-way fares from Madrid range from 2,465 to 3,200 pesetas ($19.70–$25.60); from Barcelona, 4,800 to 5,400 pesetas ($38.40–$43.20); and from Valladolid, 875 to 1,500 pesetas ($7–$12). The Burgos railway station is at the terminus of Avenida de Conde Guadalhorce, half a mile southwest of the center. To get there head for the major traffic hub in Plaza Castilla, then walk due south across the Arlazón River. For train information or a ticket, head for the RENFE office in the center of town, at Moneda, 21 (☎ **947/20-91-31**), about a block northeast of busy Plaza de Santo Domingo de Guzmán.

By Bus About 10 buses a day make the three-hour trip up from Madrid, and four buses per day make the seven-hour trip from Barcelona. A one-way fare from Madrid, depending on the bus, ranges from 1,920 to 2,750 pesetas ($15.35–$22). The bus depot in Burgos is at Calle Miranda, 4–6 (☎ **947/26-55-65**). Calle Miranda intersects the large Plaza de Vega, due south of (and across the river from) the cathedral.

By Car Burgos is well connected to its neighbors by a network of highways, but its routes to and from Barcelona (six hours away) are especially wide and modern. The road from Barcelona changes its name several times, from the A-2 to the A-68 to the E-4, but it is a superhighway all the way. From Madrid, follow the N-I north for about three hours; the highway is fast but less modern than the road from Barcelona.

VISITOR INFORMATION The tourist information office is at Plaza Alonso Martínez, 7 (☎ **947/20-31-25**). Open Monday through Friday from 9am to 2pm and 5 to 7pm, Saturday from 9am to 2pm.

VISITING THE CATHEDRAL AND THE MONASTERY

✪ **Catedral de Santa María.** Plaza de Santa Mará. ☎ **947/20-47-12.** Admission to chapels, cloisters, and treasury, 350 ptas. ($2.80). Daily 9:30am–1pm and 4–7pm.

Begun in 1221, this cathedral became one of the most celebrated in Europe. Built in diverse styles, predominantly flamboyant Gothic, it took 300 years to complete. The three main doorways are flanked by ornamented 15th-century bell towers by John of Cologne. The 16th-century Chapel of Condestable, behind the main altar, is one of the best examples of Isabelline-Gothic architecture, richly decorated with heraldic emblems, a sculptured filigree doorway, figures of apostles and saints, balconies, and an eight-sided "star" stained-glass window.

Equally elegant are the two-story 14th-century cloisters, filled with fine Spanish Gothic sculpture. The cathedral's tapestries, including one well-known Gobelin, are rich in detail. In one of the chapels you'll see an old chest linked to the legend of El Cid—it was filled with gravel but used as collateral by the warrior to trick moneylenders. The remains of El Cid himself, together with those of his wife, Doña Ximena, lie under Santa María's octagonal lanternlike dome. Finally, you may want to see the elaborate 16th-century Stairway of Gold in the north transept, the work of Diego de Siloé.

The cathedral is across the Arlazón River from the railway station, midway between the river and the Citadel.

Monasterio de las Huelgas. Calle Compás de Adentro. ☎ **947/20-16-30.** Admission 650 ptas. ($5.20); free Wed. Tues–Sat 10:30am–2pm and 4–6:30pm, Sun 10:30am–3pm.

This cloister outside Burgos has seen a lot of action. Built in the 12th century in a richly ornamented style, it was once a summer place for Castilian royalty, as well as a retreat for nuns of royal blood. Inside, the Gothic church is built in the shape of a Latin cross. Despite some unfortunate mixing of Gothic and baroque, it contains much of interest—notably some 14th- and 17th-century French tapestries. The tomb of the founder, Alfonso VIII, and his queen, daughter of England's Henry II, lies in the Choir Room.

Thirteenth-century doors lead to the cloisters, dating from that century and blending Gothic and Mudéjar styles. Despite severe damage to the ceiling, the remains of Persian peacock designs are visible. The beautiful Chapter Room contains the standard of the 12th-century Las Navas de Tolora (war booty taken from the Moors), whereas the Museo de Ricas Telas is devoted to 13th-century costumes removed from tombs. These remarkably preserved textiles give a rare look at medieval dress.

The monastery is one mile off the Valladolid Road (the turnoff is clearly marked). From Plaza Primo de Rivera in Burgos, buses for Las Huelgas leave every 20 minutes.

WHERE TO STAY

Expensive

Hotel Almirante Bonifaz. Vitoria, 22–24, 09004 Burgos. ☎ **947/20-69-43.** Fax 947/20-29-19. 79 rms. MINIBAR TV TEL. 15,500 ptas. ($124) double; 17,200 ptas. ($137.60) triple. AE, DC, MC, V.

Solidly comfortable, modern, and decorated with a contemporary kind of efficiency, this hotel attracts many of the city's visiting business people, who appreciate its low-key charm and central location. The hotel lies two blocks east of the also recommended Condestable Hotel, near the river, within the commercial heart of town. All but a few of the bedrooms are air-conditioned, and all have private baths.

Dining/Entertainment: À la carte Spanish and Castile-inspired meals are served in each of the hotel's three restaurants, the most glamorous of which is Los Sauces. There's also a bar.

Services: Room service (available from 7am to 10pm), laundry service, babysitting.

Facilities: Car rentals, business center.

Hotel del Cid. Plaza de Santa María, 8, 09003 Burgos. ☎ **947/20-87-15.** Fax 947/26-94-60. 29 rms, 3 suites. TV TEL. 14,500 ptas. ($116) double; 19,500 ptas. ($156) suite. AE, DC, MC, V. Parking 1,000 ptas. ($8).

Built in 1983 by the Alzaga family, which still owns and operates it, this establishment stands in front of the cathedral and beside their restaurant (recommended below). The restaurant is better known than the hotel, which grew up on the site of one of the first printing presses in Spain. The hotel is decorated like a 15th-century house, but it boasts 20th-century amenities, including extra-large beds and private baths in all its guest rooms, which were refurbished in 1992. A laundry and a garage are available.

✪ **Landa Palace.** Carretera Madrid-Irun (at km 236), 09001 Burgos. ☎ **947/20-63-43.** Fax 947/26-00-36. 39 rms. A/C TV TEL. 19,000 ptas. ($152) double. MC, V.

One of the greatest hotels of Castile, a member of *Relais & Châteaux*, this hotel lies some two miles (3km) south of Burgos on N-I. A romantic getaway, it is in a handsomely restored castle from the 1300s with later additions. Pilgrims once stopped here en route to Santiago de Compostela in Galicia, but they wouldn't recognize the grandeur of the place today. Decorated with tasteful antiques, the lobby sets the tone with its white marble and ornate coffered ceiling. Bedrooms are spacious and cozily inviting with antique decorations and tile floors. Marble baths are state of the art with all the extras. Although parts of the hotel look a little worn, the graciousness of the staff compensates. In back is a pool and a dining terrace where you can order some of the finest food in the area.

MODERATE

Hotel Fernán González. Calera, 17, 09002 Burgos. ☎ **947/20-94-41.** Fax 947/27-41-21. 84 rms. A/C MINIBAR TV TEL. 10,300–11,900 ptas. ($82.40–$95.20) double; 16,000–17,225 ptas. ($128–$137.80) triple. AE, DC, MC, V. Parking 850 ptas. ($6.80).

Across the Arlanzón River from the soaring bulk of the cathedral, a half-block west of Plaza de Vega, this appealing and unusual hotel incorporates a scattering of Iberian antiques and architectural oddities into its modernized decor. Built in the 1970s, it was last renovated in 1994. Several of the sitting rooms contain grandly vaulted ceilings and noble columns; others are efficiently tiled and streamlined, filled with contemporary leather-covered armchairs and chrome-and-glass tables. The guest rooms are cozy, conservative, and comfortable.

The hotel's dining room serves traditional Spanish as well as international cuisine at lunch and dinner. Bar service is available throughout the several lounges and sitting areas of the street level. There's also a late-night disco.

INEXPENSIVE

$ **Hotel España.** Paseo del Espolón, 32, 09003 Burgos. ☎ **947/20-63-40.** Fax 947/20-13-30. 69 rms. TV TEL. 8,000 ptas. ($64) double; 10,000 ptas. ($80) triple. MC, V. Closed Dec 20–Jan 20.

The best budget choice in town lies a five-minute walk southeast of the cathedral and a block south of Plaza Mayor, on a leafy promenade filled with sidewalk cafés and Castilians taking early-evening strolls. The guest rooms lack style and imagination but are completely comfortable nonetheless. The management is helpful to visitors. When the España is full, they have been known to call other hostelries for stranded tourists.

Hotel Norte y Londres. Plaza de Alonso Martínez, 10, 09003 Burgos. ☎ **947/26-41-25.** Fax 947/27-73-75. 50 rms. TV TEL. 8,500 ptas. ($68) double. AE, MC, V. Parking 1,000 ptas. ($8).

On a pleasant square a short walk northeast of the cathedral, this hotel has traces of faded grandeur with its leaded stained-glass windows, and crystal chandeliers. The building dates from the dawn of the 20th century; it was converted into a hotel in the 1950s and has flourished ever since. Bedrooms are of good size, with basic furnishings, and the large bathrooms come equipped with yesterday's finest plumbing. Breakfast is the only meal served.

WHERE TO DINE

The restaurants in the heart of Burgos—surrounding the cathedral—usually feature prices that soar as high as a Gothic spire. Every menu contains the roast lamb and suckling pig known throughout the area, or you might order *entremeses variados,* an appetizer sampler of many regional specialties.

Casa Ojeda. Vitoria, 5. ☎ **947/20-90-52.** Reservations required. Main courses 1,800–3,000 ptas. ($14.40–$24). AE, DC, MC, V. Daily 1:15–4:30pm, Mon–Sat 9–11:30pm. BURGALESE.

This top-notch restaurant combines excellent Burgalese fare, cozy decor, attentive service, and moderate prices. Moorish tiles and low ceilings set an inviting ambience that's enhanced by intimate nooks, old lanterns and fixtures, and intricate trelliswork.

Upstairs the restaurant divides into two sections: one overlooking the street and the other, the Casa del Cordón, where Ferdinand and Isabella received Columbus after his second trip to America (1497). The cookery is the best in town. À la carte dishes include roast lamb, Basque-style hake, sole Harlequin, and chicken in garlic. A house specialty is *alubias con chorizo y mirocilla* (small white beans with spicy sausages).

Mesón del Cid. Plaza de Santa María, 8. ☎ **947/20-87-15.** Reservations required. Main courses 1,100–2,100 ptas. ($8.80–$16.80); fixed-price menu 3,500 ptas. ($28). AE, DC, MC, V. Daily noon–4pm, Mon–Sat 8pm–midnight. CASTILIAN.

Once the 15th-century private home of the most powerful regional lords, today the Mesón del Cid is a restaurant serving delicious specialties. Menu selections, always fresh, are prepared according to regional traditions. You might be tempted by one of the shellfish soups, roast baby lamb with aromatic herbs, roasted stuffed peppers, the fresh fish brought in daily, or a pork, veal, or chicken dish. Try codfish house style. The restaurant lies on the square flanking the main entrance of the cathedral.

Mesón de los Infantes. Avenida Generalísimo, 2. ☎ **947/20-59-82.** Reservations recommended. Main courses 900–2,800 ptas. ($7.20–$22.40); fixed-price menu 1,800 ptas. ($14.40). AE, DC, MC, V. Daily noon–4:30pm and 8pm–midnight. CASTILIAN/BASQUE.

Just below the gate leading into the Plaza de Santa María, this restaurant serves good food amid elegant Castilian decor. Many of the chef's specialties are based on recipes in use in Castile for centuries. The roast suckling pig is everybody's favorite, and you can also order *cocido madrileño,* assorted shellfish, river crabs Burgalese style, and beef tail with potatoes. Kidneys are sautéed in sherry, and a wide list of game is often featured, including hare, partridge, rabbit, and pigeon. Grills and roasts are also crowd-pleasers.

Rincón de España. Nuño Rasura, 11. ☎ **947/20-59-55.** Reservations required. Main courses 1,200–2,500 ptas. ($9.60–$20); fixed-price menus 1,500–3,000 ptas. ($12–$24). AE, DC, MC, V. Daily 1–4pm and 8pm–midnight; closed Tues in winter. SPANISH.

This restaurant, about one block southwest of the cathedral, draws many discerning visitors. You can eat in a rustic dining room or outdoors under a large awning closed off by glass when the weather threatens. The restaurant offers *platos combinados,* as well as a more extensive à la carte menu. Some special dishes include black pudding sausage from Burgos with peppers, barbecued lamb cutlets with potatoes, and roast chicken with sweet peppers. The food here is good, the portions are large, and the vegetables are fresh.

AN EASY SIDE TRIP TO SANTO DOMINGO DE LA CALZADA

Some 42 miles (67.5km) east of Burgos, and easily visited on a day trip, lies Santo Domingo de la Calzada. The crowning achievement of the town, which grew as a stopover for pilgrims en route to Santiago de Compostela, is the 13th-century **cathedral,** a national landmark. For the most part Gothic in style, it nevertheless contains a hodgepodge of architectural elements—Romanesque chapels, a Renaissance choir, and a freestanding baroque tower. St. Dominic, for whom the city is named, is buried in the crypt. A centuries-old legend is attached to the cathedral: Supposedly a rooster stood up and crowed after it had been cooked to protest the innocence of a pilgrim who had been accused of theft and sentenced to hang. To this day, a live cock and hen are kept in a cage up on the church wall, and you can often hear the rooster crowing at mass. The cathedral is open daily from 9am to 2pm and 4 to 8:30pm. Motorists can reach Santo Domingo de la Calzada by following either of the traffic arteries paralleling the river, heading east from Burgos Cathedral until signs indicate N-120.

8

Extremadura

The westernmost region of Spain has always been known as "the land beyond the River Douro," evoking how remote it is. It extends from the Gredos and Gata mountain ranges all the way to Andalusia and from Castile to the Portuguese frontier. An area with a varied landscape, it has both plains and mountains, meadows with holm and cork oaks, and fields of stone and lime. Extremadura (not to be confused with the Portuguese province of Estremadura) includes the provinces of Badajoz and Cáceres.

Ancient civilizations were established here, including those of the Celts, Romans, and Visigoths, but the world knows Extremadura best as the land of the conquistadors. Famous sons included Cortés, Pizarro, Balboa, and many others less well known but also important, such as Francisco de Orellana and Hernando de Soto. Many of these men were driven from their homeland by economic necessity, finding it hard to make a living in this dry, sun-parched province. Some sent back money to their native land to finance the building of mansions and public structures that stand today as monuments to their long-ago adventures in the Americas.

Many of Extremadura's previous conquerors have left enduring monuments as well, including, for example, the Roman ruins in Mérida. Arab ruins are found in Badajoz, and medieval palaces stand in Cáceres.

A number of Spaniards come here to hunt. Fishing and water sports are also popular in the many reservoirs in the region. Horseback riding along ancient trails is another pastime. Because summer is intensely hot here, spring and fall are the best times to visit.

EXPLORING THE REGION BY CAR

The itinerary below assumes that you'll start in Madrid or Toledo, driving southwest.

Day 1 Head for Guadalupe, which can be your overnight stopover. It was here that Columbus showed up in 1496 with two American Indian servants dressed in feathered costumes. He wanted to have them baptized. Visit its Real Monasterio de Santa María de Guadalupe, which is filled with artistic treasures, and try to spend the night at Parador Nacional Zurbarán.

Day 2 After a final look in the morning at Guadalupe, journey west to Trujillo, birthplace of Francisco Pizarro, the conqueror of

Extremadura

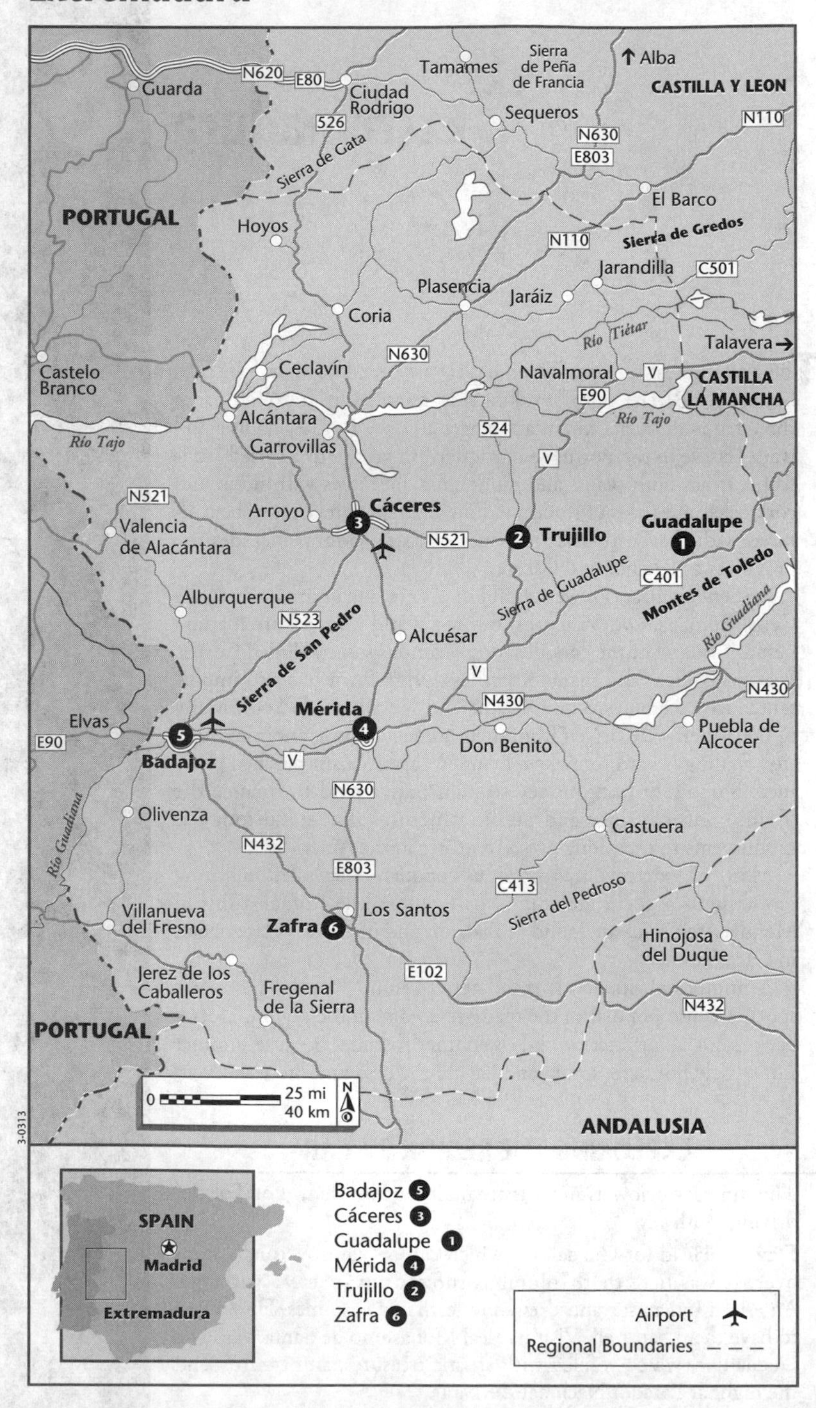

Tamames
Sierra de Peña de Francia
Alba
CASTILLA Y LEON
Guarda
N620
E80
Ciudad Rodrigo
526
Sequeros
N630
E803
N110
Sierra de Gata
El Barco
PORTUGAL
Hoyos
N110
Sierra de Gredos
Jarandilla
C501
Plasencia
Jaráiz
Coria
Río Tiétar
Talavera
N630
Castelo Branco
Ceclavín
Navalmoral
V
CASTILLA LA MANCHA
E90
Alcántara
Río Tajo
524
Río Tajo
Garrovillas
V
N521
Cáceres
Arroyo
Guadalupe
Valencia de Alacántara
N521
Trujillo
C401
Sierra de Guadalupe
Montes de Toledo
Alburquerque
N523
Sierra de San Pedro
Alcuésar
Río Guadiana
V
N430
N430
Elvas
Mérida
Puebla de Alcocer
E90
Badajoz
Don Benito
V
N630
Olivenza
Río Guadiana
N432
Castuera
E803
C413
Sierra del Pedroso
Villanueva del Fresno
Los Santos
Zafra
Hinojosa del Duque
Jerez de los Caballeros
E102
Fregenal de la Sierra
N432
PORTUGAL
0
25 mi
40 km
N
ANDALUSIA
3-0313
SPAIN
Madrid
Extremadura
Badajoz 5
Cáceres 3
Guadalupe 1
Mérida 4
Trujillo 2
Zafra 6
Airport
Regional Boundaries

Land of the Conquistadors

It's estimated that some 15,000 Extremeños (from a total population of 400,000) went to seek gold in the New World. The most fabled of these adventurers were Hernán Cortés (from Medellín) in Mexico; Francisco Pizarro (from Trujillo) in Peru; Vasco Núñez de Balboa (from Jerez de los Caballeros) in Panama, from where he first sighted the Pacific Ocean; Hernando de Soto (from Barcarrota) in Florida, proceeding on to discover the Mississippi River; and Francisco Orellana (from Trujillo) in Ecuador and the Amazon.

Because of the conquistadors, the names of Extremaduran villages are sprinkled through the Americas, as exemplified by the Guadalupe Mountains (Texas), Albuquerque (New Mexico), Trujillo (Peru), Mérida (Mexico), and Medellín (Colombia).

Because Extremeños faced such a hard time making a living from the harsh land of their ancestry, they often turned elsewhere for their fortune. One of the reasons for the poverty is that even today huge ranches are owned by absentee landlords. These ranches are called *latifundios,* and often farmers and their families live on these ranches, paying the owners for the privilege of grazing a few goats or growing some foodstuff in the dry climate. A system of *mayorazgo* (still in effect) granted all the family property to the eldest son. The other sons—called *secundinos*—were left penniless, and often set sail for the New World to seek their gold.

Many of the conquistadors died or else stayed in the New World, but others who had grown rich there returned to the land of their birth and built magnificent homes, villas, and ranches, many of which still stand today.

The situation was put very bluntly by Bernal Díaz, who joined the Cortés expedition to Mexico. "We came here to serve God and the king," he wrote, "and to get rich."

Peru. The town looks like one time forgot, and you can spend a whole day here wandering around making discoveries on your own, but be sure to visit the Plaza Mayor in the heart of Trujillo, with its seignorial mansions. A statue of Pizarro, a twin to one in Lima, stands here. Opt for a room for the night at the Parador Nacional de Trujillo.

Day 3 Make the short drive west from Trujillo to Cáceres. You'll want to check into a hotel since, as one of the best-preserved walled cities in Spain, Cáceres will take a day or more to explore. It's also home to Gothic and Renaissance seignorial mansions unequaled in all of Spain. This city was mentioned in guidebooks back in the 18th century, and it's been declared a Spanish National Monument. UNESCO has added it to its World Heritage Sites. It will be your most rewarding stopover in Extremadura.

Day 4 Drive south to Mérida, where you'll find Spain's best Roman ruins in a town established in 25 B.C. In time this town became Emerita Augusta, the capital of the vast province of Lusitania, covering much of Iberia. Approaching the city you'll see the long Roman bridge constructed to span two forks of the Guadiana River. Mérida's showpiece, however, is the 6,000-seat Roman theater at the eastern edge of town. Classical Greek and Latin dramas are performed in the theater in late June and early July. Also be sure to visit the Museo Nacional de Arte Romano, which houses the best collection of Roman artifacts in Spain and the town's Roman amphitheater, which dates from the 1st century B.C. and was once flooded for "sea battles." Consider an overnight at Parador Vía de la Plata.

Day 5 Those with a day to spare can head south now to the town of Zafra for an afternoon's exploration and then an overnight stopover in Parador Hernán Cortés. White-walled Zafra, the largest city in southern Extremadura, has such an Andalusian feeling it's often called "Little Seville."

Day 6 Either continue southeast to Córdoba and the attractions of Andalusia or make for the border town of Badajoz, crossing into Portugal and driving toward the sights of Lisbon.

1 Guadalupe

117 miles (188km) W of Toledo, 140 miles (225km) SW of Madrid

Guadalupe lies in the province of Cáceres, 1,500 feet above sea level. The village has a certain beauty and much local color. Everything of interest lies within a three-minute walk from the point where buses deposit you, at Avenida Don Blas Perez, also known as Carretera de Cáceres.

Around the corner and a few paces downhill is the Plaza Mayor, which contains the Town Hall (which is where many visitors go to ask questions in lieu of a tourist office).

The village is best visited in spring, when the balconies of its whitewashed houses burst into bloom with flowers. Wander at your leisure through the twisting, narrow streets, some no more than alleyways. The buildings are so close together that in summer you can walk in the shade of the steeply pitched sienna-colored tile roofs. Celebrated for its shrine to the Virgin, Guadalupe is viewed by the religious-souvenir industry as a major outlet.

GETTING THERE **By Bus** There are two buses every day to and from Madrid's Estación Sur, a three-hour ride away. The road is poor, but the route through the surrounding regions is savagely beautiful. In Guadalupe, the buses park on either side of the street, a few paces uphill from the Town Hall. Phone Empresa Doalde in Madrid (☎ **91/468-76-80**) for schedules. A one-way ticket from Madrid to Guadalupe is 1,860 pesetas ($14.90).

By Car One narrow highway goes through Guadalupe. Most maps don't give it a number; look on a map in the direction of the town of Navalmoral de la Mata. From Madrid, take the narrow, winding C-401 southwest from Toledo, turning north in the direction of Navalmoral de la Mata after seeing signs for Navalmoral de la Mata and Guadalupe. Driving time from Madrid is between 3½ and 4½ hours, depending on how well you fare with the bad roads.

SEEING THE MONASTERY

✪ **Real de Santa María de Guadalupe.** Plaza de Juan Carlos, 1. ☎ **927/36-70-00.** Admission to museum and sacristy, 300 ptas. ($2.40) adults, 100 ptas. (80¢) children 7–14, free for children 6 and under. Daily 9:30am–1pm and 3:30–6pm.

In 1325 a farmer searching for a stray cow reportedly spotted a statue of the Virgin in the soil. In time, this statue became venerated throughout the world, honored in Spain by Isabella, Columbus, and Cervantes. Known as the Dark Virgin of Guadalupe, it is said to have been carved by St. Luke. A shrine was commissioned by Alfonso XI to commemorate the statue, and tributes poured in from all over the world, making Guadalupe one of the wealthiest foundations in Christendom. Though the building was abandoned in 1835, it was restored by the Franciscans beginning in 1908. You can see the Virgin in a small alcove above the altar.

The church is noted for the wrought-iron railings in its naves. Be sure to see the museum devoted to ecclesiastical vestments and to the choir books produced by 16th-century miniaturists. In the magnificently decorated sacristy are eight richly imaginative 17th-century masterpieces by Zurbarán. The 16th-century Gothic cloister is flamboyant, with two galleries. The pièce de résistance is the stunning Mudéjar cloister, with its brick-and-tile Gothic-Mudéjar shrine dating from 1405; the Moorish fountain is from the 14th century.

WHERE TO STAY

Hospedería Real Monasterio. Plaza Juan Carlos, 1, 10140 Guadalupe. ☎ **927/36-70-00.** Fax 927/36-71-77. 46 rms, 1 suite. A/C TEL. 6,900 ptas. ($55.20) double; 9,300 ptas. ($74.40) triple; 10,900 ptas. ($87.20) quad; 15,750 ptas. ($126) suite. MC, V. Closed Jan 12–Feb 12.

Once a way station for pilgrims visiting the shrine, the Hospedería used to provide lodging for a small donation. Times have changed, but the prices remain moderate at this two-star hotel in the center of town, which is the second best place to stay in town after the parador. Some of the guest rooms contain high-vaulted ceilings. There is a bar. The regional meals served in the restaurant are generally good. Top it off with a home-brewed *licor de Guadalupe.*

✪ **Parador Nacional Zurbarán.** Marqués de la Romana, 12, 10140 Guadalupe. ☎ **927/36-70-75.** Fax 927/36-70-76. 39 rms, 1 suite. A/C MINIBAR TV TEL. 12,500 ptas. ($100) double; 13,500 ptas. ($108) suite. AE, DC, MC, V. Parking 700 ptas. ($5.60).

Located in a scenic spot in the center of the village, the area's most luxurious accommodation is housed in a 16th-century building with a beautiful garden. Queen Isabella once stayed here, and the place often saw meetings between royal representatives and explorers, who signed their contracts here before setting out for the New World. The house is named after Francisco de Zurbarán, the great 17th-century painter who was born in the nearby town of Fuente de Cantos. There is a Zurbarán painting in one of the salons, along with ancient maps and engravings—many of them valuable works of art. Bedrooms are comfortable and partially decorated with reproduction medieval furnishings. The attractive restaurant serves good regional food, both lunch and dinner. Try such local dishes as herb-flavored roast kid or pork Mudéjar style. The facilities include a swimming pool, bar, garage, and tennis court.

WHERE TO DINE

Both of the hotels recommended above also have good restaurants.

$ **Mesón el Cordero.** Alfonso Onceno, 27. ☎ **927/36-71-31.** Reservations recommended. Main courses 1,450–1,950 ptas. ($11.60–$15.60); fixed-price menu 1,900 ptas. ($15.20). DC, MC, V. Tues–Sun 1–4pm and 7–11pm. Closed Feb 1–15. SPANISH.

Miguel and Angelita run Guadalupe's best independent restaurant, named for their specialty, *asado de cordero* (roast lamb flavored with garlic and thyme). The couple has operated this restaurant for 20 years and enjoy a devoted local following, which is recommendation enough. You might begin with another of their specialties, *sopas guadalupanas,* then follow with partridge "from the countryside" if you have a taste for game. The house dessert is a creamy custard, *flan casero.*

2 Trujillo

152 miles (245km) SW of Madrid, 28 miles (45km) E of Cáceres

Dating from the 13th century, the walled town of Trujillo is celebrated for the colonizers and conquerors born here. Among the illustrious natives were Francisco

Pizarro, conqueror of Peru, whose family palace on Plaza Mayor was built with gold from the New World, and Francisco de Orellana, the founder of Guayaquil, Equador and the first European to explore the Amazon. Other Trujillano history makers were Francisco de las Casas, who accompanied Hernán Cortés in his conquest of Mexico and founded the city of Trujillo in Honduras; Diego García de Paredes, who founded Trujillo in Venezuela; Nuño de Chaves, founder of Santa Cruz de la Sierra in Bolivia; and several hundred others whose names are found throughout maps of North, Central, and South America. There is a saying that 20 American countries were "born" here.

Celts, Romans, Moors, and Christians have inhabited Trujillo. The original town, lying above today's modern one, was built on a granite ledge on the hillside. It is centered around the Plaza Mayor, one of the artistic landmarks of Spain. A Moorish castle and a variety of 16th- and 17th-century palaces, manor houses, towers, churches, and arcades encircle the plaza and overlook a bronze equestrian statue of Pizarro by American artists Mary Harriman and Charles Runse. Steep, narrow streets and shadowy little corners evoke bygone times when explorers set out from here on their history-making adventures.

GETTING THERE **By Bus** There are nine buses per day to and from Madrid (trip time: 3½ or 4½ hours, depending on whether it's local or *expreso*). There are also six buses running daily from Cáceres, 45 minutes away, and six from Badajoz. A one-way ticket from Madrid to Trujillo costs 1,980 pesetas ($15.85); from Cárceres, 395 pesetas ($3.15); and from Badajoz, 1,210 pesetas ($9.70). Trujillo's bus station, Calle Marqués Albayda (☎ **927/32-12-02**), lies in the south part of town on a side street that intersects with Calle de la Encarnación.

By Car Trujillo lies at a network of large and small roads connecting it to Cáceres, via the N-521, and both Lisbon and Madrid, via the N-V superhighway. Driving time from Madrid is around four hours.

VISITOR INFORMATION The tourist information office is at Plaza Mayor (☎ **927/32-26-77**). Open April through October daily from 9am to 2pm and 5 to 7pm; off-season daily from 9am to 2pm and 4 to 6pm.

EXPLORING THE PLAZA AND BEYOND

✪ Plaza Mayor

The heart of Trujillo, this is one of the outstanding architectural sights in Extremadura. It is dominated by a statue honoring Francisco Pizarro, who almost single-handedly destroyed the Inca civilization of Peru. The statue is an exact double of one standing in Lima. Many of the buildings on this square were financed with wealth brought back from the New World.

The most prominent structure on the square is the **Ayuntamiento Viejo** (Old Town Hall), with three tiers of arches, each tier squatter than the one below.

The **Iglesia de San Martín** stands behind the statue dedicated to Pizarro. This granite church, originally from the 15th century, was reconstructed in the 16th century in Renaissance style. Inside are an impressive nave, several tombs, and a rare 18th-century organ that's still in working condition.

While you are on the square, observe the unusual facade of the **Casa de las Cadenas,** a 12th-century house across which a heavy chain is draped. This was a symbol that Philip II had granted the Orellana family immunity from heavy taxes.

You can then visit the **Palacio de los Duques de San Carlos,** a 16th-century ducal residence turned into a convent. Ring the bell to gain entry any time daily from 9am to 1pm and 3 to 7pm. A donation of at least 100 pesetas (80¢) is appreciated, and a resident will show you around; appropriate dress (no shorts or bare shoulders) is required. The facade has Renaissance sculptured figures, and the two-level courtyard inside is even more impressive.

The **Palacio de la Conquista,** also on the square, is one of the most grandiose mansions in Trujillo. Originally constructed by Hernán Pizarro, the present structure was built by his son-in-law to commemorate the exploits of this explorer, who accompanied his half-brother, Francisco, to Peru.

Iglesia de Santa María. Calle de Ballesteros. No phone. Admission 100 ptas. (80¢). Mon–Sat 9am–2pm and 4–7:30pm; on Sun, mass held at 11am.

This Gothic building is the largest church in Trujillo, having been built over the ruins of a Moorish mosque. Ferdinand and Isabella once attended mass in this church, with its outstanding Renaissance choir. Its proudest treasure is a *retablo* with two dozen panels painted by Fernando Gallego (seen at the altar). Also here is the tomb of Diego García de Paredes, the "Samson of Extremadura," who is said to have single-handedly defended a bridge against an attacking French army with only a gigantic sword. To reach the church, go through one of the gates at Plaza Mayor, Puerta de San Andrés, and take Calle de las Palomas through the old town.

Castillo. Crowning the hilltop. Free admission. Dawn to dusk; many visitors find it most dramatic at sunset.

Constructed by the Arabs on the site of a Roman fortress, the castle stands at the summit of the granite hill on which Trujillo was founded. Once at the castle, you can climb its battlements and walk along the ramparts, enjoying a panoramic view of the austere countryside of Extremadura. Later, you can go below and see the dungeons. It is said that the Virgin Mary appeared here in 1232, giving the Christians renewed courage to free the city from Arab domination.

WHERE TO STAY

Las Cigüeñas. Avenida de Madrid, s/n, Carretera N-V, 10200 Trujillo. ☎ **927/32-12-50.** Fax 927/32-13-00. 75 rms, 3 suites. A/C MINIBAR TV TEL. 9,600 ptas. ($76.80) double; 12,000 ptas. ($96) suite. AE, DC, MC, V. Free parking.

Located just east of the town center, and well suited to motorists, this is the second best place to stay in Trujillo. It doesn't have the charm of the parador (see below), but it's definitely cheaper. The hotel was built in two different sections in 1971, with a major enlargement in 1983. A roadside hotel with a garden, it offers functional but clean and comfortable bedrooms. Its restaurant specializes in regional cuisine. There is also a bar. You'll find Las Cigüeñas on the main highway from Madrid, about a mile before Trujillo.

✪ **Parador Nacional de Trujillo.** Calle de Santa Beatriz de Silva, 10200 Trujillo. ☎ **927/32-13-50.** Fax 927/32-13-66. 44 rms, 1 suite. A/C MINIBAR TV TEL. 15,000 ptas. ($120) double; 18,500 ptas. ($148) suite. AE, DC, MC, V.

Housed in the 1533 Convent of Santa Clara, this centrally located parador, about one block south of Avenida de la Coronación, is a gem of Trujillo-style medieval and Renaissance architecture that's now faithfully restored. It was converted into a parador in 1984. The beautifully decorated guest rooms, once nuns' cells, have canopied beds and spacious marble baths. The gardens and fruit trees of the Renaissance cloister are inviting, and there is a swimming pool in the courtyard of a new section that blends with the original convent architecture. You can have breakfast in the old refectory and dinner in what was once a long, vaulted chapel. Try the *caldereta extremeña,* a stew made with baby lamb or baby goat.

WHERE TO DINE

Both hotels recommended above also have good restaurants serving regional cuisine.

Ⓢ Mesón la Troya. Plaza Mayor, 10. ☎ **927/32-13-64.** Reservations recommended. Fixed-price menu 1,900 ptas. ($15.20). MC, V. Daily 1–4:30pm and 9–11:30pm. EXTREMADURAN.

Locals and visitors alike are drawn to this centrally located restaurant featuring the regional cuisine of Extremadura—and doing the province proud. Have a dry sherry in the bar, which was designed to resemble the facade of a Spanish house. This cozy provincial theme also flows into the dining rooms, with their white walls (decorated with ceramic plates), potted plants, and red tiles. Few people leave hungry after devouring the set menu, with its more than ample portions; food items change daily. Local dishes include *prueba de cerdo* (garlic-flavored pork casserole) and *carne con tomate* (beef cooked in tomato sauce). A table is always reserved for the village priest, who comes here for breakfast, lunch, and dinner and has done so for 20 years.

Ⓢ Pizarro. Plaza Mayor, 13. ☎ **927/32-02-55.** Reservations recommended. Main courses 900–1,650 ptas. ($7.20–$13.20); *menú del día* 1,300 ptas. ($10.40). AE, DC, MC, V. Wed–Sun 1:30–4pm and 8:30–10:30pm. EXTREMADURAN.

Locals cite this centrally located hostal as the best place to go for regional-style Extremaduran cookery. The same family has owned and operated the place since 1919. Built in 1864, the inn is set on the town's main square and named for its famous son. Regional wines accompany meals that invariably include ham from acorn-fed pigs. You might begin with asparagus with mayonnaise sauce, then follow with *asado de cordero* (roast lamb flavored with herbs and garlic) or Roman-style fried *merluza* (hake). The kitchen's game specialty is *estofado de perdices* (partridge casserole).

3 Cáceres

185 miles (298km) SW of Madrid, 159 miles (256km) N of Seville

A national landmark and the capital of Extremadura, Cáceres is encircled by old city walls and has several seignorial palaces and towers, many financed by gold sent from the Americas by the conquistadors. Allow about two hours to explore the city center.

One of six cities in Spain designated as World Heritage Sites by UNESCO, Cáceres was founded in the 1st century B.C. by the Romans, as "Norba Caesarina," but its present-day name is derived from *Alcazares,* meaning fortified citadel. After the Romans, it was settled by all cultures that have made the south of Spain the unique cultural melting pot of native, Western, and Eastern influences it is today. The contemporary city offers a unique blend of the traces these successive invaders left behind.

On a casual stroll through the city's cobblestone streets, your attention will surely be drawn at first to the massive walls that enclose the old, upper town. These are a mixture of Roman and Arab engineering, and their state of preservation is excellent. The next likely eye-catcher is the Plaza Mayor. It is remarkably free from most of the blemishes and scarring effects that city planning and overregulation have made so common in other historically important sites. Passing through El Arco de la Estrella (Arch of the Star), you will then catch the most advantageous angle of Santa María Cathedral, a fine example of 15th-century ecclesiastic Gothic style. Cuesta dela Compañía street leads to San Mateo Square and to two adjoining *plazuelas,* which embody the old flavor of Cáceres. At the first of these, Las Veletas, is the Archaeological Museum, where some priceless prehistoric and Roman pieces are housed, as well as the famous *Aljibe* (Arab well). At the second, San Pablo, is the Casa de las Cigüeñas (storks), the only palace whose tower is intact, despite an order by Queen Isabella at the turn of the 15th century to reduce the height of all such strategic locations for military reasons.

An unusual and suggestive trait of the city is the large number of storks that can be found nesting on most of the rooftops and bell towers in the town. This is a revealing sign of how Cáceres has managed to preserve not only its landmarks but also an environmentally sound balance between people and nature. The contemporary city has kept up with the times and its inhabitants are a hospitable and lively people who proudly relish a bustling nightlife which, like their Plaza Mayor, goes quite undisturbed by city hall.

GETTING THERE **By Train** Cáceres has the best rail connections in the province, with seven trains per day from Madrid. Trip time ranges from 4 to 5 hours, and a one-way ticket costs from 2,065 to 3,400 pesetas ($16.50–$27.20). There is also one train per day from Lisbon; the trip time is 4½ hours and a one-way fare is 3,100 pesetas ($24.80). One train per day also runs from Seville, taking 4 hours and costing 1,940 pesetas ($15.50). The station in Cáceres is on Avenida Alemania (☎ **927/22-50-61**), near the main highway heading south (Carretera de Sevilla). A green-and-white bus shuttles passengers about once an hour from the railway and bus stations (across the street from one another; board the shuttle outside the bus station) to the busiest traffic junction in the new city, Plaza de América. From there it's a 10 minute walk to the edge of the old town.

By Bus Bus connections are more frequent than train connections. From the city bus station, on the busy Carretera de Sevilla (☎ **927/23-25-50**), buses arrive and depart 8 to 12 times a day for Madrid and Seville (5 and 4½ hours, respectively). Other buses travel between two and five times a day to and from Guadalupe, Trujillo, Mérida, Valladolid, Córdoba, and Salamanca. For information on reaching the new town from the bus station, see "By Train," above.

By Car Driving time from Madrid is about five hours. Most motorists approach Cáceres from eastern Spain via the N-V superhighway until they reach Trujillo. There, they exit onto the N-521, driving another 28 miles (45km) west to Cáceres.

VISITOR INFORMATION The tourist information office is on Plaza Mayor (☎ **927/24-63-47**). Open Monday through Friday from 9am to 2pm and 4 to 6pm, Saturday and Sunday from 9:30am to 2pm.

EXPLORING THE OLD CITY

The modern city lies southwest of *barrio antiguo,* **Cáceres Viejo,** which is enclosed by ramparts. The heart of the old city lies between **Plaza de Santa María** and, a few blocks to the south, **Plaza San Mateo.** Plaza Santa María, an irregularly shaped, rather elongated square, is one of the major sights. On each of its sides are the honey-brown facades of buildings once inhabited by the nobility.

On the far side of the square rises the **Catedral de Santa María,** which is basically Gothic in architecture, although many Renaissance embellishments were added. Completed some time in the 1500s, this church is the cathedral of Cáceres, and it contains the remains of many of the conquistadors. It has three Gothic aisles of almost equal height. Look at the carved retable at the high altar, dating from the 16th century. (Insert coins to light it up.)

About 30 towers from the city's medieval walls remain, all of them heavily restored. Originally much taller, the towers reflected the pride and independence of their builders; when Queen Isabella took over, however, she ordered them "cut down to size."

The largest tower is at **Plaza del General Mola.** Beside it stands the **Estrella Arco (Star Arch),** constructed by Manuel Churriguera in the 18th century. To its right you'll see the **Torre del Horno,** a mud-brick adobe structure left from the Moorish occupation.

At the highest point of the old city and near its center is the 14th-century **Iglesia de San Mateo** (St. Matthew), which has a plateresque portal and a rather plain nave (except for the plateresque tombs, which add a decorative touch). The church lies at the edge of Plaza San Mateo.

Next to it stands the **Casa de las Cigüeñas (Storks' House),** dating from the late 15th century. Its slender tower is all that remains of the battlements. The building now serves as a military headquarters and is not open to the public.

The **Church of Santiago** was begun in the 12th century and restored in the 16th century. It possesses a reredos carved in 1557 by Alonso de Berruguete and a 15th-century figure of Christ. The church lies outside the ramparts, about a block to the north of Arco de Socorro (Socorro East Gate). To reach it, exit the gate, enter Plaza Socorro, then walk down Calle Godoy. The Church of Santiago is on your right.

La Casa de los Toledo-Montezuma was built by Juan Cano de Saavedra with money from the dowry of his wife, the daughter of Montezuma. The house is set into the northern corner of the medieval ramparts, about a block to the north of Plaza de Santa María.

On the site of the old Alcázar is the **Casa de las Veletas (Weather Vane House),** Plaza de las Veletas (☎ **927/24-72-34**), which houses a provincial archaeological museum. Its baroque facade, ancient Moorish cistern, five naves and horseshoe arches, and patio and paneling from the 17th century have been preserved. The museum displays Celtic and Visigothic remains, Roman and Gothic artifacts, and a numismatic collection. Admission is 200 ptas. ($1.60), and the museum is open Tuesday to Saturday from 9:30am–2:30pm, and Sunday from 10:15am to 2:30pm.

WHERE TO STAY

Hotel Alcántara. Virgen de Guadalupe, 14, 10001 Cáceres. ☎ **927/22-89-00.** Fax 927/22-39-04. 66 rms, 3 suites. A/C MINIBAR TV TEL. 11,100 ptas. ($88.80) double; 16,000 ptas. ($128) suite. AE, DC, MC, V. Parking 800 ptas. ($6.40).

Located in the commercial center of town, this seven-story blandly modern building opened in 1966 and has been renovated at least twice since. Nevertheless, its heyday has long past. (Try first for the Extremadura across the street, which has superior rooms.) It is convenient for exploring the old town. Guest rooms are comfortably furnished and well maintained. The hotel restaurant serves a traditional *menú del día.*

Hotel Extremadura. Avenida Virgen de Guadalupe, 5, 10001 Cáceres. ☎ **927/22-16-00.** Fax 927/21-10-95. 64 rms, 4 suites. A/C TV TEL. 8,900 ptas. ($71.20) double; 14,900 ptas. ($119.20) suite. AE, DC, MC, V. Free parking.

Angular but comfortable, this clean and uncomplicated 1960s hotel offers some of the most straightforward accommodations in town. Located about half a mile southwest of the historic center, in a bustling commercial district, it offers air-conditioned relief from the heat, as well as a much-appreciated swimming pool. Prices are fair for what you get. The hotel's restaurant, Alazán, serves Spanish and international food. There is also a bar.

Services: Room service (available from 7am to midnight), laundry, concierge.

Facilities: Outdoor swimming pool, in-house tour operator/travel agent, car rentals.

✪ **Meliá Cáceres.** Plaza San Juan, 11, 10003 Cáceres. ☎ **927/21-58-00.** Fax 927/21-40-70. 86 rms. A/C TV TEL. 16,500 ptas. ($132) double. AE, DC, MC, V.

The Meliá hotel chain continues to show up the government parador system by opening superior lodgings in towns long dominated by a parador. Although the Parador de Cáceres is fine in every way, the Meliá is superior—both in service and amenities. This converted Renaissance palace is located just south of the Plaza del Géneral Mola, by the entrance to the old town. Its bedrooms are better appointed, sunnier, and more spacious than those at the parador. Everything is tastefully converted, and there's lots of exposed stone, along with indirect lighting and sleek modern furnishings. The cuisine is also superior to that at the parador; you get international dishes along with some of the better regional specialties of the Extremadura plain.

Parador de Cáceres. Calle Ancha, 6, 10001 Cáceres. ☎ **927/21-17-59.** Fax 927/21-17-29. 30 rms, 1 suite. A/C MINIBAR TV TEL. 15,000 ptas. ($120) double; 22,000 ptas. ($176) suite. AE, DC, MC, V. Free parking on streets.

This state-operated parador lies within what was originally conceived as a palace in the 15th century. Built in a severe, somewhat austere style, it enjoys a tranquil location and a well-scrubbed, durable format composed of exposed stone, white plaster, and tile or stone floors. Pristine white corridors lead to dignified bedrooms, outfitted in a starkly appealing combination of white walls and dark-grained, somewhat bulky furniture inspired by the unfussy decorative traditions of Extremadura. Suits of armor adorn some of the public areas, giving the place a vaguely feudal feel, but the patios that open onto masses of potted plants and flowers are quite welcoming. The restaurant serves a quite good regional cuisine. There's also a bar and cafeteria catering to general sightseers; it's open daily from 11:30am to 11:30pm and is the most convenient place in town to stop in for snacks at odd hours.

WHERE TO DINE

The gastronomic pleasures to be found at the parador and at many other places in Cáceres afford a novel experience to the most seasoned traveler. You may wish to try the famous *cuchifrito,* a suckling pig stewed in pepper, orange, and vinegar sauce, or the *caldereta de cordero,* lamb with pepper and almonds. A more daring choice would be *jabalí la carcereña,* a wild boar dish marinated in red wine and herbs. The most characteristic dessert of all of Extremadura is *técula mécula,* a very ancient example of the region's marzipan confectionery—which, like most things in Cáceres, has been passed down from one generation to the next for centuries.

✪ **Atrio.** Avenuda de España, 30. ☎ **927/24-29-28.** Reservations recommended. Main courses 1,800–2,600 ptas. ($14.40–$20.80). DC, MC, V. Daily 12:30–3pm, Mon–Sat 8pm–midnight. SPANISH/CONTINENTAL.

Atrio serves the finest cuisine in the province—not just in Cáceres. Even hard-to-please Michelin grants this place a star. It lies in a shopping mall cul-de-sac. On the inside, the decor is elegant and somewhat unusual for this part of Spain—all streamlined and sleek in white and sunflower yellow. The chef steers a skillful course between rich, regional flavors and continental fare. The menu changes frequently to take advantage of the best of the various seasons. Prices can go much higher than those indicated above if truffles are added to your dish. Service is the finest in the area—in all, it's a professional and deluxe operation that comes as a surprise in such a provincial city.

El Figón de Eustaquio. Plaza San Juan, 12. ☎ **927/24-81-94.** Reservations recommended. Main courses 1,000–2,600 ptas. ($8–$20.80); fixed-price menus 1,700–2,600 ptas. ($13.60–$20.80). AE, DC, MC, V. Daily 10am–4pm and 8pm–midnight. EXTREMADURAN.

El Figón, a pleasant place serving local Extremaduran cuisine, has been satisfying locals since 1948. You'll notice the four Blanco brothers who run the place doing practically everything. This includes preparing the amazingly varied dishes—for example, honey soup, *solomillo* (filet of beef), and trout Extremaduran style (covered in ham), as well as typical Spanish specialties. The air-conditioned interior has a rustic decor. El Figón lies west of the western ramparts of the old city, near the intersection of Avenida Virgen de Guadalupe and Plaza San Juan.

4 Mérida

44 miles (71km) S of Cáceres, 35 miles (56km) E of Badajoz

Mérida, known as Augusta Emerita when it was founded in 25 B.C., lay at the crossroads of the Roman roads linking Toledo and Lisbon and Salamanca and Seville. At one time the capital of Lusitania (the Latin name for the combined kingdoms of Spain and Portugal), Mérida was one of the most splendid cities in Iberia, ranking as a town of major importance in the Roman Empire; in fact, it was once called a miniature Rome. Its monuments, temples, and public works make it the site of some of the finest Roman ruins in Spain, and, as such, it is the tourist capital of Extremadura. Old Mérida can be covered on foot—in fact, that is the only way to see it. Pay scant attention to the dull modern suburb across the Guadiana River, which skirts the town with its sluggish waters.

GETTING THERE **By Train** Trains depart and arrive from the RENFE station on the Calle Cardero (☎ **924/31-81-09**), about half a mile north of the Plaza de España. Each day there are five trains to and from Cáceres (trip time: 1 hour), five trains to and from Madrid (4 hours), six to nine to and from Seville (3 hours), and eight to and from Badajoz (1 hour). On a regular train a one-way ticket from Madrid costs 2,700 pesetas ($21.60); on the faster TALGO train the one-way fare is 3,200 pesetas ($25.60)

By Bus The bus station is on Avenida de la Libertad (☎ **924/37-14-04**), close to the train station. Every day, there are nine buses to and from Madrid (5½ hours), six to nine to and from Seville (3 hours), five to and from Cáceres (2 hours), and eight to Badajoz (1 hour).

By Car Take the N-V superhighway from Madrid or Lisbon. Driving time from Madrid is approximately 5 hours; from Lisbon, about 4½ hours. Park in front of the Roman theater and explore the town on foot.

VISITOR INFORMATION The tourist information office is at Pedro María Plano (☎ **924/31-53-53**). Open April through October Monday through Friday from 9am to 1:45pm and 5 to 6:45pm, Saturday 9:15am to 1:45pm. Off-season hours are Monday through Friday from 9am to 2pm and 4 to 6pm, Saturday and Sunday from 9:15am to 1:45pm. Those are just the official hours—don't expect the staff to interpret them too literally.

SEEING THE SIGHTS

The **Roman bridge** over the Guadiana was the longest in Roman Spain—about half a mile—and consisted of 64 arches. It was constructed of granite under either Trajan or Augustus, then restored by the Visigoths in 686. Philip II ordered further refurbishment in 1610; work was also done in the 19th century. The bridge crosses the river south of the center of Old Mérida, its length increased because of the way it spans two forks of the river, including an island in midstream. In 1993 it was restored and turned into a pedestrian walkway. A semicircular suspension bridge for cars was constructed to carry the heavy traffic and save the bridge for future generations. Before the restoration and change, this bridge served as a main access road into Mérida, witnessing transportation evolve from hooves and feet to trucks and automobiles.

Another sight of interest is the old hippodrome, or **Circus Maximus,** which could seat about 30,000 spectators watching chariot races. The Roman masonry was carted off to use in other buildings, and today the site looks more like a parking lot. Excavations have uncovered rooms that may have housed gladiators. The site of the former circus lies at the end of Avenida Extremadura, on the northeastern outskirts of the old town, about half a mile north of the Roman bridge and a 10-minute walk east of the railway station.

The **Arco Trajano (Trajan's Arch)** lies near the heart of the Old Town, beside Calle Trajano, about a block south of the Parador Vía de la Plata. An unadorned triumphal arch, it measures 16 yards high and 10 yards across.

The **Acueducto de los Milagros** is the most intact of the town's two remaining Roman aqueducts, this one bringing water from Proserpina, three miles (5km) away. From the aqueducts, water was fed into two artificially created lakes, Cornalvo and Proserpina. The aqueduct is northwest of the old town, lying to the right of the road to Cáceres, just beyond the railway tracks. Ten arches still stand.

The latest monument to be excavated is the **Temple of Diana** (dedicated to Caesar Augustus). Squeezed between houses on a narrow residential street, it was converted in the 17th century into the private residence of a nobleman, who used four of the original Corinthian columns in his architectural plans. The temple lies at the junction of Calle Sagasta and Calle Romero Léal in the center of town.

While in the area, you can also explore the 13th-century **Iglesia de Santa María la Mayor,** Plaza de España. It has a 16th-century chapel and is graced with Romanesque and plateresque features. It stands on the west side of the square.

✪ **Teatro Romano.** José Ramón Melida, s/n. ☎ **924/31-25-30.** Admission 600 ptas. ($4.80) adults (includes admission to Anfiteatro Romano), free for children. Daily 9am–1:45pm and 5–6:45pm.

The Roman theater, one of the best-preserved Roman ruins in the world, was built by Agrippa (Augustus's son-in-law) in 18 B.C. to house an audience of 6,000 people. Modeled after the great theaters of Rome, it was constructed by dry-stone methods, a remarkable achievement. During the reign of Hadrian (2nd century A.D.), a tall stage wall was adorned with statues and colonnades. Behind the stage, visitors today can explore excavations of various rooms. From the end of June to early July, they can enjoy a season of classical plays.

Anfiteatro Romano. Calle José Ramón Melida, s/n. ☎ **924/31-25-30.** Admission included in Teatro Romano ticket (see above). Daily 9am–1:45pm and 5–6:45pm.

At the height of its glory, in the 1st century B.C., the amphitheater could seat 14,000 to 15,000 spectators. Chariot races were held here, along with gladiator combats and mock sea battles, for which the arena would be flooded. Many of the seats were placed dangerously close to the bloodshed. You can visit some of the rooms that housed the wild animals and gladiators waiting to go into combat.

✪ **Museo Nacional de Arte Romano.** Calle José Ramón Melida, s/n. ☎ **924/31-16-90.** Admission 400 ptas. ($3.20) adults, 200 ptas. ($1.60) students, free for children. Tues–Sat 10am–2pm and 5–7pm, Sun 10am–2pm.

Located in a modern building adjacent to the ancient Roman amphitheater, to which it is connected by an underground tunnel, this museum is acclaimed as the greatest repository of Roman artifacts left in Spain. Not only does it contain more than

30,000 artifacts from Augusta Emerita, capital of the Roman province of Lusitania, but it also incorporates part of a Roman road, discovered in the early 1980s during the construction of the building. Many of the museum's sculptures came from the excavations of the Roman theater and amphitheater. You'll see displays of mosaics, figures, pottery, glassware, coins, and bronze objects. The museum is built of red brick in the form of a Roman basilica.

Alcazaba. Plaza de España. ☎ **924/31-25-30.** Admission 300 ptas. ($2.40). Apr–Sept, Mon–Sat 9am–2pm and 5–7pm, Sun 9am–2pm; Oct–Mar, Mon 9am–1pm; Tues–Sat 9am–1pm and 3–6pm.

On the northern bank of the Guadiana River, beside the northern end of the Roman bridge (which it was meant to protect), stands the Alcázar, known as the Conventual or the Alcazaba. Built in the 9th century by the Moors, who used fragments left over from Roman and Visigothic occupations, the square structure was later granted to the Order of Santiago.

Museo Arqueológico de Arte Visigodo. Plaza de España. ☎ **924/31-16-90.** Free admission. June–Sept, Tues–Sat 10am–2pm and 5–7pm, Sun 10am–2pm; Oct–May, Tues–Sat 10am–2pm and 4–6pm, Sun 10am–2pm.

In front of Trajan's Arch is this archaeological museum, housing a treasure trove of artifacts left by the onetime-conquering Visigoths. Look for the two statues of Wild Men in one of the alcoves.

WHERE TO STAY

$ **Hotel Emperatriz.** Plaza de España, 19, 06800 Mérida. ☎ **924/31-31-11.** Fax 924/31-33-05. 43 rms, 2 suites. A/C TEL. 10,950 ptas. ($87.60) double; 11,700 ptas. ($93.60) suite. AE, MC, V.

A former 16th-century palace, the Emperatriz housed a long line of celebrated guests in its day, from Kings Philip II and III of Spain to Queen Isabella of Portugal and Charles V, the Holy Roman Emperor. Its intricate tiled gallery foyer is in the Moorish style. All the guest rooms are functionally furnished and comfortable, but try to get one facing the plaza for an unusual view of the occasional storks' nests built on the eaves and cornices of the surrounding buildings. Many of the rooms have grown seedy over the years, whereas others have been renovated (request one of the restored rooms). Late-night noise can be a problem.

The restaurant serves many intriguing Extremaduran specialties, including a soothing gazpacho made with white garlic and *tencas fritas* (fried tench), a typical fish of the region. Later you can visit the Emperatriz's nightclub and bar. A garden stands in the center of this good-value three-star hotel, located in the center of town, just north of the ruins of the Alcazaba.

Nova Roma. Súarez Somonte, 42, 06800 Mérida. ☎ **924/31-12-61.** Fax 924/30-01-60. 55 rms. A/C TV TEL. 10,450 ptas. ($83.60) double. AE, DC, MC, V. Parking 1,000 ptas. ($8).

Lacking the charm of the Parador Vía de la Plata (see below), the 1991 Nova Roma wins hands-down for those with more modern taste. Clean, comfortable, and functionally furnished, it is a good value for this heavily frequented tourist town. The hotel also runs a reasonably priced restaurant offering a *menú del día* with many regional dishes. The Nova Roma is west of the Teatro Romano and north of Plaza de Toros (bullring).

✪ Parador Vía de la Plata. Plaza de la Constitución, 3, 06800 Mérida. ☎ **924/31-38-00.** Fax 924/31-92-08. 81 rms, 1 suite. A/C MINIBAR TV TEL. 16,500 ptas. ($132) double; 28,000 ptas. ($224) suite. AE, DC, MC, V.

This parador is in the heart of town, on the Plaza de la Constitución, in the former Convento de los Frailes de Jesus (dating from the 16th century). A salon has been installed in the cloister, and a central garden is studded with shrubbery and flowers. Old stone stairs lead to the bedrooms. The place has had a long and turbulent history and was once a prison. In the 1960s two dictators met here: Franco of Spain and Salazar of Portugal. An elevator plummeted to the ground as El Caudillo was entertaining his Portuguese comrade—probably an assassination attempt on either Franco or Salazar (or both). In addition to its bar and garage, the parador has an excellent restaurant, serving both regional and national dishes.

Tryp Medea. Avenida de Portugal, s/n, 06900 Mérida. ☎ **924/37-24-00.** Fax 924/37-30-20. 126 rms. A/C MINIBAR TV TEL. 14,400 ptas. ($115.20) double; 19,075 ptas. ($152.60) triple. AE, DC, MC, V. Parking 800 ptas. ($6.40). Bus: 4 or 6.

Located a 15-minute walk west of the town's historic center, on the opposite bank of the Guadiana River, this hotel opened in 1993 and was immediately judged the finest hotel in Extremadura. A member of the nationwide Tryp chain, the four-story hotel amply employs white marble within its lobby and bedrooms. Lots of mirrors, stylish postmodern furniture crafted from locally made wrought iron, and numerous modern accessories decorate the rooms, many of which offer views over the historic core of Mérida. On the premises is an outdoor swimming pool, a health club/gymnasium, squash courts, a sauna, and a helpful, multilingual staff. There's a bar, and a restaurant, El Encenar (named after a type of tree that is indigenous to Extremadura).

WHERE TO DINE

In addition to the independent restaurants listed below, the hotels recommended above have good restaurants.

$ Briz. Félix Valverde Lillo, 5. ☎ **924/31-93-07.** Main courses 850–2,000 ptas. ($6.80–$16); fixed-price menu 1,350 ptas. ($10.80). MC, V. Mon–Sat 1:30–4 pm and 9–11:30 pm. EXTREMADURAN.

There is almost universal agreement, even among the locals, that the set menu at Briz represents the best value in town—not only reasonable in price but also very filling. Briz is known for its Extremaduran regional dishes, and has been feeding locals since 1949. Main dishes include lamb stew (heavily flavored) and *perdiz in salsa* (a gamey partridge casserole), which might be preceded by an appetizer of peppery sausage mixed into a medley of artichokes. Peppery veal steak and fried filet of goat are other specialties. Strong, hearty wines accompany the dishes. A meal here will qualify you as an Extremeño. You'll find Briz across from the post office.

Restaurante Nicolás. Félix Valverde Lillo, 13. ☎ **924/31-96-10.** Reservations recommended. Main courses 1,000–1,500 ptas. ($8–$12); fixed-price menu 2,000 ptas. ($16). AE, DC, MC, V. Daily noon–5 pm, Mon–Sat 9 pm–midnight. Closed Sept 8–22. SPANISH.

Transformed from an old, run-down house in 1985, this ranks as the most charming restaurant in town. If the lower dining room isn't to your liking, you'll find seating upstairs, as well as a pleasant garden for outdoor meals. Menu specialties are made with care from fresh ingredients. You might enjoy fresh shellfish, roast baby goat, carefully seasoned roast lamb, and flavorful concoctions of sole, salmon, and monkfish. Roast partridge is the game specialty. Nicolás is located opposite the post office.

5 Badajoz

57 miles (92km) SW of Cáceres, 39 miles (63km) E of Mérida, 254 miles (409km) SW of Madrid

The capital of Spain's largest province, Badajoz stands on the banks of the Guadiana River near the once-turbulent Portuguese border. A Moorish fortress and an old Roman bridge are two reminders of the past. Sightseeing here is lackluster, but Badajoz does have some local color, provided mainly by its huge ramparts and its narrow medieval streets. Its fortified site is best appreciated if you drive to Badajoz from the north. Park outside and walk into town; along the way you'll pass the 13th-century Gothic cathedral.

GETTING THERE **By Plane** Almost daily flights from Madrid fly into the Aeropuerto de Badajoz, Carretera Madrid-Lisboa, km 19 (☎ **924/21-04-00**). On Tuesday and Thursday, there are also flights from Barcelona.

By Train Four trains daily arrive from Madrid (trip time: 5 to 8 hours). Eight trains per day arrive from Mérida (1½ hours), and three from Cáceres (2½ hours). The railway station is situated at the terminus of Carolina Coronado in Badajoz (☎ **924/27-11-70**), a 15-minute walk northwest of the center of town.

By Bus From Madrid, 10 buses daily make the 4-hour trip; from Seville, there are 5 daily buses (4½ hours). From Mérida, there are 8 buses daily (45 minutes). The bus station (☎ **924/25-86-61**) is at Calzadilla Maestre, south of town. Take bus number 3 from the station to the town center, the Plaza de España.

By Car Badajoz sits astride the superhighway N-V, which connects Madrid with Lisbon. The E-803 connects it with Seville. Driving time from Madrid is around 4 hours; from Seville the time is about 3½ hours.

VISITOR INFORMATION The tourist information office is at Plaza de la Libertad, 3 (☎ **924/22-27-63**). Open Monday through Friday from 9am to 2pm and 4 to 6pm, Saturday and Sunday from 9am to 2pm.

WHERE TO STAY

Gran Hotel Zurbarán. Paseo Castelar, s/n, 06001 Badajoz. ☎ **924/22-37-41.** Fax 924/22-01-42. 214 rms, 8 suites. A/C TV TEL. 16,750 ptas. ($134) double; 27,500 ptas. ($220) suite. AE, DC, MC, V. Parking 1,000 ptas. ($8).

Set above the heavy ramparts that flank the southern bank of the River Guadiana, this modern but slightly dated four-star hotel enjoys one of the most scenic positions in town, overlooking the welcome verdancy of the Parque de Castelar. The public rooms are decorated with lots of metal trim and a kind of 1970s-era pizzazz, and the guest rooms are comfortably equipped and have been recently remodeled. The service is attentive.

Dining/Entertainment: An in-house restaurant serves à la carte meals. There is also a bar and a disco.

Services: Concierge, laundry, room service, babysitting.

Facilities: Outdoor pool, tennis courts, large garden with stately trees and flowers, in-house news kiosk and bookstore, shopping arcade.

Hotel Lisboa. Avenida de Elvas, 13, 06006 Badajoz. ☎ **924/27-29-00.** Fax 924/27-22-50. 176 rms. A/C TV TEL. 7,500 ptas. ($60) double. MC, V. Parking 600 ptas. ($4.80).

One of Badajoz's major hotels, this eight-floor establishment is located about a half-mile west of the town center, near the access roads of traffic coming in from Lisbon. Built in 1978, and appealing to many business travelers en route between Madrid and Lisbon, it offers uncomplicated modern rooms with conservative furnishings, and an efficient staff. The hotel contains a bar, a garage, and an economical restaurant.

Hotel Río. Adolfo Diaz Ambrona, 13, 06006 Badajoz. ☎ **924/27-26-00.** Fax 924/27-38-74. 84 rms. A/C MINIBAR TV TEL. 11,500 ptas. ($92) double. AE, DC, MC, V. Free parking. Bus: Urbano 2 or 6.

Located near a bridge on the highway connecting Lisbon and Madrid, the Hotel Río offers views of a eucalyptus grove and the river. The amenities include an outdoor pool, a parking garage, a disco pub/restaurant, and a garden; the functional guest rooms are comfortably furnished and well maintained. The hotel attracts many of the Portuguese who come over for the night for "a taste of Spain."

WHERE TO DINE

✪ **Aldeberán.** Avenida de Elvas, s/n, Urbanización Guadiana. ☎ **924/27-42-61.** Reservations recommended. Main courses 2,200–2,850 ptas. ($17.60–$22.80); fixed-price menu 4,500 ptas. ($36). AE, DC, MC, V. Mon–Sat 1:30–3:45 and 9–11:45pm. SPANISH/EXTREMADURAN.

Established in 1990 within a modern building overlooking the river, on the highway about a mile west of Badajoz's center, Aldeberán is the best restaurant in the entire area. It prides itself on its Extremaduran origins, having adopted the name of a race of local bulls (*aldeberán*). Although a range of fish and meat dishes are offered, the menu features succulent pork dishes prepared from *pata negra* (black-footed) pigs, one of the specialties of the region. Offerings include *solomillo ibérico*, a tender pork filet carefully seasoned and usually served with spinach; portions of wafer-thin cured ham, served au naturel or flavorfully mixed into salads of very fresh greens; hake in green sauce; and several different preparations of sole and monkfish. A signature dessert is ripe peaches flambéed in honey sauce and served with mint-flavored crème fraîche.

Los Gabrieles. Vicente Barrantes, 21. ☎ **924/22-00-01.** Reservations recommended. Main courses 900–1,700 ptas. ($7.20–$13.60); fixed-price menu 990 ptas. ($7.90). AE, DC, MC, V. Daily 1–4:30pm and 8–11pm. EXTREMADURAN.

Los Gabrieles has flourished as the personal domain of three generations of the Palaez family since it was established in 1952 (in a 1900 building) near the cathedral. Today, the granddaughter of the founder concocts well-flavored regional specialties from strictly fresh ingredients in the kitchen, while her husband directs the staff in the turn-of-the-century dining room. Such Extremaduran specialties as roasted partridge, lamb roasted with herbs, soups, stews, omelets, and endless cups of coffee and glasses of wine will happily sate any appetite. One section of the restaurant is devoted to a café and bar.

Mesón el Tronco. Calle Muñoz Torrero, 16. ☎ **924/22-20-76.** Reservations recommended. Main courses 850–1,800 ptas. ($6.80–$14.40); fixed-price menu 1,350 ptas. ($10.80). AE, DC, MC, V. Mon–Sat 9am–4pm, Tues–Sat 7pm–midnight. EXTREMADURAN.

You might not suspect an attractive restaurant exists here when you encounter the popular bar near the front door, but the excellent tapas will hint at the delicacies available in the back room. The owner offers traditional Extremaduran dishes, as well as a changing repertoire of daily specials. Menu items include gazpacho, *cocido* (stew) of the region, and lamb cutlets, all at affordable prices and served in air-conditioned comfort. Mesón el Tronco is in the center of town, two blocks west of the cathedral.

EASY SIDE TRIPS FROM MÉRIDA AND BADAJOZ

Jerez de los Caballeros makes an interesting journey from either Badajoz (46½ miles [75km] south on the N-432) or (61½ miles [99km] southwest on the N-360). It's a small town of white houses clustered on a hillside, with the cathedral on the summit. The **birthplace of Balboa,** the first European to discover the Pacific, is nearby—a modest whitewashed house at Capitán Cortés, 10. A statue honors the explorer in one of the town's small squares. Jerez de los Caballeros, with many belfries and towers, including the **Torre Sagrienta** (Bloody Tower), takes its name, traditions, and ambience from the Caballeros del Templo (Knights Templars), who were given the town after it was taken from the Moors in 1230.

Medellín, 25 miles (40km) east of Mérida and 62 miles (100km) east of Badajoz, is the little town where Hernán Cortés, conqueror of Mexico, was born. From the approach you'll see the old whitewashed buildings on the opposite side of the Guadiana River, with the ruins of medieval Medellín Castle dominating the skyline. A 17th-century stone bridge crosses the river into the town, where you'll find a monument to Cortés in the main cobblestoned plaza. From either Mérida or Badajoz, take the N-V superhighway heading to Madrid; exit at the C-520, the road into Medellín.

6 Zafra

38 miles (61km) S of Mérida, 107 miles (172km) N of Seville

One of the most interesting stopovers in Lower Extremadura, the white-walled town of Zafra is filled with old Moorish streets and squares. The cattle fair of San Miguel, on October 4, draws cattle breeders from all over the region. The 1457 **castle** of the dukes of Feria, the most important in the province, boasts both a sumptuous 16th-century Herreran patio and the Sala Dorada, with its richly paneled ceiling. The place is now a government parador (see below). You'll want to spend time on the central square, the arcaded 18th-century **Plaza Mayor,** and its satellite, the 16th-century **Plaza Vieja (Old Square).** These are the two most important sights in Zafra, along with the **Nuestra Señora de la Candelaria,** a church with nine panels by Zurbarán, displayed on the retable in a chapel designed by Churriguera. The church, constructed in the Gothic-Renaissance style, has a red-brick belfry. Admission is free. It's open Monday through Friday from 10:30am to 1pm and 7 to 8:30pm and Sunday from 11am to 12:30pm.

GETTING THERE **By Bus** One bus a day arrives from Mérida; a one-way ticket costs 950 pesetas ($7.60).

By Car Zafra lies at the point where the highway from Seville (E-803) splits, heading east to Mérida and Cáceres and west to Badajoz. Driving there is easy. There's also a direct road from Córdoba.

VISITOR INFORMATION The tourist information office is at Plaza de España (☎ **924/55-10-36**), open Monday through Friday from 11am to 2pm and 6 to 8pm, Saturday from 11pm to 1:30pm.

WHERE TO STAY & DINE

Huerta Honda. López Asme, 32, 06300 Zafra. ☎ **924/55-41-00.** Fax 924/55-25-04. 38 rms (27 with bath). A/C MINIBAR TV TEL. 5,800 ptas. ($46.40) double without bath; 12,500 ptas. ($100) double with bath. AE, MC, V.

Views of the citadel and the old town are to be had from the modern, recently renovated bedrooms of this Andalusian-style hotel in front of the Plaza del Alcázar. There's a disco, as well as a garden and a pretty patio for midafternoon drinks. Under the same management, at number 36 on the same street, is the restaurant Barbacana, a well-recommended regional dining room, offering French and Basque cuisine.

Parador Hernán Cortés. Plaza Corazón de María, 7, 06300 Zafra. ☎ **924/55-45-40.** Fax 924/55-10-18. 45 rms, 3 suites. A/C MINIBAR TV TEL. 13,500 ptas. ($108) double; 18,000 ptas. ($144) suite. AE, DC, MC, V. Free parking.

This government-run parador—located in a restored castle near the Plaza de España—is named after Cortés, who stayed here with the dukes of Feria before his departure for the New World. The castle was originally built in 1457, on a square plan with four round towers. The interior, beautiful but restrained, contains the chapel of the Alcázar, with an octagonal Gothic dome. In addition to being decorated in splendid taste, the Hernan Cortés is quite comfortable, boasting a patio, a garden, and a swimming pool. The magnificent-looking dining room offers regional meals; a bar and a large lounge are also on the premises.

9 Andalusia

This once-great stronghold of Muslim Spain is rich in history and tradition, containing some of the country's most celebrated sightseeing treasures: the world-famous Mezquita (mosque) in Córdoba, the Alhambra in Granada, and the great Gothic cathedral in Seville. It also has smaller towns just waiting to be discovered—Úbeda, castle-dominated Jaén, gorge-split Ronda, sherry-producing Jerez de la Frontera, and the gleaming white port city of Cádiz. Give Andalusia at least a week and you'll still have only skimmed the surface of its many offerings.

This dry, mountainous region also embraces the Costa del Sol (Málaga, Marbella, and Torremolinos), a popular strip of Spain that is covered separately in the following chapter. Go to the Costa del Sol for beach resorts, nightlife, and relaxation; visit Andalusia for its architectural wonders and beauty.

Crime alert: Anyone driving south into Andalusia and the Costa del Sol should be wary of thieves. Daylight robberies are commonplace, especially in Seville, Córdoba, and Granada. It is not unusual for a car to be broken into while tourists are enjoying lunch in a restaurant. Some establishments have hired guards (a service for which you should tip, of course). Under no circumstances should you ever leave passports and traveler's checks unguarded in a car.

EXPLORING THE REGION BY CAR

The itinerary below begins in Madrid, heading south into Andalusia.

Day 1 From Madrid head for Jaén for the night, which can be your gateway to Andalusia. If you have the time, explore its Catedral de Santa María, its Museo Provincial, and its three-in-one attraction, Centro Cultural Palacio de Villardompardo. Have dinner in the parador, which commands a panoramic view of the area.

Day 2 Explore what you missed of Jaén in the morning, then drive to Baeza and Úbeda. These are two of the most charming and unspoiled towns of Andalusia. (It's not that they're loaded with attractions, but the architectural wonder of the towns themselves is appealing.) Overnight, if you can get a reservation, stay at Úbeda's Parador Nacional del Condestabe Dávalos.

Day 3 Drive south from Jaén to Granada and check into a hotel. There is so much to see and do here that in a short amount of time you can take in only a part of it. Perhaps visit the old Arab quarter,

Andalusia

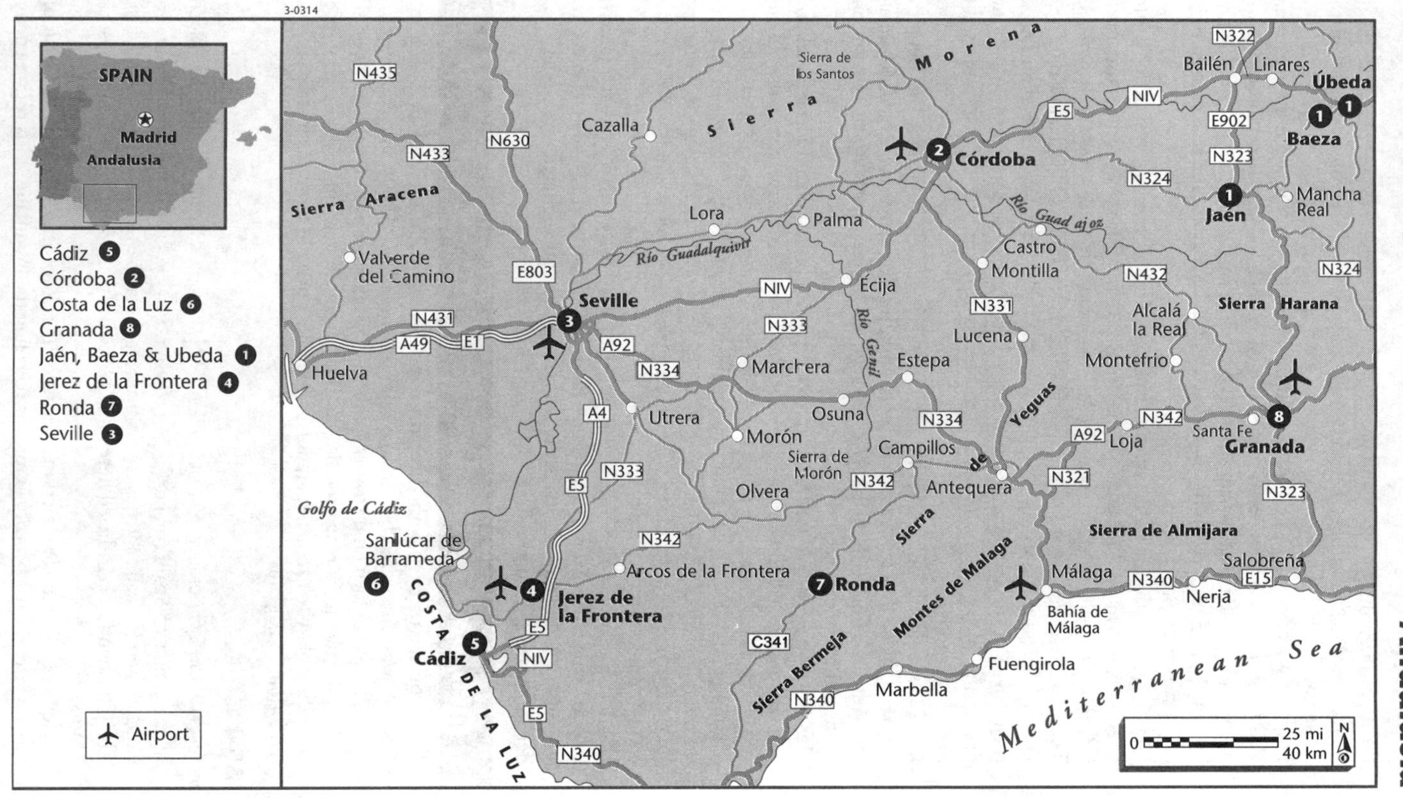

3-0314
SPAIN
Madrid
Andalusia
Cádiz 5
Córdoba 2
Costa de la Luz 6
Granada 8
Jaén, Baeza & Ubeda 1
Jerez de la Frontera 4
Ronda 7
Seville 3
Airport
Sierra Morena
Sierra de los Santos
N435
N433
N630
Cazalla
Sierra Aracena
Lora
Palma
Río Guadalquivir
Valverde del Camino
E803
Seville
N431
A49
E1
Huelva
A92
N334
A4
Utrera
N333
E5
Golfo de Cádiz
Sanlúcar de Barrameda
COSTA DE LA LUZ
Jerez de la Frontera
Cádiz
NIV
N340
N342
Arcos de la Frontera
Córdoba
Écija
Río Genil
Marchera
Osuna
Morón
Sierra de Morón
Olvera
Estepa
Campillos
Sierra de Yeguas
Antequera
Ronda
Sierra
Montes de Malaga
Sierra Bermeja
C341
Marbella
Fuengirola
Málaga
Bahía de Málaga
Mediterranean Sea
N331
Lucena
Castro
Montilla
Río Guad ajoz
N432
N321
N324
N322
Bailén
Linares
Úbeda
E902
Baeza
N323
Jaén
Mancha Real
Sierra Harana
Alcalá la Real
Montefrío
Loja
Santa Fe
Granada
Sierra de Almijara
Salobreña
Nerja
E15
0
25 mi
40 km
N

the Albaicín, in the afternoon and go shopping in the Alsaicería, the old Moorish silk market next to the cathedral in the lower city. While here you can also visit the cathedral.

Day 4 We've saved the best for last. In the morning and for part of the afternoon, visit Granada's two major attractions, the Alhambra and the Generalife. This will occupy the greater part of your day. Have lunch in the old town at the Parador Nacional San Francisco. In the evening, while still based in Granada, enjoy a night of gypsy flamenco.

Day 5 Go northwest from Granada toward Córdoba, arriving in time for a late-afternoon visit to the Mezquita, its major attraction. Visit some of the museums of Córdoba, including the Museo de Bellas Artes and the Museo de Julio Romero de Torres. Have dinner at one of the typical restaurants, such as El Caballo Rojo.

Day 6 Spend the morning exploring the sights of Córdoba you missed on Day 5, then drive west to Seville for the afternoon. If you arrive in time, explore the cathedral and go for a walk in the city's Barrio de Santa Cruz. Save the rest of the sights for the following day.

Day 7 While still based in Seville, explore the city's many attractions, including the Alcázar, Giralda Tower (which you can climb), the Hospital de la Santa Caridad, and the Museo Provincial de Bellas Artes de Sevilla. Opt for a night of flamenco in one of the old quarters.

Day 8 Drive south to Cádiz for an overnight stop, but en route have lunch and visit one of the sherry bodegas at Jerez de la Frontera. You'll arrive late in the old port city of Cádiz, but don't fear. After a walk around, a meal at a seafood restaurant, and a sampling of its colorful local life, you will have had the best of Cádiz and can press on the following day to other attractions. Cádiz is not as richly endowed in attractions as such cities as Córdoba or Seville, and you may opt to skip if you don't have enough time.

Day 9 After exploring Cádiz, return to Madrid, or drive to Algeciras and take the ferry to Tangier in Morocco. Another alternative is to head east toward Algeciras, stopping at Gibraltar, before visiting some of the resort highlights along the Costa del Sol: Marbella, Torremolinos, Málaga, and Nerja.

1 Jaén, Baeza & Úbeda

The province of Jaén, with three principal cities—Jaén, the capital; Baeza; and Úbeda—was discovered by international tourists in the 1960s. For years, visitors whizzed through Jaén on their way south to Granada or bypassed it altogether on the southwest route to Córdoba and Seville. But the government improved the province's hotel outlook with excellent paradors, which now provide some of the finest accommodations in Andalusia.

JAÉN

60 miles (97km) E of Córdoba, 60 miles (97km) N of Granada, 210 miles (338km) S of Madrid

In the center of Spain's major olive-growing district, Jaén is sandwiched between Córdoba and Granada and has always been a gateway between Castile and Andalusia. The Christian forces gathered here in 1492, before marching on Granada to oust the Moors.

Jaén's bustling modern section is of little interest to visitors, but the **Moorish old town,** where the narrow cobblestoned streets hug the mountainside, is reason enough to visit. A hilltop castle, now converted into a first-rate parador, dominates the city. On a clear day you can see the snow-covered peaks of the Sierra Nevada.

The city of Jaén is at the center of a large province of 5,189 square miles (13,491 sq. km), framed by mountains: the Sierra Morena to the north, the Segura and Cazorla ranges to the east, and those of Huelma, Noalejo, and Valdepeñas to the south. To the west, plains widen into the fertile Guadalquivir Valley. The landscape is rugged and irregular. Jaén province comprises three well-defined districts: the Sierra de Cazorla, a land of wild scenery; the plains of Bailén, Ajona, and Arjonilla, filled with wheat fields, vineyards, and old olive trees; and the valleys of the tributaries of the Guadalquivir.

GETTING THERE **By Train** It's easier to leave Jaén than it is to get there, because trains to Jaén run only from south to north. Northbound trains—including two daily to Madrid's Atocha Railway Station—arrive and depart from Jaén's RENFE station on the Paseo de la Estación (☎ **953/27-02-02**), north of the center of town. If you're traveling from north to south, however, it isn't quite so easy. Most southbound trains from Madrid, and all trains heading south to Seville and the rest of Andalusia, stop only at a larger railway junction that lies inconveniently in the hamlet of Espeluy, 22 miles (35.5km) to the north. From Espeluy, trains are sometimes funneled a short ride to the east, to the railway junction midway between Linares (31 miles [50km] from Jaén) and Baeza (the Estación de Linares—Baeza). Consult the Jaén tourist office or the railway station for advice on your particular routing.

By Bus The bus terminal is at Plaza Coca de la Piñera (☎ **953/25-01-06**), one block south of the central Parque de la Victoria. Either directly or after a transfer at Baeza, 30 miles (48km) to the north, buses travel 8 times a day to Granada (2 hours away), 11 times to Úbeda (1½ hours), four times to Córdoba (4½ hours), and three times to Seville (5 hours).

By Car Four important highways, plus several provincial roads, converge on Jaén from four directions. From Madrid, follow the N-IV (E-5) to N-323 (E-902).

VISITOR INFORMATION The tourist information office is at Calle Arquitecto Bergés, 1 (☎ **953/22-27-37**). Open April through October, Monday through Friday from 8:15am to 2:15pm; off-season, Monday through Friday from 8:30am to 2:30pm, Saturday 10am to 12:30pm.

WHAT TO SEE & DO

Catedral de Santa María. Plaza de la Catedral. ☎ **953/27-52-33.** Free admission to cathedral and museum. Cathedral, daily 8:30am–1pm and 4:30–8pm (closes at 7pm in winter); museum, Sat–Sun 11am–1pm. Bus: 8 or 10.

The formality and grandeur of Jaén's cathedral stand witness to the city's importance in days gone by. Begun in 1555 and completed in 1802, it is a honey-colored blend of Gothic, baroque, and Renaissance styles, but mainly Renaissance. The interior, with its richly carved choir stalls, is dominated by a huge dome. The cathedral museum contains an important collection of historical objects in two underground chambers, including paintings by Ribera. The cathedral stands southwest of the Plaza de la Constitución.

Iglesia de la Magdalena. Calle de la Magdalena. ☎ **953/25-60-19.** Free admission. Daily 6am–8pm.

Of the many churches worth visiting in Jaén, La Magdalena is the oldest and most interesting. This Gothic church was once an Arab mosque.

Museo Provincial. Paseo de la Estación, 29. ☎ **953/25-03-20.** Admission 100 ptas. (80¢). Tues–Fri 10am–2pm and 5–8pm, Sat–Sun 10am–2pm.

The Provincial Museum's collection includes Roman mosaics, a Mudéjar arch, and many ceramics from the early Iberian, Greek, and Roman periods. On the upper floor is an exhibition of Pedro Berruguete paintings, including *Christ at the Column.* Look also for the Paleo-Christian sarcophagus from Martos. The museum is between the bus and train stations.

Centro Cultural Palacio de Villardompardo. Plaza de Santa Luisa de Marillac, s/n. ☎ **953/23-62-92.** Free admission. Tues–Fri 10am–2pm and 5–8pm (closes at 7pm in winter), Sat–Sun 10am–2pm. You must go on foot: In the old quarter of Jaén, follow signs indicating either Baños Arabes or Barrio de la Magdalena.

This is a three-in-one attraction, including some former Arab baths (known as *hamman*), a Museo de Artes y Costumbres Populares (folk art and crafts), and a Museo Internacional de Arte Naif (with works by self-taught artists from all over the world). The hours (see above) are the same for all three attractions, and none charges admission.

Underneath the palace, which lies near Calle San Juan and the Chapel of St. Andrew (San Andrés), are the former Arab baths. These represent some of the most important Moorish architecture from the 11th century ever discovered in Spain—in fact, they are the most significant ruins of Arab baths in the country. You can visit a warm room, a hot room, and a cold room—the latter having a barrel vault and 12 star-shaped chandeliers. Later you can go upstairs to see the folk art and the Naif collection that opened in 1990.

Where to Stay

✪ **Parador Castillo de Santa Catalina.** Castillo de Santa Catalina, 23000 Jaén. ☎ **953/23-00-00.** Fax 953/23-09-30. 45 rms. A/C MINIBAR TV TEL. 16,500 ptas. ($132) double. AE, DC, MC, V. Free parking. Follow Carretera al Castillo y Neveraol.

This castle, three miles (4.8km) to the east on the hill overlooking the city, is one of the government's showplace paradors, and staying here is reason enough to visit Jaén. In the 10th century the castle was a Muslim fortress, surrounded by high protective walls and approached by a steep, winding road. The castle is still reached by the same road; visitors enter through a three-story-high baronial hallway, and a polite staff shows them to their balconied bedrooms (doubles only), tastefully furnished and comfortable, with spick-and-span tile baths.

Dining at the castle is dramatic—the high-vaulted restaurant looks like a small cathedral with its wrought-iron chandeliers and stone arches, plus a raised hearth and a collection of copper kettles and ceramics. On either side of the lofty room, arched windows open onto a terrace or a fabulous view of town. Lunch or dinner here includes typical Jaén dishes—usually made with the olives for which the area is famous—and regional wine.

Xauen. Plaza Deán Mazas, 3, 23001 Jaén. ☎ **953/26-40-11.** 35 rms. A/C TV TEL. 7,000 ptas. ($56) double. No credit cards. Parking 1,500 ptas. ($12).

Breakfast only is served at this family-run hotel, which opened in 1979, one block west of Plaza de la Constitución. The handcrafted detailing of the building and its central location make it an attractive choice, although its modest appointments hardly compete with the parador. The guest rooms are simply furnished but comfortable. Motorists might have to park far away from the entrance.

Where to Dine

Consider a meal in the luxurious hilltop parador commanding a view of Jaén (see above). It's one of the loveliest spots in the area.

The Jockey Club. Paseo de la Estación, 20. ☎ **953/25-10-18.** Reservations required Fri–Sat dinner. Main courses 1,600–3,500 ptas. ($12.80–$28); fixed-price menu 2,650 ptas. ($21.20). AE, DC, MC, V. Mon–Sat 1–4pm and 8pm–midnight. Closed Aug. SPANISH.

The leading restaurant in town is the moderately priced Jockey Club, whose owner works hard to maintain a comfortable ambience and a well-prepared cuisine. Main dishes include monkfish, Milanese-style rice, salmon with green sauce, and a full range of meats and fish. You'll find the Jockey Club in the center of town, south of Plaza de la Constitución.

Nelson. Paseo de la Estación, 33. ☎ **953/22-92-01.** Reservations required. Main courses 1,350–2,100 ptas. ($10.80–$16.80); fixed-price menu 1,500 ptas. ($12). AE, DC, MC, V. Mon–Sat 1:30–4:30pm and 8pm–midnight. Closed Aug. SPANISH.

On a pedestrian walkway near the railway station, Plaza de las Batallas, and the Museo Provincial, this restaurant relies on fresh produce and the gruff charm of the owners, the Ordóñez brothers, José and Salvador. An impressive array of tapas greets you at the bar, where you can pause for predinner drinks. In the air-conditioned dining room, full meals might include such specialties as roast goat baked with savory spices, filet steak grilled in olive oil and garlic, escabeche of fish, hake stewed with eels, and grilled lamb chops. Although cookery is only standard, fresh ingredients are used.

BAEZA

28 miles (45km) NE of Jaén, 191 miles (307km) S of Madrid

Historic Baeza (known to the Romans as Vilvatia), with its Gothic and plateresque buildings and cobblestoned streets, is one of the best-preserved old towns in Spain. At twilight, lanterns hang on walls of plastered stone, flickering against the darkening sky and lighting the narrow streets. The town had its heyday in the 16th and 17th centuries, and in the Visigothic period it was the seat of a bishop.

GETTING THERE **By Train** The nearest important railway junction, receiving trains from Madrid and most of Andalusia, is the Estación Linares-Baeza (☎ **953/65-02-02**), 8½ miles (14km) west of Baeza's center. For information about which trains arrive there, refer to "By Train" in the section on Jaén, above.

By Bus There are three buses a day to Úbeda; the ride is 15 minutes long. From Jaén, there are eight buses per day (trip time: 1 hour). For more information, call **953/74-04-68.**

By Car Baeza lies east of the N-V, the superhighway linking Madrid with Granada. Highway 321/322, which runs through Baeza, links Córdoba with Valencia.

VISITOR INFORMATION The tourist information office is at Plaza del Pópulo (☎ **953/74-04-44**). Open Monday through Friday from 9am to 2:30pm.

WHAT TO SEE & DO

Entering Baeza from Jaén, you'll approach the main square, **Plaza del Pópulo,** a two-story open colonnade—and a good point to begin exploring. The buildings here date in part from the 16th century. One of the most interesting houses the tourist office (see above), where you can obtain a map to help guide you through Baeza. Look for the fountain containing four half-effaced lions, the Fuente de los Leones, which may have been brought here from the Roman town of Cantulo.

Head south along the Cuesta de San Gil to reach the Gothic and Renaissance **cathedral,** Plaza de la Fuente de Santa María (no phone), constructed in the 16th century on the foundations of an earlier mosque. The Puerta de la Luna is in Arab-Gothic style. In the interior, remodeled by Andrés de Vandelvira and his pupils, look for the carved wood and the brilliant painted *rejas* (iron screens). The Gold Chapel is especially outstanding. The cathedral is open daily from 10am to 1pm and 4 to 7pm; admission is free.

After leaving the cathedral, continue up the Cuesta de San Felipe to the **Palacio de Jabalquinto,** a beautiful example of civil architecture in the flamboyant Gothic style. Juan Alfonso de Benavides, a relative of King Ferdinand, ordered it built. Its facade is filled with decorative elements, and there is a simple Renaissance-style courtyard with marble columns. Inside, two lions guard the stairway, heavily decorated in the baroque style.

WHERE TO STAY

$ Hotel Juanito. Plaza del Arca del Agua, s/n, 23400 Baeza. ☎ **953/74-00-40.** Fax 953/74-23-24. 37 rms. A/C TV TEL. 5,400 ptas. ($43.20) double. V. Free parking.

This establishment, known mainly for its restaurant (see below), is also a suitable choice for an overnight stopover. Built originally in the 1970s, it was renovated and enlarged in 1992. The guest rooms (half of which have a TV) are unpretentious but clean and comfortable. The Hotel Juanito stands on the outskirts of Baeza, toward Úbeda.

WHERE TO DINE

Casa Juanito. Plaza del Arca del Agua, s/n. ☎ **953/74-00-40.** Reservations required Fri–Sat. Main courses 1,200–3,600 ptas. ($9.60–$28.80). V. Daily 1:30–4pm, Tues–Sat 8:30–11pm. Closed Nov 1–15. SPANISH.

Owners Juan Antonío and Luisa Salcedo serve regional specialties from Andalusia and La Mancha. Devotees of the "lost art" of Jaén cookery, they revive ancient recipes in their frequently changing "suggestions for the day." Game is served in season, and many vegetable dishes are made with ham. Among the savory and well-prepared menu items are *habas* beans, filet of beef with tomatoes and peppers, partridge in pastry crust, and codfish house style.

$ El Sali. Pasaje Cardenal Benavides, 15. ☎ **953/74-13-65.** Reservations not required. Main courses 900–2,200 ptas. ($7.20–$17.60); fixed-price menu 1,600 ptas. ($12.80). AE, DC, MC, V. Daily 1–4pm, Thurs–Tues 8–11pm. Closed Sept 16–Oct 10. SPANISH/ANDALUSIAN.

The setting of this restaurant is a modern building erected in the 1980s in the town center, adjacent to Plaza del Pópulo. Diners in air-conditioned comfort enjoy what many locals regard as the most reasonable set menu in town. The owners serve not only the cuisine of Andalusia but also certain dishes from around Spain. They are known for their fresh vegetables, as exemplified by *la pipirana,* a cold medley of vegetables with tuna, accented with boiled eggs, fresh tomatoes, onions, and spices (only in summer). The atmosphere is relaxed and the service cordial; the portions are generous. You won't leave feeling hungry or overcharged.

ÚBEDA

6 miles (10km) NE of Jaén, 194 miles (312km) S of Madrid

A former stronghold of the Arabs, Úbeda, often called the "Florence of Andalusia," is a Spanish National Landmark filled with golden-brown Renaissance palaces and tile-roofed whitewashed houses. The best way to discover Úbeda's charm is to wander its narrow cobblestone streets.

The government long ago created a parador here in a renovated ducal palace—you might stop for lunch if you're not pressed for time. Allow time for a stroll through Úbeda's shops, which sell, among other items, leathercraft goods and esparto grass carpets.

The palaces and churches of the city are almost endless. You might begin your tour at the centrally located **Plaza de Vázquez de Molina,** which is flanked by several mansions, including the Casa de las Cadenas, now the Town Hall. For centuries the mansions have been decaying, but many are now being restored. Most are not open to the public.

GETTING THERE **By Train** The nearest train station is the Linares-Baeza station (☎ **953/65-02-02**). For information on trains to and from the station, refer to the Jaén section (see above).

By Bus There are buses seven times daily to Baeza, less than six miles (9.6km) away, and to Jaén. Six buses per day go to the busy railway station at Linares-Baeza, where a train can take you virtually anywhere in Spain. Bus service to and from Córdoba, Seville, and Granada (at least once a day) is also available. Úbeda's bus station lies in the heart of the modern town, on Calle San José (☎ **953/75-21-57**), where signs will point you on a downhill walk to the *zona monumental.*

By Car Turn off the Madrid-Córdoba road and head east for Linares, then on to Úbeda, a detour of 26 miles (42km).

VISITOR INFORMATION The tourist information office is at Plaza de los Caídos, 2 (☎ **953/75-08-97**). Open Monday through Friday from 9am to 2:30pm, Saturday from 11am to 2pm.

What to See & Do

Iglesia el Salvador. Plaza de Vázquez de Molina. No phone. Free admission. Daily 9am–1pm and 5–7pm.

One of the grandest examples of Spanish Renaissance architecture, this church was designed in 1536 by Diego de Siloé. The richly embellished portal is mere window dressing for the wealth of decoration inside the church, including a sacristy designed by Andréas de Vandelvira and a single nave with gold-and-blue vaulting. The many sculptures and altarpieces and the spectacular rose windows are of special interest.

Iglesia de San Pablo. Plaza 1 de Mayo. No phone. Free admission. Daily 9am–1pm and 7–9pm.

This church, in the center of the old town, is almost as fascinating as the Iglesia El Salvador. The Gothic San Pablo is famous for its 16th-century south portal in the Isabelline style and its chapels.

Hospital de Santiago. Calle Santiago. No phone. Free admission. Daily 9am–1pm and 5–7pm.

On the western edge of town, off the Calle del Obispo Coros, stands the Hospital of Santiago, completed in 1575 and still in use. Built by Andrés de Vandelvira, "the Christopher Wren of Úbeda," over the years it has earned a reputation as the "Escorial of Andalusia."

Iglesia de Santa María de Los Reales Alcázares. Arroyo de Santa María. ☎ **953/75-07-77.** Free admission. Daily 9am–1pm and 5–7pm.

Another intriguing Úbeda church is Santa María de los Reales Alcázares, on the site of a former Arab mosque. The cloisters, with their fan vaulting, are Gothic; the interior, with its tiled and painted ceiling, blends the Gothic and Mudéjar styles. Also inside the church you'll find a gruesome statue of a mutilated Christ. Santa María is in the center of town, opposite the Ayuntamiento (Town Hall). This church is currently under restoration—check with the tourist office to see if it has reopened before heading there.

WHERE TO STAY

Hotel Consuelo. Avenida Ramón y Cajal, 12, 23400 Úbeda. ☎ **953/75-08-40.** Fax 953/75-68-34. 36 rms, 3 suites. A/C MINIBAR TV TEL. 5,500 ptas. ($44) double; from 7,500 ptas. ($60) suite. V. Parking 700 ptas. ($5.60).

Frankly, if there's room at the parador near the bus station (see below), there isn't much reason for you to go elsewhere. But if you must, head for this comfortable and utilitarian three-story building across from the Instituto Ensenanza Media. The hotel was built in the late 1960s and renovated in 1991. It doesn't serve breakfast, so its patrons head out for coffee at one of the nearby cafés. The guest rooms are basic but clean.

Hotel la Paz. Calle Andalucía, 1, 23400 Úbeda. ☎ **953/75-21-46.** Fax 953/75-08-48. 46 rms, 4 suites. A/C TV TEL. 5,800 ptas. ($46.40) double. AE, DC, MC, V. Parking 800 ptas. ($6.40).

Set on a sharply angled street corner in the heart of the commercial district, opposite a statue to a military hero, this seven-story hotel contains comfortably unpretentious bedrooms. Each bedroom is decorated in a simplified Iberian style of dignified wood furniture, with either pure white or papered walls. Built in 1971, the hotel was renovated in 1994. The street-level El Olivo restaurant opens directly onto the sidewalk and does a thriving business with the local community. There's also a simple snack restaurant for coffee and drinks, plus a bar. Services include laundry and babysitting.

✪ **Parador Nacional del Condestabe Dávalos.** Plaza de Vázquez de Molina, 1, 23400 Úbeda. ☎ **953/75-03-45.** Fax 953/75-12-59. 31 rms, 1 suite. A/C MINIBAR TV TEL. 16,500 ptas. ($132) double; 20,400 ptas. ($163.20) suite. AE, DC, MC, V.

In the heart of town on the most central square, near the Town Hall, stands this 16th-century palace turned parador, which shares an old paved plaza with the Iglesia El Salvador and its dazzling facade. The formal entrance to the Renaissance palace leads to an enclosed patio, encircled by two levels of Moorish arches, where palms and potted plants stand on the tile floors. The guest rooms, doubles only, are nearly two stories high, with beamed ceilings and tall windows. Antiques and reproductions adorn the rooms, and the beds are comfortable.

Before lunch or dinner, stop in at the low-beamed wine cellar, with its stone arches, provincial stools and tables, and giant kegs of wine. Dinner is served in a tastefully decorated ground-floor room, where a costumed staff serves traditional Spanish dishes.

WHERE TO DINE

The parador (see above) is the best place to dine for miles around. For dinner, try the stuffed partridge or baby lamb chops. The restaurants scattered around Calle Ramón y Cajal are unremarkable.

2 Córdoba

65 miles (105 km) W of Jáen, 260 miles (419km) SW of Madrid

Ten centuries ago Córdoba was one of the greatest cities in the world, with a population of 900,000. The capital of Muslim Spain, it was Europe's largest city and a cultural and intellectual center. This seat of the Western Caliphate flourished with public baths, mosques, a great library, and palaces. But greedy, sacking hordes have since passed through, tearing down ancient buildings and carting off art treasures. Despite these assaults, Córdoba still retains traces of its former glory—enough to challenge Seville and Granada as the most fascinating city in Andalusia.

Today this provincial capital is known chiefly for its mosque, but it abounds with other artistic and architectural riches, especially its domestic dwellings. The old Arab and Jewish quarters are famous for their narrow streets lined with whitewashed homes boasting flower-filled patios and balconies, and it's perfectly acceptable to walk along gazing into the courtyards. This isn't an invasion of privacy: The citizens of Córdoba take pride in showing off their patios as part of the city's tradition. And don't forget to bring along a good pair of walking shoes, as the only way to explore the monumental heart of the city is on foot.

ESSENTIALS

GETTING THERE **By Train** Córdoba is a railway junction for routes to the rest of both Andalusia and Spain. There are about 22 TALGO and AVE trains daily between Córdoba and Madrid (1½ to 2 hours). Other, slower trains (*tranvías*) take 5 to 8 hours for the same transit. There are also 25 trains from Seville every day (1½ hours). The main railway station is on the town's northern periphery, at Avenida de América, 130, near the corner of Avenida de Cervantes. For information, call **957/49-02-02.** To reach the heart of the old town, head south on Avenida de Cervantes or Avenida del Gran Capitán. If you want to buy a ticket or to get departure times and prices only, you can go to the RENFE office at Ronda de los Tejares, 10 (**☎ 957/47-58-54**).

By Bus There are several different bus companies, each of which maintains a separate terminal. The town's most important bus terminal is operated by the Alsina-Graells Sur Company, Avenida Medina Azahara, 29 (**☎ 957/23-64-74**), on the western outskirts of town (just west of the gardens beside Paseo de la Victoria).

From the bus terminal operated by Empresa Bacoma, Avenida de Cervantes, 22 (**☎ 957/45-64-14**), a short walk south of the railway station, there are three buses per day to and from Seville (a 2-hour and 3-hour trip, respectively) and five daily buses to Jaén (3 hours). Buses arrive here from Madrid (5½ hours).

By Car Córdoba lies astride the N-IV (E-5) connecting Madrid with Seville. Don't think of entering the complicated maze of streets in the old town by car. You'll inevitably get lost and find no place to park.

VISITOR INFORMATION The tourist information office is at Calle Torrijos, 10 (**☎ 957/47-12-35**). Open Monday through Saturday from 10am to 7pm and Sunday from 10am to 2pm.

WHAT TO SEE & DO

The Mezquita, now a cathedral, is the principal reason for visiting Córdoba, but the old Alcázar, an ancient synagogue, museums, and galleries will round out your day (see below). There's a lot to absorb, and visitors with more time may want to spend at least two days here.

Among the many sights is Córdoba's **Roman bridge (Puente Romano),** believed to date from the time of Augustus. It's hardly Roman anymore because none of its 16 supporting arches is original. The sculptor Bernabé Gómez del Río erected a statue of St. Raphael in the middle of the bridge in 1651. The Roman bridge crosses the Guadalquivir River about one block south of the Mezquita.

✪ **Mezquita-Catedral de Córdoba.** Calle Cardenal Herrero, s/n. **☎ 957/47-05-12.** Admission 750 ptas. ($6) adults, 375 ptas. ($3) children under 13. Apr–Sept, daily 10am–7pm; Oct–Mar, daily 10am–1:30pm and 3:30–5:30pm.

Dating from the 8th century, the Mezquita was the crowning Muslim architectural achievement in the West, rivaled only by the mosque at Mecca. It is a fantastic labyrinth of red-and-white, peppermint-striped pillars. To the astonishment of visitors, a cathedral sits awkwardly in the middle of the mosque, disturbing the purity of the lines. The 16th-century cathedral, a blend of many styles, is impressive in its own right, with an intricately carved ceiling and baroque choir stalls. Additional ill-conceived annexes later turned the Mezquita into an architectural oddity. Its most interesting feature is the mihrab, a domed shrine of Byzantine mosaics that once housed the Koran.

After exploring the interior, stroll through the Courtyard of the Orange Trees, which has a beautiful fountain. The hardy can climb a 16th-century tower built here on the base of a Moorish minaret to catch a panoramic view of Córdoba and its environs.

The Mezquita is south of the train station, just north of the Roman bridge.

✪ **Alcázar de los Reyes Cristianos.** Amador de los Ríos, s/n. ☎ **957/42-01-51.** Admission 425 ptas. ($3.40) adults, 150 ptas. ($1.20) children. May–Sept, Tues–Sat 10am–2pm and 6–8pm, Sun 10am–2pm; Oct–Apr, Tues–Sat, 10am–2pm and 4:30–6:30pm, Sun 10am–2pm. Gardens illuminated May–Sept 10pm–1am. Bus: 3 or 12.

Commissioned in 1328 by Alfonso XI (the "Just"), the Alcázar of the Christian Kings is a fine example of military architecture. Ferdinand and Isabella governed Castile from this fortress on the river as they prepared to reconquer Granada, the last Moorish stronghold in Spain. Columbus journeyed here to fill Isabella's ears with his plans for discovery.

Located two blocks southwest of the Mezquita, the quadrangular building is notable for powerful walls and a trio of towers—the Tower of the Lions, the Tower of Allegiance, and the Tower of the River. The Tower of the Lions contains intricately decorated ogival ceilings that are the most notable example of Gothic architecture in Andalusia.

The beautiful gardens, illuminated at night, and the Moorish baths are celebrated attractions. The Patio Morisco is a lovely spot, its pavement decorated with the arms of León and Castile. A distinguished Roman sarcophagus is representative of 2nd- and 3rd-century funeral art. The Roman mosaics are also outstanding—especially a unique piece dedicated to Polyphemus and Galatea.

Sinagoga. Calle de los Judíos. ☎ **957/20-29-28.** Admission 75 ptas. (60¢). Tues–Sat 10am–2pm and 3:30–5:30pm, Sun 10am–1:30pm. Bus: 3 or 12.

In Córdoba you'll find one of Spain's few remaining pre-Inquisition synagogues, built in 1350 in the Barrio de la Judería (Jewish Quarter), two blocks west of the northern wall of the Mezquita. The synagogue is noted particularly for its stucco-work; the east wall contains a large orifice where the Tabernacle was once placed (inside, the scrolls of the Pentateuch were kept). After the Jews were expelled from Spain, the synagogue was turned into a hospital, until it became a Catholic chapel in 1588.

Museo de Bellas Artes de Córdoba. Plazuela del Potro, 1. ☎ **957/47-33-45.** Admission 250 ptas. ($2) adults, free for children 11 and under. June 15–Sept 15, Tues–Sat 10am–2pm and 6–8pm, Sun 10am–1:30pm; Sept 16–June 14, Tues–Sat 10am–2pm and 5–7pm, Sun 10am–1:30pm. Bus: 3, 4, 7, or 12.

As you cross Plazuela del Potro to reach the Fine Arts Museum, notice the fountain at one end of the square. Built in 1557, it is of a young stallion with forelegs raised, holding the shield of Córdoba.

Housed in an old hospital on the plaza, the Fine Arts Museum contains medieval Andalusian paintings, examples of Spanish baroque art, and works by many of Spain's important 19th- and 20th-century painters, including Goya. The museum is east of the Mezquita, about a block south of the Church of St. Francis (San Francisco).

Museo de Julio Romero de Torres. Plazuela del Potro. ☎ **957/49-19-09.** Admission 425 ptas. ($3.40) adults, 210 ptas. ($1.70) children under 18, free for adults over 75. Free on Tues. Oct–Apr, Tues–Sat 9:30am–1:30pm; May–Sept, Tues–Sat 9:30am–1:30pm and 5–8pm, Sun 9:30am–1:30pm.

Across the patio from the Fine Arts Museum, this museum honors Julio Romero de Torres, a Córdoba-born artist who died in 1930. It contains his celebrated *Oranges and Lemons.* Other notable works include *The Little Girl Who Sells Fuel, Sin,* and *A Dedication to the Art of the Bullfight.* A corner of Romero's Madrid studio has been reproduced in one of the rooms, displaying the paintings left unfinished at his death.

Museo Municipal de Arte Táurino. Plaza de las Bulas (also called Plaza Maimónides). ☎ **957/47-20-00.** Admission 425 ptas. ($3.40), free for children under 18. May–Sept, Tues–Sat 9:30am–1:30pm and 5–8pm, Sun 9:30am–1:30pm; Oct–Apr, Tues–Sat 9:30am–1:30pm and 4–7pm, Sun 9:30am–1:30pm. Bus: 3 or 12.

Memorabilia of great bullfights are housed here in the Jewish Quarter in a 16th-century building, inaugurated in 1983 as an appendage to the Museo Municipal de Arte Cordobesas. Its ample galleries recall Córdoba's great bullfighters with "suits of lights," pictures, trophies, posters, even stuffed bulls' heads. You'll see Manolete in repose and the blood-smeared uniform of El Cordobés—both of these famous matadors came from Córdoba. The museum is located about a block northwest of the Mezquita, midway between the mosque and the synagogue.

Torre de la Calahorra. Avenida de la Confederación, Puente Romano. ☎ **957/29-39-29.** Admission to museum, 400 ptas. ($3.20) adults, 300 ptas. ($2.40) children; multimedia presentation, 400 ptas. ($3.20) adults, 300 ptas. ($2.40) children. May–Sept, daily 10am–2pm and 5:30–8:30pm; Oct–Apr, daily 10:30am–6pm. Bus: 12.

Across the river, at the southern end of the Roman bridge, stands the Tower of the Calahorra. Commissioned by Henry II of Trastamara in 1369 to protect him from his brother, Peter I, it now houses a town museum where visitors can take a self-guided tour with headsets. One room houses wax figures of Córdoba's famous philosophers, including Averro's and Maimónides. Other rooms exhibit a miniature model of the Alhambra, at Granada, complete with water fountains; a miniature Mezquita; and a display of Arab musical instruments. Finally, you can climb to the top of the tower for some panoramic views of the Roman bridge, the river, and the cathedral/mosque.

✪ **Museo Arqueológico Provincial.** Plaza Jerónimo Paz. ☎ **957/47-10-76.** Admission 250 ptas. ($2). Tues–Sat 10am–2pm and 5–7pm, Sun 10am–1:30pm.

Córdoba's Archaeological Museum, two blocks northeast of the Mezquita, is one of the most important in Spain. Housed in a palace dating from 1505, it displays artifacts left behind by the various peoples and conquerors who have swept through the province. There are Paleolithic and Neolithic items, Iberian hand weapons and ceramics, and Roman sculptures, bronzes, ceramics, inscriptions, and mosaics. Especially interesting are the Visigothic artifacts. The most outstanding collection, however, is devoted to Arabic art and spans the entire Muslim occupation. Take a few minutes to relax in one of the patios, with its fountains and ponds.

Palacio Museo de Viana. Plaza de Don Gome, 2. ☎ **957/48-22-75.** Palace admission 400 ptas. ($3.20); patios 200 ptas. ($1.60). June–Sept, Thurs–Tues 9am–2pm; Oct–May, Thurs–Tues 10am–1pm and 4–6pm. Closed June 1–15.

The public has seldom had access to Córdoba's palaces, but that's changed with the opening of this museum. Visitors are shown into a carriage house, where the elegant vehicles of another era are displayed. Note the intricate leather decoration on the carriages and the leather wall hangings, some of which date from the period of the Reconquest; there's also a collection of leather paintings. You can wander at leisure through the garden and patios. The palace lies four blocks southeast of Plaza de Colón on the northeastern edge of the old quarter.

A NEARBY ATTRACTION

Ruinas de Medina Azahara. Carretera Palma de Río, km 8. ☎ **957/32-91-30.** Admission 250 ptas. ($2). Sept 16–May 15, Tues–Sat 10am–2pm and 4–6:30pm, Sun 10am–2pm; May 16–Sept 15, Tues–Sat 10am–2pm and 6–8:30pm, Sun 10am–2pm. Bus: A bus leaves from the station on Calle de la Bodega, but it lets you off about 2 miles (3km) from the site.

This place, a kind of Moorish Versailles just outside Córdoba, was constructed in the 10th century by the first caliph of Andalus, Abd ar-Rahman III. He named it after the favorite of his harem, nicknamed "the brilliant." Thousands of workers and animals slaved to build this mammoth pleasure palace, said to have contained 300 baths and 400 houses. Over the years the site was plundered for building materials; in fact, it might have been viewed as a "quarry" for the region. Some of its materials, so it is claimed, went to build the Alcázar in Seville. The Royal House, rendezvous point for the ministers, has been reconstructed. The principal salon remains in fragments, though, and you have to imagine it in its majesty. Just beyond the Royal House lie the ruins of a mosque constructed to face Mecca. The Berbers sacked the place in 1013.

SHOPPING

In Moorish times Córdoba was famous for its leather, known as "cordwainer." Highly valued in 15th-century Europe, this leather was studded with gold and silver ornaments, then painted with embossed designs (*guadamaci*). Large panels of it often served in lieu of tapestries. Today the industry has fallen into decline, and the market is filled mostly with cheap imitations.

Arte Zoco. Calle de los Júdios, s/n. ☎ **957/29-62-62.**

This is the largest and most comprehensive association of craftspeople in Córdoba. Established in the Jewish Quarter as a business cooperative in the mid-l980s, it assembles into one premises the creative output of about a dozen artisans, whose media include leather, wood, silver, crystal, terra-cotta, and iron. About a half-dozen of the artisans maintain their studios, which can be visited, on the premises, allowing visitors to check out the techniques and tools they use to pursue their crafts. Inventory manages to incorporate a medley of new, iconoclastic and avant-garde designs, in addition to well-made representatives of styles that have endured for thousands of years. Of special interest is the revival of the *Califar* pottery first introduced to Córdoba during the regimes of the Muslim caliphs. The shop is open Monday through Friday from 9:30am to 8pm, Saturday and Sunday from 9:30am to 2pm. The workshops and studios of the various artisans open and close according to the whims of their occupants, but are usually maintained Monday through Friday from 10am to 2pm and 5:30 to 8pm.

El Corte Inglés. Ronda de los Tejares, 32. ☎ **957/47-02-67.**

In the early 1990s, Spain's most respected department store chain bought the premises of a less elegant competitor (Galerias Preciados) and radically revised the merchandise and the marketing plans. Today, you'll find the most cooperative and internationally minded department store in Córdoba, with racks of virtually anything a traveler or a homeowner could possibly want. At least some of the staff speaks English. It's open Monday through Saturday from 10am to 10pm.

Libreria Seferad. Calle Romero, 4. ☎ **957/29-62-62.**

Set across from Córdoba's oldest synagogue, this is a cubbyhole-sized, highly evocative outlet selling articles that might revive a new sense of nostalgia and respect for the Sephardic culture of medieval Europe. Inventory includes cassette tapes of Sephardic music and chants, pottery fashioned into traditional Sephardic designs, filigreed silver ornaments, and references to Ladino, the medieval Iberian dialect spoken by Jews throughout the Diaspora. Inventory is limited, and hours are erratic, usually Monday through Friday from 10am to 2pm and 5 to 8pm.

Meryan. Calleja de Las Flores, 2. ☎ **957/47-59-02.**

This shop, on one of the most colorful streets in the city, is run by Angel López-Obrero and his two skilled sons. In the 250-year-old building, you can see the artisans plying their craft. Most items must be custom-ordered, but there are some ready-made pieces for sale, including cigarette boxes, jewel cases, attaché cases, book and folio covers, and ottoman covers. Open Monday through Friday from 9am to 8pm and Saturday from 9am to 2pm.

OUTDOOR ACTIVITIES

Bullfights The Plaza de Toros on Grand Vía del Parque stages its major bullfights in May, although fights are also presented at other times of the year. Watch for local announcements. Most hotels will arrange tickets for you, ranging in price (in general) from 1,000 to 2,000 pesetas ($8–$16).

Golf The best golf is found 5½ miles (9 km) north of town at Club de Golf Los Villares, Vía Avenida del Brilliante (☎ **957/35-02-08**). This is an excellent 18-hole golf course that's a bit of a resort, with tennis courts and a swimming pool, along with a restaurant. Nonmembers who make reservations are welcome to use the facilities.

Horseback Riding The best riding is at the Club Hipico (Riding Club), at Carretera Santa María de Trassiera (☎ **957/27-16-28**), which grants temporary membership.

Jogging To avoid heavy town traffic, do your early morning jogging at Jardines de la Victoria. Try to go before 10am in summer; after that the day becomes too hot.

Swimming Head for the Costa del Sol (see next chapter) or stay at a hotel with a pool, including Meliá Córdoba and Parador de la Arruzafa (see below). There's also a pool at the golf club (see above).

Tennis The Parador de la Arruzafa (see below) has courts for its guests; otherwise the golf club (see above) is a good choice.

WHERE TO STAY

Córdoba, at the peak of its summer season, has too few hotels to meet the demand—so reserve as far in advance as possible.

VERY EXPENSIVE

✪ **El Conquistador Hotel.** Magistral González Francés, 15, 14003 Córdoba. ☎ **957/48-11-02.** Fax 957/47-46-77. 98 rms, 3 suites. A/C TV TEL. 15,500 ptas. ($124) double; from 22,000 ptas. ($176) suite. AE, DC, MC, V. Parking 1,200 ptas. ($9.60). Bus: 12.

Built centuries ago as a private villa, this first-class three-story hotel was tastefully renovated in 1986 into one of the most attractive in town, with triple rows of stone-trimmed windows and ornate iron balustrades. It sits opposite an unused rear entrance to the Mezquita. The marble-and-granite lobby opens into an interior courtyard filled with seasonal flowers, a pair of splashing fountains, and a symmetrical stone arcade. The quality, size, and comfort of the bedrooms—each with a black-and-white marble floor and a private bath—have earned the hotel four stars, a government designation.

Dining/Entertainment: There is no restaurant, but a coffee shop and a bar serve snacks and drinks.

Services: Babysitting, room service, laundry/valet.

Facilities: Garage, sauna, solarium, car-rental facilities.

✪ **Hotel Meliá Córdoba.** Jardines de la Victoria, 14004 Córdoba. ☎ **800/336-3542** in the U.S., or 957/29-80-66. Fax 957/29-81-47. 142 rms, 5 suites. A/C MINIBAR TV TEL. 15,600 ptas. ($124.80) double; 19,000 ptas. ($152) suite. AE, DC, MC, V. Parking 1,500 ptas. ($12). Bus: 12.

Originally built in 1955, in one of Córdoba's most desirable locations, the Meliá was the first of the town's modern hotels, fulfilling what was regarded as a serious lack of hotel accommodations. Today, it's the most visible and prominent hotel in town, especially since a major renovation in 1991 improved much of its infrastructure, although a lack of effective soundproofing lets a lot of extra noise into the bedrooms. The Meliá offers a very large lobby, enough distractions and amenities to please most tastes, and an enviable setting at the southwestern tip of the city's best-known park. Its distinguishing feature is its flower-filled terrace. The bedrooms, all with private baths, are cool, contemporary, and comfortable, often with balconies and views over nearby fountains. However, many of them are a bit too dark for our tastes. The cathedral, the historic district, and the modern commercial heart of Córdoba lie within easy walking distance.

Dining/Entertainment: The Palace restaurant serves international food in gracefully modern surroundings. An adjacent bar does an active business with the city's business community.

Services: Laundry/valet, concierge, room service (available from 10am to midnight).

Facilities: Car rentals, shopping, boutiques, outdoor swimming pool, barbershop.

Expensive

Hotel Gran Capitán. Avenida de América, 5, 14008 Córdoba. ☎ **957/47-02-50.** Fax 957/47-46-43. 92 rms. A/C TV TEL. 13,200–18,400 ptas. ($105.60–$147.20) double. AE, DC, MC, V. Parking 1,750 ptas. ($14).

Set about two-thirds of a mile north of the Mezquita, on a broad avenue near the railway station, this efficiently modern hotel is a member of the Tryp chain. The bedrooms are comfortably furnished in a contemporary international style, with tightly soundproofed windows and contemporary tile baths.

Dining/Entertainment: The restaurant, La Reja, serves local and international food as part of its three-course, fixed-price lunches and dinners. There's also a bar.

Services: 24-hour room service, laundry, concierge, babysitting.

Facilities: Car rentals, sauna, and a pool.

$ **Parador Nacional de la Arruzafa.** Avenida de la Arruzafa, 33, 14012 Córdoba. ☎ **957/27-59-00.** Fax 957/28-04-09. 90 rms, 6 suites. A/C MINIBAR TV TEL. 15,000 ptas. ($120) double; 18,500 ptas. ($148) suite. AE, DC, MC, V. Free parking.

Lying 2½ miles (4km) outside town in a suburb called El Brillante, this parador—named after an Arab word meaning "palm grove"—offers the conveniences and facilities of a luxurious resort hotel at reasonable rates. Occupying the site of a former caliphate palace, it's one of the finest paradors in Spain, with both a view and a swimming pool. The spacious guest rooms have been furnished with fine dark-wood pieces, and some have balconies for eating breakfast or relaxing over a drink. All have private baths.

Dining/Entertainment: The restaurant serves regional specialties, which include *salmorejo* (a chilled vegetable soup that's a variation of gazpacho), stewed oxtail, and a local cake called *pastel cordobés.*

Services: The government staff is a bit sleepy, but offers room service, laundry/valet, babysitting.

Facilities: Swimming pool, tennis court.

MODERATE

Hotel González. Manríquez, 3, 14003 Córdoba. ☎ **957/47-98-19.** Fax 957/48-61-87. 17 rms. A/C TEL. 9,750 ptas. ($78) double; 12,450 ptas. ($99.60) triple; 16,600 ptas. ($132.80) quad. Rates include breakfast. AE, DC, MC, V. Parking 1,400 ptas. ($11.20).

Within walking distance of the major monuments of Córdoba, the González is a clean, decent hotel but not a lot more. The guest rooms are well kept, functionally furnished, and comfortable. In the hotel's restaurant, also excellent, you can sample both regional and national specialties. Readers have praised the staff's attitude. One claimed, "They solve problems like magicians, take your car to the parking lot and back, and even teach you Spanish."

Hotel Residencia el Califa. Lope de Hoces, 14, 14004 Córdoba. ☎ **800/528-1234** in the U.S. and Canada, or 957/29-94-00. Fax 957/29-57-16. 68 rms, 2 suites. A/C TV TEL. 11,500 ptas. ($92) double; 15,000 ptas. ($120) suite. Rates include breakfast. AE, MC, V. Parking 1,100 ptas. ($8.80). Bus: 12.

Attracting mainly a Spanish clientele, this centrally located hotel lies a short walk northwest of the Mezquita. Although rather impersonal and a bit austere, it is generally good value. Built in 1974, it rises three floors and is serviced by two elevators. Inside, the hotel has russet-colored marble floors, velour wall coverings, a spacious lounge, and a TV that seems to broadcast soccer matches perpetually. Upstairs, guest rooms are reasonably comfortable and furnished in a functional modern style. In lieu of a restaurant, the hotel maintains a snack bar; there's also a bar, plus a parking garage.

Hotel Selu. Calle Eduardo Dato, 7, 14003 Córdoba. ☎ **957/47-65-00.** Fax 957/47-83-76. 118 rms. A/C MINIBAR TV TEL. 10,165 ptas. ($81.30) double. Rates include breakfast. AE, DC, MC, V. Parking 1,100 ptas. ($8.80).

In a commercial part of town near Paseo de la Victoria, the Selu was constructed in 1969, in a four-story design, and renovated in 1991. Guests meet a helpful staff near the reception desk, where public rooms have masses of plants, dozens of velvet-covered armchairs, and a huge photograph of the Moorish columns of the Mezquita, which soften the angular lines. The hotel contains functional bedrooms that are not special in any way but reasonably comfortable. There's an in-house parking garage. Only breakfast is served.

Sol Gallos. Medina Azahara, 7, 14005 Córdoba. ☎ **800/336-3542** in the U.S., or 957/23-55-00. Fax 957/23-16-36. 114 rms. A/C TV TEL. 9,900–10,365 ptas. ($79.20–$82.90) double; 11,900 ptas. ($95.20) triple. AE, DC, MC, V.

Half a block from a wide, tree-shaded boulevard on the western edge of town, this aging 1970s hotel stands eight floors high, crowned by an informal roof garden. The hotel is a favorite of both groups and commercial travelers. The comfortable but small guest rooms have many extra comforts, such as balconies, and the outdoor swimming pool is a pleasure during the summer. The hotel also offers a restaurant, a drinking lounge, and a spacious public lobby.

INEXPENSIVE

Hostal el Triunfo. Corregidor Luís de la Cerda, 79, 14003 Córdoba. ☎ **957/47-55-00.** Fax 957/48-68-50. 58 rms. A/C TV TEL. 5,800 ptas. ($46.40) double; 6,900 ptas. ($55.20) triple. AE, DC, MC, V. Parking 1,500 ptas. ($12). Bus: 12.

Opposite the mosque, a block from the northern bank of the Guadalquivir River, this is a real find—a simple hotel with a formal entranceway, a pleasant white-walled lounge, and comfortable, well-furnished rooms. Built in the late 1970s, the El Triunfo was renovated in 1992. It offers polite and efficient service. The three-floor hotel has no elevator; its only other drawback is that the bells of the Mezquita may make it difficult to sleep.

Hotel Riviera. Plaza de Aladreros, 5, 14001 Córdoba. ☎ **957/47-30-00.** Fax 957/47-60-18. 30 rms. A/C TV TEL. 4,900–5,800 ptas. ($39.20–$46.40) double; 6,075–7,000 ptas. ($48.60–$56) triple. AE, DC.

The genial owner of this modern hotel is likely to be behind the reception desk when you arrive. His establishment—set on a triangular plaza in a commercial section of town a short walk south of the train station—offers very clean "no-frills" accommodations. No meals are served, but many cafés are within walking distance.

WHERE TO DINE

By all means, shake free of your hotel for at least one meal a day in Córdoba. The restaurants are not just places at which to have a quick bite. Some combine food with flamenco—so make an evening of it.

✪ **La Almudaina.** Plaza de los Santos Mártires, 1. ☎ **957/47-43-42.** Reservations required. Main courses 1,800–2,500 ptas. ($14.40–$20); fixed-price menus 3,000–5,000 ptas. ($24–$40). AE, DC, MC, V. Daily noon–5pm, Mon–Sat 8:30pm–midnight. Closed Sun in July–Aug. Bus: 12. SPANISH/FRENCH.

The owners of this historic restaurant near the Alcázar deserve as much credit for their renovations of a decrepit 15th-century palace as they do for the excellent cuisine produced by their bustling kitchen. Fronting the river in what used to be the Jewish Quarter, La Almudaina is one of the most attractive eateries in Andalusia, where you can dine in one of the lace-curtained salons or on a glass-roofed central courtyard. Specialties include salmon crêpes; a wide array of fish, such as hake with shrimp sauce; and meats, such as pork loin in wine sauce. For dessert, try the not-too-sweet chocolate crêpe. The cuisine's success is in its use of very fresh ingredients that are deftly handled by the kitchen and not overcooked or overspiced.

✪ **El Caballo Rojo.** Cardinal Herrero, 28, Plaza de la Hoguera. ☎ **957/47-53-75.** Reservations required. Main courses 1,600–3,000 ptas. ($12.80–$24). AE, DC, MC, V. Daily 1–4:30pm and 8pm–midnight. Bus: 12. SPANISH.

This restaurant is the most popular in Andalusia, and except for the Almudaina (see above), it remains the best in Córdoba, although often overrun by tourists. The place has a noise level no other restaurant here matches, but the skilled waiters still seem to cope with all demands. Within walking distance of the Mezquita in the old town, it is down a long open-air passageway flanked by potted geraniums and vines. Stop in the restaurant's popular bar for a preprandial drink, then take the iron-railed stairs to the upper dining room, where a typical meal might include gazpacho, a main dish of chicken, then ice cream and sangría. (The ice cream, incidentally, is likely to be homemade pistachio.) Try a variation on the usual gazpacho—almond-flavored broth with apple pieces. In addition to Andalusian dishes, the chef offers both Sephardic and Mozarabic specialties, an example of the latter being monkfish prepared with pine nuts, currants, carrots, and cream. Real aficionados come here for the *rabo de toro* (stew made with the tail of an ox or a bull). The cookery is robust and flavorsome.

El Churrasco. Romero, 16. ☎ **957/29-08-19.** Reservations required. Main courses 1,400–2,800 ptas. ($11.20–$22.40); fixed-price menu 5,000–7,000 ptas. ($40–$56). AE, DC, MC, V. Daily 2–5:30pm and 7:45pm–midnight. Closed Aug. Bus: 12. SPANISH.

Housed in an ancient stone-fronted building in the Jewish Quarter just northwest of the Mezquita, El Churrasco serves elegant meals in five different dining rooms on two floors. You'll pass a bar and an open grill before reaching a ground-floor dining room that resembles a Moorish courtyard, with rounded arches and a splashing fountain. Upstairs, more formal rooms display the owner's riveting collection of paintings. You can enjoy such good-tasting specialties as grilled filet of beef with whiskey sauce, succulent roast lamb, grilled salmon, and monkfish in a pine-nut sauce—all accompanied by good service—but the signature dish here is the charcoal-grilled pork loin.

Ciro's. Paseo de la Victoria, 19. ☎ **957/29-04-64.** Reservations recommended. Main courses 1,800–2,500 ptas. ($14.40–$20); fixed-price menu 2,600 ptas. ($20.80). AE, DC, MC, V. Daily 1–5pm and 8pm–midnight. Closed Sun in summer. ANDALUSIAN.

Once a simple cafeteria, Ciro's has been transformed into an accommodating, comfortably air-conditioned restaurant. The proprietors mix good service with modern and Andalusian-style cuisine. The menu includes such savory dishes as a salmon-and-anchovy pudding, stuffed sweet peppers, hake in shrimp sauce, veal in red wine, and an array of dessert sorbets. Ciro's lies directly south of the rail station, about a quarter of a mile northwest of the Mezquita.

Restaurante Da Vinci. Plaza de Los Chirinos, 6. ☎ **957/47-75-17.** Reservations required. Main courses 600–1,800 ptas. ($4.80–$14.40); *menú del día* 1,600 ptas. ($12.80). V. Daily 1:30–4:30pm and 8pm–midnight. ITALIAN/INTERNATIONAL.

Situated in a quiet neighborhood a block off the city's main boulevard, Calle Cruz Conde, this ranks as one of the leading restaurants in town. Before heading into the dining room; stop for a drink in the comfortable bar near the entrance, where many guests order from a selection of tempting tapas. Both the cuisine and the decor are a blend of Andalusian, international, and Italian influences, arranged in a curious but pleasing mishmash of traditions. Menu items include a choice of roast meats (veal, pork, beefsteak, and lamb), a variety of pastas and salads, and many kinds of fish and seafood, especially hake, monkfish, squid, and salmon. This is standard Andalusian fare, with no innovation and little flair, but it's still good.

CÓRDOBA AFTER DARK

La Canoa. Pasaje Ronda Los Tejares, 18–20. ☎ **957/47-17-61.**

The rustic interior decorated with wine-barrel tables and Carthusian cellar decor appeals to La Canoa's many customers. A glass of wine or beer here will be more of a rapid pick-me-up than something to linger over for hours. You can order a ration of Serrano ham or a hefty platter of cheese if you're hungry. La Canoa, located between the Plaza de Colón and the Paseo de la Victoria, is open Monday through Saturday from noon to 4pm and 8pm to midnight. It's closed for two weeks in August. Tapas range in price from 150 to 1,500 pesetas ($1.20–$12).

Casa Rubio. Puerta de Almodóvar, 5. ☎ **957/29-00-64.**

You must push back a thick curtain to enter this dimly lit enclave of pre-Franco Spain. Once inside, you'll find a gruff but accommodating welcome at the rectangular bar or in one of a pair of rooms partially covered with Andalusian tiles. Our preferred place is within a plant-festooned inner courtyard, where iron tables and a handful of chairs wobble only slightly on the uneven flooring. Casa Rubio is open Thursday through Tuesday from 7am to 4pm and 7:30pm to midnight. An order of tapas will range from 100 to 300 pesetas (80¢ to $2.40).

3 Seville

341 miles (549km) SW of Madrid, 135 miles (217km) NW of Málaga

Sometimes a city becomes famous for its beauty and romance. Seville (called *Sevilla* in Spain), the capital of Andalusia, is such a place. In spite of its sultry heat in summer and its many problems, such as rising unemployment and street crime, it remains one of the most charming Spanish cities.

Don Juan and Carmen—aided by Mozart and Bizet—have given Seville a romantic reputation. Because of the acclaim of *Don Giovanni* and *Carmen,* not to mention *The Barber of Seville,* debunkers have risen to challenge this reputation. But if a visitor can see only two Spanish cities in a lifetime, they should be Seville and Toledo.

All the images associated with Andalusia—orange trees, mantillas, lovesick toreros, flower-filled patios, and castanet-rattling gypsies—come to life in Seville. But it's not just a tourist city; it's a substantial river port, and it contains some of the most important artistic works and architectural monuments in Spain.

Unlike most Spanish cities, Seville has fared rather well under most of its conquerors—the Romans, Arabs, and Christians. Pedro the Cruel and Ferdinand and Isabella held court here. When Spain entered its 16th-century golden age, Seville funneled gold from the New World into the rest of the country. Columbus docked here after his journey to America.

Be warned, however, that driving here is a nightmare: Seville was planned for the horse and buggy rather than for the car, and nearly all the streets run one way toward the Guadalquivir River. Locating a hard-to-find restaurant or a hidden little square might require patience and even a little luck.

ESSENTIALS

GETTING THERE **By Plane** From Seville's San Pablo Airport, Calle Almirante Lobo (☎ **95/451-53-20**), Iberia flies several times a day to and from Madrid (and elsewhere via Madrid). It also flies several times a week to and from Alicante, Grand Canary Island, Lisbon, Barcelona, Palma de Majorca, Tenerife, Santiago de Compostela, and (once a week) Zaragoza. The airport lies about six miles (9.6km) from the center of the city, along the highway leading to Carmona.

By Train Train service into Seville is now centralized into the Estación Santa Justa, Avenida Kansas City, s/n (☎ **95/454-02-02** for information and reservations). Buses C1 and C2 take you from this train station to the bus station at Prado de San Sebastián, and bus EA runs to and from the airport. The high-speed AVE train has reduced travel time from Madrid to Seville to 2½ hours. The train makes 12 trips daily, with a stop in Córdoba. Ten trains a day connect Seville and Córdoba; the AVE train takes 50 minutes and a *TALGO* takes 1½ hours. Three trains a day run to Málaga, taking 3 to 4 hours, depending on the train; there are also three trains per day to Granada (4 to 5 hours).

Seville

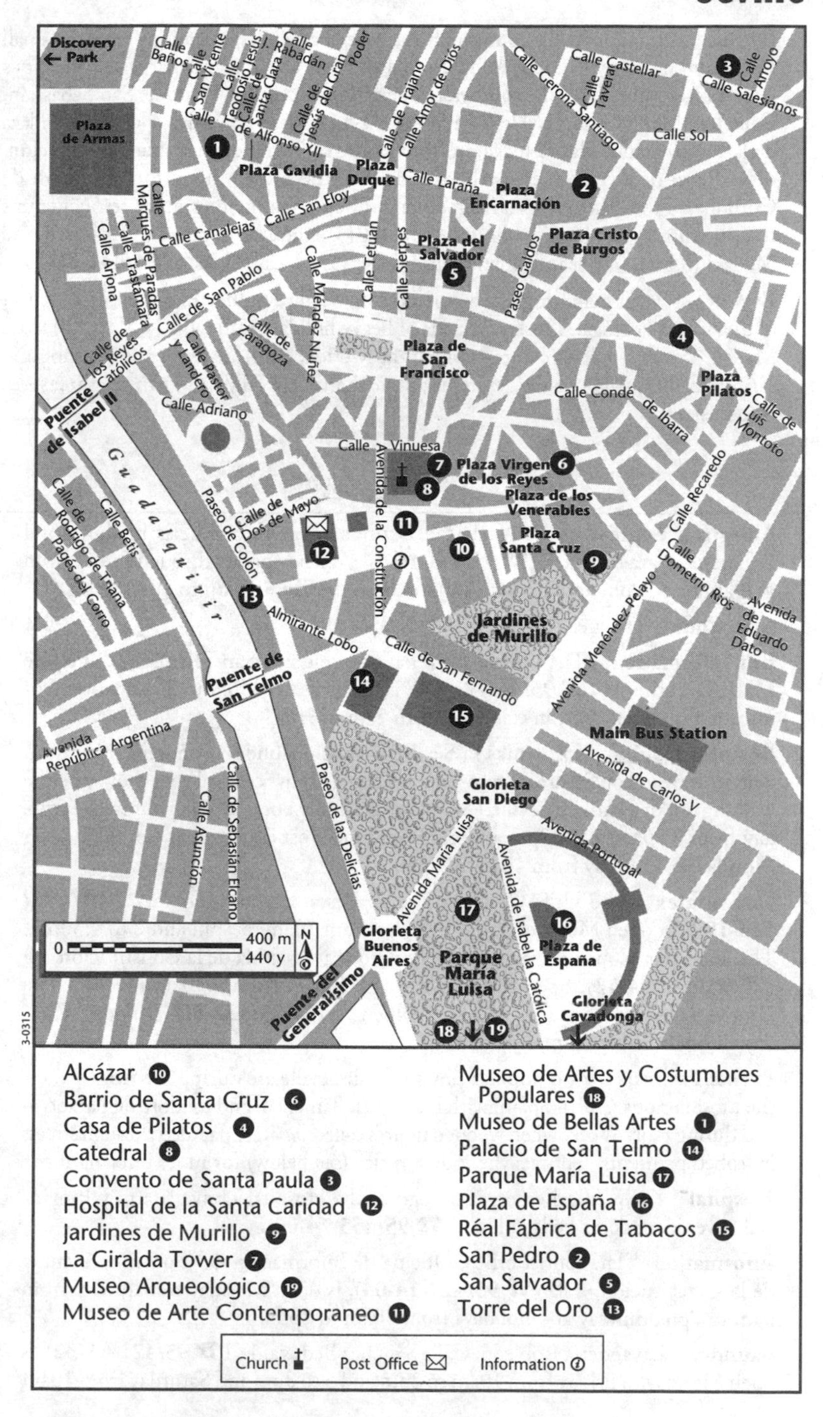

Discovery Park
Plaza de Armas
Calle Baños
Calle San Vicente
Calle Teodosio
Calle de Jesús
Calle de Santa Clara
J. Rabadán
Calle de Jesús del Gran Poder
Calle de Alfonso XII
Plaza Gavidia
Plaza Duque
Calle de Trajano
Calle Amor de Diós
Calle Gerona
Calle Castellar
Calle Tavera
Santiago
Calle Arroyo
Calle Salesianos
Calle Sol
Calle Laraña
Plaza Encarnación
Calle San Eloy
Calle Canalejas
Calle Marqués de Paradas
Calle Trastámara
Calle Arjona
Calle Méndez Nuñez
Calle Tetuan
Calle Sierpes
Plaza del Salvador
Paseo Galdos
Plaza Cristo de Burgos
Calle de San Pablo
Calle de Zaragoza
Calle de los Reyes Católicos
Calle Pastor y Landero
Plaza de San Francisco
Calle Condé de Ibarra
Plaza Pilatos
Calle de Luis Montoto
Calle Adriano
Puente de Isabel II
Guadalquivir
Calle Vinuesa
Avenida de la Constitución
Plaza Virgen de los Reyes
Plaza de los Venerables
Plaza Santa Cruz
Calle Recaredo
Calle Dometrio Rios
Avenida de Eduardo Dato
Calle de Rodrigo de Triana
Calle Pagés del Corro
Calle Betis
Paseo de Colón
Calle de Dos de Mayo
Almirante Lobo
Jardines de Murillo
Avenida Menéndez Pelayo
Calle de San Fernando
Puente de San Telmo
Main Bus Station
Avenida de Carlos V
Avenida República Argentina
Glorieta San Diego
Avenida Portugal
Calle Asunción
Calle de Sebasián Elcano
Paseo de las Delicias
Avenida María Luisa
Avenida de Isabel la Católica
Glorieta Buenos Aires
Parque María Luisa
Plaza de España
Glorieta Cavadonga
Puente del Generalísimo
0
400 m
440 y
N
3-0315
Alcázar 10
Barrio de Santa Cruz 6
Casa de Pilatos 4
Catedral 8
Convento de Santa Paula 3
Hospital de la Santa Caridad 12
Jardines de Murillo 9
La Giralda Tower 7
Museo Arqueológico 19
Museo de Arte Contemporaneo 11
Museo de Artes y Costumbres Populares 18
Museo de Bellas Artes 1
Palacio de San Telmo 14
Parque María Luisa 17
Plaza de España 16
Réal Fábrica de Tabacos 15
San Pedro 2
San Salvador 5
Torre del Oro 13
Church
Post Office
Information

By Bus Although Seville confusingly has several satellite bus stations servicing small towns and nearby villages of Andalusia, most buses arrive and depart from the city's largest bus terminal, on the southeast edge of the old city, at Prado de San Sebastián, Calle José María Osborne, 11 (☎ **95/441-71-11**). Many lines also converge on Plaza de la Encarnación, Plaza Nueva, in front of the cathedral on Avenida Constitución, or at Plaza de Armas (across the street from the old train station, Estación de Córdoba). From there, buses from several different companies make frequent runs to and from Córdoba (2½ hours), Málaga (3½ hours), Granada (4 hours), and Madrid (8 hours). For information and ticket prices, call Alsina at **95/441-88-11.**

By Car Several major highways converge on Seville, connecting it with all the rest of Spain and Portugal. During periods of heavy holiday traffic, the N-V (E-90) from Madrid through Extremadura—which, at Mérida, connects with the southbound N630 (E-803)—is usually less congested than the N-IV (E-5) through eastern Andalusia.

FAST FACTS: Seville

American Express The American Express office in Seville is in the Hotel Inglaterra, Plaza Nueva, 7 (☎ **95/421-16-17**), open Monday through Friday from 9:30am to 1:30pm and 4:30 to 7:30pm, Saturday from 10am to 1pm.

Area Code The area code for Seville is **95.**

Bus Information The Central Bus Station, Prado de San Sebastián, Calle José María Osborne, 11 (☎ **95/441-71-11**), is the place to go for bus information. For information here, you can call daily from 7am to 9pm.

Business Hours Most banks in Seville are open Monday through Friday from 9am to 2pm and on Saturday from 9am to noon. (Always conceal your money before walking out of a bank in Seville.) Shops are generally open Monday through Saturday from 9:30am to 1:30pm and 4:30 to 8pm. Most department stores are open Monday to Saturday from 10am to 8pm.

Consulates The U.S. Consulate is at Paseo de las Delicias, 7 (☎ **95/423-18-83**), open Monday through Friday from 10am to 1pm and 2 to 4:30pm. The Canadian Consulate is on the second floor at Avenida de la Constitución, 30 (☎ **95/422-94-13**), open Monday through Friday from 9:30am to 1pm. The United Kingdom Consulate is at Plaza Nueva, 8 (☎ **95/422-88-75**), open Monday through Friday from 8am to 3pm.

Events/Festivals Two popular times to visit Seville are during the April Fair—the most famous *feria* in Spain, with bullfights, flamenco, and folklore on parade—and during Holy Week, when wooden figures called *pasos* are paraded through streets by robed penitents. Contact the tourist office (see below) for more information.

Hospital For medical emergencies, go to the Hospital Universitario y Provincial, Avenida Doctor Fedriani, s/n (☎ **95/455-74-00).**

Information The tourist office, Oficina de Información del Turismo, Avenida de la Constitución, 21B (☎ **95/422-14-04**), is open Monday to Saturday from 9am to 7pm, Sunday and holidays from 10am to 2pm.

Laundry Lavandería Robledo, Calle Sánchez Bedoya, 18 (☎ **95/421-81-32**), is open Monday to Friday from 10am to 2pm and 5 to 8pm and Saturday from 10am to 2pm.

Police The police station is located on Avenida Paseo de las Delicias (☎ **95/461-54-50**).

Post Office The post office is at Avenida de la Constitución, 32 (☎ **95/421-95-85**). Hours are Monday to Friday from 8:30am to 8:30pm, Saturday from 9:30am to 2pm.

Safety With massive unemployment, the city has been hit by a crime wave in recent years. María Luisa Park is especially dangerous, as is the highway leading to Jerez de la Frontera and Cádiz. Dangling cameras and purses are especially vulnerable. Don't leave cars unguarded with your luggage inside. Regrettably, some daring attacks are made—as they are in U.S. cities—when passengers stop for traffic signals.

Taxis Call Tele Taxi at **95/462-22-22** or Radio Taxi at **95/458-00-00.** Cabs are metered and charge 52 pesetas (40¢) per kilometer.

Telephone/Telex The telephone office is at Plaza Gavidia, 7 (for telephone service information, call **003**). To send wires by phone, call **95/422-20-00.**

WHAT TO SEE & DO

THE TOP ATTRACTIONS

Seville has a wide range of palaces, churches, cathedrals, towers, and historic hospitals. Since it would take a week or two to visit all of them, we have narrowed the sights down to the very top attractions plus a few additional ones. The only way to explore Seville is on foot, with a good map in hand—but remember to be alert to muggers.

✪ **Catedral.** Plaza del Triunfo, Avenida de la Constitución. ☎ **95/421-49-71.** Admission (including visit to Giralda Tower) 500 ptas. ($4). Daily 11am–5pm.

The largest Gothic building in the world, and the third-largest church in Europe after St. Peter's in Rome and St. Paul's in London, this church was designed by builders with a stated goal—that "those who come after us will take us for madmen." Construction began in the late 1400s and took centuries to complete.

Built on the site of an ancient mosque, the cathedral claims to contain the remains of Columbus, with his tomb mounted on four statues.

Works of art abound, many of them architectural, such as the 15th-century stained-glass windows, the iron screens (*rejas*) closing off the chapels, the elaborate 15th-century choir stalls, and the Gothic reredos above the main altar. During Corpus Christi and the Immaculate Conception observances, altar boys with castanets dance in front of the high altar. In the Treasury are works by Goya, Murillo, and Zurbarán; here, in glass cases, a touch of the macabre shows up in the display of skulls.

After touring the dark interior, emerge into the sunlight of the Patio of Orange Trees, with its fresh citrus scents and chirping birds.

Warning: Shorts and T-shirts are definitely not allowed.

Giralda Tower. Plaza del Triunfo. Admission included in admission to cathedral (above). Same hours as cathedral (above).

Just as Big Ben symbolizes London, La Giralda conjures up Seville—this Moorish tower, next to the cathedral, is the city's most famous monument. Erected as a minaret in the 12th century, it has seen later additions, such as 16th-century bells. To climb it is to take the walk of a lifetime. There are no steps—you ascend an endless ramp. If you make it to the top, you'll have a dazzling view of Seville. Entrance is through the cathedral.

✪ **Alcázar.** Plaza del Triunfo, s/n. ☎ **422-71-63.** Admission 700 ptas. ($5.60). Tues–Sat 10:30am–5pm, Sun 10am–1pm.

This magnificent 14th-century Mudéjar palace, north of the cathedral, was built by Pedro the Cruel. It is the oldest royal residence in Europe still in use: On visits to Seville, King Juan Carlos stays here. From the Dolls' Court to the Maidens' Court through the domed Ambassadors' Room, it contains some of the finest work of Sevillian artisans. In many ways, it evokes the Alhambra at Granada. Ferdinand and Isabella, who at one time lived in the Alcázar and influenced its architectural evolution, welcomed Columbus here on his return from America. On the top floor, the Oratory of the Catholic Monarchs has a fine altar in polychrome tiles made by Pisano in 1504.

The well-kept gardens, filled with beautiful flowers, shrubbery, and fruit trees, are alone worth the visit.

EL PARQUE DE LOS DESCUBRIMIENTOS (DISCOVERY PARK)

Isla de la Cartuja. ☎ **95/446-16-16.** "Strolling ticket" (access to park and its gardens) 500 ptas. ($4); "super ticket" (adds access to pavilions) 4,000 ptas. ($32) adults, 3,000 ptas. ($24) children. June 7–Oct 12, Tues–Thurs, park 8pm–2am, pavilions 8pm–midnight; Fri–Sat, park 11:30am–4am, pavilions 8pm–midnight; Sun, park 11:30am–1am, pavilions noon–8pm. Apr 25–June 6 and Oct 13–Dec 21, Thurs, park 8pm–2am, pavilions 8pm–midnight; Fri–Sat, park 11:30am–2am, pavilions noon–8pm; Sun, park 11:30am–midnight, pavilions noon–8pm. Dec 22–Apr 24, Fri–Sat, park 11:30am–midnight, pavilions noon–8pm; Sun, park 11:30am–midnight, pavilions 11:30am–midnight. Bus: C2 from the center of Seville.

On the 540-acre island of La Cartuja in the Guadalquivir River, site of Expo '92, the government opened a theme park in 1993. Although closed in 1996 for restoration, it is slated to be open in the summer of 1997, when prices and hours (stated above) may be readjusted slightly. Call for information before heading here. Eight new bridges now join the island to Seville. The theme park itself takes up 168 acres of the site and incorporates some of the more acclaimed attractions at Expo. Among them are the Pavilion of Navigation, tracing the history of maritime exploration from its beginnings to the present; the Pavilion of Nature, containing flora and fauna from all over the world; and eight other pavilions, representing the autonomous regions of Spain.

Puerto de Indias is the re-creation of a 15th-century port, with small shops and evocative taverns, along with silversmiths, cobblers, welders, and other tradespersons. Replicas of Christopher Columbus's ships in 1492, the *Pinta, Niña,* and *Santa María,* are docked here. The Children's Park offers a host of entertainment, including puppet shows and water slides.

The audiovisual offerings are said to equal or top those of any theme park in the world. The computer-controlled Digital Planetarium, for example, housed in the Pavilion of the Universe, is the only one of its kind in the world—images are projected onto a 60-foot dome, taking viewers on a ride through the universe.

Buses, cable cars, a monorail, catamarans, trolley cars, and rowboats are some of the transportation available to haul visitors around. Other facilities and attractions include concerts, plays, dance clubs, 2 parades and a circus daily, a lazer-sound show with fireworks, 12 foodstalls, 15 family restaurants, 7 tapas bars, and 2 deluxe restaurants.

Impressions

Seville doesn't have an ambiance. It is ambiance.

—James A. Michener

Seville is a pleasant city, famous for oranges and women.

—Lord Byron

Hospital de la Santa Caridad. Calle Temprado, 3. ☎ **95/422-32-22.** Admission 300 ptas. ($2.40). Mon–Sat 10am–1pm and 3:30–6pm, Sun 10:30am–12:30pm.

This 17th-century hospital is intricately linked to the legend of Miguel Manara, portrayed by Dumas and Mérimée as a scandalous Don Juan. It was once thought that he built this institution to atone for his sins, but this has been disproved. The death of Manara's beautiful young wife in 1661 caused such grief that he retired from society and entered the "Charity Brotherhood," burying corpses of the sick and diseased as well as condemned and executed criminals. Today the members of this brotherhood continue to look after the poor, the old, and invalids who have no one else to help them.

Nuns will show you through the festive orange-and-sienna courtyard. The baroque chapel contains works by the 17th-century Spanish painters Murillo and Valdés-Leál. As you're leaving the chapel, look over the exit door for the macabre picture of an archbishop being devoured by maggots.

Torre del Oro. Paseo de Cristóbal Colón. ☎ **95/422-24-19.** Admission 100 ptas. (80¢). Tues–Fri 10am–2pm, Sat–Sun 10am–1pm.

The 12-sided Tower of Gold, dating from the 13th century, overlooks the Guadalquivir River. Originally it was covered with gold tiles, but someone long ago made off with them. Recently restored, the tower has been turned into a maritime museum, Museo Náutico, displaying drawings and engravings of the port of Seville in its golden heyday.

Casa de Pilatos. Plaza Pilatos, 1. ☎ **95/422-50-55.** Admission, museum 1,000 ptas. ($8); patio and gardens 500 ptas. ($4). Museum, daily 10am–2pm and 4–6pm; patio and gardens, daily 9am–7pm.

This 16th-century Andalusian palace of the dukes of Medinaceli recaptures the splendor of the past, combining Gothic, Mudéjar, and plateresque styles in its courtyards, fountains, and salons. According to tradition, this is a reproduction of Pilate's House in Jerusalem. Don't miss the two old carriages or the rooms filled with Greek and Roman statues. The collection of paintings includes works by Carreño, Pantoja de la Cruz, Sebastiano del Piombo, Lucas Jordán, Batalloli, Pacheco, and Goya. The palace lies about a seven-minute walk northeast of the cathedral on the northern edge of Barrio de Santa Cruz, in a warren of labyrinthine streets whose traffic is funneled through the nearby Calle de Aguiles.

Archivo General de Indias. Avenida de la Constitución, s/n. ☎ **95/421-12-34.** Free admission. Mon–Fri 10am–1pm.

The great architect of Philip II's El Escorial, Juan de Herrera, was also the architect of this building, originally the Lonja (Stock Exchange), located next to the cathedral. Construction on the Archivo General de Indias lasted from 1584 to 1646. In the 17th century it was headquarters for the Academy of Seville, which was founded in part by the great Spanish artist Murillo.

In 1785, during the reign of Charles III, the building was turned over for use as a general records office for the Indies. That led to today's Archivo General de Indias, said to contain some four million antique documents, even letters exchanged between patron Queen Isabella and explorer Columbus (he detailing his discoveries and impressions). These very rare documents are locked in air-conditioned storage to keep them from disintegrating. Special permission has to be acquired before examining some of them. Many treasure hunters come here hoping to learn details of where Spanish galleons laden with gold went down off the coast of the Americas. On display in glass cases are fascinating documents in which the dreams of the early explorers come alive again.

✪ **Museo Provincial de Bellas Artes de Sevilla.** Plaza del Museo, 9. ☎ **95/422-18-29.** Admission 250 ptas. ($2), free for students. Tues–Sun 9am–3pm. Bus: 21, 24, 30, or 31.

This lovely old convent off Calle de Alfonso XII houses one of the most important Spanish art collections. A whole gallery is devoted to two paintings by El Greco, and works by Zurbarán are exhibited; however, the devoutly religious paintings of the Seville-born Murillo are the highlights. An entire wing is given over to macabre paintings by the 17th-century artist Valdés-Leál. His painting of John the Baptist's head on a platter includes the knife—in case you didn't get "the point." The top floor, which displays modern paintings, is less interesting.

More Attractions

✪ **Barrio de Santa Cruz** What was once a ghetto for Spanish Jews, who were forced out of Spain in the late 15th century in the wake of the Inquisition, is today the most colorful district of Seville. Near the old walls of the Alcázar, winding medieval streets with names like *Vida* (Life) and *Muerte* (Death) open onto pocket-sized plazas. Flower-filled balconies with draping bougainvillea and potted geraniums jut out over this labyrinth, shading you from the hot Andalusian summer sun. Feel free to look through numerous wrought-iron gates into patios filled with fountains and plants. In the evening it's common to see Sevillians sitting outside drinking icy sangría under the glow of lanterns.

Although the district as a whole is recommended for sightseeing, seek out in particular the **Casa de Murillo (Murillo's House),** Santa Teresa, 8 (☎ **95/421-75-35**). Bartolomé Esteban Murillo, the great Spanish painter known for his religious works, was born in Seville in 1617. He spent his last years in this house in Santa Cruz, dying in 1682. Five minor paintings of the artist are on display. The furnishings, although not owned by the artist, are period pieces. Admission is 250 pesetas ($2), and the house is open Tuesday through Saturday 10am to 2pm and 6 to 8pm.

To enter the Barrio Santa Cruz, turn right after leaving the Patio de Banderas exit of the Alcázar. Turn right again at Plaza de la Alianza, going down Calle Rodrigo Caro to Plaza de Doña Elvira. Use caution when strolling through the area, particularly at night; many robberies have occurred here.

Parque María Luisa This park, dedicated to María Luisa, sister of Isabella II, was once the grounds of the Palacio de San Telmo, Avenida de Roma. The palace, whose baroque facade is visible behind the deluxe Alfonso XIII Hotel, today houses a seminary. The former private royal park is now open to the public.

Running south along the Guadalquivir River, the park attracts those who want to take boat rides, walk along paths bordered by flowers, jog, or go bicycling. The most romantic way to traverse it is by rented horse and carriage, but this can be expensive, depending on your negotiation with the driver.

In 1929 Seville was to host the Spanish American Exhibition, and many pavilions from other countries were erected here. The worldwide depression put a damper on the exhibition, but the pavilions still stand.

Exercise caution while walking through this park. Many muggings have been reported.

Plaza de América Another landmark Sevillian square, Plaza de América represents city planning at its best: Here you can walk through gardens planted with roses, enjoying the lily ponds and the fountains and feeling the protective shade of the palms. And here you'll find a trio of elaborate buildings left over from the world exhibition that never materialized—in the center, the home of the government headquarters of Andalusia; on either side, two minor museums worth visiting only if you have time to spare.

The **Museo Arqueológico Provincial,** Plaza de América, s/n (☎ **95/423-24-01**), contains many artifacts from prehistoric times and the days of the Romans, Visigoths, and Moors. It's open Tuesday to Sunday from 10am to 2pm. Admission is 250 pesetas ($2) for adults and free for students and children. Buses 30, 31, and 34 go there.

Nearby is the **Museo de Artes y Costumbres Populares,** Plaza de América, s/n (☎ **95/423-25-76**), displaying folkloric costumes, musical instruments, *cordobán* saddles, weaponry, and farm implements that document the life of the Andalusian people. It's open Tuesday through Saturday from 9:30am to 2:30pm, but closed on holidays. Admission is 250 pesetas ($2) for adults and free for children and students.

Plaza de España The major building left from the exhibition at the Parque María Luisa (see above) is a half-moon-shaped structure in Renaissance style, set on this landmark square of Seville. The architect, Anibal González, not only designed but supervised the building of this immense structure; today it is a government office building. At a canal here you can rent rowboats for excursions into the park, or you can walk across bridges spanning the canal. Set into a curved wall are alcoves, each focusing on characteristics of one of Spain's 50 provinces, as depicted in tile murals.

Real Fábrica de Tabacos When Carmen waltzed out of the tobacco factory in the first act of Bizet's opera, she made its 18th-century original in Seville world famous. The old tobacco factory was constructed between 1750 and 1766, and a hundred years later, it employed 10,000 *cigarreras,* of which Carmen was one in the opera. (She rolled her cigars on her thighs.) In the 19th century, these tobacco women made up the largest female workforce in Spain. Many visitors arriving today, in fact, ask guides to take them to "Carmen's tobacco factory." The building, the second largest in Spain and located on Calle San Fernando near the city's landmark luxury hotel, the Alfonso XIII, is still there. But the Real Fábrica de Tabacos is now part of the Universidad de Sevilla. Look for signs of its former role, however, in the bas-reliefs of tobacco plants and Indians over the main entrances. You'll also see bas-reliefs of Columbus and Cortés. Then you can wander through the grounds for a look at student life, Sevillian style. The factory is directly south of the Alcázar gardens.

SHOPPING

ART GALLERIES

Rafael Ortíz. Marmolles, 12. ☎ **95/421-48-74.**

This is one of the most respected art galleries in Seville, specializing in contemporary paintings, usually from Iberian artists. Exhibitions change frequently, and because of canniness of this emporium's judgments, inventories sell out quickly. It's open Monday through Saturday from 10am to 1:30pm and 4:30 to 8:30pm.

Books

The English Bookshop. Marqués de Nervion. ☎ **95/465-57-54.**

Smaller than many of the other book emporiums in Seville, this is the kind of place where you can find tomes on gardening, political discourse, philosophy, and pop fiction, all gathered into one cozy place. Open Monday through Saturday from 10am to 1:45pm and 4:30 to 8:30pm.

Libreria Vértice. San Fernando, 33. ☎ **95/421-16-54.**

Set conveniently close to Seville's university, this store stocks books in a polyglot of languages. Inventory ranges from the esoteric and professorial to Spanish romances of the soap-opera and bubblegum genre. Open Monday through Saturday from 10am to 1:30pm and 4:30 to 8:30pm.

Ceramics

Martian. Calle Sierpes, 74. ☎ **95/421-34-13.**

Set close to Seville's Town Hall, this outfit sells a wide array of painted tiles and ceramics, the kind that invariably look better when transported away from the store and displayed within your home. The inventory includes vases, plates, cups, serving dishes, and statues, all made in or near Seville. Many of the pieces exhibit ancient geometric patterns of Andalusia. Other floral motifs are rooted in Spanish traditions of the 18th century. Open Monday through Saturday from 10am to 1:30pm and 4:30 to 8:30pm.

El Postigo. Arfe, s/n. ☎ **95/421-39-76.**

Set in the town center, near the cathedral, this contains one of the biggest selections in town of the ceramics for which Andalusia is famous. Some of the pieces are much, much too big to fit into your suitcase; others—especially the hand-painted tiles—make charming souvenirs that can be packed with your luggage. Open Monday through Saturday from 10am to 2pm, Monday through Friday from 5 to 8pm.

Department Stores

El Corte Inglés. Plaza Duque, 10. ☎ **95/422-19-31.**

This is the best of the several department stores clustered in Seville's commercial center. A well-accessorized branch of a nationwide chain, it features multilingual translators and rack after rack of every conceivable kind of merchandise for the well-stocked home, kitchen, and closet. If you're in the market for the brightly colored *feria* costumes worn by young girls during Seville's holidays, there's an impressive selection of the folkloric accessories that make Andalusia memorable. Open Monday through Saturday from 10am to 9pm.

Fans

Casa Rubio. Sierpes, 56. ☎ **95/422-68-72.**

Carmen fluttered her fan and broke hearts in ways that Andalusian maidens have done with their *caballeros* for centuries. Casa Rubio stocks one of the city's largest supplies, ranging from the austere and dramatic to some of the most florid and fanciful aids to coquetry available in Spain. Open Monday through Saturday from 10am to 1:45pm and 5 to 8pm.

Fashion

Econos. Avenida de la Constitución. ☎ **95/422-14-08.**

It's an excellent example of a small, idiosyncratic boutique loaded with fashion accessories that can be used by everyone from teenaged girls to mature women. Silk scarves, costume jewelry, and an assortment of T-shirts with logos lettered in varying degrees of tastelessness—it's all here. Much of the merchandise represents the new, youthful perceptions of post-*movida* Spain. Open Monday through Saturday from 10am to 2pm, Monday through Friday from 5 to 8pm.

Marks & Spencer. Plaza Duque, 6. ☎ **95/456-49-49.**

This is the Seville branch of a gigantic, upper-middle-bracket chain of clothiers based in London. As such, it caters to British expatriates and retirees based in the hills around Seville. Clothing is conservative and well made, with greater emphasis on warm-weather garb than you'd find in equivalent branches in foggy old England. Open Monday through Saturday from 10am to 9pm.

Nicole Miller. Albareda, 16. ☎ **95/456-36-14.**

This is one of the best addresses in Seville for women who want to avoid the anonymity of El Corte Inglés, benefit from a solicitous staff, and gain access to fashion statements from Spain and the rest of Europe. Open Monday through Saturday from 10am to 2pm, Monday through Friday from 5 to 8pm.

Perdales. Cuna, 23. ☎ **95/421-37-09.**

As one of the most prestigious purveyors of flamenco dresses and *feria* costumes in Seville, this shop outfits many of the region's professional performers. Much of its merchadise is akin to couture; other items are less expensive and sold off the rack. Open Monday through Saturday from 10am to 2pm, Monday through Friday from 5 to 8pm.

Vittorio & Lucchino. Sierpes, 87. ☎ **95/422-71-51.**

This outfit has gained a reputation as a purveyor of stylish clothing, often based on Italian models, to well-heeled women of Andalusia. If you've already exhausted the inventories of the boutiques within El Corte Inglés and not found the diaphanous and alluring garment you're looking for, this place will probably have it. Open Monday through Saturday from 10am to 2pm, Monday through Friday from 5 to 8pm.

Gifts

Artesania Textil. Sierpes, 70. ☎ **95/456-28-40.**

This shop specializes in the nubbly and roughly textured textiles that reflect the earthiness of contemporary Spanish art. Weavings—some using linen, others the rough fibers of Spanish sheep—are the specialty here. Examples include placemats, tablecloths, blankets, shawls, and wall hangings. Open Monday through Saturday from 10am to 2pm, Monday through Friday from 5 to 8pm.

Matador. Avenida de la Constitución, 28. ☎ **95/422-62-47.**

Souvenirs of the city, T-shirts, hammered wrought-iron whatnots, and ceramics—this store carries these and about a dozen other types of unpretentious gift items you might want to display in your private space back home. Open Monday through Saturday from 10am to 2pm, Monday through Friday from 5 to 8pm.

Venecia. Cuna, 51. ☎ **95/422-99-94.**

The venue here is upscale, and the inventory includes lots of items you can certainly do without, but might not want to. Crystal, art objects, and fanciful accoutrements to the good life as envisioned by bourgeois Spain can all be found here. Open Monday through Saturday from 10am to 2pm, Monday through Friday from 5 to 8:15pm.

Jewelry

Joyero Abrines. Sierpes, 47. ☎ **95/422-84-55.**

This is the kind of place where grooms have bought engagement and wedding rings for their brides for generations, and where generations of girlfriends have selected watches and cigarette lighters for the *hombres* of their dreams. There's another branch of this well-known store at Calle de la Asunsión, 28 (☎ **95/427-42-44**). Both are open Monday through Saturday from 10am to 2pm, Monday through Friday from 5 to 8:15pm.

Music

Virgin Megastore. Sierpes, 81. ☎ **95/421-21-11.**

This is one of the few stores in Seville that favors the rock-and-roll motif of the rest of Europe and North America without entirely rejecting the Andalusian aesthetic. If you're looking for anything from an esoteric and obscure recording of a 19th-century *zarzuela* to the punk-rock electronic vibes of an underground band in London, this place is likely to have it. It also sells computer games (having brought Nintendo to Andalusia) and a limited roster of books. Open Monday through Friday from 10am to 2pm, Saturday from 10am to 9pm.

Riding Gear

Arcab. Paseo Cristobal Colon, 8. ☎ **95/456-14-11.**

Few other cities in Spain identify their holidays and traditions with horse riding as closely as Seville does. If you're passionately interested in horses (or know someone who is) this place can provide an array of Andalusian-style riding costumes, harnesses, saddles, bridles, and buckles that will make you and your mount feel like direct descendents of the conquistadors. Open Monday through Friday from 10am to 2pm, Saturday from 10am to 9pm.

WHERE TO STAY

During Holy Week and the Seville Fair, hotels often double, even triple, their rates. Price increases are often not announced until the last minute. If you're going to be in Seville at these times, arrive with an iron-clad reservation and an agreement about the price before checking in.

Very Expensive

✪ **Hotel Alfonso XIII.** San Fernando, 2, 41004 Sevilla. ☎ **800/221-2340** in the U.S. and Canada, or 95/422-28-50. Fax 95/421-60-33. 130 rms, 18 suites. A/C MINIBAR TV TEL. 38,000–56,000 ptas. ($304–$448) double; from 82,000 ptas. ($656) suite. AE, DC, MC, V. Parking 4,800 ptas. ($38.40).

Set at the southwestern corner of the gardens that front Seville's famous Alcázar, in the historic heart of town, this five-story rococo building is one of the three or four most legendary hotels in Spain. As such, it is obviously the premier addresses in Seville. Built as an aristocratic shelter for patrons of the Iberoamerican Exposition of 1929 and named after the then-king of Spain, it reigns as a superornate and superexpensive bastion of glamour. Built in the Mudéjar/Andalusian revival style, it contains hallways that glitter with hand-painted tiles, acres of marble and mahogany, antique furniture embellished with intricately embossed leather, and a floor plan and spaciousness that are nothing short of majestic.

Dining/Entertainment: The San Fernando restaurant offers Italian and continental cuisine. A lobby bar features midday coffee amid potted palms and memorials to another age, its blue, white, and yellow tiles reflecting the colors of Seville.

Services: 24-hour room service, laundry/valet, concierge, car rentals with or without drivers, babysitting.

Facilities: Spectacular garden, designed in the Andalusian style; outdoor pool; tennis courts; shops; arcade-enclosed courtyard with potted flowers and splashing fountain.

Expensive

Hotel Inglaterra. Plaza Nueva, 7, 41001 Sevilla. ☎ **800/528-1234** in the U.S. and Canada, or 95/422-49-70. Fax 95/456-13-36. 116 rms. A/C TV TEL. Jan–Mar and May–Dec 17,000–22,000 ptas. ($136–$176) double; Apr 21,000–25,000 ptas. ($168–$200) double. AE, DC, MC, V. Parking 1,500 ptas. ($12).

Established in 1857 and since modernized into a comfortably glossy seven-story contemporary design, this eminently respectable and rather staid hotel lies a five-minute walk southwest of the cathedral, occupying one entire side of a palm-fringed plaza. Much of its interior is sheathed with acres of white or gray marble, and the furnishings include ample use of Spanish leather and floral-patterned fabrics. Despite their modernity, the bedrooms nonetheless evoke old-fashioned touches of Iberian gentility. The best rooms lie on the fifth floor.

Dining/Entertainment: One floor above street level, overlooking the mosaic pavements of Plaza Nueva, the hotel's sunny restaurant serves well-prepared fixed-price meals from a frequently changing international menu. There's also an in-house cocktail lounge that seems favored by local businesspeople.

Services: 24-hour room service, laundry/valet service, concierge, babysitting.

Facilities: Car-rental facilities, business center.

Hotel Meliá Sevilla. Doctor Pedro de Castro, 1, 41004 Sevilla. ☎ **800/336-3542** in the U.S., or 95/442-26-11. Fax 95/442-16-08. 361 rms, 5 suites. A/C MINIBAR TV TEL. 17,750 ptas. ($142) double; from 26,500 ptas. ($212) suite. AE, DC, MC, V. Parking 1,350 ptas. ($10.80).

Located a short walk east of the Plaza de España, near the Parque María Luisa, this is the most elegant, tasteful, and international of the modern skyscraper hotels of Seville. It opened in 1987, rising 11 floors. A member of the Meliá chain, it incorporates acres of white marble as well as several dozen shopping boutiques and private apartments into its L-shaped floor plan. The guest-room decor is contemporary and comfortable, and each unit offers a private bath. Rooms at the back lack views. The Meliá was a favorite of the planners of the massive Expo, which transformed the face of both Seville and Andalusia. The hotel lacks the personal touch provided by the staff at Alfonso XIII, but its rooms are superior to those at the Inglaterra.

Dining/Entertainment: The Giralda Restaurant serves three-course fixed-price lunches and dinners. There's also a large and stylish piano bar, Corona, plus an informal coffee shop, Las Salinas.

Services: 24-hour room service, laundry, babysitting on request.

Facilities: Business center, car rentals, outdoor swimming pool with a section reserved for children, sauna, arcade of shops and boutiques, several flowering outdoor terraces.

Hotel Tryp Colón. Canalejas 1, 41001 Sevilla. ☎ **95/422-29-00.** Fax 95/422-09-38. 204 rms, 14 suites. A/C MINIBAR TV TEL. 24,200–38,200 ptas. ($193.60–$305.60) double; 82,050–117,200 ptas. ($656.40–$937.60) suite. AE, DC, MC, V. Parking 2,200 ptas. ($17.60).

Set about a quarter-mile northwest of the Giralda and about two blocks southeast of the Fine Arts Museum (Museo Provincial de Bellas Artes), this hotel is Seville's closest rival—in prestige and architectural allure—to the legendary Alfonso XIII. Originally built around the turn of the century and overhauled in 1988, it retains such features as a massive stained-glass dome stretching over the lobby, staircases worthy of a

Spanish baron, formal service, and all the niceties of a good expensive hotel. The bedrooms, all with private baths, are conservative and traditional, although some are in need of an overhaul.

Dining/Entertainment: El Burladero restaurant serves lunches and dinners (see "Where to Dine," below). There's also a bar that lures self-styled Hemingways and seems to be favored by visiting bullfighters, journalists, and politicians.

Services: 24-hour room service, concierge, babysitting, laundry/valet.

Facilities: Sauna, car-rental facilities, shopping boutiques.

✪ **Radisson Principe de Asturias Plaza Hotel Sevilla.** Isla de la Cartuja, 41018 Sevilla. ☎ **800/333-3333** in the U.S, or 95/446-22-22. Fax 95/446-04-28. 285 rms, 18 suites. A/C MINIBAR TV TEL. Mon–Thurs 21,000 ptas. ($168) double; 65,000 ptas. ($520) suite. Fri–Sun 14,000 ptas. ($112) double; 35,000 ptas. ($280) suite. Rates include breakfast. AE, DC, MC, V. Free parking.

Named after the son and designated heir of King Juan Carlos I, Don Felipe de Borbón, Principe de Asturias (his title is something akin to Britain's Prince of Wales), this hotel was expressly built to house the surge of visitors at the Seville Expo of 1992. The only hotel located at the former site of Expo itself, facing the Guadalquivir River, it lies a five-minute taxi ride from the center of Seville. The location seems a bit isolated and sad now that the excitement of Expo is long gone; the hotel is often underbooked. It was designed in three hypermodern ring-shaped modules, each four stories tall and all interconnected by passageways leading to the public rooms. Designated as a five-star luxury hotel, this Radisson was reserved during Expo for visiting dignitaries and heads of state. Its designers intended its perpetual use, at the end of the party, as one of the city's most visible hotels—sort of a modern-day counterpart to the Alfonso XIII (which was designed for use by dignitaries during Seville's International Exposition of 1929).

Dining/Entertainment: The Restaurante Colón serves gourmet versions of regional cuisine. The lobby bar and the Cartura Bar offer soothing libations, sometimes to live piano music.

Services: 24-hour room service, concierge, laundry/valet, limousine pickups, babysitting.

Facilities: Business center, conference facilities, outdoor swimming pool, in-house florist, shops, currency exchange, car rentals, trilingual TV channels, health club with sauna, massage, gymnasium, squash courts.

MODERATE

$ **Bécquer.** Calle Reyes Católicos, 4, 41001 Sevilla. ☎ **95/422-89-00.** Fax 95/421-44-00. 120 rms. A/C TV TEL. 11,000 ptas. ($88) double. AE, DC, MC, V. Parking 1,200 ptas. ($9.60). Bus: 21, 24, 30, or 31.

A short walk from the action of the Seville bullring (Maestranza) and only two blocks from the river, the Bécquer lies on a street of cafés where you can order tapas (appetizers) and drink Andalusian wine. The Museo Provincial de Bellas Artes (previously recommended) also lies nearby. Built in the 1970s, the hotel was enlarged and much renovated in the late 1980s. It occupies the site of a mansion and retains many objets d'art rescued before the building was demolished. Guests register in a wood-paneled lobby before being shown to one of the bedrooms, which are functionally furnished, well kept, and reasonably comfortable—in all, a good value in a pricey city. All have private baths. Only breakfast is served, but you'll find a bar and lounge, as well as a garage.

Hotel Alcázar. Menéndez y Pelayo, 10, 41004 Sevilla. ☎ **95/441-20-11.** Fax 495/442-16-59. 100 rms. A/C TV TEL. 13,000 ptas. ($104) double. Rates include breakfast. AE, DC, MC, V. Parking 1,000 ptas. ($8).

On the wide and busy Boulevard Menéndez y Pelayo, across from the Jardines de Alcázon, this pleasantly contemporary hotel is sheltered behind a facade of brown brick. Built in 1964, the hotel was last renovated in 1991, but even with improvements it is still no match for the Doña María (see below). Slabs of striated gray marble cool the reception area in the lobby, next to which you'll find a Spanish restaurant and bar. Above, three latticed structures resemble a trio of *miradores.* The medium-size guest rooms have functional modern furniture and private baths.

Hotel Doña María. Don Remondo, 19, 41004 Sevilla. ☎ **95/422-49-90.** Fax 95/421-95-46. 60 rms. A/C TV TEL. Jan–Feb and July–Aug 12,000 ptas. ($96) double; Mar–June and Sept–Dec 16,500 ptas. ($132) double. AE, DC, MC, V. Parking 1,200 ptas. ($9.60).

Its location a few steps from the cathedral creates a dramatic view from the Doña María's rooftop terrace. Staying at this four-star, four-story hotel represents a worthwhile investment, partly because of the tasteful Iberian antiques in the stone lobby and upper hallways. The ornate neoclassical entryway is offset with a pure white facade and iron balconies, which hint at the building's origin in the 1840s as a private villa. Amid the flowering plants on the upper floor, you'll find a swimming pool ringed with garden-style lattices and antique wrought-iron railings. Each of the one-of-a-kind bedrooms offers a private bath and is well furnished and comfortable, although some are rather small. A few have four-poster beds, others a handful of antique reproductions. Light sleepers might find the noise of the church bells jarring. Breakfast is the only meal served. The sleepy staff, however, needs to perk up.

Residencia y Restaurante Fernando III. San José, 21, 41001 Sevilla. ☎ **95/421-77-08.** Fax 95/422-02-46. 157 rms. A/C TV TEL. 16,000 ptas. ($128) double. AE, DC, MC, V. Parking 1,000 ptas. ($8).

You'll find the Fernando III on a narrow, quiet street at the edge of the Barrio de Santa Cruz, near the northern periphery of the Murillo Gardens. Its vast lobby and baronial dining hall are reminiscent of a luxurious South American hacienda. The building is modern, constructed around 1970 with marble and hardwood detailing; it is coolly and sparsely furnished with leather chairs, plants, and wrought-iron accents. Many of the accommodations—medium in size, comfortably furnished, and well maintained—offer balconies filled with cascading plants; all have private baths. There is a TV salon as well as a paneled bar. The hotel's restaurant features a regional Andalusian cuisine on its set menu.

INEXPENSIVE

Hostal Goya. Mateus Gago, 31, 41004 Sevilla. ☎ **95/421-11-70.** Fax 95/456-02-88. 20 rms (10 with bath). Jan–Mar and May–Dec 5,500 ptas. ($44) double without bath; 6,200 ptas. ($49.60) double with bath. Apr 6,200 ptas. ($49.60) double without bath; 7,000 ptas. ($56) double with bath. No credit cards. Parking 1,500 ptas. ($12)

Its location in a narrow-fronted town house in the oldest part of the barrio is one of the Goya's strongest virtues. The building's gold-and-white facade, ornate iron railings, and picture-postcard demeanor are all noteworthy. Bedrooms are cozy and simple, without phones or TVs. Guests congregate in the marble-floored ground-level salon, where a skylight floods the couches and comfortable chairs with sunlight. No meals are served. Reserve well in advance.

Hotel América. Jesús del Gran Poder, 2, 41002 Sevilla. ☎ **95/422-09-51.** Fax 95/421-06-26. 100 rms. A/C MINIBAR TV TEL. 11,000 ptas. ($88) double; 15,000 ptas. ($120) triple. AE, DC, MC, V. Parking 2,000 ptas. ($16) nearby.

Built in 1976 and partially renovated in 1994, this hotel contains rather small bedrooms but keeps the place spick-and-span. Superior features include wall-to-wall carpeting and, in winter, an individual heat control that works. Relax in the TV lounge or order a drink in the Duque Bar. Near the hotel is a parking garage for 600 cars. There isn't a major restaurant, but the América does offer a tearoom, snack bar, and cafeteria that serves regional and international cuisine. The hotel is set on the northern side of the Plaza del Duque. One of Spain's major department stores, El Corte Inglés, opens onto the same square.

Hostal Ducal. Plaza de la Encarnación, 19, 41003 Sevilla. ☎ **95/421-51-07.** Fax 95/422-89-99. 51 rms. A/C TEL. 6,250–10,500 ptas. ($50–$84) double. AE, DC, MC, V.

In this fairly modern hotel the guest rooms are modest but comfortable, with provincial and utilitarian furnishings and central heating for those Sevillian winters. A continental breakfast can be brought to your room, but no other meals are served. The location, near El Corte Inglés department store, is handy to many specialty shops.

Residencia Murillo. Calle Lope de Rueda, 7–9, 41004 Sevilla. ☎ **95/421-60-95.** Fax 95/421-96-16. 57 rms. TEL. 7,000 ptas. ($56) double; 8,500 ptas. ($68) triple. AE, DC, MC, V. Parking 1,000 ptas. ($8) nearby.

Tucked away on a narrow street in the heart of Santa Cruz, the old quarter, the Residencia Murillo (named after the artist who used to live in this district) is almost next to the gardens of the Alcázar. Inside, the lounges harbor some fine architectural characteristics and antique reproductions; behind a grilled screen is a retreat for drinks. Many of the rooms we inspected were cheerless and gloomy, so have a look before checking in. Like all of Seville's hotels, the Murillo is in a noisy area.

You can reach this residencia from the Menéndez y Pelayo, a wide avenue west of the Parque María Luisa, where a sign will take you through the Murillo Gardens on the left. Motorists should try to park in Plaza de Santa Cruz. Then walk two blocks to the hotel, which will send a bellhop back to the car to pick up your suitcases. If there are two in your party, station a guard at the car, and if you're going out at night, call for an inexpensive taxi to take you instead of strolling through the streets of the old quarter—it's less romantic but a lot safer.

NEARBY

✪ **Hacienda Benazuza.** Calle Virgen de las Nieves, s/n, 41800 Sanlúcar la Major, Seville. ☎ **95/570-33-44.** Fax 95/570-3410. 26 rooms, 18 suites. A/C MINIBAR TV TEL. 33,000–40,000 ptas. ($264–$320) double. Fri–Sun, breakfast free. Suite 40,000–90,000 ptas. ($284–$639) seven days a week, plus breakfast. AE, DC, MC, V. Free parking. Closed July 15–Aug 31. From Seville, follow the signs for Huelva and head south on the A-49 highway, exiting at exit no. 6.

Set on a hillside above the agrarian hamlet of Sanlúcar la Mayor, 12 miles (19km) south of Seville, this legendary manor house is surrounded by 40 acres of olive groves and its own farmland. Its ownership has been a cross-section of every major cultural influence that has swept through Andalusia since its foundations were laid in the 10th century by the Moors. After the Catholic conquest of southern Spain, the site became a much-feared stronghold of the fanatically religious *Caballeros de Santiago.*

In 1992 the property was bought by Basque-born entrepreneur Rafael Elejabeitia, who, after spending many millions of pesetas, transformed the premises into one of Andalusia's most charming hotels. Careful attention was paid to preserving the ancient Moorish irrigation system, whose many reflecting pools nourish the gardens. All but a few of the bedrooms lie within the estate's main building, and each is individually furnished with Andalusian antiques and Moorish trappings, representative of the original construction.

Dining/Entertainment: The most formal of the hotel's three restaurants is La Alquería, where first-class service and Andalusian and international cuisine culminate in "surprise menus." El Patio is an indoor-outdoor affair overlooking the estate's red-brick patio and palm trees. (Both of the above serve lunch and dinner daily, and are open to nonresidents who reserve in advance.) A lunch buffet beside the swimming pool, where everyone seems to show up in bathing suits and jewelry, is offered in La Alberca.

Services: Laundry, 24-hour room service, and a concierge well trained to procure almost anything.

Facilities: Tennis courts with a resident pro, paddle tennis courts, golf range, billiard room, outdoor pool. A mini-museum of Andalusian agriculture lies within an antique building originally designed as an olive press. Many other sporting options lie within driving distance, and can be arranged by the concierge staff.

WHERE TO DINE

VERY EXPENSIVE

✪ **Egaña Oriza.** San Fernando, 41. ☎ **95/422-72-11.** Reservations required. Main courses 2,150–3,800 ptas. ($17.20–$30.40); three-course fixed-price menu 5,000 ptas. ($40). AE, DC, MC, V. Restaurant, Mon–Fri 1:30–3:30pm, Mon–Sat 9–11:30pm; bar, daily 9am–midnight. Closed Aug. BASQUE/INTERNATIONAL.

Set within the conservatory of a restored mansion adjacent to the Murillo Gardens is Seville's most stylish and best restaurant. Much of its reputation stems from its role as one of the few game specialists in Andalusia—a province that is otherwise devoted to seafood. The restaurant was established by Basque-born owner and chef José Mari Egaña, who managed to combine his passion for hunting with his flair for cooking his catch. Many of the ingredients that go into the dishes presented on the menu were trapped or shot within Andalusia, a region whose potential for sports shooting is underutilized, according to Sr. Egaña. The view from the dining room encompasses a garden and a wall that formed part of the fortications of Muslim Seville.

The availability of many specialties depends on the season, but might include fresh vegetable soup studded with morsels of confit of duck, gazpacho with prawns, steak with foie gras in grape sauce, casserole of wild boar with cherries and raisins, quenelles of duck in a potato nest with apple purée, stewed mountain sheep cooked with figs, rice with stewed thrush, and woodcock flamed in Spanish brandy. The wine list provides an ample supply of hearty Spanish reds to accompany these dishes. Dessert might feature a chocolate tart slathered with freshly whipped cream. Sr. Egaña's wife, Mercedes, runs the establishment's two-story dining room.

EXPENSIVE

El Burladero. In the Hotel Tryp Colón, Canalejas, 1. ☎ **95/422-29-00.** Reservations recommended. Main courses 2,000–4,000 ptas. ($16–$32); fixed-price menus 4,100–4,500 ptas. ($32.80–$36). AE, DC, MC, V. Daily 1:30–4:30pm and 9–midnight. Closed Aug. CONTINENTAL.

Set within one of Seville's most prominent hotels, this restaurant is awash with the memorabilia and paraphernalia of the bullfighting trade. The wall tiles that decorate parts of the interior were removed from one of the pavilions at the 1929 Seville World's Fair, and the photographs adorning the walls are a veritable history of bullfighting. (The restaurant, incidentally, is named after the wooden barricade—*el burladero*—behind which bullfighters in an arena can escape from the charge of an enraged bull.) The restaurant boasts a popular bar, where a wide assortment of Sevillanos meet and mingle before their meals.

Menu specialties include upscale interpretations of local country dishes, with an attractive mix of items from other regions of Spain as well. Examples include *bacalao al horno con patatas* (baked salt cod with potatoes and saffron sauce); roasted shoulder of lamb stuffed with a deboned bull's tail and served in a richly aromatic sauce; clams with white kidney beans; a local version of *cocido,* a boiled amalgam of sausages, meats, chickpeas, and vegetables; and a stew of eel meat heavily laced with garlic and spices. Dishes from other parts of Europe might include truffled filet steak in puff pastry, duck liver, and salmon cooked in lemon-flavored dill sauce.

Casa Robles. Calle Alvarez Quintero, 58. ☎ **95/456-32-72.** Reservations recommended. Main courses 1,200–2,200 ptas. ($9.60–$17.60); fixed-price menus 4,800–10,500 ptas. ($38.40–$84). AE, DC, MC, V. Daily 1–4:30pm and 8pm–1am. ANDALUSIAN.

Praised by local residents as well as by temporary visitors, this restaurant began its life as an unpretentious bar and bodega in 1954. Over the years, thanks to a staff directed by owner-chef Juan Robles and his children, it developed into a courteous but bustling restaurant scattered over two floors of a building a short walk from the cathedral. Amid an all-Andalusian decor, you can enjoy such dishes as fish soup in the Andalusian style, lubina con naranjas (whitefish with Sevillana oranges), hake baked with strips of Serrano ham, and many kinds of fresh fish. The dessert list is long, diverse, and very tempting.

Moderate

La Albahaca. Plaza de Santa Cruz, 12. ☎ **95/422-07-14.** Reservations recommended. Main courses 1,800–3,000 ptas. ($14.40–$24); fixed-price menus 4,500–5,500 ptas. ($36–$44). AE, DC, MC, V. Mon–Sat noon–4pm and 8pm–midnight. BASQUE/FRENCH.

Located on a prominent square in the Barrio de Santa Cruz, this restaurant with an open-air terrace offers a limited but savory menu that has become a favorite of Sevillians. Specialties include a salad of carpaccio of codfish with fresh asparagus and herbs, seafood soup, shellfish bisque, grilled lamb chops, partridge braised in sherry, salmon in *papillote,* wrapped in parchment and chocolate pudding for dessert. The restaurant is in a seignorial home built in 1929.

$ Enrique Becerra. Gamazo, 2. ☎ **95/421-30-49.** Reservations recommended. Main courses 1,600–2,000 ptas. ($12.80–$16). AE, DC, MC, V. Mon–Sat 1–5pm and 8pm–midnight. ANDALUSIAN.

On our latest visit, this restaurant off Plaza Nueva and near the cathedral provided one of our best meals. The restaurant takes its name from its owner, a smart and helpful host, who installed it in a late-19th-century building. A popular tapas bar and Andalusian dining spot, it offers an intimate setting and a hearty welcome that leaves you with the feeling that your business is really appreciated. While perusing the menu, you can sip dry Tío Pepe and nibble herb-cured olives with lemon peel. The gazpacho here is among the city's best, and the sangría is served ice cold. Specialties include hake *real,* sea bream Bilbaon style, and a wide range of meat and fish dishes. Many vegetarian dishes are also featured.

La Isla. Arfe 25. ☎ **95/421-26-31.** Reservations recommended. Main courses 2,000–3,000 ptas. ($16–$24). AE, DC, MC, V. Tues–Sun 1–5pm and 8pm–midnight. Closed August. SPANISH/ANDALUSIAN.

Set within two large dining rooms designed in Andalusian fashion (thick plaster walls, tile floors, and taurine memorabilia), this air-conditioned restaurant was established shortly after World War II and has done a thriving business ever since. Its seafood is trucked or flown in from either Galicia, in northern Spain, or Huelva, one of Andalusia's major ports, and is almost always extremely fresh. Menu items include *merluza a la primavera* (hake with young vegetables), *solomillo a la Castellana* (grilled beefsteak with strips of Serrano ham), chicken croquettes, and shellfish soup. The restaurant lies a short walk from the cathedral, within a very old building erected, the owners say, on foundations laid by the ancient Romans.

Mesón Don Raimundo. Argote de Molina, 26. ☎ **95/421-29-25.** Reservations recommended. Main courses 1,500–2,500 ptas. ($12–$20); fixed-price menu 2,500 ptas. ($20). AE, DC, MC, V. Daily 12:30–5pm, Mon–Sat 7:30pm–midnight. ANDALUSIAN.

Once a 17th-century convent, this is an attractively furnished restaurant whose entrance lies at the end of a flower-lined alleyway in the center of the Barrio de Santa Cruz. The interior contains lots of brick, terra-cotta, and carved columns, which support the beamed or arched high ceilings. Your meal might include fish stew or one of six kinds of soup (including one with clams and pine nuts), then fresh grilled king shrimp, a casserole of partridge in sherry sauce, or wild rabbit casserole. Some of the recipes were adapted from old Arab-Hispanic cookbooks. In winter the central fireplace imparts a warm glow to the antique copper and wrought-iron art objects; in summer the place is comfortably air-conditioned. Menus change weekly.

Río Grande. Calle Betis, 70. ☎ **95/427-39-56.** Reservations required. Main courses 1,800–2,600 ptas. ($14.40–$20.80); fixed-price menu 3,500 ptas. ($28). AE, DC, MC, V. Daily 1–5pm and 8pm–1am. Bus: 41 or 42. ANDALUSIAN.

This classic Sevillian restaurant is named for the Guadalquivir River, which its panoramic windows overlook. It sits against the bank of the river near Plaza de Cuba in front of the Torre del Oro. Some diners come here just for a view of the city monuments. A meal might include stuffed sweet pepper *flamenca,* fish-and-seafood soup seaman's style, the chef's fresh salmon, chicken-and-shellfish paella, bull tail Andalusian, and garlic chicken Giralda. You can also have a selection of fresh shellfish that's brought in daily. Large terraces contain a snack bar, the Río Grande Pub, and a bingo room. You can often watch sports events on the river in this pleasant (and English-speaking) spot.

INEXPENSIVE

$ **Hostería del Laurel.** Plaza de los Venerables, 5. ☎ **95/422-02-95.** Reservations recommended. Main courses 750–2,500 ptas. ($6–$20). AE, DC, MC, V. Daily noon–4pm and 7:30pm–midnight. ANDALUSIAN.

Located in one of the most charming buildings on tiny, difficult-to-find Plaza de los Venerables in the labyrinthian Barrio de Santa Cruz, this hideaway restaurant has iron-barred windows stuffed with plants. Inside, amid Andalusian tiles, beamed ceilings, and more plants, you'll enjoy good regional cooking. Many diners stop for a drink and tapas at the ground-floor bar before going into one of the dining rooms. The hostería is attached to a three-star hotel.

Pizzeria San Marco. Calle Mesón de Moro 6. ☎ **95/421-43-90.** Reservations recommended. Main courses 580–1,475 ptas. ($4.65–$11.80). MC, V. Tues–Sun 1:30–4:30pm and 8:30pm–12:30am. ITALIAN.

Despite the informality implied by its name, this is actually a well-managed restaurant with sit-down service and bilingual waiters. Pizza is only one of the many items featured on the menu, and often is relegated to a secondary role, as clients usually opt for any of several kinds of pastas, salmon salads, duck in orange sauce, osso buco, chicken Parmesan, and several forms of scaloppine. There's also a congenial corner for drinking, named Harry's Bar in honor of grander role models in Venice and elsewhere.

Despite the allure of the food, the real interest of the place is its setting. It lies within what was originally built, more than a thousand years ago, as an Arab bathhouse. Its interior reminds some visitors of a secularized mosque, despite the presence of a modern wing added around 1991 in anticipation of increased business from Seville's Expo celebration. The establishment lies within the Barrio de Santa Cruz, on an obscure side street running into Calle Mateus Gago.

$ La Raza. Isabel la Católica, 2. ☎ **95/423-38-30.** Reservations recommended. Main courses 1,200–2,300 ptas. ($9.60–$18.40). AE, DC, MC, V. Daily noon–5pm and 8–midnight. ANDALUSIAN.

A terrace restaurant in Parque María Luisa, La Raza is known both for its setting and its Andalusian tapas. Begin with gazpacho, then go on to one of the meat dishes, or perhaps an order of the savory paella. On Friday and Saturday there is often music to entertain guests, many of whom are American and Japanese tourists.

SEVILLE AFTER DARK

OPERA

Teatro de la Maestranza. Paseo de Colón, 22. ☎ **95/422-65-73.**

It wasn't until the 1990s that Seville got its own opera house, but it quickly became one of the world's premier venues for operatic performances. Naturally, the focus is on works inspired by Seville itself, including Verdi's *La Forza del destino* or Mozart's *Marriage of Figaro.* Jazz, classical music, and even the quintessentially Spanish *zarzuelas* (operettas) are also performed here. The opera house can't be visited except during performances. Tickets (which vary in price, depending on the event staged) can be purchased daily from 11am to 2pm and from 5 to 8pm at the box office in front of the theater.

FLAMENCO

When the moon is high in Seville and the scent of orange blossoms is in the air, it's time to wander the alleyways of Santa Cruz in search of the sound of castanets. Or take a taxi, to be on the safe side.

✪ El Patio Sevillano. Paseo de Cristóbal Colón, 11. ☎ **95/421-41-20.** Admission (including one drink) 3,500 ptas. ($28).

In central Seville on the riverbank between two historic bridges, El Patio Sevillano is a showcase for Spanish folksong and dance, performed by exotically costumed dancers. The presentation includes a wide variety of Andalusian flamenco and songs, as well as classical pieces by composers such as Falla, Albéniz, Granados, and Chueca. From March through October, there are three shows nightly, beginning at 7:30pm, 10pm, and 11:45pm. There are only two shows from November through February, beginning nightly at 7:30 and 10pm. Drinks cost from 500 to 1,000 pesetas ($4–$8).

DRINKS & TAPAS

La Alicantina. Plaza del Salvador, 2. ☎ **95/422-61-22.**

Seafood tapas—reportedly the best in town— are served against a glazed-tile decor in the typical style of Seville. Both the bar and the sidewalk tables are always filled to overflowing. The owner serves generous portions of clams marinara, fried squid, grilled shrimp, fried codfish, and clams in béchamel sauce. La Alicantina, located about five blocks north of the cathedral, is open daily from 11:30am to 3:30pm and 7:30 to 11:30pm. Tapas range upward from 300 pesetas ($2.40).

Casa Romàn. Plaza des los Venerables. ☎ **95/421-64-08.**

Tapas are said to have originated in Andalusia, and this old-fashioned bar, incongruously named Romàn, looks as if it had been dishing them up since day one—actually, since 1934. Definitely include this place on your *tasca* hopping through the old quarter. At the deli counter in front you can make your selection; you might even pick up the fixings for a picnic in the Parque María Luisa. The Casa Romàn is in the

Barrio de Santa Cruz. Open Monday through Friday from 9am to 3pm and 5:30pm to 12:30am, Saturday and Sunday from 10am to 3pm and 6:30pm to 12:30am. Tapas are priced from 550 pesetas ($4.40).

Modesto. Cano y Cueto, 5. ☎ **95/441-68-11.**

At the northern end of Murillo Gardens, opening onto a quiet square with flower boxes and an ornate iron railing, Modesto serves fabulous seafood tapas. The bar is air-conditioned, and you can choose your appetizers just by pointing. Upstairs there's a good-value restaurant, offering a meal for 2,000 pesetas ($16), including such dishes as fried squid, baby sole, grilled sea bass, and shrimp in garlic sauce. Modesto is open daily from 8pm to 2am. Tapas are priced from 200 pesetas ($1.60).

El Rinconcillo. Gerona, 40. ☎ **95/422-31-83.**

El Rinconcillo has a 1930s ambience, partly because of its real age and partly because of its owners' refusal to change one iota of the decor—this has always been one of the most famous bars in Seville. Actually, it may be the oldest bar in Seville, with a history going back to 1670. Amid dim lighting, heavy ceiling beams, and iron-based, marble-topped tables, you can enjoy a beer or a full meal along with the rest of the easygoing clientele. The bartender will mark your tab in chalk on a well-worn wooden countertop. El Rinconcillo is especially known for its salads, omelets, hams, and selection of cheeses. Look for the art nouveau tile murals. El Rinconcillo is at the northern edge of the Barrio de Santa Cruz, near the Santa Catalina Church. It's open Thursday to Tuesday from 1pm to 2am. A complete meal will cost around 2,000 pesetas ($16).

A Special Bar

✪ **Abades.** Abades, 1. ☎ **95/455-15-69.**

A converted mansion in the Barrio de Santa Cruz has been turned into a rendezvous that has been compared to "a living room in a luxurious movie set." One member of the Spanish press labeled it "wonderfully decadent, similar to the ambience created in a Visconti film." In the heart of the Jewish ghetto, it evokes the style of the Spanish Romantic era. The house dates from the 19th century, when it was constructed around a central courtyard with a fountain. Drinks and low-key conversations are the style here, and since its opening in 1980 all the visiting literati and glitterati have put in an appearance. Young men and women in jeans also patronize the place, enjoying the comfort of the sofas and wicker armchairs.

The ingredients of a special drink called *aqua de Sevilla* are a secret, but we suspect sparkling white wine, pineapple juice, and eggs (the whites and yolks mixed in separately, of course). Classical music is played in the background. Take a taxi to get here at night, as it might not be safe to wander late along the narrow streets of the barrio. In summer, it's open daily from 9pm to 4am; in winter, hours are daily from 8pm to 2:30am.

Spectator Sports

Bullfights From Easter until late October, some of the best bullfighters in Spain appear at the Maestranza bullring, on the Paseo de Colón (☎ 95/422-45-77). One of the leading bullrings in Spain, the stadium attracts matadors whose fights often receive television and newspaper coverage throughout Iberia. Unless there's a special festival going on, bullfights (*corridas*) occur on Sunday. The best bullfights are staged during April Fair celebrations. Tickets tend to be pricey, and should be purchased in advance at the ticket office (*despacho de entrades*) on Calle Adriano, beside the

Food on the Run

Lying directly east of the cathedral, **Cervecería Giralda,** Calle Mateus Gago, 1 (☎ **95/422-74-35),** is one of the least expensive dining spots near the cathedral, Alcázar, and Giralda Tower. Residents and tourists alike eat here. You can make a meal from the selection of tapas, ranging from 225 to 275 pesetas ($1.80–$2.20), or order one of the *platos combinados* (combination plates), ranging from 800 to 1,300 pesetas ($6.40–$10.40). The place is open Monday through Saturday from 9am to midnight, Sunday from 10am to midnight.

On the same street **Pizzeria El Artesano,** Calle Mateus Gago, 9 (☎ **95/421-38-58**), also lures in customers near the cathedral. Here the feature is an Andalusian version of pizza costing 525 to 725 pesetas ($4.20–$5.80). Daily hours are noon to midnight.

Lying on the "opposite side" of the Guadalquivir, away from the throngs of tourists, is the Barrio de Triana. This used to be its own little village community until Seville burst its seams and absorbed it. It still is the place to go to escape the high food tariffs on the cathedral side of the river.

El Puerto, Betis, s/n (☎ **95/427-17-25**), stands next door to the famed Río Grande restaurant. It has a multilevel alfresco terrace opening onto the river. You can get fresh seafood here, but the special buy is the chef's *cubierto* (menu of the house), costing 1,500 pesetas ($12); tapas range from 200 to 700 pesetas ($1.60–$5.60). At the cafeteria bar, you serve yourself; inside is an inexpensive restaurant with waiter service. It's open Tuesday to Sunday; lunch is served from 1 to 4pm and dinner from 8pm to midnight. (It's closed in January.) Bus: 41 or 42.

Another way to enjoy quick meals is to eat at one of the tapas bars recommended below under "Seville After Dark." Portions, called *raciones,* are usually generous, and many tourists on the run often eat standing at the bar, making a full meal out of two orders of tapas.

Maestranza bullfight stadium. You'll also find many unofficial kiosks placed strategically along the main shopping street, Calle Sierpes, selling tickets. However, they charge a 20% commission for their tickets—a lot more if they think they can get it.

EASY EXCURSIONS

CARMONA

An easy hour-long bus trip from the main terminal in Seville, Carmona is an ancient city dating from Neolithic times. Twenty-one miles (34km) east of Seville, it grew in power and prestige under the Moors, establishing ties with Castile in 1252.

Surrounded by fortified walls, Carmona has three Moorish fortresses—one a parador and, the other two, **the Alcázar de la Puerta de Córdoba** and **Alcázar de la Puerta de Sevilla.** The top attraction is **Seville Gate,** with its double Moorish arch, opposite St. Peter's Church. Note too, **Córdoba Gate** on Calle Santa María de Gracia, which was attached to the ancient Roman walls in the 17th century.

The town itself is a virtual national landmark, filled with narrow streets, whitewashed walls, and Renaissance mansions. **Plaza San Fernando** is the most important square, with many elegant 17th-century houses. The most important church is dedicated to **Santa María** and stands on the Calle Martin López. You enter a Moorish ablutionary patio before exploring the interior with its 15th-century white vaulting.

At Jorge Bonsor there's a **Roman amphitheater** as well as a **Roman necropolis** (*necrópolis Romana*), containing the remains of 1,000 families who lived in and around Carmona 2,000 years ago. Of the two important tombs, the Elephant Vault consists of three dining rooms and a kitchen. The other, the Servilia Tomb, was the size of a nobleman's villa. On site is a **Museo Arquelógico,** displaying artifacts found at the site. From April through October hours are Tuesday through Saturday from 9am to 2pm and Sunday from 10am to 2pm; off-season, Tuesday through Friday from 10am to 2pm and 4 to 6pm, Saturday and Sunday from 10am to 2pm. Admission is 225 pesetas ($1.80).

If you're driving to Carmona, exit from Seville's eastern periphery onto the N-V superhighway, following the signs to the airport, then to Carmona on the road to Madrid. The Carmona turnoff is clearly marked.

Where to Stay and Dine

✪ **Casa de Carmona.** Plaza de Lasso, 1, 41410 Carmona (Sevilla). ☎ **95/414-33-00,** or 212/686-9213 for reservations within North America. Fax 95/414-37-52. 12 rms, 18 suites. A/C MINIBAR TV TEL. 22,000 ptas. ($176) double; 26,000 ptas. ($208) suite. Add about 30% for Feria de Sevilla and Easter (Semana Santa). AE, MC, V. Free parking.

One of the most elegant and intimate hotels in Andalusia, this plushly furnished hideaway was originally built as the home of the Lasso family during the 1500s. Several years ago, a team of entrepreneurs added the many features required for a luxury hotel, all the while retaining the marble columns, massive masonry, and graceful proportions of the building's original construction. Set at the edge of the village, the hotel offers an outdoor swimming pool with a flowering terrace, an inner courtyard covered against the midsummer heat with a canvas awning, and a small exercise room. The most visible public room still maintains vestiges of its original function as a library. Each bedroom is a cozy enclave of opulent furnishings, with a distinct decor theme inspired by ancient Rome, medieval Andalusia, or Renaissance Spain.

On the premises is a restaurant whose tables are set up outdoors. Its culinary inspiration derives from modern interpretations of Andalusian and international cuisine, with meals served daily from 1 to 4pm and from 9 to 11:30pm and priced from around 4,000 pesetas ($32) each.

ITÁLICA

Lovers of Roman history will flock to Itálica (☎ **95/599-73-76**), the ruins of an ancient city 5½ miles (9km) northwest of Seville, on the major road to Lisbon, near the small town of Santiponce.

After the battle of Ilipa, Publius Cornelius Scipio Africanus founded Itálica in 206 B.C. Two of the most famous of Roman emperors, Trajan and Hadrian, were born here. Indeed, master builder Hadrian was to have a major influence on his hometown. In his reign the **amphitheater,** the ruins of which can be seen today, was among the largest in the Roman Empire. Lead pipes that carried water from the Guadalquivir River still remain. A small museum displays some of the Roman statuary found here, although the finest pieces have been shipped to Seville. Many mosaics, depicting beasts, gods, and birds, are on exhibit, and others are constantly being discovered. The ruins, including a Roman theater, can be explored for 250 pesetas ($2). The site is open April through September, Tuesday through Saturday, from 9am to 6:30pm and on Sunday from 9am to 3pm. From October through March, it's open Tuesday through Saturday from 9am to 5:30pm and on Sunday from 10am to 4pm.

If you're driving, exit from the northwest periphery of Seville, following the signs for highway E-803 in the direction of Zafra and Lisbon. But if you don't have a car,

The Legacy of al-Andalus

The Moors who once occupied Andalusia—notably Seville, Granada, and Córdoba—left more than such architectural treasures as the Giralda Tower in Seville, the great mosque in Córdoba, and the Alahambra in Granada. Their intellectual and cultural legacy still influence modern life, not only in Spain, but in the Western world.

The celebrated Arab princesses and sultans with their harems are long gone, encountered today only in the tales of Washington Irving and others. Yet from A.D. 711, the Moors (Muslims who were an ethnic mixture of Berbers, Hispano-Romans, and Arabs) occupied southern Spain for nearly eight centuries and turned it into a seat of learning. It was a time of soaring achievements in philosophy, medicine, and music.

Moorish rule brought the importation of the eggplant and the almond, as well as the Arabian steed—not to mention such breakthroughs in academia as astronomy (including charting the positions of the planets) and a new and different view of Aristotle. Arab numerals replaced the more awkward Roman system, and from the Arabs came the gift of algebra. Ibn Muadh of Jaén wrote the first European treatise on trigonometry.

Such intellectual giants emerged as the Córdoba-born Jewish philosopher Maimonides. It is said that Columbus evolved his theories about a new route to the East after hours and hours of studying the charts of Idrisi, an Arabian geographer who drew up a world map as early as 1154. Long before its use among Portuguese explorers, the compass was relied on as a navigational aid by Arabs.

Córdoba desired to shine brighter than Baghdad as a center of science and the arts. In time it attracted Abd ar-Rahman II, who introduced the fifth string to the Arab lute, leading to the development of the six-string guitar. He also ordained the way food should be eaten at mealtimes, a legacy that lives to this day. Before, everybody just helped themselves randomly to whatever had been prepared; but he devised a method where courses were served in a regimented order, ending with dessert, fruit, and nuts. Today, many of the old recipes from the Arab cupboard, such as lamb cooked with honey, are being revived by Andalusian chefs.

Of course, on the entertainment scene, the art form of flamenco can claim significant Middle Eastern influences as well. In his book *In Search of the Firedance,* James Woodall writes, "The music, the literature, the folklore, even religion, but above all the people themselves, speak of it [the epoch of al-Andalus]. It is a matter of attitude, or mentality, and it will be encountered again and again in flamenco." Arab poetry may have inspired the first ballads sung by European troubadours, which had an enormous impact on later Western literature. Also, many Spanish words today have their origins in the Arabic language, including the *alcázar* for fortress, *arroz* for rice, *naranja* for orange, and *limón* for lemon.

The Moors brought an irrigation system to Andalusia, which increased crop production; many of today's systems follow those 1,000-year-old channels. And paper first arrived in Europe through Córdoba.

Although the fanatical Isabella la Católica may have thrown a fit at the "heretical" idea, it was really a trio of people who shaped modern Spain as a nation: the Jews, the Christians, and most definitely the Arabs. The Arabs and the Jews may have been ousted by Isabella and Ferdinand at the close of the 15th century, but their influence still lingers.

take the bus marked "Calle de Santiponce" leaving from Calle Marqués de Parada near the railway station in Seville. Buses depart every hour for the 30-minute trip.

4 Jerez de la Frontera

54 miles (87km) S of Seville, 368 miles (592km) SW of Madrid, 21 miles (34km) NE of Cádiz

The charming little Andalusian town of Jerez made a name for itself in England for the thousands of casks of golden sherry it shipped there over the centuries. With origins going back nearly 3,000 years, Jerez is nonetheless a modern, progressive town with wide boulevards, although it does have an interesting old quarter. Busloads of visitors pour in every year to get those free drinks at one of the bodegas where wine is aged and bottled.

The town is pronounced "Her-*ez*" or Her-*eth,*" in Andalusian or Castilian, respectively. The French and the Moors called it various names, including Heres and Scheris, which the English corrupted to Sherry.

ESSENTIALS

GETTING THERE **By Plane** Iberia and Avianco offer flights to Jerez every Monday through Friday from Barcelona and Zaragoza; daily flights from Madrid; and several flights a week to and from Valencia, Tenerife, Palma de Majorca, and Grand Canary Island. No international flights land at Jerez. The airport lies about seven miles (11km) northeast of the city center (follow the signs to Seville). There's an Iberia ticketing and information office located at Plaza de Aluries.

By Train Trains from Madrid arrive daily. A ticket from Madrid to Jerez on the TALGO costs 7,040 pesetas ($56.30), the trip taking 4½ hours. The railway station in Jerez is at Plaza de la Estación (☎ **956/34-23-19**), at the eastern end of Calle Medina.

By Bus Bus connections are more frequent than train connections, and the location of the bus terminal is also more convenient. You'll find it on Calle Cartuja, at the corner of the Calle Madre de Díos, a 12-minute walk east of the Alcázar. About 18 buses arrive daily from Cádiz (1 hour away) and 3 per day travel from Ronda (3 hours). Seven buses a day arrive from Seville (1½ hours). Phone **956/34-10-63** for more information.

By Car Jerez lies on the highway connecting Seville with Cádiz, Algeciras, Gibraltar, and the ferryboat landing for Tangier, Morocco. There's also an overland road connecting Jerez with Granada and Málaga.

VISITOR INFORMATION The tourist information office is at Calle Larga (☎ **956/33-11-50**). To reach it from the bus terminals, take Calle Medina to Calle Honda and continue along as the road turns to the right. The English-speaking staff can provide directions, transportation suggestions, open hours, and so on for any bodega you might want to visit. You will also be given a map pinpointing the location of various bodegas. Open April through October, Monday through Friday from 8am to 3pm and 5 to 8pm, Saturday from 10am to 1:30pm; off-season, Monday through Friday from 8am to 3pm and 5 to 7pm, Saturday from 10am to 2pm.

WHAT TO SEE & DO

✪ **TOURING THE BODEGAS** Jerez is not surrounded by vineyards, as you might expect. The vineyards lie to the north and west of Jerez, within the "Sherry Triangle" marked by Jerez, Sanlúcar de Barrameda, and El Puerto de Santa María (the latter two towns on the coast). This is where top-quality *albariza* soil is to be found, the highest quality containing an average of 60% chalk, which is ideal for the cultivation of grapes used in sherry production, principally the white *Palomino de Jerez.* The ideal time to visit is September. However, visitors can count on the finest in hospitality year-round, since Jerez is widely known for the warm welcome it bestows.

There must be more than a hundred bodegas in and around Jerez, where you can not only see how sherries are made, bottled, and aged, but also get free samples. Among the most famous producers are Sandeman, Pedro Domecq, and González Byass, the maker of Tío Pepe.

On a typical visit to a bodega, you'll be shown through several buildings in which sherry and brandy are manufactured. In one building, you'll see grapes being pressed and sorted; in another, the bottling process; in a third, thousands of large oak casks. Then it's on to an attractive bar where various sherries—amber, dark gold, cream, red, sweet, and velvety—can be sampled. If either is offered, try the very dry La Ina sherry or the Fundador brandy, one of the most popular in the world.

Warning: These drinks are more potent than you might expect.

Most bodegas are open Monday through Friday only, from 10:30am to 1:30pm. Regrettably, many of them are closed in August, but many do reopen by the third week of August to prepare for the wine festival in early September.

Of the dozens of bodegas you can visit, the most popular are listed below. Some of them charge an admission fee and require a reservation.

A favorite among British visitors is **Harveys of Bristol,** Calle Arcos, 57 (**☎ 956/48-34-00**), which doesn't require a reservation. An English-speaking guide leads a two-hour tour year-round, except for the first three weeks of August. Visit Monday through Friday from 7am to 3pm, for an admission of 300 pesetas ($2.40).

You'll definitely want to visit **Williams & Humbert Limited,** Nuño de Cañas, 1 (**☎ 956/33-31-00**), which offers tours at noon and 1:30pm Monday through Friday, charging 300 pesetas ($2.40). Their premium brands include the world-famous Dry Sack Medium Sherry, Canasta Cream, Fino Pando, and Manzanilla Alegría, in addition to Gran Duque de Alba Gran Reserva Brandy. It is wise to reserve in advance.

Another famous name is **González Byass,** Manuel María González, 12 (**☎ 956/34-00-00**); admission is 375 pesetas ($3), and reservations are required. Tours depart at 10am, 11am, noon, and 1pm Monday through Friday. Equally famous is **Domecq,** Calle San Ildefonso, 3 (**☎ 956/15-15-00**), requiring a reservation but charging no admission. Tours depart at 10am, 11am, and noon Monday through Friday.

THE DANCING HORSES OF JEREZ A rival of sorts to Vienna's famous Spanish Riding School is the **Escuela Andaluza del Arte Ecuestre (Andalusian School of Equestrian Art),** Avenida Duque de Abrantes, 11 (**☎ 956/31-11-11**). In fact, the long, hard schooling that brings horse and rider into perfect harmony originated in this province. The Viennese school was started with Hispano-Arab horses sent from this region, the same breeds you can see today. Every Thursday at noon, crowds come to admire the Dancing Horses of Jerez as they perform in a show that includes local folklore. For reservations call **956/60-99-54.** Admission is 2,400 pesetas ($19.20) for adults and 975 pesetas ($7.80) for children. Bus 18 goes there.

A NEARBY ATTRACTION Since many people go to Jerez specifically to visit a bodega, August or weekend closings can be very disappointing. If this happens to you, make a trip to the nearby village of **Lebrija,** about halfway between Jerez and Seville, 8½ miles (14km) west of the main highway. Lebrija, a good spot to get a glimpse of rural Spain, is a local winemaking center where some very fine sherries originate. At one small bodega, that of Juan García, you are courteously escorted around by the owner. There are several other bodegas in Lebrija, and the local citizens will gladly point them out to you. It's all very casual—lacking the rigidity and formality attached to the bodegas of Jerez.

WHERE TO STAY

EXPENSIVE

Hotel Avenida Jerez. Avenida Alcalde Álvaro Domecq, 10, 11405 Jerez de la Frontera. ☎ **956/34-74-11.** Fax 956/33-72-96. 90 rms, 5 suites. A/C TV TEL. 14,000 ptas. ($112) double; 18,000 ptas. ($144) suite. AE, DC, MC, V. Parking 1,500 ptas. ($12).

Set very close to the commercial heart of Jerez, this hotel occupies a modern balconied structure of seven stories and is the best hotel within Jerez itself, although Montecastillo (see below) on the outskirts is a serious challenger. Inside, cool floors of polished stone, leather armchairs, and a variety of potted plants create a restful haven. The bedrooms are discreetly contemporary and decorated in neutral colors, with big windows, comfortable beds, and private baths.

Dining/Entertainment: The hotel maintains a pleasant and unpretentious cafeteria providing coffee-shop-style snacks and platters of Spanish food. There's also a bar.

Services: Room service (available daily from 7am to 11pm), babysitting, concierge, laundry/valet.

Facilities: Car-rental desk.

Hotel Royal Sherry Park. Avenida Alcalde Álvaro Domecq, 11 Bis, 11405 Jerez de la Frontera. ☎ **956/30-30-11.** Fax 956/31-13-00. 170 rms, 3 suites. A/C MINIBAR TV TEL. 15,500–22,000 ptas. ($124–$176) double; 23,000–32,000 ptas. ($184–$256) suite. AE, DC, MC, V.

Especially noted for its setting within a palm-fringed garden and for its large swimming pool, whose tiled edges attract many of its sun-loving residents, this is one of the best modern hotels in Jerez. Located on a wide and verdant boulevard north of the historic center of town, it contains a marble-floored lobby, efficiently modern public rooms, and simple but comfortable bedrooms, each with a private bath. The uniformed staff lays out a copious breakfast buffet and serves drinks at several hideaways, both indoors and within the garden.

Dining/Entertainment: El Abaco Restaurant, which spills over onto an outdoor terrace, serves flavorful international cuisine. A bar with a good selection of sherries and whiskeys lies nearby.

Services: Room service (available daily from 8am to midnight), laundry/valet, concierge, babysitting.

Facilities: Outdoor swimming pool, car rentals, shopping boutiques.

Montecastillo. Carrertera N-342, 11406 Jerez de la Frontera. ☎ **956/15-12-00.** Fax 956/15-12-90. 120 rms. A/C MINIBAR TV TEL. 19,000 ptas. ($152) double. AE, DC, MC, V. Free parking.

Giving Hotel Avenida Jerez serious competition is this deluxe country club found in the rolling hills of the sherry *campiña,* or wine country. The most tranquil retreat in the area, it has bedrooms with scenic-view balconies overlooking a Jack Nicklaus–designed 18-hole golf course. Just a 10-minute ride from the center of Jerez, the hotel is elegantly furnished and professionally run. Bedrooms are in modern and traditional design and are maintained in a state-of-the-art condition.

Dining/Entertainment: Favorite regional meals are combined with traditional Spanish and international dishes for some of the best cuisine in the area.

Services: Room service, laundry/dry cleaning, babysitting.

Facilities: In addition to the golf course, there are swimming pools and a sauna. Horseback riding and tennis are available nearby, and there are paddle tennis facilities at the adjacent and exclusive Montecastillo Country Club.

MODERATE

$ **Hotel Ávila.** Ávila, 3, 11140 Jerez de la Frontera. ☎ **956/33-48-08.** Fax 956/33-68-07. 32 rms. A/C TV TEL. 5,000–8,000 ptas. ($40–$64) double. AE, DC, MC, V. Parking 900 ptas. ($7.20) nearby.

One of the better bargains in Jerez, the Ávila is a modern, three-story building, erected in 1968 and renovated in 1987. In the commercial center of town, it lies near the post office and Plaza del Arenal. Inside, its bedrooms are clean, comfortable, and well maintained, although not special in any way.

Hotel Serit. Higueras, 7, 11402 Jerez de la Frontera. ☎ **956/34-07-00.** Fax 956/34-07-16. 35 rms. A/C TV TEL. 5,600–6,800 ptas. ($44.80–$54.40) double. AE, DC, MC, V. Parking 800 ptas. ($6.40).

The modern three-star Hotel Serit, near Plaza de la Angustias, offers bedrooms that are functionally furnished and comfortable—all at a good price. There's a pleasant bar downstairs, plus a modern breakfast lounge. Laundry and room service are provided.

WHERE TO DINE

El Bosque. Alcalde Álvaro Domecq, 26. ☎ **956/18-08-80.** Reservations required. Main courses 1,800–2,600 ptas. ($14.40–$20.80); fixed-price menus 4,500–9,500 ptas. ($36–$76). AE, DC, MC, V. Mon–Sat 1:30–5pm and 8:30pm–1am. SPANISH/INTERNATIONAL.

Less than a mile northeast of the city center, the city's most elegant restaurant was established just after World War II. A favorite of the sherry-producing aristocracy, it retains a strong emphasis on bullfighting memorabilia, which make up most of the decoration.

Order the excellent *rabo de toro* (bull's-tail stew) if you want to be a true native. You might begin with a soothing Andalusian gazpacho, then try one of the fried fish dishes, such as hake Seville style. Rice with king prawns and baby shrimp omelets are deservedly popular dishes. Occasionally, Laguna duck in honey with chestnuts and pears is a feature. Desserts are usually good, including the pistachio ice cream.

$ **Gaitán.** Calle Gaitán, 3. ☎ **956/34-58-59.** Reservations recommended. Main courses 950–2,400 ptas. ($7.60–$19.20). AE, DC, MC, V. Daily 1–4:30pm, Mon–Sat 8:30–11:30pm. ANDALUSIAN.

This small restaurant near Puerta Santa María is owned by Juan Hurtado, who has won acclaim for the food served here. Surrounded by walls displaying celebrity photographs, you can enjoy such Andalusian dishes as garlic soup, various stews, duck à la Sevillana, and fried seafood. One special dish is lamb cooked with honey, based on a recipe so ancient it goes back to the Muslim occupation of Spain. For dessert, the almond tart is a favorite.

Restaurante Tendido 6. Calle Circo, 10. ☎ **956/34-48-35.** Reservations required. Main courses 400–2,000 ptas. ($3.20–$16). AE, DC, MC, V. Mon–Sat noon–4pm and 8–11:30pm. SPANISH.

This combination restaurant and tapas bar has loyal clients who come from many walks of life. The chef creates a dignified regional cuisine that includes grilled rump steak, fish soup, and a wide array of Spanish dishes, including Basque and Castilian cuisine. There's nothing really exciting here, but the long-tested recipes are filled with flavor and the place is a good value. The Tendido is on the south side of Plaza de Toros.

EASY EXCURSIONS

MEDINA SIDONIA

This survivor of the Middle Ages is one of the most unspoiled hillside villages of Spain, about 29 miles (46.5km) east of Cádiz and 22 miles (35.5km) southeast of Jerez de la Frontera. Motorists from Jerez should follow the 440 southeast.

A village that time forgot, Medina Sidonia has cobblestoned streets, tile-roofed white buildings dotting the hillside, a Gothic church, a Moorish gate, and steep alleyways traveled by locals on donkeys. The Arab influence is everywhere. The surrounding countryside is wild and seldom visited. The pockets of fog that sometimes settle over the land will make you think you're on the Yorkshire moors.

From Medina Sidonia, it's a 2½-hour drive to the port city of Algeciras, or you can take the Jerez road back to Seville.

ARCOS DE LA FRONTERA

Twenty miles (32km) east of Jerez de la Frontera, this old Arab town—now a National Historic Monument—was built in the form of an amphitheater. Sitting on a rock and surrounded by the Guadalete River on three sides, it contains many houses that have been hollowed out of this formation. From the old city, there's a high-in-the-clouds view that some visitors consider without rival on the Iberian Peninsula.

The city is filled with whitewashed walls and narrow winding streets that disappear into steps. It holds a lot of historical interest and has a beautiful lake complete with paddleboats and a Mississippi riverboat.

The most exciting attraction is the **view from the principal square,** the Plaza del Cabildo, a rectangular esplanade overhanging a deep river cleft. You can see a Moorish castle, but it is privately owned and cannot be visited by the public. You can, however, visit the main church, located on the main square—the **Iglesia de Santa María,** constructed in 1732, a blend of Gothic, Renaissance, and baroque. Its western front—and its most outstanding architectural achievement—is in plateresque style. The second major church of town, **Iglesia de San Pedro,** standing on the northern edge of the old barrio (quarter), at the far end of the cliff, is known for its 16th- and 18th-century tower. This church, which grew up on the site of a Moorish fortress, owns works by Zurbarán and Murillo, among others. Check with the tourist office (see below) about gaining admission to these churches, as they are often closed for security reasons. Several art thefts have occurred in the area.

Even if you don't succeed in gaining entrance to the churches, it is reason enough to visit Arcos merely to wander its alleys and view its ruins from the Middle Ages. If you have to return to wherever you're going for the night, stay at least long enough to have a drink in the patio of the parador (recommended below) and take in that monumental view.

There is no train service to this little bit of paradise, but you can take a bus from Jerez de la Frontera, Seville, or Cádiz. Motorists from Jerez should follow the 342 east until they see the turnoff for Arcos.

The tourist information office is at Plaza del Cabildo (☎ **956/70-22-64**), open Monday through Friday from 9am to 2pm and 5 to 7pm, Saturday from 9am to 2pm, and Sunday from 11am to 2pm.

Where to Stay & Dine

Parador Casa del Corregidor. Plaza del Cabildo, 11630 Arcos de la Frontera. ☎ **956/70-05-00.** Fax 956/70-11-16. 24 rms. A/C MINIBAR TV TEL. 15,000 ptas. ($120) double. AE, DC, MC, V. Free parking.

The best place to stay is this government-run parador, in a restored palace in the heart of the old quarter. Built in the 1700s, it was the palace and government seat of the king's magistrate (*corregidor*) in Arcos. From the balconies, there are views of the Valley of Guadalete with its river, plains, and farms. In good weather you can take your meals (try the pork with garlic) on one of these balconies; lunch or dinner costs 3,200 pesetas ($25.60). The decor consists of tiles and antiques. The bedrooms are handsomely furnished and beautifully maintained; perhaps you'll be assigned the one where Charles de Gaulle once stayed.

5 Cádiz

76 miles (122km) S of Seville, 388 miles (625km) SW of Madrid

The oldest inhabited city in the Western world, founded in 1100 B.C., this now modern, bustling Atlantic port is a kind of Spanish Marseilles, a melting pot of Americans, Africans, and Europeans who are docking or passing through. The old quarter teems with local characters, little dives, and seaport alleyways. But despite its thriving life, the city does not hold major interest for tourists, except for the diverse cultural strains that have helped shape it. Phoenicians, Arabs, Visigoths, Romans, and Carthaginians all passed through Cádiz and left their cultural imprints. Throughout the ages this ancient port city has enjoyed varying states of prosperity, especially after the discovery of the New World.

At the end of a peninsula, Cádiz separates the Bay of Cádiz from the Atlantic, so from numerous sea walls around the town, you have views of the ocean. It was here that Columbus set out on his second voyage.

GETTING THERE **By Train** Trains arrive at Cádiz from Seville (taking 1½ to 2½ hours), Jerez de la Frontera (45 minutes), and Algeciras (6 hours). The train station is located on Avenida del Puerto (☎ **956/25-43-01**), on the southeast border of the main port.

By Bus Passengers in transit to or from Madrid usually must transfer in Seville. Buses arrive in Cádiz at two separate terminals. From Seville (11 per day; 1¼ hours), Jerez de la Frontera (8 per day), Málaga, Córdoba, and Granada, buses arrive at the Estación de Comes terminal, Plaza de la Hispanidad, 1 (☎ **956/21-17-63**), on the north side of town, a few blocks west of the main port. Far less prominent is the terminal run by the Transportes Los Amarillos, Avenida Ramón de Carranza, 31 (☎ **956/28-58-52**), several blocks to the south, which runs frequent buses to several nearby towns and villages, most of which are of interest only for local residents and workers.

By Car From Seville, the A-4 (also called E-5), a toll road, or N-IV, a toll-free road running beside it, will bring you into Cádiz.

VISITOR INFORMATION The tourist information office is at Calderón de la Barca, 1 (☎ **956/21-13-13**). Open Monday through Friday from 9am to 2pm and 5 to 8pm, Saturday from 10am to 2pm.

WHAT TO SEE & DO

Despite being one of the oldest towns in Europe, Cádiz has few remnants of antiquity. It is still worth visiting, however, especially to wander through the old quarter, which retains a special charm.

Plaza de San Juan de Dios is the ideal place to sit at a sidewalk café and people-watch in the shadow of the neoclassical **Isabellino Ayuntamiento** (Town Hall), with its outstanding chapter house. The **Oratorio de San Felipe Neri,** Santa Inés (☎ **956/21-16-12**), where the Cortés (Parliament) met in 1812 to proclaim its constitution, has an important Murillo (*Conception*) and a history museum. Admission is free, and it's open August through June, daily from 8:30 to 10am and 7:30 to 10pm. The **Hospital de Mujeros** (Women's Hospital) has a patio courtyard dating from 1740 and a chapel with El Greco's *Ecstasy of St. Francis.*

Museo de Cádiz. Plaza de Mini, s/n. ☎ **956/21-22-81.** Admission 250 ptas. ($2). Tues–Sun 9:30am–2pm.

This museum, now fully restored, contains one of Spain's most important Zurbarán collections, as well as paintings by Rubens and Murillo (including the latter's acclaimed picture of Christ). The archaeology section displays Roman, Carthaginian, and Phoenician finds, and ethnology exhibits include pottery, baskets, textiles, and leather works.

Catedral de Cádiz. Plaza Catedral. ☎ **956/28-61-54.** Admission 400 ptas. ($3.20) adults, 200 ptas. ($1.60) children. Mon–Sat 10am–1pm.

This magnificent 18th-century baroque building by architect Vicente Acero has a neoclassical interior dominated by an outstanding apse. The tomb of Cádiz-born composer Manuel de Falla lies in its splendid crypt; music lovers from all over the world come here to pay their respects. Haydn composed *The Seven Last Words of Our Savior on the Cross* for this cathedral. The treasury/museum contains a priceless collection of Spanish silver, embroidery, and paintings by Spanish, Italian, and Flemish artists.

WHERE TO STAY

Cádiz has a number of inexpensive accommodations, some of which are quite poor. However, for moderate tabs you can afford some of the finest lodgings in the city. Note that rooms are scarce during the February carnival season.

Hotel Atlántico. Duque de Nájera, 9, 11002 Cádiz. ☎ **956/22-69-05.** Fax 956/21-45-82. 147 rms, 6 suites. A/C MINIBAR TV TEL. 12,000–15,000 ptas. ($96–$120) double; 25,000 ptas. ($200) suite. AE, DC, MC, V. Parking 1,400 ptas. ($11.20).

Actually a modern resort hotel, this national parador is built on one of the loveliest beaches of the Bay of Cádiz, at the western edge of the old town. It is clearly the outstanding choice for accommodations here, dwarfing the competition. The white six-story building has a marble patio, a salon decked out in rattan and cane, and bedrooms that feature balconies with tables and chairs for relaxed ocean viewing. More than half of the rooms were renovated in 1995. The Atlántico's own swimming pool is surrounded by palm trees. The hotel also boasts a bar and a dining room known for its superb Andalusian cuisine, particularly the seafood.

$ **Regio 1.** Ana de Viya, 11, 11009 Cádiz. ☎ **956/27-93-31.** Fax 956/27-91-13. 44 rms. TV TEL. 8,500 ptas. ($68) double. AE, DC, MC, V. Parking at nearby Regio 2, 500 ptas. ($4).

Built in 1978, this aging hotel rises six stories above a location about a block inland from the harbor and Paseo Marítimo. Bedrooms are simple but airy and comfortable—nowhere near the equal of the parador (see above), but then its prices are much more reasonable. Breakfast is the only meal served. The overflow from this hotel is sometimes directed to the hotel's slightly more expensive twin, the superior Regio 2 (see below).

Regio 2. Andalucía, 79, 11008 Cádiz. ☎ **956/25-30-08.** Fax 956/25-30-09. 45 rms. A/C TV TEL. 10,000 ptas. ($80) double. AE, DC, MC, V. Free parking.

Business was successful enough in the late 1970s to justify the construction of this five-story twin of an already existing hotel, the Regio 1 (see above). Run by the same management, and sharing some of their staff and amenities in common, it was built in 1981, about 200 yards from its twin, and contains air-conditioning in each of its simple but pleasant bedrooms, which are more comfortable and in better shape than those of Regio (see above). Both hotels are a very short walk from the ocean. The Regio 2 operates a cafeteria serving *platos combinados* (combination plates) daily.

WHERE TO DINE

El Faro. Calle San Felix, 15. ☎ **956/21-10-68.** Reservations recommended. Main courses 1,200–3,000 ptas. ($9.60–$24); fixed-price menu 2,150 ptas. ($17.20). AE, DC, MC, V. Daily 1–4pm and 8:30–11:30pm. SEAFOOD.

Unless you're a devotee of seafood, this might not be your preferred restaurant in Cádiz: There's only a limited selection of meat; the main emphasis is on the array of fresh fish and shellfish available in its large dining room. (There's an additional, much smaller room to the side, usually reserved for groups of local *compadres.*) Established in 1964, and the favorite restaurant of many visitors, El Faro occupies the white-walled premises of one of the simple houses near the harborfront in Cádiz's oldest neighborhood. Menu items include fried lamb chops and beefsteak and a long list of seafood, such as seafood soup, roulades of sole with spinach, hake with green sauce, monkfish with strips of Serrano ham, and lobster.

CÁDIZ AFTER DARK

La Boîte. Edificio Isecotel, Paseo Marítimo, s/n. ☎ **956/26-13-16.**

Most dance clubs around Cádiz come and go with the seasons, but this one has stayed alive longer than many of its competitors, attracting revelers with recorded music and air-conditioning. La Boîte draws a large crowd of Andalusian youth. In the old town on an avenue running alongside Playa de la Victoria, it's open nightly from 10pm to 6am. A beer costs 500 pesetas ($4). Admission costs range from 600 to 700 pesetas ($4.80–$5.60).

El Manteca. Mariana de Pineda, 66. ☎ **956/21-36-03.** Bus: 2 or 6.

This establishment's decor recalls the bullfight, as does that of many places in Cádiz. Homemade tapas are served, many made with fresh seafood. El Manteca is open Tuesday through Saturday from noon to 5pm and 9pm to 2am, Sunday from noon to 5pm. Wine costs from 125 pesetas ($1); tapas from 200 to 350 pesetas ($1.60–$2.80).

6 Costa de la Luz

Isla Cristina, one of the coast's westernmost cities, lies 34 miles (55km) W of Huelva, 403 miles (649km) SW of Madrid; Tarifa, at the opposite end of the coast, lies 59 miles (95km) SE of Cádiz, 429 miles (691km) SW of Madrid

West of Cádiz, near Huelva and the Portuguese frontier, lies the rapidly developing Costa de la Luz (Coast of Light), which hopes to pick up the overflow from Costa del Sol. The Luz coast stretches from the mouth of the Guadiana River, forming the boundary with Portugal, to Tarifa Point on the Straits of Gibraltar. Dotting the coast are long stretches of sand, pine trees, fishing cottages, and lazy whitewashed villages. The Huelva district forms the northwestern half of Costa de la Luz. The southern half stretches from Tarifa to **Sanlúcar de Barrameda,** the spot from which Magellan, in 1519, embarked on his voyage around the globe. Columbus also made this his home port for his third journey to the New World. Sanlúcar today is widely known in Andalusia for its local sherry, Manzanilla, which you can order at any of the city's wine cellars (bodegas). If you make it to Sanlúcar, you'll find the tourist information office at Calzada de Ejército, Paseo Marítimo (☎ **956/36-61-10**), just one block inland from the beach. It's open Monday through Friday from 10am to 11am and 6 to 8pm, Saturday and Sunday from 11am to 1pm. Do not count on a great deal of guidance, however. To travel between the northern and southern portions of Costa de la Luz, you must go inland to Seville, since no roads go across the Coto Doñana and the marshland near the mouth of the Guadalquivir.

GETTING THERE By Train Huelva, the coast's most prominent city, is serviced by trains from Seville, two hours away. If you're going on to Portugal from here, you can take a bus to Ayamonte, where you can board a ferry to the "gateway" of Vila Real de Santa Antonio, the beginning of Portugal's Algarve coast.

By Bus Buses run several times a day from Seville, where connections can be made to all parts of Spain. From Huelva, about eight buses a day depart for Ayamonte and the Portuguese frontier.

By Car Huelva is easily reached in about an hour from Seville, 55 miles (88.5km) to the east, via a broad and modern highway, the E-01.

VISITOR INFORMATION The tourist information office is in Huelva at Avenida de Alemania, 12 (☎ **959/25-74-03**), open Monday through Friday from 8:30am to 7:30pm, Saturday from 9am to 2pm.

WHAT TO SEE AND DO

At **Huelva** a large statue on the west bank of the river commemorates the departure of Christopher Columbus on his third voyage of discovery; and about 4½ miles (7.2km) up on the east bank of the Tinto River, a monument marks the exact spot of his departure. His ships were anchored off this bank while they were being loaded with supplies.

South of the Huelva is the **Monasterio de la Rabida,** Palos de la Frontera (☎ **959/35-04-11**), in whose little white chapel Columbus prayed for success on the eve of his voyage. Even without its connections to Columbus, the monastery would be worth a visit for its paintings and frescoes. A guide will show you around the Mudéjar chapel, and a large portion of the old monastery, which is open daily from 10am to 1pm and 4 to 7pm. Admission is free, but donations are accepted. The monastery lies on the east bank of the Tinto. Take bus number 1 from Huelva.

WHERE TO STAY & DINE

Accommodations are severely limited along Costa de la Luz in summer, so it's crucial to arrive with a reservation. You can stay at a government-run parador east of Huelva in Mazagón (see below) or in Ayamonte, near the Portuguese frontier. Where you are unlikely to want to stay overnight is in the dreary industrial port of Huelva itself.

Ayamonte was built on the slopes of a hill on which a castle stood. It is full of beach high-rises, which, for the most part, contain vacation apartments for Spaniards in July and August. Judging by their license plates, most of these visitors come from Huelva, Seville, and Madrid, so the Costa de la Luz is more Spanish in flavor than the overrun and more international Costa del Sol.

Ayamonte has clean, wide, sandy beaches, and the waves, for the most part, are calm. Portions of the beaches are even calmer because of sand bars some 55 to 110 yards from the shore, which become virtual islands at low tide. The nearest beaches to Ayamonte are miles away at Isla Canela and Moral.

Parador Nacional Costa de la Luz. El Castillito, 21400 Ayamonte. ☎ **959/32-07-00.** Fax 959/32-07-00. 53 rms, 1 suite. A/C MINIBAR TV TEL. 10,500–15,000 ptas. ($84–$120) double; 24,000 ptas. ($192) suite. AE, DC, MC, V. Free parking. From the center of Ayamonte, signs for the parador will lead you up a winding road to the hilltop, about 1/2 mile (1km) southeast of the center.

The leading accommodation in Ayamonte, this parador opened in 1966 and was completely renovated in 1991. Commanding a sweeping view of the river and the surrounding towns along its banks—sunsets are memorable here—the parador stands about 100 feet above sea level on the site of the old castle of Ayamonte. Built in a severe modern style, with Nordic-inspired furnishings, it numbers among its facilities a swimming pool, a garden, central heating, a dining room, and a bar. Good regional meals cost from 3,200 pesetas ($25.60). Try, if it's featured, *raya en pimiento* (stingray with red pepper); *calamar relleno* (stuffed squid) is another specialty.

Parador Nacional Cristóbal Colón. Carretera de Matalascañas, s/n, 21130 Mazagón. ☎ **959/53-63-00.** Fax 959/53-62-28. 43 rms, 1 suite. A/C MINIBAR TV TEL. 15,000–16,500 ptas. ($120–$132) double; 22,000 ptas. ($176) suite. AE, DC, MC, V. Free parking. Exit from Magazón's eastern sector, following the signs to the town of Matalascañas. Take the coast road (highway 442) to the parador.

One of the best accommodations in the area is 14 miles (24km) from Huelva and 3 1/2 miles (6km) from the center of Mazagón. A rambling 1960s structure, the parador has comfortable guest rooms with balconies and terraces overlooking a tranquil, expansive garden and pine groves that slope down to the white-sand beach of Mazagón. Swimmers and sunbathers can also enjoy the large pool, and there are tennis courts. The dining room features two *menús del día,* a Spanish one at 3,200 pesetas ($25.60) and a strictly Andalusian regional one at 3,500 pesetas ($28).

7 Ronda

63 miles (101km) NE of Algeciras, 60 miles (97km) W of Málaga, 91 miles (147km) SE of Seville, 367 miles (591km) S of Madrid

This little town, high in the Serranía de Ronda Mountains (2,300 feet above sea level), is one of the oldest and most aristocratic places in Spain. The main tourist attraction is a 500-foot **gorge,** spanned by a Roman stone bridge, Puente San Miguel, over the Guadelevín River. On both sides of this "hole in the earth" are cliff-hanging houses, which look as if, with the slightest push, they would plunge into the chasm.

Ronda is an incredible sight. The road here, once difficult to navigate, is now a wide highway with guard rails. The town and the surrounding mountains were legendary hideouts for bandits and smugglers, but today the Guardia Civil has almost put an end to that occupation.

The gorge divides the town into an older part, the Moorish and aristocratic quarter, and the newer section south of the gorge, built principally after the Reconquest. The old quarter is by far the more fascinating; it contains narrow, rough streets, and buildings with a marked Moorish influence (watch for the minaret). After the lazy resort living of Costa del Sol, make a side excursion to Ronda; its unique beauty and refreshing mountain air are a tonic.

Ronda is great for the explorer. Local children may attach themselves to you as guides. For a few pesetas it might be worth it to "hire" one, since it's difficult to weave your way in and out of the narrow streets.

GETTING THERE **By Train** There are three trains daily from Málaga (2 hours), three per day from Seville (3 1/2 hours), and three per day from Granada (3 1/2 hours). Most rail routes into Ronda require a change of train in the railway junction of Bobadilla, several miles to the northeast. Ronda's railway station lies in the western edge of the new city, on the Avenida Andalucía (☎ **95/287-16-73**).

By Bus There are four buses daily between Ronda and Seville (a 2½ hour drive), and five per day from Málaga (2½ hours). The bus station in Ronda lies on the western edge of the new town, at Avenida Concepción García Redondo, 2 (☎ **95/287-22-64**).

By Car Five highways converge on Ronda from all parts of Andalusia. All five head through mountainous scenery, but the road south to Marbella, through the Sierra Palmitera, is one of the most winding and dangerous.

VISITOR INFORMATION The tourist information office is at Plaza de España, 1 (☎ **95/287-12-72**), open Monday through Friday from 9:30am to 2pm and 4:30 to 6:30pm, Saturday and Sunday form 10:15am to 6:30pm.

WHAT TO SEE & DO

The still-functioning **Baños Arabes** are reached from the turnoff to Puente San Miguel. Dating from the 13th century, the baths have glass roof-windows and hump-shaped cupolas. They are generally open Tuesday through Sunday from 10am to 2pm. Admission is free, but you should tip the caretaker who shows you around.

The **Palacio de Mondragón,** El Campillo (☎ **95/287-08-18**), was once the private home of one of the ministers to Charles III. Flanked by two Mudéjar towers, it now has a baroque facade. Inside are Moorish mosaics. Open Monday through Friday from 10am to 7pm and Saturday and Sunday from 10am to 3pm; admission is 200 pesetas ($1.60) for adults, but free for children under 14.

The **Casa del Rey Moro,** Marqués de Parada, 17, is misnamed. The House of the Moorish King was actually built in the early 1700s. However, it is believed to have been constructed over Moorish foundations. The interior is closed, but from the garden you can take an underground stairway, called La Mina, which leads you to the river, a distance of 365 steps. Christian slaves cut these steps in the 14th century to guarantee a steady water supply in case Ronda came under siege.

On the same street you'll see the 18th-century **Palacio del Marqués de Salvatierra** (☎ **95/287-38-89**). Still inhabited by a private family, this Renaissance-style mansion is open for guided tours. Tours depart every 30 minutes, provided that half a dozen people are present. It's open Monday through Wednesday and Friday and Saturday from 10am to 2pm and 5 to 7pm, Thursday and Sunday from 10am to 2pm. Admission is 200 pesetas ($1.60).

Ronda has the oldest bullring in Spain. Built in the 1700s, **Plaza de Toros** is the setting for the yearly Goyesque Corrida in honor of Ronda native son Pedro Romero, one of the greatest bullfighters of all time. If you want to know more about Ronda bullfighting, head for the **Museo Taurino** (☎ **95/287-41-32**), reached through the ring. It is open June through September daily from 10am to 7pm; October through May, daily 10am to 2pm. Admission is 225 pesetas ($1.80).

Exhibits document the exploits of the noted Romero family. Francesco invented the killing sword and the *muleta,* and his grandson, Pedro (1754–1839), killed 5,600 bulls during his 30-year career. Pedro was the inspiration for Goya's famous *Tauromaquia* series. There are also exhibits devoted to Cayetano Ordóñez, the matador immortalized by Hemingway in *The Sun Also Rises.*

A NEARBY ATTRACTION

Near Benaoján, **Cueva de la Pileta** (☎ **95/16-72-02**), 15½ miles (25km) southwest of Ronda, plus a 1¼ mile (2km) hard climb, has been compared to the Caves of Altamira in northern Spain, where prehistoric paintings were discovered toward the end of the 19th century. In a wild, beautiful area known as the Serranía de Ronda, this cave was discovered in 1905 by José Bullón Lobato, grandfather of the present owners. More than a mile in length and filled with oddly and beautifully shaped stalagmites and stalactites, the cave was found to contain five fossilized human and two animal skeletons.

In the mysterious darkness, prehistoric paintings have been discovered, depicting animals in yellow, red, black, and ochre, as well as mysterious symbols. One of the highlights of the tour is a trip to the "chamber of the fish," containing a wall painting of a great black seal-like creature about three feet long. This chamber, the innermost heart of the cave, ends in a precipice that drops vertically nearly 250 feet.

In the valley just below the cave lives a guide who will conduct you around the chambers, carrying artificial light to illuminate the paintings. Plan to spend at least an hour here. Tours are given daily from 10am to 1pm and 4 to 6pm. Admission, including the one-hour tour, is 600 pesetas ($4.80) adults, 400 pesetas ($3.20) children.

You can reach the cave most easily by car from Ronda, but those without private transport can take the train to Benaoján. The cave, whose entrance is at least 4 miles (6.5km) uphill, is located in the rocky foothills of the Sierra de Libar, midway between two tiny villages: Jimera de Libar and Benaoján. The valley that contains the cave is parallel to the valley holding Ronda, so the town of Ronda and the cave are separated by a steep range of hills, requiring a rather complicated detour either to the south or north of Ronda, then a doubling back.

WHERE TO STAY

EXPENSIVE

Parador de Ronda. Plaza de España, 29400 Ronda. ☎ **95/287-75-00.** Fax 95/287-81-88. 70 rms, 8 suites. A/C MINIBAR TV TEL. 17,500–19,000 ptas. ($140–$152) double; 21,000 ptas. ($168) suite. AE, DC, MC, V.

When this parador opened in 1994, it surpassed the Reina Victoria (see below) to become the finest accommodation in the area. It sits on a high cliff overlooking the Tajo, a fantastic gorge that cuts a swath more than 500 feet deep and 300 feet wide through the center of this mountain town. Stretching along the edge of the gorge to a bridge, Ponte Nuevo, built over the Tajo in 1761, the parador is surrounded by a footpath with scenic overlooks, offering views of the gorge and the torrents of the Guadalevín River below. The parador fronts the old food market and the original Town Hall on the town's most historic square. The guest rooms are beautifully furnished, often opening onto views of the rugged peaks that surround Ronda.

Dining/Entertainment: Overlooking the gorge, the parador dining room (open to the pubic) features a typically regional cuisine of almond soup, gazpacho, wild game dishes—whatever's good and fresh in any season. There is also a bar-cafeteria.

Services: Room service, laundry, babysitting.

Facilities: The grounds include a swimming pool.

MODERATE

Hotel Don Miguel. Villanueva, 8. ☎ **95/287-77-22.** Fax 95/287-83-77. 19 rms. A/C TV TEL. 10,000 ptas. ($80) double. AE, DC, MC, V. Closed Jan 10–24. Parking 500 ptas. ($4).

From the narrow street leading to it, this hotel presents a severely dignified white-fronted facade very similar to that of its neighbors. From the back, however, the hotel looks out over the river gorge of a steep ravine, adding drama to those bedrooms which overlook it. Set a few steps east of Plaza de España, and composed of several interconnected houses, it offers a vine-strewn patio above the river, a warmly modernized interior accented with exposed brick and varnished pine, and simple but comfortable bedrooms. The establishment's restaurant, Don Miguel, is recommended separately (see below).

Hotel Reina Victoria. Paseo Dr. Fleming, 25, 29400 Ronda. ☎ **95/287-12-40.** Fax 95/287-10-75. 86 rms, 2 suites. A/C TV TEL. 15,000 ptas. ($120) double; 20,000 ptas. ($160) suite. AE, DC, MC, V. Free parking.

On the eastern periphery of town, a short walk from the center, this country-style hotel was built in 1906 by an Englishman in honor of his recently departed monarch, Queen Victoria. It's near the bullring, with terraces that hang right over a 490-foot precipice. Hemingway frequently visited the hotel, but the Reina Victoria is known best as the place where poet Rainer Maria Rilke wrote *The Spanish Trilogy.* His third-floor room has been set aside as a museum, with first editions, manuscripts, photographs, and even a framed copy of his hotel bill. A life-sized bronze statue of the poet stands in a corner of the hotel garden.

Bedrooms are big, airy, and comfortable, some with complete living rooms containing sofas, chairs, and tables. Many also have private terraces with garden furniture. The beds are sumptuous, and the bathrooms boast all the latest improvements.

Dining here can be recommended; the food is well prepared. The hotel also contains an outdoor pool and a well-stocked bar.

$ **Hotel Residencia Polo.** Mariano Soubirón, 8, 29400 Ronda. ☎ **95/287-24-47.** Fax 95/287-24-49. 33 rms. TV TEL. 9,350 ptas. ($74.80) double. AE, DC, MC, V. Parking 700 ptas. ($5.60).

In the commercial, modern heart of Ronda, near a large shopping arcade, the Polo is run with professionalism. Its accommodations are pleasantly—not elegantly—decorated and maintained. Bedrooms are spacious, with even the closets and private bathrooms large enough for your needs. The hotel has a bar and restaurant and also offers room service.

INEXPENSIVE

Hostal Residencia Royal. Virgen de la Paz, 42, 29400 Ronda. ☎ **95/287-11-41.** Fax 95/287-81-32. 29 rms. A/C TEL. 5,300 ptas. ($42.40) double. AE, DC, MC, V.

An adequate stopover for those who want to spend the night in the modern section of town, the Residencia Royal stands near the old bull arena. Each of the basic guest rooms is reasonably comfortable; rooms in the rear, however, tend to be noisy. No breakfast is served, but clients head for any of the town's several cafés for their morning caffeine.

WHERE TO DINE

Don Miguel Restaurant. Plaza de España, 3. ☎ **95/287-10-90.** Main courses 1,000–2,400 ptas. ($8–$19.20). AE, DC, MC, V. Daily 12:30–4pm and 8–11pm. Closed Jan 10–24. ANDALUSIAN.

At the end of the bridge, facing the river, this restaurant allows visitors views of the upper gorge. It has enough tables set outside on two levels to seat 300 people, and in summer this is a bustling place. The food is good, the restrooms are clean, and the waiters are polite and speak enough English to get by. There is also a pleasant bar for drinks and tapas. Try one of the seafood selections or the house specialty, stewed bull's tail. The restaurant is run by the also recommended Hotel Don Miguel (see above).

$ **Mesón Santiago.** Marina, 3. ☎ **95/287-15-59.** Main courses 1,000–1,800 ptas. ($8–$14.40); fixed-price menus 1,200–1,500 ptas. ($9.60–$12). AE, DC, MC, V. Daily 10am–4pm. SPANISH.

Santiago Ruíz Gil operates one of the best inexpensive restaurants in Ronda, serving lunch only. A three-course *menú del día,* with bread and wine, is not a bad deal, considering the price. If you order from the *especialidades de la casa,* count on spending more. Try the *caldo de cocido,* a savory stew with large pieces of meat cooked with such vegetables as garbanzos and white beans, almost a meal in itself. You might also like the tongue cooked in wine and served with potato salad. All the servings are generous. The more expensive à la carte menu is likely to include partridge, lamb, mountain trout, and regional meats. Fresh asparagus and succulent strawberries are also available in season. Mesón Santiago is located near Plaza del Socorro.

Pedro Romero. Virgen de la Paz, 18. ☎ **95/287-11-10.** Reservations required on day of *corrida.* Main courses 1,300–2,400 ptas. ($10.40–$19.20). AE, DC, MC, V. Daily 12:30–4pm and 8–11pm. SPANISH/ANDALUSIAN.

Named after famed bullfighter Pedro Romero, this restaurant attracts aficionados of that sport. In fact, it stands opposite the ring and gets extremely busy on bullfighting days, when it's almost impossible to get a table. While seated under a stuffed bull's head, surrounded by photographs of young matadors, you might begin your meal with the classic garlic soup, then follow with a well-prepared array of meat or poultry dishes.

8 Granada

258 miles (415km) S of Madrid, 76 miles (122km) NE of Málaga

This former stronghold of Moorish Spain, in the foothills of the snowcapped Sierra Nevada range, is full of romance and folklore. Washington Irving (*Tales of the Alhambra*) used the symbol of this city, the pomegranate (*granada*), to conjure up a spirit of romance. In fact, the name probably derives from the Moorish word *Karnattah.* Some historians have suggested that it comes from Garnatha Alyehud, the name of an old Jewish ghetto.

Washington Irving may have helped publicize the glories of Granada to the English-speaking world, but in Spain the city is known for its ties to another writer: Federico García Lorca. Born in 1898, this Spanish poet and dramatist, whose masterpiece was *The House of Bernarda Alba,* was shot by soldiers in 1936 in the first months of the Spanish Civil War. During Franco's rule García Lorca's works were banned in Spain, but happily that situation has changed and he is once again honored in Granada, where he grew up.

Granada lies 2,200 feet above sea level. It sprawls over two main hills, the Alhambra and the Albaicín, and it is crossed by two rivers, the Genil and the Darro.

The Cuesta de Gomérez is one of the most important streets in Granada. It climbs uphill from Plaza Nueva, the center of the modern city, to the Alhambra. At Plaza Nueva the east-west artery, Calle de los Reyes Católicos, goes to the heart of the 19th-century city and the towers of the cathedral. The main street of Granada is the Gran Vía de Colón, the principal north-south artery.

Calle de los Reyes Católicos and the Gran Vía de Colón meet at the circular Plaza de Isabel la Católica, graced by a bronze statue of the queen offering Columbus the Santa Fe agreement, which granted the rights to the epochal voyage to the New World. Going west, Calle de los Reyes Católicos passes near the cathedral and other major sights in the "downtown" section of Granada. The street runs to Puerta Real, which is the commercial hub of Granada, with many stores, hotels, cafés, and restaurants.

ESSENTIALS

GETTING THERE **By Plane** Iberia flies to Granada once or twice daily from Barcelona and Madrid, several times a week from Palma de Majorca, three times a week from Valencia, and every Thursday from Tenerife in the Canary Islands. Granada's airport lies 10 miles (16km) west of the center of town; dial **958/22-75-92.** A convenient Iberia ticketing office lies two blocks east of the cathedral, at Plaza Isabel la Católica, 2 (☎ **958/22-75-92**). A shuttle bus departs several times daily, connecting this office with the airport.

By Train Two trains connect Granada with Madrid's Atocha Railway Station daily (taking 6 to 8 hours). Many connections to the rest of Spain are funneled through the railway junction at Bobadilla, a two-hour ride to the west. The train station is at Calle Dr. Jaime García Royo, s/n (☎ **958/27-12-72**), at the end of Avenida Andaluces.

By Bus Most of Granada's long-distance buses arrive and depart from the Baccona Company's terminal, Avenida Andaluces, 12 (☎ **958/28-42-51**). Buses arrive from Barcelona four times a day, from Valencia five times a day, and from Madrid four times a day. Buses from closer destinations in Andalusia arrive at the Alsina Graells Company's terminal, Camino de Ronda, 97 (☎ **958/25-13-58**), a small street radiating out from the larger Calle Emperatriz Eugenia. Buses arrive from Almeria seven times a day, from Córdoba seven times a day, from Málaga about a dozen times a day, and from Seville about eight times a day. Bus number 11 services both stations.

By Car Granada is connected by superhighway to both Madrid, Malága, and Seville. Many sightseers prefer to make the drive from Madrid to Granada in two days, rather than one. If that is your plan, Jaén makes a perfect stopover.

VISITOR INFORMATION The tourist information office is at Plaza de Mariana Pineda, 10 (☎ **958/22-66-88**), open Monday through Friday from 9am to 7pm, Saturday from 10am to 2pm.

WHAT TO SEE & DO

Try to spend some time walking around Old Granada. Plan on about three hours to see the most interesting sights.

The **Puerta de Elvira** is the gate through which Ferdinand and Isabella made their triumphant entry into Granada in 1492. It was once a grisly place, with the rotting heads of executed criminals hanging from its portals. The quarter surrounding the gate was the Arab section (*morería*), until all the Arabs were driven out of the city after the Reconquest.

One of the most fascinating streets in Granada is **Calle de Elvira,** west of which the Albaicín, or old Arab quarter, rises on a hill. In the 17th and 18th centuries, artisans occupied the shops and ateliers along this street and those radiating from it. Come here if you're looking for antiques.

The most-walked street in Granada is **Carrera del Darro,** running north along the Darro River. It was discovered by the Romantic artists of the 19th century; many of their etchings (subsequently engraved) of scenes along this street were widely circulated, doing much to spread the fame of Granada throughout Europe. You can still find some of these old engravings in the musty antiques shops. Carrera del Darro ends at **Paseo de los Tristes (Avenue of the Sad Ones),** so named for the funeral cortèges that used to go by here on the way to the cemetery.

On Calle de Elvira stands the **Iglesia de San Andrés,** begun in 1528, with its Mudéjar bell tower. Much of the church was destroyed in the early 19th century, but inside are several interesting pieces of art, both paintings and sculptures. Another old church in this area is the **Iglesia de Santiago,** constructed in 1501 and dedicated to St. James, patron saint of Spain. Built on the site of an Arab mosque, it was damaged in the 1884 earthquake that struck Granada. The church contains the tomb of architect Diego de Siloé (1495–1563), who did much to change the face of Granada.

Despite its name, the oldest square in Granada is **Plaza Nueva,** which, under the Muslims, was the site of the "bridge of the woodcutters." The Darro River was covered over here, but its waters still flow underneath the square (which in Franco's time was named Plaza del General Franco). On the east side of the Plaza Nueva is the 16th-century **Iglesia de Santa Ana,** built by Siloé. Inside its five-nave interior you can see a Churrigueresque reredos and coffered ceiling.

✪ **Alhambra.** Palacio de Carlos V. ☎ **958/22-75-27.** Comprehensive ticket, including Alhambra and Generalife (below), 675 ptas. ($5.40); Museo Bellas Artes, 200 ptas. ($1.60); Museo Hispano-Musulman, 200 ptas. ($1.60); illuminated visits, 675 ptas. ($5.40). Mar–Oct, daily 9am–7:45pm, floodlit visits daily 10pm–midnight; Nov–Feb, daily 9am–6pm, floodlit visits daily 8–10pm. Bus: 2.

Later enriched by Moorish occupants into a lavish palace, the Alhambra was originally constructed for defensive purposes on a hilltop's rocky outcropping above the Darro River. The modern city of Granada was built across the river from the Alhambra, about half a mile from its western foundations.

When you first see the Alhambra, you may be surprised by its somewhat somber exterior. You have to walk across the threshold to discover the true delights of this Moorish palace. Tickets are sold in the office next to the uncompleted palace of the Hapsburg king Charles V. Enter through the incongruous 14th-century Gateway to Justice. Most visitors do not need an expensive guide but will be content to stroll through the richly ornamented open-air rooms, with their lacelike walls and their courtyards with fountains. Many of the Arabic inscriptions translate as "Only Allah is conqueror."

The most-photographed part of the palace is the Court of Lions, named after its highly stylized fountain. This was the heart of the palace, the most private section, where the sultan enjoyed his harem. Opening onto the court are the Hall of the Two Sisters, where the favorite of the moment was kept, and the Gossip Room, a factory of intrigue. In the dancing room in the Hall of Kings, entertainment was provided nightly to amuse the sultan's party. Eunuchs guarded the harem but apparently not very well—one sultan, according to legend, beheaded 36 Moorish princes here because one of them was suspected of having been intimate with his favorite.

You can see the room where Washington Irving lived (in the chambers of Charles V) while he was compiling his *Tales of the Alhambra*—the best known of which is the legend of Zayda, Zorayada, and Zorahayda, the three beautiful princesses who fell in love with three captured Spanish soldiers outside "La Torre de las Infantas."

Irving credits the French with saving the Alhambra for posterity, but in fact they were responsible for blowing up seven of the towers in 1812, and it was a Spanish soldier who cut the fuse before more damage could be done. When the Duke of Wellington arrived a few years later, he chased out the chickens, the gypsies, and the transient beggars who were using the Alhambra as a tenement and set up housekeeping here himself.

Charles V may have been horrified when he saw the cathedral in the middle of the great mosque at Córdoba, but he is responsible for architectural meddling here, building a Renaissance palace at the Alhambra—which, although quite beautiful, is terribly out of place. Today it houses the **Museo Bellas Artes en la Alhambra** (☎ **958/22-48-43**), open Monday to Saturday from 9am to 1pm. It also shelters the **Museo Hispano-Musulman en la Alhambra** (☎ **958/22-62-79**), devoted to Hispanic-Muslim art and open Monday through Saturday from 9am to 7:45pm.

Note: Because of the overwhelming crowds, there is a chance you may not be admitted to the Alhambra, as the government is forced to limit the number of people who can enter. Your best bet is to go as early as possible, but, even then, some people arriving at 10am may not be admitted until 1:30pm. If you arrive after 4pm, it is unlikely you'll get in at all.

Many visitors opt for a taxi or the bus to the Alhambra. But some hardy souls enjoy the uphill climb from the cathedral, Plaza de la Lonja (signs indicate the winding roads and the steps that lead to the Alhambra). If you decide to walk, enter the Alhambra via the Cuesta de Gomérez, which, although steep, is the quickest and shortest pedestrian route. It begins at Plaza Nueva, about four blocks east of the cathedral, and goes steeply uphill to Puerta de las Granadas, the first of two gates to the Alhambra. The second, another 200 yards uphill, is Puerta de la Justicia, which accepts 90% of the touristic visits to the Alhambra. Beware of self-styled "guides" milling around the parking lot; they may just be interested in picking your pocket.

✪ **Generalife.** Alhambra, Cerro de Sol. ☎ **958/22-75-27.** Comprehensive ticket, including Alhambra and Generalife, 675 ptas. ($5.40), see above. For hours see the Alhambra, above. Exit from the Alhambra via Puerta de la Justicia, then circumnavigate the Alhambra's southern foundations until you reach the gardens of the summer palace, where Paseo de los Cipreses quickly leads you to the main building of the Generalife.

The sultans used to spend their summers in this palace (pronounced "hay-nay-rahl-*ee*-fay"), safely locked away with their harems. Built in the 13th century to overlook the Alhambra, the Generalife's glory is its gardens and courtyards. Don't expect an Alhambra in miniature: The Generalife was always meant to be a retreat, even from the splendors of the Alhambra. This palace was the setting for Irving's story of the prince locked away from love.

✪ **Catedral and Capilla Real.** Plaza de la Lonja, Gran Vía de Colón, 5. ☎ **958/22-29-59.** Admission to cathedral, 200 ptas. ($1.60); chapel, 200 ptas. ($1.60). Cathedral and chapel, daily 10:30am–1:30pm and 4–7pm (closes at 6pm in winter).

This richly ornate Spanish Renaissance cathedral, with its spectacular altar, is one of the country's architectural highlights, acclaimed for its beautiful facade and gold-and-white decor. It was begun in 1521 and completed in 1714. Behind the cathedral (entered separately) is the flamboyant Gothic Royal Chapel (☎ **958/22-92-39**), where the remains of Queen Isabella and her husband, Ferdinand, lie. It was their wish to be buried in recaptured Granada, not Castile or Aragón. The coffins are remarkably tiny—a reminder of how short they must have been. Accenting the tombs is a wrought-iron grill, a masterpiece. Occupying much larger tombs are the remains of their daughter, Joanna the Mad, and her husband, Philip the Handsome. The cathedral lies in the center of Granada, off two prominent streets, the Gran Vía de Colón and the Calle de San Jerónimo. The Capilla Real abuts the cathedral's eastern edge.

Albaicín. Bus: 7 to Calle de Pagés.

This old Arab quarter, on one of the two main hills of Granada, doesn't belong to the city of 19th-century buildings and wide boulevards. It, and the surrounding gypsy caves of Sacromonte, are holdovers from the past. The Albaicín once flourished as the residential section of the Moors, even after the city's reconquest, but it fell into decline when the Christians drove them out. This narrow labyrinth of crooked streets escaped the fate of much of Granada, which was torn down in the name of progress. Fortunately, it has been preserved, as have its cisterns, fountains, plazas, whitewashed houses, villas, and the decaying remnants of the old city gate. Here and there, you can catch a glimpse of a private patio filled with fountains and plants, a traditional elegant way of life that continues.

Impressions

One should remember Granada as one should remember a sweetheart who has died.

—Federico García Lorca

Monasterio Cartuja. Carrera Alfacar, s/n. ☎ **958/20-19-32.** Admission 350 ptas. ($2.80). Daily 10am–1pm and 4–7pm (closes at 6pm in winter). Bus: 8 from cathedral.

This 16th-century monastery, off the Albaicín on the outskirts of Granada, is sometimes called "the Christian answer to the Alhambra" because of its ornate stucco and marble and the baroque Churrigueresque fantasy in the sacristy. Its most notable paintings are by Bocanegra, its outstanding sculpture by Mora. The church of this Carthusian monastery was decorated with baroque stucco in the 17th century. The 18th-century sacristy is an excellent example of latter-day baroque style. Napoleon's armies killed St. Bruno here, and La Cartuja is said to be the only monument of its kind in the world. Sometimes one of the Carthusian monks will take you on a guided tour.

Casa-Museo Federico García Lorca. Virgen Blanca, 6, Fuentevaqueros. ☎ **958/51-64-53.** Admission 100 ptas. ($0.80). Tues–Sun, mandatory guided tours at 10am, 11am, noon, 1pm, 5pm, 6pm, and 7pm. Closed May 1.

Poet and dramatist Federico García Lorca spent many happy summers with his family here at their vacation home. He had moved to Granada in 1909, a dreamy-eyed schoolboy, and he was endlessly fascinated with its life, including the Alhambra and the gypsies, whom he was later to describe compassionately in his *Gypsy Ballads*. The house is decorated with green trim and grillwork and filled with family memorabilia, including furniture and portraits. You can look out at the Alhambra from one of its balconies. Visitors may inspect the poet's upstairs bedroom and see his oak desk, stained with ink. Look for the white stool that he carried to the terrace to watch the sun set over Granada. The house is in the Fuentevaqueros section of Granada, near the airport.

Casa Museo de Manuel de Falla. Antequeruela Alta, 11. ☎ **958/22-94-21.** Free admission. Tues–Sat 10am–3pm.

The famous Spanish composer Manuel de Falla, known for his strongly individualized works, came to live in Granada in 1919, hoping to find a retreat and inspiration. He moved into a *carmen* (local dialect for a small white house) just below the Alhambra, and in time befriended García Lorca. In 1922, on the grounds of the Alhambra, they staged the Cante Jondo Festival, the purest expression of flamenco. Today visitors can walk through the gardens of the man who wrote such works as *Nights in the Gardens of Spain* and see his collection of handcrafts and ceramics, along with other personal memorabilia.

Baños Arabes. Carrera del Darro, 31. No phone. Free admission. Daily 9am–6pm.

These Arab baths were called by the Moors the "baths of the walnut tree." Among the oldest buildings still standing in Granada, and among the best-preserved Muslim baths in Spain, they predate the Alhambra. Supposedly Visigothic and Roman building materials went into their construction. It is remarkable that they escaped destruction during the reign of the Reyes Católicos (Ferdinand and Isabella).

Casa de Castril. Museo Arqueológico, Carrera del Darro, 41. ☎ **958/22-56-40.** Admission 250 ptas. ($2). Tues–Sat 10am–2pm. Bus: 7.

This building has always been one of the most handsome Renaissance palaces in Granada. The plateresque facade of 1539 has been attributed to Diego de Siloé. In 1869 it was converted into a museum with a collection of artifacts found in the area.

SHOPPING

The Alcaicería, once the Moorish silk market, is next to the cathedral in the lower city. The narrow streets of this rebuilt village of shops are filled with vendors selling the arts and crafts of Granada province. For the souvenir hunter, the Alcaiceríca offers one of the most splendid assortments in Spain of tiles, castanets, and wire figures of Don Quixote chasing windmills. Lots of Spanish jewelry can be found here, comparing favorably with the finest Toledan work. For the window shopper, in particular, it makes a pleasant stroll.

Artesanía Albaicín (Tienda Eduardo Ferrer Lucena). Calle del Agua, 19. ☎ **958/27-90-56.**

This is one of the Arab Quarter's most enduring repositories of the intricately tooled leather for which Andalusia, land of bullfights and beef, is famous. The inventory includes useful items (purses, wallets, briefcases, coasters for those glasses of sherry you'll be consuming after your return home) as well as some truly odd items you probably won't use (or even like) after you buy them. Established in the 1980s, the shop's open daily from 11am to 3:30pm and 5 to 9:30pm.

Casa Ferrer (Tienda Eduardo Ferrer Castillo). Cuesta de Gomérez, 26. ☎ **958/22-18-32.**

This is the patriarch of music stores in Andalusia. Founded in 1875 by an ancestor of the present owner, it stocks an elegant assortment of Spanish guitars, each a work of handcrafted aesthetic and musical art. Depending on their resonance and degree of ornamentation, guitars range in price from 40,000 pesetas ($320) to 400,000 pesetas ($3,200). Open Monday through Saturday from 9:30am to 1:30pm, Monday through Friday from 4:30 to 8:30pm.

Céramica Aliatar. Plaza de Aliatar, 18. ☎ **958/27-80-89.**

Set within the Albaicín, the city's former Arab quarter, this outfit was established in the early 1980s, and ever since has been loaded with a winning assortment of Andalusian ceramics. There are ashtrays, water and wine pitchers, serving platters, dinner plates, coffee cups, and pots for the garden that are charming. Most of the inventory comes in the traditional colors of blue and white, or blue, white, and green. Open Monday through Friday from 9am to 2pm and 5 to 8pm.

Tejidos Artistocos Fortuny. Plaza Fortuny, 1. ☎ **958/22-43-27.**

A quick perusal of the merchandise here gives a good idea of what's fashionable in Andalusia in the way of curtains, knotted carpets, nubbly textured draperies, tablecloths, placemats, and textiles (sold by the meter), which might be appealing when crafted into garments after you return home. Much of the merchandise is handwoven. Open Monday through Friday from 9am to 2pm and 5:30 to 8:30pm.

OUTDOOR ACTIVITIES

Bullfighting The *corrida* isn't really very popular here. Most of the major bullfights are limited to the week of the Fiesta de Corpus Christi in mid-June or the Día de la Cruz (Day of the Cross) observed on May 3. There is also a fight on the last Sunday in September. The Plaza de Toros, the bullring, is on Avenida de Doctor Olóriz, close to the soccer stadium. On the day of the fight, tickets can be purchased in the center of town on Calle Escudo del Carmen in back of the city hall from 5 to 9pm. For more information, call **958/22-22-72.**

Hiking The tourist office (see above) will provide you with a map for hikes through the Parque de Invierno, Granada's most popular outdoor recreation and picnic area. Some trail maps follow the original route of the Muslims or snow carriers who brought ice from the mountains to the Alhambra before electricity was invented. To reach the park, take bus number 2 beyond the Alhambra to the Cementerio stop. At the cemetery here, you'll find the entrance to the park.

Jogging The best place for jogging is the Parque de Invierno (see "Hiking," above).

Skiing The slopes at Solynieve (☎ **958/24-91-00**) offer some of the best skiing in Spain. This is the southernmost ski resort on the European continent, located some 20 miles (32km) from the heart of Granada and reached along a mountain road. Solynieve climbs to a height of 11,000 feet and has snow all year. The up-to-date facilities include chairlifts and cable cars.

Swimming Most guests head for the Costa del Sol (see next chapter) when they want to go swimming, as very few hotels in Granada offer pools. There are two outdoor pools at the Neptuno Sports Complex on Calle Arabial (☎ **958/25-10-67**), in the center of town.

Tennis Hotels in Granada are too cramped for space for tennis courts, but there are some at the Neptuno Sports Complex (see "Swimming," above).

WHERE TO STAY

VERY EXPENSIVE

✪ **Parador Nacional de San Francisco.** Alhambra, 18009 Granada. ☎ **800/343-0020** in the U.S., or 958/22-14-40. Fax 958/22-22-64. 36 rms. A/C MINIBAR TV TEL. 28,000 ptas. ($224) double. AE, DC, MC, V.

The most famous parador in Spain—and the hardest to get in—is set within the grounds of the Alhambra. It's housed in an old brick building with a new annex. The decor is tasteful and the place evokes a lot of history and a rich Andalusian ambience. The parador itself is within a former convent founded by the Catholic monarchs immediately after they conquered the city in 1492. Prior to that, the building was part of the Muslim complex that included the Alhambra Palace and a mosque built in the middle of the 1300s by Caliph Yusuf I. The bodies of Ferdinand and Isabella were once placed here until their tombs could be readied in the cathedral. One side of the parador opens onto its own lovely gardens, and the other fronts the Alhambra itself. From its terrace, you will have views of the Generalife gardens and the Sacromonte caves. Accommodations are generally roomy and comfortable, receiving their last renovation in 1992. Tile baths with such extras as hair dryers add to the allure, and housekeeping is excellent. Try for a room in the older section, which is furnished with antiques; rooms in the more modern wing are less inspired. See "Where to Dine" for the parador's restaurant recommendation.

EXPENSIVE

Hotel Alhambra Palace. Peña Partida, 2. 18009 Granada. ☎ **958/22-14-68.** Fax 958/22-64-04. 121 rms, 11 suites. A/C MINIBAR TV TEL. 18,500 ptas. ($148) double; 27,500 ptas. ($220) suite. AE, DC, MC, V. Free parking. Bus: 2.

Evoking a Moorish fortress, complete with a crenellated roofline, a crowning dome, geometric tilework, and a suggestion of a minaret, this legendary hotel is a good choice. The best known of Granada's hotels, it was built in 1910 in a sort of Mudéjar Revival style in a shady, secluded spot, midway up the slope toward the Alhambra. The private rooms don't live up to the drama of the public areas, which include an Arabian Nights dining room and a glassed-in dining terrace. Have a drink in the bar with its panorama over Granada, and try for a room with a balcony opening onto that view. The court rooms are less desirable because they lack double glazing and are subject to noise at night. Many rooms are spacious and quite comfortable, whereas others are small and need some restoration. Frankly, whether you love or hate this hotel will depend on your room assignment—some are excellent, some a bit seedy. But there's nothing like this Moorish palace in all of Granada.

Hotel Carmen. Acera del Darro, 62, 18009 Granada. ☎ **958/25-83-00.** Fax 958/25-64-62. 272 rms, 11 suites. A/C MINIBAR TV TEL. 19,220 ptas. ($153.75) double; 35,000–75,000 ptas. ($280–$600) suite. AE, DC, MC, V. Parking 1,500 ptas. ($12).

Located about half a mile south of the cathedral on a wide boulevard central to the city's business district, this 1992 hotel offers good service and clean and decent accommodations, each with its own balcony and private bath. Many of the rooms are quite small, and the decor, although traditional, is quite lackluster. The public rooms include lots of polished marble and comfortable sofas scattered throughout a variety of rooms devoted to reading, card playing, or socializing. The decoration lacks style.

Dining/Entertainment: There's a dignified modern restaurant here that serves three-course fixed-price lunches and dinners, as well as a shiny cafeteria for drinks, snacks, and coffee-shop-style food. The Bar Inglés serves drinks amid hardwood paneling, leather upholstery, and patterned fabrics.

Services: Laundry, concierge, babysitting, room service.

Facilities: Disco, car rentals, business center, shopping boutiques, outdoor swimming pool.

Hotel Granada Center. Avenida Fuentenueva, s/n, 18002 Granada. ☎ **958/20-50-00.** Fax 958/28-96-96. 165 rms, 7 suites. A/C MINIBAR TV TEL. 18,700 ptas. ($149.60) double; 55,000 ptas. ($440) suite. AE, DC, MC, V. Parking 1,300 ptas. ($10.40).

One of the most recommendable modern hotels in Granada opened in 1992 adjacent to the university. Its seven-story design allowed its architects to create a marble-floored, glass-covered atrium at its center, where elevators rise like glass cages against one wall, and potted plants and armchairs are bathed in natural light from above. Bedrooms are comfortable, monochromatically decorated in neutral beige and earth tones, with ample use of postmodern furniture and slabs of polished stone, especially in the bathrooms. There's a hairdresser and in-house garage, a bar, conference facilities, and a discreetly formal restaurant, Al Zagal, serving Andalusian and international food. In general, service here could be greatly improved.

Hotel Princesa Ana. Constitución, 37, 18012 Granada. ☎ **958/28-74-47.** Fax 958/27-39-54. 59 rms, 2 suites. A/C MINIBAR TV TEL. 15,500 ptas. ($124) double; 28,500 ptas. ($228) suite. AE, DC, MC, V. Parking 1,200 ptas. ($9.60).

Set midway between the railway station and the Plaza de Toros, about 1 1/2 miles (2.5km) northwest of the Alhambra, this balconied five-story hotel welcomes guests into an interior sheathed with marble and decorated in tones of soft pink and white. Although it has been supplanted by newer four-star hotels since its construction in 1989, it maintains a well-managed allure for foreign visitors and business travelers. Bedrooms evoke a British aura, with their dark wood furnishings; the tile bathrooms with dual sinks are well maintained. On the premises is an intimate bar, plus a restaurant (La Princesa Ana) and an uncomplicated cafeteria. Frequent clients do not regret the lack of a swimming pool here because the resulting cost savings are passed on in the form of lower overnight rates.

MODERATE

Hotel Meliá Granada. Angel Ganivet, 7, 18009 Granada. ☎ **800/336-3542** in the U.S., or 958/22-74-00. Fax 958/22-74-03. 188 rms, 9 suites. A/C MINIBAR TV TEL. 16,200 ptas. ($129.60) double; 18,625 ptas. ($149) suite. AE, DC, MC, V. Parking 1,300 ptas. ($10.40).

A modern and efficient place run by the Meliá chain, about five blocks southeast of the Ayuntamiento (Town Hall), this hotel offers a comfortable format with welcome air conditioning throughout both the public and guest rooms. Furnished with either extra-wide twin or double beds, the rooms are fairly standardized, with well-chosen carpets, art on the walls, and private baths, equipped with phones and hair dryers. One floor is devoted to executive rooms, where guests receive extra pampering. If you don't get a room with a terrace, you haven't missed much, as the views are hardly interesting. Rooms opening onto the street are double glazed, and some accommodations are for persons with disabilities. The street level is punctuated with old-fashioned arcades, but once inside, you'll find a glossy and contemporary world of clean comfort, soothing monochromes, and efficient service.

Dining/Entertainment: The restaurant Mulhacen, featuring international cuisine, serves fixed-price lunches and dinners. There's also a bar.

Services: 24-hour room service, concierge, laundry service.

Facilities: Sauna and health club, hairdresser/barber, car rentals, shopping boutiques.

Hotel Rallye. Camino de Ronda, 107, 18003 Granada. ☎ **958/27-28-00.** Fax 958/27-28-62. 79 rms. A/C MINIBAR TV TEL. 14,900 ptas. ($119.20) double. AE, DC, MC, V. Parking 1,100 ptas. ($8.80). Bus: 1 or 5.

Some local residents designate this as one of the best hotels in town, and a relatively good value for the price. Originally built as a three-star hotel in 1964, it was thoroughly upgraded into a four-star format in 1990, and today rises five light-green stories above the neighborhood that surrounds it. It lies within a 15-minute walk of the cathedral, on the northern perimeter of Granada's urban center. Bedrooms are comfortable and well maintained, with light-green and white color schemes. The in-house restaurant, the Rallye, serves well-prepared meals.

Hotel Saray. Tierno Galván, s/n, 18006 Granada. ☎ **958/13-00-09.** Fax 958/12-91-61. 195 rms, 8 suites. A/C MINIBAR TV TEL. 14,480–18,100 ptas. ($115.85–$144.80) double; 20,800–26,000 ptas. ($166.40–$208) suite. AE, DC, MC, V. Parking 1,100 ptas. ($8.80).

Just a 10-minute walk south of Granada's historic center, this nine-story hotel offers a view of the Sierra Nevada range from some of its upper floors. Built in 1991, it maintains carefully designed bedrooms whose color scheme varies from one floor to another, incorporating Andalusian blues, oranges, and terra-cottas. There's a bar near the reception area, which is sheathed, like many of the other public areas, with pale orange-pink marble, and a lobby-level restaurant, the Saray. The hotel maintains its own outdoor swimming pool for use during the midsummer months.

INEXPENSIVE

$ Hotel América. Real de la Alhambra, 53, 18009 Granada. ☎ **958/22-74-71.** Fax 958/22-74-70. 13 rms, 1 suite. TEL. 10,000 ptas. ($80) double; 13,000 ptas. ($104) suite. AE, DC, MC, V. Closed Nov–Feb. Bus: 2.

Located within the ancient Alhambra walls, this is one of the small hotels of Granada. Walk through the covered entryway of this former villa into the shady patio that's lively yet intimate, with large trees, potted plants, and ferns. Other plants cascade down the white plaster walls and entwine with the ornate grillwork. Garden chairs and tables are set out for home-cooked Spanish meals. The living room of this homey little retreat is graced with a collection of regional decorative objects; some of the bedrooms have Andalusian reproductions.

Hotel Guadalupe. Alijares, s/n, 18009 Granada. ☎ **958/22-34-24.** Fax 958/22-37-98. 43 rms. A/C MINIBAR TV TEL. 8,500 ptas. ($68) double. AE, DC, MC, V. Parking 1,550 ptas. ($12.40). Bus: 2.

This four-story building, set beside an inclined road leading up to the Alhambra, stands just above the older and more famous Washington Irving Hotel, which has seen better days. It was built in 1969, but with its thick stucco walls, rounded arches, and jutting beams, it seems older. The last renovation was in 1993. The comfortably furnished bedrooms overlook the Alhambra. There's a fifth-floor à la carte restaurant, plus a pleasant bar in the lobby.

Hotel Residencia Cóndor. Constitución, 6, 18012 Granada. ☎ **958/28-37-11.** Fax 958/28-38-50. 104 rms. A/C TV TEL. 9,800 ptas. ($78.40) double. AE, DC, MC, V. Parking 1,200 ptas. ($9.60). Bus: 6, 8, 9, or 10.

The attractive design of this hotel helps make it one of Granada's best in its price range. It's in the center of town, a five-minute walk from the Alhambra and the cathedral. Many of the pleasant bedrooms have terraces, and all have light-grained contemporary furniture. The hotel's restaurant serves both Spanish and international cuisine, and there's also a cafeteria for snacks. Room service is 24 hours a day.

Hotel Victoria. Puerta Real, 3, 18005 Granada. ☎ **958/25-77-00.** Fax 958/26-31-08. 67 rms, 2 suites. A/C MINIBAR TV TEL. 9,500 ptas. ($76) double; 20,000 ptas. ($160) suite. AE, DC, MC, V. Parking 1,300 ptas. ($10.40).

Hotel Victoria, in the heart of Granada, has long been a favorite. Its domed tower and the elegant detailing around each window evoke 19th-century Paris. You'll enter a circular salmon-and-cream marble lobby. The upper hallways have intricate geometric tilework, and on the second floor there's an American bar with Ionic columns, as well as an attractively formal dining room. Many of the guest rooms have reproductions of antiques and walls upholstered in shades of terra-cotta.

Macía. Plaza Nueva, 4, 18010 Granada. ☎ **958/22-75-36.** Fax 958/22-75-33. 44 rms. TV TEL. 7,000 ptas. ($56) double. AE, DC, MC, V. Parking 1,300 ptas. ($10.40).

An attractive 1970s hotel at the bottom of the hill leading to the Alhambra, the Macía is a real bargain for what should be a three-star hotel. All the guest rooms have heating and are clean and functional; about half have air-conditioning. Breakfast is the only meal served.

WHERE TO DINE

VERY EXPENSIVE

Restaurante Cunini. Plaza de la Pescadería, 14. ☎ **958/25-07-77.** Reservations recommended. Main courses 2,200–5,500 ptas. ($17.60–$44); fixed-price menu 5,000 ptas. ($40). AE, DC, MC, V. Tues–Sun noon–4pm and 8pm–midnight. SEAFOOD.

The array of seafood specialties served at Cunini, perhaps a hundred selections, extends even to the tapas served at the long stand-up bar. Many guests move on, after a drink or two, to the paneled ground-floor restaurant, where the cuisine reflects the whole of Spain. Meals often begin with soup—perhaps sopa sevillana (with ham, shrimp, and whitefish). Also popular is a deep fry of small fish called a *fritura Cunini,* with other specialties including rice with seafood, *zarzuela* (seafood stew), smoked salmon, and grilled shrimp. Plaza de la Pescadería is adjacent to the Gran Vía de Colón, just below the cathedral.

Expensive

Carmen de San Miguel. Plaza de Torres Bermejas, 3. ☎ **958/22-67-23.** Reservations recommended. Main courses 2,000–3,100 ptas. ($16–$24.80); three-course *menú del día* 5,000–7,000 ptas. ($40–$56). AE, DC, MC, V. Mon–Sat 1:30–4:30pm and 9–11:30pm. INTERNATIONAL.

Set on the sloping incline leading up to the Alhambra, this likable restaurant offers spectacular views over the city center. Proud of its glassed-in dining room and patio-style terrace whose banks of flowers are changed seasonally, the restaurant serves specialties that include *rabo de toro* (stewed oxtail), an array of such fish dishes as grilled hake and well-seasoned *zarzuela* (seafood stew), and a shoulder of lamb (*paletilla de cordero*) stuffed with pine nuts and herbs. The food, although good, doesn't quite match the view. The wines here derive from throughout the country, with a strong selection of Riojas.

Parador Nacional San Francisco. Real de la Alhambra. ☎ **958/22-14-40.** Reservations required. Main courses 2,000–2,600 ptas. ($16–$20.80); fixed-price menu 3,800 ptas. ($30.40). AE, DC, MC, V. Daily 1–4pm and 8–11pm. Bus: 2. SPANISH.

Even if you can't afford to stay at this luxurious parador—the most famous in Spain—consider a meal here. The dining room is spacious, the service is polite, and you gaze upon the rose gardens and a distant view of the Generalife. The same set menu, which changes daily, is repeated in the evening, although you can always order à la carte. At this 16th-century convent built by the Reyes Católicos, you get not only atmosphere, but also a cuisine that features regional dishes of Andalusia and Spanish national specialties. Lunch is the preferred time to dine here, because the terrace overlooking the palace is open then. A light outdoor lunch menu of sandwiches and salads can be ordered on the à la carte menu if you don't want to partake of the heavy major Spanish repast in the heat of the day.

✪ **Ruta del Valleta.** Carretera de la Sierra Nevada, km 5.5, Cenés de la Vega. ☎ **958/48-61-34.** Reservations recommended. Main courses 2,500–3,200 ptas. ($20–$25.60); fixed-price menus 4,500–5,000 ptas. ($36–$40). AE, DC, MC, V. Daily 1–4:30pm, Mon–Sat 8pm–midnight. ANDALUSIAN/INTERNATIONAL.

Despite its origins in 1976 as an unpretentious roadhouse restaurant, this place rapidly evolved into what is usually acclaimed as the best restaurant in or around Granada. It lies within the hamlet of Cenés de la Vega, about 3½ miles northwest of Granada's center, and contains six dining rooms of various sizes, each decorated with a well-planned mixture of English and Andalusian furniture and accessories. (These include a worthy collection of hand-painted ceramics from the region, many of which hang from the ceilings.)

Its owners are a pair of Granada-born brothers, Miguel and José Pedraza, who direct a well-intentioned staff in impeccable service rituals. Menu items change with the seasons, but are likely to include roast suckling pig; roasted game birds such as pheasant and partridge, often served with Rioja wine sauce; preparations of fish and shellfish, including monkfish with Andalusian herbs and strips of Serrano ham; filet steak in a morel-studded cream sauce; and a dessert specialty of frozen rice pudding on a bed of warm chocolate sauce. The wine list is said to be the most comprehensive in the region.

MODERATE

Chikito. Plaza del Campilio, 9. ☎ **958/22-33-64.** Reservations recommended. Main courses 1,800–2,200 ptas. ($14.40–$17.60); fixed-price menu 2,000 ptas. ($16). AE, DC, MC, V. Thurs–Tues 1–4pm and 8–11:30pm. Bus: 1, 2, or 7. SPANISH.

Chikito sits across the street from the famous tree-shaded square where García Lorca met with other members of El Rinconcillo (The Little Corner), a dozen young men considered the best and the brightest in the 1920s, when they brought a brief but dazzling cultural renaissance to their hometown. The café where they met has now changed its name, but it's the same building. The present-day Chikito is both a bar and a restaurant. In fair weather, guests enjoy drinks and snacks on tables placed in the square; in winter they retreat inside to the tapas bars. There is also a complete restaurant facility, offering *sopa sevillana,* shrimp cocktail, Basque hake, baked tuna, oxtail, *zarzuela* (seafood stew), grilled swordfish, and Argentine-style veal steak. Regrettably, this literary shrine has barely civil waiters, who obviously lack patience with newcomers. You may want to skip dinner here and settle only for tapas and a glass of sherry at the bar.

Restaurante Sevilla. Calle Oficios, 12. ☎ **958/22-12-23.** Reservations recommended. Main courses 900–3,000 ptas. ($7.20–$24); fixed-price menu 1,950 ptas. ($15.60). AE, DC, MC, V. Daily 1–4pm, Mon–Sat 8–11pm. SPANISH/ANDALUSIAN.

Attracting a mixed crowd of all ages, the Sevilla is definitely *típico,* with an upbeat elegance. In the past, you might have seen El Cordobés (when he was Spain's leading bullfighter), Brigitte Bardot, or even Andrés Segovia dining here. Even before them, the place had been discovered by García Lorca, a patron in the 1930s, and Manuel de Falla. Our most recent meal here included gazpacho, Andalusian veal, and caramel custard, plus bread and the wine of Valdepeñas. To break the gazpacho monotony, try *sopa virule,* made with pine nuts and chicken breasts. For a main course, we recommend the *cordero a la pastoril* (lamb with herbs and paprika). The best dessert is bananas flambé. You can dine inside, where it is pleasantly decorated, or have a meal on the terrace. Sevilla also has a bar. You'll find the place in the center of town opposite the Royal Chapel, near Plaza Isabel la Católica.

INEXPENSIVE

Mesón Antonio. Ecce Homo, 6. ☎ **958/22-95-99.** Main courses 1,100–1,500 ptas. ($8.80–$12). AE, MC, V. Mon–Sat 2–3:30pm and 9–10:30pm. Closed July–Sept. SPANISH.

This appealing and unpretentious restaurant, established in 1980, is one floor above street level in an unassuming 1740s house, whose address sometimes requires a bit of looking. (The narrow street on which it's found lies a few steps from the landmark Campo del Príncipe.) You'll traverse a communal patio before climbing a flight of stairs to reach the simply decorated dining room. All of the specialties served here are prepared in wood-burning ovens. These might include roasted lamb in local herbs, *zarzuela* (seafood stew), several different versions of steaks, and such vegetables as fresh asparagus and roasted leeks au gratin.

$ **La Nueva Bodega.** Cetti Merlem, 9. ☎ **958/22-59-34.** Reservations required. *Platos combinados* 800–1,200 ptas. ($6.40–$9.60); main courses 1,000–1,800 ptas. ($8–$14.40); fixed-price menus 1,100–1,600 ptas. ($8.80–$12.80). AE, DC, MC, V. Daily noon–midnight. IBERIAN.

This place seems to be everyone's favorite inexpensive restaurant in Granada. You can enjoy both cafeteria and restaurant service and even order food at the bar, which is cheaper than sitting at a table. The restaurant and cafeteria specialize in *platos combinados* (combination plates). This doesn't mean that you get everything on one plate. You might be served chicken soup, followed by an omelet, then swordfish Milanese style, along with bread and a simple dessert. In addition, the restaurant offers fixed-price menus that are both filling and well prepared. Specialties are from not only Andalusia but all of Iberia, including Portugal.

Polinarío. Real de la Alhambra, 3. ☎ **958/22-29-91.** Luncheon buffet 1,350 ptas. ($10.80). No credit cards. Daily 10am–4pm; bar daily noon–7pm. Bus: 2. SPANISH.

Although its food is usually somewhat ordinary, this simple restaurant is one of only three restaurants within the walled confines of the Alhambra. (Another is the dining room within the local parador, which, while preferable, is also more expensive.) The Polinarío enjoys an enviable position within a very old building across from the Palace of Carlos V, and, as such, does a thriving lunch business every day with participants of organized tours. By the end of a hot day, the luncheon buffet might be a bit fatigued, but the Spanish cooking is adequate, and usually includes a selection of salads, soups, meats, and desserts.

GRANADA AFTER DARK

The Gypsy Caves of Sacromonte These inhabited gypsy caves are the subject of much controversy. Admittedly, they are a tourist trap, one of the most obviously commercial and shadowy rackets in Spain. Still, the caves are a potent-enough attraction, if you follow some rules.

Once thousands of gypsies lived on the "Holy Mountain," so named because of several Christians martyred here. However, many of the caves were heavily damaged in the floodlike rains of 1962, forcing hundreds of the occupants to seek shelter elsewhere. Nearly all the gypsies remaining are in one way or another involved with tourism. (Some don't even live here—they commute from modern apartments in the city.)

When evening settles over Granada, loads of visitors descend on these caves near the Albaicín, the old Arab section. In every cave you'll hear the rattle of castanets and the strumming of guitars, while everybody in the gypsy family struts his or her stuff. Popularly known as the *zambra,* this is intriguing entertainment only if you have an appreciation of the grotesque. Whenever a gypsy boy or girl comes along with genuine talent, he or she is often grabbed up and hustled off to the more expensive clubs. Those left at home can be rather pathetic in their attempts to entertain.

One of the main reasons for going is to see the caves themselves. If you're expecting primitive living, you may be in for a surprise—many are quite comfortable, with conveniences like telephones and electricity. Often they are decorated with copper and ceramic items—and the inhabitants need no encouragement to sell them to you.

If you want to see the caves, you can walk up the hill by yourself. Your approach will already be advertised before you get here. Attempts will be made to lure you inside one or another of the caves—and to get money from you. Alternatively, you can book an organized tour, arranged by one of the travel agencies in Granada. Even at the end of one of these group outings—with all expenses theoretically paid in advance—there is likely to be an attempt by the cave dwellers to extract more money from you. As soon as the *zambra* ends, hurry out of the cave as quickly as possible. Many readers have been critical of these tours.

During the *zambra,* refuse to accept a pair of castanets, even if offered under the friendly guise of having you join in the fun. If you accept them, the chances are that you'll later be asked to pay for them. Buying anything in these caves is not recommended. Leave your jewelry at your hotel, and don't take more money than you're prepared to lose.

A visit to the caves is almost always included as part of the morning and (more frequently) afternoon city tours offered every day by such companies as **Grana Vision** (☎ **958/13-58-04**). Night tours of the caves (when the caves are at their most eerie, most evocative, and, unfortunately, most larcenous) are usually offered only to those who can assemble 10 or more persons into a group. This might have changed by the time of your visit, so phone a reputable tour operator, such as Grana Vision, to learn if any newly developed options are available.

Flamenco The best flamenco show in Granada is staged at **Jardines Neptuno,** Calle Arabial, s/n (☎ **958/25-11-12**), nightly at 10:15. The acts are a bit racy, even though they have been toned down considerably for today's audiences. In addition to flamenco, performers attired in regional garb do folk dances and give guitar concerts. The show takes place in a garden setting. There's a high cover charge of 3,300 pesetas ($26.40), but it includes a drink that you can nurse all evening. It's best to take a taxi here.

10 The Costa del Sol

The mild winter climate and almost-guaranteed sunshine in summer have made this razzle-dazzle stretch of Mediterranean shoreline a year-round attraction. It begins at the western frontier harbor city of Algeciras and stretches east to the port city of Almería. Sandwiched between these two points is a steep, rugged coastline, with poor-to-fair beaches, set against the Sierra Nevada. You'll find sandy coves, whitewashed houses, olive trees, lots of new apartment houses, fishing boats, golf courses, souvenir stands, fast-food outlets, and a widely varied flora—both human and vegetable.

This coastal strip, quite frankly, no longer enjoys the chic reputation it had back in Franco's days. It is now overbuilt and spoiled, although you can still find pockets of posh, including Puerto Banús, with a yacht-clogged harbor for the rich. One advantage of the area is that, thanks to European Community money, it is easier to get around than ever before. The infamous N-340 highway from Málaga to Estepona has become a fast and safe six-lane highway. In days of yore, it was the most dangerous highway—in terms of recorded accidents—in Spain.

The coast is often better for **golf** than it is for beaches. The best resorts offering golf are Parador de Golf (☎ **95/238-12-55**), between Málaga and Torremolinos; Hotel Atalaya Park in Estepona (☎ **95/288-48-01**); Golf Hotel Guadalmina (☎ **95/288-22-11**), and in Marbella, Los Monteros (☎ **95/277-17-00**), which is the leading course. For more golfing possibilities, pick up a copy of the monthy magazine *Costa Golf* at any newsstand. Many golfers prefer to play a different course at every hotel. Usually, if you notify your hotel reception desk a day in advance, someone will phone the course of your choice to arrange a playing time.

Water-skiing and windsurfing are available in every resort, and all types of boats can be rented from various kiosks at all the main beaches. You don't have to search hard to connect yourself with any of these outfitters—chances are they'll find you!

From June through October the coast is mobbed, so make sure that you've nailed down a reservation. And keep in mind that October 12 is a national holiday—visitors should make doubly sure of their reservations at this time. At other times, innkeepers are likely to roll out the red carpet.

Many restaurants close around October 15 for a much-needed vacation. Remember, too, that many supermarkets and other facilities are closed on Sunday.

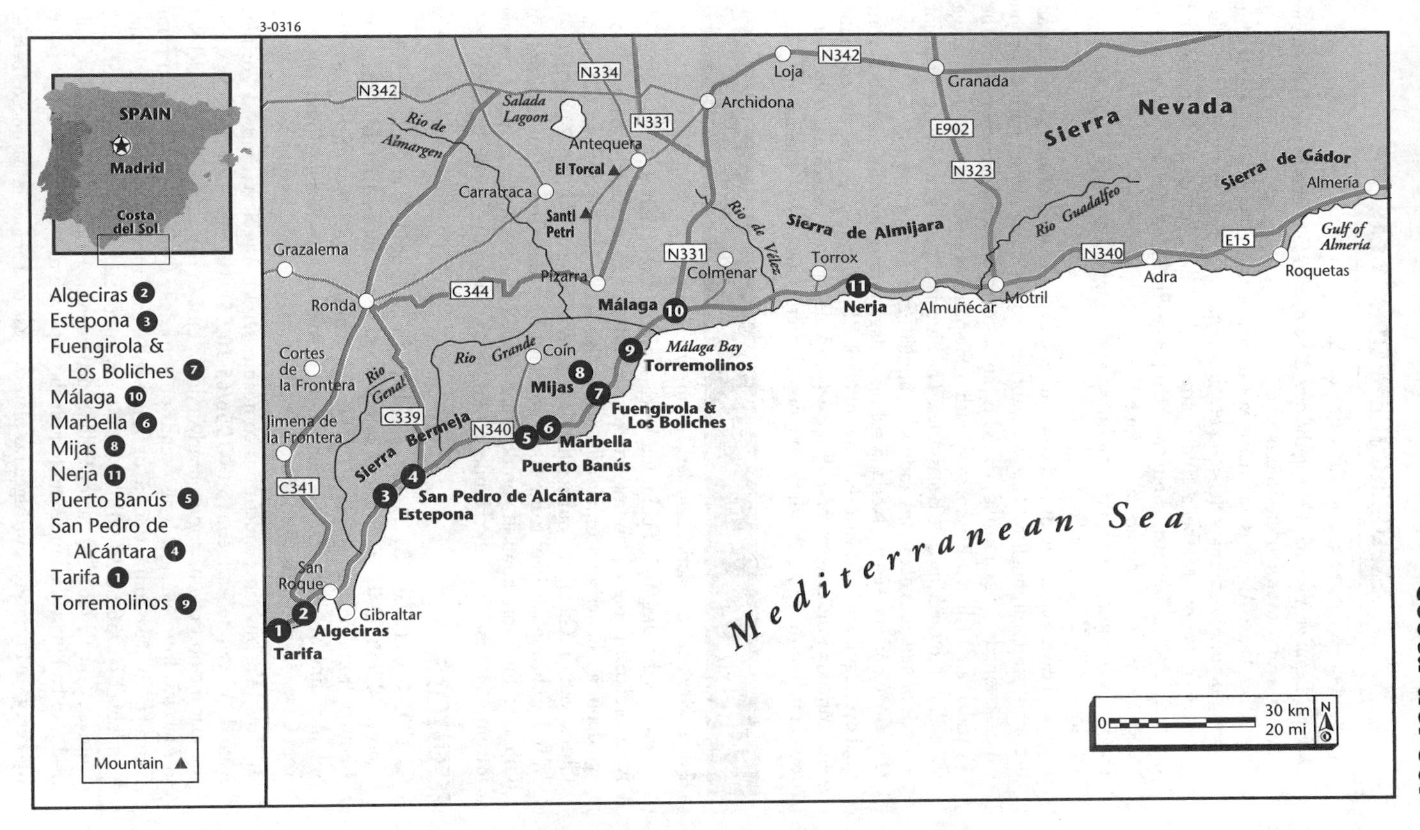
3-0316
SPAIN
Madrid
Costa del Sol
Algeciras 2
Estepona 3
Fuengirola & Los Boliches 7
Málaga 10
Marbella 6
Mijas 8
Nerja 11
Puerto Banús 5
San Pedro de Alcántara 4
Tarifa 1
Torremolinos 9
Mountain ▲
Mediterranean Sea
Sierra Nevada
Sierra de Gádor
Sierra de Almijara
Sierra Bermeja
Gulf of Almería
Málaga Bay
Salada Lagoon
Río de Vélez
Río Guadalfeo
Río Grande
Río Genal
Río de Almargen
El Torcal
Santi Petri
Almería
Roquetas
Adra
Motril
Almuñécar
Granada
Loja
Archidona
Antequera
Torrox
Colmenar
Pizarra
Carratraca
Coín
Ronda
Grazalema
Cortes de la Frontera
Jimena de la Frontera
San Roque
Gibraltar
Algeciras
Tarifa
Estepona
San Pedro de Alcántara
Puerto Banús
Marbella
Mijas
Fuengirola & Los Boliches
Torremolinos
Málaga
Nerja
E15
N340
N323
E902
N342
N331
N334
C344
C339
C341
0
30 km
20 mi
N

EXPLORING THE REGION BY CAR

Allow about six days to explore the Costa del Sol.

Day 1 Begin at Algeciras. During the day, cross over to Gibraltar to see all the main attractions. Stay overnight in Algeciras.

Day 2–3 Leave Algeciras and drive east to Marbella. This will be your only chic stopover on the coast. Enjoy the good beaches, restaurants, bars, and nightclubs. Also be sure to check out Marbella's old quarter, around the Plaza de los Naranjos and visit the "Golden Mile" strip, home to the superwealthy. Marbella hosts a famous flamenco festival in the second half of June.

Day 4 Continue east to Torremolinos for the night. For most of the year, the activity here is like a street festival.

Day 5 Leave Torremolinos and continue east to the historic city of Málaga for an overnight stop. Although Málaga is an ancient city (it was a former harbor for the Moorish kingdom of Granada), its sights can be covered in a day. These include the Alcazaba, an 11th-century fortress with a Hispano-Muslim garden; the Málaga Cathedral; and the Museo de Bellas Artes. The historic city is also known for its major festivals on religious occasions and its big annual *feria* (fair) in August.

Day 6 Continue east to Nerja, a fishing village transformed into a resort, your final overnight stop, and visit the Cave of Nerja. If you're driving, you can continue your trip along the eastern coast all the way to Valencia and Barcelona. If you must leave, the best transportation links are found by returning west to Málaga.

1 Algeciras

422 miles (679km) S of Madrid, 82 miles (132km) W of Málaga

Algeciras is the jumping-off point for Africa—its only three hours to Tangier or Spanish Morocco. If you're planning an excursion, there's an inexpensive baggage storage depot at the ferry terminal. Algeciras is also a base for day trips to **Gibraltar.** Check with the Gibraltar Tourist Office at Cathedral Square (☎ **350/749-50**), open Monday through Friday from 10am to 6pm, Saturday from 10am to 2pm, in Gibraltar, for information. If you don't have time to visit "the Rock," you can view it from Algeciras—it's only six miles (10km) away, out in the Bay of Algeciras.

ESSENTIALS

GETTING THERE **By Train** The local RENFE office is at Calle Juan de la Cierva (☎ **956/63-02-02**). From Madrid, there are two trains daily (trip time: 7 to 9 hours); from Málaga, two daily (5½ hours, running along most of the Costa del Sol, including Marbella and Torremolinos); from Seville, three daily (6 hours); and from Granada, two daily (5½ hours).

By Bus Various independent bus companies service Algeciras. Empresa Portillo, Avenida Virgen de Carmen, 15 (☎ **956/65-10-55**), 1½ blocks to the right when you exit the port complex, runs nearly a dozen buses a day along the Costa del Sol to Algeciras from Málaga. It also sends one bus daily from Madrid and two from Granada. To make connections to or from Seville, use Empresa La Valenciana, Viajes Koudubia (☎ **956/60-34-00**). Six buses a day go to Jerez de la Frontera and Seville. Empresa Comes, Hotel Octavio, Calle San Bernardo, 1 (☎ **956/65-34-56**), sells tickets to La Línea (the border station for the approach to Gibraltar).

By Ferry Most visitors in Algeciras plan to cross to Tangier in Morocco. Ferries leave every hour on the hour daily from 8am to 10pm. A Class A ticket costs 3,700

Beaches: The Good, the Bad, and the Ugly

We'd like to report that the Costa del Sol is a paradise for swimmers. Surprisingly, it isn't, although it was the allure of beaches that originally put the sun in the Costa del Sol beginning in the 1950s. The worst beaches—mainly pebbles and shingles—are found at Nerja, Málaga, and Almuñécar.

Moving westward, you encounter the gritlike and grayish sands of Torremolinos. The best beaches here are at El Bajondillo and La Carihuela (the latter bordering an old fishing village). Another good stretch of beach is found along the meandering strip between Carvajal, Los Boliches, and Fuengirola. In addition, two good beaches line both sides of Marbella, El Fuerte and La Fontanilla. However, all these beaches tend to be overcrowded, especially in July and August when mama and papa take the kids to the beach from the hinterlands. Crowding is worst on Sundays from May through October, when beaches are overrun with not just sunbathers, but family picnickers as well.

All public beaches in Spain, including those just previewed, are free. Don't expect changing facilities—perhaps a cold shower on the major beaches, and that's it.

Although not sanctioned or technically allowed by the government, many women, especially those from France, go topless on the beaches. Nudity is commonly seen on some of the less frequented beaches, although it is against the law—and you are subject to arrest by the civil guard. Nevertheless, many bathers flout Spanish law and go nude anyway. It's not advised. If you want to bare it all, head for the Costa Natura, about two miles (3km) west of Estepona. This is the site of the only "official" nudist colony along the Costa del Sol.

pesetas ($29.60) per person, while a Class B ticket goes for 2,960 pesetas ($23.70). To transport a car costs from 9,300 pesetas ($74.40) per vehicle (cars aren't transported in stormy weather). Discounts are available: 20% for Eurailpass holders, 30% for InterRail pass holders, and 50% for children.

By Car The Carretera de Cádiz (E-15/N-340) makes the run from Málaga west to Algeciras. If you're driving south from Seville (or Madrid), take highway N-IV to Cádiz, then connect with the N-340/E-5 southwest to Algeciras.

VISITOR INFORMATION The tourist information office is at Juan de la Cierva (☎ **956/57-26-36**). Open Monday through Friday from 9am to 2pm and Saturday from 10am to 1pm.

WHERE TO STAY

Hotel Alarde. Alfonso XI, 4, 11201 Algeciras. ☎ **956/66-04-08.** Fax 956/65-49-01. 70 rms. A/C MINIBAR TV TEL. 9,850 ptas. ($78.80). AE, DC, MC, V. Parking 1,000 ptas. ($8).

If you want to get away from the tacky, noisy port area, consider this three-star hotel near the Parque María Cristina—a central location in a quiet commercial section. The double rooms have balconies and Andalusian-style furnishings. The hotel also has a snack bar, a restaurant, and laundry. The restaurant, open daily, serves a good-value international/regional fixed-price menu. During our most recent stay we were impressed with both the staff and the inviting atmosphere.

Hotel Al-Mar. Avenida de la Marina, 2, 11201 Algeciras. ☎ **956/65-46-61.** Fax 956/65-45-01. 186 rms, 6 suites. A/C TV TEL. 9,000 ptas. ($72) double; from 11,000 ptas. ($88) suite. Rates include breakfast. AE, DC, MC, V. Parking 700 ptas. ($5.60).

The three-star Al-Mar—one of the best choices in town, with better rooms than the Alarde—stands near the port, where the ferries embark for Ceuta and Tangier. This large hotel boasts a blue-and-white Sevillian and Moorish decor, as well as three restaurants, a handful of bars, and lots of verdant hideaways. The guest rooms are well maintained, furnished in a slightly Andalusian style. The fourth-floor drawing room provides a panoramic view of the Rock.

Hotel Octavio. San Bernardo, 1, 11207 Algeciras. ☎ **956/65-27-00.** Fax 956/65-28-02. 77 rms. A/C MINIBAR TV TEL. 12,000 ptas. ($96) double. AE, DC, MC, V. Parking 1,000 ptas. ($8).

Conveniently located in the center of town near the railway station, the Octavio is decorated with reproductions of English antiques, which contrast sharply with the building's angular modern exterior. In Algeciras, only the Reina Cristina is a more prestigious address. The guest rooms are nicely furnished and well maintained. International drinks are served at an American-style bar. Room service is available daily from 8am to 11pm.

Hotel Reina Cristina. Paseo de la Conferencia, 11207 Algeciras. ☎ **956/60-26-22.** Fax 956/60-33-23. 168 rms, 2 suites. AC TV TEL. 13,000–17,000 ptas. ($104–$136) double; from 21,000 ptas. ($168) suite. AE, DC, MC, V. Free parking.

Set within its own park on the southern outskirts of the city, a 10-minute walk south of both the rail and bus stations, this hotel reigns without challenge as the best established and most prestigious in town. Built during the heyday of the Victorian era and accented with turrets, ornate railings, and a facade appropriately painted with pastels, the Reina Cristina offers its clientele (many of whom are British) a view of the faraway Rock of Gibraltar. On the premises are a small English-language library, a semitropical garden held in place with sturdy retaining walls, and comfortable, high-ceilinged bedrooms.

Dining/Entertainment: The hotel's two restaurants include La Parilla, the more formal à la carte restaurant, and the Andalucía, which is buffet style. There's also a bar.

Services: Room service (available daily from 7am to midnight), laundry/valet, concierge, babysitting.

Facilities: Sauna, indoor and outdoor swimming pools, and tennis courts.

WHERE TO DINE

Because Algeciras is not distinguished for its restaurants, many visitors prefer to dine at the hotels instead of taking a chance at some of the dreary little spots along the waterfront.

$ Casa Alfonso. Calle Juan de la Cierva, 4. ☎ **956/60-31-21.** Reservations not required. Main courses 550–1,000 ptas. ($4.40–$8); *menú del día* 900 ptas. ($7.20). No credit cards. Daily 9am–11pm. Closed Dec 25 and Jan 1. SPANISH.

Simple and unpretentious, this workaday restaurant was established in 1936 within a building on the southern edge of the city, near the harborfront and the tourist office. Convenient to travelers disembarking from the ferryboats from Morocco, it serves simple *menús del día* and such uncomplicated fare as bean soup, fried fish, and beefsteak with potatoes. Paella is also available, according to the arrival of the ingredients on the day of your arrival. Unnumbered buses from Cádiz and Seville stop nearby.

2 Tarifa

14 miles (22km) W of Algeciras, 443 miles (713km) S of Madrid, 61 miles (98km) SE of Cádiz

Instead of heading east from Algeciras along the Costa del Sol, we'd suggest a visit west to Tarifa, an old Moorish town that is the southernmost point in Europe. After leaving Algeciras, the roads climb steeply, and the drive to Tarifa is along one of Europe's most splendid coastal routes. In the distance you'll see Gibraltar, the straits, and the "green hills" of Africa—in fact, you can sometimes get a glimpse of houses in Ceuta and Tangier on the Moroccan coastline.

Tarifa, named for Tarik, a Moorish military hero, has retained more of its Arab character than any other town in Andalusia. Narrow cobblestoned streets lead to charming patios filled with flowers. The main square is the Plaza San Mateo.

Two factors have inhibited the development of Tarifa's beautiful three-mile (5km) white beach, the Playa de Lances: It's still a Spanish military zone, and the wind never stops blowing (43% of the time). For windsurfers, though, the strong western breezes are unbeatable. Tarifa is filled with shops renting windsurfing equipment, as well as giving advice about the best locales.

Many visitors also come to see Tarifa's historical past and wander its crumbling ramparts. The town is dominated by the **Castle of Tarifa,** site of a famous struggle in 1292 between Moors and Christians. The castle was held by Guzmán el Bueno ("the Good"). When Christians captured his nine-year-old son and demanded surrender of the garrison, Guzmán tossed the Spanish a dagger for the boy's execution, preferring "honor without a son, to a son with dishonor." Sadly, the castle is not open to the public.

GETTING THERE **By Bus** In Algeciras, Empresa Comes, Calle San Bernardo, 1 (☎ **956/65-34-56**), under the Hotel Octavio, runs several buses daily to Tarifa (trip time: 45 minutes).

By Car Take the Cádiz highway, N-340/E-5, west from Algeciras.

WHERE TO STAY & DINE

Hotel Balcón de España. La Peña, 2, Carretera Cádiz–Málaga, km 77, 11380 Tarifa. ☎ **956/68-43-26.** Fax 956/68-43-26. 38 rms. TEL. 8,000–11,500 ptas. ($64–$92) double. AE, MC, V. Closed Oct 20–Apr 1. Free parking.

The surrounding park adds a welcome calm to your stay at the Balcón de España, located five miles (8km) north of Tarifa. Although relatively modest, it is the best place to stay in the area. The hotel offers clean and well-kept accommodations, an outdoor pool, tennis courts, and a riding stable nearby. Some guests prefer to stay in outlying bungalows. In the restaurant, meals are served daily from 1 to 4pm and 8 to 11pm.

Mesón de Sancho. Carretera Cádiz-Málaga, km 94, 11380 Tarifa. ☎ **956/68-49-00.** Fax 956/68-47-21. 45 rms. MINIBAR TV TEL. 5,990–7,550 ptas. ($47.90–$60.40) double. AE, DC, MC, V. Free parking.

Ten miles (16km) southwest of Algeciras and 6½ miles (10.5km) northeast of Tarifa on the Cádiz road stands this informal hacienda-style inn, where you can swim in a pool surrounded by olive trees and terraces. The rooms are furnished in modest but contemporary style, and there is steam heating in the cooler months. In the provincial dining room, with its window walls overlooking the garden, a complete lunch or dinner goes for 1,900 pesetas ($15.20).

3 Estepona

53 miles (85km) W of Málaga, 397 miles (639km) S of Madrid, 28½ miles (46km) E of Algeciras

A town of Roman origin, Estepona is a budding beach resort, less developed than Marbella or Torremolinos but perhaps preferable for that reason. Estepona contains an interesting 15th-century parish church, with the ruins of an old aqueduct nearby (at Salduba). Its recreational port is an attraction, as are its **beaches:** Costa Natura, km 257 on the N-340, the first legal nude beach of its kind along the Costa del Sol; La Rada, two miles (3km) long; and El Cristo, only 600 yards long. After the sun goes down, stroll along the Paseo Marítimo, a broad avenue with gardens on one side, the beach on the other.

In summer the cheapest places to eat in Estepona are the *merenderos,* little dining areas set up by local fishers and their families right on the beach. Naturally, they feature seafood, including sole and sardine kebabs grilled over an open fire. You can usually order a fresh salad and fried potatoes; desserts are simple.

After your siesta, head for the tapas bars. You'll find most of them—called *freidurías* (fried-fish bars)—at the corner of the Calle de los Reyes and La Terraza. Tables spill onto the sidewalks in summer, and *gambas a la plancha* (shrimp) are the favorite (but not the cheapest) tapas to order.

GETTING THERE **By Train** The nearest rail links are in Algeciras.

By Bus Estepona is on the bus route from Algeciras to Málaga.

By Car Drive east from Algeciras along the E-5/N-340.

VISITOR INFORMATION The tourist information office is at Paseo Marítimo Pedro Manrique (☎ **95/280-09-13**). Hours are Monday through Friday from 9am to 5pm.

WHERE TO STAY

✪ **Atalaya Park Golf Hotel & Resort.** Carretera de Cádiz, km 168.5, 29688 Estepona. ☎ **95/288-48-01.** Fax 95/288-57-35. 416 rms, 32 suites. A/C MINIBAR TEL. 21,800–28,500 ptas. ($174.40–$228) double; from 39,280 ptas. ($314.25) suite. Rates include breakfast. AE, DC, MC, V. Free parking.

Located midway between Estepona and Marbella, this modern resort complex attracts sports and nature lovers to its tranquil beachside location amid 20 acres of subtropical gardens. The hotel is the largest, most opulent, and most expensive in and around Estepona. Its bedrooms, furnished in a pristine but rather elegant modern style, are well maintained and inviting. Guests have complementary use of the hotel's extensive sports facilities. Many guests from northern Europe check in here and virtually never leave the grounds until it's time to fly back home.

Dining/Entertainment: The hotel's three restaurants—each inspired by characters or episodes from Cervantes and each serving Spanish and international food—are the Don Quijote, the Sancho, and La Torre. Several bars are scattered throughout the property, and there is also a dance club.

Services: Babysitting, concierge, laundry/valet, breakfast room service.

Facilities: Sauna, health club, solarium, indoor and outdoor swimming pools, car-rental facilities, shopping boutiques, tennis, water sports center, two 18-hole golf courses nearby.

Buenavista. Avenida de España, 180, 29680 Estepona. ☎ **95/280-01-37.** 38 rms. A/C TV. 3,500–4,500 ptas. ($28–$36) double. AE, MC, V.

This comfortable little five-story residencia located beside the coastal road opened in the 1970s. It's recommended for an overnight stop or a modest holiday. The guest rooms are clean but likely to be noisy in summer because of heavy traffic nearby. Buses from Marbella stop nearby.

WHERE TO DINE

Costa del Sol. Calle San Roque, 23. ☎ **95/280-11-01.** Main courses 700–1,200 ptas. ($5.60–$9.60); fixed-price menus 800–1,200 ptas. ($6.40–$9.60). AE, MC, V. Tues–Sat noon–4pm and 8–11:30pm. FRENCH.

Its French owners have infused this restaurant with the heart and soul of their native Toulouse, creating an outpost of Gallic charm in the heart of Estepona. Set at the edge of the sea, in a modern building whose interior is outfitted in tones of scarlet and gold, it's the multilingual domain of Jean Wilhelm (who cooks) and his wife, Gerdy (who directs the staff in the dining room). Menu specialties derive from the bistro tradition of France and include onion soup, coq au vin (chicken in wine), tournedos béarnaise, mussels in Bordelaise sauce, shrimp crêpes, and cheese soufflés.

4 Puerto Banús

5 miles (8km) E of Marbella, 486 miles (782km) S of Madrid

A favorite resort for international celebrities, this marine village was created almost overnight in the traditional Mediterranean style. It's a dreamy place, a Disney World creation of what a Costa del Sol fishing village should look like, but rarely does. Yachts can be moored at your doorstep. Along the harborfront you'll find an array of expensive bars and restaurants. Wandering through the quiet back streets, you'll pass archways and patios with grilles.

GETTING THERE **By Bus** Fifteen buses a day connect Marbella to Puerto Banús.

By Car Drive east from Marbella along the E-15.

WHERE TO STAY

Hotel Marbella-Dinamar. Urbanización Nueva Andalucía, Carretera de Cádiz, km 175, 29660 Puerto Banús. ☎ **95/281-05-00.** Fax 95/281-23-46. 112 rms, 5 suites. A/C TV TEL. 23,400 ptas. ($187.20) double; 30,900 ptas. ($247.20) suite. AE, DC, MC, V. Free parking.

Distinctly Moorish in flavor and feeling, this striking and exotic resort celebrates the Arab domination of what is today Spanish Andalusia. Set just 400 yards from both the beach and the borders of Puerto Banús's congested center, it was built around 1980 with stark white walls, soaring arches, and a central courtyard containing a large, abstractly shaped swimming pool. Bedrooms each feature two large beds and a simple and airy collection of furniture and look out on either the palm trees beside the pool or the sea. The resort offers tennis courts that are floodlit at night, plus easy access to the casino at the neighboring Hotel Plaza Andalucía as well as to one of the best all-around golf courses along the Costa del Sol. There's also an indoor swimming pool suitable for year-round use. Perhaps best of all, the diversions and facilities of Puerto Banús lie within a three-minute walk.

WHERE TO DINE

$ **Dalli's Pasta Factory.** Muelle de Rivera. ☎ **95/281-24-90.** Reservations not accepted. Pastas 900–1,300 ptas. ($7.20–$10.40); meat platters 1,295–1,375 ptas. ($10.35–$11). AE, MC, V. Daily 7pm–1am. PASTA.

The light-hearted, California-inspired philosophy at Dalli's has added a new way to save pesetas in high-priced Puerto Banús. Its specialty is pasta, pasta, and more pasta, which, served with a portion of garlic bread and a carafe of house wine, is more than adequate for the gastronomic needs of many budget travelers. In a setting that's a cross between high-tech and art deco (even the owners aren't absolutely certain how to define it), you can order nutmeg-flavored ravioli with spinach filling, *penne all'arrabbiata,* lasagne, and several kinds of spaghetti. More filling are the chicken cacciatore and the scaloppine of chicken and veal. These are served with—guess what?—pasta as a side dish.

The owners, incidentally, are a trio of Roman-born brothers who were reared in England and educated in California.

Don Leone. Muelle Ribera, 45. ☎ **95/281-17-16.** Reservations recommended. Main courses 2,000–3,800 ptas. ($16–$30.40). AE, MC, V. Daily 1–4pm and 8pm–1am. Closed Nov 21–Dec 21; lunch from late June to mid-Sept. INTERNATIONAL.

Many residents in villas around Marbella drive to this luxuriously decorated dockside restaurant for dinner. It tends to get crowded at times. Begin with the house minestrone, then follow with a pasta in either Bolognese or clam sauce; lasagne is also a regular. Meat specialties include veal parmigiana and roast baby lamb, and the fish dishes are also worth a try, especially the *fritta mista del pescados,* a mixed fish fry. The food is competently prepared with fresh ingredients, although at times it fails to capture an authentic Spanish flavor. The wine list is one of the best along the coast.

Red Pepper. Muelle Ribera. ☎ **95/281-21-48.** Reservations recommended. Main courses 1,600–4,000 ptas. ($12.80–$32); fixed-price menu 3,200 ptas. ($25.60). AE, DC, MC, V. Daily noon to 1 or 3am. GREEK/INTERNATIONAL.

Run by an exuberant band of Cypriot expatriates, Red Pepper offers an array of Greek and international dishes in a sunny and sparsely furnished dining room. Selections include Hellenic chicken soup, moussaka, a variety of well-seasoned grilled meats, lots of fish, calf's liver, lamb on a skewer in the Greek fashion, and king prawns and lobster, which are the most expensive main courses since they are priced by the gram. Full meals are usually accompanied by a selection of Greek and Spanish wines. You'll find the place in the center of Paseo Marítimo.

La Taberna del Alabardero. Muelle Benabola, A2. ☎ **95/281-27-94.** Reservations required. Main courses 2,000–3,200 ptas. ($16–$25.60). AE, DC, MC, V. Daily 1–4pm and 8pm–midnight. Closed Jan 15–Feb 15. INTERNATIONAL.

This restaurant—the best in the port—lies directly on the harborfront, within full view of the hundreds of strolling pedestrians, whose numbers seem to ebb and flow like the tides. You can dine inside, but you might have more fun at one of the dozens of outdoor tables, where the only clues to the place's upper-crust status are the immaculate napery, well-disciplined waiters, and discreet twinkle of some very expensive jewelry among the blue jeans or formal attire of the fashionable clientele. An armada of private yachts bobs at anchor a few feet away. The cuisine, although good, seems secondary to the milling social scene of the see-and-be-seen set who hang out here. Meals might include crêpes stuffed with chunks of lobster and crayfish, hake and small clams served in a Basque-inspired green sauce, filet of duck's breast with green peppercorns or orange sauce, and a wide assortment of desserts.

5 San Pedro de Alcántara

43 miles (69km) W of Málaga, 42½ miles (68km) E of Algeciras

Situated between Marbella and Estepona, this interesting village contains **Roman remains** that have been officially classified as a national monument. In recent years it has been extensively developed as a resort suburb of Marbella and now offers some good hotel selections, the best of which is previewed below.

GETTING THERE **By Bus** Service is every 30 minutes from Marbella.

By Car Take the E-15 west from Marbella.

WHERE TO STAY

Golf Hotel Guadalmina. Hacienda Guadalmina, Carretera de Cádiz, 29670 San Pedro de Alcántara. ☎ **95/288-22-11.** Fax 95/288-54-48. 80 rms. A/C MINIBAR TV TEL. 23,500 ptas. ($188) double. Free parking.

At this moderately priced, large, country club–type resort, the first tee and the 18th green are both right next to the hotel. The golf course is open to both residents and nonresidents. This is an informal place, like a private world on the shores of the Mediterranean. The resort is 50 yards from the beach, 8 miles (13km) east of Marbella, and 1¼ miles (2km) from the center of San Pedro de Alcántara. You reach it by a long driveway from the coastal road. Two seawater swimming pools attract those seeking the lazy life, while the tennis courts appeal to the more energetic. The guest rooms—most opening onto the pool/recreation area and the sea—are attractive in their traditional Spanish style.

The hotel offers two excellent dining choices—one a lunch-only reed-covered poolside terrace overlooking the golf course and the sea, the other an interior room in the main building, with a sedate clubhouse aura. Informality and good food reign.

6 Marbella

37 miles (59km) W of Málaga, 28 miles (45km) W of Torremolinos, 50 miles (80km) E of Gibraltar, 47 miles (76km) E of Algeciras, 373 miles (600km) S of Madrid

Though it's packed with tourists, only slightly less popular than Torremolinos, Marbella is still the most exclusive resort along the Costa del Sol—with such bastions of posh as the Marbella Club. Despite the hordes, Marbella remains a pleasant Andalusian town at the foot of the Sierra Blanca. Traces of the past are found in its palatial town hall, its medieval ruins, and its ancient Moorish walls. Marbella's most charming area is the **old quarter,** with narrow cobblestoned streets and Arab houses, centered around the Plaza de los Naranjos.

The biggest attractions in Marbella, however, are **El Fuerte** and **La Fontanilla,** the two main beaches. There are other, more secluded beaches, but you need your own transportation to get to them.

A long-ago visitor, Queen Isabella, was said to have exclaimed *"¡Que mar tan bello!"* ("What a beautiful sea!"), and the name remained for posterity.

GETTING THERE **By Bus** Twenty buses run between Málaga and Marbella daily, plus three buses coming in from Madrid and another three buses from Barcelona.

By Car Marbella is the first major resort as you head east on the N-340/E-15 from Algeciras.

VISITOR INFORMATION The tourist information office is at Glorieta de la Fontanilla, s/n (☎ **95/277-14-42**). Open April through October, Monday through Friday from 9:30am to 9pm, Saturday from 10am to 2pm. Off-season hours are Monday through Friday from 9:30am to 8pm, Saturday from 10am to 2pm. Another tourist office is on Plaza Naranjos (☎ **95/282-35-50**); it keeps the same hours.

WHERE TO STAY

Since the setting is so ideal—with pure Mediterranean sun, sea, and sky, plus the scent of Andalusian orange blossoms in the air—some of the best hotels along the Costa del Sol are found in Marbella.

Very Expensive

✪ Marbella Club. Bulevar Príncipe Alfonso von Hohenlohe, s/n, 29600 Marbella. ☎ **95/282-22-11.** Fax 95/282-98-84. 85 rms, 34 suites, 10 bungalows. A/C MINIBAR TV TEL. 25,000–55,000 ptas. ($200–$440) double; 41,000–200,000 ptas. ($328–$1,600) suite; 120,000–250,000 ptas. ($960–$2,000) bungalows. AE, DC, MC, V. Free parking.

Until a few equally chic hotels were built along the Costa del Sol, the snobbish Marbella Club reigned almost without equal as the exclusive hangout of the world's commercial and genealogical aristocracy. Established in 1954 on land originally owned by the father of Prince Alfonso von Hohenlohe, the resort sprawls over a landscaped property that slopes from its roadside reception area down to the beach. Composed of small, ecologically conscious clusters of garden pavilions, bungalows, and small-scale annexes (none of which is higher than two stories), the Marbella basks amid some of the most well-conceived gardens along the coast. Rooms have private balconies or terraces. Today, its clientele is discreet, international, elegant, and appreciative of the resort's small scale and superb service.

Dining/Entertainment: The Marbella Club Restaurant moves from indoor shelter to an outdoor terrace according to the season (see "Where to Dine," below.) A bar is located within the garden nearby.

Services: 24-hour room service, babysitting, laundry/valet, massage, concierge well versed in the arrangement of almost anything.

Facilities: There are two swimming pools and a beach with a lunch restaurant. Golf can be arranged nearby. Tennis courts are available within a two-minute walk at thc Marbella Club's twin resort, Puente Romano.

Meliá Don Pepe. Finca Las Merinas, 29600 Marbella. ☎ **800/336-3542** in the U.S., or 95/277-03-00. Fax 95/277-99-54. 204 rms, 18 suites. A/C MINIBAR TV TEL. 23,800–56,200 ptas. ($190.40–$449.60) double; from 55,100 ptas. ($440.80) suite. AE, DC, MC, V. Free parking.

Meliá Don Pepe occupies six acres of prize-winning tropical gardens and lawns between the coastal road and the sea on a broad manmade beach set back from the road. Its well-furnished bedrooms, with private baths and wall-to-wall carpeting, face either the sea or the Sierra Blanca range. The latter rooms, however, can be noisy. The facilities are so vast that you could spend a week here and not use them all.

Dining/Entertainment: The hotel has lounges, bars, and restaurants. La Farola grill provides international à la carte cuisine.

Services: 24-hour room service, laundry/valet, babysitting.

Facilities: Three swimming pools, tennis courts, health club, Swedish sauna, Turkish baths, boutiques, yacht harbor along beach, golf course.

✪ Puente Romano. Carretera de Cádiz, km 167, 29600 Marbella. ☎ **800/448-8355** in the U.S., or 95/282-09-00. Fax 95/277-57-66. 142 rms, 67 suites. A/C MINIBAR TV TEL. 21,500–42,000 ptas. ($172–$336) double; from 27,500–56,500 ptas. ($220–$452) suite. AE, DC, MC, V. Free parking. Drive 2½ miles (4km) west of Marbella on the E-15.

This hotel was originally built as a cluster of vacation apartments, a fact that influenced the attention to detail and the landscaping that surrounds it. In the early 1970s, a group of entrepreneurs transformed it into one of the most unusual hotels in the south of Spain, sitting close to the frenetic coastal highway midway between Marbella and Puerto Banús. Although some critics have dismissed it as "more flash than class," it still enjoys a loyal following.

Once inside the complex, guests wander through a maze of arbor-covered walkways. En route they pass cascading water, masses of vines, and a subtropical garden. Each of the Andalusian-Mediterranean-style accommodations is a showcase of fabrics, accessories, and furniture, boasting a private bath, an electronic safe, and a semisheltered balcony with flowers.

Dining/Entertainment: Nestled amid the lushness are well-upholstered indoor/outdoor bars and restaurants. Three of these overlook a terra-cotta patio bordered at one end by the stones of a reconstructed Roman bridge, the only one of its kind in southern Spain. There is also a nightclub.

Services: 24-hour room service, laundry/valet, babysitting.

Facilities: The edges of the free-form swimming pool are bordered by trees and vines and a drain-away waterfall, which makes it look something like a Tahiti lagoon. There is also a sandy beach with water sports, as well as tennis courts, a cluster of boutiques, a gym, a sauna, and a solarium.

EXPENSIVE

Andalucía Plaza. Urbanización Nueva Andalucía, 29660 Apartado 21, Nueva Andalucía Marbella. ☎ **95/281-20-00.** Fax 95/281-47-92. 308 rms, 67 suites. A/C MINIBAR TV TEL. 17,500–27,500 ptas. ($140–$220) double; from 25,000 ptas. ($200) suite. Rates include American breakfast. AE, DC, MC, V. Free parking.

Originally built in 1972, the six-story Andalucía Plaza resort complex is now showing its age, but it at least offers more of a Spanish atmosphere than some of the pricey choices just considered. On the mountain side of the coastal road between Marbella and Torremolinos, twin buildings are linked by a reception lounge and formal gardens. On the sea side is the hotel's beach club. The public rooms are spacious and decorated in a bold, brassy style. Equally luxurious are the guest rooms, all with private baths and furnished with reproductions in the classic Castilian manner. The hotel is on more than a 300-foot strip of sand, four miles (6km) west of the center of Marbella and a 10-minute walk from Puerto Bánus.

Dining/Entertainment: The Cordoba restaurant serves upscale international meals. The Bar Toledo, primarily a watering hole, offers light snacks and suppers. The in-house casino is discussed under "Marbella After Dark," below.

Services: 24-hour room service, concierge, babysitting, laundry.

Facilities: The hotel's beach club includes a 300-foot strip of sand, with adjacent sunbathing terraces, tennis courts, two saunas, an open-air swimming pool, a golf course, and an enclosed all-weather pool. About half a mile away, there's a 1,000-berth marina, where the hotel will arrange the rental of a vessel for deep-sea fishing.

Don Carlos. Jardines de las Goldondrinas, Carretera de Cádiz, km 192, 29600 Marbella. ☎ **800/223-5652** in the U.S. and Canada, or 95/283-11-40. Fax 95/283-34-29. 223 rms, 15 suites. A/C MINIBAR TV TEL. 16,500–32,000 ptas. ($132–$256) double; 25,000–45,000 ptas. ($200–$360) suite. AE, DC, MC, V. Free parking.

One of the most dramatically alluring hotels along the coastline, the Don Carlos rises on a set of angled stilts above a pine forest. Between the hotel and its manicured beach, the best in Marbella, are 130 acres of award-winning gardens replete with cascades of water, a full-time staff of 22 gardeners, and thousands of subtropical plants. There's far more to this hotel than the modern tower that rises above the eastern edge of Marbella. Its low-lying terraces and elegant eating and drinking facilities attract high-powered conferences from throughout Europe as well as individual nonresident diners from along the Mediterranean coast. Each of the accommodations has its own lacquered furniture, private bath done in honey-colored marble, and satellite TV. The hotel also offers the finest tennis in the area.

Dining/Entertainment: You can dine amid splashes of bougainvillea beside an oversized swimming pool bordered with begonias and geraniums, or in La Pergola, where ficus and potted palms decorate the hundreds of lattices. A hideaway, Los Naranjos, has a sun-flooded atrium with mosses and orange trees. The grand piano on the marble dais provides diverting music. Meals, including grills and elaborate buffets, are served here and in the semi-outdoor beachfront cabaña.

Among the bars scattered around the various terraces and marble-lined hideaways of the public rooms, the most popular offers an English-inspired decor, a panoramic view of the sea, plenty of sofas, a dance floor, and a musical trio.

Services: 24-hour room service, laundry, babysitting.

Facilities: Three swimming pools, use of 5 golf courses nearby, saunas, gym, 11 tennis courts. Water sports cost extra.

✪ **Los Monteros.** Carretera de Cádiz, km 187, 29600 Marbella. ☎ **95/277-17-00.** Fax 95/282-58-46. 170 rms, 10 suites. A/C MINIBAR TV TEL. 19,600–32,000 ptas. ($156.80–$256) double; from 31,400 ptas. ($251.20) suite. Rates include breakfast. AE, DC, MC, V. Free parking.

Los Monteros, located 400 yards from a beach and 4 miles (6km) east of Marbella, is one of the most tasteful resort complexes along the Costa del Sol. Situated between the coastal road and its own private beach, it attracts those seeking intimacy and luxury. No cavernous lounges exist here; instead, many small public rooms, Andalusian/Japanese in concept, are the style. The hotel offers various salons with open fireplaces, a library, and terraces. The bedrooms are brightly decorated, with light-colored lacquered furniture, private baths, and terraces.

Dining/Entertainment: The hotel has a bar and four restaurants on different levels that open onto flower-filled patios, gardens, and fountains. Grill El Corzo is one of the finest grill rooms along the coast. Soft, romantic music is played nightly, and the cuisine is a pleasing combination of French and Spanish.

Services: 24-hour room service, babysitting, laundry/valet.

Facilities: Guests can use the nearby 18-hole golf course, Río Real, for free. Also included are several swimming pools, a beach club with a heated indoor swimming pool, 10 tennis courts, 5 squash courts, a riding club and school—plus a fully equipped gymnasium with sauna, massage, and Jacuzzi.

MODERATE

Hotel El Fuerte. El Fuerte, s/n, 29600 Marbella. ☎ **95/286-15-00.** Fax 95/282-44-11. 261 rms, 2 suites. A/C MINIBAR TV TEL. 12,300–14,400 ptas. ($98.40–$115.20) double; 30,200–36,500 ptas. ($241.60–$292) suite. AE, DC, MC, V. Parking 650 ptas. ($5.20).

This is the largest and most recommendable hotel in the center of Marbella. Set directly on the waterfront, El Fuerte has a balconied and angular facade that's divided into two separate six-story towers. Originally built in 1957, it added a wing in 1987 and was last renovated in 1994. Catering to a sedate clientele of conservative northern Europeans, it offers a palm-fringed swimming pool set across the street from a sheltered lagoon and a wide-open beach. The hotel also has a handful of terraces, some shaded by flowering arbors, which are perfect hideaways for taking a quiet drink. Inside, the public rooms contain a wide variety of tilework, certain sections of which were culled from much older buildings. Bedrooms are contemporary, with piped-in music and terraces.

The hotel offers a coffee shop plus a restaurant. The facilities for leisure activities include the above-mentioned swimming pool, a floodlit tennis court, a health club, and a squash court.

Hotel Guadalpín. Carretera Cádiz-Málaga, km 179, 29600 Marbella. ☎ **95/277-11-00.** Fax 95/277-33-34. 110 rms. TEL. 7,400–11,400 ptas. ($59.20–$91.20) double. AE, DC, MC, V. Free parking.

This aging three-star 1960s hotel is right on the coast, only 300 yards from the beach and a mile from the center of Marbella. Guests can relax around the two swimming pools or walk along the fir-lined private pathway to the Mediterranean. The dining room has large windows that overlook the patio, whereas the ranch-style lounge boasts round marble tables and leather armchairs. There's also a bar. Most accommodations have two terraces, a living room, and a bedroom furnished in "new ranch" style and centrally heated during the cooler months.

INEXPENSIVE

$ Hostal El Castillo. Plaza San Bernabé, 2, 29600 Marbella. ☎ **95/277-17-39.** 26 rms. 3,800–4,000 ptas. ($30.40–$32) double. No credit cards.

Located at the foot of the castle in the narrow streets of the old town, this small hotel opens onto a minuscule triangular area used by the adjoining convent and school as a playground. There's a small, covered courtyard, and the second-floor simple bedrooms have only inner windows. The Spartan guest rooms are scrubbed clean and contain white-tile baths. No morning meal is served, and not one word of English is spoken.

$ Hostal Munich. Calle Virgen del Pilar, 5, 29600 Marbella. ☎ **952/77-24-61.** 18 rms. TEL. 4,255 ptas. ($34.05) double. No credit cards.

Set back from the street and shielded by banana and palm trees, this unassuming three-story hostal is just a short walk from the water and the bus station. Some guest rooms have balconies, and all are simply furnished but well kept. The homey lounge is warm and inviting.

$ Residencia Finlandia. Finlandia, 12, 29600 Marbella. ☎ and fax **95/277-07-00.** 11 rms. TEL. 4,815–6,420 ptas. ($38.50–$51.35) double. AE, DC, MC, V.

Situated in the Huerta Grande, a peaceful residential section, the slightly tattered 1970s Finlandia is only a five-minute walk from the center of the old quarter and 200 yards from the beach. It's clean and well run with spacious but rather plain guest rooms and contemporary furnishings. Your bed will be turned down at night.

Residencia Lima. Antonio Belón, 2, 29600 Marbella. ☎ **95/277-05-00.** Fax 95/286-30-91. 64 rms. TEL. 8,950 ptas. ($71.60) double. AE, DC, MC, V.

Tucked away in a residential section of Marbella, right off the N-340/E-15 and near the sea, this hotel is more secluded than the others nearby. The modern eight-story structure features plain, but clean bedrooms with Spanish provincial furnishings and private balconies.

Residencia San Cristóbal. Ramón y Cajal, 3, 29600 Marbella. ☎ **95/277-12-50.** Fax 95/286-20-44. 97 rms. A/C TV TEL. 7,525–9,900 ptas. ($60.20–$79.20) double. AE, MC, V.

In the heart of Marbella, 200 yards from the beach, this 1960s five-story hotel has long, wide terraces and flower-filled window boxes. The somewhat tattered guest rooms have walnut headboards, individual overhead reading lamps, and room dividers separating the comfortable beds from the small living-room areas. An added plus is the private terrace attached to each room—a perfect spot to enjoy breakfast.

El Rodeo. Victor de la Serna, s/n, 29600 Marbella. ☎ **95/277-51-00.** Fax 95/282-33-20. 100 rms. TV TEL. 6,500–9,500 ptas. ($52–$76) double. AE, DC, MC, V.

Even though this modern hotel stands just off the main coastal road of Marbella, within walking distance of the bus station, the beach, and the old quarter—it is quiet and secluded. The facilities in the seven-story structure include a swimming pool, terrace, sunbathing area, solarium, and piano bar. Two elevators whisk you to the sunny, spacious second-floor lounges with country furnishings; there's also a bar with tropical bamboo chairs and tables. Continental breakfast is served in the cheerful breakfast room. The bedrooms are functional, with several shuttered closets, lounge chairs, and white desks. Although the hotel is open all year, the highest rates are charged from April 1 to October 31.

WHERE TO DINE

EXPENSIVE

✪ **La Hacienda.** Urbanización Hacienda Las Chapas, Carretera de Cádiz, km 193. ☎ **95/283-12-67.** Reservations recommended. Main courses 2,200–3,200 ptas. ($17.60–$25.60); fixed-price menu 6,900 ptas. ($55.20). AE, DC, MC, V. Summer, daily 8:30–11:30pm; winter, Wed–Sun 1–3:30pm and 8:30–11:30pm. Closed Nov 15–Dec 20. INTERNATIONAL.

La Hacienda, a tranquil choice eight miles (13km) east of Marbella, enjoys a reputation for serving some of the best food along the Costa del Sol. In cooler months you can dine in the rustic tavern before an open fireplace. In fair weather, meals are served on a patio partially encircled by open Romanesque arches. The chef is likely to offer foie gras with lentils, lobster croquettes (as an appetizer), and roast guinea hen with cream, minced raisins, and port. The food has a great deal of flavor, is presented with style, and is prepared with the freshest ingredients available. An iced soufflé finishes the meal quite nicely.

✪ **Marbella Club Restaurant.** The Marbella Club, Bulevar Príncipe Alfonso von Hohenlohe, s/n. ☎ **95/282-22-11.** Reservations recommended. Lunch buffet 5,400 ptas. ($43.20) per person; dinner main courses 2,900–6,900 ptas. ($23.20–$55.20). AE, DC, MC, V. Daily 1:30–4pm; summer, daily 9pm–12:30am; winter, daily 8:30–11:30pm. INTERNATIONAL.

Much of this establishment's charm derives from the willingness of the staff to move the action onto a flowering terrace in good weather. Lunch is traditionally an overflowing buffet served in the beach club. Dinners are served amid blooming flowers, flickering candles, and the strains of live music—perhaps a Spanish classical guitarist, a small chamber orchestra playing 19th-century classics, or a South American vocalist. Menu items, inspired by the cuisines of Europe, change with the season. You might begin, for example, with beef carpaccio or lobster salad delicately flavored with olive oil. Specialties include one of the coast's most savory paellas and tender veal cutlets from Ávila.

✪ **El Portalon.** Carretera de Cádiz, km 178. ☎ **95/282-78-80.** Reservations recommended. Main courses 1,800–3,000 ptas. ($14.40–$24). AE, DC, MC, V. Daily 1pm–1:30am. SPANISH/INTERNATIONAL.

This is one of Marbella's most stylish and sophisticated newcomers. It lies about a mile west of town, beside the road leading to Puerto Banús, across the road from the beach, and adjacent to the entrance to the ultra-expensive Marbella Club. Its staff is one of the most urbane and international in town, serving clients from throughout Europe with aplomb and a recognizable pride. Menu selections inlcude some of the most time-honored dishes of Iberia, such as suckling lamb and pig slowly roasted in a wood-burning oven, grilled meats, and impeccably fresh fish imported daily. Also featured are light, calorie-conscious and low-fat dishes like those you might expect to find at a sophisticated spa in northern California—for example, lobster salad, grilled sea bass with a julienne of fresh vegetables, a medley of baby lamb chops grilled over charcoal, and entrecôte of beef with fresh vegetables and red wine sauce (served on the side if you request).

Villa Tiberio. Carretera de Cádiz, km 178.5. ☎ **95/277-17-99.** Reservations recommended. Main courses 1,550–2,900 ptas. ($12.40–$23.20). AE, MC, V. Mon–Sat 7:30pm–midnight. ITALIAN.

Villa Tiberio's proximity to the upscale Marbella Club (a five-minute walk away) ensures a flow of visitors from that elite hotel. Set within what was originally built as a private villa during the 1960s, it serves the most innovative Italian food in the region. It attracts the many north European expatriates living nearby. Appetizers include slices of thinly sliced smoked beef with fresh avocados and oil-and-lemon dressing and a *fungi fantasia,* composed of a large wild mushroom stuffed with seafood and lobster sauce. Especially tempting is the *pappardelle alla Sandro*—large flat noodles studded with chunks of lobster, tomato, and garlic. Other versions come with cream, caviar, and smoked salmon. Main dishes include grilled monkfish with prawns and garlic butter, grilled filets of pork or veal with mushroom-and-cream sauce, and osso buco. Live music sometimes accompanies a meal here.

MODERATE

Balcón de la Virgen. Remedios 2. ☎ **95/277-60-92.** Reservations recommended. Main courses 750–1,700 ptas. ($6–$13.60). AE, MC, V. Daily 7pm–midnight. Closed Tues Nov–May. SPANISH.

Set in the historic core of old Marbella, this restaurant is named after a 200-year-old statue of the Virgin that adorns a wall niche surrounded by flowers and vines—the focal point of the antique house that contains it. You'll find it within a short walk of the Plaza de los Naranjos, and regardless of when you arrive, it's likely to be well patronized because of its floral charm, good food, attentive service, and reasonable prices. The menu—derived mostly from Andalusia and, to a lesser degree, the rest of Spain—features Málaga-style meat stew, baked hake with olive oil and herbs, marinated swordfish, roasted pork, and grilled filets of beef.

Hostería del Mar. Cánovas del Castillo, 1. ☎ **95/277-02-18.** Reservations recommended. Main courses 1,750–2,100 ptas. ($14–$16.80). AE, MC, V. Mon–Sat 1–4pm and 7:30pm–midnight. MEDITERRANEAN.

Hostería del Mar lies at the beginning of the bypass road that runs beside the Hotel Meliá Don Pepe. Its cuisine is known throughout the region as being both delicious and highly unusual. The Hostería has been called the most consistently good restaurant in the region—a judgment with which many loyal clients agree.

The dining room is decorated in shades of fern green and cream and accented with wooden columns, a floor colored blue and terra-cotta, decorative ceiling beams, and hand-painted porcelain. In summer, a tree-shaded patio is also set with tables. Delectable meals might include calves' sweetbreads in mustard sauce, clams stuffed with ratatouille, roast duck with a sauce made from roasted figs and cassis, Catalán-style shrimp with chicken, and a casserole of monkfish with white wine sauce, clams, and fresh asparagus. The sumptous desserts include a selection of cold soufflés.

Mesón del Museo. Plaza de los Naranjos, 11. ☎ **95/282-56-23.** Reservations recommended. Main courses 2,200–3,200 ptas. ($17.60–$25.60). AE, DC, MC, V. Mon–Sat 7:30–11:30pm. Closed Sun Dec 23–May 1, Jul, and Aug. SWEDISH/INTERNATIONAL.

Mesón del Museo is located on the upper floor of an 18th-century building that contains one of the oldest art and antiques galleries in Marbella. Although its dining room is decorated with Iberian accessories and Andalusian antiques, its menu is partially Swedish—the inspired result of the partnership of Stockholm-born Hans Jöhncke and his Chilean wife, Valeska. Menu items include smoked or marinated salmon served with mustard sauce and creamed spinach, beef Stroganoff, versions of Swedish meatballs with gravy and mashed potatoes, and top-quality sirloin filet prepared at least five different ways, including versions served with béarnaise, green pepper, Madeira, or *cabrales* (a Spanish blue cheese) sauce, as well as filets stuffed with truffles and/or foie gras. Desserts might include a homemade and very succulent pear tart with vanilla sauce.

A Marbella Tasca Crawl

The best way to keep food costs low in Marbella is to do what the Spaniards do: Take your meals in the tapas bars. You can eat well in most places for around 700 pesetas ($5.60), and Marbella boasts more holes-in-the-wall where tapas are served than virtually any other resort town in Spain. Know in advance that even if you set out with a specific site in mind, you'll likely be waylaid en route by a newer, older, bigger, smaller, brighter, or more mysterious joint.

Prices and hours are remarkably consistent: The coffee house that opens at 7am will switch to a venue of wine and tapas whenever the first client asks for it (sometimes shortly after breakfast), then continue through the day dispensing wine, sherry, and more recently, bottles of beer to accompany the food tastings. Tapas cost from 200 to 600 pesetas ($1.60–$4.80) per *ración,* though some foreign visitors configure them into *platos combinados.*

Tapas served along the Costa del Sol are principally Andalusian in origin, with an emphasis on seafood. The most famous plate, called *fritura malagueña,* offers fried fish based on the catch of the day. Sometimes *ajo blanco,* a garlicky local version of gazpacho, is served, especially in summer. Fried squid or octopus is another favorite, as are little Spanish-style herb-flavored meatballs. *Tortilla* (a fried Spanish omelet, often with potatoes) is the most popular egg dish. Other well-known tapas selections include pungent tuna, grilled shrimp, *piquillos rellenos* (red peppers stuffed with fish), *bacalao* (salted cod), or mushrooms sautéed in olive oil and garlic.

Many of the narrow streets of Marbella's historic core are lined with tapas bars, with rich pickings around La Calle del Perral and, to a somewhat lesser extent, the Calle Miguel Cana. At **Bar El Gallo,** Calle Lobatas, 44 (☎ **95/282-79-89**), a TV set blares from above the bar and locals shout at one another above the din. It's open daily from 9am to midnight. The selection will vary, according to how many drinkers beat you to it, but you can usually be assured of *tortillas,* some shellfish, sausages, stuffed mushrooms, and other eminently munchable snacks.

Looking for vegetarian tapas? A sure bet would be those prepared by the oldest vegetarian restaurant in Marbella, **Restaurante Albahaca,** Calle Lobatas, 31 (☎ **95/286-35-20**). Open daily from noon to 4pm and 7:30pm to midnight, its roster includes succulent slices of stuffed eggplant. Prices range from 275 to 580 pesetas ($2.20–$4.65) per *ración.* If you want to stay for a meal, main courses are between 600 and 1,200 pesetas ($4.80–$9.60); and a limited selection of meat and fish dishes are on hand for anyone who can't abide a meatless meal.

Santiago. Duque de Ahumada, 5. ☎ **95/277-43-39.** Reservations required. Main courses 1,200–3,200 ptas. ($9.60–$25.60). AE, DC, MC, V. Daily 12:30–5pm and 7pm–midnight. SEAFOOD/ANDALUSIAN.

As soon as you enter Santiago, the bubbling lobster tanks give you an idea of what's in store. The decor, the tapas bar near the entrance, and the summertime patio join with fresh fish dishes to make this one of the most popular eating places in town. On our most recent visit, we arrived so early for lunch that the mussels for our mussels marinara were just being delivered. The fish soup is well prepared, well spiced, and savory. The sole in champagne comes in a large serving, and the turbot can be grilled or sautéed. On a hot day, the seafood salad, garnished with lobster, shrimp, and crabmeat and served with a sharp sauce, is especially recommended. In addition to seafood, many meat dishes including pork and chicken are served. For dessert, we suggest a serving of Manchego cheese.

Inexpensive

La Gitana. Buitrago 2. ☎ **95/282-4656.** Reservations recommended. Main courses 955–2,100 ptas. ($7.65–$16.80). DC, MC, V. Daily 7:30–11:30pm. Closed Wed Dec–March. ANDALUSIAN/INTERNATIONAL.

Set on a narrow, winding street in the old pueblo of Marbella, close to the Plaza de los Naranjos, this restaurant lies within a boxy-looking, antique house whose charm derives partly from a rooftop terrace that the owners adorn with cascades of flowers throughout the summer. Other areas within the cozy place include a bar/cocktail lounge and an indoor dining area on the first floor, which the owners use in winter or during the region's rare rainfalls. Menu items derive from southern and central Spain, as well as from such northern climes as Switzerland. Specialties include young roasted lamb, served either as cutlets or in a rack with herbs; barbecued pork or beef; several kinds of baked fish, including monkfish and hake; deep-fried mushrooms with tartar sauce; and salmon—either marinated and raw or served *à la nage* (in an aromatic poaching sauce).

$ La Tricyclette. Buitrago, 14. ☎ **95/277-78-00.** Main courses 800–2,200 ptas. ($6.40–$17.60); fixed-price menu (Oct–May only) 1,800 ptas. ($14.40). AE, MC, V. Wed–Mon 7:30pm–midnight. INTERNATIONAL.

One of the more popular dining spots in Marbella, this restaurant is in a converted 18th-century home—courtyard and all—located on a narrow street in the old quarter near Plaza de los Naranjos. Sofas in the bar area provide a living-room ambience, and a stairway leads to an intimate dining room with an open patio that is delightful in the warmer months. Perhaps start with crêpes with a soft cream-cheese filling or grilled giant prawns, then move on to a delectable main dish such as roast duck in beer, filet steak with green-pepper sauce, or calves' liver cooked in sage and white wine. The wine list is extensive and reasonably priced.

A Nearby Place to Dine

El Refugio. Carretera de Ojén C-337. ☎ **95/288-10-00.** Main courses 1,500–2,100 ptas. ($12–$16.80); fixed-price menu 2,800 ptas. ($22.40). AE, DC, MC, V. Daily 1–4pm and 8–11pm. SPANISH.

If the summer heat has you down, retreat to the Sierra Blanca, just outside Ojén, where motorists come to enjoy both the mountain scenery and the cuisine at El Refugio, lying nine miles (15km) up in the hills north of Marbella. Meals are served in a rustic dining room, with an open terrace for drinks. Specialties include local versions of various spicy regional sausages, roast pork, roast chicken, grilled steaks, and in season, local pheasant. The lounge has an open fireplace and comfortable armchairs, along with a few antiques and Oriental rugs.

MARBELLA AFTER DARK

Flamenco

Ana María. Plaza del Santo Cristo, 4–5. ☎ **95/277-56-46.** Cover 2,500 ptas. ($20).

Of the many clubs that profess to specialize in flamenco within and around Marbella, this is the most reputable, the most appealing, the most authentic, and the safest for foreign visitors with a limited knowledge of Spanish. The venue includes a long and often crowded bar area selling tapas, wines, sherries, and a selection of more international libations, and a stage where a frequently changing assortment of singers, dancers, and musicians perform flamenco as well as a roster of popular songs. This is late-night entertainment—the doors don't open till 11pm, and the crowd becomes more congenial between midnight and 4am. It's closed in November and on Monday between December and March. Drinks cost from around 1,000 pesetas ($8) each.

GAMBLING

Casino Nueva Andalucía Marbella. Hotel Andalucía Plaza, Urbanización Nueva Andalucía. ☎ **95/281-40-00.** Cover to casino 600 ptas. ($4.80) and presentation of valid passport.

Set six miles (10km) west of Marbella, near Puerto Banús, this casino is on the lobby level of the previously recommended Andalucía Plaza Hotel. The designers carefully incorporated traffic flow between the facilities of the hotel and the jangle and clatter of the casino. Unlike the region's competing casino at the Hotel Torrequebrada, the Nueva Andalucía does not offer cabaret or nightclub shows. The focus, instead, is on gambling, which the mobs of visitors from northern Europe perform with abandon. Individual games include French and American roulette, blackjack, punto y banco, craps, and chemin de fer.

You can dine before or after gambling in the Casino Restaurant, which is raised a few steps above the gaming floor. Meals go for about 3,500 pesetas ($28) per person, including wine. Jackets are not required for men, but shorts and T-shirts will be frowned on. The casino is open daily from 8pm to either 4 or 5am. La Caseta Bar offers flamenco shows at 11pm on Friday and Saturday nights. Entrance is free but drinks cost from 1,800 pesetas ($14.40).

7 Fuengirola & Los Boliches

20 miles (32km) W of Málaga, 64½ miles (104km) E of Algeciras, 356½ miles (574km) S of Madrid

The twin fishing towns of Fuengirola and Los Boliches lie halfway between the more famous resorts of Marbella and Torremolinos. The promenade along the water stretches some 2½ miles (4km), with the less developed Los Boliches just half a mile from Fuengirola.

The towns don't have the facilities or drama of Torremolinos and Marbella. Except for two major luxury hotels, however, Fuengirola and Los Boliches are cheaper, and that has attracted a horde of budget-conscious European tourists.

The ruins of **San Isidro Castle** can be seen from a promontory overlooking the sea. The **Santa Amalja, Carvajal,** and **Las Gaviotas beaches** are broad, clean, and sandy. Everybody goes to the big **flea market** at Fuengirola on Tuesdays.

GETTING THERE **By Train** From Torremolinos, take the Metro at La Nogalera station (under the RENFE sign). Trains depart every 30 minutes.

By Bus Fuengirola is on the main Costa del Sol bus route from either Algeciras in the west or Málaga in the east.

By Car Take the N-340/E-15 east from Marbella.

VISITOR INFORMATION The Tourist Information Office is at Avenida Jesús Santos Rein, 6 (☎ **95/246-74-57**). Open Monday through Friday from 9:30am to 1:30pm and 4 to 7pm, Saturday from 10am to 1pm.

WHERE TO STAY

✪ **Byblos Andaluz.** Urbanización Mijas Golf, 29640 Fuengirola. ☎ **95/246-02-50.** Fax 95/247-67-83. 144 rms, 37 suites. A/C MINIBAR TV TEL. 25,000–33,500 ptas. ($200–$268) double; from 47,000 ptas. ($376) suite. AE, DC, MC, V. Free parking.

This luxurious resort is in a golf club setting three miles (5km) from Fuengirola and six miles (10km) from the beach. The grounds contain shrubbery, a white minaret, Moorish arches, tile-adorned walls, and an orange-tree patio inspired by the Alhambra grounds. The resort's two 18-hole golf courses designed by Robert Trent Jones, tennis courts, spa facilities, gymnasium, and swimming pools bask in the Andalusian sunshine. The health spa is housed in a handsome classic structure, Mijas Thalasso Palace.

The rooms and suites are elegantly and individually designed and furnished in Roman, Arabic, Andalusian, and rustic styles. Private sun terraces and lavish bathrooms add to the comfort.

Dining/Entertainment: The dining choices here include Le Nailhac, with its French gastronomic offerings; El Andaluz, with its regional and Spanish specialties; and La Fuente, offering a dietetic cuisine. Live entertainment is often presented at the San Tropez Bar, which opens onto a poolside terrace.

Services: Laundry/valet, babysitting, room service.

Facilities: Health club, sauna, solarium, two outdoor pools, three indoor pools, two golf courses, tennis.

Florida. Paseo Marítimo, s/n, 29640 Fuengirola. ☎ **95/247-61-00.** Fax 95/258-15-29. 116 rms. TV TEL. 7,000–10,300 ptas. ($56–$82.40) double. AE, DC, MC, V. Free parking.

There is a semitropical garden in front of the Florida, and guests can enjoy refreshments under a wide, vine-covered pergola. During the summer months, live music and flamenco shows are offered. Most of the comfortable guest rooms have balconies overlooking the sea or mountains, although furnishings and decor are a bit bleak and severe. The floors are tile, and plastic furniture abounds, particularly in the lounge. It's a 10-minute walk from the train station.

$ **Hostal Sedeño.** Don Jacinto, 1, 29640 Fuengirola. ☎ **95/247-47-88.** 30 rms. 3,000–4,800 ptas. ($24–$38.40) double. No credit cards.

The Sedeño is located three minutes from the beach, in the heart of town. Its modest lobby leads to a larger lounge furnished with antiques and reproductions. You pass a small open courtyard where stairs lead to the second- and third-floor balconied but basic bedrooms. These overlook a small garden with fig and palm trees, plus a terrace. There is no restaurant and not even breakfast is served, although many restaurants and cafés lie nearby.

Las Pirámides. Paseo Marítimo, 29640 Fuengirola. ☎ **95/247-06-00.** Fax 95/258-32-97. 280 rms, 40 suites. A/C MINIBAR TV TEL. 13,000–17,500 ptas. ($104–$140) double; 16,000–18,500 ptas. ($128–$148) suite. Rates include breakfast. AE, MC, V. Parking 1,000 ptas. ($8).

This resort, much favored by clients and travel groups from northern Europe, is divided into two 10-story towers capped with pyramid-shaped roofs. It's a citylike compound, set about 50 yards from the beach, with seemingly every kind of divertissement: flamenco shows on the large patio, a cozy bar and lounge, traditionally furnished sitting rooms, a coffee shop, a poolside bar, and a gallery of boutiques and tourist facilities, such as car-rental agencies. All the guest rooms have slick modern styling, as well as terraces. Room service is provided, as are laundry/valet services and babysitting.

WHERE TO DINE

Casa Vieja. Avenida de Los Boliches, 27, Los Boliches. ☎ **95/258-38-30.** Reservations recommended. Fixed-price three-course lunch (Sat–Sun only) 1,500 ptas. ($12); main dinner courses 1,275–2,100 ptas. ($10.20–$16.80). AE, MC, V. Sat–Sun 12:30–3pm, Tues–Sun 7:30–11pm. FRENCH.

Set within the thick stone walls of a cottage that was originally built in the 1870s for a local fisherman, this restaurant lies on the main street of Los Boliches, a short walk east of the center of Fuengirola. Owned and managed by London-born Jon Adams, the establishment is a favorite of the expatriate community living in the nearby hills. A flowering patio is available for outdoor dining, and there's a cozy bar for chatting with the owner. Menu items include a subtly flavored terrine of oxtail, king prawns, tournedos with béarnaise sauce, suprême of salmon, gratin of sole in puff pastry, and guinea fowl with cumin and honey-glazed turnips. The house's special dessert is a *tarte tatin,* an upside-down tart inspired by France, served with fresh cream and ice cream.

La Cazuela. Calle Miguel Márquez, 8, Fuengirola. ☎ **95/247-46-34.** Reservations recommended. Main courses 1,000–1,900 ptas. ($8–$15.20). MC, V. Daily 7pm–midnight. SPANISH/INTERNATIONAL.

Set south of the center of Fuengirola, at the edge of the road leading off to Marbella, this cozy restaurant has flourished since the 1970s. Its long-time owner, Francisco Calle, outfits his dining rooms with hand-painted, Spanish-style porcelain, and green and white accessories that match the potted plants scattered throughout the premises. The house specialty is a tender chicken Kiev, which fans cite as even better than the tasty filets of grilled beef, grilled prawns with garlic, homemade pâtés, and crayfish. A worthy beginning for any meal might be the cheese crêpes.

Don Pé. De la Cruz, 19, Fuengirola. ☎ **95/247-83-51.** Reservations recommended. Main courses 850–2,100 ptas. ($6.80–$16.80). DC, MC, V. Mon–Sat 7pm–midnight. CONTINENTAL.

In hot weather, visitors at Don Pé dine in the courtyard, where the roof can be adjusted to allow in light and air. In cold weather, a fire within the hearth illuminates the heavy ceiling beams and rustic accessories. The menu features a selection of game dishes: medallion of venison, roast filet of wild boar, and duck with orange sauce. The ingredients are imported from the forests and plains of Andalusia. Don Pé lies off the Avenida Ramón y Cajal.

La Langosta. Calle Francisco Cano, 1, Los Boliches. ☎ **95/247-50-49.** Main courses 1,290–2,990 ptas. ($10.30–$23.90); fixed-price menus 1,290–1,990 ptas. ($10.30–$15.90). AE, DC, MC, V. Mon–Sat 7:30pm–midnight. SPANISH/SEAFOOD.

Just a stone's throw from Fuengirola in the satellite community of Los Boliches is La Langosta, one of the best-recommended restaurants in the area. The stylish two-story art deco dining room comes as welcome relief from the ever-present Iberian "rustic style" that adorns so many restaurants in the region. A variety of seafood is featured on the menu (the place is just two blocks in from the beach), as well as Spanish dishes that include chicken and prawns with a medley of sauces, mussels, and salmon. Lobster is prepared thermidor style, or virtually any way you want; among the beef offerings is an especially succulent version of chateaubriand. The staff here seems particularly well trained and helpful.

El Paso. Calle Francisco Cano, 39, Los Boliches. ☎ **95/247-50-94.** Reservations recommended. Main courses 1,100–2,000 ptas. ($8.80–$16). MC, V. Daily 7pm–midnight. MEXICAN/REGIONAL.

The building that contains El Paso was originally constructed a century ago as a canning factory for sardines, with a row of fisher's cottages nearby. Today, this is the area's most popular Mexican restaurant, where a splashing fountain enlivens an outdoor patio rich with blooming flowers. (There are additional tables set up inside.) By far the most popular drink here is a frothy margarita, which might be followed by your choice of tacos, burritos, frijoles, fajitas, and guacamoles. The chef's specialty is barbecued meats.

Tomate. El Troncon, 19, Fuengirola. ☎ **95/246-35-59.** Reservations recommended. Main courses 650–1,990 ptas. ($5.20–$15.90); fixed-price menus 1,390–2,390 ptas. ($11.10–$19.10). AE, MC, V. Tues–Sun 7pm–midnight. INTERNATIONAL.

One of the most gastronomically sophisticated restaurants in town presents the best culinary traditions of northern and southern Europe. Set within the heart of Fuengirola, in a century-old town house whose dining space was added on in back, Tomate is the creative statement of German-born Michael Lienhoop. Meals might include dishes from Spain (gazpacho or filet of hake floating on a lake of mustard-flavored cream-and-herb sauce), France (*langoustines provençales*), Germany (sauerkraut with an assortment of smoked meats or pork in a sauce of red wine and mushrooms), and Scandinavia (a selection of marinated herring and marinated salmon with dill sauce).

8 Mijas

18½ miles (30km) W of Málaga, 363 miles (584km) S of Madrid

Just five miles (8km) north of coastal road N-340/E-15, this village is known as "White Mijas" because of its marble-white Andalusian-style houses. Mijas is at the foot of a mountain range near the turnoff to Fuengirola, and from its lofty height, 1,476 feet above sea level, you get a panoramic view of the Mediterranean.

Celts, Phoenicians, and Moors preceded today's intrepid tourists in visiting Mijas. The town itself—not any specific monument—is the attraction. The easiest way to get around its cobblestoned streets is to rent a burro taxi. If you find Mijas overrun with souvenir shops, head for the park at the top of Cuesta de la Villa, where you'll see the ruins of a **Moorish fortress** dating from 833. If you're in Mijas for a fiesta, you'll be attending events in the country's only square bullring.

GETTING THERE **By Bus** There's frequent bus service from the terminal at Fuengirola.

By Car At Fuengirola, take the Mijas road north.

WHERE TO STAY

✪ **Hotel Mijas.** Urbanización Tamisa, 2, 29650 Mijas. ☎ **95/248-58-00.** Fax 95/248-58-25. 100 rms, 3 suites. TV TEL. 10,000–14,000 ptas. ($80–$112) double; 20,000–28,000 ptas. ($160–$224) suite. AE, DC, MC, V. Free parking.

One of the most charming hotels on the Costa del Sol was built in the 1970s on steeply sloping land in the center of town. Designed in a four-story, Andalusian-inspired block of white walls, wrought-iron accents, and flowering terraces, it features sweeping views over the Mediterranean from most of its public areas and accommodations. Throughout, the style is sun-flooded, comfortable, and Andalusian, and the staff is tactful and hardworking. The in-house tavern is accented with enormous kegs of wine, whereas the lounge is the setting for live music on some evenings, performed amid Iberian antiques and a collection of unusual fans. The hotel's facilities include tennis courts, a swimming pool, sauna, gymnasium, boutique, facilities for games of lawn bowling, hairdresser, and a barber. If you have an aversion to climbing stairs, ask for a room on one of the lower floors, because there is no elevator.

WHERE TO DINE

Club El Padrastro. Paseo del Compás. ☎ **95/248-50-00.** Reservations recommended. Main courses 975–2,650 ptas. ($7.80–$21.20); fixed-price menus 985–1,875 ptas. ($7.90–$15). AE, DC, MC, V. Daily 12:30–4pm and 7–11pm. INTERNATIONAL.

Part of the fun of dining at El Padrastro is reaching the place. You go to the cliff side of town and, if you're athletic, walk up 77 steps; if you're not, take the elevator to the highest point. Once you get there, you'll discover that El Padrastro is the town's best dining spot, offering international cuisine on its covered terraces with panoramic views of the Mediterranean coast. You can choose whether to eat inexpensively or elaborately. If it's the latter, make it chateaubriand with a bottle of the best Spanish champagne. If you stick to regional dishes, you'll save money.

Restaurante El Capricho. Los Caños, 5. ☎ **95/248-51-11.** Reservations recommended. Main courses 1,400–2,100 ptas. ($11.20–$16.80); fixed-price lunch 1,200 ptas. ($9.60). AE, DC, MC, V. Thurs–Tues 12:30–4pm and 7–11:30pm. Closed Nov 15–Dec 15. INTERNATIONAL.

El Capricho, located in what was once an 1850s private home in the town center, draws a large English-speaking clientele, and the varied menu is geared to their tastes. Appetizers include prawn cocktail, Serrano ham, omelets, soups, and salads. Among the main dishes are sole, grilled swordfish, chicken Kiev, steak Stroganoff, and flambéed meats. You might prefer the paella Mijeña, which is excellent. Desserts range from flambéed concoctions to baked Alaska. The wine list offers good choices, including the house Riolja.

9 Torremolinos

9 miles (14km) W of Málaga, 76 miles (122km) E of Algeciras, 353 miles (568km) S of Madrid

This Mediterranean beach resort is the most famous in Spain. It's a gathering place for international visitors, a melting pot of Europeans and Americans. Many relax here after a whirlwind tour of Europe—the living's easy, the people are fun, and there are no historical monuments to visit. Thus the sleepy fishing village of Torremolinos has been engulfed in a cluster of cement-walled resort hotels. Prices are on the rise, but it nevertheless remains one of Europe's vacation bargains.

GETTING THERE **By Plane** Torremolinos is served by the nearby Málaga airport.

By Train There are frequent departures from the terminal at Málaga. For information, call **95/236-02-02.**

By Bus Buses run frequently between Málaga and Torremolinos. For information, call **95/238-24-19.**

By Car Take the N-340/E-15 west from Málaga or the N-340/E-15 east from Marbella.

VISITOR INFORMATION The tourist information office is at La Nogalera, 517 (☎ **95/238-01-66**). Open daily 8am to 3pm.

WHERE TO STAY

EXPENSIVE

Aloha Puerto Sol. Calle Salvador Allende, 45, 29620 Torremolinos. ☎ **800/336-3542** in the U.S., or 95/238-70-66. Fax 95/238-57-01. 430 rms. A/C MINIBAR TV TEL. 11,500–17,690 ptas. ($92–$141.50) double. Rates include buffet breakfast. AE, DC, MC, V.

Heralded as one of the most modern hotels along the Costa del Sol when it was built in 1972, this now-aging hotel stands on the seashore in the residential suburb of El Saltillo, on the southwestern edge of Torremolinos, beside the coastal road leading to Marbella. Away from the noise of the town center, it offers spacious rooms, all defined by the hotel as mini-suites. Each faces the sea, the Benalmádena marina, or the beach, and each contains a separate sitting area.

Amid all the accessories of a resort, guests are given a choice of two restaurants and four bars. The most popular lunchtime option is a poolside buffet that includes an all-you-can-eat medley of meats, salads, and seafood. Many guests spend their days near the two swimming pools, one of which is heated. Spanish evenings at El

Comodoro, one of the several bars on the premises, last well into the early morning hours.

Don Pablo. Paseo Marítimo, s/n, 29620 Torremolinos. ☎ **95/238-38-88.** Fax 95/238-37-83. 443 rms. A/C MINIBAR TV TEL. 14,980–19,474 ptas. ($119.85–$155.80) double. Rates include buffet breakfast. AE, DC, MC, V.

One of the most desirable hotels in Torremolinos is housed in a modern building that's located a minute from the beach and surrounded by its own garden and playground areas. There are two unusually shaped open-air swimming pools, with terraces for sunbathing and refreshments, and a large indoor pool as well. The surprise is the glamorous interior, which borrows heavily from Moorish palaces and medieval castle themes. Splashing fountains are found in the arched-tile arcades, and niches with life-size stone statues of nude figures line the grand staircase. The comfortably furnished bedrooms have sea-view terraces and private baths.

The hotel has a full day and night entertainment program, including fitness classes, dancing at night to a live band, and a disco. Piano music is played in a wood-paneled English lounge, and the hotel shows movie videos on a giant screen every night.

Hotel Cervantes. Calle las Mercedes, s/n, 29620 Torremolinos. ☎ **95/238-40-33.** Fax 95/238-48-57. 397 rms. A/C TV TEL. 12,000–15,000 ptas. ($96–$120) double. Rates include breakfast; half board 4,800 ptas. ($38.40) per person extra. AE, DC, MC, V.

The four-star Cervantes is a seven-minute walk from the beach. It has its own garden and is adjacent to a maze of patios and narrow streets of boutiques and open-air cafés. The Cervantes's self-contained facilities include a sun terrace, a sauna, massage, two pools (one covered and heated), hairdressers, a gift shop, a TV and video lounge, a card room, and games, such as billiards, table tennis, and darts.

The bedrooms have streamlined modern furniture, private baths, piped-in music, safes, TVs, and spacious terraces; many have balconies with views of the sea.

Also on the premises are a restaurant, a bar with live music and entertainment programs, and a coffee shop. In midsummer this hotel is likely to be booked with tour groups from northern Europe.

Meliá Costa del Sol. Paseo Marítimo, 19, 29620 Torremolinos. ☎ **800/336-3542** in the U.S, or 95/238-66-77. Fax 95/238-64-17. 540 rms, 18 suites. A/C TV TEL. 10,000–15,000 ptas. ($80–$120) double; 23,500–34,000 ptas. ($188–$272) suite. AE, DC, MC, V. Free parking.

There are two Meliá hotels in Torremolinos, both operated by a popular hotel chain in Spain. This one is preferred by many travelers because of its more central location (although the other Meliá is more luxurious). The guest rooms are modern and well maintained, each with a private bath. However, the hotel is popular with package-tour groups, so you may not feel a part of things if you're here alone. The facilities include a garden, swimming pool, thalassotherapy center (for medicinal seawater treatments), shopping arcade, and hairdresser. Once a week a free flamenco show is presented to house guests, and on the other six nights there is a pianist who plays for dancing couples.

Meliá Torremolinos. Carlota Alessandri, 109, 29620 Torremolinos. ☎ **800/336-3542** in the U.S., or 95/238-05-00. Fax 95/238-05-38. 275 rms, 6 suites. A/C TV TEL. 12,300–16,600 ptas. ($98.40–$132.80) double; 28,900 ptas. ($231.20) suite. AE, DC, MC, V. Closed Nov–Mar. Free parking.

This is the more luxurious of the two Meliá hotels at the resort, but farther removed from the center. The hotel deliberately lowered its official rank from five stars to four stars, which means you can enjoy the amenities and service of a five-star hotel but at lower prices. The six-story hotel, which stands in its own gardens, is located on the western outskirts of town, on the road to Cádiz. Bedrooms are generally spacious and always well furnished and maintained; many contain minibars. The public areas were renovated and upgraded in 1993. Other facilities include a swimming pool and tennis courts. Flamenco shows are occasionally presented.

Moderate

Hotel Las Palomas. Carmen Montes, 1, 29620 Torremolinos. ☎ **95/238-50-00.** Fax 95/238-64-66. 345 rms. TEL. 6,510–13,178 ptas. ($52.10–$105.40) double. AE, DC, MC, V.

Originally built during the heyday of Torremolinos's construction boom (1968), this well-managed hotel is one of the town's most attractive, surrounded by carefully tended gardens. Located near the coastal road, a one-minute walk from the beach and a ten-minute walk south of the center of town, it has an Andalusian decor in the public and guest rooms, a formal entrance, and a clientele of repeat visitors who hail mostly from France, Belgium, and Holland. Each of the rooms contains a private balcony, a tiled bathroom, and furniture inspired by southern Spain. None is air-conditioned, although many clients compensate by opening windows and balcony doors to catch the sea breezes. The hotel boasts a sauna, three swimming pools (one reserved for children), some form of entertainment going on throughout the day and early evening, a handful of shops, a hairdresser, and an unending series of lunch and dinner buffets.

Hotel los Arcos. Carlota Alessandri, 192, 29620 Torremolinos. ☎ **95/238-08-22.** Fax 95/238-02-20. 51 rms. A/C TV TEL. 9,875 ptas. ($79) double. Rates include breakfast. AE, DC, MC, V.

Built in 1958 as a grand villa evocative of Beverly Hills in the 1920s, this Spanish-style house was remodeled and modernized in the 1990s. Eclectic furnishings are placed throughout. The bedrooms are pleasant, all with balconies and garden views and half with minibars. A complete lunch or dinner is available. The hotel stands 225 yards from the beach and less than a mile (1km) from the town center.

Sidi Lago Rojo. Miami, 1, 29620 Torremolinos. ☎ **95/238-76-66.** Fax 95/238-08-91. 144 rms. A/C TV TEL. 10,000 ptas. ($80) double. AE, DC, MC, V.

Located in the heart of the fishing village of La Carihuela and the finest place to stay there, Sidi Lago Rojo stands only 150 feet from the beach and has its own gardens, swimming pool, sunbathing terraces, and refreshment bar. It offers studio-style guest rooms, doubles only, tastefully decorated with contemporary Spanish furnishings and tile baths. All the rooms have terraces with views; some have minibars. In the late evening there is disco dancing. The hotel also has a good restaurant.

Inexpensive

Hostal Los Jazmines. Lido, s/n, 29620 Torremolinos. ☎ **95/238-50-33.** Fax 95/237-27-02. 85 rms. TEL. 5,400–6,600 ptas. ($43.20–$52.80) double. AE, MC, V.

Located on one of the best beaches in Torremolinos, facing a plaza at the foot of the shady Avenida del Lido, this choice for sunseekers is replete with terraces, lawns, and an irregularly shaped swimming pool. Meals are served alfresco or inside the appealing dining room, furnished with Spanish reproductions. The bedrooms, all doubles, seem a bit impersonal, but they have their own little balconies and compact baths. From here it's a good hike up the hill to the town center.

Hotel El Pozo. Casablanca, 4, 29620 Torremolinos. ☎ and fax **95/238-06-22.** 28 rms. TV TEL. 5,000–6,000 ptas. ($40–$48) double. DC, MC, V.

This hotel isn't for light sleepers, and it's usually filled with budget travelers, including many students from the north of Europe. It's in one of the liveliest sections of town, a short walk from the train station. The lobby-level bar has an open fireplace, heavy Spanish furniture, cool white tiles, and a view of a small courtyard. From your window or terrace you can view the promenades below. The guest rooms are furnished in a simple, functional style—nothing special, but the price is right.

$ **Miami.** Aladino, 14, 29620 Torremolinos. ☎ **95/238-52-55.** 27 rms. TEL. 4,100–6,400 ptas. ($32.80–$51.20) double. No credit cards.

The Miami, near the Carihuela section, is like one of those Hollywood movie-star homes of the 1920s. Its swimming pool is isolated by high walls and private gardens. Fuchsia bougainvillea climbs over the rear patio's arches. A tile terrace is used for sunbathing and refreshments. The country-style living room contains a walk-in fireplace, while the bedrooms are furnished in a traditional and comfortable style, each with a balcony. Breakfast is the only meal served.

PLACES TO STAY NEARBY

Where Torremolinos ends and Benalmádena-Costa to the west begins is hard to say. Benalmádena-Costa has long been a resort extension on the western frontier of Torremolinos, and it's packed with hotels, restaurants, and tourist facilities.

✪ **Hotel Torrequebrada.** Carretera de Cádiz, km 220, 29630 Benalmádena. ☎ **95/244-60-00.** Fax 95/244-57-02. 317 rms, 33 suites. A/C MINIBAR TV TEL. 19,300 ptas. ($154.40) double; 27,200 ptas. ($217.60) suite. Discounts granted for stays of 5 or more days. Rates include breakfast. AE, DC, MC, V. Free parking.

In the late 1980s this became one of the largest five-star luxury hotels to rise along the Costa del Sol. Lying three miles (5km) west of Torremolinos, it opens onto its own beach and offers a wide range of facilities and attractions, including one of the largest casinos in Europe and a world-class golf course. It also has a variety of restaurants, bars, pools, gardens, a nightclub, a health club, and tennis courts—you'll almost need a floor plan to navigate your way around the complex. Nine levels of underground parking accommodate motorists. The hotel is furnished in muted Mediterranean colors, and both antique and modern furniture are used.

The hotel offers handsomely furnished and coordinated bedrooms in two 11-story towers. All accommodations have large terraces with sea views, plus private safes and baths.

A specialty restaurant, Café Royal, overlooks the gardens and the sea; it enjoys a five-fork rating for its international cuisine. At garden level, the Pavillion provides buffet and cafeteria service throughout the day. A flamenco show is presented at 10:30pm Tuesday through Saturday; the cost is 3,800 pesetas ($30.40), including two drinks.

Tritón. Avenida António Machado, 29, 29491 Benalmádena-Costa. ☎ **95/244-32-40.** Fax 95/244-26-49. 196 rms, 10 suites. A/C MINIBAR TV TEL. 20,800–22,800 ptas. ($166.40–$182.40) double; from 46,800 ptas. ($374.40) suite. Rates include breakfast. AE, DC, MC, V. Free parking.

Less than two miles (3km) north of Torremolinos, the Tritón is a beachfront Miami Beach–style resort colony in front of the marina of Benalmádena-Costa. It features a high-rise stack of guest rooms as well as an impressive pool and garden area. Surrounding the swimming pool are subtropical trees and vegetation, plus thatched sunshade umbrellas. All the rooms have private baths and wide windows opening onto sun balconies. Among the public rooms are multilevel lounges and two bars with wood paneling and handmade rustic furniture (one has stained-glass windows). For dining, there's the main restaurant with its three-tiered display of hors d'oeuvres, fruits, and desserts; a barbecue grill; plus a luncheon terrace. The Tritón also offers tennis courts, a Swedish sauna, and music in the bar with an orchestra July through August.

WHERE TO DINE NEARBY

The cuisine in Torremolinos is more American and continental European than Andalusian. The hotels often serve elaborate four-course meals, but you may want to sample the local fast-food offerings. A good spot to try is the food court called **La Nogalera,** the major gathering place in Torremolinos, located between the coast road and the beach. Head down the Calle del Cauce to this compound of modern white-washed Andalusian buildings. Open to pedestrian traffic only, it features a maze of passageways, courtyards, and patios for eating and drinking. If you're seeking anything from sandwiches to Belgian waffles to scrambled eggs to pizzas, you'll find it here.

AT LA NOGALERA

$ El Gato Viudo. La Nogalera, 8. ☎ **95/238-51-29.** Main courses 700–1,850 ptas. ($5.60–$14.80). AE, DC, MC, V. Thurs–Tues 1–4pm and 6–11:30pm. SPANISH.

Simple and amiable, this old-fashioned tavern occupies the street level and the cellar of a building off Calle San Miguel. It offers sidewalk seating for those who prefer it, and a tradition with local diners that dates back to its founding in 1960. The menu includes such good dishes as grilled fish; marinated hake; roasted pork, steak, and veal; calamari with spicy tomato sauce; grilled shrimp; and shellfish or fish soup. The atmosphere is informal, and the staff has grown accustomed over the years to coping with clients from virtually everywhere.

Golden Curry. Calle Guetaria, 6, La Nogalera, Bloque 6. ☎ **95/237-48-55.** Main courses 950–1,600 ptas. ($7.60–$12.80). AE, MC, V. Sat–Thurs 1–4pm, daily 7pm–1am. INDIAN.

Set one floor above street level, in the commercial heart of Torremolinos, this restaurant specializes in traditional Mogul dishes of India, which have been adapted and altered to suit British tastes. The two chefs and the Calcutta-born owner all worked in Indian restaurants in London prior to emigrating to Spain, and many of their patrons are Brits on holiday. Menu items include chicken Madras, chicken in onion sauce, lamb slow-cooked in spices and served with lentils, and succulent versions of prawns. Vegetarian dishes are also served, the best of which arrive as an array of small dishes.

AT LA CARIHUELA

If you want to get away from the brash high-rises and honky-tonks, head to nearby Carihuela, the old fishing village on the western outskirts of Torremolinos, where some of the best bargain restaurants are found. You can walk down a hill toward the sea to reach it.

$ Casa Prudencio. Carmen, 41, La Carihuela. ☎ **95/238-14-52.** Reservations recommended. Main courses 950–1,800 ptas. ($7.60–$14.40); fixed-price menu 1,200 ptas. ($9.60). AE, MC, V. Daily 12:30–4:30pm and 7:30pm–midnight. Closed Dec 25–Feb 15. SEAFOOD.

Tops with locals and visitors alike, this seaside restaurant just over a mile (2km) west of the center is the oldest surviving restaurant in the fishing hamlet of Carihuela. It features gazpacho, lentils, shrimp omelets, swordfish, and shish kebab. Try the special paella for a main course, followed by strawberries with whipped cream (in the late spring) for dessert. The atmosphere is cordial, and almost everyone sits together at long tables. If you want to splurge, order *lubina à la sal*—a huge boneless fish packed under a layer of salt, which is then broken open at your table.

El Roqueo. Calle del Carmen, 35, La Carihuela. ☎ **95/238-49-46.** Reservations recommended. Main courses 1,400–2,200 ptas. ($11.20–$17.60); fixed-price menu 1,350 ptas. ($10.80). AE, DC, MC, V. Wed–Mon noon–4pm and 8pm–midnight. Closed Nov. SEAFOOD.

Located right in the heart of the village, El Roqueo, which was established in 1975, is the perfect place for a seafood dinner near the sea. Begin with the savory *sopa de mariscos* (shellfish soup). Then try a specialty of the chef, a delectable fish baked in rock salt; you can also order grilled sea bass or shrimp. Top everything off with a soothing caramel custard for dessert. Some of the more expensive fish courses are priced by the gram, so order carefully.

At Playamar

El Vietnam del Sur. Playamar, Bloque, 9. ☎ **95/238-67-37.** Reservations required. Main courses 850–1,400 ptas. ($6.80–$11.20). AE, MC, V. Sun 1–4pm, Thurs–Tues 7pm–midnight. Closed Jan. VIETNAMESE.

The inexpensive food here is best shared. Chopsticks are the norm as you begin with spring rolls served with mint and a spicy sauce for dipping. The chef's specials include fried stuffed chicken wings and beef with rice noodles. The wine list is short and moderately priced. The restaurant stands in the Playamar section near the beach and has an outdoor dining terrace.

At Los Alamos

Frutos. Carretera de Cádiz, km 228, Urbanización Los Alamos. ☎ **95/238-14-50.** Reservations recommended. Main courses 1,000–2,200 ptas. ($8–$17.60); fixed-price menu 1,300 ptas. ($10.40). AE, DC, MC, V. Daily 1–4:30pm; Mon–Sat 8pm–midnight. SPANISH.

Malagueños frequent this place in droves, as they like its good old-style cooking—the cuisine is Spanish with a vengeance. The portions are large and the service is hectic. Diners enjoy the "day's catch," perhaps *rape* (monkfish), angler fish, or the increasingly rare mero (grouper). Also available are garlic-studded leg of lamb and oxtail prepared in a savory ragoût. Frutos is located next to the Los Alamos service station, 1¼ miles (2km) from the town center.

At Benalmádena-Costa

✪ **Mar de Alborán.** Alay, 5. ☎ **95/244-64-27.** Reservations recommended. Main courses 1,200–2,300 ptas. ($9.60–$18.40); *menús del día* 3,300–3,700 ptas. ($26.40–$29.60). AE, DC, MC, V. Sun and Tues–Fri 1:30–3:30pm, Tues–Sat 8:30–11:30pm. Closed Dec 22–Jan 22. BASQUE/ANDALUSIAN.

This restaurant offers an elegantly airy decor that seems appropriate for its location near the sea, just a short walk from the resort's Puerto Marina. It serves a combination of the regional specialties of both Andalusia and the Basque region of northern Spain. Menu items change with the seasons but might include cold terrine of leeks; Basque *piperadda* in puff pastry; *piquillos rellenos* (red peppers stuffed with pulverized fish in a sweet pepper sauce); *bacalao* (salted cod) "Club Ranero," served with garlic and red-pepper cream sauce; *kokotxas,* the Basque national dish of hake cheeks in green sauce with clams; anglerfish with prawns; and foie gras served with sweet Málaga wine and raisins. In season, the restaurant's game dishes are renowned. Dessert might be a frothy version of peach mousse served with purée of fruit and dark-chocolate sauce.

TORREMOLINOS AFTER DARK

Torremolinos has more nightlife activity than any other spot along the Costa del Sol. The earliest action is always at the bars, which are lively most of the night, serving drinks and tapas (Spanish hors d'oeuvres). Sometimes it seems that in Torremolinos there are more bars than people, so you shouldn't have trouble finding one you like. Note that some of the bars are open during the day as well.

DRINKS & TAPAS

Bar Central. Plaza Andalucía, Bloque 1. ☎ **95/238-27-60.**

Bar Central offers coffee, brandy, beer, cocktails, limited sandwiches, and pastries—served either inside or on a large, French-style covered terrace. It's a good spot to meet congenial people. Drinks begin at 125 pesetas ($1) for a beer or 450 pesetas ($3.60) for a hard drink. Open Monday through Saturday from 8am to 2am.

Bar El Toro. San Miguel, 32. ☎ **95/238-65-04.**

Bar El Toro, located in the very center of Torremolinos, is for bullfight aficionados. Kegs of beer, stools, and the terrace in the main shopping street make it a perfect spot for a before-dinner sherry or an after-dinner beer. Drinks at your table begin at 350 pesetas ($2.80) for a pitcher of beer or sangría. Open winter, daily 8am to 10pm; summer, daily 8am to 2am.

La Bodega. San Miguel, 40. ☎ **95/238-73-37.**

La Bodega relies on its colorful clientele and the quality of its tapas to draw customers, who seem to seek this place out above the dozens of other *tascas* within this popular tourist zone. You'll be fortunate to find space at one of the small tables, since many clients consider the bar food plentiful enough for a satisfying lunch or dinner. Once you begin to order one of the platters of fried squid, pungent tuna, grilled shrimp, or tiny brochettes of sole, you might not be able to stop. Most tapas cost 200 to 750 pesetas ($1.60–$6). A beer costs 150 pesetas ($1.20); a hard drink from 400 pesetas ($3.20). Open daily from 11:30am to midnight.

A DANCE CLUB

El Palladium. Palma de Mallorca. ☎ **95/238-42-89.** Cover 900 ptas. ($7.20), including one drink after 10pm.

Located in the town center, this well-designed nightclub is one of the most convivial in Torremolinos. Strobes, spotlights, and a sound system described as loud and distortion free set the scene. There's even a swimming pool. Expect to pay from 350 pesetas ($2.80) for a drink. Open nightly from 11pm to 6am.

THE GAY LIFE

Torremolinos has the largest cluster of gay life along the coast of southern Spain. Several bars huddle together in Pueblo Blanco, which is like a little village of its own. Although much gay and lesbian life also sprawls across La Nogalera, the restaurants there tend to attract a mixed crowd.

Men's Bar. La Nogalera, 714. ☎ **95/238-42-05.**

One of the most popular gay bars in La Nogalera is called simply "Men's Bar." Crowded most nights, it charges 300 pesetas ($2.40) for beer and stays open nightly from 10pm to 5am.

Tamora. Edificio Centro Jardín. ☎ **95/238-73-60.**

This is the leading gay disco in town. A beer goes for 350 pesetas ($2.80). Open nightly from 11pm until the last customer calls it an evening.

A Casino

Casino Torrequebrada. Carretera de Cádiz, Benalmádena-Costa. ☎ **95/244-25-45.** Admission to casino, 600 ptas. ($4.80); cabaret/nightclub, 3,800 ptas. ($30.40), which includes two drinks, both shows, and casino admission.

One of the major casinos along the Costa del Sol, this establishment is located on the lobby level of the Hotel Torrequebrada. The Torrequebrada combines a nightclub/cabaret, a restaurant, and an variety of tables devoted to blackjack, chemin de fer, punto y banco, and two kinds of roulette.

The nightclub offers a flamenco show year-round, presented at 11pm on Thursday, Friday, and Saturday nights; in midsummer, there might be more glitz and more frequent shows (ask when you get there or call). The casino is open daily from 8am to 4am. Nightclub acts begin at 10:30pm (Spanish revue) and 11:30pm (Las Vegas revue). The restaurant is open nightly from 8:30pm to 11pm.

10 Málaga

340 miles (547km) S of Madrid, 82 miles (132km) E of Algeciras

Málaga is a bustling commercial and residential center whose economy does not depend exclusively on tourism. Its chief attraction is the mild off-season climate—summer can be sticky.

Málaga's most famous citizen was Pablo Picasso, born here in 1881 at Plaza de la Merced, in the center of the city. The co-founder of cubism, who would one day paint his *Guernica* to express his horror of war, unfortunately left little of his spirit in his birthplace and only a small selection of his work.

ESSENTIALS

GETTING THERE **By Plane** None of the several airlines that fly into Spain from North America touches down in Málaga. Transfers are required in either Madrid or Barcelona, although some airlines (such as British Airways) offer nonstop flights to Málaga from other European cities, such as London.

For passengers who opt for a transfer through Madrid, the largest operator, with the greatest number of connections, is **Iberia,** the national airline of Spain. Iberia offers daily nonstop service to Madrid from New York, Miami, Los Angeles, Montreal, and Toronto, as well as nonstop service to Barcelona from New York three times per week.

Iberia offers an even greater selection of itineraries into Málaga through its affiliate airlines, which include **Binter, Viva,** and **Aviaco.** Flights on any of these airlines can be booked via Iberia's reservations line: **800/772-4642** in the U.S.

By Train Málaga maintains good rail connections with Madrid (at least five trains a day). The trip takes around four hours. Many visitors arrive by train after having explored the Andalusian city of Seville. There are three trains a day connecting Seville with Málaga, a three-hour run. For ticket prices and rail information in Málaga, call RENFE at **95/221-31-22.**

By Bus Buses from all over Spain arrive at the terminal on the Paseo de los Tilos, behind the RENFE offices. Málaga is linked by bus to all the major cities of Spain, including Madrid (seven buses per day), Barcelona (four per day), and Valencia (four per day). From Madrid, the trip is 7 hours; from Barcelona, it's 17 hours; and from Valencia, it's 12 hours. Call **95/235-00-61** in Málaga for bus information.

By Car From the resorts in the west (such as Torremolinos or Marbella), head east along the N-340/E-15 to Málaga. If you're in the east at the end of the Costa del Sol

(Almería), take the N-340E-15 west to Málaga, with a recommended stopover at Nerja.

VISITOR INFORMATION The tourist information office is at Pasaje de Chinitas, 4 (☎ **95/221-34-45**). Open Monday through Friday from 9am to 1pm.

Warning: Málaga has one of the highest crime rates in Spain. The most common complaint is purse-snatching, with an estimated 75% of the crimes committed by juveniles. Stolen passports are also a problem—if it happens to you, contact the U.S. Consulate located in El Centro Commercial Las Rampas, 1st floor, in nearby Fuengirola (☎ **95/247-48-91**), open Monday through Friday from 10am to 1pm.

SPECIAL EVENTS The most festive time in Málaga is the first week in August, when the city celebrates its reconquest by Ferdinand and Isabella in 1487. This big **feria** (fair) is the occasion for parades and bullfights. A major tree-shaded boulevard of the city, **Paseo del Parque,** is transformed into a fairground featuring amusements and restaurants.

EXPLORING THE CITY

Unlike the rest of the Costa del Sol, Málaga has several historical sites of interest to the average visitor.

Alcazaba. Plaza de la Aduana, Alcazabilla. ☎ **95/221-60-05.** Admission to museum, 30 ptas. (25¢). Museum: Apr–Sept, Tues–Fri 9:30am–1:30pm and 5–8pm, Sat 10am–1pm, Sun 10am–2pm; winter, Tues–Fri 9:30am–1:30pm and 4–7pm, Sat 10am–1pm, Sun 10am–2pm. Bus: 4, 18, 19, or 24.

The remains of this ancient Moorish palace are within easy walking distance of the city center, off Paseo del Parque (plenty of signs point the way up the hill). The fortress was erected in the 9th or 10th century, although there have been later additions and reconstructions. Ferdinand and Isabella stayed here when they reconquered the city. The Alcazaba now houses an archaeological museum, with exhibits of cultures ranging from Greek to Phoenician to Carthaginian. With government-planted orange trees and purple bougainvillea making the grounds even more beautiful, the view overlooking the city and the bay is among the best on the Costa del Sol.

Málaga Cathedral. Plaza Obispo. ☎ **95/221-59-17.** Admission 200 ptas. ($1.60). Mon–Sat 10am–12:45pm and 4–6:30pm. Closed holidays. Bus: 14, 18, 19, or 24.

This 16th-century Renaissance cathedral in Málaga's center, built on the site of a great mosque, suffered damage during the Civil War. But it remains vast and impressive, reflecting changing styles of interior architecture. Its most notable attributes are the richly ornamented choir stalls by Ortiz, Mena, and Michael. The cathedral has been declared a national monument.

Castillo de Gibralfaro. Cerro de Gibralfaro. Free admission. Daylight hours. Microbus: H, leaving hourly from cathedral.

On a hill overlooking Málaga and the Mediterranean are the ruins of an ancient Moorish castle-fortress of unknown origin. It is near the government-run parador and might easily be tied in with a luncheon visit.

Warning: Do not walk to Gibralfaro Castle from town. Readers have reported muggings along the way, and the area around the castle is dangerous. Take the bus from the cathedral (see above).

Museo de Bellas Artes. San Agustín, 8. ☎ **95/221-83-82.** Admission 250 ptas. ($2). Tues–Fri 10am–1:30pm and 5–8pm, Sat–Sun 10:30am–1:30pm. Bus: 4, 18, 19, or 24.

Behind the cathedral, this former Moorish palace houses a modest collection of paintings, including a gallery devoted to native son Pablo Picasso. In addition, it also displays works by Murillo, Ribera, and Morales, along with Andalusian antiques, mosaics, and sculptures.

WHERE TO STAY

For such a large city in a resort area, Málaga has a surprising lack of hotels. The best ones in all price ranges are documented below. *Note:* Book well in advance for all the paradors.

EXPENSIVE

Málaga Palacio. Cortina del Muelle, 1, 29015 Málaga. ☎ **95/221-51-85.** Fax 95/221-51-85. 207 rms, 16 suites. A/C MINIBAR TV TEL. 18,000 ptas. ($144) double; 25,500 ptas. ($204) suite. AE, DC, MC, V. Parking 1,000 ptas. ($8) nearby. Bus: 4, 18, 19, or 24.

The leading hotel in the town center, the Palacio opens directly onto a tree-lined esplanade near the cathedral and the harbor. The 1960s building was constructed flatiron style; it rises 15 stories and is crowned by an open-air swimming pool and refreshment bar. Most of the balconies open onto views of the port, and down below you can see turn-of-the-century carriages pulled by horses. The bedrooms are traditionally furnished and have private baths. The street-floor lounges mix antiques with more modern furnishings. Other facilities include hairdressers for both men and women, a cafeteria, and boutiques.

Parador de Málaga-Gibralfaro. Monte Gibralfaro, 29016 Málaga. ☎ **95/222-19-02.** Fax 95/222-19-04. 38 rms. A/C MINIBAR TV TEL. 15,000–24,000 ptas. ($120–$192) double. AE, DC, MC, V. Free parking. Take the coastal road, Paseo de Reding, which becomes first Avenida Casa de Pries and then Paseo de Sancha. Turn left onto Camino Nuevo and follow the small signs the rest of the way.

Restored in 1994, this is one of Spain's oldest, more tradition-laden paradors. It enjoys a scenic location high on a plateau near an old fortified castle, overlooking the city and the Mediterranean, with views of the bullring, mountains, and beaches. Originally a famous restaurant, the parador has been converted into a fine hotel with two dining rooms. The bedrooms, with their own entranceways, have private baths, living-room areas, and wide glass doors opening onto private sun terraces. The rooms are tastefully decorated with modern furnishings and reproductions of Spanish antiques.

Tryp Guadalmar. Urbanización Guadalmar, Carrertera de Cádiz, km 238, 29080 Málaga. ☎ **95/223-17-03.** Fax 95/224-0385. 190 rms, 10 suites. A/C MINIBAR TV TEL. 11,500–16,000 ptas. ($92–$128) double; 21,750–26,250 ptas. ($174–$210) suite. Rates include breakfast; children under 12 free in parents' room. AE, MC, V. Free parking.

Drenched in sunlight, and set across from a private beach two miles (3km) west of the center of Málaga, this nine-story modern hotel benefited in 1996 from a radical renovation and a takeover by the well-respected Tryp chain. Accommodations are spacious, airy, and simply furnished with chairs and tables appropriate to a beach resort, and each has a private sea-view balcony. You're likely to get heavy doses of families with children at this hotel, and there is a certain anonymity from a staff struggling with morale and too-constant exposure to the comings and goings of large numbers of vacationers. Despite that, there are advantages to staying here, including access to cribs, babysitters, and a playground for children. The in-house restaurant, La Bodega, opens onto a view of the sea and is outfitted with rustic accessories and simple furnishings. For dancing, head for La Corrida, the hotel's bar, which features live music.

Moderate

Hotel Los Naranjos. Paseo de Sancha, 35, 29016 Málaga. ☎ **95/222-43-19.** Fax 95/222-59-75. 41 rms, 1 suite. A/C MINIBAR TV TEL. 14,800 ptas. ($118.40) double; 19,900 ptas. ($159.20) suite. AE, DC, MC, V. Parking 1,276 ptas. ($10.20). Bus: 11.

Hotel Los Naranjos is one of the more reasonably priced (and safer) choices in the city. Serving breakfast only (which costs extra), this is a well-run and well-maintained hotel lying one mile from the heart of town on the eastern side of Málaga, past the Plaza de Torres (bullring). It is near the best beach in Málaga, the Baños del Carmen. The hotel offers guest rooms in contemporary styling, with private baths or showers. The public rooms are decorated in the typical Andalusian style, with colorful tiles and ornate wood carving.

Parador Nacional del Golf. Carretera de Málaga, Apartado 324, 29080 Torremolinos, Málaga. ☎ **95/238-12-55.** Fax 95/238-09-63. 60 rms. A/C MINIBAR TV TEL. 12,000–15,000 ptas. ($96–$120) double. AE, DC, MC, V. Parking 2,400 ptas. ($19.20).

A tasteful resort hotel created by the Spanish government, this hacienda-style parador is flanked by a golf course on one side and the Mediterranean on another. It's less than 2 miles (3.2km) from the airport, $6^1/_2$ miles (10.5km) from Málaga, and $2^1/_2$ miles (4km) from Torremolinos. Each bedroom has a private bath and a private balcony with a view of the golfing greens, the circular swimming pool, or the water. Some guest rooms are equipped with Jacuzzis. The furnishings are attractive. Long tile corridors lead to the air-conditioned public rooms: graciously furnished lounges, a bar, and a restaurant.

Inexpensive

$ El Cenachero. Barroso, 5, 29001 Málaga. ☎ **95/222-40-88.** 14 rms. 4,000–4,600 ptas. ($32–$36.80) double with shower; 5,000 ptas. ($40) double with bath. No credit cards. Bus: 15.

Opened in 1969, this modest little hotel is five blocks from the park (near the harbor). All the nicely carpeted but very simply and functionally furnished guest rooms are different; half have showers, the rest baths. Everything is kept clean. No meals are served.

Hostal Residencia Carlos V. Cister, 6, 29015 Málaga. ☎ **95/221-51-20.** Fax 95/221-51-29. 50 rms. TEL. 5,900–6,741 ptas. ($47.20–$53.95) double. AE, DC, MC, V. Parking 1,250 ptas. ($10). Bus: 15 from the rail station.

This hotel has a good central location near the cathedral, as well as an interesting facade decorated with wrought-iron balconies and *miradores.* The lobby is fairly dark, but this remains an old, safe haven. An elevator will take you to your room, furnished in a no-frills style, but clean and well maintained.

$ Hostal Residencia Derby. San Juan de Díos, 1, 29015 Málaga. ☎ **95/222-13-01.** 16 rms (8 with bath or shower). TEL. 3,600 ptas. ($28.80) double without bath or shower; 3,800 ptas. ($30.40) double with shower; 4,000 ptas. ($32) double with bath. No credit cards. Bus: 15.

The Derby is a real find. This fourth-floor boarding house is right in the heart of Málaga, on a main square directly north of the train station. Some of the rather basic rooms have excellent views of the Mediterranean and the port of Málaga. The hostal is quite clean. No breakfast is served.

A Luxurious Place to Stay Nearby

✪ La Bobadilla. Finca La Bobadilla, 18300 Loja (Granada), Apartado 53. ☎ **958/32-18-61.** Fax 958/32-18-10. 50 rms, 10 suites. A/C MINIBAR TV TEL. 30,600–34,800 ptas. ($244.80–$278.40) double; from 43,800 ptas. ($350.40) suite. Rates include breakfast. AE, DC, MC, V.

Free parking. From the airport at Málaga, follow the signs toward Granada, but at km 178 continue through the village of Salinas. Take the road marked Salinas/Rute but after two miles (3km) follow the signposts for the hotel to the entrance.

Located an hour's drive northeast of Málaga, La Bobadilla is the most luxurious retreat in the south of Spain. It is a secluded oasis in the foothills of the Sierra Nevada near the town of Loja, which is 44 miles (71km) north of Málaga. La Bobadilla is a 13-mile (21km) drive from Loja.

The hotel complex is built like an Andalusian village, a cluster of whitewashed *casas* constructed around a tower and a white church. Every *casa* is rented to guests, complete with a roof terrace and a balcony overlooking the olive-grove–studded district. Each accommodation is individually designed, from the least expensive doubles to the most expensive King's Suite, the latter with plenty of room for bodyguards. The hotel rents its sumptuous bedrooms to a pampered coterie of international guests. The service here is perhaps the finest in all of Spain.

The hotel village stands on a hillside, on 1,750 acres of private, unspoiled grounds. If you get bored in this lap of luxury, you can always drive to Granada, only an hour away. Should you decide to marry your companion at this resort, you'll find a chapel featuring an organ 30 feet high with 1,595 pipes.

Dining/Entertainment: Even the King of Spain has dined at La Finca, which serves both a Spanish national and an international cuisine. El Cortijo, on the other hand, specializes in a regional cuisine. Concerts, featuring flamenco, are presented on Friday and Saturday nights.

Services: Laundry/valet, 24-hour room service, massage, babysitting.

Facilities: Two tennis courts, horseback riding, archery, outdoor swimming pool, heated indoor swimming pool, Jacuzzis, Finnish sauna, Turkish steam bath, fitness club, bicycles, and beauty salon.

WHERE TO DINE

EXPENSIVE

Café de Paris. Vélez Málaga, 8. ☎ **95/222-50-43.** Reservations required. Main courses 1,800–2,500 ptas. ($14.40–$20); *menú del día* 2,500 ptas. ($20). AE, DC, MC, V. Mon–Sat 1–4pm and 8:30pm–midnight. Closed July 1–15. Bus: 13. FRENCH/SPANISH.

Café de Paris—the best restaurant on Málaga—is in La Malagueta, the district surrounding the Plaza de Toros (bullring) of Málaga. This is the domain of the proprietor and chef de cuisine, José García Cortés, who worked at many important dining rooms before carving out his own niche. Some critics have suggested that the chef's cuisine is pitched too high for the taste of the average Malagueño, at least too high for the pocketbook—particularly the caviar, game (including partridge), and foie gras.

Much of Cortés's cuisine has been adapted from classic French dishes to please the Andalusian palate. Menus are changed frequently, reflecting both the chef's imagination and the availability of produce in the Málaga markets. You might on any given night be served crêpes gratinée (filled with baby eels) or local white fish baked in salt (it doesn't sound good but is excellent). Meat Stroganoff is made here not with the usual cuts of beef but with ox meat. Save room for the creative desserts, such as a citrus-flavored sorbet made with champagne or the custard apple mousse.

MODERATE

El Chinitas. Moreno Monroy, 4. ☎ **95/221-09-72.** Main courses 1,750–2,300 ptas. ($14–$18.40). AE, DC, MC, V. Daily 1–4pm and 8pm–midnight. SPANISH.

Set in the heart of Málaga, a short walk from the tourist office, this is one of the most entrenched restaurants in town. Many of its regular patrons follow a ritual, consuming a round of tapas and drinks at the associated **Bar Orellana** next door (which maintains the same hours without the midafternoon closing) and then heading to Chinitas for a meal. The place is often filled with local residents, which is a good sign. The menu changes but might on any given night include a mixed fish fry, grilled red mullet, shrimp cocktail, grilled sirloin, or shellfish soup. The service is both fast and attentive.

Parador de Málaga-Gibralfaro. Monte Gibralfaro. ☎ **95/222-19-02.** Main courses 1,800–2,200 ptas. ($14.40–$17.60); fixed-price menu 3,500 ptas. ($28). AE, DC, MC, V. Daily 1–4pm and 8:30–11pm. Microbus: H, by the cathedral. SPANISH/INTERNATIONAL.

This government-owned restaurant sits on a mountainside high above the city and is notable especially for its view. You can look down into the heart of the Málaga bullring, among other sights. Meals are served in the attractive dining room or under the arches of two wide terraces, which provide views of the coast. Featured are hors d'oeuvres parador—your entire table literally covered with tiny dishes of tasty tidbits. Two other specialties are an omelet of chanquetes, tiny whitefish popular in this part of the country, and chicken Villaroi.

Parador Nacional del Golf. Carretta de Málaga, Apartado 324, Málaga. ☎ **95/238-12-55.** Main courses 1,800–2,000 ptas. ($14.40–$16); fixed-price menus 1,800–3,500 ptas. ($14.40–$28). AE, DC, MC, V. Daily 1:30–4pm and 8:30–11pm. SPANISH.

This government-owned restaurant has an indoor/outdoor dining room that opens onto a circular swimming pool, golf course, and private beach. The interior dining room, furnished with reproductions of antiques, has a refined country-club atmosphere. Before-lunch drinks at the sleek modern bar tempt golfers, among others, who then proceed to the covered terrace for their Spanish meals.

Refectorium. Calle Cervantes, 8. ☎ **95/221-89-90.** Reservations recommended on weekends and at all bullfights. Main courses 1,500–2,200 ptas. ($12–$17.60). AE, V. Daily 1–4pm and 9pm–2am. SPANISH.

Located behind the bullfighting ring of Málaga, this place becomes hectic during any bullfight, filling up with aficionados and, after the fight, often with the matadors themselves. But it can be visited at any time, especially when the pace here is less frantic. The cuisine has an old-fashioned flair, and the servings are generous. The typical soup of the Málaga area is *ajoblanco con uvas* (cold almond soup flavored with garlic and garnished with big muscatel grapes). For a classic opener, try a plate of garlic-flavored mushrooms seasoned with bits of ham. The fresh seafood is a delight, including *rape* (monkfish) and angler fish; lamb might be served with a saffron-flavored tomato sauce. Desserts are "like mama made," including rice pudding.

INEXPENSIVE

$ La Manchega. Marín García, 4. ☎ **95/222-21-80.** Main courses 650–1,300 ptas. ($5.20–$10.40); fixed-price menu 1,150 ptas. ($9.20). No credit cards. Daily 11am–midnight. Bus: 7 or 9. SPANISH.

This restaurant has thrived as a crowded and popular tavern since 1954. Set within a building from the 1920s on a popular pedestrian-only street in Málaga's downtown commercial zone, it offers sidewalk tables, a ground-floor bar with tile walls, and a decorator's attempt to create an indoor Andalusian courtyard. A *salon comedor* offers additional space for dining on an upper floor. Menu items include a peppery version of fish soup, shrimp omelets, Málaga-style soup, beans with Serrano ham, snails, eels, and a full selection of fish, including grilled shrimp, hake, monkfish, clams, and mussels.

✪ Parador Nacional de Nerja. Calle Almuñecar, 8, Playa de Burriana-Tablazo, 29780 Nerja. ☎ **95/252-00-50.** Fax 95/252-19-97. 73 rms. A/C MINIBAR TV TEL. 14,000–16,550 ptas. ($112–$132.40) double. AE, DC, MC, V. Free parking.

This government-owned hotel located on the outskirts of town, a five-minute walk from the center of town, takes the best of modern motel designs and blends them with a classic Spanish ambience of beamed ceilings, tile floors, and hand-loomed draperies. It's built on the edge of a cliff, around a flower-filled courtyard with a splashing fountain, and its social life centers around the large swimming pool and tennis courts. There is a sandy beach below, reached by an elevator, plus lawns and gardens. The bedrooms are spacious and furnished in an understated but tasteful style, each with a private bath. International and Spanish meals are served in the hotel restaurant.

MODERATE

Hotel Balcón de Europa. Paseo Balcón de Europa, 1,29780 Nerja. ☎ **95/252-08-00.** Fax 95/252-44-90. 85 rms, 20 suites. A/C TV TEL. 9,750–13,700 ptas. ($78–$109.60) double; 13,150–21,500 ptas. ($105.20–$172) suite. AE, DC, MC, V. Parking 750 ptas. ($6).

Occupying the best position in town at the edge of the Balcón de Europa, this 1970s hotel offers guest rooms with private balconies overlooking the water and the rocks. At a private beach nearby, parasol-shielded tables offer a place for a peaceful vista. The comfortable bedrooms are decorated with modern furniture and marble floors. There's a private garage a few steps away.

Guests can dine at the fourth-floor restaurant Azul, which offers a panoramic view, or at the beach restaurant, Nautico. An international menu is served. The Nautico is open only for lunch in winter but for both lunch and dinner in summer. The facilities include a sauna, health club, and solarium; the services include babysitting, laundry, and room service.

INEXPENSIVE

Cala-Bela. Puerta del Mar, 8, 29780 Nerja. ☎ **95/252-07-00.** Fax 95/252-07-04. 10 rms. TEL. 3,750–5,000 ptas. ($30–$40) double. AE, DC, MC, V.

Originally built as a private house in 1895, but much modernized since then, this well-positioned hotel lies only a one-minute walk from the Balcón de Europa. It offers bedrooms opening onto the sea. They may be small, but they're clean—and what a view! The lounge is charming. In the seafront dining room the food is good, so even if you're not staying at the hotel, you may want to give the restaurant a try. Enjoy the filet of pork in sherry sauce, the chef's paella, grilled crayfish, or trout with cream.

$ Hostal Mena. Alemania, 15, 29780 Nerja. ☎ **95/252-05-41.** 14 rms (8 with bath). TV. 2,500 ptas. ($20) double without bath; 4,000 ptas. ($32) double with bath. No credit cards.

This century-old little residencia near the Balcón de Europa serves no meals, but there's a lot of charm about the place, including the central hallway, whose back walls are lined with hundreds of blue and white Andalusian tiles. The family running the hostal is very helpful. The bedrooms are plain and functional but clean.

Hostal Miguel. Almirante Ferrándiz, 31, 29780 Nerja. ☎ **95/252-15-23.** Fax 95/252-34- 9 rms. 3,500 ptas. ($28) double. MC, V.

The Miguel is a pleasant, unpretentious inn that contains only nine simply furr rooms. They're housed in a 19th-century building with iron-rimmed balconie ated on a quiet back street about a three-minute walk from the Balcón de and across from the well-known Pepe Rico Restaurant. Breakfast is the o served.

WHERE TO DINE

Casa Luque. Plaza Cavana, 2. ☎ **95/252-10-04.** Reservations required. Main courses 1,200–1,900 ptas. ($9.60–$15.20); *menú degustación* 2,450 ptas. ($19.60). AE, DC, MC, V. Daily 1–4pm and 7:30pm–11:30pm. ANDALUSIAN.

With its impressive canopied and balconied facade, the Casa Luque looks like a dignified private villa, lying near the heart of town. The interior has an Andalusian courtyard, and in summer there is a sea-view terrace. Dishes are tasty and the helpings are quite filling—good value here. Meals might include Andalusian gazpacho, shoulder of ham, osso buco (braised veal shank), pork filet, hot-pepper chicken Casanova, grilled meats, or a limited selection of fish, including grilled Mediterranean grouper.

El Colono. Granada, 6. ☎ **95/252-18-26.** Reservations required. Wed and Fri, flamenco shows with fixed-price menus 2,295–2,995 ptas. ($18.35–$23.95); other nights, fixed-price lunch and dinner 1,250 ptas. ($10). No credit cards. Tues–Sun 8pm–midnight. Closed Nov 15–Dec 20. ANDALUSIAN/FRENCH.

A family place for a night of Spanish fun—that's El Colono, near the Balcón de Europa, a three-minute walk from the main bus stop at Nerja. Guitar music and flamenco dancing account for the entertainment highlights, and you can also dine here in a tavern atmosphere, enjoying set menus featuring local specialties. If you just want a glass of wine, you can still enjoy the shows (three per evening, from 8pm until "the wee hours").

Pepe Rico Restaurant. Almirante Ferrándiz, 28. ☎ **95/252-02-47.** Reservations recommended. Main courses 1,300–2,100 ptas. ($10.40–$16.80); fixed-price menu 2,800 ptas. ($22.40). DC, MC, V. Wed–Mon 12:30–3pm and 7–11pm. Closed Dec 1–15 and Jan 15–Feb 15. INTERNATIONAL.

Established in 1966, Pepe Rico is today one of the finest places for food in Nerja. It's housed in a white building with grille windows and little balconies. The rooms open onto a large rear balcony overlooking a flower-filled courtyard. Dining is in a tavern room, half wood paneled, with handmade wooden chairs, plaster walls, and ivy vines—the vines creep in from the patio, where you can order meals alfresco.

The specialty of the day, which might be a Spanish, German, Swedish, or French dish, ranges from almond-and-garlic soup to duck in Málaga wine. The list of hors d'oeuvres is impressive—including Pepe Rico salad, smoked swordfish, salmon mousse, and prawns pil-pil (with hot chile peppers). Main dishes include filet of sole Don Pepe, roast leg of lamb, prawns Café de Paris, and steak dishes. Considering the quality of the food, the prices are reasonable.

Restaurante de Miguel. Pintada, 2. ☎ **95/252-29-96.** Reservations recommended. Main courses 1,400–1,800 ptas. ($11.20–$14.40). MC, V. Daily 8pm–midnight. Closed Feb and two Mondays each month. INTERNATIONAL.

This restaurant, the best in town, was established in 1986 by the son of a Nerja resident. At first it was patronized only by local families hoping for their friend to succeed. Since then, however, mostly because of the excellent food, the place has attracted a devoted coterie of foreign visitors and expatriate residents of the Costa del Sol. It sits in the center of town near the busiest traffic intersection, behind a plate-lass aquarium loaded with fresh lobsters, fish, and shellfish. Its not-very-large r-conditioned interior is one of the most decidedly upscale places in Nerja, with ite marble floors, elegant crystal and porcelain, and crisply ironed white napery. menu lists a full array of well-prepared international dishes, including cream-of-p soup flavored with cognac, tournedos with a sauce made from goat cheese, s with Pernod and fennel, a wide selection of beef and steak dishes, and con-s composed from the cornucopia of fish from the aquarium.

$ **Restaurante Rey Alfonso.** Paseo Balcón de Europa, s/n. ☎ **95/252-09-58.** Reservations recommended. Main courses 750–1,900 ptas. ($6–$15.20); fixed-price menu 1,000 ptas. ($8). MC, V. Thurs–Tues 11am–4pm and 7–11pm. Closed Nov. SPANISH/INTERNATIONAL.

Few visitors to the Balcón de Europa realize that they're standing directly above one of the most unusual restaurants in town. You enter from the bottom of a flight of stairs that skirts the rocky base of what was originally designed in the late 19th century as a *miradore* (viewing station), which juts seaward as an extension of the town's main square. The restaurant's menu and interior decor don't hold many surprises, but the close-up view of the crashing waves makes dining here worthwhile. Have a drink at the bar if you don't want a full meal. Specialties include a well-prepared *paella valenciana,* Cuban-style rice, five different preparations of sole (from grilled to meunière), several versions of tournedos and entrecôte, beef Stroganoff, *fondue bourguignonne,* crayfish in whiskey sauce, and crêpe Suzette for dessert.

11

Valencia & the Costa Blanca

The third-largest city of Spain, Valencia, celebrated for oranges and paella, lies in the midst of a *huerta*—a fertile crescent of an alluvial plain that's irrigated by a system built centuries ago. As such, the area is a bread basket of Spain, a place where "the soil never sleeps."

For such a major city, Valencia is relatively unexplored by foreigners, but it provides an offbeat adventure for those who decide to seek out its treasures. The town has a wealth of baroque architecture, fine museums, good cuisine, and a proud but troubled history.

The Costa Blanca (White Coast) begins rather unappealingly at Valencia but improves considerably as it winds its way south toward Alicante. The overbuilt route is dotted with fishing ports and resorts known chiefly to Spanish and other European vacationers. The success of Benidorm, fitting for a long stay, began in the 1960s, when this fishing village was transformed into an international resort. Alicante, the official capital of the Costa Blanca, enjoys a reputation as a winter resort because of its mild climate. Murcia is inland, but it's on the main road to the Costa del Sol, so hordes of motorists pass through it.

EXPLORING THE REGION BY CAR

Day 1 Begin in Valencia, exploring its ancient monuments, such as the Catedral, which claims to possess the Holy Grail, and the Palacio de la Generalidid, a 16th-century edifice that now serves as headquarters for the regional government.

Day 2 Still based in Valencia, branch out on a day trip. Head north on the A-7 (also called E-15) to the old Roman ruins (ca. A.D. 2) at Sagunto or south to the rice paddies of La Albufera.

Day 3 Head south along the coast on the N-332 for an overnight stop in Benidorm, the once tiny fishing village whose 3½-mile beach coast has made it a popular tourist destination.

Day 4 Continuing on the N-332, make the short drive south to Alicante, where you can explore its monuments, including the stately Castillo de Santa Bárbara. Called Arka Leuka (White Peak) by the Greeks, it was originally erected as a fortification by the Carthaginians in 400 B.C. and provides panoramic views of Alicante.

Day 5 While in Alicante, the capital of the Costa Blanca, spend the day exploring the palm groves and the *huerta* around Elche.

Costa Blanca

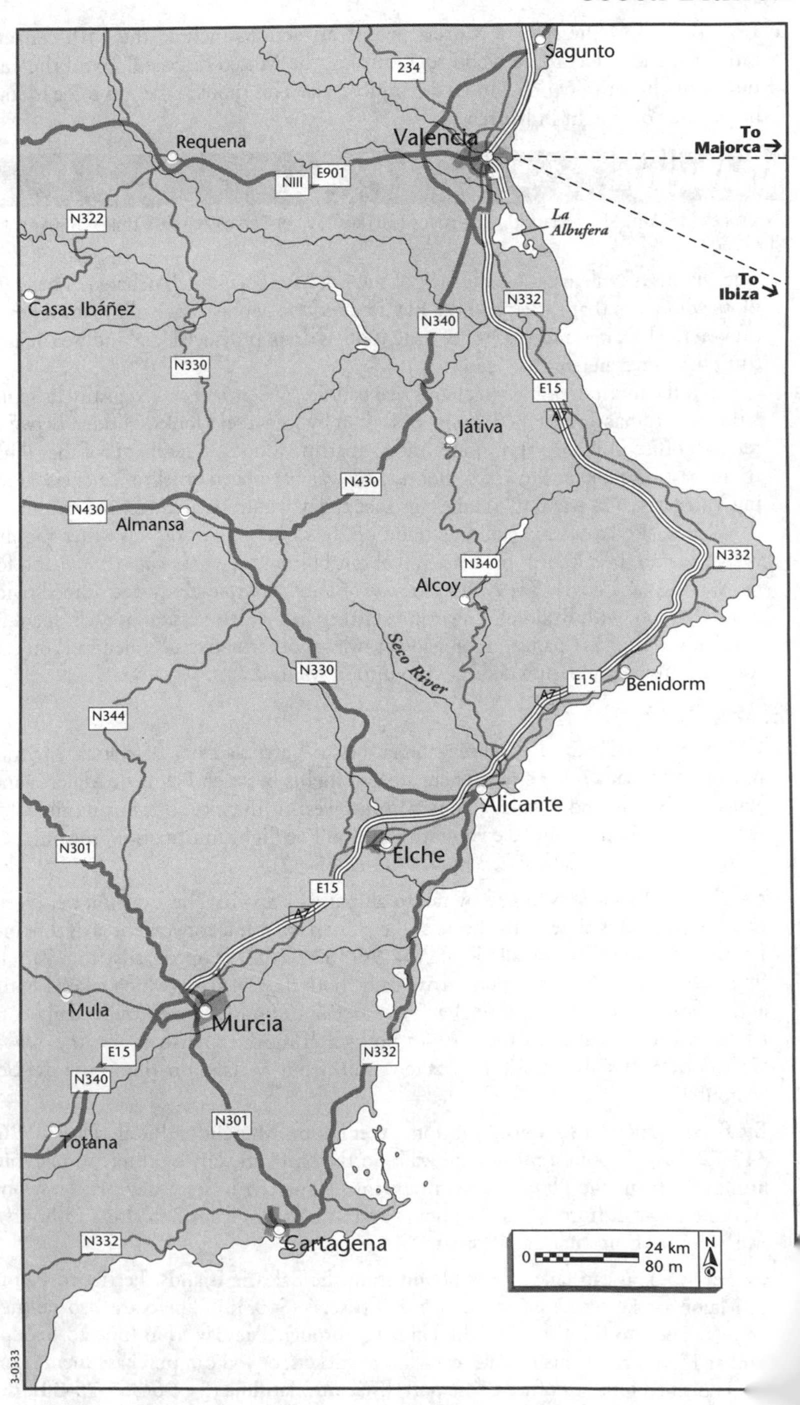

Day 6 Follow the A-7 to Murcia, whose attractions include the 14th-century cathedral, the polychrome wood sculptures of the Museo de Salzillo, and the culturally and historically rich Museo de Arqueología. This should take you three to four hours. Stay overnight in Murcia.

1 Valencia

218 miles (351km) SE of Madrid, 224 miles (361km) SW of Barcelona, 404 miles (650km) NE of Málaga.

The charms of Valencia—or the lack of them—have been much debated. There are those who claim that the city where El Cid faced the Moors is one of the most beautiful on the Mediterranean. Others write it off as drab, provincial, and industrial. The truth lies somewhere in between.

Set in the midst of orange trees and rice paddies, Valencia seems to justify its reputation as a romantic city more by its past than by its present looks. Hidden between modern office buildings and monotonous apartment houses, remnants of that illustrious past do remain. However, floods and war have been cruel to Valencia, forcing Valencianos to tear down buildings that today would be architectural treasures.

Valencia also has a strong cultural tradition. Its most famous son was writer Vicente Blasco Ibañez, best known for his novel about bullfighting, *Blood and Sand,* and for his World War I novel, *The Four Horsemen of the Apocalypse.* Both were filmed twice in Hollywood, with Rudolph Valentino starring in the first version of each. Joaquín Sorolla, the famous Spanish impressionist, was another native of Valencia. You can see his works at a museum dedicated to him in Madrid.

ESSENTIALS

GETTING THERE **By Plane** Iberia flies to Valencia from Barcelona, Madrid, Málaga, and many other cities. There are also flights between Palma de Majorca and Valencia. You'll land 9 miles (14.5km) southwest of the city, but bus number 15, which leaves hourly, will take you into the city. For flight information, the office of Iberia Airlines is at Calle Paz, 14 (☎ **96/352-75-52**).

By Train Valencia is linked by rail to all parts of Spain. The Estación del Norte (North Station) is close to the heart of the city, making it a convenient arrival point. Its information office at Calle Renfe (☎ **96/352-02-02**) is open daily from 7am to 9pm. Nine trains from Barcelona arrive daily, both the *TALGO* (which takes 4 hours and is faster and more expensive) and the *rápido* (6 hours). Seven trains daily connect Madrid to Valencia, the *TER* (5 hours and more expensive) and the *rápido* (7$^1/_2$ hours). It's also possible to take a train from Málaga on the Costa del Sol (9 hours).

By Bus Valencia's Central Station, Avenida deMénendez Pidal, 15 (☎ **96/349-72-22**), is about a 30-minute walk northwest of the city's center, so take bus number 8 from the Plaza del Ayuntamiento. Thirteen buses a day—at least one every hour—run from Madrid (5 hours away), 10 buses from Barcelona (5 hours), and 30 buses from Málaga (11 hours).

By Ferry You can take a ferry to and from the Balearic Islands. Ferries to Palma le Majorca take six hours and cost 5,040 pesetas ($40.30). There are also sailings om Valencia to Ibiza at midnight Thursday through Tuesday from June 15 to Sepnber 15. Travel agents in Valencia sell these tickets, or you can purchase them from Transmediterránea office at the port, Estación Marítima (☎ **96/367-75-80**), the of your departure. To reach the port, take bus number 4 or 19 from the Plaza untamiento.

Valencia

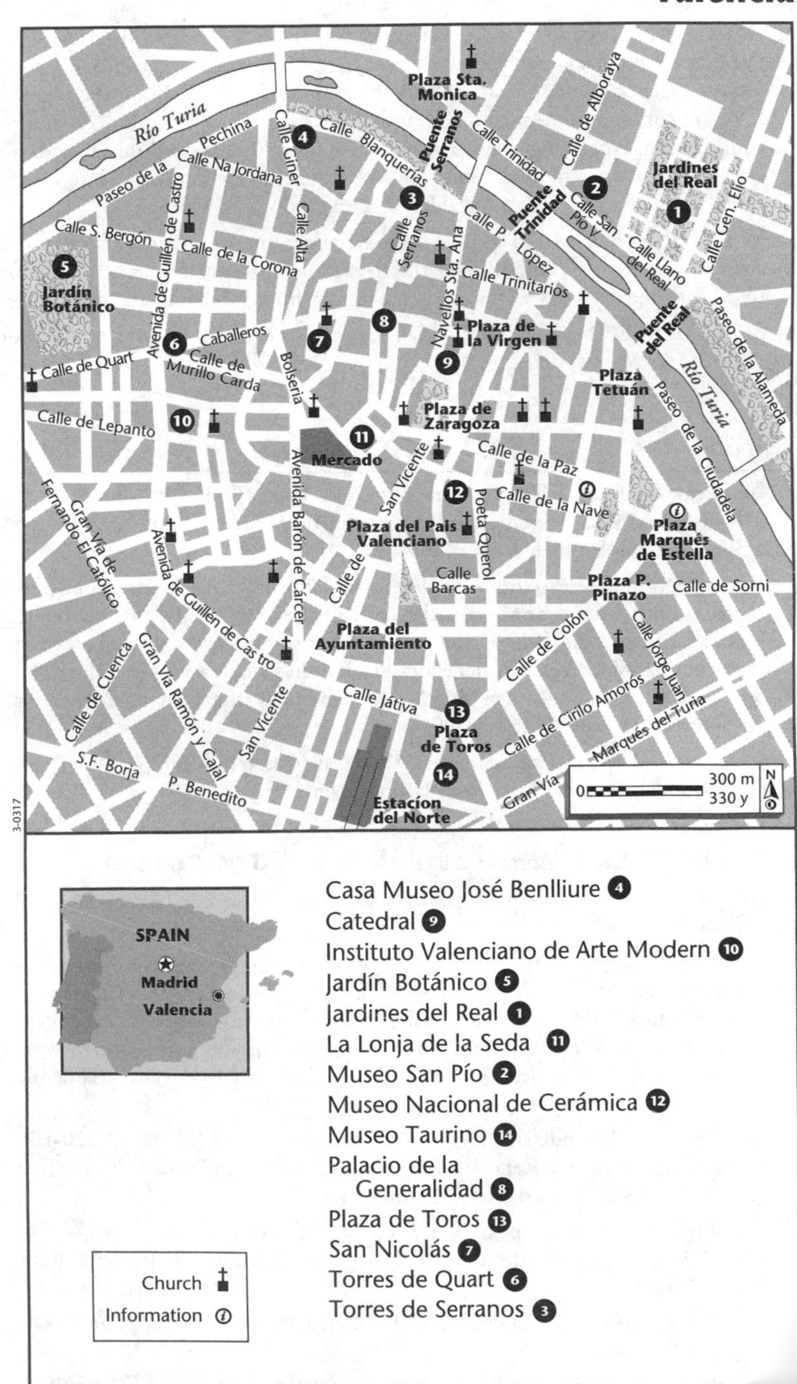

Río Turia
Plaza Sta. Monica
Puente Serranos
Calle Trinidad
Calle de Alboraya
Jardines del Real
Calle Gen. Elío
Puente Trinidad
Calle San Pío V
Calle Llano del Real
Puente del Real
Paseo de la Alameda
Paseo de la Pechina
Calle Na Jordana
Calle Giner
Calle Blanquerías
Calle S. Bergón
Avenida de Guillén de Castro
Calle de la Corona
Calle Alta
Calle Serranos
Calle P. López
Navellos Sta. Ana
Calle Trinitarios
Jardín Botánico
Caballeros
Calle de Quart
Calle de Murillo Carda
Bolsería
Plaza de la Virgen
Plaza Tetuán
Paseo de la Ciudadela
Calle de Lepanto
Plaza de Zaragoza
Mercado
Calle de la Paz
Calle de la Nave
San Vicente
Gran Vía de Fernando El Católico
Avenida Barón de Cárcer
Plaza del Pais Valenciano
Poeta Querol
Plaza Marqués de Estella
Avenida de Guillén de Cas tro
Calle de
Calle Barcas
Plaza P. Pinazo
Calle de Sorni
Plaza del Ayuntamiento
Calle de Colón
Calle Jorge Juan
Calle de Cuenca
Gran Vía Ramón y Cajal
San Vicente
Calle Játiva
Plaza de Toros
Calle de Cirilo Amorós
Marqués del Turia
S.F. Borja
P. Benedito
Estacíon del Norte
Gran Vía
0
300 m
330 y
N
3-0317
SPAIN
Madrid
Valencia
Casa Museo José Benlliure 4
Catedral 9
Instituto Valenciano de Arte Modern 10
Jardín Botánico 5
Jardines del Real 1
La Lonja de la Seda 11
Museo San Pío 2
Museo Nacional de Cerámica 12
Museo Taurino 14
Palacio de la Generalidad 8
Plaza de Toros 13
San Nicolás 7
Torres de Quart 6
Torres de Serranos 3
Church
Information

By Car The easiest route is the express highway (E-15) south from Barcelona. Connections are also made on a national highway, E-901, from Madrid, which lies northwest of Valencia. From Alicante, south of Valencia, take the E-15 express highway. If you're coming from Andalusia, the roads are longer and more difficult and not connected by express highways. You can drive from Málaga north to Granada and cut across southeastern Spain along the 342, which links with the 340 into Murcia. From there, take the road to Alicante for an easy drive into Valencia.

VISITOR INFORMATION The tourist information office is at Plaza del Ayuntamiento, 1 (☎ **96/352-54-78**). Open Monday through Friday from 8:30am to 2:15pm and 4:15 to 6:15pm, and on Saturday from 9:15am to 12:45pm.

SPECIAL EVENT The Fallas of San José is held in Valencia every March, honoring the arrival of spring.

FAST FACTS: Valencia

American Express The local agency is Duna Viajes, Calle Cirilo Amorós, 88 (☎ **96/374-15-62**), open Monday through Friday from 10am to 2pm and 4:30pm to 8pm, Saturday from 9am to 1pm.

Buses Most buses leave from Playa del Ayuntamiento, 22. Tickets can be purchased at any newstand; a one-way ticket costs 80 pesetas (65¢), and a 10-ride booklet sells for 550 pesetas ($4.40). Bus number 8 runs from Playa del Ayuntamiento to the bus station at Avenida Menéndez Pidal. A bus map is available at the EMT office at Calle En Sanz, 4, open Monday through Friday from 8am to 3:30pm. For bus information, call **96/352-83-99**.

Consulate The U.S. Consular Agency is at Calle Paz, 6 (☎ **96/351-69-73**); it's open Monday through Friday from 10am to 1pm.

Emergency Call **091** or **092.**

First Aid Assistance is provided by the Red Cross (☎ **96/360-68-00**).

Hospital Go to the Hospital Clínico Universitario, Avenida BlascoIbañez, 17 (☎ **96/386-26-00**).

Language Don't be surprised if you see signs in a language that's not Spanish—and not Catalán either. It is *valenciano,* a dialect of Catalán. Often you'll be handed a "bilingual" menu that is in Castilian Spanish and in *valenciano.* Of course, many citizens of Valencia are not caught up in this cultural resurgence, viewing the promotion of the dialect tongue as possibly damaging to the city's economic goals.

Laundry The Lavanderia El Mercat, Plaza del Mercado, 12 (☎ **96/391-20-10**), offering a self-service wash and dry, is open Monday through Friday from 10am to 2pm and 4 to 8pm, Saturday from 10am to 2pm.

Post Office The main post office, at Plaza del Ayuntamiento, 24 (☎ **96/351-67-50**), is open Monday through Friday from 8:30am to 9:30pm, Saturday from 9:30am to 2pm.

axis Call **96/370-33-33** or **96/357-13-13.** Taxi companies charge 52 pesetas)¢) per kilometer.

ephone The local telephone office at Plaza del Ayuntamiento, 24 (☎ **96/003**), en Monday through Saturday from 9am to 11pm. Making a long-distance re is much cheaper than making one from your hotel room.

EXPLORING THE CITY

Catedral (Seu). Plaza de la Reina. ☎ **96/391-81-27.** Cathedral, free; Miguelete, 100 ptas. (80¢); Museo de la Catedral, 100 ptas. (80¢). Cathedral, Mon–Sat 10am–1pm and 4:30–8pm; Miguelete, Mon–Sat 10am–12:30pm and 4:30–8pm, Sun 10am–1pm; Museo de la Catedral, Mon–Sat 10am–1pm and 4–6pm. Bus: 9, 27, 70, or 71.

For the past 500 years, the cathedral has claimed to possess the Holy Grail, the chalice used by Christ at the Last Supper. The subject of countless legends, the Grail was said to have been used by Joseph of Arimathea to collect Christ's blood as it fell from the cross. It looms large in Sir Thomas Malory's *Morte d'Arthur,* Tennyson's *Idylls of the King,* and Wagner's *Parsifal.*

Although this 1262 cathedral represents a number of styles, including Romanesque and baroque, Gothic predominates. Its huge arches have been restored, and in back is a handsome domed basilica. It was built on the site of a mosque torn down by the Catholic monarchs.

After seeing the cathedral, you can scale an uncompleted 155-foot-high Gothic tower—known as **Miguelete**—for a panoramic view of the city and the fertile *huerta* beyond, or visit the **Museo de la Catedral,** where works by Goya and Zurbarán are exhibited.

Palacio de la Generalidad. Caballeros, 2. ☎ **96/386-61-00.** Free admission. Mon–Fri 9am–2pm. Bus: 5.

Located in the old aristocratic quarter of Valencia, this Gothic palace, built in the 15th and 16th centuries, is one of the most fascinating edifaces in Spain, with its two square towers (one built as recently as 1952), its carved wooden ceilings and galleries, and its frescoes. It now serves as the headquarters of the regional government (Generalidad) and can be visited only with the permission of the Gabinete del Presidente de la Generalidad (☎ **96/386-34-61** before visiting).

La Lonja de la Seda. Plaza del Mercado. ☎ **96/391-36-08.** Free admission. Tues–Sat 9am–1:30pm, Sun 10am–2pm. Closed holidays. Bus: 4, 7, 27, 60, or 81.

This former silk exchange, completed in 1498, is the most splendid example of secular Gothic architecture in Spain. A beautiful building, La Lonja has twisted spiral columns inside and stained-glass windows.

Museu San Pío (Museu Sant Píus V). San Pío V, 9. ☎ **96/360-57-93.** Free admission. Tues–Sat 10am–2pm and 4–6pm, Sun 10am–2pm. Bus: 1, 6, 8, or 11.

This treasure house of paintings and sculptures, which stands on the north bank of the Turia River, contains a strong collection of Flemish and native Valencian artworks (note particularly those by the 14th- and 15th-century Valencian "primitives"). The most celebrated painting is a 1640 self-portrait by Velázquez, and there is a whole room devoted to Goya. Other artists exhibited include Bosch, Morales, El Greco (*St. John the Baptist*), Ribera, Murillo, Pinturicchio, and Sorolla. Of special interest is a salon displaying the works of contemporary Valencian painters and an important sculpture by Mariano Benlliure. The ground-floor archaeological collection encompasses early Iberian, Roman (including an altar to a pagan Roman emperor), and early Christian finds.

Instituto Valenciano de Arte Modern [Viam]. Calle Guillén Castro, 118. ☎ **96/386-30-00.** Admission 350 ptas. ($2.80) adults, free for children. Julio González Center, Tues–Sun 11am–8pm; Center del Carmen, Tues–Sun noon–3:30pm and 4:30–8:30pm. Bus: 5.

This giant complex, costing millions to build, consists of two sites—an ultramodern building and a 13th-century former convent. Its opening launched Valencia into prime status among the world's art capitals.

The **Julio González Center** is named for an avant-garde Spanish artist whose paintings, sculptures, and drawings form the nucleus of the institute's permanent collection. Much influenced by Picasso, González was a pioneer in iron sculpture.

The other site is the nearby **Center del Carmen,** the old convent, with cloisters from both the 14th and the 16th centuries. It contains three halls devoted to changing exhibitions of contemporary art. Other permanent exhibitions include works of Ignacio Pinazo, whose paintings and drawings mark the beginning of modernism in Valencia.

The institute is located on the western edge of the old quarter, near the Torres de Quart.

BEACHES, BULLFIGHTING & OTHER OUTDOOR ACTIVITIES

BEACHES The beaches lying to the north and south of the port, Playa de la Punta and Playa de Levante, are now too polluted for swimming. If you'd like to go to the beach, head south in the direction of El Saler, where you'll find cleaner waters.

BOATING **Real Club Náutico (Royal Nautical Club),** at Camí del Canal (☎ **96/367-90-11**), has a sailing school renting boats for scuba diving, fishing, and snorkeling. It also maintains a full yacht service facility.

BULLFIGHTING *Corridas* (bullfights) are staged for a week during the *fallas* observances in the spring (see "Spain Calendar of Events" in Chapter 3). Today, locals seem more interested in soccer than in bullfighting. Nevertheless, one of the largest rings in Spain lies adjacent to the rail station at Calle de Xátiva, 28 (☎ **96/351-93-15**).

GOLF There are four major golf courses in the area around Valencia. One of the best is **Golf El Saler** at the Parador Luis Vives (☎ **96/161-11-86**), located 11 miles (18km) south of Valencia in a panoramic setting of pine dunes. Another good course is the **Club de Campo del Bosque,** Carretera Godella, km 4, Chiva (☎ **96/180-41-42**), 2½ miles (4km) from Valencia. Yet another is the **Club de Golf Escorpión** at Bétera (☎ **96/160-12-11**), some 12 miles (19km) northwest en route to Liria. All these are 18-hole courses. There's a 9-hole course, the **Manises Golf Club,** at Manises, 7½ miles (12km) west of Valencia (☎ **96/379-08-50**).

WHERE TO STAY

Normally, Valencia maintains year-round hotel prices, but often in July and August (when Valencia can be uncomfortably hot and humid) some hoteliers will lower prices if business is slow—it never hurts to ask.

EXPENSIVE

Hotel Astoria Palace. Plaza Rodrigo Botet, 5, 46002 Valencia. ☎ **96/352-67-37.** Fax 96/352-80-78. 190 rms, 15 suites. A/C MINIBAR TV TEL. 18,600 ptas. ($148.80) double; 30,000 ptas. ($240) suite. Aug, 11,200 ptas. ($89.60) double; 22,000 ptas. ($176) suite. AE, DC, MC, V. Parking 1,200 ptas. ($9.60) nearby. Bus: 9, 10, 27, 70, or 71.

Located on a small and charming square in the heart of town, five short blocks south of the cathedral, this modern hotel contains some of the best-furnished public and private rooms in Valencia. A favorite of such Spanish stars as opera singer Montserrat Caballé, bullfighter Manuel Benitez ("El Cordobés"), and an impressive roster of writers and politicians, the Astoria is plush, well managed, and appealing. Many of the bedrooms overlook a statue of Grecian maidens and swans in the square outside, and each contains a private bath and a tasteful arrangement of dignified, conservative furniture.

Dining/Entertainment: The Vinatea restaurant serves regional and international three-course fixed-price lunches and dinners. There's also a bar.

Services: 24-hour room service, laundry and limousine service, concierge, babysitting.

Facilities: Car rentals, shopping boutiques, Jacuzzi.

Hotel Reina Victoria. Barcas, 4, 46002 Valencia. ☎ **96/352-04-87.** Fax 96/352-04-87. 97 rms. A/C MINIBAR TV TEL. July–Aug, 10,000 ptas. ($80) double; Sept–June, 19,100 ptas. ($152.80) double. AE, DC, MC, V. Parking 1,500 ptas. ($12). Bus: 4, 7, or 27.

Although it has lost some of its charm and luster in recent years, the Reina Victoria has traditionally been the most architecturally glamorous hotel in Valencia. Built in 1913 and renovated in 1988, the hotel has welcomed many distinguished guests, including Alfonso XIII and Queen Victoria (its namesake), Dalí, Manolete, Picasso, Falla, Garcia Lorca, and Miró. Bristling with neoclassical detailing and wrought-iron accents, it overlooks the flower gardens and fountains of Valencia's central square, the Plaza del Pais Valenciano. Bedrooms are furnished with conservative elegance and many modern accessories. The Bar Inglés is a popular rendezvous, and the hotel's restaurant, El Levant, serves international food in a dignified setting. There's also a cafeteria-style restaurant for less formal dining. The hotel lies in the heart of town, a five-minute walk from the railway station.

Meliá Rey Don Jaime. Avenida de Baleares, 2, 46023 Valencia. ☎ **800/336-3542** in the U.S., or 96/337-50-30. Fax 96/337-15-72. 322 rms. A/C MINIBAR TV TEL. Sept–July, 21,900 ptas. ($175.20) double; Aug and Fri–Sat in winter, 16,000 ptas. ($128) double. AE, DC, MC, V. Parking 1,400 ptas. ($11.20). Bus: 19, 41, 89, or 90.

A well-respected member of one of Spain's largest hotel chains, the Meliá towers over an urban landscape about half a mile southeast of the city's cathedral. Many guests appreciate the hotel's close proximity to the convention and concert hall (Palau de la Música) midway between the Old Town and the port. The stylish public rooms are sheathed in marble, rough stone, and tilework, whereas the bedrooms are sunny, well-maintained enclaves of contemporary style.

Dining/Entertainment: International cuisine is served in the well-recommended Restaurante Christina. Nearby, a richly paneled bar with leather sofas and armchairs evokes a private club in England.

Services: 24-hour room service, laundry/valet, concierge, babysitting.

Facilities: Business center, car-rental kiosk, solarium, outdoor swimming pool set into rooftop garden terrace.

MODERATE

Hotel Inglés. Marqués de Dos Aguas, 6, 46002 Valencia. ☎ **96/351-64-26.** Fax 96/394-02-51. 61 rms, 1 suite. A/C MINIBAR TV TEL. 12,750 ptas. ($102) double; 20,000 ptas. ($160) suite. AE, DC, MC, V. Parking 1,500 ptas. ($12). Bus: 31 or 32.

This turn-of-the-century hotel, the former palace of the Duke and Duchess of Cardona, has aged well. Located in the heart of old Valencia, it stands opposite another Churrigueresque palace. Most of its bedrooms have views of the tree-lined street below and offer old-fashioned comforts. The lounge and dining room have original decorating touches—chandeliers, gilt mirrors, provincial armchairs, and murals. The service is discreet and polite.

INEXPENSIVE

$ **Hostal Residencia Bisbal.** Pie de la Cruz, 9, 46001 Valencia. ☎ **96/391-70-84.** Fax 96/392-37-37. 17 rms. 3,800 ptas. ($30.40) double with shower; 5,400 ptas. ($43.20) double with bath. No credit cards. Parking 1,100 ptas. ($8.80). Bus: 8, 27, 29, or 81.

Conveniently located in the old city, this husband-and-wife operation has clean and simply furnished rooms. No meals are served, but you'll find many bars and restaurants nearby. The English-speaking staff is very helpful.

Sorolla. Convento de Santa Clara, 5, 46002 Valencia. ☎ **96/352-33-92.** Fax 96/352-14-65. 50 rms. A/C TV TEL. 10,500 ptas. ($84) double. AE, MC, V.

In the city center, this 1960s six-story hotel is named after Valencia's most famous artist. The guest rooms have narrow balconies and compact, utilitarian furnishings. Comfort, not style, is the key; everything, however, is clean. No meals are served. To reach the Sorolla, take any bus from the rail station.

WHERE TO DINE

EXPENSIVE

Eladio. Calle Chiva, 40. ☎ **96/384-22-44.** Reservations recommended. Main courses 1,500–3,200 ptas. ($12–$25.60). AE, DC, MC, V. Mon–Sat 1–4pm and 8–11:30pm. Closed Aug. SPANISH/INTERNATIONAL.

Borrowing from culinary models he learned during his apprenticeship in Switzerland, Eladio Rodríguez prepares flavorful cuisine based on the season's ingredients. Some clients praise him particularly for his shellfish and fish from Galicia, which might include hake, monkfish, or sea wolf, each prepared as simply or as elaborately as you want. (Many clients prefer these grilled simply over charcoal and served with garlic butter sauce.) Noteworthy are his ragoût of shellfish, anglerfish, and salmon and his recipe for octopus, derived from his native Galicia. The pastries prepared by Eladio's wife, Violette, are a suitable finish. The menu is changed daily, always based on what is fresh and available in any season. The setting is calm and pleasant, accented with touches of marble, oak, and plush upholstery.

✪ **La Hacienda.** Navarro Reverter, 12. ☎ **96/373-18-59.** Reservations recommended. Main courses 2,000–3,500 ptas. ($16–$28); *menú del día* 5,000 ptas. ($40). AE, MC, V. Mon–Sat 1:30–4pm and 9pm–midnight. VALENCIAN/INTERNATIONAL.

One of Valencia's most luxurious restaurants, the Hacienda caters to a lunch crowd of businesspeople discussing their deals and an evening crowd of conservative locals celebrating a dignified night on the town. In a dining room filled with antique furniture, gilt-framed mirrors, and pastels, you can enjoy the fine service of a time-tested staff, plus such delectable dishes as peppers stuffed with asparagus and exotic mushrooms, lobster with strips of salmon and pink peppercorns, roasted oxtail in the style of Córdoba, cold slices of roast beef with horseradish, filet of duckling with blackberry sauce, and chateaubriand topped with slices of foie gras. To accompany these dishes, the wine steward maintains an assortment of French and Spanish wines. The restaurant lies near the river and Valencia's eastern gate, about two blocks east of the historic center of town.

MODERATE

✪ **Galbis.** Marvá, 28–30, ☎ **96/380-94-73.** Reservations recommended. Main courses 1,100–1,975 ptas. ($8.80–$15.80); *menú gourmet degustación* 3,380 ptas. ($27.05); *menú la cena de picoto* 2,650 ptas. ($21.20). AE, V. Mon–Fri 1–4pm, Mon–Sat 8:30–11pm. Closed Aug 5–Sept 8. SPANISH.

Bustling, popular, and one of the most consistently crowded in town, this highly visible restaurant serves filling portions of straightforward food in an unmistakably Valencian ambience. You'll pass through a convivial bar area (where the ingredients for much of the day's cuisine might be displayed in a refrigerated case) before heading into the dining room. Specialties include a salad of roasted peppers with fresh duck meat, traditional preparations of hake and anglerfish, roast pork in savory sauce, roasted lamb with Mediterranean herbs, roasted goat in garlic sauce, and a succulent version of peppersteak. Next door, accessible via a separate entrance, the owners have established a simple cafeteria that many diners shun in favor of the better-known original restaurant. The cafeteria is open as a "day bar" for lunch only Monday through Friday from 7:30am to 5:30pm; on Saturday it is open only in the evening from 8:30pm to 2am. Inexpensive *menús del día* are served in this cafeteria/bar, costing 1,500 pesetas ($12) each. However, if someone wants one of the more glamorous—and more expensive items—offered in the restaurant, it is available on demand.

El Gourmet. Calle Taquígrafo Martí, 3. ☎ **96/395-25-09.** Reservations recommended. Main courses 1,600–2,000 ptas. ($12.80–$16); fixed-priced menu 2,500 ptas. ($20). AE, DC, MC, V. Mon–Sat 1–4pm and 9–11:30pm. Closed 1 week at Easter and in Aug. SPANISH/INTERNATIONAL.

This restaurant has welcomed clients since the 1950s. It's known as an honest establishment where well-trained waiters serve good-quality food that is not overly expensive. Set in the center of Valencia, it offers such dishes as hake with clams, partridge with herbs in puff pastry, oxtail stew, fried filets of veal or pork, scrambled eggs with eggplant and shrimp, and seasonal vegetables.

Palace Fesol. Hernán Cortés, 7. ☎ **96/352-93-23.** Reservations recommended. Main courses 1,400–2,200 ptas. ($11.20–$17.60); fixed-price menu 3,000 ptas. ($24). AE, DC, MC, V. Mon–Sun 1–3:30pm, Tues–Sat 9–11:30pm. Closed Sat and Sun June 15–Sept 15. Bus: 13. INTERNATIONAL.

Back in the post–World War I era, the Palace Fesol, known as the "bean palace," became famous for its namesake specialty, lima beans. Today, of course, many more excellent dishes grace the menu, with typical Valencian paella high on the list at lunch. You can also order several chicken dishes served with rice that go under the general name *paella,* since they are cooked in paella pans. Dinner selections include *zarzuela de mariscos* (shellfish medley), grilled red mullet and baby hake, baby lamb cutlets, and chateaubriand. Photos of film stars, bullfighters, and other celebrities line the walls. The restaurant is cooled by old-fashioned ceiling fans and is decorated with beamed ceilings, lanterns, and a hand-painted tile mosaic.

INEXPENSIVE

Foster's Hollywood. Gran Vía Marqués del Turia, 16. ☎ **96/395-15-20.** Main courses 750–1,200 ptas. ($6–$9.60). AE, DC, MC, V. Sun–Thurs 1pm–1am, Fri–Sat 1pm–2am. AMERICAN.

This is one of the many, many branches of Foster's, which opened its doors in 1971, becoming the first American restaurant in Madrid. The same format of California-style hamburgers is served in Valencia. At first, some locals encountered problems in eating the hamburgers, as would anyone not familiar with devouring food that is five inches high. The half-pound burgers are served with french fries and salad. The varied menu also includes many Tex-Mex selections such as chili con carne, as well as steaks, butterfly shrimp, freshly made pasta salads, and pizzas.

VALENCIA AFTER DARK

THE PERFORMING ARTS

The **Palau de la Música,** Paseo de la Alameda, 30 (☎ **96/337-50-20**), is a contemporary concert hall constructed in a dried-out river bed of the Turia. Opened in 1987, it stands within a sort of Hispano-Muslim venue—palm trees, "temples," and reflecting pools—between the Aragón and Angel Custudio bridges. Call to find out the day's program or ask at the tourist office (see "Essentials," above). Details of major concerts are also published in the newspapers. Ticket prices vary.

Best Buys on Porcelain, Pottery & Tiles

Valencia is the home of some of the country's best pottery. Lladró porcelain, Manises stoneware, and glassware are made or blown in the region. Local craftspeople also take pride in their *azulejos,* brightly colored ceramic tiles, first developed during the Muslim occupation of Andalusia.

In Valencia itself, the best place to buy the internationally known Lladró figurines is at Lladró, Calle Poeta Querol (☎ **96/351-16-25**). But, for the best buys, serious shoppers will want to head to the area surrounding Valencia, where hundreds of shops sell porcelain and ceramics at much lower prices than those of the high-rent stores in the heart of Valencia.

One worthy detour is Manises, located 5½ miles (9km) west of Valencia, known as a center for Valencian ceramics as well as for its *azulejos.* As a pottery center, Manises dates from the Middle Ages. Representatives from all the major kingdoms of Europe used to come here to purchase these wares, which are characterized by their distinctive blue-and-white patterns. The town is packed with factories and retail outlets hawking these ceramics. From the center of Valencia, several buses run frequently to Manises. The tourist office will give you a bus schedule.

Another good stop for the serious shopper is nearby Paterna, about 4 miles (6km) northwest of Valencia off the C-234 (it's signposted all the way). It has dozens of pottery stores with prices far below those in the center of Valencia.

Continuing farther north to the province of Castellón, the towns of Alcora, 12 miles (19km) northwest from Castellón de la Plana along the C-232, and Onda, 9 miles (15km) west along the C-223, are justly celebrated for their pottery—much of which is very reasonably priced since the "middleperson" is often eliminated. In addition to pottery, Onda has several shops selling some of the best-crafted *azulejos* in this part of Spain.

THE BAR SCENE

Barcas 7. Barcas, 7. ☎ **96/352-12-33.**

Set among banks and office buildings in the heart of town, directly north of the Estación del Norte, Barcas 7 offers drinks and tapas (including small servings of paella) at the stand-up bar. Conceivably you could stop here for your first cup of coffee at 7am and for your final "nightcap" at 1am. In the evening there is often live music. Despite the restaurant in back, where beef filet and veal dishes are house specialties, the establishment is more popular as a bar than as a restaurant, even with its incredibly rude staff. It's open daily from 7am to 1am. Drinks cost from 450 pesetas ($3.60), and tapas from 300 to 1,200 pesetas ($2.40–$9.60).

SIDE TRIPS FROM VALENCIA

LA ALBUFERA Eleven miles (17.7km) south of Valencia lies La Albufera, a land of rice paddies and reed beds. The largest wetland along the Mediterranean coast of Spain, it was called "an agreeable lagoon" in the writings of Pliny the Elder. Sand dunes separate the fresh water from the salt water.

La Albufera has been declared a national park since its lake is home to some 250 species of waterfowl, including a European version of the endangered flamingo. It abounds with such fish as mullet, tench, and eel, still caught by ancient traps. You can rent an *albuferenc* (flat-bottomed boat) from local fishers, but make sure to

The Disappearing Barraca

In the orchard lands around Valencia there were once hundreds of *barracas,* shedlike farm buildings where workers lived. Once a symbol of life in the area, they are now disappearing. *Barraca* are built of mud mixed with rice husks and strengthened with reeds to form whitewashed walls. The ground plan is rectangular, and the front wall is topped by a cross. The steep, saddleback roof provides easy drainage of the scarce, though torrential, rainwater and shelter from the summer heat.

The lower rooms of the structure are laid out in rows, and the top room (*andana*) is used as a storage area or for raising silkworms. A smaller *barraca,* used as a kitchen or for stables, is often attached to the larger one. *Barracas* can still be seen in and around Valencia at El Saler, El Palma, and in the areas of Fuente San Luis and La Punta. The tourist office in Valencia will locate these areas on a map for you.

Other interesting and also disappearing forms of architecture are found in the area around Alicante known as La Marina Alta. Here two very typical houses can be observed: the *riu-rau* and the *naia* —both with porticoes of semicircular, usually whitewashed arches and very low springers. The arched porticoes of the *riu-rau* are used as drying places for raisins, whereas those of the *naia* are the setting for family life.

negotiate prices beforehand. As you go about the lake, you can see *barracas,* whitewashed houses with thatched and steeply pitched roofs. Some of these *barracas,* standing on stilts, can be reached only by boat.

La Albufera gave the world paella, and nearly all the restaurants in the area serve this classic dish. Try **Raco de l'Olla,** Carretera de El Palma, s/n (**☎ 96/161-00-72**), eight miles (13km) south of Valencia on the El Saler road near the turnoff to El Palma. The restaurant was opened in the 1960s and since then has served paella to thousands of visitors from around the world. Most of the year it is open only for lunch, Tuesday through Sunday, from 10am to 6pm, but in July and August it is also open from 7:30pm to midnight. Meals range from 1,200 to 2,200 pesetas ($9.60–$17.60); American Express and Visa cards are accepted. It's also customary to stop in the town of El Palma to order a plate of *alli al pebre* (garlic-flavored eels) before heading north to Valencia or south to Alicante.

SAGUNTO Another popular excursion is to Sagunto, 15½ miles (25km) north of Valencia, reached by bus or rail connections. Sagunto is known for holding out nine months against Hannibal's conquering Carthaginian soldiers in 219 B.C. The Iberians set themselves on fire rather than surrender. In time, the Romans discovered the town, and later it was taken by the Visigoths and the Muslims.

Its **Roman ruins** today are just that: ruins. But it makes an interesting stopover. In the 2nd century A.D. it had an amphitheater seating 8,000, in the remains of which theatrical performances are still staged. It also has an old **Acrópolis/** *castillo* (castle); the remains of its Moorish walls and dramparts stretch for about a half mile.

The best place for food is right near the castle: **L'Armeler,** Calle Subida del Castillo, 44 (**☎ 96/266-43-82**). Meals cost 3,000 pesetas ($24) with wine; it's open Tuesday through Saturday from 1:30 to 4pm and 9:30 to 11pm. You can get both French and Spanish food in the ambience of a *vieja mansion* (old mansion). Try one of the splendid pâtés, salmon casserole, or filet steak with truffle sauce. The terrace provides a fine view.

2 Benidorm

27 miles (43km) NE of Alicante, 84 miles (135km) S of Valencia

Before its 3½ miles (6km) of beach were discovered by tourists, Benidorm was a tiny fishing village. But now summer vacationers pour in, and a new concrete hotel seems to be built every day. With its heavy European influence, Benidorm has become the most overrun beach town east of Torremolinos. It has both its fans and its detractors.

According to an 1890s guidebook, Benidorm was a "very tranquil place where drunkenness was unknown." What a change had come over the resort by the 1970s and 1980s, when it attracted a rowdy, beer-drinking crowd. Today some 180,000 people a day visit Benidorm's long beach strip.

After the bad press of the past decades, city officials are trying to clean up the act in Benidorm and make it more of an upmarket destination. Signs of the changing times are exemplified by the Aiguera Park and its amphitheater, offering such free cultural activities as dancing, jazz, soul music, and even a Russian choir.

Despite efforts to upgrade its image, Benidorm still has its high-rises and inexpensive package tours. In winter many pensioners from all over Europe, even Russia, fill up the villas and small hotels. In summer, however, the place takes on a much more youthful aura. There are two fine white sand beaches running along the resort. In Franco's day, a man could get arrested for walking without his shirt on the resort's streets, but today one of the beaches is topless.

GETTING THERE **By Train** From Alicante, there are hourly departures for Benidorm.

By Bus Buses from Valencia and Alicante to Benidorm leave almost hourly.

By Car Take the E-15 expressway south from Valencia or north from Alicante.

VISITOR INFORMATION The tourist information office is at Avenida Martínez Alejos, 16 (☎ **96/585-13-11**). It's open Monday through Saturday from 10am to 2pm and 5 to 8pm.

WHERE TO STAY

Make sure you reserve in advance between mid-June and September—if you arrive without a reservation, you'll be out of luck. During this time most hotel managers often slap the full-board requirement onto their rates. The way to beat this is to book into one of the rare residencias in Benidorm, which serve breakfast only.

Don Pancho. Avenida del Mediterráneo, 39, 03500 Benidorm. ☎ **96/585-29-50.** Fax 96/586-77-79. 251 rms. A/C TV TEL. 10,300–16,200 ptas. ($82.40–$129.60) double. AE, DC, MC, V.

One of the best hotels in Benidorm, Don Pancho is a high-rise set a short walk from the beach. Its inviting lobby has a Spanish-colonial/Aztec decor, and each of the well-furnished, well-maintained bedrooms opens onto a small balcony. Each room is a double, although it can be rented for single use. Facilities include a swimming pool and a lighted tennis court.

Gran Hotel Delfín. Playa de Poniente (La Cala), 03500 Benidorm. ☎ **96/585-34-00.** Fax 96/585-71-54. 99 rms. A/C TV TEL. 14,450–18,300 ptas. ($115.60–$146.40) double. AE, DC, MC, V. Closed Oct–Mar. Free parking.

Located about two miles (3km) west of the center of town, away from the traffic-clogged mayhem that sometimes overwhelms the center of Benidorm, this 1960s hotel lies beside the very popular Poniente Beach. It is the resort's finest hotel, catering to a sun-loving crowd of vacationers who appreciate its airy spaciousness and lack of formality. Bedrooms are sparsely decorated, with masonry floors and much-used furniture, some in a darkly stained Iberian style.

Dining/Entertainment: The in-house restaurant, El Delfín, serves fixed-price *menús del día.* There are also two bars, one of which serves drinks near the pool.

Services: Room service (available daily from 7am to 11pm), laundry/valet, concierge, babysitting.

Facilities: Outdoor swimming pool set into large and verdant garden, tennis courts.

Hotel Brisa. Playa de Levante, 03500 Benidorm. ☎ **96/585-54-00.** 70 rms. TEL. July–Aug (with obligatory half board), 14,000 ptas. ($112) double; Sept–June (including breakfast), 8,000 ptas. ($64) double. V.

Set immediately opposite one of the town's most popular beaches, this hotel is a five-story modern building with a swimming pool, a small garden, and clean and sunny bedrooms, simply furnished with sturdy furniture and tile floors. This is very much a beach hotel, where many of the clients bring uncomplicated wardrobes, and in some cases their children, in anticipation of lazy days on the beach. There's at least one bar on the premises, and an airy, sun-flooded dining room. In summer a large percentage of the clients are from northern Europe.

$ **Hotel Canfali.** Plaza de San Jaime, 5, 03500 Benidorm. ☎ **96/585-08-18.** Fax 96/585-08-18. 39 rms. TEL. 6,000–9,000 ptas. ($48–$72) double. Rates include breakfast. No credit cards.

A seaside villa between the Playa de Levante and the Playa de Poniente, the Canfali ranks as one of the best small hotels in the town. Originally built in 1950, it was enlarged in 1992. Its position is a scene-stealer—on a low cliff at the end of the esplanade, with a staircase winding down to the beach. The best rooms have balconies with sea views. Although the hotel is spacious and comfortable, its decor is undistinguished, its bedrooms functional. Terraces overlook the sea, a perfect spot for morning coffee.

Hotel Cimbel. Europa, 1, 03500 Benidorm. ☎ **96/585-21-00.** Fax 96/586-06-61. 134 rms. A/C TV TEL. 12,000–21,000 ptas. ($96–$168) double. Rates include breakfast. AE, DC, MC, V. Parking 1,300 ptas. ($10.40). Bus: 1, 2, 3, 4, or 5.

Situated on one of the most popular beaches in town, this hotel especially appeals to sun worshipers, who step virtually from the lobby onto the sand. The guest rooms are functionally furnished but comfortable. The hotel restaurant serves a *menú del día* that often features fresh catches. Guests will enjoy the swimming pool and can order drinks in a *sala des noches,* a nighttime gathering spot where they can listen to music. Also on the premises are a dance hall, a cafeteria, and safety deposit boxes.

WHERE TO DINE

Pérgola. Acantillado-Edificio Coblanca, 10, Rincón de Loix. ☎ **96/585-38-00.** Reservations recommended. Main courses 1,800–2,300 ptas. ($14.40–$18.40). AE, V. Mon–Sun 1–4pm and 8–11:30pm. Closed Dec 15–Feb 1. SPANISH/INTERNATIONAL.

Of the many buildings along the seafront at the Playa de Levante, this is the one that is nearest the center of Benidorm. Established in 1979, it offers a sweeping view over the bay, an airy and stylish interior, and a flower-strewn terrace for warm-weather lunches and dinners. Food is skillfully prepared and includes seafood crêpes with clams, a combination platter of hake with salmon drizzled in crabmeat sauce, stuffe crabs, stewed codfish with a confit of garlic, breast of duck with pears, and rack of beef with mustard sauce.

Tiffany's. Avenida del Mediterráneo, 51. ☎ **96/585-44-68.** Reservations recommended. Main courses 1,550–2,300 ptas. ($12.40–$18.40). AE, MC, V. Daily 7:30pm–midnight. Closed Jan 10–Feb 10. SPANISH/INTERNATIONAL.

Tiffany's, one of the town's better restaurants, has attracted visitors since the 1970s. Meals are served with a well-rehearsed dignity and the occasional sound of a live pianist. The food offerings change with the seasons and the availability of the ingredients. Your meal might include a roulade of filet of sole stuffed with caviar and shrimp, tournedos "Tiffany" with foie gras and truffles, a choice of fish or veal dishes, and a dessert of homemade chocolate éclairs with warm chocolate sauce.

BENIDORM AFTER DARK

Benidorm Palace. Carretera de Diputación, s/n, Rincón de Loix. ☎ **96/585-16-60.** Cover 2,975 ptas. ($23.80).

The best nightclub in the region, located in the Rincón de Loix, the Benidorm Palace features the latest music and a large dance floor. It has the biggest stage in Europe, 130 feet (40m) wide. The stage is filled with 50 international artists, often entertaining an audience of 1,500. Shows have ranged from "Hurrah for Hollywood" to Russian dancers. Always count on glamorous dancing women. There are expansive bars and ample seating. It's open Tuesday through Saturday from 9pm to 2am; closed in January. Drinks run 500 pesetas ($4).

Casino Costa Blanca. Carretera Nacional, km 114. ☎ **96/589-27-12.** Admission to casino, 600 ptas. ($4.80). Passports must be presented.

Located about 4½ miles (7km) from Benidorm, beside the highway leading to Alicante, this establishment offers gambling in a modern building surrounded by the rolling hills of the Costa Blanca. Most visitors come to try their hand at roulette (both the French and the American versions), blackjack, and boules. An on-site restaurant, Costa Blanca, serves à la carte Spanish meals from 3,000 pesetas ($24) per person every evening from 9pm to 1am. The casino's open nightly from 8pm to 4am.

3 Alicante

50 miles (80km) N of Murcia, 25 miles (40km) S of Benidorm, 107 miles (172km) S of Valencia, 259 miles (417km) SE of Madrid

Alicante, capital of the Costa Blanca, is considered by many to be the best all-around city in Spain, since it's popular in both summer and winter. As you walk its esplanades, you almost feel as if you were in Africa: Women in caftans and peddlers hawking carvings from Senegal or elsewhere often populate the waterfront.

San Juan, the largest beach in Alicante, lies a short distance from the capital. It's lined with villas, hotels, and restaurants. The bay of Alicante has two capes, and on the bay is **Postiguet Beach.** The bay stretches all the way to the **Cape of Santa Pola,** a town with two good beaches, a 14th-century castle, and several seafood restaurants.

ESSENTIALS

GETTING THERE **By Plane** Alicante's Internacional El Altet Airport (☎ **96/690-90-00**) is 12 miles (19.3km) from the city. There are usually as many as six daily flights from Madrid, about three flights per week from Seville, and three weekly from Barcelona. Also, three flights arrive here weekly from Ibiza and Málaga (on the Costa del Sol). Thirteen buses daily connect the city to the airport; the fare is 125 pesetas ($1). The Iberia Airlines ticket office is at the airport (☎ **96/520-60-00**).

By Train There are five trains a day from Valencia (trip time: 3 hours), five trains a day from Barcelona (11 hours), and six a day from Madrid (9 hours). The RENFE office is at the Estación Término, Avenida Salamanca (☎ **96/592-02-02**).

By Bus Different bus lines from various parts of the coast converge at the terminus, Calle Portugal, 17 (☎ **96/513-07-00**). There is frequent service—almost hourly—from Benidorm (see above) and from Valencia (four hours away). Buses also run from Madrid, a five- to six-hour trip.

By Car Take the E-15 expressway south along the coast from Valencia. The expressway and the N-340 run northeast from Murcia.

By Ferry There are ferry connections four times per day by Transmediterránea to Ibiza (3 hours). Call the office in Valencia for tickets and information (☎ **96/367-75-80**). Marítima de Denia, Estacion Marítima (☎ **96/578-40-11**), offers daily service to Ibiza (7 hours) and Formentera (10 hours) twice weekly.

VISITOR INFORMATION The tourist information office is at Explanada d'Espanya, 2 (☎ **96/520-00-00**), and is open Monday through Friday from 10am to 7pm and on Saturday from 10am to 2pm and 3 to 7pm. For medical assistance, go to the Hospital Clínico, Calle Alicante Sant Joan (☎ **96/590-87-00**). If you need an ambulance, call **96/511-46-76;** in case of emergency, dial **091;** to reach the city police, call **96/514-22-22.**

WHAT TO SEE & DO

With its wide, palm-lined avenues, this town was made for walking. The magnificent **Explanada d'Espanya,** extending around part of the yacht harbor, includes a great promenade of mosaic sidewalks under the palms. All the boulevards are clean and lined with unlimited shopping facilities, including Alicante's leading department store, Galerías Preciados, where you can find bargains without being trampled by mobs, as in Madrid. Alicante is known for its parks, gardens, and lines of palm trees, and it offers several old plazas, some paved with marble.

The **Castillo de San Fernando** has a panoramic view and can be visited during the day. High on a hill, the more stately **Castillo de Santa Bárbara** (☎ **96/526-31-31**) towers over the bay and provincial capital. The Greeks called the fort Akra Leuka (White Peak). Its original defenses were erected by the Carthaginians in 400 B.C. and were later used by the Romans and the Arabs. The grand scale of this fortress is evident in its moats, drawbridges, tunneled entrances, guardrooms, bakery, cisterns, underground storerooms, hospitals, batteries, powder stores, barracks, high breastworks, deep dungeons, and the Matanza Tower and the Keep. From the top of the castle there's a panoramic view over land and sea (the castle is reachable by road or an elevator, boarded at the Explanda d'Espanya). Admission is 200 pesetas ($1.60) by elevator. In winter the castle is open daily from 9am to 7pm; in summer it's open daily from 10am to 8pm.

On the slopes of the Castillo de Santa Bárbara is the **Barrio de Santa Cruz.** Lying behind the cathedral and forming part of the **Villa Vieja** (as the old quarter c Alicante is called), it is a colorful section with wrought-iron grilles on the windov banks of flowers, and a view of the entire harbor.

Alicante isn't all ancient. Facing the Iglesia Santa Maria, the **Museu Colecci del Segle XX,** Plaza de Santa Maria, 3 (☎ **96/514-07-68**), is housed in the oldest building but contains modern art. Constructed as a granary in 1685, stored building features works by Miró, Calder, Cocteau, Vasarély, Dalí, Pic Tápies. Other notable artists include Braque, Chagall, Giacometti, Kandi Zadkine. You'll also see a musical score by Manuel de Falla. The museum in 1977 from the donation of a private collection by the painter/sculptor Eusebio Sempere, whose works are also on display. It is open May through September, Tuesday through Saturday, from 10:30am to 1:30pm and 6 to 9pm; October through April, Tuesday through Saturday, from 10am to 1pm and 5 to 8pm. Sunday hours year-round are from 10am to 1pm. Admission is free.

WHERE TO STAY

EXPENSIVE

Hotel Meliá Alicante. Playa de El Postiguet, 03001 Alicante. ☎ **800/336-3542** in the U.S., or 96/520-50-00. Fax 96/520-47-56. 535 rms, 10 suites. A/C MINIBAR TV TEL. 14,400–18,000 ptas. ($115.20–$144) double; 24,350 ptas. ($194.80) suite. AE, DC, MC, V. Parking 1,000 ptas. ($8).

Built in 1973 on a spit of landfill jutting into the Mediterranean, midway between the main harbor and the very popular El Postiguet beach, this hotel is so massive in size that it almost dwarfs every other establishment in town. Bedrooms are painted in clear, sunny colors and contain private baths and balconies, usually with sweeping panoramas of either the rows of moored sailboats in the nearby marina or over the beach. The public rooms are contemporary, with lots of marble.

Dining/Entertainment: The two in-house restaurants serve à la carte meals. There is also a bar near the pool and an indoor bar with a piano player, plus a *sala de fiestas* where drinking, conversation, and dancing occur.

Services: Concierge, laundry, 24-hour room service, babysitting.

Facilities: Outdoor swimming pools.

Hotel Tryp Gran Sol. Rambla Méndez Nuñez, 3, 03002 Alicante. ☎ **800/272-8674** in the U.S., or 96/520-30-00. Fax 96/521-14-39. 144 rms, 4 suites. A/C MINIBAR TV TEL. 10,500 ptas. ($84) double; 16,000 ptas. ($128) suite. AE, DC, MC, V. Parking 1,200 ptas. ($9.60).

Set in the heart of the tourist zone, a block from the beachfront Paseo Marítimo, this 1970 hotel towers conspicuously above most of the buildings in town. A member of the widely known Tryp chain, it offers simple and uncomplicated bedrooms with unimaginative but comfortable furnishings, plus private bathrooms accented with tiles and/or marble. One-third of the rooms have been recently renovated.

Dining/Entertainment: The Ramblas Restaurant lies adjacent to a popular bar. Both of these are on the building's 26th floor, where big windows offer sweeping views of the town and coastline.

Services: Room service until midnight, laundry service, concierge, babysitter.

Facilities: Car rentals, reading room, game room, TV room, meeting facilities.

MODERATE

Hotel Residencia Covadonga. Plaza de los Luceros, 17, 03004 Alicante. ☎ **96/520-28-44.** Fax 96/521-43-97. 83 rms, 4 suites. A/C TV TEL. 8,000 ptas. ($64) double; from 9,400 ptas. ($75.20) suite. AE, DC, MC, V. Parking 1,000 ptas. ($8). Bus: 5, A, B, or D.

Convenient to attractions, the railway station, buses, and the airport, the Covadonga offers spacious rooms and good service. The public rooms are large and inviting. There's no restaurant, but you'll find many places to dine nearby.

el Residencia San Remo. Navas, 30, 03001 Alicante. ☎ **96/520-95-00.** Fax 96/ 6-68. 28 rms (22 with bath). TV TEL. 3,500–4,500 ptas. ($28–$36) double without bath, -5,500 ptas. ($36–$44) double with bath. AE, DC, MC, V. Parking 1,500 ptas. ($12).

te-plastered seven-floor building, the San Remo offers clean, unpretentious some with balconies. Breakfast is the only meal served. The welcome is warm, price is right. Room service is provided from 8am to 8pm.

Palas. Cervantes, 5, 03002 Alicante. ☎ **96/520-92-11.** Fax 96/514-01-21. 40 rms. A/C TEL. 9,000 ptas. ($72) double. AE, DC, MC, V. Parking 800 ptas. ($6.40).

This charmer has a lot of old-fashioned style. Many guests like its location—near the seafront at the eastern end of the Explanada d'Espanya—along with its personal service. Several public areas are graced with chandeliers and antiques. The bedrooms are pleasantly furnished and well maintained.

Portugal. Calle Portugal, 26, 03003 Alicante. ☎ **96/592-92-44.** 18 rms (5 with bath). 4,000 ptas. ($32) double with sink; 4,500 ptas. ($36) double with bath. No credit cards. Parking 1,000 ptas. ($8).

The Portugal is a two-story hotel, located one block from the bus station, about four blocks from the railway station, and a three-minute walk from the harbor. The accommodations, furnished in tasteful modern style, are immaculate but rather basic.

WHERE TO DINE

The characteristic dish of Alicante is rice, served in many different ways. The most typical sauce is *aïoli,* a kind of mayonnaise made from oil and garlic. Dessert selections offer the greatest variety on the Costa Blanca, with *turrón de Alicante* (Spanish nougat) the most popular of all.

La Dársena. Muelle del Puerto (Explanada d'Espanya). ☎ **96/520-75-89.** Reservations required at lunch. Main courses 1,500–2,600 ptas. ($12–$20.80); fixed-price menu 4,200 ptas. ($33.60). AE, DC, MC, V. Mon–Sun 1–4pm, Tues–Sun 8:30–11:30pm. SPANISH.

Paella is the best choice on the menu at this popular place located off the Explanada d'Espanya, overlooking the harbor. Some 20 other rice dishes are commendable as well—for example, *arroz con pieles de bacalao* (rice with dried codfish). Try the crab soup flavored with Armagnac or the tart made with tuna and spinach.

Delfín. Explanada d'Espanya, 14. ☎ **96/521-49-11.** Reservations recommended. Main courses 2,000–2,600 ptas. ($16–$20.80); *menú del día* 3,700 ptas. ($29.60). AE, DC, MC, V. Daily 1–5 pm and 8pm–midnight. MEDITERRANEAN.

Set on the town's most visible promenade, this restaurant, established in 1961, offers an upstairs dining room, where hushed service, lots of mirrors, and views over the town's harbor and yacht basin complement the attentive service and culinary style. The service is first class, the ingredients fresh, and the dishes savory and well flavored. Menu specialties might include smoked salmon served on toast with a gratin of shrimp, filet steak grilled with a goat-cheese topping, sauté of sweetbreads flavored with foie gras and strips of duck meat, crêpes stuffed with seafood, paella, and an array of tempting pastries rolled from table to table on a trolley.

Nou Manolín. Calle Villegas, 3. ☎ **96/520-0368.** Reservations recommended. Main courses 1,800–2,200 ptas. ($14.40–$17.60). AE, DC, MC, V. Daily 1–4pm and 8:30pm–midnight. REGIONAL/SPANISH.

When it was established in 1972, the founder of this restaurant named it after an almost-forgotten neighborhood bar (El Manolín) that his grandfather had maintained before the Spanish Civil War. The Nou Manolín's street level contains a busy bar area, but diners usually gravitate to the upstairs dining room, where tiled walls an uniformed waiters contribute to the ambience of an elegant *tasca.* Menu items inclu many kinds of fish cooked in a salt crust, as well as a delectable paella, several ki of stew, fresh shellfish, and a wide selection of Iberian wines.

Restaurante El Jumillano. César Elquezábel, 64. ☎ **96/521-17-64.** Reservations mended. Main courses 1,950–2,600 ptas. ($15.60–$20.80); fixed-price menu 3,500 pta AE, DC, MC, V. Mon–Sat 1–4pm and 8pm–midnight; Sun noon–4pm. Bus: D or F. SP

This was a humble wine bar when it opened in 1936 near the old city. The original wine-and-tapas bar is still going strong, but the food has improved immeasurably. Today the original owner's sons (Juan José and Miguel Pérez Mejías) offer a cornucopia of succulent food, including fresh fish laid out in the dining room on the sun-bleached planks of an antique fishing boat. Many of the menu items are derived from locally inspired recipes. The specialties include a "festival of canapes," slices of cured ham served with fresh melon, shellfish soup with mussels, Alicante stew, pig's trotters, a savory filet of beef seasoned with garlic, and a full gamut of grilled hake, sea bass, and shellfish.

4 Elche

13 miles (21 km) SW of Alicante, 35 miles (56km) NE of Murcia, 252 miles (406km) SE of Madrid

Situated between Alicante and Murcia, the little town of Elche is famous for its age-old mystery play, lush groves of date palms, and shoe and sandal making. The play is reputedly the oldest dramatic liturgy performed in Europe. On August 14 and 15 for the last six centuries, the ✪ **Mystery of Elche** has celebrated the Assumption of the Virgin. Songs are performed in an ancient form of Catalán. Admission is free, but it's hard to get a seat unless you book in advance through the tourist office (see below). The play is performed at the Church of Santa María, which dates from the 17th century.

Unless you visit at the time of the mystery play, the town's date palms will hold the most appeal. The palm forest is unrivaled in Europe—some 600,000 trees said to have been originally planted by Phoenician (perhaps Greek) seafarers. The Moors created the irrigation system which maintains the palms, 1,000 years ago. Stroll through the **Huerto del Cura (Priest's Grove),** open daily from 9am to 6pm, to see the palm garden and collection of tropical flowers and cacti. In the garden look for the Palmera del Cura (Priest's Palm), from the 1840s, with seven branches sprouting from its trunk. In the grove you will see one of the most famous ladies of Spain, *La Dama de Elche.* This is a replica—the original 500 B.C. limestone bust, discovered in 1897, is now on display in the National Archaeological Museum in Madrid.

GETTING THERE **By Train** The central train station is the Estación Parque, Plaza Alfonso XII. Trains arrive almost hourly from Alicante.

By Bus The bus station is at Avenida de la Libertat. Buses travel between Alicante and Elche on the hour.

By Car Take the N-340 highway from Alicante and proceed southwest.

VISITOR INFORMATION The tourist information office is at Passeig de l'Estació (☎ **96/545-27-47**). Open Monday through Friday from 10:30am to 2pm and 4 to 6pm, Saturday and Sunday from 10:30am to 1:30pm.

WHERE TO STAY

Don Jaime. Juan Carlos Primera, 5, 03203 Elche. ☎ **96/545-38-40.** Fax 96/542-64-36. 4 rms. TEL. 5,885 ptas. ($47.10) double. MC, V. Parking 1,750 ptas. ($14).

Although it doesn't have the glamour of the parador Huerto del Cura (see below) and rated only two stars by the government, this five-story hotel near the town center easy on the purse. The hotel was built in 1960, and the well-maintained guest ms are comfortable rather than stylish. During performances of the *Mystery of* , prices rise about 25%. There's no restaurant, but there are a number of places nearby.

✪ **Huerto del Cura.** Porta de La Morera, 14, 03200 Elche. ☎ **96/545-80-40.** Fax 96/542-19-10. 70 rms, 3 suites. A/C MINIBAR TV TEL. 16,000–18,000 ptas. ($128–$144) double; 40,000 ptas. ($320) suite. AE, DC, MC, V. Parking 1,000 ptas. ($8).

Huerto del Cura stands in the so-called Priest's Grove, and from your bedroom you'll have panoramic views of the palm trees. The privately owned parador consists of a number of cabins in the grove. Although the rates are high, staying here is a unique experience—everything beautifully furnished and immaculately kept, the service impeccable. A swimming pool under the palms separates the cabins from the main hotel building. A tennis court, sauna, solarium, and cafeteria also grace the grounds. There is an attractive bar and a four-fork dining room, Els Capellans.

WHERE TO DINE

Parque Municipal. Paseo Alfonso XIII, s/n. ☎ **96/545-34-15.** Reservations recommended. Main courses 1,300–1,800 ptas. ($10.40–$14.40); fixed-price menu 1,300 ptas. ($10.40). MC, V. Daily 1–4pm and daily 8–11pm. SPANISH/INTERNATIONAL.

A large open-air restaurant and café right in the middle of a public park, the Parque Municipal is a good place to go for decent food and relaxed service. Many regional dishes appear on the menu; try one of the savory rice dishes as a main course, followed by "cake of Elche." Two specialties here are paella and Mediterranean sea bass, sailor's style.

Restaurante La Finca. Partida de Perleta, 1–7. ☎ **96/545-60-07.** Reservations recommended. Main courses 1,800–2,300 ptas. ($14.40–$18.40); fixed-price menus 3,600–4,500 ptas. ($28.80–$36). AE, DC, MC, V. Tues–Sun 1–5pm, Tues–Sat 8:30pm–midnight. SPANISH.

Located in the *campo* (countryside) near the Elche football stadium, three miles (5km) south of town along the Carretera de El Alted, La Finca opened in 1984 and has attracted customers ever since with its good food. The menu changes frequently, based on the season and what's fresh. Both fish and meat are prepared in creative ways, although time-tested recipes are used as well. Try tuna-stuffed peppers, if featured, or veal kidneys with potatoes. Chocolate mousse might be available for dessert.

5 Murcia

52 miles (83km) SW of Alicante, 245 miles (409km) SE of Madrid, 159 miles (256km) SW of Valencia

This ancient Moorish city of sienna-colored buildings is an inland provincial capital on the main road between Valencia and Granada. It lies on the Segura River.

ESSENTIALS

GETTING THERE **By Train** From Alicante, 18 trains arrive daily (trip time: 1½ hours); from Barcelona, 2 daily (11 hours); and from Madrid, 3 daily (5 to 8¼ hours). From the Estación del Carmen, Calle Industria, s/n (☎ **968/25-21-54**), take bus number 11 to the heart of the city.

By Bus Buses pull in at Calle San Andrés (☎ **968/29-22-11**), behind the Museo Salzillo. The information window here is open daily from 8am to 10pm. Frequent service is possible from Granada (4 to 5 hours), Cádiz (12½ hours), Córdob (9 hours), Valencia (3¾ hours), and Seville (9¾ hours).

By Car Take the N-340 southwest from Alicante.

VISITOR INFORMATION The tourist information office is at Alejз Seiquer, 4 (☎ **968/21-37-16**). Open Monday through Friday from 9am tc Saturday from 5 to 7pm.

SPECIAL EVENTS Murcia's **Holy Week celebration,** from Palm Sunday to Easter Sunday, is an ideal time to visit. Its processions are spectacular, with about 3,000 people taking part, and some sculptures of Salzillo (see below) are carried through the streets. Musicians blow horns so big they have to be carried on wheels.

EXPLORING THE CITY

Although it suffered much from fire and bombardment during the Spanish Civil War, the city abounds in grand houses built in the 18th century. But the principal artistic treasure is the **cathedral,** Plaza Cardenal Belluga (☎ **968/21-63-44**), a bastardized medley of Gothic, baroque, and Renaissance. Begun in the 1300s, its bell tower was built at four different periods by four different architects. You can climb the tower for a view of Murcia and the enveloping fertile *huerta* (plain). The Capilla de los Vélez, off the ambulatory, is the most interesting chapel. You can see works by the famous local sculptor, Francisco Salzillo (1707–83), as well as the golden crown of the Virgen de la Fuensanta, patroness of Murcia. To reach the museum, go through the north transept. You can visit it daily from 10am to 1pm and 5 to 8pm; admission is 200 pesetas ($1.60). The cathedral is open daily from 7am to 1pm and 5 to 8pm.

The other major sight is the **Museo de Salzillo,** San Andrés, 1 (☎ **968/29-18-93**). The son of an Italian sculptor father and a Spanish mother, Salzillo won fame with his sculptures done in polychrome wood. This museum displays his finest work, plus many terra-cotta figurines based on biblical scenes. It is open Tuesday through Saturday from 9:30am to 1pm and 4 to 7pm, Sunday from 9:30am to 1pm. Admission is 200 pesetas ($1.60).

Another attraction is the **Museo de Arqueología,** Calle Gran Vía Alfonso, X El Sabio, 7 (☎ **968/23-46-02**), one of the best in Spain. Through artifacts—mosaics, fragments of pottery, Roman coins, ceramics, and various other objects—it traces life in Murcia province from prehistoric times. The two most important collections are devoted to objects from the Hispano-Moorish period of the 12th to the 14th century and to Spanish ceramics of the 17th and 18th centuries. Hours are July through August, Monday through Friday from 10am to 2pm, and September through June, Monday through Friday from 9am to 2pm and 5 to 8pm and Saturday from 11am to 2pm. Admission is 75 pesetas (60¢).

WHERE TO STAY

Hotel Conde de Floridablanca. Princesa, 18, 30002 Murcia. ☎ **968/21-46-26.** Fax 968/21-32-15. 85 rms, 5 suites. A/C MINIBAR TV TEL. 12,000 ptas. ($96) double; 15,000 ptas. ($120) suite. AE, DC, MC, V. Parking 1,200 ptas. ($9.60). Bus: 2, 5, 6, or 11.

Rising from the center of the Barrio del Carmen, near the cathedral, this hotel is ideally suited for explorations of the old city. Originally built in 1972, it was thoroughly renovated and enlarged in 1992. The building is attractively decorated in a conservatively modern style, with comfortable and appealing bedrooms, which include use of a safe. The hotel serves breakfast, and a newly added bar and restaurant offer dinner and drinks.

Hotel Hispano 1. Trapería, 8, 30001 Murcia. ☎ **968/21-61-52.** Fax 968/21-68-59. rms. TV TEL. 4,500 ptas. ($36) double. AE, DC, MC, V. Bus: 2, 5, 6, or 11.

n older version of Hispano 2 (see below), run by the same people, this good-value el is still reliable after all these years. It stands right at the cathedral. The well-kept t rooms are functional and homey. The hotel also has a restaurant serving a rel cuisine.

Hotel Hispano 2. Calle Radio Murcia, 3, 30001 Murcia. ☎ **968/21-61-52.** Fax 968/21-68-59. 35 rms. A/C MINIBAR TV TEL. 12,000 ptas. ($96) double. AE, DC, MC, V. Parking 1,000 ptas. ($8). Bus: 2, 5, 6, or 11.

The older Hispano 1 (see above) proved so successful that the owners inaugurated this version in the late 1970s. Bedrooms are comfortably furnished and superior to those at the older sibling. The family-run hotel-restaurant offers well-prepared regional food and tapas.

Hotel Meliá 7 Coronas. Paseo de Garay, 5, 30000 Murcia. ☎ **800/336-3542** in the U.S., or 968/21-77-72. Fax 968/22-12-94. 150 rms. A/C MINIBAR TV TEL. 14,500–18,200 ptas. ($116–$145.60) double. AE, DC, MC, V. Parking 1,000 ptas. ($8). Bus: 2, 5, 6, or 11.

Set within a 15-minute walk east of the cathedral, near the gardens abutting the northern edge of the Río Segura, this angular 1971 hotel offers comfortable bedrooms and a cool, refreshing terrace with bar service and a legion of flowering plants. A member of the well-recommended nationwide chain, this is the finest hotel in town.

Dining/Entertainment: The in-house restaurant serves à la carte Spanish and continental meals. There's also a bar.

Services: Concierge, laundry service, babysitting.

Residencia Rincón de Pepe. Plaza de Apóstoles, 34, 30002 Murcia. ☎ **968/21-22-39.** Fax 968/22-17-44. 116 rms. A/C MINIBAR TV TEL. 17,600 ptas. ($140.80) double. AE, DC, MC, V. Parking 1,250 ptas. ($10).

This modern hotel hidden on a narrow street in the heart of the old quarter is attached to a well-known restaurant, Rincón de Pepe (see below). Once beyond its entranceway, which is accented with marble, glass, and plants, you'll discover a good-sized lounge as well as a bar. The bedrooms are up-to-date with many built-in conveniences.

A Resort Nearby

✪ **Hyatt La Manga Club Resort.** Los Belones, 30385 Cartagena, Murcia. ☎ **800/228-9000** or 968/13-72-34. 185 rms, 7 suites (in the Hotel Príncipe Felipe), and 70 apartments (in the Las Lomas apartment complex). A/C MINIBAR TV TEL. 28,500–35,000 ptas. ($228–$280) double; 50,000 ptas. ($400) suite; 13,500–18,700 ptas. ($108–$149.60) studio apartment; 15,500–26,600 ptas. ($124–$212.80) one- to-three-bedroom apartment. AE, DC, MC, V. Free parking.

One of the best resorts in Spain is located inland from the coast, near the eastern extremity of Andalusia. Nestled within 1,400 acres (grounds that are larger than the land controlled by the Principality of Monaco), it's the only resort in Europe with three championship golf courses. It also features a comprehensive array of sport facilities. The decor is inspired by the aristocratic private villas of Andalusia. Families usually opt for one of the airy, four-star, Andalusian-style apartments within the Los Lomos complex, where 50 apartments (as well as about 20 time-share units not accessible to the public) are configured into a re-creation of an Andalusian pueblo. Couples and clients staying for a week or less tend to gravitate toward the five-star accommodations in the resort's architectural showcase, the Príncipe Felipe, named for the sons of King Juan Carlos.

Dining/Entertainment: The Ampola restaurant has views over the rolling terrain of the golf courses. Other dining venues include a Mexican restaurant, an Italian pizza and pasta restaurant, and a jazz bar.

Services: Babysitting, 24-hour room service, hairdressing, laundry/valet, concierge.

Facilities: Three championship golf courses, a health and fitness club, a children's camp with facilities for supervision and babysitting, golf and tennis pro shops, a tennis center with 18 tennis courts (all but 4 have lights), and 4 outdoor swimming pools. A beach with its own watersports facilities and kiosks lies within a 10-minute shuttlebus drive.

WHERE TO DINE

Acuario. Plaza Puxmaria, 1. ☎ **968/21-99-55.** Reservations recommended. Main courses 1,350–2,200 ptas. ($10.80–$17.60); fixed-price menu 3,200 ptas. ($25.60). AE, DC, MC, V. Mon–Sat 1–4pm and 8pm–midnight. Closed 2 weeks in Aug. Bus: 2, 5, 6, or 11. MURCIAN/INTERNATIONAL.

Located near the cathedral, this restaurant allows you to dine in air-conditioned comfort. Since it opened in 1987, it has long been known for both its excellent Murcian cuisine and its selection of international dishes. Begin perhaps with the pâté of salmon, following with such dishes as *merluza* (hake) in sherry sauce, a tender tournedos, or the chef's specialty, eggplant cooked with Serrano ham and mushrooms. If featured, the lemon soufflé is delectable.

Rincón de Pepe. Plaza de Apóstoles, 34. ☎ **968/21-22-39.** Reservations recommended. Main courses 1,800–3,500 ptas. ($14.40-$28). AE, DC, MC, V. Daily noon–4pm, Mon–Sat 8pm–midnight. Closed Aug. Bus: 3, 4, or 8. SPANISH/INTERNATIONAL.

Many visitors won't leave town without going to this culinary landmark set up in the mid-1920s. It rates as the best restaurant in town, and you can dine here at a wide range of price levels, depending on what you order. Specialties change frequently, since every effort is made to produce a menu with seasonal variations. You might enjoy pig's trotters and white beans, spring lamb kidneys in sherry, or white beans with partridge. The shellfish selection includes Carril clams, a platter of assorted grilled seafood and fish, and grilled red prawns from Aguilas. Among the meat and poultry specialties are roast spring lamb Murcian style and duck in orange sauce.

TAPAS

Good tapas are served at **La Tapa,** Plaza de las Flores (☎ **968/21-13-17**), daily from 7am to midnight. An interesting end to a walk through the old city (it's located on one of the oldest town squares), La Tapa offers beer on tap as well as its savory selection of tapas for 125 to 200 pesetas ($1–$1.60). There is a big terrace on which you can enjoy your food and drink.

Settling into Barcelona

12

Blessed with rich and fertile soil, an excellent harbor, and a hardworking population, Barcelona has always prospered. At a time when Madrid was still a dusty and unknown Castilian backwater, Barcelona was a powerful, diverse capital, one influenced more by the Mediterranean empires that conquered it than by the cultures of the arid Iberian plains to the west. Carthage, Rome, Charlemagne-era France—each overran Catalonia, and each left an indelible mark on the region's nascent identity.

The Catalán people have clung fiercely to their unique culture—a culture that, earlier in this century, Franco systematically tried to eradicate. But Catalonia has endured, becoming a semiautonomous region of Spain (with Catalán its official language). And Barcelona, the region's lodestar, has come into its own. The city's most powerful monuments are those that open a window onto its history: from the intricately carved edifices that comprise the medieval Gothic Quarter; to the curvilinear *modernismo* that inspired Gaudí's Sagrada Familia; to seminal surrealist works of Picasso and Miró, found in museums that peg Barcelona as a crucial incubator for 20th-century art.

As if the attractions of Barcelona weren't enough, it stands on the doorstep of some of the great playgrounds and vacation retreats of Europe: the Balearic Islands to the east, the Costa Brava (Wild Coast) to the north, the Penedés wine country to the west, the Roman city of Tarragona, the monastery at Montserrat, and such Costa Dorada resort towns as Sitges, to the south.

Despite its allure, Barcelona grapples with problems common to many major cities—the increasing polarization of rich and poor, a rising tide of drug abuse, and an escalating crime rate. But in reaction to a rash of negative publicity, city authorities have, with some degree of success, brought crime under control, at least within the tourist zones.

A revitalized Barcelona eagerly prepared for and welcomed thousands of visitors as part of the 1992 Summer Olympic Games. But the action didn't end when the last medal was handed out. Barcelona turned its multimillion-dollar building projects into permanently expanded facilities for sports and tourism. Its modern $150-million terminal at El Prat de Llobregat Airport can accommodate 12 million passengers a year; and the restructuring of Barcelona is called "Post Olympica"—a race to the 21st century.

1 Catalonian Culture

Barcelona (which was described in the Middle Ages as "the head and trunk of Catalonia") has always thrived on contacts and commerce with countries beyond Spain's borders. From its earliest days, the city has been linked more closely to France and the rest of Europe than to Iberia. And each of the military and financial empires that swept through and across the collective consciousness of Catalonia left its cultural legacy.

ARCHITECTURE Like many other cities in Spain, Barcelona claims its share of Neolithic dolmens and ruins from the Roman and Moorish periods. Monuments survive from the Middle Ages, when the Romanesque solidity of no-nonsense barrel vaults (sometimes with ribbing), narrow windows, and a fortified design were widely used.

In the 11th and 12th centuries, a religious fervor swept through Europe and pilgrims began to flock through Barcelona on their way west to Santiago de Compostela, bringing with them the influence of French building styles and a need for new and larger churches. The style that emerged (called Catalonian Gothic) had softer lines and more elaborate ornamentation. Appropriate for both civic and religious buildings, it called for ogival (pointed) arches, intricate stone carvings, large interior columns, exterior buttresses, and vast rose windows set with colored glass. One of Barcelona's purest and most-loved examples of this style is the Church of Santa María del Mar, north of the city's harborfront.

The Barcelona that visitors best remember, however, is the Barcelona of *modernismo*—an art nouveau movement that, from about 1890 to 1910, put the city on the architectural map. A highly articulate school of Catalán architects blended Pre-Raphaelite voluptuousness and Catalonian romanticism, heavily laced with a yearning for the curved lines and organic forms easily recognized in nature.

The movement's most famous architect was Antoni Gaudí. The chimneys of his buildings look like half-melted mounds of chocolate twisted into erratic spirals, and his horizontal lines flow, rather than lie, over vertical supports. Some of Gaudí's most distinctive creations include the Casa Milá, the Casa Batlló, Parc Güell and the surrounding neighborhood, and the landmark Temple Expiatori de la Sagrada Familia (never completed).

Other modernist architects of this era looked to medieval models for inspiration, particularly the fortified castles and sculpted gargoyles and dragons of the 12th-century counts of Barcelona. Examples include Domènech i Montaner and Puig i Cadafalch, whose elegant mansions and concert halls seemed perfectly suited to the enlightened and sophisticated prosperity of the 19th-century Catalonian bourgeoisie. Fortunately, a 19th-century economic boom neatly coincided with the profusion of geniuses who suddenly emerged in the building business. Some of the elaborately beautiful villas of Barcelona and nearby Sitges were commissioned by entrepreneurs whose fortunes had been made in the fields and mines of the New World.

The expansion—first initiated in 1858—of Barcelona into the northern Eixample district laid the groundwork, as it were, for the buildings designed by the *modernismo* architects. The gridlike pattern of streets in the Exiample was intersected, in surprisingly modern motifs, with broad diagonals. Although opposed by local landowners and never endowed with the detail of its original design, it provided a carefully planned and elegant path in which a growing city could showcase its finest buildings.

Consistent with the general artistic stagnation of Spain during the Franco era (1939–75), the 1950s saw a tremendous increase in the number of anonymous housing projects around the periphery of Barcelona. Since the death of Franco, the renaissance of *la movida* (the movement) has enhanced all aspects of Spain's artistic life; new and more creative designs for buildings are once again being executed.

ART From the cave paintings discovered at Lérida to the giants of the 20th century, such as Picasso, Dalí, and Miró, Catalonia has had a long artistic tradition. It is the center of plastic arts in Spain.

Barcelona entered the world art pages with its Catalonian Gothic sculpture, which held sway from the 13th to the 15th century and produced such renowned masters as Bartomeu and Pere Johan. Sculptors working with Italian masters brought the Renaissance to Barcelona, but few great Catalonian legacies remain from this period. The rise of baroque art in the 17th and 18th centuries saw Catalonia filled with several impressive examples but nothing worth a special pilgrimage.

In the neoclassical period of the 18th century, Catalonia, and particularly Barcelona, arose from an artistic slumber. Art schools opened in the city and foreign painters arrived, exerting considerable influence. The 19th century produced many Catalonian artists who, it might be said, followed the general European trends of the time without forging any major creative breakthroughs.

The 20th century brought renewed artistic ferment in Barcelona, as reflected by the arrival of Málaga-born Pablo Picasso (the city today is the site of a major Picasso museum). The great surrealist painters of the Spanish school, Joan Miró (who also has a museum in Barcelona) and Salvador Dalí (whose museum is along the Costa Brava, north of Barcelona), also came to the Catalonian capital.

Many Catalán sculptors also achieved acclaim in this century, including Casanovas, Llimon, and Blay. The Spanish Civil War brought a cultural stagnation, yet against all odds many a Catalán artist continued to make bold statements. Antoni Tàpies was a major artist of this period (one of the newest museums in Barcelona is devoted to his work). Among the various schools formed in Spain at the time was the neofigurative band, which included such artists as Váquez Díaz and Pancho Cossio. Antonio López, dubbed a hyperrealist, went on to international acclaim.

Today, toward the end of the 20th century, many Barcelona artists are making major names for themselves, and their works are sold in the most prestigious galleries of the Western world.

LITERATURE & LANGUAGE Catalonia, a region lying midway between France and Castilian Spain, is united by a common language, Catalán. The linguistic separateness of the region is arguably the single most important element in the sometimes obsessive independence of its people. Modern linguists attribute the earliest division of Catalán from Castilian to two phenomena: The first was the cultural links and trade ties between ancient Barcina and the neighboring Roman colony of Provence, which shaped the Catalán tongue along Provençal and Languedocian models. The second major event was the invasion of the eastern Pyrenees by Charlemagne in the late 800s and the designation of Catalonia as a Frankish march (buffer zone) between Christian Europe and a Moorish-dominated Iberia.

Contemporaneous with the troubadour tradition of courtly love so popular in Provence and neighboring Languedoc during the 1100s and the 1200s, a handful of

Impressions

Although the great adventures that befell me there occasioned me no great pleasure, but rather much grief, I bore them the better for having seen the city [Barcelona].

—Don Quixote

courtly minstrels composed similar poems in Catalán and recited them at banquets for the amusement of the lords of Barcelona. By the late 1200s, Catalonia's literature became better defined, thanks to the works of Peter the Ceremonious, Desciot, and Mutaner and to the religious treatises of Arnau de Vilanova. The best-remembered of them all was a socially prominent physician and mystic theologican, a true Renaissance man born 200 years too soon, Ramón Llull. In addition to poetry and the composition of a scientific encyclopedia, he worked in what has been called an early form of the novel, describing a medieval urban landscape filled with what later generations would have labeled bourgeois characters. Llull also coined many words of his own (or recorded existing words for the first time), thereby enriching the Catalán language.

The most prolific period of Catalán literature was the late 1300s and early 1400s, a period critics view as an early articulate expression of the humanism that later swept through the rest of Europe in better-developed forms. Authors from this period include Bernat Metge, Febrer, Ausias March, Ruís de Corella, and Jordi de Sant Jordi. About a century later, Catalán literature received a tremendous boost from the most important and venerated writer in Spanish history, Miguel de Cervantes (1547–1616), who lavishly praised a Catalán epic written about a century before his birth—the chivalric poem *Tirant lo Blanch* by Joanot Martorell.

From about 1500 to about 1810, Catalán literature was severely eclipsed by the brilliant works being written in Castilian. The capital of the Spanish Empire shifted to Madrid, and it was both fiscally and politically expedient to mimic Castilian, rather than Catalán, models. A more cynical view suggests that this era marked the beginning of the suppression of Catalonian culture, with the simultaneous relegation to obscurity of works that otherwise might have been celebrated.

The 19th century, however, brought economic prosperity to hardworking Catalonia, where the bourgeois middle class enjoyed a financial boom that made it the envy of Spain. Prosperity and the resulting *renaixença* (renaissance) of Catalonian culture produced a form of romanticism exemplified by Jacint Verdaguer and Angel Guimerà (in dramatics), Milà i Fontanals (in poetry), Narcís Oller (described as a naturalist), and Santiago Rusinñol (a modernist). Writing was considered inappropriate for women at this time, but Catalonia nevertheless produced a female novelist, Caterina Albert, who wrote under the pseudonym Victor Catala.

During the early 20th century, there was a strong emphasis on literary style and form. In the same way that the Parisians applauded the sophistication of Marcel Proust, Cataláns read and appreciated such stylists as Eugeni d'Ors and such poets as Carles Riba (*Elégies de Bierville*) and Joan Salvat-Papasseit.

In the 1950s, despite the suppression of the Catalonian language by Franco, such works as *Béarn* by Lorenc Villalonga, *La Plaça del Diamant* by Mercé Rodoreda, and *Els Payesos* by Josep Plá were enthusiastically received by international critics.

MUSIC & DANCE The counts of Barcelona, so we are told, were great music lovers, and the Catalán appreciation of music continues to this day. Richard Strauss arrived to dedicate the musical center, the Palau de la Música Catalana, in 1908.

In addition to importing the great talents of Europe for its listening pleasure, the people of Catalonia also create music. Many of their own artists and composers have gone on to international acclaim in their fields, Pablo Casals being the most notable.

But few artistic traditions enjoy the renown of the *sardana,* the national dance of the Catalláns. This is really a street dance, accompanied by *coblas* (brass bands). You can perform a *sardana* almost anywhere and at any time, provided you get some like-minded people to join you. Age doesn't matter—everybody joins in the spontaneous outburst. The roots of the dance are not known. Some claim that it originated on one of the Greek islands and was brought to Barcelona by seafarers; others say that it came from the Italian island of Sardinia, which would at least account for its name. To see this dance, go to the Plaça de Sant Jaume in the Barri Gótic of Barcelona on a Sunday morning.

2 Orientation

GETTING THERE

BY PLANE During the months prior to the 1992 Olympics, airlines scrambled to provide nonstop transatlantic service to Barcelona. In the post-Olympic world, however, most passengers must first change aircraft in Madrid. The only exception is **TWA,** which has maintained its nonstop transatlantic service from New York to Barcelona long after other carriers, including Iberia, discontinued theirs. Passengers originating in such European capitals as London, Paris, and Rome, can fly nonstop to Barcelona (usually on their national airlines), but most passengers, for whatever reason, opt for transit through Madrid. For more information on flying into Madrid, refer to "Getting There" in Chapter 3.

Within Spain, the most likely carrier is **Iberia,** which offers peak-hour shuttle flights at 15-minute intervals between Madrid and Barcelona. Service from Madrid to Barcelona at less congested times of the day averages around one flight every 30 to 40 minutes. Iberia also offers flights between Barcelona and Valencia, Granada, Seville, and Bilbao. Within Barcelona, you can arrange ticketing at one of two Iberia offices. The easiest to find lies a few blocks north of the sprawling Plaça de Catalunya, at Passeig de Gràcia, 30 (☎ **93/412-47-48;** metro: Passeig de Gràcia).

El Prat de Llobregat, 08820 Prat de Llobregat (☎ **93/298-38-38**), the Barcelona airport, lies 7½ miles (12km) southwest of the city. The route to the center of town is carefully signposted. A train runs daily between the airport and Barcelona's Estació Central de Barcelona-Sants from 6:14am (the first airport departure) to 10:44pm (the last city departure). The 21-minute trip costs 290 pesetas ($2.30) Monday through Friday and 335 pesetas ($2.70) Saturday and Sunday. If your hotel lies near Plaça de Catalunya, you might opt instead for an Aerobús that runs daily every 15 minutes between 5:30am and 10pm. The fare is 435 pesetas ($3.50). A taxi from the airport into central Barcelona will cost approximately 2,000 to 2,500 pesetas ($16–$20).

BY TRAIN A train called the Barcelona-TALGO provides rail service between Paris and Barcelona in 11½ hours. For many other connections from the mainland of Europe, it is necessary to change trains at Port Bou, on the French-Spanish border. Most trains issue seat and sleeper reservations.

Trains departing from the **Estació de Franca,** Avenida Marqués de L'Argentera (metro: Barceloneta, L3), cover long distances within Spain as well as international routes, carrying a total of 20,000 passengers daily. There are express night trains to Paris, Zurich, Milan, and Geneva. Every international route served by the state-owned RENFE railway company uses the Estació de Franca, including some of its most luxurious express trains, such as the *Pau Casals* and the *TALGO Catalán.*

This totally modernized 1929 station includes a huge screen with updated information on train departures and arrivals, personalized ticket dispatching, a passenger attention center, a tourism information center, showers, internal baggage control, a first-aid center, as well as centers for hotel reservations and car rentals. But it is much more than a departure point: The station has an elegant restaurant, a cafeteria, a book-and-record store, a jazz club, and even a disco. The Estació de Franca is just steps away from Ciutadella Park, the zoo, and the port and is near Vila Olímpica.

From this station you can book tickets to the major cities of Spain: Madrid (5 TALGOS trains per day, 7 hours; and 3 *rápidos,* 10 hours), Seville (2 trains daily, 10½ hours), and Valencia (11 daily, 4 hours).

RENFE also has a terminal at **Estació Central de Barcelona-Sants,** Plaça de Països Catalanes (metro: Sants-Estació).

For general RENFE information, call **93/490-02-02.**

BY BUS Bus travel to Barcelona is possible but not popular—it's slow. Coach services do not operate regularly from the major capitals of western Europe to Barcelona. **Eurolines Limited,** 23 Crawley Rd., Luton LU1 1HX, Bedfordshire, England (☎ **01582/404-511** or **0171/730-8235**), can arrange your trip from London to Barcelona.

Enatcar, Estació del Nord (☎ **93/245-25-28**), operates five buses per day to Madrid (trip time: 8 hours) and 10 buses per day to Valencia (trip time: 4½ hours). A one-way ticket to Madrid costs 2,690 pesetas ($21.50); to Valencia, 2,650 pesetas ($21.20). For bus travel to one of the beach resorts along the Costa Brava (see Chapter 15), go to **Sarfa,** Estació del Nord (☎ **93/265-11-58**), which operates buses from Barcelona to such resorts as Tossa de Mar. Trip time is usually two hours.

BY CAR From France (the usual road approach to Barcelona), the major access route is at the eastern end of the Pyrenees. You have a choice of the express highway (E-15) or the more scenic coastal road. But be warned: If you take the scenic coastal road in July and August, you will often encounter bumper-to-bumper traffic. From France, you can also approach Barcelona via Toulouse. Cross the border into Spain at Puigcerdá (frontier stations are there), near the principality of Andorra. From there, take the N-152 to Barcelona.

From Madrid, take the N-2 to Zaragoza, then the A-2 to El Vendrell, followed by the A-7 motorway to Barcelona. From the Costa Blanca or Costa del Sol, take the E-15 north from Valencia along the eastern Mediterranean coast.

BY FERRY **Transmediterránea,** Muelle de Barcelona Estación Maritima (☎ **93/443-25-32**), operates daily voyages to the Balearic island of Majorca (trip time: 8 hours) and also to Minorca (trip time: 9 hours). In summer, it's important to have a reservation as far in advance as possible, because of overcrowding.

VISITOR INFORMATION

A conveniently located tourist office is the **Patronat de Turisme,** Gran Vía de les Corts Catalanes, 658 (☎ **93/301-74-43;** metro: Urquinaona or Plaça de Catalunya). It's open Monday through Saturday from 9am to 7pm. There's also an office at the airport, **El Prat de Llobregat** (☎ **93/478-47-04**), which you'll pass as you clear Customs. Summer hours are Monday through Saturday from 9:30am to 8pm; off-season hours are Monday through Saturday from 9:30am to 8pm; year-round, it's open on Sunday from 9:30am to 2pm.

There's another office at the **Estació Central de Barcelona-Sants,** Plaça Països Catalanes (☎ **93/491-44-31;** metro: Sants-Estació). In summer it is open daily from 8am to 8pm; off-season, Monday through Friday from 8am to 8pm and Saturday and Sunday from 8am to 2pm. At these offices, you can pick up maps and information.

CITY LAYOUT

MAIN SQUARES, STREETS & ARTERIES The **Plaça de Catalunya** (Plaza de Catalunña in Spanish) is the city's heart; the world-famous Rambles (*Ramblas* in Spanish) are its arteries. Les Rambles begin at the Plaça Portal de la Pau, with its 164-foot-high monument to Columbus and a panoramic view of the port, and stretch north to the Plaça de Catalunya, with its fountains and trees. Along this wide promenade you'll find bookshops and newsstands, stalls selling birds and flowers, and benches or café tables and chairs, where you can sit and watch the passing parade.

At the end of the Rambles is the **Barri Xinés** (Barrio Chino in Spanish, Chinese Quarter in English), which has enjoyed notoriety as a haven of prostitution and drugs, populated in Jean Genet's *The Thief's Journal* by "whores, thieves, pimps, and beggars." Still a dangerous district, it is best viewed during the day, if at all.

Off the Rambles lies **Plaça Reial** (Plaza Real in Spanish), the most harmoniously proportioned square in Barcelona. Come here on Sunday morning to see the stamp and coin collectors peddle their wares.

The major wide boulevards of Barcelona are the **Avinguda** (Avenida in Spanish) **Diagonal** and **Passeig** (Paseo in Spanish) **de Colom,** and an elegant shopping street, the **Passeig de Gràcia.**

A short walk from the Rambles will take you to the **Passeig del Moll de la Fusta,** a waterfront promenade developed in the 1990s, with some of the finest (but not the cheapest) restaurants in Barcelona. If you can't afford the high prices, come here at least for a drink in the open air and take in a view of the harbor.

To the east is the old port of the city, called **La Barceloneta,** which dates from the 18th century. This strip of land between the port and the sea has traditionally been a good place for seafood.

The **Barri Gòtic** (Barrio Gótico in Spanish, Gothic Quarter in English) lies to the east of the Rambles. This is the site of the city's oldest buildings, including the cathedral.

North of Plaça de Catalunya, the **Eixample** unfolds. An area of wide boulevards, in contrast to the Gothic Quarter, it contains two major roads leading out of Barcelona, the previously mentioned Avinguda Diagonal and Gran Vía de les Corts Catalanes. Another major area, Gràcia, lies north of the Eixample.

Montjuïc, one of the mountains of Barcelona, begins at Plaça d'Espanya, a traffic rotary. This was the setting for the 1992 Summer Olympic Games and is today the site of Vila Olímpica (see below). The other mountain is Tibidabo, in the northwest, which boasts great views of the city and the Mediterranean. It contains an amusement park.

FINDING AN ADDRESS/MAPS Finding an address in Barcelona can be a problem. The city is characterized by long boulevards and a complicated maze of narrow, twisting streets. Therefore, knowing the street number is all-important. If you see the designation *s/n* it means that the building is without a number (*sin número*). Therefore, it's crucial to learn the cross street if you're seeking a specific establishment.

The rule about street numbers is that there is no rule. On most streets, numbering begins on one side and runs up that side until the end, then runs in the opposite direction on the other side. Therefore, number 40 could be opposite 408. But there are many exceptions. Sometimes street numbers on buildings in the older quarters have been obscured by the patina of time.

Arm yourself with a good map before setting out. Those given away free by tourist offices and hotels aren't adequate, since they don't label the little streets. The best map for exploring Barcelona, published by **Falk,** is available at most bookstores and newsstands, such as those found along the Les Rambles. This pocket map includes all the streets, with an index of how to find them.

NEIGHBORHOODS IN BRIEF

Barri Gòtic The section rises to the north of Passeig de Colom, with its Columbus Monument, and is bordered on its east by a major artery, Via Laietana, which begins at La Barceloneta at Plaça d'Antoni López and runs north to Plaça d'Urquinaona. Les Rambles are the western border of the Gothic Quarter, and on the northern edge is the Ronda de Sant Pere, which intersects with Plaça de Catalunya and the Passeig de Gràcia. The heart of this medieval quarter is the Plaça de Sant Jaume, which was a major crossroads in the old Roman city. Many of the structures in the old section are ancient, including the ruins of a Roman temple dedicated to Augustus. Antiques stores, restaurants, cafés, museums, some hotels, and bookstores fill the place today. It is also the headquarters of the Generalitat, seat of the Catalán government.

Les Rambles The most famous promenade in Spain, ranking with Madrid's Paseo del Prado, was once a drainage channel. These days, street entertainers, flower vendors, news vendors, café patrons, and strollers flow along its length. Les Rambles (L*as* Rambl*as* in Spanish) is actually composed of five different sections, each a particular *rambla,* with names like Rambla de Canaletes, Rambla dels Estudis, Rambla de Sant Josep, Rambla dels Caputxins, and Rambla de Santa Mònica. The pedestrian esplanade is shaded, as it makes its way from the Plaça de Catalunya to the port—all the way to the Columbus Monument. Along the way you'll pass the Gran Teatre del Liceu, on Rambla dels Caputxins, one of the most magnificent opera houses in the world until it caught fire. Miró did a sidewalk mosaic at the Plaça de la Boqueria. During the stagnation of the Franco era, this street grew seedier and seedier. But the opening of the Ramada Renaissance hotel and the restoration of many buildings have brought energy and hope for the street.

Barri Xinés This isn't "Chinatown," as most people assume—in fact, historians are unsure just how the neighborhood got its name. For decades it's had an unsavory reputation, known for its houses of prostitution. Franco outlawed prostitution in 1956, but apparently no one ever told the denizens of this district of narrow, often murky, old streets and dark corners. Petty thieves, drug dealers, and purse snatchers are just some of the neighborhood characters. Nighttime is dangerous, so exercise caution; still, most visitors like to take a quick look to see what all the excitement is about. Just off Les Rambles, the area lies primarily between the waterfront and Carrer de l'Hospital.

Barri de la Ribera Another *barrio* that stagnated for years but is now well into a renaissance, the Barri de la Ribera is adjacent to the Barri Gòtic, going east to Passeig de Picasso, which borders the Parc de la Ciutadella. The centerpiece of this district is the Museu Picasso, housed in the 15th-century Palau Agüilar, at Montcada, 15. Numerous art galleries have opened around the museum, and the old quarter is fashionable. Many mansions in this area were built at the time of one of the major maritime expansions in Barcelona's history, principally in the 1200s and 1300s. Most of these grand homes still stand along Carrer de Montcada and other nearby streets.

La Barceloneta & the Harborfront Although Barcelona was founded on seagoing tradition, its waterfront was in decay for years. Today, it's bursting with activity along the waterfront promenade, Passeig del Moll de la Fusta. The best way to get a bird's-eye view of the area is to take an elevator to the top of the Columbus Monument in Plaça Portal de la Pau.

In the vicinity of the monument were the Reials Drassanes, or royal shipyards, a booming place of industry during Barcelona's maritime heyday in the Middle Ages. Years before Columbus landed in the New World, ships sailed around the world from here, flying the traditional yellow-and-red flag of Catalonia.

To the east lies a mainly artificial peninsula called La Barceloneta (Little Barcelona), formerly a fishing district, dating mainly from the 18th century. It's now filled with seafood restaurants. The blocks here are long and surprisingly narrow—architects planned them that way so that each room in every building fronted a street. Many bus lines terminate at the Passeig Nacional here, site of the Barcelona Aquarium.

Eixample (Ensanche) To the north of the Plaça de Catalunya lies the Eixample, or Ensanche, the section of Barcelona that grew beyond the old medieval walls. This great period of "extension," or enlargement (*eixample* in Catalán), came mainly in the 19th century. Avenues form a grid of perpendicular streets, cut across by a majestic boulevard—Passeig de Gràcia, a posh shopping street ideal for leisurely promenades. The area's main traffic artery is Avinguda Diagonal, which links the expressway and the heart of this congested city.

The Eixample possesses some of the most original buildings any architect ever designed—not just those by Gaudí, but ones by others as well. The area was the center of Barcelona's *modernismo* movement. And of course, Gaudí's Sagrada Familia is one of the major attractions.

Montjuïc & Tibidabo Montjuïc, called Hill of the Jews after a Jewish necropolis there, gained prominence in 1929 as the site of the World's Fair and again in 1992 as the site of the Summer Olympic Games. Its major attraction is the Poble Espanyol (Spanish Village), a five-acre site constructed for the World's Fair, where examples of Spanish art and architecture are displayed against the backdrop of a traditional Spanish village. Tibidabo (1,650 feet) is where you should go for your final look at Barcelona. On a clear day you can see the mountains of Majorca (the most famous of the Balearic Islands). Reached by train, tram, and cable car, Tibidabo is the most popular Sunday excursion in Barcelona.

Pedralbes Pedralbes is where the wealthy people live, some in stylish blocks of apartment houses, others in 19th-century villas behind ornamental fences, and still others in stunning *modernismo* structures. Set in a park, the Palau de Pedralbes (at Avinguda Diagonal, 686) was constructed in the 1920s as a gift from the city to Alfonxo XIII, the grandfather of today's King Juan Carlos. The king abdicated and fled in 1931, never making much use of the palace. Today it has a new life, housing a museum of carriages and a group of European paintings called the Colecció Cambó.

Vila Olímpica This seafront property contains the tallest buildings in the city. The revitalized site, in the post–Olympic Games era, is the setting for numerous showrooms for imported cars, designer clothing stores, restaurants, and business offices. The "village" was the center of the 1992 games. A regular city-in-miniature is taking shape, complete with banks, art galleries, nightclubs, bars, even pastry shops.

3 Getting Around

Discounts To save money on public transportation, buy one of two transportation cards, each good for 10 trips; **Tarjeta T-1,** costing 650 pesetas ($5.20), is good for the metro, bus, Montjuïc funicular, and Tramvía Blau, which runs from the Passeig de Sant Gervasi/Avinguda del Tibidabo to the bottom part of the funicular to Tibidabo. **Tarjeta T-2,** for 625 pesetas ($5), is good on everything but the bus.

Passes (*abonos temporales*) are available at the office of **Transports Metropolita de Barcelona,** Plaça de Catalunya, open Monday to Friday from 8am to 7pm and Saturday from 8am to 1pm.

To save money on sightseeing tours during the summer, take a ride on **Bus Turistic,** which passes by a dozen of the most popular sights. You can get on and off the bus as you please and also ride the Tibidabo funicular and the Montjuïc cable car and funicular for the price of a single ticket. Tickets, which may be purchased on the bus or at the transportation booth at Plaça de Catalunya, cost 850 pesetas ($6.80) for a half day or 1,200 pesetas ($9.60) for a full day.

By Subway Barcelona's metro system consists of five main lines; it crisscrosses the city more frequently and with greater efficiency than the bus network. Two commuter trains also service the city, fanning out to the suburbs. Service is Monday through Friday from 5am to 11pm, Saturday from 5am to 1am, and Sunday and holidays from 6am to 1am. A one-way fare is 135 pesetas ($1.10). The entrance to each metro station is marked with a red diamond. The major station for all subway lines is Plaça de Catalunya.

By Bus Some 50 bus lines traverse the city, and as always, you don't want to ride them at rush hour. The driver issues a ticket as you board at the front. Most buses operate daily from 6:30am to 10pm; some night buses go along the principal arteries from 10pm to 4am. Buses are color-coded—red ones cut through the city center during the day, and blue ones do the job at night. A one-way fare is 135 pesetas ($1.10) or 150 pesetas ($1.20) on Sundays and holidays.

By Taxi Each yellow-and-black taxi bears the letters *SP* (*servicio público*) on both its front and its rear. A lit green light on the roof and a "Libre" sign in the window indicate that the taxi is free to pick up passengers. The basic rate begins at 250 pesetas ($2). Check to make sure you're not paying the fare of a previously departed passenger; taxi drivers have been known to "forget" to turn back the meter. For each additional kilometer in the slow-moving traffic, you are assessed 110 to 118 pesetas (90¢–95¢). Supplements might also be added—125 pesetas ($1) for a large suitcase, for instance. Rides to the airport carry a supplement of 300 pesetas ($2.40). For a taxi, call **93/330-08-04, 93/300-38-11,** or **93/358-11-11.**

By Bicycle Ever wonder why you see so few people riding bicycles in Barcelona? As in Madrid, heavy pollution from traffic and pedestrian-clogged narrow streets of the inner city make riding a bicycle very difficult. It's better to walk.

By Car Driving is next to impossible in congested Barcelona, and it's potentially dangerous. Besides, it's unlikely that you'd ever find a place to park. Try other means of getting around. Save your car rentals for one-day excursions from the Catalonian capital to such places as Sitges and Tarragona to the south, Montserrat to the west, or the resorts of the Costa Brava to the north.

All three of the major U.S.-based car-rental firms are represented in Barcelona, both at the airport and at downtown offices. The company with the longest hours and some of the most favorable rates is **Budget,** Travesera de Gràcia, 71 (☎ **93/201-21-99**), open Monday through Friday without a midday break, from 8am to 8pm. Hours on Saturday and Sunday are 9am to 1pm.

Other contenders include **Avis,** Carrer de Casanova, 209 (☎ **93/209-95-33**), open Monday through Friday 9am to 1pm and 4 to 7pm, and Saturday 8am to 1pm. **Hertz** maintains its office at Tuset, 10 (☎ **93/217-80-76**); it's open Monday through Friday from 8am to 2pm and 4–7pm, Saturday from 9am to 1pm. Both Hertz and Avis are closed on Sunday, forcing clients of those companies to trek out to the airport to pick up or return their cars.

Remember that it's usually cheaper and easier to arrange your car rental before leaving the U.S. by calling one of the firms' toll-free numbers. For more information on car rentals in Spain, refer to the section on car rentals in "Getting Around" in Chapter 3.

Barcelona Metro

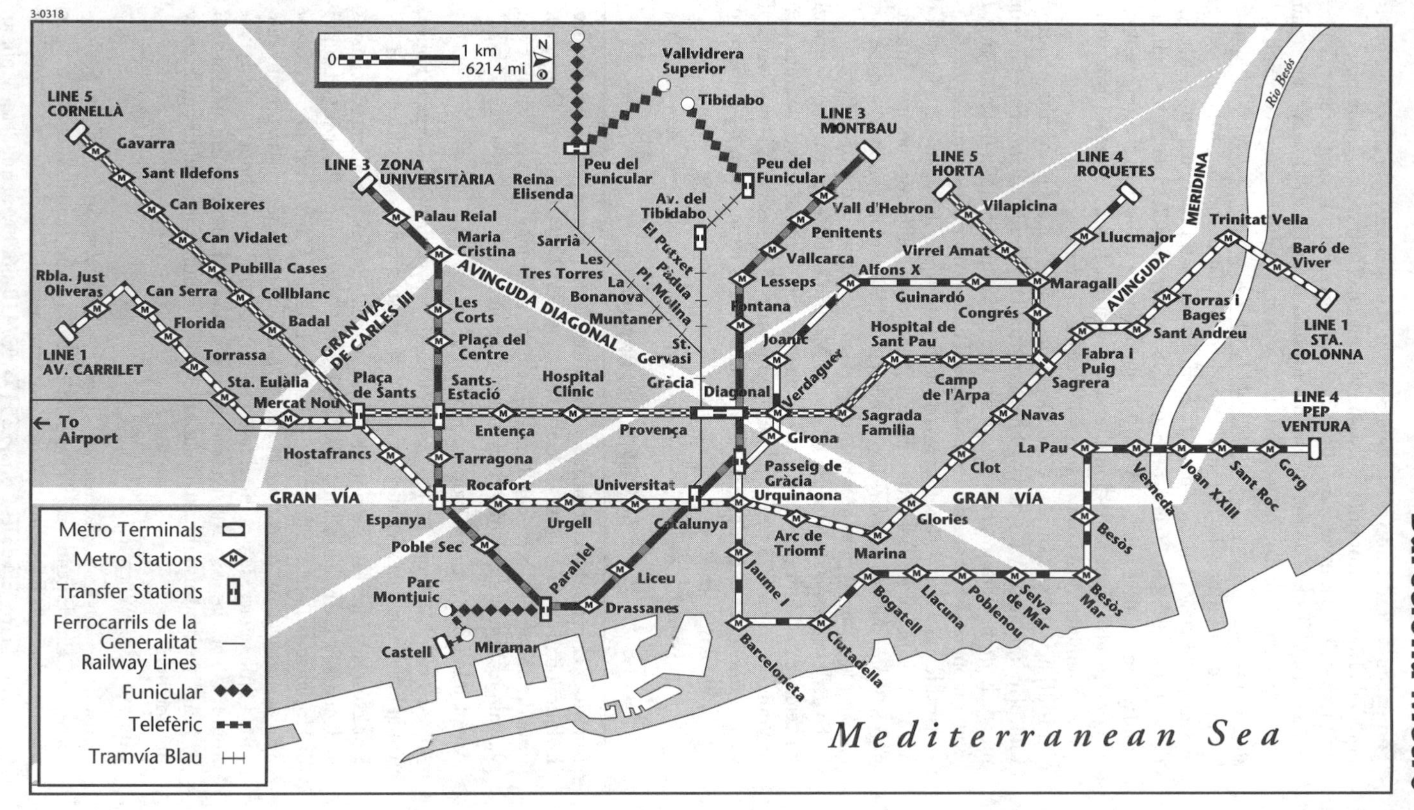

Funiculars & Rail Links At some point in your journey, you may want to visit both Tibidabo and Montjuïc. There are various links to these mountaintops.

A train called **Tramvía Blau (Blue Streetcar)** goes from Passeig de Sant Gervasi/ Avinguda del Tibidabo to the bottom of the funicular to Tibidabo every 3 to 15 minutes. It operates Monday through Saturday from 7am to 10pm and Sunday and holidays from 7am to 10:30pm. The one-way fare is 250 pesetas ($2). At the end of the run, you can continue the rest of the way by funicular to the top, at 1,650 feet, for a panoramic view of Barcelona. The funicular operates every half hour Monday through Friday from 7:05am to 9:43pm, Saturday from 7:15am to 9:45pm, and Sunday and holidays from 7:15 to 10:15am and 8:45 to 9:45pm. During peak visiting hours (10:15am to 8:45pm) service is increased, with a funicular departing every 15 minutes. A one-way fare is 400 pesetas ($3.20).

Montjüic, the site of the 1992 Olympics, can be reached by the Montjuïc funicular, linking up with subway line 3 at Parallel. The funicular operates in summer daily from 11am to 8pm, charging a fare of 325 pesetas ($2.60) round-trip. In winter it operates on Saturday, Sunday, and holidays from 10:45am to 2pm.

A **cable car** linking the upper part of the Montjuïc funicular with Castell de Montjuïc is in service from June through September, daily from noon to 3pm and 4 to 8:30pm; the one-way fare is 350 pesetas ($2.80). In off-season it operates only on Saturday, Sunday, and holidays from 11am to 2:45pm and 4 to 7:30pm.

To get to these places, you can board the **Montjuïc telèferic,** which runs from La Barceloneta to Montjuïc. Service from June through September is daily from 11am to 9pm; the fare is 575 pesetas ($4.60) round-trip, 375 pesetas ($3) one way. Off-season hours are Saturday, Sunday, and holidays from 11am to 2:45pm and 4 to 7:30pm.

FAST FACTS: Barcelona

American Express For your mail or banking needs, the American Express office in Barcelona is at Passeig de Gràcia, 101 (☎ **93/217-00-70;** metro: Diagonal), near the corner of Carrer del Rosselló. It's open Monday through Friday from 9:30am to 6pm and Saturday from 10am to noon.

Area Code The area code for Barcelona is **93.**

Babysitters Most major hotels can arrange for babysitters with adequate notice. You'll have to make a special request for an English-speaking babysitter.

Bookstores The best selection of English-language books, including travel maps and guides, is LAIE, Pau Claris, 85 (☎ **93/318-17-39;** metro: Plaça de Catalunya or Urquinaona), one block from the Gran Vía de les Corts Catalanes. It's open Monday through Saturday from 10am to 9pm. The bookshop has an upstairs café with a little terrace, serving breakfast, lunch (salad bar), even dinners. Meals cost from 1,650 pesetas ($13.20). The café is open Monday through Saturday from 9am to 1am. The shop also presents cultural events, including art exhibits and literary presentations.

Climate See "When to Go" in Chapter 3.

Consulates For embassies, refer to Chapter 3, "Fast Facts: Spain." The U.S. Consulate, at Reina Elisenda, 23 (☎ **93/280-22-27;** train: Reina Elisenda), is open Monday through Friday from 9am to 12:30pm and 3 to 5pm. The Canadian Consulate, Travessera de les Corts, 265 (☎ **93/410-66-99;** metro: Plaça Molina), is open Monday through Friday from 9am to 2pm and 3 to 5:30pm. The U.K. Consulate, Avinguda Diagonal, 477 (☎ **93/419-90-44;** metro: Hospital Clinic), is open Monday through Friday from 9am to 2pm and from 4 to 5pm. The Australian Consulate is at Gran Vía Carlos III, 98, ninth floor (☎ **93/330-04-96;** metro: María Cristina), and is open Monday through Friday from 10am to noon.

Currency Exchange Most banks will exchange currency Monday to Friday from 8:30am to 2pm and Saturday from 8:30am to 1pm. A major *oficina de cambio* (exchange office) is operated at the Estació Central de Barcelona-Sants, the principal rail station for Barcelona. It's open Monday through Saturday from 8:30am to 10pm, Sunday from 8:30am to 2pm and 4:30 to 10pm. Exchange offices are also available at Barcelona's airport, El Prat de Llobregat, open daily from 7am to 11pm.

Dentist Call Clinica Dental Beonadex, Paseo Bona Nova, 69, third floor (☎ **93/418-44-33**), for an appointment. It is open Monday from 4 to 9pm and Tuesday through Friday from 8am to 3pm.

Doctors See "Hospitals," below.

Drugstores The most central one is Farmacía Manuel Nadal i Casas, Rambla de Canaletes, 121 (☎ **93/317-49-42;** metro: Plaça de Catalunya), open Monday to Friday from 9am to 1:30pm and 4:30 to 8pm, Saturday from 9am to 1:30pm. Various pharmacies take turns staying open late at night. Pharmacies that aren't open post names and addresses of pharmacies in the area that are open.

Emergencies Fire, **080;** police, **092;** ambulance, **061.**

Eyeglasses Complete service is provided by Optica 2000, Santa Anna, 2 (☎ **93/302-12-47;** metro: Plaça de Catalunya), open Monday through Saturday from 9:30am to 2pm and 4:30 to 8pm.

Hairdresser A few steps from Les Rambles is Peluqueria Santos, Santa Anna, 6 (☎ **93/317-54-87;** metro: Plaça de Catalunya)—for both *señoras y caballeros.* Located one floor above street level, the shop receives clients Monday through Saturday from 9am to 7pm.

Hospitals Barcelona has many hospitals and clinics, including Hospital Clínic, and Hospital de la Santa Creu i Sant Pau, at the intersection of Carrer Cartagena and Carrer Sant Antoni Maria Claret (☎ **93/291-90-00;** metro: Hospital de Sant Pau).

Laundromats Ask at your hotel for the one nearest you, or try one of the following. *Lavandería Brasilia,* Avinguda Meridiana, 322 (☎ **93/352-72-05;** metro: Plaça de Catalunya), is open Monday through Friday from 9:30am to 1:30pm and 4 to 8pm. Also centrally located is *Lavandería Yolanda,* Carrer Carma, 114 (☎ **93/329-43-68;** metro: Liceu, at Les Rambles). It is open Monday through Friday from 9am to 1:30pm and 4 to 8pm, Saturday from 9am to 1:30pm.

Libraries There's an American Studies library with an English-language collection at the Instituto de Estudios Norteamericanos, Vía Augusta, 123 (☎ **93/200-75-51**). It has a large selection of U.S. magazines and newspapers, as well as circulation and reference sections. Open Monday through Friday from 11am to 2pm and 4 to 9pm; closed August. Take the FFCC commuter train to Plaça Molina.

Lost Property To recover lost property, go to Objects Perduts, Carrer Ciutat, 9 (☎ **93/402-31-61;** metro: Jaume I), Monday to Friday from 9:30am to 1:30pm. If you've lost property on public transport, contact the office in the metro station at Plaça de Catalunya (☎ **93/318-52-93**).

Luggage Storage/Lockers The train station, Estació Central de Barcelona-Sants (☎ **93/491-44-31**), has lockers for 400 to 600 pesetas ($3.20–$4.80) per day. You can obtain locker space daily from 7am to 11pm.

Newspapers/Magazines The *International Herald-Tribune* is sold at major hotels and nearly all the news kiosks along Les Rambles. Sometimes you can also obtain copies of *USA Today* or one of the London newspapers, such as the *Times.* The two leading daily newspapers of Barcelona, which often list cultural events, are *El Periódico* and *a Vanguardia.*

Police See "Emergencies," above.

Post Office The main post office is at Plaça d'Antoni López (☎ **93/318-38-31;** metro: Jaume I). It's open Monday through Friday from 8am to 10pm and Saturday from 8am to 8pm.

Radio/TV If your hotel room has a radio or a TV set (unlikely in budget accommodations), you can often get Britain's BBC World Service. Otherwise, what you'll see in the TV lounges of most budget hotels are Spanish broadcasts of international soccer and rugby competitions and perhaps a bullfight. Deluxe and some first-class hotels subscribe to CNN. Two national TV channels (1 and 2) transmit broadcasts in Spanish, and two regional channels (3 and 33) broadcast in Catalán; there are also some private TV channels. If you're listening to radio, tune in to the Spanish music program, "Segunda Programa," with everything from classical music to jazz—nights only.

Restrooms Some public restrooms are available, including those at popular tourist spots, such as Tibidabo and Montjuïc. You'll also find restrooms at the major museums of Barcelona, at all train stations and airports, and at metro stations. The major department stores, such as El Corté Ingles, also have good restrooms. Otherwise, out on the streets you may be a bit hard-pressed. Sanitation is questionable in some of the public facilities. If you use the facilities of a café or tavern, it is customary to make a small purchase at the bar, even if only a glass of mineral water.

Safety Be particularly careful with cameras, purses, and wallets, all favorite targets of thieves and pickpockets in Barcelona; particularly on the world-famous Rambles. The southern part of Les Rambles, near the waterfront, is the most dangerous section, especially at night. Proceed with caution.

Shoe Repairs Simago, Rambla dels Estudis, 113 (☎ **93/302-48-24;** metro: Plaça de Catalunya or Liceu), in the basement, is open for repairs Monday through Saturday from 9am to 9pm.

Taxes See "Shopping" in Chapter 5 for details on VAT (or IVA in Spanish).

Taxis See "Getting Around," earlier in this chapter.

Telegrams/Telex These can be sent at the main post office (see above). You can send telex and fax messages at all major and many budget hotels.

Telephone Dial **003** for local operator information within Barcelona. For elsewhere in Spain, dial **009.** Most local calls cost 15 pesetas (10¢). Hotels impose various surcharges on phone calls, especially long distance, either in Spain or abroad. It's cheaper to go to the central telephone office at Fontanella, 4, off the Plaça de Catalunya (metro: Plaça de Catalunya), open Monday through Saturday from 8:30am to 9pm.

Transit Information For general RENFE (train) information, dial **93/490-02-02.** For details about airport information, call **93/298-38-38.**

4 Accommodations

Barcelona hotels have never been better—nor as plentiful. In the wake of the 1992 Olympics, old palaces were restored and converted into hotels, and long seedy and tarnished hotels were completely renovated in time for the games. The final result is an abundance of good hotels in all price ranges. Regrettably, the first-class and deluxe hotels are vastly overpriced, in the view of many visitors from less expensive parts of the world. For top-grade comfort, you'll pay, and pay dearly, in the Barcelona of the 1990s.

Safety is an important factor to consider when choosing a hotel in Barcelona. Some of the least expensive hotels are not in good locations. A popular area for the budget-conscious traveler is the Barri Gòtic, located in the heart of town. You'll live and eat less expensively here than in any other part of Barcelona. But you should be especially careful when returning to your hotel late at night.

More modern, but also more expensive, accommodations can be found north of Les Rambles and the Barri Gòtic in the Eixample district, centered around the metro stops Plaça de Catalunya and Universitat. Many of the buildings are in the *modernismo* style (that is, turn-of-the-century art nouveau), but sometimes the elevators and plumbing tend to be of the same vintage. The Eixample is a desirable and safe neighborhood, especially along its wide boulevards. Noise is the only problem you might encounter.

Farther north still, above the Avinguda Diagonal, you'll enter the Grácia area, where you can enjoy Catalán neighborhood life. You'll be a bit away from the main attractions, but they can be reached by public transportation.

Hotels judged very expensive charge from 28,000 pesetas ($224) and up per day for a double room; those considered expensive ask from 17,500 to 30,000 pesetas ($140–$240) for a double; and those viewed as moderate charge from 12,000 to 20,000 pesetas ($96–$160) for a double. Hotels asking under 12,000 pesetas ($96) for a double are considered inexpensive.

Many of Barcelona's hotels were built before the invention of the automobile, and even those that weren't rarely found space for a garage. When parking is available at the hotel, the price is indicated; otherwise, the hotel staff will direct you to a garage somewhere in the general vicinity. Expect to pay from 1,800 pesetas ($14.40) for 24 hours; you might as well park your car, as you can't see traffic-congested Barcelona comfortably by automobile—rely on your trusty feet and public transportation instead.

CIUTAT VELLA

"Old City" in Catalán, Ciutat Vella forms the monumental heartland of Barcelona, taking in Les Rambles, Plaça de Sant Jaume, Via Laietana, Passeig Nacional, and Passeig de Colom. It contains some of the city's best hotel bargains, which exist in older structures. Most of the glamorous—and more expensive—hotels are in Sur Diagonal (see below).

VERY EXPENSIVE

✪ **Le Meridien Barcelona.** Rambles, 111, 08002 Barcelona. ☎ **800/543-4300** in the U.S., or 93/318-62-00. Fax 93/301-77-76. 200 rms, 8 suites. A/C MINIBAR TV TEL. 29,000–38,000 ptas. ($232–$304) double; suites from 48,000 ptas. ($384). AE, DC, MC, V. Metro: Liceu or Plaça de Catalunya.

This is the finest hotel in the old town of Barcelona, as Michael Jackson and other former guests will surely agree. It is superior in both amenities and comfort to its two

Accommodations in Central Barcelona

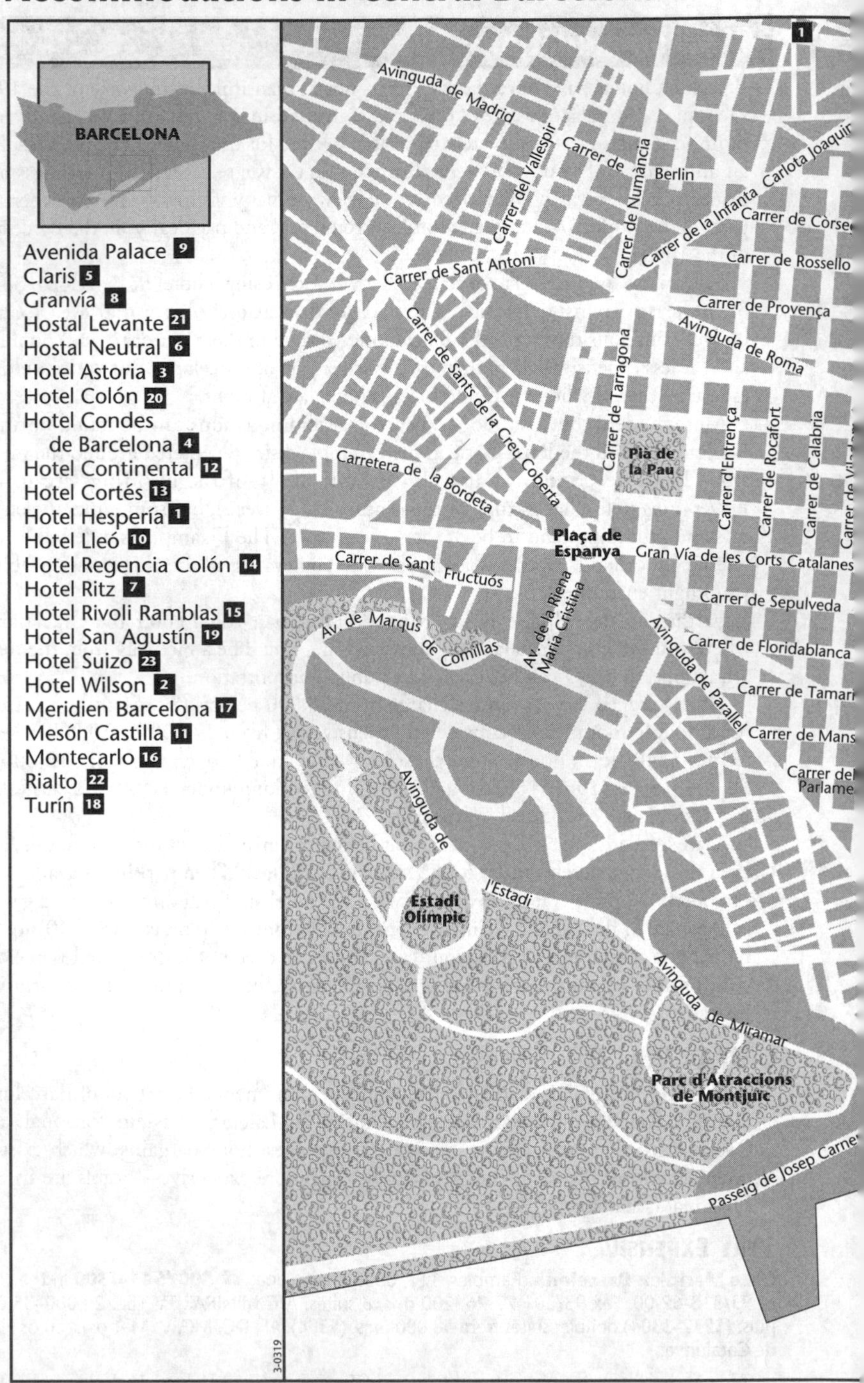

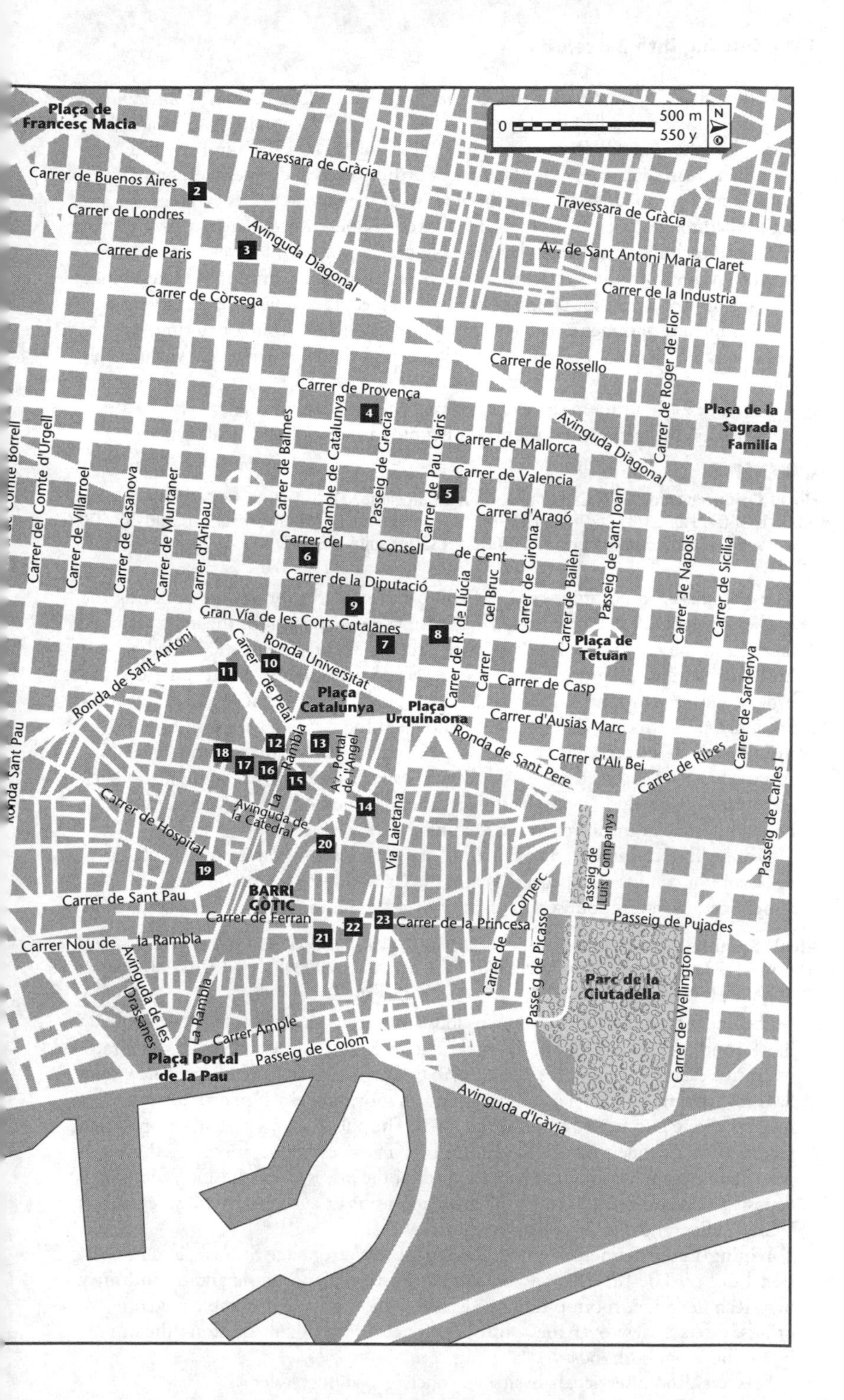
Plaça de Francesc Macia
0
500 m
550 y
N
Travessara de Gràcia
Carrer de Buenos Aires
Carrer de Londres
Carrer de Paris
Avinguda Diagonal
Carrer de Còrsega
Travessara de Gràcia
Av. de Sant Antoni Maria Claret
Carrer de la Industria
Carrer de Rossello
Carrer de Roger de Flor
Carrer de Provença
Plaça de la Sagrada Familia
Carrer de Mallorca
Avinguda Diagonal
Carrer de Valencia
Carrer d'Aragó
Carrer del Comte d'Urgell
Carrer de Villarroel
Carrer de Casanova
Carrer de Muntaner
Carrer d'Aribau
Carrer de Balmes
Ramble de Catalunya
Passeig de Gracia
Carrer de Pau Claris
Carrer del Consell de Cent
Carrer de la Diputació
Gran Vía de les Corts Catalanes
Carrer de R. de Llúcia
Carrer del Bruc
Carrer de Girona
Carrer de Bailèn
Passeig de Sant Joan
Carrer de Napols
Carrer de Sicilia
Plaça de Tetuan
Ronda de Sant Antoni
Carrer de Pelai
Ronda Universitat
Plaça Catalunya
Plaça Urquinaona
Carrer de Casp
Carrer d'Ausias Marc
Ronda de Sant Pere
Carrer d'Alı Bei
Carrer de Ribes
Carrer de Sardenya
Ronda Sant Pau
La Rambla
Av. Portal de l'Angel
Via Laietana
Avinguda de la Catedral
Carrer de Hospital
Passeig de Carles I
Passeig de Lluís Companys
Carrer de Sant Pau
BARRI GÒTIC
Carrer de Ferran
Carrer de la Princesa
Carrer de Comerc
Passeig de Pujades
Carrer Nou de la Rambla
Avinguda de les Drassanes
La Rambla
Passeig de Picasso
Parc de la Ciutadella
Carrer de Wellington
Carrer Ample
Plaça Portal de la Pau
Passeig de Colom
Avinguda d'Icàvia
2
3
4
5
6
7
8
9
10
11
12
13
14
15
16
17
18
19
20
21
22
23

closest rivals in the area: Colón and Rivoli Ramblas. Built in the classic *modernismo* style in 1956, it was called the Hotel Manila. Then it was completely renovated and opened as the Ramada Renaissance in 1988. Finally, in 1991 the French-owned Meridien chain took over. It is a medley of artful pastels and tasteful decorating. Its guest rooms are spacious and comfortable, with such amenities as extra-large beds, heated bathroom floors, 18-channel TVs, three in-house videos, hair dryers, and two phones in each room; all rooms have double-glazed windows. However, that doesn't prevent noise from the Les Rambles from reaching the rooms. The Renaissance Club—the executive floor popular with businesspeople—provides extra amenities.

Dining/Entertainment: The chic lobby bar, open daily from 7 to 11pm, has live piano music. The main restaurant, Le Patio, serves a fine continental and Catalán cuisine.

Services: 24-hour room service, laundry, concierge, babysitting.

Facilities: Business center, rooms for people with disabilities, small gym.

Expensive

Hotel Colón. Avenida de la Catedral, 7, 08002 Barcelona. ☎ **800/845-0636** in the U.S., or 93/301-14-04. Fax 93/317-29-15. 136 rms, 11 suites. A/C MINIBAR TV TEL. 20,500–32,500 ptas. ($164–$260) double; from 37,000 ptas. ($296) suite. AE, DC, MC, V. Bus: 16, 17, 19, or 45.

The Colón is an appropriate choice if you plan to spend a lot of time exploring the medieval neighborhoods of Barcelona. Blessed with what might be the most dramatic location in the city, immediately opposite the main entrance to the cathedral, this hotel sits behind a dignified neoclassical facade graced with carved pilasters and ornamental wrought-iron balustrades. Inside, you'll find conservative and slightly old-fashioned public rooms, a helpful staff, and guest rooms filled with comfortable furniture and, despite recent renovations, an appealingly dowdy kind of charm. Although not all rooms have views, they all have private baths. The rooms in back are quieter. Sixth-floor rooms with balconies overlooking the square are the most desirable. Some of the lower rooms are rather dark.

Dining/Entertainment: The hotel maintains two well-recommended restaurants, the Grill (for continental specialties) and the Carabela (for Catalán specialties).

Services: 24-hour room service, laundry/valet, limousine, concierge, babysitting.

Rivoli Ramblas. Rambla dels Estudis, 128, 08002 Barcelona. ☎ **93/302-66-43.** Fax 93/317-50-53. 78 rms, 9 suites. A/C MINIBAR TV TEL. 24,000–26,000 ptas. ($192–$208) double; from 36,000 ptas. ($288) suite. AE, DC, MC, V. Metro: Plaça de Catalunya.

Set behind a dignified, art deco town house on the upper section of the Rambles, a block south of the Plaça de Catalunya, this recently renovated hotel incorporates many fine examples of avant-garde Catalán design into its stylish interior. The Colón has more tradition and style, and the Meridien more modern comfort; however, this remains choice number three in the old town. The public rooms glisten with polished marble and a pristinely contrived minimalism. The guest rooms are carpeted, soundproof, and elegant, although rather cramped for the prices charged. Along with safety deposit boxes and private baths, the guest rooms boast such electronic amenities as VCRs, radios, and TVs with satellite hookups.

Dining/Entertainment: Le Brut Restaurant serves regional, Spanish, and international dishes. The Blue Moon cocktail bar features piano music and a soothingly high-tech design. A rooftop terrace, decked with flowers and suitable for coffee or drinks, offers a view over the rooftops of one of Barcelona's most architecturally interesting neighborhoods.

Services: Room service, babysitting, concierge, laundry/valet.

Facilities: Small health club/fitness center, sauna, solarium, car rentals, shopping boutiques.

MODERATE

Hotel Lleó. Pelal, 22–24, 08001 Barcelona. ☎ **93/318-13-12.** Fax 93/412-26-57. 76 rms. A/C MINIBAR TV TEL. 12,000 ptas. ($96) double. AE, DC, MC, V. Parking 2,000 ptas. ($16) nearby. Metro: Plaça de Catalunya or Universitat.

Solid, well run, and conservative, this hotel occupies the premises of an 1840s building on a busy commercial street in one of the most central neighborhoods in town. Completely renovated in 1992 in time for the Olympics, it offers clean, streamlined, and comfortable bedrooms, each equipped with a lock-box and comfortable, functional furniture. There's a restaurant on one of the upper floors. For the price, this is a good, standard, functional choice, but not a lot more.

$ **Hotel Regencia Colón.** Carrer Sagristans, 13–17, 08002 Barcelona. ☎ **93/318-98-58.** Fax 93/317-28-22. 55 rms. A/C MINIBAR TV TEL. 15,500 ptas. ($124) double; 19,000 ptas. ($152) triple. Rates include breakfast. AE, DC, MC, V. Metro: Jaume 1 or Urquinaona.

This stately stone six-story building stands directly behind the more prestigious, superior, and more expensive Hotel Colón—both lie in the shadow of the cathedral. It's attractive to tour groups. The formal lobby seems a bit dour, but the well-maintained rooms are comfortable and often roomy, albeit worn. Rooms are insulated against sound, and 40 of them have full tub baths (the remainder have showers). All have piped-in music. The hotel's location at the edge of the Barri Gòtic is a plus. Considering the prices charged and what you get, the hotel is a good value for Barcelona.

INEXPENSIVE

Granvía. Gran Vía de les Cortes Catalanes, 642, 08007 Barcelona. ☎ **93/318-19-00.** Fax 93/318-99-97. 50 rms. A/C MINIBAR TV TEL. 11,500 ptas. ($92) double. AE, DC, MC, V. Parking 2,100 ptas. ($16.80). Metro: Plaça de Catalunya.

A grand hotel on one of the most fashionable boulevards in Barcelona, the Granvía has public rooms that reflect the opulence of the 1860s—chandeliers, gilt mirrors, and French provincial furniture—and a grand balustraded staircase. Although the traditional bedrooms contain interesting antique reproductions, they are comfortable rather than luxurious. The courtyard, graced with a fountain and palm trees, is set with tables for alfresco drinks; in the garden room off the courtyard, continental breakfast is served. Centrally heated in the winter, the hotel has one drawback: the noise. Street sounds might disturb the light sleeper.

$ **Hostal Levante.** Baïxada de Sant Miguel, 2, 08002 Barcelona. ☎ **93/317-95-65.** 38 rms (7 with bath). 3,500 ptas. ($28) double without bath; 4,500 ptas. ($36) double with bath. No credit cards. Metro: Liceu or Jaume 1.

This is one of the nicest and most reasonably priced places to stay in Barcelona. In a quiet, imposing building more than two centuries old, it stands just a short distance from the Plaça de Sant Jaume, in the center of the Barri Gòtic. The units are clean and comfortable, and there is central heating. The staff speaks English. No meals are served.

$ **Hostal Neutral.** Rambla de Catalunya, 42, 08007 Barcelona. ☎ **93/487-63-90.** Fax 93/487-40-28. 35 rms. TEL. 3,950–4,950 ptas. ($31.60–$39.60) double; 4,725–6,210 ptas. ($37.80–$49.70) triple. MC, V. Metro: Passeig de Gràcia.

An older pension, but very recommendable, the hostal has a reputation for its cleanliness and efficiency. As the name suggests, the small rooms here are neutral—but comfortable nevertheless, although furnished with a medley of odds and ends. Colorful antique floor tiling brightens some of the high-ceilinged rooms. Breakfast is served in a salon with a coffered ceiling, and there's a large TV room nearby. English is spoken. The entrance is one flight up.

Hotel Continental. Rambla de Canaletes, 138, 08002 Barcelona. ☎ **93/301-25-70.** Fax 93/302-73-60. 36 rms. MINIBAR TV TEL. 8,650–9,900 ptas. ($69.20–$79.20) double; 9,900 ptas. ($79.20) triple; 10,850–12,600 ptas. ($86.80–$100.80) quad. Rates include buffet breakfast. AE, DC, MC, V. Metro: Plaça de Catalunya.

This hotel lies on the upper two floors of a commercial building in a safer section of the upper Rambles. The flowery, slightly faded reception area is clean and accented with 19th-century statues. The rooms are pleasant and modern, and 10 have semicircular balconies overlooking the Rambles. Though the decor in some of the bedrooms seems to shout "Laura Ashley gone mad," everything is clean and comfortable. Amenities include safe deposits and hair dryers. A buffet breakfast is served daily from 6am to noon.

Hotel Cortés. Santa Anna, 25, 08002 Barcelona. ☎ **93/317-91-12.** Fax 93/302-78-70. 46 rms. TV TEL. 7,970 ptas. ($63.75) double. Rates include breakfast. AE, DC, MC, V. Metro: Plaça de Catalunya.

A short walk from the cathedral, the Cortés was originally built around 1910 and, like many of its competitors in Barcelona, was thoroughly renovated in time for the 1992 Olympics. It competes effectively against the Continental. Bedrooms are scattered over five floors, and about half overlook a quiet central courtyard, the other half open onto the street. The hotel's ground floor contains a simple, unpretentious restaurant and bar, where breakfast is served and where clients can enjoy a beer throughout the day and night.

Hotel San Agustín. Plaça de San Agustín, 3, 08001 Barcelona. ☎ **93/318-16-58.** Fax 93/317-29-28. 77 rms. A/C TV TEL. Mon–Fri 8,900 ptas. ($71.20) double; Sat–Sun 8,000 ptas. ($64) double. Rates include breakfast. AE, MC, V. Metro: Plaça de Catalunya.

This tastefully renovated five-story hotel stands in the center of the old city—near the covered produce markets overlooking the brick walls of an unfinished Romanesque church. Bedrooms are comfortable and modern, containing such amenities as piped-in music and safety deposit boxes. Some rooms are specially equipped for persons with disabilities. The hotel also runs a good restaurant offering reasonably priced meals.

Hotel Suizo. Plaça de l'Angel, 12, 08010 Barcelona. ☎ **93/315-41-11.** Fax 93/315-38-19. 48 rms. A/C MINIBAR TV TEL. 11,550 ptas. ($92.40) double. AE, DC, MC, V. Parking 1,800 ptas. ($14.40) nearby. Metro: Jaume I.

A few blocks from the cathedral in a 19th-century building, the Hotel Suizo has an elaborate Belle Epoque–style bar where drinks and snacks are served. A Gargallo hotel, it is a sibling of the Rialto (see below). The Suizo doesn't have the roomy hallways of the Rialto, but its public rooms are more attractively furnished and inviting. The reception area is pleasantly modern. Bedrooms have antique-patterned wallpaper, Spanish furniture, and private baths. The staff is polite and helpful.

✪ **Mesón Castilla.** Valldoncella, 5, 08002 Barcelona. ☎ **93/318-21-82.** Fax 93/412-40-20. 56 rms. A/C TEL. 9,500 ptas. ($76) double. AE, DC, MC, V. Parking 1,500 ptas. ($12). Metro: Plaça de Catalunya or Plaça Universitat.

This two-star hotel, a former apartment building, has a Castilian facade, with a wealth of art nouveau detailing, and the high-ceilinged lobby is filled with cabriole-legged chairs. Owned and operated by the Spanish hotel chain HUSA, the Castilla is clean, charming, and well maintained. Its nearest rival is the Regencia Colón, to which it is comparable in atmosphere and government ratings. It is far superior to either the Cortés or Continental. The rooms are comfortable—beds have ornate Catalán-style headboards—and some open onto large terraces. Breakfast is the only meal served, but it is a fine buffet, with ham, cheese, and eggs. One reader found the location of the hotel "fantastic," right in the center of Barcelona, close to the Rambles.

Montecarlo. Rambla dels Estudis, 124, 08002 Barcelona. ☎ **93/412-04-04.** Fax 93/318-73-23. 76 rms. A/C MINIBAR TV TEL. Mon–Thurs, 12,000 ptas. ($96) double; 15,000 ptas. ($120) triple. Fri–Sun, 10,000 ptas. ($80) double; 12,700 ptas. ($101.60) triple. AE, DC, MC, V. Parking 1,900 ptas. ($15.20). Metro: Plaça de Catalunya.

This hotel, set beside the wide and sloping promenade of the Rambles, was originally built around 200 years ago as an opulent and aristocratic private home, with superior comfort to such previously recommended competitors as the Lleó. In the 1930s, it was transformed into the comfortably unpretentious hotel you'll find today. Each of the bedrooms is efficiently decorated and comfortable, most of them renovated around 1989. Double-glazed windows help keep out some of the noise. Public areas include some of the building's original accessories, with carved doors, a baronial fireplace, and crystal chandeliers.

Rialto. Ferran, 40–42, 08002 Barcelona. ☎ **93/318-52-12.** Fax 93/315-38-19. 141 rms. A/C MINIBAR TEL. 11,500 ptas. ($92) double. AE, DC, MC, V. Parking 1,800 ptas. ($14.40) nearby. Metro: Jaume 1.

One of the best choices in the Barri Gòtic, this hotel is part of the Gargallo chain, which also owns the Hotel Suizo. The three-star Rialto is furnished with Catalán flair and style; completely overhauled in 1985, it offers clean, well-maintained, and comfortably furnished guest rooms with private baths. There is a cafeteria.

Turín. Carrer Pintor Fortuny, 9–11, 08001 Barcelona. ☎ **93/302-48-12.** Fax 93/302-10-05. 60 rms. A/C TV TEL. 8,000 ptas. ($64) double; 10,000 ptas. ($80) triple. AE, DC, MC, V. Parking 1,800 ptas. ($14.40). Metro: Plaça de Catalunya.

This neat and well-run three-star hotel is in a terra-cotta grillwork building located in a shopping district. It offers small, streamlined accommodations with balconies. An elevator will take you to your room. The Turín also offers a restaurant, specializing in grilled meats and fresh fish. It's a clean, safe choice, comparable to the Lleó, but in its price range inferior in atmosphere to the Mesón Castilla.

SUR DIAGONAL

VERY EXPENSIVE

Barcelona Hilton. Diagonal, 589, 08014 Barcelona. ☎ **800/445-8667** in the U.S. and Canada, or 93/419-22-33. Fax 93/405-25-73. 275 rms, 15 suites. A/C MINIBAR TV TEL. 32,000 ptas. ($256) double; from 40,000 ptas. ($320) suite. AE, DC, MC, V. Parking 2,900 ptas. ($23.20). Metro: María Cristina.

Opened in 1990 as one of the most publicized hotels in Barcelona, this five-star property lies in a desirable position on one of the most famous and elegant boulevards. Opposite the gates to the fairgrounds of Barcelona (beyond that, to the Olympic Stadium), this is a huge seven-floor corner structure, with a massive tower placed on top of it. It hides behind a rather lackluster white marble facade. The lobby is sleek with lots of marble, and public lounges are furnished with black leather and velvet chairs. The patio is undistinguished and rather minimalist. Most bedrooms are fairly large and finely equipped, although none are set aside for nonsmokers. Furnishings are

Family-Friendly Hotels

Hotel Colón *(see p. 402)* Opposite the cathedral in the Gothic Quarter, this hotel has been compared to a country home. Families ask for—and often get—spacious rooms.

Hotel Hespería *(see p. 410)* At the northern edge of the city, this hotel has gardens and a safe neighborhood setting. The rooms are generous enough in size for an extra bed.

Hotel Princesa Sofía *(see p. 409)* Although primarily a business-oriented hotel, the Princesa Sofía has excellent babysitting services, as well as two pools (one indoor and one outdoor), making it ideal for the business traveler and his or her family.

standard Hilton, but with suitable amenities such as private safes. Bathrooms are also well equipped with such features as large mirrors and hair dryers.

Dining/Entertainment: The Restaurant Cristal Garden serves well-prepared international and Spanish menus in a relaxed but polished setting. A bar/lounge lies nearby. Night owls head for a popular local disco, Up & Down, a short walk from the hotel.

Services: 24-hour room service, laundry/valet, concierge, translation and secretarial services, express checkout, limousine service, babysitting.

Facilities: The hotel maintains a cooperative relationship with a well-equipped health club half a mile away. Tennis courts are a mile away, and the hotel can arrange golf at a course 16 miles away. Shopping boutiques and a news kiosk are on the premises.

✪ **Claris.** Carrer de Pau Claris, 150, 08009 Barcelona. ☎ **800/888-4747** in the U.S., or 93/487-62-62. Fax 93/487-87-36. 121 rms, 38 suites. A/C MINIBAR TV TEL. Mon–Thurs 31,850 ptas. ($254.80) double; from 35,100 ptas. ($280.80) suite. Fri–Sun 17,800 ptas. ($142.40) double; from 22,800 ptas. ($182.40) suite. Fri–Sun rates include breakfast. AE, DC, MC, V. Parking 1,750 ptas. ($14). Metro: Passeig de Gràcia.

One of the most unusual hotels built in Barcelona since the 1930s, this postmodern hotel is the only five-star grand *luxe* hotel in the city center. It incorporates vast quantities of teak, marble, steel, and glass with the historically important facade of a landmark 19th-century building (the Verdruna Palace). We think the Ritz (see below) is number one, but many hotel critics hail the Claris as the stellar choice. It opened in 1992, in time for the Barcelona Olympics, in a seven-story format that includes a swimming pool and garden on its roof, a mini-museum of Egyptian antiquities on its second floor, and two restaurants, one of which specializes in different brands of caviar. Each of the bedrooms is painted an iconoclastic shade of blue-violet and combines unusual art objects with state-of-the-art electronic accessories. (Art objects, depending on the inspiration of the decorator, include Turkish kilims, English antiques, Hindu sculptures, Egyptian stone carvings, and engravings inspired by Napoleon's campaigns in Egypt.) Committed to celebrating many facets of Catalán culture, the hotel's owner and developer, art dealer Jordi Clos, named his hotel after the 19th-century Catalán writer Pau Claris.

Dining/Entertainment: On site is the Restaurante Claris, where Catalán meals in the Ampurdan style are served. Also on the premises is a restaurant sponsored by the international caviar emporium, Caviar Caspa, where sturgeon eggs from many different distributors compete for gastronomic attention with an array of smoked meats, smoked fish, and bubbly wines. The restaurant's forte is light but elegant lunches and suppers.

Services: Laundry/valet, babysitting, room service.

Facilities: Swimming pool, sauna, currency exchange.

✪ **Hotel Ritz.** Gran Vía de les Corts Catalanes, 668, 08010 Barcelona. ☎ **800/223-1230** in the U.S., or 93/318-52-00. Fax 93/318-01-48. 155 rms, 6 suites. A/C MINIBAR TV TEL. 43,000–52,000 ptas. ($344–$416) double; from 126,000 ptas. ($1,008) suite. AE, DC, MC, V. Parking 3,000 ptas. ($24). Metro: Passeig de Gràcia.

Acknowledged as the finest, most prestigious, and most architecturally distinguished hotel in Barcelona, the Ritz was built in art deco style in 1919. Richly remodeled during the late 1980s, it has welcomed more millionaires, famous people, and aristocrats (with their official and unofficial consorts) than any other hotel in northeastern Spain. One of the finest features is the cream-and-gilt neoclassical lobby, whose marble floors and potted palms are flooded with sunlight from an overhead glass canopy, and where afternoon tea is served to the strains of a string quartet. Bedrooms are as formal, high-ceilinged, and richly furnished as you'd expect, sometimes with Regency furniture and bathrooms accented with mosaics and bathtubs inspired by those in ancient Rome.

Dining/Entertainment: The elegant Restaurante Diana serves French and Catalán cuisine amid soaring ceilings, crystal chandeliers, and formally dressed waiters (see separate recommendation below). Nearby lies the elegantly paneled Bar Parilla, where music from a grand piano will soothe your frazzled nerves while you enjoy the deep leather upholstery and gilded cove moldings.

Services: 24-hour room service, laundry, limousine service, concierge, babysitting.

Facilities: Business center, car rentals, handful of shopping kiosks and boutiques.

Rey Juan Carlos I. Avinguda Diagonal, 661, 08028 Barcelona. ☎ **800/448-8355** in the U.S., or 93/448-08-08. Fax 93/448-06-07. 375 rms, 37 suites. A/C MINIBAR TV TEL. Mon–Thurs 37,000 ptas. ($296) double; 63,000 ptas. ($504) suite. Fri–Sun 16,200 ptas. ($129.60) double; 44,000 ptas. ($352) suite. AE, DC, MC, V. Free parking for guests, otherwise 2,500 ptas. ($20) per day. Metro: Palau Reial.

Named for the Spanish king, who attended its opening and who has visited it several times since, this is the only five-star choice that competes effectively against the Ritz and Claris. Opened in 1992, in time for the Olympics, it rises 17 stories from a position at the northern end of the Diagonal, within a prestigious neighborhood known for its corporate headquarters and banks. The design includes a soaring inner atrium, at one end of which a bank of glass-sided elevators glide silently up and down. Bedrooms contain many electronic extras, conservatively comfortable furnishings, and in many cases, views out over Barcelona to the sea.

Dining/Entertainment: The hotel's most elegant restaurant is Chez Vous, a glamorous and panoramic locale with impeccable service and French/Catalán meals. Saturday night, a dinner dance offers a live orchestra accompanied by a set price menu. There's also a Japanese restaurant (Kokoro) and the Café Polo, which serves an endless series of buffets at lunch and dinner. The gardens surrounding the hotel contain fountains, flowering shrubs, and the Café Terraza.

Services: 24-hour room service, laundry, concierge staff.

Facilities: Swimming pool, health club, jogging track, men's and women's hairdresser, car-rental facilities, business center.

EXPENSIVE

Avenida Palace. Gran Vía de les Corts Catalanes, 605 (at corner of Passeig de Gràcia), 08007 Barcelona. ☎ **93/301-96-00.** Fax 93/318-12-34. 147 rms, 18 suites. A/C MINIBAR TV TEL.

20,000 ptas. ($160) double; from 35,000 ptas. ($280) suite. AE, DC, MC, V. Parking 2,000 ptas. ($16). Metro: Plaça de Catalunya.

Set in an enviable 19th-century neighborhood filled with elegant shops and apartment buildings, this hotel lies behind a pair of mock-fortified towers that were built (like the hotel) in 1952. Despite its relative modernity, it evokes an Old World sense of charm, partly because of the attentive staff, scattering of flowers and antiques, and 1950s-era accessories that fill its well-upholstered public rooms. Bedrooms, all with private baths, are solidly traditional and quiet, and some are set aside for nonsmokers, a rarity in Spain.

Dining/Entertainment: The hotel has an elegantly proportioned dining room, El Restaurante Pinateca, which serves lunch and dinner Monday through Friday. The bar/lounge contains potted palms, a scattering of interesting antiques, and a sense of graciousness.

Services: Concierge, translation and secretarial services, currency exchange, hairdresser/barber, room service, express checkout, babysitting.

✪ **Hotel Condes de Barcelona.** Passeig de Gràcia, 73–75, 08008 Barcelona. ☎ **93/488-22-00.** Fax 93/488-06-14. 181 rms, 2 suites. A/C MINIBAR TV TEL. 19,000 ptas. ($152) double; 25,000–40,000 ptas. ($200–$320) suite. AE, DC, MC, V. Metro: Passeig de Gràcia.

Located off the architecturally splendid Passeig de Gràcia, this four-star hotel, originally designed to be a private villa (1895), is one of Barcelona's most glamorous. Business was so good it opened a 74-room extension, which regrettably lacks the elan of the original core. It boasts a unique neomedieval facade, influenced by Gaudí's *modernismo* movement. During recent renovation, just enough hints of high-tech furnishings were added to make the lobby exciting, but everything else has the original opulence. The curved lobby-level bar and its adjacent restaurant add a touch of art deco. All the comfortable salmon-, green-, or peach-colored guest rooms contain marble baths, reproductions of Spanish paintings, and soundproof windows. Some rooms are beginning to show a post-Olympian wear and tear.

Dining/Entertainment: In times past you might have seen the late Conde de Barcelona, father of King Juan Carlos, passing through on the way to a refreshing snack in the Café Condal, featuring regional dishes. Guests also enjoy the piano bar, including, on occasions, the Baron von Thyssen and his Catalán-born wife, who sold their fabulous art collection to Madrid.

Services: Laundry, babysitting, room service.

Facilities: Outdoor swimming pool.

Hotel Meliá Barcelona Sarrià. Avinguda Sarrià, 50, 08029 Barcelona. ☎ **800/336-3542** in the U.S., or 93/410-60-60. Fax 93/321-51-79. 295 rms, 20 suites. A/C MINIBAR TV TEL. 26,000 ptas. ($208) double; from 40,000 ptas. ($320) suite. AE, DC, MC, V. Parking 2,300 ptas. ($18.40). Metro: Hospital Clínic.

Located just a block away from the junction of the Avinguda Sarría and the Avinguda Diagonal, right in the modern business heart of Barcelona, this five-star hotel originally opened in 1976. Some of its rooms were renovated as late as 1993, but others are beginning to look a bit worn. It offers comfortably upholstered and carpeted bedrooms in a neutral international modern style. The hotel—a member of the nationwide Spanish chain Meliá—caters both to the business traveler and the vacationer.

Dining/Entertainment: The hotel restaurant serves both Catalán and international dishes, and a cocktail bar provides not only drinks but also piano music six nights a week.

Services: 24-hour room service, concierge, laundry/valet, executive floor, private parking, and babysitting on request.

Facilities: Business center, one of the best-equipped health clubs in Barcelona.

Hotel Princesa Sofía. Plaça de Pius XII, 4, 08028 Barcelona. ☎ **93/330-71-11.** Fax 93/330-76-21. 481 rms, 24 suites. A/C MINIBAR TV TEL. 20,000 ptas. ($160) double; from 40,000 ptas. ($320) suite. AE, DC, MC, V. Parking 1,800 ptas. ($14.40). Metro: Palau Reial or María Cristina.

Set beside the Avinguda Diagonal, about a block east of the Palau Reial and about two miles (3km) northwest of Barcelona's historic center, the high-rise Princesa Sofía is perhaps the busiest, most business-oriented, and most international of the large-volume modern hotels in Barcelona. It's much better than the Hilton. Although it was a five-star hotel when it opened, its new government rating of four stars is more in keeping with the reality here. The hotel was built in 1975 and renovated during the early 1990s. Packed with glamorous grace notes (including a branch of Régine's disco in the basement) and named after the wife of the Spanish monarch, the Princesa Sofía is the venue for dozens of daily conferences and social events. The guest rooms contain comfortable traditional furniture, often with a vaguely British feel.

Dining/Entertainment: Le Gourmet restaurant serves continental and Catalán meals, but the fare is lackluster. L'Emporda is slightly less expensive, and an in-house coffee shop, El Snack 2002, is open until midnight. Also on the premises is a bar.

Services: 24-hour room service, laundry/valet, concierge, in-house branch of Iberia Airlines, babysitting.

Facilities: An upscale shopping boutique, barber/hairdresser, car rentals, amply equipped gym and health club, sauna, indoor and outdoor swimming pools, several well-conceived gardens, extensive conference and meeting facilities, and an unusually well-managed business center offering translation (English and French) and secretarial services.

Moderate

✪ **Hotel Astoria.** París, 203, 08036 Barcelona. ☎ **93/209-83-11.** Fax 93/202-30-08. 114 rms. A/C MINIBAR TV TEL. 8,000–16,200 ptas. ($64–$129.60) double. AE, DC, MC, V. Metro: Diagonal.

One of our favorite hotels, the Astoria has an art deco facade that makes it appear older than it is. The high ceilings, geometric designs, and brass-studded detailings in the public rooms could be Moorish or Andalusian. Each of the comfortable bedrooms is soundproofed; half have been renovated with slick louvered closets and glistening white paint. The more old-fashioned rooms have warm textures of exposed cedar and elegant, pristine modern accessories.

Hotel Derby/Hotel Gran Derby. Loreto, 21–25, and Loreto, 28, 08029 Barcelona. ☎ **93/322-32-15.** Fax 93/410-08-62. 111 rms, 40 suites. A/C MINIBAR TV TEL. 9,000–17,350 ptas. ($72–$138.80) double; 11,500–17,850 ptas. ($92–$142.80) suite. AE, DC, MC, V. Parking 1,800 ptas. ($14.40). Metro: Hospital Clínic.

Divided into two separate buildings, these twin hotels (owned and managed by the same corporation) lie in a tranquil neighborhood about two blocks south of the busy intersection of the Avinguda Diagonal and Avinguda Sarría. The Derby offers 111 conventional hotel rooms, whereas the Gran Derby (across the street) contains 40 suites, many of which have small balconies overlooking a flowered courtyard. (All drinking, dining, and entertainment facilities lie in the larger of the two establishments, the Derby.) A team of English-inspired designers imported a British aesthetic into these hotels, and the pleasing results include well-oiled hardwood panels, soft lighting, and comfortably upholstered armchairs. Less British in feel than the public rooms, the guest rooms and suites are outfitted with simple furniture in a variety of decorative styles, each comfortable and quiet.

Dining/Entertainment: Although the hotel does not have a full-fledged restaurant, it contains a dignified but unpretentious coffee shop, The Times, which serves Spanish, British, and international food. The Scotch Bar, an upscale watering hole, has won several Spanish awards for the diversity of its cocktails.

Services: Concierge, laundry, babysitting.

NORTE DIAGONAL

MODERATE

Hotel Hespería. Los Vergós, 20, 08017 Barcelona. ☎ **93/204-55-51.** Fax 93/204-43-92. 139 rms. A/C MINIBAR TV TEL. Mon–Thurs 14,500 ptas. ($116) double. Fri–Sun 9,500 ptas. ($76) double. AE, DC, MC, V. Parking 1,450 ptas. ($11.60). Metro: Tres Torres.

This hotel, on the northern edge of the city, a 12-minute taxi ride from the center, is surrounded by the verdant gardens of one of Barcelona's most pleasant residential neighborhoods. Built in the late 1980s, the hotel was renovated before the 1992 Olympics. You'll pass a Japanese rock garden to reach the stone-floored reception area, with its adjacent bar. Sunlight floods the monochromatic interiors of the bedrooms—all doubles, although singles can be rented at the prices above. The uniformed staff offers fine service. A restaurant on the premises serves a regional cuisine.

INEXPENSIVE

Hotel Wilson. Avinguda Diagonal, 568, 08021 Barcelona. ☎ **93/209-25-11.** Fax 93/200-83-70. 51 rms, 6 suites. A/C MINIBAR TV TEL. 12,000 ptas. ($96) double; from 21,500 ptas. ($172) suite. AE, DC, MC, V. Metro: Diagonal.

Set in a neighborhood rich with architectural curiosities, this comfortable hotel is a member of the nationwide HUSA chain. The small lobby isn't indicative of the rest of the building, which on the second floor opens into a large and sunny coffee shop/bar/TV lounge. The guest rooms are well kept. Laundry services are provided.

VILA OLÍMPICA

EXPENSIVE

Hotel Arts. Carrer de la Marina, 19–21, 08005 Barcelona. ☎ **800/241-3333** in the U.S., or 93/221-10-00. Fax 93/221-10-70. 397 rms, 56 suites. A/C MINIBAR TV TEL. Mon–Thurs 25,000–26,000 ptas. ($200–$208) double; from 30,000 ptas. ($240) suites. Fri–Sun 20,000 ptas. ($160) double; from 30,000 ptas. ($240) suites. AE, DC, MC, V. Parking 2,500 ptas. ($20). Metro: Ciutadella–Vila Olímpica.

This is the only hotel in Europe managed by the luxury-conscious Ritz-Carlton chain, the first of what the company hopes will be a string of hotels across the European continent. It occupies 33 floors of one of the tallest buildings in Spain, a 44-floor postmodern tower whose upper floors contain the private condominiums of some of Iberia's most gossiped-about aristocrats and financiers. The location is about 1½ miles southwest of Barcelona's historic core, adjacent to the sea and the Olympic Village. Although some rooms were occupied by athletes and Olympic administrators in 1992, the hotel didn't become fully operational until 1994. Its decor is contemporary and elegant, including a large lobby sheathed in slabs of soft gray and yellow marble, and bedrooms outfitted in pastel shades of yellow or blue. Views from the bedrooms sweep out over the skyline of Barcelona and the Mediterranean. The staff is youthful, well trained, polite, and hardworking, each the product of months of training by Ritz-Carlton.

Dining/Entertainment: Three in-house restaurants include the Newport Room, which pays homage to new American cuisine and the seafaring pleasures of New England; the Café Veranda, a light and airy indoor/outdoor restaurant; and the Goyesca, which serves Spanish food and shellfish in a Catalán setting.

Services: 24-hour room service, laundry, concierge staff who can arrange almost anything.

Facilities: Fitness center, outdoor pool, business center. Adjacent to the hotel is an upscale cluster of many different luxury boutiques operated by the Japanese retailer Sogo.

5 Dining

Finding an economical restaurant in Barcelona is easier than finding an inexpensive, safe hotel. There are sometimes as many as eight places per block, if you include tapas bars as well as restaurants. Reservations are seldom needed, except in the most expensive and popular places.

The Barri Gòtic offers the cheapest meals. There are also many low-cost restaurants in and around the Carrer de Montcada, site of the Picasso museum. Dining rooms in the Eixample tend to be more formal, more expensive, but less adventurous.

However, if you're not a budget traveler and can afford to dine in first-class and deluxe restaurants, in Barcelona you'll find some of the grandest culinary experiences in Europe. The widely diversified Catalán cuisine reaches its pinnacle in Barcelona, and many of the finest dishes feature fresh seafood. But you don't get just Catalán fare here, as the city is also rich in the cuisines of all the major regions of Spain, including Castile and Andalusia. Because of Barcelona's proximity to France, many of the finer restaurants also serve French or French-inspired dishes, the latter often with a distinctly Catalán flavor.

CIUTAT VELLA

EXPENSIVE

✪ **Agut d'Avignon.** Trinitat, 3. ☎ **93/302-60-34.** Reservations required. Main courses 1,800–4,200 ptas. ($14.40–$33.60). AE, MC, V. Daily 1–3:30pm and 9–11:30pm. Metro: Jaume I or Liceu. CATALÁN.

Founded in 1962, one of our favorite restaurants in Barcelona is located near the Plaça Reial, in a tiny alleyway (the cross street is Calle d'Avinyó). The restaurant explosion in Barcelona has toppled Agut d'Avignon from its once stellar position, but it's still going strong, still drawing in habitués. The restaurant attracts the leading politicians, writers, journalists, financiers, industrialists, and artists of Barcelona—even the king and various ministers of the cabinet, along with the visiting presidents from other countries. Since 1983, the restaurant has been run by Mercedes Giralt Salinas and her son, Javier Falagán Giralt. A small 19th-century vestibule leads to the multilevel dining area, which has two balconies and a main hall; the whole of it evokes a hunting lodge. You might need help translating the Catalán menu. Specialties—all prepared according to traditional recipes—are likely to include acorn-squash soup served in its shell; fisherman soup with garlic toast; haddock stuffed with shellfish, sole with *nyoca* (a medley of different nuts), large shrimps with *aïoli* (a garlicky mayonnaise sauce), duck with figs, chicken with shrimp, and filet steak in a sherry sauce.

Casa Leopoldo. Carrer Sant Rafael, 24. ☎ **93/441-30-14.** Reservations required. Main courses 1,800–8,500 ptas. ($14.40–$68). AE, DC, MC, V. Tues–Sun 1–4pm, Tues–Sat 9–11pm. Closed Aug. Metro: Liceu. SEAFOOD.

Dining in Central Barcelona

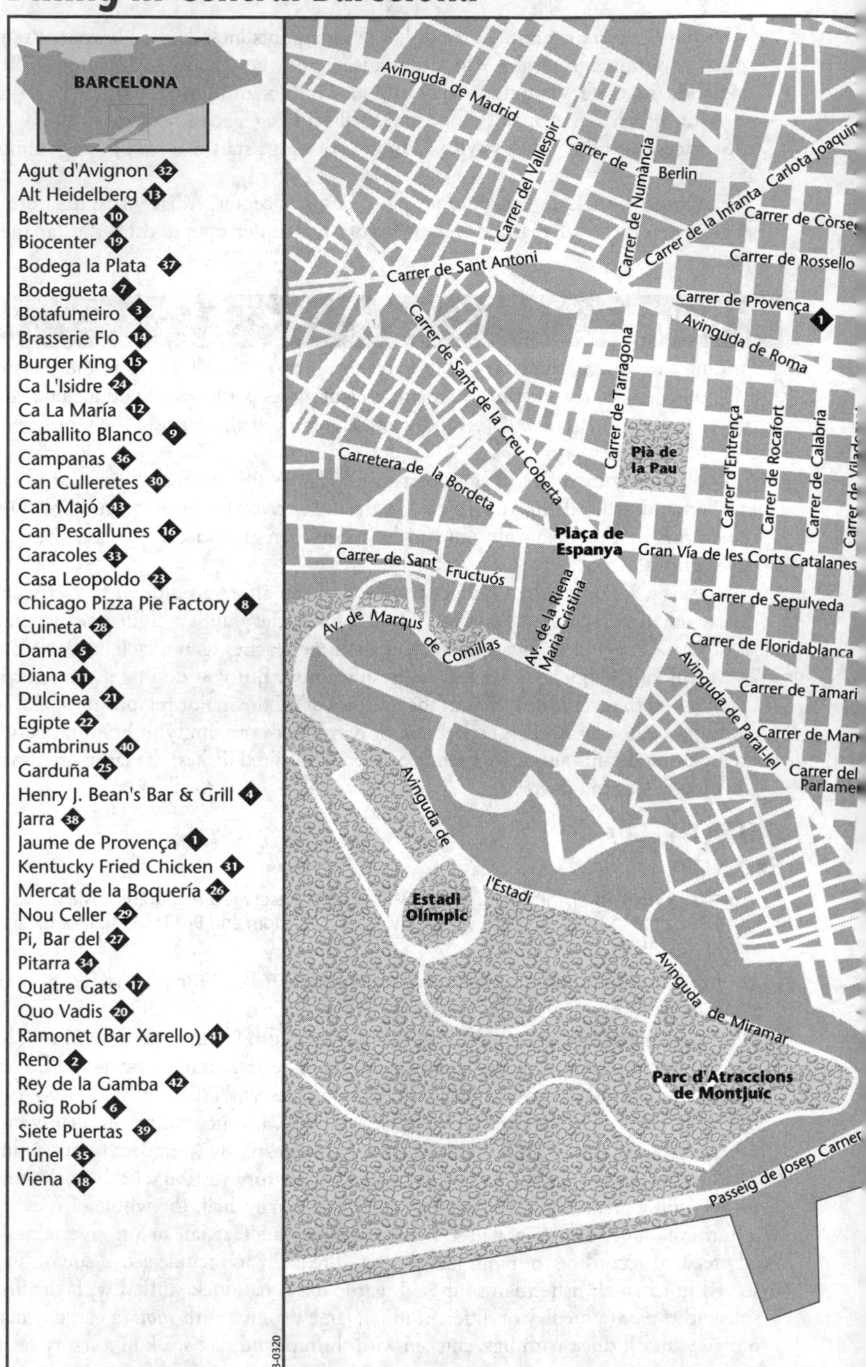

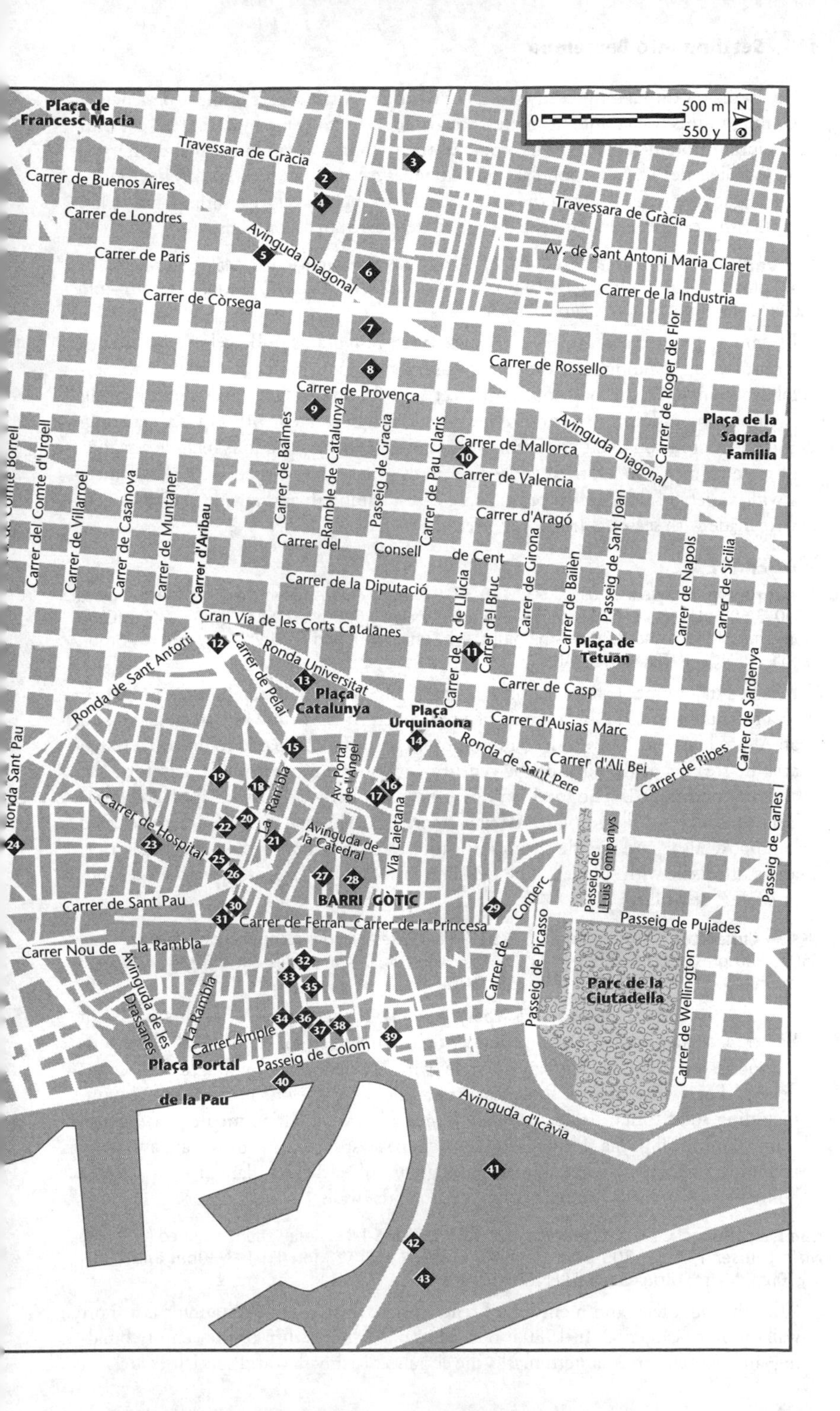

500 m
550 y
0
N
Plaça de Francesc Macia
Travessara de Gràcia
Carrer de Buenos Aires
Carrer de Londres
Carrer de Paris
Avinguda Diagonal
Carrer de Còrsega
Travessara de Gràcia
Av. de Sant Antoni Maria Claret
Carrer de la Industria
Carrer de Roger de Flor
Carrer de Rossello
Carrer de Provença
Rambla de Catalunya
Passeig de Gracia
Carrer de Pau Claris
Carrer de Mallorca
Avinguda Diagonal
Plaça de la Sagrada Familia
Carrer de Valencia
Carrer d'Aragó
Carrer del Comte d'Urgell
Carrer de Villarroel
Carrer de Casanova
Carrer de Muntaner
Carrer d'Aribau
Carrer de Balmes
Carrer del Consell de Cent
Carrer de la Diputació
Carrer de R. de Llúcia
Carrer del Bruc
Carrer de Girona
Carrer de Bailèn
Passeig de Sant Joan
Carrer de Napols
Carrer de Sicilia
Gran Vía de les Corts Catalanes
Ronda de Sant Antoni
Carrer de Pelai
Ronda Universitat
Plaça Catalunya
Plaça de Tetuan
Carrer de Casp
Plaça Urquinaona
Carrer d'Ausias Marc
Ronda de Sant Pere
Carrer d'Ali Bei
Carrer de Ribes
Carrer de Sardenya
Ronda Sant Pau
Av. Portal de l'Angel
La Rambla
Carrer de Hospital
Avinguda de la Catedral
Via Laietana
Passeig de Lluís Companys
Passeig de Carles I
BARRI GÒTIC
Carrer de Sant Pau
Carrer de Ferran
Carrer de la Princesa
Carrer de Comerç
Passeig de Picasso
Passeig de Pujades
Carrer Nou de la Rambla
Avinguda de les Drassanes
La Rambla
Parc de la Ciutadella
Carrer de Wellington
Carrer Ample
Passeig de Colom
Plaça Portal de la Pau
Avinguda d'Icàvia
1
2
3
4
5
6
7
8
9
10
11
12
13
14
15
16
17
18
19
20
21
22
23
24
25
26
27
28
29
30
31
32
33
34
35
36
37
38
39
40
41
42
43

An excursion through the seedy streets of the Barri Xinés is part of the experience of coming to this restaurant. At night, though, it's safer to come by taxi. This colorful restaurant (founded in 1939) has some of the freshest seafood in town and caters to a loyal clientele. There's a popular stand-up tapas bar in front, then two dining rooms, one slightly more formal than the other. Specialties include eel with shrimp, barnacles, cuttlefish, seafood soup with shellfish, and deep-fried inch-long eels.

Quo Vadis. Carme, 7. ☎ **93/302-40-72.** Reservations recommended. Main courses 1,650–3,500 ptas. ($13.20–$28); *menú del día* 3,750 ptas. ($30). AE, DC, MC, V. Mon–Sat 1:15–4pm and 8:30–11:30pm. Metro: Liceu. SPANISH/CONTINENTAL.

Elegant and impeccable, this is one of the finest restaurants in Barcelona. Set within a century-old building near the open stalls of the Boquería food market, it was established in 1967 and has done a discreet but thriving business ever since. Seating is within any of four different dining rooms, each decorated with exposed paneling and a veneer of conservative charm. Personalized culinary creations include a ragoût of seasonal mushrooms; fried goose liver with prunes; filet of beef with wine sauce; a wide variety of fish, grilled or, in some cases, flambéed; and a wide choice of desserts made with seasonal fruits imported from all over Spain.

Moderate

Brasserie Flo. Jonqueras, 10. ☎ **93/319-31-02.** Reservations recommended. Main courses 1,800–3,600 ptas. ($14.40–$28.80); fixed-price menu 3,090 ptas. ($24.70). AE, DC, MC, V. Mon–Thurs 1–4pm and 8:30pm–midnight, Fri–Sun 1–4pm and 8:30pm–1am. Metro: Urquinaona. FRENCH/INTERNATIONAL.

Installed in a former textiles factory, this handsomely restored warehouse was opened as a restaurant in 1982 by a group of Frenchmen. It is as close as Barcelona gets to an Alsace brasserie. The art deco dining room has been compared to one on a transatlantic steamer at the turn of the century—it's spacious, palm-filled, comfortable, and air-conditioned. The food isn't overlooked either—begin with fresh foie gras. The specialty is a large plate of *choucroute* (sauerkraut) served with a steamed hamhock. Also good are the shrimp in garlic, salmon tartare with vodka, black rice, and stuffed sole with spinach. These dishes, each familiar fare, are nevertheless solid, satisfying, and filling.

Ⓢ Can Culleretes. Quintana, 5. ☎ **93/317-64-85.** Reservations recommended. Main courses 850–1,900 ptas. ($6.80–$15.20). DC, V. Tues–Sun 1:30–4pm, Tues–Sat 9–11pm. Closed 3 weeks in July. Metro: Liceu. Bus: 14 or 59. CATALÁN.

Founded in 1786 as a *pastelería* (pastry shop) in the Barri Gòtic, this oldest of Barcelona restaurants still retains many original architectural features. All three dining rooms are decorated in Catalán style, with tile dadoes and wrought-iron chandeliers. The well-prepared food features authentic dishes of northeastern Spain, including sole Roman style, *zarzuela a la marinara* (shellfish medley), *canalones* (cannelloni), and paella. From October to January, special game dishes are available, including *perdiz* (partridge). Signed photographs of celebrities, flamenco artists, and bullfighters who have visited this *casa* decorate the walls.

Can Pescallunes. Carrer Magdalenas, 23. ☎ **93/318-54-83.** Reservations required for lunch. Main courses 1,800–2,300 ptas. ($14.40–$18.40). MC, V. Mon–Fri 1–3:30pm and 8:30–10:30pm. Metro: Urquinaona. FRENCH/CATALÁN.

With the look, feel, and menu of a French bistro, this 10-table restaurant is a short walk from the cathedral. In 1980 it opened its doors in this turn-of-the-century building; an elaborate street lantern marks the entrance. Richly flavorful specialties are *rape* (monkfish) with clams and tomatoes, a smooth vichyssoise, chateaubriand with béarnaise sauce, sole cooked in cider, steak tartare, and dessert crêpes with Cointreau. The specials change daily, and the prices remain a model of temperance.

Los Caracoles. Escudellers, 14. ☎ **93/302-31-85.** Reservations required. Main courses 1,500–3,600 ptas. ($12–$28.80). AE, DC, MC, V. Daily 1pm–midnight. Metro: Drassanes. CATALÁN/SPANISH.

Set in a labyrinth of narrow cobblestoned streets, Los Caracoles is the port's most colorful and popular restaurant—and it has been since 1835. It has won acclaim for its spit-roasted chicken and for its namesake, snails. A long, angular bar is located up front, with a two-level restaurant in back. You can watch the busy preparations in the kitchen, where dried herbs, smoked ham shanks, and garlic bouquets hang from the ceiling. In summer, tables are placed outside. The excellent food features all sorts of Spanish and Catalán specialties. Everybody from Richard Nixon to John Wayne, has stopped in, and Salvador Dalí was a devoted patron. Today's clientele may not be as legendary, but people keep coming in hordes to dine. Tourists often make this their number one restaurant stop in Barcelona, but it is not a tourist trap—Los Caracoles delivers the same aromatic and robust food it always did. We doubt if it has ever updated a recipe. The cookery is "the way it was."

La Cuineta. Paradis, 4. ☎ **93/315-01-11.** Reservations recommended. Main courses 2,000–3,200 ptas. ($16–$25.60); fixed-price menu 2,500 ptas. ($20). AE, DC, MC, V. Daily 1–4pm and 8pm–midnight. Metro: Jaume I. CATALÁN.

A well-established restaurant near the center of the Catalán government, this is a culinary highlight of the Barri Gòtic. The restaurant is decorated in typical regional style and favors local cuisine. The fixed-price menu is a good value, or you can order à la carte. The most expensive appetizer is *bellota* (acorn-fed ham), but we suggest that you settle instead for a market-fresh Catalán dish.

Egipte. Carrer Jerusalem, 3. ☎ **93/317-74-80.** Reservations recommended. Main courses 1,200–2,400 ptas. ($9.60–$19.20); fixed-price menu 950–3,000 ptas. ($7.60–$24). AE, DC, MC, V. Mon–Sat 1–4pm and 8pm–midnight. Metro: Liceu. CATALÁN/SPANISH.

A favorite among the locals, this tiny place, located right behind the central marketplace, jumps day and night. The excellent menu includes spinach vol-au-vent (traditionally served with an egg on top), *lengua de ternera* (tongue), and *berengeras* (stuffed eggplant), a chef's specialty. The local favorite is codfish in cream sauce. The ingredients are fresh, and the price is right. Expect hearty market food and a total lack of pretension.

Els 4 Gats. Montsió, 3. ☎ **93/302-41-40.** Reservations required Sat–Sun. Main courses 1,200–2,800 ptas. ($9.60–$22.40); fixed-price menu 1,800 ptas. ($14.40). AE, MC, V. Mon–Sat 1–4pm and 9pm–midnight; café, daily 8am–2am. Metro: Plaça de Catalunya. CATALÁN.

A Barcelona legend since 1897, the Four Cats was the favorite of Picasso and other artists, who once hung their works on its walls. Located on a narrow cobblestoned street near the cathedral, the fin de siècle café was the setting for poetry readings by Joán Maragall, piano concerts by Isaac Albéniz and Ernie Granados, and murals by Ramón Casa. It was a base for members of the *modernismo* movement and played a major role in the intellectual and bohemian life of the city. In Catalán slang, the name of the restaurant translates as "just a few people."

Today a bar that's become a popular meeting place in the heart of the Barri Gòtic, it was long ago restored but retains its fine old look. The fixed-price meal, offered every day but Sunday, rates as one of the best bargains in town, considering the locale. The good food is prepared in an unpretentious style of Catalán cooking called *cuina de mercat* (based on whatever looked fresh at the market that day). The constantly changing menu reflects the seasons. No hot food is served on Sunday.

INEXPENSIVE

Biocenter. Pintor Fortuny, 25. ☎ **93/301-45-83.** Main courses 900–1,000 ptas. ($7.20–$8). Fixed-price menu 1,075 ptas. ($8.60). No credit cards. Bar, Mon–Sat 9am–11pm; food, Mon–Sat 1–5pm. Metro: Plaça de Catalunya. VEGETARIAN.

This is the largest and best-known vegetarian restaurant in Barcelona, the creation of Catalonia-born entrepreneur Pep Cañameras, who is likely to be directing the service from his position behind the bar in front. Many clients, vegetarians or not, congregate over drinks in the front room. Some continue on for meals in one of two ground-floor dining rooms, whose walls are decorated with the paintings and artworks of the owner and his colleagues. There's a salad bar, an array of vegetarian casseroles, such soups as gazpacho or lentil, and a changing selection of seasonal vegetables. No meat and no fish of any kind are served.

$ Garduña. Morera, 17–19. ☎ **93/302-43-23.** Reservations recommended. Main courses 1,200–2,800 ptas. ($9.60–$22.40); fixed-price menus 975 ptas. ($7.80) and 1,375 ptas. ($11). AE, MC, V. Daily 1–4pm, Mon–Sat 8pm–midnight. Metro: Liceu. CATALÁN.

This is the most famous restaurant within Barcelona's covered food market, La Boquería. Originally conceived as a hotel, it eliminated its bedrooms in the 1970s and ever since has concentrated on serving food. Battered, somewhat ramshackle, and a bit claustrophobic, it nonetheless enjoys a fashionable reputation among actors, sculptors, writers, and painters who appreciate a blue-collar atmosphere that might have been designated as bohemian in an earlier era. Because of its position near the back of the market, you'll pass endless rows of fresh produce, cheese, and meats before you reach it, a fact that adds to its allure. You can dine downstairs, near a crowded bar, or a bit more formally upstairs. Food is ultra-fresh (the chefs don't have to travel far for the ingredients) and might include "hors d'oeuvres of the sea," *canalones* (cannelloni) Rossini, grilled hake with herbs, *rape* (monkfish) *marinera,* paella, brochettes of veal, filet steak with green peppercorns, seafood rice, or a *zarzuela* (stew) of fresh fish with spices.

$ Nou Celler. Princesa, 16. ☎ **93/310-47-73.** Reservations required. Main courses 600–1,800 ptas. ($4.80–$14.40). MC, V. Sun–Fri 8am–midnight. Closed June 15–July 15. Metro: Jaume I. CATALÁN/SPANISH.

Near the Picasso Museum, this establishment is perfect for either a bodega-type meal or a cup of coffee. Country artifacts hang from the beamed ceiling and plaster walls. The back entrance, at Barra de Ferro, 3, is at the quieter end of the place, where dozens of original artworks are arranged into a collage. The dining room offers such "Franco era" food as fish soup, Catalán soup, *zarzuela* (a medley of seafood), paella, hake, and other classic dishes.

$ Pitarra. Avinyó, 56. ☎ **93/301-16-47.** Reservations required. Main courses 950–2,000 ptas. ($7.60–$16); fixed-price lunch 1,100 ptas. ($8.80). AE, DC, MC, V. Mon–Sat 1–4pm and 8:30–11pm. Metro: Liceu. CATALÁN.

Founded in 1890, this restaurant in the Barri Gòtic was named after the 19th-century Catalán playwright who lived and wrote his plays and poetry here in the back room. Try the grilled fish chowder or a Catalán salad, followed by grilled salmon or squid Málaga style. Valencian paella is another specialty. The cuisine does not even pretend to be imaginative but strictly adheres to time-tested recipes—"the type of food we ate when growing up," in the words of one diner.

SUR DIAGONAL

VERY EXPENSIVE

Beltxenea. Majorca, 275. ☎ **93/215-30-24.** Reservations recommended. Main courses 2,500–5,500 ptas. ($20–$44); *menú degustación* 6,900 ptas. ($55.20). AE, DC, MC, V. Mon–Fri 1:30–4pm, Mon–Sat 8:30–11:30pm. Closed 2 weeks in Aug. Metro: Passeig de Gràcia. BASQUE.

Set in a building originally designed in the late 19th century as a *modernismo* Eixample apartment building, this restaurant celebrates the nuances and subtleties of Basque cuisine. Since the Basques are noted as the finest chefs in Spain, this is a grand cuisine indeed and is also one of the most elegantly and comfortably furnished restaurants in Barcelona. Save a visit here for that special night—it's worth the money. Within a dignified dining room with parquet floors and nautical accessories, you can enjoy a cuisine that is affected by the inspiration of the chef and the availability of ingredients. Examples include hake served either fried with garlic or garnished with clams and served with fish broth. Roast lamb, grilled rabbit, and pheasant are well prepared and succulent, as are the desserts. Summer dining is possible outside in the formal garden.

✪ **Ca l'Isidre.** Les Flors, 12. ☎ **93/441-11-39.** Reservations required. Main courses 2,200–3,800 ptas. ($17.60–$30.40). AE, MC, V. Mon–Sat 1:30–4pm and 8:30–11:30pm. Closed Aug. Metro: Parallel. CATALÁN.

In spite of its seedy location (take a cab at night!), this is perhaps the most sophisticated Catalán bistro in Barcelona, drawing such patrons as King Juan Carlos and Queen Sofía. Opened in 1970, it was also visited by Julio Iglesias and the famous Catalonian band leader, Xavier Cugat. Isidre Gironés, helped by his wife, Montserrat, is known for his fresh Catalán cuisine. Flowers decorate the restaurant, along with artwork, and the array of food is beautifully prepared and served. Try spider crabs and shrimp, a gourmand salad with foie gras, sweetbreads with port and flap mushrooms, or carpaccio of veal Harry's Bar style. The selection of Spanish and Catalán wines is excellent.

EXPENSIVE

✪ **La Dama.** Diagonal, 423. ☎ **93/202-06-86.** Reservations required. Main courses 1,800–4,000 ptas. ($14.40–$32); fixed-price menus 4,750–7,500 ptas. ($38-$60). AE, DC, MC, V. Daily 1–4pm and 8:30–11:30pm. Metro: Provença. CATALÁN/INTERNATIONAL.

This is one of the few restaurants in Barcelona that deserves—and gets—a Michelin star. Located one floor above street level in one of the grandly iconoclastic 19th-century buildings for which Barcelona is famous, this stylish and well-managed restaurant serves a clientele of local residents and civic dignitaries with impeccable taste and confidence. You'll take an art nouveau elevator (or the sinuous stairs) up one flight to reach the dining room. The specialties might include roast filet of goat, salmon steak served with vinegar derived from *cava* (sparkling wine) and onions, confit of duckling, cream-of-potato soup flavored with caviar, a salad of crayfish with orange-flavored vinegar, an abundant seasonal platter of autumn mushrooms, and succulent preparations of lamb, fish, shellfish, beef, and veal. The building that contains the restaurant, designed by the *modernismo* architect Manuel Sayrach, lies three blocks west of the intersection of Avinguda Diagonal and Passeig de Grácia.

✪ **Jaume de Provença.** Provença, 88. ☎ **93/430-00-29.** Reservations recommended. Main courses 1,950–3,000 ptas. ($15.60–$24). AE, DC, MC, V. Tues–Sun 1–4pm, Tues–Sat 9–11:30pm. Closed Easter week and Aug. Metro: Estació-Sants. CATALÁN/FRENCH.

Family-Friendly Restaurants

Fast Food Places *(see p. 423)* Burger King, The Chicago Pizza Pie Factory *(see p. 423)*, and Kentucky Fried Chicken *(see p. 423)* are good bets for fast food that the kids will enjoy.

Henry J. Bean's Bar and Grill *(see p. 421)* This place has sit-down meals that the kids will love.

Dulcinea *(see p. 425)* This makes a great refueling stop any time of the day—guaranteed to satisfy any chocoholic.

Poble Espanyol *(see p. 434)* A good introduction to Spanish food. All the restaurants in the "Spanish Village" serve comparable food at comparable prices—let the kids choose what to eat.

Located a few steps away from the Estació Central de Barcelona-Sants railway station at the western end of the Eixample, this is a small, cozy, and personalized restaurant with a country-rustic decor. It is the only restaurant in the Diagonal that offers food to equal that of La Dama. The young-at-heart clientele is served by a polite and hardworking staff. Named after its owner/chef Jaume Bargués, it features modern interpretations of traditional Catalán and southern French cuisine. Examples include a gratin of clams with spinach, a salad of two different species of lobster, small packets of foie gras and truffles, pig's trotters with plums and truffles, crabmeat lasagne, cod with saffron sauce, sole with mushrooms in a port-wine sauce, and a dessert specialty of orange mousse, whose presentation is an artistic statement in its own right. This establishment, incidentally, was launched during the 1940s by Jaume's forebears, who acquiesced to their talented offspring's new and successful culinary theories.

Restaurante Diana. In the Hotel Ritz, Gran Vía de les Corts Catalanes, 668. ☎ **93/318-52-00.** Reservations recommended. Main courses 2,000–3,800 ptas. ($16–$30.40); fixed-price menu Mon–Fri 3,250 ptas. ($26); fixed-price menu Sat–Sun 4,450 ptas. ($35.60). AE, DC, MC, V. Daily 1:30–4pm and 8:30–11pm. Metro: Arc del Triomf. FRENCH.

At least part of the allure of dining here involves the chance to visit the most legendary hotel in Barcelona. Located on the lobby level of the Ritz, the restaurant is filled with French furnishings and accessories amid a gilt-and-blue color scheme. The polite and well-trained staff serves such dishes as seafood salad flavored with saffron; filets of sole layered with lobster; filet mignon braised in cognac, cream, and peppercorn sauce; turbot in white-wine sauce; and a wide array of delectable desserts. The cuisine is of a high international standard, although the restaurant doesn't quite reach the sublime culinary experience of La Dama or Jaume de Provença.

INEXPENSIVE

Ca La María. Tallers, 76. ☎ **93/318-89-93.** Reservations recommended Sat–Sun. Main courses 925–1,550 ptas. ($7.40–$12.40). AE, DC, MC, V. Mon–Sun 1:30–4pm, Tues–Sat 8:30–11pm. Metro: Universitat. CATALÁN.

This small blue-and-green-tiled bistro (only 18 tables) is on a quiet square opposite a Byzantine-style church near the Plaça de la Universitat. Look for the constantly changing daily specials. This is not a place for haute cuisine. A bit battered in looks, the restaurant serves endearingly homelike food—providing you grew up in a family of Catalán cooks. These dishes, which despite their simple origins, are often surprisingly tasty, as exemplified by the baby squid with onions and tomatoes, anglerfish with burnt garlic, and a veal sirloin cooked to taste.

El Caballito Blanco. Majorca, 196. ☎ **93/453-10-33.** Reservations not required. Main courses 875–3,900 ptas. ($7–$31.20). AE, MC, V. Tues–Sun 1–3:45pm, Tues–Sat 9–10:45pm. Closed Aug. Metro: Hospital Clínic. SEAFOOD/INTERNATIONAL.

This old Barcelona standby, famous for its seafood, has long been popular among locals. The fluorescent-lit dining area does not offer much atmosphere, but the food is good, varied, and relatively inexpensive. The "Little White Horse," in the Passeig de Gràcia area, features a huge selection, including monkfish, mussels marinara, and shrimp with garlic. If you don't want fish, try the grilled lamb cutlets. Several different pâtés and salads are offered. There's a bar to the left of the dining area.

NORTE DIAGONAL

VERY EXPENSIVE

✪ **Botafumeiro.** Gran de Gràcia, 81. ☎ **93/218-42-30.** Reservations recommended for dining rooms, not necessary for meals at the bar. Main courses 2,500–5,800 ptas. ($20–$46.40); fixed-price menus 8,000–9,000 ptas. ($64–$72). AE, DC, MC, V. Mon–Sat 1pm–1am, Sun 1–5pm. Metro: Enrique Cuiraga. SEAFOOD.

Although the competition is severe, this *restaurante marisqueria* consistently puts Barcelona's finest seafood on the table. Much of the allure of this place comes from the attention to details paid by the white-jacketed staff, who prepare a table setting at the establishment's bar for anyone who prefers to dine there. If you do choose to venture to the rear, you'll find a series of attractive dining rooms outfitted with light-grained panels, white napery, polished brass, potted plants, and paintings by Galician artists. These rooms are noted for the ease with which business deals seem to be arranged during the lunch hour, when international business people often make it their favorite rendezvous. The King of Spain is sometimes a patron.

Menu items include some of the most legendary seafood in Barcelona, prepared ultrafresh in a glistening and ultramodern kitchen that's visible from parts of the dining room. The establishment prides itself on its fresh and saltwater fish, clams, mussels, lobster, crayfish, scallops, and several varieties of crustaceans that you may never have seen before. Stored live in holding tanks or in enormous crates near the restaurant's entrance, many of the creatures are flown in every day from Galicia, home of owner Moncho Neira. In contrast to the hundred-or-so fish dishes (which might include *zarzuelas,* paellas, and grills), the menu lists only four or five meat dishes, including three kinds of steak, veal, and a traditional version of pork with turnips. The wine list offers a wide array of *cavas* from Catalonia and highly drinkable choices from Galicia.

EXPENSIVE

✪ **Neichel.** Pedralbes, 16. ☎ **93/203-84-08.** Reservations required. Main courses 2,300–3,800 ptas. ($18.40–$30.40). AE, DC, MC, V. Mon–Sat 1–4pm and 8:30–11pm. Closed Aug and all holidays. Metro: Palau Reial or María Cristina. FRENCH.

Owned and operated by Alsatian-born Jean Louis Neichel, who has been called "the most brilliant ambassador French cuisine has ever had within Spain," this restaurant serves a clientele whose credentials might best be described as stratospheric. Outfitted in cool tones of gray and pastel, with its main decoration derived from a bank of windows opening onto greenery, Neichel is vastly and almost obsessively concerned with gastronomy—the savory presentation of some of the most talked-about preparations of seafood, fowl, and sweets in Spain.

Your meal might include a "mosaic" of foie gras with vegetables, a salad composed of fresh asparagus, strips of salmon marinated in sesame and served with *escabeche* (vinaigrette) sauce, slices of raw and smoked salmon stuffed with caviar, a prize-winning terrine of seacrab floating on a lavishly decorated bed of cold seafood sauce, escalope of turbot served with *coulis* (puree) of sea urchins, fricassee of Bresse chicken served with spiny lobsters, sea bass with a mousseline of truffles, Spanish milk-fed lamb served with the juice of Boletus mushrooms, a ragoút of sole containing fresh asparagus and Iranian caviar, rack of lamb gratinéed within an herb-flavored pastry crust, and an array of well-flavored game birds obtained in season from hunters throughout Catalonia and France. Both the selection of European cheeses and the changing array of freshly made desserts are nothing short of spectacular.

Reno. Tuset, 27. ☎ **93/200-91-29.** Reservations required. Main courses 1,200–3,500 ptas. ($9.60–$28). AE, DC, MC, V. Sun–Fri 1–4pm and 8:30–11:30pm. Metro: Diagonal. CATALÁN/FRENCH.

One of the finest and most enduring haute cuisine restaurants in Barcelona, Reno boasts an impeccably mannered staff (formal but not intimidating) and an understated modern decor accented with black leather and oversized mirrors. A discreet row of sidewalk-to-ceiling windows hung with fine-mesh lace shelters diners from the prying eyes of those on the octagonal plaza outside. Specialties, influenced by the seasons and by the traditions of France, might include partridge simmered in wine or port sauce, a platter of assorted smoked fish (each painstakingly smoked on the premises), hake with anchovy sauce, filet of sole either stuffed with foie gras and truffles or grilled with anchovy sauce, Catalán-style civet of lobster, roast duck with a sauce of honey and sherry vinegar, and an appetizing array of pastries wheeled from table to table on a trolley. Dessert might also be one of several kinds of crêpes flambéed at your table. The restaurant, incidentally, was established in 1954 by the father of the present owner.

Roig Robí. Séneca, 20. ☎ **93/218-92-22.** Reservations required. Main courses 1,950–3,250 ptas. ($15.60–$26). AE, DC, MC, V. Mon–Sat 1:30–4pm and 9–11:30pm. Metro: Diagonal. CATALÁN/FRENCH.

Excellent food from an imaginative kitchen and a warm welcome keep patrons coming back here, although we're not as excited about this restaurant as we once were. It remains, however, one of the city's most dependable choices for reliable cuisine. Begin by ordering an aperitif from the L-shaped oaken bar. Then head down a long corridor to a pair of flower-filled dining rooms. In warm weather, glass doors open onto a walled courtyard, ringed with cascades of ivy and shaded with willows and mimosa. Menu items include fresh beans with pine-nut sauce, hake al Roig Robí, codfish salad with pintos, lobster salad, ravioli stuffed with spring herbs, three different preparations of hake, chicken stuffed with foie gras, and a cockscomb salad, the latter a dish too adventuresome for many palates.

✪ **Via Veneto.** Granduxer, 10–12. ☎ **93/200-72-44.** Reservations required. Main courses 2,200–3,990 ptas. ($17.60–$31.90). AE, DC, MC, V. Mon–Fri 1:15–4pm, Mon–Sat 8:45pm–midnight. Metro: La Bonanova. CATALÁN/INTERNATIONAL.

With a soothing and dignified decor of calming colors and baroque swirls, this restaurant is known for its solid respectability and consistently well-prepared cuisine. Set a short walk from the Plaça de Francesc Macia, it offers such dishes as a tartare of fresh fish with caviar, roasted salt cod with potatoes, veal kidney with truffle sauce, loin of roast suckling pig with baby vegetables of the season, and filet steak served in a brandy, cream, and peppercorn sauce. Innovative and imaginative Catalán recipes are always being invented here. The cuisine is finely crafted based on superb local products. There's a wide array of wines to accompany any meal. Dessert might be a richly textured combination of melted chocolate, cherries, Armagnac, and vanilla ice cream.

MODERATE

Arcs de Sant Gervasi. Santaló, 103. ☎ **93/201-92-77.** Reservations recommended. Main courses 1,900–2,400 ptas. ($15.20–$19.20). AE, DC, MC, V. Tues–Sun 1–4:30pm, Tues–Sat 9pm–midnight. Metro: Muntaner. CATALÁN.

North of the old town, Arcs de Sant Gervasi is sleekly decorated with such trappings as black lacquer chairs. A nearby gallery fills the walls with pictures that are for sale. To begin, try cream-of-crab soup or Palafrugell "black rice." For a main dish, order tender slices of veal served with wild mushrooms in a delectable cognac-flavored sauce; the kid cutlets are also juicy and superb. For dessert, try the scooped-out pineapple filled with chopped fresh fruit and *crema catalana* (caramel pudding).

Henry J. Bean's Bar and Grill. Carrer La Granada del Penedés, 14–16. ☎ **93/218-29-98.** Main courses 1,295–3,000 ptas. ($10.35–$24). AE, DC, MC, V. Daily 1pm–1am. Metro: Diagonal. AMERICAN.

Food is cheap, plentiful, and savory in this unassuming restaurant filled with Americana. Have a great smokehouse burger or perhaps chili con carne, stuffed mushrooms, nachos, or barbecued baby back ribs. No meal is complete without pecan or mud pie for dessert. Half-price drinks are de rigueur during happy hour, between 6 and 9pm and all night Wednesday.

MOLL DE LA FUSTA & BARCELONETA

EXPENSIVE

Can Majó. Almirante Aixada, 23. ☎ **93/221-54-55.** Reservations recommended. Main courses 1,800–3,500 ptas. ($14.40–$28); fixed-price menu 6,000 ptas. ($48). AE, DC, MC, V. Tues–Sun 1:30–4:30pm and 9–11:30pm. Metro: Barceloneta. SEAFOOD.

Located in the old fishing quarter of Barceloneta, Can Majo attracts many people from the fancier quarters, who journey down here for a great seafood dinner. The Suárez-Majo family welcome you; they're still operating a business where their grandmother first opened a bar. Try a house specialty, *pelada* (Catalán for *paella*), perhaps starting with *entremeses* (hors d'oeuvres), from which you can select barnacles, oysters, prawns, whelks, clams, and crab—virtually whatever was caught that day. The clams with white beans are recommended. The classic all-vegetable gazpacho comes with fresh mussels and shrimp.

Ramonet (Bar Xarello). Carrer Maquinista, 17. ☎ **93/319-30-64.** Reservations recommended. Main courses 1,800–3,950 ptas. ($14.40–$31.60); fixed-price menus 4,200–5,950 ptas. ($33.60–$47.60). AE, DC, MC, V. Daily 10am–4pm and 8pm–midnight. Closed Aug 10–Sept 10. Metro: Barceloneta. SEAFOOD.

Located in a Catalán-style villa near the seaport, this rather expensive restaurant serves a large variety of fresh seafood, and has done so since 1763. The front room, with stand-up tables for seafood tapas, beer, and regional wine, is often crowded. In the two dining rooms in back, lined with wooden tables, you can choose from a wide variety of fish—shrimp, hake, and monkfish are almost always available. Other specialties include a portion of pungent anchovies, grilled mushrooms, black rice, braised artichokes, and a tortilla with spinach and beans. Mussels "from the beach" are also sold.

MODERATE

Gambrinus. Passeig del Moll de la Fusta. ☎ **93/221-96-07.** Reservations required. Main courses from 1,000 ptas. ($8). AE, DC, MC, V. Thurs–Sun 12:30–4pm and 7pm–midnight. Metro: Drassanes. SEAFOOD.

Although this restaurant is respected for the well-prepared food served within, much of its fame derives from the enormous statue perched on its roof. Made of polychromed fiberglass by Javier Mariscal (creator of the 1992 Olympic mascot), the statue depicts a giant lobster whose waving tentacles and threatening claws attract looks of amazement from pedestrians and motorists.

Set beside the sea, in a low-slung modern building with lots of glass, the restaurant has outdoor tables set on a pier, shaded with parasols. Menu items are priced from relatively inexpensive to very expensive, as, for example, anything made with lobster or pricey shellfish. Meals can include such dishes as fish soup, fresh oysters, fried squid, shellfish paella, and various cuts and filets of grilled fish, depending on the day's catch. Many visitors opt for a drink at the boat-shaped bar before or after their meal.

Siete Puertas (also known as 7 Portes). Passeig d'Isabel II, 14. ☎ **93/319-30-33.** Reservations required. Main courses 825–3,320 ptas. ($6.60–$26.55). AE, DC, MC, V. Daily 1pm–midnight. Metro: Barceloneta. SEAFOOD.

This is a lunchtime favorite for businesspeople (the Stock Exchange is across the way) and an evening favorite for in-the-know clients who have made it their preferred restaurant in Catalonia. It's been going since 1836. Regional dishes—the portions are enormous—include fresh herring with onions and potatoes, a different paella daily (sometimes with shellfish, for example, or with rabbit), and a wide array of fresh fish, succulent oysters, and an herb-laden stew of black beans with pork or white beans with sausage.

El Túnel. Ample, 33–35. ☎ **93/315-27-59.** Reservations recommended for lunch. Main courses 1,200–2,500 ptas. ($9.60–$20). AE, DC, MC, V. Tues–Sun 1:30–4pm, Tues–Sat 6–around 11:30pm. Closed Aug. Metro: San Jaume. CATALÁN.

This long-established restaurant features a delectable fish soup, cannelloni with truffles, kidney beans with shrimp, roast kid, fish stew, and filet of beef with peppers. The food is umcomplicated but delicious. The service is eager, the wine cellar extensive. El Túnel lies close to the general post office.

WEST OF TIBIDABO

La Balsa. Infanta Isabel, 4. ☎ **93/211-50-48.** Reservations required. Main courses 1,500–2,600 ptas. ($12–$20.80); fixed-price lunch 3,000 ptas. ($24); fixed-price dinner 5,500–6,950 ptas. ($44–$55.60). AE, DC, V. Tues–Sat 2–3:30pm, Mon–Sat 9–11:30pm. Closed Easter week, reduced menu in Aug. Transportation: Taxi. INTERNATIONAL.

Poised on the uppermost level of a circular tower that was originally built as a water cistern, La Balsa offers a view over most of the surrounding cityscape. To reach it you must climb up to what was originally intended as the structure's rooftop. Glassed-in walls, awnings, and a verdant mass of potted plants create the decor. You're likely to be greeted by owner and founder Mercedes López before being seated. Menu items emerge from a cramped but well-organized kitchen several floors below. (The waiters here are reputedly the most athletic in Barcelona because they must run up and down the stairs carrying steaming platters.) Often booked several days in advance, the restaurant serves such dishes as a salad of broad beans (*judías verdes* with strips of salmon in lemon-flavored vinaigrette, stewed veal with wild mushrooms, a salad of warm lentils with anchovies, pickled fresh salmon with chives, undercooked magret

Fast Food & Picnic Fare

For those travelers who miss good old American food, don't fret—there are plenty of fast-food joints. It may not be as adventurous as trying authentic Spanish cuisine, but you'll definitely please the kids.

Burger King, Rambla de Canaletes, 135 (☎ **93/302-54-29;** metro: Plaça de Catalunya), is open Sunday through Friday, 10am to midnight; Saturday, 10am to 1am. A burger, fries, and a drink costs 550 to 1,000 pesetas ($4.40–$8).

Chicago Pizza Pie Factory, Carrer de Provença, 300 (☎ **93/215-94-15;** metro: Passeig de Gràcia), offers pizzas for 1,250 to 3,000 pesetas ($10–$24), the latter big enough for four. It's open daily from 1pm to 1am; happy hour runs from 6 to 9pm.

Kentucky Fried Chicken, Ferran, 2 (☎ **93/412-51-54;** metro: Drassanes), is open Monday through Thursday, 11am to 11pm; Friday through Sunday, 11am to midnight. A bucket containing six pieces of chicken, enough for a meal for two, costs 1,075 pesetas ($8.60).

Viena, Rambla dels Estudis, 115 (☎ **93/317-14-92;** metro: Plaça de Catalunya), is Barcelona's most elegant fast-food place. Waiters wearing Viennese vests serve croissants with Roquefort for breakfast and, later in the day, toasted ham sandwiches, hamburgers with onions, and pasta with tomato sauce. Meals cost from 1,500 pesetas ($12). Service is Monday through Saturday, 9am to 1am; Sunday, 2pm to midnight.

The best place in all Barcelona to buy the makings of your picnic is **Mercat de la Boquería,** in the center of the Les Rambles (metro: Liceu). This is the old marketplace of Barcelona. You'll jostle elbows with butchers and fish mongers in bloodied smocks and see salespeople selling cheeses and sausages. Much of the food is uncooked, but hundreds of items are already prepared and you can even buy a bottle of wine or mineral water.

Now for where to have your picnic. Right in the heart of Barcelona is the **Parc de la Ciutadella** (see "Parks & Gardens" in Chapter 13), at the southeast section of the district known as the Barri de la Ribera, site of the Picasso Museum. After lunch, take the kids to the park zoo and later go out on the lake in a rented rowboat.

It's more scenic to picnic in **Montjuïc,** site of several events at the 1992 Summer Olympics. After your picnic, you can enjoy the amusement park or walk through the Poble Espanyol, a re-created Spanish village.

(breast) of duck served with fresh and lightly poached foie gras, and baked hake (flown in frequently from faraway Galicia) prepared in squid-ink sauce.

TASCAS

The bars listed below are known for their tapas; for further recommendations, refer to the "Barcelona After Dark" section of Chapter 13.

Alt Heidelberg. Ronda Universitat, 5. ☎ **93/318-10-32.** Tapas 250–750 ptas. ($2–$6); combination plates 1,000–1,450 ptas. ($8–$11.60). MC, V. Mon–Fri 8am–1:30am, Sat–Sun noon–2am. Metro: Universitat. GERMAN/TAPAS.

Since the 1930s, this has been an institution in Barcelona, offering German beer on tap, a good selection of German sausages, and Spanish tapas. You can also enjoy full meals here—sauerkraut garni is a specialty.

Bar del Pi. Plaça Sant Josep Oriol, 1. ☎ **93/302-21-23.** Tapas 250–550 ptas. ($2–$4.40). No credit cards. Mon–Fri 9am–11pm, Sat 9:30am–10pm, Sun 10am–10pm. Metro: Liceu. TAPAS.

One of the most famous bars in the Barri Gòtic, this establishment lies midway between two medieval squares, opening onto Església del Pi. You can sit inside at one of the cramped bentwood tables or stand at the crowded bar. In warm weather, take a table beneath the single plane tree on this landmark square. Tapas are limited; most visitors come to drink coffee, beer, or wine.

Bar Turó. Tenor Viñas, 1. ☎ **93/200-69-53.** Tapas 300–1,500 ptas. ($2.40–$12). No credit cards. Daily 9am–1am. Metro: Muntaner. TAPAS.

Set in an affluent residential neighborhood north of the old town, Bar Turó serves some of the best tapas in town. In summer you can either sit outside or retreat to the narrow confines of the inside bar. There you can select from about 20 different kinds of tapas, including Russian salad, fried squid, and Serrano ham.

Bodega la Plata. Mercè, 28. ☎ **93/315-10-09.** Tapas 180–300 ptas. ($1.45–$2.40). No credit cards. Mon–Sat 9pm–11pm. Metro: Barceloneta. TAPAS.

Part of a trio of famous bodegas on this narrow medieval street, La Plata occupies a corner building whose two open sides allow richly aromatic cooking odors to permeate the neighborhood. This bodega contains a marble-topped bar and overcrowded tables. The culinary specialty is *raciones* (small plates) of deep-fried sardines (head and all). You can make a meal with two servings of these, coupled with the house's tomato, onion, and fresh anchovy salad.

Bodegueta. Rambla de Catalunya, 100. ☎ **93/215-48-94.** Tapas from 160 ptas. ($1.30). No credit cards. Mon–Sat 8am–2am, Sun 6:30pm–2am. Metro: Diagonal. TAPAS.

Founded in 1940, this old wine tavern specializes in Catalán sausage meats. Everything can be washed down with inexpensive Spanish wines. Beer costs 125 pesetas ($1); wine goes for 100 pesetas (80¢).

Las Campanas [Casa Marcos]. Mercè, 21. ☎ **93/315-06-09.** Tapas from 250 ptas. ($2). No credit cards. Thurs–Tues noon–2am. Metro: Barceloneta. TAPAS.

No sign announces its name—from the street Las Campanas looks like a storehouse for cured hams and wine bottles. At a long and narrow stand-up bar, patrons flock here for a *chorizo* (spicy sausage), which is then pinioned between two pieces of bread. Sausages are usually eaten with beer or red wine. The place opened in 1952, and nothing has changed since. A tape recorder plays nostalgic favorites, everything from Edith Piaf to the Andrews Sisters.

Casa Tejada. Tenor Viñas, 3. ☎ **93/200-73-41.** Tapas 275–2,150 ptas. ($2.20–$17.20). V. Daily 9am–2am. Metro: Muntaner. TAPAS.

Covered with rough stucco and decorated with hanging hams, Casa Tejada (established in 1964) offers some of Barcelona's best tapas. Arranged behind a glass display case, they include such dishes as marinated fresh tuna, German-style potato salad, five preparations of squid (including one that's stuffed), and ham salad. For variety, quantity, and quality, this place is hard to beat. There's outdoor dining in summer.

Jamón Jamón. Mestre Nicolau, 4. ☎ **93/209-41-03.** Tapas 1,200–1,600 ptas. ($9.60–$12.80). No credit cards. Mon–Sat 9am–midnight. Metro: Muntaner. TAPAS.

Located north of Avinguda Diagonal, near Plaça de Francesc Maria, this establishment has a modern interior of gray granite and chrome, a deliberate contrast to the traditional pork products that are the specialty of this *tasca.* Entire hams from Huelva, deep in the south of Andalusia, are impaled on steel braces. The ham is laboriously carved and trimmed before you into paper-thin slices.

La Jarra. Mercè, 9. ☎ **93/315-17-59.** Tapas 200–352 ptas. ($1.60–$2.80). No credit cards. Thurs–Tues 10:30am–1am. Metro: Barceloneta. TAPAS.

La Jarra occupies a tile-covered L-shaped room that's somewhat bleak in appearance, yet residents claim it is one of the most authentic tapas bars in the old town. You can order a *ración* of marinated mushrooms or well-seasoned artichokes Rioja style, but the culinary star is the ever-present haunch of *jamón canario* (Canary Island ham), which is carved before your eyes into lean, succulent morsels served with boiled potatoes, olive oil, and lots of salt. It resembles roast pork in flavor and appearance.

Rey de la Gamba. Joan de Borbo, 53. ☎ **93/221-75-98.** Tapas 800–1,850 ptas. ($6.40–$14.80). MC, V. Daily 10am–1am. Metro: Barceloneta. TAPAS/SHELLFISH.

The name of this place means "king of prawns," but this restaurant could also be called the House of Mussels since it sells more of that shellfish. In the old fishing village of Barceloneta, dating from the 18th century, this place packs them in, especially on weekends. A wide array of seafood is sold, along with cured ham—the combination is considered a tradition.

A SPECIAL PLACE FOR DESSERT

Dulcinea. Via Petrixol, 2. ☎ **93/302-68-24.** Cup of chocolate 325 ptas. ($2.60). No credit cards. Daily 9am–1pm and 5–9pm. Closed late July to mid-Aug. Metro: Plaça de Catalunya or Liceu. CHOCOLATE.

At this, the most famous chocolate shop in Barcelona, the specialty is *melindros* (sugar-topped soft-sided biscuits), which the regulars who flock here love to dunk into the very thick hot chocolate—so thick, in fact, that imbibing it feels like eating a melted chocolate bar.

13 Barcelona Attractions

Barcelona, long a Mediterranean center of commerce, is fast emerging as one of the focal points of European tourism, a role that reached its zenith during the 1992 Olympic Games. Spain's second-largest city is also its most cosmopolitan and avant-garde.

Because its rich history extends back for centuries, Barcelona is filled with landmark buildings and world-class museums offering many sightseeing opportunities. These include Antoni Gaudí's Sagrada Familia, the Museu Picasso, the Gothic cathedral, and Les Rambles, the famous tree-lined promenade cutting through the heart of the old quarter.

The capital of Catalonia, Barcelona sits at the northeast end of the Costa Brava, Spain's gateway to the Mediterranean. A half-hour flight east will land you on one of the Balearic Islands—Majorca, Ibiza, or Minorca. You can also branch out from Barcelona to one of the cities of historic interest in its environs, including the old Roman city of Tarragona or the monastery at Montserrat (see Chapter 14).

To begin, however, you will want to take in the artistic and intellectual aura of this unique seafaring city. Residents take justifiable pride in their Catalán heritage, and they are eager to share it with you. Many of these sights can be covered on foot, and this chapter includes two walking tours.

An array of nightlife (Barcelona is a *big* bar town), shopping possibilities, and sports programs are also covered in this chapter, along with some organized tours, special events, and trips to Catalonia's wine country. It makes for some serious sightseeing; you'll need plenty of time to take it all in.

SUGGESTED ITINERARIES

If You Have 1 Day

Spend the morning following the walking tour of the **Barri Gòtic** (see below), taking in the highlights of this ancient district. In the afternoon visit Antoni Gaudí's unfinished cathedral, **La Sagrada Familia,** before returning to the heart of the city for a walk down Les Rambles. To cap your day, take the funicular to the fountains at Montjuïc or go to the top of Tibidabo for an outstanding view of Barcelona and its harbor.

If You Have 2 Days

Spend Day 1 as described above. On Day 2 visit the **Museu Picasso,** housed in two Gothic mansions. Then stroll through the surrounding district, the **Barri de la Ribera,** which is filled with Renaissance mansions. Follow this with a ride to the top of the **Columbus Monument** for a panoramic view of the harborfront. Have a seafood lunch at La Barceloneta, and in the afternoon stroll up Les Rambles again. For the rest of the afternoon explore Montjuïc and visit the Museu d'Art de Catalunya. End the day with a meal at Los Caracoles, the most famous restaurant in the old city, just off Les Rambles.

If You Have 3 Days

Spend Days 1 and 2 as described above. On Day 3, make a pilgrimage to the monastery of **Montserrat** to see the venerated Black Virgin and a host of artistic and scenic attractions. Try to time your visit to hear the 50-member boys' choir.

If You Have 5 Days

Spend your first three days as described above. On Day 4 take a morning walk in *modernismo* Barcelona and have lunch on the pier. In the afternoon visit Montjuïc again to tour the **Fundació Joan Miró** and walk through the **Poble Espanyol,** a miniature village created for the 1929 World's Fair. On Day 5 take another excursion from the city. If you're interested in history, visit the former Roman city of **Tarragona** to the south. If you want to **unwind on a beach,** head south to Sitges or north to Tossa de Mar, on the Costa Brava.

1 The Top Attractions

✪ **La Sagrada Familia.** Majorca, 401. ☎ **93/455-02-47.** Admission 750 ptas. ($6), including 12-minute video on Gaudí's religious and secular works; additional 200 ptas. ($1.60) for elevator to the top (about 200 feet). Jan–Feb and Nov–Dec, daily 9am–6pm; Mar–Apr and Oct, daily 9am–7pm; May and Sept, daily 9am–8pm; June–Aug, daily 9am–9pm. Metro: Sagrada Familia.

Gaudí's incomplete masterpiece is one of the more idiosyncratic creations of Spain—if you have time to see only one Catalán landmark, make it this one. Begun in 1882 and still incomplete at Gaudí's death in 1926, this incredible cathedral—the Church of the Holy Family—is a bizarre wonder. The languid, amorphous structure embodies the essence of Gaudí's style, which some have described as art nouveau run rampant. Work continues on the structure but without any sure idea of what Gaudí intended. Some say that the cathedral will be completed by the mid-21st century.

✪ **Catedral de Barcelona.** Plaça de la Seu, s/n. ☎ **93/315-15-54.** Admission to cathedral, free; museum, 100 ptas. (80¢). Cathedral, daily 8am–1:30pm and 4–7:30pm; cloister museum, daily 10am–1pm. Metro: Jaume I.

Barcelona's cathedral stands as a celebrated example of Catalonian Gothic architecture. Except for the 19th-century west facade, the basilica was begun at the end of the 13th century and completed in the mid-15th century. The three naves, cleaned and illuminated, have splendid Gothic details. With its large bell towers, blending of medieval and Renaissance styles, beautiful cloister, high altar, side chapels, sculptured choir, and Gothic arches, it ranks as one of the most impressive cathedrals in Spain. Vaulted galleries in the cloister surround a garden of magnolias, medlars, and palm trees; the galleries are further enhanced by forged iron grilles. The historian Cirici called this place the loveliest oasis in Barcelona. The cloister, illuminated on Saturdays and fiesta days, also contains a museum of medieval art. The most notable work displayed is the 15th-century *La Pietat* of Bartolomé Bermejo. At noon on

Barcelona Attractions

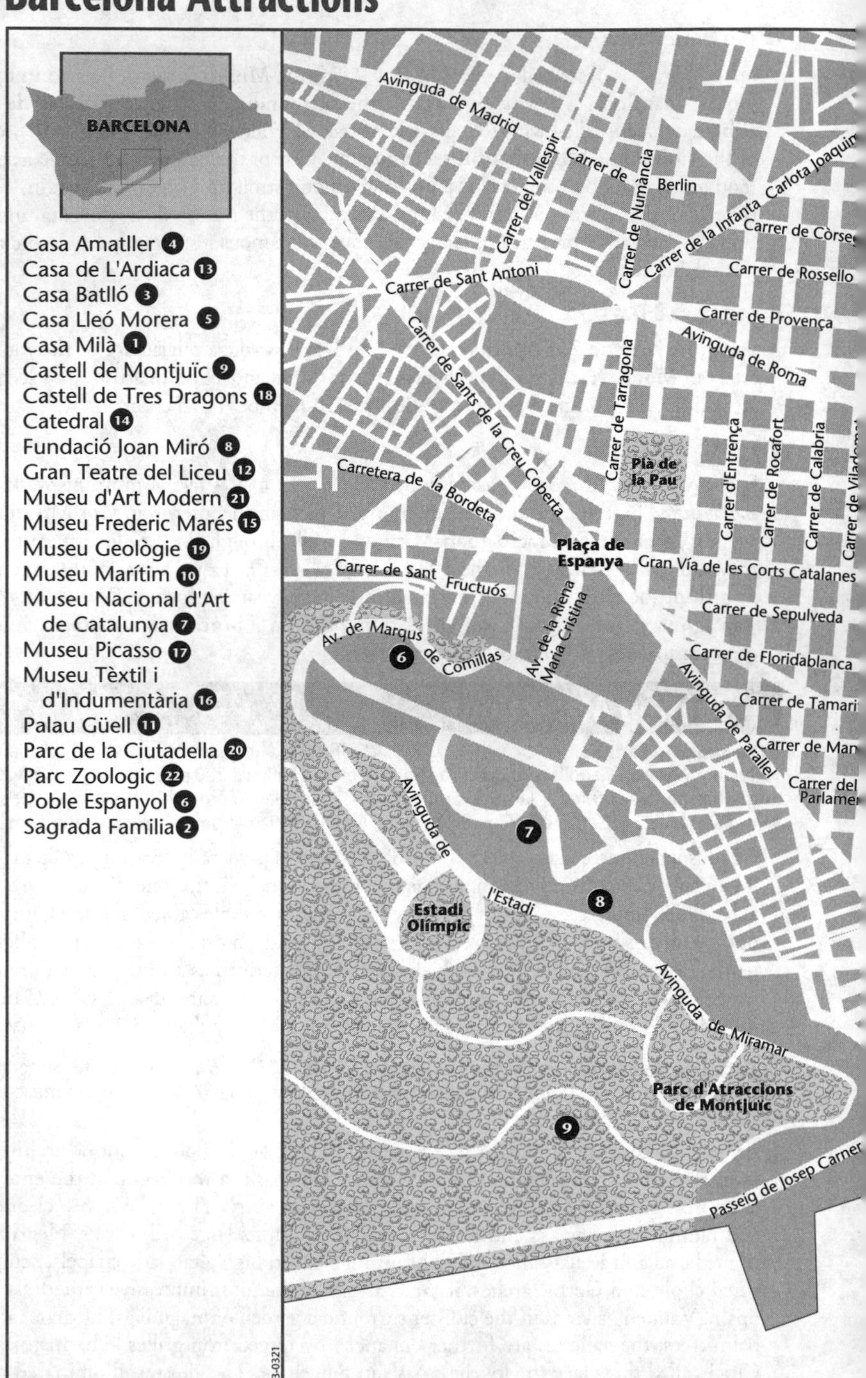

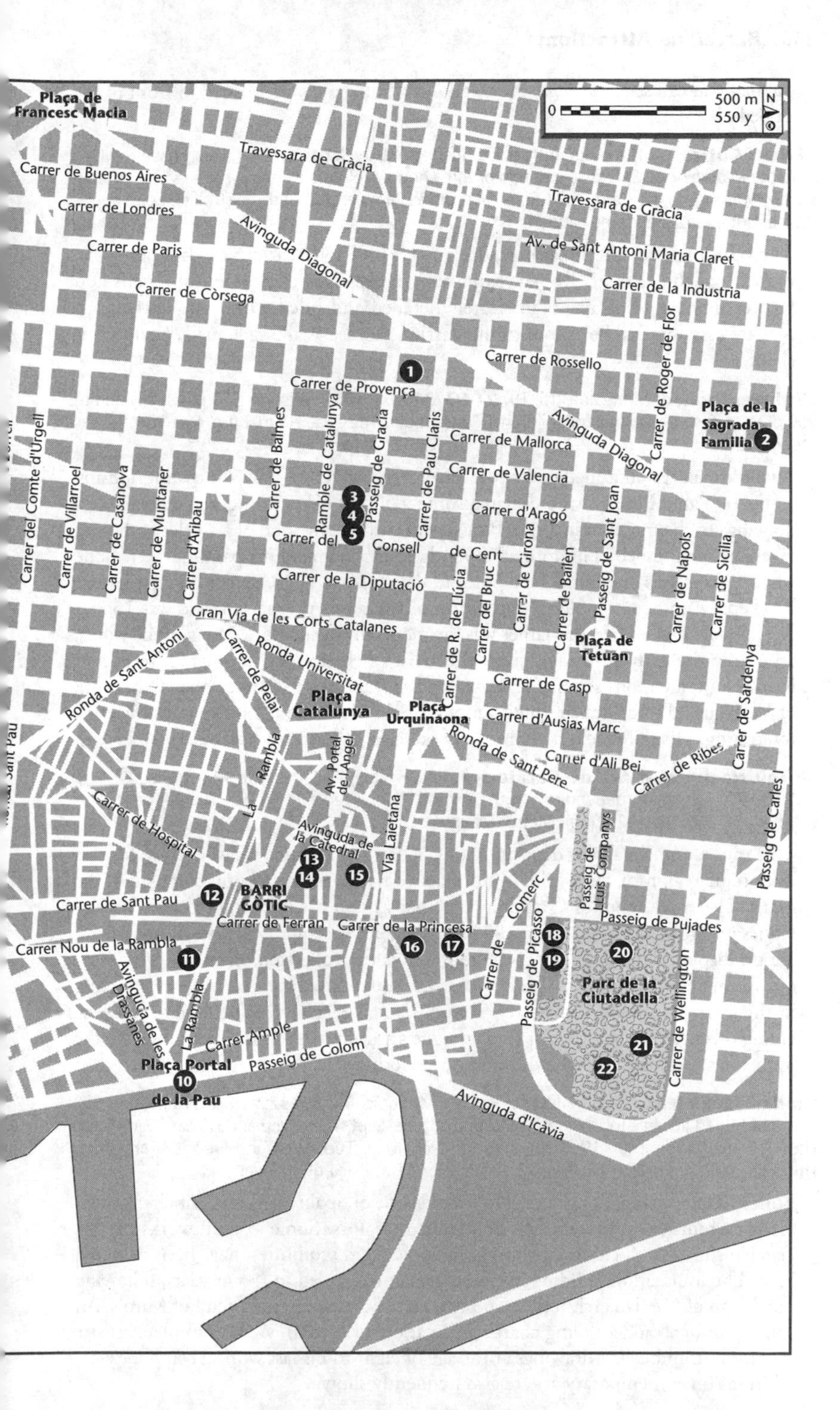

Plaça de Francesc Macia
500 m
550 y
N
Travessara de Gràcia
Carrer de Buenos Aires
Carrer de Londres
Avinguda Diagonal
Carrer de Paris
Carrer de Còrsega
Av. de Sant Antoni Maria Claret
Carrer de la Industria
Carrer de Rossello
Carrer de Roger de Flor
Carrer de Provença
Plaça de la Sagrada Familia
Carrer de Mallorca
Carrer de Valencia
Carrer d'Aragó
Carrer del Consell de Cent
Carrer de la Diputació
Carrer del Comte d'Urgell
Carrer de Villarroel
Carrer de Casanova
Carrer de Muntaner
Carrer d'Aribau
Carrer de Balmes
Rambla de Catalunya
Passeig de Gracia
Carrer de Pau Claris
Carrer de R. de Llúcia
Carrer del Bruc
Carrer de Girona
Carrer de Bailèn
Passeig de Sant Joan
Carrer de Napols
Carrer de Sicilia
Gran Vía de les Corts Catalanes
Plaça de Tetuan
Ronda de Sant Antoni
Carrer de Pelai
Ronda Universitat
Plaça Catalunya
Plaça Urquinaona
Carrer de Casp
Carrer d'Ausias Marc
Carrer de Sardenya
Ronda de Sant Pere
Carrer d'Ali Bei
Carrer de Ribes
Passeig de Carles I
La Rambla
Av. Portal de l'Angel
Via Laietana
Carrer de Hospital
Avinguda de la Catedral
Passeig de Lluís Companys
Carrer de Sant Pau
BARRI GÒTIC
Carrer de Ferran
Carrer de la Princesa
Carrer de Comerc
Passeig de Pujades
Passeig de Picasso
Carrer Nou de la Rambla
Avinguda de les Drassanes
Parc de la Ciutadella
Carrer de Wellington
La Rambla
Carrer Ample
Plaça Portal de la Pau
Passeig de Colom
Avinguda d'Icàvia

Sunday you can see a *sardana,* the Catalonian folk dance, performed in front of the cathedral.

✪ **Barri Gòtic.** This is the old aristocratic quarter of Barcelona, parts of which have survived from the Middle Ages. Spend at least two or three hours exploring its narrow streets and squares; start by walking up the Carrer del Carme, east of Les Rambles. A nighttime stroll takes on added drama, but exercise extreme caution.

The buildings, for the most part, are austere and sober, the cathedral being the crowning achievement. Roman ruins and the vestiges of 3rd-century walls add further interest. This area is intricately detailed and filled with many attractions that are easy to miss. For a tour of the Barri Gòtic, see Walking Tour 1, later in this chapter.

✪ **Museu Picasso.** Montcada, 15–19. ☎ **93/319-63-10.** Admission 500 ptas. ($4) adults, 250 ptas. ($2) students, free for children 17 and under. Tues–Sat 10am–8pm, Sun 10am–3pm. Metro: Jaume I.

Two old palaces on a medieval street have been converted into a museum housing works by Pablo Picasso, who donated some 2,500 of his paintings, engravings, and drawings to the museum in 1970. Picasso was particularly fond of Barcelona, the city where he spent much of his formative youth. In fact, some of the paintings were done when Picasso was only nine. One portrait, dating from 1896, depicts his stern aunt, Tía Pepa. Another, completed at the turn of the century, when Picasso was 16, depicts *Science and Charity* (his father was the model for the doctor). Many of the works, especially the early paintings, show the artist's debt to van Gogh, El Greco, and Rembrandt; a famous series, *Las Meninas* (1957), is said to "impersonate" the work of Velázquez. From Picasso's blue period, the *La Vie* drawings are perhaps the most interesting. His notebooks contain many sketches of Barcelona scenes.

Museu Nacional d'Art de Catalunya. Palau Nacional, Parc de Montjuïc. ☎ **93/423-71-99.** Admission depending on the exhibit. Tues–Wed and Fri–Sat 10am–7pm, Thurs 10am–9pm, Sun 10am–2:30pm. Metro: Espanya.

This museum is the major depository of Catalán art, a virtual treasure trove for this important region of the world. With massive renovations recently completed, the National Art Museum of Catalonia is perhaps the most important center for Romanesque art in the world. Over 100 pieces, including sculptures, icons, and frescoes, are on display. The highlight of the museum is the collection of murals from various Romanesque churches. The frescoes and murals are displayed in apses, much as in the churches in which they were found. Each is placed in sequential order, providing the viewer with a tour of Romanesque art from its primitive beginnings to the more advanced, late Romanesque and early Gothic era.

Fundació Joan Miró. Plaça de Neptú, Parc de Montjuïc. ☎ **93/329-19-08.** Admission 600 ptas. ($4.80) adults, free for children 9 and under. June–Sept, Tues–Wed and Fri–Sat 10am–8pm, Thurs 10am–9:30pm, Sun 10:30am–2:30pm; Nov–May, Tues–Wed and Fri–Sat 11am–7pm, Thurs 11am–9:30pm, Sun 10:30am–2:30pm. Bus: 61 at Plaça d'Espanya.

Born in 1893, Joan Miró went on to become one of Spain's greatest painters, known for his whimsical abstract forms and brilliant colors. Some 10,000 works by this Catalán surrealist, including paintings, graphics, and sculptures, have been collected here. The foundation building has been greatly expanded in recent years, following the design of Catalán architect Josep Lluís Sert, a close personal friend of Miró's. An exhibition in a modern wing charts (in a variety of media) Miró's complete artistic evolution from his first drawings at the age of eight to his last works. Temporary exhibitions on contemporary art are also frequently shown.

Frommer's Favorite Barcelona Experiences

A Walk Through the Barri Gòtic. You'll pass through 15 centuries of history in one district.

Watching the Sardana. The national dance of Catalonia is performed at noon at the Plaça de San Jaume, in front of the cathedral.

A Trip to the Top of Montjuïc. This stop will provide enough amusement to fill three days.

Soaking Up Bar Culture. Bars in all shapes and sizes are the chic places to go at night—Barcelona has more than any other city in Spain.

Drinking Cava in a Xampanyería. Enjoy a glass of bubbly, Barcelona style. The wines are excellent, and Cataláns swear that their cavas taste better than French champagne.

A Tour of Barcelona's Harbor. Stroll from the pier in front of the Columbus Monument to the breakwater.

Exploring the Museum Picasso. Examine the artistic evolution of a genius from the age of nine.

Marveling at La Sagrada Familia. Gaudí's "sand-castle cathedral" is a testimony to the architect's talent and religious belief.

A Trip to Poble Espanyol. This is an artificial village, to be sure, but it gives you a chance to see the architecture of all of Spain without leaving Barcelona.

2 More Attractions

Museu Frederic Marès. Plaça de Sant Iú, 5–6. ☎ **93/310-58-00.** Admission 300 ptas. ($2.40) adults, free for children under 16. Tues–Sat 10am–5pm, Sun 10am–2pm. Metro: Jaume I. Bus: 17, 19, or 45.

One of the biggest repositories of medieval sculpture in the region is the Frederic Marès Museum, located just behind the cathedral. It's housed in an ancient palace whose interior courtyards, chiseled stone, and soaring ceilings are impressive in their own right, an ideal setting for the hundreds of polychrome sculptures. The sculpture section dates from pre-Roman times to the 20th century. Also housed in the same building is the Museu Sentimental, a collection of everyday items that help to illustrate life in Barcelona during the past two centuries. Admission to both museums is included in the ticket price.

Center of Contemporary Culture of Barcelona (CCCB). Montalegre, 5. ☎ **93/412-07-81.** Admission 500 ptas. ($4) adults, 300 ptas. ($2.40) students and adults over 65, free for children under 16. Tues–Sat 11am–2pm and 4pm–8pm, Sun 10am–3pm. Metro: Catalunya.

Located in the Ciutat Vella, the Center of Contemporary Culture of Barcelona focuses on the city itself as its subject. It explores Barcelona's culture, history, and present role as a modern European city.

Museu Marítim. Avinguda de las Drassanes, s/n. ☎ **93/318-32-45.** Admission 600 ptas. ($4.80) adults, free for children 14 and under. Tues–Sun 10am–7pm. Closed holidays. Metro: Drassanes. Bus: 14, 18, 36, 38, or 57.

Located in the former Royal Shipyards (Drassanes Reials), this 13th-century Gothic complex was used for the construction of ships for the Catalano-Aragonese rulers. The most outstanding exhibition here is a reconstruction of *La Galería Real* of Don Juan of Austria, a lavish royal galley. Another special exhibit features a map by Gabriel de Vallseca that was owned by explorer Amerìgo Vespucci.

Museu de la Ciència (Science Museum). Teodor Roviralta, 55. ☎ **93/212-60-50.** Admission to museum and planetarium, 725 ptas. ($5.80) adults, 650 ptas. ($5.20) children 16 and under. Tues–Sun 10am–8pm. Bus: 17, 22, 58, or 73.

The Museu de la Ciència of the "La Caixa" Foundation is one of the most popular in Barcelona, with more than 500,000 people visiting annually. Its modern design and hands-on activities have made it the most important science museum in Spain and a major cultural attraction.

Visitors can touch, listen, watch, and participate in a variety of hands-on exhibits. From the beauty of marine life to the magic of holograms, the museum offers a world of science to discover. Watch the world turn beneath the Foucault Pendulum; ride on a human gyroscope; hear a friend whisper from 65 feet (20m) away; feel an earthquake; or use the tools of a scientist to examine intricate life-forms with microscopes and video cameras.

More than 300 exhibits explore the wonders of science, from optics to space travel to life sciences. In the Optics and Perception exhibits visitors can interact with prisms, lenses, and holograms and walk inside a kaleidoscope. In the Living Planet area baby sharks swim, a tornado swirls, and plants magically change their form when touched.

In the Mechanics exhibit, visitors can lift an 88-pound (40kg) weight with little effort. The use of lasers and musical instruments provides a fun way to learn about sound and light waves. Throughout the exhibits, there are computers to help you delve deeper into various topics. Visitors can also walk inside a submarine and make weather measurements in a working weather station. For those who want to explore new worlds, there are Planetarium shows where the beauty of the night sky surrounds the audience.

Fundació Antoni Tàpies. Aragó, 255. ☎ **93/487-03-15.** Admission 500 ptas. ($4) adults, 250 ptas. ($2) children 10–18, free for children under 10. Tues–Sun 11am–8pm. Metro: Passeig de Gràcia.

When it opened in 1990, this became the third museum in Barcelona devoted to the work of a single artist. In 1984 the Catalán artist Antoni Tàpies set up the foundation bearing his name, and the city of Barcelona donated an ideal site: the old Montaner i Simon publishing house near the Passeig de Gràcia in the 19th-century Eixample district. One of the landmark buildings of Barcelona, the brick-and-iron structure was built between 1881 and 1884 by that exponent of Catalán art nouveau, architect Lluís Domènech i Montaner. The core of the museum is a collection of works by Tàpies (most contributed by the artist himself), covering the different stages of his career as it evolved into abstract expressionism. Here you can see the entire spectrum of mediums in which he worked: painting, assemblage, sculpture, drawing, and ceramics. His associations with Picasso and Miró are apparent. The largest of all the works by Tàpies is on top of the building itself: a gigantic sculpture made from 9,000 feet of metal wiring and tubing, entitled *Cloud and Chair.*

Museu d'Art Modern. Plaça d'Armes, Parc de la Ciutadella. ☎ **93/319-57-28.** Admission 300 ptas. ($2.40) adults, 200 ptas. ($1.60) students and adults over 65, free for children 16 and under. Tues–Sat 10am–7pm, Sun 10am–2pm. Closed Jan 1 and Dec 25. Metro: Arc de Triomf. Bus: 14, 16, 17, 39, or 40.

This museum shares a wing of the Palau de la Ciutadella with the Catalonian parliament. Constructed in the 1700s, it was once used as an arsenal, forming part of Barcelona's defenses. It later became a royal residence before being turned into a museum early in this century. Its collection of art focuses on the early 20th century and features the work of Catalán artists, including Martí Alsina, Vayreda, Casas, Fortuny, and Rusiñol. The collection also encompasses some 19th-century Romantic and neoclassical works, as well as *modernismo* furniture (including designs by architect Puig i Cadafalch).

Monestir de Pedralbes. Baixada del Monestir, 9. ☎ **93/203-92-82.** Admission 300 ptas. ($2.40) adults, 150 ptas. ($1.20) students and seniors 65 or older, free for children 16 or under. Tues–Sun 10am–2pm. Metro: Reina Elisenda. Bus: 22, 63, 64, 75, or 114.

One of the oldest buildings in Pedralbes (the city's wealthiest residential area) is this monastery, founded in 1326 by Elisenda de Montcada, Queen of Jaume II. Still a convent, the establishment is also the mausoleum of the queen, who is buried in its Gothic church. Walk through the cloisters, with nearly two dozen arches on each side, rising three stories high. A small chapel contains the chief treasure of the monastery, murals by Ferrer Bassa, who was considered the major artist of Catalonia in the 1300s.

This monastery was considered a minor attraction of Barcelona until 1993, when 72 paintings and 8 sculptures from the famed Thyssen-Bornemisza collection went on permanent display here. Among the more outstanding works of art are Fra Angelico's *The Virgin of Humility* and 20 paintings from the early German Renaissance period. Italian Renaissance paintings range from the end of the 15th century to the middle of the 16th century, as exemplified by works from Dosso Dossi, Lorenzo Lotto, Tintoretto, Veronese, and Titian. The baroque era is also represented, including such old masters as Rubens, Zurbarán, and Velázquez.

Museu Arqueològic. Passeig de Santa Madrona, 39–41, Parc de Montjuïc. ☎ **93/423-21-49.** Admission 200 ptas. ($1.60) adults (Sun free), free for children. Tues–Sat 9:30am–1:30pm and 3:30–7pm, Sun 9:30am–2pm. Metro: Espanya. Bus: 55.

Occupying the former Palace of Graphic Arts, built for the 1929 World's Fair, the Museu Arqueològic reflects the long history of this Mediterranean port city, beginning with prehistoric Iberian artifacts. The collection includes articles from the Greek, Roman (glass, ceramics, mosaics, bronzes), and Carthaginian periods. Some of the more interesting relics were excavated in the ancient Greco-Roman city of Empúries in Catalonia; other parts of the collection came from the Balearic Islands.

Museu d'Art Comtemporani de Barcelona. Plaça dels Angels, 1. ☎ **93/412-08-10.** Admission 600 ptas. ($4.80) adults, free for children. Tues–Fri noon–8pm, Sat 10am–8pm, Sun 10am–3pm. Metro: Plaça de Catalunya.

A soaring, glistening edifice in Barcelona's shabby Raval district, the Museum of Contemporary Art is to Barcelona what the Pompidou Center is to Paris. Designed by American architect Richard Meier, the building itself is a work of art, manipulating sunlight to offer brilliant, natural interior lighting. On display in the 74,000 square feet of exhibit space is the work of such modern luminaries as Tápies, Klee, Miró, and many others. The museum has a library, book shop, and cafeteria.

Museu de les Arts Decoratives. Palau Reial de Pedralbes, Avinguda Diagonal, 686. ☎ **93/280-50-24.** Admission 500 ptas. ($4), Wed 250 ptas. ($2), free 1st Sun of every month. Tues–Sun 10am–3pm. Metro: Palau Reial. Bus: 7, 63, 67, 68, or 75.

Set in a beautiful park, this palace was constructed as a municipal gift to King Alfonso XIII. He didn't get to make much use of it, however, as he was forced into exile in 1931. Today it houses a collection of objets d'art, furniture, jewelry, and glassware from the 14th century to the present. More than 200 pieces, all of Spanish origin, are on display.

Museu Egipci de Barcelona. Rambla de Catalunya, 57–59. ☎ **93/488-01-88.** Admission 600 ptas. ($4.80) adults, 500 ptas. ($4) children. Mon–Sat 10am–2pm and 4–7pm. Guided tours on Sat. Closed holidays. Metro: Passeig de Gràcia.

Spain's only museum dedicated specifically to Egyptology, it contains more than 250 pieces from founder Jordi Clos's personal collection. On display are sacrophagi, jewelry, hieroglyphics, and various sculptures and artworks. Exhibits pay close attention to the everyday life of ancient Egyptians, including details regarding education, social customs, religion, and food. The museum possesses its own lab for restorations. A library with more than 3,000 works is open to the public.

Museu d'Història de la Ciutat. Plaça del Rei. ☎ **93/315-11-11.** Admission 500 ptas. ($4). Tues–Sat 10am–2pm and 4–8pm, Sun 10am–2pm. Bus: 16, 17, 19, 22, or 45.

Connected to the Royal Palace (see below), this museum traces the history of the city from its early days as a Roman colony to its role as the city of the 1992 Summer Olympics. The museum is housed in a Catalán-Mediterranean mansion from the 1400s called the Padellás House. Many of the exhibits date from Roman days, with much else from medieval times.

Palau Reial (Royal Palace). Plaça del Rei. ☎ **93/315-11-11.** Admission 500 ptas. ($4). Mon 3:30–8pm, Tues–Sat 9am–8pm, Sun 9am–1:30pm. Bus: 16, 17, 19, 22, or 45.

Former palace of the counts of Barcelona, this later became the residence of the kings of Aragón—hence, the name of its plaza (Kings' Square). It is believed that Columbus was received here by Isabella and Ferdinand when he returned from his first voyage to the New World. Here, some believe, the monarchs got their first look at a Native American. The Saló del Tinell, a banqueting hall with a wood-paneled ceiling held up by half a dozen arches, dates from the 14th century. The hall dates from the 14th century. Rising five stories above the hall is the Torre del Reí Martí, a series of porticoed galleries.

Poble Espanyol. Marqués de Comilias, Parc de Montjuïc. ☎ **93/325-78-66.** Admission 950 ptas. ($7.60) adults and children over 6, free for children 6 and under; audiovisual hall, 400 ptas. ($3.20) extra, free for children 6 and under. Mon 9am–8pm, Tues–Thurs 9am–2pm, Fri–Sat 9am–3pm, Sun 9am–2pm. Metro: Espanya, then free red double-decker bus.

In this re-created Spanish village, built for the 1929 World's Fair, various regional architectural styles, from the Levante to Galicia, are reproduced—in all, 115 life-size reproductions of buildings and monuments, ranging from the 10th through the 20th centuries. At the entranceway, for example, stands a facsimile of the gateway to the walled city of Ávila. The center of the village has an outdoor café where you can sit and have drinks. Numerous shops sell crafts and souvenir items from all of the provinces, and in some of them you can see artists at work, printing fabric and blowing glass. Ever since the 1992 Olympics, the village has offered 14 restaurants of varying styles, one disco, and eight musical bars. In addition, visitors can see an audiovisual presentation about Barcelona and Catalonia in general.

Monument à Colom (Columbus Monument). Portal de la Pau. ☎ **93/302-52-34.** Admission 225 ptas. ($1.80) adults, 125 ptas. ($1) children 4–12, free for children 3 and under. Sept 25–May 31, Mon–Fri 10am–1:30pm and 3:30–6:30pm, Sat–Sun and holidays 10am–6:30pm; June 1–Sept 24, daily 9am–9pm. Closed Jan 1, Jan 6, and Dec 25–26. Metro: Drassanes.

This monument to Christopher Columbus was erected at the harborfront of Barcelona on the occasion of the Universal Exhibition of 1888. It is divided into three parts, the first being a circular structure, raised by four stairways (19½ feet wide) and eight iron heraldic lions. On the plinth are eight bronze bas-reliefs depicting the principal feats of Columbus. (The originals were destroyed; the present ones are copies.) The second part is the base of the column, consisting of an eight-sided polygon, four sides of which act as buttresses; each side contains sculptures. The third part is formed by the column itself, Corinthian in style and rising 167 feet. The capital boasts representations of Europe, Asia, Africa, and America—all linked together. Finally, over a princely crown and a hemisphere recalling the newly discovered part of the globe, is a 25-foot-high bronze statue of Columbus himself by Rafael Ataché. Inside the iron column, an elevator ascends to the mirador. From there, a panoramic view of Barcelona and its harbor unfolds.

Torre de Collserola. Carretera de Vallvidrera, Turó de la Vilana. ☎ **93/211-79-42.** Admission 500 ptas. ($4). Wed–Sun 11am–8pm. Funicular goes to a point near the tower's carpark; from there, free minivans make frequent runs up the mountain to the tower's base.

Some city planners considered this the most ambitious building project of the 1992 Olympics. When it was perceived that Barcelona lacked a state-of-the-art television transmitter, a team of engineers whipped up plans for a space-age needle. Completed within 24 months of its initiation, its pinnacle rises 940 feet above the city's highest mountain ridge, the Collserola, beaming TV signals throughout the rest of Europe. Open now as a tourist attraction, the tower offers panoramic views over Catalonia, and an insight into some of the most bizarre engineering in town. Trussed with cables radiating outward to massive steel anchors, the tower perches delicately atop an alarmingly narrow vertical post only 14 feet wide. A high-speed elevator carries visitors from deep inside the mountain (where there's a cafeteria) to an observation platform 1,820 feet above the sea level of the (very visible) Mediterranean.

PARKS & GARDENS

Barcelona isn't just museums; much of its life takes place outside, in its unique parks and gardens, through which you'll want to stroll. The **Parc Güell** (☎ **93/424-38-09**), was begun by Gaudí as a real-estate venture for a friend, the wealthy, well-known Catalán industrialist Count Eusebi Güell, but it was never completed. Only two houses were constructed, but it makes for an interesting excursion nonetheless. The city took over the property in 1926 and turned it into a public park. It is open May through September, daily from 10am to 9pm; October through April, daily from 10am to 6pm. Admission is free. To reach the park, take bus 24, 25, 31, or 74.

One of the houses, **Casa-Museu Gaudí,** Carrer del Carmel, 28 (☎ **93/284-64-46**), contains models, furniture, drawings, and other memorabilia of the architect. Gaudí, however, did not design the house. Ramón Berenguer claimed that honor. Admission is 150 pesetas ($1.20). The museum can be visited October through March, Sunday through Friday from 10am to 2pm and 4 to 8pm. April through September, it is open Sunday through Friday from 10am to 2pm and 4 to 9pm.

Gaudí completed several of the public areas, which today look like a surrealist Disneyland, complete with a mosaic pagoda and a lizard fountain spitting water. Originally, Gaudí planned to make this a model community of 60 dwellings, somewhat like the arrangement of a Greek theater. A central grand plaza with its market below was built, as well as an undulating bench decorated with ceramic fragments. The bizarre Doric columns of the would-be market are hollow, part of Gaudí's drainage system.

Another attraction, **Tibidabo Mountain,** offers the finest panoramic view of Barcelona. A funicular takes you up 1,600 feet to the summit. The ideal time to visit this summit (the culmination of the Sierra de Collcerola) north of the port is at sunset, when the city lights are on. An amusement park—with Ferris wheels swinging over Barcelona—has been opened here. (For more information on this Parc d'Atraccions, see "Especially for Kids," below.) There's also a church, called Sacred Heart, in this carnival-like setting, plus restaurants and mountaintop hotels. From Plaça de Catalunya, take a bus to Avinguda del Tibidabo, where you can board a special bus that will transport you to the funicular. Hop aboard to scale the mountain. The funicular runs daily from 7:15am to 9:45pm and costs 400 pesetas ($3.20) each way.

Located in the south of the city, the mountain park of **Montjuïc** (Montjuch in Spanish) has splashing fountains, gardens, outdoor restaurants, and museums, making for quite an outing. The re-created Spanish village, the Poble Espanyol, and the Joan Miró Foundation are also within the park. There are many walks and vantage points for viewing the Barcelona skyline.

The park was the site of several events during the 1992 Summer Olympics. An illuminated fountain display, the Fuentes Luminosas at Plaça de la Font Magica, near the Plaça d'Espanya, is on view from 8 to 11pm every Saturday and Sunday from October through May, and from 9pm to midnight on Thursday, Saturday, and Sunday from June through September. See individual attractions in the park for various hours of opening. To reach the top, take bus number 61 from Plaça d'Espanya or the Montjuïc funicular.

The **Parc de la Ciutadella,** Avenida Wellington, s/n (☎ **93/221-25-06**), gets its name, Park of the Citadel, because it is the site of a former fortress that defended the city. After Philip V won the War of the Spanish Succession (Barcelona was on the losing side), he got his revenge. He ordered that the "traitorous" residential suburb be leveled. In its place rose a citadel. In the mid-19th century it, too, was leveled, though some of the architectural evidence of that past remains in a governor's palace and an arsenal. Today most of the park is filled with lakes, gardens, and promenades, but it includes a zoo (see "Especially for Kids," below) and the Museu d'Art Modern (see "More Attractions," above). Gaudí is said to have contributed to the monumental "great fountain" in the park when he was a student. The park is open, without charge, daily from 8am to 9pm. To reach the park, take the metro to Ciutadella.

The **Parc de Joan Miró,** lying near the Plaça de Espanya, is dedicated to one of the most famous artists of Catalonia, Joan Miró. It occupies an entire city block. One of the parks added in the 1990s and one of Barcelona's most popular, it is often called Parc de l'Escorxador (slaughterhouse), a reference to what the park used to be. Its main features are an esplanade and a pond from which a sculpture by Miró, *Woman and Bird,* rises up. Palm, pine, and eucalyptus trees, as well as playgrounds and pergolas, complete the picture. To reach the park, take the metro to Espanya. It is open throughout the day.

3 Especially for Kids

The Cataláns have a great affection for children, and although many of the attractions of Barcelona are for adults only, there is an array of amusements designed for the young or the young at heart.

Children from three to seven have their own special place at the **Museu de la Ciència,** Teodor Roviralta, 55 (☎ **93/212-60-50**). Clik del Nens is a playground of science. Children walk on a giant piano, make bubbles, lift a hippopotamus, or enter an air tunnel. They observe, experiment, and examine nature in an environment created just for them. Special one-hour guided sessions are given daily. (For further details, see Section 2,"More Attractions," earlier in this chapter.)

Also described in Section 2 is the Poble Espanyol, Marqués de Comillas, Parc de Montjuïc (☎ 93/325-78-66). Kids compare a visit here to a Spanish version of

Disneyland. Frequent fiestas enliven the place, and it's fun for everybody, young and old.

Parc Zoologic. Parc de la Ciutadella. ☎ **93/221-25-06.** Admission 1,000 ptas. ($8) adults, free for children under 3. Summer, daily 9:30am–7:30pm; off-season, daily 10am–5pm. Metro: Ciutadella.

Modern, with barless enclosures, this ranks as Spain's top zoo. One of the most unusual attractions is the famous albino gorilla, Snowflake (Copito de Nieve), the only one of its kind in captivity in the world. The main entrances to the Ciutadella Park are via the Passeig de Pujades and Passeig de Picasso.

Parc d'Atraccions (Montjuïc). Parc de Montjuïc. ☎ **93/441-70-24.** Admission 600 ptas. ($4.80); ticket for all rides, 1,800 ptas. ($14.40). Oct–Mar, Sat–Sun 11:30am–8pm; Apr–May, Sat–Sun 11am–9pm; June–Aug, Tues–Fri 5pm–10pm, Sat 6pm–1am, Sun noon–11pm; Sept, days and hours vary. Metro: Paral-lel, then take funicular.

This place becomes a festival in summer, with open-air concerts and more than three dozen rides for the kids. Everything is set against a wide view of Barcelona and its harbor. Children love the nightly illuminated fountain displays and the music.

Parc d'Atraccions (Tibidabo). Plaça Tibidabo, 3–4, Cumbre del Tibidabo. ☎ **93/211-79-42.** Ticket for all rides 1,800 ptas. ($14.40), 300 ptas. ($2.40) seniors (65 or older), free for children under 5. May to mid-June, Wed–Sun noon–8pm; mid-June to Sept, Tues–Sun noon–8pm; off-season, Sat–Sun and holidays 11am–8pm. Ferrocarrils de la Generalitat to Avinguda Tibidabo to Tramvía Blau, then take funicular.

On top of Tibidabo, this park combines tradition with modernity—rides from the beginning of the century complete with 1990s novelties. In summer the place takes on a carnival-like atmosphere.

4 Special-Interest Sightseeing

ARCHITECTURE

Architecture enthusiasts will find a wealth of fascinating sights in Barcelona. The **Casa Milà,** Passeig de Gràcia, 92 (☎ **93/484-59-80;** metro: Diagonal), commonly called La Pedrera, is the most famous apartment-house complex in Spain. Antoni Gaudí's imagination went wild when planning its construction; he even included vegetable and fruit shapes in his sculptural designs. Controversial and much criticized upon its completion, today it stands as a classic example of *modernismo* architecture. The entire building was restored in 1996. The ironwork around the balconies forms an intricate maze, and the main gate has windowpanes shaped like turtle shells. The rooftop is filled with phantasmagorical chimneys known in Spanish as *espantabrujas* (witch-scarers). Tours of the famous rooftops are available Tuesday to Saturday at 10am, 11am, noon, and 1pm, but they have to be arranged in advance by calling the number above. Tours are free, but a tip is expected. From the rooftop, you'll also have a view of Gaudí's unfinished cathedral, La Sagrada Familia.

Casa Lleó Morera, Passeig de Gràcia, 35 (no phone; metro: Passeig de Gràcia), lying between the Carrer del Consell de Cent and the Carrer d' Aragó, is one of the most famous buildings of the *modernismo* movement. It is one of the trio of structures called the Mançana de la Discòrdia (Block of Discord), an allusion to the mythical judgment of Paris. Three of the most famous *modernismo* architects of Barcelona, including Gaudí, competed with their various works along this block. In florid *modernismo* design, the Casa Lleó, designed by Domènech i Montaner in 1905, was considered extremely revolutionary in its day. Perhaps that assessment still stands. Today the building is private; no visits to the interior are possible.

Constructed in a cubical design, with a Dutch gable, the **Casa Amatller,** Passeig de Gràcia, 41 (☎ **93/216-01-75;** metro: Passeig de Gràcia), was created by Puig i Cadafalch in 1900. It stands in sharp contrast to its neighbor, the Gaudí-designed Casa Batlló. The architecture of the Casa Amatller, actually imposed on an older structure, is a vision of ceramic, wrought iron, and sculptures. Admission to the Gothic-style interior is free. It is open Monday through Friday from 9am to 2pm.

Next door to the Casa Amatller, the **Casa Batlló,** Passeig de Gràcia, 43(☎ **93/216-01-12;** metro: Passeig de Gràcia), was designed by Gaudí in 1905. Using "sensuous" curves in iron and stone, the architect gave the facade a lavish baroque exuberance. The balconies have been compared to "sculpted waves." The upper part of the facade evokes animal forms, and delicate tiles spread across the design—a polychromatic exterior extraordinaire. The downstairs building is the headquarters of an insurance company. Although visitors are not always welcome, many tourists walk inside for a view of Gaudí's interior, which is basically as he designed it. Since this *is* a place of business, be discreet.

Casa de la Ciutat/Ayuntamiento, Plaça de Sant Jaume (☎ **93/402-73-62;** metro: Jaume I), originally constructed at the end of the 14th century, is considered one of the best examples of Gothic civil architecture in the Catalán-Mediterranean style. Across this landmark square from the Palau de la Generalitat, it has been endlessly renovated and changed since its original construction. Behind a neoclassical facade, the building has a splendid courtyard and staircase. Its major architectural highlights are the 15th-century Salón de Ciento (Room of the 100 Jurors) and the Salón de las Cronicas (Room of the Chronicles), the latter decorated with black marble. The Salón de Ciento, in particular, represents a medley of styles. You can enter the building Saturday and Sunday from 10am to 2pm or by special arrangement; it is closed from mid-December to mid-January.

OLYMPICS

Galeria Olímpico. Passeig Olimpic, s/n, lower level. ☎ **93/426-06-60.** Admission 375 ptas. ($3). Apr–Sept, Tues–Sat 10am–2pm and 4–8pm, Sun 10am–2pm; Oct–Mar, Tues–Sat 10am–1pm and 4–6pm, Sun 10am–2pm. Metro: Espanya. Bus: 9, 13.

An enthusiastic celebration of the 1992 Olympic Games in Barcelona, this is one of the few museums in Europe exclusively devoted to sports and sports statistics. Its exhibits include photos, costumes, and memorabilia, with heavy emphasis on the events' pageantry, the number of visitors who attended, and the fame the events brought to Barcelona. Of interest to statisticians, civic planners, and sports buffs, the gallery contains audiovisual information about the building programs that prepared the city for the onslaught of visitors. There are also conference facilities, an auditorium, video recordings of athletic events, and archives. In the cellar of the Olympic Stadium's southeastern perimeter, the museum is most easily reached by entering the stadium's southern gate (Porta Sud).

WALKING TOUR 1
Gothic Quarter

Start: Plaça Nova.
Finish: Plaça de la Seu.
Time: 3 hours.
Best Times: Any sunny day.
Worst Times: Mon–Sat 7–9am and 5–7pm because of traffic.

Walking Tour—Gothic Quarter

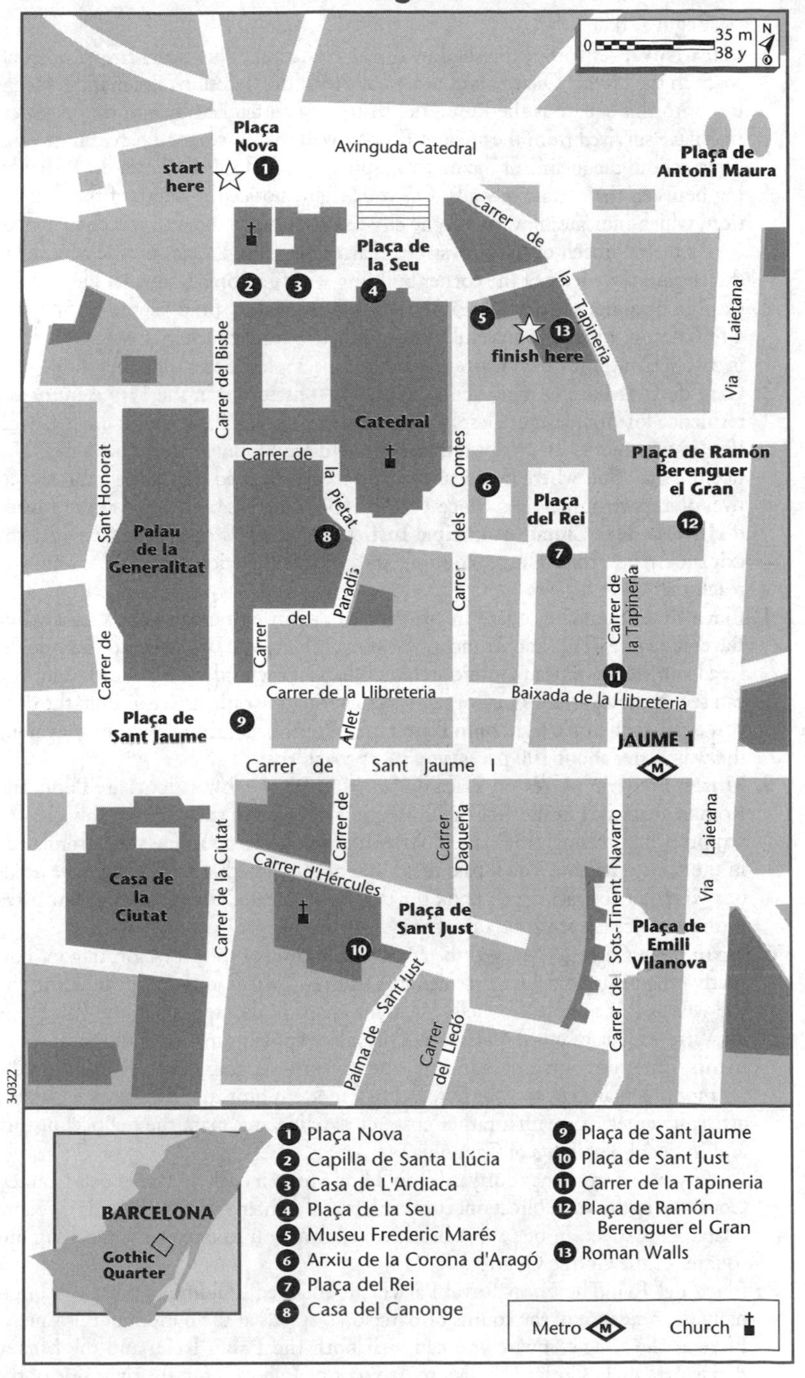

Begin at the:

1. **Plaça Nova,** set within the shadow of the cathedral. This is the largest open-air space in the Gothic Quarter and the usual site of the Barcelona flea market. Opening onto this square is the Portal del Bisbe, a gate flanked by two round towers that have survived from the ancient Roman wall that once stood here. From Plaça Nova, climb the incline of the narrow asphalt-covered street (Carrer del Bisbe) lying between these massive walls. On your right, notice the depth of the foundation, which indicates how much the city has risen since the wall was constructed.

   At the approach of the first street, Carrer de Santa Llúcia, turn left, noticing the elegant simplicity of the corner building with its Romanesque facade, the:
2. **Capilla de Santa Llúcia (☎ 93/315-15-54),** open daily from 9am to 1:15pm and 4 to 6:45pm. Its solidly graceful portal and barrel-vaulted interior were completed in 1268. Continue down Carrer de Santa Llúcia a few paces, noticing the:
3. **Casa de L'Ardiaca (Archdeacon's House),** constructed in the 15th century as a residence for Archdeacon Despla. The Gothic building has sculptural reliefs with Renaissance motifs. In its cloisterlike courtyard are a fountain and a palm tree. Notice the mail slot, where five swallows and a turtle carved into stone await the arrival of important messages. Since 1919 this building has been home to the **Museu d'Història de la Ciutat (Municipal Institute of the History of the City).** As you exit the Archdeacon's House, continue in the same direction several steps until you reach the:
4. **Plaça de la Seu,** the square in front of the main entrance to the **Catedral de Barcelona** (see "The Top Attractions," above). Here you can stand and admire the facade of Mediterranean Gothic architecture. On each side of Plaça de la Seu, you can see the remains of Roman walls. After touring the cathedral, exit from the door you entered and turn right onto Carrer dels Comtes, admiring the gargoyles along the way. After about 100 paces, you'll approach the:
5. **Museu Frederic Marés** on Plaça de Sant Iú. On the lower floors are Punic and Roman artifacts, but most of the museum is devoted to the works of this Catalán sculptor. Exit through the same door you entered and continue your promenade in the same direction. You'll pass the portal of the cathedral's side, where the heads of two rather abstract angels flank the throne of a seated female saint. A few paces farther, notice the stone facade of the:
6. **Arxiu de la Carona d'Aragó,** the archives building of the crown of Aragón. Formerly called Palacio del Lugarteniente (Deputy's Palace), this Gothic building was the work of Antonio Carbonell. On some maps it also appears as the Palacio de los Virreyes (Palace of the Viceroys). The palace contains medieval and royal documents. Enter its courtyard, admiring the century-old grapevines. Then climb the 11 monumental steps to your left, facing a modern bronze sculpture by a Catalán artist. It represents, with a rather abstract dateline and map, the political history and imperial highlights of Catalonia.

   As you exit from the courtyard, you'll find yourself back on Carrer dels Comtes. Continue in the same direction, turning left at the intersection of Baixada de Santa Clara. This street, in one short block, will bring you to one of the most famous squares of the Gothic Quarter:
7. **Plaça del Rei.** The Great Royal Palace, an enlarged building of what was originally the residence of the counts of Barcelona, stands at the bottom of this square. Here at the King's Square you can visit both the **Palau Reial** and the **Museu d'Història de la Ciutat** (see "More Attractions," above). On the right side of the square stands the **Palatine Chapel of Santa Agata,** a 14th-century Gothic temple

that is part of the Palau Reial. In this chapel is preserved the altarpiece of the Lord High Constable, a 15th-century work by Jaume Huguet.

Retrace your steps up Baixada de Santa Clara, crossing Carrer dels Comtes, and continue straight to Carrer de la Pietat, which will skirt the semicircular, massively buttressed rear of the cathedral. With the buttresses of the cathedral's rear to your right, pass the 14th-century:

8. **Casa del Canonge (House of the Canon),** opening onto Carrer Arzobispo Irurita. This building was erected in the Gothic style and restored in 1929; escutcheons from the 15th and 16th centuries remain. Notice the heraldic symbols of medieval Barcelona on the building's stone plaques—twin towers supported by winged goats with lion's feet. On the same facade, also notice the depiction of twin angels. The building today is used as a women's training school, the Escola Professional per a la Doña.

Continue walking along Carrer de la Pietat, which makes a sudden sharp left. Notice the carved *Pietà* above the Gothic portal leading into the rear of the cathedral. Continue walking straight. One block later, turn left onto Carrer del Bisbe and continue downhill. Your path will lead you beneath one of the most charming bridges in Spain. Carved into lacy patterns of stonework, it connects the Casa del Canonge with Palau de la Generalitat.

Continue walking until Carrer del Bisbe opens into:

9. **Plaça de Sant Jaume,** in many ways the political heart of Catalán culture. Across this square, constructed at what was once a major junction for two Roman streets, race politicians and bureaucrats intent on Catalonian government affairs. On Sunday evenings you can witness the *sardana,* the national dance of Catalonia. Many bars and restaurants stand on side streets leading from this square. Standing in the square, with your back to the street you just left (Carrer del Bisbe), you'll see, immediately on your right, the Doric portico of the **Palau de la Generalitat,** the parliament of Catalonia. With its large courtyard and open-air stairway, along with twin arched galleries, this exquisite work in the Catalonian Gothic style began construction in the era of Jaume I. A special feature of the building is the Chapel of St. George, built in flamboyant Gothic style between 1432 and 1435 and enlarged in 1620 with the addition of vaulting and a cupola with hanging capitals. The back of the building encloses an orangery courtyard begun in 1532. In the Salón Dorado, the Proclamation of the Republic was signed. The palace bell tower houses a carillon on which both old and popular music is played each day at noon. Across the square are the Ionic columns of the **Casa de la Ciutat/Ayuntamiento,** the Town Hall of Barcelona (see "Special-Interest Sightseeing," earlier in this chapter).

With your back to Carrer del Bisbe, turn left onto the narrow and very ancient Carrer de la Llibreteria. Two thousand years ago, this was one of the two roads that marked the Roman center of town. Walk uphill on Carrer de la Llibreteria for about 1½ blocks.

TAKE A BREAK **Mesón del Café,** Llibreteria, 16 (☎ **93/315-07-54**), founded in 1909, specializes in coffee and cappuccino. It is one of the oldest coffeehouses in the neighborhood, sometimes crowding 50 people into its tiny precincts. Some regulars perch on stools at the bar and order breakfast. Coffee costs 100 pesetas (80¢), and a cappuccino goes for 235 pesetas ($1.90). The café is open Monday to Saturday from 7am to 11pm.

Retrace your steps along Carrer de la Llibreteria and once again enter the Plaça de Sant Jaume. Facing the Town Hall, take the street that parallels its left side,

Carrer de la Ciutat. Note the elegant stonework on the building's side, which is carved in a style radically different from the building's neoclassical facade. At the first left, turn onto Carrer d'Hercules, and walk along it for one block until you enter the quiet, somewhat faded beauty of:

10. Plaça de Sant Just, dominated by the entrance to the Església dels Sants Just i Pastor (☎ **93/301-73-33**). Visiting hours are erratic; you'll find that its doors are usually closed except during Sunday mass. Above the entrance portal, an enthroned Virgin is flanked by a pair of protective angels. The Latin inscription hails her as Virgo Nigra et Pulchra, Nostra Patrona Pia (Black and Beautiful Virgin, Our Holy Patroness). This church dates from the 14th century, although work continued into the 16th. Some authorities claim that the church—in an earlier manifestation of the present structure—is the oldest in Barcelona.

Opposite the facade of the church, at Plaça de Sant Just, 4, is an aristocratic town house covered with faded but still elegant frescoes of angels cavorting among garlands, an example of the artistry, taste, and wealth of a bygone era. With your back to the Black Virgin, turn right onto the narrow cobblestoned street, Carrer del Lledo, which begins at the far end of the square. One short block later, turn left onto Baixada de Cassador. As you descend the steep slope of this narrow street, notice the blue-and-white covering of the House of the Blue Tiles at the bottom of the hill.

Turn left onto Carrer del Sots Tinent Navarro. The massive gray-stone wall rising on your left is the base of an ancient Roman fort. Note the red bricks of a 13th-century palace on top of the Roman wall. The solitary Corinthian column rising from the base is another reminder of Barcelona's Roman past.

Continue on to Plaça d'Emili Vilanova. Near the top of the Roman wall, note the pair of delicate columns of a Gothic window. Continue another block to the cross street, Carrer Jaume I. Cross it and approach Plaça de l'Angel. Continue walking to the:

11. Carrer de la Tapineria. For centuries, Catalonia has been the center of Spain's footwear industry. In medieval times, this was the street of the shoemakers. In fact, the industry is so entrenched that there is even a museum devoted to antique footwear, the **Museu del Calcat Antic,** Plaça Sant Felip Neri, 5 (☎ **93/301-45-33**), open Monday through Saturday from 11am to 2pm and 4 to 7pm, Sunday from 11am to 2pm.

In one short block Carrer de la Tapineria leads to:

12. Plaça de Ramón Berenguer el Gran. An equestrian statue dedicated to this hero (1096–1131) is ringed with the gravel of a semicircular park, whose backdrop is formed by the walls of the ancient Roman fort and, nearby, a Gothic tower.

Traverse the park, crossing in front of the equestrian statue, until you once again reach the edge of the Roman wall as you head toward the park's distant end. There Carrer de la Tapineria will lead you on a path paralleling the ancient:

13. Roman Walls, one of Barcelona's most important treasures from its past. The walls, known as *Las Murallas* in Spanish, were constructed between A.D. 270 and 310. The walls followed a rectangular course, and were built so that their fortified sections would face the sea. By the 11th and 12th centuries, Barcelona had long outgrown their confines. Jaume I ordered the opening of the Roman Walls, and the burgeoning growth that ensued virtually destroyed them, except for the foundations you see today.

Continue your promenade, but turn left at the narrow Baixada de la Canonja. A short walk down this cobblestoned alleyway will return you to **Plaça de la Seu,** not far from where you began this tour.

WALKING TOUR 2
Barcelona Harborfront

Start: Plaça Portal de la Pau.
Finish: Parc de la Ciutadella.
Time: 2 hours.
Best Times: Any sunny day.
Worst Times: Mon–Sat 7–9am and 5–7 because of traffic.

This tour begins near the harborfront at the end of Les Rambles in the shadow of the Columbus Monument at:

1. **Plaça Portal de la Pau.** Here at the base of the Columbus Monument, look at the quartet of nymphs seeming to offer laurel garlands to whoever approaches. If you haven't already done so, you may want to take the elevator to the top for a bird's-eye view of the harborfront you are about to traverse.

   Afterward, head east along:

2. **Passeig de Colom,** which, at this point, is raised on stilts high above a yacht basin. The waterside promenade adjacent to the yacht basin, far below you on your right, is called:

3. **Passeig del Moll de la Fusta,** originally the timber wharf. It stands as an excellent symbol of the recovery of Barcelona's formerly seedy waterfront. Several bars and restaurants enliven this balcony over the Mediterranean, from which one can descend via bridges to the level of a pedestrian wharf, where palm trees arise from the cobbled pavement.

   Continue along Passeig de Colom until you reach the slightly faded but very grand:

4. **Plaça del Duc de Mendinaceli,** on the inland (left) side of the boulevard. When traffic permits, cross Passeig de Colom, perhaps resting a moment on one of the park benches in the square, whose focal point is a column ringed with mermen (half fish, half men). Continue walking east, passing pigeons, children, and grandparents sunning themselves.

   You can now begin a brisk seven-block stroll eastward along the left side (the inland one) of Passeig de Colom. After about 2½ blocks, glance to your right at an enormous sculpture of a lobster waving a claw from atop the low-slung modern restaurant called Gambrinus. The lobster, crafted from fiberglass by a local sculptor, has become one of Barcelona's conversation pieces.

   You will eventually reach a monumental square called:

5. **Plaça d'Antoni López,** whose northern end is dominated by the Barcelona Post Office (Correos y Telegrafos). Cross Carrer de la Fustería, heading toward the front side of the post office, then pass in front of the building, traversing the busy Via Laietana, which borders the post office's eastern edge.

   Continue to walk straight, always east. The quiet street you'll enter is Carrer del Consolat del Mar, more interesting than the broader Passeig d'Isabel II, which runs parallel and a short distance to the right. Walk east along Carrer del Consolat del Mar. The neoclassical doorway on your right marks the entrance to:

6. **La Lonja,** the stock exchange of Barcelona. It has a central courtyard with allegorical statues. The stock exchange dates from the 14th century. Once it was a fine arts school attended by Picasso and Miró.

   A half block later, Carrer del Consolat del Mar opens onto:

7. **Plaça del Palau,** a gracefully proportioned square reminiscent of another era's political and cultural glory. Midway down the length of this square, head north (left) on Carrer de l'Espasería, at the end of which you'll come upon:

8. Santa María del Mar, in Plaça de Santa María, a Catalonian Gothic church with a soaring interior dating from the 14th century. After your visit, turn left as you exit, then left again, so that your footsteps along Carrer de Santa María flank the southern exterior of the church.

A half block later, Carrer de Santa María opens onto one of the most bizarre monuments in Barcelona:

9. Carrer del Fossar de los Moreres. Occupying most of the medieval square that contains it, the plaza incorporates a sprawling and steeply inclined red-brick pavement, fronted by a low wall of reddish porphyry, inscribed with a memorial to Catalonian martyrs who died in an uprising against Castilian Spain in 1714. As you enter the square, note on your left a narrow street.

TAKE A BREAK **Pâtissería Güell La Mallorquina,** Plaça de Les Olles, 7 (☎ **93/319-39-83**), was established in 1878 in a 16th-century building on this narrow street. Sample the *llunes,* half-moon-shaped pastries filled with almonds and sprinkled with powdered sugar. Or take out an order of *coques,* sprinkled with sugar and topped with pine nuts. All pastries are made on the premises, and the dough is rolled out on marble tables. You can stop in here and buy pastries on Monday and Wednesday through Saturday from 8am to 2pm and from 5 to 8:30pm, Sunday from 8am to 3pm.

Return to the square of the martyrs and continue walking along Carrer de Santa María until you reach the rear of the Church of Santa María del Mar, where you'll notice the massive buttresses. You have arrived at:

10. Passeig del Born, one of the colorful old squares of Barcelona and the residence of some appealing and nostalgic bars. But this square doesn't come alive until much later at night.

Turn left after one very short block onto Placeta de Montcada, which narrows after about 30 paces and changes its name to:

11. Carrer de Montcada, which represents the aristocratic heart of Barcelona during the height of its prestige and power. Notice the semifortified palace at number 20, which served during the 18th century as the Barcelona residence of the Catalonian ambassador from Great Britain. Also note the nine gargoyles adding visual interest to the fourth and uppermost floor of the palace, whose forbidding exterior seems even more severe because of the narrow street containing it.

A few steps later, on your right, is the:

12. Galería Maeght, Montcada, 25 (☎ **93/310-42-45**), established by the children of the couple who created one of the most famous museums of modern art in Europe, the Foundation Maeght in St-Paul-de-Vence in France. Many well-known and unknown painters are exhibited under the gallery's brick vaults, and works are for sale. The showrooms are open Tuesday to Saturday from 10am to 2pm and 4 to 8pm.

As you leave the gallery, turn right and continue walking until you reach the:

13. Museu de Textil i d'Indumentaria, Montcada, 12 (☎ **93/310-45-16**), occupying two 13th-century Gothic palaces. Many of the articles in this textile and costume museum are Egyptian and Hispano-Muslim. Textiles range from the Gothic era to the 20th century; many of the garments are liturgical. It is open Tuesday through Saturday from 10am to 5pm, Sunday and holidays from 10am to 2pm. Admission is 300 pesetas ($2.40).

Walking Tour—Barcelona Harborfront

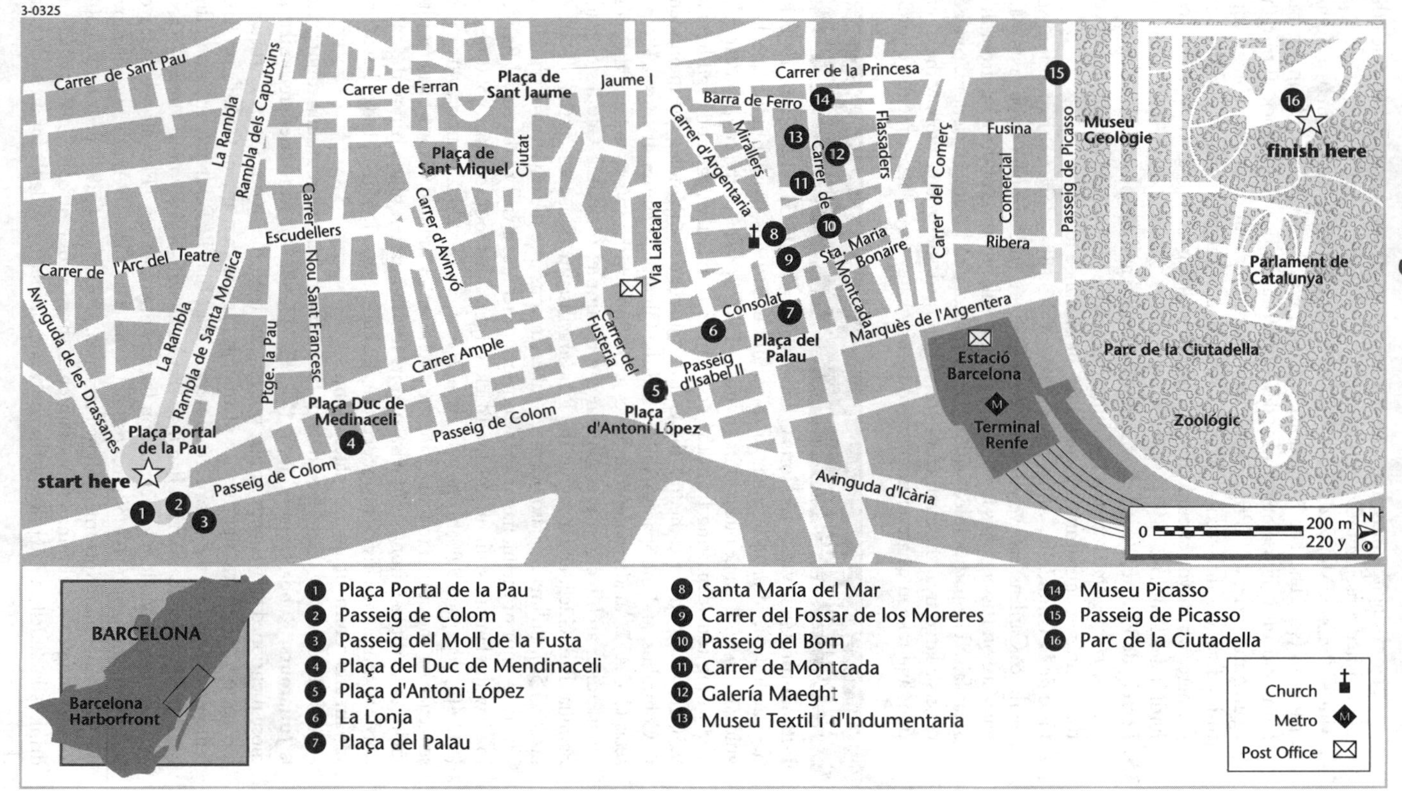

3-0325
Carrer de Sant Pau
Carrer de Ferran
Plaça de Sant Jaume
Jaume I
Carrer de la Princesa
Barra de Ferro
La Rambla
Rambla dels Caputxins
Plaça de Sant Miquel
Ciutat
Carrer d'Argentaria
Mirallers
Carrer de Montcada
Flassaders
Carrer del Comerç
Fusina
Comercial
Ribera
Passeig de Picasso
Museu Geològie
finish here
Parlament de Catalunya
Carrer Escudellers
Carrer d'Avinyó
Via Laietana
Sta. Maria
Bonaire
Carrer de l'Arc del Teatre
Avinguda de les Drassanes
La Rambla
Rambla de Santa Monica
Ptge. la Pau
Nou Sant Francesc
Carrer del Fusteria
Consolat
Marquès de l'Argentera
Carrer Ample
Passeig d'Isabel II
Plaça del Palau
Estació Barcelona
Terminal Renfe
Parc de la Ciutadella
Zoològic
Plaça Duc de Medinaceli
Plaça d'Antoni López
Passeig de Colom
Plaça Portal de la Pau
start here
Passeig de Colom
Avinguda d'Icària
0
200 m
220 y
N
BARCELONA
Barcelona Harborfront
1 Plaça Portal de la Pau
2 Passeig de Colom
3 Passeig del Moll de la Fusta
4 Plaça del Duc de Mendinaceli
5 Plaça d'Antoni López
6 La Lonja
7 Plaça del Palau
8 Santa María del Mar
9 Carrer del Fossar de los Moreres
10 Passeig del Born
11 Carrer de Montcada
12 Galería Maeght
13 Museu Textil i d'Indumentaria
14 Museu Picasso
15 Passeig de Picasso
16 Parc de la Ciutadella
Church
Metro
Post Office

After exiting the museum, turn left and continue walking until you reach the most visited museum in Barcelona, the:

14. **Museu Picasso,** Montcada, 15–19 (☎ **93/319-63-10**), ensconced in two Gothic mansions (see "The Top Attractions," above, for more details). Exit from the museum and turn right along Carrer de Montcada. In one short block, turn right again onto Carrer de la Princesa and walk straight for four blocks, traversing a confusing five-way intersection. You'll soon arrive at the wide and busy Carrer del Comerç, which you should cross. Continue walking along Carrer de la Princesa until it dead-ends at:

15. **Passeig de Picasso,** designed by architects Amadó and Domènech. A sculpture by Tàpies, *Homage to Picasso,* is the centerpiece. Cross Passeig de Picasso and notice the ornate wrought-iron gates guarding the entrance to the:

16. **Parc de la Ciutadella,** which was the site of the 1888 Universal Exposition (see "Parks & Gardens," above, for more details). If you enter the park through its main entrance on Passeig Lluís Companys, you can still see some of the relics from that great fair. The park is filled with museums, a zoo, and many attractions. Since it covers a large area, these attractions are signposted, and you can follow the directions and take in whatever interests you—or whatever you have time to explore.

5 Organized Tours

Pullmantur, Gran Vía de les Corts Catalanes, 635 (☎ **93/317-12-97;** metro: Plaça de Catalunya), offers a number of tours and excursions (with English-speaking guides)—in both Barcelona and its environs. For a preview of the city, you can take a morning tour departing from the company's terminal at the above address at 9:30am, taking in the cathedral, the Gothic Quarter, Les Rambles, the monument to Columbus, and the Spanish Village and the Olympic Stadium. It costs 4,180 pesetas ($33.45). An afternoon tour leaves at 3:30pm, with visits to some of the most outstanding architectural examples in the Eixample, including Gaudí's Sagrada Familia, Parc Güell, and a stop at the Picasso Museum. This tour costs 4,190 pesetas ($33.50). Pullmantur also offers several excursions into the environs of Barcelona. The daily tour of the monastery of Montserrat includes a visit to the Royal Basilica to view the famous sculpture of the Black Virgin. This tour, costing 5,300 pesetas ($42.40), departs at 9:30am and returns at 2:30pm to Barcelona's harbor, where passengers have the option to remain for the afternoon. A full-day Girona-Figueres tour includes a visit to Girona's cathedral and its Jewish quarter, plus a trip to the Salvador Dalí museum. This excursion, costing 10,700 pesetas ($85.60), leaves Barcelona at 9am and returns at approximately 6pm.

Another company that offers tours of Barcelona and the surrounding countryside is **Juliatours,** Ronda Universitat, 5 (☎ **93/317-64-54**). Itineraries are similar to those mentioned above, with similar prices. One tour, the "Visita Ciudad Artistica," focuses on the artistic significance of the city. It passes many of Gaudí's brilliant buildings, including the Casa Lleó Morera, Casa Milá (La Perdrera), and his unfinished masterpiece, La Sagrada Familia. Also included is a visit to the Museu Picasso or Museu d'Art Modern, depending on the day of your tour. This tour, which leaves at 3:30pm and returns at 6:30pm, costs 4,180 pesetas ($33.45). Another popular tour is the "Panorámica Nocturna y Show Flamenco." At a cost of 7,950 pesetas ($63.60), this evening tour culiminates in a flamenco show at one of Barcelona's *tablaos.* A drink is included in the price of the tour, and dinner is available for an additional charge.

6 Outdoor Activities

BULLFIGHTING The Catalâns of Barcelona do not pursue this "art" with as much fervor as do the Castilians of Madrid. Nevertheless, you may want to attend one of the *corridas*. Bullfights are held from April through September, usually on Sunday at 6pm at Plaça de Toros Monumental, Gran Vía de les Corts Catalanes (☎ **93/245-58-04**). Purchase tickets in advance from the office at Muntaner, 24 (☎ **93/453-38-21**). Tickets cost 2,100 to 12,000 pesetas ($16.80–$96).

A FITNESS CENTER The city's most obvious fitness center lies adjacent to the Olympic Stadium, within an indoor-outdoor complex whose main allure is its beautifully designed pair of swimming pools. Built for the 1992 Summer Olympics, the facility contains a health club and gym open to members of the public for 1,100 pesetas ($8.80) for a full day's pass. For the address, opening hours, and a description, refer to the Piscina Bernardo Picornell in "Swimming," below.

GOLF One of the city's best courses, **Club de Golf Vallromanas,** Afueras, s/n, Vallromanas (Barcelona) (☎ **93/572-90-64**), is within a 20-minute drive north of the town center. Nonmembers who reserve tee-off times in advance are welcome to play for a greens fees of 6,000 pesetas ($48) on weekdays and 12,000 pesetas ($96) on weekends. The club is open Wednesday to Monday from 9am to 8:30pm.

JOGGING In the heart of Barcelona, the **Parc de la Ciutadella** (see "Parks & Gardens," in Section 2) is the jogger's favorite. You can also use the paths surrounding Montjuïc.

SQUASH Your best bet is the **Squash Club Barcelona,** Doctor Gregoria Maranon, 17 (☎ **93/334-02-58;** metro: Universitat), which accepts nonmembers and is open Monday through Friday from 9am to midnight, Saturday from 10am to 10pm, and Sunday from 10am to 8pm. Squash courts can be rented by anyone for 1,330 pesetas ($10.65) per half hour of play time. There are 15 courts in all. The swimming pool and gym, however, are reserved for members.

SWIMMING Most city residents head out to the beaches of Sitges when they feel like swimming, but if you're looking for a not-very-crowded pool, you'll find one at the **Esportiu Piscina DeStampa,** Calle Rosich, s/n, in the Hospitalete district (☎ **93/334-56-00**). It's open Monday through Friday, 1 to 3pm and 7 to 9pm; Saturday, 10am to 2pm and 4 to 8pm; and Sunday, 10am to 2pm. Monday through Friday admission is 315 pesetas ($2.50); Saturday and Sunday, it's 365 pesetas ($2.90).

A much better choice, however, allows you to swim where some of the events of the 1992 Summer Olympics took place, at **Piscina Bernardo Picornell,** Avinguda de Estadi, 30–40, on Montjuïc (☎ **93/423-40-41**). Set adjacent to the Olympic Stadium, it incorporates two of the best and most state-of-the-art swimming pools in Spain, each custom-built for the 1992 Olympics, and now open to the public Monday through Friday from 7am to midnight, Saturday from 7am to 9pm, and Sunday from 7:30am to 2:30pm. (One pool is outdoors; the other is indoors.) Entrance costs 600 pesetas ($4.80) and allows full use throughout the day of whichever pool is open, plus the gymnasium, the sauna, and the Jacuzzis. Bus number 61 makes frequent runs from the Plaça d'Espanya.

TENNIS The neighborhoods of Barcelona don't contain as many tennis courts as you might have expected from a city of its size. The ones that do exist are organized in often unexpected places, usually in a cluster of two or three courts. Many of them are private; others are associated with hotels or some of the city's schools and universities. One of city's largest clubs is technically private, but sometimes allows qualified players to use their facilities for an hour if the courts aren't busy. The **Open Tennis Club** (also known as Club Open) (☎ **93/379-42-46**), is in the village of Castel de Fels, 3 1/2 miles (5.5km) beyond the airport, beside the road leading to Sitges. (Signs will guide you from the highway.) If space is not available at the time of your call, your hotel concierge, the Barcelona tourist office, or the operators at phone line "010" might be able to tell you of other courts allowing short-term access to nonmembers.

7 Shopping

Barcelonans look more to Paris than to Madrid for their fashions and style and, of course, create much of their style themselves. *Moda joven* (young fashion) is all the rage in Barcelona.

If your time and budget are limited, you may want to patronize Barcelona's major department store, El Corte Inglés, for an overview of Catalán merchandise at reasonable prices. Barcelona is filled with boutiques, but clothing is an expensive item here, even though the city has been a textile center for centuries.

Markets (see below) are very popular in Barcelona and are suitable places to search for good buys.

THE SHOPPING SCENE If you're a window shopper, stroll along the **Passeig de Gràcia** from the Avinguda Diagonal to the Plaça de Catalunya. Along the way, you'll see some of the most elegant and expensive shops in Barcelona, plus an assortment of splendid turn-of-the-century buildings and cafés, many with outdoor tables.

Another shopping expedition is to the **Mercat de la Boquería,** Rambla, 101 (☎ **93/318-25-84**), near Carrer del Carme. Here you'll see a wide array of straw bags and regional products, along with a handsome display of the food that you are likely to be eating later in a local restaurant: fruits, vegetables (artfully displayed), breads, cheeses, meats, and fish. Venders sell their wares Monday through Saturday from 7am to 8pm.

In the **old quarter** the principal shopping streets are all five Rambles, plus Carrer del Pi, Carrer de la Palla, and Avinguda Portal de l'Angel, to cite only some of the major ones. Moving north in the Eixample are Passeig de Catalunya, Passeig de Gràcia, and Rambla de Catalunya. Going even farther north, Avinguda Diagonal is a major shopping boulevard. Other prominent shopping streets include Bori i Fontesta, Via Augusta, Carrer Muntaner, Travessera de Gràcia, and Carrer de Balmes.

In general, shopping hours are Monday to Saturday from 9am to 8pm. Some smaller shops close from 1:30 to 4pm.

The **American Visitors Bureau,** Gran Vía, 591 (☎ **93/301-01-50**), between Rambla de Catalunya and Calle de Balmes, will pack and ship your purchases and gifts and even handle excess luggage and personal effects. The company also operates a travel agency here, booking flights and hotel accommodations for those needing it. It's open Monday through Friday from 9am to 1pm and 4 to 7pm, Saturday from 9am to 1pm.

Watch for summer sales (*rebajas*) in late July and August. Merchandise is often heavily discounted by stores getting rid of their summer stock before fall.

SHOPPING A TO Z

Barcelona, a city of design and fashion, offers a wealth of shopping opportunities. In general, prices tend to be slightly lower than those in London, Paris, and Rome.

In addition to modern, attractively designed, and stylish clothing, shoes and decorative objects are often good buys. In the city of Miró, Tàpies, and Picasso, art is a major business, and the reason so many gallery owners from around the world come to visit. You'll find dozens of galleries, especially in the Barri Gòtic and around the Picasso Museum. Barcelona is also noted for its flea markets, where good purchases are always available if you search hard enough.

Antiques abound here, but rising prices have put them beyond the means of the average shopper. However, the list below includes some shops where you can look, if nothing else. Most shoppers from abroad settle happily for handcrafts, and the city is rich in offerings, ranging from simple pottery to handmade furniture. Barcelona has been in the business of creating and designing jewelry since the 17th century, and its offerings in this field are of the widest possible range—as are the prices.

What follows is only a limited selection of some of the hundreds of shops in Barcelona.

ANTIQUES

Artur Ramón Anticuario. Carrer de la Palla, 25. ☎ **93/302-59-70.** Metro: Jaume I.

One of the finest antiques stores in Barcelona is this three-level emporium with high ceilings and a medieval kind of grace. Set on a narrow flagstone-covered street near Plaza del Pi (the center of the antiques district), it stands opposite a tiny square, the Placeta al Carrer de la Palla, whose foundations were laid by the Romans. The store, which has been operated by four generations of men named Artur Ramón, contains everything from Romanesque works to Picasso pieces. The prices are high, as you'd expect, for items of quality and lasting value. Open Monday through Saturday from 10am to 1:30pm and 5 to 8pm.

El Bulevard des Antiquaris. Passeig de Gràcia, 55. No central phone. Metro: Passeig de Gràcia.

This 70-unit shopping complex, just off one of the town's most aristocratic avenues, has a huge collection of art and antiques, assembled in a series of boutiques. There's a café/bar on the upper level. Summer hours are Monday to Friday from 9:30am to 8:30pm; winter hours, Monday from 4:30 to 8:30pm and Tuesday to Saturday from 10:30am to 8:30pm. Some boutiques, however, keep "short" hours.

Urbana. Còrsega, 258. ☎ **93/218-70-36.** Metro: Hospital Sant Pau.

Urbana sells an array of architectural remnants (usually from torn-down mansions), antique furniture, and reproductions of brass hardware. There are antique and reproduction marble mantlepieces, wrought-iron gates and garden seats, even carved wood fireplaces with the *modernismo* look. It's an impressive, albeit costly, array of merchandise rescued from the architectural glory of yesteryear. Open Monday through Friday from 10am to 2pm and 4:30 to 8pm.

CAMERAS

Casa Arpi. Rambla dels Caputxins, 38. ☎ **93/301-74-04.** Metro: Liceu.

This is one of the most famous camera shops in Spain. A multilingual staff will guide you to the best buys in new and used cameras, including familiar brand-name products. The firm also does quality processing, ready within 24 to 48 hours. Open Monday through Saturday from 9:30am to 1:30pm and 4:30 to 8pm.

DEPARTMENT STORES

El Corte Inglés. Plaça de Catalunya, 14. ☎ **93/302-12-12.** Metro: Plaça de Catalunya.

Part of the largest and most glamorous department store chain in Spain, this store sells a wide variety of merchandise, ranging from Spanish handcrafts to high-fashion items, from Spanish or Catalán records to food. The store also has restaurants and cafés and offers a number of consumer-related services, such as a travel agent. It has a department that will arrange the mailing of your purchases back home. Open Monday through Friday from 10am to 9:30pm.

DESIGNER HOUSEWARES

Vincón. Passeig de Gràcia, 96. ☎ **93/215-60-50.** Metro: Passeig de Gràcia.

Fernando Amat's Vincón is the best in the city, with 10,000 products—everything from household items to the best in Spanish contemporary furnishings. Housed in the former home of artist Ramón Casas, with gilded columns and mosaic-inlaid floors, the showroom is filled with the best Spain has, with each item personally selected because of its quality and craft. The window display alone is worth the trek there: Expect *anything.* Open Monday through Saturday from 10am to 1:30pm and 5 to 8pm.

FABRICS & WEAVINGS

Coses de Casa. Plaça de Sant Josep Oriol, 5. ☎ **93/302-73-28.** Metro: Jaume I.

Appealing fabrics and weavings are displayed in this 19th-century store. Many are handwoven in Majorca, their boldly geometric patterns inspired by Arab motifs of centuries ago. The fabric, for the most part, is 50% cotton, 50% linen; much of it would make excellent upholstery material. Open Monday through Friday from 9:45am to 1:30pm and 4:30 to 8pm; Saturday from 10am to 2pm and 5 to 8pm.

FASHION

Groc. Ramble de Catalunya, 100. ☎ **93/215-74-74.** Metro: Plaça de Catalunya.

Designs for both women and men are sold here. One of the most stylish shops in Barcelona, it is expensive but filled with high-quality apparel made from the finest of natural fibers. The men's store is downstairs, the women's store one flight up. Open Monday through Saturday from 10am to 2pm and 4:30 to 8pm. The men's department is closed Monday from 10am to 2pm, the women's department is closed Saturday from 4:30 to 8pm. The entire store is closed in August.

Roser-Francesc. Roger de Llúria, 87. ☎ **93/215-78-67.** Metro: Urquinaona.

With an inventory scattered over two floors of a narrow storefront in the Eixample district, this establishment is the quintessential boutique. It stocks only a limited selection of casually elegant clothes for both men and women, each chosen carefully with an alert consciousness of what is currently fashionable in Rome, Paris, Düsseldorf, and Los Angeles. Most of the garments are crafted from cotton, and are ideal for such warm-weather resorts as Sitges, a short car ride to the south of Barcelona. Open Monday through Saturday from 10am to 2:30pm and 4:30 to 8:30pm.

GALLERIES

Art Picasso. Tapineria, 10. ☎ **93/310-49-57.** Metro: Jaume I.

Here you can get good lithographic reproductions of works by Picasso, Miró, and Dalí, as well as T-shirts emblazoned with the designs of these masters. Tiles sold here often carry their provocatively painted scenes. Open Monday through Saturday from 9:30am to 8pm and Sunday from 9:30am to 3pm.

Sala Parés. Petritxol, 5. ☎ **93/318-70-20.** Metro: Plaça de Catalunya.

Established in 1840, this is the finest art gallery in the city, recognizing and promoting the work of many Spanish and Catalán painters and sculptors who have gone on to acclaim. The Maragall family has been the "talent" recognizing all this budding genius. Paintings are displayed in a two-story amphitheater, whose high-tech steel balconies are supported by a quartet of steel columns evocative of Gaudí. Exhibitions of the most avant-garde art in Barcelona change about every three weeks. Open Monday through Saturday from 10:30am to 2pm and 4:30 to 8:30pm, Sunday from 11am to 2pm.

GIFTS

Beardsley. Petritxol, 12. ☎ **93/301-05-76.** Metro: Plaça de Catalunya.

Named after the Victorian English illustrator, this store is on the same street where the works of Picasso and Dalí were exhibited before they became world famous. The wide array of gifts, perhaps the finest selection in Barcelona, includes a little bit of everything—dried flowers, writing supplies, silver dishes, unusual bags and purchases, and lots more. Open Monday through Friday from 9:30am to 1:30pm and 4:30 to 8pm, Saturday from 10am to 2pm and 5 to 8pm.

LEATHER

Loewe. Passeig de Gràcia, 35. ☎ **93/216-04-00.** Metro: Passeig de Gràcia.

The biggest branch in Barcelona of this prestigious nationwide leather-goods chain is in one of the best-known *modernismo* buildings in the city. Everything is top-notch, from the elegantly spacious showroom to the expensive merchandise to the helpful salespeople. The company exports its goods to branches throughout Asia, Europe, and North America. Open Monday through Saturday from 9:30am to 2pm and 4:30 to 8pm.

MARKETS

El Encants antiques market is held every Monday, Wednesday, Friday, and Saturday in Plaça de les Glóries Catalanes (metro: Glóries). There are no specific times—go any time during the day to survey the selection.

Coins and postage stamps are traded and sold in **Plaça Reial** on Sunday from 10am to 2pm. The location is off the southern flank of Les Rambles (metro: Drassanes).

A book-and-coin market is held at the **Ronda Sant Antoní** every Sunday from 10am to 2pm (metro: Universitat).

MUSIC

Casa Beethoven. Rambles, 97. ☎ **93/301-48-26.** Metro: Liceu.

Probably the most complete collection of sheet music in town can be found here. In a narrow store established in 1920, the collection naturally focuses on the works of Spanish and Catalán composers. Music lovers might make some rare discoveries here. Open Monday through Friday from 9am to 1:30pm and 4 to 8pm, Saturday from 9am to 1:30pm and 5 to 8pm.

PORCELAIN

Kastoria 2. Avinguda Catedra, 6–8. ☎ **93/310-04-11.** Metro: Plaça de Catalunya.

This large store near the cathedral carries many kinds of leather goods, including purses, suitcases, coats, and jackets. But most people come here to look at its famous Lladró porcelain—they are authorized dealers and have a big selection. Open Monday through Saturday from 10am to 2pm and 3 to 8pm and Sunday from 10am to 2pm.

Pottery

Artesana I Coses. Placeta de Montcada, 2. ☎ **93/319-54-13.** Metro: Jaume I.

Here you'll find pottery and porcelain from every major region of Spain. Most of the pieces are heavy and thick-sided—designs in use in the country for centuries. Open Monday through Saturday from 10:30am to 2pm and 4:30 to 8pm.

Itaca. Carrer Ferran, 26. ☎ **93/301-30-44.** Metro: Liceu.

Here you'll find a wide array of handmade pottery, not only from Catalonia and other parts of Spain, but also from Portugal, Mexico, and Morocco. The merchandise has been selected for its basic purity, integrity, and simplicity. Open Monday through Friday from 10am to 2pm and 4:30 to 8pm, Saturday from 10am to 2pm and 5 to 8:30pm.

Shopping Centers/Malls

The landscape of Barcelona has exploded since the mid-l980s with the construction of several American-style shopping malls, some of which are too far from the city's historic core to be convenient to most foreign visitors. Here's a description, however, of some of the city's best.

Centre Comercial Barcelona Glories. Avenida Diagonal, 208. ☎ **93/486-06-39.** Metro: Glories.

Built in 1995, this is the largest shopping center in downtown Barcelona, a three-story emporium of the good life as based on California models, but crammed into a distinctly urban neighborhood. More than 100 shops are contained within: some posh, others much less so. Although there's a typical shopping-mall anonymity to some aspects of this place, you'll still be able to find virtually anything you might have forgotten while packing for your trip. It's open Monday through Saturday from 10am to 10pm.

Diagonal Center (Illa). Avinguda Diagonal, 557. ☎ **93/444-00-00.** Metro: María Cristina.

Smaller than the above-mentioned Centre Comercial Barcelona Glories, with about half the number of shops, this two-story mall contains stores devoted to luxury products, as well as a scattering of bars, cafés, and simple but cheerful restaurants favored by office workers and shoppers. Built in the early 1990s, it even has an area devoted to video games, where teenagers can make as much electronic noise as they want while their guardians go shopping. It's open Monday through Saturday from 10am to 9pm.

Maremagnum. Moll d'Espanya, s/n. ☎ **93/225-81-00.** Metro: Drassanes.

The best thing about this place is its position adjacent to the waterfront of Barcelona's historic seacoast, plus the fact that it's well suited to outdoor promenades. Built in the early 1990s near the Columbus Monument, it contains a handful of shops selling touristy items and lots of cafés, bars, and places to sit. You might get the idea that only a few of the people who come here are really interested in shopping, despite the fact that the place defines itself as a shopping mall.

Poble Espanyol. Marqués de Comilias, Parc de Montjuïc. ☎ **93/325-78-66.** Metro: Espanya, then free red double-decker bus to Montjuïc.

This is not technically a shopping mall but a "village" (see "More Attractions," earlier in this chapter) with about 35 stores selling typical folk crafts from every part of Spain: glassware, leather goods, pottery, paintings, and carvings—you name it. Stores keep various hours, but you can visit any time during the day.

STRAW PRODUCTS

La Manual Alpargatera. Aviño, 7. ☎ **93/301-01-72.** Metro: Jaume I or Liceu.

In addition to its large inventory of straw products, such as hats and bags, this shop is known mainly for its footwear, called *espadrilles* (*alpargatas* in Spanish). This basic rope-soled shoe (said to go back 1,000 years) is made on the premises. Some Cataláns wear only espadrilles when performing the *sardana,* their national dance. To find La Manual Alpargatera, turn off Les Rambles at Carrer Ferran, walk two blocks, and make a right. Open Monday through Saturday from 9:30am to 1:30pm and 4:30 to 8pm.

UMBRELLAS

Julio Gomez. Rambla de Sant Josep, 104 (also called Rambla de las Flors). ☎ **93/301-33-26.** Metro: Liceu.

For more than a century, Julio Gomez has rung up umbrella sales here. In a workshop out back, women labor over these unique umbrellas or lace-trimmed silk or cotton parasols. There are also Spanish fans, walking sticks capped with silver, and other memorabilia—all adding up to an evocative piece of shopping nostalgia. Open Monday through Saturday from 9:30am to 1:30pm and 4 to 8pm.

8 Barcelona After Dark

Barcelona comes alive at night—the funicular ride to Tibidabo or the illuminated fountains of Montjuïc are especially popular. During the Franco era, the center of club life was the cabaret-packed district near the south of Les Rambles, an area, incidentally, known for nighttime muggings—so use caution if you go there. But the most fashionable clubs long ago deserted this seedy area and have opened in nearly every major district of the city.

Your best source of local information is a little magazine called *Guía del Ocio,* which previews "La Semana de Barcelona" (This Week in Barcelona). It's in Spanish, but most of its listings will probably be comprehensible. The magazine is sold at virtually every news kiosk along Les Rambles.

Nightlife begins for Barcelonans with a promenade (*paseo*) along Les Rambles in the early evening, usually from 5 to 7pm. Then things quiet down a bit, until a second surge of energy brings out Les Rambles crowds again, from 9 to 11pm. After that the esplanade clears out quite a bit.

If you've been scared off by press reports of Les Rambles between the Plaça de Catalunya and the Columbus Monument, you'll feel safer along the Rambla de Catalunya, in the Eixample, north of the Plaça de Catalunya. This street and its offshoots are lively at night, with many cafés and bars.

The array of nighttime diversions in Barcelona is staggering. There is something to interest almost everyone and to fit most pocketbooks. For families, the amusement parks are the most-frequented venues. Sometimes locals opt for an evening in the *tascas* (taverns) or pubs, perhaps settling for a bottle of wine at a café, an easy and inexpensive way to spend an evening of people watching. Serious drinking in pubs and cafés begins by 10 or 11pm. But for the most fashionable bars and discos, Barcelonans delay their entrances until at least 1am.

Cultural events are big in the Catalonian repertoire, and the old-fashioned dance halls, too, still survive in some places. Although disco has waned in some parts of the world, it is still going strong in Barcelona. Decaying movie houses, abandoned garages, and long-closed vaudeville theaters have been taken over and restored to become nightlife venues for *la movida,* that after-dark movement that sweeps across the city until dawn.

Flamenco isn't the rage here that it is in Seville and Madrid, but it still has its devotees. The city is also filled with jazz afficionados. Best of all, the old tradition of the music hall with vaudeville lives on in Barcelona.

SPECIAL EVENTS & DISCOUNTS In the summer you'll see plenty of free entertainment just by walking the streets—everything from opera to monkey acts. Les Rambles are a particularly good place to watch.

There is almost always a **festival** happening in the city, and many of the events can be enjoyed for free. The tourist office can give you details of when and where.

Some **theaters** advertise discount or half-price nights. Check in the weekly *Guía del Ocio.*

THE PERFORMING ARTS

Culture is deeply ingrained in the Catalán soul. The performing arts are strong here—some, in fact, taking place on the street, especially along Les Rambles. Crowds will often gather around a singer or mime. A city square will suddenly come alive on Saturday night with a spontaneous festival—"tempestuous, surging, irrepressible life and brio," is how the writer Rose MacCauley described it.

Long a city of the arts, Barcelona experienced a cultural decline during the Franco years, but now it is filled once again with the best opera, symphonic, and choral music.

The **Gran Teatre del Liceu,** Rambla dels Caputxins (metro: Liceu), was a monument to Belle Epoque extravagance, a 2,700-seat century opera house and one of the grandest theaters in the world. It was designed by Catalán architect Josep Oriol Mestves. In January of 1994, the opera house was gutted by fire, which shocked Catalonia, many of whose citizens regarded this place as the citadel of their culture. To borrow from Shakespeare, the old Liceu now belongs to the "Bare ruin'd choirs, where late the sweet birds sang." The government of Catalonia has vowed that "the Liceu will be rebuilt—right here, in the same place, and just as it was." Even as Barcelona debates the future of this world-famous opera house, visitors to the city view its ruins as a sightseeing oddity. Stay tuned for future developments.

CLASSICAL MUSIC

Palau de la Música Catalán. Sant Francest de Paula, 2. ☎ **93/268-10-00.** Ticket prices depend on event.

In a city chock-full of architectural highlights, this one stands out. In 1908 Lluís Domènech i Montaner, a Catalán architect, designed this structure, including stained glass, ceramics, statuary, and ornate lamps, among other elements. It stands today, restored, as a classic example of *modernismo.* Concerts and leading recitals are presented here. The box office is open Monday through Friday from 10am to 9pm, Saturday from 3 to 9pm.

THEATER

Theater is presented in the Catalán language and therefore will not be of interest to most visitors. However, for those who speak the language, or perhaps who are fluent in Spanish, here are some recommendations.

Companyia Flotats. Teatre Poliorama, Rambla dels Estudis, 115. ☎ **93/317-75-99.** Tickets 1,500–2,500 ptas. ($12–$20). Closed Aug. Metro: Liceu.

This leading company is directed by Josep Maria Flotats, an actor-director who was trained in the tradition of theater repertory, working in such theaters in Paris as the

Théâtre de la Villa and the Comédie-Français. He founded his own company in Barcelona, where he presents both classic and contemporary plays.

Mercat de Los Flors. Lleida, 59. ☎ **93/426-18-75.** Tickets 1,100–2,500 ptas. ($8.80–$20). Metro: Espanya.

Housed in a building constructed for the 1929 International Exhibition at Montjuïc is this other major Catalán theater. Peter Brook first used it as a theater for a 1983 presentation of *Carmen.* Innovators in drama, dance, and music are showcased here, as are modern dance companies from Europe, including troupes from Italy and France. The 999-seat house also has a restaurant overlooking the rooftops of the city.

Teatre Lliure. Montseny, 47. ☎ **93/218-92-51.** Tickets Tues–Thurs, 1,600 ptas. ($12.80); Fri–Sun, 2,000 ptas. ($16). Metro: Passeig de Gràcia.

This self-styled free theater is the leading Catalán-language theater in Barcelona. Once a workers' union, since 1976 the building has been the headquarters of a theater co-operative. Its directors are famous in Barcelona for their bold presentations here, including works by Bertolt Brecht, Luigi Pirandello, Jean Genêt (who wrote about Barcelona), and even Molière and Shakespeare. New dramas by Catalán playwrights are also presented. The house seats from 200 to 350.

FLAMENCO

El Tablao de Carmen. Poble Espanyol de Montjuïc. ☎ **93/325-68-95.** Dinner and show, 7,500 ptas. ($60); drink and show, 4,000 ptas. ($32).

This club provides a highly rated flamenco cabaret in the re-created village. You can go early and explore the village if you wish and even have dinner here. This place has long been a tourist favorite. The club is open Tuesday through Sunday from 8pm to past midnight. During the week, it sometimes closes around 1am, but often stays open until 2 or 3am on weekends, depending on business. The first show is always at 9:30pm; the second show on Tuesday to Thursday and Sunday is at 11:30pm, on Friday and Saturday midnight. Reservations are encouraged.

Tablao Flamenco Cordobés. Les Rambles, 35. ☎ **93/317-66-53.** Dinner and show, 7,500 ptas. ($60); one drink and show, 4,000 ptas. ($32). Metro: Drassanes.

At the southern end of Les Rambles, a short walk from the harborfront, you'll hear the strum of the guitar, the sound of hands clapping rhythmically, and the haunting sound of the flamenco, a tradition here since 1968. Head upstairs to an Andalusian-style room where performances take place with the traditional *cuadro flamenco* —singers, dancers, and guitarist. Cordobés is said to be the best showcase for flamenco in Barcelona. November 1 through March 31 (except for one week in December), the show with dinner begins at 8:30pm and the show without dinner at 10pm. April 1 through October 31 and December 25 through December 31, four shows are offered nightly with dinner, at 8pm and 9:45pm; without dinner at 9:30pm and 11:15pm. Reservations are required. It's closed in January.

THE CLUB & MUSIC SCENE

CABARET

Arnau. Avinguda del Paral-lel, 60. ☎ **93/442-28-04.** Cover 2,500 ptas. ($20), including first drink. Metro: Paral-lel.

A veteran at surviving the many changes that have affected the worlds of cabaret and entertainment since its heyday in the 1970s, this place has managed to keep up with the times and the demands of the marketplace. Shows mingle touches of Catalán folklore with glitz and glitter, hints of family nostalgia, and doses of melodrama. At presstime, the theme of the shows was based on a cabaret version of the *Rocky*

Horror Picture Show. Two shows are presented every night, at 9pm and midnight. Drinks cost from 600 pesetas ($4.80) each.

Bodega Bohemia. Lancaster, 2. ☎ **93/302-50-61.** Metro: Liceu.

This cabaret extraordinaire, off Les Rambles, is a Barcelona institution, and everybody who is anybody has been here. The Bodega Bohemia rates as high camp—a talent showcase for theatrical personalities whose joints aren't so flexible but who perform with bracing dignity. Curiously, most audiences fill up with young people, who cheer, boo, catcall, and scream with laughter—and the old-timers on stage love it. The show stretches on forever. In all, it's an incredible entertainment bargain if your tastes lean slightly to the bizarre. Hard drinks cost 1,000 to 1,500 pesetas ($8–$12). The street outside is none too safe; take a taxi right to the door. Open daily from 11pm to 4am.

Dance Clubs & Discos

Estudio 54. Avinguda del Paral-lel, 64. ☎ **93/329-54-54.** Cover 1,200 ptas. ($9.60). Metro: Paral-lel.

Barcelona's version of New York's ill-fated and long-defunct Studio 54 continues to jump with a slightly faded version of the same energy as its namesake. It lies on the opposite side of the Barri Xinés from Les Rambles. Inside, you'll find a creative array of lighting effects and an energetic dance floor that thrives on eccentric styles of personal expression. The place is at its most appealing Thurday through Saturday from 11:30pm to 5am. Drinks begin at 850 pesetas ($6.80) each.

Up and Down. Numancia Diagonal, 179. ☎ **93/280-29-22.** Cover 2,000 ptas. ($16), including first drink. Metro: Sants Estació.

The chic atmosphere of this disco attracts the elite of Barcelona, spanning a generation gap. The more mature patrons, specifically the black-tie, post-opera crowd, head for the upstairs section, leaving the downstairs to the loud music and "flaming youth." Up and Down is the most cosmopolitan disco in Barcelona, with a carefully planned ambience, impeccable service, and a welcoming atmosphere. Every critic who comes here comments on the piquant, sassy antics of the waiters, whose theatricality is part of the carnival-like atmosphere pervading this place. The disco is enhanced by audiovisual techniques; the decor is black and white. Dress can be your own selection, but men must always—regardless of their outfit—wear a tie.

Technically, this is a private club and you can be turned away at the door. The restaurant is open Monday through Saturday from 10pm to 2am, serving meals costing from 4,500 pesetas ($36). The disco is open Tuesday through Saturday from 12:30am to anytime between 5am and 6:30am, depending on business. Drinks in the disco cost 1,400 pesetas ($11.20) for a beer or from 1,900 pesetas ($15.20) for a hard drink.

A Dance Hall

La Paloma. Tigre, 27. ☎ **93/301-68-97.** Cover 400–800 ptas. ($3.20–$6.40). Metro: Universitat.

Those feeling nostalgic may want to drop in on the most famous dance hall of Barcelona. It was young in 1903. The iron for the famed Barcelona statue of Columbus was smelted in La Paloma before it became the dance hall it is today. Remember the fox trot? The mambo? If not, learn about them at La Paloma, where they're still danced, along with the tango, the cha-cha, and the bolero. Tuesday is boxing night: A boxing match actually takes place in a ringed-off area of the dance floor. Live orchestras provide the music for this old hall with its faded but flamboyant trappings, including gilded plaster angels, crystal chandeliers, and opera-red draperies. "Matinees" are from 6 to 9:30pm; night dances are from 11:30pm to 5am. Drinks cost from 800 pesetas ($6.40).

THE BAR SCENE

In addition to the bars listed below, several Barcelona tapas bars are recommended in the "Dining" section of Chapter 12.

PUBS & BARS

El Born. Passeig del Born, 26. ☎ **93/319-53-33.** Metro: Jaume I.

Facing a rural-looking square, this place, once a fish store, has been cleverly converted. There are a few tables near the front, but our preferred spot is the inner room, decorated with rattan furniture, ceramic jugs, books, and modern paintings. Music here could be anything from Louis Armstrong to classic rock-and-roll. Dinner can also be had at the upstairs buffet. The room is somewhat cramped, but there you'll find a simple but tasty collection of fish, meat, and vegetable dishes, all carefully laid out; a full dinner without wine costs around 3,000 pesetas ($24). Beer costs 350 pesetas ($2.80); wine, 200 pesetas ($1.60). Open Monday through Saturday from 7:30am to 2:30am.

Café Bar Padam. Rauric, 9. ☎ **93/302-50-62.** Metro: Liceu.

The tapas served here are derived from time-honored Catalán culinary traditions, but the clientele and decor are modern, hip, and often gay. The bar is on a narrow street in the Ciutat Vella, about three blocks east of the Rambla dels Caputxins. The only color in the black-and-white rooms comes from fresh flowers and modern paintings. Tapas include fresh anchovies and tuna, plus cheese platters. Jazz is sometimes featured. Open Monday to Saturday from 7pm to 2am.

Cocktail Bar Boadas. Tallers, 1. ☎ **93/318-95-92.** Metro: Plaça de Catalunya.

This intimate and conservative bar is usually filled with regulars. Established in 1933, it lies near the top of Les Rambles. Many visitors stop here for a pre-dinner drink and snack before wandering to one of the district's many restaurants. You can choose among a wide array of Caribbean rums, Russian vodkas, and English gins—the skilled bartenders know how to mix them all. The place is especially well known for its daiquiris. Open daily from noon to 2am.

Dirty Dick's, Taberna Inglesa. Carrer Marc Aureli, 2. ☎ **93/200-89-52.** Metro: Muntaner.

An English-style pub behind an inwardly curving bay window in a residential part of town, Dirty Dick's has an interior of dark paneling and exposed brick, with banquettes for quiet conversation. If you sit at the bar, you'll be faced with a tempting array of tiny sandwiches that taste as good as they look. The pub is set at the crossing of Vía Augusta, a main thoroughfare leading through the district. Open daily from 6pm to 2:30am.

Pub 240. Aribau, 240. ☎ **93/209-09-67.** Cover 2,500 ptas. ($20).

This elegant bar, which bears absolutely no resemblance to an English pub, is arranged in three sections: a bar, a small amphitheater, and a lounge for talking and listening to music. Rock and South American folk music are played here, and the place is jammed almost every night. Open daily from 7pm to 5am.

Zig-Zag Bar. Platón, 13. ☎ **93/201-62-07.** Metro: Muntaner.

Favored by actors, models, cinematographers, and photographers, this bar claims to have inaugurated Barcelona's trend toward high-tech minimalism in its watering holes. Owned by the same entrepreneurs who developed the state-of-the-art nightclub Otto Zutz, it offers an unusual chance to see Spain's *movida* in action. Open Monday through Thursday from 7:30pm to 2:30am, Friday and Saturday from 7:30pm to 3am. Beer costs 450 pesetas ($3.60); a hard drink, 850 pesetas ($6.80).

SPECIALTY BARS

CHAMPAGNE BARS

The growing popularity of champagne bars during the 1980s was an indication of Spain's increasing cosmopolitanism. The Catalάns call their own version of champagne *cava.* In Spanish, champagne bars are called *champanerías,* and in Catalán the name is *xampanyerías.* These Spanish wines are often excellent, said by some to be better than their French counterparts. With more than 50 companies producing *cava* in Spain and with each bottling up to a dozen different grades of wine, the best way to learn about Spanish champagne is either to visit the vineyard or to sample the products at a *xampanyería.*

Champagne bars usually open at 7pm and stay open into the wee hours of the morning. Tapas are served, ranging from caviar to smoked fish to frozen chocolate truffles. Most establishments sell only a limited array of house *cavas* by the glass—you'll be offered a choice of *brut* or *brut nature* (*brut* is slightly sweeter). More esoteric *cavas* must be purchased by the bottle. The most acclaimed brands include Mont-Marçal, Gramona, Mestres, Parxet, Torello, and Recaredo.

La Cava del Palau. Verdaguer I Callis, 10. ☎ **93/310-09-38.** Metro: Urquinaona.

Located in an old part of Barcelona, this large champagne bar is a favorite of the after-concert crowd (the Palace of Music is just around the corner). Live music is sometimes presented, accompanied by a wide assortment of cheeses, cold cuts, pâtés, and fresh anchovies. Open Monday through Friday from 1:30 to 4pm and 8pm to 2am, Saturday from 8pm to 2am.

Xampanyería Casablanca. Bonavista, 6. ☎ **93/237-63-99.** Metro: Passeig de Gràcia.

Someone had to fashion a champagne bar after the Bogart-Bergman film, and this is it. Four kinds of house *cava* are served by the glass. The staff also serves a good selection of tapas, especially pâtés. The Casablanca is close to the Passeig de Gràcia. Open Sunday through Thursday from 6:45pm to 2:30am and Friday and Saturday from 6:45pm to 3am.

Xampú Xampany. Gran Vía de los Corts Catalanes, 702. ☎ **93/265-04-83.** Metro: Girona.

At the corner of the Plaça de Tetuan, this *champanería* offers a variety of hors d'oeuvres in addition to the wine. Abstract paintings, touches of high tech, bouquets of flowers, and a pastel color scheme create the decor. Open daily from 6:30pm to 3:30am.

GRAND CHIC BARS

In Barcelona they speak of a "bar boom"—the weekly entertainment guide, *Guía del Ocio,* has estimated that 500 new bars opened before the 1992 Olympics. A staff writer said, "The city has put her ambition and energy into designing bars and hopping from bar to bar. The inauguration of a new watering hole interests people more than any other social, cultural, or artistic event." The bars are stylish and often avant-garde in design. We'll sample only a few of the better ones, but know that there are literally hundreds more.

Nick Havanna. Roselló, 208. ☎ **93/237-54-05.** Cover Fri–Sat 900 ptas. ($7.20), including first drink; no cover Sun–Thurs. Metro: Diagonal.

Like a high-tech cathedral, it has a soaring ceiling, supported by vaguely ecclesiastical concrete columns, off which radiate four arms. There's a serpentine-shaped curve of two different bars upholstered in black-and-white cowhide, plus a bank of at least 30 different video scenes. To keep patrons in touch with world events between drinks, a Spanish-language teletype machine chatters out news events. Some women have admitted to detouring to the men's room for a view of the famous mirrored waterfall cascading into the urinal. This has become one of Barcelona's most-talked-about and most-frequented watering holes. It's hip and happening—so dress accordingly, and go late or you'll have the place to yourself. Open daily from 11pm to 5:30am.

Otto Zutz Club. Carrer Lincoln, 15. ☎ **93/238-07-22.** Cover 2,000 ptas. ($16). Metro: Passeig de Gràcia or Fontana.

Sheathed in one of the most carefully planned neoindustrial decors in Spain, this nightspot is the last word in hip and a magnet for the city's artists and night people. Facetiously named after a German optician and the recipient of millions of pesetas worth of interior drama, it sits behind an angular facade that reminds some visitors of a monument to some mid-20th-century megalomaniac. Originally built to house a textile factory, the building contains a labyrinth of metal staircases decorated in shades of blue, highlighted with endless spotlights and warmed with lots of exposed wood. On the uppermost floor, a high tech restaurant serves supper-club food (brochettes, light pastas, and platters of smoked fish) for around 3,000 pesetas ($24) for a full meal. Open Tuesday through Saturday from 11pm to 6am—but don't even think of showing up before midnight.

Ticktacktoe. Roger de Llúria, 40. ☎ **93/318-99-47.** Metro: Passeig de Gràcia.

In the Eixample district, this bar/restaurant is one of the most-talked-about rendezvous spots in the city. The decor is definitely tongue-in-cheek—everything from a marble whale to a bar in the form of a female breast. Frequented by TV personalities, Ticktacktoe draws a fashionable crowd, most of whom are under 35. At the snooker and the billiards tables, regular competitions are held. The bar is open Monday through Thursday from 8pm to midnight, Friday and Saturday from 8pm to 1am; the restaurant, from 1 to 4pm and 8:30pm to midnight. Closed from August 15 to 30.

Zsa Zsa. Rosellò, 156. ☎ **93/453-85-66.** Metro: Provença.

This is a favorite bar with journalists, writers, and advertising executives, who mingle, drink, converse, and make or break deals. A light system creates endlessly different patterns that seem to change with the mood of the crowd. Chrome columns capped with stereo speakers dot the room like a high-tech forest. Open daily from 7pm to 3am.

Nostalgia Bars

Bar Pastis. Calle Santa Mònica, 4. ☎ **93/318-79-80.** Metro: Drassanes.

Just off the southern end of Les Rambles, this tiny bar was opened in 1947 by Carme Pericás and Quime Ballester, two Valencianos. They made it a shrine to Edith Piaf, and her songs are still played on an old phonograph in back of the bar. If you look at the dusty art in this dimly lit place, you'll see some of Piaf. But mainly the decor consists of paintings by Quime Ballester, who had a dark, rather morbid vision of the world. You can order four different kinds of pastis in this "corner of Montmartre." Outside the window, check out the view, usually a parade of transvestite hookers. The crowd is likely to include almost anyone, especially people who used to be called "bohemians"; they live on in this bar of yesterday. Live music is performed Sunday through Thursday. Go after 11:30pm. Open Monday, Wednesday, and Thursday from 7:30pm to 2:30am, Friday and Saturday from 7:30pm to 3am, and Sunday from 6:30pm to 1:30am.

Els Quatre Gats. Montsió, 3. ☎ **93/302-41-40.** Metro: Urquinaona.

The Four Cats has been called "the best bar in Barcelona" (see also the restaurant listing in Chapter 12). In 1897 Pere Romeu and three of his friends, painters Ramón Casas, Santiago Rusiñol, and Miguel Utrillo, opened a café for artists and writers at the edge of the Barri Gòtic. Early in the history of the café, they staged a one-man show for a young artist, Pablo Picasso, but he didn't sell a single painting. However, Picasso stayed around to design the art nouveau cover of the menu. The café folded in 1903, becoming a private club and art school and attracting Joan Miró.

In 1978 two Cataláns reopened the café in the Casa Martí, a building designed by Josep Puig i Cadafalch, one of the leading architects of *modernismo.* The café displays works by major modern Catalán painters, including Tàpies. You can come in to drink coffee at the café, taste some wine, eat a full meal—and even try, if you dare, a potent Marc de Champagne, an eau-de-vie distilled from the local *cava.* The café is open daily from 8am to 2am.

GAY & LESBIAN BARS

Chaps. Avinguda Diagonal, 365. ☎ **93/215-53-65.** Metro: Diagonal.

Gay residents of Barcelona refer to this saloon-style watering hole as the premier leather bar of Catalonia. But, in fact, the dress code usually steers more toward boots and jeans than leather and chains. Set behind a pair of swinging doors evocative of the old American West, Chaps contains two different bar areas. Open daily 7pm to 3am.

El Convento. Carrer Bruniquer, 59 (Plaça Joanic). No phone. Cover 1,100 ptas. ($8.80), including first drink. Metro: Joanic.

This may be like no disco you've ever seen. The decoration is like a church, with depictions of the Virgin Mary and even candles adding to the ecclesiastical atmosphere. But the clientele consists of mainly young gay males in a party mood. Often shows and organized parties are presented here. A novelty, to say the least. Hours are daily from midnight to 6am.

Martin's Disco. Passeig de Gràcia, 130. ☎ **93/218-71-67.** Cover 1,000 ptas. ($8), including first drink. Metro: Passeig de Gràcia.

Behind a pair of unmarked doors, in a neighborhood of art nouveau buildings, this is one of the more popular gay discos in Barcelona. Within a series of all-black rooms, you'll wander through a landscape of men's erotic art, upended oil drums (used as cocktail tables), and the disembodied front-end chassis of yellow cars set amid the angular surfaces of the drinking and dancing areas. Another bar supplies drinks to a large room where films are shown. Open daily from midnight to 6am.

Santanassa. Carrer Aribau, 27. ☎ **93/451-00-52.** Cover Fri–Sat 1,000 ptas. ($8), including first drink; no cover Sun–Thurs. Metro: Universidad.

This is a regular staple on Barcelona's gay circuit, with at least one bar, a dance floor, provocative art, and a clientele whose percentage of gay women has greatly increased in the past several years. Open nightly from 11pm to 3am.

MORE ENTERTAINMENT

MOVIES Recent cinematic releases from Paris, New York, Rome, Hollywood, and even Madrid come quickly to Barcelona, where an avid audience often waits in long lines for tickets. Most foreign films are dubbed into Catalán, unless they're indicated as *VO* (original version). Movie listings are published in *Guía de Ocio,* available at any newsstand along Les Rambles.

If you're a movie buff, the best time to be in Barcelona is June and early July for the annual film festival.

A CASINO Midway between the coastal resorts of Sitges and Villanueva, about 25 miles (40km) southwest of Barcelona and about 2 miles (3km) north of Sitges, stands the **Gran Casino de Barcelona,** Sant Pere (San Pedro) de Ribes (☎ **93/893-36-66**). The major casino in all of Catalonia, it is housed in a villa originally built during the 1800s. Elegant, with gardens, it attracts restaurant clients as well as gamblers. A set menu in the restaurant (reservations recommended) costs 5,000 pesetas ($40), and drinks go for around 700 pesetas ($5.60) each. For admission to the casino, you'll pay 550 pesetas ($4.40) and must show your passport. The casino is open year-round Sunday through Thursday from 5pm to 4am, Friday and Saturday from 5pm to 5am.

9 Easy Excursions

The major one-day excursions, such as those to the monastery of Montserrat or to the resorts north along the Costa Brava, are covered in Chapters 14 and 15. However, if you've got a day to spare, you might also want to consider the following jaunt.

PENEDÉS WINERIES

From the Penedés wineries comes the famous *cava* (Catalán champagne), which can be sampled in the champagne bars of Barcelona. You can see where this wine originates by journeying 25 miles (40km) from Barcelona, via highway A-2, to Exit 27. There are also daily trains to Sant Sadurní d'Anoia, home to 66 *cava* firms. Trains depart from Barcelona Sants.

The firm best equipped to receive visitors is **Codorníu** (☎ **93/818-32-32),** the largest producer of *cava* (some 40 million bottles a year). Codorníu is ideally visited by car because of unreliable public transportation. However, it's sometimes possible to get a taxi from the station at Sant Sadurní d'Anoia.

Groups are welcomed at Codorníu (there must be at least four). It's not necessary to make an appointment before showing up. Tours are presented in English, among other languages, and take 1½ hours; they visit some of the 10 miles (16km) of underground cellars by electric cart. Take a sweater, even on a hot day. A former pressing section has been turned into a museum, exhibiting wine-making instruments through the ages. The museum is housed in a building designed by the great *modernismo* architect Puig i Cadafalch—one reason King Juan Carlos has declared the plant a national historic and artistic monument.

The tour ends with a *cava* tasting. Tours are conducted Monday through Friday at 8am, 12:30pm, and 3:45pm. Call the number above for more information. The ideal time for a visit is for the autumn grape harvest. Codorníu is closed in August.

CARDONA

Another popular excursion from Barcelona is to Cardona, 60 miles (97km) northwest of Barcelona. Take the N-11 west, then go north on Route 150 to Manresa. Cardona, reached along Route 1410, lies northwest of Manresa, a distance of 20 miles (32km).

The home of the dukes of Cardona, the town is known for its canonical church, **Sant Vicenç de Cardona,** placed inside the walls of the castle. The church was consecrated in 1040. The great Catalán architect Josep Puig i Cadafalch wrote, "There are few elements in Catalán architecture of the 12th century that cannot be found in Cardona, and nowhere better harmonized." The church reflects the Lombard style of architecture. The castle (now a parador—see below) was the most important fortress in Catalonia.

Where to Stay & Dine

Parador Nacional Duques de Cardona. Castillo de Carona, s/n, 08261 Cardona. ☎ **93/869-12-75.** Fax 93/869-16-36. 56 rms, 2 suites. A/C TV TEL. 9,000–12,000 ptas. ($72–$96) double; 13,765–17,600 ptas. ($110.10–$140.80) suite. AE, DC, MC, V. Free parking.

Sitting atop a cone-shaped mountain that towers 330 feet above Cardona, this restored castle opened as a four-star parador in 1976. Once the seat of Ludovici Pio (Louis the Pious) and a stronghold against the Moors, it was later expanded and strengthened by Guifré el Pilós (Wilfred the Hairy). In the 9th century the palace went to Don Ramón Folch, nephew of Charlemagne. The massive fortress proved impregnable to all but the inroads of time, and several ancient buildings in this hilltop complex have been restored and made part of the parador.

The spacious accommodations, some with minibars, are furnished with canopied beds with hand-carved wood and woven bedspreads and curtains. The bedrooms command panoramic views. The public rooms are decorated with antique furniture, tapestries, and paintings of various periods. The bar is in a former castle dungeon, with meals served in the lone stone-arched medieval dining room where the counts once took their repasts. Offered on the menu are regional dishes costing 3,200 pesetas ($25.60) for a complete meal. Try the Catalán bouillabaisse, accompanied by wines whose taste would be familiar to the Romans. Service is daily from 1 to 4pm and 8 to 10:30pm.

14 Catalonia

From Barcelona you can take several one-day excursions. The most popular is to the Benedictine monastery of Montserrat, northwest of Barcelona. To the south, the Roman city of Tarragona has been neglected by visitors but is particularly interesting to those who appreciate history. Beach lovers should head for the resort of Sitges.

About six million people live in Catalonia, and twice that many visit every year. It is one of Europe's "playgrounds," with its beaches along the Costa Brava (see Chapter 15) and the Costa Dorada, centered around Sitges. Tarragona is the capital of its own province, and Barcelona, of course, is the hub of Catalonia (see Chapters 12 and 13).

The province of Catalonia forms a triangle bordered by the French frontier to the north, the Mediterranean Sea to the east, and the province of Aragón to the west. The northern coastline is rugged, whereas the Costa Dorada is flatter, with miles of sandy beaches as well as a mild, sunny climate.

Pilgrims may go to Montserrat for its scenery and religious associations, and history buffs to Tarragona for its Roman ruins, but folks head to the Costa Dorada just for fun. This seashore, named for its strips of golden sand, extends along the coastlines of Barcelona and Tarragona provinces. Avid beachcombers sometimes traverse the entire coast.

One popular stretch is La Maresme, extending from Río Tordera to Barcelona, a distance of 40 miles (64.5km). Allow at least 2½ hours to cover it without stops. The Tarragonese coastline extends from Barcelona to the Ebro River, a distance of 120 miles (193km); a trip along it will take a whole day. Highlights along this coast include Costa de Garraf, a series of creeks skirted by the corniche road after Castelldefels; Sitges; and Tarragona. One of the most beautiful stretches of the coast is Cape Salou, lying south of Tarragona in a setting of pinewoods.

We'll begin our tour through this history-rich part of Catalonia by going not along the coast, but rather inland to the Sierra de Montserrat, which has views more spectacular than any along the coast. Wagner used it as the setting for his opera *Parsifal.* The serrated outline made by the sierra's steep cliffs led the Catalonians to call it *montserrat* (sawtooth mountain). It is the religious center of Catalonia. Thousands of pilgrims annually visit the town's monastery, with its Black Virgin.

A Journey to Andorra

Charlemagne gave this "country" its independence in 784, and with amused condescension, Napoleon let Andorra keep its autonomy. The principality of Andorra is now ruled by two co-princes, the president of France and the Spanish archbishop of Seo d'Urgell.

Less than 200 square miles (322 sq km) in size, Andorra is a storybook land of breathtaking scenery—cavernous valleys, snowcapped peaks, rugged pastureland, and deep gorges. It's popular for summer excursions and recently as a winter ski resort as well.

Because of its isolation—sandwiched between France and Spain high in the eastern Pyrenees—Andorra retained one of the most insular peasant cultures in Europe until as late as 1945. But since the 1950s, tourists have increased from a trickle to a flood—12 million every year, in fact. This has wreaked havoc with Andorra's economy, although opinions are sharply divided on what the deluge has done to the country overall.

Some suggest that Andorra has ruined its mountain setting with urban sprawl, because taxis, crowds, and advertising have transformed the once-rustic principality into a busy center of trading and commerce. At first glance, the route into the country from Spain looks like a used-car lot, and its traffic jams are legendary. New hotels and hundreds of shops have opened in the past decade to accommodate the French and Spanish pouring across the frontiers to buy duty-free merchandise. A magazine once called Andorra "Europe's feudal discount shopping center." In addition, gasoline is cheap here.

Warning: Border guards check very carefully for undeclared goods.

Most people make their base in the capital, Andorra-la-Vella (in Spanish, Andorra-la-Vieja) or the adjoining town, Les Escaldes, where there are plenty of shops, bars, and hotels. Shuttles run between the towns, but most shoppers prefer to walk. Most of the major hotels and restaurants are on the main street of Andorra-la-Vella (Avinguda Meritxell) or on the main street of Les Escaldes (Avinguda Carlemany). French francs and Spanish pesetas may be used interchangeably, and hotel, restaurant, and shop prices are quoted in both currencies.

But unless you've come just to shop, you will want to leave the capital for a look at this tiny principality. Two nearby villages, La Massana and Ordino, can be visited by car or by bus (leaving about every 30 minutes from the station in Andorra-la-Vella). Buses cross the country from south to north and vice versa. The drive to Andorra will take you through some of the finest mountain scenery in Europe, with a backdrop of peaks, vineyards, and rushing brooks. From Barcelona, drive via Puigcerda to La Seu d'Urgell. From here on the C-145, it's a quick 6 miles (10 km) to the border of this autonomous principality, one of the world's smallest countries.

The Monestir de Poblet in Tarragona is the other major monastery of Catalonia. It, too, is a world-class attraction.

EXPLORING THE REGION BY CAR

Day 1 From Barcelona the most important pilgrimage site is to Montserrat, sitting atop a 4,000-foot mountain 7 miles (11km) long. It's a major pilgrimage site in

Catalonia

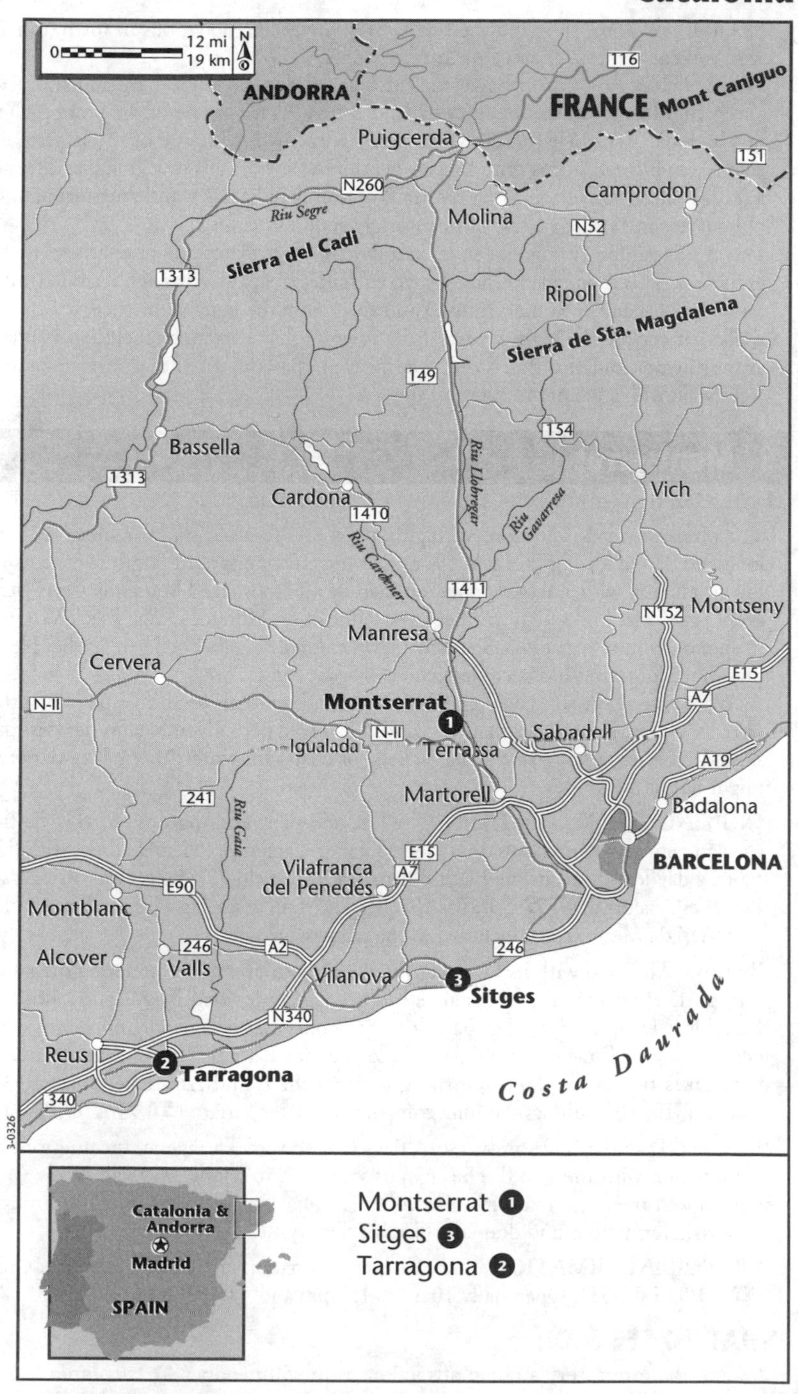
12 mi
19 km
N
ANDORRA
FRANCE
Mont Caniguo
116
151
Puigcerda
N260
Riu Segre
Molina
Camprodon
N52
Sierra del Cadi
1313
Ripoll
Sierra de Sta. Magdalena
149
154
Bassella
1313
Cardona
1410
Riu Cardener
Riu Llobregat
Riu Gavarresa
Vich
1411
Montseny
N152
Manresa
Cervera
E15
A7
N-II
Montserrat
Sabadell
Igualada
N-II
Terrassa
A19
241
Riu Gaia
Martorell
Badalona
BARCELONA
E15
Vilafranca
del Penedés
A7
E90
Montblanc
246
A2
246
Alcover
Valls
Vilanova
Sitges
N340
Reus
Tarragona
340
Costa Daurada
3-0326
Catalonia &
Andorra
Madrid
SPAIN
Montserrat 1
Sitges 3
Tarragona 2

Spain. If you'd like to spend the night, there are accommodations in town; otherwise you can return to Barcelona in the evening.

Day 2 Head south from Barcelona for a day at Sitges. (If you have an extra day, and would like to unwind, you can spend it here, as it has one of the best beaches in Catalonia.) This Mediterranean seaside resort town, with one of the largest gay colonies in Europe, opens onto a sandy beach (La Ribera), 1 1/2 miles long, and fronts a flower-lined promenade along the sea. You can spend a day wandering through its old quarter and visiting a trio of surprisingly good museums.

Day 3 Head for Tarragona, either as a day trip from Barcelona or as an overnight excursion. This is one of the "undiscovered" cities of Spain, although it's filled with attractions—namely Roman ruins. You can explore the remains of ancient Roman walls that enclose the highest part of the town. Other attractions include a Roman amphitheater and the Balcó del Mediterráni (Balcony of the Mediterranean), a cliffwalk with a panoramic view of the sea.

1 Montserrat

35 miles (56km) NW of Barcelona, 368 miles (592km) E of Madrid

The monastery at Montserrat, sitting atop a 4,000-foot mountain 7 miles (11km) long and 3 1/2 miles (5.5km) wide, is one of the most important pilgrimage spots in Spain, ranking with Zaragoza and Santiago de Compostela. Thousands travel here every year to see and touch the medieval statue of La Moreneta (The Black Virgin), the patron saint of Catalonia. So many newly married couples flock here for her blessings that Montserrat has become Spain's Niagara Falls.

Avoid visiting on Sunday, if possible. Thousands of locals pour in, especially if the weather is nice. Remember that the winds blow cold here. Even in summer, visitors should take along warm sweaters, jackets, or coats. In winter, thermal underwear might not be a bad idea.

GETTING THERE **By Train** The best and most exciting way to go is via the Catalán railway—Ferrocarrils de la Generalitat de Catalunya (Manresa line), with five trains a day leaving from the Plaça d'Espanya in Barcelona. The central office is at Plaça de Catalunya, 1 (☎ **93/205-15-15**). The train connects with an aerial cableway (Aeri de Montserrat), included in the rail passage.

By Bus The train with its funicular tie-in has taken over as the preferred means of transport. However, a long-distance bus service is provided by Autocars Julià in Barcelona. Daily service from Barcelona to Montserrat is generally operated, with departures near Estacio Central de Barcelona-Sants, Plaça de Països Catalanes. One bus makes the trip at 9am, returning at 5pm; the round-trip ticket costs 1,290 pesetas ($10.30). Contact the Julià company at Carrer Viriato (☎ **93/490-40-00**).

By Car Take the N-2 southwest of Barcelona toward Tarragona, turning west at the junction with the N-11. The signposts and exit to Montserrat will be on your right. From the main road, it's nine miles (14.5km) up to the monastery through eerie rock formations and dramatic Catalán scenery.

VISITOR INFORMATION The tourist information office is at Plaça de la Creu (☎ **93/835-02-51**). Open daily 10am to 1:45pm and 3 to 5:30pm.

WHAT TO SEE & DO

One of the **monastery's** noted attractions is the 50-member ✪ **Escolanía** (boys' choir), one of the oldest and most renowned in Europe, dating from the 13th century. At 1pm daily you can hear them singing *Salve Regina* and the *Virolai* (hymn of Montserrat) in the basilica. The basilica is open daily from 8 to 10:30am and noon to 6:30pm. Admission is free. To view the Black Virgin, a statue from the 12th or 13th century, enter the church through a side door to the right. At the Plaça de Santa María you can also visit the **Museu de Montserrat** (☎ **93/835-02-51**), known for its collection of ecclesiastical paintings, including works by Caravaggio and El Greco. Modern Spanish and Catalán artists are also represented (see Picasso's early *El Viejo Pescador,* dating from 1895). Works by Dalí and such French impressionists as Monet, Sisley, and Degas are also shown. The collection of ancient artifacts is also interesting. And look for the crocodile mummy, at least 2,000 years old. Charging 400 pesetas ($3.20) admission, the museum is open daily from 10:30am to 2pm and 3 to 6pm.

The nine-minute funicular ride to the 4,119-foot-high peak, Sant Jeroni, makes for an exciting trip. The funicular operates about every 20 minutes in April through October, daily from 10am to 6:40pm. The cost is 700 pesetas ($5.60) round-trip. From the top, you'll see not only the whole of Catalonia but also the Pyrenees and the islands of Majorca and Ibiza.

You can also make an excursion to **Santa Cova (Holy Grotto),** the alleged site of the discovery of the Black Virgin. The grotto dates from the 17th century and was built in the shape of a cross. Many famous Catalán artists, such as Puig i Cadafalch and Gaudí, exhibited religious works on the road to the shrine. You go halfway by funicular but must complete the trip on foot.

The chapel is open April through October, daily from 9am to 6:30pm; off-season hours are daily 10am to 5:30pm. The funicular operates from April through October only, every 15 minutes daily from 10am to 7pm, at a cost of 300 pesetas ($2.40) round-trip.

WHERE TO STAY & DINE

Few people spend the night here, but most visitors will want at least one meal. If you don't want to spend a lot, purchase a picnic in Barcelona or ask your hotel to pack a meal.

Abat Cisneros. Plaça de Monestir, 08691 Montserrat. ☎ **93/835-02-01.** Fax 93/828-40-06. 41 rms. TV TEL. 8,400 ptas. ($67.20) double. AE, DC, MC, V. Parking 500 ptas. ($4).

Set on the main square of Montserrat, this is a well-maintained modern hotel with few pretensions and a history of family management dating back to 1958. Bedrooms are simple and clean. The in-house restaurant offers fixed-price meals for around 2,675 pesetas ($21.40) per person. Many regional dishes of Catalonia are served. The hotel's name is derived from a title given to the head of any Benedictine monastery during the Middle Ages.

2 Tarragona

60 miles (97km) S of Barcelona, 344 miles (554km) E of Madrid

The ancient Roman port city of Tarragona, on a rocky bluff above the Mediterranean, is one of the grandest, but most neglected, sightseeing centers in Spain. Despite its Roman and medieval remains, it is the "second" modern city of Catalonia.

The Romans captured Tarragona in 218 B.C., and during their rule the city sheltered one million people behind its 40-mile-long (64km-long) city walls. One of the four capitals of Catalonia when it was an ancient principality, and once the home of Julius Caesar, Tarragona today consists of an old quarter filled with interesting buildings, particularly the houses with connecting balconies. The upper walled town is mainly medieval, whereas the town below is newer.

In the new town, walk along Rambla Nova, a wide and fashionable boulevard, the main artery of life. Running parallel with Rambla Nova to the east is the Rambla Vella, which marks the beginning of the old town. The city has a bullring, good hotels, and beaches. The Romans were the first to designate Tarragona a resort town.

After seeing the attractions listed below, cap off your day with a stroll along the Balcó del Mediterrani (the Balcony of the Mediterranean), where the vistas are especially beautiful at sunset.

GETTING THERE **By Train** Daily, 32 trains make the 1½-hour trip to and from the Barcelona-Sants station. Five trains per day make the 8-hour trip from Madrid. In Tarragona, the RENFE office is in the train station, Plaza de España, s/n (☎ **977/24-02-02**).

By Bus From Barcelona, there are four buses per day to Tarragona (1½ hours). The cost is 830 pesetas ($6.65) one way. Call **977/22-20-72** in Tarragona for more information.

By Car Take the A-2 southwest from Barcelona to the A-7, then take the N-340. The route is well signposted. This is a fast toll road.

VISITOR INFORMATION The tourist information office is at Fortuny, 4 (☎ **977/23-34-15**). Open Monday through Friday from 9am to 3pm and 4 to 7pm, Saturday from 9am to 2pm.

WHAT TO SEE & DO

Passeig Arqueològic. Plaça del Pallol. ☎ **977/24-57-96.** Admission 420 ptas. ($3.35). Oct–May, Mon–Sat 10am–1pm and 3–7pm, Sun and holidays 10am–2pm; June–Sept, Mon–Sat 9am–8pm, Sun and holidays 10am–2pm. Bus: 1.

At the far end of Plaça del Pallol, an archway leads to this half-mile walkway along the ancient ramparts, built by the Romans on top of cyclopean boulders. The ramparts have been much altered over the years, especially in medieval times and in the 1600s. There are pleasant views from many points along the way.

Catedral. Plaça de la Seu. ☎ **977/23-86-85.** Free admission to cathedral, museum, 300 ptas. ($2.40). Mar 16–June 30, daily 10am–12:30pm and 4–6:45pm; July 1–Oct 15, daily 10am–7pm; Oct 16–Nov 15, daily 10am–12:30pm and 3–6pm; Nov 16–Mar 15, daily 10am–1:45pm. Bus: 1.

Situated at the highest point of Tarragona is this 12th-century cathedral, whose architecture represents the transition from Romanesque to Gothic. It has an enormous vaulted entrance, fine stained-glass windows, Romanesque cloisters, and an open choir. In the main apse, observe the altarpiece of St. Thecla, patron of Tarragona, carved by Pere Joan in 1430. Two flamboyant doors open into the chevet. The east gallery is the Museu Diocesà, with a collection of Catalán art.

Amfiteatre Romà. Parc del Milagro. Admission 400 ptas. ($3.20). Apr–Sept, Tues–Sat 9am–8pm, Sun 9am–3pm; Oct–Mar, Tues–Sat 9am–5:30pm, Sun 9am–3pm. Bus: 1.

At the foot of Miracle Park and dramatically carved from the cliff that rises from the beach, the Roman amphitheater recalls the days in the 2nd century when thousands of Romans gathered here for amusement.

Necròpolis. Passeig de la Indepèndencia, 15. ☎ **977/21-11-75.** Admission to Necròpolis plus museum 300 ptas. ($2.40). Mid-June to mid-Sept, Tues–Sat 10am–1pm and 4:30–8pm, Sun and holidays 10am–2pm; off-season, Tues–Sat 10am–1:30pm and 4–7pm, Sun and holidays 10am–2pm. Bus: 1.

This is one of the most important burial grounds in Spain, used by the Christians from the 3rd through the 5th centuries. It stands outside town next to a tobacco factory whose construction led to its discovery in 1923. While on the grounds, visit the Museu Paleocristià, which contains a number of sarcophagi and other objects discovered during the excavations.

Museu Nacional Arqueològic. Plaça del Rei, 5. ☎ **977/23-62-09.** Admission 300 ptas. ($2.40). June 16–Oct 15, Tues–Sat 10am–2pm and 4–7pm, Sun 10am–2pm; Oct 16–June 15, Tues–Sat 10am–1pm and 4:30–8pm, Sun 10am–2pm. Bus: 1.

The Archaeology Museum, overlooking the sea, houses a collection of Roman relics—mosaics, ceramics, coins, silver, sculpture, and more. The outstanding attraction here is the *Head of Medusa,* with its penetrating stare.

WHERE TO STAY

EXPENSIVE

Hotel Imperial Tarraco. Paseo de las Palmeras/Rambla Vella, 43003 Tarragona. ☎ **977/23-30-40.** Fax 977/21-65-66. 145 rms, 25 suites. A/C MINIBAR TV TEL. 16,500–31,500 ptas. ($132–$252) double; 32,500–54,000 ptas. ($260–$432) suite. Rates include breakfast. AE, DC, MC, V. Free parking. Bus: 1.

Located about a quarter-mile south of the cathedral, atop an oceanfront cliff whose panoramas include a sweeping view of both the sea and the Roman ruins, this hotel is the finest in town. Designed in the form of a crescent, it has guest rooms that usually angle out to sea and almost always include small balconies. The accommodations, all with private baths, are furnished with uncomplicated modern furniture and are, in fact, a bit plain. The public rooms contain lots of polished white marble, Oriental carpets, and leather furniture. The staff responds well to the demands of both traveling businesspeople and art lovers on sightseeing excursions.

Dining/Entertainment: The hotel contains both a bar and a restaurant. Some Catalonian regional dishes are featured, although the food is rather standard.

Services: Room service, laundry, concierge, hairdresser, babysitting.

Facilities: Outdoor pool, tennis courts, pleasant garden.

MODERATE

Hotel Lauria. Rambla Nova, 20, 43004 Tarragona. ☎ **977/23-67-12.** Fax 977/23-67-00. 72 rms. A/C TV TEL. 9,500–10,000 ptas. ($76–$80) double. AE, DC, MC, V. Parking 1,000 ptas. ($8). Bus: 1.

Set less than half a block north of the town's popular seaside promenade (Paseo de les Palmeres), beside the tree-lined Rambla, this straightforward three-star hotel offers unpretentious, functional, and clean bedrooms, each of which has been recently modernized. For years considered the leading hotel of town, until its replacement by newcomers, it still draws a loyal clientele of repeat visitors. The rooms in back open onto a view of the sea, a garden, and the hotel's swimming pool. Only the public rooms are air-conditioned.

Dining/Entertainment: There is no full-fledged restaurant on the premises, but the staff happily directs clients to nearby eateries. The ground floor contains an informal pizzeria.

Services: Room service (daily 7am to midnight), laundry, concierge, babysitting.

Facilities: Outdoor swimming pool, bar, car rentals.

Hotel Urbis. Carrer Reding, 20 bis, 43001 Tarragona. ☎ **800/528-1234** in the U.S. and Canada, or 977/24-01-16. Fax 977/24-36-54. 44 rms. A/C MINIBAR TV TEL. 11,449–13,322 ptas. ($91.60–$106.60) double. Rates include buffet breakfast. AE, MC, V. Parking 1,300 ptas. ($9.20). Bus: 3.

The rooms at this hotel off the Plaça de Corsini are three-star quality and much improved in recent years, with such added amenities as safes. The hotel also offers a restaurant with an English menu. The nearby tourist office will give you a map for exploring Tarragona.

INEXPENSIVE

Hotel Astari. Vía Augusta, 95, 43003 Tarragona. ☎ **977/23-69-00.** Fax 977/23-69-11. 83 rms. TV TEL. 6,630–7,800 ptas. ($53.05–$62.40) double. Closed Oct 31–May 2. Bus: 3.

In-the-know travelers in search of peace and quiet on the Mediterranean come to the Astari, which opened its doors back in 1959 and was last renovated in 1992. This five-story resort hotel on the Barcelona road offers fresh and airy, but rather plain, accommodations; a swimming pool; and a solarium. The Astari has long balconies and terraces, one favorite spot being the outer flagstone terrace with its umbrella tables set among willows, orange trees, and geranium bushes. There is a cafeteria as well as a cocktail lounge. This is the only hotel in Tarragona with garage space for each guest's car.

Nuría. Vía Augusta, 217, 43007 Tarragona. ☎ **977/23-50-11.** Fax 977/24-41-36. 61 rms. TV TEL. 6,000 ptas. ($48) double. MC, V. Closed Nov–Mar. Parking 950 ptas. ($7.60). Bus: 1 or 9.

Built near the beach in 1967, this five-floor modern building offers neat, pleasant rooms, most with balconies. You can dine in the sunny restaurant, where the specialty is *romesco,* a kind of *zarzuela* (seafood medley).

WHERE TO DINE

$ Barquet. Gasometro, 16. ☎ **977/24-00-23.** Reservations recommended. Main courses 1,100–3,500 ptas. ($8.80–$28); *menú del día* 1,100 ptas. ($8.80). AE, DC, MC, V. Mon–Sat 1–4pm and 8–11:30pm. Closed Aug. CATALÁN/SEAFOOD.

Set in the center of town, within a five-minute walk from the cathedral, this restaurant specializes in seafood and shellfish prepared in the Catalán style. It was established in 1950 in the cellar of a relatively modern building and today is run by the third generation of its original owners. Within a pair of dining rooms, comfortably outfitted in nautical themes, you can enjoy such dishes as *sopa de pescados* Tarragona style, *romesco* (ragoût) of sea bass with herbs, a local assemblage of fried finned creatures identified for many hundreds of years as *fideos rossejats,* several different preparations of sole and hake, and, if you're not interested in seafood, a choice of grilled veal, chicken, or beef. The list of Spanish and Catalán wines will complement any meal here. The staff is well-trained, polite, and proud of their Catalán antecedents.

$ Cafetería Arimany. Rambla Nova, 43–45. ☎ **977/23-79-31.** Main courses 1,200–2,200 ptas. ($9.60–$17.60); fixed-price menu 1,450 ptas. ($11.60). AE, DC, MC, V. Daily 8am–1am. Bus: 1. CATALÁN/INTERNATIONAL.

When this central and popular cafeteria opens its doors at 8am, visitors and locals alike pour in for breakfast. Others come back for lunch, and some finish with a good-value dinner. You can eat here inexpensively or for more money, depending on your appetite. The shrimp in garlic oil is outstanding. Try the fresh fish of the day, based on the local catch, or else squid cooked Roman style. The dessert specialty is "Pau Casals," named after a native Catalonian, the late musician Pablo Casals. It is a chocolate cake served with a hot chocolate sauce. Another bakery specialty is *maginet,* the typical cookie of Tarragona.

Sol-Ric. Vía Augusta, 227. ☎ **977/23-20-32.** Main courses 1,800–2,200 ptas. ($14.40–$17.60); fixed-price menu 1,500 ptas. ($12). AE, MC, V. Tues–Sat 1–4pm, Tues–Sun 8:30–11pm. Closed mid-Dec to mid-Jan. CATALÁN.

The Beaches of Costa Dorada

For some 131 miles (212km) running along the entire coastline of the province of Tarragona, from Cunit as far as Les Cases d'Alcanar, there is a series of excellent beaches and impressive cliffs, along with beautiful pine-covered headlands. In the city of Tarragona itself there is El Miracle beach, and a little farther north can be found the beaches of L'Arrabassade, Savinosa, Dels Capellans, and the Llarga. At the end of the latter stands La Punta de la Mora, which has a 16th-century watchtower. The small towns of Altafulla and Torredembarra, both complete with castles, stand next to these beaches and are the location of many hotels and urban developments.

Farther north again are the two magnificent beaches of Comarruga and Sant Salvador. The first is particularly cosmopolitan, whereas the second is more secluded. Lastly come the beaches of Calafell, Segur, and Cunit, all with modern tourist complexes. You'll also find the small towns of Creixell, Sant Vicenç de Calders, and Clarà, which have wooded hills in the background.

South of Tarragona the coastline forms a wide arc that stretches for miles and includes La Pineda beach. El Recó beach fronts the Cape of Salou where, in among its coves, hills, and hidden-away corners, many hotels and residential centers are located. The natural port of Salou is nowadays a center for international tourism.

Continuing south toward Valencia, you next come to Cambrils, a maritime town with an excellent beach and an important fishing port. In the background stand the impressive Colldejou and Llaberia mountains. Farther south are the beaches of Mont-roig and L'Hospitalet, as well as the small town of L'Ametlla de Mar with its small fishing port.

After passing the Balaguer massif the traveler eventually reaches the delta of the River Ebro, a wide lowland area covering more than 300 miles (500km), opening like a fan into the sea. This is an area of rice fields, crisscrossed by branches of the River Ebro and by an enormous number of irrigation channels. There are also some lagoons here that, because of their immense size, are ideal as hunting and fishing grounds. Moreover, there are some beaches over several miles in length and others in small, hidden-away estuaries. Two important towns in the region are Amposta, located on the River Ebro itself, and Sant Carles de la Ràpita, a 19th-century port town favored by King Carlos III.

The Costa Dorada finishes at its most southwesterly point at the plain of Alcanar, a large area given over to the cultivation of oranges and other similar crops. Its beaches, along with the small hamlet of Les Cases d'Alcanar, mark the end of the Tarragona section of the Costa Dorada.

Many guests remember the service here long after memories of the good cuisine have faded. Dating from 1859, the place has a rustic ambience, replete with antique farm implements hanging from the walls. There is also an outdoor terrace as well as a central fireplace, usually blazing in winter. The chef prepares oven-baked hake with potatoes, tournedos with Roquefort, seafood stew, and several exotic fish dishes, among other specialties.

EXCURSIONS FROM TARRAGONA

If you rent a car, you can visit two attractions within a 30- to 45-minute drive from Tarragona. The first stop is the **Monestir de Poblet,** Plaça Corona d'Aragó, 11,

E-43448 Poblet (☎ **977/87-00-89**), 29 miles (46.5km) northwest of Tarragona, one of the most intriguing monasteries in Spain. Its most exciting features are the oddly designed tombs of the old kings of Aragón and Catalonia. Constructed in the 12th and 13th centuries and still in use, Poblet's cathedral-like church reflects both Romanesque and Gothic architectural styles. Cistercian monks live here, passing their days writing, studying, working a printing press, farming, and helping to restore the building, which suffered heavy damage during the 1835 revolution. Admission to the monastery is 400 pesetas ($3.20) for adults and 200 pesetas ($1.60) for children. It's open Monday through Friday from 10am to 12:30pm and 3 to 6pm, Saturday and Sunday from 10am to 12:30pm and 2:30 to 5pm.

About three miles (4.8km) farther, you can explore an unspoiled medieval Spanish town, **Montblanch.** At its entrance, a map pinpoints the principal artistic and architectural treasures—and there are many. Walk, don't drive, along the narrow, winding streets.

3 Sitges

25 miles (40km) S of Barcelona, 370 miles (596km) E of Madrid

Sitges is one of the most frequented resorts of southern Europe, the brightest spot on the Costa Dorada. It is crowded in summer, mostly with affluent young northern Europeans, many of them gay. For years the resort was patronized largely by prosperous middle-class industrialists from Barcelona, but those rather staid days have gone; Sitges is as lively today as Benidorm and Torremolinos down the coast, but it's nowhere near as tacky.

Sitges has long been known as a city of culture, thanks in part to resident artist, playwright, and Bohemian mystic Santiago Rusiñol. The 19th-century *modernismo* movement began largely at Sitges, and the town remained the scene of artistic encounters and demonstrations long after the movement waned. Sitges continued as a resort of artists, attracting such giants as Salvador Dalí and poet Federico García Lorca. The Spanish Civil War (1936–39) erased what has come to be called the "golden age" of Sitges. Although other artists and writers arrived in the decades to follow, none had the name or the impact of those who had gone before.

GETTING THERE **By Train** RENFE runs trains from Barcelona-Sants to Sitges, a 50-minute trip. Call **93/490-02-02** in Barcelona for information about schedules. Four trains leave Barcelona per hour.

By Car Sitges is a 45-minute drive from Barcelona along the C-246, a coastal road. An express highway, the A-7, opened in 1991. The coastal road is more scenic, but it can be extremely slow on weekends because of the heavy traffic, as all of Barcelona seemingly heads for the beaches.

Visitor Information The tourist information office is at Carrer Sínis Morera, 1 (☎ **93/811-76-30**). Open June through September 15, daily from 9am to 9pm; September 16 through May, Monday through Friday from 9am to 2pm and 4 to 6:30pm, Saturday from 10am to 1pm.

SPECIAL EVENTS The **Carnaval** at Sitges is one of the outstanding events on the Catalán calendar. For more than a century, the town has celebrated the days prior to the beginning of Lent. Fancy dress, floats, feathered outfits, and sequins all make this an exciting event. The party begins on the Thursday before Lent with the arrival of the king of the "Carnestoltes" and ends with the "Burial of a Sardine" on Ash Wednesday. Activities reach their flamboyant best on Sant Bonaventura, where gay people hold their own celebrations.

WHAT TO SEE & DO

The old part of Sitges used to be a fortified medieval enclosure. The castle is now the seat of the town government. The local parish church, called *La Punta* (The Point) and built next to the sea on top of a promontory, presides over an extensive maritime esplanade, where people parade in the early evening. Behind the side of the church are the Museu Cau Ferrat and the Museu Maricel (see below).

The Beaches It is the beaches that attract most visitors to Sitges. They have showers, bathing cabins, and stalls. Kiosks rent such items as motorboats and air cushions for fun on the water. Beaches on the eastern end and those inside the town center are the most peaceful—for example, **Aiguadoiç** and **Els Balomins.** The **Playa San Sebastián, Fragata Beach,** and the **"Beach of the Boats"** (under the church and next to the yacht club) are the area's family beaches. Most young people go to the **Playa de la Ribera,** to the west.

All along the coast women can go topless. Farther west are the most solitary beaches, where the scene grows more racy, especially along the **Playas del Muerto,** where two tiny nude beaches lie between Sitges and Vilanova i la Geltrú. A shuttle bus runs between the cathedral and Golf Terramar. From Golf Terramar, go along the road to the club L'Atlántida, then walk along the railway. The first beach draws nudists of every sexual persuasion, and the second is almost solely gay. Be advised that lots of action takes place in the woods in back of these beaches.

Beaches aside, Sitges has some interesting museums.

Museu Cau Ferrat. Carrer del Fonollar. ☎ **93/894-03-64.** Admission 400 ptas. ($3.20) adults, 200 ptas. ($1.60) students, free for children under 16; combination ticket for three museums listed 600 ptas. ($4.80). June 21–Sept 11, Tues–Sat 9:30am–2pm and 4–8pm, Sun 9:30am–2pm; Sept 12–June 20, Tues–Fri 9:30am–2pm and 4–6pm, Sat 9:30am–2pm and 4–8pm, Sun 9:30am–2pm.

Catalán artist Santiago Rusiñol combined two 16th-century cottages to make this house, where he lived and worked and which upon his death (1931) he willed to Sitges along with his art collection. More than anyone else, Rusiñol made Sitges a popular resort. The museum collection includes two paintings by El Greco and several small Picassos, including *The Bullfight.* A number of Rusiñol's works are also on display.

Museu Maricel. Carrer del Fonallar. ☎ **93/894-03-64.** Admission 300 ptas. ($2.40) adults, 150 ptas. ($1.20) students, free for children under 16; admission included in combination ticket (see above). June 21–Sept 11, Tues–Sat 9:30am–2pm and 4–8pm, Sun 9:30am–2pm; Sept 12–June 20, Tues–Fri 9:30am–2pm and 4–6pm, Sat 9:30am–2pm and 4–8pm, Sun 9:30am–2pm.

Opened by the King and Queen of Spain, the Museu Maricel contains art donated by Dr. Jesús Pérez Rosales. The palace, owned by American Charles Deering when it was built right after World War I, is in two parts connected by a small bridge. The museum has a good collection of Gothic and Romantic paintings and sculptures, as well as many fine Catalán ceramics. There are also three noteworthy works by Santiago Rebull and an allegorical painting of World War I by José María Sert.

Museu Romàntic ("Can Llopis"). Sant Gaudenci, 1. ☎ **93/894-29-69.** Admission 300 ptas. ($2.40) adults, 150 ptas. ($1.20) students, free for children under 16; admission included in combination ticket (see above). June 21–Sept 11, Tues–Sat 9:30am–2pm and 4–8pm, Sun 9:30am–2pm; Sept 12–June 20, Tues–Fri 9:30am–2pm and 4–6pm, Sat 9:30am–2pm and 4–8pm, Sun 9:30am–2pm.

This museum re-creates the daily life of a Sitges landowning family in the 18th and 19th centuries. The family rooms, furniture, and household objects are most

The Enigmatic Figure of Modernismo

Cau Ferrat was the house-cum-studio of artist and writer Santiago Rusiñol. Born in Barcelona in 1861, he was one of the most enigmatic figures of Catalán *modernismo,* or art nouveau, a literary and artistic trend that represented a spiritualist reaction to 19th-century positivism. He died in Aranjuez in 1931.

On return from a trip to Italy in 1892, he bought a couple of terraced fisher's cottages that had been built on the edge of a rocky coastline. Then he commissioned the architect Francesc Rogent to build a new house on the ground where the cottages stood.

Rusiñol described Cau Ferrat as a "refuge for those whose heart no longer feels the warmth it needs, a place to rest the spirit that has become weary from the toil of life, a hermitage near the sea for those injured by indifference and a hostel for the pilgrims of Holy Poetry."

Today, the collection at Cau Ferrat that arouses most interest is the painting and drawing collection. Works by the most outstanding artists of the *modernismo* period can be seen here—such artists as Ramon Casas, Aleix Clapés, Pere Ferran, Joan Llimona, Arcadi Mas i Fontdevila, Isidre Nonell, Darió de Regoyos, Miquel Utrillo, and Ignacio Zuloaga. There are also works by younger artists such as Herman Anglada i Camarasa and Picasso. Rusiñol's work is represented by a wide range of styles, from realism to symbolism.

Cau Ferrat is a treasure chest containing a large number of private objects, objects that are inseparable from the private and social life of its creator. There are portraits of friends Casellas, Eleonora Duse, Casas, Utrillo, and Benito Pérez Galdós.

The writer, Josep Pla defined Rusiñol as a "man who was horrified by industrial civilization, who postulated freedom in all domains, who tended to replace reality by literature and reason by sentiments, fascinated by nature and gardens, who searched for vagrancy and melancholy, sentimental expression, who valued the inaccessible, death and nihilism, dreams and indecision."

An outstanding painter and a renowned satirical writer, novelist, and dramatist, Rusiñol lived in Paris when impressionism made its appearance. In his own artwork he employed many elements of impressionism as far as technique, light, and color were concerned. However, he portrayed his own private and lyrical world. Rusiñol considered painting to be a spiritual language that transmitted his poetry rather than a medium that reflected the real world.

interesting. You'll also find wine cellars, and an important collection of antique dolls (upstairs).

WHERE TO STAY

In spite of a building spree, Sitges is unprepared for the large numbers of tourists who flock here in July and August. By mid-October just about everything—including hotels, restaurants, and bars—slows down considerably or closes altogether.

EXPENSIVE

Hotel Calípolis. Avenida Sofia, 2–4, 00870 Sitges. ☎ **93/894-15-00.** Fax 93/894-07-64. 164 rms, 6 suites. A/C MINIBAR TV TEL. 11,500–17,000 ptas. ($92–$136) double; 15,000–23,500 ptas. ($120–$188). AE, DC, MC, V. Parking (available June 15–Sept 15) 1,500 ptas. ($12).

Built in 1964 and renovated at great expense in 1990, this 11-story hotel fits in a gently undulating curve against the resort's beachfront and seaside promenade.

Bedrooms contain expansive balconies, individual safes, satellite TV hookups, marble-sheathed bathrooms, and a comfortably conservative decor of contemporary furniture. Most offer sea views; the remainder offer views of the mountains.

Dining/Entertainment: The hotel restaurant includes a flowering outdoor terrace and offers formal service, very crisp linens, and both international and Catalonian specialties. There's also a bar.

Services: Concierge, babysitting.

Facilities: Car rentals, excursions to nearby tennis courts and golf courses, horseback riding, sailing, and trips to nearby historic monasteries can be arranged. The parking lot is available only during the congested summer months; the lot closes when street parking becomes available again in the fall.

Meliá Gran Sitges. El Puerto de Aiguadolç, 08870 Sitges. ☎ **800/336-3542** in the U.S., or 93/811-08-11. Fax 93/894-90-97. 294 rms, 13 suites. A/C MINIBAR TV TEL. Mon–Thurs 20,000 ptas. ($160) double; Fri–Sun 12,000 ptas. ($96) double; suites from 30,000 ptas. ($240) throughout week. Weekend rates include breakfast. AE, DC, MC, V. Parking 1,500 ptas. ($12).

Designed with steeply sloping sides, reminiscent of a pair of interconnected Aztec pyramids, this hotel was built in 1992 as housing for spectators and participants in the Barcelona Olympics. Angled to curve around two sides of a large swimming pool and set a few yards from the beach, the hotel contains a white-marble lobby with what feels like the largest window in Spain, overlooking a view of the mountains. Each bedroom is outfitted in shades of blue and includes many of the electronic amenities you'd expect and a large, furnished veranda for sunbathing. The in-house restaurant, Norai, offers international and Catalonian cuisine. Many guests at this hotel are here to participate in any of dozens of conferences and conventions held frequently within the establishment's battery of high-tech convention facilities. It's about a 15-minute walk east of the center of Sitges, near the access roads leading to Barcelona.

MODERATE

El Galeón. Sant Francesc, 44, 08870 Sitges. ☎ **93/894-06-12.** Fax 93/894-63-35. 47 rms. TEL. 10,500 ptas. ($84) double. Rates include breakfast. MC, V. Closed Oct 20–Apr. Parking 1,200 ptas. ($9.60).

A leading three-star hotel only a short walk from both the beach and the Plaça d'Espanya, this well-styled hostelry blends a bit of the old Spain with the new. The small public rooms feel cozy, whereas the good-sized guest rooms, accented with wood grain, have a more streamlined aura. The hotel offers a swimming pool and a patio in the rear. Advance reservations are necessary.

Hotel Platjador. Passeig de la Ribera, 35, 08870 Sitges. ☎ **93/894-50-54.** Fax 93/894-63-35. 59 rms. TV TEL. 5,500–11,300 ptas. ($44–$90.40) double. Rates include breakfast. MC, V. Closed Nov–Apr.

One of the best hotels in town, the Platjador, on the esplanade fronting the beach, has comfortably furnished and recently restored guest rooms, all with private baths and many with big French doors opening onto balconies and sea views. There is also a swimming pool. The dining room, facing the beach, is known for its good cuisine, including gazpacho, paella, fresh fish, and flan for dessert.

INEXPENSIVE

Hotel El Cid. San José, 39 bis, 08870 Sitges. ☎ **93/894-18-42.** Fax 93/894-6335. 77 rms. TEL. 4,600–7,500 ptas. ($36.80–$60) double. Rates include continental breakfast. MC, V. Closed Nov–June.

El Cid's exterior suggests Castile and inside, appropriately enough, you'll find beamed ceilings, natural stone walls, heavy wrought-iron chandeliers, and leather chairs. The same theme is carried out in the rear dining room and in the pleasantly furnished bedrooms. Breakfast is the only meal served. The hotel has a top-floor swimming pool and solarium. El Cid lies off the Passeig de Vilanova in the center of town.

$ **Hotel Romàntic de Sitges.** Carrer de Sant Isidre, 33, 08870 Sitges. ☎ **93/894-83-75.** Fax 93/894-81-67. 55 rms. TEL. 9,000–11,600 ptas. ($72–$92.80) double. Rates include breakfast. MC, V. Closed Nov–Mar 15.

Made up of three beautifully restored 19th-century villas, this hotel lies only a short walk from both the beach and the train station. The romantic bar is an international rendezvous, and the public rooms are filled with artworks. You can have breakfast either in the dining room or in the garden filled with mulberry trees. Overflow guests are housed in a nearby annex, the Hotel de la Renaixença.

Hotel Subur. Passeig de la Ribera, s/n, 08870 Sitges. ☎ **93/894-00-66.** Fax 93/894-69-86. 96 rms. A/C MINIBAR TV TEL. 9,750–12,250 ptas. ($78–$98) double. Rates include breakfast. AE, DC, MC, V. Parking 1,000 ptas. ($8).

The first hotel built in Sitges (in 1916), the Subur was later torn down and reconstructed in 1960 and last renovated in 1992. Today, as always, it occupies a prominent position in the center of town on the seafront. Its rooms are well furnished, with balconies opening onto the Mediterranean. The dining room, decorated with fine woods, lays a bountiful table of both regional and international dishes. The hotel remains open all year, even during the cooler months.

$ **Sitges Park Hotel.** Carrer Jesús, 16, 08870 Sitges. ☎ **93/894-02-50.** Fax 95/894-08-39. 85 rms. A/C TV TEL. 6,800–10,900 ptas. ($54.40–$87.20) double. AE, DC, MC, V. Closed Dec–Feb.

Outside, the Sitges Park has an 1880s red-brick facade. Inside, past the desk, a beautiful garden with palm trees and a swimming pool awaits. This, in fact, was once a private villa, owned by a family who made their fortune in Cuba. You'll find a good restaurant downstairs, and you can have your coffee or drinks indoors or outdoors at the café/bar, surveying the landmark Catalán tower on the premises. The hotel is about 50 yards from the bus station.

WHERE TO DINE

EXPENSIVE

El Velero. Passeig de la Ribera, 38. ☎ **93/894-20-51.** Reservations required. Main courses 1,900–3,500 ptas. ($15.20–$28); fixed-price menu 2,850 ptas. ($22.80). AE, DC, MC, V. Daily 1:30–4pm and 8:30–11:30pm. SEAFOOD.

This is one of the leading restaurants of Sitges, occupying a position along the beachfront promenade. The most desirable tables are found on the "glass greenhouse" terrace, opening onto the esplanade, although there is a more glamorous restaurant inside. Try a soup such as clam and truffle or white fish, followed by a main dish such as paella marinara (with seafood) or suprême of salmon in pine-nut sauce. The restaurant is named after a type of pleasure boat.

MODERATE

$ **Chez Jeanette.** Sant Pau, 23. ☎ **93/894-00-48.** Reservations recommended. Main courses 1,200–2,600 ptas. ($9.60–$20.80); *menú del día* 1,350–1,700 ptas. ($10.80–$13.60). AE, DC, MC, V. Thurs–Tues 1–4pm and 8–11pm. Closed Dec 20–Jan 15. CATALÁN.

A Frenchwoman, Jeanette, established her Catalán-style restaurant here in 1975. She has since died, but her culinary tradition continues. Patrons flock to a rustic atmosphere created by textured stucco walls and a regional tavern decor. Set back on a restaurant-flanked street a short walk from the beach, it draws both straight and gay clients. From the standard menu, you can order such dishes as onion soup, *rape* (monkfish) with whiskey, and entrecôte with Roquefort sauce. There are also several *platos del día* (plates of the day). The chef is proudest of his *parilla pescada,* a mixed grill of fresh fish from the Mediterranean.

$ Els 4 Gats. Sant Pau, 13. ☎ **93/894-19-15.** Reservations recommended. Main courses 2,200–3,500 ptas. ($17.60–$28); *menú del día* 1,900 ptas. ($15.20). AE, DC, MC, V. Wed–Mon 1–3:30pm and 8:30–11pm. Closed Nov–Mar. CATALÁN.

When it was established in the early 1960s as a bar and café, it adopted the name of one of Catalonia's most historic cafés, Els 4 Gats, a Barcelona hangout that had been a favorite of Picasso. By 1968 the newcomer was firmly established as one of the leading restaurants in Sitges, serving a well-received *cocina del mercado,* based on whatever was fresh and available that day in the local markets. Within a setting accented with paintings and varnished paneling, you can enjoy fresh grilled fish, garlic soup, lamb cutlets with local herbs, roast chicken in wine sauce, and veal kidneys in sherry sauce. Set on a side street near the sea, the restaurant is a few steps from the beachfront Passeig de la Ribera.

Fragata. Passeig de la Ribera, 1. ☎ **93/894-10-86.** Reservations recommended. Main dishes 975–3,200 ptas. ($7.80–$25.60). AE, DC, MC, V. Daily 1–4:30pm and 8:30–11:30pm. SEAFOOD.

Although its simple interior offers little more than well-scrubbed floors, tables with crisp napery, and air-conditioning, some of the most delectable seafood specialties in town are served here, and hundreds of loyal customers come to appreciate the fresh, authentic cuisine. Specialties include seafood soup, a mixed grill of fresh fish, codfish salad, mussels marinara, several preparations of squid and octopus, plus some flavorful meat dishes, such as grilled lamb cutlets.

Mare Nostrum. Passeig de la Ribera, 60. ☎ **93/894-33-93.** Reservations required. Main courses 1,200–2,200 ptas. ($9.60–$17.60). AE, DC, MC, V. Thurs–Tues 1–4:30pm and 8:30–11pm. Closed Dec 15–Feb 1. SEAFOOD.

This landmark restaurant was established in 1950 during the height of the Franco era and has flourished ever since. The building was constructed in the 1890s as a private home. The dining room has a waterfront view, and in warm weather tables are placed outside. The menu includes a full range of seafood dishes, among them grilled fish specialties and steamed hake with champagne. The fish soup is particularly delectable. Next door, the restaurant's café, resting under a blue beamed ceiling, serves ice cream, milk shakes, sandwiches, a selection of tapas, and three varieties of sangría, including one with champagne and fruit.

La Masía. Paseo Vilanova, 164. ☎ **93/894-10-76.** Reservations required. Main courses 950–2,400 ptas. ($7.60–$19.20); *menú del día* 1,400 ptas. ($11.20). AE, DC, MC, V. Daily 1–4pm and 8:30–11:30pm. CATALÁN.

The provincial decor complements the imaginative regional specialties for which this place has been known since 1972. They include several preparations of codfish, roast suckling lamb well seasoned with herbs, *pollo a los hijos* ("brother's chicken," a regional dish), a wide array of fresh fish and shellfish, and monkfish with aïoli—the chef's pride. Every Catalonian's favorite dessert is *crème catalán* (caramel pudding). If you prefer to dine outdoors, you can sit in the pleasant garden adjacent to the main dining room.

Oliver's. Isla de Cuba, 39. ☎ **93/894-35-16.** Reservations required. Main courses 1,100–2,200 ptas. ($8.80–$17.60). MC, V. Sat–Sun 1–4pm, Tues–Sun 8:30pm–midnight. CATALÁN/INTERNATIONAL.

On the northern fringe of the old town, directly south of the Plaça de Maristany, this angular bistro-style establishment is decorated like a regional tavern with local paintings. It makes a good choice for dinner, unless you insist on being on the beachfront esplanade, five minutes away. The wines are reasonably priced, and the seafood is excellent—look for the chef's daily specials. Also try the grilled salmon, entrecôte flavored with herbs of Provence, grilled goat cutlets, or a daily soup prepared with fresh ingredients.

SITGES AFTER DARK

One of the best ways to spend the night in Sitges is to walk the waterfront esplanade, have a leisurely dinner, then retire at about 11pm to one of the open-air cafés for a nightcap and some serious people-watching. Few local dives can compete with "the scene" taking place on the streets.

If you're straight, you'll have to hunt to find a bar that isn't gay. There are so many gay bars, in fact, that a map is distributed pinpointing their locales. Nine of them are concentrated on Sant Bonaventura in the center of town, a five-minute walk from the beach (near the Museu Romàntic). If you grow bored with the action in one place, you just have to walk down the street to find another. Drink prices run about the same in all the clubs.

Mediterráneo. Sant Bonaventura, 6. No phone.

This leading—also the largest—gay disco and bar in Sitges has a formal Iberian garden and sleek modern styling. And upstairs in this restored 1690s house just east of the **Plaça d'Espanya,** there are pool tables and a covered terrace. The club, which on a summer night can be filled to overflowing, is open only from May through October, Monday through Thursday, from 10pm to 3am, until 3:30am Friday and Saturday.

Ricky's Disco. Sant Pau, 25. ☎ **93/894-96-81.** Cover 1,100 ptas. ($8.80).

This is one of the resort's most popular and crowded discos, catering to a mix of gay and straight clients. In business since the 1970s, it is set back from the beach on a narrow street noted for its inexpensive restaurants and folkloric color. The music inside is recorded, and the crowd reflects the international origins of many clients at this resort. The place is open every night from midnight to 6am. It's closed in November.

Girona & the Costa Brava

15

The Costa Brava (Wild Coast) is a 95-mile (153km) stretch of coastline—the northernmost Mediterranean seafront in Spain—that begins north of Barcelona at Blanes and stretches toward the French border. Visit this area in May, June, September, or October and avoid July and August, when tour groups from northern Europe book virtually all the hotel rooms.

Undiscovered little fishing villages along the coast long ago bloomed into resort towns. Tossa de Mar is the most delightful of these. Lloret de Mar is also immensely popular but too commercial for many tastes. The most unspoiled spot is remote Cadaqués. Some of the smaller villages also make excellent stops.

If you want to visit the Costa Brava but simply cannot secure a room in high season, consider taking a day trip by car from Barcelona or booking one of the daily organized tours that leave from that city. Allow plenty of time for driving. In summer the traffic jams can be fierce, and the roads between towns difficult and winding.

If you visit the coast in summer without a hotel reservation, you'll stand a fair chance of getting a room in Girona, the capital of the province and one of the most interesting medieval cities in Spain.

EXPLORING THE REGION BY CAR

Day 1 Drive north from Barcelona, stopping at the coastal resort of either Lloret de Mar or Tossa de Mar for a two-day stay at the beach.

Day 2 While based in Tossa or Lloret, explore the environs if you have a car, or stay and enjoy the joie de vivre of these fun-loving towns. If you're staying at Lloret, go to Tossa to explore its old quarter.

Day 3 Leave Tossa or Lloret and continue to drive along the coast to Figueres to see the Dalí Museum, one of the most popular attractions in Spain. Stay overnight in the gourmet citadel of Figueres, or drive over to Cadaqués on the far eastern coast, where Dalí used to live, and spend the night there.

Day 4 Drive south again on the N-11 or the A-17 to the provincial capital of Girona. See what you can before nightfall, and the following morning take a walk through the monumental district.

Day 5 Return to Barcelona.

1 Girona

60 miles (97km) NE of Barcelona, 56 miles (90km) S of the French city of Perpignan

Split by the Onyar River, this sleepy medieval city attracts crowds of tourists darting inland from the Costa Brava for the day.

One of the most important historical sites in Spain, Girona was founded by the Romans. Later, it was a Moorish stronghold. Later still, it reputedly withstood three invasions by Napoleon's troops (1809). For that and other past sieges, Girona is often called "The City of a Thousand Sieges."

For orientation purposes, go to the ancient stone footbridge across the Onyar. From there, you'll have the finest view. Bring good walking shoes, as the only way to discover the particular charm of this medieval city is on foot. You can wander for hours through the **Call,** the labyrinthine old quarter, with its narrow, steep alleyways and lanes and its ancient stone houses, which form a rampart chain along the Onyar. Much of Girona can be appreciated from the outside, but it does contain some important attractions you'll want to see on the inside.

GETTING THERE **By Train** More than 30 trains per day run between Girona and Barcelona from 6:08am to 9:26pm, including two TALGOS. Trip time is 1 to 1½ hours, depending on the train. Trains arrive in Girona at the Plaça Espanya (☎ **972/20-70-93** for information).

By Bus From the Costa Brava, you can take one of the SARFA buses (☎ **972/20-17-96** in Girona) to Girona. Three per day depart from Tossa de Mar (see below). Fills de Rafael Mas (☎ **972/21-32-27** in Girona), another bus company, makes four runs per day between Girona and Lloret de Mar. Barcelona Bus (☎ **972/20-24-32** in Girona) also operates express buses between Girona and Barcelona at the rate of 6 to 13 per day, depending on the season and demand.

By Car From Barcelona or the French border, connect with the main north-south route (A-7), taking the turnoff to Girona. From Barcelona, take the A-2 north to reach the A-7.

VISITOR INFORMATION The tourist information office is at **Rambla de la Libertat** (☎ **972/22-65-75**). Open Monday through Friday from 8am to 8pm, Saturday from 8am to 2pm and 4 to 8pm, Sunday from 9am to 2pm.

EXPLORING THE MEDIEVAL CITY

Catedral. Plaça de la Catedral. ☎ **972/21-44-26.** Free admission to cathedral; cloister and museum 300 ptas. ($2.40). Cathedral, daily 9am–1pm and during cloister and museum visiting hours; cloister and museum, July–Sept, Tues–Sat 10am–8pm, Sun 10am–2pm; Oct–Dec and Feb, Tues–Sat 10am–2pm and 4–6pm, Sun 10am–2pm; Mar–June, Tues–Sat 10am–2pm and 4–7pm, Sun 10am–2pm. Closed Jan.

The major attraction of Girona is its magnificent cathedral, reached by climbing a 17th-century baroque staircase of 90 steep steps. The 14th-century cathedral represents many architectural styles, including Gothic and Romanesque, but it is most notably Catalán baroque. The facade that you see as you climb those long stairs dates from the 17th and 18th centuries; from a cornice atop it, there rises a bell tower crowned by a dome with a bronze angel weathervane. Enter the main door of the cathedral and go into the nave, which, at 75 feet, is the broadest in the world of Gothic architecture.

The cathedral contains many works of art, displayed for the most part in its museum. Its prize exhibit is a tapestry of the Creation, a unique piece of 11th- or 12th-century Romanesque embroidery depicting humans and animals in the Garden

Girona & the Costa Brava

The Jews of Girona

The Jews form part of Girona's cultural heritage. From 890 to 1492, they were a strong community in the city. It is believed that early settlers from Jerusalem formed the nucleus of the first colony. They were forced to live ghetto style in the Call, their early settlements grouped around the Plaça dels Apòstols.

In the Middle Ages, the Jewish community of Girona achieved considerable importance. It was here that the most important Cabala school in western Europe was developed in the 13th century, largely under the guidance of Rabbi Mossé ben Bahman, or Ramban, its best-known representative.

In 1492, the year Columbus landed in America, his patrons, Ferdinand and Isabella, expelled all Jews from Spain, thus ending this once-flourishing colony.

The Bonastruc ça Porta Center, Calle Sant Llorenç (☎ **972/21-67-61**), will soon open a Catalán Museum of Jewish Culture and the Nahmanides Institute for Jewish Studies, on the site where the 15th-century synagogue was located. Meanwhile, it houses temporary exhibitions relating to Jewish history and art. It is open April through October, Monday through Saturday from 10am to 9pm and on Sunday from 10am to 2pm. In winter, the hours are daily from 10am to 6pm.

The Municipal Archives house an important collection of fragments of Jewish manuscripts dating from the 13th and 14th centuries. The Archaeological Museum contains more than 20 medieval gravestones and Hebrew inscriptions, found in the old Jewish cemetery.

Since 1995, Girona has held the status of secretary of the Red de Juderías 9 de España, a network of towns and cities within Spain whose common aim is to foster awareness of Jewish culture in the community.

of Eden. The other major work displayed is one of the world's rarest manuscripts—the 10th-century *Códex del Beatus,* which contains an illustrated commentary on the Book of the Apocalypse.

From the cathedral's Chapel of Hope a door leads to a Romanesque cloister from the 12th and 13th centuries, with an unusual trapezoidal layout. The cloister gallery, with a double colonnade, has a series of biblical scenes that are the prize jewel of western Catalán Romanesque art. From the cloister you can view the 12th-century Torre de Carlemany (Charlemagne's Tower).

Museu d'Art. Pujada de la Catedral, 12. ☎ **972/20-95-36.** Admission 200 ptas. ($1.60) adults; free for students, adults over 65, and children; free on Sun and holidays. Mar–Sept, Tues–Sat 10am–7pm, Sun 10am–2pm; Oct–Feb, Tues–Sat 10am–6pm, Sun 10am–2pm.

Located in a former Romanesque and Gothic episcopal palace (Palau Episcopal) next to the cathedral, this museum displays artworks spanning 10 centuries (once housed in the old Diocesan Museum and the Provincial Museum). Stop in the throne room to view the altarpiece of Sant Pere of Púbol by Bernat Martorell and that of Sant Miguel de Crüilles by Lluís Borrassa. Both of these works, from the 15th century, are exemplary pieces of Catalán Gothic painting. The museum is also proud of its altar stone of Sant Pere de Roda, which dates from the 10th and 11th centuries; this work in wood and stone, depicting figures and legends, was once covered in embossed silver. The 12th-century *Crüilles Timber* is a unique piece of Romanesque polychrome wood. *Our Lady of Besalù,* from the 15th century, is one of the best Virgins carved in alabaster.

Banys Arabs. Carrer Ferran el Catòlic. ☎ **972/21-32-62.** Admission 100 ptas. (80¢). Apr–Sept, Mon–Sat 10am–7pm, Sun 10am–2pm; Oct–Mar, daily 10am–2pm. Closed Jan 1, Jan 6, Easter, and Dec 25–26.

In the old quarter of the city are the 12th-century Arab baths, an example of Romanesque civic architecture. Visit the *caldarium* (hot bath), with its paved floor, and the *frigidarium* (cold bath), with its central octagonal pool surrounded by pillars that support a prismlike structure in the overhead window. The Moorish baths were heavily restored in 1929, but they give you an idea of what the old ones were like.

Museu Arqueològic. Sant Pere de Galligants, Santa Llúcia, 1. ☎ **972/20-26-32.** Admission 125 ptas. ($1). Tues–Sat 10am–1pm and 4:30–7pm, Sun 10am–1pm.

Housed in a Romanesque church and cloister from the 11th and 12th centuries, this museum illustrates the history of the country from the Paleolithic to the Visigothic period, using artifacts discovered in nearby excavations. The monastery itself ranks as one of the best examples of Catalán Romanesque architecture. In the cloister, note some Hebrew inscriptions from gravestones of the old Jewish cemetery.

Museu d'História de la Ciutat. Carrer de la Força. ☎ **972/22-22-29.** Free admission. Tues–Sat 10am–2pm and 5–7pm, Sun 10am–2pm.

Housed in the old 18th-century Capuchin Convent de Sant Antoni, this collection dates from the time of Puig d'en Roca (Catalonia's oldest prehistoric site) to the present. It includes Girona's (and Spain's) first electric streetlights. Additional displays of tools, technical materials, and the accoutrements of passing lifestyles make up a kind of municipal résumé. From the original Capuchin convent there remains the cemetery used for drying corpses before mumifying them (one of the three of this type left in the world).

Església de Sant Feliu. Pujada de Sant Feliu. ☎ **972/20-14-07.** Free admission. Daily 8am–8pm.

This 14th- to 17th-century church was built over what may have been the tomb of Feliu of Africa, martyred during Diocletian's persecution at the beginning of the 4th century. Important in the architectural history of Catalonia, the church has pillars and arches in the Romanesque style and a Gothic central nave. The bell tower, one of the Girona skyline's most characteristic features, has eight pinnacles and one central tower, each supported on a solid octagonal base. The main facade of the church is baroque. The interior contains some exceptional works, including a high altarpiece from the 16th century and an alabaster *Reclining Christo* from the 14th century. Notice the eight pagan and Christian sarcophagi set in the walls of the presbytery, the two oldest of which are from the 2nd century A.D. One shows Pluto carrying Persephone off to the depths of the earth.

WHERE TO STAY

MODERATE

Costabella. Avenida de Francia, 61, 17007 Girona. ☎ **972/20-25-24.** Fax 972/20-22-03. 46 rms. A/C MINIBAR TV TEL. 11,850 ptas. ($94.80) double. AE, DC, MC, V. Parking 975 ptas. ($7.80).

Built in the 1960s, and renovated in 1989, this hotel lies about 2 miles (3km) north of Girona's center, beside the N-11 highway leading to Figueres, near the town's largest hospital. Bedrooms are comfortable, outfitted in pastel colors, and conservatively modern. The in-house restaurant serves fixed-price meals, and breakfast is a generous buffet.

Hotel Sol Girona. Carrer Barcelona 112, 17003 Girona. ☎ **800/336-3542** in the U.S., or 972/24-32-32. Fax 972/24-32-33. 114 rms, 1 suite. A/C MINIBAR TV TEL. 12,900 ptas. ($103.20) double; 19,500 ptas. ($156) suite. AE, DC, MC, V. Parking 990 ptas. ($7.90).

Set a short drive southwest of Girona's historic center, in an industrial and commercial neighborhood with heavy traffic, this member of the widely known Sol chain is the most prestigious hotel in town, a position it has maintained since it opened in 1989. A favorite of both businesspeople and visiting art lovers, it offers calm, quiet, and tastefully comfortable accommodations, many with king-size beds and all with elegant bathrooms amply stocked with toiletries.

The hotel lies immediately adjacent to one of Girona's largest shopping malls, which provides lots of diversions. An in-house restaurant serves international and continental cuisine, and there is an adjacent bar. Services include a concierge, laundry, babysitting, and 24-hour room service.

Hotel Ultonia. Avinguda Jaume I, 22, 17001 Girona. ☎ **972/20-38-50.** Fax 972/20-33-34. 45 rms. A/C MINIBAR TV TEL. 9,500–11,000 ptas. ($76–$88) double. AE, DC, MC, V. Parking 800 ptas. ($6.40) nearby.

A three-star hotel just a short walk from the Plaça de la Independència, the Ultonia was restored in 1993 and is now better than ever. Ever since the late 1950s it has been a favorite with business travelers, but today it attracts more tourists, as it lies close to the historical district. Bedrooms are compact and furnished in modern style; double-glazed windows keep out the noise. Some of the rooms opening onto the avenue have tiny balconies. In just 8 to 12 minutes, you can cross the Onyar into the medieval quarter. Guests enjoy a breakfast buffet in the morning, but no other meals are served.

Novotel Girona. Carretera del Aeropuerto, 17457 Riudellots de la Selva (Girona). ☎ **800/221-4542** in the U.S., or 972/47-71-00. Fax 972/47-72-96. 79 rms, 2 suites. A/C TV TEL. 11,800–12,600 ptas. ($94.40–$100.80) double; 16,000 ptas. ($128) suite. Children under 16 free in parents' room. AE, DC, MC, V. Free parking. Take exit 8 from the A-7 motorway, signposted a few miles west of the Girona city center.

Low-slung and modern and set within a sunny, tree-dotted park, this member of the French-based chain offers some of the most consistently reliable accommodations and best values in the region. Located beside the A-7 motorway, just south of the Girona airport and a short drive west of the city center, Novotel Girona offers comfortable and efficient bedrooms with soundproofed windows, large writing tables, and a simple modern decor much appreciated by both families and businesspeople.

The clean and modern restaurant Le Grill serves à la carte meals daily from 6am to midnight. There's also a bar. Room service is offered from 6am to midnight daily, plus there's a concierge and laundry service. Car rentals can be arranged at the hotel, and guests enjoy the outdoor pool set within a garden and the tennis court.

INEXPENSIVE

Condal. Joan Maragall, 10, 17002 Girona. ☎ and fax **972/20-44-62.** 38 rms. 5,300 ptas. ($42.40) double. V.

Located near the rail and bus stations west of the old town, this third-class 1960s hotel is, in the words of one frequent visitor, "aggressively simple." As such, it's recommended to bargain hunters only. The lounge and reception area are small; there is no service elevator; and no meals (not even breakfast) are served—but these are minor concerns. The bedrooms are clean and functional, and some of them open onto pleasant views.

Hotel Peninsular. Carrer Nou, 3, 17001 Girona. ☎ **972/20-38-00.** Fax 972/21-04-92. 60 rms. TEL. 5,600 ptas. ($44.80) double. AE, DC, MC, V. Parking 800 ptas. ($6.40) nearby.

Devoid of any significant architectural character, this one-star hotel provides clean but uncontroversial accommodations in a location near the cathedral and the river. Bedrooms, which benefited from a 1990 renovation, are scattered over five different floors. The hotel is better for short-term stopovers than for prolonged stays. No meals other than breakfast are served, but 24-hour room service is available.

A Nearby Place to Stay

✪ **Hostal de la Gavina.** Plaça de la Rosaleda, 17248 S'Agaro (Girona). ☎ **972/32-11-00.** Fax 972/32-15-73. 64 rms, 10 suites. A/C MINIBAR TV TEL. 21,000–38,000 ptas. ($168–$304) double; 32,000–95,000 ptas. ($256–$760) suite. AE, DC, MC, V. Closed Nov–Apr. Parking 1,600 ptas. ($12.80) garage, free outside.

Since it was established in the early 1980s, the Hostal de la Gavina has attracted some of the most glamorous people in the world, including King Juan Carlos I, Elizabeth Taylor, and a host of celebrities from northern Europe. It lies on a peninsula jutting seaward from the center of S'Agaro, within a thick-walled Iberian villa that was originally built as the private home of the Ansesa family (the owners of the hotel) in 1932. The public rooms, the main restaurant, and most of the accommodations are contained within the resort's main building, which has been much enlarged and modified since its original construction. Many of the paneled public rooms are enclaves of taste and style. A large and very modern swimming pool is a short walk away, above the town's public beach. Adjacent to the pool is a beach house, containing a Jacuzzi, a handful of boutiques, and a daytime restaurant.

Dining/Entertainment: The daytime restaurant is Las Conchas, which serves fresh salads, brochettes, and light platters beside the pool. More formal evening meals are served in the main building, in the Candlelight Restaurant, which features well-prepared international specialties and an outdoor patio. There are also two bars.

Services: 24-hour room service, hairdresser, massage, laundry/valet, concierge.

Facilities: Two tennis courts, paddle tennis courts, two bars, masses of well-tended gardens, Jacuzzi, swimming pool.

Where to Dine

$ **Bronsoms.** Sant Francesc, 7. ☎ **972/21-24-93.** Reservations recommended. Main courses 850–1,850 ptas. ($6.80–$14.80); fixed-price menu 900 ptas. ($7.20). AE, MC, V. Tues–Sun 1–4pm and 8–11:30pm. CATALÁN.

Set in the heart of the old town, within an 1890s building that was originally a private home, this restaurant is one of the most consistently reliable in Girona. The subject of recent praise from newspapers as far away as Madrid, it has been under its present management since 1982, perfecting the art of serving a Catalán-based *cocina del mercado*—that is, cooking with whatever market-fresh ingredients are available each day. The frequently ordered house specialties include paella, *arroz negre* ("black rice," tinted with squid ink and studded with shellfish), filet of beef served with your choice of either pepper sauce or Roquefort sauce, and several preparations of Iberian ham.

2 Lloret de Mar

62 miles (100km) S of the French border, 42 miles (68km) N of Barcelona

Although it has a good half-moon-shaped sandy beach, Lloret is neither chic nor sophisticated, and most of the people who come here are low-income Europeans. The competition for cheap rooms is fierce.

Lloret de Mar has grown at a phenomenal rate from a small fishing village with just a few hotels to a bustling resort with more hotels than anyone could count. And more keep opening up, although there are never enough in July and August. The accommodations are typical of those in the Costa Brava towns, running the gamut from impersonal modern box-type structures to vintage whitewashed, flowerpot-adorned buildings on the narrow streets of the old town. There are even a few pockets of posh, including the Hotel Roger de Flor (see below). The area has rich vegetation, attractive scenery, and a mild climate.

GETTING THERE **By Train & Bus** From Barcelona, take a train to Blanes, then take a bus five miles (8km) to Lloret.

By Car Head north from Barcelona along the A-19.

VISITOR INFORMATION The tourist information office is at Plaça de la Vila, 1 (☎ **972/36-47-35**). Open daily from 9am to 1pm and 4 to 8pm.

WHERE TO STAY

Many of the hotels—particularly the three-star establishments—are booked solidly by tour groups. Here are some possibilities if you reserve in advance.

Hotel Excelsior. Passeig Mossèn Jacinto Verdaguer, 16, 17310 Lloret de Mar. ☎ **972/36-61-76.** Fax 972/37-16-54. 45 rms. TEL. July–Sept (including obligatory half board), 7,250 ptas. ($58) per person; Oct–June, 6,100 ptas. ($48.80) double. AE, DC, MC, V. Closed Oct 31–Mar 20. Parking 1,000 ptas. ($8).

This well-managed three-star hotel attracts a beach-oriented clientele from Spain and northern Europe, many of whom have returned every summer since the hotel opened in 1978. The Excelsior sits almost directly on the beach, rising six floors above the esplanade, and contains an elevator. All but a handful of bedrooms offer either full-frontal or lateral views of the sea, and some have TVs. The furniture is modern and uninspiring, but Mediterranean food in the dining room is well prepared, and clients seem generally content with the services provided. During midsummer, half board is obligatory.

Hotel Marsol. Passeig Jacint Verdaguer, 7, 17310 Lloret de Mar. ☎ **972/36-57-54.** Fax 972/37-22-05. 100 rms. A/C MINIBAR TV TEL. 7,000–11,600 ptas. ($56–$92.80) double. Rates include breakfast. AE, DC, MC, V.

Completely refurbished and vastly improved in 1992, this medium-size hotel opens directly onto beachfront action. Its chief drawing card is its rooftop swimming pool along with sauna and solarium. Favored by an essentially European clientele, it offers sleekly modern bedrooms, each with satellite TV, air-conditioning, radio, personal safe, soundproof windows, and minibar. Occupying the ground floor is a cafeteria serving drinks and snacks, plus a restaurant, Els Dofins, overlooking a palm-shaded plaza.

✪ **Hotel Roger de Flor.** Turó de l'Estelat, s/n, 17310 Lloret de Mar. ☎ **972/36-48-00.** Fax 972/37-16-37. 96 rms, 2 suites. TV TEL. 15,550–25,000 ptas. ($124.40–$200) double; 30,000–36,000 ptas. ($240–$288) suite. AE, DC, MC, V. Free parking.

This much-enlarged older hotel, sections of which are reminiscent of a dignified private villa, is a pleasant diversion from the aging and unimaginative slabs of concrete filling other sections of the resort. Set at the eastern edge of town, within its own verdant park and garden (whose only access is from the Carretera de Tossa, a busy inland boulevard), it offers some of the most pleasant and panoramic views of any hotel in town. Potted geraniums, climbing masses of bougainvillea, and evenly spaced rows of palms add elegance to the combinations of new and old architecture. Bedrooms are high-ceilinged, modern, and simple yet comfortable. The public rooms contain plenty of exposed wood and spill out onto a partially covered terrace, which functions as a centerpiece for the dining and drinking facilities.

Dining/Entertainment: The modern and panoramic L'Estelat restaurant, near an airy and comfortable bar, serves international food.

Services: Room service (offered from 8am to 10:30pm), laundry, concierge, babysitting.

Facilities: Car rentals, simple shopping boutique, outdoor swimming pool filled with pumped-in seawater set within the garden, tennis courts, billiard room, and a card lounge.

✪ **Hotel Santa Marta.** Playa de Santa Cristina, 17310 Lloret de Mar. ☎ **972/36-49-04.** Fax 972/36-92-80. 76 rms, 2 suites. TEL. 13,000–31,000 ptas. ($104–$248) double; 21,000–44,000 ptas. ($168–$352) suite. Full board 17,000–26,000 ptas. ($136–$208) per person. AE, DC, MC, V. Closed Dec 23–Jan 31.

This tranquil hotel is a short walk above a crescent-shaped bay favored by swimmers, nestled amid a sun-flooded grove of pines. Most rooms offer private balconies overlooking either the sea or a pleasant garden, and about two-thirds contain minibars, TVs, and air-conditioning. Both the public rooms and the bedrooms are attractively paneled and filled with traditional furniture. The hotel lies in a quiet but desirable seaside neighborhood, about 1 1/2 miles (2km) west of the commercial center of town.

Dining/Entertainment: The Restaurante Santa Marta is recommended separately below. An airy bar is nearby.

Services: Laundry/valet, concierge, babysitting.

Facilities: Car-rental kiosk, solarium.

Xaine Hotel. Vila, 55, 17310 Lloret de Mar. ☎ **972/36-50-08.** Fax 972/37-11-68. 165 rms. June–Sept (including obligatory half board), 6,500–8,500 ptas. ($52–$68) double; off-season, 3,500 ptas. ($28) double. AE, DC, MC, V. Closed Nov–Apr.

Larger than you might think from a quick glance, this hotel was opened in 1959 within the noisy and congested center of town, about two blocks inland from the beach. Many of its simple but clean bedrooms contain balconies overlooking the commercial center of Lloret. Rooms show a lot of wear and tear, but the place is still heavily booked because of its low prices. Facilities include an outdoor swimming pool, a sauna, a solarium, and a cafeteria. Laundry service is available.

WHERE TO DINE

Restaurante Santa Marta. In the Hotel Santa Marta, Playa de Santa Cristina. ☎ **972/36-49-04.** Reservations recommended. Main courses 1,900–2,600 ptas. ($15.20–$20.80); fixed-price menu 5,775 ptas. ($46.20). AE, DC, MC, V. Daily 1:30–3:30pm and 8:30–10:30pm. Closed Dec 23–Jan 31. INTERNATIONAL/CATALÁN.

Set within a previously recommended hotel lying about 1 1/2 miles (2km) west of the commercial center of town, this pleasantly sunny enclave offers a sweeping view of the beaches and the sea—and well-prepared food. Menu specialties vary with the seasons but might include pâté of wild mushrooms in a special sauce, smoked salmon with hollandaise on toast, medallions of monkfish served with a mousseline of garlic, a ragoût of giant shrimp with broad beans, a filet of beef Stroganoff, and a regionally inspired cassolette of chicken prepared with cloves.

Ⓢ **El Trull.** Cala Canyelles, s/n. ☎ **972/36-49-28.** Main courses 1,150–3,300 ptas. ($9.20–$26.40); fixed-price menus 1,550–3,950 ptas. ($12.40–$31.60). AE, DC, MC, V. Daily 1–4pm and 8pm–midnight. SEAFOOD.

Since its establishment in 1975, this restaurant has attracted hordes of Spanish clients, who appreciate the two-mile (3km) trek north of Lloret into the nearby hills.

Set in the modern suburb of Urbanización Playa Canyelles, El Trull positions its tables within view of a well-kept garden and a (sometimes crowded) swimming pool. The food is some of the best in the neighborhood. Menu items focus on seafood, prepared in the Catalán style, and include fish soup; a fish stew heavily laced with lobster; many variations of hake, monkfish, and clams; and an omelet "surprise." (The waiter will tell you the ingredients if you ask.)

LLORET DE MAR AFTER DARK

Casino Lloret de Mar. Calle Esports, 1. ☎ **972/36-65-12.** Admission 550 ptas. ($4.40).

Games of chance include French and American roulette, blackjack, and chemin de fer, among others. There is a restaurant, buffet dining room, bar-boîte, and dance club, along with a swimming pool. Drinks cost around 750 pesetas ($6). Bring your passport. The casino lies southwest of Lloret de Mar, beside the coastal road leading to Blanes and Barcelona. Drive or take a taxi at night. Hours are Monday through Friday from 5pm to 4am and Saturday and Sunday from 5pm to 4:30am.

Hollywood. Calle Esports, 5. ☎ **972/36-74-63.**

This dance club at the edge of town is the place to be and be seen. Look for it on the corner of Carrer Girona. It's open nightly from 10pm to 5am, and drinks cost 700 peseas ($5.60).

3 Tossa de Mar

56 miles (90km) N of Barcelona, 7½ miles (12km) NE of Lloret de Mar

This gleaming white town, with its 12th-century walls and labyrinthine old quarter, fishing boats, and fairly good sands, is the most attractive base for a Costa Brava vacation. It seems to have more joie de vivre than its competitors. The battlements and towers of Tossa were featured in the 1951 Ava Gardner and James Mason movie *Pandora and the Flying Dutchman,* which is still sometimes shown on late-night television.

In the 18th and 19th centuries Tossa survived as a port center, growing rich on the cork industry. But that declined in the 20th century, and many of its citizens emigrated to America. Yet in the 1950s, thanks in part to the Ava Gardner movie, tourists began to discover the charms of Tossa and a new industry was born.

To experience these charms, walk through the 12th-century walled town, known as **Vila Vella,** built on the site of a Roman villa from the 1st century A.D. Enter through the Torre de les Hores.

Tossa was once a secret haunt for artists and writers—Marc Chagall called it a blue paradise. It has two main beaches, **Mar Gran** and **La Bauma.** The coast near Tossa—north and south—offers even more possibilities.

As one of few resorts to have withstood exploitation and retained most of its allure, Tossa enjoys a broad base of international visitors—so many, in fact, that it can no longer shelter them all. In spring and fall, finding a room may be a snap, but in summer it's next to impossible unless reservations are made far in advance.

GETTING THERE **By Bus** Direct bus service is offered from Blanes and Lloret. Tossa de Mar is also on the main Barcelona-Palafruggel route. Service from Barcelona is daily from 7:40am to 7:10pm, taking 1½ hours. For information call **972/36-42-36** or **972/34-09-03.**

By Car Head north from Barcelona along the A-19.

VISITOR INFORMATION The tourist information office is at Avinguda El Pelegrí, 25 (☎ **972/34-01-08**). Open April through October, Monday through Saturday from 9am to 9pm, Sunday 10am to 1pm; off-season, Monday through Friday from 10am to 1pm and 4 to 7pm, Saturday from 10am to 1pm.

WHERE TO STAY

VERY EXPENSIVE

Grand Hotel Reymar. Platja de Mar Menuda, 17320 Tossa de Mar. ☎ **972/34-03-12.** Fax 972/34-15-04. 148 rms, 18 suites. A/C MINIBAR TV TEL. 22,600–24,600 ptas. ($180.80–$196.80) double; 17,000 ptas. ($136) per person in suite. AE, DC, MC, V. Closed Nov–Apr. Parking 1,000 ptas. ($8).

A triumph of engineering because of its unusual position on a jagged rock above the edge of the sea, this gracefully contoured building was constructed in the 1960s and renovated in the early 1990s. Located a 10-minute walk southeast of the historic walls of the old town, the Reymar offers several levels of expansive terraces ideal for sunbathing away from the crowds below, plus a wide variety of indoor/outdoor dining and drinking areas. Each of these has big windows, expansive views, and a clientele devoted to relaxing in the streaming Iberian sunlight. Each bedroom has a balcony, a sea view, a safety-deposit box, a TV with satellite reception, a marble-covered bathroom, and a combination of modern wood-grained and painted furniture.

Dining/Entertainment: The hotel contains four restaurants (one open in midsummer only) and at least four bars scattered amid the terraces and beachfronts. There's also a dance club.

Services: 24-hour room service, laundry/valet, concierge, babysitting.

Facilities: Outdoor swimming pool, Jacuzzi, solarium, car rentals, children's playground, tennis courts.

EXPENSIVE

Mar Menuda. Platja de Mar Menuda, 17320 Tossa de Mar. ☎ **800/528-1234** or 972/34-10-00. Fax 972/34-00-87. 50 rms. 11,000 ptas. ($88) double. AE, DC, MC, V. Closed Jan 8–Mar 1. Parking 1,000 ptas. ($8) garage, free on street.

This rustically decorated Mediterranean-style hotel offers a pool, tennis courts, a garden, and a big parking lot. A restaurant serves competently prepared meals. Rooms are pleasant and comfortably furnished, all with private baths and 10 with air-conditioning, minibars, TVs, and phones (naturally these are booked first).

MODERATE

$ **Hotel Avenida.** Avinguda de La Palma, 5, 17320 Tossa de Mar. ☎ **972/34-07-56.** Fax 972/34-22-70. 50 rms. 5,600–9,000 ptas. ($44.80–$72) double. Rates include breakfast. AE, MC, V. Closed Nov–Easter.

This pleasant, well-maintained four-story hotel, located near the village church, about one block from the beach, is one of the best values in town. The lobby level contains a sunny dining room and a modern bar. The comfortable but very functionally furnished bedrooms, all doubles, have private terraces.

Hotel Diana. Plaza de España, 6, 17320 Tossa de Mar. ☎ **972/34-18-86.** Fax 972/34-11-03. 21 rms. 6,050–9,350 ptas. ($48.40–$74.80) double. AE, DC, MC, V. Closed Nov–Apr.

Set back from the esplanade, this two-star hotel is a former villa designed in part by students of Gaudí. It boasts the most elegant fireplace on the Costa Brava. The inner patio—with its towering palms, vines and flowers, and fountains—is almost as popular with guests as the sandy "frontyard" beach. The spacious rooms contain fine traditional furnishings; many open onto private balconies.

Hotel Vora la Mar. Avinguda de La Palma, 14, 17320 Tossa de Mar. ☎ **972/34-03-54.** Fax 972/34-11-03. 60 rms. TEL. 6,050–9,000 ptas. ($48.40–$72) double. AE, DC, MC, V. Closed Nov–Apr. Free parking 5 minutes from hotel.

Located on a quiet street a block away from the beach, this hotel was built in the 1950s and renovated in the 1970s. It has an outdoor café, a garden, and a dining room. The terrazzo-floored bedrooms are comfortable, many with balconies, but the furnishings are a little tired.

INEXPENSIVE

Hotel Cap d'Or. Passeig de Vila Vella, 1, 17320 Tossa de Mar. ☎ **972/34-00-81.** 11 rms. 5,600–7,200 ptas. ($44.80–$57.60) double. MC, V. Closed Nov–Mar.

Perched on the waterfront on a quiet edge of town, this 1790s building, originally a fish store, nestles against the stone walls and towers of the village castle. Built of rugged stone itself, the Cap d'Or is like an old country inn and seaside hotel combined. It is both neat and well-run. The Old World dining room, with its ceiling beams and ladder-back chairs, has a pleasant sea view. Although the hotel is a bed-and-breakfast, it does have a tearoom, offering sandwiches, ice cream, milkshakes, sangría, and coffee daily from 9am to midnight.

Hotel Neptuno. La Guardia, 52, 17320 Tossa de Mar. ☎ **972/34-01-43.** Fax 972/34-19-33. 126 rms. June–Sept (including half board), 8,600 ptas. ($68.80) double; off-season (including breakfast), 5,500 ptas. ($44) double. AE, DC, MC, V. Closed Oct–Apr.

The popular Neptuno sits on a quiet residential hillside northwest of Vila Vella, somewhat removed from the seaside promenade and the bustle of Tossa de Mar's inner core. The hotel, originally built in the 1960s, was renovated and enlarged in the late 1980s. Inside, antiques are mixed with modern furniture, creating a personalized decor; the beamed-ceiling dining room is charming, and the bedrooms are tastefully lighthearted, modern, and sunny. A small swimming pool with its own terraced garden has a view of the sloping forest next door. This place is a longtime favorite with northern Europeans, who often book it solid during July and August.

Hotel Tonet. Plaça de l'Església, 1, 17320 Tossa de Mar. ☎ **972/34-02-37.** 36 rms. June–Sept (including half board), 7,500 ptas. ($60) double; off-season, 4,300–4,700 ptas. ($34.40–$37.60) double. AE, DC, MC, V. Parking 800–1,000 ptas. ($6.40–$8) nearby.

Established in the early 1960s, in the earliest days of the region's tourist boom, this simple family-run pension is one of the resort's oldest hotels. Renovated since then, it lies on a central plaza surrounded by narrow streets. It maintains the ambience of a country inn, with upper-floor terraces where guests can relax or have breakfast amid potted vines and other plants. There's a somewhat sleepy bar on the premises where tapas and snacks are served, and a simple dining room for clients taking half board. Bedrooms are rustically simple, with wooden headboards and furniture. Tonet maintains its own brand of well-entrenched Iberian charm.

WHERE TO DINE

Bahía. Passeig del Mar, 19. ☎ **972/34-03-22.** Reservations recommended. Main courses 950–2,500 ptas. ($7.60–$20); *menú del día* 1,850–3,250 ptas. ($14.80–$26). AE, DC, MC, V. Daily 1–4pm and 7:30–9pm. Closed Dec 1–15. CATALÁN.

Set adjacent to the sea, Bahía is a well-known restaurant with a much-awarded chef and a history of feeding hungry vacationers that dates back to its founding in 1953. Menu favorites are for the most part based on time-honored Catalán traditions and include *simitomba* (a grilled platter of fish), baked monkfish, and an array of grilled fish—including salmonete (red mullet), dorada, and calamari—depending on what's available from local fisherfolk. (Most fish served here are caught locally.)

Can Tonet. Plaça de l'Església, 2. ☎ **972/34-05-11.** Main courses 1,000–3,200 ptas. ($8–$25.60); *menú del día* 1,550 ptas. ($12.40). AE, DC, MC, V. Daily 12:30–4pm and 8–11:30pm. CATALÁN.

Perched beside one of the most secluded, charming squares of the old town, this restaurant occupies what was originally built in the 1600s as a dormitory for local field hands. Established in 1979, Can Tonet has been one of the best-value and most-popular restaurants in Tossa de Mar ever since, known for its Catalán cuisine and fresh seafood. It has an extensive menu that includes paella, Tossa crayfish, grilled shrimp, and *zarzuela* (fish stew). At night the chef keeps the pizza oven going. Diners can eat at outside café tables or in the tavernlike dining room with its old beams and brass chandeliers.

Es Molí. Carrer Tarull, 5. ☎ **972/34-14-14.** Reservations recommended. Main courses 1,200–3,500 ptas. ($9.60–$28); fixed-price menus 2,250–4,500 ptas. ($18–$36). AE, DC, MC, V. Daily 1–3:30pm and 7:30–11:30pm. Closed Jan 15–Feb 15. CATALÁN.

The most beautiful—and the best—restaurant in Tossa is located behind the church, set in the courtyard of a stone-walled windmill built in 1856. You'll dine beneath one of three arcades, each facing a three-tiered fountain. There is also a cluster of iron tables near the garden for those who prefer the sunlight. Among the specialties are an elaborately presented platter of local grilled fish, a delightful sole amandine, fisher's cream soup, salad Es Molí (garnished with seaweed), hazelnut cream soup, hake and shrimp in garlic sauce, crayfish flambéed with Calvados, and a long list of well-chosen wines. The impeccably dressed waiters serve with a flourish.

TOSSA DE MAR AFTER DARK

In Tossa de Mar's fast-changing nightlife, there is little stability or reliability. However, one club that's been in business for a while is the **Ely Club,** Calle Bernat (☎ **972/34-00-09**). Fans from all over the Costa Brava come here to dance to up-to-date tunes. Daily hours are 10pm to 5am. In July and August, admission is 1,200 pesetas ($9.60), which includes your first drink. From September to June, admission and your first drink cost only 500 pesetas ($4). The Ely Club is in the center of town between the two local cinemas.

4 Figueres

136 miles (219km) N of Barcelona, 23 miles (37km) E of Girona

As the heart of Catalonia, Figueres once played a role in Spanish history. Philip V wed Maria Luisa of Savoy here in 1701 in the church of San Pedro, thereby paving the way for the War of the Spanish Succession. But that historical fact is relatively forgotten today: The town is better known as the birthplace of surrealist artist Salvador Dalí in 1904.

There are two reasons for visiting Figueres—one of the best restaurants in Spain and the Dalí Museum.

GETTING THERE **By Train** RENFE has hourly train service between Barcelona and Figueres. All trains between Barcelona and France stop here.

By Bus It's better and faster to take the train if you're coming from Barcelona. But if you're in Cadaqués (see below), there are five daily SARFA buses making the 45-minute trip.

By Car Figueres is a 40-minute ride from Cadaqués. Take the excellent north-south highway, the A-7, either south from the French border at La Jonquera or north from Barcelona, exiting at the major turnoff to Figueres.

The Mad, Mad World of Salvador Dalí

Salvador Dalí (1904–89) became one of the leading exponents of surrealism, depicting irrational imagery of dreams and delirium in a meticulously detailed style. Famous for his eccentricity, he was called "outrageous, talented, relentlessly self-promoting, and unfailingly quotable." At his death at age 84, he was the last survivor of the three famous *enfants terribles* of Spain (García Lorca and Luís Buñuel were the other two).

Dalí was born in Figueres, and it was here too that he died. Most of his works are in the Theater-Museum, built by the artist himself around the former theater where his first exhibition was held. Dalí was also buried in the Theater-Museum, next door to the church that witnessed both his christening and his funeral—the first and last acts of a perfectly planned scenario.

Salvador Felipe Jacinto Dalí i Domènech, the son of a highly respected notary, was born on May 11 in a house on Carrer Monturiol in Figueres. In 1922 he registered at the School of Fine Arts in Madrid and went to live at the prestigious Residencia de Estudiantes. There, his friendship with Federico García Lorca and Luís Buñuel had a more enduring effect on his artistic future than his studies at the school. As a result of his undisciplined behavior and the attitude of his father, who clashed with the Primo de Rivera dictatorship over a matter related to elections, the young Dalí spent a month in prison.

In the summer of 1929, the artist René Magritte along with the poet Paul Éluard and his wife, Gala, came to stay at Cadaqués, and their visit caused sweeping changes in Dalí's life. The young painter became enamored with Éluard's wife; he left his family and fled with Gala to Paris, where he became an enthusiastic member of the surrealist movement. Some of his most famous paintings— *The Great Masturbator, Lugubrious Game,* and *Portrait of Paul Éluard* —date back to his life at Portlligat, the small Costa Brava town where he lived and worked off and on during the 30s.

VISITOR INFORMATION The tourist information office is at the Plaça del Sol (☎ **972/50-31-55**). Open June 21 through September, Monday through Saturday from 8:30am to 8pm; October until Easter, Monday through Friday 8:30am to 3pm; and Easter until June 20, Monday through Friday 8:30am to 3pm and 4:30 to 8pm, Saturday 9am to 1pm.

SEEING THE DALÍ MUSEUM

✪ **Teatre Museu Dalí.** Plaça de Gala-Dalí, 5 ☎ **972/51-17-96.** Admission Oct–June, 700 ptas. ($5.60) adults, 400 ptas. ($3.20) students and adults over 65, free for children under 9; July–Sept, 1,000 ptas. ($8) adults, 700 ptas. ($5.60) students and adults over 65, free for children under 9. July–Sept, Tues–Sun 9am–8pm; Oct–June, Tues–Sun 10:30am–6pm. Visits available various nights in July and Aug; call for information.

The internationally known Dalí was as famous for his surrealist and often erotic imagery as he was for his flamboyance and exhibitionism. At the Figueres museum, located in the center of town beside the Rambla, you'll find his paintings, watercolors, gouaches, charcoals, and pastels, along with graphics and sculptures, many rendered with seductive and meticulously detailed imagery. His wide-ranging subject matter encompassed such repulsive issues as putrefaction and castration. You'll see, for instance, *The Happy Horse,* a grotesque and lurid purple beast that the artist painted during one of his long exiles at Port Lligat. A tour of the museum is an experience.

Following Dalí's break with the tenets of the surrealist movement, his work underwent a radical change, with a return to classicism and what he called his mystical and nuclear phase. He became one of the most fashionable painters in the United States, and the surrealist poet André Breton baptized him with the anagram "Avida Dollars." Dalí wrote a partly fictitious autobiography entitled *The Secret Life of Salvador Dalí* and *Hidden Faces,* a novel containing autobiographical elements. These two short literary digressions earned him still greater prestige and wealth, as did his collaborations in the world of the cinema (such as the dream set for Alfred Hitchcock's *Spellbound,* 1945) and in those of the theater, opera, and ballet.

On August 8, 1958, Dalí and Gala were married according to the rites of the Catholic church in a ceremony performed in the strictest secrecy at the shrine of Els Àngels, just a few miles from Girona.

During the 1960s, Dalí painted some very large works, such as *The Battle of Tetuan.* Another important work painted at this period is *Perpignan Railway Station,* a veritable revelation of his paranoid-critical method that relates this center of Dalí's mythological universe to his obsession with painter Jean-François Millet's *The Angelus.*

In 1979 his health began to decline. After failing to recover from an attack of influenza in New York, he retired to Portlligat in a state of depression. When Gala died, he moved to Púbol, where, obsessed by the theory of catastrophes, he painted his last works, until suffering severe burns in a fire that nearly cost him his life. On his recovery he moved to the Torre Galatea, a building that he had bought as an extension to the museum in Figueres. There he lived for five more years, hardly ever leaving his room. He was buried at his own request beneath the dome of the Theater-Museum.

When a catalog was prepared, Dalí said with a perfectly straight face, "It is necessary that all of the people who come out of the museum have false information."

WHERE TO STAY

Ampurdán. Antigua Carretera de Francia, s/n (N-II), 17600 Figueres. ☎ **972/50-05-62.** Fax 972/50-93-58. 39 rms, 3 suites. A/C TV TEL. 10,550–11,400 ptas. ($84.40–$91.20) double; 14,000–17,000 ptas. ($112–$136) suite. AE, DC, MC, V. Parking 1,100 ptas. ($8.80).

Although the restaurant is a gastronomic landmark (see below), the hotel associated with it provides reasonably priced accommodations for those passing between France and Spain, usually on business. It does not lie near the beach, it does not have a pool, and although rooms are comfortable and distinguished, it is not designed as a place for long-term sojourns. It has three floors of rooms.

$ **Hotel Bon Retorn.** Carretera Nacional IIA, km 3, 17600 Figueres. ☎ **972/50-46-23.** Fax 972/67-39-79. 50 rms. A/C TV TEL. 9,000 ptas. ($72) double. AE, DC, MC, V. Parking 900 ptas. ($7.20). Take a taxi from the rail station or take A-17 to exit 4 (Figueres south) and head toward town on Carretera Nacional IIA.

Located near the edge of the national highway, 1½ miles (2.5km) south of Figueres, this family-owned hotel features a large and relaxing bar, a children's garden, and a sunny restaurant with an outdoor terrace. The hotel also has a private enclosed garage. The rooms are rustically furnished and comfortable, some with minibars.

Hotel Pirineos. Ronda de Barcelona, 1, 17600 Figueres. ☎ **972/50-03-12.** Fax 972/50-07-66. 53 rms. TV TEL. 6,500 ptas. ($52) double. AE, DC, MC, V. Parking 856 ptas. ($6.85).

This pleasant hotel, near the main road leading to the center of town, is a five-minute walk from the Dalí Museum. The hotel's restaurant takes up most of the ground floor, and there's also a bar. Many of the comfortable rooms have balconies, but furnishings are rather plain.

WHERE TO DINE

✪ **Ampurdán.** Antigua Carretera de Francia, s/n (N-II). ☎ **972/50-05-62.** Reservations required. Main courses 2,500–4,000 ptas. ($20–$32); fixed-price menu 4,100 ptas. ($32.80). AE, DC, MC, V. Daily 12:45–3:30pm and 8:30–10:30pm. CATALÁN.

At this restaurant, you'll probably have your finest meal in Catalonia. See above for its hotel recommendation. Don't judge the place by its appearance, which is ordinary, if not institutional-looking—there's nothing ordinary about the cuisine, as all the food-loving French who cross the border to dine here will tell you. This family-run restaurant, half a mile north of the center of town, also gained a reputation early on among U.S. servicemen in the area for subtly prepared game and fish dishes. In time, Salvador Dalí (who wrote his own cookbook) and Josep Pla, perhaps the country's greatest 20th-century writer, became fans. The appetizers are the finest along the Costa Brava, including such selections as duck foie gras with Armagnac, warm pâté of rape (monkfish) with garlic mousseline, and fish soup with fennel. The outstanding fish dishes include cuttlefish in Catalán sauce, suprême of sea bass with flan made with fennel and anchovy, and filet of red mullet with basil. Among the meat selections are the chef's special roast duck, beef filet in red-wine sauce with onion marmalade, and goose in a delectable mushroom sauce.

$ **Durán.** Carrer Lasauca, 5, 17600 Figueres. ☎ **972/50-12-50.** Fax 972/50-26-09. Reservations required. Main courses 2,000–3,500 ptas. ($16–$28); fixed-price menus 2,400–3,725 ptas. ($19.20–$29.80). AE, DC, MC, V. Daily 12:15–3:30pm and 8:15–11:30pm. CATALÁN.

This popular place for a top-notch meal in the provinces had Dalí as a loyal patron. You can start with the salad Catalán, made with radishes, boiled egg, ham pâté, tuna fish, tomato, and fresh crisp salad greens. Other specialties include steak with Roquefort, *zarzuela* (fish stew), and *filetes de lenguado a la naranja* (sole in orange sauce). Like the Ampurdán (see above), the Durán specializes in game. Try, if it's available, the grilled rabbit on a plank, served with white wine. The french fries here, unlike those in most of Spain, are crisp and excellent. Finish off with a rich dessert or at least an espresso.

You can also stay at the Durán, in one of its 65 well-furnished rooms, each with private bath, air-conditioning, TV, and phone. A double goes for 8,500 pesetas ($68).

5 Cadaqués

122 miles (196km) N of Barcelona, 19 miles (31km) E of Figueres

This little village is still unspoiled and remote, despite the publicity it received when Salvador Dalí lived in the next village of Lligat in a split-level house surmounted by a giant egg. The last resort on the Costa Brava before the French border, Cadaqués is reached by a small winding road, twisting over the mountains from Rosas, the nearest major center. When you get to Cadaqués, you really feel you're off the beaten path. The village winds around half a dozen small coves, with a narrow street running along the water's edge. This street has no railing, so exercise caution.

Scenically, Cadaqués is a knockout—with crystal-blue water; fishing boats on the sandy beaches; old whitewashed houses; narrow, twisting streets; and a 16th-century parish up on a hill.

GETTING THERE **By Bus** Two to five buses per day run from Figueres to Cadaqués. Trip time is 1¼ hours. The service is operated by SARFA (☎ **972/25-87-13**).

VISITOR INFORMATION The tourist information office is at Cotxe, 2 (☎ **972/25-83-15**). It's open Monday through Saturday from 10:30am to 1pm and 4 to 7pm.

WHERE TO STAY

$ **Hostal Marina.** Rivera Sant Vincent, 3, 17488 Cadaqués. ☎ **972/25-81-99.** 27 rms (23 with bath). 6,500 ptas. ($52) double with bath. AE, MC, V. Closed Jan–Mar.

This simple, centrally located hotel near the beach is the oldest in town. It offers clean, no-frills bedrooms at a good price. All of the singles are without bath, but doubles have baths. Breakfast is the only meal served.

$ **Hostal S'Aguarda.** Carretera de Port Lligat, 28, 17488 Cadaqués. ☎ **972/25-80-82.** Fax 972/25-87-56. 28 rms. A/C TV TEL. 10,500–17,850 ptas. ($84–$142.80) double. Rates include full board. AE, DC, MC, V. Closed Nov. Free parking.

Situated on the road winding above Cadaqués on the way to Port Lligat, this hostal has a panoramic view of the village's harbor and medieval church. Each of the modern, airy accommodations opens onto a flower-decked terrace. The rooms have tile floors and simple furniture. A swimming pool, solarium, and tennis courts are located on the hotel grounds.

Hotel Playa Sol. Platja Planch, 3, 17488 Cadaqués. ☎ **972/25-81-00.** Fax 972/25-80-54. 50 rms. TV TEL. 11,900–17,900 ptas. ($95.20–$143.20) double. AE, DC, MC, V. Closed Jan–Feb. Parking 800–1,200 ptas. ($6.40–$9.60).

Located in a relatively quiet section of the port along the bay, this 1950s hotel has, arguably, the best view of the stone church at the distant edge of the harbor. The balconied building is constructed of brick and terra-cotta tiles. Its bedrooms are comfortably furnished. Twenty-five rooms are air-conditioned. The hotel doesn't have a restaurant, but it does offer a cafeteria as well as an outdoor pool.

Hotel Port Lligat. Salvador Dalí, 17488 Cadaqués. ☎ **972/25-81-62.** Fax 972/25-86-43. 30 rms. TEL. 6,600–11,600 ptas. ($52.80–$92.80) double. Rates include breakfast. V. Closed Nov.

Many visitors find the relative isolation of this hotel—at the end of a winding gravel road a half mile outside Cadaqués—to be its most alluring feature. The terrace overlooks an idyllic harbor and an unusual house once occupied by Salvador Dalí. The gallery adjoining the reception lobby features a changing series of surrealist paintings. Also on the premises are a swimming pool with cabanas and a snack bar. The airy bedrooms, all doubles, have tile floors, exposed wood, and balconies.

WHERE TO DINE

Don Quijote. Caridad Seriñana, 5. ☎ **972/25-81-41.** Reservations recommended. Main courses 1,800–2,600 ptas. ($14.40–$20.80). DC, MC, V. Daily noon–midnight. Closed Nov–Mar. CATALÁN.

Located on the road leading into the village, this intimate bistro has a large vine-covered garden in front. You can dine either inside or alfresco. The à la carte specialties include lamb chops, pepper steak, *zarzuela* (seafood stew), and gazpacho. The Don Quijote cup, a mixed dessert, is the best way to end a meal.

Es Trull. Port Ditxos, s/n. ☎ **972/25-81-96.** Reservations recommended. Main courses 780–2,950 ptas. ($6.25–$23.60); fixed-price menus 1,100–1,700 ptas. ($8.80–$13.60). AE, MC, V. Daily 12:30–4pm and 7–11pm. Closed Nov–Easter. SEAFOOD.

On the harborside street in the center of town, this cedar-shingled cafeteria is named for the ancient olive press that dominates the interior. A filling fixed-price meal is served. According to the chef, if it comes from the sea and can be eaten, he will prepare it with that special Catalán flair. You might, for example, prefer mussels in a marinara sauce or grilled hake. Rice dishes are also a specialty, not only paella, but also "black rice" colored with squid ink and rice with calamari and shrimp. Natural baby clams are yet another dining delight.

✪ **La Galiota.** Carrer Narciso Monturiol, 9. ☎ **972/25-81-87.** Reservations required. Main courses 1,800–2,600 ptas. ($14.40–$20.80); fixed-price menu 1,600 ptas. ($12.80). AE, DC, MC, V. Daily 2–3:30pm and 9–11pm. Closed Mon–Fri in Nov–May. CATALÁN/FRENCH.

Dozens of surrealist paintings, including some by Dalí, adorn the walls of this award-winning restaurant, the finest in town. Located on a sloping street below the cathedral, the place has a downstairs sitting room and a dining room converted from what was a private house. The cuisine is not at all pretentious. The secret of the chef is in selecting only the freshest of ingredients and preparing them in a way that enhances their natural flavors. The roast leg of lamb, flavored with garlic, is a specialty. The menu changes with the season but always features the best of French and Catalán fare. The marinated salmon is excellent, as are the sea bass and the sole with orange sauce.

$ **Sa Gambina.** Riba Nemeslo Llorens, s/n. ☎ **972/25-81-27.** Reservations recommended. Main courses 1,200–2,300 ptas. ($9.60–$18.40); fixed-price menus 1,300–1,600 ptas. ($10.40–$12.80). AE, MC, V. Daily noon–4pm and 7–11pm. CATALÁN.

This restaurant, with its regional ambience and cavelike dining room, is located on the waterfront and serves reasonably good food at moderate prices. It's been a local favorite since the 1960s. A Catalán salad (tomato, lettuce, peppers, *butifarra* [pork sausage], onions, and olives) is a good choice, as is the delectable paella or the good-tasting fish soup. The shrimp (*gambas*), for which the place is named, are always reliable. You might also try the fish soufflé.

CADAQUÉS AFTER DARK

Es Porró. Portal de la Font, 1. ☎ **972/25-80-82.**

Although small, Es Porró is the most popular dance club in town. It's open daily from 11pm to 4:30am. In the off-season, it is likely to be open only on weekends—check locally. But in midsummer it seems to be thriving every night. Expect to pay around 750 pesetas ($6) for a drink.

L'Hostal. Paseo, 8A. ☎ **972/25-80-00.**

This distinctive place has attracted some of the most glamorous names of the art and music worlds. Some music critics have called it the second-best jazz club in Europe, and it certainly rates as the best club along the coast. It's a Dixieland bar par excellence, run by the most sophisticated entrepreneurial team in town. Habitués still remember when Salvador Dalí escorted Mick Jagger here, much to the delight of Colombian writer Gabriel García Marquez. In fact, the bar's logo was designed by Dalí himself. Heightening the ambience are the dripping candles, the high ceilings, and the heavy Spanish furniture. The best music is usually performed late at night. Open daily from noon to 5am. Entrance is free. Beer costs from 350 to 650 pesetas ($2.80–$5.20); whiskey, 850 to 1,000 pesetas ($6.80–$8).

16

Aragón

Landlocked Aragón, along with Navarre, forms the northeastern quadrant of Spain. It is an ancient land, composed of three provinces: Zaragoza; remote Teruel, which is farther south; and Huesca, in the north as you move toward the Pyrenees. These are also the names of the provinces' three major cities.

Most of Aragón constitutes *terra incognita* for the average tourist—which is unfortunate, since Aragón is one of the most history-rich regions of the country. You can visit it as an extension of your trip to Castile, to the west, or as a segment of your trek through Catalonia, to the east. Huesca, close to the mountains, is ideal for a summer visit—unlike most of Aragón, especially its fiercely hot southern section, which has Spain's worst climate. Winter is often bitterly cold, but spring and autumn are ideal.

Aragón is known best for two former residents: Catherine of Aragón, who foolishly married Henry VIII of England, and Ferdinand of Aragón, whose marriage to Isabella, Queen of Castile and León in the 15th century, led to the unification of Spain.

Aragón also prides itself on its exceptional Mudéjar architecture and on its bullfighting tradition. In September many villages in the region have their own *encierros,* when bulls run through the streets. What they don't have is the good promotion that Hemingway gave the festival at Pamplona, in the neighboring province of Navarre. On the other hand, they aren't plagued with wine-drunk tourists—the curse of the Pamplona festival. In folklore, Aragón is known for the *jota,* a bounding, leaping dance performed by men and women since at least the 1700s.

Aragón's capital, Zaragoza, is the most-visited destination because it lies on the main route between Madrid and Barcelona. If you're driving from Madrid to Barcelona (or vice versa), make a detour to Zaragoza. If you get interested in Aragón while there, stick around to explore this ancient land.

EXPLORING THE REGION BY CAR

Days 1–2 Travel to Zaragoza from either Madrid (on the N-11) or Barcelona (on the E-90), arriving late in the afternoon. Sample some of the *tascas* (taverns) and nightlife of the city before retiring. In the morning, take a stroll around Zaragoza and visit its major

Aragón

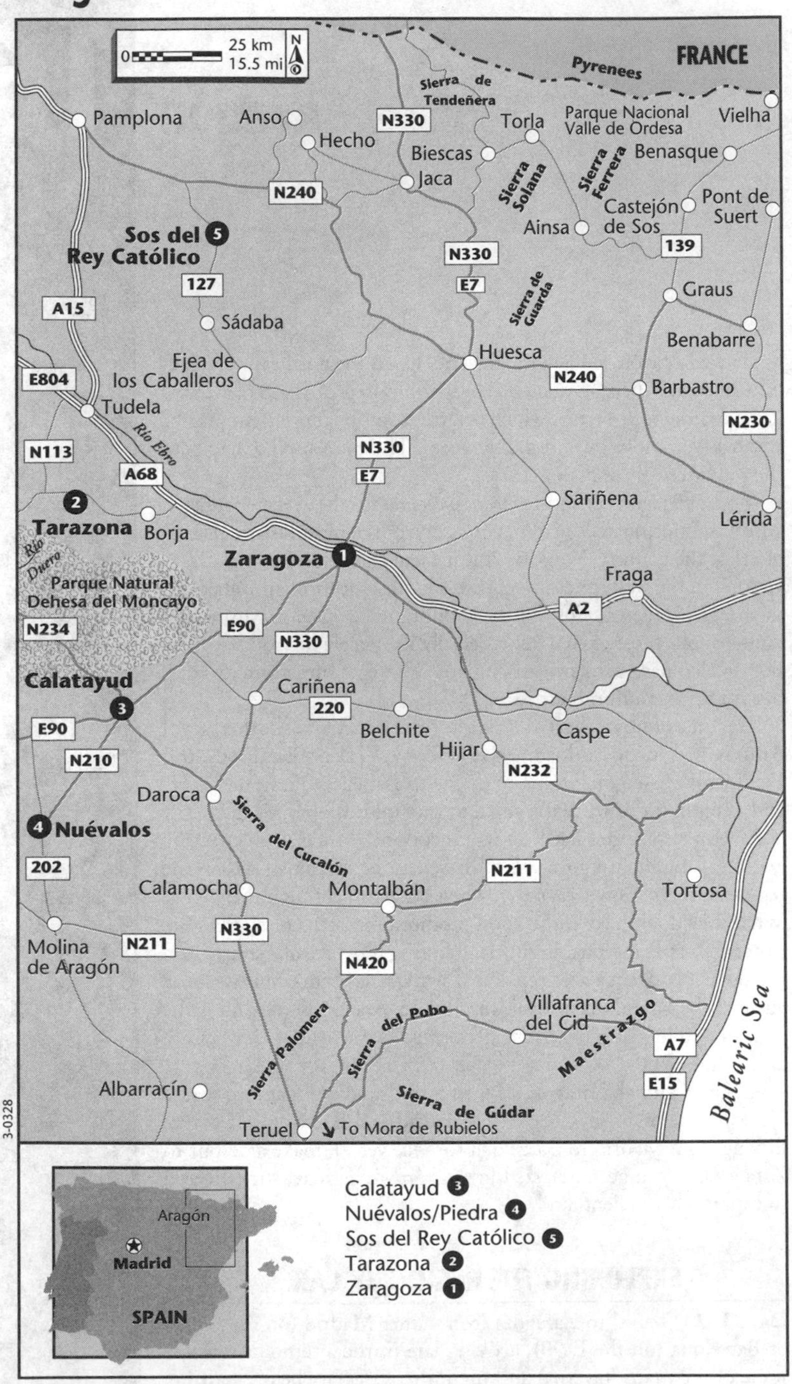
25 km
15.5 mi
N
FRANCE
Pyrenees
Sierra de Tendeñera
Pamplona
Anso
Hecho
N330
Torla
Parque Nacional Valle de Ordesa
Vielha
Biescas
Jaca
Benasque
Sierra Solana
Sierra Ferrera
N240
Castejón de Sos
Pont de Suert
Ainsa
Sos del Rey Católico
N330
139
E7
127
Graus
Sierra de Guarda
A15
Sádaba
Benabarre
Ejea de los Caballeros
Huesca
E804
N240
Barbastro
Tudela
Río Ebro
N230
N113
N330
E7
A68
Sariñena
Tarazona
Borja
Lérida
Río Duero
Zaragoza
Fraga
Parque Natural Dehesa del Moncayo
A2
N234
E90
N330
Calatayud
Cariñena
220
Belchite
Caspe
E90
Hijar
N210
N232
Daroca
Sierra del Cucalón
Nuévalos
202
N211
Tortosa
Calamocha
Montalbán
N330
Molina de Aragón
N211
N420
Villafranca del Cid
Maestrazgo
Sierra Palomera
Sierra del Pobo
A7
E15
Balearic Sea
Albarracín
Sierra de Gúdar
Teruel
To Mora de Rubielos
3-0328
Aragón
Madrid
SPAIN
Calatayud 3
Nuévalos/Piedra 4
Sos del Rey Católico 5
Tarazona 2
Zaragoza 1

monuments. In the afternoon, if you have a car, consider at least one of the "Easy Excursions" from Zaragoza (see below).

Day 3 Strike out on "the Mudéjar trail," driving west on A-68/E-804 and then following the N-122 west to Tarazona. Continue on to Calatayud by taking C 101 south until it hits N-234; from there, follow the signs for Calatayud. If time remains, visit Nuévalos (follow the signs from Calatayud) and spend the night at the Monasterio de Piedra (reservation required; see below). If that's full, there are other accommodations in the area.

Day 4 Take the N-234 to Daroca for about two hours of sightseeing, then head north to spend the night in Sos del Rey Católico. (To reach Sos del Rey Católico, take the N-330 northeast to Zaragoza, then the N-123 to Huesca, then the N-240 in the direction of Pamplona. At the town of Liedena, head south and follow the signs.)

1 Zaragoza

200 miles (322km) NE of Madrid, 190 miles (306km) W of Barcelona

Zaragoza ("Tha-ra-*go*-tha") is halfway between Madrid and Barcelona. This provincial capital, the seat of the ancient kingdom of Aragón, is a bustling, prosperous, commercial city of wide boulevards and arcades.

Zaragoza has not one, but two, cathedrals and ranks with Santiago de Compostela in Galicia as a pilgrimage center. According to legend, the Virgin Mary appeared to St. James, patron saint of Spain, on the banks of the Ebro River and ordered him to build a church there.

Zaragoza lies in the center of a rich *huerta,* or plain. Its history goes back to the Romans, who called it Caesar Augusta. Today, Zaragoza is a city of more than three-quarters of a million people, just less than 75% of the entire population in Aragón.

Some 40,000 students at the University of Zaragoza have brought a joie de vivre to this once-staid city. Cafés, theaters, restaurants, music bars, and *tascas* have boomed in recent years, and more monuments have been restored and opened to the public.

One of the city's big festivities is the Fiesta de la Virgen del Pilar, held the week of October 12, with top-name bullfighters, religious processions, and general merriment.

GETTING THERE **By Plane** Aviaco has direct flights to Zaragoza from Madrid and Barcelona. From the airport in Zaragoza, you can get a bus to the Plaza de San Francisco. The Iberia office in Zaragoza is at Canfranc, 22–24 (☎ **976/21-82-54**).

By Train From Barcelona, 9 to 12 trains arrive daily, and from Madrid there are 12 per day. The trip takes 4½ hours from Barcelona and 3 to 4 hours from Madrid. The RENFE office in Zaragoza is at Calle Anselo Clavet, 13 (☎ **976/28-02-02**), just off Paseo de la Independencia.

By Bus There is one direct bus a day running between Zaragoza and Barcelona (7 hours away).

By Car Zaragoza is easily reached on the E-90 (A-2) east from Madrid or west from Barcelona.

VISITOR INFORMATION The tourist information office is at Torrcón de la Zuda—Glorieta Pio XII (☎ **976/39-35-37**), next to the Roman wall. Open Monday through Friday 8:30am to 2:45pm and 3:30 to 8pm, Saturday and Sunday from 10am to 1:30pm.

WHAT TO SEE & DO

Catedral de Nuestra Señora del Pilar. Plaza de las Catedrales. ☎ **976/39-74-97.** Free admission to cathedral; museum, 150 ptas. ($1.20). Cathedral, daily 5:45am–9:30pm; museum, daily 9am–2pm and 4–6pm. Bus: 22 or 23.

This 16th- and 17th-century basilica, on the banks of the Ebro River, is in an almost Oriental style with its domes and towers. Thousands of the faithful travel here annually to pay homage to the tiny statue of the Virgin del Pilar in the Holy Chapel. The name of the cathedral, El Pilar, comes from the pillar upon which the Virgin is supposed to have stood when she asked Santiago (St. James) to build the church.

During the second week of October, the church is a backdrop for an important festival devoted to Our Lady of the Pillar, which combines parades, bullfights, fireworks, flower offerings, and street dancing. Also of interest within the church are frescoes painted by Goya, who was born nearby.

You can also visit the Museo del Pilar, which houses the jewelry collection used to adorn the Pilar statue, as well as sketches by Goya and other artists, including Bayeu. Much of the collection is ancient, including an 18th-century ivory horn.

La Seo del Salvador. Plaza de la Seo. ☎ **976/29-12-38.** Museum admission 150 ptas. ($1.20). Museum, daily 9am–2pm and 4–6pm. Bus: 21, 22, 29, 32, 35, 36, 43, 44, 45.

This Gothic-Mudéjar church, built between 1380 and 1550, is more impressive than El Pilar (see above). It has a rich baroque and plateresque facade and is a particularly fine example of Aragonese Gothic architecture. Among its more important features are the main altar and a fine collection of French and Flemish tapestries from the 15th to the 17th centuries, which are housed in the adjacent museum. The baroque cupolas in the Temple of Pilar were decorated by Goya and Bayeu. Keep in mind that an ongoing restoration project has restricted access to the church.

Palacio de la Aljafería. Aljafería, Calle Los Diputados. ☎ **976/28-95-28.** Free admission. Tues–Sat 10am–2pm and 4–8pm, Sun 10–2pm. Bus: 32, 33, or 36.

This most unusual sight, a Moorish palace in Aragón, has been restored by the parliament and preserved as a national monument. Reminiscent of Cordoban architecture, the palace was built in the 11th century for Moorish kings but has seen considerable alterations and additions since then, particularly when Ferdinand and Isabella lived here.

Museo de Zaragoza. Plaza de los Sitios, 6. ☎ **976/22-21-81.** Admission 200 ptas. ($1.60). Tues–Sun 9am–2pm. Bus: 30, 35, or 40.

This museum is installed in a 1908 building that has 10 ground-floor rooms devoted to exhibits from the prehistoric to the Muslim period. The Roman legacy (rooms 4 to 8) has sculptures (the head of Augustus), mosaics, and ceramics. The fine arts section includes paintings by Goya (room 20); see his self-portrait. In the next room you'll find his drawings of *Los Caprichos (The Whims).* Also displayed is a Goya portrait of Carlos IV and his wife. The museum lies directly north of the Paseo de Marino Moreno.

Museo Camón Aznar. Espoz y Mina, 23. ☎ **976/39-73-28.** Admission 100 ptas. (80¢). Tues–Sun 11am–2pm, Tues–Sat 6–9pm. Bus: 22 or 23.

One block from El Pilar (see above), occupying a Renaissance palace, this museum has 3 floors and 23 rooms, each filled with artwork. On the second floor is a sketch of María Sarmiento that Velázquez made for his masterpiece *Las Meninas (The Maids of Honor),* which hangs in the Prado in Madrid. The Bayeu brothers (Francisco and Ramón) are represented by several works, as is Goya. His collection includes an important self-portrait, a version of his *Los Caprichos (The Whims), La Tauromaquia (The Tauromachy), Los Desastres de la Guerra (The Disasters of War),* and *Los Disparates (The Follies).*

Museo Pablo Gargallo. Plaza de San Felipe, 3. ☎ **976/39-20-58.** Free admission; passport required; no cameras. Tues–Sat 10am–1pm and 5–9pm, Sun 11am–4pm. Bus: 22 or 23.

The museum honors eponymous sculptor Pablo Gargallo, born in Maella in 1881. It is installed in a beautiful Aragonese Renaissance-style palace (1659), which was declared a national monument in 1963. Gargallo, influential in the art world of the 1920s, is represented by 100 original works, ranging from *Dr. Petit's Fireplace* (1904) to *Great Prophet,* a bronze piece from 1933. The museum is located in the center, a five-minute walk south of El Pilar. For reasons not announced by security, a passport or some other form of picture ID is needed before you're admitted to the museum, and you can't take your camera inside.

WHERE TO STAY

MODERATE

Boston. Camino de las Torres, 28, 50008 Zaragoza. ☎ **976/59-91-92.** Fax 976/59-04-46. 297 rms, 16 suites. A/C MINIBAR TV TEL. 16,000–19,000 ptas. ($128–$152) double; 23,000–80,000 ptas. ($184–$640) suite. AE, DC, MC, V. Parking 1,700 ptas. ($13.60). Bus: 29.

Set in the heart of Zaragoza's modern business district, a 15-minute walk from the medieval neighborhoods that most foreign visitors search out, this eight-story hotel was opened in 1992. Named in honor of Boston, Massachussetts, where the building's architect earned his degree, it's the city's best hotel and one of the tallest buildings in town. Many of its public areas are sheathed in layers of beige marble, occasionally accented with wood paneling. Throughout, the style is ultra-modern, even futuristic, strongly infused with postmodern design and American-derived ideas. The in-house restaurant, one floor below the lobby level, is named Niagara and serves filling fixed-price meals. On the premises is a health club with a sauna. Room service is available 24 hours a day.

Gran Hotel. Joaquín Costa 5, 50001 Zaragoza. ☎ **976/22-19-01.** Fax 976/23-67-13. 120 rms, 20 suites. A/C MINIBAR TV TEL. 16,900 ptas. ($135.20) double; from 27,500 ptas. ($220) suite. AE, DC, MC, V. Parking 1,500 ptas. ($12).

Located half a mile south of the cathedral, behind one of the most beautiful Hispano–art deco facades in town, this hotel is the most historic and the most charming in Zaragoza. Established by King Alfonso XIII in 1929, the Gran offers a domed rotunda for conversation and an array of formal public rooms and conference facilities with crystal chandeliers and classic furniture. Bedrooms have been restored into a neutral, traditional international style, yet they retain the high ceilings and spaciousness of their original design, as well as occasional touches of art deco. A favorite of the business community, the hotel offers excellent service and many hideaways for quiet drinks and dialogue.

Hemingway and one of his biographers, A. E. Hotchner, stayed at the Gran when they were in Zaragoza.

Dining/Entertainment: The hotel's restaurants include the very elegant La Ontina, where three-course fixed-price lunches and dinners are served daily. Current newspapers are available along with the drinks served in the bar, an enclave that some visitors consider their favorite spot.

Services: 24-hour room service, laundry, concierge.

Hotel Goya. Calle Cinco de Marzo, 5, 50004 Zaragoza. ☎ **976/22-93-31.** Fax 976/23-21-54. 148 rms. A/C TV TEL. 13,650 ptas. ($109.20) double. AE, DC, MC, V. Parking 1,200 ptas. ($9.60). Bus: 22.

Just off the Paseo de la Independencia, near the Plaza de España in the city center, this hotel (rebuilt in 1986) has excellent bedrooms that in some respects equal the much more expensive accommodations at the Gran (see above). True to its namesake, the hotel displays copies of Goya's paintings throughout the multilevel lobby, which is decorated in black marble and wood paneling.

Hotel Palafox. Calle Casa Jiménez, s/n. 50004 Zaragoza. ☎ **976/23-77-00.** Fax 976/23-47-05. 180 rms, 4 suites. A/C MINIBAR TV TEL. 16,000 ptas. ($128) double; 24,000 ptas. ($192) suite. AE, DC, MC, V. Parking 1,200 ptas. ($9.60). Bus: 22.

Affiliated with the also recommended Hotel Goya, this is a more modern version, with sleek Spanish styling. One of the top four hotels in town, it looks somewhat like an apartment house. It was inaugurated in 1982 and has been rated five stars by the government. A favorite of business travelers, it is frequently the venue for such local events as fashion shows. A rooftop swimming pool is a magnet during the long, hot Aragonese summer. Bedrooms have sleek traditional styling (often leather armchairs) and are well maintained and comfortable. The hotel restaurant, Puerto Sanco, serves a traditional Aragonese cuisine. Other services and facilities include a sauna, massage, and 24-hour room service.

Rey Alfonso I. Calle Coso, 17–19, 50003 Zaragoza. ☎ **976/39-48-50.** Fax 976/39-96-40. 117 rms. A/C MINIBAR TV TEL. 8,650–12,400 ptas. ($69.20–$99.20) double. AE, DC, MC, V. Parking 1,150 ptas. ($9.20). Bus: 22.

This clean, efficient place is a favorite with businesspeople, who prefer its location in the commercial heart of town. A prominent arcade marks the entrance. The hotel has a popular countertop-service snack bar and, in the basement, a comfortably modern restaurant. A helpful crew of veteran, good-natured doormen help visitors with their luggage. The rooms are furnished with comfortable modern furniture.

INEXPENSIVE

$ **Hotel Sauce.** Calle Espoz y Mina, 33, 50003 Zaragoza. ☎ **976/39-01-00.** Fax 976/39-85-97. 37 rms. A/C TV TEL. 7,900 ptas. ($63.20) double. AE, MC, V. Parking 1,100 ptas. ($8.80). Bus: 22.

Lying in the historic and artistic old town, right off the Calle de Don Jaime I, this rates as one of the best bargains in a high-priced city. The decor is cozy, the staff helpful. The guest rooms are small but comfortably furnished and well maintained.

WHERE TO DINE

Los Borrachos. Paseo de Sagasta, 64. ☎ **976/27-50-36.** Reservations recommended. Main courses 1,800–4,300 ptas. ($14.40–$34.40). AE, MC, V. Daily 1–4pm and 8pm–midnight. SPANISH/FRENCH.

Solid, dignified, and committed to preserving a discreet and old-fashioned kind of service, this restaurant occupies a formal set of dining rooms in a location near the heart of town. Menu items may include such dishes as a combination platter of hake with lobster, wild boar with wine sauce, filet of beef with a pepper-cognac sauce, roasted pheasant or rabbit, and an asparagus mousse accented with strips of Serrano ham. This restaurant's name, incidentally, translates as "The Drunkards," and was taken from the characters in a famous Velásquez painting.

Gurrea. San Ignacio de Loyola, 14. ☎ **976/23-31-61.** Reservations recommended. Main courses 2,000–3,000 ptas. ($16–$24); fixed-price menu 4,000 ptas. ($32). AE, DC, MC, V. Daily 1–5pm, Mon–Sat 9pm–12:30am. SPANISH/INTERNATIONAL.

This is probably the most enduring restaurant in Zaragoza, committed to maintaining its reputation for good service, an attractive setting, and a time-honored cuisine. It's a favorite of the lunching business community and the venue, supposedly, of many successfully completed deals. Quality ingredients are fashioned into good-tasting and often delectable dishes, which are beautifully presented. Menu items might include goosemeat terrine, duck with orange sauce, chateaubriand with foie-gras sauce, hake served with fruit sauce, venison meatballs (in season) with truffles, wild mushrooms with goose liver, and filet mignon in curry sauce—plus a succulent array of desserts.

La Mar. Plaza Aragón, 12. ☎ **976/21-22-64.** Reservations recommended. Main courses 1,000–2,600 ptas. ($8–$20.80), fixed-price menu 4,500 ptas. ($36). AE, MC, V. Mon–Sat 1:30–4pm and 9–11:30pm. SEAFOOD.

Established in 1985 within what was originally (1890) a private house, this is one of the better seafood restaurants in town. Service is leisurely, but if you're in the mood for a prolonged meal, the menu will include a full range of seasonal vegetables, peppers stuffed with seafood mousse, *dorada* cooked in a salt crust, baked sea bream, turbot with clams, grilled hake or monkfish, grilled squid, shellfish soup or shellfish rice, and—if you're not in the mood for fish—grilled beefsteak with several kinds of sauces.

La Rinconada de Lorenzo. Calle La Salle, 3. ☎ **976/55-51-08.** Reservations required. Main courses 2,700–3,500 ptas. ($21.60–$28); fixed-price menu 2,200 ptas. ($17.60). AE, DC, MC, V. Daily 1–4pm and 8–11:30pm. Bus: 40 or 45. ARAGONESE.

This restaurant, one of the best in town, offers unusual dishes such as fried rabbit with snails. Oven-roasted lamb or lamb hock can be ordered in advance, but lamb skewers are always available. The chef prepares several versions of *migas* (fried breadcrumbs) flavored with a number of different ingredients, including grapes and ham. Giant asparagus spears are often served. Even though Zaragoza is inland, fresh fish is always on the menu: hake, grilled sole, sea bream, and salmon, for example. Desserts are all homemade, including rice pudding, chocolate mousse with cream, and fig ice cream with nuts. Red, white, and rosé wines from Aragón help wash everything down smoothly.

ZARAGOZA AFTER DARK

Casa Amadico. Jordán de Urriés, 3. ☎ **976/29-10-41.** Bus: 22.

This popular hangout is located near Plaza del Pilar, on one of the smallest streets in the city. Local government workers and businesspeople come here after work for the tasty seafood tapas. Oysters come in three different sizes, or perhaps you'll be tempted by the smoked salmon, lobster, or Serrano ham. It's open Tuesday to Sunday from 1 to 4pm and 7pm to midnight, but closed in August. A glass of wine costs 100 pesetas (80¢); tapas range from 100 to 550 pesetas (80¢–$4.40) as does a glass of beer.

Casa Luís. Romea, 8. ☎ **976/29-11-67.** Bus: 22.

This tiled-and-oak bar is one of the more interesting places in the barrio of La Magdalena. The array of tapas served here—some of the best around—includes fresh oysters, shrimp, and razor clams "in little bundles." It's open daily from 1 to 4pm and again from 7pm to midnight. A glass of wine will cost 75 pesetas (60¢); tapas are 100 to 550 pesetas (80¢–$4.40).

EASY EXCURSIONS FROM ZARAGOZA

Goya aficionados (male ones only) can visit the **Cartuja de Aula Dei** (☎ **976/15-42-11**), a 16th-century Carthusian monastery seven miles (11km) north of

Zaragoza in Montañana. The young Goya, an Aragonese, completed one of his first important commissions here in 1774, a series of 11 murals depicting scenes from the lives of Christ and Mary. During the Napoleonic invasion, the murals suffered badly, but restoration has since been done. In this strictly-run Carthusian community, only men are admitted. Visiting times are Tuesday and Thursday from 11am to 1pm and 6 to 7pm, Saturday from 10:30am to 1pm. From Zaragoza, bus number 28 departs about every half hour to the site (trip time: 20 minutes), with a one-way ticket costing 70 pesetas (55¢). Catch the bus at the stop near the Roman walls. You can also drive; take E-90 east out of town and follow the signs for Montañana.

Goya fans—of both genders this time—can also go south from Zaragoza to the little village of **Fuendetodos,** the birthplace of Goya in 1746. A small two-room cottage in the village (not his actual birthplace, however), was restored in 1985 and turned into a museum, **Casa de Goya,** Zuloaga, 3 (☎ **976/14-38-30**). You're shown transparencies of his most important works. It is open Tuesday through Sunday from 11am to 2pm and 4 to 7pm. Admission is 300 pesetas ($2.40). Take the N-330 south to the town of Muel, then go 11 miles south (18km) to Villanueva del Huerve. Bear east on the A-220 and continue for 5 miles (8km) to Fuendetodos. From Zaragoza, Autobuses Tervel Zaragoza, Calle Juan Pablo Bonet, 13–15 (☎ **976/27-61-79**) carries passengers to the village.

2 Tarazona

54½ miles (88km) W of Zaragoza, 182 miles (293km) NE of Madrid

To call this town the "Toledo of Aragón" may be a bit much, but it does deserve the name "Mudéjar City." Lying about halfway along the principal route connecting Zaragoza to the province of Soria, it is laid out in tiers above the quays of the Queiles River. Once the kings of Aragón lived here, and before that the place was known to the Romans. You can walk through the old barrio with its tall facades and narrow medieval streets.

GETTING THERE **By Bus** From Zaragoza four buses leave daily for Tarazona (1½ hours away).

By Car Drive west from Zaragoza along the A-68, connecting with the N-122 to Tarazona.

VISITOR INFORMATION The tourist information office is at Iglesias, 5 (☎ **976/64-00-74**). Open daily from 9am to 1pm and from 5 to 7pm. Hours vary slightly on holidays, when it is open from 10am to 1pm.

WHAT TO SEE & DO

Tarazona's major attraction is its Gothic **cathedral,** begun in 1152 but essentially reconstructed in the 15th and 16th centuries. However, the Aragonese Mudéjar style is still much in evidence, especially as reflected in the lantern tower and belfry. The dome resembles that of the old cathedral in Zaragoza. The church was closed at press time for renovations, but is expected to reopen in 1998.

The town is also known for its 16th-century **Ayuntamiento (Town Hall),** which has reliefs across its facade depicting the retaking of Granada by Ferdinand and Isabella. The monument stands on Plaza de España in the older upper town, on a hill overlooking the river. Take the Ruta Turística from here up to the church of Santa Magdalena, with a Mudéjar tower that forms the chief landmark of the town's skyline; its mirador opens onto a panoramic view. Continuing up the hill, you reach **La Concepción,** another church with a narrow brick tower.

WHERE TO STAY & DINE

Brujas de Bécquer. Teresa Cajal, 30, 50500 Tarazona. ☎ **976/64-04-00** or 976/64-04-04. Fax 976/64-01-98. 57 rms. A/C TV TEL. 4,200–5,825 ptas. ($33.60–$46.60) double. AE, DC, MC, V. Parking garage 750 ptas. ($6).

Half a mile southeast of town, beside the road leading to Zaragoza, you'll find this unpretentious modern hotel, which was built in 1972 and renovated 20 years later. Rooms are modest but comfortable. The dining room serves fixed-price meals for around 1,400 pesetas ($11.20) each, every day from 1 to 4pm and 8 to 10:30pm. Reservations are almost never needed. The hotel, incidentally, was named in honor of a 19th-century Seville-born patriot (Gustavo Adolfo Bécquer) who praised the beauties of Aragón in some of his poetry.

3 Calatayud

53 miles (85km) W of Zaragoza, 146 miles (235km) NE of Madrid

The Romans founded this town, only to abandon it some time during the 2nd century, and it wasn't until the arrival of the Muslims in the 8th century that it was repopulated. The Moors were routed in 1120 by the conquering Catholic forces, who allowed some of the inhabitants to stay. But they were made virtual slaves and forced to live in a *morería* (Moorish ghetto). Some of the Moorish influence can still be seen in the town. Many 14th- and 15th-century church towers in Calatayud are reminiscent of minarets.

GETTING THERE **By Train** Calatayud lies on the main rail line linking Madrid to Zaragoza. There are 12 trains a day from Madrid, 9 from Zaragoza, and 3 from Barcelona.

By Bus There are three to four buses a day from Zaragoza (1¼ hours away).

By Car Calatayud is on the E-90 linking Madrid with Zaragoza.

VISITOR INFORMATION The tourist information office is at Plaza del Fuerte, s/n (☎ **976/88-63-22**). Open Monday through Friday from 9am to 5pm.

WHAT TO SEE & DO

The major attraction of Calatayud is **Santa María la Mayor,** Calle de Opispo Arrué, a brick church built in Aragonese style, with an ornate plateresque-Mudéjar facade and an exceptionally harmonious octagonal belfry. Nearby, on the Calle Datao, the **Iglesia de San Pedro de los Francos** might be called the "leaning tower" of Calatayud. This is a fine example of the Mudéjar style.

A walk along the Calle Unión leads to **La Parraguía de San Andrés,** with an elegant and graceful Mudéjar belfry.

Strike a path through the old Moorish quarter up the hill to the ruins of the castle that dominated Qal'at Ayyub (the old Arab name for the town). Once you're there, a panoramic view unfolds.

East of Calatayud, excavations continue to uncover the **Roman city of Bibilis,** lying on the Mérida-Zaragoza highway. It was the birthplace of Roman satirist Martial (ca. A.D. 40–104).

WHERE TO STAY & DINE

Hotel Calatayud. Autovia de Aragón Salida, km 237, 50300 Calatayud. ☎ **976/88-13-23.** Fax 976/88-54-38. 63 rms. TV TEL. 7,650 ptas. ($61.20) double. AE, MC, V. Parking 250 ptas. ($2).

Of a lackluster lot, this low-slung, modern hotel is your best bet in town. Set about a mile (1.6 km) east of Calatayud, on the N-II highway to Zaragoza, the hotel contains acceptable bedrooms with simple furnishings. It also offers a garden and a popular restaurant and bar, the only air-conditioned areas in the entire building.

AN EASY EXCURSION TO DAROCA

From Calatayud, take the N-234 southeast 25 miles (40km) to **Daroca.** Once a Roman military outpost known as Agiria, it was eventually taken by the Moors, who called it Kalat-Daruca. Moorish clans fought over the town bitterly, paving the way for its eventual takeover in 1122 by King Alfonso I of Aragón. Daroca is a gem of a town, known for its period architecture, including Roman, Mudéjar, Romanesque, and Gothic. It is visited mainly for the ruins of its walls, with 114 towers. An attempt in the 15th century to restore them was abandoned because of the enormity of the task. Some of the gates are in better shape, particularly Puerta Baja, flanked by twin towers and bearing the coat-of-arms of Carlos I. Other attractions include a beautiful fountain, Fuente de Veine Caños (20 spouts), lying just outside the walls, and a half-mile tunnel carved into a mountain to carry off flood waters, an unusual feat of engineering for the 16th century.

4 Nuévalos/Piedra

73 miles (118km) W of Zaragoza, 143 miles (230km) E of Madrid

The town of Nuévalos, with its one paved road, isn't much of a lure, but thousands of visitors from all over the world flock to the ✪ **Monasterio de Piedra,** called the garden district of Aragón (see review below).

GETTING THERE **By Train** From Madrid, train connections reach Alhama de Aragón. Take a taxi from there to the monastery.

By Car From Zaragoza, head southwest on the N-II through Calatayud. At the little town of Ateca, take the left turnoff, which is signposted for Nuévalos and the Monasterio de Piedra, and drive for 14 miles (22.5km). If you're driving from Madrid, take the N-II and turn east at the spa town of Alhama de Aragón.

WHAT TO SEE & DO

In Nuévalos, the major attraction is the ✪ **Monasterio de Piedra.** *Piedra* means "rock" in Spanish, and after the "badlands" of Aragón, you expect bleak, rocky terrain. Instead, you have a virtual Garden of Eden, with a 197-foot waterfall. It was here in 1194 that Cistercian monks built a charter house on the banks of the Piedra River. The monks are long gone, having departed in 1835, and their former quarters have been reconstructed and turned into a hotel (see below).

Two pathways, marked in either blue or red, meander through the grounds. Views are offered from any number of levels. Tunnels and stairways, dating from the 19th century, are the work of Juan Federico Mutadas, who created a park here. Slippery steps lead down to an iris grotto, just one of many quiet, secluded retreats. It is said that the original monks inhabited the site because they wanted a "foretaste of paradise." To be honest, they were also escaping the court intrigues at the powerful Monestir de Poblet in Tarragona province. The monastery at Piedra lies only 2 miles (3.2km) from the hillside village of Nuévalos. You can wander through the monastery grounds daily from 9am to 8pm in summer (closed at 5pm in winter) for an admission charge of 775 pesetas ($6.20) for adults, 475 pesetas ($3.80) for children.

For either rooms or meals, **Monasterio de Piedra,** 50201 Nuévalos (☎ **976/84-90-11**), is one of the showplaces of Aragón, and a meal in the great hall is a medieval event. The room has been tastefully decorated and is a perfect backdrop for the good-tasting Aragonese fare. Meals start at 2,500 pesetas ($20), and service is daily from 1 to 4pm and 9pm to midnight. On weekends, the dining room can get crowded. The grounds include a swimming pool, tennis courts, and, naturally, a garden, with little log bridges and masses of flowering plants and trees. The beautifully maintained bedrooms (all doubles), for which you should reserve well in advance, have phones but no other amenities. Some open onto terraces. Doubles cost 9,000 to 10,000 pesetas ($72–$80).

5 Sos del Rey Católico

262 miles (422km) N of Madrid, 37 miles (60km) SW of Pamplona

In northern Aragón, Sos del Rey Católico formed one of the Cinco Villas of Aragón, stretching along a 56-mile (90km) frontier with Navarre. These villages, in the far-distant part of northern Aragón, also included Tauste, Ejea, Uncastillo, and Sabada. Despite their small size, they were raised to the status of towns by Philip V, who was grateful for their assistance and loyalty in the War of Spanish Succession (1701–13).

The most visited town is Sos del Rey Católico, so named because it was the birthplace of Ferdinand, the Catholic king, in 1452. He entered the world's history books after his marriage to Isabella of Castile and León. Locals will point out the Palacio de Sada, where the future king is said to have been born. The town is more interesting than its minor monuments, and you can explore it at will, wandering its narrow cobbled streets and stopping at any place that attracts your fancy. The kings of Aragón fortified this village on the Navarre border with a thick wall. Much of that medieval character has been preserved—enough so that the village has been declared a national monument.

GETTING THERE **By Bus** From Zaragoza to Sos, 2 1/4 hours away, there is a daily bus at 6:30pm, returning at 7am the next morning.

By Car From Zaragoza, take the N-330 to Huesca. Continue on N-330 to Jaca, then bear west on the N-240 towards Pamplona. Turn south at the cutoff to Sanguesa.

WHERE TO STAY & DINE

Parador Fernando de Aragón. Sianz de Vicuña, 1, 50680 Sos del Rey Católico. ☎ **948/88-80-11.** Fax 948/88-81-00. 66 rms. A/C MINIBAR TV TEL. 12,500 ptas. ($100) double. AE, DC, MC, V. Closed Dec–Jan. Parking 750 ptas. ($6).

This member of the government-owned parador network is unusual because of the care that was taken to blend a six-story building into its medieval setting. Built in 1975 on much older foundations, it's composed mostly of stone and wood timbers, with lots of interior paneling and antique-looking accessories. Despite its location in the heart of the village, sweeping views open from some of the bedroom windows onto the nearby countryside. Accommodations are dignified, clean, and comfortable. Hearty Aragonese food is served in the restaurant, where *menús del día* cost 2,500 pesetas ($20) each. Service is daily from 1 to 4pm and from 8 to 10:30pm.

17

Navarre & La Rioja

The ancient land of Navarre (*Navarra* in Spanish; *Nafarroa* in Basque) shares with France an 81-mile (130km) frontier, with nine crossing points. As such, it is an important link between Iberia and the rest of the continent. Lying east of Castile, Navarre is a single province with a strong Basque tradition.

As a border region, Navarre has had a rough time in history, and to this day the remains of lonely castles and fortified walled towns bear witness to that. But somehow this kingdom, one of the most ancient on the peninsula, has managed to preserve its own government and identity. Romans, Christians, Muslims, and Jews have all influenced Navarre, and its architecture is as diverse as its landscape. It is also a province rich in folklore. Pagan rites were blended into Christian traditions to form a mythology that lives even today in Navarre's many festivals. Dancers and singers wear the famous red berets; the *jota* is the most celebrated folk dance; and the best-known sport is *pelota,* sometimes called jai alai in other parts of the world.

Navarre is rich in natural attractions, although most foreign visitors miss them when they visit just for the Fiesta de San Fermín in July, to see the running of the bulls through the streets of Pamplona (Iruña in Basque), Navarre's capital and major city. Even if you do visit just for the festival, try to explore some of the panoramic Pyrenean landscape.

Adjoining Navarre is La Rioja, the smallest region of mainland Spain—bordered not only by Navarre but also by Castile and Aragón. Extending along the Ebro River, this province has far greater influence than its tiny dimensions would suggest, because it is one of the most important wine-growing districts of Europe. The land is generally split into two sections: Rioja Alta, which gets a lot of rainfall and has a mild climate, and Rioja Baja, which is much hotter and more arid, more like Aragón. The capital of the province, Logroño, a city of some 200,000, links the two regions.

The most visited towns are the capital of Logroño and Haro, the latter known for its wineries. Santo Domingo de la Calzada was a major stop on the pilgrims' route, and Nájera was once the capital of the kings of Navarre. Now, little more than a village, it lies along the Najerilla River. From that river's valleys comes about a third of all Rioja wine production. From the 15th to the 30th of September, the Wine Harvest Festival takes place throughout La Rioja. Barefoot locals stomp upon grapes spilling from oaken casks, and area

Navarre & La Rioja

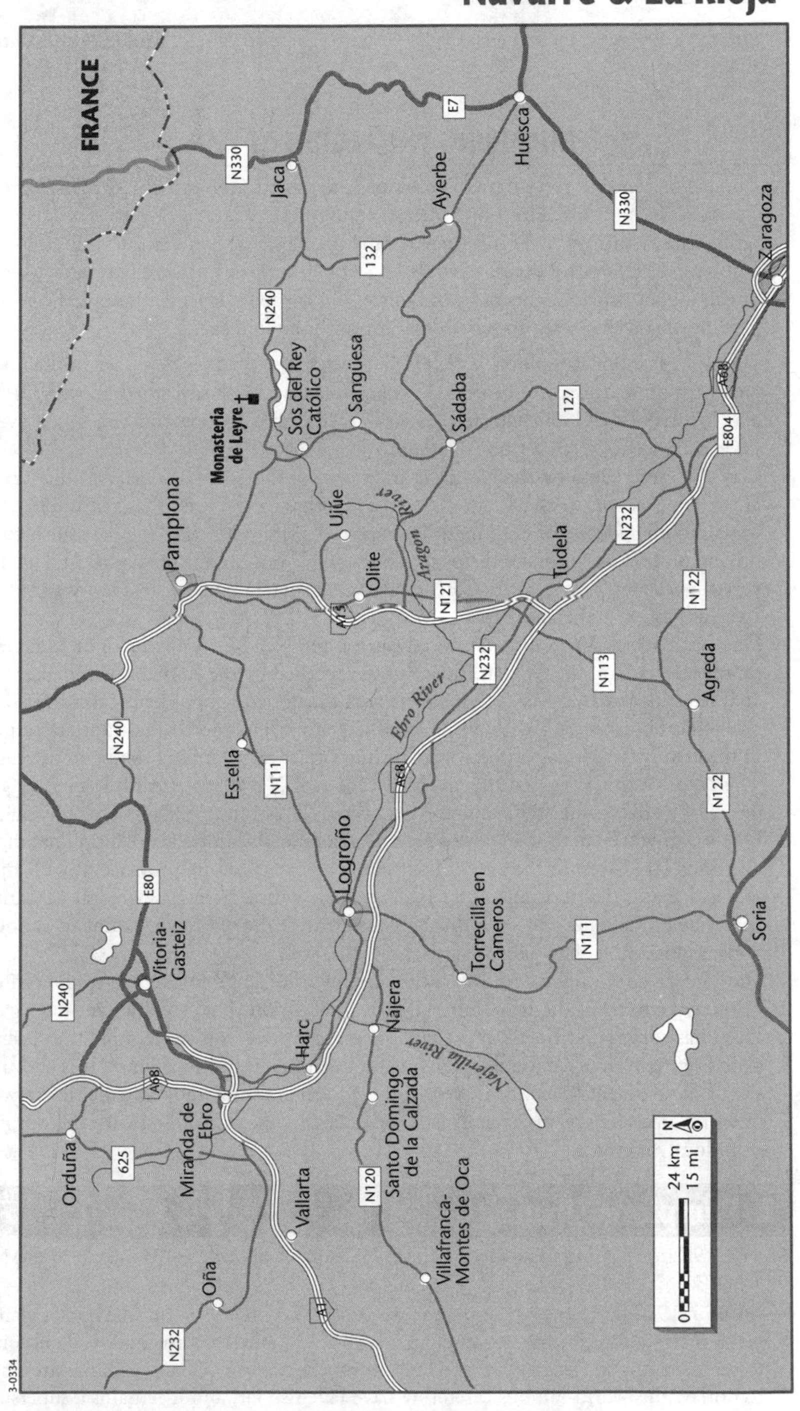
FRANCE
N330
Jaca
E7
Huesca
Ayerbe
132
N240
Sos del Rey Católico
Sangüesa
Monasteria de Leyre
127
Sádaba
Pamplona
Ujúe
Aragon River
Olite
A15
N121
Tudela
N232
N330
Zaragoza
A68
E804
N122
N113
Agreda
Ebro River
A68
N240
Estella
N111
Logroño
E80
Vitoria-Gasteiz
Torrecilla en Cameros
N111
Soria
N122
N240
Haro
Nájera
Najerilla River
A68
Miranda de Ebro
Orduña
625
Santo Domingo de la Calzada
N120
Vallarta
Villafranca-Montes de Oca
Oña
A1
N232
0
24 km
15 mi
N
3-0334

vineyards showcase their wares. Other activities include dances, parades, music, and bullfights.

EXPLORING THE REGION BY CAR

The major center for visitors is Pamplona, the most important city of the Spanish Pyrenees. It is immortalized in Ernest Hemingway's *The Sun Also Rises,* which describes the running of the bulls there during the Fiesta de San Fermín, July 6–14. If you have a car, you can base yourself in a hotel there and make day trips to check out all the tourist highlights of the province. But if you're dependent on public transportation, you may want to stay in various towns and villages.

Day 1 Head for Pamplona, which is an intriguing city to visit even when the bulls aren't running. You can wander its ancient streets and visit its cathedral, with 14th- and 15th-century Gothic cloisters, as well as its Museo de Navarra. You might even have a chance to watch a game of *pelota.*

Day 2 Head south on the N-121 to the towns of Olite and Tudela. At Olite there aren't major sights to check out—it is the "Gothic town" itself that's of interest. It was a favorite address of the kings of Navarre. Try for a lunch at the parador before driving on to Tudela, where there are some suitable options for the night. At Tudela, you can visit the 12th-century Catedral de Santa Ana, famous for its Doorway of the Last Judgment, and explore its old town.

Day 3 Backtrack to Olite, and head east on the NA-132 to the town of Sangüesa on the left bank of the Aragón River. Once occupied by the Romans, this makes for an interesting stopover. As in Olite, there aren't major attractions here—it is the town itself that holds interest with all its antique charm. The most important attraction in the area is the Monasterio de San Salvador of Leyre, 10 miles (16km) to the east. The crypt of this 11th-century spiritual center of Navarre is one of Spain's major pieces of Romanesque architecture. After visiting it, return to Sangüesa for the night.

Day 4 If you have time in your schedule, take the N-240 back to Pamplona, then take the N-111 west to the city of Logroño. The capital of the province of La Rioja, this is a major distribution center for the area's wines. Visit its Catedral de Santa María de la Redonda and walk through the heart of the old town, calling at various bodegas to sample the wines.

Day 5 Head northwest on the A-68 (southwest of Logroño) to Haro, the center of the wine tours of the Rioja Alta district. In addition to its wineries and bodegas, Haro has some good hotels and plenty of places where you can sample the special dishes of the region—naturally with an accompaniment of Rioja wines. It is also the site of the Battle of Wine, held every June 29—an amusing, mock-medieval "brawl" in which opposing teams splatter each other with wine skins filled with the output from local vineyards.

1 Pamplona (Iruña)

56 miles (90km) SE of San Sebastián, 239 miles (385km) NE of Madrid, 104 miles (167km) NE of Zaragoza

It was in 1927 that Ernest Hemingway wrote *The Sun Also Rises.* But the book's glamour remains undiminished for foreigners who read it and then rush off to Pamplona to see the running (*encierro*) of the bulls during the Fiesta de San Fermín. Attempts to outlaw this world-famous ceremony have failed so far, and it remains a superstar attraction, particularly among bullfighting aficionados. The riotous Festival of San Fermín usually begins on July 6 and lasts through the 14th. Fireworks and Basque flute concerts are only some of the spectacles that give added color to the fiesta, where the wine flows. Those who want to know they'll have a bed after watching the *encierro* should reserve years in advance at one of the city's handful of hotels or boarding houses or stay in San Sebastián or some other neighboring town and visit Pamplona during the day.

Pamplona is more than just a city where an annual festival takes place. Long the most significant town in Spain's Pyrenean region, it was also a major stopover for those traveling either of two frontier roads: the Roncesvalles Pass or the Velate Pass. Once a fortified city, it was for centuries the capital of the ancient kingdom of Navarre.

In its historical core, the Pamplona of legend lives on, but the city has been engulfed by modern real-estate development. The saving grace of "new Pamplona" is La Taconera, a spacious "green lung" of fountain-filled gardens and parkland, lying west of the old quarter, where you will see students from the University of Navarre.

Pamplona became the capital of Navarre in the 10th century. Its golden age was during the reign of Charles III (called "the Noble"), who gave it its cathedral, in which he was eventually buried. Over the years the city has been the scene of many battles, with various factions struggling for control. Those who lived in the old quarter, the Navarrería, wanted to be allied with Castile, whereas those on the outskirts favored a French connection. Obviously, Castile eventually won out, although some citizens of Navarre today want Pamplona to be part of a newly created country of the Basque lands.

GETTING THERE **By Plane** The gateway for air travel to Navarre is Pamplona. The city is served by two weekday Aviaco flights from both Madrid and Barcelona; international connections can be made from either city. Arrivals are at Aeropuerto de Noaín (☎ **948/31-71-82**), four miles (6km) from the city center and accessible only by taxi.

By Train Three trains a day arrive from Madrid (trip time: 5 to 6 hours) and two to three from Barcelona (7 to 9 hours). Pamplona also has three daily train connections from San Sebastián to the north (1¾ hours) and four to seven daily from Zaragoza to the south (2 to 3 hours). For information, call **948/13-02-02.**

By Bus Buses connect Pamplona with several major Spanish cities: four per day from Barcelona (5½ hours), seven to nine per day from Zaragoza (3½ hours), and seven per day from San Sebastián (1½ hours). Call **948/22-38-54** for information.

By Car The A-15 Navarra national highway begins on the outskirts of Pamplona and runs south to join the A-68, midway between Zaragoza and Logroño. The N-240 connects San Sebastián with Pamplona.

VISITOR INFORMATION The tourist information office is at Duque de Ahumada, 3 (☎ **948/22-07-41**). Open Monday through Friday from 10am to 2pm and 4 to 7pm, Saturday and Sunday from 10am to 2pm.

SEEING THE SIGHTS

The heart of Pamplona is the **Plaza del Castillo,** built in 1847. It was the former Plaza de Toros (bullring). Expanded in 1932, it is today the seat of the provincial government, which has a certain amount of autonomy. This elegant tree-lined *paseo* becomes a virtual communal bedroom during the Festival of San Fermín.

The narrow streets of the old quarter extend from three sides of the square. The present bullring, the **Plaza de Toros,** lies just east and south of this square alongside the Paseo Hemingway. Running parallel to the east of the square is the **Calle Estafeta,** a narrow street that is the site of the running of the bulls. With its bars and

The Running of the Bulls

Beginning at noon on July 6 and continuing nonstop through July 14, the ✪ **Fiesta de San Fermín** is one of the most attended events in Europe, drawing thousands of tourists, who overtax the severely limited facilities of Pamplona. Get up early (or don't go to bed in the first place)—the bulls run every day at 8am sharp. To watch, be in position behind the barricades along the Calle Estafeta no later than 6am. Only the able-bodied and sober should plan to run. Women are not permitted to run (although many defy this ban each year).

There simply aren't enough beds or bullfight tickets to go around, and scalpers have a field day. Technically, tickets for a good seat in the ring go on sale at 8pm the night before the *corrida,* and tickets for standing room go on sale at 4pm on the day of the bullfight. But all of the tickets are sold out, and since it is impossible to obtain them through a travel agent beforehand, tourists have to use scalpers.

The fiesta draws half a million visitors, many of whom camp in the city parks. Temporary facilities are set up, but there are never enough beds. Hotel reservations should be confirmed at least six months beforehand. If you look respectable, some Pamplonicos may rent you a room. Be aware, however, that they may gouge you for the highest price they think you're willing to pay, and your "room" may turn out to be a dirty floor shared with others in a rotten part of the city. The tourist office will not make any recommendations during the festival—you're basically on your own. Many young visitors sleep on the grounds of the Ciudadela and Plaza Fueros traffic ring, but you could be mugged. Oldtime visitors to Pamplona advise that it's better to sleep in a group, on top of your belongings, and during the day, when it's safer than under a cloud of darkness. If you can't find a room, check your valuables at the bus station on the Calle Conde Oliveto (where there are also showers—free, but cold).

As for bars and restaurants, ignore all of the times given below. Most establishments operate around the clock at this time.

A Couple of Warnings: (1) Some people go to the festival not to watch the bulls but to pick pockets. (2) Don't take needless risks, such as leaping from a building in the hope that friends below will catch you. Many people do this each year, and not all are caught.

tascas, it attracts university students and is lively all year, even without a festival. During the festival it is the most frequented place in town next to the Plaza del Castillo. The bulls are also run through the barricaded streets of Santo Domingo and Mercaderes.

Catedral. Plaza de la Catedral. ☎ **948/22-56-79.** Free admission to cathedral; museum, 350 ptas. ($2.80). Mid-May to mid-Oct, daily 10:30am–1:30pm and 4–6pm. Off-season, daily 8–11:30am and 6–8pm.

The most important sight in Pamplona is the cathedral, dating from the late 14th century on the site of a former Romanesque basilica. The present facade, a mix of neoclassical and baroque, was the work of Ventura Rodríguez, architect to Charles III. The interior is Gothic, with lots of fan vaulting. In the center is the alabaster tomb of Charles III and his Castilian wife, Queen Leonor; it was done in 1416 by Flemish sculptor Janin de Lomme. The 14th- and 15th-century Gothic cloisters are a highlight of the cathedral. The Barbazán Chapel, off the east gallery, is noted for its vaulting. The Museo Diocesano, housed in the cathedral's refectory and kitchen, displays religious objects.

Museo de Navarra. Cuesta de Santa Domingo, s/n. ☎ **948/22-78-31.** Admission 300 ptas. ($2.40). Tues–Sat 9:30am–2pm and 5–7pm, Sun 11am–2pm.

The major museum of Pamplona is housed in a 16th-century hospital, the Nuestra Señora de la Misericordia, located close to the river. It has rich collections of both Roman artifacts, including some 2nd-century mosaics, and Romanesque art, plus an important Goya portrait of the Marqués de San Adrián. Gothic and Renaissance paintings are on the second floor. Murals from the 13th century are also a highlight.

ATTENDING A PELOTA MATCH

While in Pamplona, you might want to head about 3½ miles (6km) outside of town to Frontón Euskal-Jai Berri (☎ **948/33-11-59**), along the Avenida de Francia, to check out a professional *pelota* (jai alai) match. Game times are Thursday, Saturday, and Sunday at 4pm. Four matches are usually played on game days, and tickets can be purchased at any time during the sets. Admission to the bleachers is 1,200 to 1,600 pesetas ($9.60–$12.80). Betting is for aficionados only.

WHERE TO STAY

During the Festival of San Fermín, prices are three to four times higher than those listed below. In some instances a hotel will commit itself to prices it will charge at *Fiesta* (the original name of *The Sun Also Rises* when it was first published in Britain). Other owners charge pretty much what they think they can get, and they can get a lot. Therefore, agree on the price when making a reservation, if you've been able to get a reservation in the first place. At other times of the year, Pamplona is a reasonably priced tourist destination.

EXPENSIVE

Hotel Tres Reyes. Jardines de la Taconera, s/n, 31001 Pamplona. ☎ **800/448-8355** in the U.S., or 948/22-66-00. Fax 948/22-29-30. 160 rms, 8 suites. A/C MINIBAR TV TEL. 18,600 ptas. ($148.80) double; 32,500 ptas. ($260) suite. Festival, 32,400 ptas. ($259.20) double; 51,500 ptas. ($412) suite. AE, DC, MC, V. Parking 1,500 ptas. ($12) indoors; free outside.

Located a short walk west of the old town, just two blocks north of the ancient citadel, this is one of the finest hotels in town, surpassed only by Iruña Park. Modern, with a cement-balconied 10-story facade that curves around a pleasant garden, it provides tasteful and airy bedrooms with contemporary furnishings, lots of sunlight, and private baths. Many have balconies, and all are welcome refuges from the intensity of the local festivities.

Dining/Entertainment: The Grill Tres Reyes serves an excellently prepared Basque and Navarre cuisine. There's also a bar and an inexpensive cafeteria.

Services: 24-hour room service, laundry, concierge, babysitting, daily exercise classes.

Facilities: Car rentals; shopping boutiques; health club with sauna, gymnasium, squash courts, and massage facilities; heated outdoor swimming pool.

Iruña Park Hotel. Ronda Ermitagaña, s/n, 31008 Pamplona. ☎ **800/448-8335** in the U.S., or 948/17-32-00. Fax 948/17-23-87. 219 rms, 6 suites. A/C MINIBAR TV TEL. 18,500 ptas. ($148) double; 30,000 ptas. ($240) suite. AE, DC, MC, V. Parking 1,190 ptas. ($9.50).

A short walk west of the Parque de la Ciudadela, behind a facade of mirrored glass and white masonry, this is the largest and most convention-conscious, as well as the best, hotel in town. A large staff maintains the blandly furnished but comfortable bedrooms, some of which are suitable for persons with disabilities. The public rooms are modern and glossy, with deep armchairs and big windows.

Dining/Entertainment: The Royal Restaurant serves regional and international cuisine. There's also a bar.

Services: Room service (daily from 7am to 11pm), concierge, babysitting, laundry.

Facilities: Car rentals, sauna, solarium, business center.

MODERATE

Avenida. Zaragoza, 5, 31000 Pamplona. ☎ **948/24-54-54.** Fax 948/23-23-23. 24 rms. MINIBAR TV TEL. 13,900 ptas. ($111.20) double. AE, MC, V. Parking 1,100 ptas. ($8.80).

One of the best inns in town, this small, well-run place opened in 1989. The guest rooms are well furnished and maintained; some are even better than the inn's three-star rating suggests. Furnishings tend toward the sleek and modern, and local watercolors add a warm touch. Sixteen units are air-conditioned. Full lunches and dinners are served in the restaurant Leyre, known for its regional cuisine. There's also a cafeteria on the premises, serving snacks and drinks daily from 7:30am to 11pm.

Hotel Orhi. Leyre, 7, 31002 Pamplona. ☎ **948/22-85-00.** Fax 948/22-83-18. 55 rms. MINIBAR TV TEL. 14,000 ptas. ($112) double. AE, DC, MC, V. Parking 80 ptas. (65¢) nearby in municipal lot. Bus: 11.

Conveniently located in the town center, a few steps from the bus station, the Orhi was built around 1965 and renovated in 1996. It's been consistently popular with bull breeders and with matadors and their fans. Bedrooms are comfortable but simple, with sturdy furniture and high ceilings. A restaurant and a popular bar are on the premises.

Hotel Sancho Ramírez. Calle Sancho Ramírez, 11, 31008 Pamplona. ☎ **948/27-17-12.** Fax 948/17-11-43. 86 rms. A/C MINIBAR TV TEL. 13,850 ptas. ($110.80) double. AE, DC, MC, V. Bus: 7.

Built in 1981 and last renovated in 1990, the Sancho Ramírez has quickly drawn business away from its older competitors. Each of the reasonably priced units has a streamlined and contemporary decor; some contain minibars. The hotel restaurant serves a regional cuisine.

Maisonnave. Nueva, 20, 31001 Pamplona. ☎ **948/22-26-00.** Fax 948/22-01-66. 152 rms. MINIBAR TV TEL. 13,500 ptas. ($108) double. AE, DC, MC, V. Parking 1,200 ptas. ($9.60). Bus: 5, 9, or 10.

Located in the historic old town of Pamplona, west of the Plaza del Castillo and within easy walking distance of the *tascas* and restaurants, this place is solidly booked for the fiesta. You must reserve at least six months in advance—and then say a prayer. Rooms have been completely renovated, each well furnished, well maintained, and comfortable although blandly standardized. The hotel also offers a Navarrese restaurant serving a regional and Spanish national cuisine.

La Perla. Plaza del Castillo, 1, 31001 Pamplona. ☎ **948/22-77-06.** 67 rms, 8 suites. 9,150–12,200 ptas. ($73.20–$97.60) double; 19,150 ptas. ($153.20) suite. AE, DC, MC, V.

Opened in 1880 and last renovated in 1970, this is not the most prepossessing hotel in town—far from it. But at the festival it becomes the most desirable place to stay, because it opens onto the main square of Pamplona and overlooks Calle Estafeta, the straightaway of the *encerrio* through which the bulls run. The guest rooms are often furnished with an old-fashioned flair, and in days of yore they sheltered everybody from Ernest Hemingway to U.S. Senator Henry Cabot Lodge.

INEXPENSIVE

Residencia Eslava. Plaza Virgen de la O, 7, or Calle Recoletas, 20, 31001 Pamplona. ☎ **948/22-22-70.** Fax 948/22-51-57. 28 rms. TV TEL. 9,500 ptas. ($76) double. AE, DC, MC, V. Bus: 9.

Located right off Plaza de Recoletas, a 10-minute walk from the bus station, this renovated hotel manages to combine the spirit of old and new Spain. Its small living room resembles the drawing room of a distinguished Spanish house. All the average-size guest rooms are tastefully decorated; some have balconies with views of the city walls and the balconies beyond. A cellar lounge offers drinks.

WHERE TO DINE

EXPENSIVE

Alhambra. Calle Bergamín, 7. ☎ **948/24-50-07.** Reservations recommended. Main courses 1,875–2,875 ptas. ($15–$23); fixed-price menus 3,850–5,850 ptas. ($30.80–$46.80). AE, DC, MC, V. Mon–Sat 1–3:30pm and 9–11:30pm. NAVARRESE/SPANISH.

One of the best-known and most stable restaurants in Pamplona, Alhambra, a 16-minute walk from the cathedral, was established shortly after World War II. Since 1985, it has been directed by a well-trained group of new owners. Set within two paneled dining rooms, the restaurant features a complete selection of local wines and regional specialties, including carefully deboned sardines, grilled and served with truffles; grilled filet of hake with local herbs; and selected cuts of filet steak with sauces made from local mushrooms and garlic.

✪ **Europa.** Calle Espoz y Mina, 11. ☎ **948/22-18-00.** Reservations recommended. Main courses 2,200–3,200 ptas. ($17.60–$25.60); *menú del día* 3,000 ptas. ($24). AE, DC, MC, V. Mon–Sat 1–3:30pm and 9–11pm. SPANISH.

Located in the center of Pamplona, near the Plaza del Castillo, this is the best restaurant in the entire region—except for Josetxo (see below), with whom it is in a neck-to-neck race. Both have Michelin stars, which are rare in this part of Europe. Known for its creative interpretations of regional recipes, this restaurant occupies several intimate, recently renovated dining rooms within what was originally built in the 1930s as a private house. The chef and culinary artist is Pamplona-born Pilar Idoate, who prepares food based on seasonal availability of ingredients. Examples include baked potatoes stuffed with truffles and minced crayfish, roulades of sole with mountain herbs, filet steaks with Roquefort dressing, and such game dishes as venison and pheasant. Desserts include an orange mousse with a *marquesa de chocolate.*

✪ **Hartza.** Juan de Labrit, 19. ☎ **948/22-45-68.** Reservations recommended. Main courses 3,200–3,800 ptas. ($25.60–$30.40). AE, DC, MC, V. Tues–Sun 1:30–3:30pm, Tues–Sat 9–11:30pm. Closed Aug and 10 days at Christmas. NAVARRESE.

One of the oldest bodegas in town, this popular restaurant has flourished at this location near the bullring since the 1870s. Amazingly for such a small city, it too has a Michelin star, and is a rival in almost every way with Josetxo and Europa. The chef's touch is delicate, and although Hartza doesn't attempt as many dishes as Josetxo, what its chefs prepare is sublime and inventive. There's a summer garden for outdoor dining, plus a street-level bar. The portions are generous (and expensive); specialties change with the seasons but might include a well-seasoned vegetable soup, stuffed peppers, tournedos, hake and eel, and a selection of regional cheeses. The interior is air-conditioned during the hottest summer months.

✪ **Josetxo.** Plaza Principe de Viana, 1. ☎ **948/22-20-97.** Reservations recommended on weekends. Main courses 2,000–4,000 ptas. ($16–$32). AE, DC, V. Mon–Sat 1–3:30pm and 9–11pm. Closed Holy Week and Aug. BASQUE.

The finest, grandest, and most prestigious restaurant in town, Josexto is run by a civic-minded local family with more than 30 years' experience in the restaurant trade. The chef has a magic combination: inventiveness and a solid technique, backed up by the very freshest ingredients. Specialties vary with the seasons but might include cream-of-crabmeat soup, puff pastry stuffed with shellfish, lobster salad, a panaché of fresh vegetables with Serrano ham, sea bass cooked in white wine, several variations of goose pâté, and several dishes concocted from rabbit and trout. Dessert might be a tart of chocolate truffles layered with orange-flavored cream. The restaurant lies beside a busy traffic circle, four blocks south of the Plaza del Castillo.

Las Pocholas. Paseo de Sarasate, 6. ☎ **948/22-22-14.** Reservations required. Main courses 1,900–3,500 ptas. ($15.20–$28). AE, DC, MC, V. Mon–Sat 1–3:30pm and 9–11pm. Closed Aug. INTERNATIONAL.

This restaurant west of the Plaza del Castillo is well known for its good food and elegant air-conditioned dining salons. You can enjoy salt-cured cod with lobster chunks in garlic sauce, sea bass baked in red wine, a champagne-laden filet of sole, seasonal game dishes, a superb roast pork, and temptingly elaborate desserts.

INEXPENSIVE

$ Estafeta. Estafeta, 57. ☎ **948/22-16-05.** Reservations not accepted. Main courses 600–1,200 ptas. ($4.80–$9.60); fixed-price menu 1,000 ptas. ($8). AE, V. Daily 12:30–4pm, Fri–Sat 8:30–11:30pm. NAVARRESE.

During the festival, this self-service cafeteria west of Plaza del Castillo seems to be everybody's favorite budget restaurant. It's cheap and clean. Go as early as possible in the evening—the dishes are cooked at the same time and everything tastes fresher and better the earlier you dine. Drawing everybody from young American students to retired pensioners in Pamplona, the Estafeta is a relaxed, informal place with wholesome and filling food, including fresh hake, salt cod, squid, and trout in the style of Navarre.

PAMPLONA AFTER DARK

Café Iruña. Plaza del Castillo, 44. ☎ **948/22-42-93.**

This art deco bar and café, dating from 1888, has an outdoor terrace that is popular in summer. The winter crowd is likely to congregate around the bar, ordering combination plates and snacks in addition to drinks. The place thrives as a café/bar daily from 8am to 1am; however, it becomes more of a restaurant during the lunch hour. Platters of hot food are served to many of the local office workers and day laborers. There is no *menú del día,* but a full lunch, served daily from 1 to 3:30pm, costs from 1,500 to 2,000 pesetas ($12–$16). Beer goes for 160 pesetas ($1.30) at the bar, slightly more at a table.

Cafeteria El Molino. Bayona, 13. ☎ **948/25-10-90.**

This cafeteria, centrally located in the commercial Barrio San Juan, doubles as a popular tapas bar. Late in the evening its ambience becomes more youthful, lighthearted, and animated. The huge assortment of tapas includes fried shrimp, squid, anchovies, fish croquettes, and Russian salad. Tapas begin at 150 pesetas ($1.20), and most orders don't exceed 175 pesetas ($1.40), although some of the more expensive ones peak at 400 pesetas ($3.20). Open Monday through Saturday from 8am to 1am and Sunday from 9am to 1am.

2 Olite

27 miles (43km) S of Pamplona, 229 miles (369km) N of Madrid

A historical city, Olite sits in a rich agricultural belt with a Mediterranean climate of short winters and long hot summers. Cornfields and vineyards, along with large villages, pepper the countryside. It is also the center of a wine-making industry carried on by cooperative cellars. These wine merchants hold a local festival each year from September 14 to 18.

ESSENTIALS

GETTING THERE **By Train** Two to three trains per day run to Olite, taking 35 minutes one way. For rail information, call **948/70-06-28.**

By Bus Two companies, Conda (☎ **948/82-03-42)** and La Tafallesa (☎ **948/70-09-79**), run buses to Olite at the rate of 6 to 12 per day. The trip takes 45 minutes.

By Car Take the A-15 expressway south from Pamplona.

VISITOR INFORMATION The tourist information office is at Castillo Palacio, s/n (☎ **948/71-24-34**). It's open Monday through Friday from 10am to 2pm and 4 to 7pm, Saturday and Sunday from 10am to 2pm.

EXPLORING THE TOWN

In the 15th century, this "Gothic town" was a favorite address of the kings of Navarre. Charles III put Olite on the map, ordering that the **Palacio Real,** Plaza Carlos III el Noble, be built in 1406. The oldest towers and lookouts make visiting it a bit of an adventure. From April through September, hours are daily from 10am to 2pm and 5 to 8pm; October through March, daily 10am to 6pm. Admission is 300 pesetas ($2.40) for adults, 200 pesetas ($1.60) for children.

Next to the castle stands a Gothic church, **Iglesia de Santa María la Real,** with a splendid 12th-century doorway decorated with flowers.

WHERE TO STAY & DINE

Parador Príncipe de Viana. Plaza de los Teobaldos, 2, 31390 Olite. ☎ **948/74-00-00.** Fax 948/74-02-01. 43 rms. A/C MINIBAR TV TEL. 12,000–16,500 ptas. ($96–$132) double. AE, DC, MC, V. Free parking.

This parador in the center of town lies within one of the wings of the Palacio Real (see above). Surrounded by watchtowers, thick walls, and massive buttresses, the building is one of the most impressive sights in town. Only 12 accommodations, however, lie within the parador's medieval core, and these go for a premium over their very comfortable counterparts, which lie in a new wing, added to the castle in 1963, when it became a parador. Regardless of their location within the compound, the bedrooms are severely dignified and quite comfortable.

Even if you're visiting just for the day, consider a meal here, which might include grilled ribs or rabbit with snails. The chef takes pride in his regional offerings. Meals cost from 3,200 pesetas ($25.60). The restaurant is open daily from 1 to 4pm and 8:30 to 11pm.

SIDE TRIPS: UJÚE & A HISTORIC MONASTERY

High up on a mountain of the same name, **Ujúe,** a short drive east along a secondary road from Olite, seems to be from the Middle Ages. Built as a defensive town, it has cobblestoned streets and stone houses clustered around its fortress **Church of Santa María,** dating from the 12th to the 14th century. The heart of King Charles II ("the Bad") was placed to rest here. The church towers open onto views of the countryside, extending to Olite in the west and the Pyrenees in the east.

On the Sunday after St. Mark's Day (April 25), Ujúe is an important pilgrimage center for the people of the area, many of whom, barefoot and wearing tunics, carry large crosses. They come to Ujúe to worship Santa María, depicted on a Romanesque statue dating from 1190. It was plated in silver in the second half of the 15th century.

Motorists may want to consider yet another excursion from Olite, to the **Monastero del la Oliva,** 21 miles (34km) south of Olite. It was founded by King García Ramírez in 1164 and is an excellent example of Cistercian architecture. This monastery, one of the first to be constructed by French monks outside of France, once had great influence; its most notable feature is its 14th-century Gothic cloisters. The church, which dates from the late 12th century, is even more impressive than the cloisters. It has a distinguished portal and two rose windows. Pillars and pointed arches fill its interior. From April to September it's open daily from 9am to 8pm; October to March, daily from 9am to 6pm.

3 Tudela

52 miles (84km) S of Pamplona, 196 miles (316km) N of Madrid

In the center of the food belt of the Ribera or Ebro Valley, the ancient city of Tudela, with a population of only 30,000, is the second largest in Navarre. Situated on the right bank of the Ebro, it had a long history as a city where Jews, Arabs, and Christians lived and worked together. The Muslims made it a dependency of the caliphate at Córdoba, a period of domination that lasted until 1119. The city had a large Moorish quarter, the *morería,* and many old brick houses are in the Mudéjar style. King Sancho VII ("the Strong"), who defeated the Saracens, chose Tudela as his favorite residence in 1251. It has been a bishopric since the 18th century.

ESSENTIALS

GETTING THERE **By Train** Tudela lies on the southern rail line south of Pamplona. Two RENFE trains pass through here, one connecting La Rioja to Zaragoza via Castejón de Ebro. Another train links Zaragoza to Vitoria-Gasteiz via Pamplona. For more information and schedules (subject to change), call **948/82-06-46.**

By Bus Conda buses (☎ **948/22-10-26**) go to Tudela from Pamplona at the rate of seven to nine per day (trip time: 1½ hours).

By Car Take the A-15 south from Pamplona.

VISITOR INFORMATION The tourist information office is at Carrera Gaztambide, 11 (☎ **948/82-15-39**), open Monday through Friday from 10am to 2pm and 4 to 7pm, Saturday and Sunday from 10am to 2pm.

SEEING THE CATHEDRAL

Begin your exploration at the central Plaza de los Fueros, from where you can wander through a maze of narrow alleys that were laid out during the Moorish occupation. At the square called Plaza Vieja, visit Tudela's most important monument, the **Catedral de Santa Ana,** which is open Tuesday through Saturday from 9am to 1pm and 4 to 7pm, Sunday from 9am to 1pm. Constructed in the 12th and 13th centuries, it has an outstanding work of art on its facade, the Doorway of the Last Judgment, with about 120 groups of figures. Creation is depicted, but the artisans were truly inspired in showing the horrors of hell. The church contains many Gothic works of art, such as choir stalls from the 1500s. Several chapels are richly decorated, including one dedicated to Our Lady of Hope, with masterpieces from the 15th century. The main altar contains an exceptional *retablo* painted by Pedro Díaz de Oviedo. The small but choice cloisters, however, are the highlight of the tour.

Dating from the 12th and 13th centuries, they contain many Romanesque arches. Capitals on the columns include scenes from the New Testament.

WHERE TO STAY

Hotel Tudela. Avenida Zaragoza, 56, 31500 Tudela. ☎ **948/41-08-02.** Fax 948/41-09-72. 51 rms. A/C MINIBAR TV TEL. 9,500 ptas. ($76) double. AE, DC, MC, V. Free parking.

Set directly in front of the bullring (Plaza de Toros), this hotel was built in the 1930s and then tripled in size in two separate stages between 1989 and 1992. Today, with five floors, it's the best hotel in town, modern and functional, with a polite and helpful staff. The in-house restaurant draws a lively crowd, especially before and after bullfights, and serves well-prepared food (see separate recommendation below).

Morase. Paseo de Invierno, 2, 31500 Tudela. ☎ **948/82-17-00.** Fax 948/87-17-04. 11 rms. A/C MINIBAR TV TEL. 8,000 ptas. ($64) double. AE, DC, MC, V. Parking 1,000 ptas. ($8).

Not only is this one of the best places to stay in town, but it's also the leading restaurant (see below). Built in 1963 and completely renovated in 1986, it's small but very comfortable. The guest rooms are furnished in a modern style and have many conveniences.

WHERE TO DINE

Hotel Tudela. Avenida Zaragoza, 56. ☎ **948/41-08-02.** Reservations recommended. Main courses 1,800–2,200 ptas. ($14.40–$17.60); fixed-price menu 1,250 ptas. ($10). AE, MC, V. Daily 1–3:30pm, Mon–Sat 8–11pm. NAVARRESE.

Previously recommended as a place to stay, this is also one of the leading restaurants in the city. It offers typical and fresh products of the Ribera region, along with some magnificent fish and grilled meat. Try the omelet with codfish or the baked monkfish. You can also order beefsteak, followed by homemade pastries and desserts. And sample such wines as Viña Magaña. You can dine in air-conditioned comfort and will find parking on the premises.

Morase. Paseo de Invierno, 2. ☎ **948/82-17-00.** Reservations recommended. Main courses 1,100–2,200 ptas. ($8.80–$17.60); *menú del día* 2,150 ptas. ($17.20). AE, DC, MC, V. Daily 1–4pm, Mon–Sat 8:30 –11pm. Closed Aug 1–7. NAVARRESE.

The finest dining room in town, the Morase is a special delight when the first of the asparagus comes in, as the region's product is praised by gastronomes all over Spain. The specialties sound conventional but are well prepared, including a "pastel" of vegetables and hake baked with garlic. The lamb from Navarre is delectable, as is roast pork with herbs or red peppers stuffed with purée of seafood. Set on the banks of the Ebro, the restaurant offers a garden, an air-conditioned dining room, and adequate parking.

4 Sangüesa

253 miles (407km) N of Madrid, 29 miles (47km) SE of Pamplona

Sangüesa stands on the left bank of the Aragón River, at the Aragonese frontier. If after visiting the town you want to spend the night in the area, drive nine miles (14.5km) across the border south to Sos del Rey Católico, one of the most charming towns of Aragón; it boasts an excellent parador. With fewer than 5,000 inhabitants, Sangüesa is the largest town on the eastern side of the middle zone of Navarre.

Sangüesa was long a trading center. Today it is the hub of a large agricultural area, where grapes and cereals are produced on irrigated land. A "monumental town" in its own right, Sangüesa also serves as a base for a number of excursions in the area, including visits to some of Navarre's major attractions, such as the monastery at Leyre and Javier Castle.

Long known to the Romans, Sangüesa was later involved in the battle against Muslim domination in the 10th century. It has seen many wars, including occupation by supporters of Archduke Charles of Austria in 1710 and many a skirmish during the Carlist struggles of the 19th century. On several occasions, it has been the seat of the parliament of Navarre. Pilgrims crossing northern Spain to Santiago de Compostela stopped at Sangüesa.

ESSENTIALS

GETTING THERE **By Bus** Two to three buses bound for Sangüesa leave from Pamplona daily; the trip takes 45 minutes one way. For information, call **948/87-02-09.**

By Car From Pamplona, take the N-240, a secondary road, to Sangüesa.

VISITOR INFORMATION The tourist information office is at Calle Alfonso el Batallador, 20 (☎ **948/87-03-29**). Open Monday through Friday from 10am to 2pm and 4 to 7pm, Saturday and Sunday from 10am to 2pm.

SEEING THE CHURCHES

Iglesia de Santa María stands at the far end of town beside the river. Begun in the 12th century, it has a doorway from the 12th and 13th centuries that is one of the outstanding works of Romanesque art. The south portal, filled with remarkably carved sculptures, is Santa María's most outstanding feature. The vestry contains a 4½-foot-high processional monstrance from the 15th century.

The nearby **Iglesia de Santiago** is a late traditional Romanesque structure from the 12th and 13th centuries. It has a battlement-type tower and contains an impressive array of Gothic sculpture, which was discovered under the church only in 1964. Look for the bizarre statue of St. James atop a big conch.

WHERE TO STAY & DINE

$ **Yamaguchy.** Cerretera de Javier, s/n, 31400 Sangüesa, ☎ **948/87-01-27.** Fax 948/87-07-00. 40 rms. A/C TV TEL. 7,200 ptas. ($57.60) double. AE, DC, MC, V. Free parking.

The best place to stay (from an extremely limited choice) is this hotel ¼ mile (.40km) outside town on the road to Javier. In summer its most attractive feature is its swimming pool. Bedrooms are in a functional modern style, but they're clean and comfortable.

Meals costing from 2,700 pesetas ($21.60) are available daily from 1 to 3:30pm and 8:30 to 11pm. The many Navarrese dishes served include lamb stew and steak. You can also sample some of the award-winning red and rosé wines from local wine cellars.

SIDE TRIPS TO LEYRE & JAVIER CASTLE

The **Monasterio de San Salvador of Leyre** (☎ **948/88-40-11**) is 10 miles (16km) east of Sangüesa, perched on the side of a mountain of the same name, overlooking the Yesa Dam. Of major historical and artistic interest, the main body of the monastery was constructed between the 11th and the 15th centuries on the site of a primitive pre-Romanesque church; in time, it became the spiritual center of Navarre. Many kings, including Sancho III, made it their pantheon. Its crypt, consecrated in 1057, ranks as one of the country's major works of Romanesque art.

When the church was reconstructed by the Cistercians in the 13th century, they kept the bays of the old Romanesque church. The 12th-century west portal is outstanding and richly adorned. Called the Porta Speciosa, it is covered with intricate carvings; in one section, Jesus and his disciples are depicted atop mythical creatures. Some of the other artistic treasures of this once-great monastery are displayed at the Museo de Navarra in Pamplona.

When Navarre joined with Aragón, the power of Leyre declined. Finally, in the 19th century, the monastery was abandoned. It wasn't until 1954 that a Benedictine order came here and began the difficult restoration.

The monastery lies 2$^1/_2$ miles (4km) from Yesa, which itself is on N-240, the major road linking Pamplona, Sangüesa, and Huesca. Take the N-240 into Yesa, then follow an uphill road signposted "Leyre, 4 km" to reach the monastery. Visits are possible Monday through Friday from 10:30am to 2pm and 4 to 7pm, Sunday from 10:30 to 11:15am, 1 to 2pm, and 4 to 7pm. Admission is 150 pesetas ($1.20) for adults and 50 pesetas (40¢) for children.

At Leyre you'll also find one of the most unusual accommodations in Navarre, the **Hospedería,** Monasterio de Leyre, 31410 Leyre (☎ **948/88-41-00;** fax 948/88-41-37). This two-star inn with 32 rooms (all with private baths and phone) was created from the annexes constructed by the Benedictines in the 1700s. The guest rooms open onto views of the Yesa Reservoir. The rate is 8,500 pesetas ($68) for a double room, and parking is free. The hotel restaurant serves good Navarrese fare in a rustic setting. Meals go for 1,800 pesetas ($14.40). The restaurant is open daily from 1 to 3:30pm and 8:30 to 10:30pm. Credit cards (AE, DC, MC, V) are accepted. The Hospedería is closed December 25 through January 1.

The second major excursion possible in the area is to **Castillo de Javier** (☎ **948/88-40-00**), five miles (8km) from Sangüesa. The castle dates from the 11th century, but owes its present look to restoration work carried out in 1952. Francisco Javier (Xavier), patron of Navarre, was born here on April 7, 1506. Along with Ignatius Loyola, he founded the order of the Society of Jesus (the Jesuits) in the mid-16th century. The castle houses a magnificent 13th-century crucifix, and thousands of the faithful congregate at Javier on two consecutive Sundays in March. This is the most popular pilgrimage in Navarre. Known as the Javierada, it pays homage to Francisco Javier, who was canonized in 1622.

During your visit to the castle, visit the oratory, the guard chamber, the great hall, and the saint's bedroom. The castle is teeming with interesting art, including a 15th-century fresco called the *Dance of Death.* To get to the castle, take the N-240 to Yesa, then follow an unmarked road that's signposted for Castillo de Javier. It's open daily from 9am to 1pm and 4 to 7pm. Admission is free.

For food and lodging, go to the tranquil **Hotel El Mesón,** Zona Turistica, s/n, 31411 Javier (☎ **948/88-40-35;** fax 948/88-42-26), right in the center of the hamlet of Javier, on the same unmarked road the castle is on. Management rents eight comfortably furnished bedrooms, but the hotel is closed December 15 through February. Doubles go for 5,800 pesetas ($46.40), and parking is free. The hotel's restaurant offers the best food in the area, with a fixed-price menu going for 1,650 pesetas ($13.20).

5 Logroño

205 miles (330km) N of Madrid, 57 miles (92km) W of Pamplona

The capital of the province of La Rioja, Logroño is also the major distribution center for the area's wines and agricultural products. Because La Rioja is so small, Logroño could be your base for touring all the major attractions of the province. Although much of Logroño is modern and dull, it does have an old quarter known to the pilgrims crossing this region to visit the tomb of St. James at Santiago de Compostela.

ESSENTIALS

GETTING THERE **By Train** There are five daily RENFE trains from Barcelona (trip time: 6 to 7½ hours) and two per day from Madrid (5 hours). From Bilbao in the north, three trains arrive per day (3 hours). For information, call **941/23-17-37.**

By Bus Five buses arrive daily from Pamplona (trip time: 2 hours) and from Madrid (5 hours). For information, call **941/23-59-83.**

By Car Take the N-111 southwest from Pamplona or the A-68 northwest form Zaragoza.

VISITOR INFORMATION The tourist office is at Calle Miguel Villanueva, 10 (☎ **941/29-12-60**). Open June through October, Monday through Saturday from 10am to 2pm and 4:30 to 7:30pm, Sunday from 10am to 2pm; November through May, Monday through Friday from 9am to 2pm.

SEEING THE SIGHTS

The **Catedral de Santa María de la Redonda,** Plaza del Mercado (☎ **941/25-76-11**), has vaulting from the 1400s, but the baroque facade dates from 1742. Inside, you can visit its 1762 Chapel of Our Lady of the Angels, built in an octagonal shape with rococo adornments. Constructed on top of an earlier Romanesque church, today's cathedral is known for its broad naves and twin towers. Open daily from 8am to 1pm and 6:30 to 8:30pm.

From the square on which the cathedral sits, walk up Calle de la Sagasta until you reach the 12th-century **Iglesia de Santa María de Palacio,** Marqués de San Nicolás, once part of a royal palace. The palace part dates from 1130, when Alfonso VII offered his residence to the Order of the Holy Sepulchre. Most of what he left is long gone, of course, but there is still a pyramid-shaped spire from the 13th century.

Walk through the heart of Logroño, exploring the gardens of the broad **Paseo del Espolón.** In the late afternoon, all the residents turn out for their *paseo.*

While in Logroño, you can visit the **Bodegas Olarra,** Poligono Independencia de Cantabria, s/n (☎ **941/23-52-99**), open Monday through Friday from 9am to 1pm and 3 to 7pm. Reserve in advance for a tour. It produces wines under the Otonal and Olarra labels.

WHERE TO STAY

Hotel Murrieta. Marqués de Murrieta, 1, 26005 Logroño. ☎ **941/22-41-50.** Fax 941/22-32-13. 111 rms. MINIBAR TV TEL. 9,350 ptas. ($74.80) double. AE, MC, V. Parking 1,400 ptas. ($11.20).

Set at the western border of the historic part of town, a block north of the Gran Vía, this 1980s cement-sided hotel offers comfortable, pristinely decorated rooms and relatively good value. The public rooms, all modernized in 1991, are outfitted with colored marble, deep carpeting, and tasteful upholstery.

Efficient and unpretentious, the Murrieta restaurant serves both regional and Spanish food, along with an appealing collection of Rioja wines. Uncomplicated à la carte lunches and dinners are served in the hotel's cafeteria.

Room service is available from 7:30am to midnight; other extras include laundry, babysitting, and car rentals.

$ La Numantina. Calle Sagasta, 4, 26001 Logroño. ☎ **941/25-41-11.** 17 rms. TEL. 4,300–4,700 ptas. ($34.40–$37.60) double. AE, MC, V. Closed Dec 24–Jan 8.

This rather simple hotel, one of the best bargains in town, lies on a street central to both the historic core and the commercial district. Its basic rooms are clean and reasonably comfortable. No breakfast is served, but you can buy pastries at a shop across the street.

Paris. Avenida La Rioja, 8, 26000 Logroño. ☎ **941/22-87-50.** 36 rms. TEL. 5,700–6,300 ptas. ($45.60–$50.40) double. No credit cards.

One of the town's bargain accommodations lies within what was originally built during the 1920s as a private house. Renovated during the 1980s, it is near the police station and attracts many employees of the wine industry who are in Logroño on business. Bedrooms are outfitted in a basic modern style—absolutely no personality but suitable for an overnight stop. No meals are served, but many cafés populate the neighborhood.

WHERE TO DINE

Asador La Chata. Carnicerías, 3. ☎ **941/25-12-96.** Reservations required. Main courses 1,250–1,900 ptas. ($10–$15.20); fixed-price menu 3,000 ptas. ($24). DC, MC, V. Daily 1:30–4pm, Wed–Sat 9–11pm. RIOJANA.

This delightful dining choice is reeking with ambience and a sense of Old Navarre. Founded in 1821, it occupies a building close to the town's cathedral. Its tactful owners define it as an *asador,* which means that it specializes in wood-roasted meat dishes, in this case in the style of the region. Although lunch is an everyday event, and much patronized by workers in the local wine trade, dinner is served only four evenings a week. Because of the establishment's small size (only 40 seats), advance reservations are essential. Within the wood-paneled dining room, ringed with artifacts of the wine trade, you can enjoy the two house specialties: fresh asparagus prepared with strips of locally cured ham, and *cabrito asado* (roast baby goat with herbs). Meats are succulently tender.

$ **Casa Emilio.** Pérez Galdós, 18. ☎ **941/25-88-44.** Reservations recommended. Main courses 1,800–2,200 ptas. ($14.40–$17.60); *menú del día* 3,000 ptas. ($24). AE, DC, MC, V. Mon–Sat 1:30–4pm and 9–11:30pm. Closed Aug. RIOJANA.

An ample bar greets you as you enter Casa Emilio, which serves primarily roasts, especially goat and beef. In air-conditioned comfort, you can also enjoy peppers stuffed with codfish or baked hake. From the well-stocked wine cellar come some of the finest Rioja wines. Casa Emilio lies south of the old town, directly west of the major boulevard, Vara de Rey.

Las Cubanas. San Agustín, 17. ☎ **941/22-00-50.** Reservations recommended. Main courses 1,500–2,300 ptas. ($12–$18.40). MC, V. Mon–Sat 1–4pm, Mon–Fri 9–11pm. Closed July 15–30 and Sept 15–30. RIOJANA.

This family-owned establishment located in the center of the old town, west of the police station and three minutes from the cathedral, succeeds in maintaining a happy balance between quality and price. The cuisine is based on fresh seasonal ingredients; try the veal with mushrooms. The restaurant is air-conditioned.

✪ **La Merced.** Marqués de San Nicolas, 109. ☎ **941/22-11-66.** Reservations required. Main courses 1,900–3,600 ptas. ($15.20–$28.80). AE, DC, MC, V. Mon–Sat 1:15–3:30pm and 9–11pm. Closed Aug 1–21. RIOJANA/INTERNATIONAL.

This restaurant occupies the street level and two upper floors of the 18th-century palace of the Marqués of Covarrubias. It is the most elegant and refined dining choice in the entire region, often attracting some of the world's great wine connoisseurs, who also have demanding palates when it comes to cuisine. Merced generally pleases.

Much of the decoration inside is in the original baroque style of the palace. The wines in its collection are especially well represented in the Rioja category. The chefs offer a modern interpretation of regional cuisine. The cookery is savory and based on a splendid repertoire of market-fresh ingredients—never destroyed by oversaucing. Your meal might include steamed sea bass with truffle sauce, roast lamb with potatoes, sweet peppers stuffed with spicy meat, or fresh seasonal vegetables. The dessert special is a succulent version of caramelized apples with chocolate sauce and cream.

6 Haro

223 miles (359km) N of Madrid, 30 miles (48km) NE of Logroño

Center of the wine tours of the Rioja Alta district, the region around Haro has been compared to Tuscany. Come here to taste the wine at the bodegas, as the international wine merchants do all year long (but especially after the autumn harvest).

ESSENTIALS

GETTING THERE **By Train** Four to five RENFE trains (☎ **941/31-15-97**) run daily from Logroño (trip time 1 hour one way). There are also four to five connections per day from Zaragoza; the trip takes 3¹/₂ hours one way.

By Bus Five to six buses per day run to Haro from Logroño. Trip time is 45 minutes to 1 hour one way.

By Car Take the A-68 expressway (south of Logroño) northwest to the turnoff for Haro.

VISITOR INFORMATION The tourist information office is at Plaza Hermanos Florentino Rodríguez, s/n (☎ **941/31-27-26**). Open Monday through Saturday from 10am to 2pm and 4:30 to 7:30pm, Sunday from 10am to 2pm.

SEEING THE SIGHTS & VISITING THE BODEGAS

The town itself deserves a look before you head for the bodegas. Its old quarter is filled with mansions, some from the 16th century; the most interesting ones lie along **Calle del Castillo.** At the center of the old quarter is the major architectural landmark of the town, the **Iglesia de San Tomás,** Plaza de la Iglesia. Distinguished by its wedding-cake tower and plateresque south portal, the 16th-century church has a Gothic interior.

You could spend at least three days touring the wineries in the town, but chances are that a few visits will satisfy your curiosity. The **Bodegas Muga,** Barrio de la Estación, s/n (☎ **941/31-04-98**), near the rail station, offers tours (usually in Spanish) of its wine cellars, Monday through Friday at 11am and 4pm.

You can also visit the **Compañia Vinícola del Norte de España,** Avenida Costa del Vino, 21 (☎ **941/31-06-50**), which is open Monday through Friday from 9am to 1pm and 3 to 6:30pm; it's closed from mid-August to mid-September. It dates from the 1870s, and its cellars have some vintages more than 100 years old.

Finally, pay a visit to **Rioja Alta,** Avenida Vizcaya, s/n (☎ **941/31-03-46**), not far from the Muga. It's open Monday through Friday from 8:30am to 1:30pm and 4 to 6pm (closed from mid-August to mid-September). Visits must be arranged in advance.

If you arrive in Haro in August or the first two weeks in September, when many of the bodegas are closed, settle instead for drinking wine in the *tascas* that line the streets between Parroquía and Plaza de la Par. After a night spent there, you'll forget all about the bodega tours. Some of the finest wines in Spain are sold at these *tascas,* along with tapas—all at reasonable prices.

WHERE TO STAY

Los Agustinos. Calle San Agustin, 2, 26200 Haro. ☎ **941/31-13-08.** Fax 941/30-31-48. 60 rms, 2 suites. A/C TV TEL. 12,500 ptas. ($100) double; 24,200 ptas. ($193.60) suite. AE, DC, MC, V. Parking 700 ptas. ($5.60).

A former Augustinian convent has been turned into a four-star hotel in the center of Haro. Since its restoration and reopening in 1990, it has become the most desirable place to stay in a town that has always had too few accommodations. Owned by a Basque chain of hotels, it lies in a "zone of tranquillity." The bedrooms are well appointed and comfortable. The restaurant serves good-tasting regional meals, accompanied by selections from a well-stocked cellar of Rioja wines.

Iturrimurri. Carretera N-124, km 41, s/n, 26200 Haro. ☎ **941/31-12-13.** Fax 941/31-17-21. 36 rms. A/C MINIBAR TV TEL. 9,900 ptas. ($79.20) double. AE, MC, V. Free parking.

Lying half a mile southeast of the city on the highway, this is the "second choice" hotel in Haro. The comfortable rooms are attractively furnished, many with impressive views. There is an animated cafeteria, as well as a large dining room serving regional meals accompanied by Rioja wines. Ample parking facilities are also provided. In summer the garden and the swimming pool are compelling reasons to stay here.

WHERE TO DINE

Beethoven I, II, y III. Santo Tomás, 3–5, ☎ **941/31-11-81.** Reservations required in summer. Main courses 1,800–2,200 ptas. ($14.40–$17.60); fixed-price menus 1,600–2,000 ptas. ($12.80–$16). MC, V. Wed–Sun 1:30–4pm, Wed–Mon 9–11:30pm. Closed July 1–15 and Dec. RIOJANA/BASQUE.

The premier restaurant of Haro, located in the center of town, is actually three restaurants, standing beside each other. Each offers good food and value. One of them is a large old house where a bar has been installed. Have a drink here, then perhaps move next door to sample the more modern dining rooms at Beethoven II or III. They're justifiably famous for their platters of wild mushrooms, which owner Carlos Aquirre raises himself. Try the stuffed filet of sole, vegetable stew, or wild pheasant, finishing off with an apple tart. The interiors are air-conditioned. The wine cellars are among the finest in the area.

Terete. Arana, 17. ☎ **941/31-00-23.** Reservations recommended. Main courses 3,000–4,000 ptas. ($24–$32); fixed-price menu 1,500 ptas. ($12). AE, DC, MC, V. Tues–Sun 1:15–4pm, Tues–Sat 8:30–11pm. Closed Oct. RIOJANA.

This place has been a *horno asado* (restaurant specializing in roasts) since 1867 and is beloved by locals for its roast suckling pig. The service is discreet, the food both savory and succulent—the kitchen has had a long time to learn the secrets of roasting meats. The dishes are all prepared according to traditional regional recipes. When the fresh asparagus comes in, that is reason enough to dine here. The local peaches in season make the best dessert. Naturally, the finest of Rioja wines are served. Terete is located in the center of Haro.

18 Basque Country

The Basques are the oldest traceable ethnic group in Europe. Their language, called Euskera, predates any of the commonly spoken Romance languages, and its origins, like that of the Basque race itself, are lost in obscurity. Perhaps the Basques were descended from the original Iberians, who lived in Spain before the arrival of the Celts some 3,500 years ago. Conqueror after conqueror, Roman to Visigoth to Moor, may have driven these people into the Pyrenees, where they stayed and carved out a life for themselves—filled with tradition and customs practiced to this day.

The region is called Euskadi, which in Basque means "collection of Basques." In a very narrow sense it refers to three provinces of Spain: Guipúzcoa (whose capital San Sebastián, the number-one sightseeing destination in Euskadi, features La Concha, one of Spain's best-loved and most popular stretches of sand), Viscaya (whose capital is industrial Bilbao), and Alava (with its capital at Vitoria). But to Basque nationalists, who dream of forging a new nation that will one day unite all the Basque lands, Euskadi also refers to the northern part of Navarre and three provinces in France, including the famed resort of Biarritz.

The three current Basque provinces occupy the eastern part of the Cantabrian Mountains, between the Pyrenees and the valley of the Nervión. They maintained a large degree of independence until the 19th century, when they finally gave in to control from Castile, which recognized their ancient rights and privileges until 1876.

As a badge of pride, Basques wear a *boina,* a beret of red, blue, or white woolen cloth. Today, more than ever, the wearing of the *boina* is also a political statement. In recent years, more and more graffiti have appeared. You'll see such slogans as *Euskadi Ta Askatasuna* ("Freedom for Basques") painted virtually everywhere. Although most of the people are friendly, hospitable, and welcoming, a small but violent minority has given the land much bad publicity. Politics, however, rarely needs to concern the foreign traveler intent on having a vacation in these lands, which remain some of the most beautiful in Spain.

Basque Country

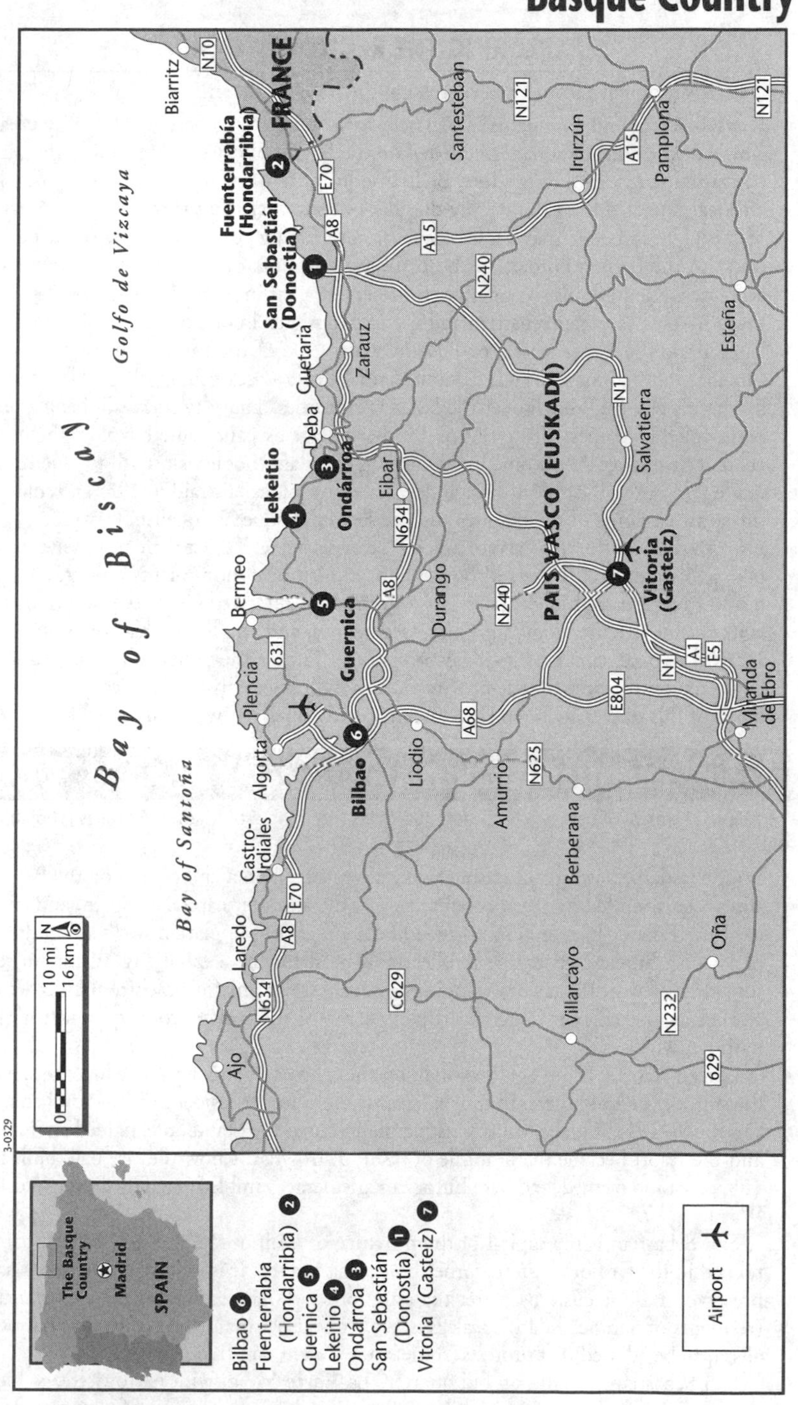

EXPLORING THE REGION BY CAR

Most visitors arrive from France, crossing the border at Irún.

Days 1–2 Spend two nights in San Sebastián, enjoying its beaches and lively tapas crawls through the old quarter. Situated on the Bay of Biscay, it is surrounded by verdant mountainsides and exudes a Belle Epoque aura. Its moderate climate makes it an ideal retreat during the steamy dog days of summer. You might take a day trip or overnight to Fuenterrabía, a seaside resort and fishing port that, because of its proximity to the French border, has been subject to numerous attacks throughout the centuries. Fuenterrabía has many well-preserved villas in its medieval quarter.

Days 3–4 Leave San Sebastián and spend two nights in one of the little fishing villages along the Costa Vasca, or Basque coast. One of the most desirable places is Ondárroa, which for some is the quintessential Costa Vasca fishing village. Here town life hasn't changed much over the last few centuries. Laundry lines still hang from plant-filled balconies. Using this or another village as your center, explore the others that lie nearby. Allow time for a morning or an afternoon visit south to Guernica, made famous by Picasso. Although devastated by a Nazi air raid in 1937, it remains the spiritual home of the Basques and the seat of Basque nationalism.

Day 5 Bilbao, the "Chicago of Spain," deserves a day. To get there from Guernica, take 635 south to A-8 west. Although light in historical monuments, this gray-hued bastion of industrial might possesses a number of interesting secrets. Among them is its cuisine: try the restaurant Guría (see below), and you'll see what we mean.

Day 6 If time remains, take the A-68 south to Vitoria, the capital of Alava, the most neglected of the three Basque provinces. Although once considered "sleepy," the students of this university town keep taverns rowdy until the wee hours.

1 San Sebastián (Donostia)

13 miles (21km) W of the French border, 300 miles (483km) N of Madrid, 62 miles (100km) E of Bilbao

San Sebastián (Donostia in Basque)—ideally situated on a choice spot on the Bay of Biscay, surrounded by green mountains—is the summer capital of Spain, and here the Belle Epoque lives on. From June to September the population swells as hundreds of Spanish bureaucrats escape the heat and head for this capital city. A tasteful resort, it has few of the tawdry trappings associated with major beachfront cities. It is also an ideal excursion center for trips to some of the Basque country's most fascinating towns.

Queen Isabella II put San Sebastián on the map as a tourist resort when she spent the summer of 1845 there. In time it became the summer residence of the royal court. On July 8, 1912, Queen María Cristina inaugurated the grand hotel named after her, and the resort became the pinnacle of fashion. In what is now the city hall, built in 1887, a casino opened, and here European aristocrats gambled in safety during World War I.

San Sebastián is the capital of the province of Guipúzcoa, the smallest in Spain, tucked in the far northeastern corner bordering France. It is said that Guipúzcoa has preserved Basque customs better than any other province. Half of the *donostiarras* (residents of San Sebastián) speak Euskera. It is also a major seat of Basque nationalism, so be advised that protests, sometimes violent, are frequent.

San Sebastián contains an old quarter, **La Parte Vieja,** with narrow streets, hidden plazas, and medieval houses, but it is primarily a modern city of elegant shops, wide boulevards, sidewalk cafés, and restaurants.

Basking in the Basque Culture

The *Pays Basque,* or *Euskadi* (Basque country), is home to a unique culture rich in folklore, charm, and a sense of national destiny. Enterprising and seafaring, the Basques trace their roots to a pre-Indo–European people whose origins aren't fully known. The Basques resisted the incursions of both the ancient Romans and the Moors and later became known throughout Europe for their commercial zeal, capacity for hard work, and culinary skill.

The Basque language is a linguistic riddle that has puzzled ethnologists for years; its grammar, syntax, and vocabulary are in no way related to those of any other European language. Depending on the dialect being spoken, the language is known as Uskara, Euskara, or Eskuara. Although on the wane since the beginning of this century, the Basque language is now enjoying a modest renaissance.

Geographically, the Basque country straddles the western foothills of the Pyrenees, so the Basque people live in both France and Spain—but mostly in the latter. During the Spanish Civil War (1936–39) the Basques were on the Republican side and were defeated by Franco. Oppression during the Franco years has led to deep-seated resentment against the policies of Madrid.

The Basque separatist movement Euskadi ta Azkatasuna (Basque Nation and Liberty) and the French organization Enbata (Ocean Wind) engaged (unsuccessfully) in guerrilla activity in 1968 to secure a united Basque state. Despite the relative calm of recent years, many Basque nationalists fervently wish that the Basque people could be united into one autonomous state instead of being divided between France and Spain.

La Concha is the most famous beach, where it seems half the population of Spain and France spend their days under striped canopies when they're not dashing into the refreshingly cool waters of the bay. The shell-shaped La Concha is half-encircled by a promenade, where crowds mill during the evening. The adjoining beach is the **Playa de Ondarreta.** The climate here is more Atlantic than Mediterranean.

San Sebastián has a good but insufficient choice of hotels in summer, plus an excellent number of Basque restaurants, most of which are expensive. Its chief drawback is overcrowding—it is overpopulated in July, and there is no space at all in August.

Bullfights, art and film festivals, sporting events, and cultural activities keep San Sebastián hopping during the summer season.

ESSENTIALS

GETTING THERE **By Plane** From Madrid, Iberia Airlines offers two daily flights to San Sebastián, plus one daily flight from Barcelona. The domestic airport is at nearby Fuenterrabía. From Fuenterrabía buses run to the center of San Sebastián every 12 minutes from 7:48am to 10pm. Phone **943/66-85-00** for flight information.

By Train From Madrid, RENFE runs trains to the French border at Irún, many of which stop in San Sebastián (a 6- to 7-hour trip). An overnight train from Paris to Madrid also stops in San Sebastián—just in time for breakfast (and San Sebastián's cafés serve the best croissants south of the Pyrenees). RENFE also provides overnight train service from Barcelona to San Sebastián and on to Bilbao. For RENFE information, call **943/28-35-99.**

By Bus San Sebastián is well linked by a bus network to many of Spain's major cities, although if you're in Madrid, it's more convenient to take a train. Nine to 29 buses a day connect San Sebastián to Bilbao (trip time: 1 1/4 hours); 3 daily buses arrive from Barcelona (7 hours); 5 buses run daily from Pamplona (1 1/2 hours). These routes are covered by several private bus companies. The tourist office (see below) distributes an information pamphlet outlining various routes, the companies that service these runs, and telephone numbers to call for schedules.

By Car From Madrid, take the N-1 toll road north to Burgos, then take the A-1 to Miranda de Ebro. From there, continue on the A-68 north to Bilbao and then the A-8 east to San Sebastián. From Pamplona, take the A-15 north to the N-1 route, which will take you into San Sebastián.

VISITOR INFORMATION The tourist information office is at Calle Reina Regente, s/n (☎ **943/48-11-66**). Open Monday through Saturday from 9am to 2pm and 3:30 to 7pm, Sunday from 10am to 1pm.

SPECIAL EVENTS Two weeklong events draw visitors from around the world. In mid-August, San Sebastián stages its annual carnival, **Aste Nagusia,** a joyous celebration of traditional Basque music and dance, along with fireworks, cooking competitions, and sports events. In mid-September, the San Sebastián **International Film Festival** draws luminaries from America and Europe. The actual dates of these festivals vary from year to year, so check with the tourist office (see above). Also, in the second half of July, San Sebastián hosts a jazz festival, Jazzaldia.

ENJOYING THE TOWN

People come to San Sebastián for fun and to take a promenade along the Paseo de la Concha. The monuments, such as they are, can easily be viewed before lunch.

Museo de San Telmo, Plaza Zuloaga, 1 (☎ **943/42-49-70**), housed in a 16th-century Dominican monastery, contains an impressive collection of Basque artifacts dating from unrecorded Iberian times. The display includes works by Zuloaga (*Torreillos en Turégano,* for example), "golden age" artists such as El Greco and Ribera, and a large number of Basque painters. Standing in the old town at the base of Monte Urgull, the museum is open Tuesday through Saturday from 10am to 1:30pm and 4 to 7pm, Sunday 10am to 1:30pm. Admission is free.

The **Paseo Nuevo** is a wide promenade that almost encircles **Monte Urgull,** one of the two mountains between which San Sebastián is nestled (Monte Igueldo is the other one). A ride along this promenade opens onto panoramic vistas of the Bay of Biscay. The *paseo* comes to an end at the **Palacio del Mar,** Muelle, 34 (☎ **943/42-49-77**), an oceanographic museum and aquarium. Here you can see the skeleton of the last whale caught in the Bay of Biscay, in 1878. The museum is open Tuesday through Saturday from 10am to 1:30pm and 5 to 8:30pm, Sunday from 11am to 2pm. Admission is 400 pesetas ($3.20) for adults, 100 pesetas (80¢) for children ages 5 to 12, and free for children 4 and under.

Other sights include **El Palacio de Miramar,** which stands on its own hill opening onto La Concha. In the background is the residential district of Antiguo. Queen María Cristina, after whom the grandest hotel in the north of Spain is named, opened this palace in 1893, but by the turbulent 1930s it had fallen into disrepair. The city council took it over in 1971, and renovations continue. You can visit daily in summer from 8am to 8:30pm and daily in winter from 8am to 6pm. Because you can't go inside the palace, you must settle for a look at the lawns and gardens. The palace stands on land splitting the two major beaches of San Sebastián: Playa de la Concha and Playa de Ondarreta.

Another palace of interest is the **Palacio de Ayete,** which was constructed by the Duke of Bailéen in 1878 and became the summer home of King Alfonso XIII and his queen, María Cristina, until their own Palacio Miramar (see above) was completed. Standing in 250,000 square feet of parkland, the palace also served as the summer home of Franco from 1940 until 1975. The residence remains closed to the public, but you can wander through the beautiful grounds daily in summer from 10am to 5pm. To reach it, take bus number 19 to Ayete from Plaza de Guipúzcoa.

Finally, to get the best view of the city take the funicular to the top of Monte Igueldo, where from the belvedere you get a fabulous view of the bay and the Cantabrian coastline. From June 25 through September 25, the funicular runs Monday through Friday from 10am to 9pm and on Saturday and Sunday from 10am to 10pm. Off-season service is daily from 11am to 8pm. A round-trip fare costs 170 pesetas ($1.35). It's also possible to drive up. In spring the air is scented with honey-suckle.

WHERE TO STAY

If you book well in advance, you'll find many good hotel values, but in season most hoteliers may insist that you take at least half board (breakfast plus one main meal).

VERY EXPENSIVE

✪ **Hotel María Cristina.** Paseo República Argentina, 4, 20004 San Sebastián. ☎ **800/221-2340** in the U.S., or 943/42-49-00. Fax 943/42-39-14. 109 rms, 30 suites. A/C MINIBAR TEL. 24,900–29,000 ptas. ($199.20–$232) double; 35,000–80,000 ptas. ($280–$640) suite. AE, DC, MC, V. Parking 2,000 ptas. ($16).

One of the most spectacular Belle Epoque hotels in Spain, enviably positioned in the heart of town midway between the bay and Río Urumea, this is the most visible and prestigious hotel in town. It received its first guests in 1912. Set behind a facade of chiseled stone and ornate ironwork, the Cristina was once the preferred hotel of virtually every titled aristocrat in France and Spain. It was richly remodeled in 1987. The public rooms are opulent with ormolu, Cuban mahogany, acres of onyx and exotic marbles, and rosewood marquetry. The guest rooms are appropriately lavish, with equally lavish rates. Today the clientele includes starlets, film directors, and a crowd of newly monied moguls—but the legends live on anyway.

Dining/Entertainment: The main dining room, the restaurant Easo, serves Basque and international food in three-course fixed-price lunches and dinners. The hotel also contains one of the most beautiful bars in town, the Gritti, where a pianist sometimes performs.

Services: 24-hour room service, babysitting, laundry/valet, concierge.

Facilities: Car rentals (with or without driver), business center.

EXPENSIVE

Hotel de Londres y de Inglaterra. Zubleta, 2, 20007 San Sebastián. ☎ **943/42-69-89.** Fax 943/42-00-31. 127 rms, 18 suites. A/C MINIBAR TV TEL. 17,900–20,000 ptas. ($143.20–$160) double; 22,000–27,000 ptas. ($176–$216) suite. AE, DC, MC, V.

Beside the northern edge of the town's most popular beach, the Playa de la Concha, this venerable 19th-century hotel is one of the most enduring and stylish in town, although a bit of a comedown after the María Cristina. Views from many of the balconies encompass the beach and a handful of rocky offshore islands. The traditional-style public rooms contain deep armchairs and big windows. Completely renovated in the past few years, the hotel has comfortably conservative guest rooms with a vaguely English decor, individual safes, and modern marble bathrooms.

Dining/Entertainment: La Brasserie Mari Galant serves both Basque and international cuisine. A bar lies adjacent to it, and there's also the street-level Swing Bar to attract sun-worshipping passersby.

Services: Room service (from 1 to 4pm and 8:30 to 11pm), laundry/valet, concierge, babysitting, in-house tour operator/travel agent.

Facilities: Car rentals, easy access to the Kursaal Casino (not affiliated with the hotel), cafeteria, and bingo parlor.

MODERATE

Hotel San Sebastián. Avenida Zumalacárregui, 20, 20008 San Sebastián. ☎ **943/21-44-00.** Fax 943/21-72-99. 92 rms, 2 suites. MINIBAR TV TEL. 13,000–15,000 ptas. ($104–$120) double; 23,000 ptas. ($184) suite. AE, DC, MC, V. Parking 1,200 ptas. ($9.60). Bus: 5.

Located only a short distance from Ondarreta beach, near the edge of the city on the main road to Bilbao, this modern hotel has a swimming pool in a pleasant garden, as well as an informal restaurant, a disco, two bars, and one coffee bar. The rooms are comfortable and attractively furnished. The place is a serviceable but not exciting stopover.

Monte Igueldo. Paseo del Faro, 134, Monte Igueldo, 20008 San Sebastián. ☎ **943/21-02-11.** Fax 943/21-50-28. 125 rms. A/C TV TEL. 15,500–17,000 ptas. ($124–$136) double. Extra bed 5,500 ptas. ($44). AE, DC, MC, V. Free parking. Bus: Igueldo.

This first-class hotel is perched like a castle on the top of the mountain overlooking San Sebastián, only a 10-minute drive from the center of town. The public rooms, bedrooms, and pool terrace all boast a panoramic view of the Cantabrian coast. Each of the streamlined, modern rooms has a private balcony. Ample parking is provided. A restaurant serves Spanish and international cuisine; there is also a bar on the premises.

Niza. Zubieta, 56, 20007 San Sebastián. ☎ **943/42-66-63.** Fax 943/42-66-63. 41 rms. TV TEL. 14,200 ptas. ($113.60) double. AE, DC, MC, V. Bus: 5 or 6.

This charming little hotel, which opens onto the Playa de la Concha, has character and is favored by those who like to be near the beach and the esplanade. It has modern furnishings in the bedrooms and antiques in the public lounges. The petit salon, for example, contains an Oriental rug, Directoire chairs, a tall grandfather clock, and a rosewood breakfront. In direct contrast are the basic rooms, with wooden headboards, white walls, and wall-to-wall carpeting. There's a pizzeria in the cellar, plus a bar overlooking the sea.

INEXPENSIVE

Codina. Zumalacárregui, 21, 20008 San Sebastián. ☎ **943/21-22-00.** Fax 943/21-25-23. 77 rms. TV TEL. July–Sept (including half board), 15,500 ptas. ($124) double; Oct–June, 9,800 ptas. ($78.40) double. AE, DC, MC, V. Parking 1,000 ptas. ($8). Bus: 5.

Near an attractive residential district and close to a beach, this modern building is designed so that all of the comfortably furnished, compact rooms have a view of the bay. On the wide, busy boulevard you'll find a popular café and bar. A Basque cuisine is served.

$ **Hostal Bahía.** Calle San Martín, 54B, 20007 San Sebastián. ☎ **943/46-92-11.** Fax 943/46-39-14. 59 rms. TV TEL. 6,900–9,300 ptas. ($55.20–$74.40) double. Rates include breakfast. MC, V. Bus: 5, 6, 7, 8, or 9.

A good-value little hotel just one block from the beach near a string of other hotels, the Bahía features guest rooms of varying sizes: Some are large enough to contain sofas and armchairs; others fall into the cubicle category. Many North Americans stay at the hostal and take public transportation to Pamplona for the running of the bulls.

Hotel Parma. Paseo de Salamanca, 10, 20003 San Sebastián. ☎ **943/42-88-93.** Fax 943/42-40-82. 27 rms. TEL. 10,800–19,400 ptas. ($86.40–$107.20) double. AE, DC, MC, V. Bus: 5, 6, 8, 9, 21, or 28.

This modern, clean hotel in the center of town has beautiful views of the ocean. The Parma has up-to-date rooms cozily furnished in wood, with good, modern bathrooms. There is also a downstairs snack bar as well as a pleasant TV lobby, with armchairs and sofas. Breakfast is the only meal served.

WHERE TO DINE

EXPENSIVE

✪ **Akelare.** Paseo del Padre Orkolaga, 56. ☎ **943/21-20-52.** Reservations strongly recommended. Main courses 2,950–4,400 ptas. ($23.60–$35.20); *menú degustación* 7,500 ptas. ($60). AE, DC, MC, V. Tues–Sun 1–3:30pm, Tues–Sat 8:30–11pm. Closed Jan 21–Feb 23 and Oct 3–19. BASQUE.

A visit to Akelare is a must for any dedicated aficionado of gourmet food in Spain. Owner/chef Pedro Subijana's preparations have influenced a generation of chefs and defined—perhaps more than any other—the entire philosophy of *la nueva cocina vasco* (modern Basque cuisine). Established in 1974, the restaurant lies on the western edge of San Sebastián, within a hexagonal villa originally built as a catering hall for weddings and christenings. Inside, a sweeping view through large windows encompasses the mists and raging currents of the Bay of Biscay far below. The plushly upholstered modern decor, with its hospitable fireplace, is an appropriate foil for dishes inspired by the Basque *caserios* (farmsteads).

The perfect beginning to any meal here is puff pastry filled with filets of anchovies, accompanied by a glass of chilled *fino* sherry. Traditional dishes might include fish cooked on a griddle with garlic and parsley; beans accompanied by bacon, *chorizo,* and pork ribs; baked rice with clams; or a special *marmitako* (fisherman's stew). More innovative are the snails with watercress sauce; boiled cabbage stuffed with duckmeat and served with purée of celery; a warm salad of bonito fish served with a basil, lemon, chervil, and vinegar sauce; and filet of duck with an assortment of exotic seasonal mushrooms. On occasion, Subijana—who won the 1983 National Prize for Gastronomy, which is awarded to the best chef in Spain—may venture into the dining room to gauge the reaction to his inventions and to offer advice about the day's menu. The name of the restaurant, incidentally, translates from the Basque as "Witches' Sabbath."

✪ **Arzak.** Alto de Miracruz, 21. ☎ **943/28-55-93.** Reservations required. Main courses 2,800–4,400 ptas. ($22.40–$35.20); fixed-price menu 8,300 ptas. ($66.40). AE, DC, MC, V. Tues–Sun 1–3:30pm, Tues–Sat 8:30–11:30pm. Closed June 15–July 3. BASQUE.

One of the most famous restaurants in the Basque world (an honor it shares with Akelare, see above), this legendary restaurant occupies the lavishly renovated childhood home of owner/chef Juan Mari Arzak. Well known in San Sebastián for his role in preparing a meal for Queen Elizabeth II of Britain (for which he later received an invitation to Buckingham Palace), Arzak combines staples of the Basque culinary legacy with many new creations of his own. Begin, perhaps, with a selection of fresh oysters or, even more elegant, natural foie gras. Crayfish is regularly featured as an appetizer, as is the chef's special *sopa de pescado* (fish soup). For a main course, consider *merluza* (hake) in a vinaigrette with onions and small squid. On the back of the menu is a list of classic dishes that have won the most praise among visitors since the restaurant's opening—everything from stuffed sweet peppers with a fish mousse to pheasant or partridge. For dessert, the orange flan with cream might just be the best version you've ever had. The restaurant is on the main road leading from the center of town to the French border.

✪ **Casa Nicolasa.** Calle Aldamar, 4. ☎ **943/42-17-62.** Reservations required. Main courses 7,000–9,000 ptas. ($56–$72); *menú del chef* 5,100 ptas. ($40.80). AE, DC, MC, V. Mon–Sat 1–3:30pm, Tues–Sat 8:30–11:30pm. Closed Jan 21–Feb 13. BASQUE.

Members of all-male eating clubs (a Basque tradition going back to the 19th century) have assured us that Casa Nicolasa serves the best cuisine at San Sebastián. That would be difficult to prove, especially in a city where international food critics have rated Arzak and Akelare even higher (see above). Nevertheless, Casa Nicolasa surfaces very close to the top.

In the heart of the resort, at the edge of the old town by the Mercado la Brecha, the restaurant features a refined cuisine and impeccable service. Diners are made to feel like guests being served by a proper butler. Master chef José Juan Castillo seems to believe that gastronomy should be elevated to a high art—and he does that convincingly here.

Señor Castillo is greatly aided by his wife, the gracious Ana María. Many of the dishes served here have stood the test of time; others reflect the free-reign culinary imagination of the 1990s. The foie gras is homemade and is the smoothest, albeit the most expensive, way to begin a meal here. *Rape* (monkfish) is prepared in various creative ways and, we have found, is one of the most satisfying main courses. Save room for dessert, as the pastry selections are one of the outstanding features of the kitchen.

When business is at its peak in August and September, the restaurant is likely to open Monday night for dinner as well.

✪ **Martín Berasategui.** Loidi Kalea 4, Lasarte. ☎ **943/36-64-71.** Reservations required. Main courses 4,000–7,500 ptas. ($32–$60); "tasting menus" (without wine, tax, or service) 3,000 ptas. ($24), 5,000 ptas. ($40), and 7,500 ptas. ($60). AE, MC, V. Tues–Sun 12:30–4pm and Tues–Sat 8:30–11:30pm. Closed 2 weeks at Christmas. BASQUE.

Just when you thought the dining situation in San Sebastián couldn't stand any more starred chefs, along comes a youngster, Martín Berasategui, with a cuisine that has excited food critics throughout Europe. Trained by his mother, who cooked for local fishers for a small fee, Berasategui opened his restaurant on the outskirts of town, and the world has literally flocked to his door ever since.

His cuisine is subtle and pure, and he uses butter and cream for desserts only. The hors d'oeuvres are among the best we've ever sampled in the region—everything from a curl of cider-marinated mackerel with fried anchovies in olive oil to morsels of rare tuna belly grilled over wooden charcoal. For a main dish, opt for such delectable choices as hake with baby clams or a refreshing gazpacho of langoustines. If you try one of the "tasting menus," you'll get a summation of Berasategui's cuisine—perhaps pan-seared lambs' brains surrounded by baby salad greens and a fat and juicy slice of duck liver. The chef's attention to detail is fantastic. For example, for a soup (*Porrusalda*) made with, among other ingredients, fresh sea eel and ribbons of smoked eel, Berasategui collects the moisture the eels give off when smoked which he then mixes back into the savory broth!

✪ **Panier Fleuri.** Paseo de Salamanca, 1. ☎ **943/42-42-05.** Reservations required. Main courses 2,000–4,200 ptas. ($16–$33.60); fixed-price menu 5,500 ptas. ($44). AE, DC, MC, V. Thurs–Tues 1–3:30pm, Mon–Tues and Thurs–Sat 8:30–11pm. Closed June 1–24 and Dec 24–31. BASQUE/INTERNATIONAL.

Yet another celebrated restaurant in San Sebastián, this citadel of good cuisine serves Basque dishes with a definite French flavor and flair, typical of the resort of Biarritz across the border in France. The third generation of the Fombedilla family of chefs has had a long time to perfect their cuisine and their special offerings. Service is discreet and elegant, and diners here have a chance to learn why Basque food preparation is regarded as among the finest in Europe.

The setting alone is rewarding, in a formal dining room opening onto the pounding surf at the mouth of the Urumea River.

The chef, Tatus Fombellida, once won the National Prize for Gastronomy in Spain, and critics of San Sebastián cuisine claim she's better than ever. Her *faisan* (pheasant) and *becada asada* (roast woodcock) have been hailed as among the finest game dishes at the resort. Another delectable offering is sole baked with spinach and presented with a freshly made hollandaise sauce, similar to what you might find in one of the better restaurants of Florence. Finish off this rich fare with perhaps a lemon sorbet with champagne.

Even better known than the cuisine is the wine cellar, containing many vintage bottles. The wine steward will guide you through an often perplexing selection, including mellow versions of such wines as Remelluri, Barón de Oña, and Viña Albina.

MODERATE

Juanito Kojua. Puerto, 14. ☎ **943/42-01-80.** Reservations required. Main courses 1,900–3,000 ptas. ($15.20–$24); fixed-price menus 2,800–3,200 ptas. ($22.40–$25.60). AE, DC, MC, V. Daily 1–3:30pm, Mon–Sat 8:30–11:30pm. SEAFOOD.

This little seafood restaurant in the old town, off Plaza de la Constitución, has no decor to speak of, but it has become famous throughout Spain. There's always a wait, but it's worth it. There are two dining areas on the main floor, behind a narrow bar (perfect for an appetizer while you're waiting for your table), plus one downstairs—all of them air-conditioned in summer. Specialties may include paella, half a *besugo* (sea bream), *rape* (monkfish) *l'americana,* and *lubina* (sea bass). The meats are good, too, but it's best to stick to the fresh fish dishes.

Salduba. Pescadería, 6. ☎ **943/42-56-27.** Reservations recommended. Main courses 1,700–2,200 ptas. ($13.60–$17.60); fixed-price menu 3,500 ptas. ($28). AE, DC, MC, V. Mon–Sun 1–4pm, Mon–Sat 8–11pm. Closed Nov. BASQUE.

Opened shortly after the end of World War II, this well-established restaurant owes much of its popularity to the owners, who oversee the cooking. Specialties include Basque hake, herb-laden fish soup, a confit of duckling, and a platter stacked high with the "fruits of the sea"—as well as succulent beef, veal, and pork dishes and various desserts. There are several dining rooms. Salduba lies on the edge of the old town, a five-minute walk from the beach.

✪ **Urepel.** Paseo de Salamanca, 3. ☎ **943/42-40-40.** Reservations required. Main courses 1,800–2,800 ptas. ($14.40–$22.40). AE, DC, MC, V. Mon–Sat 1–3:30pm, Mon and Wed–Sat 8:30–11pm. Closed Holy Week, June 1–23, and Dec 24–Jan 6. BASQUE/INTERNATIONAL.

Standing close to one of its major competitors, the equally rewarding Panier Fleuri (see above), Urepel lies near the mouth of the Urumea River, at the edge of the old town. Its interior is not as elegant as the establishments reviewed above, but fans of this place aren't bothered by that at all. They're here for the cuisine.

The chef demands impeccable ingredients to concoct a menu of traditional Basque fare, and serves only the freshest and best produce along with the finest cuts of meat and "harvests of the sea." The Basque palate, at least according to legend, is the most discriminating in Spain, and few complaints are heard here. The restaurant is the domain of Tomás Almandoz, one of the outstanding chefs in the north of Spain.

Seafood dominates the menu, as it should in this region of the world, and it's deftly handled by the kitchen staff. The fish is often served with delicate sauces, and the main courses are made even better by an emphasis on fresh and perfectly prepared vegetables. *Rape* (monkfish), *dorada* (John Dory), and *cigalas* (crayfish) are likely to turn up on the menu. Somewhat of a rarity in San Sebastián, you can also order goose or duck. One specialty is *pato de caserio fileteado a la naranja* (regional-style duck flavored with oranges).

One local food critic got so carried away with the dessert cart and its presentation that she claimed, "It would take Velázquez to arrange a pastry so artfully"—a gross exaggeration, of course, but an indication of how highly regarded this place is. We prefer it in the evening instead of at midday, when many of the tables are reserved by local businesspersons and government officials.

INEXPENSIVE

La Oka. Calle San Martín, 43. ☎ **943/46-38-84.** Main courses 750–1,400 ptas. ($6–$11.20); fixed-price menu 1,250 ptas. ($10). V. Daily 1–3:30pm, Fri–Sat 8–11pm. Closed last 3 weeks in Dec. BASQUE.

Don't come to La Oka, near the beach in the center of town, looking for glamour. If, on the other hand, you're looking for an inexpensive self-service cafeteria, this is the place. Some critics, in fact, rate it the best self-service cafeteria in Spain. The diners represent a cross section of the city's office workers. The Basque cooking is hearty and plentiful. You can also order a very good Valencia-style paella here.

SAN SEBASTIÁN AFTER DARK

The best evening entertainment in San Sebastián is to go tapas tasting in the old quarter of town. Throughout the rest of Spain this is known as a *tapeo,* or tapas crawl. In San Sebastián it's called a *poteo-ir-de pinchos,* or searching out morsels on toothpicks. Groups of young people often spend their evenings on some 20 streets in the old town, each leading toward Monte Urgull, the port, or La Brecha marketplace. The Alameda del Bulervar, the "popular grove," is the most upscale of these streets; the Calle Fermín Calveton, one of the most popular. You'll find plenty of these places on your own, but here are some to get you going.

Bar Asador Ganbara. Calle San Jerónimo, 21. ☎ **943/42-25-75.**

Decorated with a flair in light-colored wood, this place is a tapas lover's delight. The dishes are well prepared, using market-fresh ingredients. Try the house specialty and the chef's pride: small melt-in-your-mouth croissants filled with cheese, egg, bacon, and Serrano ham. Also sample the spider crab and prawns with mayonnaise. Tapas run 150 to 190 pesetas ($1.20–$1.50); drinks from 175 pesetas ($1.40). In addition to its bar service, the establishment also runs a restaurant in a separate section, offering a fixed-price menu at 2,500 pesetas ($20). The bar is open Tuesday through Sunday from 11am to 2:45pm and 6 to 11:45pm. The restaurant is open Tuesday through Sunday from 1 to 3:30pm and 8 to 11:45pm. Calle San Jerónimo runs at right angles to Calle Fermín Calveton.

Casa Alcalde. Mayor, 19. ☎ **943/42-62-16.**

The tasty tapas served at the Casa Alcalde, just a five-minute walk from the Parque Alderdi Eder, are thinly sliced ham, cheeses, and shellfish dishes. The different varieties are all neatly displayed, and priced from 175 to 225 pesetas ($1.40–$1.80). You can also have full meals in a small restaurant at the back, for 1,500 to 2,200 pesetas ($12–$17.60). Open daily from 10am to 11pm.

Casa Valles. Reyes Católicos, 10. ☎ **943/45-22-10.**

The variety of tapas and wines offered here seems endless. Go to hang out with the locals and feast on tidbits guaranteed to spoil your dinner. Most tapas cost 130 pesetas ($1.05), with a beer going for 150 pesetas ($1.20). In addition, a *menú del día* is offered for 3,000 pesetas ($24). Casa Valles is in the center of town behind the cathedral. Open Thursday through Tuesday from 8:30 to 11pm (closed in late June and late December).

✪ **La Cepa.** 31 de Agosto, 7–9. ☎ **943/42-63-94.**

Many locals say that La Cepa, located on the northern edge of the old town, serves the best tapas in town, and the Jabugo ham is one proof of this claim. Try the grilled squid or the salt-cod-and-green-pepper omelet. You can also order dinner here—a daily changing menu that costs 2,000 pesetas ($16) in the peak summer season and 1,700 pesetas ($13.60) off-season. Tapas begin at 100 pesetas (80¢) but could go up to 1,500 pesetas ($12) for a small portion of Jabugo ham. A glass of wine costs 85 pesetas (70¢). A former bullfighter known as Barberito is fondly remembered by his wife and children, who still own and operate La Cepa. Open Thursday through Tuesday from 11am to midnight.

EXPLORING THE ENVIRONS: SIDE TRIPS FROM SAN SEBASTIÁN

One of the reasons for coming to San Sebastián is to use it as a base for touring the environs. Driving is best because bus connections are awkward or nonexistent.

PASAI DONIBANE

On the east bank of a natural harbor 6½ miles (10.5km) from San Sebastián, Pasai Donibane is one of the most typical of Basque fishing villages. Once it was known by its Spanish name, Pasajes de San Juan. Many visitors come here to dine. The village, with its codfish-packing factories, is on a sheltered harbor; fishing boats are tied up at the wharf. The architecture is appealing: five- and six-story balconied tenement-like buildings in different colors.

Victor Hugo lived here in the summer of 1846 (it hasn't changed much since) at building number 63 on the narrow main street, San Juan.

In summer, don't take a car into the village. Parking is difficult, the medieval streets are one-way, and the wait at traffic signals is long because all southbound traffic has to clear the street before northbound motorists have the right of way.

A bus leaves every 15 minutes from the Calle Aldamar in San Sebastián for **Pasajes de San Pedro,** Pasai Donibane's neighboring fishing village. From there, it's possible to walk to Pasai Donibane. Buses head back to San Sebastián from Pasajes de San Pedro at a quarter to the hour all day long.

A Good Place to Dine

Txulotxo. San Juan, 82, Pasai Donibane. ☎ **943/52-39-52.** Reservations recommended. Main courses 1,200–2,000 ptas. ($9.60–$16); *menú del día* 1,500 ptas. ($12). AE, V. Wed–Mon 1:30–4:30pm, Wed–Sat and Mon 8:30–11:30pm. Closed Oct 15–Nov 15. BASQUE.

Right on the waterfront, this old stone building with a glass-enclosed dining room overlooking the harbor is one of the most authentic and typical of Basque restaurants. The house specialties are made from fish that is delivered daily. For openers, try the *sopa de pescado* (fish soup) or a mixture of *entremeses variados* (hors d'oeuvres). Although pasta dishes are featured, most diners opt for one of the good-tasting seafood selections, perhaps hake in green sauce or perfectly grilled shrimp. The grilled monkfish with clams and shrimp is also done to perfection.

LOYOLA

Surrounded by mountain scenery, Loyola, 34 miles (55km) southwest of San Sebastián, is the birthplace of St. Ignatius, the founder of the Jesuits. He was born in 1491, died in 1556, and was canonized in 1622. The sanctuary at Loyola is the most visited attraction outside the city.

There are large pilgrimages to Loyola for the annual celebration on St. Ignatius Day, July 31. The activity is centered at the **Monastery of San Ignacio de Loyola,** an immense structure built by the Jesuits in the 1700s around the Loyola family manor house near Azpeitia. An International Festival of Romantic Music is held here during the first week of August.

The **basilica** is the work of Italian architect Fontana. Surrounded by a 118-foot-high cupola by Churriguera, it is circular in design.

From 12:30 to 3:30pm daily, visitors can enter the **Santa Casa,** site of the former Loyola manor house, with its 15th-century tower. The rooms in which the saint was born and in which he convalesced have been converted into richly decorated chapels. At the entrance you can rent a tape detailing Loyola's life, and dioramas are shown at the end of the tour.

Six buses a day leave from Plaza Guipúzcoa, 2, San Sebastián, for Loyola (the first departing at 8:30am and the last at 8pm). Buses return about every two hours.

2 Fuenterrabía (Hondarribía)

14 miles (23km) E of San Sebastián, 317 miles (510km) N of Madrid, 11 miles (18km) W of St-Jean-de-Luz (France)

A big seaside resort and fishing port, Fuenterrabía (Hondarribía in Basque) lies near the French frontier, and for that reason it has been subject to frequent attacks over the centuries. In theory, it was supposed to guard the access to Spain, but sometimes it didn't perform that task too well.

ESSENTIALS

GETTING THERE **By Train** Fuenterrabía does not have a train station, but it is serviced by the station in nearby Irún (☎ **943/61-96-70** for information). Buses depart Irún's Plaza de San Juan for Fuentarrabía at 10- to 15-minute intervals. Irún is the "end of the line" for trains in northern Spain. East of Irún, you must board French trains.

By Bus Buses run every 15 minutes from Plaza Guipúzcoa in San Sebastián to Fuenterrabía, one hour away.

By Car Take the A-8 east to the French border, turning toward the coast at the exit sign for Fuenterrabía.

VISITOR INFORMATION The office of tourism at Calle Javier Ugarte, 6 (☎ **943/64-54-58**), is open April through September daily from 9am to 6:30pm; off-season, Monday through Friday from 9am to 1:30pm and 4 to 6:30pm, Saturday from 10am to 2pm.

EXPLORING THE TOWN & ENVIRONS

The most interesting part of town is the **medieval quarter** in the upper market. Some of the villas here date from the early 17th century. The fishing district, in the lower part of town, is called **La Marina:** old homes, painted boats, and the general marine atmosphere attract many visitors. Because restaurants in Fuenterrabía tend to be very expensive, you can fill up here on seafood tapas in the many taverns along the waterfront. The beach at Fuenterrabía is wide and sandy, and many prefer it to the more famous ones at San Sebastián.

Wander for an hour or two around the old quarter, taking in the Calle Mayor, Calle Tiendas y Pampinot, and Calle Obispo. The **Castillo de Carlos V,** standing at the Plaza de las Armas, has been turned into one of the smallest and most desirable paradors in Spain (see below). It's hard to get a room here unless you reserve well in advance, but you can visit the well-stocked bar over the entrance hall.

Sancho Abarca, a king of Navarre in the 10th century, is supposed to have founded the original castle that stood on this spot. The present look owes more to Charles V in the 16th century. You can still see the battle scars on the castle that date from the time of the Napoleonic invasion of Spain.

The most impressive church in the old quarter is the **Iglesia de Santa María,** a Gothic structure that was vastly restored in the 17th century and given a baroque tower. The proxy wedding of Louis XIV and the Infanta María Teresa took place here in June 1660.

If you have a car, you can take some interesting trips in the area, especially to **Cabo Higuer,** a promontory with panoramic views, reached by going 2½ miles (4km) north. Leave by the harbor and beach road. You can see the French coast and the town of Hendaye from this cape.

You can also head west out of town along the **Jaizkibel Road,** which many motorists prefer at sunset. After going three miles (5km), you'll reach the shrine of the Virgin of Guadalupe, where another panoramic view unfolds. From here you can see the French Basque coast. Even better views await you if you continue along to the Hostal Jaizkibel. If you stay on this road, you will come to the little fishing village of Pasai Donibane (see "Side Trips from San Sebastián" above), 11 miles (18km) away.

WHERE TO STAY

✪ **Hotel Pampinot.** Kale Nagusia, Calle Mayor, 3, 20280 Fuenterrabía. ☎ **943/64-06-00.** Fax 943/64-51-28. 8 rms, 3 suites. TV TEL. 10,000–17,000 ptas. ($80–$136) double; from 17,000 ptas. ($136) suite. DC, MC, V. Closed Nov.

If the walls here could talk, they would probably reveal more tales than those of any other hotel in the region. Originally built as an aristocratic mansion in 1587, it housed for a night the Infanta María Teresa. She was headed toward France to marry the Sun King, Louis XIV. Today, it presents a richly textured stone facade with Renaissance detailing and heraldic symbols to one of the most historic and quiet streets of the old town. Inside, an antique sense of elegance is conveyed by beamed ceilings, exposed stonework, parquet flooring, and ornate ironwork. The guest rooms are traditional and charming, with a mixture of antique and reproduction furniture.

Dining/Entertainment: Although breakfast is the only meal served, the staff can direct you to a choice of nearby eateries.

Services: Laundry, concierge, babysitting.

Facilities: Car rentals.

Jáuregui. San Pedro, 28, 20280 Fuenterrabía. ☎ **943/64-14-00.** Fax 943/64-44-04. 53 rms. MINIBAR TV TEL. 12,500 ptas. ($100) AE, DC, MC, V. Parking 1,000 ptas. ($8).

Opened in 1981 in the center of the old village, this is a good choice for moderately priced accommodations. The modern interior boasts comfortable accessories, and the hotel also has a garage—a definite plus, since parking in Fuenterrabía is virtually impossible. Each of the rooms is well furnished and maintained; thoughtful extras include a hair dryer in each bathroom, a safe in every room, and a shoeshine machine on each floor. Only breakfast is served.

Parador de Hondarribía. Plaza de Armas, 20280 Fuenterrabía. ☎ **943/64-55-00.** Fax 943/64-21-53. 36 rms. TEL. 15,000–16,500 ptas. ($120–$132) double. AE, DC, MC, V. Free parking.

This beautifully restored 10th-century castle situated on a hill in the center of the old town was once used by Emperor Charles V as a border fortification. The building itself is impressive, and so are the taste and imagination of the restoration: Antiques, old weapons, and standards hang from the high-vaulted ceilings. Some of the comfortable provincial-style rooms open onto the Bay of Biscay. Breakfast is the only meal served. Ample parking is available out front. It's best to reserve a room here well in advance.

WHERE TO DINE

✪ **Ramón Roteta.** Villa Alnara. ☎ **943/64-16-93.** Reservations recommended. Main courses 2,200–3,200 ptas. ($17.60–$25.60). AE, MC, V. Fri–Wed 1:30–3:30pm, Mon–Wed and Fri–Sat 8:30–11:30pm.

Named after its owner and founder, this attractively furnished restaurant is one of Europe's most consistently respected purveyors of traditional Basque cuisine. Contained within what was originally a 1920s private villa, it lies in the southern outskirts of town, near the local parador and the city limits of Irún. Menu specialties include a terrine of green vegetables and fish served with red-pepper–flavored vinaigrette, baked sea crabs with tiny potatoes and onions, fresh pasta with seafood, and the dessert specialty, a mandarin-orange tart flavored with rose petals. The villa is surrounded by a pleasantly unstructured garden.

Sebastián. Mayor, 7. ☎ **943/64-01-67.** Reservations required. Main courses 1,400–2,900 ptas. ($11.20–$23.20); fixed-price menus 4,000–4,500 ptas. ($32–$36). AE, MC, V. Tues–Sun 1–3:30pm, Tues–Sat 8:30–11pm. Closed Nov. BASQUE.

Lying within the oldest district of Fuenterrabía, close to the castle, this restaurant offers modern cuisine, well presented and using top-notch ingredients appropriate to the season. The two floors of the restaurant feature thick masonry walls, among which are scattered an array of 18th-century paintings. Try one of the specialties: foie gras of duckling Basque style, terrine of fresh mushrooms, or medallions of sole and salmon with seafood sauce.

3 Ondárroa

30 miles (48km) W of San Sebastián, 38 miles (61km) E of Bilbao, 265 miles (427km) N of Madrid

Ondárroa is described as a *pueblo típico,* a typical Basque fishing village. It is also the area's largest fishing port. Lying on a spit of land, it stands between a hill and a loop of the Artibay River. Laundry hangs from the windows of the little plant-filled balconied Basque houses, and most of the residents are engaged in canning and fish salting, if not fishing. The local church looks like a ship's prow at one end. Around the snug harbor you'll find many little places to drink and dine after taking a stroll through the village.

GETTING THERE **By Bus** From San Sebastián, Ondárroa is serviced by buses that run along the Costa Vasca.

By Car Head west from San Sebastián along the coastal road.

WHERE TO STAY

Hotel/Restaurant Vega. Calle Antigua, 8, 48700 Ondárroa. ☎ **94/683-00-02.** 22 rms (5 with bath). 5,000 ptas. ($40) double without bath; 6,000 ptas. ($48) double with bath. AE, V. Free parking.

This establishment in the center of town is a real find, offering comfortable and simple rooms for reasonable prices year-round. It is the only hotel of note in town, and the setting is pleasant.

The dining room serves a well-prepared *menú del día,* which typically includes veal, fish, fried beef, and fish soup. The restaurant is open daily from 1:30 to 3:30pm and 8 to 11pm (Friday to Wednesday in winter); it's closed for the month of October.

WHERE TO DINE

Restaurante Penalty. Eribera, 32. ☎ **94/683-00-00.** Reservations required. Main courses 1,800–2,300 ptas. ($14.40–$18.40). AE, MC, V. Thurs–Tues 1:30–3:30pm and 8:30–11pm. Closed Dec and Jan. SEAFOOD.

This small restaurant, with a limited number of tables, stands at a crossroads at the edge of town. Meals might include a house recipe for hake that is simply heavenly, plus other fish specialties. The *sopa de pescado* (fish soup) invariably makes a good choice for a beginning to a fine meal.

4 Lekeitio

38 miles (61km) W of San Sebastián, 37 miles (60km) E of Bilbao, 280 miles (451km) N of Madrid

This unspoiled Basque fishing village, which everybody talks about, is most often visited on a day trip. There are those who consider it "more authentic" than Ondárroa. Situated at the foot of Mount Calvario, Lekeitio opens onto a deeply indented bay. Queen Isabella II first gave the town prominence when she spent time here in the 19th century. Fishing may have diminished in recent years, but Lekeitio is still home to some of the Basque coast's trawlers. The island of San Nicolás converts the bay into a naturally protected harbor, a phenomenon that led to the village's growth.

GETTING THERE **By Bus** Seven buses a day connect Lekeitio with Bilbao (45 minutes away), and four buses a day run from San Sebastián (1 1/2 hours away).

By Car From Ondárroa, take the coastal road northwest along the Costa Vasca.

WHAT TO SEE & DO

A beach lies across from the harbor, but the one at Carraspio, farther along the bay, is considered safer. Note the 15th-century church "guarding" the harbor. Three tiers of flying buttresses characterize this monument, which has a baroque belfry. Go inside to the third south chapel, off the right nave, to see a remarkable altarpiece, *The Road to Calvary,* which was erected in a flamboyant Gothic style.

The town is noted for its **festivals,** including the feast day of Saints Peter and Paul on June 29, at which a *Kaxarranca,* a Basque folk dance, takes place. A dancer leaps about on top of a trunk carried through the streets by some hearty Basque fishers. Even better known is the controversial Jaiak San Antolín, or goose festival, on September 1 to 8. A gruesome custom, it involves hanging live geese in the harbor. Youths leap from row boats to grab the greased necks of the geese. Both youth and goose are dunked into the water, using a system of pulleys, until the youth cries uncle or the neck of the goose is wrenched off. Perhaps you'll want to skip this one. The candlelit march through the streets, with everyone dressed in white, does not mourn the unfortunate geese but signals the end of the festival.

A GOOD PLACE TO DINE

$ **Restaurante Egaña.** Santa Catalina, 4. ☎ **94/684-01-03.** Main courses 850–1,400 ptas. ($6.80–$11.20); *menú del día* 975 ptas. ($7.80). AE, V. Tues–Sun 1–4pm and 8–10pm. SEAFOOD.

Fans of Basque seafood can get their fill in this spacious, breezy dining room on the upper side of the village. The portions are large and generous, and the price is right. The place is unfussy and unpretentious: You are here to eat without frills. The menu depends on the catch of the day. Try the Basque-style hake.

5 Guernica

266 miles (428km) N of Madrid, 52 miles (84km) W of San Sebastián

The subject of Picasso's most famous painting (returned to Spain from the United States and displayed at the Thyssen-Bornemisza Museum in Madrid), Guernica, the spiritual home of the Basques and the seat of Basque nationalism, was destroyed in a Nazi air raid on April 26, 1937. It was the site of a revered oak tree, under whose branches Basques had elected their officials since medieval times. No one knows how many died during the 3½-hour attack—estimates range from 200 to 2,000. The bombers reduced the town to rubble, but a mighty symbol of independence was born.

The town has been attractively rebuilt, close to its former style. The chimes of a church bell ring softly, and laughing children play in the street. In the midst of this peace, however, you'll suddenly come upon a sign: "Souvenirs . . . Remember."

GETTING THERE **By Train** From San Sebastián, trains run three times daily to Guernica; change at Amorebieta. Trains also depart Bilbao for Guernica every hour throughout the day and evening.

By Bus Vascongados, at Estación de Amara in San Sebastián, runs buses to Bilbao, with connections to Guernica. Inquire at the station. From Bilbao, CAV, Plaza Encarnación, 7 (☎ **94/433-12-79**), operates 10 buses per day to Guernica Monday through Friday and 5 buses per day on the weekends. The trip time is 45 minutes.

By Car From Bilbao, head east along the A-8 superhighway; cut north on the 6315 and follow the signs for Guernica. From San Sebastián, drive west along A-8, and cut north on the 6315. A more scenic, but slightly longer, route involves driving west from San Sebastián on the A-8, and branching off on the coastal road to Ondárroa. Continue on as the road turns south and follow the signs to Guernica.

VISITING THE CASA DE JUNTAS

The former Basque parliament, the Casa de Juntas (or *Juntetxea*), is the principal attraction in the town. It contains a historical display of Guernica and is open daily from 10am to 2pm and 4 to 7pm in summer (to 6pm in winter). Admission is free. Outside are the remains of the ancient communal oak tree, symbol of Basque independence; it was not uprooted by Hitler's bombs. From the train station, head up the Calle Urioste.

A NEARBY PLACE TO DINE

Asador Zaldua. Sabino Arana, 10. ☎ **94/687-08-71.** Reservations required in summer. Main courses 1,600–2,400 ptas. ($12.80–$19.20); *menú del día* 2,600 ptas. ($20.80). AE, DC, MC, V. Daily 1:30–3:30pm, Mon–Sat 8:30–11pm. Closed mid-Dec to Jan 5. BASQUE.

Most of the specialties served here come from the blazing grill, whose turning spits are visible from the dining room. A wide array of seafood and fish is also available, some dishes baked to a flaky goodness in a layer of rock salt. The lobster salad is worth the trip here. The restaurant is 5½ miles (9km) north of the center of town on the road to Bermeo.

6 Bilbao

246 miles (396km) N of Madrid, 62 miles (100km) W of San Sebastián

Bilbao is often described as an "ugly, gray, decaying, smokestack city," and so it is—in part. But it has a number of interesting secrets to reveal, as well as good-quality cuisine, and it is a rail hub and a center for exploring some of the best attractions in the Basque country if you're dependent on public transport. Most of its own attractions can be viewed in a day.

Bilbao is Spain's sixth-largest city, its biggest port (with hundreds of skycranes), the industrial hub of the north, and the political capital of the Basques. Shipping, shipbuilding, and steelmaking have made it prosperous. Many bankers and industrialists live here. Its commercial heart contains skyscrapers and hums with activity. Among cities of the Basque region, it has the highest population (around 450,000); the metropolitan area, including the suburbs and many surrounding towns, boasts one million inhabitants.

Bilbao has a wide-open feeling, extending more than five miles (8km) across the valley of the Nervión River, one of Spain's most polluted waterways. Many buildings wear a layer of grime. Some visitors compare Bilbao to England—not the England of hills and vales, but rather the sooty postindustrial sprawl of an English port town. (Because of the interconnected interests of coal and iron, in fact, there has always been English commerce here, and even English schools and pubs.) Surrounding the city's central core are slums and heavily polluting factories. There's a feeling of decay here, not to mention political unrest from the Basque separatist movement. These factors, plus the frequent rainfall, do not place Bilbao on the major touristic maps of Europe or even of Spain.

The city was established by a charter dated June 15, 1300, which converted it from a village (*pueblo*), ruled by local feudal duke Don Diego López de Haro, into a city. Aided by water power and the transportation potential of the Nervión River, it grew and grew, most of its fame and glory coming during the industrial expansion of the 19th century. Many grand homes and villas for industrialists were constructed at that time. (Its wealthiest suburb is Neguri.) The most famous son of Bilbao was Miguel de Unamuno, the writer and educator, more closely associated with Salamanca.

The hardworking Basques of Bilbao, who have a rough-and-ready, no-nonsense approach to life, like to have a good time. **Festivals** often fill the calendar, the biggest and most widely publicized being La Semana Grande, dedicated to the Virgin of Begoña and lasting from mid-August until early September. During the celebration, the Nervión River is the site of many flotillas and regattas. July 25 brings the festival of Bilbao's patron saint, Santiago (St. James), and July 31 is the holiday devoted to the region's patron saint, St. Ignatius.

ESSENTIALS

GETTING THERE **By Plane** Bilbao Airport (☎ **94/486-93-00**) is five miles (8km) north of the city, near the town of Erandio. From the airport into town take red bus A3247. Flights arrive from Madrid, Barcelona, Alicante, Arrecife, Fuenteventura, Las Palmas, Málaga, Palma, Santiago de Compostela, Sevilla, Tenerife, Valencia, Vigo, Brussels, Frankfurt, Lisbon, London, Milan, Paris, and Zurich. Iberia's main booking office in Bilbao is at Ercilla, 20 (☎ **94/424-10-94**); it's open Monday through Friday from 9am to 1:45pm and 5 to 6:45pm.

By Train The RENFE Station, Estación de Abando (☎ **94/423-86-23**), is on the Hurtado de Amézaga, just off the Plaza de España, in Bilbao. From here, you can catch short-distance trains within the metropolitan area of Bilbao and long-distance trains to most parts of Spain. Two trains per day run to and from Madrid (trip time: 6 hours on the afternoon train, 7 hours on the night train). Two trains per day run to and from Barcelona (11 hours), and two trains per day run to and from Galicia (12 hours). There are also two night trains per week to and from the Mediterranean Coast: one toward Alicante and Valencia (daily during the summer months) and the other toward Málaga (three times per week in the summer).

By Bus PESA, Calle Hurtado de Amézaga (☎ **94/416-94-79**), at the Estación Abando, operates more than a dozen buses per day to and from San Sebastián (trip time: 1¼ hours). ANSA, Calle Autonomía, 17 (☎ **94/444-31-00**), has nine buses per day from Madrid (trip time: 5 hours). It also has four buses per day to and from Barcelona (7 hours). If you'd like to explore either Lekeitio or Guernica (see above) by bus, use the services of CAV, Plaza Encarnación, 7 (☎ **94/433-12-79**). Seven buses per day go to Lekeitio Monday through Saturday and two on Sunday. Trip time is 45 minutes. Ten buses run each weekday to Guernica (trip time: 45 minutes). On weekends, only five buses per day go to Guernica.

By Car Bilbao lies beside the A-8, linking the cities of Spain's northern Atlantic seacoast to the western edge of France. It is connected by superhighway to both Barcelona and Madrid.

VISITOR INFORMATION The tourist information office is at Plaza Arriaga, s/n (☎ **94/416-00-22**). It's open Monday through Friday from 9am to 1:30pm and 4 to 8pm, Saturday from 9am to 2pm, and Sunday from 10am to 2pm. The Post Office is at Alameda de Urquijo, 19 (☎ **94/422-05-48**) and is open Monday through Friday from 8:30am to 8:30pm, Saturday from 9:30am to 2pm.

CITY LAYOUT The River Nervión meanders through Bilbao, whose historic core was built inside one of its loops, with water protecting it on three sides. Most of the important shops, banks, and tourist facilities lie within a short walk of the **Gran Vía,** running east-west through the heart of town. The old quarter lies east of the modern commercial center, across the river.

SEEING THE SIGHTS

Guggenheim Museum. Muella Evaristo Churruca, 1. ☎ **94/423-27-99.** Admission 700 ptas. ($5.60) adults, 350 ptas. ($2.80) seniors and students, free for children 12 and under. Tues–Wed 11am–8pm, Thurs–Sat 11am–9pm, Sun 11am–3pm. Closed Jan 1, Good Friday, July 31, Aug 15, and Dec 25.

The newest and biggest attraction in Bilbao will be the Guggenheim Museum, at the intersection of the bridge called Puente de la Salve and the Nervión River. The 349,000-square-foot colossus is slated to open in the summer of 1997 and is one of the focal points of a $1.5 billion redevelopment plan for the city. The Frank Gehry design features a 165-foot high atrium—more than one-and-a-half times the height of the rotunda of Frank Lloyd Wright's Guggenheim Museum in New York. Stretching under the aforementioned bridge and incorporating it in its design, the museum reanimates the promenade with its towering roof, reminiscent of a blossoming "metallic flower." The museum will be devoted to American and European art of the 20th century, featuring the works of such renowned artists as Kandinsky, Mondrian, Picasso, Ernst, Pollock, Lichtenstein, Oldenburg, Serra, and others. It is envisioned as an international center of modern and contemporary art.

Museo de Bellas Artes. Plaza del Museo, 2. ☎ **94/441-95-36.** Free admission. Tues–Sat 10am–1:30pm and 4–7:30pm, Sun 10am–2pm.

This is one of Spain's most important art museums, containing both medieval and modern works, including paintings by Velázquez, Goya, Zurbarán, and El Greco. Among the works of non-Spanish artists are *The Money Changers* by the Flemish painter Quentin Massys and *The Lamentation over Christ* by Anthony van Dyck. In its modern wing, the museum contains works by Gauguin, Picasso, Léger, Sorolla, and American Mary Cassatt. The gallery is particularly strong in 19th- and 20th-century Basque artists, the foremost of which is the modern sculptor Chillida, who created a massive piece entitled *Monument to Iron.* If you tire of looking at the art, you can walk in the English-inspired gardens around the museum.

Euskal Arkeologia. Etnografia Eta Kondaira-Museoa, Cruz, 4. ☎ **94/415-54-23.** Free admission. Tues–Sat 10:30am–1:30pm and 4–7pm, Sun 10:30am–1:30pm.

In the center of the old quarter, south of Calle Esperanza Ascao, this museum—devoted to Basque archaeology, ethnology, and history—is contained within a centuries-old Jesuit cloister. Some of the exhibits showcase Basque commercial life during the 16th century. You see everything from ship models to shipbuilding tools, along with reconstructions of rooms illustrating political and social life. Basque gravestones are also on view. In addition, you'll see the equipment used to play the popular Basque game of *pelota.*

CASCO VIEJO (OLD QUARTER)

East side of Nervión River.

Despite the fact that Bilbao was established around 1300, it is curiously scarce in medieval monuments. It does have this old quarter, however, site of its most intriguing bars and restaurants. The custom is to go here at night and bar-hop, ordering small cups of beer or wine. A small glass of wine is called a *chiquiteo.*

The old quarter of Bilbao is connected to the much larger modern section on the opposite bank by four bridges. A few paces north of the old quarter's center lie the graceful arches, 64 in all, enclosing Plaza Nueva, also called Plaza de los Martires, completed in 1830.

The entire *barrio* has been declared a national landmark. It originally defined an area around seven streets, but it long ago spilled beyond that limitation. Its most important church is the **Church of St. Nicolás.** Behind this church you'll find an elevator on Calle Esperanza Ascao, which, if working, carries sightseers to the upper town. You can also climb 64 steps from Plaza Unamuno. From there it's a short walk to the **Basílica de Begoña,** built largely in the early 1500s. Inside the dimly lit church, there is a brightly illuminated depiction of the Virgin, dressed in long, flowing robes. She is the patroness of the province. Also displayed are some enormous paintings by Luca Giordano.

While in the old town, you might also visit the **Cathedral of Santiago,** Plaza Santiago, which was originally built in the 14th century, then restored in the 16th century after a fire. The facade was later rebuilt in the 19th century. On Sundays you might also take in the flea market, starting at 8am, on the streets of the old quarter.

To reach the old town on foot, the only way to explore it, take the Puente del Arenal from the Gran Vía, the main street of Bilbao.

WHERE TO STAY

Avenida. Zumalacárregui, 40, 48007 Bilbao. ☎ **94/412-43-00.** Fax 94/411-46-17. 116 rms. TV TEL. 11,500 ptas. ($92) double. AE, MC, V. Free parking. Bus: 48.

For those who want to be away from the center, and don't mind a bus or taxi ride or two, this is a welcoming choice. It lies in the Barrio de Begoña, near one of the major religious monuments of Bilbao, the Basílica de Begoña. The five-story hotel was built in the late 1960s. Rooms, furnished in a sober, functional modern style, are well kept and maintained. The hotel has a garden and a helpful staff. During special fairs in Bilbao, rates are increased by at least 10%.

Gran Hotel Ercilla. Ercilla, 37–39, 48011 Bilbao. ☎ **94/410-20-00.** Fax 94/443-93-35. 338 rms, 7 suites. A/C MINIBAR TV TEL. 20,225 ptas. ($161.80) double; 21,850 ptas. ($174.80) triple; 40,775 ptas. ($326.20) suite. AE, DC, MC, V. Parking 1,625 ptas. ($13).

Soaring high above the buildings surrounding it and located in the heart of Bilbao's business district, this is a tastefully decorated bastion of attentive service and good living. The guest rooms are conservative and comfortably furnished. Completely renovated in 1989 and 1990, the Ercilla is one of Bilbao's most desirable hotels, usually the preferred choice of Spanish politicians, movie stars, and journalists away from home.

Dining/Entertainment: The restaurant, Bermeo, specializing in Basque cuisine, is known as one of the best restaurants in Bilbao (see "Where to Dine," below). Adjacent to it is an American-inspired bar (with an English-inspired decor) providing a peaceful haven with its richly grained hardwood paneling. There is also an informal and stylishly modern snack bar, the Ercilla (open daily from 7am to 2am), plus a high-tech, high-energy disco, the Bocaccio.

Services: 24-hour room service, concierge, laundry/valet, babysitting.

Facilities: Business center, car rental, safety-deposit boxes, boutiques.

✪ **Hotel López de Haro.** Obispo Orueta, 2, 48000 Bilbao. ☎ **94/423-55-00.** Fax 94/423-45-00. 49 rms, 5 suites. A/C MINIBAR TV TEL. 15,750–26,500 ptas. ($126–$212) double; from 30,865 ptas. ($246.90) suite. AE, DC, MC, V. Parking 1,950 ptas. ($15.60).

Situated behind a discreet facade of chiseled gray stone and filled with English touches, this six-story elegant 1990 hotel features marble flooring, hardwood paneling, and a uniformed staff. The comfortable guest rooms each contain flowered or striped upholstery, a modern bath, and wall-to-wall carpeting or hardwood floors.

Dining/Entertainment: The hotel has two restaurants, one of which, Club Nautico, is recommended below in "Where to Dine." Both provide gracious havens for good food and service. A luxurious English-inspired cocktail bar lies nearby.

Services: 24-hour room service, laundry/valet, limousines available, concierge, babysitting.

Facilities: Car rentals.

Roquefer. Lotería, 2–4, 48005 Bilbao. ☎ **94/415-07-55.** 18 rms (6 with bath). 3,000 ptas. ($24) double without bath; 4,000 ptas. ($32) double with bath. No credit cards.

If you'd like to live in the old quarter and avoid the high prices of business-client hotels, this is a basic choice, suitable for a stopover. Rooms are simple and furnished in a functional style. You'll be in the center of the *tasca* and restaurant district for nighttime prowls. To reach the hotel, take the bridge, the Puente del Arenal, across the river to the old town.

WHERE TO DINE

EXPENSIVE

Guría. Gran Vía de López de Haro, 66. ☎ **94/441-05-43.** Reservations required. Main courses 1,800–4,600 ptas. ($14.40–$36.80); fixed-price menus 5,800–8,000 ptas. ($46.40–$64). AE, DC, MC, V. Mon–Sat 1:30–4pm and 8:30pm–midnight. Closed last week of July and first week of Aug. BASQUE.

One of the most venerated restaurants of Bilbao, the air-conditioned Guría is expensive—and worth it, say its devotees. The chef shows care and concern for his guests, serving only market-fresh ingredients. He is celebrated for his *Bacalao* (codfish), which he prepares in many ways. Try his sea bass with saffron as an alternative or his loin of beef cooked in sherry. A slightly caloric but divine dessert is *espuma de chocolat.*

✪ **Bermeo.** Gran Hotel Ercilla, Ercilla, 37. ☎ **94/410-20-00.** Reservations required. Main courses 1,975–3,675 ptas. ($15.80–$29.40); fixed-price menu 5,500 ptas. ($39.10). AE, DC, MC, V. Sun–Fri 1–3:30pm, Mon–Sat 8:30–11:30pm. BASQUE.

One of the finest hotel restaurants in all of Spain and one of the finest representatives of Basque cuisine anywhere in the world, the Bermeo caters to a clientele of the Basque world's most influential politicians, writers, and social luminaries. Contained within the modern walls of one of Bilbao's tallest hotels, the establishment is decorated with richly conservative, glowing wood panels; crisp linens; and copies of 19th-century antiques. The service from the uniformed and formal staff is impeccable. Menu items change with the seasons but might include a salad of lettuce hearts in saffron dressing with smoked salmon, homemade foie gras scented with essence of bay leaves, fresh thistles sautéed with ham, five preparations of codfish, stewed partridge with glazed shallots, and filets of duckling with green peppercorns. For dessert, try the truffled figs or a slice of bilberry pie with cream.

✪ **Club Nautico.** In the Hotel López de Haro, Obispo Orueta, 2. ☎ **94/423-55-00.** Reservations recommended. Main courses 1,950–7,000 ptas. ($15.60–$56); fixed-price menus 5,000–10,500 ptas. ($40–$84). AE, DC, MC, V. Mon–Fri 1–3:30pm, Mon–Sun 8:30–11:30pm. BASQUE.

One of the finest and most prestigious restaurants in the Basque world, the elegantly decorated Club Nautico lies within a previously recommended hotel. The chefs are former protégés of Alberto Zuluaga, one of the most publicized culinary luminaries of northern Spain, who ran the kitchen here for years. The restaurant offers a uniformed staff and formal tables set with some of the finest china, crystal, and silverware available. Menu specialties include succulent local artichokes stuffed with foie gras, poached eggs with beluga caviar and oyster sauce, lobster sautéed with artichokes and balsamic vinegar, baked sea bass with béarnaise sauce, sautéed scallops with truffle sauce, and roast beef with a purée of radishes. A superb selection of Spanish and international wines are available by either the glass or the bottle.

Moderate

Matxinbenta. Ladesma, 26. ☎ **94/424-84-95.** Reservations required. Main courses 2,000–2,600 ptas. ($16–$20.80); *menú del día* 4,000 ptas. ($32). AE, DC, MC, V. Mon–Sat 1–4pm and 8–11:30pm. BASQUE.

Serving some of the finest Basque food in the city since the 1950s, this restaurant, one block north of the Gran Vía, is popular for business lunches or dinners. Specialties include fresh tuna in piquant tomato sauce and a local version of ratatouille known as *piperada.* You can also order veal cutlets cooked in port wine and finish with a mint-flavored fresh-fruit cocktail. The service is excellent.

Inexpensive

Restaurante Begoña. Virgen de Begoña, s/n. ☎ **94/412-72-57.** Reservations recommended. Main courses 1,300–2,800 ptas. ($10.40–$22.40). AE, MC, V. Mon–Sat 1:30–3:30pm and 8–11pm. Closed Aug. Bus: 48. BASQUE.

At this tranquil choice, near the famous Basílica de Begoña, lying on the eastern bank of the river, the chef imaginatively combines classic dishes with modern ones.

Specialties include stuffed onions, loin of pork, and sea bass with fines herbs. This restaurant offers good value, serving quality food at reasonable prices. The wine cellar offers prestigious vintages at competitive rates, and the service is attentive.

7 Vitoria (Gasteiz)

41 miles (66km) S of Bilbao, 71 miles (114km) SW of San Sebastián, 218 miles (351km) N of Madrid

Quiet and sleepy until the early 1980s, Vitoria was chosen as headquarters of the Basque region's autonomous government. In honor of that occasion, it revived the name *Gasteiz,* by which it was known when founded in 1181 by King Sancho of Navarre. Far more enduring, however, has been the name *Vitoria,* a battle site revered by the English. On June 21, 1813, Wellington won here against the occupying forces of Napoleon. A statue dedicated to the Iron Duke stands today on the neoclassical Plaza de la Virgen Blanca.

Shortly after its founding, the city became a rich center for the wool and iron trades, and this wealth paid for the fine churches and palaces in the medieval quarter. Many of the city's buildings are made of gray-gold stone. There is a university, whose students keep the taverns rowdy until the wee hours.

ESSENTIALS

GETTING THERE **By Plane** Aeropuerto Vitoria-Foronda (☎ **945/16-35-00**) lies five miles (8km) northwest of the town center and has direct air links to Madrid on Iberia Airlines. For flight information, call Iberia at **945/27-40-00** daily from 7am to 11pm.

By Train From San Sebastián, 16 trains daily make the two-hour trip to Vitoria. For information, call **945/23-02-02.**

By Bus From San Sebastián, roughly four buses daily make the 1½-hour trip. Bus connections are also possible through Bilbao (8 to 12 buses daily make the 1-hour trip).

By Car Take the E-5 north from Madrid to Burgos, cutting northwest until you see the turnoff for Vitoria. (Note that along its more northerly stretches this superhighway is identified as both E-5 and A-1.)

VISITOR INFORMATION The tourist information office is at Parque de la Florida (☎ **945/13-13-21**). It is open Monday through Thursday from 9am to 1:30pm and 3 to 7pm, Friday from 8am to 7pm, and Saturday from 9am to 1pm.

SEEING THE SIGHTS

The most important sight in Vitoria is the **medieval district,** whose Gothic buildings were constructed on a series of steps and terraces. Most of the streets are arranged in concentric ovals and are named after medieval artisan guilds. The northern end is marked by the Cathedral of Santa María, its southern flank by the Church of San Miguel.

One of the most interesting streets in the *barrio* is **Calle Cuchillaría,** which contains many medieval buildings. You can enter the courtyard at number 24, the Casa del Cordón, which was constructed in different stages from the 13th to the 16th century. Number 58, the Bendana Palace, built in the 15th century, has a fine ornate staircase set into its courtyard.

The **Cathedral of Santa María** (the "old" cathedral), Calle Fray Zacaras, was built in the 14th century in the Gothic style. It contains a good art collection, with paintings that imitate various schools, including those of van Dyck, Caravaggio, and Rubens, as well as several tombs carved in a highly decorated plateresque style. Santa María lies at the northern edge of the old town.

This cathedral is not to be confused with the town's enormous "new" cathedral on Avenida Magdalena (just north of the Jardines la Florida), which is built in a neo-Gothic style.

The major historic square is the **Plaza de la Virgen Blanca,** a short walk south of the medieval quarter. Its neoclassical balconies overlook the statue of Wellington. The square is named after the late-Gothic polychrome statue of the Virgen Blanca (the town's patron) that adorns the portico of the 13th-century **Church of San Miguel,** which stands on the square's upper edge. The 17th-century altarpiece inside was carved by Gregoria Hernández.

At **Plaza de España** (also known as Plaza Nueva), a satellite square a short walk away, the student population of Vitoria congregates to drink.

Vitoria has some minor museums, which are free. **Museo de Arqueología de Álava,** Correría, 116 (☎ **945/14-23-10**), behind a half-timbered facade, exhibits artifacts, such as pottery shards and statues, that were unearthed from digs in the area. Some of these are from Celto-Iberian days; others from the Roman era. The museum is open Tuesday through Friday from 10am to 2pm and 4 to 6:30pm, Saturday from 11am to 2pm.

Museo de Bellas Artes de Álava, Palacio de Agustín, Paseo de Fray Francisco, 8 (☎ **945/23-17-77**), has a collection of several unusual weapons, a *Crucifixion* and portraits of Saints Peter and Paul by Ribera, and a triptych by the Master of Ávila. It is open Tuesday through Friday from 11am to 2pm and 4 to 6:30pm, Saturday and Sunday from 11am to 2pm.

WHERE TO STAY

$ Achuri. Rioja, 11, 01005 Vitoria. ☎ **945/25-58-00.** Fax 945/26-40-74. 40 rms. TV TEL. 6,000 ptas. ($48) DC, MC, V.

This is an attractively priced modern hotel with a welcoming style. Located a short walk from the train station, it offers tidy and comfortably furnished bedrooms and laundry service. Breakfast is the only meal available, but you'll find several places serving food in the vicinity.

$ Hotel Dato. Eduardo Dato, 28, 01005 Vitoria. ☎ **945/23-23-20.** Fax 945/23-23-20. 14 rms. TV TEL. 4,986 ptas. ($39.90) double. AE, DC, MC, V. Parking meters on street.

Three blocks south of the southern extremity of the old town in the pedestrian zone, this hotel has firmly established itself as the best budget accommodation in town. It has modern decor and amenities but only a few bedrooms—so reservations are wise. No breakfast is served.

Hotel General Álava. Gasteiz, 79, 01009 Vitoria. ☎ **945/22-22-00.** Fax 945/24-83-95. 113 rms, 1 suite. TV TEL. 11,500–12,500 ptas. ($92–$100) double; 21,000 ptas. ($168) suite. AE, DC, MC, V. Parking 950 ptas. ($7.60).

Named after a local hero—a Spanish general who won an important battle against the French in 1815—this hotel is one of the best and most comfortably furnished in town. Built in 1975, it attracts scores of business travelers from throughout Spain. It does not maintain a formal restaurant, but rather a well-managed bistro (open only Monday through Friday) and a bar. The hotel is a 10-minute walk west of the town center, near the junction of Calle Chile.

Hotel Residencia Gasteiz. Avenida Gasteiz, 45, 01009 Vitoria. ☎ **945/22-81-00.** Fax 945/22-62-58. 150 rms, 4 suites. A/C MINIBAR TV TEL. Mon–Thurs, 16,200 ptas. ($129.60) double;

27,000 ptas. ($216) suite. Fri–Sun, room and suite prices reduced 50%. AE, DC, MC, V. Parking 1,300 ptas. ($10.40).

Located on the eastern flank of the broad, tree-lined boulevard that circumnavigates the old town, this is the most modern and solidly reliable hotel around. Built in 1982, it was completely renovated in 1994. Although not architecturally distinguished, it serves as the preferred meeting point for the city's business community, offering conservative bedrooms with uncomplicated furnishings and a series of comfortable (albeit undramatic) public rooms.

Dining/Entertainment: The Restaurante Artagnan, specializing in Basque and international cuisine, serves a set menu and à la carte dinners. The restaurant is closed every Sunday and from August 10 to September 10. There is also an American-inspired bar (which doubles as a cafeteria during the day), as well as a disco.

Services: Room service (daily from 7am to midnight), laundry, concierge, babysitting.

Facilities: Car rentals.

WHERE TO DINE

As in Bilbao, tasca hopping before dinner, with the consumption of many small glasses (*chiquiteos*) of beer or wine at many different bars and taverns, is popular and fun. There are a number of places on the Avenida de Gasteiz.

Mesa. Calle Chile, 1. ☎ **945/22-84-94.** Reservations recommended. Main courses 1,100–1,950 ptas. ($8.80–$15.60); *menús de la casa* 1,800 ptas. ($14.40). AE, MC, V. Thurs–Tues 1–3:30pm and 9–11:30pm. Closed Aug 10–Sept 10. BASQUE.

For price and value, this ranks as one of the most competitive and worthwhile restaurants in town. In air-conditioned comfort you can partake of a number of Basque specialties, none better than the notable *merluza* (hake), the fish so beloved by Basque chefs. Fresh fish and a well-chosen selection of meats are presented nightly. The service is attentive.

El Portalón. Correría, 151. ☎ **945/14-27-55.** Reservations recommended. Main courses 1,450–3,000 ptas. ($11.60–$24); fixed-price menu 2,950 ptas. ($23.60). AE, MC, V. Mon–Sat 1–3:30pm and 9pm–midnight. Closed Aug 10–Sept 1. BASQUE.

This is the finest and most interesting restaurant in town. It was originally built in the late 1400s as a tavern and post office near what was, at the time, one of the only bridges leading in and out of Vitoria. Rich with patina and a sense of history, the restaurant prides itself on serving extremely fresh fish from the nearby Gulf of Biscay, always prepared in traditional Basque style. Cream and butter are rarely used here. Menu items include a salad of endive with shellfish, vegetarian crêpes, a traditional hake dish known as *merluza koxkera,* ragoúts of fish and/or shellfish, and many variations of monkfish, turbot, and eel.

19 Cantabria & Asturias

Part of "Green Spain," the provinces of Cantabria and Asturias are historic lands that boast attractions ranging from the fishing villages of the Cantabrian and Asturian coastlines to the Picos de Europa, a magnificent stretch of snowcapped mountains.

Cantabria, settled in prehistoric times, was colonized by the Romans. The Muslims were less successful in their invasion. Many Christians, protected by the mountains, found refuge here during the long centuries of Moorish domination. Much religious architecture remains from this period, particularly Romanesque. Cantabria was once part of the Castilla y León district of Spain, but is now an autonomous region with its own government.

Most of the tourism is confined to the northern coastal strip; much of the inland mountainous area is poor and unpopulated. If you venture away from the coast, you'll usually need a rental car, because public transport is inadequate at best. Santander, a rail terminus, makes the best center for touring the region; it also has the most tourist facilities. From Santander, you can get virtually anywhere in the province in a three-hour drive.

The principality of Asturias lies between Cantabria in the east and Galicia in the west. It reaches its scenic (and topographical) peak in the Picos de Europa, where the first Spanish national park was inaugurated. With green valleys, fishing villages, and forests, Asturias is a land for all seasons.

The coastline of Asturias constitutes one of the major sightseeing attractions in northern Spain. Called the Costa Verde, it begins in the east at San Vicente de la Barquera and stretches almost 90 miles (145km) to Gijón. Allow about six hours to drive it without stops. The western coast, beginning at Gijón, goes all the way to Ribadeo, a border town with Galicia—a distance of 112 miles (180km). This rocky coastline, studded with fishing villages and containing narrow estuaries and small beaches, is one of the most spectacular stretches of scenery in Spain. It takes all day to explore.

Asturias is an ancient land, as prehistoric cave paintings in the area demonstrate. Iron Age Celtic tribes resisted the Romans, as Asturians proudly point out to this day. They also resisted the Moors, who subjugated the rest of Spain. The Battle of Covadonga in 722 represented the Moors' first major setback after their arrival in Iberia some 11 years previously.

The Asturians are still staunchly independent. In 1934 Francisco Franco, then an ambitious young general, arrived with his Moroccan troops to suppress an uprising by miners who had declared an independent Socialist republic. His Nationalist forces returned again and again to destroy such Asturian cities as Gijón for their fierce resistance during the Spanish Civil War.

EXPLORING THE REGION BY CAR

Cantabria and Asturias can be part of a car or train ride across the northern rim of Spain. After visiting the Basque country in the east, you can head west along E-70 to the Cantabrian coastline.

Day 1 Spend the day in Laredo, after a stop for lunch in Castro-Urdiales (both towns are on the E-70).

Days 2–3 Continue west on E-70 and spend two nights in Santander. You'll need a day to explore the single most rewarding sightseeing target in the province: the medieval town of Santillana del Mar, reached by a secondary road just off the E-70 (follow the signs). Don't overlook a visit to the Cuevas de Altamira, on the outskirts of Santillana.

Day 4 Leave Santander by returning to Santillana and driving west along the coastal highway, and pay a morning visit to the seaside town of Comillas (to look at the Catalán *modernismo* architecture). Have a seafood lunch farther west at San Vicente de la Barquera, another seaside town, before getting back on westbound E-70. At Unquera, on the border between Cantabria and Asturias, head southbound on N-621 into the Picos de Europa. Take the N-621 through scenic landscapes alongside the Deva River until you reach the town of Potes, 24 miles (39km) inland. Stay overnight in or around Potes.

Day 5 Continue your drive through the Picos de Europa, taking N-621 to Rianos, where you'll pick up N-637. Drive northwest, admiring the rugged scenery as you go. Plan to spend the night in the Picos district at Cangas de Onís.

Day 6 From Cangas, take a secondary road signposted to the coastal hamlet of Colunga, where you'll pick up the N-632—a winding but scenic coast road. Head west to Gijón for another overnight stop.

Day 7 Take the A-66 to Oviedo, and spend the day exploring the capital of Asturias. Sleep over here.

Day 8 Head west from Oviedo along the N-634 to reach the old port city of Luarca. Have lunch here and, if time is up, conclude your tour and return to Oviedo, where rail and train connections can be made to Madrid. If time permits, continue west along the N-634 coastal road to Ribadeo, a border town between Galicia and Asturias and a gateway to the province of Galicia.

1 Laredo

37 miles (60km) W of Bilbao, 30 miles (48km) E of Santander, 265 miles (427km) N of Madrid

To an American, "the streets of Laredo" means the gun-slinging Old West. To a Spaniard it means an ancient maritime town on the eastern Cantabrian coast that has been turned into a major summer resort, with hundreds of apartments and villas along its three miles (5km) of beach. The Playa de la Salvé lies to the west and the Playa de Oriñón to the east.

On the last Friday of August, the annual **Battle of Flowers** draws thousands of visitors to watch bloom-adorned floats parade through the old town.

Cantabria & Asturias

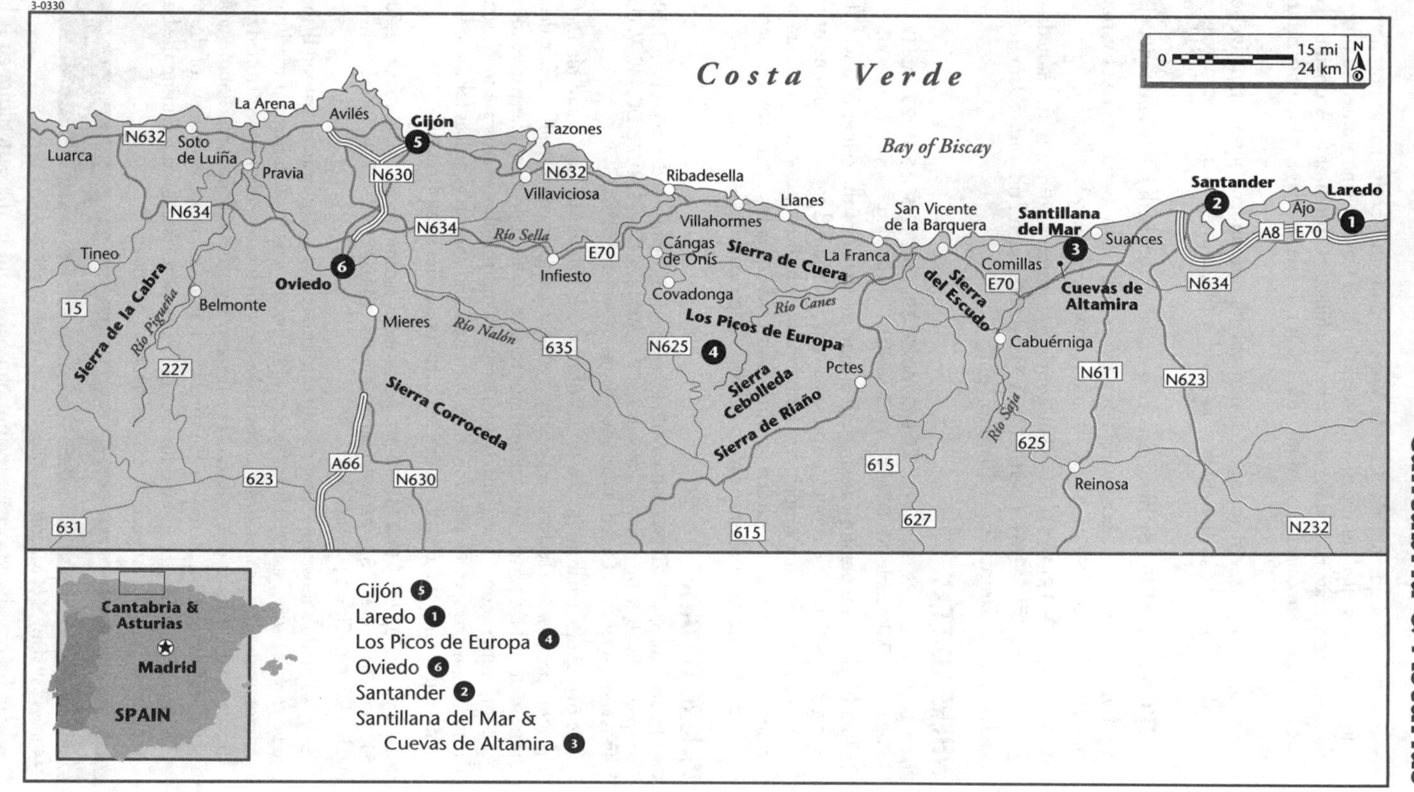

The medieval quarter, the **Puebla Vieja,** retains the traditional atmosphere of Laredo. It was walled on orders of Alfonso VIII of Castile, who wanted to protect the town from pirate raids along the coast. The hillside **Church of La Asunción,** dating from the 13th century, overlooks the harbor. It has five naves and rather bizarre capitals.

If you're driving west to Santoña, note the big monument honoring native son Juan de la Cosa, the cartographer who sailed with Columbus on his first voyage to America.

GETTING THERE **By Bus** Service is available from both Bilbao and Santander.

By Car From Bilbao, head west along the coastal highway (identified at various points as either the A-8 or the E-70), and follow the signs to Laredo.

VISITOR INFORMATION The tourist information office is at Alameda de Miramar, s/n (☎ **942/61-10-96**). Open Monday through Friday from 9am to 3pm and 4 to 8pm, Saturday from 10am to 1pm.

WHERE TO STAY

Risco. La Arenosa, 2, 39770 Laredo. ☎ **942/60-50-30.** Fax 942/60-50-55. 25 rms. TV TEL. 12,000 ptas. ($96) double. AE, DC, MC, V. Closed Jan. Free parking.

On a hillside overlooking Laredo, half a mile southeast of the center of town, this aging 1960s hotel opens onto impressive views of the old town and of one of the nearby beaches. It offers simple, very functionally furnished bedrooms, each clean and comfortable, as well as a garden in which scattered tables are placed for food service (see the restaurant recommendation below). Ample parking is provided.

WHERE TO DINE

Camarote. Vitoria, s/n. ☎ **942/60-67-07.** Reservations recommended. Main courses 1,700–2,500 ptas. ($13.60–$20); fixed-price menus 2,500–3,500 ptas. ($20–$28). AE, DC, MC, V. Daily 1–4pm and 8–11:30pm. Closed Jan and Sun dinner in winter. SEAFOOD.

The owner of Camarote (in the center of town) is Felipe Manjarrés, and his *chef de cuisine* specializes in seafood, especially fresh fish as opposed to shellfish. The decor is tasteful and attractive, and the outdoor terrace makes a pleasant alternative to the indoor dining room. The spinach with crayfish and the cheese tarts are truly excellent. Original recipes are used for salads with ham and shrimp as well as for those with tuna and fresh fruit. Try the grilled sea bream or a filet steak Rossini.

Risco. La Arenosa, 2. ☎ **942/60-50-30.** Reservations recommended. Main courses 1,700–2,600 ptas. ($13.60–$20.80); *menú del día* 5,500 ptas. ($44). AE, DC, MC, V. Tues–Sun 1–4pm and 8–11:30pm. Closed Jan. SEAFOOD.

This is Laredo's most appealing restaurant, known for its innovative seafood dishes. The *chef de cuisine,* assisted by a battery of helpers, prepares such items as marinated salmon with pink peppercorns, scrambled eggs with lobster, and peppers stuffed with minced pig's trotters or crabmeat. For dessert, try a fresh-fruit sorbet. Some tables are set up in the garden, or you can dine in a traditional room with views of the sea. The restaurant is on the ground floor of the Risco hotel (see above). During the busy months of July and August, it remains open on Monday.

2 Santander

244 miles (393km) N of Madrid, 72 miles (116km) NW of Bilbao

Santander has always been a rival of San Sebastián, in the east, although it has never attained the premier status of that Basque resort. It did, however, become a royal residence from 1913 to 1930, after city officials presented an English-style Magdalena Palace to Alfonso XIII and his queen, Victoria Eugenia.

An ancient city, Santander was damaged by a 1941 fire, which destroyed the old quarter and most of its dwellings. It was rebuilt along original lines, with wide boulevards, a waterfront promenade, sidewalk cafés, shops, restaurants, and hotels.

The **Music and Dance Festival** in August is one of the most important artistic events in Spain (accommodations are very hard to find during this time). At times, this festival coincides with religious celebrations honoring Santiago, the patron saint of Spain.

Santander is an education center in summer as well. Courses are offered at the once-royal palace, now the Menéndez Pelayo International University. Students and teachers from North America and Europe come here to study and enjoy the area.

Most visitors to Santander head for **El Sardinero,** a resort less than 1 1/2 miles (2.4km) from the city. Buses and trolleys make the short run between the city center and El Sardinero both day and night. Besides hotels and restaurants, Santander has three beaches: the **Playa de Castaneda,** the **Playa del Sardinero,** and the **Playa de la Concha,** where people stretch out under candy-striped umbrellas.

If these beaches get too crowded, take a 15-minute boat ride to **El Puntal,** a beautiful beach that is rarely crowded, even in August.

If you don't like crowds or beaches, go up to the lighthouse, a little more than 1 1/4 mile (2km) from El Sardinero, where the views are wide-ranging. A restaurant serves both indoor and outdoor snacks. Here, you can hike along the green cliffs or loll in the grass.

GETTING THERE **By Plane** Daily flights from Madrid and Barcelona land at Aeropuerto de Santander (☎ **942/20-21-00**), a little more than four miles (6.5km) from the town center, accessible by taxi only.

By Train There are three trains daily from Madrid (5 hours away); a one-way fare costs 3,550 pesetas ($28.40). Four trains a day travel from Bilbao (3 hours). For rail information call **942/28-02-02.**

By Bus Buses arrive at Plaza Estaciones (☎ **942/21-19-95**). There are 19 connections a day to and from Bilbao (trip time: 3 hours), a one-way ticket costing 865 pesetas ($6.90). Six buses a day arrive from Madrid (6 hours), costing from 3,115 to 4,400 pesetas ($24.90–$35.20), depending on the bus.

By Car The N-634 continues west from Laredo to Santander, with an N-635 turn-off to reach the resort.

VISITOR INFORMATION The tourist information office is at Estación Maritima, s/n (☎ **942/31-07-08**). Open Monday through Friday from 9am to 1pm and 4 to 7pm.

WHAT TO SEE & DO

Catedral. Somorrostro, s/n. ☎ **942/22-60-24.** Free admission. Daily 10am–1pm and 4–6pm.

Greatly damaged in the 1941 fire, this restored fortresslike 13th-century cathedral holds the tomb of historian/writer Marcelino Menéndez y Pelayo (1856–1912), Santander's most illustrious man of letters. The 12th-century crypt with a trio of low-slung aisles, untouched by fire, can be entered through the south portico. The Gothic cloister was restored after the fire. Roman ruins were discovered beneath the north aisle in 1983.

Museo Provincial de Prehistoria y Arqueología de Cantabria. Calle Casimiro Sainz, 4. ☎ **942/20-71-05.** Free admission. Tues–Sat 10am–1pm and 4–7pm, Sun 11am–2pm.

This museum has some interesting artifacts discovered in the Cantabrian province—not only Roman but also some unusual prehistoric finds. Since it is unlikely that you'll be allowed to visit the Cuevas de Altamira (see Section 3 later in this chapter), come here to see objects and photographs from these prehistoric caves with their remarkable paintings. Some of the items on display date from 15,000 years ago.

Museo Municipal de Bellas Artes. Calle Rubío, 6. ☎ **942/23-94-85.** Free admission. Mon–Fri 10am–1pm and 5–8pm, Sat 10am–1pm.

Located near the Ayuntamiento (Town Hall), the Municipal Museum of Fine Arts has some interesting Goyas, notably his portrait of Ferdinand VII, commissioned by the city, and his series of etchings called *Disasters of War.* You can also see some of his continuing series of *Caprichos* (Whims). See also Zurbarán's *Mystic Scene* and an array of works by Flemish, Spanish, and Italian artists, many of them contemporary.

Biblioteca Menéndez y Pelayo. Calle Rubío, 4. ☎ **942/23-45-34.** Free admission. Mon 9am–1:30pm, Tues–Thurs 9am–2pm and 4–9:30pm.

Located in the same building as the Municipal Museum is this 45,000-volume library amassed by Menéndez y Pelayo and left to Santander upon his death in 1912. Guided tours are available. Opposite the building is the Casa Museo, which displays this great man's study and shows how modestly he lived.

WHERE TO STAY

Santander is loaded with good-value hotels, from its year-round city hotels to its summer villas at El Sardinero. It gets crowded, so try to reserve well in advance.

IN TOWN

Hotel Ciudad de Santander. Menéndez Pelayo, 13–15, 39006 Santander. ☎ **942/22-79-65.** Fax 942/21-73-03. 60 rms, 2 suites. A/C MINIBAR TEL. 14,200–17,800 ptas. ($113.60–$142.40) double; 17,800–22,000 ptas. ($142.40–$176) suite. AE, DC, MC, V. Parking 600 ptas. ($4.80) outdoors, 1,200 ptas. ($9.60) indoors. Bus: 5.

Located about eight blocks north of Santander's busiest seaside promenade (the Paseo de Pereda) in the heart of the city's commercial heartland, this white-sided rectangular hotel was built in 1989, rising five floors. Although it is the best address within the city itself, for true luxury check into Real at El Sardinero (see below). The big-windowed lobby has marble floors, honey-colored wooden paneling, and modern accessories. Bedrooms are monochromatic, reflecting themes similar to that of the lobby, with fully equipped bathrooms and conveniently proportioned writing desks.

Dining/Entertainment: The hotel contains an informal snack bar, plus a stone-and-glass-sheathed restaurant serving three-course fixed-price lunches and dinners.

Services: Room service (daily 7am to midnight), laundry/valet, concierge.

Facilities: Car rentals.

Hotel México. Calderón de la Barca, 3, 39002 Santander. ☎ **942/21-24-50.** Fax 942/22-92-38. 35 rms. TV TEL. 6,500–9,500 ptas. ($52–$76) double. MC, V.

Only a block from the rail station, this is one of your best budget bets in the heart of the city, ideal for those without transportation who don't want to range far afield of the hotel, especially if they have luggage. The exterior may not be too enticing, but the atmosphere improves inside this family-operated inn. Even though it's in a congested area, street noises seem at a minimum, and the rooms are well cared for and comfortably furnished. Often they are in the old-fashioned architectural style of northern Spain, with glassed-in balconies and tall ceilings. Breakfast, the only meal served, is offered in a formal room with Queen Anne chairs and oak wainscoting. The manager speaks English.

AT EL SARDINERO

✪ **Hotel Real.** Paseo Pérez Galdós, 28, 39005 Santander. ☎ **942/27-25-50.** Fax 942/27-45-73. 114 rms, 9 suites. A/C MINIBAR TV TEL. 21,000–36,000 ptas. ($168–$288) double; 40,000–130,000 ptas. ($320–$1,040) suite. AE, DC, MC, V. Free parking. Bus: 1, 2, 5, or 7.

Architecturally noteworthy as the first building in the entire region constructed of reinforced concrete, the Real was built in 1917 to house the entourage of courtiers who accompanied King Alfonso XIII on his midsummer vacations to Santander. Purchased and completely renovated by the prestigious HUSA chain in 1987, it is once again one of the most elegant hotels in northern Spain, filled with updated reminders of a more gracious age. Located about 2 miles (3km) east of the commercial center of town, near the site of the Royal Palace on a hillside above the Magdalena Beach, the Real contains richly conservative bedrooms, most with views of the sea and all with many comfort-inducing amenities.

Dining/Entertainment: The El Puntal Restaurant serves regional and international three-course fixed-price lunches and dinners. Nearby lies a cocktail lounge accented with potted palms and high ceilings, and boasting a well-mannered staff.

Services: 24-hour room service, concierge, babysitting, laundry/valet.

Facilities: Car rentals, golfing available nearby.

Hotel Rhin. Avenida Reina Victoria, 153, 39005 Santander. ☎ **942/27-43-00.** Fax 942/27-86-53. 95 rms. A/C TV TEL. 11,000–17,000 ptas. ($88–$136) double. AE, DC, MC, V. Parking 800 ptas. ($6.40). Bus: 1, 2, 5, or 7.

Built in the early 1970s and renovated last in 1995, this hotel has panoramic views of the city's beaches. Following massive renovation, the hotel has improved considerably and has earned a four-star rating from the government. Bedrooms are handsome and very comfortable, and housekeeping is fastidious. On the premises there are both a cafeteria and a restaurant, serving international cuisine, although food is not one of the reasons to stay here. Laundry service and room service are provided. Although it's at the beach, the hotel is open all year.

WHERE TO DINE

Most visitors to Santander dine at their hotels or boardinghouses, which sometimes offer better value for the money and more efficient service than city restaurants. For variety, however, here are a few suggestions.

IN TOWN

Bodega Cigaleña. Daoíz y Velarde, 19. ☎ **942/21-30-62.** Main courses 1,100–2,600 ptas. ($8.80–$20.80); fixed-price menu 2,700 ptas. ($21.60). AE, DC, MC, V. Mon–Sat noon–4pm and 7:30pm–midnight. Closed June 20–July 1, Oct 20–Nov 20. Bus: 5. CANTABRIAN.

Popular with the young set in Santander, this Castilian bodega in the city center serves typical regional cuisine in a rustic decor—hanging hams, large wine kegs, and provincial tables. The set menu changes every day. A sample meal might be *sopa de pescado* (fish soup), shellfish paella, the fruit of the season, bread, and wine. The Cigaleña offers a good choice of wines from an old Castilian town near Valladolid. Ask to see its Museo del Vino.

Cañadío. Gómez Oreña, 15. ☎ **942/31-41-49.** Reservations recommended Fri–Sat. Main courses 1,800–2,800 ptas. ($14.40–$22.40); fixed-price menu 1,550 ptas. ($12.40). AE, DC, MC, V. Mon–Sat 1–4pm and 9pm–12:30am. Bus: 5. BASQUE/INTERNATIONAL.

This pleasant, centrally located restaurant off Plaza Cañadío has a deserved reputation for serving some of the best specialties in the region. Featured may be shrimp flan, hake in *cava* (Catalán champagne) sauce, and escalopes of ham with cheese. The bar, where drinks and light snacks are served, is open daily from 11am to midnight.

AT EL SARDINERO

La Sardina de Plata. Doctor Fleming, 3–4. ☎ **942/27-10-35.** Reservations required. Main courses 2,000–3,100 ptas. ($16–$24.80); fixed-price menu 2,400 ptas. ($19.20). Wed–Mon 1:30–4pm, Wed–Sat and Mon 8:30pm–midnight. AE, DC, MC, V. Bus: 1, 2, 5, or 7. SEAFOOD.

In a warren of small streets in the center of the old city, this nautically designed restaurant serves an imaginative cuisine highlighted by several delicate sauces. Menu selections might include such enticing dishes as cheese mousse, beef filet with truffles and cognac, and an unusually seasoned fish salad. There is also an extensive wine list. The service is courteous and efficient.

SANTANDER AFTER DARK

Gran Casino del Sardinero. Plaza de Italia. ☎ **942/27-60-54.** Admission 500 ptas. ($4). Bus: 1, 2, 5, or 7.

This is the most exciting nighttime diversion, offering such games as blackjack and chemin de fer. Be sure to bring your passport. The casino serves dinner from 9pm to 1am, costing 3,000 pesetas ($24). It's open daily from 8pm to 4am.

Lisboa. Plaza de Italia. ☎ **942/27-10-20.** Bus: 1, 2, 5, or 7.

Located within the city casino, this bar/restaurant/café draws gamblers taking a break from the tables as well as visitors looking for action of another sort. Many residents drop in for breakfast. Beer and mixed drinks are served. In summer it's especially crowded. It's open daily from 10am to 3:30am.

3 Santillana del Mar & Cuevas de Altamira

18 miles (29km) SW of Santander, 244 miles (393km) N of Madrid

Among the most perfectly preserved medieval villages in Europe, ✪ **Santillana del Mar,** a Spanish national landmark, was once a famous place of pilgrimage. A monastery housed the relics of St. Juliana, a martyr in Asia Minor who refused to surrender her virginity to her husband. Pilgrims, especially the *grandees* of Castile, came to worship at this site. The name Santillana is a contraction of Santa Juliana. The "del Mar" is misleading, as Santillana is not on the water but inland.

Jean-Paul Sartre called Santillana "the prettiest village in Spain," and we wouldn't want to dispute his judgment. In spite of all the tour buses, Santillana still retains its medieval atmosphere and is still very much a village of dairy farmers.

Wander on foot throughout the village, taking in its principal sites, including **Plaza de Ramón Pelayo** (sometimes called Plaza Mayor). Here the Parador de Santillana (see below) has been installed in the old Barreda Bracho residence.

A 15th-century tower, facing Calle de Juan Infante, is known for its pointed arched doorway. A walk along Calle de las Lindas (Street of Beautiful Women) doesn't live up to its promise, but includes many of the oldest buildings in Santillana and two towers dating from the 14th and 15th centuries. Calle del Rio gets its name from a stream running through town to a central fountain.

GETTING THERE **By Bus** La Cantábrica (☎ **942/72-08-22**) operates six buses a day from Santander, but cuts back to four between September and June. Trip time is 45 minutes.

By Car Take the N-611 out of Santander to reach the C-6316 cutoff to Santillana.

VISITOR INFORMATION The tourist information office is at Plaza Mayor (☎ **942/81-82-51**). Open daily from 9:30am to 1pm and 4 to 7pm.

WHAT TO SEE & DO

Visit the 800-year-old cathedral, the **Colegiata de Santillana,** Calle Santo Domingo, which shelters the tomb of the patron saint of the village, Juliana, and walk through its interesting cloister. Other treasures include 1,000-year-old documents and a 17th-century Mexican silver altarpiece. The cathedral is open April through October daily from 9am to 1pm and 4 to 7:30pm; off-season, daily from 10am to 1pm and 4 to 6pm. Admission, including entrance to the Convent of the Poor Clares, is 100 pesetas (80¢).

At the other end of the main street the 400-year-old Convent of the Poor Clares **(Museo Diocesano)** (☎ **942/81-80-04**) houses a rich art collection that was inspired by a Madrid art professor who encouraged the nuns to collect and restore religious paintings and statues damaged or abandoned during the Spanish Civil War. The collection is constantly growing. It's open daily from 10am to 1pm and 4 to 8pm (closing at 6pm in winter). Admission is 100 pesetas (80¢).

WHERE TO STAY

EXPENSIVE

✪ **Parador de Santillana.** Plaza de Ramón Pelayo, 8, 39330 Santillana del Mar. ☎ **942/81-80-00.** Fax 942/81-83-91. 56 rms. MINIBAR TV TEL. 14,500–16,500 ptas. ($116–$132) double. AE, DC, MC, V.

A 400-year-old former palace filled with many beautiful antiques, this parador is one of the most popular, and one of the best, in Spain. The public rooms are elegantly informal. The hand-hewn plank floor, the old brass chandeliers, and the refectory tables with their bowls of fresh flowers enhance the atmosphere. Large portraits of knights in armor hang in a gallery. Most of the guest rooms are unusually large, with antiques and windows on two sides; many have views of a small garden. The large baths contain all sorts of conveniences, including terry-cloth robes. Note that the third-floor rooms are very small. Four-course evening meals and luncheons—rather standard fare—are served in the great dining hall.

MODERATE

Hotel Altamira. Calle Cantón, 1, 39330 Santillana del Mar. ☎ **942/81-80-25.** Fax 942/84-01-36. 32 rms. TV TEL. 10,300 ptas. ($82.40) double. AE, DC, MC, V.

This three-star hotel in the center of the village is a 400-year-old former palace, and it is the best place to stay if you can't get into the government-run parador (see above). Although not as impressive as the parador, it often takes the overflow in its comfortable, well-maintained guest rooms. You can get a complete meal at the Castilian-inspired restaurant.

Hostal-Residencia Emperador. Avenida le Dorat, 12, 39330 Santillana del Mar. ☎ **942/81-80-54.** 5 rms. TV. 4,000–6,800 ptas. ($32–$54.40) double. No credit cards.

In the historic district, this residencia offers simply furnished but clean and reasonably comfortable rooms. For such a modest place, the hospitality is gracious. Because of the Emperador's small size, it can be difficult to get a room from June 15 to September 1.

Los Infantes. Avenida L'Dorat, 1, 39330 Santillana del Mar. ☎ **942/81-81-00.** Fax 942/84-01-03. 50 rms. TV TEL. 6,000–14,000 ptas. ($48–$112) double. AE, DC, MC, V.

This three-star hotel, although not as charming as the Altamira (see above), is a comfortable choice. Located in an 18th-century building on the main road leading into the village, the Infantes has successfully kept the old flavor of Santillana: beamed ceilings and lounges furnished with tapestries, antiques, clocks, and paintings. The rooms are pleasant and simple, with wall-to-wall carpeting; two have small balconies. A restaurant serves international cuisine.

WHERE TO DINE

Los Blasones. Plaza de la Gándara, s/n. ☎ **942/81-80-70.** Reservations recommended. Main courses 1,400–2,000 ptas. ($11.20–$16); fixed-price menu 2,500 ptas. ($20). AE, MC, V. Daily 1–4pm and 8–11pm. Closed Dec–Feb. CANTABRIAN.

Located in the center of town on the Plaza de la Gándara, this bar-cum-restaurant is a local hangout, and also serves the best food in town among the independent restaurants. It's in a rustic building made of stone. Barbecue selections are featured. The chef's specialty is *solomillo al queso de Treviso* (sirloin with cheese sauce). Try also the perfectly grilled hake or the tasty stuffed peppers.

AN EASY EXCURSION TO THE CAVES

About 1½ miles (2.5km) from Santillana del Mar are the ✪ **Cuevas de Altamira** (☎ **942/81-80-05**), famous for prehistoric paintings dating from the end of the Ice Age, paintings that have led those caves to be called the "Sistine Chapel of prehistoric art."

These ancient depictions of bison and horses, painted vividly in reds and blacks on the cave ceilings, were not discovered until the late 19th century. Once their authenticity was established, scholars and laypeople alike flocked to see these works of art, which provide a fragile link to our remote ancestors.

Severe damage was caused by the bacteria that so many visitors brought with them, so now the Research Center and Museum of Altamira allows only 20 visitors per day June through September (no children under 13) and 5 visitors per day October through May. Admission is 400 pesetas ($3.20). If you wish to visit, write to this address one year in advance asking permission to see the main cave and specifying the number in your party and the desired date: **Centro de Investigación y Museo de Altamira,** 39330 Santillana del Mar, Cantabria, Spain.

Reservations are not necessary for visits to the nearby **Cave of the Stalactites** and the little admission-free museum at the site, open Monday through Saturday from 10am to 1pm and 4 to 6pm, Sunday from 10am to 1pm. There you can see reproductions of the caves' artwork and buy color slides that show the subtleties of color employed. You'll also see pictures of what the bacteria did to these priceless paintings. To reach the area, you need to go by car or on foot because there is no bus service.

4 Los Picos de Europa

Potes: 71 miles (114km) W of Santander, 247 miles (398km) N of Madrid; Cangas de Onís: 91 miles (147km) W of Santander, 260 miles (419km) N of Madrid

These mountains are technically part of the Cordillera Cantábrica, which runs parallel to the northern coastline of Spain. In the narrow and vertiginous band known as Los Picos de Europa, they are by far at their most dramatic.

They are the most famous and most legend-riddled mountains in Spain. Rising more than 8,500 feet, they are not high by alpine standards, but their proximity to the sea makes their height especially awesome. During the Middle Ages, they were passable only with great difficulty. (Much earlier, the ancient Romans constructed a north-south road whose stones are still visible in some places.) The abundance of wildlife, the medieval battles that occurred here, and the dramatically rocky heights have all contributed to the "twice-told tales" that are an essential part of the entire principality of Asturias.

The position of Los Picos defined the medieval borders between Asturias, Santander, and León. Covering a distance of only 24 miles (39km) at their longest point, they are geologically and botanically different from anything else in the region. Thousands of years ago, busy glaciers created massive and forbidding limestone cliffs, which today challenge the most dedicated and intrepid rock climbers in Europe.

Even hill climbers should never underestimate the dangers of walking here. Many of the slopes are covered with loosely compacted shale, making good treads and hiking boots necessary. For amateurs, only well-established paths are safe: Setting out on their own for uncharted vistas has left many neophytes stranded. In summer, temperatures can get hot and humid, and sudden downpours sweeping in from the frequently rainy coastline are common in any season. Hiking is not recommended between October and May. Excursions by car and the walking tour contained in Driving Tour 3, below, are possible in any season.

The Picos are divided by swiftly flowing rivers into three regions: From east to west, they are Andara, Urrieles, and Cornion.

GETTING THERE **By Car** By far the best way to see this region is by car. Most drivers arrive in the region on the N-621 highway, heading southwest from Santander, or on the same highway northeast from the cities of north central Spain (especially León and Valladolid). This highway connects many of the region's best vistas in a straight line. It also defines the region's eastern boundary. If you're driving east from Oviedo, you'll take the N-6312, in which case the first town of any importance will be Cangas de Onís.

By Bus Travel by bus is much less convenient but possible if you have lots of time and have had your fill of the rich architecture of the Spanish heartland. The region's touristic hubs are the towns of Panes and Potes, both of which receive bus service (two buses per day in summer, one per day in winter) from both Santander and León. More frequent buses (five per day) come to Potes from the coastal town of Unquera (which lies along the coastal train lines). From Oviedo, there are two buses daily to the district's easternmost town of Cangas; these continue a short distance farther southeast to Covadonga. Within the region, a small local bus runs once a day, according to an erratic schedule, along the northern rim of the Picos, connecting Cangas de Onís with Las Arenas. Frankly, bus service in this region is too time consuming for most visitors.

THREE DRIVING TOURS

If you have a car, the number and variety of tours within this region are almost endless, but for the purposes of this guide, we have organized the region into three motor tours. Any of them, with their side excursions, could fill an entire day; if you're rushed and omit some of the side excursions, you'll spend half a day.

DRIVING TOUR 1: From Panes to Potes

18 miles (29km); 1 hour

This drive, except for one optional detour, extends entirely along one of the region's best roads, the N-621, which links León and Valladolid to Santander. The drive is most noteworthy for its views of the ravine containing the Deva River, a ravine so steep that direct sunlight rarely penetrates it.

About two-thirds of the way to Potes, signs will point you on a detour to:

1. **The village of Lebana,** half a mile off the main road. Here you'll find the church of **Nuestra Señora de Lebana,** built in the 10th century in the Mozarabic style, surrounded by a copse of trees at the base of tall cliffs. Some people consider it the best example of "Arabized" Christian architecture in Europe, with Islamic-inspired geometric motifs. If it isn't open, knock at the door of the first house you see as you enter the village—the home of the guardian, who will unlock the church if she's around. For this, she will expect a tip. If she's not around, content yourself with admiring the church from the outside, noting its spectacular natural setting. Continuing for about another five miles (8km), you'll reach the village of:
2. **Potes,** a charming place with well-kept alpine houses against a backdrop of jagged mountains. Two miles (3.2km) southwest of Potes, near Turiano, stands the:
3. **Monastery of Santo Toribio de Liébana,** dating from the 17th century. Restored to the style it enjoyed at the peak of its vast power, a transitional Romanesque, it contains what is reputed to be a splinter from the True Cross, brought from Jerusalem in the 8th century by the Bishop of Astorga. The monastery is also famous as the former home of Beatus de Liébana, the 8th-century author of *Commentary on the Apocalypse,* one of medieval Spain's most famous ecclesiastical documents. Today the building remains a functioning monastery. Ring the bell during daylight hours, and one of the brothers will let you enter if you are properly attired.

   At the end of a winding and breathtakingly beautiful road to the west of Potes lies the:
4. **Parador del Río Deva,** where you can spend the night or stop for lunch only. Doubles cost 9,500 to 11,500 pesetas ($76–$92), including breakfast. The drive to:
5. **Fuente-Dé** will, for the most part, follow the path of the Deva River. Once you're here, a *teleférico* will carry you 2,000 feet up to an observation platform above a wind-scoured rock face. In summer this cable car operates daily in July and August from 9am to 8pm; from September through June hours are daily 10am to 6pm. Round-trip fare is 1,200 pesetas ($9.60). At the top you can walk three miles (4.8km) along a footpath to the rustic **Refugio de Aliva,** open between June 15 and September 15. Doubles cost 7,500 to 8,500 pesetas ($60–$68). If you opt for just a meal or a snack at the hostal's simple restaurant, remember to allow enough time to return to the *teleférico* before its last trip down. If you plan on taking the next driving tour (below), then head back to Potes.

DRIVING TOUR 2: From Potes to Cangas de Onís

93 miles (150km); 4 hours

This tour includes not only the Quiviesa Valley and some of the region's most vertiginous mountain passes, but also some of its most verdant fields and most elevated pastures. You might stop at an occasional village, but most of the time you will be going through deserted countryside. Your route will take you under several tunnels and high above mountain streams set deep into gorges. The occasional belvederes signposted along the way always deliver on their promise of spectacular views.

1. **Potes** (see "Driving Tour 1" above) is your starting point. Take the N-621 southwest to Riaño. At Riaño, turn north for a brief ride on N-625. Then take:
2. **A winding, panoramic route** through the heart of the region by driving northwest on N-637. After a day of vistas, the first really important place you'll reach is:
3. **Cangas de Onís,** the westernmost town in the region, where you can get a clean hotel room and a solid meal after a trek through the mountains. The biggest attraction in Cangas de Onís is an ivy-covered **Roman bridge,** lying west of the center, spanning the Sella River. Also of interest is the **Capilla de Santa Cruz,** immediately west of the center. One of the earliest Christian sites in Spain (and a holy spot many centuries before that), it was originally constructed in the 8th century over a Celtic dolmen and rebuilt in the 15th century.

   A mile northwest of Cangas de Onís, beside the road leading to Arriondas, stands the:
4. **Monastery of San Pedro,** a Benedictine monastery in the village of **Villanueva.** The church that you see was originally built in the 17th century, when it enclosed within its premises the ruins of a much older Romanesque church. Combining a blend of baroque opulence and Romanesque simplicity, it has some unusual carved capitals showing the unhappy end of the medieval King Favila, supposedly devoured by a Cantabrian bear.

DRIVING TOUR 3: From Cangas de Onís to Panes

35 miles (56km); 1 hour

This tour travels along the relatively straight C-6312 from the western to the eastern entrance to the Picos de Europa region. A number of unusual excursions could easily stretch this into an all-day outing.

From Cangas de Onís, heading west about 1 mile (1.6km), you'll reach the turnoff to:

1. **El Buxu Cueva.** Inside the cave are a limited number of prehistoric rock engravings and charcoal drawings, somewhat disappointingly small. Only 25 persons per day are allowed inside (respiration erodes the drawings), so unless you get there early, you won't get in. It's open Wednesday through Sunday from 10am to 2pm and 4 to 6:30pm. Admission is 200 pesetas ($1.60).

   Four miles (6.5km) east, signs point south in the direction of:
2. **Covadonga,** revered as the birthplace of Christian Spain. It is about six miles (9.6km) off the main highway. A battle here in A.D. 718 pitted a ragged band of Christian Visigoths against a small band of Muslims. The resulting victory established the first niche of Christian Europe in a Moorish Iberia.

   The town's most important monument is **La Santa Cueva,** a cave containing the sarcophagus of Pelayo (d. 737), king of the Visigothic Christians, and an enormous neo-Romanesque basilica, built between 1886 and 1901, commemorating the Christianization of Spain. At the end of the long boulevard that funnels into the base of the church stands a statue of Pelayo.

   Return to the highway and continue east. You'll come to the village of Las Estazadas; then after another seven miles (11km) you'll reach:
3. **Las Arenas de Cabrales** (some maps refer to it as Arenas). This is the headquarters of a cheese-producing region whose Cabrales, a blue-veined cheese made from ewes' milk, is avidly consumed throughout Spain.

Drive three miles (4.8km) south from Arenas, following signs to the village of:

4. **Puente de Poncebos** (known on some maps as Poncebos). Here, the road ends abruptly (except perhaps for four-wheel-drive vehicles). This village is set several miles downstream from the source of Spain's most famous salmon-fishing river, the Cares, which flows from its source near the more southerly village of Cain through deep ravines.

   A Trek Through the Divine Gorge Beginning at Poncebos, a footpath has been cut into the ravine on either side of the Cares River. It is one of the engineering marvels of Spain, known for centuries as "The Divine Gorge." It crosses the ravine many times over footbridges and sometimes through tunnels chiseled into the rock face beside the water, making a hike along the banks of this river a memorable outing. You can climb up the riverbed from Poncebos, overland to the village of Cain, a total distance of seven miles (11km). Allow between three and four hours. At Cain, you can take a taxi back to where you left your car in Poncebos if you don't want to retrace your steps.

   After your trek up the riverbed, continue your drive on to the village of:

5. **Panes,** a distance of 14 miles (22km), to the eastern extremity of the Picos de Europa.

WHERE TO STAY & DINE

Accommodations are extremely limited in these mountain towns. If you're planning an overnight stop, make sure you have a reservation. Most taverns will serve you food during regular opening hours without a reservation.

IN CANGAS DE ONÍS

Hotel Aultre Naray. Peruyes-Cangas de Onís, 33547 Asturias. ☎ **98/584-08-08.** Fax 98/584-0448. 10 rms. TV TEL. 7,400–9,500 ptas. ($59.20–$76) double. No credit cards. Free parking.

A small hotel of character, this establishment, which opened in 1995, is an Asturian country house dating back to 1873. Its robust masonry work is typical of the last century, and it boasts a beautiful stone archway in the entrance. The decoration came from an interior design workshop in Madrid, resulting in a harmonious blend of traditional architecture with current design trends. The hotel has well-furnished bedrooms, each with a private bath. Four of the accommodations have sloping ceilings. There's also a cozy sitting room with a fireplace for guests, a bar and dining room, and a garden. The hotel is set in the foothills of the Escapa mountain range, enjoying a panoramic view of these mountains and of an oak forest on the banks of the River Sella. The area is a perfect place for fishing; hiking in the mountains and canoeing are other popular diversions.

La Palmera. Soto de Cangas. ☎ **98/594-00-96.** Main courses 1,000–2,000 ptas. ($8–$16); *menús del día* 900–1,100 ptas. ($7.20–$8.80). No credit cards. Daily 1–5pm and 8–11:30pm. ASTURIAN.

When the weather is right, you can dine outside here, enjoying some mountain air with the mountain food. Sometimes this place is overrun, but on other occasions you can have a meal in peace. The menu features game from the surrounding mountains, along with filet of beef, lamb chops, and salmon in green sauce. Try the local mountain cheese. La Palmera lies two miles (3km) east of Cangas de Onís on the road to Covadonga.

In Cosgaya

Hotel del Oso. Carretera Espinama, s/n, 39539 Cosgaya. ☎ **942/73-30-18.** Fax 942/73-30-36. 36 rms. TEL. 7,000–8,900 ptas. ($56–$71.20) double. AE, DC, MC, V. Free parking. From Potes, take the road signposted to Espinama 9 miles (14.5km) south.

This well-run little hotel is located in two buildings set next to the banks of the Deva River, beside the road leading from Potes to the parador and cable car at Fuente-Dé. The place is ringed with natural beauty. Its bedrooms are well furnished and maintained, and meals are taken at the Mesón del Oso (see below).

$ Mesón del Oso. Carretera Espinama, s/n. ☎ **942/73-04-18.** Main courses 1,100–2,000 ptas. ($8.80–$16). DC, MC, V. Daily 1–4pm and 9–11pm. Closed Jan 7–Feb 15. From Potes, take the route south toward Espinama 9 miles (14.5km). ASTURIAN.

Open to the public since 1981, this stone-built place is named after the bear that supposedly devoured Favilia, an 8th-century king of Asturias. Here, at the birthplace of the Christian warrior King Pelayo, you can enjoy Lebaniega cuisine, reflecting the bounty of mountain, stream, and sea. The portions are generous. Try trout from the Deva River, grilled tuna, roast suckling pig, or a mountain stew called *cocida lebaniego,* whose recipe derives from local lore and tradition. Dessert might be a fruit-based tart. There's also an outdoor terrace.

In Covadonga

Hotel Pelayo. 33589 Covadonga. ☎ **98/584-60-61.** Fax 98/584-60-54. 43 rms, 2 suites. TV TEL. 7,900–13,000 ptas. ($63.20–$104) double; 10,500–17,000 ptas. ($84–$136) suite. AE, MC, V. Closed Dec 15–Feb 1. Free parking. Drive east and then south from Cangas de Onís, following the signs for Covadonga and the hotel.

There's no street address for this place, but it lies in the shadow of the large 19th-century basilica that dominates the village. The view from its windows takes in a panoramic landscape. Guests come here to enjoy the mountain air, and many pilgrims check in while visiting religious shrines in the area. The place has a somewhat dated, but nevertheless appealing, family atmosphere. The rooms are comfortable and well furnished. The facilities include a parking lot, a garden, and a restaurant offering well-prepared lunch or dinner for 2,000 pesetas ($16).

In Fuente-Dé

Parador del Río Deva. At 3.5km de Espinama, 39588 Espinama. ☎ **942/73-00-01.** Fax 942/73-66-54. 78 rms. TV TEL. 9,500–11,500 ptas. ($76–$92) double. AE, DC, MC, V. Free parking. Drive 16 miles (26km) west of Potes.

The finest place to stay in the area, this government-run parador opens onto panoramic vistas of the Picos de Europa. Opened in 1975, it lies at the end of the major road through the Liébana region. Hunters in autumn and mountain climbers in summer often fill its attractively decorated and comfortably furnished bedrooms. The place has a pleasant bar, and its restaurant serves good regional cuisine, with a *menú del día* costing 3,200 pesetas ($25.60).

In Potes

$ Restaurant Martín. Roscabao, s/n. ☎ **942/73-02-33.** Main courses 1,200–2,200 ptas. ($9.60–$17.60); fixed-price menu 1,200 ptas. ($9.60). V. Daily 1–4pm and 8:30–11pm. Closed Jan. ASTURIAN.

This family-run establishment in the center of Potes is filled with regional charm and spirit. They prepare garbanzos (chickpeas) with bits of *chorizo* sausage. Other vegetables and the rich produce of the region appear on the seasonally adjusted menu, as well as game from the Picos and fish from the Cantabrian coast. The dessert choices comprise more than a dozen tarts and pastries.

5 Gijón (Xixón)

294 miles (473km) N of Madrid, 119 miles (192km) W of Santander, 18 miles (29km) E of Oviedo

The major port of Asturias and its largest city is also a summer resort and an industrial center rolled into one. As a port, Gijón (pronounced "hee-*hon*") is said to predate the Romans. The Visigoths came through here, and in the 8th century the Moors also wandered through the area, but none of those would-be conquerors made much of an impression on Gijón.

The best part of the city to explore is the *barrio* of **Cimadevilla,** with its maze of alleys and leaning houses. This section, jutting into the ocean to the north of the new town, spills over an elevated piece of land known as Santa Catalina. Santa Catalina forms a headland at the west end of the **Playa San Lorenzo,** stretching for about 1½ miles (2km); this beach has good facilities and is sandy. After time at the beach you can stroll through the **Parque Isabel la Católica** at its eastern end.

The most exciting time to be in Gijón is on **Asturias Day,** the first Sunday in August. This fiesta is celebrated with parade floats, traditional folk dancing, and lots of music. But summers here tend to be festive even without a festival. Vacationers are fond of patronizing the cider taverns (*chigres*), eating grilled sardines, and joining in sing-alongs in the portside *tascas.* Be aware that you can get as drunk on cider as you can on beer, maybe somewhat faster.

Gijón is short on major monuments. The city was the birthplace of Gaspar Melchor de Jovellanos (1744–1811), one of Spain's most prominent men of letters, as well as an agrarian reformer and liberal economist. Manuel de Godoy, the notorious minister, ordered that Jovellanos be held prisoner for seven years in Bellver Castle on Majorca. In Gijón his birthplace has been restored and turned into the **Museo-Casa Natal de Jovellanos,** Plaza de Jovellanos, open Tuesday through Saturday from 10am to 2pm and 4 to 8pm. Admission is free.

GETTING THERE **By Plane** Gijón doesn't have an airport, but Iberia flies to the airport at Ranón, 26 miles (42km) away, a facility it shares with Oviedo-bound passengers.

By Train Gijón has good rail links and makes a good gateway into Asturias. Three trains a day make the 6½- to 8½-hour trip from Madrid. León is a convenient rail hub for reaching Gijón because nine trains per day make the 2- to 3-hour trip between these cities. You can also take the narrow-gauge FEVE from Bilbao.

By Bus Six buses a day connect Gijón with Madrid (5½ hours away), and two buses per day run to and from Santander (4½ hours away). Four buses a day go to León (2 hours away).

By Car From Santander in the east, continue west along the N-634. At Ribadesella, you can take the turnoff to the 632, which is the coastal road that will take you to Gijón. This is the scenic route. To save time, continue on the N-634 until you reach the outskirts of Oviedo, then cut north on A-66, the expressway highway to Gijón.

VISITOR INFORMATION The tourist information office is at Marqués de San Estebán, 1 (☎ **98/534-60-46**). Open Monday through Friday from 9am to 2pm and 4 to 7pm, Saturday and Sunday from 11am to 2pm.

WHERE TO STAY

EXPENSIVE

Parador El Molino Viejo (Parador de Gijón). Parque Isabel la Católica, s/n, 33203 Gijón. ☎ **800/223-1356** in the U.S., or 98/537-05-11. Fax 98/537-02-33. 40 rms. A/C TV TEL. 13,500–16,500 ptas. ($108–$132) double. AE, DC, MC, V. Free parking. Bus: 4 or 11.

Next to the verdant confines of Gijón's most visible park, about half a mile east of the town center and an easy walk from the popular beach Playa San Lorenzo, this is the premier place to stay. Awarded four stars by the government (which also runs it), it was constructed around the core of an 18th-century cider mill. The parador is surrounded by a garden strewn with tables, beside a stream sheltering colonies of swans. It contains a marble-sheathed reception area, an unpretentious restaurant, and a cider bar that, on weekends, is quite popular with local residents. The guest rooms are somewhat cramped and surprisingly simple for a four-star hotel; however, they're tastefully restored with well-scrubbed wooden floors, thick shutters, traditional furniture, and larger-than-usual baths.

MODERATE

Begoña. Carretera de la Costa, 44, 33205 Gijón. ☎ **98/514-72-11.** Fax 98/539-82-22. 249 rms. TV TEL. 9,520–10,890 ptas. ($76.15–$87.10) double. AE, DC, V. Parking 1,300 ptas. ($10.40). Bus: 4 or 11.

This functional modern hotel with much-appreciated parking has rooms that are well furnished and comfortable, plus efficient chamber service to keep everything clean. Regional and national dishes, with many seafood concoctions, are served in the Begoña's restaurant, where meals begin at 2,000 pesetas ($16). The hotel lies on the southern outskirts of the new town, one block north of Avenida Manuel Llaneza, the major traffic artery from the southwest.

La Casona de Jovellanos. Plaza de Jovellanos, 1, 33201 Gijón. ☎ **98/534-12-64.** Fax 98/535-61-51. 13 rms. TV TEL. 8,750–13,400 ptas. ($70–$107.20) double. AE, MC, V. Parking 1,000 ptas. ($8) nearby. Bus: 4 or 11.

This venerable hotel stands on the rocky peninsula that was the site of the oldest part of fortified Gijón, a short distance south of the Parque Santa Catalina. It contains only a few bedrooms, so reservations are imperative. The rooms themselves are attractively furnished and well maintained. The hotel was built on foundations three centuries old. In 1794 the writer Jovellanos established the Asturian Royal Institute of Marine Life and Mineralogy here, and it was later transformed into a hotel, lying within walking distance of the beach and yacht basin.

Hernán Cortés. Fernández Vallín, 5, 33205 Gijón. ☎ **98/534-60-00.** Fax 98/535-56-45. 109 rms. MINIBAR TV TEL. 10,800 ptas. ($86.40) double. AE, DC, MC, V. Parking 1,250 ptas. ($10) nearby. Bus: 4 or 11.

About one block east of Plaza del 6 de Agosto, midway between Playa San Lorenzo and the harbor, the Cortés is one of the finest hotels in town. Although it was recently renovated, its guest rooms still retain a bit of the allure of yesteryear and provide such thoughtful extras as shoe-shine equipment. The facilities include a disco, convention rooms, and ample parking. The Cortés doesn't have a restaurant, but it does offer a nighttime cafeteria for snacks and light meals. The proprietors will serve lunch or dinner from a neighboring restaurant in your room.

WHERE TO DINE

$ Casa Justo (Chigre Asturianu). Hermanos Feigueroso, 50. ☎ **98/538-63-57.** Reservations recommended. Main courses 1,500–2,500 ptas. ($12–$20); fixed-price menus

1,250–1,500 ptas. ($10–$12). AE, MC, V. Fri–Wed 1pm–1am. Closed 3 weeks in June (dates vary). Bus: 4 or 11. ASTURIAN.

Housed within a very old cider press, for years this place has been called Chigre Asturianu, but most locals still refer to it by its old designation. Renovations have added well-designed dining rooms and kitchens to what used to be a large and drafty building. The cuisine is based primarily on fish and shellfish but with plenty of Asturian regional dishes as well. Try octopus with potatoes, grilled fresh John Dory, or veal chops. There is a full array of wines. Here, too, you can sample that Roquefort-like cheese, Cabrales, made in the Picos de Europa. The Casa Justo lies south of the old town near Campo Sagrada on the road to Pola de Siero.

Casa Tino. Alfredo Truán, 9. ☎ **98/534-13-87.** Reservations recommended. Main courses 1,600–2,200 ptas. ($12.80–$17.60); *menú del día* 1,250 ptas. ($10). AE, V. Fri–Wed 1:30–3:30pm and 8:30–11:30pm. Bus: 4 or 11. ASTURIAN.

Quality combined with quantity, at reasonable prices, is the hallmark of this restaurant, located near the police station, north of Manuel Llaneza and west of the Paseo de Begoña. Each day the chef prepares a different stew—sometimes fish and sometimes meat. The place is packed with chattering diners every evening, many of them habitués. Sample the white beans of the region cooked with pork, stewed hake, or marinated beefsteak, perhaps finishing with one of the fruit tarts.

Casa Victor. Carmen, 11. ☎ **98/534-83-10.** Reservations recommended. Main courses 1,800–2,800 ptas. ($14.40–$22.40); fixed-price menu 1,800 ptas. ($14.40). AE, MC, V. Mon–Sat 1:30–3:30pm and 8:30–11:30pm. Closed Nov. Bus: 4 or 11. SEAFOOD.

Owner and sometime chef Victor Bango is a bit of a legend. He oversees the buying and preparation of the fresh fish for which this place is famous. The successful young people of Gijón enjoy the tavernlike atmosphere here, as well as the imaginative dishes—a mousse made from the roe of sea urchins, for example, is all the rage in Asturias these days. Well-chosen wines accompany such other menu items as octopus served with fresh vegetables and grilled steak. Casa Victor is located by the dockyards.

6 Oviedo (Uviéu)

126 miles (203km) W of Santander, 276 miles (444km) N of Madrid

Oviedo is the capital of Asturias. Despite its high concentration of industry and mining, the area has unspoiled scenery. Only 16 miles (26km) from the coast, Oviedo is very pleasant in summer, when much of Spain is unbearably hot. It also makes an ideal base for excursions along the "Green Coast."

A peaceful city today, Oviedo has had a long and violent history. Razed in the 8th century during the Reconquest, it was rebuilt in an architectural style known as Asturian pre-Romanesque, which predated many of the greatest achievements under the Moors. Remarkably, this architectural movement was in flower when the rest of Europe lay under the black cloud of the Dark Ages.

As late as the 1930s Oviedo was suffering violent upheavals. An insurrection in the mining areas on October 5, 1934, led to a seizure of the town by miners, who set up a revolutionary government. The subsequent fighting led to the destruction of many historical monuments. The cathedral was also damaged, and the university was set on fire. Even more destruction came during the Spanish Civil War.

GETTING THERE **By Plane** Oviedo doesn't have an airport. The nearest one is at Ranón, 32 miles (51.5km) away, which it shares with Gijón-bound passengers.

By Train From Madrid, there are three trains per day. Call RENFE at **98/525-02-02** for information.

By Bus One bus per day arrives from Santander. Eleven buses pull in daily from Madrid. For bus schedules, call **98/528-12-00.**

By Car From the east or west, take the N-634 across the coast of northern Spain. From the south, take the N-630 or the A-66 from León.

VISITOR INFORMATION The tourist information office is at Plaza de Alfonso II el Casto (☎ **98/521-33-85**). Open October through May, Monday through Friday from 9am to 2pm and 4 to 7pm, Saturday and Sunday from 11am to 4pm; June through September, Monday through Friday from 9:30am to 1:30pm and 4:30 to 8pm, Saturday from 9am to 2pm, and Sunday from 11am to 2pm.

WHAT TO SEE & DO

Oviedo has been rebuilt into a modern city around the Parque de San Francisco. It still contains some historical and artistic monuments, however, the most important being the **cathedral** on the Plaza de Alfonso II el Casto (☎ **98/522-10-33**), a Gothic building begun in 1348 and completed at the end of the 15th century (except for the spire, which dates from 1556). Inside is an altarpiece in the florid Gothic style, dating from the 14th and 15th centuries. The cathedral's 9th-century **Cámara Santa (Holy Chamber)** is famous for the Cross of Don Pelayo, the Cross of the Victory, and the Cross of the Angels, the finest specimens of Asturian art in the world. Admission to the cathedral is free, but entrance to the Holy Chamber is 300 pesetas ($2.40) for adults and 100 pesetas (80¢) for children 10 to 15; children under 10 are free. The cathedral is open May through October, Monday through Saturday from 10am to 1pm and 4 to 7pm; November through April, Monday through Saturday from 10am to 1pm and 4 to 6pm. Take bus number 1.

Behind the cathedral, the **Museo Arqueológico,** Calle San Vicente, 5 (☎ **98/521-54-05**), in a former convent dating from the 15th century, houses prehistoric relics discovered in Asturias, pre-Romanesque sculptures, a numismatic display, and old musical instruments. It's open Tuesday through Saturday from 10am to 1:30pm and 4 to 6pm, Sunday from 11am to 1pm. Admission is free.

Standing above Oviedo, on Monte Naranco, are two of the most famous examples of Asturian pre-Romanesque architecture. **Santa María del Naranco** (☎ **98/529-67-55**), originally a 9th-century palace and hunting lodge of Ramiro I, offers views of Oviedo and the snowcapped Picos de Europa. Once containing baths and private apartments, it was converted into a church in the 12th century. Intricate stonework depicts hunting scenes, and barrel vaulting rests on a network of blind arches. The open porticoes at both ends were 200 years ahead of their time architecturally. The church is open April through September, daily from 9:30am to 1pm and 3 to 7pm; October through March, daily from 10am to 1pm and 3 to 5pm. Admission is 200 pesetas ($1.60).

Lying about 100 yards away is **San Miguel de Lillo** (☎ **98/529-56-85**). It, too, was built by Ramiro I as a royal chapel, and was no doubt a magnificent specimen of Asturian pre-Romanesque until 15th-century "architects" marred its grace. The stone carvings that remain, however, are exemplary. Most of the sculptures have been transferred to the archaeological museum in town.

The church is open daily from 10am to 1pm Monday through Saturday, also from 3 to 7pm. Admission is 250 pesetas ($2) Tuesday through Sunday, free on Mondays.

Secrets of the Green Coast

Shopping in Oviedo This city doesn't immediately come to mind when you're planning a trip to Spain. But serious shoppers know that it offers some of the best outlets in Spain for handbags and shoes. For a number of finest boutiques, head for the intersection of Uria and Gil de Jaz. In this district and on adjoining side streets you'll find some of the country's best-known designer boutiques, selling the exact merchandise that goes at far higher prices in such cities as Madrid and Barcelona. Many artisans in this district make their own products—selling, for example, a variety of calfskin goods and hand-sewn leather. You'll also come across good sales on Asturian ceramicware.

Endangered Wildlife As you're touring the majestic Picos de Europa (see our driving tours) be on the lookout for some of the rarest wildlife remaining in Europe. The Picos de Europa is the domain of some endangered species that have all but disappeared elsewhere. On the beech-covered slopes of these mountains and in gorges laden with jasmine, you might spot the increasingly rare Asturcon. This is a shaggy and rather chubby wild horse that's so small it first looks like a toy horse. Another endangered species is the Iberian brown bear—but if you see one, keep your distance. The park is also the home of the sure-footed chamois goat. Many bird-watchers "flock" here every year to see rare birds of prey that include peregrine falcons, buzzards, and golden eagles. There are also some rare butterflies. All of this wildlife, of course, is strictly protected by the government.

Ask at the tourist office for its 45-minute walking tour from the center of Oviedo to the churches. Also check that the churches will be open at the time of your visit.

WHERE TO STAY

EXPENSIVE

✪ Hotel de la Reconquista. Gil de Jaz, 16, 33004 Oviedo. ☎ **98/524-11-00.** Fax 98/524-11-66. 131 rms, 11 suites. A/C MINIBAR TV TEL. 21,600–27,000 ptas. ($172.80–$216) double; from 32,000 ptas. ($256) suite. AE, DC, MC, V. Parking 1,600 ptas. ($12.80). Bus: 1, 2, or 3.

Named after a subject dear to the hearts of the Catholic monarchs (the ejection of the Muslims from Iberia), this is one of the most prestigious hotels in Spain. Originally built between 1754 and 1777 as an orphanage and hospital, it received visits from Queen Isabella II in 1858 and a reworking of its baroque stonework during a restoration in 1958. The Reconquista was converted into a hotel in 1973 after the outlay of massive amounts of cash. Despite the growth of the city, it remains the second-largest building in Oviedo.

Today, the interior boasts a combination of modern and reproduction furniture, as well as a scattering of ecclesiastical paintings and antiques. The spacious guest rooms contain private baths and are outfitted in antique styles, with views of the old town or of a series of elegantly antique interior courtyards. The hotel lies two blocks north of the largest park in the town center, the Campo San Francisco.

Dining/Entertainment: Rey Casto, a cafeteria/restaurant, offers both regional and national dishes. In addition there is a bar, plus a lounge bar with live piano music.

Services: 24-hour room service, concierge, currency exchange, safe-deposit boxes, doctor on call, babysitting upon request.

Facilities: Sauna, hairdresser, shopping boutiques, business center.

MODERATE

Clarín. Caveda, 23, 33002 Oviedo. ☎ **98/522-72-72.** Fax 98/522-80-18. 47 rms. MINIBAR TV TEL. 12,900 ptas. ($103.20) double. AE, MC, V. Bus: 1, 2, or 3.

This recently built modern hotel in the old quarter is noted for its tasteful decor, with comfortable, inviting, and well-maintained rooms. On the premises you'll find a cozy and well-managed cafeteria but no restaurant. The hotel stands right in the middle of the historic district within walking distance of many of the attractions.

Hotel La Gruta. Alto de Buenavista, s/n, 33006 Oviedo. ☎ **98/523-24-50.** Fax 98/525-31-41. 105 rms. TV TEL. 10,900 ptas. ($87.20) double. AE, DC, MC, V. Free parking. Bus: 1.

In this family-run hotel just outside the city limits, the rooms are comfortably but simply furnished, many with views of the surrounding countryside. Amenities include safety-deposit boxes. Regional cuisine is served in the on-premises restaurant.

Hotel Principado. Calle San Francisco, 6, 33003 Oviedo. ☎ **98/521-77-92.** Fax 98/521-39-46. 63 rms, 4 suites. MINIBAR TV TEL. 14,000 ptas. ($112) double; 16,000 ptas. ($128) suite. AE, DC, MC, V. Parking 700 ptas. ($5.60).

The well-managed Principado stands opposite the university. Guests have access to an underground parking garage, easing the problem of parking in the center of town. The guest rooms are comfortably furnished and well maintained. The dining room, featuring a regional menu, serves nonguests as well as guests. Although built in 1951, the hotel was completely renovated in 1991.

A NEARBY PLACE TO STAY

If you're driving to La Coruña and Santiago de Compostela, you may want to stop in the little town of Cornellana (Salas), 24 miles (39km) west of Oviedo on the route to Luarca.

Hotel La Fuente. Carretera N-634, 33876 Cornellana. ☎ **98/583-40-42.** 19 rms. TV. 6,000 ptas. ($48) double; 7,500 ptas. ($60) triple. MC, V. Closed Sept 20–Oct 2. Free parking. Take the N-634 west to Cornellana.

This little inn, located on the N-634, has a sitting room on each floor as well as a bath. Bedrooms are simply furnished but comfortable. In the dining room overlooking the garden you can order a three-course *menú del día.*

WHERE TO DINE

$ Cabo Peñas. Melquiades Alvarez, 24. ☎ **98/522-03-20.** Main courses 950–2,300 ptas. ($7.60–$18.40). AE, DC, MC, V. Daily 1–4pm and 8pm–midnight. Bus: 1. ASTURIAN.

The most atmospheric and *típico* place in town, Cabo Peñas, near the train station, is one of the few fast-food places that attract the gastronomes of Oviedo. At the dining room in the rear, diners perch on high stools placed around wood tables. They can begin with tapas before going on to order a *plato del día* (plate of the day). Deli-type cold cuts are featured, including boiled pork shoulder, and the huge steaks are often served with cheese sauce.

Casa Conrado. Argüelles, 1. ☎ **98/522-39-19.** Reservations required. Main courses 1,600–2,750 ptas. ($12.80–$22); fixed-price menu 2,950 ptas. ($23.60). AE, DC, MC, V. Mon–Sat 1–4pm and 9pm–midnight. Closed Aug. Bus: 1. ASTURIAN.

Almost as solidly established as the cathedral nearby, this restaurant offers good-tasting and hearty Asturian stews, seafood platters, seafood soups, several preparations of hake, including one cooked in cider, escalopes of veal with champagne, and a full range of desserts. It is a local favorite and a long-established culinary tradition. The service is attentive.

✪ **Casa Fermín.** Calle San Francisco, 8. ☎ **98/521-64-52.** Reservations recommended. Main courses 1,500–2,850 ptas. ($12–$22.80); fixed-price menus 4,500–5,000 ptas. ($32–$35.50). DC, MC, V. Mon–Sat 1–4pm and 8:30–11:30pm. Bus: 1 or 2. ASTURIAN/INTERNATIONAL.

The chef here prepares the best regional cuisine in town in a building near the university and the cathedral. To order its most classic dish, ask for *fabada asturiana,* a bean dish with Asturian black pudding and Avilés ham. A tasty hake cooked in cider is another suggestion. In season (October through March), venison is the specialty. Try also the traditional Cabrales cheese of the province. The Casa Fermín lies directly east of the Parque de San Francisco.

El Raitán. Trascorrales, 6. ☎ **98/521-42-18.** Reservations recommended. Fixed-price menu 3,500 ptas. ($28). AE, MC, V. Mon–Sat 1:30–4pm and 9pm–midnight. Bus: 1. ASTURIAN.

This restaurant south of the cathedral, serving a set menu, bases all its dishes on regional ingredients, with meals accompanied by wines from La Rioja. A large array of well-prepared choices is available for each course. Each day the chef presents nine classic regional dishes that change with the season. The place has a tavern setting with overhead beams—atmospheric and intimate.

Galicia 20

Set "atop" Portugal in the northwest corner of Spain, Galicia is a rainswept land of grass and granite, much of its coastline gouged out by fjordlike inlets. It is a land steeped in Celtic tradition—in many areas its citizens, called *gallegos,* speak their own language (not a dialect of Spanish, they insist, but a combination of Portuguese and Spanish). Galicia consists of four provinces: La Coruña (including Santiago de Compostela), Pontevedra, Lugo, and Ortense.

The Romans, who arrived after having conquered practically everything else in Europe, made quite an impression on the region. The Roman walls around the city of Lugo and the Tower of Hercules at La Coruña are part of that legacy. The Moors came this way, too, and did a lot of damage along the way. But finding the natives none too friendly and other battlefields more promising, they moved on.

Nothing did more to put Galicia on the tourist map than the Santiago Road. It is the oldest, most traveled, and most famous route on the old continent. To guarantee a place in heaven, pilgrims journeyed to the tomb of Santiago (St. James), patron saint of Spain. They trekked across the Pyrenees by the thousands, risking their lives in transit. The Pilgrims' Way to Santiago contributed to the development and spread of Romanesque art and architecture. Pilgrimages to the shrine lessened as medieval culture itself began its decline.

EXPLORING THE REGION BY CAR

If you're touring the northern coast of Spain, you'll enter Galicia at the border town of Ribadeo.

Day 1 Take the corniche road (Highway 642) along the northwestern coast to explore the Rías Altas, or fjord district, of Galicia. Spend the night at La Coruña, where, if you arrive early enough, you'll get to spend some time on the beach. Depending on your schedule, you can also explore some of the sights, such as the Jardín de San Carlos, although Santiago (coming up) is much more interesting for general sightseeing.

Day 2 After a morning tour of La Coruña, continue south along E-1/A-9, cutting west on Highway 543 to Santiago de Compostela, the destination of the medieval pilgrim. Stay overnight here after visiting the old town and the cathedral.

Day 3 Follow signs along a secondary road to Padrón, then hook up again with the E-1, taking it south to Pontevedra, a provincial capital, for the night. If you're not in a hurry, between Padrón and Pontevedra stay on the winding coastal road (the 550) and detour along the *rías* of the Rías Bajas country, which offers the most dramatic fjord scenery in Galicia. Pontevedra itself is of minor tourist interest, except for its old quarter and the Basilica de Santa María in Mayor. However, it makes a good stop because it's the site of the Parador Nacional Casa del Barón.

Day 4 Leave Pontevedra after seeing its old quarter and drive northeast along the N-541 and the N-640 to another provincial capital, Lugo. (Be aware that on the 14-mile stretch between Cerdeo and Lalin the road will be identified only by signposts pointing toward Lalin and Lugo.) After a visit to its old Roman walls, the next morning you can take the national highway (N-VI) to Madrid.

1 La Coruña

375 miles (604km) NW of Madrid, 96 miles (155km) N of Vigo

Despite the fact that La Coruña (Corunna in English and A Coruña in Galician) is an ancient city, it does not have a wealth of historical and architectural monuments. Celts, Phoenicians, and Romans all occupied the port, and it is another of the legendary cities that claims Hercules as its founder.

The great event in the history of La Coruña occurred in 1588, when Philip II's Invincible Armada sailed from here to England. Only half of the ships made it back to Spain. The following year, Sir Francis Drake and his ships attacked the port in reprisal.

GETTING THERE **By Plane** There are five flights a week from Madrid to La Coruña Airport. Serviced only by Aviaco, the Aeropuerto de Alvedro (☎ **981/23-22-40**) is six miles (10km) from the heart of the city.

By Train From Madrid (via Orense and Zamora), there is express service two times a day (trip time: 8½ hours). Arrivals are at the La Coruña Station on Calle Joaquín Planelles (☎ **981/23-03-09**). For the RENFE office, call **981/15-02-02.**

By Bus From Santiago, there's frequent daily bus service leaving from the station on the Calle Caballeros (☎ **981/23-96-44**). Four buses a day connect Madrid and La Coruña (trip time: 9 hours). A one-way ticket from Madrid is 4,830 pesetas ($38.65).

By Car La Coruña is reached from Madrid by the N-VI. You can also follow the coastal highway, the N-634, which runs all the way across the northern rim of Spain from San Sebastián to the east.

VISITOR INFORMATION The tourist information office is at Dársena de la Marina, s/n (☎ **981/22-18-22**). The office is open Monday through Friday from 9am to 2pm and 4:30 to 6:30pm, Saturday from 10:30am to 1pm.

WHAT TO SEE & DO

La Coruña's old town is ideal for strolling around and stopping at any of the historic churches and mansions. **Plaza de María Pita**—named after the 16th-century Spanish Joan of Arc—divides the old town from the new. María Pita was a La Coruña housewife who is said to have spotted the approach of Drake's troops. Risking her own life, she fired a cannon shot to alert the citizens to an imminent invasion. For that act of heroism, she is revered to this day. Drake, on the other hand, is still a hated name in these parts.

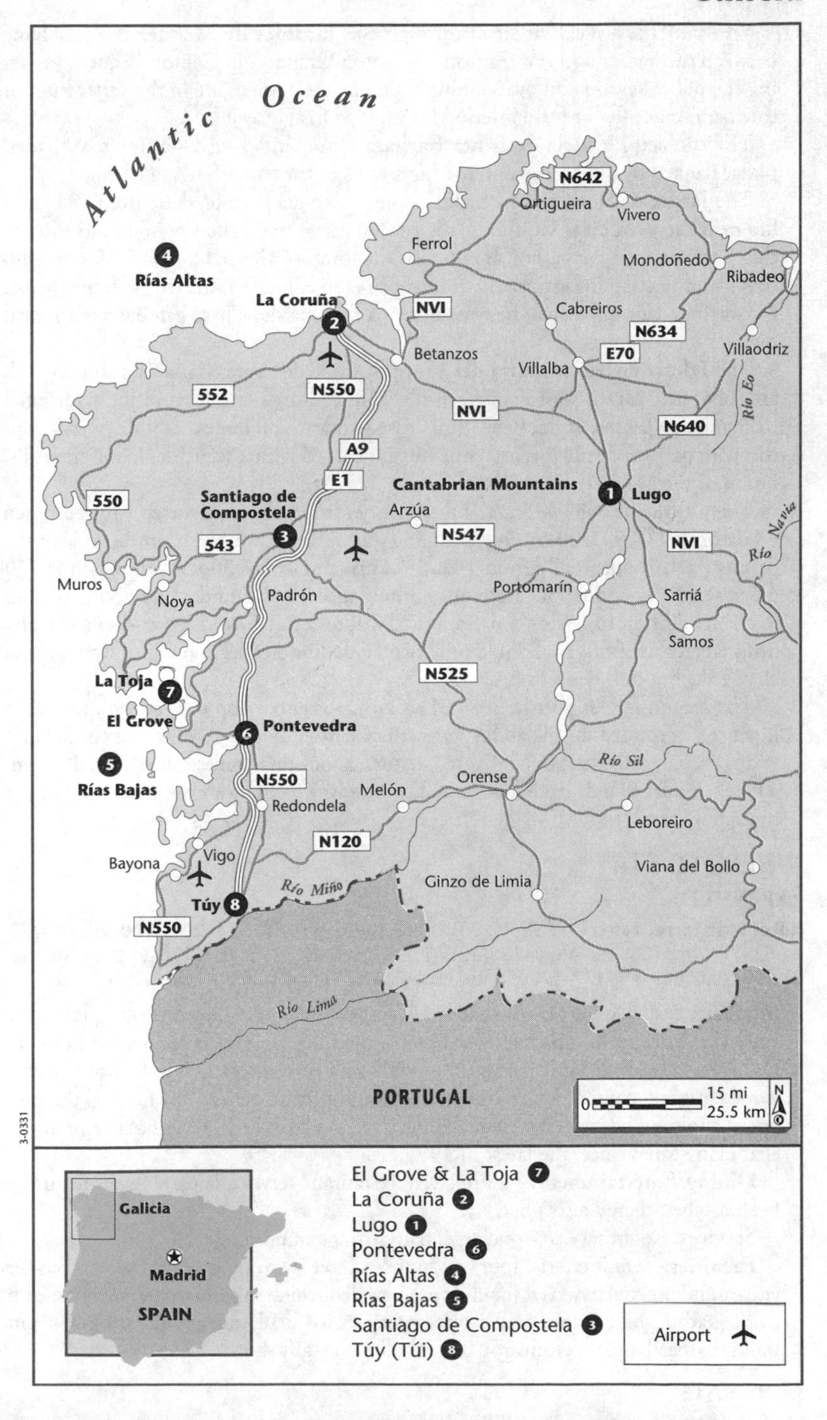
Atlantic Ocean
Rías Altas
La Coruña
Ferrol
Ortigueira
N642
Vivero
Mondoñedo
Ribadeo
Cabreiros
NVI
N634
Betanzos
Villalba
E70
Villaodriz
Río Eo
552
N550
NVI
N640
A9
E1
550
Santiago de Compostela
Cantabrian Mountains
Lugo
Arzúa
N547
543
NVI
Río Navia
Muros
Noya
Padrón
Portomarín
Sarriá
Samos
La Toja
N525
El Grove
Pontevedra
Río Sil
Rías Bajas
N550
Orense
Melón
Redondela
Leboreiro
N120
Bayona
Vigo
Viana del Bollo
Río Miño
Ginzo de Limia
Túy
N550
Río Lima
PORTUGAL
0
15 mi
25.5 km
N
3-0331
Galicia
Madrid
SPAIN
El Grove & La Toja 7
La Coruña 2
Lugo 1
Pontevedra 6
Rías Altas 4
Rías Bajas 5
Santiago de Compostela 3
Túy (Túi) 8
Airport

You can take a pleasant stroll through the **Jardines de Méndez Núñez,** lying between the harbor and Los Cantones (Cantón Grande and Cantón Pequeño). Facing the police station and overlooking the port, the gardens are in the very center of town and make for a restful interlude during your sightseeing.

The cobbled **Plazuela de Santa Bárbara** also merits a visit—a tiny tree-shaded plaza, flanked by old houses and the high walls of the Santa Bárbara convent.

The **Jardín de San Carlos,** reached along Paseo del Parrote, dates from 1843 and lies near the Casa de la Cultura. This garden grew up on the site of an old fortress that once guarded the harbor. It contains the tomb of General Sir John Moore, who fought unsuccessfully against the troops of Napoleon. He retreated with his British forces to La Coruña, where he was shot in a final battle. These gardens are an ideal picnic spot.

The **Iglesia de Santa María del Campo,** Calle de Santa María, is a church with an elaborately carved west door from the 13th century—modeled in the traditional Romanesque-Gothic style. Beneath its rose window you'll see a Gothic portal from the 13th or 14th century. The tympanum is carved with a scene depicting the Adoration of the Magi.

The Castillo de San Antón, a 16th-century fort, is now the **Museo Arqueológico e Histórico** (☎ **981/20-59-94**), standing out in the bay on the southeast side of the peninsula. It is open daily from 10am to 2pm and 4 to 7:30pm. Admission is 250 pesetas ($2) for adults, but free for children aged 13 and under and adults 66 and over. In addition to having a panoramic location on its own islet, it displays many unusual artifacts from La Coruña province, including a collection of pre-Roman jewelry. Take bus number 3 or 3A.

The second-largest port in Spain, La Coruña is also a popular vacation resort, so it gets very crowded in July and August. Riazor Beach, right in town, is a good, fairly wide beach, but the best one is Santa Cristina, about three miles (5km) outside town. There's regular round-trip bus service. The best way to go, however, is via the steamer that plies the bay.

WHERE TO STAY

EXPENSIVE

Hotel Finisterre. Paseo del Parrote, 20, 15001 La Coruña. ☎ **981/20-54-00.** Fax 981/20-84-62. 117 rms, 10 suites. A/C MINIBAR TV TEL. 14,500–17,325 ptas. ($116–$138.60) double; 21,500–25,000 ptas. ($172–$200) suite. AE, DC, MC, V. Free parking. Bus: 1, 2, 3, or 5.

Immediately above the port, a short walk east of the tourist information office at the edge of the old town, this high-rise hotel is the finest and most panoramic in town. Bedrooms are small but comfortable, with wall-to-wall carpeting, lots of exposed wood, brightly contemporary upholsteries, and private baths. The hotel is the preferred choice of business travelers. Although it was built in 1947, it has been remodeled many times since, the latest in 1991.

Dining/Entertainment: La Finisterre restaurant serves à la carte meals featuring fresh catches; there's also a bar.

Services: Room service, concierge, babysitting, laundry.

Facilities: Tennis courts, four outdoor seawater swimming pools (two heated for year-round use, one reserved for children), garden, children's nursery, gym and health club, skating rink, sauna, ample opportunities for brisk and invigorating seafront walks, barber/hairdresser, nearby basketball court, gift shop.

MODERATE

Ciudad de La Coruña. Ciudad Residencial La Torre, Poligono de Adormideras, s/n, 15002 La Coruña. ☎ **981/21-11-00.** Fax 981/22-46-10. 123 rms, 9 suites. A/C MINIBAR TV TEL.

10,400–13,200 ptas. ($83.20–$105.60) double; 14,300–17,600 ptas. ($114.40–$140.80) suite. AE, DC, MC, V. Free parking. Bus: 3 or 3A.

On the northwestern tip of the peninsula, surrounded by sea grasses and dunes, this three-star establishment is cordoned off from the apartment-house complexes that surround it by a wide swath of green. Built in the early 1980s, the hotel features a swimming pool; a big-windowed bar; a gym with sauna, whirlpool, and solarium; and a ground-floor restaurant. Each attractively modern guest room contains a kitchenette and a private bath. In the hotel restaurant, fixed-price meals are served, and there is also a bar-style cafeteria serving coffee, drinks, and snacks.

Hotel Atlántico. Jardines de Méndez Nuñez, s/n, 15006 La Coruña. ☎ **981/22-65-00.** Fax 981/20-10-71. 195 rms, 5 suites. TV TEL. 12,500–14,500 ptas. ($100–$116) double; 15,000–17,000 ptas. ($120–$136) suite. AE, DC, MC, V. Parking 1,000 ptas. ($8). Bus: 1, 2, or 3.

This convenient, comfortable hotel with a contemporary design contrasts with the lavishly ornate 19th-century park surrounding it. Crowds of Galicians promenade here in fine weather. The Atlántico is in the building that also houses the city's casino, a modern restaurant, and a disco. The well-furnished guest rooms, all with private baths, are among the best in town.

Residencia Riazor. Barrie de la Maza, 29, 15004 La Coruña. ☎ **981/25-34-00.** Fax 981/25-34-01. 176 rms. MINIBAR TV TEL. 9,400–11,500 ptas. ($75.20–$92) double. AE, DC, MC, V. Parking 850 ptas. ($6.80). Bus: 5, 20, or 22.

This 12-story 1960s hotel is right on the beach and was last renovated in 1993. It has a glass-enclosed lounge on the second floor and a snack bar/cafeteria. The guest rooms are functional and lack style, but they are clean and comfortable and have private baths. Room service is available until 11pm.

INEXPENSIVE

Almirante. Paseo de Ronda, 54, 15011 La Coruña. ☎ **981/25-96-00.** 20 rms. TV TEL. 5,700 ptas. ($45.60) double. AE, MC, V. Parking 500 ptas. ($4). Bus: 7, 14, or 14A.

There are few amenities here—just good, clean rooms, all doubles, at a real bargain price. There is no restaurant, but a continental breakfast is served in the cafeteria. Room service is available. The location is a bonus: just one minute from the beach.

$ **Hotel España.** Juana de Vega, 7, 15004 La Coruña. ☎ **981/22-45-06.** Fax 981/20-02-79. 84 rms. TV TEL. 5,800–7,800 ptas. ($46.40–$62.40) double. AE, DC, MC, V. Parking 1,000 ptas. ($8). Bus: 1, 2, or 23.

This pleasant but somewhat lackluster choice, just a few steps from the gazebos and roses of the Jardines de Méndez Núñez, has a narrow reception area, a comfortable series of long sitting rooms, and modern, simply furnished bedrooms. The cafeteria offers combination platters. The hotel has a bar and provides laundry service.

WHERE TO DINE

Two or so blocks from the waterfront, there are several restaurants that specialize in Galician cuisine. It is customary to go window shopping for food here. The restaurants along two of the principal streets—Calle de la Estrella and Calle de los Olmos—have display counters in front of their establishments. Most of the establishments charge comparable prices.

✪ **Casa Pardo.** Novoa Santos, 15. ☎ **981/28-71-78.** Reservations recommended. Main courses 1,750–2,900 ptas. ($14–$23.20); fixed-price menu 3,000 ptas. ($24). AE, DC, MC, V. Mon–Sat 1:30–4pm and 9pm–midnight. GALICIAN.

Located near the Palacio de Congresos south of the old town, this restaurant is justly acclaimed as the finest dining room in the city. Under the direction of Eduardo

Pardo, the restaurant offers both a traditional cuisine and innovative seafood dishes. Fresh shellfish and fish dishes, everything from oysters to salmon, are prepared here with skill. The Galician turbot is delectable. Seafood items aren't the only selections on the menu—meat and vegetable dishes are also well prepared. The kitchen seems always aware of the necessity of securing fresh ingredients—both from field and shore. The first-rate service matches the cuisine. Patrons of this well-entrenched dining room prefer such wines as Terras Gauda and Viña Costeira.

El Coral. Calle Estrella, 2–4. ☎ **981/22-10-82.** Reservations recommended. Main courses 1,600–2,900 ptas. ($12.80–$23.20); fixed-price menus 2,600–3,600 ptas. ($20.80–$28.80). AE, DC, MC, V. Daily 1–4pm and 9pm–midnight. Closed Sun night except July–Aug. Bus: 1, 2, 5, or 17. GALICIAN/SEAFOOD/INTERNATIONAL.

This is our favorite and one of the most popular dining spots at the port. In business since 1954, it offers polite service, cleanliness, and Galician cookery prepared with distinction. This restaurant specializes in shellfish, fish, meats, and Galician wines. The chef's specialty is *turbante de mariscos* (shellfish). You might also try the *calamares rellenos* (stuffed squid). A popular main course is *lubina* (sea bass) *al horno.* A pitcher (1 liter) of Ribero wine makes a good choice, and you can also order Condados and Rioja wines.

$ Taverna Pil-Pil. Paralela a Orillamar, s/n. ☎ **981/21-27-12.** Reservations recommended. Main courses 950–1,800 ptas. ($7.60–$14.40). No credit cards. Tues–Sat 1–4:30pm and 8pm–12:30am. Closed Sept 15–Oct 15. Bus: 3 or 3A. GALICIAN.

In spite of its size, this small tavern has a fine culinary tradition and serves many elegant, moderately priced wines like the Albariño white. Host Luis Moya purchases fresh ingredients, often seafood, and handles them deftly in the kitchen. Try a mussel omelet as an appetizer, followed by one of the main courses, perhaps smoked salmon, concluding with a velvety chocolate mousse. The place is on the road leading to the Torre de Hércules.

2 Santiago de Compostela

381 miles (613km) NW of Madrid, 46 miles (74km) S of La Coruña

All roads in Spain used to lead to this northwestern pilgrimage city. In addition to being the third-largest holy city of the Christian world, Santiago de Compostela is both a university town and a marketplace for Galician farmers.

But it was the pilgrims who made the city famous. A pilgrimage to the tomb of the beheaded apostle, St. James, was a high point for the faithful—peasant and prince alike—who journeyed here from all over Europe, often under difficult, sometimes life-threatening conditions.

Santiago de Compostela's link with legend began in A.D. 813, when an urn was discovered containing, it was believed, the remains of St. James. A temple was erected over the spot, but the poor saint wasn't allowed to remain in peace. Wars, a long and mysterious disappearance, and an equally mysterious "rediscovery" followed.

Aside from its religious connections, Santiago de Compostela, with its flagstone streets, churches, and shrines, is one of the most romantic and historic of Spain's great cities and has been declared a national landmark. It also has the dubious distinction of being the rainiest city in Spain, but the showers tend to arrive and end suddenly. Locals claim that the rain only makes their city more beautiful.

GETTING THERE **By Plane** From Madrid, Iberia has daily flights to Santiago, and there are also daily flights from Barcelona. The only international airport in

The Oldest Hotel in the World

The oldest hotel in the world has been fortifying the weary bodies and souls of travelers for nearly five centuries. In 1499 the Catholic Kings founded the Hospital Real (Royal Hospice) in Santiago de Compostela to serve as a respite for the hundreds of thousands of pilgrims who came to pay homage to the shrine of Saint James. Known today as Hostal de Los Reyes Católicos, the same structure proudly stands as the world's most ancient hotel, and certainly one of the most luxurious, offering its guests a truly unique hotel experience.

During the Middle Ages, Santiago prevailed, together with Jerusalem and Rome, as one of the three holy cities of Christendom. The cult of Santiago (Saint James), the son of Zebedee and the brother of John the Evangelist, drew hordes of pilgrims who trekked across northern Spain in search of the tomb of the saint. The route to Santiago proved long, arduous, and dangerous; the pilgrims who did arrive came weary and fatigued. Having made the pilgrimage themselves, the Catholic monarchs experienced firsthand the dearth of decent accommodations along the way. Hence the decision by Ferdinand and Isabella to construct monasteries and hospitals to house and protect visitors, the best of such efforts culminating in this prominent structure.

Construction on the Hospital Real began in the 15th century and continued through the 18th century. Set on the magnificent Obradoiro Plaza, this grand edifice shares the square with the impressive cathedral of Santiago, with its blend of architectural styles. In addition to its luxury rooms, this five-star hotel boasts a concert and an exhibition room surrounded by various cloisters in different styles. The hotel doorway reflects the plateresque style, and the windows display rich baroque detailing.

Architecturally, the old part of the city stopped developing in the baroque period and, as a result, its buildings exude an aura of impressive grandeur—in fact, a sense of mysticism permeates Santiago. It is fitting, then, that one of Spain's great monumental cities should be home to one of the country's most luxurious, historically significant hotels, let alone one of the world's oldest.

Galicia is east of Santiago de Compostela at Labacolla (☎ **981/54-75-00** for flight information). It lies seven miles (11km) from the center on the road to Lugo.

By Train From La Coruña, 14 trains make the one-hour trip daily at a cost of 480 pesetas ($3.85). Two trains arrive daily from Madrid. The eight-hour trip costs 5,200 pesetas ($41.60). Call **981/52-02-02** for information.

By Bus Buses leave on the hour, connecting La Coruña with Santiago (1½ hours away) and cost 4,900 pesetas ($39.20). Two buses arrive in Santiago daily from Madrid (8 to 9 hours). The trip costs 5,440 pesetas ($43.50). Phone **981/58-77-00** for schedules.

By Car Take the expressway highway (A-9/E-50) south from La Coruña to reach Santiago. From Madrid, the N-VI runs to Galicia. From Lugo, head south along the N-640.

VISITOR INFORMATION The tourist information office is at Rúa del Villar, 43 (☎ **981/58-40-81**). Office hours are Monday through Friday from 10am to 2pm and 4 to 7pm, Saturday from 11am to 1pm and 5 to 7pm, and Sunday and holidays from 11am to 1pm.

WHAT TO SEE & DO

The highlight at Santiago de Compostela is undoubtedly the cathedral, and you should take at least two hours to see it. Afterward, take a stroll through this enchanting town, which has a number of other interesting monuments as well as many stately mansions along Rúa de Villar and Rúa Nueva.

The ✪ **cathedral,** Plaza del Obradoiro (☎ **981/58-35-48**), begun in the 11th century, is the crowning achievement of Spanish Romanesque, even though it actually reflects a number of styles. Some of the architecture is spectacular. The Pórtico de la Gloria, carved by Mateo in the late 12th century, ranks among the finest produced in Europe at that time; the altar, with its blend of Gothic simplicity and baroque decor, is also extraordinary. The floor plan of the cathedral resembles a cross. It has three naves and several chapels and cloisters. You can visit the crypt, where a silver urn contains what are believed to be the remains of the Apostle St. James. A cathedral museum displays tapestries and archaeological fragments. Next door, the **Palacio de Gelmírez,** an archbishop's palace built during the 12th century, is another outstanding example of Romanesque architecture. Admission to the cathedral is free; to the cloisters, 400 pesetas ($3.20); to the Palacio de Gelmírez, 200 pesetas ($1.60). Hours for the cathedral are daily from 7am to 9pm; for the museum, daily from 10:30am to 1:30pm and 4 to 6:30pm; for the Palacio de Gelmírez, July through September daily from 10:30am to 1:30pm and 4 to 7pm.

Most of the other impressive buildings are also on Plaza del Obradoiro, also called Plaza de España. Next door to the cathedral is **Los Reyes Católicos,** now a parador (see "Where to Stay," below), formerly a royal hospice and, in the 15th century, a pilgrims' hospice. It was designed by Enrique de Egas, Isabella and Ferdinand's favorite architect. Tours (daily from 10am to 1pm and 4 to 7pm; ☎ **981/58-22-00** for information) visit the cloistered courtyard with its beautiful 16th- to 18th-century fountains and the main chapel with its beamed ceiling; however, you must have a guide from the cathedral in attendance.

Monasterio de San Martín Pinario, Plaza de la Immaculada, founded in 899 by monks and rebuilt in the 17th century, remains one of the most important monasteries in Galicia. Its large facade was built in the Compostela baroque style, with massive Doric columns. The interior has a richly ornamented Churrigueresque high altar and choir stalls that are truly works of art.

One of the most important squares in the old town is **Plaza de la Quintana,** to the left of the cathedral's Goldsmith's Doorway. This is a favorite square with students, who often perch on the flight of broad steps that connect the rear of the cathedral to the walls of a convent. The square is dominated by **Casa de la Canónica,** the former residence of the canon, which has wrought-iron window bars, lending it a rather severe appearance.

South of the square is the Renaissance-style **Plaza de las Platerías (Silversmiths' Square),** which has an elaborate fountain.

The **Centro Galego de Arte Contemporaneau,** Rue Valle-Inclan, s/n (☎ **981/546-621**), is the Galician Center of Contemporary Art, highlighting artworks from regional, national, and international artists. The center displays with changing exhibits the works of contemporary artists and also hosts retrospectives. Until the opening of this center, contemporary art had virtually no place in the city's agenda, which emphasized the ancient or the antique. Inaugurated in 1993 by Portuguese architect Álvaro Siza, the building is a stark exterior study in slabs of granite. Among the several exhibition rooms is a terrace for open-air exhibits, affording a panoramic view of the old quarter of Santiago. The admission-free museum is open Tuesday through Saturday from 11am to 8pm and Sunday from 11am to 2pm.

Farther afield, visit the Romanesque **Santa María del Sar,** on Calle Castron d'Ouro, half a mile down Calle de Sar, which starts at Patio de Madre. This collegiate church is one of the architectural gems of the Romanesque style in Galicia. Its walls and columns are on a 15-degree slant, thought to be attributable to either a fragile foundation or an architect's fancy. Visit the charming cloister with its slender columns. The church is open Monday through Saturday from 10am to 1pm and 4 to 7pm. Admission is 50 pesetas (40¢).

Cap off your day with a walk along **Paseo de la Herradura,** the gardens southwest of the old town, from where you'll have an all-encompassing view of the cathedral and the old city.

WHERE TO STAY

VERY EXPENSIVE

✪ Hostal de Los Reyes Católicos. Plaza de España, 1, 15705 Santiago de Compostela. ☎ **981/58-22-00.** Fax 981/56-30-94. 130 rms, 6 suites. MINIBAR TV TEL. 24,000 ptas. ($192) double; from 50,000 ptas. ($400) suite. AE, DC, MC, V. Parking 1,700 ptas. ($13.60). Bus: 4, 21, 25, 26, 33, or 34.

This former 16th-century hospice, founded by Ferdinand and Isabella, has been turned into one of the most spectacular hotels in Europe. Next to the cathedral, it also served as a resting place and hospital for pilgrims visiting the tomb of St. James. Even if you don't stay here, you should stop in and see it, but only on a guided tour (see above).

The hotel has four huge open-air courtyards, each with its own covered walk, gardens, and fountains. In addition, there are great halls, French grillwork, copies of paintings by El Greco, and a large collection of antiques. The Gothic chapel is the setting for weekly concerts.

There is a full range of accommodations, everything from Franco's former bedchamber to small rooms. Many of the palatial rooms have ornate canopied beds draped in embroidered red velvet. Hand-carved chests, gilt mirrors, and oil paintings—along with private baths—enhance the air of luxury.

Dining/Entertainment: The hotel's formal dining room, Libredon, serves both Galician and international cuisine. There is also an elegant bar.

Services: Room service, laundry.

Facilities: Car rentals, hairdresser.

EXPENSIVE

Hotel Araguaney. Calle Alfredo Brañas, 5, 15701 Santiago de Compostela. ☎ **981/59-59-00.** Fax 981/59-02-87. 68 rms, 5 suites. A/C MINIBAR TV TEL. 19,250–24,200 ptas. ($154–$193.60) double; from 30,000 ptas. ($240) suite. AE, DC, MC, V. Parking 1,390 ptas. ($11.10). Bus: 4, 21, 25, 26, 33, or 34.

Located in Santiago's commercial and residential zone, about eight blocks southwest of the cathedral, this is a comfortable hotel whose streamlined walls contain some of the most up-to-date dining, drinking, and conference facilities in town. The modern guest rooms, all with private baths, are quite stylish.

Dining/Entertainment: The Restaurante Luis XVI and the Restaurante 3 Conchas (O'Portón) serve fixed-price lunches and dinners. The comfortable hotel bar offers an array of international drinks and Spanish brandies. The hotel also contains one of the most frequented discos in Galicia.

Services: Room service (daily from 7am to 4pm and 9pm to midnight), concierge, babysitting, in-house tour operator, laundry/valet.

Facilities: Large and well-maintained swimming pool, sauna, shopping boutiques, business center, car rentals.

MODERATE

Hotel Compostela. Hórreo, 1, 15702 Santiago de Compostela. ☎ **981/58-57-00.** Fax 981/56-32-69. 99 rms, 1 suite. MINIBAR TV TEL. 14,800 ptas. ($118.40) double; 18,500 ptas. ($148) triple; 20,000 ptas. ($160) suite for two. AE, DC, MC, V. Bus: 10.

This hotel is conveniently located just a few short blocks from the cathedral, but it is also, unfortunately, close to the heavily trafficked city center. It has a grand granite facade, which belies the modern interior and bedrooms filled with clean, angular, machine-made furniture. A pleasant dining room and a café/bar are on the premises, offering a fixed-price lunch or dinner. The hotel was completely renovated in 1995.

Hotel del Peregrino. Rosalía de Castro, s/n, 15706 Santiago de Compostela. ☎ **981/52-18-50.** Fax 981/52-17-77. 150 rms, 7 suites. MINIBAR TV TEL. 16,950 ptas. ($135.60) double; 20,000 ptas. ($160) suite. AE, DC, MC, V. Free parking. Bus: 1 or 2.

This four-star hotel at the edge of town off the main road is preferred by many people traveling to this remote part of Spain. It has a good restaurant serving regional cuisine, a bar and snack bar, a rear garden with a swimming pool, and a disco. The decor is restrained and tasteful; the bedrooms are modern and well furnished.

Hotel Gelmírez. Hórreo, 92, 15702 Santiago de Compostela. ☎ **981/56-11-00.** Fax 981/56-32-69. 138 rms. TV TEL. 7,680–10,175 ptas. ($61.45–$81.40) double. AE, DC, MC, V. Bus: 10.

This soaring concrete structure near the train station is one of the largest hotels in the region. Built in the early 1970s, it has a comfortable and pleasant interior far more attractive than its plain facade suggests. The guest rooms are furnished in a functional modern style—nothing special, but clean and comfortable. On the premises is a bistro/cafeteria/bar, offering *platos combinados* (combination plates), along with a wide array of drinks.

INEXPENSIVE

Hostal Residencia Alameda. San Clemente, 32, 15705 Santiago de Compostela. ☎ **981/58-81-00.** 20 rms. TV TEL. 4,900 ptas. ($39.20) double without bath; 6,500 ptas. ($52) double with bath. AE, MC, V. Parking 700 ptas. ($5.60). Bus: 10.

Located on the second floor of a 1970s building in the cathedral district, the Alameda has comfortable, immaculate rooms, although in a very simple boardinghouse style. The staff here is courteous and efficient. Ample parking is available, adjacent to the hostal. The Alameda serves breakfast only.

Hotel Maycar. Doctor Teijeiro, 15, 15701 Santiago de Compostela. ☎ **981/56-34-44.** 40 rms. TEL. 4,800–7,000 ptas. ($38.40–$56) double. No credit cards. Bus: 10 from train station.

This simple two-star hotel stands not far from the busy central Plaza de Galicia. The marble-trimmed lobby is unpretentious, and there is an elevator. The rooms are well maintained but very spartan. Breakfast is the only meal served.

Hotel Universal. Plaza de Galicia, 2, 15706 Santiago de Compostela. ☎ **981/58-58-00.** 54 rms. TV TEL. 6,675–8,250 ptas. ($53.40–$66) double. Rates include breakfast. AE, DC, MC, V.

Located south of the Fuente de San Antonio, just outside the center of the city, this is a pleasant and comfortable hotel despite its drab 1970s concrete facade. It has a modernized lobby, and there is a TV lounge on the premises. The aging guest rooms are furnished in a simple modern style. Breakfast is the only meal served.

Where to Dine

Alameda. Porta Faxeira, 15. ☎ **981/58-66-57.** Reservations recommended in summer. Main courses 1,800–3,000 ptas. ($14.40–$24); fixed-price menus 2,600–3,000 ptas. ($20.80–$24). AE, DC, MC, V. Daily 1–4pm and 8pm–midnight. GALICIAN.

Since 1954 the constant stream of diners, both foreign and local, indicates the popularity of this government-rated "two-fork" restaurant, located opposite the Parque de Alameda. There is a stylish cafeteria/snack bar on the ground floor, great for light meals and drinks; guests can sit at sidewalk tables in fair weather. The fare includes many Galician specialties, and the chef is noted for his paella. Start with the *caldo gallego* (Galician soup) and follow with another regional specialty, *lacón con grelos* (hamhock with greens). The *necoras* (spider crabs) are also a real gourmet delight.

Anexo Vilas. Avenida de Villagarcía, 21. ☎ **981/59-86-37.** Reservations recommended. Main courses 2,100–3,600 ptas. ($16.80–$28.80); fixed-price menu 4,500 ptas. ($36). AE, DC, MC, V. Tues–Sun 1–4pm and 8pm–midnight. Bus: 4, 21, or 25. GALICIAN.

Although this restaurant is located at the edge of the old quarter, on a drab street off Avenida de Donallo Romero, it's worth seeking out. It looks like a country tavern, and, in fact, the *tasca* in front is one of the most popular in the area, especially with locals. It's a family-run place with conscientious service. A few of the Galician dishes served here are based on meat (the filet of beef with sherry sauce is especially good), but the real specialties are seafood creations, such as fish soup, hake, and grilled shrimp.

Restaurante Vílas. Rosalía de Castro, 88. ☎ **981/59-21-70.** Reservations required. Main courses 1,850–3,200 ptas. ($14.80–$25.60); fixed-price menus 4,500–5,000 ptas. ($32–$35.50). AE, DC, MC, V. Mon–Sat 1–4pm and 8pm–midnight. SEAFOOD.

Located on the outskirts of the old town on the road to Pontevedra, this reliable Spanish tavern, housed in a three-story town house, has a devoted clientele, many from industry, politics, and the arts. Beyond the large bar near the entrance and display cases filled with fresh fish, you'll find the baronial stone-trimmed dining room. A wide variety of fish is available—fresh sardines, three different preparations of salmon, a *zarzuela* (seafood stew), and eels. Two kinds of paella are served, and nonfish dishes such as partridge and rabbit also grace the menu. The restaurant was founded in 1915 as a little eating house. Back then, it was on the outskirts of town, but the place was enveloped by the city long ago. It stands on a street named after the illustrious female poet of Galicia. Today, the restaurant is run by the grandsons of the original founders.

La Tacita d'Juan. Hórreo, 31. ☎ **981/56-32-55.** Reservations recommended. Main courses 1,300–2,800 ptas. ($10.40–$22.40). AE, DC, MC, V. Mon–Sat 12:30–4pm and 8–11pm. Closed Aug 1–15. Bus: 10. GALICIAN.

A favorite place for business lunches, five minutes from the train station, this restaurant offers *caldo gallego,* fish soup, artichokes with ham, Basque-style eels, shellfish cocktail, and a wide array of fish platters. Two special meat courses are the hamhock with greens and *fabada asturiana,* the famous stew of Asturias. The portions are generous, and the service is attentive.

Toñi Vicente. Calle Rosalía de Castro, 24. ☎ **981/59-41-00.** Reservations recommended. Main courses 2,000–3,800 ptas. ($16–$30.40); fixed-price menus 3,200–5,500 ptas. ($25.60–$44). AE, DC, MC, V. Mon–Sat 1:30–4pm and 9pm–midnight. Closed 3 weeks in Feb. INTERNATIONAL.

Set in the heart of town, on two floors of a building erected around 1950, this is the most flamboyantly international (and the finest) restaurant in Santiago or for miles around. Within dining rooms accented with a neoclassical overlay and a color scheme of blue and salmon, you can enjoy the celebrated cuisine of Toñi Vicente. Menu items change with the availability of the ingredients, but are likely to include such delectable dishes as a warm seafood salad with herbs, escalopes of veal with a confit of onions, turbot with chive sauce, unusual preparations of seasonal game dishes, and for dessert, a tart made with Galician pears.

3 Rías Altas

In Norway they're called fjords; in Brittany, *abers;* in Scotland, lochs; and in Galicia, *rías.* These are inlets cut into the Galician coastline by the turbulent Atlantic pounding against its shores. Rías Altas is a relatively modern name applied to all the estuaries on the northern Galicia coast, from Ribadeo (the gateway to Galicia on the border with Asturias) to La Coruña (the big Atlantic seaport of northwest Spain). The part that begins at Ribadeo—part of Lugo province—is also called Marina Lucense. Four estuaries form the Artabro Gulf: La Coruña, Betanzoa, Ares, and Ferrol. All four converge on a single point, where Marola crag rises.

FROM RIBADEO TO LA CORUÑA

From Ribadeo, take the corniche road west (N-634) until you reach the Ría de Foz. About 1½ miles (2.5km) south of the Foz-Barreiros highway, perched somewhat in isolation on a hill, stands the **Iglesia de San Martín de Mondoñeda,** part of a monastery that dates from 1112.

The little town of **Foz** itself is a fishing village and also a summer beach resort. Its beaches are separated by a cliff. You might stop here for lunch.

From Foz cut northwest along the coastal highway (C-642) going through **Burela,** another fishing village. You can make a slight detour south to **Sargadelos,** which is a ceramics center. You can purchase the famous Galician pottery here much more cheaply than elsewhere in Spain.

Back on the coastal road (C-642) at Burela, continue west approaching Ría de Vivero and the historic village of **Vivero.** Part of its medieval walls and an old gate, Puerta de Carlos V, have been preserved. The town has many old churches of interest, including the Gothic-style Iglesia San Francisco. Vivero—a summer resort, attracting vacationers to its beach, the Playa Covas—makes a good lunch stop.

The road continues northwest to **Vicedo,** passing such beaches as Xillo and Aerealong. Excellent vistas of the estuary greet you. Oxen can be seen plowing the cornfields.

Driving on, you'll notice the coastline becoming more sawtoothed. Eventually you reach **Ortigueira,** a major fishing village at the head of the *ría* from which it takes its name. A Celtic folk festival is staged here at the end of August.

From here you can continue south along the C-642 to **El Ferrol,** which used to be called El Caudillo, in honor of the late dictator Francisco Franco, who was born here and who used to spend part of his summers in this area. El Ferrol is one of the major shipbuilding centers of Spain, and since the 18th century it has also been a center of the Spanish navy. It's a grimy town, but it lies on one of the region's most beautiful *rías.* In spite of its parador, few tourists will want to linger at El Ferrol (also spelled O Ferrol).

From El Ferrol, the C-642 continues south, passing through the small town of **Puentedeume** (also spelled Pontedeume), on the Rías Ares. Historically, it was the center of the counts of Andrade. The last remains of their 14th-century palace can be seen, along with the ruins of a 13th-century castle rising to the east.

Shortly below Betanzos, head west along the N-VI until you reach La Coruña. The entire trip from Ribadeo is roughly 150 miles (242km) and takes at least four hours.

WHERE TO DINE ALONG THE COAST

Nito. Playa de Area, Vivero. ☎ **982/56-09-87.** Reservations recommended. Main courses 1,600–2,800 ptas. ($12.80–$22.40); fixed-price menu 1,800 ptas. ($14.40). AE, MC, V. Daily 1–4pm and 8pm–midnight. Closed Sun night in winter. SEAFOOD.

Established in the early 1970s, this restaurant lies in the center of the Vivero, only a hundred yards from the beach, with a sweeping view of the Atlantic. It starts serving dinner early for Spain (8pm). The restaurant maintains a balance between its prices and the quality of its ingredients, and you get unpretentious but flavorful food. Shellfish, priced according to weight, is the specialty, but you can also order grilled sea bream or perhaps a house-style beefsteak. Most diners begin their meal with a bowl of *caldo gallego* (Galician broth). A full range of wines also is offered. Diners wishing to eat outside can sit on a garden-view terrace.

FROM LA CORUÑA TO CAPE FISTERRA

This next drive—"to the end of the world"—takes you from La Coruña to Cape Fisterra (called Cabo Fisterra on most maps). It's a 90-mile (145km) trip that will take at least three hours. For the ancients, Cape Fisterra was the end of the world as they knew it.

This route takes you along **A Costa da Morte** (La Costa de la Muerte—The Coast of Death), so called because of the numerous shipwrecks that have occurred here.

Leaving La Coruña, take the coastal road west (Highway 552), heading first to the road junction of **Carballo,** a distance of 22 miles (35.5km). From this little town, many of the small coastal harbors will be within an easy drive. **Malpica,** to the northwest, is the most interesting, with its own beach. An offshore seabird sanctuary exists there, and Malpica itself was a former whaling port. From Malpica, continue to the tiny village of **Corme** at Punta Roncudo. This sheltered fishing village draws the summer beach fans, as there are many isolated sand dunes.

From Corme, continue along the winding roads to the whitewashed village of **Camariñas,** which stands on the *ría* of the same name. A road here leads all the way to the lighthouse at Cabo Vilán. Camariñas is known as a village of expert lacemakers, and you'll see the work for sale at many places.

The road now leads to **Mugia** (shown on some maps as Muxia), below which stands the lighthouse at Cabo Touriñan. Continue driving south along clearly signposted coastal roads that are sometimes perched almost precariously on clifftops overlooking the sea. They will lead you to **Corcubión,** a village with a Romanesque church. From here, follow signs which lead you along a lonely southbound secondary road to the "end of the line," **Cabo Fisterra,** for a panoramic view. The sunsets from here are among the most spectacular in the world. The Roman poet Horace said it best: "The brilliant skylight of the sun drags behind it the black night over the fruitful breasts of earth."

4 Rías Bajas

After Cabo Fisterra, some of the most dramatic coastal scenery in Spain flanks the coastal highway, 550, following the edge of one of the most torturous shorelines in Europe. The four estuaries, collectively called the ✪ **Rías Bajas,** face the Atlantic from Cape Silleiro to Baiona to Point Louro in Muros. Two of these are in the province of Pontevedra (Ría de Pontevedra and Ría de Vigo); one is in the province of La Coruña (Ría de Muros y Noya); and one (Ría de Arousa) divides its shores between the two provinces. The 20-mile (32km) Vigo estuary is the longest, stretching from Ponte Sampasio to Baiona.

FROM MUROS TO SANTA UXEA DE RIBEIRA

The seaside town of **Muros** has many old houses and a harbor, but **Noya** (also spelled Noia), to the southeast, is more impressive. If you don't have a car but would like to see at least one or two *ría* fishing villages, you can do so at either Noya or Muros: Both lie on a bus route connecting them with Santiago de Compostela. Eleven buses per day leave from Santiago heading for Noya, and nine run to Muros. Some of the tiny little villages and beaches are also connected by bus routes.

If you do drive, the entire trip is only 47 miles; at a leisurely pace it should take you two hours. Noya is known for its braided straw hats with black bands. It has a number of interesting, handsome old churches, including the 14th-century **Igrexa de Santa María** (with tombstones dating from the 10th century) and the **Igrexa de San Francisco.** A lot of good beaches lie on the northern bank of the *ría* near Muros. Noya might be your best bet for a lunch stop.

From Noya, the coast road (highway 550) continues west to **Porto do Son.** You can take a detour to Cabo de Corrubedo, with its lighthouse, before continuing on to **Santa Uxea de Ribeira** at the southern tip. Ribeira is a fishing port and a canning center. At Santa Uxea de Ribeira you'll see the **Ría de Arousa,** the largest and deepest of the inlets.

From Ribeira, continue east along the southern coastal road to **A Puebla de Caramiñal.** From here, take a signposted route six miles (9.6km) inland into the mountains, to admire the most magnificent panorama in all of *rías* country—the **Mirador de la Curota,** at 1,634 feet. The four inlets of the Rías Bajas can, under the right conditions, be seen from the belvedere. In clear weather you can also view Cape Fisterra.

Back on the C-550, drive as far as Padrón, where, it is claimed, the legendary sea vessel arrived bringing Santiago (St. James) to Spain. Padrón was also the home of romantic poet Rosalía de Castro (1837–85), sometimes called the Emily Dickinson of Spain. Her house, the **Casa Museo de Rosalía de Castro,** Carretera de Herbrón (☎ **981/81-12-04**), is open to the public Tuesday through Sunday from 9:30am to 1:30pm. Admission is 200 pesetas ($1.60). Padrón also makes a good lunch stop.

From Padrón, follow the alleged trail of the body of St. James north along the N-550 to Santiago de Compostela or take the N-550 south to Pontevedra.

WHERE TO STAY & DINE

Ⓢ Ceboleiro II. Galicia, 15, Noya. ☎ **981/82-05-31.** Fax 981/82-44-97. Main courses 900–2,000 ptas. ($7.20–$16). AE, DC, MC, V. Daily 1–4pm and 9pm–midnight. Closed Dec 20–Jan 15. SEAFOOD.

For about a century, this inn has provided food and accommodations to passersby. Set in the heart of Noya, it is owned and managed by three generations of the Fernández family. It offers hearty food from the sea, prepared in conservative but flavorful ways that usually correspond to the culinary traditions of Galicia and northern Portugal. The menu almost always includes several versions of hake, shellfish soup, several kinds of rice studded with fish or shellfish, pork and beef dishes, and among other desserts, an apple tart. The establishment also contains 13 simple but comfortable accommodations, each with private bathroom, TV, and telephone. Doubles cost from 6,000 to 8,000 pesetas ($48–$64).

Chef Rivera. Enlace Parque, 7, Padrón. ☎ **981/81-04-13.** Fax 981/81-14-54. Reservations recommended. Main courses 1,000–2,300 ptas. ($8–$18.40); fixed-price menus 1,800–2,400 ptas. ($14.40–$19.20). AE, DC, MC, V. Daily 1–4pm and 9pm–midnight. Closed Sun night in winter. FRENCH.

The name of the owner, to everyone in town, is simply El Chef. His cuisine is innovative but also based on traditional continental recipes. His wife, Pierrette, attends to service in the dining room, which resembles an English pub with its dark, warm colors and leather upholstery. Try the shellfish soup or stew or the house-style monkfish. The restaurant is known for its *pimientos de Padrón.* Tiny green peppers are sautéed with olive oil—there's nothing unusual about that; the trick is that about one in five of those peppers is hot. Finish with lemon mousse. The couple also rents 20 simply furnished guest rooms, at 4,850 pesetas ($38.80) for a double.

5 Pontevedra

36 miles (58km) S of Santiago de Compostela, 521 miles (839km) NW of Madrid

An aristocratic old Spanish town on the Lérez River and the capital of Pontevedra province, the city of Pontevedra still has vestiges of an ancient wall that once encircled the town. In medieval days, the town was called Pontis Veteris (Old Bridge).

Some of the best Gallego seamen lived in Pontevedra in the Middle Ages. Sheltered at the end of the Pontevedra Ría, the city was a bustling port and foreign merchants mingled with local traders, seamen, and fishers. It was the home of Pedro Sarmiento de Gamboa, the 16th-century navigator and cosmographer who wrote *Voyage to the Magellan Straits.* In the 18th century the Lérez delta silted up and the busy commerce moved elsewhere, mainly to Vigo. Pontevedra entered a period of decline, which may account for its significant old section. Had it been a more prosperous town, the people might have torn down the buildings to rebuild.

The old *barrio*—a maze of colonnaded squares and cobbled alleyways—lies between Calle Michelena and Calle del Arzobispo Malvar, stretching to Calle Cobián and the river. The old mansions are called *pazos,* and they speak of former marine glory, since it was the sea that provided the money to build them. Seek out such charming squares as Plaza de la Leña, Plaza de Mugártegui, and Plaza de Teucro.

GETTING THERE **By Train** From Santiago de Compostela in the north, 11 trains per day make the one-hour trip to Pontevedra at a cost of 555 pesetas ($4.45) one way. RENFE has an office on Calle Gondomar, 3 (☎ **986/85-13-13**), where you can get information. The actual rail and bus stations (☎ **986/85-13-13** for information about transportation in the area), lie half a mile from the center on Alféreces Provisionales.

By Bus Pontevedra has good links to major Galician cities. From Vigo in the south, the bus traveling time is only 1/2 hour if you take one of the 12 inland expresses leaving from Vigo daily. From Santiago de Compostela in the north, a bus leaves every hour during the day for Pontevedra (1 hour away).

By Car From Santiago de Compostela, head south along the N-550 to reach Pontevedra.

VISITOR INFORMATION The tourist information office is at General Mola, 3 (☎ **986/85-08-14**). Open Monday through Friday from 9:30am to 2pm and 5 to 7pm, Saturday from 10am to 12:30pm.

SPECIAL EVENT A Rapa das Bestas (The Capture of the Beasts) is held every year in the beginning of July. In the hills of nearby San Lorenzo de Sabuceno, wild horses are rounded up and herded into a corral, in a ritual that evokes the Wild West. For information, contact the Office of Tourism in Pontevedra (phone number above).

WHAT TO SEE & DO

In the old quarter, the major attraction is the **Basílica de Santa María in Mayor,** Arzobispo Malvar, with its avocado-green patina, dating from the 16th century. This is a plateresque church constructed with funds provided by the mariners' guild. Its most remarkable feature is its west front, which was carved to resemble an altarpiece. At the top is a depiction of the Crucifixion.

The **Museo Provincial,** Pasantería, 10 (☎ **986/85-14-55**), with a hodgepodge of everything from the Pontevedra attic, contains displays ranging from prehistoric artifacts to a still life by Zurbarán. Many of the exhibits are maritime-oriented, and there is also a valuable collection of jewelry. Hours are June through September, Tuesday through Saturday 10am to 2:15pm and 5 to 10:45pm; October through May, Tuesday through Saturday 10am to 1:30pm and 5 to 10pm; Sunday (year-round) and holidays 11am to 1pm. Admission is 200 pesetas ($1.60); free for European Union citizens. The museum opens onto a major square in the old town, the Plaza de Leña (Square of Wood).

Iglesia de San Francisco, Plaza de la Herrería, is another church of note. Its Gothic facade opens onto gardens. It was founded in the 14th century and contains a sculpture of Don Payo Gómez Charino, noted for his part in the 1248 Reconquest of Seville, when it was wrested from Muslim domination.

Directly south, the gardens lead to the 18th-century **Capilla de la Peregrina,** Plaza Peregrina, with a narrow half-moon facade connected to a rotunda and crowned by a pair of towers. It was constructed by followers of the cult of the Pilgrim Virgin, which was launched in Galicia sometime in the 17th century.

WHERE TO STAY

EXPENSIVE

Hotel Rías Bajas. Daniel de la Sota, 7, 36001 Pontevedra. ☎ **986/85-51-00.** Fax 986/85-51-00. 93 rms, 7 suites. MINIBAR TV TEL. 12,000 ptas. ($96) double; 13,000 ptas. ($104) suite. AE, DC, MC, V. Parking 600 ptas. ($4.80).

On a busy street corner near Plaza de Galicia in the commercial center, this 1960s hotel is more comfortable than you might expect, judging from the outside. The largest hotel in town, it is often used for community political meetings and press conferences. The lobby, of stone and wood paneling, has been designed to look like an English club. Bedrooms are comfortable and well maintained, with private baths. The hotel doesn't have a restaurant but does offer a cafeteria.

Hotel Virgen del Camino. Virgen del Camino, 55, 36001 Pontevedra. ☎ **986/85-59-00.** Fax 986/85-09-00. 53 rms. TV TEL. 7,900–10,500 ptas. ($63.20–$84) double. AE, DC, MC, V. Parking 500 ptas. ($4).

On a relatively quiet street off the C-531, at the edge of the suburbs, this balconied stucco hotel contains a comfortable English-style pub as well as spacious sitting rooms. The bedrooms have wall-to-wall carpeting and private baths, plus central heating in winter. The best doubles contain separate salons and sitting rooms. A cafeteria serves fixed-price meals. There is also a laundry service on the premises.

✪ **Parador Nacional Casa del Barón.** Plaza de Maceda, s/n, 36002 Pontevedra. ☎ **986/85-58-00.** Fax 986/85-21-95. 47 rms. MINIBAR TV TEL. 11,500–12,500 ptas. ($92–$100) double. AE, DC, MC, V.

The parador is located in the old quarter of Pontevedra, in a well-preserved 16th-century palace near the Basílica de Santa María la Mayor. Built on either 13th- or 14th-century foundations, this hotel became one of Spain's first paradors when it opened in 1955. The interior has been maintained very much as the old *pazo* (manor house) looked. It includes a quaint old kitchen, or *lar* ("heart"), typical of Galician country houses and furnished with characteristic items. Off the vestibule is a courtyard dominated by a large old stone staircase. Many of the accommodations, all with private baths, are large enough to include sitting areas; the beds are comfortable, the furnishings attractive. Many of the rooms overlook the walled-in formal garden. Both lunch and dinner are served. Most dishes, such as a casserole of shrimp with tomato sauce, are well prepared, and regionally influenced. It's just four miles (6km) from the beach.

MODERATE

Hotel Comercio. Augusto González Besada, 3, 36001 Pontevedra. ☎ **986/85-12-17.** Fax 986/85-99-91. 40 rms. A/C TV TEL. 6,500 ptas. ($52) double. AE, DC, V. Bus: 14 or 20 from train station.

This tall hotel, with its modern facade and art deco–inspired café and bar, is an acceptable choice in its price category. The guest rooms are fairly comfortable, but only functional in style. A restaurant serves both lunch and dinner, with many regional specialties offered.

WHERE TO DINE

Casa Román. Augusto García Sánchez, 12. ☎ **986/84-35-60.** Main courses 1,000–3,200 ptas. ($8–$25.60); fixed-price menus 3,500–4,000 ptas. ($28–$32). AE, DC, MC, V. Daily 1:30–4pm, Mon–Sat 9pm–midnight. Closed Sun night Sept–Jun. SEAFOOD.

Known for the quality of its food, this well-established restaurant is on the street level of a brick apartment building in a leafy downtown development known as Campolongo, near Plaza de Galicia. To reach the dining room, you pass through a tavern. In addition to lobster (which you can see in the window), a wide array of well-prepared fish and shellfish dishes are served here, including sea bass, squid, sole, crab, lobsters, and tuna.

Doña Antonia. Soportales de la Herrería, 9. ☎ **986/84-72-74.** Reservations required. Main courses 1,600–2,800 ptas. ($12.80–$22.40); *menú del día* 4,000 ptas. ($32). AE, MC, V. Mon–Sat 1:30–4pm and 9–11:30pm. GALICIAN.

Without question, Pontevedra's best restaurant is Doña Antonia, located under a stone arcade on one of the town's oldest streets, east of the Jardines Vincenti. You climb one flight to reach the pink-and-white dining room. In such a provincial town, it is surprising to come across a restaurant of such sophistication and refinement. Although a few readers have sometimes reported a disappointing meal, most diners are filled with joy at this discovery. There's a pristine freshness to the dishes prepared with fish just caught off the coast. The reward for all this culinary vigilance is a loyal clientele of contented food lovers. Menu items include baked suckling lamb, scaloppine with port, rolled filet of salmon, and kiwi sorbet.

6 Lugo

314 miles (506km) NW of Madrid, 60 miles (97km) SE of La Coruña

Lugo has known many conquerors. The former Celtic-Iberian settlement fell to the Romans, and centuries later the Moors used the land and its people to grow crops for them. Today, Lugo is one of the four provincial capitals of Galicia. It is generally neglected by those taking the Pilgrims' Way to Santiago de Compostela. However, it makes a rewarding detour for a morning or afternoon of sightseeing.

GETTING THERE **By Train** Lugo lies on the rail link with Madrid. Two trains per day arrive from La Coruña.

By Bus Lugo has bus links with most of the major towns in the northwest, including Oviedo, with one per day making the 5-hour trip, and Orense, with five per day making the 2½-hour trip.

By Car The N-VI connects Lugo with La Coruña as well as, at some distance, Madrid.

VISITOR INFORMATION The tourist information office is at Plaza de España, 27 (☎ **982/23-13-61**). It is open Monday through Friday from 9:30am to 1:30pm and 4:30 to 6pm, Saturday from 10am to 1:30pm.

WHAT TO SEE & DO

Lugo, split by the Miño River, is surrounded by a thick 1¼-mile (2km) ✪ **Roman wall,** the best preserved in the country. The wall is about 33 feet high and contains a total of 85 round towers; a sentry path can be approached by steps at the various town gates. Your best bet is to enter the old town at Puerto de Santiago, the most interesting of the ancient gates, and begin a most impressive promenade—what may well be one of the highlights of your tour of Galicia.

Along the way you'll come to the **cathedral,** built in 1129 and notable for its trio of landmark towers. Standing at the Plaza Santa María, it has many Romanesque architectural features, such as its nave, but it was subsequently given a Gothic overlay. Further remodeling took place in the 18th century, when many features were added, such as the Chapel of the Wide-Eyed Virgin (*Ojos Grandes*) at the east end, with a baroque rotunda. The highlight of the cathedral is a 13th-century porch at the north end, which provides shelter for a Romanesque sculpted *Jesus Christ in His Majesty.* The figure rises over a capital and seems to hang in space. At the far end of the transept rise huge wood-built altarpieces in the Renaissance style.

As you wander about—and that is far preferable to going inside the many monuments—you'll traverse the cobblestoned, colonnaded medieval streets and interesting squares of the old town, especially behind the cathedral. The 18th-century **Episcopal Palace**—called a *pazo* in Galicia—faces the north side of the cathedral and opens onto Plaza Santa María. From the palace, old alleys behind it lead to a tiny nugget, **Plaza del Campo,** one of the most charming squares of Lugo, flanked with ancient houses and graced with a fountain at its core.

Or from the bishop's palace at the Plaza Santa María, you can take Calle Cantones to Plaza de España, where you will be greeted with the **Ayuntamiento (Town Hall),** built in a flowery rococo style.

From the Town Hall, follow Calle de la Reina north to the **Iglesia de San Francisco,** a church said to have been founded by St. Francis upon his return from a pilgrimage west to the tomb of St. James. The cloister of the church, entered at Plaza de la Soledad, s/n, has been turned into the **Museo Provincial** (☎ **982/24-21-12**). Many artifacts, including sundials from Celtic and Roman days, are found in this museum, along with folkloric displays. In July and August it is open Monday through Friday from 11am to 2pm and 5 to 8pm, Saturday 10:30am to 2pm. From September through June, it is open Monday through Saturday from 10:30am to 2pm and 4:30 to 8:30pm, Sunday 11am to 2pm. Admission is free.

WHERE TO STAY

EXPENSIVE

Gran Hotel Lugo. Avenida Ramón Ferreiro, 21, 27002 Lugo. ☎ **982/22-41-52.** Fax 982/24-16-60. 156 rms, 12 suites. A/C MINIBAR TV TEL. 14,050–14,600 ptas. ($112.40–$116.80) double; 19,600–20,200 ptas. ($156.80–$161.60) suite. AE, DC, MC, V. Parking 850 ptas. ($6.80). Bus: 1, 2, 3, or 4.

About half a mile west of the ancient city walls in a leafy residential neighborhood, this hotel is large, modern, and the best in town, far superior with more comfortable bedrooms than its closest competitor, the Méndez Núñez. Its guest rooms are conservative and comfortable, with marble and/or tile private baths and restful monochromatic colors.

Dining/Entertainment: The Os Marisqueiros restaurant serves regional and international three-course fixed-price lunches and dinners. Live music is sometimes performed in the Atalaya Bar. Snack 2003 is a coffee shop/snack bar, and La Oca is a combination pizzeria and pub.

Services: Room service (daily from 8am to midnight), laundry, concierge, babysitting.

Facilities: Business center, car rentals, shopping boutiques, bingo hall, swimming pool.

MODERATE

$ Hotel Jorje Primero. La Campiña, 27923 Lugo. ☎ **982/22-34-55.** Fax 982/25-01-07. 29 rms. TV TEL. 5,400 ptas. ($43.20) double. Free parking.

If you're driving, this little hotel about two miles (3km) north of town on the Carretera N-640 is one of your best bets, particularly if you're arriving from neighboring Asturias. The old building has a bit of charm, whereas the well-maintained bedrooms are filled with modern comforts. You can enjoy the scenery as you dine in the hotel restaurant, which serves regional fare.

Méndez Núñez. Raiña, 1, 27002 Lugo. ☎ **982/23-07-11.** Fax 982/22-97-38. 86 rms. TEL. 6,500–8,500 ptas. ($52–$68) double. MC, V. Parking 130 ptas. ($1.05) per hour in nearby garage. Bus: 1, 2, 3, or 4.

Just around the corner from Plaza Mayor, this hotel was built in 1888 and named in honor of a then-famous Spanish general who had just won an important battle against revolutionaries in Cuba. Rebuilt and modernized in 1970, the hotel is today one of the best-managed in town, although not as highly rated as the Gran Hotel Lugo. Bedrooms are well maintained and comfortable. No meals other than breakfast are served, but many restaurants and cafés lie within the neighborhood. The hotel is especially convenient for exploring the medieval streets of the town's old quarter.

WHERE TO DINE

Campos. Rúa Nova, 4. ☎ **982/22-07-43.** Reservations recommended. Main courses 1,500–2,000 ptas. ($12–$16); fixed-price menus 1,950–2,250 ptas. ($15.60–$18). AE, DC, MC, V. Daily noon–4:30pm and 7:30pm–midnight. Bus: 1, 2, 3, or 4. GALICIAN.

In the old quarter, immediately adjacent to Plaza del Campo, this well-acclaimed restaurant is the creation of Amparo Yañez and his son, Manuel. Together, they offer imaginative combinations of fresh ingredients that are deftly prepared and much appreciated by their loyal clients. Winner of the 1995 Gran Cocineros de Galicia award, they feature seasonal game dishes, especially local pheasant, along with fresh fish, such as grouper with almonds. The best dessert is fresh local strawberries with honey and cream.

Ferreiros. Rúa Nueva, 1. ☎ **982/22-97-28.** Reservations recommended. Main courses 1,600–2,400 ptas. ($12.80–$19.20); *menús del día* 1,600–1,900 ptas. ($12.80–$15.20). MC, V. Thurs–Tues 1–4pm and 8pm–midnight. Bus: 1, 2, 3, or 4. GALICIAN.

In business since the 1920s, this longtime favorite near the cathedral must be doing something right. In fact, it offers well-prepared and old-fashioned regional fare with a certain unpretentious flair. The portions are generous, and the food is fresh. The many shellfish dishes featured are the most expensive items on the menu. You can also order a big slab of rib of beef or monkfish prepared in different ways.

Mesón de Alberto. Calle de la Cruz, 4. ☎ **982/22-83-10.** Reservations recommended. Main courses 1,600–2,600 ptas. ($12.80–$20.80); fixed-price menu 2,500 ptas. ($20). AE, DC, MC, V. Mon–Sat 1–4pm and 8pm–midnight. Bus: 1, 2, 3, or 4. GALICIAN.

Alberto García is the culinary star of Lugo, and with good reason. Ably assisted by his wife, Flor, he offers a well-chosen menu of imaginative fish and meat dishes and the best wine cellar in Lugo. In style the place resembles a rustic tavern, with a stand-up bar serving tapas, plus a handful of dining tables. The overflow is directed either to a somewhat more formal dining room beside the tavern or to the second floor. Try Alberto's salad with eel and an exotic vinegar, monkfish served with a mountain cheese (Cabrales from Asturias), or beefsteak for two, prepared with his "secret" sauce. Mesón de Alberto stands one block north of the cathedral in the old quarter.

7 El Grove & La Toja

395 miles (636km) NW of Madrid, 20 miles (32km) W of Pontevedra, 45 miles (72km) S of Santiago de Compostela

A summer resort and fishing village, **El Grove** is on a peninsula west of Pontevedra, with some five miles (8km) of beaches of varying quality. It juts out into the Ría de Arousa, a large inlet at the mouth of Ulla River. The village, sheltered from Atlantic gales because of its eastern position, has become more commercial than many visitors would like, but it is still renowned for its fine cuisine. A shellfish festival is held here every October.

La Toja (A Toxa in Galician), an island linked to El Grove by a bridge, is a famous spa and the most fashionable resort in Galicia, known for its sports and leisure activities. The casino and the golf course are both very popular. The island is covered with pine trees and surrounded by some of the finest scenery in Spain.

La Toja first became known for health-giving properties when, according to legend, the owner of a sick donkey left it on the island to die. The donkey recovered, and its cure was attributed to the waters of an island spring.

GETTING THERE **By Train** The train from Santiago de Compostela goes as far as Vilagarcía de Arousa; take the bus from there. For train schedules, call the station in Santiago de Compostela (**☎981/52-02-02**) for information.

By Bus From Pontevedra, buses heading for Ponte Vilagarcía de Arousa stop at La Toja. Call the transportation information number in Pontevedra (**☎ 986/85-13-13**) for details.

By Car From Pontevedra, take the 550 coastal road east via Sanxenxo. From Santiago de Compostela, expressway A-9 leads to Caldas de Reis, where you turn off onto the 550, heading west to the coast.

WHERE TO STAY AND DINE IN EL GROVE

Hotel Amandi. Castelao, 94, 36989 El Grove. ☎ **986/73-19-42.** Fax 986/73-16-43. 30 rms. TEL. 9,700 ptas. ($77.60) double. Rates include breakfast. MC, V. Closed Nov.

This stylish and tasteful hotel is a brisk 10-minute walk from the bridge that connects El Grove with La Toja. The rooms, most with TVs, are decorated with antique reproductions; the majority have tiny terraces with ornate cast-iron balustrades and sea views. Breakfast is the only meal served.

La Pousada del Mar. Castelao, 202. ☎ **986/73-01-06.** Reservations required July–Aug. Main courses 1,300–2,600 ptas. ($10.40–$20.80); fixed-price menu 3,600 ptas. ($28.80). AE, DC, MC, V. Daily 1–4pm, Mon–Sat 8:30pm–midnight. Closed Dec 10–Feb 1. SEAFOOD.

This warm, inviting place near the bridge leading to La Toja is the best dining spot outside those at the hotels. At times you can watch women digging for oysters in the river in front. The chef, naturally, specializes in fish, including a wide selection of shellfish. Among the specialties are a savory soup, an outstanding shellfish paella, hake Galician style, and fresh grilled salmon. For dessert, try the *flan de la casa.*

WHERE TO STAY IN LA TOJA

Hotel Louxo. 36991 Isla de la A Toxa. ☎ **986/73-02-00.** Fax 986/73-27-91. 115 rms. MINIBAR TV TEL. 16,900 ptas. ($135.20) double. Rates include breakfast. AE, DC, MC, V. Closed Nov–May. Free parking.

Set on flatlands a few paces from the town's ornate casino is this modern white building, sheltered from the Atlantic winds. It offers clean, stylish, modern accommodations. The many ground-floor public rooms have rows of comfortable seating areas and sweeping views over the nearby tidal flats. The hotel also serves an outstanding menu, with an emphasis on fresh fish.

8 Túy (Túi)

18 miles (29km) S of Vigo, 30 miles (48km) S of Pontevedra

A frontier town first settled by the Romans, Túy is a short distance from Portugal, located near the two-tiered road-and-rail bridge (over the Miño River) that links the two countries. The bridge was designed by Alexandre-Gustave Eiffel. For motorists coming from Portugal's Valenca do Minho, Túy is their introduction to Spain.

GETTING THERE **By Train** Trains run daily for the 1½- to 2-hour trip from Vigo to Túy.

By Bus From Vigo, buses run south to Túy hourly, taking 1 hour.

By Car From Vigo, head south along the A-9 expressway until you see the turnoff for Túy.

VISITOR INFORMATION The tourist information office is at Puente Tripes, Avenida de Portugal (☎ **986/60-17-89**), open Monday through Friday from 9am to 1pm and 4 to 6pm, Saturday from 10am to 2:30pm.

WHAT TO SEE & DO

The winding streets of the old quarter lead to the **cathedral,** a national art treasure that dominates the *zona monumentale.* The acropolis-like cathedral-fortress, built in 1170, wasn't used for religious purposes until the early 13th century. Its principal portal, ogival in style, is exceptional. What is astounding about this cathedral is that later architects respected the original Romanesque and Gothic style and didn't make changes in its design. If you have time, you may want to visit the Romanesque-style **Church of San Bartolomé,** on the outskirts of town, and the **Church of Santo Domingo,** a beautiful example of Gothic style (look for the bas-reliefs in the cloister). The latter church stands next to the Parque de Santo Domingo. Walls built over Roman fortifications surround Túy.

WHERE TO STAY & DINE

Parador Nacional de San Telmo. Avenida de Portugal, s/n, 36700 Túy. ☎ **986/60-03-09.** Fax 986/60-21-63. 30 rms, 2 suites. A/C MINIBAR TV TEL. 9,500–12,500 ptas. ($76–$100) double; 13,500–17,500 ptas. ($108–$140) suite. AE, DC, MC, V. Free parking.

Advance reservations are essential if you want to stay in this elegant, fortress-style hacienda located four streets north of the Miño River crossing. Built in 1968, the inn, with its cantilevered roof, was designed to blend in with the architectural spirit of the province, emphasizing local stone and natural woods. Brass chandeliers, paintings by well-known *gallegos,* and antiques combined with reproductions furnish the public rooms. In the main living room are a large inglenook fireplace, a tall banjo-shaped grandfather clock, hand-knotted rugs, 18th-century paintings, hand-hewn benches, and comfortable armchairs. Not to be forgotten are the swimming pool and tennis courts also on the premises.

The bedrooms are sober in style, but comfortable, and offer views across a colonnaded courtyard to the river and hills. They are furnished with Castilian-style pieces, and the tiled baths are modern. The dignified dining room has a high wooden ceiling and tall windows that offer a fine view of the surrounding hills. Even if you are not a hotel guest, it is worth dining on the regional cuisine served here. The hors d'oeuvres—served while you wait in the bar—consist of almost a dozen little dishes. The fish dishes are excellent, especially (when available) lamprey, as well as salmon, shad, and trout. Homemade cakes are offered for dessert.

21 The Balearic Islands

The Balearic Islands (*Los Baleares*), an archipelago composed of the major islands of Majorca, Minorca, and Ibiza, plus the diminutive Formentera, Cabrera, and the uninhabited Dragonera, lie off the coast of Spain, between France and the coast of northern Africa. Because of the group's location along the Mediterranean's major shipping lanes, the islands have known many rulers and occupying forces—Carthaginians, Greeks, Romans, Vandals, and Moors. But despite a trove of Bronze Age megaliths and some fine Punic artifacts, the invaders who have left the largest imprint on Balearic culture are the hordes of sun-seeking tourists who descend year after year upon the archipelago.

After the expulsion of the Moors in 1229, by Jaume I, the islands flourished as the kingdom of Majorca. When they were integrated into the kingdom of Castile in the mid-14th century, they experienced a massive decline. The early 19th century provided a renaissance for the islands; artists such as George Sand and her lover Chopin, and later the poet Robert Graves established the islands, especially Majorca and Ibiza, as a haven for musicians, writers, and artists (read Sand's book *A Winter in Majorca*). Gradually the artist colony attracted tourists of all dispositions.

Today the Balearics are administrated by an autonomous government, *Govern Balear.* Majorca, the largest island, is the most commercial. It has both benefited and suffered from its huge tourist boom. Many of its scenic expanses have given way to sprawling hotels and fast-food joints. Unabashed, uninhibited Ibiza, world-renowned for its decadent ways, attracts the international party crowd, as well as visitors who come to the island for its tamer offerings, such as white-sand beaches and sky-blue waters. The smallest of the major islands, Minorca, the last to succumb to the tourist invasion, is the most serene. It is less touristy than Majorca and Ibiza, and for that reason, it is now experiencing an anti-tourist tourist boom.

Although long delayed, the government of the islands now sees the damage caused by overdevelopment of Majorca and Ibiza from the 1960s through the 1980s. Under new guidelines, some 35% of this island group is now safeguarded from exploitation by builders.

Very few visitors have time to explore all three islands, so you'll have to decide early which one is for you. Many vacationers include one of the Balearic Islands as a "tag-on" on a visit to Barcelona, while others view them as destinations unto themselves.

The Best Beaches of the Balearics

The golden sands of Majorca are typified in the beaches of Ca'n Pastilla and El Arenal, although they are the major destination of package tours and tend to be overcrowded. Tourist facilities also line the shores of Cala Mayor and Sant Agustí, both good beaches, as is Playa Magaluf, the longest beach on the Calvía coast. Cala de San Vicente, four miles (6km) north of Pollença, is a beautiful beach bordered by a pine grove and towering cliffs. Sandy stretches of golden sand beaches lie between Cala Pi and Cala Murta in Formentor near the tip of the northern coast.

The Ciudad de Ibiza boasts Playa Talamanca in the north and Ses Figueretes and Playa d'en Bossa in the south, two outstanding beaches. Las Salinas, in the south, near the old salt flats, also offers excellent sands. Playa Cavallet and Aigües Blanques attract the nude sunbathers. Other good beaches include Cala Bassa, Port des Torrent, Cala Tarida, and Cala Conta—all within a short bus or boat ride from San Antonio de Portmany. The long sandy cove of Cala Llonga, south of Santa Eulalia del Rio, and the white sandy beach of El Cana to the north, are sacred to Ibiza's sun worshipers. In Formentara, Playa de Mitjorn stretches three miles (5km) and is relatively uncrowded. The pure white sand of Es Pujols—set against a backdrop of pines and dunes—is the most popular of Ibiza's beaches and deservedly so.

One of the best beaches in the Balearics is found on the island of Minorca: Cala'n Porter, seven miles (11km) west of Mahón—towering promontories guard the slender estuary where this spectacular beach is found. Another of Minorca's treasures, Cala de Santa Galdana, is located 14 miles (22.5km) south of Ciudadela. Its gentle bay and excellent sandy beach affords the most scenic spot on the island. Ila d'en Colom, an island in the Mahón bay, is bordered with great beaches, but is reachable only by boat.

1 Majorca

The largest of the Balearic archipelago, Majorca (Morca in Spanish) is the most touristy of the Mediterranean islands, drawing millions of visitors each year. The most prominent tourist is Juan Carlos, King of Spain, who comes with his family to their summer residence, Marivent, in Cala Mayor.

About 130 miles (209km) from Barcelona and 90 (145km) from Valencia, Majorca has a coastline of 310 miles (500km). The beautiful island is an explorer's paradise in its exterior, although horribly overbuilt along certain coastal regions. The north is mountainous, whereas the fertile southern flatlands offer a landscape of olive and almond groves, occasionally interrupted by windmills.

The island has much to offer—fine beaches, little harbors, hidden mountain villages, and historical sights. Both the English and the Americans alike have settled in, buying either homes or apartments, but the "Chopin Heights Real Estate Development" is a bit much! (Chopin and his mistress, George Sand, were in the legendary vanguard of the tourists to Majorca. They spent a few months on the island in 1838.)

July and August are high season for Majorca; *never* arrive on the island then without a reservation. It's possible to swim comfortably from roughly June to October, at which time it becomes too cold except for hardy Scandinavians and Germans used to the chilly waters.

The Balearic Islands

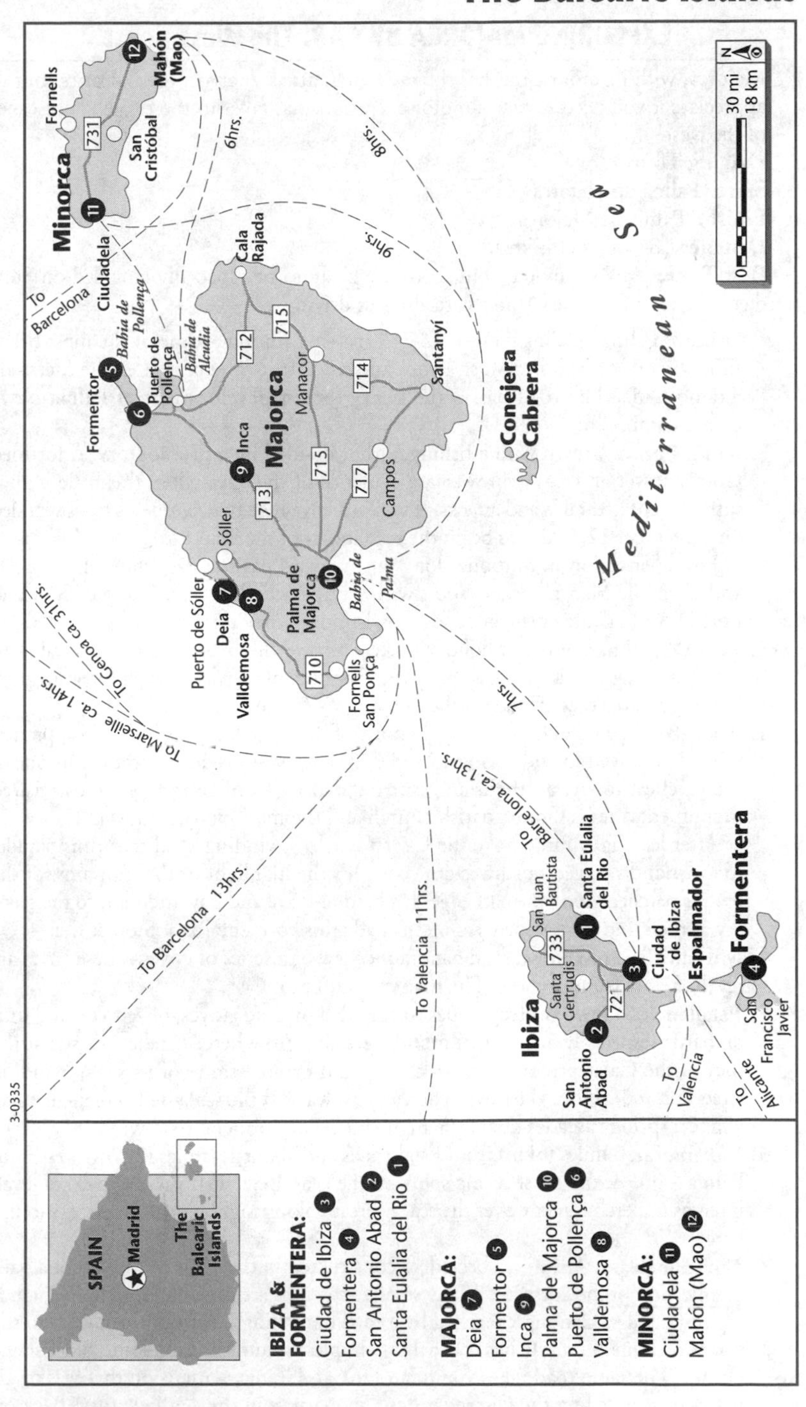

EXPLORING MAJORCA BY CAR: The West Coast

Majorca, with its mountains, has the most dramatic scenery in the Balearics. But to appreciate it you need to take a motor excursion that takes in the rugged landscapes of the west.

Driving Tour

Start: Palma de Majorca.

Finish: Palma de Majorca.

Distance: 88 miles (142km).

Best Time: Any sunny day, but roads are likely to be especially crowded on Sunday, when many of the islanders are also out driving.

Leave Palma heading west on C-719, passing through some of the most beautiful scenery of Majorca. Just a short distance from the seas rises the Sierra de Tramontana. The road passes the heavy tourist development of Palma Nova before coming to:

1. **Santa Ponça,** a town with a fishing harbor divided by a promontory. A fortified Gothic tower and a watchtower are evidence of the days when this little harbor suffered repeated raids and attacks. It was in a cove here that Jaume I's troops landed on September 12, 1229, to begin the reconquest of the island from the Muslims.

   From Santa Ponça, continue along the highway, passing Paguera, Cala Fornells, and Camp de Mar, all beauty spots with sandy coves. Between Camp de Mar and Port D'Andratx are corniche roads, a twisting journey to:

2. **Port D'Andratx.** Summer holiday makers mingle with fishers in this natural port, which is set against a backdrop of pines. Once the place was a haven for smugglers. Leaving the port, continue northeast along C-719 to reach:

3. **Andratx,** three miles (5km) away. Because of the frequent raids by Turkish pirates, this town moved inland. Lying 19 miles (31km) west of Palma, Andratx is one of the loveliest towns on the island, surrounded by fortifications. Its most visited monuments are its Gothic parish church and the mansion of Son Mas.

   After leaving Andratx take the C-710 north, a winding road that runs parallel to the island's jagged northwestern coast. It's the highlight of the trip; most of the road is perched along the cliff edge. It's hard to drive and pay attention to the scenery at the same time. Pine trees often shade this corniche road. Stop at the:

4. **Mirador Ricardo Roca,** for a panoramic view of a series of coves. These coves are reached only from the seas. The road continues to:

5. **Estallenchs,** a town of steep slopes surrounded by pine groves, olive trees, and fruit orchards (especially apricot). Almond trees also grow here. Estallenchs sits at the foot of the Galatzo mountain peak. Stop and explore some of its steep, winding streets on foot. From the town, you can also walk to the Cala de Estallenchs cove, where a spring cascades down the high cliffs. The corniche road winds to:

6. **Bañalbufar,** 5 miles (8km) from Estallenchs and about 16 miles (26km) west from Palma—one of the most scenic spots on the island. Set 110 yards above sea level, it seems to perch directly over the sea. A breathtaking highlight of Majorca is found here—

7. **Mirador de Ses Animes,** a belvedere constructed in the 17th century with a panoramic view of the coastline. Many small excursions are possible from here, including to Port d'es Canonge, reached by a road branching out from the C-710 to the north of Bañalbufar. It has a beach, a simple restaurant, and some old fishers' houses. The same road takes you inland to San Granja, a mansion that was originally constructed by the Cistercians as a monastery in the 13th century. Back on the C-710, continue to:

Driving Tour of Majorca

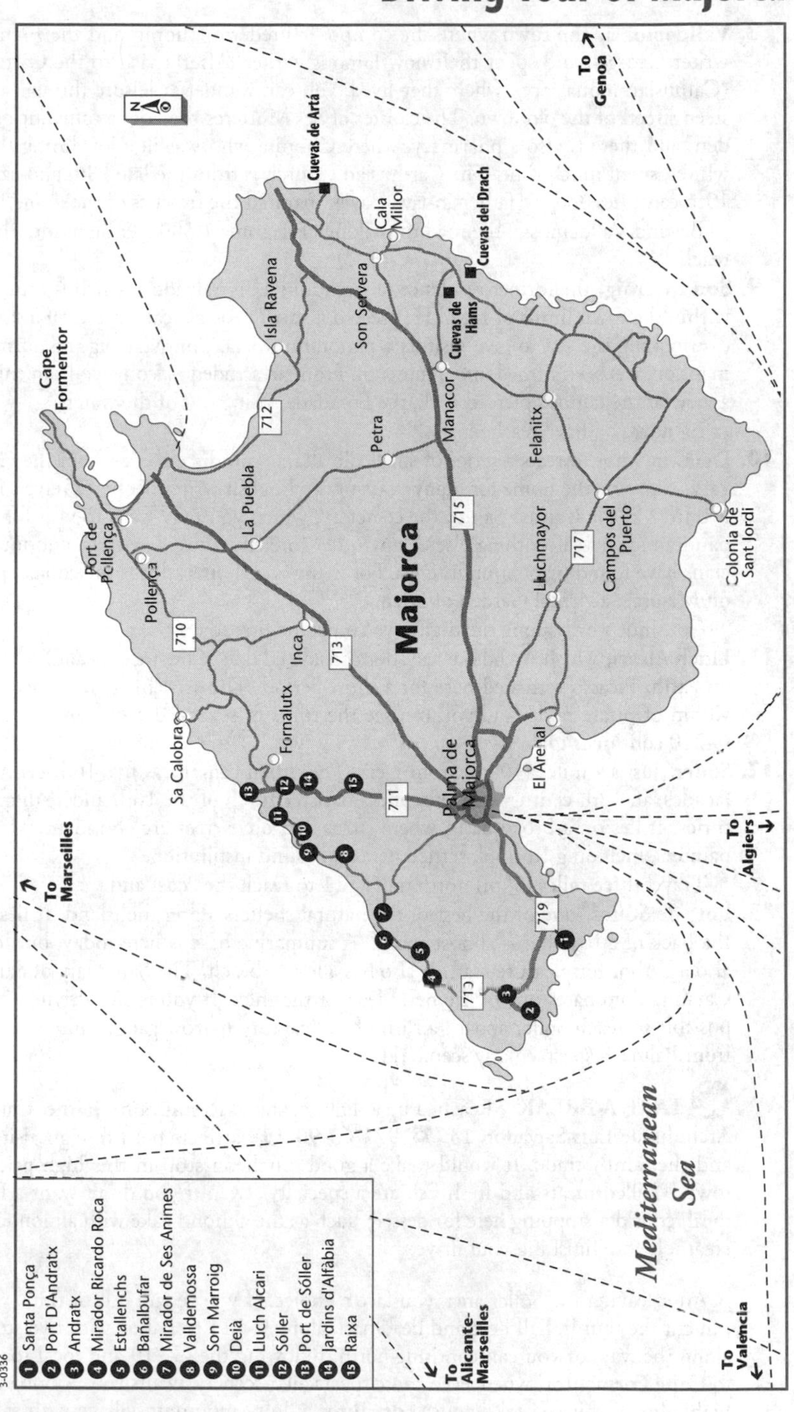

8. Valldemossa, the town where the composer Frédéric Chopin and the French writer George Sand spent their now-famous winter. After a visit to the Cartuja (Cathusian monastery), where they lived, you can wander at leisure through the steep streets of the old town. The cloister of Ses Murteres provides a romantic garden, and there is also a pharmacy, where Chopin, who was ill a lot during that winter, spent much time. The Carthusian Church is from the late 18th and early 19th centuries. Goya's father-in-law, Bayeu, painted the frescoes of the dome.

Beyond Valldemossa, the road runs along cliffs some 1,300 feet high until they reach:

9. Son Marroig, the former residence of Archduke Luis Salvador, which is actually within the town limits of Deià. He erected a small neoclassical temple on a slope overlooking the sea to give visitors a panoramic vista. Son Marroig, his former mansion, has been turned into a museum. From an arcaded balcony, you can enjoy a view of the famous pierced rock, the Foradada, rising out of the water.

By now you have reached:

10. Deià, in whose streets a series of small tile altars reproduce scenes from the Calvary. This was the home for many years of the English writer, Robert Graves. He is buried at the Campo Santo, the cemetery, which you may want to visit for its panoramic view, if nothing else. Many other foreign painters, writers, and musicians have found inspiration in Deià. For living and dining, this is the choice spot on Majorca, a virtual Garden of Eden.

Continue north along the highway. You come first to:

11. Lluch Alcari, which Archduke Salvador considered one of the most beautiful spots on earth. Picasso retreated here for a short period. The settlement was once the victim of pirate raids, and you can see the ruins of several defense towers. The C-710 continues to:

12. Sóller, just six miles (10km) from Deià. The urban center has five 16th-century facades, an 18th-century convent, and a parish church of the 16th and 17th centuries. It lies on a broad basin where citrus and olive trees are abundant. Many painters, including Rusiñol, settled here and found inspiration.

Travel three miles (5km) north on C-711 to reach the coast and:

13. Port de Sóller, one of the best of the natural shelters along the island. It lies at the back of a bay that is almost round. A submarine base is here today, but it is also a harbor for pleasure craft. It also has a lovely beach. The Sanctuary of Santa Catalina dominates one of the best views of the inlet. If you're not driving, it is possible to reach Sóller aboard a turn-of-the-century narrow gauge railroad train from Palma, a spectacularly scenic ride.

TAKE A BREAK Reached up a flight of stairs, **Restaurante Jaime,** Carrer Archiduque Luis Salvador, 13 (☎ **971/63-90-29**), attracts both foreign visitors and the family trade. It would make a good luncheon stop in this high-priced town. Grilled meats and fresh fish are a specialty. Even if you don't want a full meal, consider stopping here for dessert, such as the almond cake with almond ice cream, before finishing your drive.

After leaving the Sóller area, you face a choice. If you've run out of time, you can cut the tour in half here and head back along C-711 to Palma with two stops along the way, or you can continue north, following the C-710 and local roads, to **Cape Formentor,** where even more spectacular scenery awaits you. Among the highlights of this coastal detour: **Fornalutx,** a lofty mountain village with steep cobbled streets, Moorish-tiled roofs, and groves of almond trees; the splendid, hair-raising road to the harbor village of **Sa Calobra,** plunging to the sea one minute, then climbing arduously past olive groves, oaks, and jagged boulders; and the 13th-century **Monasterio de Lluch,** some 28 miles (45km) north of Palma, which is home to the Black Virgin of Lluch, the island's patron saint. The well-known "boys' choir of white voices" sings there daily at noon and again at twilight.

Those ending the tour at this point can head south along C-711 with a stopover at:

14. **Jardins d'Alfàbia,** a former Muslim residence. This estate is located in the foothills of the sierra and includes both a palace and romantic gardens. The gardens are richly planted, and you can wander among pergolas, a pavilion, and ponds. Inside the palace you can see a good collection of Majorcan furniture and an Arabic coffered ceiling. The gardens are open April through October, Monday through Saturday from 9:30am to 6:30pm; November through March, Monday through Saturday from 9:30am to 5pm. Admission is 450 pesetas ($3.60).

    From Alfàbia, the highway becomes straight and Palma lies just 11 miles (18km) away. But before reaching the capital, consider a final stop at:

15. **Raixa,** another charming place, built on the site of an old Muslim hamlet. It stands one mile (1.6km) outside the village of Buñola ("small vineyard"). The present building was once the estate of Cardinal Despuif and his family who constructed it in the Italian style near the end of the 1700s. Ruins from Roman excavations are found on the grounds. Rusiñol came here, painting the place several times. It keeps the same hours as Alfàbia (see above).

    After Raixa, the route leads directly to the northern outskirts of Palma.

ESSENTIALS

GETTING THERE At certain times of the year the trip by boat or plane can be pleasant. But in August the routes to Palma must surely qualify as the major bottleneck in Europe. Don't travel without advance reservations, and be sure you have a return plane ticket if you come in August—otherwise you may not get off the island until September!

By Plane Both Iberia (☎ **971/71-63-29**) and Aviaco (☎ **971/26-02-73**) fly to Palma's Aeroport Son San Juan (☎ **971/26-42-10**) from Barcelona, Valencia, and Madrid. There are daily planes from Madrid and Valencia. Barcelona, the major gateway to the Balearics, has several daily flights in summer; the number depends on the volume. Countless charter flights also make the run. Bookings are very tight in August, and delays of at least 24 hours, sometimes more, are common. If you're flying—say, Iberia—on a transatlantic flight from New York to either Madrid or Barcelona, you should have Majorca written into your ticket before your departure if you plan to visit the Balearics as part of your Spanish itinerary. Bus number 17 will take you to the Plaça Espanya in the center of Palma from 7am to 11:30pm daily; the cost is 230 pesetas ($1.84). A metered cab costs between 1,500 and 2,000 pesetas ($12–$16) for the 25-minute drive into the city center.

By Ferry **Transmediterránea,** Estación Marítim in Palma (☎ **971/40-06-15** for schedules) operates eight vessels a day from Barcelona, taking 8 hours and costing from 6,305 pesetas ($50.45) for one-way passage. There are also six ferries per week from Valencia, taking 8½ hours and costing 6,305 pesetas ($50.45) one way. In Barcelona, tickets can be booked at the Transmediterránea office at Estación Marítim (☎ **93/443-25-32**), and in Valencia at the office at Avinguda Manuel Soto Ingeniero 15 (☎ **96/367-65-12**). Any travel agent in Spain can also book you a seat. Schedules and departure times (subject to change) should always be checked and double-checked.

VISITOR INFORMATION The National Tourist Office is located in Palma at Plaça Reyna, 2 (☎ **971/71-22-16**). It is open Monday through Friday from 9am to 1:30pm and 3 to 8pm, Saturday from 9am to 1pm.

GETTING AROUND In Palma, you can get around on foot (the only way, really), especially if you plan to sightsee or shop in the Old Town. Likewise, you can explore the Paseo on foot. Otherwise, you can make limited use of taxis for getting around Palma or use one of the buses that cuts across the city. Out on the island, you'll have to depend mainly on buses or rented cars for transportation.

By Bus At the tourist office (see "Visitor Information," above), you can pick up a bus schedule that explains island routes. Or call **Emprese Municipal de Transportes** (☎ **971/29-57-00** or **971/43-10-24**). This company runs city buses from Estació Central D'Autobus, Plaça Espanya, the main terminal. The standard one-way fare is 140 pesetas ($1.10) within Palma; at the station you can purchase a booklet good for 10 rides, costing 590 pesetas ($4.70).

Bus service to other parts of Palma is offered by private companies; again, the tourist office can supply you with information and schedules.

The most popular destinations (Valldemossa, Deià, Sóller, and Port de Sóller) are offered by **Bus Nord Balean,** Carrer Arxiduc Luís Salvador 1 (☎ **971/42-71-87**) in Palma. **Autocares Majorca,** Plaça Espanya (☎ **971/55-07-30**), runs buses to the eastern coast, including Porto Cristo.

By Train **Ferrocarril de Sóller,** Carrer Eusebio Estada, 1 (☎ **971/75-20-52**), off Plaça Espanya, has train service, passing through majestic mountain scenery, to Sóller. Trains run from 9am to 7pm, and a one-way ticket costs 380 pesetas ($3.05). A "tourist train" leaves daily at 10:40am and costs 735 pesetas ($5.90) before reaching Sóller. The only thing special about this route is a 10-minute stop at Mirador del Pujol d'en Banya—a privilege for which you pay dearly. The tourist train itself, however, is a worthy sightseeing trip. Privately owned, it was constructed by orange growers early in this century and still uses the carriages of the Belle Epoque days.

Another train runs to Inca; it's often called "the leather express" because most passengers are on board to buy inexpensive leather goods in the Inca shops. This line is the **Ferrocarriles de Majorca,** and it too leaves from Plaça Espanya (☎ **971/75-22-24** for more information and schedules). The train ride is only 35 minutes, and departures are at the rate of 20 per day Monday through Saturday and 16 per day on Sunday. A one-way fare costs 230 pesetas ($1.85).

By Bike & Moped Contact **RTR Bike Rental,** Joan Miró, 338, in Palma (☎ **971/40-25-85**), daily from 9am to 9pm. Mopeds cost 2,675 pesetas ($21.40) per day.

By Taxi For a radio taxi, call **971/75-54-40** or **971/40-14-14.**

By Car If you plan to stay in Palma, you don't need a car. The city is extremely traffic clogged. Scarcity of parking is another reason not to have a car. If you'd like to take our driving tour, you can rent cars at such companies as the Spanish-owned **Atesa** at Passeig Marítim (☎ **971/45-66-02**), where rentals begin at 6,400 pesetas ($51.20) per day. **Avis** at Passeig Marítim (☎ **971/73-07-20**) is also well stocked with cars; their rates start at 7,500 pesetas ($60) per day. Both Atesa and Avis also maintain offices at the airport. Reservations, however, should always be made in advance, especially in summer.

PALMA DE MAJORCA

Palma, on the southern tip of the island, is the seat of the autonomous government of the Balearic Islands, as well as the center for most of Majorca's hotels, restaurants, and nightclubs. The Moors constructed Palma in the style of a Casbah, or walled city. Its roots are still visible, although obscured by the high-rise hotels that have cropped up.

Old Palma is typified by the area immediately surrounding the cathedral. Mazes of narrow alleys and cobblestone streets echo the era when Palma was one of the chief ports in the Mediterranean.

Today Palma is a bustling city, whose massive tourist industry has more than made up for its decline as a major seaport. It's estimated that nearly half of the population of the island lives in Palma. Majorca itself attracts the largest number of visitors of any place in Spain. The islanders call Palma simply *Ciutat,* ("City") and it is the largest of the Balearic ports, its bay often clogged with yachts. Arrival by sea is the most impressive, with the skyline characterized by Bellver Castle and the bulk of the cathedral.

FAST FACTS: PALMA

Business Hours Most shops open Monday through Friday from 9:30am to 1:30pm and 4:30 to 8pm, Saturday from 9:30am to 1:30pm. However, department stores are generally open Monday through Saturday from 10am to 8pm. Most banks are in business from 9am to 2pm only. Keep in mind, though, that hours change with the tourist season.

Consulates The **U.S. Consulate,** Avinguda Jaime III, 26 (☎ **971/72-26-60**), is open from 4 to 7pm Monday through Friday. The **British Consulate,** Plaça Mayor, 3 (☎ **971/71-24-45**), is open in summer from 9am to 2pm Monday through Friday and in winter from 9am to 3pm Monday through Friday.

Emergencies Dial 091 or 092.

Holidays Majorca observes the same holidays as the rest of Spain, but also celebrates June 29, the Feast of St. Peter, the patron saint of all fishers.

Mail The central post office is at Carrer Constitució, 6 (☎ **971/72-18-67**). Hours are Monday through Friday from 9am to 1pm and 4 to 7pm.

Medical In an emergency, try **Centro Médico,** Passeig Marítim, 16 (☎ **971/23-00-23**). This is a private facility.

Newspapers Major foreign newspapers, including the *International Herald Tribune,* are for sale at most major newsstands.

Telephones It's expensive to call from hotel rooms. Go instead to the central phone office at Avinguda Jaume III, 20, open Monday through Saturday from 9:30am to 1:30pm and 5 to 9pm.

WHAT TO SEE & DO

Most visitors don't spend time exploring the historical sights in Palma, but there are a number of places to see if you wish to break the monotony of going to the beach every day.

✪ **Catedral.** Carrer Palau Reial. ☎ **971/72-31-30.** Free admission to cathedral; museum and treasury, 300 ptas. ($2.40). Cathedral, Mon–Fri 10am–12:30pm and 4–6:30pm, Sat 10am–1:30pm; museum and treasury, Mon–Fri 10am–12:30pm and 4–6:30pm, Sat 10am–2pm. Bus: 15.

This graceful Catalonian-Gothic cathedral—called La Seu —stands in the old town overlooking the seaside. It was begun during the reign of Jaume II (1276–1311) and completed in 1601. Its central vault is 144 feet high, its columns rising 65 feet. There is a scalloped-edged, wrought-iron baldachin by Gaudí over the main altar. The treasury contains pieces of the True Cross and relics of St. Sebastián, patron saint of Palma.

Castell de Bellver. Between Palma and Illetas. ☎ **971/73-06-57.** Admission 350 ptas. ($2.80) adults, free for children. Daily 8:30am–5:30pm. Museum closed Sun. Bus: 3, 4, 21, or 22.

Erected in 1309, this hilltop round castle was once the summer palace of the kings of Majorca—during the short period when there were kings of Majorca. The castle, which was a fortress with a double moat, is well preserved and now houses the Museu Municipal, which is devoted to archaeological objects and old coins. It's really, however, the view from here that is the chief attraction. In fact, the name, Bellver, means beautiful view.

Llotja. Passeig Sagrera. ☎ **971/71-17-05.** Free admission. Tues–Sat 11am–2pm and 5–9pm, Sun 11am–2pm. Bus: 15.

This 15th-century Gothic structure is a leftover from the wealthy mercantile days of Majorca. La Lonja (its Spanish name) was, roughly, an exchange or guild. Exhibitions here are announced in local newspapers.

Banys Arabs. Carrer Serra, 7, ☎ **971/72-15-49.** Admission 100 ptas. (80¢). Daily 9:30am–8pm. Bus: 15.

You can spend hours exploring the narrow streets of the medieval quarter (*Barri Gòtic*) east of the cathedral. Along the way, you may want to visit the Moorish baths, which date from the 10th century. These baths are the only complete remaining Moorish-constructed buildings in Palma, evoking what life was like in the heyday of the caliphate. In one room a dome is supported by 12 columns.

Palau de l'Almudaina. Carrer Palau Reial. ☎ **971/72-71-45.** Admission 450 ptas. ($3.60) adults, 250 ptas. ($2) children; free on Wed. Apr–Oct, Mon–Sat 10am–2pm and 4–6:30pm; off-season, Mon–Sat 10:30am–2pm and 4–6pm. Closed holidays. Bus: 15.

The Muslims who ruled the island erected this splendid fortress surrounded by Moorish-style gardens and fountains opposite the cathedral. During the short-lived reign of the kings of Majorca, it was converted into a royal residence that evokes the Alcázar at Málaga. Now it is one of the most popular attractions of Palma and houses a museum displaying antiques, arts, suits of armor, and Gobelin tapestries. Panoramic views of the harbor of Palma can be seen from here.

Poble Espanyol. Carrer Capitán Mesquida Veny, 39. ☎ **971/28-77-08.** Admission 500 ptas. ($4) adults, 400 ptas. ($3.20) children. Daily 9am–7pm. Bus: 5.

This is a touristy collection of buildings evoking Spain in miniature and is similar to the already-described Poble Espanyol in Barcelona. Bullfights are held in its *corrida* on summer Sundays. There are mock representations of such famous structures as the Alhambra in Granada, the Torre de Oro in Seville, and El Greco's House in Toledo.

Marineland. Costa d'en Blanes. ☎ **971/67-51-25.** Admission 1,600 ptas. ($12.80) adults, 875 ptas. ($7) children 3–12, free for children 2 and under. Daily 9:30am–5pm. Closed Nov 20–Dec 26. Direct bus, marked Marineland, from Palma rail station.

Eleven miles (18km) west of Palma, just off the coast road en route to Palma Nova, this attraction offers a variety of amusements—dolphin, sea lion, and parrot shows are given daily. There's also a Polynesian pearl diving demonstration and a mini zoo. You'll find a cafeteria, picnic area, and children's playground, as well as beach facilities.

ORGANIZED TOURS

Viajes Sidetours, Passeig Marítim, 16, (☎ **971/28-39-00**), offers numerous full- and half-day excursions throughout Palma and the surrounding countryside. The full-day excursion to Valldemossa and Sóller takes visitors through the monastery where former island residents Chopin and his lover George Sand spent their scandalous winter. After leaving the monastery, the tour explores the peaks of the Sierra Mallorquina, then makes its way to the seaside town of Sóller. A visit to the Arabian gardens of Raixa or Alfàbia is included in the 5,000-peseta ($40) cost of the tour.

Another full-day tour of the mountainous western side of the island is conducted by train and boat, including a ride on one of Europe's oldest railways to the town of Sóller and the Monasterio de Lluch, as well as a boat ride between the port of Sóller and La Calobra. Tours cost 6,240 pesetas ($49.90). The eastern coast of Majorca is explored in the Caves of Drach and Hams tour. A concert on the world's largest underground lake (Lake Martel), tours through the caves, a stop at an olive wood works, and a visit to the Majorica Pearl Factory are all covered in the 4,915-peseta ($39.30) cost. Days and times of departure vary.

OUTDOOR ACTIVITIES

Beaches There is a beach fairly close to the cathedral in Palma, but some readers have been discouraged from swimming here because of foul-smelling, although covered, sewers nearby. The closest public beach is **Playa Nova,** a 35-minute bus ride from downtown Palma. Some hotels, however, have private beaches. If you head east, you reach the beaches of **Ca'n Pastilla.** The beaches at **El Arenal** are very well equipped with tourist facilities and have golden sands as well. Going to the southwest, you find good but often crowded beaches at **Cala Mayor** and **Sant Agustí** (see also "The Best Beaches of the Balearics," above).

You can swim from late June through October; don't believe the promoters who try to sell you on mild Majorcan winters in January and February—it can get downright cold. Spring and fall can be heaven-sent, and in summer the coastal areas are pleasantly cooled by sea breezes.

Biking The best places for biking on the island are C'an Picafort, Alcúdia, and Port de Pollença because they are relatively flat. These centers are found along the north coast. Most roads have special bike lanes on the island, as it's a popular sport here. For rentals, go to **RTR Bike Rental,** Joan Miró, 338 (☎ **971/40-25-85**), where mopeds rent for 2,675 pesetas ($21.40) per day.

Boat Trips In summer, there are boat excursions, some starting from the Paseo Marítimo in Palma and others at Ca'n Pastilla and in El Arenal. You can travel to San Telmo and the island of Cabrera, even to beach parties on faraway strands. For information on such trips, ask your hotel receptionist or contact the tourist office (see "Visitor Information," above).

Golf Majorca is a golfer's dream. The best course is the Son Vida Club de Golf, Urbanización son Vida about eight miles (13km) east of Palma along the Andrade highway. This 18-hole course is shared by the guests of the island's two best hotels, Arabella Golf Hotel and the Son Vida. However, the course is open to all players who call for reservations (☎ **971/23-76-20**). Greens fees are 5,750 pesetas ($46) for 18 holes.

Hiking Because of its hilly terrain, this sport is better pursued on Majorca than on Ibiza or Minorca. The mountains of the northwest, the Serra de Tramuntana, are best for exploring. The tourist office (see above) will provide you with a free booklet called "20 Hiking Excursions on the Island of Majorca," which includes detailed maps and itineraries.

Horseback Riding The best stables on the island are at The Riding School of Majorca, at km 12 on the Palma-Sóller road. Call **971/61-31-57** to make arrangements and get directions from wherever you are on the island.

Tennis If your hotel doesn't have a court, head for the **Tennis Center,** Plaça de Santa Ponçay (☎ **971/69-04-14**).

Water Sports Most beaches have outfitters who will rent you windsurfers and dinghies. The best diving operation is **Escuba Palma,** Carrer Jaume I, s/n (☎ **971/69-49-68**). Divers here are highly skilled and will take you to the most intriguing sights underwater if you are a qualified diver.

Shopping

Shopping in Palma offers handcrafts, elegant leather goods, Majorcan pearls, and fine needlework. The best shopping is on the following streets: San Miguel, Carrer Sindicato, Jaume II, Jaume III, Caller Platería, Vía Roman, and Passeig des Borne, plus the streets radiating from the Borne all the way to Plaça Cort, where the city hall stands. Most shops close on Saturday afternoon and Sunday.

Casa Bonet. Plaça Federico Chopin, 2. ☎ **971/72-21-17.**

Elegant boudoirs throughout Europe are furnished with finely textured needlework from this famous store, which was founded in 1860. Each of the sheets, tablecloths, napkins, and pillowcases is made in Majorca from fine linen or cotton (also, for the less expensive items, from acrylic). Many are hand-embroidered, using ancient designs and floral motifs popularized by this establishment. Casa Bonet specializes in mail orders, and a complete catalog is available.

Loewe. Passeig des Born, 2. ☎ **971/71-52-75.**

Majorca's outlet of Spain's premier showroom for fine leather, Loewe offers elegant accessories for men and women, fine luggage, as well as, chic apparel for women.

Passy. Avinguda Jaume III, 6. ☎ **971/72-56-86.**

This is the purveyor of quality, locally made shoes, handbags, and accessories. There are also shops located at San Miguel, 53 (☎ **971/72-56-86**), and Tous y Ferrer, 8 (☎ **971/71-73-38**).

Perlas Majorica. Avinguda Jaume III, 11. ☎ **971/72-52-68.**

This is the authorized agency for the authentic Majorcan pearl, an elegant shop with fanciful wrought-iron and gates. The pearl producers employ hundreds of artisans to make and design their stunning jewelry, and they offer a decade-long guarantee for their products. Pearls come in varied sizes and settings, of course.

Pink. Avinguda Jaume III, 3. ☎ **971/72-23-33.**

At this supplier of luxury leather goods, the wares are a bit funkier than those found at Loewe. Pink caters to a bold clientele, and designs can be custom made.

Yanko. Carrer Unión, 3. ☎ **971/72-27-88.**

Most of the high-fashion shoes and leather goods in this glossy showroom are made in a factory in central Majorca. Here, you'll find displays of shoes, luggage, and leather and suede items at reasonable prices.

Where to Stay

Majorca has a staggering number of hotels and boarding houses. But hold onto your reservations, for even that quantity is vastly inadequate in summer, particularly August. We strongly advise against going to Majorca during peak summer season without a reservation.

Some of our hotel recommendations in Palma are in El Terreno section, the heart of the nighttime district. Don't book into one of these hotels unless you like plenty of action, until late at night. More conservative readers may find it unsavory. If you seek seclusion, check our other suggestions.

Palma's suburbs, notably Cala Mayor, about 2¹/₂ miles (4km) from the center, and San Agustín, about 3 miles (5km) from town, continue to sprawl. In the area El Arenal, part of Playas de Palma, there is a huge concentration of hotels. The beaches at El Arenal are quite good, but many readers have complained of the "Coney Island atmosphere." We have a number of hotel recommendations in these suburbs for those who don't mind staying outside of the city center.

Very Expensive

✪ **Arabella Golf Hotel.** Carrer de la Vinagrella, 07013 Palma de Majorca. ☎ **971/79-99-99.** Fax 971/79-99-97. 70 rms, 24 suites. A/C MINIBAR TV TEL. 80,920–95,600 ptas. ($647.35–$764.80) double; 103,800–117,600 ptas. ($830.40–$940.80) suite. Rates include half board. AE, DC, MC, V. Bus: 7.

This hotel joined the ranks of Majorca's most opulent hostelries in 1992, when the German-based Arabella chain bought the rolling land it sits on, as well as the Son Vida Hotel (which can be reached after a brisk 10-minute walk) and its 18-hole golf course. All three entities lie within an area whose ecology is fiercely protected, about three miles (5km) northwest of the center of Palma. Don't come here expecting raucous good times on the beach; the resort is elegant and rather staid, its focal point a sprawling outdoor swimming pool, one of the most appealing on the island. There's no health club, and no shuttle to the beach, though many visitors drive to the several nearby beaches.

The complex is low-slung, intensely landscaped, and offers views over the golf course (not of the sea) from many of its bedrooms. Accommodations include white walls, dark-stained furnishings, wall-to-wall carpeting, and in all but the least expensive accommodations, a balcony or veranda.

Dining/Entertainment: The Plat d'Or restaurant expects men to wear jackets and ties in the evening. The grill room is somewhat less formal yet very, very stylish. The three bars are staffed with an impeccably trained team used to dealing with well-heeled guests from all over the world.

Services: Room service, concierge, shuttle limousine to and from the airport.

Facilities: Beauty salon/barbershop, plus complete sports facilities: golf, five tennis courts, mini-golf, windsurfing, waterskiing, Turkish bath, sauna, whirlpool, horseback riding stables, and one of the only bullrings within any hotel in Spain.

Hotel Son Vida. Urbanización Son Vida, 07013 Palma de Majorca. ☎ **800/223-6800** in the U.S., or 971/79-00-00. Fax 971/79-00-17. 171 rms, 11 suites. A/C MINIBAR TV TEL. 34,450 ptas. ($275.60) double; 66,500 ptas. ($532) suite. Rates include breakfast. AE, DC, MC, V. Bus: 7.

Set in a 13th-century castle in the Son Vida hills, on a secluded hilltop several miles from Palma, this hotel commands the most panoramic views on the island. Many rooms are also located in a modern wing, which is a pleasing reproduction of a Spanish hacienda. Inside, the public rooms are swathed in sumptuous fabrics, Oriental rugs, and chandeliers. Guest rooms in the new building are not quite as distinctive as those in the castle. Many rooms have private balconies or terraces.

Dining/Entertainment: The restaurant serves an excellent international cuisine, enhanced by an extensive wine list. A piano bar is the ideal location for an after-dinner drink.

Services: 24-hour room service, shuttles to town and the beach.

Facilities: Outdoor pool, tennis courts, golf course, fitness center, covered pool, solarium, Turkish bath, whirlpool, sauna, massage.

Expensive

✪ **Casa Galesa.** Miramar, 8, 07012 Palma de Majorca. ☎ **971/71-54-00.** Fax 971/72-15-79. 5 rms, 7 suites. A/C MINIBAR TV TEL. 24,650 ptas. ($197.20) double; 27,000–32,000 ptas. ($216–$256) suite. AE, MC, V. Closed 1 week at Christmas. Parking 1,500 ptas. ($12).

For generations, this 15th-century townhouse languished as a decaying apartment building that faced the side of the cathedral. Beginning in 1993, an entrepreneurial couple from Cardiff, Wales, restored the place, salvaging the original marble floors and stained-glass windows, sheathing the walls of the public areas with silk, and adding discreetly concealed modern amenities. Today, the setting is the most alluring in all of Palma, loaded with a worthy collection of English and Spanish antiques and paintings, and accented throughout with bouquets of flowers. Most rooms overlook an enclosed courtyard draped with potted plants and climbing vines. The owners, Christopher and Vivien Pollard, are cosmopolitan and savvy managers, whose warm welcome and hearty breakfast buffet are a large part of the hotel's allure.

Sol Palas Atenea. Passeig Ingeniero Gabriel Roca, 29, 07014, Palma de Majorca. ☎ **971/28-14-00.** Fax 971/45-19-89. 362 rms, 8 suites. A/C MINIBAR TV TEL. 23,000 ptas. ($184) double; 27,800 ptas. ($222.40) suite. Rates include breakfast. AE, DC, MC, V. Bus: 1.

Another member of the Sol chain, this modern hotel offers extensive leisure amenities to complement its services for the business traveler. The hotel overlooks the Bay of Palma, within walking distance of the town's major restaurants and shops. Spacious guest rooms are endowed with terraces, many overlooking the harbor or Bellver Castle. An entire floor is designed for the special needs of the business traveler.

Dining/Entertainment: A dining room and a café serve fine food. For evening entertainment you can choose from a piano bar, an outdoor terrace bar, or a nightclub.

Services: 24-hour room service, Club Elite floor for executives.

Facilities: Outdoor and indoor pools, sauna, massage, Jacuzzi, solarium, beauty salon, shops.

Moderate

Hotel-Residencia Almudaina. Avinguda Jaume III, 9, 07012 Palma de Majorca. ☎ **971/72-73-40.** Fax 971/72-25-99. 80 rms. A/C TEL. 10,750 ptas. ($86) double. Rates include breakfast. AE, DC, MC, V. Free parking. Bus: 1 or 13.

Located on the main commercial street in Palma, this simple hotel offers comfortable, clean, quite basic rooms. Because of its location, many of the rooms are quite loud; the quietest rooms are in the rear. Some have terraces and glass doors that let in ample sunlight. The service is helpful. The Almudaina has a cafeteria.

Hotel Saratoga. Passeig Majorca, 6, 07012 Palma de Majorca. ☎ **971/72-72-40.** Fax 971/72-73-12. 187 rms. A/C MINIBAR TV TEL. 11,950–13,975 ptas. ($95.60–$111.80) double. Rates include breakfast. V. Bus: 50 from airport.

Under the arches of an arcade beside the old city's medieval moat stands the entrance to the Hotel Saratoga. Constructed in 1962 and renovated in 1992, the hotel features bright, well-furnished guest rooms, many of which have balconies or terraces with views of the bay and city of Palma. The hotel has two pools—a small wading pool in the courtyard and a large rooftop pool. The Saratoga contains a dining room and a seventh-floor bar, where live music and dances are presented.

Sol Bellver. Passeig Ingeniero Gabriel Roca, 11, 07014 Palma de Majorca. ☎ **800/448-8355** in the U.S., or 971/73-51-42. Fax 971/73-14-51. 389 rms. A/C TV TEL. 19,046 ptas. ($152.35) double. Rates include breakfast. AE, DC, MC, V. Bus: 1.

This high-rise harborfront hotel offers clean, comfortable rooms. Public rooms are well decorated, especially the marble-floored lobby. All accommodations have terraces that afford a view of the marina or the cathedral. Guests can relax by the outdoor pool which overlooks the bay; on chillier days the water is heated. You can enjoy fine international cuisine in the dining room, followed by a visit to the nightclub for dancing or a nightcap in the cozy cocktail bar.

Inexpensive

Costa Azul. Passeig Marítim, 7, 07014 Palma de Majorca. ☎ **971/73-19-40.** Fax 971/73-19-71. 130 rms. TEL. 9,560 ptas ($76.50) double. Rates include breakfast. AE, DC, MC, V. Bus: 3 or 21.

This is the bargain oasis for those wanting a room overlooking the yacht-clogged harbor. It is not glamorous, but it does offer good value. A short taxi ride will deposit you at night on the Plaça Gomila in El Terreno with its after-dark diversions. Barren, well-worn rooms are clean, but furnished in very modest style. On the ground floor is a bar and restaurant, very Iberian in decor, offering buffet meals three times a day. A tiny pool on the third floor is heated for winter visitors, often booked in here on package tours from England.

Hotel Jaume III. Passeig Majorca, 14B, 07012 Palma de Majorca. ☎ **971/72-59-43.** Fax 971/75-88-40. 88 rms. TV TEL. 10,500 ptas. ($84) double. AE, DC, MC, V. Bus: 8.

This modern hotel has a pleasant contemporary lobby, a cafeteria, and a ground-floor café that usually spills out onto the sidewalk. All of the double rooms have sun terraces and basic contemporary furnishings. The hotel stands at the end of the major shopping street of Palma.

Hotel Majórica. Carrer Garita, 3, 07015 Palma de Majorca. ☎ **971/40-02-61.** Fax 971/40-33-58. 153 rms. TEL. 9,000–15,000 ptas. ($72–$120) double. Rates include breakfast. AE, DC, MC, V. Bus: 3, 20, 21, or 22.

This modern hotel, in the hills overlooking Palma Bay, offers airy, pleasantly furnished guest rooms, many with views of the marina. Facilities include a swimming pool and solarium. The hotel contains a restaurant and two bars, one by the pool for sunbathers. A minibus takes guests to the beach or into the center of Palma.

Hotel Rosamar. Joan Miró, 74, 07015 Palma de Majorca. ☎ **971/73-27-23.** Fax 971/28-38-28. 40 rms. 4,400–4,900 ptas. ($35.20–39.20) double. MC, V. Bus: 3, 4, 21, or 22.

Hotel Rosamar, right on the main road in the boom-town El Terreno district, is popular with Germans and Scandinavians. Fresh, clean bedrooms have balconies overlooking a front patio surrounded by tall palm trees—the focus of the social life of the young, lively crowd that frequents the Rosamar. There's a stand-up bar off the lobby.

At Illetas

This suburb of Palma lies immediately west of the center.

Hotel Bon Sol. Paseo de Illetas, 30, 07015 Illetas. ☎ **971/40-21-11.** Fax 971/40-25-59. 120 rms, 10 suites. A/C MINIBAR TV TEL. 18,160–26,250 ptas. ($145.30–$210) double; 22,660–32,800 ptas. ($181.30–$262.40) suite. Rates include half board. AE, DC, MC, V. Closed Jan.

Set across from a beach, about four miles (6km) west of Palma, this four-star hotel was built in 1953 and renovated many times since in successful efforts to keep up with the times. It charges less than equivalent hotels, and as such, is quite popular with vacationing families, who consume their meals within the airy, somewhat spartan dining room. The establishment's core is a four-story, white-sided masonry tower, with some of the suites clustered into a simple collection of outlying villas. The hotel overlooks a garden, adjacent to the sea, with three swimming pools (two of them filled with seawater) and two tennis courts. Bedrooms are larger than you might expect, efficient but comfortable and well suited to beachfront holidays.

Hotel Meliá de Mar. Paseo Illetas, 15, 07015 Calvia. ☎ **971/40-25-11.** Fax 971/40-58-52. 133 rms, 11 suites. A/C MINIBAR TV TEL. 28,000–32,000 ptas. ($224–$256) double; 73,500–86,100 ptas. ($588–$688.80) suite. AE, DC, MC, V. Free parking.

Originally built in 1964, and renovated most recently in 1988, the Meliá de Mar is one of the most comfortable—and for its category, one of the most expensive—in Palma. This seven-story, four-star hotel is close to the beach and sports one of the largest gardens of any resort in the neighborhood. The marble-floored lobby and light, summery furniture provide a cool refuge from the hot sun and a calm, deliberately uneventful setting that's evocative of some of the spa hotels of central Europe. Swimming is available within a sheltered cove. A bar and a large, airy restaurant boast lots of space between tables and flavorful, but not particularly fussy, food. The grounds have tennis and and handball courts.

At Portocolom

This hotel lies on the eastern coast, reached by going east from Palma along C-717, then cutting north at the signposted directions.

✪ **Hotel Villa Hermosa/Restaurant Vista Hermosa.** Carretera Felanitx-Portocolom, km 6, 07670 Portocolom. ☎ **971/82-49-60.** Fax 971/82-45-92. 6 rms, 4 suites. A/C MINIBAR TV TEL. 33,500 ptas. ($268) double; 45,000 ptas. ($360) suite. Rates include breakfast. AE, MC, V. From Portocolom, follow signs to roads leading northeast to Felanitx.

This is one of the newest and most creative five-star hotels on Majorca—a 1993 adaptation of what was originally a 19th-century farm. Don't expect an old-fashioned venue, as the building and outbuildings were recently reconstructed to profit from views that soar from the high-altitude hillside. Evocative of a severe, dignified monastery, set on elaborate terraces cut into the rocky hillside, the building (which has only 10 accommodations and a quite deliberate sense of privacy) wraps around a large, heated swimming pool. The in-house restaurant, Vista Hermosa, is its convivial nerve center. Even if you aren't staying, you won't be alone if you opt for a meal—it's been booked solid virtually every night for at least a year. Meals are served daily from 1 to 3:30pm and from 7 to 10:30pm. Menu items are continental and sophisticated: magret of duck flambéed in Calvados; loin of pork with basil and bacon, and fresh salmon with a confit of tomatoes. You'll find two tennis courts on the premises, and a small health club. Thankfully isolated from the often overcrowded coast near Palma, it has sweeping views that incorporate some of the most panoramic sunsets on the island.

Where to Dine

The most typical main dish of Majorca is *lomo,* or pork loin, and it appears as the specialty in any restaurant offering Majoran cuisine. *Lomo con col* is a method of preparation where the loin is enveloped in cabbage leaves and served with a sauce made with tomatoes, grapes, pine nuts, and bay leaf.

A sausage, *sabrasada,* is made with pure pork and red peppers. Paprika gives it its characteristic bright red color. *Sopas mallorquínas* can mean almost anything, but basically it is mixed greens in a soup flavored with olive oil and thickened with bread. When *garbanzos* (chickpeas) and meat are added, it becomes a meal in itself.

The best known vegetable dish is *el tumbet,* a kind of cake with a layer of potato and another of lightly sautéed eggplant. Everything is covered with a tomato sauce and peppers, then boiled for a while. Eggplant, often served stuffed with meat or fish, is one of the island's vegetable mainstays. *Frito mallorquín* might include anything, but basically is a dish of fried onions and potatoes, mixed with red peppers, diced lambs' liver, "lights," and fennel. It's zesty to say the least.

Of all the islands in the Balearics, only Majorca produces wine. But this wine isn't exported. The red wine bottled around Felanitx and Binissalem adds Franja Roja and Viña Paumina to your wine list. Most of the wine, however, comes from Spain. *Café carajillo* is a Majorcan specialty—coffee with cognac.

Expensive

Diplomatic. Carrer Palau Reial, 5. ☎ **971/72-64-82.** Reservations recommended. Main courses 3,500–4,000 ptas. ($28–$32); fixed-price menu 1,600 ptas. ($12.80). AE, MC, V. Mon–Fri 12:30–4pm and 7:30–11pm, Sat 9pm–12:30am. Bus: 1, 3, or 15. CONTINENTAL.

In the center of Palma, near the cathedral, this restaurant is an ideal spot for just about anything, from tapas to a full meal. Set in a white, stuccoed medieval building with exposed beams, Diplomatic's intimate atmosphere lends to the enjoyment of a unique continental cuisine. Start with pâté with green peppercorns. Next try sole with almonds, steak tartare, or the filet mignon in port wine. Owner and wine connoisseur Juan Contesti, will be happy to help you select a vintage from his cellar to accompany your meal.

✪ **Koldo Royo.** Avinguda Gabriel Roca, 3. ☎ **971/45-70-21.** Reservations required. Main courses 1,250–3,000 ptas. ($10–$24); set menu (lunch only) 2,350 ptas. ($18.80). AE, MC, V. Mon–Fri 1:30–3:30pm, Mon–Sat 8:30–11:30pm. BASQUE.

This is the premier outlet on Majorca for savory Basque cuisine; if you're baffled by the unusual dishes on the menu, a staff member will assist you. This big-windowed establishment lies about three-fourths of a mile south of Palma's cathedral, adjacent to a marina and one of the island's most popular beaches. Menu items run the gamut of Basque seafood dishes, including baked hake, tripe, lamprey eel, and roasted pork. Meal after meal, Koldo Royo serves the best food within Palma itself.

Lonja del Pescado (Casa Eduardo). Muelle Viejo, s/n. ☎ **971/72-11-82.** Reservations required. Main courses 2,000–6,500 ptas. ($16–$52); fixed price menu 3,000 ptas. ($24). AE, MC, V. Tues–Sat 1–3:30pm and 8–11pm. Bus: 1 or 4. SEAFOOD.

This no-frills restaurant serves the catch of the day, taken directly from the boat to the kitchen. Specialties include seafood paella and *zarzuela* (a fish stew). It's also possible to get fresh lobster. The rest of the menu consists of various types of fish, most prepared in the Majorcan style.

La Lubina. Muelle Viejo. ☎ **971/72-33-50.** Reservations recommended. Main courses 3,000–8,000 ptas. ($24–$64). AE, DC, MC, V. Daily noon–4pm and 8pm–midnight. Bus: 1, 4, or 21. SEAFOOD.

La Lubina's location on the old pier makes it the purveyor of the freshest seafood in Palma. Begin with an aperitif in the tiled bar, and then dine in either the formal dining room or the more casual, enclosed terrace. Although the menu consists mainly of seafood, La Lubina is known for its unique preparation and presentation. *Caldereta* (lobster served in an almond broth) is an excellent choice. Try the traditional Majorcan fish *en papillote* (encrusted with salt) or the grilled swordfish.

✪ **Mediterráneo 1930.** Passeig Marítim, 33. ☎ **971/45-88-77.** Reservations recommended. Main courses 2,000–6,500 ptas. ($16–$52); fixed price menu 1,900 ptas. ($15.20). AE, MC, V. Daily 1–4pm and 8pm–1am. Bus: 1. SEAFOOD.

Located next to the Hotel Meliá Victoria, this is one of two top restaurants in Palma, though not as good as Koldo Royo. The interior is brash art deco with a distinctly

Mediterranean spirit. The menu relies heavily on seafood, but numerous meat dishes add to the selection. Owners Juan and Mary Martí have assured a chic, refined dining experience.

Porto Pí. Joan Miró, 174. ☎ **971/40-00-87.** Reservations required. Main courses 4,000–5,000 ptas. ($32–40). AE, DC, MC, V. Mon–Sat 1:30–3:30pm and 8:30–11:30pm. Bus: Palma-Illetas. FRENCH/BASQUE.

This restaurant, a favorite of King Juan Carlos, occupies an elegant 19th-century mansion above the yacht harbor at the west end of Palma. Contemporary paintings complement the decor, and there is an outdoor terrace. The food has a French/Basque influence. Specialties change with the season but might include house-style fish *en papillote* and quail stuffed with foie gras cooked in a wine sauce. Game is a specialty in winter.

✪ **Tristán.** Port Portals, Portals Nous. ☎ **971/67-55-47.** Reservations required. Main courses 1,200–4,000 ptas. ($9.60–$32). AE, DC, MC, V. Tues–Sun 1–3:30pm and 8:30–11pm. Closed mid-Nov to mid-Dec. Bus: 22. NOUVELLE CUISINE.

Several miles southwest of Palma, Tristán overlooks the marina of Port Portals. This is the finest restaurant in the Balearics, winning a coveted two stars from Michelin, a designation previously unheard of in the archipelago. The sophisticated menu varies depending on what was best in the market that day. Selections may include pigeon in rice paper, a medley of Mediterranean vegetables, or the catch of the day, usually prepared in Majorcan style. But this is mere recitation. What it doesn't prepare you for is the exceptional burst of flavor when you sample the chef's wares. Tristán remains the gastronomic reason for visiting Majorca in the first place.

Moderate

Arroseria Catranca. Passeig Marítim, 13. ☎ **971/73-74-47.** Reservations recommended. Main courses 2,000–4,000 ptas. ($16–$32); AE, DC, MC, V. Tues–Sun 1–4pm and 8pm–midnight. Bus: 1. SEAFOOD.

In a sophisticated setting overlooking the port, Arroseria Catranca serves a seafood menu, with some pork and beef dishes—and, as the name implies, rice. More than 15 different rice dishes are served, most with local seafood in the recipe. Try the *parillada*, an array of grilled seafood or the *merluza al estilo waleska* (hake and lobster medallions smothered in a white cream sauce).

Caballito del Mar (Little Seahorse). Passeig de Sagrera, 5. ☎ **971/72-10-74.** Reservations recommended. Main courses 1,500–4,500 ptas. ($12–36). AE, DC, MC, V. Mon–Sat 8–11:30pm. Bus 5 or 22. MAJORCAN.

Although there are several ouudoor tables, many guests prefer to dine inside, because of the lively spirit of this popular place along the seafront. The decor is vaguely nautical, and the activity is sometimes frenzied, but that's part of its charm. The food is well prepared from fresh ingredients; specialties include a Majorcan version of bouillabaisse, a *zarzuela* (fish stew), assorted grilled fish (our favorite), oysters in season, red bream baked in salt, or sea bass with fennel. If you want something other than seafood, try the duck in orange sauce.

Done Peppone. Carrer Bayarte, 14. ☎ **971/45-42-42.** Reservations recommended Fri–Sat nights. Main courses 1,100–2,000 ptas. ($8.80–16). AE, DC, MC, V. Tues–Sat 1:30–3:30pm, Mon–Sat 8:30pm–midnight. Bus: 3 or 21. ITALIAN.

Near the Plaça del Progreso, this is the best place on the island for savory Italian cuisine. Begin with the selection of antipasti, then go on to one of the pastas or main courses, including linguini in a sauce made with shellfish, carpaccio, osso buco, and other courses. In summer the terrace roof is rolled back.

Es Parlament. Carrer Conquistador, 11. ☎ **971/72-60-26.** Reservations recommended. Main courses 1,100–3,500 ptas. ($8.80–28). No credit cards. Mon–Sat 1–4pm and 8–11pm. Closed Aug. Bus: 15. MAJORCAN/VALENCIAN.

Es Parlament is noted for serving the island's finest paella. The chef is proud of the various paella dishes, including "blindman's paella," made without bones or shells, and "black paella," with the added ingredient of squid ink providing both coloring and extra flavoring. The restaurant, with its Belle Epoque ambience, is housed in the Balearic Autonomous Parliament building.

Inexpensive

Bon Lloc. San Feliu, 7. ☎ **971/71-86-17.** Reservations required. Four-course *menú del diá* 1,200 ptas. ($9.60). No credit cards. Tues–Fri 1–4pm, Sat 1:30–4pm. Bus: 1. VEGETARIAN.

Located near Passeig des Born, this simple restaurant, decorated with New Age paraphernalia, serves tasty vegetarian cuisine. Lloc offers only a four-course *menú del diá,* which changes daily. Most dishes are consistently savory, although occasionally some are too bland.

La Casita. Joan Miró, 68. ☎ **971/73-75-57.** Reservations recommended. Main courses 800–2,500 ptas. ($6.40–$20); fixed price menu 1,000 ptas. ($8). MC, V. Wed–Mon 1–4pm, Wed–Sun 7pm–midnight. Bus: 3. FRENCH/AMERICAN.

La Casita serves French and American specialties, although the American influence is a bit hard to decipher. The ceiling fans, exposed wood, and paintings by John Winn-Morgan contribute to the ambience. À la carte dishes include French onion soup, tournedos with mushroom sauce, trout almondine, pepper steak, and potato pancakes. For dessert, try the homemade apple pie.

Cellar Pagés. Carrer Felipe Bauzá, 2. ☎ **971/72-60-36.** Reservations not accepted. Main courses 1,500–1,700 ptas. ($12–13.60); fixed price menu 1,000 ptas. ($8). AE, DC, MC, V. Mon–Sat 1–4pm, Mon–Fri 8:30–11pm. Bus: 15. MAJORCAN.

The set menu here can include soup, noodles, or gazpacho; steak or fish; and dessert, bread, and wine. From the à la carte menu you can select the fish of the day, which most guests prefer grilled. Other dishes include the classic kidneys in sherry or a roast chicken. Admittedly, this isn't the best cooking on the island, but the price is right. The rustic setting is cramped and intimate, with original paintings on the white stucco walls. The location is 75 yards west from the cathedral, a short walk from Plaça de la Reina.

$ Mesón Ca'n Pedro. Carrer Rector Vives, 4. Génova. ☎ **971/40-24-79.** Reservations recommended. Main courses 800–3,000 ptas. ($6.40–$24). DC, MC, V. Daily 1pm–1am. Bus: 4. MAJORCAN.

Once dubbed "the most *Mallorquín* eatery" on the island, this *mesón* in a Palma hilltop suburb has a bustling, animated atmosphere. It's a local favorite, its success owing in no small part to low prices. Try the *cabrito* (kid) or the roast lamb. One regional dish worth sampling is savory snails prepared with fennel and served with helpings of *aïoli.*

Svarta Pannan. Carrer Brondo, 5. ☎ **971/72-10-39.** Reservations recommended. Main courses 750–2,100 ptas. ($6–16.80). AE, DC, MC, V. Mon–Fri noon–4pm and 6:30–10:30pm, Sat noon–10:30pm. Bus: 15. INTERNATIONAL.

In the center of Palma, on a narrow traffic-clogged street off the Plaça Pío XII, this restaurant serves a variety of international specialties guaranteed to stave off homesickness. The Swede can have *frikadeller* (meatballs) and the American can order a burger. Herring with onion and potatoes is always our favorite beginning, followed by Wiener schnitzel. Show up early, it's likely to be crowded.

A Special Treat

Dating from 1700, **Ca'n Juan de S'aigo,** Carrer Sans, 10 (☎ **971/71-07-59**), is the oldest ice-cream parlor on the island. Correspondingly elegant and Old World, it serves its homemade ice creams (try the almond), pastries, cakes, *ensaimadas,* fine coffee, and several kinds of hot chocolate amid marble-top tables, lots of wood, beautiful tile floors, and an indoor garden with a fountain.

PALMA AFTER DARK

The Club & Music Scene

As Majorca's largest settlement, Palma contains more dance clubs and hangout bars than anywhere else on the island. Granted, you'll find worthy sites to mingle along the island's northern tier, but for the gregarious, laser-and-strobe-lit club you'd expect in urban settings of mainland Europe, you'll have to boogie in Palma. Here are three that are currently packing them in.

B.C.M.. Avinguda Olivera, s/n. ☎ **971/68-38-69.** Cover 1,500 ptas. ($12), including first drink.

This is the busiest, most lighthearted, and most cosmopolitan disco in Majorca, featuring a sprawling, three-story premises that offers a different sound system on each floor, giving you a wide variety of musical styles. If you're young, eager to mingle, and like to dance, this place is for you. Strobe lights and lasers (the most technologically up-to-date on the island) quickly break down cultural differences among those who show up. From October through May, it's open Thursday through Saturday from 11pm to at least 4am. From June through September, it's open nightly during the same hours.

Riu Palace. Carrer Llaut, s/n, El Arenal. ☎ **971/26-57-04.** Cover 1,600 ptas. ($12.80), including first drink.

This nightclub (in El Arenal, on the eastern fringes of the bay) has a bit more Catalán flavor than its internationalized competitors, and it attracts a clientele in their 20s and early 30s from virtually everywhere in Europe. It lies near the sands of a three-mile beach that's mobbed during the day and dotted with trysting friends or companions late at night. Palma hipsters cite it as *the* place to go on Sunday nights.

Tito's Palace. Passeig Marítim. ☎ **971/73-00-17.** Cover 1,500 ptas. ($12), including first drink.

Set directly on the beach, close to a dense concentration of hotels and visitors from Europe's mainland, this is a polycultural, polylingual hangout where most of the party gathers on a terrace overlooking the Mediterranean. Between June and September, it's open every night of the week between 11pm and at least 4am. The rest of the year, it's open only on Friday and Saturday, from 11pm to 4am.

Other Entertainment

Abaco. Carrer San Juan, 1. ☎ **971/71-49-39.**

This is the most opulently decorated nightclub in Spain—a cross between a harem and a czarist Russian church. The bar is decorated with a trove of European decorative arts. The place is packed, with many customers congregating in a beautiful courtyard, which has exotic caged birds, fountains, more sculpture than the eye can absorb, extravagant bouquets, and hundreds of flickering candles. All this exoticism is enchanced by the lushly romantic music (Ravel's *Bolero,* at our last visit) piped in through the sound system. Whether you view this as a bar, a museum, or a sociological survey, be sure to go. The bar is open daily from 9pm to 2:30am February through December only.

Broadway Discoteque & Bar. Joan Miró, 36. ☎ **971/28-52-73.** Cover 2,500 ptas. ($20), including first drink.

This intimate theater-club features scantily clad dancers and magicians. Several shows a night are performed, growing more risqué and erotic as the night progresses. Many "performers" incorporate flamenco and magic into their acts. The last show of the night is the raunchiest and not recommended for the prudish. The club is open daily from 11pm to 6am, with shows starting at midnight.

Zorbas. Avinguda Son Rigo, 4. ☎ **971/26-66-64.**

This place is fun, youthful, well decorated, and often interesting, although the fickle crowd has long since deserted it for trendier oases (see above). An eclectic crowd from across Europe dances to recorded music. Admission is free but you must order one drink. Open daily 10:30pm to 4:30am April through September.

A Casino

Casino de Majorca. Urbanización Sol de Mallarca, s/n, Costa del Calvía. ☎ **971/13-00-00.** Cover 650 ptas. ($5.20); floor show without drinks, 4,800–7,200 ptas. ($38.40–$57.60).

Located at the end of the Andraitx motorway (Cala Figuera turnoff), this is the spot for gambling, dining, or watching a show. If you bring your passport, you can play American or French roulette, blackjack, dice, and slot machines. A "Las Vegas" floor show is presented nightly at 11pm. The casino is open April through October daily 8pm to 5am; off-season Sunday through Thursday 8pm to 4am and Friday and Saturday 8pm to 5am.

VALLDEMOSSA & DEIÀ (DEYÁ)

Valldemossa is the site of the ✪ **Cartoixa Reial,** Plaça de las Cartujas, s/n (☎ **971/61-21-06**), where George Sand and the tubercular Frédéric Chopin wintered in 1838 and 1839. The monastery was founded in the 14th century, but the present buildings are from the 17th and 18th centuries. After monks abandoned the dwelling, the cells were rented to guests, which led to the appearance of Sand and Chopin, who managed to shock the conservative locals. They occupied cells 2 and 4. The only belongings left are a small painting and a French piano. The peasants burned most of it after the couple returned to the mainland, fearing they'd catch Chopin's tuberculosis. It may be visited Monday through Saturday from 9:30am to 1pm and 3 to 6pm for 1,000 pesetas ($8) adults, free for children under 10. Off-season it shuts down an hour earlier.

It's also possible to visit the **Palau del Rei Sancho,** next door to the monastery, on the same ticket. This is a Moorish retreat built by one of the island kings. You're given a guided tour of the palace by a woman in Majorcan dress.

From Valldemossa, continue through the mountains following the signposts for 6½ miles (10.5km) to Deià. But before your approach to the village, consider a stopover at **San Marroig** (☎ **972/63-91-58**), at the 26km mark on the highway. Now a museum, this was once the estate of Archduke Luis Salvador. Born in 1847, the archduke fled court life and found refuge here with his young bride in 1870. A tower on the estate is from the 1500s. Many of his personal furnishings and mementos, such as photographs, are still here. His ceramic collection is also on display. The estate is surrounded by lovely gardens, and there are many panoramic views on the property.

It is open Monday through Saturday from 9:30am to 1:30pm and 3 to 8pm (closing at 6pm in winter). Admission is 350 pesetas ($2.80).

Set against a backdrop of olive-green mountains, **Deià (Deyá)** is peaceful and serene, with its stone houses and creeping bougainvillea. It has long had a special meaning for artists, notably Robert Graves, the English poet and novelist (*I, Claudius* and *Claudius the God)* who once lived here, until his death in 1985. He is buried in the local cemetery.

After walking through the old streets, you can stand on a rock overlooking the sea and watch the sun set over a field of silvery olive trees and orange and lemon groves. Then you'll know why painters come here to live on the slopes of a 4,000 foot mountain.

GETTING THERE Valldemossa lacks basic services, including a tourist office. It is connected to a bus service from Palma, however. Bus Nord Balear (☎ **971/42-71-87**) goes to Valldemossa five times daily for a one-way fare of 180 pesetas ($1.45). Buses leave from Palma at the bar at Carrer Arxiduc Salvador, 1.

To reach Deià by public transportation from Palma, 17 miles (27km) away, just stay on the bus that stops in Valldemossa. If you're driving from Palma, take the Carretera Valldemossa-Deià to Valldemossa; from there, you can continue on to Deià. Those with cars may want to consider one of the idyllic accommodations offered in this little Majorcan village, which has very few tourist facilities outside of the hotels.

Where to Stay

Deià offers some of the most tranquil and stunning retreats on Majorca—La Residencia and Es Molí—but it has a number of inexpensive little boarding houses as well.

Expensive

✪ **Hotel Es Molí.** Carretera de Valldemossa, s/n, 07179 Deià. ☎ **971/63-90-00.** Fax 971/63-93-33. 84 rms, 3 suites. A/C MINIBAR TEL. 21,400–25,400 ptas. ($171.20–$203.20) double; 43,800–47,000 ptas. ($350.40–$376) suite. Supplement for a balcony 3,000 ptas. ($24) per room per day. Rates include breakfast; half board 2,100 ptas. ($16.80) extra per person per day. AE, DC, MC, V. Closed early Nov to late Apr. Free parking.

One of the best-recommended and most spectacular hotels on Majorca originated in the 1880s as a severely dignified manor house in the rocky highlands above Deià, home of the landowners who controlled access to the town's freshwater springs. In 1966 the manor house was augmented with two annexes, transforming this luxurious four-star hotel. Bedrooms are stylish, monochromatic, and impeccably maintained, often with access to a private veranda overlooking the gardens or the faraway village. Some hardy souls make it a point to hike for 30 minutes to the public beach at Deià Bay; others wait for the shuttlebus to take them to the hotel's private beach, four miles away.

Dining/Entertainment: The in-house restaurant, Ca'n Quet, has a stone-and-timber veranda with a view looking down the hillside (see recommendation under "Where to Dine," below).

Services: Room service, concierge; definite emphasis on multilingual, multicultural catering to clients and their needs.

Facilities: One of the most appealing swimming pools in Majorca, fed from the freshwater springs that used to sustain the village; private beach 4 miles from hotel; tennis court on premises.

✪ **La Residencia.** Son Moragues, s/n, 07179 Deià. ☎ **971/63-90-11.** Fax 971/63-93-70. 52 rms, 1 suite. A/C TEL. 19,500–41,000 ptas. ($156–$328) double; 33,000–81,000 ptas. ($264–$648) suite. Rates include breakfast. AE, MC, V. Free parking.

This is the most stylish, hip, elegant hotel on Majorca, a reknowned hostelry that became even more famous in the early 1990s when it was acquired by British businessman Richard Branson. The ambience is luxurious but unpretentious at these two tawny, stone, 16th-century manor houses, surrounded by 13 acres of rocky Mediterranean gardens. Guests have included everyone from Queen Sofia and the Emperor of Japan to America's rock-and-roll elite. Bedrooms are outfitted with simple and rustic antiques, terra-cotta floors, romantic-looking four-poster beds, and in some cases, beamed ceilings. Open hearths, deep leather sofas, wrought-iron candelabra, and a supremely accommodating staff make this hotel internationally famous. Although it's technically defined as a four-star resort and a Relais & Châteaux, only the lack of such room amenities as minibars and TVs prevent it from reaching five-star status.

Dining/Entertainment: The more formal of the resort's two restaurants, El Olivo, lies within and around an antique olive press. Its award-winning cuisine is usually concocted from fresh local ingredients. The bar evokes the private salon of an arts-conscious landowner interested in abstract and surreal paintings. A less formal Mediterranean bistro, Son Fony, operates from both beside the pool (at lunch in summer) and within a bistro-like Mediterranean area near the pool.

Services: Room service (8am to midnight), a concierge well versed in acquiring virtually anything.

Facilities: Elliptical, 100-foot swimming pool lined with subtropical plants and bougainvillea; tennis court. Access to the beach, less than a mile away as the crow flies, requires a winding downhill minivan ride.

Inexpensive

Hotel Costa d'Or. Lluch Alcari, s/n, 07179 Deià. ☎ **971/63-90-25.** Fax 971/63-93-47. 30 rms. 4,500 ptas. ($36) double. Rates include breakfast. MC, V. Closed Nov–May.

This former villa, one mile (1.6km) north of Deià on the road to Sóller, has the best possible view of the vine-covered hills, and the rugged coast beyond. Surrounded by private gardens filled with fig trees, date palms, and orange groves, this old-fashioned hotel is furnished with odds-and-ends furniture, but it's clean and comfortable. Most rooms have good views. Good, home-cooked meals are served in the restaurant.

Where to Dine

El Olivo at La Residencia (see above) is one of the top three dining choices on the entire island, and you may opt to dine there even if you aren't a pampered guest at this hotel.

$ **Ca'n Costa.** Carretera Valldemossa-Deià, s/n. ☎ **971/61-22-63.** Reservations recommended. Main courses 1,000–2,000 ptas. ($8–16). AE, DC, MC, V. Wed–Mon noon–4pm and 7:30–11pm. MAJORCAN/INTERNATIONAL.

This restaurant specializes in Majorcan cuisine, but includes some continental dishes to please the mostly foreign patronage. The owner has selected only the finest of wines from the island itself, which he has wisely combined with some good vintages from Rioja. The hearty regional fare includes roast pork loin with mushrooms "from the fields" and even thrush enveloped in cabbage. Try for a seat on the outdoor patio, with a panoramic vista of the coast.

C'an Jaime. Carrer Arxiduc Luis Salvador, 13. ☎ **971/63-90-29.** Reservations recommended. Main courses 1,000–1,600 ptas. ($8–12.80). No credit cards. Tues–Sun noon–3pm and 7–10:30pm. Closed 2 weeks in May and 2 weeks in Nov. MAJORCAN.

Prices in Deià tend to be expensive, but this reasonably priced restaurant offers a good-quality cuisine. Local families come here to dine, mingling with the foreign visitors. They usually begin with *sopa mallorquínas* (Majorcan soup), perhaps followed with *arroz brut.* The specialty is always pork loin, stuffed with spicy sausage, pine nuts, and raisins and then rolled in cabbage leaves.

Ca'n Quet. Carretera de Valldemossa-Sóller. ☎ **971/63-91-96.** Reservations required. Main courses 1,800–3,000 ptas. ($14.40–24). AE, MC, V. Daily 1–3:30pm and 8–11pm. Closed Oct–Apr. INTERNATIONAL.

This restaurant, belonging to Es Molí (see above), is one of the most sought-after dining spots on the island. Set on a series of terraces above a winding road leading out of town, the building is well scrubbed, modern, and stylish, but with an undeniably romantic air. Cascades of pink geraniums ring its terraces, and if you wander along the sloping pathways you'll find groves of orange and lemon trees, roses, and a swimming pool ringed with neoclassical balustrades.

There is a spacious and sunny bar, an elegant indoor dining room with a blazing fire in winter, and alfresco dining on the upper terrace under an arbor. The food is well prepared and the portions generous. Meals can include a salad of marinated fish, a terrine of fresh vegetables, fish crêpes, shellfish stew, duck with sherry sauce, and an ever-changing selection of fresh fish.

INCA

About 17 miles (27 km) north of Palma is Inca, the island's second largest city and Majorca's market and agricultural center.

Thursday is market day for farming equipment and livestock, but visitors will be more interested in the variety of low-priced leather goods—shoes, purses, jackets, and coats—sold here. In general, stores in Inca selling these leather goods are open Monday through Friday from 9:30am to 7pm and on Saturday from 9:30am to noon.

Modernization has deprived Inca of its original charm, but the parish church of Santa María la Mayor and the convent of San Jerónimo hold some interest, as does the original Son Fuster Inn, a reminder of an earlier, simpler era.

GETTING THERE **By Train** From Palma, trains (☎ **971/50-00-59**) run Monday through Saturday at the rate of 20 per day and 16 on Sunday. Trip time is only 35 minutes.

By Car Inca lies on C-713, the road leading to the Pollença-Formentor region.

WHERE TO DINE

Cellar Ca'n Amer. Carrer Miguel Durán. ☎ **971/50-12-61.** Fixed-price menu 2,000 ptas. ($16). AE, MC, V. Mon–Sat 1–5pm and 7pm–midnight, Sun 5pm–midnight. MAJORCAN.

If you can stay for lunch or dinner, we recommend this charming spot. In this building dating from 1850, you'll find the most authentic *cueva* dining on the island. The container of local wine, which everyone here seems to drink, is tapped from one of the dozens of casks that line the stone walls of the vaults. The interconnected dining rooms are furnished with wooden tables and rustic artifacts. A polite staff serves large portions of Majorcan specialties, including *lechona frit* (a mélange of minced pork offal fried and seasoned), bread and vegetable soup, Majorcan codfish, thrush wrapped in cabbage leaves, and the chef's version of roast suckling pig with a bitter but tasty sauce. There is also an array of fresh seafood and fish.

PORT DE POLLENÇA/FORMENTOR

Beside a sheltered bay and between Cape Formentor to the north and Cape del Pinar to the south lies Port de Pollença, amid two hills: Calvary to the west and Puig to the east. From the town, the best views of the resort and the bay are from Calvary Chapel. The bay provides excellent waterskiing and sailing. The location is 40 miles (65 km) north of Palma.

A series of low-rise hotels, private homes, restaurants, and snack bars line the very attractive beach, which is somewhat narrow at its northwestern end but has some of the island's finest, whitest sand and warmest, clearest water. For several miles along the bay there is a pleasant pedestrian promenade. There is only one luxury hotel in the area, however, and that is out on the Formentor Peninsula.

Tons of fine white sand were imported to the beach at the southeastern end of Pollença Bay to create a broad ribbon of sunbathing space that stretches for several miles along the bay's waters. Windsurfing, waterskiing, and scuba diving are among the water sports offered in the area.

Cabo de Formentor, "the devil's tail," can be reached from Port de Pollença via a spectacular road, twisting along to the lighthouse at the cape's end. Formentor is Majorca's fjord country—a dramatic landscape of mountains, pine trees, rock, and sea, plus some of the best beaches in Majorca. In Cape Formentor, you'll see *miradores,* or lookout windows, which provide panoramic views.

GETTING THERE By Bus Five buses a day leaving the Plaça Espanya in Palma, pass through Inca, and continue onto Port de Pollença.

By Car You can continue on from Deià (see above), along the C-710, or from Inca on the C-713 all the way to Pollença.

VISITOR INFORMATION The local tourist office (☎ **971/89-26-15**) on Carrer Formentor, behind Hotel Deià, is open May through October, Monday through Friday from 9am to 1pm and 4 to 7pm, Saturday from 9am to 1pm. It's closed off-season.

WHAT TO SEE & DO

The plunging cliffs and rocky coves of Majorca's northwestern coast are a stunning prelude to Port de Pollença. From the **Mirador de (del) Colomer** is an expansive view of the striking California-like coast that stretches from Punta de la Nau to Punta de la Troneta and includes El Colomer (Pigeon's Rock), named for the nests in its cave.

But it is the 12½-mile (20km) stretch of winding, at times vertiginous, road leading from Port de Pollença to the tip of the **Formentor Peninsula** that delivers the island's most intoxicating scenic visions. Cliffs over 650 feet high and spectacular rock-rimmed coves embrace intense turquoise waters. About halfway along this road is the **Cala de Pi de la Posada,** where you will find the Hotel Formentor and a lovely bathing beach. Continuing on to the end you'll come to the lighthouse at **Cabo de Formentor.**

Wednesday is **market day** in Port de Pollença, so head for the town square (there's only one) from 8am to 1pm and browse through the fresh produce, leather goods, embroidered tablecloths, ceramics, and more. Bargaining is part of the fun. Sunday is market day in the town of Pollença.

Alcúdia Bay is a long stretch of narrow, sandy beach with beautiful water backed by countless hotels, whose crowds rather overwhelm the beach in peak season. The nightlife is more abundant and varied here than in Port de Pollença.

Between Port de Alcúdia and Ca'n Picafort is the **Parc Natural de S'Albufera,** Carrertera Alcúdia-Artá, km 27, 07458 C'an Picafort (no phone). A wetlands area of lagoons, dunes, and canals covering some 1,975 acres, it attracts bird-watchers and other nature enthusiasts. To date, more than 200 species of birds have been sighted here, among them herons, owls, ospreys, and warblers. The best times to visit are spring and fall, when migratory birds abound. Spring, too, offers a marvelous display of flora. The park is open daily, except Christmas, from October 1 to March 30 from 9am to 5pm, and from April 1 to September 30 from 9am to 7pm. Visits are free, but you must get a permit at the reception center, where all motorized vehicles must be left. Binoculars are available for rent. The reception center has further information.

In the town of Pollença, about four miles (6km) from Port Pollença, is an 18th-century stairway leading up to an *ermita* (hermitage). Consisting of 365 stairs, it is known as the **Monte Calvario** (Calvary), but you can also reach the top by car via Carrer de las Cruces, which is lined with 10-foot-high concrete crosses.

Cala San Vicente, between Pollença and Port de Pollença, is a pleasant, small sandy cove with some notable surf. Several small hotels and restaurants provide the necessary amenities.

Exploring the Outdoors

Various companies offer tours of Pollença Bay, and many provide glass-bottom boats for viewing the varied aquatic creatures and plants. Many of these boats leave from Port de Pollença's Estación Marítim several times daily during the summer months, with less frequent departures in winter. Your hotel concierge or the marina can provide you with a schedule.

To arrange fishing expeditions or other water sport excursions, contact **Borrás Excursiones,** Port de Pollença (☎ **971/53-11-43**). **Bellini,** Carrer Médico Llopis, 9, Port de Pollença (☎ **971/53-32-95**) offers windsurfers, catamarans, and other small sailboats. They rent the equipment and provide instruction, but only from April through October.

An excellent way to experience and explore the area around Port de Pollença is on horseback. **Rancho Grande,** Carrer Polença (☎ **971/86-54-80**), organizes guided tours through the surrounding countryside.

Where to Stay: Puerto Pollença

Hotel Illa d'Or. Passeig Colón 265, 07470 Port de Pollença. ☎ **971/86-51-00.** Fax 971/86-42-13. 112 rms, 8 suites. A/C TEL. 12,000–19,500 ptas. ($96–$156) double; 14,000–21,500 ptas. ($112–$172) suite. Rates include breakfast. AE, DC, MC, V. Closed late Nov to early Feb.

Originally built in 1929, and enlarged and improved several times since then, this four-story hotel sits at the relatively isolated northwestern edge of Pollença Bay—far from the heavily congested, touristed region around Palma. Decorated in a mixture of colonial Spanish and English reproductions, it offers a seafront terrace with a view of the mountains and airy, simply furnished bedrooms. There's no swimming pool on the premises, but since the beach is just a few steps away, no one seems to care. A bar and a restaurant set the scene for socializing.

$ **Hotel Miramar.** Passeig Anglada Camarasa, 39, 07470 Port de Pollença. ☎ **971/53-33-30.** Fax 971/86-40-75. 69 rms. A/C TEL. 6,800 ptas. ($54.40) double. Rates include breakfast. AE, DC, V. Closed Nov–Mar.

This centrally located hotel is one of the grandly old-fashioned hostelries in town, in a desirable position across the coastal road from the beach. It has ornate front columns supporting a formal balustrade, tiled eaves, and several jardinieres. The lobby is furnished with antiques, and the formal dining room has views of the seas. Some rooms have private verandas overlooking the flower-filled courtyard in back. All the rooms are comfortably furnished and well maintained.

Hotel Pollentía. Passeig de Londres, s/n, 07470 Port de Pollença. ☎ **971/86-52-00.** Fax 971/53-12-00. 76 rms. TEL. 7,000 ptas. ($56) double. MC, V. Closed Dec–Mar.

This hotel is located half a mile from the commercial center of the resort, behind a screen of foliage. It's our favorite hotel in town, partly because of its cool, airy spaciousness and partly because of the genial reception. The steps leading to the formal modern lobby are banked with dozens of terra-cotta pots overflowing with ivy and geraniums. The reception area has Majorcan glass chandeliers, and many of the well-furnished rooms have private terraces. Guests have access to a private terrace overlooking the Mediterranean, and the dining room offers a fine fixed-price meal of regional dishes.

WHERE TO STAY: CABO DE FORMENTOR

✪ **Hotel Formentor.** Platja de Formentor, 07470 Port de Pollença. ☎ **971/86-53-00.** Fax 971/86-51-55. 103 rms, 24 suites. A/C MINIBAR TV TEL. 20,240–37,620 ptas. ($161.90–$300.95) double; 33,850–55,670 ptas. ($270.80–$445.35) suite. Rates include breakfast; half board 6,500 ptas. ($52) per person extra. AE, DC, MC, V. Closed early Jan to early Mar.

Set on an isolated, sprawling, intensely manicured expanse of scrub-covered peninsula that once served as a private farm, the Hotel Formentor is one of Europe's most spectacular and exclusive hotels. Far from the maddening crowds of Palma, on the island's northern tip, it's elegant and unpretentious. Most of it lies within a long, low-slung three-story building that's more modern-looking than its 1920s origins would imply. It has hosted an awesomely impressive roster of guests, including a 1995 summit meeting of the heads of state for all the countries in the European Union. Stage and film stars, and such religious icons as Tibet's Dalai Llama appear regularly. Accommodations are classically modern, spacious, and supremely comfortable, with some of the more expensive units containing reproductions of Iberian antiques that include elaborately carved beds. Terraced gardens descend gracefully to the resort's private beach.

WHERE TO DINE: PORT DE POLLENÇA

Corb Mari. Passeig Anglada Camarasa, 91. ☎ **971/53-10-40.** Reservations recommended. Main courses 1,000–4,000 ptas. ($8–$32); fixed-price menu 1,850 ptas. ($14.80). AE, DC, MC, V. Tues–Sun 1–3:30pm and 7–10:30pm. Closed Dec–Jan. MAJORCAN.

At Corb Mari, the best restaurant in town, you can dine in the outdoor courtyard or in the simple, tiled dining room. The menu consists largely of fish and meat. It is prepared over a flame fueled by the local Majorcan oak, *encina.* Specialties of the house include lobster, T-bone steaks, a succulent mixed grill of lamb chops, oysters, ribs of beef, and sherry-flavored kidneys. Occasionally a wild rabbit dish appears on the menu.

Stay Restaurant. Muelle Nuevo, Estació Marítima, s/n. ☎ **971/86-40-13.** Reservations recommended July–Aug. Main courses 1,700–2,600 ptas. ($13.60–$20.80); fixed-price menu 3,450 ptas. ($27.60). MC, V. Daily noon–4pm and 7:30–10:30pm. SPANISH/INTERNATIONAL.

Stay offers a unique menu that changes about every two months. Recipes depend on what's available at the market. Main courses include fresh salmon filets in a white wine sauce, roasted duck with a green peppercorn sauce, grilled fillet of beef with a wild mushroom sauce, and our favorite, the *parrillada de mariscos,* a platter of assorted grilled fish and seafood. Finish your meal with a strudel of fresh figs, almonds, and raisins smothered in a hot vanilla sauce.

Where to Dine: Pollença

✪ **Daus.** Escalonada Calvari, 10. ☎ **971/53-28-67.** Reservations recommended. Main courses 1,700–2,500 ptas. ($13.60–$20); fixed-price menu 2,850 ptas. ($22.80). MC, V. Wed–Mon 12:30–3pm and 7:30–11pm. MAJORCAN/SPANISH.

Located in the town of Pollença several miles from Port de Pollença, Daus sits at the bottom end of the 365 steps of Pollença's Monte Calvario (see "What to See & Do" above). If you're in the mood for a romantic meal, this is the place to come. The entranceway, adorned with a white drape and a large urn with a candle, sets the tone. The stone ceilings of its two dining areas recall its former function as the *bodega* (wine cellar) of the Jesuits. Soft, live classical music accompanies dinner on Wednesdays, Fridays, and Sundays except in July and August. You get all this and good food, too, as well as sophisticated service. The menu changes every few months; selections may include such excellently prepared fare as Majorcan rabbit, roast lamb, or sea bass stuffed with shrimp. We especially enjoy the *arroz negro,* rice with shrimp and cuttlefish in its own ink.

Majorca's East Coast: The *Cava* Route

Exploring the east coast of Majorca is often called the *cava* route because of the caves that stud the coastline. Though there are scores, we'll include only the most important ones; other places mentioned are Manacor, where cultured Majorcan pearls are manufactured, and Petra, home of Fray Junípero Serra, founder of many California missions. In general, the east coast of Majorca doesn't have the dramatic scenery of the west coast, but has worthy attractions in its own right.

Leave Palma on the freeway, but turn onto Carrertera C-715 in the direction of Manacor. About 35 miles (56km) east of Palma, you come to your first stop, Petra.

Petra

Founded by Jaume II, Petra grew up over the ruins of a Roman settlement. This was the birthplace of Father Junípero Serra (1713–84), the Franciscan priest who founded the missions in California that eventually grew into San Diego, Monterey, and San Francisco. A statue commemorates him at the Capitol building in Washington, D.C., and you will also see a statue of Father Serra in this, his native village.

The **Museo Beato Junípero Serra,** Carrer Barracar (☎ **971/56-11-49**) gives you an idea of how the island people lived in the 18th century. The property was bought and fixed up by the San Francisco Rotary Club, who then presented it as a gift to the citizens of Petra in 1972. The museum, which lies 500 yards from the center of the village, is open every day of the year but doesn't keep regular hours. Visits are by appointment only. Admission is free, but donations are encouraged.

Manacor

The C-715 continues east to Manacor, the town where the famous artificial pearls of Majorca are manufactured. The trade name for the pearls is "Perlas Majorica," so avoid such knock-offs as "Majorca" or "Majorca." You can visit the factories where the pearls are made, and purchase some if that is your desire.

The largest of these is **Perlas Majorica,** Vía Roma, 52 (☎ **971/55-02-00**), which offers organized tours. On the road to Palma at the edge of town, it is open Monday through Friday from 9am to 1pm and 2:30 to 7pm. On Saturday and Sunday, it is open from 10am to 1pm. Admission is free. They'll explain how the pearls are made (from fish scales that simulate the sheen of a real pearl). From shaping to polishing, some 300 artisans are employed. They are now used to being inspected by foreign visitors while at work. Perlas Majorica carry a 10-year guarantee.

CUEVAS DEL DRACH

From Manacor, take the road southeast to the sea—about 7½ miles (12km)—and the town of **Porto Cristo,** 38 miles (61km) east of Palma. Go a half mile south of town to **Cuevas del Drach (Caves of the Dragon)** (**☎ 971/82-07-53**), which contains an underground forest of stalactites and stalagmites as well as five subterranean lakes, where you can listen to a concert and later go boating à la Jules Verne. The roof appears to glitter with endless icicles. Martel Lake, 581 feet long, is the largest underground lake in the world. E. A. Martel, a French speleologist who charted the then mysterious caves in 1896, described it better than anyone: "As far as the eye can see, marble cascades, organ pipes, lace draperies, pendants or brilliants, hang suspended from the walls and roof." Tours depart daily, every hour from 10 am to 7 pm. Admission is 800 pesetas ($6.40).

If you don't have a car, you can take one of the four daily buses that leave from the railroad station in Palma (inquire at the tourist bureau in Palma for times of departure). The buses pass through Manacor on the way to Porto Cristo.

CUEVAS DEL HAM

Discovered in 1906, these caves, which in Majorcan mean "fish hooks," lie half a mile from Porto Cristo on the road to Manacor. The **Cuevas del Ham** (**☎ 971/82-09-88**) are far less impressive than the Cuevas del Drach, and can be skipped if you're rushed. They are open daily all year from 10am to 3:30pm, charging 1,100 pesetas ($8.80) admission for adults, but nothing for children under 12. These caves contain white stalactites and follow the course of an underground river. There is a link to the sea, so the water level inside the cave's pools rises and falls according to the tides.

✪ CUEVAS DE ARTÁ

Near Platja de Canyamel (Playa de Cañamel on some maps), Cuevas de Artá (**☎ 971/56-32-93**) lies on the stretch of land closing Canyamel Bay to the north. They are reached by a corniche road. These caves are said to be the inspiration for the Jules Verne tale *Journey to the Center of the Earth,* published in 1864. Formed by seawater erosion, the caves lie about 35 yards above sea level, and some of the "rooms" rise about 150 feet.

You enter an impressive vestibule. The black on the walls came from the torches used to light the caves for early tourists in the 1800s. There follows the *Reina de las Columnas* (Queen of the Columns), rising about 72 feet tall, then a lower room whose Dantesque appearance has led to it being called "Inferno." It is followed by a field of stalagmites and stalactites, the "Purgatory rooms," which eventually lead to the "theater" and "paradise."

Once used by pirates, centuries ago the caves provided a haven for *moriscos* fleeing the persecution of Jaume I. The stairs in the cave were built for Isabella II for her 1860 visit. In time, such luminaries as Sarah Bernhardt, Alexandre Dumas, and Victor Hugo, arrived for the tour. Tours depart daily, every half-hour from 10am to 5pm. Admission is 900 pesetas ($7.20).

2 Ibiza & Formentera

Ibiza was once a virtually unknown and unvisited island; Majorca, its bigger neighbor, got all the business. But in the 1950s, Ibiza's art colony began to thrive, and in the 1960s it became the European resort most favored by that era's "flower children." A New York art student once wrote, "Even those who come to Ibiza (Ee-*bee*-tha) for the 'wrong' reason (to work!) eventually are seduced by the island's easy life. Little chores like picking up the mail from the post office stretch into day-long missions." Today, Ibiza is overrun by middle-class package-tour tourists, mainly from England, France, Germany, and Scandinavia.

At 225 square miles, it is the third largest of the Balearic Islands. Physically, Ibiza has a jagged coastline, some fine beaches, whitewashed houses, secluded bays, cliffs, and a hilly terrain dotted with fig and olive trees. Warmer than Majorca, it's a better choice for a winter holiday, but it can be sweltering in July and August. Thousands of tourists descend on the island in summer, greatly taxing the island's limited water supply.

Many liberated travelers still arrive dreaming of soft drugs and hard sex. Both exist in great abundance, but there are dangers. It's common to pick up the local paper and read the list of the latest group of people deported because of *irresponsibilidad economica* (no money) or *conducta antisocial* (drunk and disorderly conduct). Many young travelers, frankly, have forsaken Ibiza, taking a ferry 40 minutes away (and just three miles as the crow flies) to the tiny island of Formentera, where they find less harassment (although anyone looking suspicious will be checked out here too). Formentera is the most southern of the Balearic Islands, and because of limited accommodations, restaurants, and nightlife, it is most often visited on a day trip from Ibiza.

Eivissa is the local (Catalán) name for Ibiza. Catalán is the most common language of the island, but it is a dialectal variation—called *eivissenc* or *ibicenco*. The same language is spoken on Formentera.

GETTING THERE Again, as with Palma, if you come in July and August, be sure you have a return ticket and a reservation. Stories of passengers who were stranded for days in Ibiza in midsummer are legend.

By Plane **Iberia** (☎ **971/30-25-80**) flies into Es Cordola International Airport, located 3½ miles (5.5km) from Ciudad de Ibiza. Four daily flights connect Ibiza with Palma de Majorca, and five flights a day arrive from Barcelona. It's also possible to take one of two daily flights from Valencia or one of four from Madrid.

By Ferry **Transmediterránea,** Avinguda B.V. Ramón (☎ **971/31-41-73**), operates a ferry service to Barcelona at the rate of five per week, costing 6,305 pesetas ($50.45) for a one-way ticket. Six boats per week also depart from Valencia, with a one-way ticket going for 5,260 pesetas ($42.10). From Palma, there's one ferry per week; it costs 4,600 pesetas ($37.30) one way. Check with travel agents in Barcelona, Valencia, or Palma regarding ferry schedules. You can also book tickets through any agent.

GETTING AROUND If you land at Es Cordola airport outside Ciudad de Ibiza, you will find bus service for the 3½-mile (9km) ride into town. Sometimes taxis are shared. In Ciudad de Ibiza, buses leave for the airport from Avinguda Isidor Macabich, 24 (by the ticket kiosk), every hour on the hour daily from 7am to 10pm.

Once in Ibiza, you'll have to walk, but the city is compact and can be covered on foot. There are buses, however, leaving for the nearby beaches. The two main bus terminals are at Avinguda Isidor Macabich, 20 and 42.

One of the most popular means of getting around the island, especially in the south, is by a moped or bicycle. Rental arrangements can be made through **Moto Sud,** Avinguda de la Paz, s/n (☎ **971/30-24-42**). Mopeds cost from 3,000 pesetas ($24) per day.

If you'd like to rent a car, both **Hertz** and **Avis** have offices at the airport.

VISITOR INFORMATION The tourist information office is located at Vara de Rey, 13, in Ciudad de Ibiza (☎ **971/30-19-00**). It is open Monday through Friday from 9:30am to 1:30pm and 5 to 7pm, Saturday from 10:30am to 1pm.

CIUDAD DE IBIZA

Ciudad de Ibiza, the island's capital, was founded by the Carthaginians 2,500 years ago. Today the town consists of a lively marina district around the harbor and an old town (*D'Alt Vila*) with narrow, cobblestone streets and flat-roofed, whitewashed houses. The marina is usually clogged with yachts, whereas the district's main street, Vara de Rey, is a constant spectacle of people—from old fishermen and an occasional native Ibizan woman swathed in black to the ubiquitous, scantily clad tourist. The marina district is also fun to wander about with its art galleries, dance clubs, boutiques, bars, and restaurants.

Much of the medieval character of the old town has been preserved, in spite of massive development elsewhere. Many houses have Gothic styling and open onto spacious courtyards. These houses, some of which are 500 years old, are often festooned with geraniums and bougainvillea. The old quarter is entered through the Puerta de la Tablas, flanked by Roman statues.

Plaça Desamparadors, crowded with open-air restaurants and market stalls, lies at the top of the town. Traffic leaves town through the Portal Nou.

WHAT TO SEE & DO

Although Ibiza is primarily a destination for sun and fun, there are also two sightseeing attractions worth a special visit.

Museu D'Alt Vila (Museum of Archaeology). Plaça de Catedral, 3. ☎ **971/31-12-31.** Admission 450 ptas. ($3.60). Mon–Sat 10am–1pm and 4–7pm. Closed holidays.

Located in D'Alt Vila, Ibiza's old town, this museum in a former arsenal houses the world's most important collection of Punic remains. It contains pottery and other artifacts from prehistoric sites in Formentera and Ibiza, and Punic terra-cotta figurines and other items from the sanctuaries of Illa Plana (7th to 5th centuries B.C.) and Cuieram (4th to 2nd centuries B.C.). Also on display are vases, figurines, and other Carthaginian artifacts found in the island's burial grounds. Examples of Roman epigraphs, sculpture, and small glass bottles are included in the exhibit. Other displays include Moorish artifacts (10th to 13th centuries A.D.), various Christian wooden and stone sculptures, plus 14th- to 16th-century ceramics.

Museu Puig d'Es Molins. Vía Romana, 31. ☎ **971/30-17-71.** Admission 450 ptas. (same ticket as for museum above). Mon–Sat 10am–1pm.

This museum, at the foot of the necropolis of Puig d'Es Molins, contains a collection of Punic (Phoenician) relics, including hand-painted vases from the 7th and 6th centuries B.C., Carthaginian amulets, Punic terra-cotta figurines and busts, and a collection of coins found on the island. Many objects here were discovered in the area that served as a cemetery for the city's inhabitants from 654 B.C., the accepted date for the founding of Ibiza, to the 3rd century A.D. The necropolis is about 550 yards from the center of the city.

OUTDOOR ACTIVITIES

Beaches These strips of sand, of course, are the allure of Ibiza—that and its unique lifestyle, which often combines high fashion with the worst sort of packaged tourism. The very chic and the very unchic are both attracted to the island.

The most popular (and overcrowded) beaches are Playa Talamanca in the north and Ses Figueretes (also called Playa Figueretes) in the south. Beach sophisticates often seek out remoter spots, including many where it is commonplace to sunbathe completely nude. The best beaches are connected by boats and buses. The remoter ones require a private car or private boat. Both Playa Talamanca and Ses Figueretes are near Ciudad de Ibiza, as is another popular beach, Playa d'en Bossa lying to the south.

To avoid the hordes here, keep going until you reach Las Salinas, near the old salt flats farther south. Here beaches include Playa Cavallet, one of the officially designated nudist strands, although nudism doesn't always follow official designations laid down by Ibizan law.

The most horrendously overcrowded beach in Ibiza is Playa San Antonio at San Antonio de Portmany—if it got any worse, you'd have to stand up instead of lie down! However, a boat or bus will take you to several beaches southwest of the town, all of which are far less congested. These include Cala Bassa, Port des Torrent, Cala Tarida, and Cala Conta.

Santa Eulalia de Rio, site of the third major tourist development in Ibiza, has a less crowded beach, but it's also less impressive. If you stay in this east coast town, you can find a better beach at Cala Llonga in the south or at one of the beaches along the north, including Playa d'es Caná and Cala Lleña. These beaches are among the finest on Ibiza.

If you venture to the north coast, you'll discover more good beaches at the tourist developments of Portinatz, which is at the very northern tip, and at Puerto de San Miguel, which lies north of the small town of San Miguel. The quickest way to reach San Miguel from Ciudad de Ibiza is to go inland via Santa Gerturdis, and then north. Along the way, you'll pass Rio de Santa Eulalia, the only river in the Balearics.

Sports & Fitness **Ahmara, Centro Deportivo,** Carretera Sant Josep (2.7km), on the road to Sant Josep (☎ **971/30-77-62**), offers the best collection of health equipment on the island, along with a swimming pool, hot tub, sauna, and even a Turkish bath with massage. There's a restaurant, grill, and bar, plus four squash courts. Badminton and indoor football are also played here. Tennis courts (and lessons) are also available.

Tennis In addition to Ahmara (mentioned above), you'll find five public tennis courts at Port Sant Miquel (☎ **971/33-30-19**).

SHOPPING

Fashion has been an important Ibiza industry since the late 1960s, when a nonconformist fashion philosophy took hold, combining elements of the traditional *pitiusa* attire of the natives and the natural, free-flowing garments of the hippies who flocked here in the 1960s. In recent years Ibizan designs have become much more sophisticated and complex, but the individualistic spirit has not wavered.

Joy Borne. Carrer Josep Verdera, 14. ☎ **971/31-09-72.**

This is the premier place on the island to purchase outrageous clothes and funky accessories. Designs may be embellished with feathers, sequins, or other eye-catching accents. Customers of Joy Borne can purchase the daring, outlandish garb that has become synonymous with fashion in Ibiza.

Lucky Lizard. Mestre Joan Mayans, 2. ☎ **971/31-47-06.**

Lucky Lizard is Ibiza's foremost purveyor of funky accessories and bold but chic footwear. Beverly Feldman's daring designs are created for those who prefer to take a fashion risk.

Pedro's. Carrer Aníbal, 8. ☎ **971/31-30-26.**

At the corner of Conde Rosselón, master artisan Pedro Planells creates hand-sewn, original leather goods. Many items can be custom-made. Pedro creates stylish accessories, as well as home furnishings in leather and silver. Well-heeled clients have included everyone from international celebrities to King Juan Carlos. Pedro's does not keep set hours, and during the off-season, hours and days vary.

Sandal Shop. Plaça De Vila, 2. ☎ **971/30-54-75.**

The Sandal Shop sells high quality leather goods, made by a cast of local artisans. One-of-a-kind accessories, including bejeweled belts and leather bags, are designed for individual clients. Custom-made sandals can be created to suit personal fashion tastes.

Where to Stay

The chances of finding space in peak summer months are dismal, more so than in any Mediterranean resort in Spain. At other overcrowded resorts, such as those on the Costa Brava and Costa del Sol, a visitor—faced with the no-vacancy sign—can always press on or go inland to find a room for the night. But in Ibiza, because of infrequent transportation, a visitor without a reservation in July and August can land in a trap. You may end up sleeping on the beach on an air mattress (if the police let you; there are camping areas), even though your pockets are bulging with pesetas.

The island is not always prepared for its hordes of international tourists. The hotels can't be built fast enough. Many of the hastily erected ones sprouting up in San Antonio de Portmany, Santa Eulalia del Rio—even on the outskirts of Ciudad de Ibiza—are more frame than picture.

At most resorts you can write ahead to make a reservation. But at hotel after hotel on the island of Ibiza, you can't do this. Individual bookings in most establishments range from the horrifically difficult to the impossible. In many cases hoteliers don't bother to answer requests for space in summer. Armed with a nice fat contract from a British tour group, they're not interested in the plight of the stranded pilgrim.

So if you're set on going to Ibiza during the summer, book through a package tour to ensure an iron-clad reservation. In the less-busy months, however, using your credit card to reserve a room is enough to guarantee a hotel room upon your arrival.

In Town

In town, hotels are limited and often lack style and amenities, except for the following recommendations.

Hotel Royal Plaza. Carrer Pedro Francés, 27–29, 07800 Ibiza. ☎ **800/528-1234** in the U.S., or 971/31-00-00. Fax 971/31-40-95. 117 rms, 5 suites. A/C MINIBAR TV TEL. 11,900–20,600 ptas. ($95.20–$164.80) double; 21,600–38,500 ptas. ($172.80–$308) suite. AE, DC, MC, V.

Located three blocks from the port, this six-story modern hotel offers in-town convenience plus a casual, resortlike atmosphere. For those who wish to stay within Ciudad de Ibiza, this is the premier choice. The marble reception lobby exudes elegance. Well-appointed accommodations are carpeted; most have private terraces. The rooftop pool offers a sunbathing platform, with commanding views of the port and town of Ibiza.

Dining/Entertainment: During the summer months, the Plaza Snack Bar/Restaurant serves good meals; snacks are available daily from 11:30am to midnight and meals from 1:30 to 4pm and 8:30 to 11:30pm. The hotel's bar is open daily from 8am to 11pm.

Services: Room service (daily 8am to midnight), laundry, currency exchange. **Facilities:** Rooftop pool, conference room, car rentals.

Moderate

El Corsario. Carrer Ponent, 5, 07800 Ibiza. ☎ **971/30-12-48.** Fax 971/39-19-53. 14 rms, 1 suite. 10,500–12,500 ptas. ($84–$100) double; 20,000 ptas. ($160) suite. AE, DC, MC, V. Closed Nov–Mar.

After your taxi deposits you near the church below, you'll have to walk the last 500 feet up a hill to reach this hotel, located within a labyrinth of cobblestone pedestrian walkways. The house was founded in 1570, and it is rumored that its terraces were built by corsairs. The modest rooms are pleasant and clean, often containing antiques. Some overlook an enclosed garden of trailing bougainvillea and cultivated flowers. The hotel's restaurant is one of the most romantic places to dine (see the restaurant recommendations below). No parking is available.

Hostal Residencia Montesol. Vara de Rey, 2, 07800 Ibiza. ☎ **971/31-01-61.** 55 rms. TEL. 9,300 ptas. ($74.40) double. MC, V.

Located next to the Café Montesol, Hostal Montesol—short on charm—offers clean, convenient accommodations. Its proximity to the marina affords panoramic views of the sea. The simple rooms are outfitted with rather sterile white-tiled floors and comfortable but uninspired furnishings.

Inexpensive

Hostal Aragón. Carrer Aragón, 54, 07800 Ibiza. ☎ **971/30-60-60.** 8 rms (with sink only). 6,000 ptas. ($48) double. No credit cards.

Lleo Marchuet is often cited for running one of the finest and most reasonably priced "one-star" hotels in town. No meals are served, but many cafés and restaurants are within walking distance. Climb one flight of stairs to enter this simple but clean environment. Rooms are modestly furnished, but the welcome compensates. Arrangements can be made to accommodate families of four, and TV is available upon request.

Sol y Brisa. Avinguda B.V. Ramón, 15, 07800 Ibiza. ☎ **971/31-08-18.** 20 rms (with sink only). 2,600 ptas. ($20.80) double. No credit cards.

This is an utterly basic hostelry, yet it is clean and well maintained, and the owners are helpful. Young people on low budgets are especially fond of this place, which attracts a lot of American students in summer. Bedrooms are tiny, containing tile floors, which somehow make them seem cooler in July and August. Two courtyards are filled with plants in the old style of an *ibicenco* house.

In Playa de Ses Figueretes

On the edge of town, a number of modern beach hotels have been erected that are far superior to the ones in the city. With few exceptions, most are booked solidly in summer by tour groups.

Cénit. Arxiduc Lluís Salvador, 07800 Ibiza. ☎ **971/30-14-04.** Fax 971/30-07-54. 62 rms. TEL. 7,500 ptas. ($60) double. AE, DC, MC, V. Closed Nov–Mar.

Although way down in pecking order from Los Molinos (see below), this is still the bargain place to stay here. Circular in shape, the hotel looks like a quartered wedding cake. In the pueblo style, each floor has been staggered so as to provide a terrace for the rooms above. The accommodations are routine, but comfortable. The curved dining room, with its picture windows, is a pleasant place to enjoy a continental breakfast. The Cénit, which has a pool, is perched on a hillside, a short walk from the beach.

Los Molinos. Ramón Muntaner, 60, 07800 Ibiza. ☎ **971/30-22-50.** Fax 971/30-25-04. 154 rms. A/C TV TEL. 16,500 ptas. ($132) double. AE, DC, V. Parking 1,500 ptas. ($12).

This modern resort—a favorite with "snowbirds" from the north of Europe—situated less than a mile from Ibiza town, is the finest hotel in Ses Figueretes. Nestled between the water and a medieval village, Los Molinos offers its clientele resort life combined with proximity to town. The accommodations, most with private terraces facing the sea, are comfortably furnished, with safes, carpets, and twin beds pushed together European style. Public areas include a dining room with views of the Mediterranean, two bars, and a café providing snacks throughout the day. The hotel has two pools (one is heated).

WHERE TO DINE

It's hard to find authentic Ibizan cookery. The clientele and often the chefs are mainly from Europe, and the menu choices cater almost exclusively to their tastes.

Because of the lack of agriculture in some parts of the island, fish has always been the mainstay of the diet of these Mediterranean people. But budget travelers may be put off by the price of some of this fare. Once the cheapest item you could order on a menu, fish is now one of the most expensive. The fish is sautéed, baked, or broiled and might be blended in a fisher's rice, *arros à la pescadora. Parrillada* and *zarzuela* are two stewlike dishes containing a wide assortment of fish.

As in Majorca, the pig is important in the diet. Some islanders feed figs to these animals to sweeten their meat, meat that is turned into such pungent cooked sausages as *sobrasadas* or *longanizas.*

A local dish, occasionally offered on some menus, is a *sofrit pages,* a stew made with three kinds of meat and poultry—chicken, pork, and lamb—then cooked with pepper, cloves, cinnamon, and garlic. One of the best seafood plates is *borrida de rajada,* crayfish in an almond sauce.

The most famous dessert is *flaó,* a kind of cheesecake to which mint and anisette are added for flavoring. *Greixonera* is a spiced pudding, and *maccarrones de San Juan* is cinnamon- and lemon-flavored milk baked with cheese.

Wines are shipped over from the mainland; however, islanders make alcohol-based herbal concoctions. These include *rumaniseta,* made from rosemary, and *frigola,* golden in color and very sweet, with a strong aroma coming from wild thyme. A rather bitter aperitif known as *balo* comes from locally grown carob. For special occasions, islanders treasure *hierbas ibicencas,* made with numerous local herbs, including anise.

El Brasero. Carrer Barcelona, 4. ☎ **971/31-14-69.** Reservations required. Main courses 1,800–3,000 ptas. ($14.40–$24). MC, V. Daily 8pm–midnight. Closed Nov 15–Mar. INTERNATIONAL.

This is one of the best-known and most popular places on the island, catering to a wide range of tastes. The cookery is robust and filled with flavor—chicken salad, grilled meats, asparagus gratiné, duckling with honey, beef filet in hot sauce, and a steamy fish stew. There is also a sidewalk café section. It is elegantly decorated in a black-and-white bistro style.

El Corsario. Carrer Ponent, 5. ☎ **971/30-12-48.** Reservations required. Main courses 1,500–3,000 ptas. ($12–$24). MC, V. Daily 8–11pm. Closed Nov–Apr. INTERNATIONAL.

Although we've reviewed its accommodations above, the dining room, with its panoramic view, is so romantic that it deserves special mention. This 400-year-old flower-draped villa is near the hilltop fortress. Your taxi will deposit you about 500 feet down the hill in a square fronting an old church, and you must climb the slippery cobblestones to reach it. There's a stand-up bar, two pleasant dining rooms with a handful of neatly laid tables, and a view of the harbor. Menu specialties include various kinds of pasta, two different preparations of lamb, and especially fresh fish brought up from the harbor. The cookery is rather home style and well prepared, especially if you stick to the fish dishes.

El Portalón. Plaça dels Desamparats, 1–2. ☎ **971/30-39-01.** Reservations recommended. Main courses 2,000–3,800 ptas. ($16–$30). AE, MC, V. Mon–Sat 12:30–3:30pm, daily 8pm–12:30am. Closed mid-Jan to mid-Feb. SPANISH/INTERNATIONAL.

Before you hit the bars (go very late, as is the fashion), dine here, in the old town. Alfresco courtyard dining is a lure, as is an often handsome crowd. El Portalón attracts gay as well as straight couples, usually European. The food is a combination of Spanish, Catalán, and continental. It's expensive, but worth the extra pesetas.

S'Oficina. Avinguda d'Espanya, 6. ☎ **971/30-00-16.** Reservations recommended. Main courses 1,800–6,000 ptas. ($14.40–$48). AE, DC, MC, V. Mon–Fri 1:30–4pm, daily 8:30pm–12:30am. Closed Dec. BASQUE.

One of the better restaurants in the city center, S'Oficina serves large portions—perhaps a combination shellfish and shrimp platter, hake with shellfish sauce, veal dishes, or a seafish soup. You might begin with a terrine of foie gras, and follow with sea bass in Calvados. Although a relatively simple restaurant, the food is surprisingly sophisticated. The interior is air-conditioned and there is also a garden and terrace.

Ciudad de Ibiza After Dark

Casino de Ibiza. Passeig Juan Carlos I (Passeig Marítim). ☎ **971/31-33-12.** Casino entrance, 500 ptas. ($4); dinner and show 5,000–6,000 ptas. ($40–$48).

Here gamblers will find the usual gaming tables and slot machines in a quiet, modern setting. You need your passport to get in. The adjoining nightclub offers live cabaret entertainment several nights a week from May through October. It opens at 9:30pm, and the show begins at 10:15pm. The slot-machine room is open daily from 6pm to 6am in summer and to 5am in winter. The casino's hours are daily from 10pm to 5am in summer and to 4am in winter.

Montesol. Vara de Rey, 2. ☎ **971/31-01-61.**

The crowd at this hotel bar, a short walk from the harbor on the main street, is likely to include both the well-established foreign community, the newly arrived social climbers, and Spaniards along for the view. In many ways this is the greatest multi-ring circus in town, made more pleasant by the well-prepared tapas and the generous drinks. If you enjoy people-watching, sit at one of the sidewalk tables. Inside, you'll find an interior of white tiles, mirrors, and tones of brown and pink. Montesol is open daily from 8am to midnight.

Pacha. Passeig Marítim, s/n. ☎ **971/31-36-12.** Cover 3,000 ptas. ($24).

Frequented by beautiful people of all ages in their ultrachic clothes and kinky coifs, this spacious split-level disco near the casino (see above) has several dance floors and numerous bars. In summer, overheated dancers can cool off in the swimming pool. The music, primarily droning disco and rap, evokes a pounding cadence of jackhammers. Open May through October, daily from midnight to 6am; November through April, Friday and Saturday from midnight to 6am.

The Gay Scene

Ibiza attracts more gay men than any other island resort in Europe. The nude beach— *playa natural* —is at **Es Cavallet,** south of Ciudad de Ibiza. It contains a gay section at the far end with lots of "in back of the bushes" action near the Bar Chirin Gay.

At night, Ciudad de Ibiza is the scene of the most action. There may be more tourists at San Antonio de Portmany, but it has been the scene of some gay-bashing.

Most of the gay clubs in Ciudad de Ibiza are situated either in the old town, near the Ayuntamiento (Town Hall) or grouped along Carrer de la Virgen.

Catwalk, Carrer de la Virgen, 42 (☎ **971/31-42-79**), is a hot gay bar, open daily from 9pm to 3am.

Crisco, Carrer Ignacio Riquer, 2 (☎ **971/30-17-19**), lies in D'Alt Vila, the old quarter. It is closed from January through March, but otherwise open nightly from 10pm to 4am. The club is for those who wear jeans, cut their hair short, and preferably have a mustache. The air conditioning comes in handy for those who show up on a hot night in leather. All ages go here, and X-rated video shows are presented in the dark room downstairs.

Exis, Carrer de la Virgen, 57 (no phone), offers perfectly made cocktails and soothing tropical drinks. If you're feeling elegant, ask for a bottle of Catalán *cueva* (champagne). It is open daily from April through October from 8pm to 4am. It has a terrace and garden and stages shows (often drag) once a week.

SAN ANTONIO DE PORTMANY

Known as Portus Magnus to the Romans and before that a Bronze Age settlement, this thriving town was discovered in the 1950s by foreigners and has remained popular ever since. Tourism here is "mega-mass." The town today goes by two names—San Antonio de Portmany for Spanish speakers or Sant Antoni de Portmany for Catalán speakers.

In summer you have as much chance of finding a room here as you would of booking a reservation on the last flight to the moon if the earth were on fire. Virtually all the hotels have a direct pipeline to tour-group agencies in northern Europe, and the individual traveler probably won't get the time of day. If you're determined to stay in the area during peak travel season, your best bet is to try and arrange a package tour.

The resort, with a 14th-century parish church, is built on an attractive bay. Avoid the impossibly overcrowded narrow strip of sand at San Antonio itself. Take a ferry or bus to one of the major beaches, including Cala Gració, one mile (1.6km) to the north, set against a backdrop of pines, or Port des Torrent, three miles (5km) southwest. Cala Bassa in the south is also popular. San Antonia overlooks the Isla Conejera, an uninhabited rock island. With its hordes of visitors, San Antonio has a joie de vivre, plus lots of mildly entertaining nightlife. Even if you're staying in Ibiza or Santa Eulalia, you may want to hop over for the day or evening.

But San Antonio is not for the conservative. It's not unusual to see topless (or bottomless) women on the beach—and even topless in dance clubs. Note, however, that even though marijuana is common here, buying and selling it is strictly against the law.

When visiting hooligans have had too much cheap booze and *vino,* San Antonio can get dangerous. In the earlier part of the evening, however, you may want to patronize one of the bars or open-air terraces around Avinguda Doctor Fleming.

GETTING THERE **By Bus** Buses leave from Ciudad de Ibiza every 30 minutes.

VISITOR INFORMATION The tourist information office is at Passeig de Pontes (☎ **971/34-33-63**). It's open Monday through Friday from 10am to 8:30pm and Saturday and Sunday from 9:30am to 1pm May through October. Off-season hours are Monday through Saturday from 9:30am to 1pm.

What to See & Do

Throughout the day boats leave from Passeig de Ses Fonts. They will take you to Cala Bassa, a sandy beach on a thin strip, for 115 pesetas (90¢) one way, or to Cala Conta, a slightly rocky beach, for 125 pesetas ($1). If you negotiate, they'll also take you along the coastline northwest to the far point of Portinatx. This is virtually the only way to see the coastline, since there isn't a road running along it, and most visitors agree it's the most beautiful coastline of Ibiza.

North of the waterfront, the chief attraction is **Sa Cova de Santa Agnès,** a national monument and an object of eerie devotion. This has been a place of sacred worship ever since a sailor prayed to Santa Agnès during a rough storm and was saved. The sailor, to show his gratitude, placed a figure of the saint in this dark hole. It's become a place of pilgrimage ever since, and it's open free on Monday and again on Saturday from 9am to noon.

If you have rented a car you can also explore **Cueva de Ses Fontanelles,** north of Platja Calad Salada, where faintly colorful prehistoric paintings decorate the walls. The site is usually open daily from 9am to 5pm (but don't count on it), and admission is free.

Offshore at the popular southern beach of Cala d'Hort is the intriguing **Es Vedrá rock,** where, in times of hardship and hunger, the Ibicencos would go, at great personal risk, to gather seagull eggs for survival. A Carmelite priest once recorded mystical revelations and meetings with "unearthly beings surrounded by light" while meditating on the island. Gigantic circles of light, up to 165 feet in diameter, have allegedly emerged from the sea here at times, discouraging fishers from working the area. It is said that a strong magnetic force emanating from Es Vedrá attracts such strange phenomena. Photographers and romantics take note: After June 15 the sunrise here is especially dramatic, illuminating Es Vedrá while the surrounding hills remain in darkness.

Where to Stay

The prospect of finding a room here in July and August is bleak—some Brits reserve a year in advance. British package tourists virtually occupy the crescent beach and busy harbor all during the warm months. You'll stand a better chance of finding lodgings in Ciudad de Ibiza.

Expensive

Hotel Village. Urbanización Caló den Real (along the road to Cala Tarida), 07830 Sant Josep, Ibiza. ☎ **971/80-00-34.** Fax 971/80-80-27. 20 rms, 3 suites. MINIBAR TV TEL. 21,000–24,500 ptas. ($168–$196) double; 35,000 ptas. ($280) suite. Rates include breakfast. AE, DC, MC, V.

Located 15 miles west of Ibiza Town, this small, elegant hotel is one of our favorite refuges on the island. Just beyond the gleaming white marble lobby sits a cozy bar, ideal for aperitifs. Guest rooms, also done in white marble, have terraces, most facing the sea, but several open onto the mountains. A walkway leads down the hill to the rocky beach, where guests can lounge in the sun and enjoy a drink at the beachside bar.

Dining/Entertainment: International cuisine with a Spanish influence is served in the elegant dining room.

Services: Room service.

Facilities: Tennis courts, fitness center, whirlpool, sauna, putting green.

Les Jardins de Palerm. Apartado, 62, 07830 San José, Ibiza. ☎ **971/80-03-18.** Fax 971/80-04-53. 8 rms, 1 suite. TV TEL 16,000–42,000 ptas. ($128–$336) double; 42,000 ptas. ($336) suite. Rates include breakfast. AE, DC, MC, V. Closed Nov–Feb.

This intimate little hotel, located outside of the village of San José, is constructed in the style of a 17th-century hacienda. Patios and garden terraces scattered throughout the grounds are ideal locations for sunbathing or just enjoying a lazy Ibiza afternoon. A large outdoor pool is perfect for an afternoon dip. The accommodations are rustic, with beamed ceilings, antiques, and ceiling fans. Each has its own terrace. The popular restaurant is a local hangout, so reservations are a must. Prices change every month—the lowest price quoted above is charged in the cool months of March, the highest tariff for the hot month of August.

Pikes. Apartado 104, 07820 San Antonio, Ibiza. ☎ **971/34-22-22.** Fax 971/34-23-12. 22 units. A/C MINIBAR TV TEL. 18,000–33,000 ptas. ($144–$264) double; 28,000–90,000 ptas. ($224–$720) suite. Rates include breakfast. AE, DC, MC, V. Children under 12 must be accompanied by a nanny.

Originally a farm or *finca,* this 600-year-old compound has been transformed into a luxurious playground for well-heeled travelers and celebrities from around the world. Touted for its "sophisticated informality," Pikes boasts rooms with sensuous interiors, including king-size beds and oversized bathtubs. The hotel provides activities and entertainment for its guests ranging from flamenco shows to costume balls. The Pikes also provides a VIP card that allows VIP entrance to most of the area's clubs and casinos.

Dining/Entertainment: The hotel's restaurant serves an international cuisine in a series of intimate dining rooms. A poolside bar is provided for sunbathers.

Services: 24-hour room service, massage, laundry, VIP card.

Facilities: Car rental, boat charter, beauty salon, outdoor pool, sauna, solarium, tennis court, Jacuzzi, fitness center; management will arrange boating, golfing, and horseback riding.

Moderate

Arenal Hotel. Avinguda Doctor Fleming, 16, 07820 San Antonio. ☎ **971/34-01-12.** Fax 971/34-25-65. 131 rms. TEL. 9,800 ptas. ($78.40) double. DC, MC, V.

This selection ranks among the top hotels in San Antonio de Portmany, offering value comparable to that of more expensively priced neighbors. During high season groups take over, but in October and from April to mid-May you can generally get a reservation if you write two weeks in advance. Off-season, all you need to do is arrive.

Located at the edge of town on its own private beach, the Arenal is a four-story establishment with a swimming pool. The rooms are simple and attractive, furnished in contemporary style with comfortable beds and a balcony opening onto the sea or the little front garden lawn with palm trees.

Inexpensive

Hotel Tropical. Cervantes, s/n, 07820 San Antonio. ☎ **971/34-00-50.** 142 rms. TEL. 8,200 ptas. ($65.60) double. Rates include half board. AE, DC, MC, V. Closed Nov–Mar.

Located away from the port area in a commercial section of town, this hotel's garden and swimming pool are across the street from the hotel's main building. The recreation area is like a small public park with dozens of reclining chairs and some billiard tables. The hotel was built in the early 1960s with a russet and white-marbled lobby filled with armchairs. The Tropical is rated as one of the best hotels in the center, with comfortably furnished, modernized but rather bland bedrooms.

Where to Dine

Many of Ibiza's restaurants are tucked away in quiet coves or in the countryside, so you really need a car to sample the full range of the island's culinary savoir-faire.

Expensive

✪ **Cana Juana.** Sant José, 9 miles (14km) from Ibiza Town, on road to San José. ☎ **971/80-01-58.** Reservations recommended. Main courses 1,200–3,600 ptas. ($9.60–$28.80). AE, DC, MC, V. Daily 1:30–3:30pm and 8pm–midnight. Closed Oct 16–Dec 29. INTERNATIONAL.

This centuries-old country villa has been converted into the finest restaurant on the island. The menu is composed of Catalán specialties: main courses may include codfish with spinach, raisins, and pine nuts; *confit de canard* (duck) served with beans; potatoes with sea-urchin sauce; *dorada* (John Dory) with vinegar, olive oil, garlic, and lamb's lettuce. The cellar features an extensive selection of Spanish wines, with a vintage to complement any meal.

Moderate

Restaurante/Bar Rias Baixas. Carrer Ignacio Riguer, 4. ☎ **971/34-04-80.** Reservations required. Main courses 1,900–3,000 ptas. ($15.20–$24). AE, DC, MC, V. Tues–Sun 8pm–midnight. Closed mid-Dec to Jan. GALICIAN.

This rustic air-conditioned Iberian dining room, with its stucco arches, beamed ceiling, and open fireplace is an apt setting for the Galician specialties served here. Seafood, flown in fresh every day from northern Spain, is the restaurant's specialty—mussels, Galician clams, crabmeat soup, *caldo gallego* (Galician broth), trout meunière, and Bilbao-style eels, each accompanied by a selection of Galician wine. Good-tasting beef, pork, and veal dishes are also available.

Sa Capella. Carretera de Santa Inés 0.5km. ☎ **971/34-00-57.** Reservations recommended. Main courses 1,900–2,500 ptas. ($15.20–$20). MC, V. Daily 8pm–midnight. Closed Nov–Mar. IBICENCO.

This restaurant is set in a 600-year-old chapel with stone vaulting, rose windows, radiating alcoves, balconies, and chandeliers that can be lowered on pulleys from the overhead masonry. You pass beneath an arbor of magenta-colored bougainvillea and are ushered to your table by a waiter dressed in red-and-white traditional Ibizan costume. Meals include fisher's soup, seafood cocktail, sole meunière, eels Bilbao-style, Basque-style *rape* (monkfish), marinated mussels, rabbit, and pepper steak. Each dish is individually prepared, filled with flavor, and beautifully served. This dining choice deservedly has a devoted following.

Inexpensive

El Rincón de Pepe. Sant Mateu, 6. ☎ **971/34-06-97.** Tapas 500–700 ptas. ($4–$5.60); main courses 800–2,000 ptas. ($6.40–$16). Daily 11am–1:30am. TAPAS/SNACKS.

This friendly, simple café, primarily a place for tapas and light snacks, also serves a menu that includes Spanish dishes, as well as hamburgers, hot dogs, and a variety of fresh salads. The food is simple and good, the atmosphere convivial, and the bar an attractive arrangement in tile and wood.

THE NORTHERN COAST

The north remains largely untainted by the scourge of mass tourism, except for a handful of coves. Here you'll find some of the island's prettiest countryside, with fields of olive, almond, and carob trees and the occasional *finca* raising melons or grapes.

WHAT TO SEE & DO

Off the road leading into Port de Sant Miquel (Puerto de San Miguel) is the **Cova de Can Merca,** about 300 feet from the Hotel Galeón. There is a fine view of the bay from the snack bar. After a stunning descent down stairs that cling to the face of the cliff, you enter a cave that's more than 100,000 years old and forms its stalactites and stalagmites at the rate of about a quarter inch (1cm) per 100 years. A favored hiding place for smugglers and their goods in former days, today it's a beautifully orchestrated surrealistic experience—including a sound-and-light display—not unlike walking through a Dalí painting. Many of the limestone formations are delicate miniatures. The half-hour tour is conducted in several languages for groups of up to 70. From Holy Week to the end of October, tours are offered daily every half hour from 10am to 7pm. Admission is 650 pesetas ($5.20) for adults and 350 pesetas ($2.80) for children.

At the island's northern tip is **Portinatx,** a pretty series of beaches and bays now marred by a string of souvenir shops and haphazardly built hotels. For a taste of its original, rugged beauty, go past all the construction to the jagged coast along the open sea.

Every Saturday throughout the year there is a **flea market** just beyond Sant Carles (San Carlos) on the road to Santa Eulalia (you'll know where it is by all the cars parked along the road). Open from about 10am until 8 or 9pm, it offers all kinds of clothing (both antique and new), accessories, crafts, and the usual odds and ends.

If you want to escape to a lovely beach that remains a stranger to hotel construction, head for **Playa Benirras** just north of Port de Sant Miquel. An unpaved but passable road leads out to this small, calm, pretty cove, where lounge chairs are available and pedal boats are for rent. There are also snack bars and restaurants here.

A beautiful drive is that from Sant Carles (San Carlos) along the coast to Cala Sant Vicent (San Vicente).

Where to Stay

The hotel offerings are more limited in the north than in the traditional pockets of tourism in the south and west. Nevertheless, the island's finest hotel, the five-star Hacienda, is here, above Na Xamena Bay. Port de Sant Miquel, Cala Sant Vicent, and Portinatx—once tranquil, seaside havens—have become increasingly pockmarked with package-tour hotels.

Very Expensive

✪ **Hotel Hacienda.** Na Xamena, 07815 San Miguel (Apartado 423), Ibiza. ☎ **71/33-45-00.** Fax 971/33-45-14. 53 rms, 10 suites. A/C MINIBAR TV TEL. 19,000–39,600 ptas. ($152–$316.80) double; 24,500–41,800 ptas. ($196–$334.40) suite. AE, DC, MC, V. Closed Nov to mid-Apr.

Located 14 miles (22km) northwest of Ciudad de Ibiza, this Moorish villa, set on a promontory overlooking Na Xamena Bay, is the top destination on Ibiza for well-heeled travelers and celebrities seeking leisure and sanctuary. Luxury, informality, privacy, and personal service—the Hacienda has it all. Public rooms are full of various cubbyholes, ideal for cozying up to a book or travel companion. Diners gather at tables beside the large outdoor pool during the warmer months. Spacious guest rooms are individualized, decorated with four-poster beds, sumptuous carpets, and balconies that overlook the Mediterranean. Many rooms have marble baths and private Jacuzzis.

Dining/Entertainment: The hotel has an excellent terrace restaurant providing panoramic vistas of the surrounding cliffs and sea. An indoor restaurant serves à la carte menus. A bar offers snacks, and a pub/disco is available for evening entertainment.

Services: Room service, massage, laundry.

Facilities: Three swimming pools (including one for children), a tennis court, billiard room, beauty salon, bicycle rentals, horseback riding, boat rentals, fishing excursions arranged on request.

Inexpensive

Hotel Galeón. Puerto de San Miguel, 07815 Sant Joan de Labritja, Ibiza. ☎ **971/33-45-34.** 184 rms. 11,000 ptas. ($88) double. Rates include breakfast. AE, DC, MC, V. Closed Nov–Apr.

One of two hotels overlooking the little bay, this basic hotel offers simple, clean, comfortable guest rooms. Accommodations have terraces with views of the sea. Tennis courts and water sports are available. The hotel's restaurant serves a good but rather uninspired cuisine.

SANTA EULALIA DEL RIO

Once patronized by expatriate artists from the capital, nine miles (14km) to the south, Santa Eulalia del Rio now attracts mostly middle-class northern Europeans.

Santa Eulalia is at the foot of the Puig de Missa, on the estuary of the only river in the Balearics. The principal monument in town is a fortress church standing on a hilltop, or *puig*. Dating from the 16th century, it has an ornate Gothic altar screen.

Santa Eulalia is relatively free of the sometimes plastic quality of San Antonio. Visitors often have a better chance of finding accommodations here than in the other two major towns.

GETTING THERE **By Bus** During the day buses run between Ciudad de Ibiza and Santa Eulalia del Rio every 30 minutes.

By Boat Fourteen boats a day run between Ciudad de Ibiza and Santa Eulalia del Rio. The boat ride takes 45 minutes.

VISITOR INFORMATION The tourist information office is at Carrer Mariano Riquer Wallis (☎ **971/33-07-28**), open Monday through Friday from 9:30am to 1:30pm and 5 to 7:30pm, Saturday from 9:30am to 1:30pm.

WHAT TO SEE & DO

You can reach the famous northern beaches from Santa Eulalia either by bus or boat, departing from the harborfront near the boat basin. **Aigües Blanques** is one of the best beaches, lying six miles (10km) north. (It's legal to go nude there.) It's reached by four buses a day. A long, sandy cove, **Cala Llonga,** lies three miles (5km) south and is reached by ten buses a day. Cala Llonga fronts a bevy of package-tour hotels, so it's likely to be crowded. Boats also depart Santa Eulalia for Cala Llonga every 30 minutes from 9am to 6pm. **Es Caná** is a white-sand beach, three miles (5km) north of town; boats and buses leave every 30 minutes from 8am to 9pm. Four buses a day also depart for **Cala Llenya** and **Cala Nova.**

WHERE TO STAY

Expensive

Hotel S'Argamassa Sol. Urbanización S'Argamassa, 07182 Santa Eulalia del Rio. ☎ **971/33-00-51.** Fax 971/33-00-76. 230 rms. TEL. 14,000 ptas. ($112) double. AE, DC, MC, V. Closed Nov–Apr.

Two miles (3km) outside Santa Eulalia del Rio, near Roman ruins, the Hotel S'Argamassa is a well-run, family-oriented resort. The hotel is a short walk from the beach and maintains its own small pier. All guest rooms have terraces with sea views. Accommodations are comfortable; many have been recently renovated. The hotel provides an outdoor pool, bowling alley, playground, tennis courts, and a game room. For evening entertainment, music and dancing are offered in the lounge or cocktails at the poolside bar.

Moderate

Hotel Ses Estaques. Ses Estaques, 07840 Santa Eulalia del Rio. ☎ **971/33-00-69.** Fax 971/33-04-86. 165 rms. TEL. 7,140–11,590 ptas. ($57.10–$92.70) double. Rates include breakfast. AE, DC, MC, V. Closed Nov–Apr.

A much-favored hotel in this resort, close to the seashore at the edge of town, the Ses Estaques is open only in the good weather months. A beautiful garden filled with roses, palms, and ivy surrounds it, and the swimming pool is edged with pines and a poolside snackbar. Inside, it's filled with extra touches and hideaway corners of charm. There's an aquarium in the spacious lobby, a pleasant tropical restaurant on the beach a short walk away, and a tennis court. Each of the comfortable terrazzo-floored bedrooms has a balcony with a view of the garden or the sea.

Hotel Tres Torres. Ses Estaques, s/n, 07840 Santa Eulalia del Rio. ☎ **971/33-03-26.** Fax 971/33-20-85. 114 rms, 4 suites. TEL. 9,000–11,500 ptas. ($72–$92) double; 14,000 ptas. ($112) suite. Rates include breakfast. AE, DC, MC, V. Closed Nov–Apr.

A stylish modern hotel, where many of the comfortable balconied rooms overlook the two swimming pools, Hotel Tres Torres has a disco and a comfortable lobby filled with neo-Victorian wicker chairs. An airy and sunny dining room offers a view of the water.

Inexpensive

Hotel Riomar. Playa Dels Pins, s/n, 07840 Santa Eulalia del Rio. ☎ **971/33-03-27.** 120 rms. TEL. 7,500 ptas. ($60) double. No credit cards.

Built on the beach, this hotel has six floors of good-sized, nicely furnished bedrooms, each opening onto a small balcony. Try to get one of the sea-view rooms. Meals here offer only standard fare but are reasonably priced.

Where to Dine

Doña Margarita. Passeig Marítim, s/n. ☎ **971/33-06-55.** Reservations required. Main courses 1,000–3,000 ptas. ($8–$24). AE, DC. Tues–Sun 1–4pm, daily 7:30–11:30pm. Closed Nov. SPANISH.

This large, simple, yet surprisingly elegant restaurant on the Passeig Marítim serves very good food. The solidly traditional menu seems to please the many locals who come here to dine in the air-conditioned restaurant or on the panoramic sea-view terraces. The dishes include mussels marinara, paella, filet of beef with peppers and asparagus gratiné, salmon with green peppercorns, calves' kidneys with fried onions, and beef stew. The extensive menu changes greatly from day to day, depending on market offerings. The fish dishes are more market-sensitive.

El Naranjo. Carrer San José, 31. ☎ **971/33-03-24.** Reservations required. Main courses 1,900–2,300 ptas. ($15.20–$18.40). AE, MC, V. Tues–Sun 7–11:30pm. Closed Nov–Feb. CONTINENTAL.

This chic nighttime rendezvous is altogether the most beautiful courtyard in town. Many refer to this place as "The Orange Tree," its name in English. The orange tree patio, with its flowering bougainvillea vines, has such appeal that many diners don't mind its out-of-the-way location (in town, several blocks from the water). If your table isn't ready when you arrive, enjoy an aperitif in the cozy bar. The menu items are beautifully prepared and served. One newspaper called the chef "an artist." Dishes include fresh fish and duckling in red-currant-and-pepper sauce. Begin with *las tres mousses* (three mousses) as an appetizer, finishing with the lemon tart for dessert.

FORMENTERA

For years, Formentera was known as the "forgotten Balearic." The smallest of the archipelago, it's a 30-square-mile, flat limestone plain. In the east it is flanked by La Mola, a peak rising 615 feet, and in the west it is protected by Berberia at 315 feet.

The Romans called it Frumentaria (meaning "wheat granary"), when they oversaw it as a booming little agricultural center. But that was then: a shortage of water and strong winds has allowed only meager vegetation to grow, notably some fig trees and fields of wild rosemary (which seem to be home to thousands of green lizards).

A few hearty goats live on the island, and, like Ibiza, Formentera has a salt industry. Its year-round population of 5,000 swells in summer, mostly with day trippers from Ibiza. Limited hotels have kept development in check, and most visitors come over for the day to enjoy the beaches, where they often swim without bathing suits and sunbathe along the excellent stretches of sand. British and Germans form the majority of tourists—that is, those who actually spend the night.

On the ferry ride over from Ibiza, you pass Isla Ahorcados, or hanged men's island, where criminals from Ibiza were once strung up, and the more reassuring Isla Espalmador, with its sandy beaches. Carry some seasickness pills, as the ferry crossing can be turbulent.

ESSENTIALS

GETTING THERE **By Ferry** Formentera is serviced by up to 29 boat passages a day in summer and by about a dozen per day in winter. Boats depart from Ciudad de Ibiza, on Ibiza's southern coast, for La Savina (La Sabina), two miles (3km) north of the island's capital and largest settlement, Sant Francesc (San Francisco Javier). Depending on the design of the boat you select, passage across the three-mile (5km) channel separating the islands takes between 35 and 75 minutes. For information on Formentera, call **971/34-28-71,** although it's usually easier to ask the staff at virtually any hotel on the island, who are all usually well versed in the hours of ferryboats to and from Ibiza.

GETTING AROUND As ferryboats arrive at the quays of La Savina, taxis line up at the pier. One-way passage to such points as Es Pujols and Playa de Mitjorn costs 1,000 pesetas ($8) and 2,000 pesetas ($16), respectively, although it's always wise to negotiate or predetermine the fare before the journey begins. To call a taxi in Sant Francesc, dial **971/32-20-16;** in Pujols, **971/32-80-16;** and in La Savina, **971/32-20-02.** Regardless of when and where you call for a taxi, be prepared to wait.

Car rentals can be arranged through Avis (☎ **971/32-28-17**), whose kiosk lies at La Savina, close to where you'll disembark from the ferryboats.

If you wear protection from the often harsh sun, you might enjoy seeing Formentera by a bicycle or a motor scooter. These can be rented from **Moto-Rent** in La Savina (☎ **971/32-02-84**) or in Pujols (☎ **971/32-24-88**). Motor scooters rent for 2,000 pesetas ($16) a day; bicycles for around 550 pesetas ($4.40) a day.

VISITOR INFORMATION The tourist office at Formentera is **Es Puhols,** Plaça Constitució, 1, in Port de la Savina (☎ **971/32-20-57**), open Monday through Friday from 10am to 2pm and 5 to 7pm, Saturday from 10am to 2pm.

WHAT TO SEE & DO

Beaches, beaches, and more beaches—that's why visitors come here. You can see the ocean from any point on the island. Some say the island has the best beaches in the Mediterranean—an opinion with much merit. Formentera has been declared a "World Treasure" by UNESCO, one of four places so honored because of its special character as an ecological and wildlife preserve. This implies an indirect control by UNESCO of activities that could jeopardize the island's ecological well-being.

Meanwhile, day trippers from Ibiza have fun sampling its long, sedate beaches and solitary coves before returning to Ibiza's ebullience in the evening.

The island is virtually ringed with beaches, so selecting the one that you think will appeal to you is about the only problem you'll face—that and whether or not you should wear a bathing suit.

Playa de Mitjorn, on the southern coast, is three miles (5km) long and obviously there are many uncrowded sections. This is the principal area for nude sunbathing. A few bars and hotels occupy the relatively undeveloped stretch of sand. You can make **Es Copinyars,** the name of one of the beachfronts, your stop for lunch, as it has a number of restaurants and snack bars.

At **Es Calo,** along the northern coast, west of El Pilar, there are some small boarding houses, called *hostales.* From this point, you can see the lighthouse of La Mola, which was featured in Jules Verne's *Journey Round the Solar System,* and, if weather conditions are right, Majorca.

Sant Ferran serves the beach of **Es Pujols,** darling of the package-tour operators. This is the most crowded beach on Formentera, and you may want to avoid it. The beaches, however, are pure white sand, with a backdrop of dunes and pine trees. It's also a place to go windsurfing and is the site of several tourist amenities. The beach is protected by the Punta Prima headland.

Westward, **Cala Sahona** is another popular tourist spot, lying near the lighthouse on Cabo Berberia. Often pleasure vessels anchor here on what is the most beautiful cove in Formentera.

WHERE TO STAY

Accommodations are scarce and you must arrive with an iron-clad reservation should you want to spend the night or a longer time.

Club La Mola. Apartado 23, Sant Ferran, 07871 Playa de Mitjorn, Formentera. ☎ **971/32-70-69.** 329 rms. 13,500–17,000 ptas. ($108–$136) double. AE, DC, MC, V. Closed mid-Oct to Apr.

Located at Es Arenals, this hotel is one of the best equipped on the island, and during the summer it is usually packed. Opening onto the longest beach on the island, La Mola is constructed in the style of a Spanish village. Rooms are comfortable and well furnished. Facilities include two swimming pools, tennis courts, much equipment for water sports, a gym, a garden, mini-golf, and a disco. The restaurant serves Spanish and continental meals, but it's only standard fare.

Club Punta Prima. Punta Prima, 07871 Sant Ferran. ☎ **971/32-82-44.** Fax 971/32-81-28. 64 rms, 40 suites. TV TEL. 17,400 ptas. ($139.20) double; 21,400 ptas. ($171.20) suite. Rates include half board. AE, MC, V. Closed Nov–Apr.

Built in 1987 in a low-slung, two-story format that hugs the coastline, a short walk from the beach, this is the best and best-accessorized hotel on Formentera, with a loyal clientele from northern Europe, which tends to return year after year. Bedrooms are comfortably furnished and well maintained—the best Formentera has to offer. Virtually everyone checks in here on the half-board plan, indulging in meals that are, more often than not, served as an ongoing series of buffets. Great attention has been paid to the enhancement and preservation of the site's isolated natural beauty.

Sa Volta. Apartado 71, Sant Ferran, 07871 Es Pujols, Formentera. ☎ **971/32-81-25.** Fax 971/32-82-28. 25 rms. TEL. 9,000 ptas. ($72) double. Rates include breakfast. AE, DC, MC, V.

This is a small hostal with good, clean but very modest rooms, charging reasonable prices. It has a cafeteria but no restaurant. However, you are in the midst of many cafés, restaurants, and nightlife possibilities, because this is "the tourist belt" of Formentera. Reserve well in advance; it's hard to get a room here. The word is out.

Where to Dine

Es Molí del Sal. Ses Illetes (al Noroeste). ☎ **908/13-67-73** (note different area code from rest of Balearics). Reservations required. Main courses 1,200–2,500 ptas. ($9.60–$20). AE, MC, V. Daily 12:30–11pm. Closed Nov–Apr. SPANISH/CATALÁN.

Near the salt flats, this restaurant, the island's best, is in a restored windmill. It opens onto Platja de Ses Illetes, that slender northern tip of Formentera, which is the most desirable beachfront on the island. A small restaurant, it specializes in fresh fish and lobster and seems to please everybody. The cookery, although hardly spectacular, is good, simple fare prepared with fresh ingredients. The view of the sea and of Ibiza is panoramic.

3 Minorca

Minorca (also written Menorca) is one of the most beautiful islands in the Mediterranean; miles of lovely beaches have made it a longtime favorite vacation spot for Europeans.

Barely 9 miles (14.5km) wide and less than 32 miles (52km) long, its principal city is Mahón (also called Maó), population 25,000, set on a rocky bluff overlooking the great port, which was fought over for centuries by the British, French, and Spanish.

After Majorca, it is the second largest of the Spanish Balearic Islands, but it has more beaches than Majorca, Ibiza, and Formentera combined—they range from miles-long silver or golden crescents of sand to rocky bays, or *calas,* reminiscent of Norwegian fjords.

The beaches along 135 miles (218km) of pine-fringed coastline are the island's greatest attraction, though many of its beaches and coves are not connected by roads. Nude bathing is commonplace, although the practice is officially illegal. Golf, tennis, and sailing are available at reasonable fees, and windsurfing is offered at all major beaches.

With about 60,000 permanent inhabitants, Minorca plays host to about half a million visitors a year. But it is not overrun with tourist developments and has none of the junky excess that has plagued Ibiza and Majorca for years.

Unlike those islands, Minorca is not utterly dependent on tourism; it has some industry, including leatherwork, costume jewelry making, dairy farming, and even gin manufacturing. Life here is quieter and more relaxed; it is not a place to go for glittering nightlife. Some clubs in Ibiza *open* only at 4 in the morning, whereas on Minorca nearly everybody, local and visitor alike, is in bed well before then.

In addition to trips to the beach, there are some fascinating things to do for those interested in history, archaeology, music, and art. Many artists live in Minorca, and exhibitions of their work are listed regularly in the local paper. The Cathedral of Santa María in Mahón has one of the great pipe organs of Europe, and world-famous organists have appeared here, giving free concerts.

In the south some 1,600 archaeological sites were found, dating back to prehistoric times. Of the mysterious monuments unearthed, the most spectacular are the *taulas,* Stonehenge-type structures made from two slabs of rock forming the letter "T." Known only on Minorca, these megalithic structures are often more than 12 feet high.

GETTING THERE Minorca, lying off the eastern coast of Spain and northeast of Majorca, is reached by air or sea. The most popular method of reaching Minorca, certainly the quickest, is to fly, though you can take a ferry from mainland Spain or from the other two major Balearic Islands, Ibiza and Majorca.

It is always good to arrive with everything arranged in advance—hotel rooms, car rentals, ferry or airplane tickets. In July and August, reservations are vital, because of the limited hotel and transportation facilities.

By Plane The **Minorca International Airport** (☎ **971/15-70-00** for information) lies two miles (3km) outside the capital city of Mahón. It receives dozens of charter flights, mainly from Germany, Italy, the Scandinavian countries, and Britain. However, both **Iberia** and **Aviaco** (☎ **971/36-90-15** for information on both airlines) also operate regularly scheduled domestic flights from Barcelona, Palma de Majorca, and even Madrid.

By Ferry Regular service, which operates frequently in the summer, connects Minorca with Barcelona, Palma de Majorca, and Ibiza. From Barcelona, the journey takes seven to eight hours aboard moderately luxurious lines. If you're on a real budget but still want a decent night's sleep, bunk in a four-person cabin, which is about the same price as a chair in the lounge. Meals can be purchased in a self-service restaurant on board or else brought along if you're on a strict budget.

The ferry service is operated by **Transmediterránea,** whose offices in Mahón are at Estació Marítima, along Moll (Andén) de Ponent (☎ **971/36-60-50**), open from 8:30am to 1pm and 4 to 6pm Monday through Friday. Saturday hours are from 8:30am to noon, and Sunday hours from 3 to 6:30pm. However, any travel agency in Barcelona or Palma, even Ibiza, can book you a ticket; you need not go directly to one of the company's offices.

GETTING AROUND **By Bus** **Transportes Menorca (TMSA),** Carrer Joseph M. Quadrado, 7 (☎ **971/36-03-61**), off Plaça s'Esplanada in Mahón, operates bus service around the island. The tourist office (see Mahón "Visitor Information" below) has complete bus schedules for the island.

By Car A good local company is **British Car-Hire G.B. International,** Plaça s'Esplanada in Mahón (☎ **971/36-24-32**), with rentals beginning at 3,000 pesetas ($24) per day. The Spanish-owned **Atesa** (☎ **971/36-62-13**) operates a desk at the airport, charging from 6,500 pesetas ($52) for its cheaper models. **Avis** (☎ **971/36-15-76**) also operates out of the airport, asking from 8,000 pesetas ($64) for its cheapest cars. Car-rental firms on the island will deliver a vehicle either to the airport upon your arrival or later after you check into your hotel—but you must specify in advance.

By Taxi To summon a local taxi, call **971/36-12-83** or **971/36-28-91.** The taxi stop is at Plaça s'Esplanada in Mahón. Typical fares—say, from Mahón to the beaches at Cala'n Porter—are 1,650 pesetas ($13.20) one way.

By Bike & Moped Try **Just Bicicletas,** Carrer Infanta, 19 (☎ **971/36-47-51**), in Mahón.

MAHÓN (MAÓ)

Mahón and neighboring Villacarlos still show traces of British occupation—gorgeous Georgian architecture and Chippendale reproductions. There's also Golden Farm, the magnificent mansion north of the capital, overlooking Mahón harbor, where in October 1799 Admiral Lord Nelson enjoyed a brief rest and, according to local legend, hid out with his lady love, Emma Hamilton. But actually, Nelson was here alone working on *Sketches of My Life.*

The largest city on the island, Mahón is an east coast port. In the Minorcan language, it is called Maó. Mahón lent its name to one of the world's most popular sauces, mayonnaise.

Mahón was built on the site of an old castle standing on a cliff overlooking one of Europe's finest natural harbors, some 3 1/2 miles (5.5km) long. The castle and the town wall erected to dissuade pirates are long gone, except for the archway of San Roque.

The first Christian king from the mainland, Alfonso II, established a base in the harbor in 1287. It became known as **Isla del Rey** (Island of the King). When the British constructed a hospital here to tend to wounded soldiers, it was called "Bloody Island."

Since 1722, when the seat of government was moved here from Ciudadela, Mahón has been the capital of Minorca.

GETTING THERE **By Taxi** From the airport (see above), you must take a taxi into Mahón, as there is no bus link.

By Bus Mahón is the bus transport depot for the island, with departures from Plaça s'Esplanada in the heart of town. The most popular run—six buses per day—is to Ciudadela, but there are also connections to other parts of the island. The tourist office (see "Visitor Information," below) distributes a list of schedules, and the list is also published in the local newspaper *Menorca Diario Insular*. Tickets are purchased once you're aboard. Make sure you carry some change.

VISITOR INFORMATION The tourist office is at Plaça s'Esplanada, 40 (**☎ 971/36-37-90**), open Monday through Friday from 8am to 3pm and 5 to 7pm, Saturday from 9:30am to 1pm.

City Layout

The heart of Mahón is the **Plaça de la Constitució,** with its Town Hall from the 18th century, constructed in an English Palladian style.

Plaça s'Esplanada, seat of the tourist office and the bus departure point, is actually the main square. Here on Sundays locals gather to enjoy ice cream, the best in the Balearics. In summer, a market is held on Tuesday and Saturday from 9am to 2pm. Island artisans from all over the island sell their wares at that time.

The northern boundary of the city is formed by the **Puerto de Mahón,** which has many restaurants and shops, lying along Muelle Comercial.

Mahón is not a beach town, but has some accommodations, and is the center of the best shopping and nightclubs. The closest beaches for swimming are those at **Es Grau** and **Cala Mesquida.**

Villacarlos stretches east along the port, a virtual extension of the capital, and it doesn't have beaches either. Several good restaurants line the harbor leading toward Villacarlos. When the British founded this village, now a southeast suburb of Mahón, they called it Georgetown.

What to See & Do

Most people don't take sightseeing too seriously in Mahón, as they are here mainly to enjoy the views of the port, to dine, or to shop. Even so, you may want to visit the **Església de Santa María la Major,** Plaça Constitució. It was founded in 1287 by the Christian conqueror Alfonso III, who wanted to celebrate the Reconquest. Over the years, the original Gothic structure has been much altered, and it was rebuilt in 1772. Its organ is celebrated, having been constructed in 1810 by Johan Kyburz, a Swiss artisan. Admiral Collingwood brought it to Mahón during the Napoleonic wars. It has four keyboards and more than 3,000 pipes. A music festival in July and August "showcases" the organ, whose melodic sounds can be heard even as you sit drinking in a nearby café.

An hour-long **catamaran tour** of the port with submarine-like views of underwater life is offered Monday through Saturday, with seven tours a day, costing 800 pesetas ($6.40) for adults and 400 pesetas ($3.20) for children under 11. Tickets can be purchased at Xoriguer Gin Distillery, Moll de Ponent, 93 (☎ **971/36-21-97**).

You can also visit the **Xoriguer Gin Distillery** on the harborfront at Moll de Ponent, 93 (see above). Here giant copper vats simmer over wood-fed fires. Later, after watching the process by which the famed Minorcan gin is made, you can taste more than a dozen brews. The distillery and a store selling the products, including some potent liqueurs, is open Monday through Friday 8am to 7pm and Saturday 9am to 1pm.

Prehistoric Monuments From Mahón you can take excursions to some of the prehistoric relics in the area. One of these, signposted off the Mahón-Villacarlos highway, is **Trepucó,** where you'll find both a 13-foot *taula* and a *talayot* (circular stone tower). The megalithic monuments stand on the road to San Lluís, only about a mile from Mahón. Of all the prehistoric remains on the island, this is the easiest to visit. It was excavated by Margaret Murray and a team from Cambridge University in the 1930s.

Another legacy of prehistoric people can be visited at km 4 (a stone marker) off the Mahón-Ciudadela highway. The trail to **Talatí de Dalt** is signposted. Your path will lead to this *taula* with subterranean caves.

Another impressive prehistoric monument is **Torre d'en Gaumés,** nine miles (14.5km) from Mahón off the route to Son Bou (the path is signposted). You can take a bus from Mahón to Son Bou if you don't have a car. This megalithic settlement spreads over many acres, including both *taulas* and *talayots,* along with some ancient caves in which people once lived. The exact location is two miles (3km) south of Alayor off the road to Son Bou.

The restored **Naveta d'es Tudons** is accessible three miles (5km) east of Ciudadela, just to the south of the road to Mahón. This is the best-preserved and the most significant prehistoric collection of megalithic monuments on Minorca. Its *naveta* (a boat-shaped monument thought to be a dwelling or a burial chamber) is said to be among the oldest monuments constructed by humans in Europe. Archaeologists have found the remains of many bodies at this site, along with a collection of prehistoric artifacts, including pottery, decorative jewelry, and weapons—although these have been removed to museums. The site is more easily visited if you're staying in Ciudadela.

OUTDOOR ACTIVITIES

Beaches **Cala'n Porter,** seven miles (11km) west of Mahón, is one of the most spectacular beaches on the island. It's a sandy beach at a narrow estuary inlet protected by high promontories. Thinly scattered houses perch upon a cliff. You can drop in on a bar here during the day, where refreshments are "obligatory." **La Cova d'en Xoroi,** ancient troglodyte habitations overlooking the sea from the upper part of the cliffs, can also be visited (see below).

Going around the cliff face you'll discover more caves at **Cala Caves.** People still live in some of these caves. There are boat trips to see them from Cala'n Porter.

North of Mahón on the road to Fornells you'll encounter many beachside settlements. Close to Mahón and already being overly exploited is **Cala Mesquida,** one of the best beaches. To reach it turn off the road to Cala Llonga and follow the signs to "Playa."

The next fork in the road takes you to **Es Grau,** another fine beach. Along the way you see the salt marshes of S'Albufera, abundant in migrant birds. Reached by bus from Mahón, Es Grau, lying five miles (8km) north of Mahón, opens onto a sandy bay and gets very crowded in July and August. From Es Grau you can take a boat to **Illa d'en Colom,** an island in the bay with some good beaches. There are several bars at Es Grau for "refueling."

South of Mahón is the little town of San Lluís and the large sandy beach to the east, **Punta Prima.** Patronized heavily by occupants of the local *urbanizaciones,* this beach is serviced by buses from Mahón, with six departures daily. The same buses will take you to the attractive "necklace" of beaches, the **Platges de Son Bou,** on the southern shore. Many tourist facilities are found here (see below).

Golf The only course is **Urbanización Son Parc** (☎ **971/36-88-06**), a traditional nine-hole course that recently added another nine holes.

Horseback Riding For an equestrian tour of the island (subject to demand), call **Es Fornás** at **971/36-44-22** in Mahón. Both beginner and advanced riders are accommodated. Tours by carriage can also be arranged by Es Fornás.

Windsurfing & Sailing The best possibilities are at Fornells Bay, which is a mile wide and several miles long. The best outfitter is **Windsurfing Fornells** (☎ **971/37-66-36** for more information).

SHOPPING

Looky Boutique. Carrer de Ses Moreres, 43. ☎ **971/36-06-48.**

This shop is Minorca's outlet for chic, elegant leather accessories, which are produced in the company's factory in Ciudadela. The shop sells exquisite handbags, shoes, and leather clothing for men and women. Open Monday through Friday from 9am to 1pm and 5 to 8:30pm, Saturday from 9am to 1pm. Other locations include a shop in Ciudadela, at José María Quadradro, 10 (☎ **971/38-19-32**), and in Fornells, at Passeig Marítim, 23 (☎ **971/37-65-45**).

Patricia. Carrer de Ses Moreres, 31. ☎ **971/36-91-78.**

Another of Minorca's outlets for fine leather goods, Patricia sells locally produced jackets, suits, skirts, and accessories. Other shops are located at Camino Santandria/Ronda Baleares (☎ **971/38-50-56**) in Ciudadela, and Carrer Poeta Gumersindo Riera, 1 (☎ **971/37-65-73**). All three shops are open Monday through Friday from 9:30am to 1:30pm and 5 to 8pm, Saturday from 9:30am to 1:30pm.

Es Portal. Sa Ravaleta, 23. ☎ **971/36-30-36.**

Es Portal supplies Minorca's chic men and women with fashions from such cutting-edge designers as Moschino, Versace, Christian Lacroix, Dolce & Gabbana, and Armand Basi. Designs by Ibiza favorite Armin Henemann are also featured. Sophisticated accessories and shoes are also available. Summer hours are Monday through Friday from 10am to 1:30pm; off-season, Monday through Friday from 10am to 1:30pm and 5 to 8:30pm, Saturday from 10am to 1:30pm.

WHERE TO STAY

Expensive

Hotel Port Mahón. Avinguda Fort de L'Eau, 07701 Mahón. ☎ **971/36-26-00.** Fax 971/36-26-50. 72 rms, 2 suites. A/C TV TEL. 9,000–24,000 ptas. ($72–$192) double; 20,000–38,000 ptas. ($160–$304) suite for two. Rates include breakfast. AE, DC, MC, V.

Perched on a steep hillside above the harbor, this hotel looks like a large Georgian villa, whose charms are largely of another era. It is, without question, the most traditional accommodation in Minorca, located in a residential neighborhood. It's one of the few large hotels that stays open all year, and half of its rooms are usually reserved for tour groups. Some guests have been coming here since the 1950s, which indicates the age level of many of the patrons.

There is a pervading sense of calm and unhurried comfort in the airy stone-floored public areas. The bedrooms overlook the harbor, the bougainvillea-filled garden, or the quiet street outside. Each has an ornate balcony with louvered shutters and potted flowers. Elegant touches abound, like the stone cherub riding a carved snail that splashes water into a swimming pool.

The dining room, a popular spot for visitors, serves good-tasting regional and international meals daily from 1 to 3pm and 8 to 10pm.

Moderate

Hotel Capri. Sant Esteve, 8, 07703 Mahón. ☎ **971/36-14-00.** Fax 971/35-08-53. 75 rms. A/C TV TEL. 12,000 ptas. ($96) double. AE, DC, MC, V.

If you don't stay at the more expensive and superior Hotel Port Mahón (see above), this comfortable, modern hotel, conveniently situated in the heart of Mahón, is the next best choice. Each well-furnished room has a private terrace and piped-in music. The hotel has an inviting lounge, a snack bar, and a cafeteria, but no full restaurant. The Capri, unlike many hotels on the island, is open year-round. The hotel is geared more to businesspeople than tourists and offers no pool but includes such extras as room service until midnight, turndown service, and babysitting upon request.

Hotel del Almirante (Collingwood House). Carretera de Villacarlos, s/n, 07700 Mahón. ☎ **971/36-27-00.** Fax 971/36-27-04. 40 rms. 6,300–13,120 ptas. ($50.40–$104.95) double. Rates include breakfast. No credit cards. Closed Nov–Apr.

This hotel was originally built in the late 18th century for Admiral Collingwood, a close friend of Lord Nelson. Later it served as a convent, as the home of a German sculptor, and until the end of World War II, the German embassy. Architecturally, it reflects a number of styles: Italianate, Georgian, and Minorcan.

In 1964 it was restored and enlarged into a hotel. The reception area, with its 18th-century staircase, is decorated with numerous oil paintings and, like the rest of the public rooms, successfully mixes antiques with British memorabilia. Facilities include a bar, a game room, a swimming pool, and a tennis court. Guests are housed in the main building or in one of the more modern bungalow accommodations. The rooms are a mixed bag—you don't really know what you get until the maid opens the door. But all are clean and well kept, and many rooms have terraces overlooking the Bay of Mahón. The British love it here.

Inexpensive

Hostal Reynes. Carrer d'es Comerc, 26, 07700 Mahón. ☎ **971/36-40-59.** 27 rms. 3,200 ptas. ($25.60) double. Rates include breakfast. No credit cards.

On a quiet, narrow street in the town center near the cathedral, this is a cozy, well-maintained, family-run and very inexpensive hotel. Wide hallways lead to the simple but clean bedrooms that occupy three floors of the building. Meals are served in a well-scrubbed dining room with windows overlooking the street.

NEARBY ACCOMMODATIONS

In San Lluís

$ **Biniali.** Carretera S'Uestrà, Binibeca, 50, 07710 Sant Lluís. ☎ **971/15-17-24.** Fax 971/35-11-47. 10 rms. 14,850 ptas. ($118.80) double. AE, DC, MC, V. Closed late Oct–Mar.

This is one of the most charming hotels and restaurants in Minorca, about a mile south of San Lluís on the island's southwestern coastal road to Binibeca. The house, surrounded by English-style gardens, was originally the home of a prosperous Minorcan farmer in the 18th century. The comfortable bedrooms are decorated with a scattering of antiques, seven with terraces, and two with separate salons. A few of the rooms are air-conditioned. There is also a small outdoor swimming pool.

Many nonresidents visit for meals. Tables are set out under an arcade, overlooking the roses and geraniums in the garden, or in one of the charmingly old-fashioned dining rooms. Specialties include filet steak in port with truffle sauce, monkfish in a wild mushroom sauce, baked potato filled with lobster, magret (breast) of duck in a sweet and sour currant sauce, and a selection of Minorcan cheeses. The restaurant is open daily from 1:30 to 3pm and 8 to 11pm.

All in all, this is a retreat offering lots of peace, comfort, and quaintness within easy reach of Binibeca beach and the facilities and activities of Mahón.

Where to Dine

Fish and seafood form most of the basis of the Minorcan diet. The sea harvest is abundant along the long coastline. The most elegant dish— *la caldereta de langosta* —consists of pieces of lobster blended with onion, tomato, pepper, and garlic, and flavored with a herb liqueur. This is a favorite dish of King Juan Carlos when he visits Minorca.

Shellfish paella is another much-consumed dish, as is *escupinas* ("warty Venus"), a shellfish from Mahón. Thrushes with cabbage (*tordos con col*) are served in autumn. A peasant dish, *pa amb oli,* often precedes a meal. This is bread flavored with salt and olive oil and rubbed with fresh tomato.

Wine for the Minorcan table is brought in from mainland Spain, but gin is made on the island, a legacy from the days of the British occupation. You can drink the gin by itself or mix it with lemon and ice (if the latter, ask the bartender for *palloza*). Mixed with soda or lemonade, the gin drink is called a *pomada.*

Expensive

Gregal. Moll de Llevant. ☎ **971/36-66-06.** Reservations recommended. Main courses 1,200–4,000 ptas. ($9.60–$32). AE, DC, MC, V. Daily noon–3:30pm and 7:30–11:30pm. SEAFOOD/INTERNATIONAL.

Seafood is the specialty of this small, friendly restaurant. The decor is simple; checkered tablecloths and exposed beams lend a rustic air to the interior. The catch of the day is often on display. Included on the menu are several meat and fowl dishes, most with Catalán or French influences. Along with traditional Spanish plates, a selection of international dishes appear as well. Greek specialties, including *taramosalata,* moussaka, and *dolmades,* are excellent choices.

✪ **Jàgaro.** Moll de Llevant. ☎ **971/36-23-90.** Reservations recommended. Main courses 1,500–4,000 ptas. ($12–$32); *menús del día* 2,000 ptas. ($16) and 3,000 ptas. ($24). AE, DC, MC, V. Daily noon–4pm and 7pm–midnight. MEDITERRANEAN.

The menu, specializing in seafood, is Minorca's most eclectic and interesting. Begin with *ensalada templada con cigalitos y setas,* a mix of warm prawns and wild mushrooms served on a bed of lettuce, or Jàgaro's interpretation of gazpacho, flavored with shrimp and melon. The *mosaico de verduras,* a plate of grilled fresh vegetables is also an excellent choice. Main courses may include *carparcho de mero* (grouper) served with a tangy green-mustard sauce, *caldereta de langosta* (lobster stew), or *ortigas* (sea anemones). The seafood offerings are extensive. Most fish is prepared *al horno* (baked) or *al espalda* (baked in wine and topped with a garlic sauce). Although Jàgaro focuses on seafood, meat dishes including duck magret (breast) in orange sauce and foie gras with sweet-and-sour sauce are especially appealing. The extensive wine list assures a vintage to accompany any meal. For dessert, try one of the homemade ice creams or sorbets.

Rocamar. Cala Fonduco, 32, 07720 Es Castell. ☎ **971/36-56-01.** Fax 971/36-52-99. Reservations recommended. Main courses 2,000–4,000 ptas ($16–$32); fixed-price menus 2,000–3,500 ptas. ($16–$28). AE, DC, MC, V. Tues–Sun 1–4pm and 8:30–11pm. Closed Nov. INTERNATIONAL.

This restaurant is famous on Minorca. You reach it by following a narrow rutted road parallel to the harbor. The beamed and paneled restaurant on the upper floor has views overlooking the harbor. Although some locals claim the cooking was more glorious in the past, it still shines—especially when the chef treats sublime products with simplicity.

Dishes might include almond soup, marinated salmon with shellfish, magret (breast) of duckling in port wine, or beef filet with mustard sauce. Don't overlook the pleasant street-level snackbar (it's actually a restaurant in its own right). This establishment also offers 22 simple bedrooms (most of which are booked by English tour groups). Rooms rent for 5,000 pesetas ($40) for a double.

Moderate

✪ **Pilar.** Des Forn, 61. ☎ **971/36-68-17.** Reservations recommended. Main courses 850–2,400 ptas. ($6.80–$19.20). MC, V. Tues–Sat 1:30–3:30pm, Mon–Sat 8:30–11:30pm. Closed Jan–Feb. MINORCAN/MEDITERRANEAN.

At this small, stylish restaurant in the center of Mahón, you'll feel you're dining in somebody's home. Even the small kitchen where owner-chef Teodoro Beurrun works culinary wonders looks more like a domestic kitchen than a restaurant kitchen. There are about half a dozen tables indoors and another half a dozen spread around the rear patio in summer. A smattering of antique furnishings and impressionistic artworks contribute to the coziness.

The menu is understandably limited, but that does not apply to the quality and care taken in preparation. The market-fresh cuisine is largely Menorquín with innovative variations. Try the *berenjenas rellenas* (stuffed eggplant) and *conejo a la menorquina* (rabbit in an onion-and-thyme sauce), *calamares rellenos* (stuffed squid), and *cap roig* (scorpion fish). For dessert, try the homemade *pastel de nueces con chocolate* (walnut cake with chocolate).

Inexpensive

American Bar. Plaça Reial, 8. ☎ **971/36-18-22.** Main courses 550–1,350 ptas. ($4.40–$10.80). No credit cards. Mon–Sat 7am–11pm, Sun 7am–2pm. INTERNATIONAL.

For years, this has been the traditional international meeting place in Mahón. Many come here for drinks on its pleasant terrace, but you can also order food, eating inside or alfresco. Several typical Catalán dishes are featured along with an assortment of sandwiches, hamburgers, and Italian pasta dishes. It's also a great place to take the kids, as it serves the famous ice cream made on the island, most often using fresh fruit.

$ **Bar Restaurant España.** Carrer Victori, 48–50. ☎ **971/36-32-99.** Reservations recommended. Main courses 900–1,100 ptas. ($7.20–$8.80); *menús del día* 900–975 ptas. ($7.20–$7.80). MC, V. Daily 1–4:30pm and 7:30–11:30pm. Closed Jan. SPANISH.

The Bar Restaurant España, one of the oldest restaurants on the island, offers outstanding food at reasonable prices. Patrons are usually vacationing Europeans; the menu appeals to a wide variety of palates. Well-prepared items may include *cigalas a la americana,* prawns served in a spicy sauce or various fish and meat dishes with a distinctively Spanish flair.

La Tropical. Carrer Lluna, 36. ☎ **971/36-05-56.** Main courses 650–2,500 ptas. ($5.20–$20); *menú del día* 1,400 ptas. ($11.20). MC, V. Daily 8am–midnight. SPANISH/MINORCAN/INTERNATIONAL.

La Tropical is a three-in-one eatery. You can have snacks at the bar, *platos combinados* (combination plates) in the informal dining room, or full-fledged restaurant fare in the more formal dining area. The restaurant offers a good selection of Minorcan specialties, including a reasonably priced and savory fish-and-shellfish *caldereta* (stew). There is also a daily market menu and an assorted selection of Spanish and international dishes.

CIUDADELA (CIUTADELLA DE MENORCA)

27 miles (44km) W of Mahón.

At the western end of the island, Ciudadela has a typically Mediterranean air about it. Lining the narrow streets of the old city are noble mansions of the 17th and 18th centuries and numerous churches. It was the capital until 1722, when the British chose Mahón instead, largely because its harbor channel is eminently more navigable than the one at Ciudadela. Subsequently, the British built the main island road to link the two cities.

Like Mahón, Ciudadela perches high above its harbor, which is smaller than Mahón's. The seat of Minorca's bishopric, Ciudadela pontificates whereas Mahón administrates.

Known as Medina Minurka under the Muslims, Ciudadela retains some Moorish traces despite the 1558 Turkish invasion and destruction of the city. An obelisk in memory of the city's futile defense against that invasion stands in the pigeon-filled Plaça d'es Born (Plaza del Born), the city's main square overlooking the port.

Getting There **By Taxi** From the airport, you must take a taxi to Ciudadela, as there is no bus link.

By Bus From Mahón six buses go back and forth every day. Departures are from Plaça s'Esplanada in Mahón.

VISITOR INFORMATION The tourist office is at Plaça d'es Born (☎ **971/38-26-93**), open Monday through Friday from 9:30am to 1:30pm and 5 to 7pm, Saturday from 9:30am to 1pm.

What to See & Do

The center of Ciudadela is Plaça d'es Born, site of tourist information. When the town was known to Jaume I, this was the center of life. Back then Ciudadela was completely walled to protect itself from pirate incursions, which were a serious threat from the 13th century on. Much of the present look of this square, and of Ciudadela itself, is thanks to its "demotion" in 1722, when the capital was transferred to Mahón. For centuries that checked urban development in Ciudadela, and many buildings now stand that might have been torn down to make way for "progress."

Plaça d'es Born looks over the port from the north. Once it was known as Plaza Generalíssmo, honoring the dictator Franco. The square was built around the obelisk that remembers the hopeless struggle of the town against the invading Turks. The Turks entered the city in 1558 and caused much destruction. On the west side of the square is the Ayuntamiento (Town Hall).

To the southwest of the square stands **Iglesia de San Francisco.** This is a 14th-century Gothic building, with some excellent carved wood altars. The town once had a magnificent opera house, Casa Salort, but that cultural note sounds no more, as it's been turned into a somewhat seedy old movie palace. Another once splendid palace,

Palacio de Torre-Saura, also opens onto the square. Still owner occupied, this place was constructed in the 1800s.

The **cathedral,** Plaça Pio XII, was ordered built by the conquering Alfonso III on the site of the former mosque. Gothic in style, it appears fortress-like. The facade of the church, in the neoclassical style, was added in 1813. The church suffered heavy damage in 1936, during the Spanish Civil War, but has since been restored.

Ciudadela is at its liveliest at the **port,** where you'll find an array of little shops, bars, restaurants, sailboats, and some impressive yachts in summer. **Carrer Quadrando** is another street worth walking, as it is lined with shops and arcades.

The Moorish influence still lingers in a block of whitewashed houses in the **Voltes,** lying off the Plaça s'Esplanada. In Ciudadela the local people still meet at **Plaça d'Alfons III,** the square honoring their long-ago liberator.

OUTDOOR ACTIVITIES

Beaches In Ciudadela, buses depart from Plaça d'Artrutx for most coastal destinations, including the best beaches. Of these, **Cala Santandria,** two miles (3km) to the south, is known for its white sands. This is a sheltered beach near a creek, and in the background are rock caves, which were inhabited in prehistoric times. The coves of **En Forcat, Blanes,** and **Brut** are near Ciudadela.

Cala de Santa Galdana, not reached by public transport, is the most stunning in the area, lying 14 (22.5km) miles south of Ciudadela. The bay here is tranquil and ringed with a beach of fine golden sand. Tall bare cliffs rise in the background, and the air is perfumed with the smell of pine trees. The road to this beach, unlike so many others on Minorca, is a good one.

WHERE TO STAY

Expensive

Hotel Patricia. Passeig Sant Nicolau, 90, 07760 Ciudadela. ☎ **971/38-55-11.** Fax 971/48-11-20. 40 rms, 4 junior suites. A/C MINIBAR TV TEL. 15,200 ptas. ($121.60) double; 17,200 ptas. ($137.60) junior suite. AE, DC, MC, V. Closed Nov–Feb. Free parking on street.

Built in 1988 in a three-story, centrally located position that business travelers tend to find convenient, this is Ciudadela's most respected and most luxurious hotel. Set near the Plaça d'es Born, a half-mile from the nearest beach (Playa de La Caleta), it has a polite and hardworking staff well versed on the island's facilities and geography. Bedrooms are comfortable, carpeted, outfitted pleasantly in pastels, and have large bathrooms. There's no full-fledged restaurant within this hotel, but you can get simple platters of food, coffee, beer, and wine at the in-house *cafetería.*

Moderate

Hotel Almirante Farragut. Urbanización Los Delfines, Cala'n Forcat, 07760 Ciudadela. ☎ **971/38-28-00.** Fax 971/38-51-18. 472 rms. A/C TV TEL. 4,630–17,100 ptas. ($37.05–$136.80) double. Rates include breakfast. MC, V. Closed Nov–Apr.

Located three miles (5km) outside Ciudadela, beside a small rock-lined inlet, this four-story building is one of the best hotels in the development of Los Delfines, a cluster of resort hotels initiated in the 1970s and 1980s. Public rooms are airy, large, sparsely furnished, and appropriate to the hotel's role as a warm-weather beach resort with an international clientele, often from England and Germany. Guest rooms are pleasant and standardized in both their amenities and furnishings. Each has a balcony or terrace, usually overlooking either the rocky inlet or the open sea. Prices vary widely according to season, but lodgings that the hotel identifies as suites are nothing more than larger-than-usual double rooms.

Facilities include two saltwater pools for adults, one pool for children, two *cafeterías* (snack bars), a disco, a TV and video room, two tennis courts, mini-golf, shops, a beauty parlor, a supermarket, and an independently operated school for scuba divers. The hotel, incidentally, was named for U.S. Admiral Farragut, a 19th-century U.S. naval officer whose grandparents lived in one of the nearby villages.

Hotel Esmeralda. Cami Sant Nicolau 171, 07760 Ciudadela. ☎ **971/38-02-50.** Fax 971/38-02-58. 161 rms. 8,100–11,600 ptas. ($64.80–$92.80) double. Rates include breakfast; half board 1,450 ptas. ($11.60) extra per person. AE, DC, MC, V. Closed Nov–Apr. Free parking.

This is a simple, respectable three-star hotel, built in the 1960s and set near the entrance to the mouth of Ciudadela's harbor. It lies within a 10-minute walk from the commercial heart of town, close to the better-accessorized Patricia Hotel, and rising three floors. Guest rooms are large but sparsely furnished, but bathrooms are big and bright. In many cases, rooms have terraces and sea views. There's a pool on the premises, and the beach is within a five-minute walk.

Inexpensive

Hostal Residencia Ciutadella. Carrer Sant Eloy, 07701 Ciudadela. ☎ and fax **971/38-34-62.** 17 rms. TEL. 5,000 ptas. ($40) double; 9,500 ptas. ($76) triple. Rates include breakfast. AE, MC, V.

Near Plaça d'Alfons III, on a quiet street just off the main shopping artery, this small hotel offers comfortable, convenient accommodations. Tiled floors and floor-length windows provide an airy atmosphere. Furniture is covered in fresh, floral fabrics. Beware, this three-story hotel has no elevator.

Hotels Cala Bona & Mar Blava. Avinguda del Mar, 14–16, 07760 Ciudadela. ☎ **971/38-00-16.** Fax 971/48-20-70. 44 rms. TEL. 4,500–5,500 ptas. ($36–$44) double. No credit cards. Closed Nov–Mar.

These two hotels stand just a short walk from the town center, with views overlooking the little bay. Stairs lead down to a little beach, with a larger beach just five minutes away. Guest rooms are clean and comfortable; almost all have views facing the water. The rooms at the Mar Blava are smaller than those at the Cala Bona. The hotels share an outdoor pool, bar, and outdoor terrace. A restaurant serves snacks and light meals.

A Nearby Place to Stay

Hotel Los Cóndores Sol. Playa Santo Tomás, s/n, 07749 San Cristóbal. ☎ **971/37-00-50.** Fax 971/37-03-48. 188 rms. TEL. 16,700–22,244 ptas. ($133.60–$177.95) double. Rates include half board. AE, DC, MC, V. Closed late Oct to Apr 30.

This hotel gives the impression of a large well-maintained hacienda, complete with lacy iron balconies and louvered shutters. Surrounded by lawns and flowering shrubs, the hotel has a swimming pool, a private beach, and a sweeping view of rocky islets. Many guests make their balconies an extension of their bedrooms, reading, sitting, and talking within sight of the sea.

Where to Dine

The port of Ciudadela offers a wide selection of restaurants for all palates and prices. Beyond that, there are some commendable choices in and around town.

Moderate

✪ **Casa Manolo.** Marina 117. ☎ **971/38-00-03.** Reservations required in summer. Main courses 850–2,400 ptas. ($6.80–$19.20); fixed-price menus 1,800–2,500 ptas. ($14.40–$20). AE, DC, MC, V. Daily 1–4:30pm and 7:30–11:30pm. Closed Sun mid-Nov to mid-Feb. SPANISH/MINORCAN.

Located at the port, across from the spot where the larger yachts anchor, Casa Manolo is a favorite of the yachting crowd. You can dine indoors in a room carved out of stone, or alfresco, on the intimate terrace. King Juan Carlos has been seen here enjoying the elegant atmosphere and outstanding cuisine. The menu consists mainly of fresh seafood and lobster dishes. The specialty of the house is *arroz de pescado caldoso,* a dish resembling paella, but with more of a focus on fish. The *caldereta de langosta,* a lobster-based bouillabaisse, is one of our favorites. The hardworking and affable owner, Sra. Maria Postores, supervises all aspects of your dining experience.

Cas Quintu. Plaça d'Alfons III, 4. ☎ **971/38-10-02.** Main courses 850–3,750 ptas. ($6.80–$30); fixed-price menu 1,070 ptas. ($8.55). AE, DC, MC, V. Daily 9am–2am. SPANISH/MINORCAN.

One of the most solidly entrenched restaurants in town, thriving since the early 1960s from a position on an ornate square in the most historic core of town, Cas Quintu offers both indoor and outdoor tables that afford vantage points for observations of the passing crowd. You can order drinks and light food in the café daily from 9am to 2pm. This establishment's selection of tapas is among the best in town. Full meals are served outdoors or in one of a pair of charming and stylish rooms in back. Specialties include a zesty squid sautéed in butter, several different preparations of beefsteak, a perfect sole meunière, and a mixed grill of fish based on the catch of the day.

Es Caliu Grill. Carretera Cala Blanca. ☎ **971/38-01-65.** Main courses 600–2,000 ptas. ($4.80–$16). DC, MC, V. May–Oct, daily 1–4pm and 7:30pm–12:30am; off-season, Fri–Sun 1–4pm and 7:30pm–12:30am. SPANISH.

One and a half miles (2.5km) south of Ciudadela, along the main road between Cala Santandria and Cala Blanca, Es Caliu is the place to come when you've had your fill of seafood. Specializing in grilled meats of the freshest quality, it offers lamb, veal, pork, rabbit, quail, and spit-roasted suckling pig. But beyond fine food, you get a special ambience. Above the bar hang hams and garlic braids, and off to the side are stacked wine barrels. The family-style tables and benches are made of cut and polished logs. The outdoor terrace is roofed and smothered with cascading flowers; indoors there are two rustic dining areas, one with a fireplace.

Inexpensive

Bar Triton. Muelle Ciutadella. ☎ **971/38-00-02.** Tapas and *platos combinados* 500–2,500 ptas. ($4–$20). AE, MC, V. Daily 4pm –3am. TAPAS.

The best place for tapas, Triton, in the port, offers a wide range of snacks, including sausages, *tortillas* (Spanish omelets), meatballs, and a dozen or so seafood tapas, among them octopus, stuffed squid, and *escupiñas* (Minorcan clams). On the wall inside are photos and illustrations of the port before it was a haven for vacationers. As in those days, fishers still make up an important part of the clientele, and you'll often find the locals engaged in a friendly afternoon game of cards.

El Comilon. Plaça Colóm 47. ☎ **971/38-09-22.** Couscous 1,950 ptas. ($15.60) per person; crêpes 600–950 ptas. ($4.80–$7.60). V. Mon–Sat 1pm–midnight. Closed late Oct to early May. CRÊPES/COUSCOUS.

In 1996 this restaurant radically changed its agenda, discarding a deeply entrenched policy of serving fish and shellfish and switching to a cheaper and much less formal roster of crêpes. These are served in both sweet and savory versions, and include 40 different kinds of fillings ranging from ham, cheese, and broccoli to the kind of dessert crêpes you'd consume after a main course of Algerian-style couscous. This, the staple dish of North Africa, comes in only one tried-and-true version, with chunks of vegetables, chickpeas, lamb, and chicken served over a bed of semolina wheat. There are about a dozen tables inside, as well as additional tables within an interior courtyard lined with potted plants. The place is proud of its role as the only restaurant serving couscous in all of Minorca, and proud that its version is based on the culinary traditions of Algeria.

La Granja. Plaça de s'Esplanada (Plaça Colóm), 48. ☎ **971/38-40-81.** Tapas 300–425 ptas. ($2.40–$3.40). No credit cards. Mon–Sat 10am–1 or 4am (depending on crowd). TAPAS.

A gathering place for locals and tourists alike, this hangout offers a variety of fresh tapas and sandwiches; you can enjoy them in the rather raucous interior or at the calmer outdoor tables. A glass of Jerez (sherry), the perfect accompaniment to tapas, costs from 120 to 150 pesetas ($.95–$1.20). Platters of tapas can be purchased for 325 to 800 pesetas ($2.60–$6.40), depending on your selection.

Ciudadela After Dark

Café El Molino. Plaça d'Alfons III. ☎ **971/38-00-00.**

This is one of our favorite bars, a hangout near the Avinguda de la Constitució. It has attracted virtually every drinker in town since it was established in 1905, within the circular premises of what was originally built as a windmill in 1794. It provides a rustic but richly international contrast to the busy square it borders, and boasts the unusual distinction of having monumental walls and vaulted ceilings that are a lot older than those of the buildings that surround it. The clientele includes visiting foreigners and local fishers, and the venue changes from that of an early-morning café, whose opening is timed to coincide with the departure of fishing boats, to a late-night bar. Keeping long hours, it is open daily from 5:30am to 2am.

CENTRAL & SOUTHERN MINORCA

Topographically and climatically, this is the more tranquil part of the island. The beaches are more accessible, and the winds blow less strongly—as a result, tourism has taken a firmer foothold here than in the north. Santo Tomás, Cala Galdana, Platges de Son Bou, Cala Bosch, and Punta Prima are some of the focal points for travelers.

What to See & Do

Es Mercadal, a town of several thousand inhabitants at the foot of Monte Toro, is an ensemble of white houses with grace notes of color. Among its claims to local fame are two types of almond confectionery— *carquinyols* (small, hard cookies) and *amargos* (a kind of macaroon). The place to get both is **Pastelería Villalonga Ca's Sucrer,** Plaça Constitución, 11, Es Mercadal (☎ **971/37-57-75**), open Tuesday through Saturday from 9:30am to 1:30pm and from 5 to 8:30pm, also open on Sunday in winter from 11am to 2pm.

From Es Mercadal, you can take a road 2½ miles (4km) up to **Monte Toro,** the island's tallest mountain at 1,170 feet, crowned with a sanctuary that is a place of pilgrimage for Minorcans. The winding road leads to a panoramic view of the island's rolling green countryside dotted with *fincas* (farm estates), trim fields, and stands of trees. From this vantage point you can also clearly see the contrast between the flatter southern part of the island and the hilly northern region. The hilltop sanctuary includes a small, simple church with an ornate gilded altar displaying the image (reportedly found nearby in 1290) of the Virgin Mare de Déu d'el Toro, the island's patron saint. In 1936 the church was destroyed, but the statue was saved from the flames and a new church built. The church is open daily from early morning to sunset; admission is free. In the courtyard of the sanctuary is a bronze monument to those

Minorcans who left in the 18th century, while the island was still a British colony, to colonize Spanish settlements in North America. The large statue of Christ commemorates the dead in the Spanish Civil War. There is a snack bar with a pleasant terrace here.

Platges de Son Bou is a stunning beach pockmarked by two outsize hotels. Although still enchanting, the mile-long, narrow beach and clear, turquoise waters are now often crowded, even in the off-season; in July and August they're best avoided. At the eastern end of the beach just beyond the two monster hotels are the ruins of a Paleo-Christian basilica, most probably dating from the 5th or 6th century. Visible in the cliffs beyond are cave dwellings, some of which appear quite prosperous, with painted facades and shades to keep out the noonday sun.

To the east in Cala'n Porter is a most unique nightspot. Embedded in a series of caves within a sheer cliff face rising from the sea, **La Cova d'en Xoroi** (☎ **971/37-72-36**) is a conglomeration of bars, terraces, intimate nooks and crannies, and a disco floor. For sheer drama, the setting is without equal. As you walk down the entrance stairway, all magnificently unfolds before you. Then you come to the dance floor overlooking the sea at the cliff's edge—there's no window, just a railing. Prehistoric vessels were found inside these caves, which, according to legend, were once the refuge of a Moor called Xoroi, who had abducted a local maid and made his home here with her and their family. You can visit this unusual spot during the day as well, from 11am to 9pm. Admission is 400 pesetas ($3.20) and includes refreshments. In the evening, from 11pm to 5am, La Cova d'en Xoroi transforms into a disco. Admission is 1,500 pesetas ($12) including your first drink. Drinks cost from 600 to 1,000 pesetas ($4.80–$8).

WHERE TO STAY

Most of the hotels in this area cater almost exclusively to tour groups.

Los Gavilanes Sol. Urbanización Cala Galdana, s/n, 07750 Ferreries. ☎ **971/37-31-75.** Fax 971/37-31-75. 355 rms, 9 suites. 10,900 ptas. ($87.20) double; 12,000 ptas. ($96) suite. Rates include breakfast. AE, DC, MC, V. Closed Nov–Apr.

A large resort hotel, the Gavilanes Sol is fully equipped with swimming pools, discos, restaurants, and bars. It's atop a steep slope overlooking one of the most perfect beaches in the Mediterranean, and it's surrounded by a grove of pines and palmettos. The original beauty of Cala Galdana has been substantially marred by tourist construction, but you can enjoy the best end of its sandy, crescent-shaped beach and turquoise waters by staying here. Each of the sizable, functionally furnished rooms has a balcony.

Many of the clients here are on group tours from England, so the sweeping lobby-level terraces and the pub take on a British flavor. The hotel also has a restaurant, a swimming pool, and a children's playground.

✪ **Hotel Santo Tomás.** Playa Santo Tomás, 07749 Es Migjorn Gran. ☎ **971/37-00-25.** Fax 971/37-02-04. 84 rms, 5 suites. A/C MINIBAR TV TEL. 17,500 ptas. ($140) double; 22,000 ptas. ($176) suite. Rates include half board. AE, DC, MC, V. Closed Nov–Apr.

One of our favorite hotels on Minorca, Santo Tomás offers the best quality and comfort on the island; it's the only four-star hotel on the beach. Public areas are airy and spacious. Accommodations are comfortable, and amenities include hair dryers and radios. Most rooms have a terrace that faces the sea. On the premises, guests will find a large swimming pool, surrounded by thatched umbrellas, providing shelter from the sun. A seaside bar offers refreshments, and guests may also use a mini-golf course. Various water sports can be arranged.

Where to Dine

Some of the best dining in this area is offered in the inland villages rather than along the coast. Es Mercadal, in particular, has a few choice restaurants.

✪ **Ca N'Olga.** Pont Na Macarrana (near the Carrer d'es Sol), Es Mercadal. ☎ **971/37-54-59.** Reservations recommended on weekends. Main courses 1,100–3,000 ptas. ($8.80–$24). AE, DC, MC, V. Mar–May and Oct–Dec, Fri–Sun 1:30–3pm and 7:45–11pm; June–Sept, Fri–Sun 7:45–11:30pm. Closed Jan–Feb. MINORCAN/INTERNATIONAL.

A stylish, sophisticated spot that attracts a similar clientele, Ca N'Olga is warm, winsome, and intimate. Occupying a typical white-stucco Minorcan house some 150 years old, this restaurant offers dining on a pretty outdoor patio or at a handful of indoor tables.

The eclectic menu changes frequently with the market offerings. It is likely to include quail with onion-and-sherry vinegar and osso buco. Some standard dishes that tend to appear regularly are *cap roig* (scorpion fish), *cabrito* (baby goat), some kind of fish terrine, and mussels au gratin. Among the homemade desserts you'll often find a velvety smooth fig ice cream and chestnut pudding.

Costa Sur. Playa de Santo Tomás. ☎ **971/37-03-26.** Main courses 750–2,500 ptas. ($6–$20). AE, MC, V. Daily 7–11pm. Closed Nov–Apr. INTERNATIONAL.

The sophisticated aspirations of Costa Sur are hampered by its rather stark decor. The well-planned menu is equally divided between seafood and meat dishes, and the house rightly prides itself on its cheese soufflé, salmon crêpes, pepper steak, and suquet de rape (monkfish stew). It also serves a smattering of succulent pasta dishes.

$ **58, S'Engolidor.** Carrer Major, 3, Es Migjorn Gran. ☎ **971/37-01-93.** Reservations required Sat–Sun Jun–Aug. Main courses 1,100–1,400 ptas. ($8.80–$11.20). MC, V. May–Oct, Tues–Sun 8–11pm; off-season, Fri–Sat 8–10:30pm, Sun 1:30–3:30pm. Closed Jan. MINORCAN.

In the village of Es Migjorn Gran (San Cristóbal), between Es Mercadal and Santo Tomás, lies this relatively undiscovered restaurant. Except for a small sign on the door, it could be mistaken for any other house on this quiet, side street. The building dates from 1740, with sections added throughout the years. The interior is simple: stark white walls accented with various works of art. The dining area consists of several small rooms, with only a few tables each. You can also dine outdoors in one of the small patio areas; many overlook the owner's small vegetable garden. The menu consists of various Minorcan specialties, including *olaigua,* eggplant stuffed with fish, rabbit and wild-mushroom stew, and roast lamb. Owner José Luis will rent you a cozy room for the night. A room for two, with breakfast included, costs 4,500 pesetas ($36) per night.

Molí d'es Reco. Es Mercadal. ☎ **971/37-53-92.** Reservations recommended in summer. Main courses 1,000–2,800 ptas. ($8–$22.40); *menú del día* 1,500 ptas. ($12). AE, MC, V. Daily 1–4pm and 7–11pm. MINORCAN.

Easily spotted by the windmill that inspired its name, Molí d'es Reco has a pleasant outdoor patio but a rather plain indoor dining area. Overall, the place is a bit touristy, but if offers hearty Minorcan fare including stuffed eggplant, *oliaigua amb tomatecs* (a soup with tomato, onion, parsley, green pepper, and garlic), snails with spider crab, partridge with cabbage, and *calamares a la menorquina* (stuffed squid with an almond-cream sauce).

Sa Plaça. Carrer d'Enmig (also Avinguda de la Constitución), 2, Es Mercadal. ☎ **971/37-50-48.** Main courses 850–1,800 ptas. ($6.80–$14.40); Mon–Sat fixed-price menu 1,000 ptas. ($8), Sun 1,200 ptas. ($9.60). MC, V. Daily 5:30am–1am. MINORCAN.

Keeping the longest hours of any place in the area, this is a simple and unpretentious place, offering a respite from the heat, comfortable chairs, and a reassuring array of tapas filled with flavor and accompanied by either sherry or beer. The management likes to define this spot as a simple *cafetería,* or bistro, rather than a full-fledged restaurant. The venue is ideal if only for coffee or a midafternoon pick-me-up. Portions are filling and flavorful, and the cost is right.

FORNELLS & THE NORTHERN COAST

The road leading north from Es Mercadal to Fornells runs through some of the island's finer scenery. Mass tourism hotels, so far, have not discovered this place, although there are several good dining choices. On the northern coast, the tiny town of Fornells snuggles around a bay filled with boats and windsurfers and lined with restaurants and a few shops. Built around four defense fortifications—the Talaia de la Mola (now destroyed), the Tower of Fornells at the harbor mouth, the fortress of the Island of Las Sargantanas (the Lizards) situated in the middle of the harbor, and the now-ruined Castle of San Jorge or San Antonion—Fornells today is a flourishing fishing village noted for its upscale restaurants featuring savory lobster *calderetas.*

WHAT TO SEE & DO

West of Fornells is **Platja Binimella,** a beautiful beach (unofficially nudist) that's easily accessible by car. Its long, curving, sandy cove is peacefully set against undulating hills. A snack bar is the sole concession to civilization.

By far the most splendid panorama here is that from the promontory at **Cap de Cavalleria,** the northernmost tip of the island, marked by a lighthouse. Getting here requires some effort, however. At a bend in the road leading to Platja Binimella, a signpost indicates the turnoff to Cap de Cavalleria through a closed gate leading to a dirt road. The closed gate is typical of many of the roads leading to Minorca's undeveloped beaches. All the beaches in Spain, however, are public, so no one may impede access to them—although landowners may discourage visitors by making access difficult. The prevailing custom is simply to open the gate, go on through, and close it behind you. It is important that you close the gate, because often these gates keep livestock confined to certain areas. As you follow the long dirt road (negotiable in a regular car or on a motorbike) out to Cap de Cavelleria, you'll come across several more sets of gates and travel through countryside that's somewhat reminiscent of the Scottish highlands, with cultivated fields and scattered, grand *fincas,* or farmsteads. Shortly before the lighthouse is a "parking area" down to the left. You'll have to pick your way across the scrub and rocks for the views. The best one is from a circular tower in ruins up to the right of the lighthouse. Now brace yourself for a vista encompassing the whole of Minorca—a symphony of dramatic cliffs and jewel-blue water.

WHERE TO STAY

Hostal S'Algaret. Plaça S'Algaret, 7, 07748 Fornells. ☎ **971/37-65-52.** 23 rms. A/C TEL. 11,250 ptas. ($90) double. Rates include breakfast. AE, MC, V. Closed Nov–Mar.

This is for escapists only. It's really like an unpretentious inn. It's also a bit sleepy, so don't expect a lot in the way of hotel services. But adventurous do-it-yourself types often book the modest and very simply furnished guest rooms, which are clean and reasonably comfortable. Floors are tiled, the furnishings basic but the spacious modern baths are alluring. There are sizable terraces opening onto views as well. If your expectations aren't high, you might go for this one. No one complains when the reasonable bill is presented, either.

Where to Dine

Fornells is noted for its fine seafood restaurants specializing in the Minorcan *calderetas* (seafood stews). King Juan Carlos has been know to sail in here when he wants to savor some, and in peak summer season people phone up their favorite Fornells restaurant days in advance with their orders.

✪ **Es Pla.** Pasage des Pla, Fornells. ☎ **971/37-66-55.** Reservations recommended July–Aug. Main courses 1,800–2,400 ptas. ($14.40–$19.20); *menú del día* 2,700 ptas. ($21.60). AE, MC, V. Daily 1–3:30pm and 7:30–10:30pm. MINORCAN/SEAFOOD.

If any restaurant in Minorca deserves a comparison to the grand Roman watering holes of *La Dolce Vita,* it would be this one, where King Juan Carlos and his family have come to dine several times, but not within recent memory. Stylish, airy, and elegant in a way that reflects the seagoing life of the island, it has thrived here since the 1960s, on a wood-floored porch that lies only about six feet above the swell of the surf. Large and informal, it has a long, stainless-steel bar area and an indoor-outdoor design. Menu items include a long roster of perfectly prepared fish, meat, and shellfish, but the acknowledged culinary winner—and the most frequently ordered dish—is paella with crayfish, priced at 6,000 pesetas ($48) per person, or more, depending on market conditions.

S'Algaret. Plaça S'Algaret, 7, Fornells. ☎ **971/37-65-52.** Tapas 225–375 ptas. ($1.80–$3) per *ración* (serving); *platos combinados* (combination plates) 1,000–1,300 ptas. ($8–$10.40). AE, DC, MC, V. Daily noon–4pm and 8–11pm. TAPAS.

Adjacent to the hostal of the same name (see above), S'Algaret is much frequented by locals and is one of the few economical alternatives for eating in Fornells (here you eat instead of "dine"). The venue is sleepy, quiet, small in scale, and unpretentious. You can nibble on good-tasting tapas, sandwiches, a varied selection of *tortillas* (Spanish omelets), and a smattering of *platos combinados* (combination plates), the ingredients of which change daily.

Appendix

A Basic Phrases & Vocabulary

English	Spanish	Pronunciation
Hello	**Buenos días**	*bway*-noss *dee*-ahss
How are you?	**¿Como está usted?**	*koh*-moh ess-*tah* oo-*steth*
Very well	**Muy bien**	mwee byen
Thank you	**Gracias**	*gra*-theeahss
Good-bye	**Adiós**	ad-*dyohss*
Please	**Por favor**	pohr fah-*bohr*
Yes	**Sí**	see
No	**No**	noh
Excuse me	**Pardóneme**	pahr-*doh*-neh-may
Give me	**Deme**	*day*-may
Where is…?	**¿Donde está?**	*dohn*-day ess-*tah*
the station	**la estación**	la ess-tah-*thyohn*
a hotel	**un hotel**	oon oh-*tel*
a restaurant	**un restaurante**	oon res-tow-*rahn*-tay
the toilet	**el servicio**	el ser-*vee*-thee-o
To the right	**A la derecha**	ah lah day-*ray*-chuh
To the left	**A la izquierda**	ah lah eeth-*kyehr*-duh
Straight ahead	**Adelante**	ah-day-*lahn*-tay
I would like…	**Quiero**	*kyehr*-oh
to eat	**comer**	ko-*mayr*
a room	**una habitación**	*oo*-nah ah-bee-tah-*thyon*
How much?	**¿Cuánto?**	*kwahn*-toh
The check	**La cuenta**	la *kwen*-tah
When	**¿Cuándo?**	*kwan*-doh
Yesterday	**Ayer**	ah-*yeyr*
Today	**Hoy**	oy
Tomorrow	**Mañana**	mah-*nyah*-nah
Breakfast	**Desayuno**	deh-sai-*yoo*-noh
Lunch	**Comida**	ko-*mee*-dah
Dinner	**Cena**	*thay*-nah

NUMBERS

1 uno (*oo*-noh)
2 dos (dose)
3 tres (trayss)
4 cuatro (*kwah*-troh)
5 cinco (*theen*-koh)
6 seis (sayss)
7 siete (*syeh*-tay)
8 ocho (*oh*-choh)
9 nueve (*nway*-bay)
10 diez (dyeth)
11 once (*ohn*-thay)
12 doce (*doh*-thay)
13 trece (*tray*-thay)
14 catorce (kah-*tor*-thay)
15 quince (*keen*-thay)
16 dieciséis (dyeth-ee-*sayss*)
17 diecisiete (dyeth-ee-*sye*-tay)
18 dieciocho (dyeth-ee-*oh*-choh)
19 diecinueve (dyeth-ee-*nyway*-bay)
20 veinte (*bayn*-tey)
30 treinta (*trayn*-tah)
40 cuarenta (kwah-*ren*-tah)
50 cincuenta (theen-*kwhen*-tah)
60 sesenta (say-*sen*-tah)
70 setenta (say-*ten*-tah)
80 ochenta (oh-*chayn*-tah)
90 noventa (noh-*ben*-tah)
100 cien/ciento (thyen/thyen-toe)

B Menu Savvy

Alliolo Sauce made from garlic and olive oil

Arroz amb feseola i naps Rice with beans and turnips

Arroz con costra Rice dish of chicken, rabbit, sausages, black pudding, chickpeas, spices, and pork meatballs—everything "hidden" under a layer of beaten egg crust.

Arroz empedrado Rice cooked with tomatoes and cod and a top layer of white beans

Bacalao al ajo arriero Cod-and-garlic dish named after Leonese mule drivers

Bacalao al pil-pil Cod with garlic and chile peppers

Bacalao a la vizcaina Cod with dried peppers and onion

Bajoques farcides Peppers stuffed with rice, pork, tomatoes, and spices

Butifarra Catalonian sausage made with blood, spices, and eggs

Caldereta Stew or a stew pot

Caldereta extremeña Kid or goat stew

Caldillo de perro "Dog soup," made with onions, fresh fish, and orange juice

Caldo gallego Soup made with cabbage, potatoes, beans, and various meat flavorings

Caseolada Potato-and-vegetable stew with bacon and ribs

Chanfaina salmantina Rice, giblets, lamb sweetbreads, and pieces of *chorizo*

Chilindrón Sauce made from tomatoes, peppers, garlic, and *chorizo*

Chorizo spicy pork sausage

Cochifrito navarro Small pieces of fried lamb

Cocido español Spanish stew

Cocido madrileña Chickpea stew of Madrid, with potatoes, cabbage, turnips, beef, marrow, bacon, *chorizo,* and black pudding

Cocido de pelotas Stew of minced meat wrapped in cabbage leaves and cooked with poultry, bacon, chickpeas, potatoes, and spices

Empanada Crusted pie of Galicia, with a variety of fillings

Escudella Catalán version of chickpea stew

Fabada White bean stew of Asturias

Habas a la catalana Stew of broad beans, herbs, and spices

Judías blancas Haricot beans

Judías negras Runner beans

Lacón con grelos Salted ham with turnip tops

Magras con tomate Slices of slightly fried ham dipped in tomato sauce

Mar y cielo "Sea and heaven," made with sausages, rabbit, shrimp, and fish

Merluza a la gallega Galician hake with onion, potatoes, and herbs

Merluza a la sidra Hake cooked with cider

Morcilla Black sausage akin to black pudding

Paella alicantina Rice dish made with chicken and rabbit

Pato a la naranja Duck with orange, an old Valencian dish

Pericana Cod, olive oil, dry peppers, and garlic

Picada Sauce made from nuts, parsley, garlic, saffron, and cinnamon

Pilota Ball made of meat, parsley, bread crumbs, and eggs

Pinchito Small kebab

Pisto manchego Vegetable stew from La Mancha

Pollos a la chilindrón Chicken cooked in a tomato, onion, and pepper sauce

Romesco Mediterranean sauce, with olive oil, red pepper, bread, garlic, and maybe cognac

Salsa verde Green sauce to accompany fish

Samfaina Sauce made from tomatoes, eggplant, onions, and zucchini

Sangría Drink made with fruit, brandy, and wine

Sofrito Sauce made from peppers, onions, garlic, tomatoes, and olive oil

Sopa de ajo castellana Garlic soup with ham, bread, eggs, and spices

Sopa castellanas Bread, broth, ham, and sometimes a poached egg and garlic

Tapas Small dishes or appetizers served with drinks at a tavern

Tortilla de patatas Spanish omelet with potatoes

Trucha a la navarra Trout fried with a piece of ham

Turrón Almond paste

Zarzuela Fish stew

C Glossary of Architectural Terms

Alcazaba Moorish fortress

Alcázar Moorish fortified palace

Ayuntamiento Town hall

Azulejo Painted glass tiles, popular in Mudéjar work and later architecture, especially in Andalusia, Valencia, and Portugal

Barrio (**Barri** in Catalán) City neighborhood or district

Churrigueresque Floridly ornate baroque style of the late 17th and early 18th centuries in the style of Spanish sculptor and architect José Churriguera (1665–1725)

Ciudadela Citadel

Cortijo Andalusian country house or villa

Granja Farm or farmhouse

Isabeline Gothic Architectural style popular in the late 15th century, roughly corresponding to the English perpendicular

Judería Jewish quarter

Lonja Merchants' exchange or marketplace

Medina Walled center of a Moorish city, traditionally centered around a mosque

Mezquita Mosque

Mirador Scenic overlook or belvedere, or a glassed-in panoramic balcony sheltering its occupants from the wind

Mirhab Prayer niche in a mosque, by Koranic law facing Mecca

Mudéjar Moorish-influenced architecture, usually "Christianized" and adopted as Spain's most prevalent architectural style from the 12th to the 16th century

Plateresque Heavily ornamented Gothic style widely used in Spain and Portugal during the 16th century. Its name derives from the repoussé floral patterns hammered into 16th-century silver (*la plata*), which were imitated in low relief carvings in stone

Plaza Mayor Square at the center of many Spanish cities, often enclosed, arcaded, and enhanced with cafés or fountains

Plaza de Toros Bullring

Puerta Portal or gate

Reja Iron grilles, either those covering the exterior windows of buildings or the decorative dividers in churches

Retablo Carved and/or painted altarpiece

Index

Frommer's Complete Travel Guides

(Comprehensive guides to destinations around the world, with selections in all price ranges—from deluxe to budget)

Acapulco/Ixtapa/Taxco
Alaska
Amsterdam
Arizona
Atlanta
Australia
Austria
Bahamas
Bangkok
Barcelona, Madrid & Seville
Belgium, Holland & Luxembourg
Berlin
Bermuda
Boston
Budapest & the Best of Hungary
California
Canada
Cancún, Cozumel & the Yucatán
Caribbean
Caribbean Cruises & Ports of Call
Caribbean Ports of Call
Carolinas & Georgia
Chicago
Colorado
Costa Rica
Denver, Boulder & Colorado Springs
Dublin
England
Florida
France
Germany
Greece
Hawaii
Hong Kong
Honolulu/Waikiki/Oahu
Ireland
Italy
Jamaica/Barbados
Japan
Las Vegas
London
Los Angeles
Maryland & Delaware
Maui
Mexico
Mexico City
Miami & the Keys
Montana & Wyoming
Montréal & Québec City
Munich & the Bavarian Alps
Nashville & Memphis
Nepal
New England
New Mexico
New Orleans
New York City
Northern New England
Nova Scotia, New Brunswick & Prince Edward Island
Paris
Philadelphia & the Amish Country
Portugal
Prague & the Best of the Czech Republic
Puerto Rico
Puerto Vallarta, Manzanillo & Guadalajara
Rome
San Antonio & Austin
San Diego
San Francisco
Santa Fe, Taos & Albuquerque
Scandinavia
Scotland
Seattle & Portland
South Pacific
Spain
Switzerland
Thailand
Tokyo
Toronto
U.S.A.
Utah
Vancouver & Victoria
Vienna
Virgin Islands
Virginia
Walt Disney World & Orlando
Washington, D.C.
Washington & Oregon

FROMMER'S FRUGAL TRAVELER'S GUIDES

(The grown-up guides to budget travel, offering dream vacations at down-to-earth prices)

Australia from $45 a Day
Berlin from $50 a Day
California from $60 a Day
Caribbean from $60 a Day
Costa Rica & Belize from $35 a Day
Eastern Europe from $30 a Day
England from $50 a Day
Europe from $50 a Day
Florida from $50 a Day
Greece from $45 a Day
Hawaii from $60 a Day
India from $40 a Day
Ireland from $45 a Day
Italy from $50 a Day
Israel from $45 a Day
London from $60 a Day
Mexico from $35 a Day
New York from $70 a Day
New Zealand from $45 a Day
Paris from $65 a Day
Washington, D.C. from $50 a Day

FROMMER'S PORTABLE GUIDES

(Pocket-size guides for travelers who want everything in a nutshell)

Charleston & Savannah
Las Vegas
New Orleans
San Francisco

FROMMER'S IRREVERENT GUIDES

(Wickedly honest guides for sophisticated travelers)

Amsterdam
Chicago
London
Manhattan
Miami
New Orleans
Paris
San Francisco
Santa Fe
U.S. Virgin Islands
Walt Disney World
Washington, D.C.

FROMMER'S AMERICA ON WHEELS

(Everything you need for a successful road trip, including full-color road maps and ratings for every hotel)

California & Nevada
Florida
Mid-Atlantic
Midwest & the Great Lakes
New England & New York
Northwest & Great Plains
South Central &Texas
Southeast
Southwest

FROMMER'S BY NIGHT GUIDES

(The series for those who know that life begins after dark)

Amsterdam
Chicago
Las Vegas
London
Los Angeles
Miami
New Orleans
New York
Paris
San Francisco